PREFACE

History

It happens to me all the time: I hear a new acronym. I worry that everyone knows something important that I should know. (Where do they learn these things? Why don't I have time to read as much as they must?) I don't know who to ask for an explanation, or I never get an explanation I understand. I don't even know what it stands for, or where to look it up.

I never intended to write a book. I am a data communications consultant, and I read magazines constantly. Realizing that I was not remembering most of what I carefully read, I began by writing down expansions of acronyms. Then I started recording juicy factoids and descriptions. Then things sort of got out of control.

Here is the result. Over several years it has grown to critical mass (and maintaining it is a big part of what I do every day). I hope you find it a fast and convenient way to get a basic or updated grasp of that newest acronym.

This book is not intended to be the definitive or authoritative work on any of the topics inside. It is a fast and condensed way to get up-to-speed on topics that you have heard mentioned by colleagues or seen in magazines and in advertisements but have not had the time to track. The many cross-references at the end of each entry show that it all (sort of) fits together.

Also, this is not intended to be your very first introduction to computer terms. For example, you need to already know what a PC is, what a bit and byte are, and the difference between a floppy and a hard disk drive.

Contents

Although there are over 1,000 entries here, they generally have one of the following themes:

▲ *Data Communication APIs (Application Program Interfaces)*: One of the reasons I find data communications so interesting is that it is a combination of hardware, application software, and operating system, each of which typically comes from a different company. The links between these components must therefore be well defined and, ideally, standardized. These software links are typically function calls, subroutines, software interrupts, and libraries, and are called APIs.

▲ *Wireless Communication*: For certain niche requirements, wireless communication (voice and data) is a big deal and becoming more so every day. There are many competing, complementary, and developing technologies.

▲ *The Internet and TCP/IP*: Of course, these are very trendy and important topics. Many related issues, such as network management and security, are also covered.

▲ *PC hardware*: The standard Intel-architecture personal computer is everywhere. Important PC issues, such as processor and bus types, interrupts, and disk drive interfaces are covered. I know there are lots of other kinds of "personal computers" that are better, smarter, or were developed before the Intel-architecture PC, but the book has to have *some* focus. So in this book, "PC" means a computer with an Intel processor, or a processor that is able to natively run programs compiled for Intel-architecture computers.

▲ *LANs (Local Area Networks)*: Networking within buildings is always getting faster and more heavily loaded. No longer is it simply that IBM shops use Token Ring and everyone else uses 10-Mbits/s Ethernet. The various types of LANs being deployed, developed, and standardized, as well as cabling and connectors, are presented.

▲ *WANs (Wide Area Networks)*: Data communication between buildings (and over any distance) has many limitations (costs, speeds, delays) that drive design and therefore business decisions. The types of WANs, interfaces, and modems and data sets are all part of the knowledge base required to use WANs effectively.

▲ *Multimedia:* There is a merging of computers, video, audio, data, and voice. You can no longer be a specialist in just one area. Many topics are presented, such as video standards, music concepts, and the networking requirements to carry this type of traffic.

Using This Book

Within these areas the coverage is quite broad. Of course, finding the right entry may be a task (at least for paper versions of this book). Some finding tips follow.

Unlike many glossaries, this one mixes acronyms with phrases, since it is not always clear when something is an acronym or not. For example:

▲ BISYNC is more like an abbreviation

▲ PING, TWAIN, and YAHOO are acronyms (some would say) but are not usually written that way

The sort order is:

1. Numbers first

2. Then spaces and special characters (such as -, /, *, and .—these are all considered as spaces for the purposes of sorting)

3. Letters next

So *Frame Relay* comes before *FT1*, which comes before *FTAM*, and *X.25* comes several entries before *X/Open*, which is before *X-stone*, which is before *X Terminal*, which is before *XAPIA*.

If you can't find a topic, try only part of the phrase:

▲ Instead of *Trumpet WinSock*, try *WinSock*

▲ Instead of *IEEE 1284* try *1284*

▲ Instead of *QCIF* try *CIF*

If you can't find a topic, try something related. For example, instead of *Floppy Diskette Drive*, try *Disk Drive*.

One of the needless complexities of data communications is that there are often several terms used for the same thing. For example, an Ethernet *multiport repeater* is usually simply called a *repeater*—or a *concentrator*—or a *hub*. The entries in this dictionary provide other popular terms, and cross-references are usually provided to the main entry for the less-often used terms.

There is a statistic that Eskimos have something like 13 words for snow. Well, computer people have about that many terms for the desktop computer on your desk. Just like people that each speak the same two languages often switch languages in mid-sentence (because it just felt right), there are subtle reasons why so many terms are used: PC (typically indicates an Intel-type processor in the box), workstation (typically high-powered, used to mean only running UNIX, but now may be running a different operating system), node (any device on a LAN, including a printer), host (typically any device which uses the TCP/IP protocol, but may mean a mainframe too), machine (usually a larger computer, used by someone who has great respect for hardware), computer (very generic), processor or CPU (thinking only about the guts of the box) and terminal (used to denote fixed-function terminals—only a keyboard and screen—with no local processing capability, but now can mean a low-end PC or one used for routine business tasks). Of course, there are many more colorful terms for the box on your desk, but those are usually used only when it is not working to your satisfaction.

Conventions

▲ A goal of this book is to explain acronyms, so the priority is always on putting the information in the entry for a term's acronym. Continuing with the example above, the entry for FTAM will begin with its expansion (File Transfer, Access, and Management), and then the explanation. In the alphabetical place for "File Transfer, Access, and Management," the entry says simply "See FTAM." If a term has no acronym (such as Frame Relay), then the explanation is in the entry for Frame Relay.

▲ After an acronym becomes accepted and widely used, its creator often augments the technology or changes their business so that the acronym isn't as descriptive or as accurate as it once was. They then insist that the acronym is in fact just another technical term that doesn't stand for anything. In these cases, the acronym is listed as (for example) "Previously Digital Versatile Disk". AT&T and OLE are other examples. Another reason vendors may insist that some letters are not acronyms (even though they really look like an acronym—such as MMX) is to ensure that the letters can be trademarked.

▲ Hexadecimal numbers are subscripted, for example, $D000_{16}$.

▲ The prefixes "k" and "M" are binary (2^{10} and 2^{20}, respectively), when referring to data storage. For example, 1 kbyte is 1×2^{10}, which is $1,024_{10}$ (base 10) bytes; 1 Mbyte of memory is $1,024 \times 1,024 = 1,048,576_{10}$ bytes.

▲ "k" and "M" are decimal (10^3 and 10^6, respectively) when referring to frequencies or data transfer rates. For example, 8 kHz is 8,000 cycles per second; 9.6 kbits/s is 9,600 bits/s; 1.544 Mbits/s is 1,544,000 bits/s.

▲ While many magazines abbreviate *byte* as "B", and *bit* as "b" (as in kb/s or MB/s, or even kBps), these are not official international abbreviations (see the entry for **SI**). In this book, byte and bit are never abbreviated (so kbyte/s and Mbyte/s are used).

▲ The `courier` font is used for things computers read and say, such as, file names and computer commands and output.

▲ *Italic* is used for emphasis and to keep a group of words or a phrase together (for example, *zero bit stuffing* or *Adobe Type Manager*). Typically, these are important key words that are related to the technology being discussed. The words may be more fully described elsewhere in the book, in which case they (or their acronym) will be mentioned at the end of that entry (for example, *See* **ATM** *and* **POSTSCRIPT PAGE DESCRIPTION LANGUAGE**).

▲ SMALL CAPITAL letters are used for acronyms, such as PC and ISDN.

▲ For additional or updated information, the Uniform Resource Locator (URL) for relevant World Wide Web (WWW) servers are often referenced. These references will always start with "http" (HyperText Transfer Protocol) and will be in *sans serif italic*. For example, *http://www.ieee.org*.

▲ References to directories and files on ftp sites are given in Web Browser format. For example, *ftp://rtfm.mit.edu/pub/usenet-by-group/* means that on the ftp site `rtfm.mit.edu`, there is a subdirectory `/pub/usenet-by-group`.

▲ When a table breaks across pages, there is a "*table continued on next page*" line at the bottom of the first part and the table heads repeat at the top of the second part.

Where to Go from Here

We are trying an experiment with this book—the entire book (including the tables and graphics) is Internet-accessible (for free) at http://www.ora.com/ reference/dictionary/. All the book's cross-references (to other entries) and URL references (for additional information) are hypertext hot links. For your browsing pleasure, the home page is a form into which you enter the term or acronym. Click away, and watch this book come alive!

We hope that you find this helpful not only for your own reference, but also for online technical documents you may be writing—you don't need to write your own glossary of technical terms, just reference the appropriate entries from this book.

While I certainly hope that this book (and its online version) remains an important reference for you, new technologies, standards (and acronyms!) are being developed every day. It is important to have a wide variety of information sources to keep up. Here are some ways I track what is going on.

Magazines

Magazines are amazing. Of all the sources of information available to me, magazines are the most important. Pick two technical ones, and subscribe to them. Read every issue. Flip through every page, reading only articles and advertisements that are important to you and your job. My favorite two magazines are:

▲ *PC Magazine*. Unfortunately, it's huge (400 pages, twice a month), but it usually does a professional job of evaluating products and has good coverage of PC Hardware and some data communications coverage as well. It is at *http://www.pcmag.com* and on almost every magazine stand. Fill out the subscription card or phone to request the magazine's network edition (it has additional articles and advertising concerning networking). The article index is searchable through what the magazine calls Ziffnet, which is reachable from CompuServe, for an additional monthly charge.

▲ *Data Communications Magazine*. It used to be a great, somewhat expensive magazine; now it is a great free magazine (for qualifying subscribers). It has first-class coverage of data communications issues. Phone 1-800-525-5003 or 609-426-7070 and ask them to mail or fax you a subscription request form. Better yet, visit their web site (at *http://www.data.com*). It has all their articles categorized and on-line.

You need to flip through every page because you never know when there will be one of those fantastic tutorial articles that fully explains a technology or mentions some new acronym or feature that you don't need today but will need to know about tomorrow.

Vendor World Wide Web (WWW) Pages

The progression from having a salesman visit to discussing a product with a knowledgeable inside sales person to asking for a brochure to be mailed out to using a faxback service has now gone to checking a vendor's WWW server for product information. Even for general information, vendor web sites (such as *http://www.3com.com*) are very good at explaining new technologies—if they can't explain what their products do, then why would you buy their stuff?. I have included many references for relevant WWW servers, but the search engines are important to. I usually use altavista or yahoo, but there are many, some of which are listed below:

▲ Digital Equipment Corporation's Altavista at *http://www.altavista.digital.com*

▲ Yahoo at *http://www.yahoo.com*

▲ Excite at *http://www.excite.com*

▲ Global Network Navigator at *http://www.gnn.com/wr*

▲ Lycos at *http://www.lycos.com*

▲ OpenText at *http://www.opentext.com*

▲ WebCrawler at *http://www.webcrawler.com*

Links to lots of search engines are at *http://www.stpt.com*, *http://ds2.internic.net/tools/* and *http://www.netscape.com/escapes/internet_search.html*.

Also, there are some great pointer pages, such as the following:

▲ The Lawrence Livermore National Laboratory's *Telecommunications Page* at *http://www-atp.llnl.gov/atp/telecom.html* and their all-encompassing pointer page to everything about data communications at *http://www-atp.llnl.gov/atp/standards.html*

▲ The University of Michigan's *Telecom Information Resources* page at the site *http://ippsweb.ipps.lsa.umich.edu/telecom/telecom-info.html*

▲ The University of Texas' *Access to Network Information* page at the site *http://mojo.ots.utexas.edu/netinfo*

▲ The *Data Communications and Networking Links* page at *http://www.racal.com/networking.html*

Of course, most anything mainstream in the area of computers and communications is a standard of some sort. See the entry for **STANDARDS** for more information.

The many FAQs online are excellent and are loaded with expert and practical information. Try *http://www.faqs.org*, and see the entry in this dictionary for **FAQ** further information.

Vendors are usually a useful source of information:

▲ Stelcom Inc., an Internet service provider, has a home page of *Electronics Manufacturers on the Net* at

http://www.webscope.com/elx/.

▲ The entry for **CARRIER** has links to telephone companies' home pages, most of which have some information on their telecommunications offerings.

Finally, there are acronym servers at *http://www.yahoo.com/Reference/Acronyms* and *http://curia.ucc.ie/cgi-bin/acronym*, and the "Jargon file" is at *http://www.ccil.org/jargon/jargon-toc.html*.

Usenet Newsgroups

With about 20,000 newsgroups, Usenet has a newsgroup for almost any topic. Use your news reader's newsgroup search function (which searches the text of each newsgroup's one-line description). Many newsgroups have FAQs that are constantly updated and periodically posted in the newsgroup. Often, posted news items will refer to the site that has the most-recent FAQ for that newsgroup. It is becoming popular for FAQs to be in HTML, and therefore easily viewed and retrieved using your WWW browser. See the entries for **FAQ** and **USENET** for more details and links. For real-time help, IRC can sometimes be useful. See the entry for **IRC**.

Standards

Many technologies are completely described by their standards or RFCs (*request for comments*). I have included references to these when possible, and the entries for Standards and RFCs describe how to obtain these documents.

Also in the entry for Standards are several references to "Master" WWW pages of extensive references to other specialty sites of communications-oriented information.

Books

Although books are expensive and usually best as detailed references, they can be great sources of information. I am astonished (and overwhelmed) by the excellent technical quality and range of topics available in everyday bookstores. This kind of information never used to be available at all, let alone at your local bookstore.

If your local bookstore does not have what you need, a university or college bookstore, or a bookstore specializing in computer books, is a good place to go. Nothing can beat looking through an expensive book before purchasing it.

Some bookstores have their inventory database available on the Internet and allow searches by subject—and display the book's price and which stores have the book in stock. Having a knowledgeable staff and accepting credit card orders by telephone are also good features for a bookstore to have. Computer Literacy Bookshops is one bookstore that does all this, and has many on-line book reviews too. They are at *http://www.clbooks.com*

The Internet

As you can see from the many references to the world wide web in both this preface and throughout this book, the Internet is crucial to keeping up with technology and getting vendor information, technical support, and software updates. The entry for **ISP** has some further information on connecting to the Internet.

Monthly Reports and Newsletters

Many very specialized monthly reports and newsletters are available. These typically cost $200 to $400 per year, and are a bargain if they target your area of interest.

For example, to keep up to date on the wide variety of Canadian telecommunications issues (regulatory, competition, wireless, costs, and management), Angus Telemanagement is superb (phone: 905-686-5050, WWW: *http://www.angustel.ca*).

Courses

Some people learn technology best from a real, live person. Taking a course may then be a good idea. I happen to teach courses for Learning Tree International (*http://www.learningtree.com*), and my honest opinion is that their courses and instructors are first-rate (of course, you could argue that I may be biased, but I wouldn't be teaching for them if they did not have a high-quality product).

Input

Finally—everyone is an expert in something. What we want to know is some of what everyone else knows. I hope this book helps you with that goal. Although thousands of hours have gone into this effort, there are going to be oversights, omissions, and outright mistakes. Also, technology is a frustratingly moving target to put into print. I welcome your comments and input.

Mitchell Shnier, P. Eng.
Toronto, Canada

NUMBERS

10BASE-F

A local area network that transmits data at 10 Mbits/s over fiber-optic cable.

An 802.3 media option that supports 10 Mbits/s Ethernet over optical fiber. The following table summarizes the characteristics of the three options, along with the 802.3 FOIRL option.

Media Option	Name	Intended Use	Characteristics
10BASE-FB	Fiber backbone	Repeater-to-repeater links only	2-km maximum segment length, 15 repeater maximum cascade, must be built into repeater (no external transceivers)
10BASE-FL	Fiber link	Workstation-to-repeater and repeater-to-repeater links	2-km maximum segment length, 5 repeater maximum cascade, can connect to FOIRL transceivers (with FOIRL limits)
10BASE-FP	Fiber passive	Workstation-to-repeater and repeater-to-repeater links	Passive hubs, 500-m maximum segment length, no limit on number of hub ports but 33 ports currently available
FOIRL	Fiber-optic inter-repeater link	Repeater-to-repeater links	1-km maximum segment length, 4 repeater maximum cascade

All use 62.5/125 μm fiber-optic cable with ST connectors and a 800-nm to 910-nm (infrared) light source.

The 10BASE-FB option has a feature to detect jabbering transmitters and can automatically enable a backup link.

See **S10BASET**, **S802.3**, and **ETHERNET**.

10BASE-T

A local area network that transmits data at 10 Mbits/s over copper cabling.

An 802.3 media option that supports 10 Mbits/s Ethernet over UTP. While 2 10BASE-T devices can be directly connected together (usually only for testing), 10BASE-T devices are

100BASE-FX

typically each connected to their own port on a concentrator (also called a hub or multi-port repeater), or a switch.

A nonstandardized full-duplex version (sometimes called full duplex switched Ethernet, FDSE) was developed by Kalpana and is supported by Compaq and a few other vendors. A standard version of FDSE is to be called 802.3x.

See **S100BASET**, **S802.3**, **CABLE**, **CONNECTOR ETHERNET**, and **SWITCHED LAN**.

100BASE-FX

A local area network that transmits data at 100 Mbits/s over fiber-optic cable.

A full- or half-duplex version of 100BASE-T *Fast Ethernet* that uses two strands of multimode optical fiber. Configuration rules are as follows:

▲ If only one repeater (concentrator): 225 m from repeater to switch, bridge, or router (making a 100 + 225 = 325 m network diameter)

▲ If no repeaters (workstation to switch or switch to switch): 450 m (if half-duplex 100BASE-FX) or 2 km (if full-duplex 100BASE-FX)

The distance rules are illustrated in the following figure.

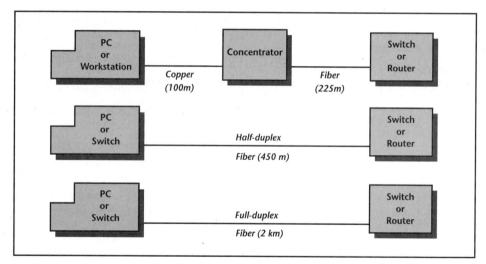

100BASE-FX-1

See **S100BASET**.

100BASE-T
100 Mbits/s Baseband Modulation on Twisted Pair

A local area network that transmits data at 100 Mbits/s, which is also called *Fast Ethernet*. It is standardized in 802.3u, and was first released in June 1995.

An implementation of 802.3 "Ethernet" that uses 10 times the user bit rate (100 Mbits/s), one-tenth the interframe gap (0.96 μs), different bit encoding but otherwise is identical to

10BASE-T (same frame format and minimum and maximum lengths, same collision detection scheme, same connector and pin-out, and sometimes the same Ethernet drivers can be used too).

Four media options are defined: 100BASE-T2 (not widely available), 100BASE-T4 (not very popular), 100BASE-TX (most popular), and 100BASE-FX.

Does not have the reliability features of FDDI (no secondary channel or dual-homing) nor the isochronous capability of ATM.

Does not support prioritization or multimedia (though 3Com's PACE technology is supposed to provide this capability), but Ethernet users should find it easier to migrate to (and interconnect to) 100BASE-T than to 100VG-AnyLAN, since 100BASE-T does not require changes to upper-layer software or SNMP MIBs (some vendors even allow 10BASE-T drivers to be used).

Developed and promoted by the *Fast Ethernet Alliance* (which was formed in 1993, and had 75 vendor-members in 1995), whose main members are 3Com, Intel, Standard Microsystems (SMC), Sun Microsystems, Bay Networks (which is the name of the company created by the merging of SynOptics Communications and Wellfleet Communications), and Cabletron Systems. Also supported by Cisco Systems (through their ownership of Kalpana), Digital Equipment Corporation, and even IBM.

The following table summarizes the characteristics of 100BASE-T, 100VG-AnyLAN, and FDDI.

Technology	Speed (Mbits/s)	Suited to	Comments
100BASE-T	100	Desktop	Low-cost, easiest to upgrade from Ethernet
100VG-AnyLAN	100	Desktop	Low-cost, deterministic, does not have as wide internetworking and trouble-shooting equipment support as 100BASE-T
FDDI	100	Desktop or backbone	Uses fiber, STP or UTP, dual ring architecture adds reliability, available now, strong management capabilities
ATM	25 to 622	LAN and WAN	Only solution with isochronous channel for voice and video, highest speed and cost

Designed for to-the-desktop rather than the backbone (though 100BASE-TX's and 100BASE-FX's support for full-duplex operation may result in backbone use).

An autonegotiation (which 3Com calls *NWay*) function built into adapters permits dual-speed (10BASE-T and 100BASE-T) adapters to automatically sense and use the highest speed that is supported by both ends. On power-up, the adapter sends *fast link pulse* burst (in contrast, 10BASE-T devices' link pulses are 100 ns wide—which is one bit-time—sent every 16 to 24 ms). If the concentrator or switch also supports 100BASE-T, it will respond with fast link pulses, and the adapter will then use its 100BASE-T mode of operation. Otherwise, operation will be at 10 Mbits/s.

100BASE-T2

Autonegotiation (see **S100BASETX**) uses *parallel detection* to determine whether the adapter supports full- or half-duplex operation and for determining which media (100BASE-TX or 100BASE-T4) option is being used. Full-duplex can only be used on switched links where there are no other devices sharing the bandwidth (shared hubs must have collision detection enabled, so full-duplex operation cannot be used on them).

A link-by-link flow-control feature enables a receiver to signal a transmitter that it is busy; if the transmitter is not the originator of the data, then it must relay the flow-control back to the transmitter. End-to-end flow control requires the switches at the ends of a link to communicate to regulate the data from an end station.

The Fast Ethernet Consortium is at *http://www.iol.unh.edu/consortiums/fe/fast_ethernet_ consortium.html*. Some further information is at *http://wwwhost.ots.utexas.edu/ethernet/ descript-100quickref.html*. A site with lots of pointers to sites related to 100BASE-T (and some 100VG-AnyLAN too) is *http://www.alumni.caltech.edu/~dank/fe*.

See **100BASE-T2, 100BASE-T4, 100BASE-TX, 100BASE-FX, 100VG-ANYLAN, ETHERNET, FDDI, GIGABIT ETHERNET, ISOCHRONOUS, LAN, MULTIMEDIA, PACE, SWITCHED LAN**, and **UTP**.

100BASE-T2

A local area network that transmits data at 100 Mbits/s over 2 pairs of Category 3 (or 4 or 5) UTP copper cabling.

Full-duplex transmission is supported. Both pairs of the cable are used for both transmission and reception. Digital signal processing (DSP) is used to accommodate installation and cable problems (such as untwisting too much of a pair, or delay skew in the cable)— by measuring and cancelling the effects of echoes (due to impedance mismatches), signal distortion, interference and crosstalk. It even allows two 100BASE-T2, or one 100BASE-T2 and one 100BASE-TX, signals in the same 4-pair cable.

To be standardized in IEEE 802.3y.

See **S100BASET, DSP, PARALLEL**, and **UTP**.

100BASE-T4

A local area network that transmits data at 100 Mbits/s over up to 100 m of UTP copper cabling.

A half-duplex-only version of 100BASE-T that uses four pairs of a Category 3, 4, or 5 UTP cable. Transmission uses three pairs simultaneously (to reduce the bit rate on each). The fourth pair is used for collision detect (see the following table).

	Pair Function When Workstation Is ...	
Pair	Transmitting	Receiving
1	Transmits data to hub	Receives data from hub
2	Receives collision detect indication from hub	Receives data from hub
3	Transmits data to hub	Transmits collision detect indication to hub
4	Transmits data to hub	Receives data from hub

Bit encoding is 8B/6T—this means that 8 bits are represented by six ternary (three-state) symbols. Each transmitting pair runs at 25 Mbaud, and 6 baud intervals represent 8 bits. The bit rate of each pair is therefore $25 \times \frac{8}{6} = 33\frac{1}{3}$ Mbits/s. The three transmitting pairs together therefore have a bit rate of 100 Mbits/s.

100BASE-T4 has been slower (compared to 100BASE-TX) to be available for the following reasons:

▲ Whereas 100BASE-TX uses the bit encoding and transmission method developed for FDDI's TP-PMD (greatly facilitating the design of the ICs), 100BASE-T4 required new design and development for this interface.

▲ 100BASE-T4 was offered largely to compete with 100VG-AnyLAN's similar capability of using Category 3 UTP cabling. Vendors waited to see whether anybody really bought any 100VG-AnyLAN to see if there was any competitive reason or market demand for 100 Mbit/s transmission over Category 3 cabling.

While 100BASE-T4 was developed so that less-expensive Category 3 cable can be used (compared to the Category 5 cable for 100BASE-TX), the Category 3 cable must have very low *skew*. Skew is the difference (between the fastest and slowest pars) of the signal propagation delay through the cable. A maximum of 50 ns is specified (this is for 100 m of cable, including the connection hardware, over a range of temperatures).

100BASE-T4 is standardized in IEEE 802.3u.

See **S100BASET**, and **ENCODING**.

100BASE-TX

A type of Ethernet local area network that transmits data at 100 Mbits/s over copper cabling.

A full- or half-duplex version of 100BASE-T that uses two pairs of IBM-type STP or Category 5 UTP cable. The *Multilevel Transmit* bit-encoding scheme (called MLT-3) is the same as that used for FDDI's TP-PMD.

The maximum Category 5 cable length (either station-to-station or hub-to-station) is 100 m. A simplified equation showing the maximum distance (in meters) between two stations (including the distance between the hubs between the stations) is as follows:

$$\text{total cable length} = [400 - (\text{repeaters} \times 95)] \text{ m}$$

Usually, there will be two repeaters (hubs), and the two hub-to-station cables will be up to 100 m, so there can be up to 10 m between the repeaters. The maximum network diameter is therefore 210 m.

The intent was that it should be easy to install 100BASE-TX because many sites have Category 5 UTP already installed for 10BASE-T networks. The problem is that many installations have components that are not Category 5 (such as patch panels), so installation may be a substantial problem.

See **S100BASET**, **ENCODING**, **FDDI**, **LAN**, and **UTP**.

1000BASE-T

See **GIGABIT ETHERNET**.

100VG-ANYLAN
100 Mbits/s on Voice-Grade Unshielded Twisted Pair Cable for Any (Ethernet or Token Ring) Local Area Network

A local area network that transmits data at 100 Mbits/s over copper cabling.

A 100 Mbits/s half-duplex LAN standard promoted by AT&T, Hewlett-Packard, and IBM, hoped to be the successor to both Ethernet and Token Ring (for example, it can handle Token Ring size frames, whereas 100BASE-T cannot). Hubs must be configured for *either* Ethernet *or* Token Ring frames. A 100VG-AnyLAN Hub (and therefore LAN segment) cannot carry both types simultaneously; a router is needed to connect two 100VG-AnyLANs that have different frame types.

A new *media access control* scheme (and therefore frame type) called *demand priority* (sometimes called the *demand priority access method*—DPAM) provides two priority levels:

▲ *Isochronous* and therefore high-priority traffic (typically constant-bit-rate traffic from digitized voice or video) gets priority over regular traffic, making transmission more deterministic than 100BASE-T and therefore suitable for multimedia (however, on lightly-loaded networks, 100BASE-T can transmit sooner, since it does not need to wait to be polled by the hub)

▲ *Asynchronous* (normal-priority) traffic is carried only if there is capacity left over for it

Hubs provide controlled LAN access for their directly connected stations, which request LAN access by using a round-robin (within priority levels) scheme that polls stations, and gives them (one at a time) permission to send one frame. Stations with lower-priority messages will receive a priority boost if their messages have been waiting 250 µs or more (because of the high-priority traffic hogging all the bandwidth).

The normal polling for low-priority messages is interrupted (after any current frame is handled) as soon as any station has a high-priority frame ready to transmit. If a low-priority request has been waiting too long, the hub temporarily assigns it a high priority. This ensures that high-priority stations cannot completely hog all the bandwidth.

Typically, hub ports can be manually designated as having low- or high-priority traffic. Also, the adapter drivers can usually be configured to generate low- or high-priority traffic. Eventually, applications will be able to specify (on a per-frame basis) whether frames are low- or high-priority.

Hubs are cascaded below a *root hub*. When the root hub gives permission to a lower-level hub to transmit, the lower-level hub can send *one* frame received from *each* of the lower-level hub's ports.

A maximum of five hubs between any two stations is allowed. These are typically arranged as a *root hub* at the top level, which has connections to other stations and *second-level* hubs. The second-level hubs connect to other stations, and to *third-level* hubs, which in turn connect to stations.

The maximum link lengths (either station-to-hub or hub-to-hub) are as follows:

▲ 100 m, using all four pairs of a Category 3, 4, or 5 UTP cable (using *quartet signaling*, which splits the data among four pairs of conductors)

▲ 150 m, using two pairs of STP or Category 5 UTP cable (still in development)

▲ 2,000 m, using single-mode or multimode fiber-optic cable (still in development)

The maximum network diameter is as follows:

▲ 500 m over Category 3 UTP (up to five hubs can be between any two stations)

▲ 1,200 m over Category 5 UTP

▲ 4,000 m over multimode fiber-optic cable (a maximum of one hub between stations)

Products usually support both standard 10 Mbits/s 10BASE-T Ethernet and 100 Mbits/s 100VG-AnyLAN (either manually configured or automatically switching between the two), though separate connectors are usually used, so the cable must manually be moved to the 100VG-AnyLAN port to upgrade. In contrast, 100BASE-T boards have a single connector which supports both 10BASE-T and 100BASE-TX, and the switching is usually done automatically.

100VG-AnyLAN is standardized in IEEE 802.12, and is sometimes called *demand priority*. Competes with 100BASE-T (which cannot carry Token Ring frames but sometimes uses existing 10BASE-T drivers, simplifying upgrades).

The 100VG-AnyLAN forum had 24 vendor-members in 1995. In addition to Hewlett-Packard and IBM, it includes AT&T, Cisco, Compaq, Newbridge, Proteon, Puredata, Texas Instruments and Thomas-Conrad.

See **S100BASET**, **ISOCHRONOUS**, **LAN**, **MULTIMEDIA**, and **UTP**.

1284

A standard documenting the existing operation of PC parallel ports and, most important, several additional capabilities.

IEEE Standard 1284 defines several enhancements and modes for a PC's parallel port (also called the *centronics port*), including support for bidirectional communications. The following tables describe these modes.

Mode	Capabilities	Transfer Rate (kbytes/s)	Suited to
Compatibility	8-bit output to printer Limited printer status monitoring Programmed and interrupt-based I/O Handshaking with printer for flow control	100 to 200 output only	Original PC and centronics use (see **PARALLEL PORT**).

(table continued on next page)

Mode	Capabilities	Transfer Rate (kbytes/s)	Suited to
4-bit or nibble	4-bit input (two sequential transfers to transfer a byte from printer) *Compatibility Mode* used for Output Programmed and interrupt-based I/O	40 to 60 input	Printers or other applications in which the 4 input status bits can be used to input data to the PC.
8-bit or byte	8-bit input from printer Compatibility mode used for output Programmed and interrupt-based I/O	80 to 300 input	Printers but also other types of peripherals (such as disk or LAN interfaces) that require faster input to the PC. Implemented in most PCs manufactured after 1991 to 1993. A direction bit in the printer port registers controls the port's direction.
ECP	8-bit output and 8-bit input Programmed, interrupt-based, and DMA-based I/O (typically using DMA channel 1) 16-byte (or more) FIFO	More than 2,000	Highest-speed block transfers; for example, to printers or from scanners. Includes support for RLE data compression (2 bytes can represent up to 128 repeated bytes).
EPP	8-bit output and 8-bit input Programmed and interrupt-based I/O	Up to 2,000	Interactive communications. For example, to LAN adapters or to CD-ROM, disk, and tape drives. This is the most powerful and flexible mode.

ECP (*Extended Capabilities Port*) mode provides the fastest data transfer but is best-suited to simpler transfers. Windows 95 supports ECP mode, as do Hewlett-Packard LaserJet 4 and 5 series of printers. EPP (*Enhanced Parallel Port*) provides more complex control features. EPP is typically the best configuration choice, unless the port is connected to a device that requires only ECP (for example, most printers support only ECP).

The standard's emphasis is on the signaling format, pin assignments, and error detection and correction procedures (that is, what goes on outside of the PC). The BIOS functions, software interface, and control of the ports are not specified, so vendor-specific utilities and software will be required to configure the ports.

Three types of connectors are defined, as shown in the following table.

Connector Type	Description	Maximum Cable Length (m)	Comments
A	A DB-25 *subminiature D-shell* connector (as is also used by the incompatible EIA-232 Serial COM ports on a PC)	2[a]	Standard PC parallel port, used at the PC end. Female connector on PC. (EIA-232 uses a male connector on the PC.)
B	Traditional 36-pin centronics connector (is 5 cm wide)	2[a]	Standard PC parallel port, used at the printer end.
C	36-pin miniature centronics connector (is about 3 cm wide)	10[b]	New connector (and pin assignment) and interface voltages defined for higher-speed and greater-distance printer connections. Both ends must use Type C connectors and voltages. With the appropriate cable, a Type C connector can be connected to Type A and B PC ports, providing only Type A and B cable distances.

a. The standard gives this as an example distance that will work. Hewlett-Packard allows up to 2 or 3 m, depending on the cable used.
b. The standard actually specifies the only maximum cable propagation delay (58 ns), which works out to a length of just over 10 m for the velocity of propagation for typical cables.

The standard defines two levels of *compliance*, as shown in the following table.

Compliance Level	Interface	Comments
I	Type A and B connectors and existing (*Level 1*) voltages	That is, existing PC parallel ports.
II	Type C connectors and new high-performance interfaces (which use *Level 2* voltages)	Expected to be implemented on new PCs. Level 2 voltages require Type C connectors and work over greater cable distances (when connected to other Level 2 devices) or over Level 1 distances (when connected to Level 1 devices).

A 1284 parallel port powers-on to *compatibility mode*. The 1284 standard defines the negotiation process between software in the PC and a peripheral attached to the parallel port to determine which of the five modes the port should be switched to (it will be left in compatibility mode if there is no response). The PC can request certain modes, and the peripheral replies with the mode it chooses. Each of the modes defines the new functionality of the interface signals. Modes can be switched quickly. For example, the interface will be switched between compatibility and nibble for each transfer for an interactive "half-duplex" exchange of data.

1284-compliant devices need to implement only compatibility and nibble modes (that is, byte, ECP, and EPP modes are optional). Therefore printers with a standard centronics port that also support nibble mode (so the printer can send information back to the PC, 4 bits at a time) are IEEE 1284 compliant.

For example, a Hewlett-Packard LaserJet 4 Printer is IEEE 1284 compliant. HP calls this *Bi-Tronics* support. Bi-Tronics:

▲ Basically means support for nibble mode

▲ Does not support EPP (HP will likely never support this, since ECP is more suited to printer communications)

▲ Does not support ECP either (though HP has stated that future printers will include ECP support as part of their IEEE 1284 compliance)

To summarize all of these modes, parallel ports will be used in up to four ways, as shown in the following table.

Port Support	IEEE 1284 Modes Used	Used For
Traditional PC parallel port	Compatibility	Sending data to (and only to) printers
HP Bi-Tronics	Compatibility and nibble	Sending data to printers and receiving printer status information from a printer
Extended capabilities port	ECP	Highest-speed data transfers to and from printers
Enhanced parallel port	Byte and EPP	Disk, tape, and CD-ROM drives

Another optional feature is *device ID*, in which the PC requests the peripheral to reply with an ASCII string (which begins with the string's length count). The string is a series of ;-delimited key: and *value* sequences (there can be more than one *value* for each key; multiple *values* are separated by a ,). If device ID is supported, then the MANUFACTURER, MODEL and COMMAND SET (optionally abbreviated as MFG, MDL, and CMD) keys must be part of the reply (vendors can add any others they want). For example,

`MFG:Hewlett-Packard; MDL:LaserJet 4; CMD:PCL, PostScript;`

"IEEE Std 1284-1994 compliant" cables are required for use with all modes and compliance levels. The standard specifies (among other things) the cable:

▲ Be clearly and permanently labeled "IEEE Std 1284-1994 compliant"

▲ Be 18-pair cable, with a foil *and* braid shield that is bonded 360° around to metal connector shells (at both ends of the cable)

▲ Shield coverage, grounding, pair twists per meter, impedance, and maximum attenuation

▲ Pin-out, including which ground pin wires are to be twisted to which control and data signal pin wires

The IEEE 1284 cable provides reliable bidirectional communications and support for the highest-speed (that is, ECP mode) data transfer. The optional Type C ports provide extended distance.

The following table summarizes the IEEE 1284 features available, according to which components of IEEE 1284 are implemented.

IEEE 1284 Feature	IEEE 1284 Component*		
	Compliant cable	Host computer operating system and parallel port supports ECP	Host computer and peripheral supports Type C connector and Level 2 voltages
Bidirectional data transfer	✓		
High-speed operation	✓	✓	
10 m cable distance support	✓		✓
All IEEE 1284 features can be supported	✓	✓	✓

* A ✓ indicates that this component must be implemented to support the feature.

See **COMPATIBLE, COMPLIANT, DB25, DMA, ECP, EPP, IRQ, PARALLEL PORT, PIO,** and **RLE.**

1394
IEEE 1394 Standard for a High Performance Serial Bus

A technology initially developed and promoted by Apple for a shared media (cable daisy-chains to each device), full-duplex, serial, peripheral-sharing bus. Intended to connect computers to consumer electronics devices, such as video and audio recorders and players.

Apple's trademarked name for it is FireWire, and it supports speeds of 100 Mbits/s, 200 Mbits/s, and 400 Mbits/s. Devices that communicate at different speeds can be simultaneously connected to the cable (so long as pairs of communicating devices use the same speed). The recommended maximum length of cable is 4.5 m between devices. A maximum of 63 devices (called *nodes*) can be directly connected (each device has a 6-bit physical identification number), and the total cable length can be up to 72 m. Bridges can be used to increase the number of buses to a maximum of 1,023 (each device also has a 10-bit bus ID), so up to 64,449 devices can be interconnected. Each device has a 64-bit *device address*, which includes the above 6-bit and 10-bit addresses. The remaining 48 bits per device can be used memory addressing, so each device can have up to 2^{48} bytes (256 Tbytes) of storage.

This would permit a single port on a computer to support many peripherals. Isochronous data transmission is supported, so 1394 is well-suited to real-time multimedia applications.

Intended for home computers and higher-end consumer applications, such as digitized video (many DV—*digital video* camcorders support it) recording and editing, photography, as well as disk drive interfaces (so it competes with SCSI).

The bus has a node designated the *root*, which has certain control responsibilities. The root can either be elected automatically when the bus is initialized, or can be forced to be a specific node (likely your PC). The non-root nodes are either *branches* (if they have more than one connection active), or *leaves* (if only a single connection is active).

One of the functions performed by the root is that of *cycle master*, which gets top priority access to the bus. It provides a common clock for the other devices on the bus, and for the isochronous data transfers.

There may also be a *bus manager*. This has responsibility for power management and some optimization functions.

The *isochronous resource manager* allocates time slots (out of a pool of 64 channel numbers) to nodes requesting to be *talkers*. The cycle master sends a *cycle start* timing message (typically) every 125 µs. At most, 80% of the cycle (100 µs) is reserved for isochronous traffic. The remainder of the cycle is then available for asynchronous traffic. Nodes with isochronous data to send, and that have been assigned a channel number arbitrate for transmission time first (right after each cycle start message), and the node closest to the root will get permission to transmit first. Each farther node with an assigned channel number and with isochronous traffic to send subsequently gets permission to transmit. Then nodes with asynchronous traffic arbitrate for permission to transmit.

The manager functions may all be performed by the same device, or by different devices.

Devices typically have 1 to 3 ports, and any device can be plugged-in to any other device (with the restrictions that there can be a maximum of 16 hops between any two devices and devices cannot be connected in a loop). Hot-plugging is allowed, so devices can be connected and disconnected at any time. Addresses are assigned automatically when devices are plugged-in, so there are no addresses to manually set.

Two types of communication are supported (each supporting variable-length packets), as the following describes.

▲ *Asynchronous communications* are sent to a specific address, and acknowledgments are used for error-detection. Traffic that does not require very high data rates, and is not time-sensitive, is well-suited to this type of communication (such as some control information).

▲ *Isochronous communications* broadcasts data at regular intervals, and acknowledgments are not used. This mode is designed to carry digitized video and audio.

The packets of data are sent in multiples of 32 bits, called *quadlets*. Packets begin with at least two quadlets of header (followed by a CRC for error-detection) followed by a variable number of payload quadlets (which is followed by a payload CRC). Asynchronous packet headers are at least 4 quadlets in length, because of the 64-bit address and other bits, such as the priority. Isochronous packets may have only a 2-quadlet header, as the only address required is the channel number.

A 6-pin connector is used. The cable used is round, and contains the following:

▲ Twisted Pair A (TPA) uses red and green wires and has an overall shield. It uses a balanced, differential voltage (for noise immunity), and carries bidirectional data using NRZ encoding. The actual voltage used is 172 to 265 mV.

▲ Twisted Pair B (TPB) uses blue and orange wires, carries a strobe which changes state whenever two consecutive data bits (on the other pair) are the same—this is called *data-strobe encoding*, and ensures that either the data or strobe pair changes state at each bit edge. This strobe pair is also shielded.

▲ The black and white wires provide power to smaller devices. VP carries up to 1.5 amps at 8 to 40 volts DC, and VG is ground. An AV connector and cable, which has no power wires, may be added to the standard in the future.

▲ An overall shield is insulated from the pair shields, and is bonded to the connector shells.

IEEE 1394 is also called high-speed serial bus, IEC 1883, and P-1394 (during the standard development process). Other companies assisting in the development include; Texas Instruments, Molex, Adaptec, Western Digital, and the IBM PC Company.

Promoted by the 1394 Trade Association (at *http://www.1394ta.org/*), which consists of Apple and consumer electronics vendors. Will compete with (and cost and do more than) DDC (which is based on ACCESS.bus and promoted by monitor manufacturers) and USB (promoted by Intel, Microsoft, and major PC vendors).

Other information is available at *http://firewire.org/aboutta/new.html*, *http://www.ti.com/sc/1394/* and *ftp://ftp.symbios.com/pub/standards/io/1394*.

Development began in 1988. In December 1996, IEEE standard 1394 was approved. Future enhancements planned are support for 800 and 1,600 Mbits/s.

See **BUS**, **CRC**, **DDC**, **DV**, **ENCODING**, **EVC**, **IEC**, **ISOCHRONOUS**, **MULTIMEDIA**, **SCSI1**, **SERIAL BUS**, **USB**, **V.35**, and **VIDEO**.

16550

A popular integrated circuit for handling the serial data communications for a PC's COM ports.

Refers to the National Semiconductor 16550AFN UART (or a work-alike), which has a built-in 16-byte receive buffer so that multitasking operating systems (such as Microsoft Windows, which gives higher priority to foreground task disk accesses) and MS-DOS 6 (when its SMARTDRV disk caching program flushes its delayed writes to disk) can reliably receive data at speeds above 9,600 bits/s. That is, the data is buffered (temporarily stored) in the UART while characters are being received, but the operating system is not able to read it out of the UART.

For example, a V.34 modem (28,800 bits/s) or V.34+ (33,600 bits/s) using V.42*bis* data compression (which typically provides up to a 4:1 compression ratio) should use a serial port speed of 115,200 bits/s. At this speed, a character is received every 86.8 μs. If the CPU is busy doing something else for much longer than this (even the older 8250 UART can receive a second character while waiting for the first to be read), then characters will be overwritten in the UART and therefore lost.

Data communications software utilizing the 16550 can be more efficient than using the 8250, since the 16550 can be programmed by the communications software to *interrupt* only after 1, 4, 8, or 14 characters have been received by the UART, so fewer interrupts are necessary (this reduces the CPU time needed to support the communications, since more characters are read per interrupt). Setting this too high however, requires that the CPU respond very quickly to the interrupt, as there won't be many more buffer places to hold characters received after the interrupt. Therefore, the setting is usually user-settable.

Also, a 16-byte *transmit* buffer allows the processor to write many bytes per interrupt (when the UART has transmitted almost all its bytes), so the processor does not need to be interrupted after every character has been sent.

Software (either the communications program, or the operating system) must have software support for the 16550's buffering feature (to enable the buffering), since the 16550 powers up to act like the older 8250. This was the National Semiconductor's INS8250, and was used in the first IBM PCs, making it the de facto standard.

The 16450 was an implementation of an 8250 that could support faster bit rates—the 8250 had a maximum speed of about 56,000 bits/s, and the 16450 could run at 115,200 bits/s. However, both the 8250 and 16450 have only a 1-byte receive and transmit buffer, making them useless for applications requiring both faster bit rates while working under multitasking operating systems (which is what most people want nowadays). Most current communications programs, and Windows 95 and NT have built-in support for the 16550.

The 16552 has 2 16550-type UARTs on a single IC.

PCs have a 1,843,200 Hz clock signal for the UARTs, and this is divided by a hardware counter to lower speeds which are provided to the UARTs. The UARTs then divide this by 16 to generate the bit rate clock—UARTs need the "×16" higher speed clock so they can have better resolution in locating the center of each bit of a character once they receive the leading edge of the start bit. The original PC hardware counter divided the 1,843,200 Hz clock by 12 (resulting in 153,600 Hz) to provide bit rates from 110 to 9,600 bits/s (by dividing that by 87 through 1). Newer communication software can set the hardware divider to 1 (instead of 12), to provide bit rates up to 115,200 bits/s.

The newer 16650 UART (sometimes called a 16C650) has a 4× clock-multiplier circuit to produce bit rates of up to 460,800 bits/s, while still using the standard PC 1,843,200 Hz communications clock signal (with the hardware divider set to 1). The 16650 also has a 32-byte buffer to allow even more characters to be received before the CPU must read them.

The newer-still 16750 UARTs have 64-byte buffers.

See **ESP**, **EIA/TIA232**, **IRQ**, and **UART**.

3172 Interconnect Controller

A communications device first popular in the early 1990s for IBM mainframe computers that provides TCP/IP capability.

A rack-mount PS/2 PC running OS/2 that (with expensive IBM software and a $25,000 Bus-and-Tag or ESCON channel attachment card, for a total cost of about $28,000) provides TCP/IP and APPN connectivity for IBM mainframes (and does not require an FEP).

Supports Ethernet, Token Ring, FDDI, ATM, frame relay, and SDLC connections (for a price).

The 3172 does some TCP/IP and APPN processing in order to reduce the load on the mainframe (so it is sometimes called an "offload host"). Typical prices are $10,000 to $100,000.

The function of the 3172 is now often provided by channel-attached routers (such as Cisco Systems' 7000 series).

See **APPN, CHANNEL, ESCON, FEP, TCP-IP,** and **TN3270.**

3174 AND 3274
3174 Establishment (or Enterprise) Controller
or Network Processor, and 3274

A communications device for IBM mainframe computers that provides connectivity for fixed-function computer terminals.

An IBM *cluster controller* (sometimes called a *communications controller*) that supports up to 32 (a BISYNC limitation) or 253 (an SNA limitation) 3270-series terminals and printers. It is connected to a mainframe (if *channel-attached*) or, more commonly, to an FEP (usually through a 9,600- to 56,000-bits/s SDLC link).

A 3299 can increase the number of terminals and sessions. The 3274 was introduced in 1977. The newer 3174 supports:

▲ Higher-speed SDLC or frame relay links (up to 256 kbits/s) and Token Ring and Ethernet connections to FEPs

▲ Optional channel attachment, so an FEP is not needed to connect to the mainframe (this provides faster response times for the 3174-connected users but results in additional mainframe CPU loading)

See **S3299, CHANNEL, CUT, DFT, FEP, PU 2, PU 4,** and **SDLC.**

3270

The type of fixed-function (sometimes called page-mode or block-mode, since they send a full screen of text when you press the transmit key) computer terminals used with IBM mainframe computers.

A family of IBM terminals and support equipment. The 3278 series was introduced in the late 1970s and supports various sizes of monochrome character displays, as shown in the following table.

3270 Model (horizontal characters × vertical rows)	Display Size
2	80×24
3	80×32
4	80×43
5	132×27

The 3279 series support color and graphics. The 3290's screen can be split into four quarters, and a separate session can be established on each. The 3178 is a more modern terminal. The 3287 is a printer.

Due to the characteristic green phosphor color of the terminals most commonly used, mainframe character-based applications are often called *green screen*—especially when accessed from a terminal emulation window on a UNIX or Windows workstation.

Data communication is at 2.358 Mbits/s through up to 1,525 m of RG-62A/U coaxial cable.

See **S347X**, **CUT**, **DFT**, **LU 2**, **LU 3**, **RJE**, and **TN3270**.

3299

A communications device for an IBM mainframe computer.

A multiplexer that uses one of the coax terminal connections supported by the 3x74, and provides up to eight five-session DFT connections (therefore up to 40 sessions per 3299) on the 3299. This does not enable the 3x74 to support any *more* connections, it simply provides them on the 3299.

See **S3174 AND 3274**.

347x

The type of fixed-function computer terminals used with IBM mainframe computers.

A series of newer 3270 terminals. For example, the 3471-1 model 2 is 80 columns, and the 3472-4 model 5 supports 132 columns of text.

See **S3270**.

37x5

See **FEP**.

3780

See **RJE**.

3COM
Computers, Communications, and Compatibility

A big company that makes Ethernet and other data communications hardware.

The company co-founded by Ethernet inventor Robert M. Metcalfe (in 1979, after he left Xerox Corp.'s Palo Alto Research Center—PARC, and later DEC), to commercialize Ethernet. He left 3Com in 1990 after a disagreement over whether 3Com should emphasize LAN software (it had been reselling Microsoft's and IBM's LAN Manager, as 3+Open)—which he wanted to continue, or network infrastructure (LAN adapters and concentrators, and so on)—which was favored by his successor, Eric Benhamou.

The company operates a WWW server at *http://www.3com.com/*.

See **ETHERNET**.

486DX

Intel's PC central processing unit that was popular between about 1990 and 1994.

A standard 168-pinned 486 with a built-in math coprocessor. Includes an 8-kbyte unified Level 1 cache (instructions and data share the same cache). Since this relatively small cache results in a low *hit rate* (the percentage of times that the required instructions or data are in the cache), an external (Level 2) cache is usually included in motherboard designs. These will usually be 64 to 512 kbytes in size.

These processors can often be replaced by an OverDrive (clock-doubled DX2) or Pentium processor to provide faster CPU operations.

See **CACHE**, **DX4**, **INTEL**, **OVERDRIVE**, and **PC**.

486DX2

Intel's PC central processing unit that was popular between about 1991 and 1995.

A clock-doubled 486 that runs internally at twice the speed at which it runs externally. For example, a 486DX2-66-based system would have a motherboard that runs at 33 MHz, and internal CPU operations (math and instructions running out of the internal 8 kbyte Level 1 cache) would run at 66 MHz.

A 238-pin upgrade socket usually built into these PCs will accept a 32-bit bus version of the Pentium CPU (called the P24T).

See **INTEL**, **OVERDRIVE**, **PC**, and **PENTIUM**.

486DX4

See **DX4**.

486SX

Intel's PC central processing unit that was popular between about 1990 and 1993.

For Intel 486 CPUs, the *SX* suffix means that it does not have a built-in math coprocessor (or that it is disabled, as it was found to be defective after manufacture). Computers based on the 486SX therefore can cost less, with little user impact, since most software seldom uses the floating-point math operations that math coprocessors handle.

Has a 32-bit internal and external data bus and an 8-kbyte cache, just as the 486DX does. These systems usually have a socket that can accept a 487SX math coprocessor to upgrade the system to hardware math capability (rather than having the main CPU perform the math in software, a process that is much slower).

An OverDrive chip can usually be installed into the 487SX socket to provide faster main CPU operations (this disables the original 486SX).

See **INTEL** and **PC**.

486SX2

Intel's PC central processing unit that was popular between about 1991 and 1994.

A clock-doubled 486SX. For example, it runs at 25 MHz externally and 50 MHz internally.

See **INTEL** and **PC**.

5250

The type of fixed-function computer terminal used with IBM's AS/400 minicomputers.

A polled, page-mode terminal. Up to seven terminals can be daisy-chained (or connected by using a T-connector) on up to 1,500 m of twin-ax cable (which is like coax, but has a 110 Ω; twisted pair in the center). The terminals communicate at 1 Mbits/s. The cable is directly connected to either an AS/400, or to a 5394 workstation controller, which is then connected to the AS/400 through a WAN link at up to 64 kbits/s.

See **LU 7** and **PU 2.1**.

56k Modem
56 KBIT/S MODEM

A "modem" technology that sends data (from your PC to the network) using V.34+ (up to 33.6 kbits/s), but can receive data at up to 56,000 bits/s (using a method based on direct PCM encoding that is not analog modulation/demodulation, so is not really being a modem in that direction).

Two, so far non-standardized, methods to receive the data have been proposed, as listed below:

▲ US Robotics' (now owned by 3Com Corporation) method is called x2.

▲ Lucent Technologies and Rockwell Semiconductor Systems Inc. have proposed a method called *K*56Flex. This is supported by Ascend Communications, Ind. and Cisco Systems, Inc.

Since the method used must be compatible with that used at wherever you are dialing in to (such as your Internet Service Provider), there is a need for one method to be standardized. Modem manufacturers hope that by using *flash memory* and *digital signal processing* in the modem, they will be able to sell modems now, and update the modulation method in the future.

In addition to the need for a single standard, other problems include the following:

▲ Due to EMI and maximum signal strength regulations, the maximum actual data rate is limited to about 53.3 kbits/s.

▲ Robbed-bit signalling on the digital T1 circuits further reduces the bit rate that can be carried to a theoretical maximum of 50.8 kbits/s. And typical analog telephone line quality further reduces the bit rate. The end result is that initial devices have a typical maximum throughput of 40 to 45 kbits/s. (As for any recent modem, data compression increases this throughput for compressible data.)

▲ Also, company (and hotel) PBXs typically prevent the PCM encoding method from working, so your 56k Modem acts as a standard 33.6 kbit/s modem (in both directions) when calling through a PBX. One way of explaining this is that the additional analog to digital conversions add noise to the signal, reducing its information carrying capacity.

At the central site, a digitally-connected (using ISDN or channelized T1) dial-in router (or RAS) accepts the calls from the 56k Modems. That is, you don't get the benefit of the 56 kbit/s if the remote user dials into another 56 kbit/s Modem connected to an analog telephone line at the central location. The central location must be digitally connected to the network so that there is only one digital to analog conversion of the data sent from the central site to the remote user with the 56 kbit/s Modem, and this is at the central office nearest the remote modem user. Also, since an ISDN PRI or T1 is used at the central site (which has a capacity for 23 or 24 simultaneous incoming calls), it is only cost-effective to use 56 kbit/s Modems in larger installations.

US Robotics and Rockwell have web sites at *http://www.usr.com* and *http://www.nb.rockwell.com*. A procedure for testing whether your current phone line will support a 56K modem is at *http://x2.usr.com/linetest1.html*. The Open 56K Forum has a web site at *http://www.open56k.org*. Just to keep things confusing, you can also check *http://www.56k.com* and *http://www.k56.org*.

See **DSP**, **EMI**, **FLASH**, **MODEM**, and **PBX**.

800

The dialing prefix that provides usually toll-free (that is, toll-free to the caller; the callee pays the long-distance charge) long-distance service. A long time ago, this service was called *Wide Area Telephone Service* (WATS). Much of the world outside of North America calls the service *FreePhone*.

Approximately 40% (in 1996) of all U.S. long-distance voice calls are 800 calls, and the service has become so popular that all 7.71 million available 800 numbers were exhausted by April 1996 (and AT&T's 800 call revenue exceeded its regular long-distance for the first time in 1996). Of the reserved expansion codes, it was felt that the 888 code sounded the nicest, so new 800 numbers are actually 888 numbers. The 877 code will begin to be assigned in April 1998, as all numbers in the 888 codes are expected to be assigned by then. After that the 866, 855, 844, 833 and 822 codes will be assigned (in that order).

The *Industry Numbering Committee* has allocated the 880 and 881 area codes for calls from Canada and the Caribbean to U.S. destinations when the call recipients only want to pay for the U.S. portion of the long distance call. The caller pays the remainder (a pre-recorded message before the call is completed alerts caller to this charge). Calls to 1 880 numbers go to the corresponding 1 800 number, and calls to 1 881 numbers go to the corresponding 1 888 number.

800 numbers for the U.S. and Canada are administered by Database Service Management Inc., who provide numbers to carriers. They follow rules, for example; how long a discontinued number must remain inactive before being reassigned, and how many numbers a carrier can reserve, awaiting assignment to new customers.

The international version of 800 service is called international freephone service (IFS), and the international "800 number" is called a universal international freephone number (UIFN).

To search for an AT&T "1 800" number (complete with links to company's home pages), try AT&T's WWW server at *http://www.tollfree.att.net/dir800/*.

See **DN**, **DTMF2**, **POTS**, and **UIFN**.

802.1h

IEEE's standard for *translational bridging*, which is used to convert (for example) Ethernet frames to FDDI frames. Among other things, the conversion requires changing the packet headers and trailers.

See **ETHERNET** and **FDDI**.

802.1p

See **COS2** (*Class of Service*).

802.2

A format used for the frames of data sent on Ethernet, Token Ring, and other types of local area networks.

The LAN frame format standardized by the IEEE and used for OSI, NetWare 4.0, and LLC2. Other common frame formats are SNAP and Ethernet II.

See **S802.3**.

802.3

More commonly called Ethernet. The most popular type of local area network. However, Ethernet is a misnomer, since Ethernet was the name of the predecessor, which has minor but important differences.

It uses *Carrier Sense* (before transmitting, stations ensure that no other stations are already transmitting) and *Multiple Access* (any station can transmit) with *Collision Detection* (by detecting collisions, stations detect when the LAN is getting heavily loaded and adjust their transmitting algorithm). Hence 802.3's access method is often abbreviated CSMA/CD.

Several frame formats are used, as shown in the following table.

Frame Format	Used by	Comments
802.2	NetWare 3.12 NetWare 4.*x* IBM's LLC2	DSAP field identifies the upper-layer protocol.
802.3	NetWare 3.11 and earlier	Uses the checksum field of the IPX (network layer) header to identify the upper-layer protocol.
Ethernet II	Apple's EtherTalk Phase 1 DEC's DECnet DEC's LAT Older TCP/IP	Original frame format used on Ethernet. Type field identifies the upper-layer protocol.
SNAP	Apple's EtherTalk Phase 2 Newer TCP/IP	5-byte overhead used to identify the protocol.

Although an Ethernet segment (concentrator) can carry any number of frame formats simultaneously, each pair of communicating stations must use the same frame format.

See **S802.2**, **S802.3x**, **CSMACD**, **ETHERNET**, **ETHERNET II**, **LAN**, **MAC**, **PACE**, and **SNAP**.

802.3x

The IEEE standard for full-duplex and flow-control support for Ethernet LANs such as Gigabit Ethernet.

IEEE 802.3x was ratified in March 1997.

See **S802.3**, **ETHERNET**, and **GIGABIT ETHERNET**.

802.5

See **TOKEN RING**.

802.6

See **MAN**.

802.9a

An enhancement to Ethernet to support multimedia traffic.

An effort first proposed (in 1992) by Apple, IBM, and National Semiconductor for a 16.208-Mbits/s LAN that supports multimedia (a total of 16.144 Mbits/s is used for data and multimedia traffic, and an additional 64 kbits/s for ISDN D-channel type signalling). Video conferencing and CTI are expected to be the main applications. The bandwidth is allocated as follows.

▲ 10 Mbits/s is reserved for standard Ethernet asynchronous data. This is called an ISDN P channel.

▲ 6.144 Mbytes/s is divided into 96 64-kbits/s, full-duplex, circuit-switched, isochronous channels to be used for the multimedia traffic (or standard voice telephone calls). Stations can aggregate (using *inverse multiplexing*) multiple 64 kbit/s channels as required for their application. Instead of Ethernet traffic, the 10 Mbit/s P channel can also be used for isochronous traffic, providing a total of 248 64 kbit/s isochronous channels per iso-Ethernet concentrator.

▲ 64 kbits/s is reserved for D-channel signalling to set-up and clear the 64 kbit/s multimedia connections (using standard ISDN Q.931 protocols).

Users basically get a combination of 10BASE-T Ethernet and ISDN BRI all in one LAN adapter and cable connection.

The 64-kbits/s channels are intended to be connected to, and synchronized with, the clock speed of ISDN B-and D-channels. The 96 64 kbit/s channels plus the one 64 kbit/s signalling channel are called an ISDN C channel).

Iso-Ethernet requires new concentrators (hubs), which typically have a T1 or ISDN PRI (which supports TAPI) for connection to the outside world. While iso-Ethernet supports standard Ethernet traffic (and iso-Ethernet concentrators support standard 10BASE-T LAN adapters), to get the neato new iso-Ethernet features, stations must have new iso-Ethernet LAN adapters.

Autonegotiation (as is used for 100BASE-T to determine whether full-duplex is supported) automatically determines whether standard 10BASE-T, 10BASE-T plus isochronous, or all isochronous is being used. Each port of a concentrator supports all three modes, so the user LAN adapters determine the mode used for their connections.

Since typical video conferencing systems require two to six 64-kbits/s channels per connection, 802.9a will support 16 to 48 simultaneous multimedia connections in addition to the 10 Mbits/s traditional Ethernet.

While iso-Ethernet has a higher data rate than standard 10 Mbits/s Ethernet, iso-Ethernet uses a more efficient bit encoding scheme, so Category 3 cabling can still be used (two pairs are required, one for transmit, the other for receive—powering ISDN devices through the network is not widely supported yet). The encoding scheme is FDDI's 4B/5B scheme, where 4 data bits are encoded into 5 symbols. In contrast, 10BASE-T uses Manchester encoding, which has 1 data bit encoded into two symbols.

Officially called *Isochronous Ethernet Integrated Services*, but also called *iso-Ethernet*, and *isoEnet*. Standardized by the IEEE in late 1995, but probably a dead technology now that people want data rates faster than 10 Mbits/s.

Promoted by the Isochronous Networking Communication Alliance, which includes Ascom Nexion Inc., AT&T, L.M. Ericsson Business Networks AB, IBM, Incite, Luxcom, National Semiconductor Corp., and Siemens.

See **S100BASET**, **CTI**, **ENCODING**, **INVERSE MULTIPLEXER**, **ISDN**, **ISOCHRONOUS**, **MULTIMEDIA**, and **TAPI**.

802.10

An enhancement to Ethernet that addresses some security concerns.

Addresses *secure data exchange* on LANs as well as virtual LANs. End-stations negotiate encryption and authentication parameters at Layer 2 (the MAC layer).

Bridges and/or Ethernet adapters add and check a 16- to 20-byte header added to each frame (between the MAC header and the payload data) that identifies which virtual LAN is to receive the frame (this is also called *colorizing* the frame). A 32-bit *group identifier* (or VLAN ID) in the header ensures that frames are seen only by members of the same group.

The specification also describes segmentation and reassembly of frames (to facilitate carrying frames over networks that have different maximum frame sizes).

See **AUTHENTICATION**, **ENCRYPTION**, and **VLAN**.

802.11 Wireless LAN Standard

The IEEE standard for wireless LANs operating in the 2.4000 to 2.4835-GHz ISM frequency band (plus other optional frequency bands, and infrared too).

Some features of the standard are:

▲ Both frequency-hopping and direct-sequence spread spectrum radio frequency (RF) transmission, and infrared light transmission (using *pulse-position modulation*—PPM) are "media" options. This is the physical layer (PHY) part of the standard.

▲ The CSMA/CA access method is used (and a single frame format is specified), for both Ethernet and Token Ring traffic. The access point (device that connects a LAN to an

802.11 wireless network) converts between the LAN used and 802.11's access method and frame format. This is the link layer (*media access control—MAC*) part of the standard.

▲ Since CSMA/CA is somewhat similar to CSMA/CD, 802.11 is sometimes called *wireless Ethernet.*

▲ The actual bit-rate can be either 1 Mbit/s or 2 Mbits/s (either set by the user, or selected by the equipment according to what conditions permit—the lower speed will have greater range, and fewer retransmissions in noisy environments). Actual user data throughput will be lower due to protocol overhead, retransmissions, network latency and other factors. A raw bit-rate of 2 Mbit/s will typically result in a user data throughput of 0.5 Mbit/s to 1 Mbit/s for short messages, and 1 Mbit/s to 1.5 Mbit/s for long messages.

▲ Encryption called the *Wired Equivalent Privacy* (WEP) algorithm. This is handled by the adapter card, not software in the PC. The method based on work licensed from RSA Data Security Inc.

▲ Range (for RF) in a typical office environment is expected to be 60 m to 100 m, but is very dependent on the building materials (for example, open office partitions versus steel reinforced concrete walls).

▲ *Power management* support, where access points store frames destined for computers which are in a temporary power-down mode. The access points periodically broadcast a message indicating the addresses of computers for which they have stored frames, and transmit the frames once the computers become available.

▲ The maximum transmit power level is 1 watt (which is the same as saying 30 dBm, since "dBm" is decibels relative to 1 mW, and 30 dBm is a factor of 10^3 greater than this). This is an FCC restriction. Receivers must be sensitive enough to receive signals as "quiet" as –80 dBm. Receivers with more than one antenna provide better reception.

▲ After a station reserves the channel and transmits the message, it expects an immediate acknowledgment. If this is not received, the message is retransmitted.

While infrared transmission (which typically costs more, and has less range than RF) and trunking applications (such as connecting two buildings as a point-to-point connection) are supported, it is expected that 802.11 will be most widely implemented for connecting to multiple end-user devices, such as PDAs and portable PCs (this is called *access*), using RF.

So far, the standard does not support *roaming* (the ability to move from the range of one access point to another, without interrupting data transmission)—so Lucent Technologies and some other vendors have produced the *Interoperability Access Point Protocol* (IAPP), to handle roaming.

802.11 will likely include both hub-based and peer-to-peer capability. The physical layer options will likely include direct-sequence spread-spectrum, frequency-hopping spread-spectrum, narrowband microwave, and diffuse infrared transmission.

The frequency-hopping option will support 22 channels (each of which can support a network of users).

While 802.11 would have provided the most compatibility if only one type of RF transmission was supported, vendors who had products of each type insisted that their type be in the standard, so the only way to get the standard developed was to include both types of

transmission. So rather than having no standard for wireless LANs, there are now two (which provides greater user choice, at the expense of incompatibilities).

Lucent Technologies has a web site on their 802.11 wireless products at *http:// www.wavelan.com*.

See **CSMACA**, **ISM**, **PCCA**, **PDA**, **RSA**, **SST**, **SWATS**, and **WIRELESS**.

802.12

See **S100VG ANYLAN**.

802.14

The IEEE group working on a standard for cable TV–based data communications. *Cable modems* are used to connect between the user equipment (which may use an Ethernet interface) and the CATV network. Using *radio frequency* RF for carrying data (regardless of the actual bit rates) used to be called *broadband*, but broadband is now usually used to indicate really high speed data communications, as in "Broadband ISDN".

Cable modem bit-rates are usually between 500 kbits/s and 30 Mbits/s, but this is typically shared among many users.

See **B-ISDN**, and **CATV**.

80386DX

Intel's PC central processing unit that was popular from 1987 to 1993.

A standard 80386. Has a 32-bit data bus and a 32-bit address bus.

See **INTEL** and **PC**.

80386SX

Intel's PC central processing unit that was popular from 1987 to 1992.

For Intel 80386 CPUs (which are 32-bit internally, allowing up to 4 Gbytes of virtual memory), the *SX* suffix means that it has a 16-bit data bus (which provides slower memory and peripheral access than a 32-bit bus would) and a 24-bit address bus (limiting physical memory to 16 Mbytes). Computers based on the 80386SX, therefore, can cost less while providing full 80386 software compatibility.

See **INTEL** and **PC**.

80486DX4

See **DX4**, **INTEL**, and **PC**.

80487SX

The math coprocessor that can be added to a 486SX-based system to provide hardware math capability (such as faster multiplication and division).

See **S486SX**, **INTEL**, and **PC**.

8514/a

IBM's high-resolution graphics (1,024 × 768, interlaced) standard for PCs. Faster than VGA but no longer used.

See **VGA** and **XGA**.

88open

A failed effort by Motorola to get its 88000 RISC processor accepted. Realizing that a single company could not compete with Intel in a getting a new processor designed and accepted, Motorola then worked with Apple and IBM on the PowerPC instead.

See **MOTOROLA**, **POWERPC**, and **RISC**.

8B/10B

A data encoding and transmission scheme patented by IBM and used for its ESCON data links (which connect IBM's mainframe computers to frontend processors).

Eight data bits are sent in 10 bits to provide the following:

▲ Error detection (called *disparity control*).

▲ Frame delimiting with data transparency (that is, you can send any bit pattern and still have a way to mark the beginning and end of a frame).

▲ Clock recovery: signal transitions assist the receiver in finding the center of each bit, even if many contiguous ones (or zeros) are sent and the sender has a slightly different transmission rate. The encoding scheme used is called RLE(0,4), which denotes *run length encoding* with a minimum run length (contiguous sequence of all 1s or all 0s) of 1 bit, and a maximum of 5 (there will be no more than 5 sequential 0 bits or 5 sequential 1 bits).

▲ DC voltage balance (on average, the signal spends an equal time positive and negative; this is required if the signal is to be coupled through a transformer), to eliminate transformer core saturation.

Also used for fibre channel (and therefore Gigabit Ethernet), SSA and some ATM implementations (manufacturers license the technology from IBM).

See **ATM** (*Asynchronous Transfer Mode*), **ENCODING**, **ESCON**, **FEP**, **FIBRE CHANNEL**, **GIGABIT ETHERNET**, **MAINFRAME**, and **SSA**.

A

A/UX

Apple's UNIX-like operating system implementation.

Instead of this, most Apple Macintosh computers run Apple's Macintosh operating system (Mac OS), such as System 6.*x* or 7.*x*.

See **APPLE** and **UNIX**.

ACAP
Application Configuration Access Protocol

A protocol to be used between an e-mail client (such as that you run on your PC) and an e-mail post office (such as that at your ISP or at your company). It builds on the capabilities of IMAP4 to provide additional features such as shared address book, calendaring and scheduling data. Also, simultaneous administration of multiple post offices is supported.

See **IMAP**, **ISP**, and **SMTP**.

ACCESS.bus

A lower-speed (than a LAN) limited-distance data communications method. The intent is to replace the PC's limited number of ports and specialized nature of those ports with a general-purpose, single port that can support many peripherals simultaneously.

A daisy-chain method of connecting low-speed I/O devices (such as mice, trackballs, modems, bar-code readers, printers, and a keyboard) to a computer. Used by VESA's DDC standard.

Up to 125 devices (seven-bit device addresses, minus the host and broadcast address) over a total cable length of 8 m is supported. Uses two-pair (ground/+5 volt power on one pair and clock and data on the other pair), stranded, shielded cable and modular jack–like connectors (they have locking tabs on each side of the connector).

To support the daisy-chaining, devices may have two connectors or may use a T-connector.

Data rates of up to 100 kbits/s are specified (in version 2.2 of the standard, though, the technology could support 400 kbits/s), and each device can use a different data rate.

All communication is either to or from the host computer (and not directly between two peripherals). Messages are from zero to 127 bytes in length plus the:

▲ Leading destination address byte

▲ Source address byte

▲ Length byte (the most significant bit of the length byte is 1 to indicate *control* and 0 to indicate *data* messages)

▲ Trailing bitwise `exclusive-or` checksum byte

Hot plugging (new devices can be connected while the computer is operating) is supported, as well as *auto-addressing* (devices are automatically assigned unique addresses). A new adapter card would be required for existing PCs.

Six host-computer-to-device control messages have been defined:

▲ `Reset`: to device's power-on state and default ACCESS.bus address

▲ `Identification request`: query device for its identification string

▲ `Assign address`: assign device with specified identification string to specified ACCESS.bus address

▲ `Capabilities request`: query device for the section of its capabilities response string, starting at the specified offset

▲ `Enable application report`: Enable or disable device to send application reports to the host computer

▲ `Presence check`: check whether a device is present at the specified ACCESS.bus address

Three device-to-host-computer control messages have been defined:

▲ `Attention`: informs host computer that device has completed its power-on reset and needs to be configured

▲ `Identification reply`: contains the device's unique identification string (which has information such as keyboard character set or mouse resolution)

▲ `Capabilities reply`: contains the section of the device's capabilities response, starting at the specified offset

The capabilities string is ASCII information based on keywords that are part of either the *base protocol* (apply to all types of devices) or the *application protocol* (apply to devices only of that type, such as keyboard, locator, or text).

Software drivers are required to provide the interface between application programs and the ACCESS.bus communications hardware in a PC.

Based on the Inter-Integrated Circuit (I^2C) serial bus developed by Philips Semiconductors and Signetics and supported by DEC.

Initially defined and developed by DEC. The ACCESS.bus Industry Group (ABIG) is currently promoting the effort. It now seems that ACCESS.bus is too slow, and USB will be more popular (even ACCESS.bus developers Philips and DEC support USB).

See **S1394, ASCII, CHECKSUM, DISPLAY DATA CHANNEL, SERIAL BUS, SYSTEM MANAGEMENT BUS, UNIVERSAL SERIAL BUS**, and **VIDEO ELECTRONICS STANDARDS ASSOCIATION**.

ACE
Advanced Computing Environment

A proposed standard platform effort, initially intended to compete with Intel. The group fell apart when Compaq withdrew its support and other things such as the PowerPC happened. The platform was to support OSF's UNIX, SCO's ODT, and Microsoft's Windows NT.

Initially backed by a consortium including DEC, Compaq, Microsoft, Silicon Graphics, and SCO. Initially required either the MIPS RISC (initially the R3000) or later the Intel 80386SX (or later) processor. This loss of potential market resulted in significant financial difficulties for MIPS, so Silicon Graphics (which depends on the MIPS processors) had to buy MIPS.

See **CHRP, DEC, MIPS TECHNOLOGIES INC., OSF, POWERPC, PREP, SANTA CRUZ OPERATION, INC.,** and **UNIPLEXED INFORMATION AND COMPUTING SYSTEM.**

Acrobat

A method of exchanging documents so that they still look nice; that is, they maintain their font sizes and character attributes, such as underlining, bolding, and spacing.

Adobe System Inc.'s technology to support transportable documents (called *portable document files*, which are 7-bit ASCII) that maintain their appearance and character spacing even if the destination machine does not have the required font built in.

The document (generated with Adobe's *Exchange* utility, which appears as a printer driver, or from any PostScript file, using Adobe's *Distiller* utility) includes descriptions of its fonts to enable Adobe's *Multiple Master* fonts to be used to approximate the required font.

Using Adobe's *Reader* (its file viewer program) provides display-only capability, though the text can be exported to a word processor (losing the font information).

Is a subset of PostScript, and was formerly called Carousel.

More information is available at *http://www.adobe.com*.

See **ADOBE, AMERICAN STANDARD, ATM1** (*Adobe Type Manager*), **MULTIPLE MASTER, POSTSCRIPT PAGE DESCRIPTION LANGUAGE, POSTSCRIPT TYPE 1 FONTS,** and **POSTSCRIPT TYPE 3 FONTS.**

Adaptation Layer

Software that provides and matches services between two communications protocol layers in a protocol suite.

In ATM, the ATM adaption layer (AAL) is a communications protocol layer that provides services such as the following:

▲ Takes the packet of data, as provided by the user equipment, and appends a 48-byte *convergence trailer*, which includes a 2-byte packet length field and a 32-bit CRC, for the entire packet.

▲ Chops the AAL 5 *protocol data unit* (PDU) into 48-byte *service data units* (SDUs). This is called segmentation—and at the other end, it is undone by reassembly. So this process is called *segmentation and reassembly* (SAR). The convergence trailer goes into the last cell of the packet, and a bit in the cell header is set, designating the cell as SDU-type=1 (all other cells of the packet are SDU-type=0).

▲ Adds a 5-byte cell header to each SDU, which indicates the virtual circuit identifier.

▲ Sends the cells into the ATM network.

Depending on the AAL, other functions may also be performed, such as adding sequence numbers or other information for multiplexing and error control.

See **ATM** (*Asynchronous Transfer Mode*), and **CRC**.

ADB
Apple Desktop Bus

The bus used by Apple Macintosh computers for the connection of the keyboard and mouse to the computer. Up to 16 devices can be on the bus, communicating at up to 90 kbits/s.

A great low-end serial bus, but too limited for future higher-speed applications.

See **S1394**, **GEOPORT**, and **SERIAL BUS**.

Adobe

A company that developed a very successful page description language and designs nice fonts.

The company is named after the Adobe River, which is near where the company was founded (in California, where else?).

Adobe has a WWW server at *http://www.adobe.com/*.

See **ATM1** (*Adobe Type Manager*), **POSTSCRIPT PAGE DESCRIPTION LANGUAGE**, **POSTSCRIPT TYPE 1 FONTS**, and **POSTSCRIPT TYPE 3 FONTS**.

ADPCM
Adaptive Differential Pulse Code Modulation

A method of digitizing speech; that is, turning the analog signal (which can have any amplitude and frequency, within a range) into a series of binary ones and zeros.

Standard PCM represents each instantaneous voltage sample as an absolute 8-bit value specifying the amplitude. *Differential PCM* specifies the difference from the previous sample—which requires fewer bits. *Adaptive differential PCM* dynamically adjusts the step size (the difference in amplitude represented by the bits) of the bits to more accurately represent very loud or very quiet signals—providing a further reduction in the number of bits required to represent a signal.

Generally, for voice signals, ADPCM at 32,000 bits/s (such as G.721) provides the same quality signal as 64,000 bit/s PCM (such as G.711).

While the use of PCM is imperceptible to humans, it cannot carry higher-speed modem and fax transmissions. Therefore, modem traffic should not be digitized using ADPCM.

See **FAX**, **G.711**, **G.721**, **G.722**, **G.726**, **MODEM**, and **PCM**.

ADSL
Asymmetric Digital Subscriber Line

A method of sending high-speed data (fast enough to carry digitized movies, for example) over the existing pair of wires from a telephone company's central office to most residences.

A line-encoding scheme (that uses both *carrier amplitude* and *carrier phase* modulation—called *CAP*) that provides the following:

▲ A *downstream channel*. This is a high-speed, one-way (from the network to your house) data channel at 1, 2, 3 or 4 times 1.536 Mbits/s (the maximum speed depends on the cable length to the CO, and the wire diameter). 1.536 Mbit/s is the speed required to carry the data for 24 timeslots at 64 kbits/s each. And it is the speed of a full T1, minus the framing bit overhead that users don't get to use anyway. This is enough for MPEG-compressed full-motion, full-color movies, or really fast downloads from the Internet. In Europe, this channel would carry 1 or 2 E1 circuits, at 2.048 Mbits/s each.

▲ The *duplex*, or *upstream channel* provides full-duplex transmission at 16 kbits/s or (optionally) 64 kbits/s. In addition, another full-duplex channel may be supported that runs at one of the following speeds: 160 (the ISDN U interface speed), 384 (6 B channels, and good for video conferencing), 544 (both a U interface and video conference speeds) or 576 kbits/s. These channels can be subdivided in many ways to provide several simultaneous services (Internet access, leased-line data links, utility meter reading, burglar alarm monitoring, and so on).

▲ Filters will be used so that the lower 4 kHz is available for standard POTS (voice, group 3 Fax, and so on) even if the ADSL part fails.

Most users (clients) download (digitized movies, surfing the Internet, and so on) more than they upload (that is, they receive more than they send—despite the sage advice that it is better to give than to receive). Therefore, sinc it is more fun if you can receive faster (even at the expense of sending slower), the technology is optimized to provide faster download than upload speeds—hence the "asymmetric" in the name.

ADSL was designed to run over a single twisted copper pair (ideally, the one that already exists between your home and the central office). The table below shows the maximum bit rates and distances of cable (between the central office and your house) that can be supported for the downstream channel (assuming a straight run of cable, with no *bridge taps*—where a second cable is connected somewhere in the middle of the first):

Downstream Speed (Mbits/s)	Wire Diameter		Maximum Cable Distance	
	AWG	mm	km	Miles
1.536 or 2.048	24	0.5	5.5	18,000
	26	0.4	4.6	15,000
6.144	24	0.5	3.7	12,000
	26	0.4	2.7	9,000

An important use is expected to be providing digital, compressed video (to replace cable TV) and standard two-way telephone service on the existing telephone drop to a house. Other uses will be for LAN connection.

ADSL modems will be able to perform some error correction, but this adds about a 20 ms delay to transmitted data. Since LAN protocols typically have their own error correction, and may not be able to tolerate the added 20 ms delay, the ADSL modem error correction can be turned off.

ADSL has been very slow in being implemented because the ADSL modems have been too expensive, and there has been no widespread agreement on which implementation of ADSL to adopt. One version is standardized as ANSI T1E1.413. It uses *discrete multitone* (DMT) modulation, and divides 1.1 MHz of spectrum into 256 4-kHz channels, and runs each channel at whatever bit-rate the quality of the line supports at that frequency. This produces about a 6 Mbit/s downstream channel, and up to 640 kbit/s upstream). One technical reason for the speed asymmetry is that signals from a CO to a customer site are all the same amplitude (and decrease in amplitude with increasing cable distance from the CO equally), so the cross-talk between them is not too great. However, customers are varying distances from the CO, and they all transmit at the same signal strength. When these signals are combined into larger cable bundles, signals from more distant customers will be much quieter than signals from customers closer to the CO, so the distant customers will receive much more cross-talk (relative to their signal's strength). Lowering the bit-rate from customers towards the CO is one way to mitigate this (also, the upstream channels use lower frequencies than the downstream channels, since lower frequencies have less cross-talk). As an aside, in cellular telephone networks, handsets closer to base station cell sites transmit at a lower power (through commands sent to them from the base stations) to both reduce the interference with other more distant handsets, and to extend the handset's battery life.

Another modulation method (*carrierless amplitude phase*—CAP) may be added to that standard, as it is more widely installed (largely because it is much less expensive to implement). Also, provision for more than one device at the customer premises may be added.

Both the DMT and CAP methods (which are forms of quadrature amplitude modulation—QAM) are patented, and manufacturers must pay royalties. A different QAM method (which is in the public domain, and does not require the payment of royalties to anyone) called QAM, has also been proposed.

Since cable modems have been slow to becoming available (that is, providing digital service using your cable TV coaxial cable), there has been little reason for telephone companies to invest in ADSL implementations (so they just talk about it instead).

AT&T's version of ADSL-type technology is called *Rate Adaptive Digital Subscriber Line* (RADSL). It also uses a single copper pair, and provides a 600 kbits/s to 7 Mbit/s downstream and 128 kbit/s to 1 Mbit/s upstream data rate. As the name suggests, the speeds depend on the length (3.6 to 5.5 km, which is 12,000 to 18,000 feet) and quality of the specific copper pair to the CO.

HDSL provides a similar (but symmetric) capability.

All the DSL technologies are point-to-point—that is, you are at one end, and the other end is at your telephone company's central office. It is not itself a switched service, though the

Advantage Networks

DSL circuit can provide high-speed access to a switched service, such as an ISP that could connect you to anywhere on the Internet.

The term ADSL was first used by Bellcore in 1989. The ADSL Forum was formed in 1994, and has a WWW server at *http://www.adsl.com*. The DMT technology was developed by Amati Communications Corporation, who are at *http://www.amati.com*. Some information on DSL technologies in general is at *http://www.telechoice.com/xdslnewz*.

See **BELLCORE**, **CATV**, **C.O.**, **E1**, **HDSL**, **MPEG**, **MULTIMEDIA**, **POTS**, **T1**, and **VIDEO**.

Advantage Networks

The marketing name for DEC's protocol software.

DEC's newer name for what it used to call DECnet Phase V, since in addition to being DECnet and OSI, it supports DECnet Phase IV, Pathworks (DEC's customization of Microsoft's LAN Manager), TCP/IP, IPX, and SNA. Runs over FDDI in addition to Ethernet.

See **DEC** and **NAS**.

AFP
AppleTalk Filing Protocol

Apple Computer's AppleTalk LAN protocol for sharing files.

See **APPLE**.

AGP
Accelerated Graphics Port

Intel's specification and implementation of method to directly transfer graphics data from system DRAM (that is, your 64 Mbytes, or whatever, of memory) to a graphics adapter (sometimes called a graphics accelerator or video adapter), without using the PCI bus (which is already loaded enough with disk drive and LAN traffic). As shown in the following figure, AGP is an additional port on the system chip set (which is required for all processors).

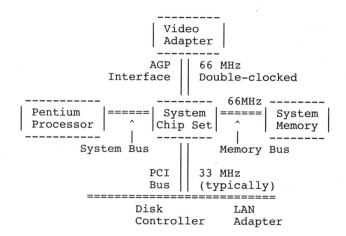

It is intended to provide faster support for 3-dimensional graphics and full-motion video. Some features and advantages are:

▲ It is a point-to-point connection (that is, not a bus, so only one graphics adapter can be supported per AGP port) based on a 66.6 MHz PCI revision 2.1 bus, with a 32-bit data bus. By transferring data on both the rising and falling edge of the bus clock (sometimes called *double-clocking* or "2x"), the data transfer rate is up to 533 Mbytes/s (133.2 MHz bus operation, and 4-byte transfers).

▲ Transformations (such as image scaling or rotating) can be carried out in system memory, under the control of the graphics adapter. Since AGP is a bus master, this can be done with no involvement of the main system CPU.

▲ Since the PCs main PCI bus is not used, this reduces the loading on that bus, freeing capacity for other transfer functions, such as reading your disk drive.

▲ System DRAM (rather than separate DRAM on the video adapter) is used for graphics data (such as textures that are too big, or too infrequently used to be stored in the main *frame buffer* memory (that actually stores the image being displayed)—which is often 4 Mbytes—on the graphics adapter board itself). This shared approach provides more efficient use of memory (not all AGP implementations allow the video adapter to directly access system DRAM).

▲ An additional unidirectional (graphics adapter to system DRAM) 8-bit bus provides *side band signalling* (or *sideband addressing*—SBA) to indicate whether transferred information is address or data.

In addition to the hardware support required (an AGP video adapter and motherboard), the operating system and video adapter driver software must provide support—and the application program must utilize the new AGP capabilities (such as 3-dimensional texture mapping)—to get the performance benefits of AGP.

AGP enables lower-cost (typically only 4 Mbytes of RAM are needed on the video adapter) higher-performance graphics processing (such as texture rendering). But for really high-performance (at greater cost), having more memory (such as 16 Mbytes) on the graphics adapter, and doing all texture rendering locally on the graphics adapter is fastest (basically, why go to system memory when you can do it all on-board).

Intel first announced AGP in the spring of 1996, and the first implementation of it was part of the Pentium II's Slot 1 interface, and became available in late 1997.

The specification is available at *http://www.teleport.com/~agfxport/*.

See **PCI**, **PENTIUM II**, and **USDA**.

Airplane Magazine Syndrome

Things that happen because an executive (who usually doesn't read such dangerous literature) reads an article about the "latest technology", in a magazine he got on an airplane. Expecting that he just learned a big secret that he must act on instantly, he changes the course of mighty projects to ensure he does not get bulldozed by his competition (who probably already are working on the new stuff).

Projects then get changed without due consideration of the technology, time gets wasted, and generally, all the technical people (who knew full well about the new technology, but were ignoring it because it was not ready for prime time) get upset.

See (*Everything in this book*).

AIX
Advanced Interactive Executive

IBM's UNIX-like operating system, which runs on IBM's RISC System/6000 (RS/6000) workstations. The first version was based on UNIX System V Release 2 (current versions on SVR3.2).

AIX/ESA is a version for IBM's System/370 and System/390 mainframe computers and is based on OSF/1.

See **IBM**, **MAINFRAME**, **OPERATING SYSTEM**, **OSF/1**, **POWERPC**, **RISC**, **SVR4**, and **UNIX**.

Alpha AXP

DEC's RISC-based central processing unit, developed to replace the CISC-based processor previously used in DEC's VAXes and workstations.

DEC's RISC architecture. Features include the following:

▲ Designed from the beginning to be 64-bit everything (buses, registers, and so on), unlike most other processors, which began as 16- or 32-bit and were redesigned to be 64-bit, usually with the requirement that they be compatible with the earlier 16- or 32-bit mode (which complicates the design and probably reduces 64-bit performance)

▲ Runs OpenVMS, OSF/1, and Microsoft's Windows NT, using *Physical Architecture Layer* (PAL) software code, which permits the processor to be configured for efficiently running different operating systems

▲ Has 1.68 million transistors and runs on 3.3 v

▲ Superscalar

The three types of Alpha processor families were designed for different markets:

▲ 21066: Lower-cost desktop PCs, since it includes a built-in cache, DRAM, and 32-bit PCI I/O controller and runs at 33 MHz externally. Cache and DRAM share the same 64-bit bus. The 166 MHz version was first announced in March 1994. 166 and 233 MHz versions of the 21066A were announced in March 1995.

▲ 21064: The first Alpha AXP, higher-performance (nonmultiplexed address and data bus). The first version ran at 150 MHz and was announced September 1992. The 200 MHz version was announced in July 1993. 225 and 275 MHz versions of the 21064A were announced in July 1994, and 300 MHz versions in December 1995. Later versions have a clock speed of 333 MHz.

▲ The 21068 was first announced in March 1994 and ran at 66 MHz.

▲ 21164: Highest performance. Includes a 64-bit PCI interface and 128-bit internal and external data buses. The 266 MHz version was announced in January 1995, the 300 MHz version in March 1995, the 333 MHz version in December 1995, the 366 and

400 MHz version in June 1996, and later versions have a clock speed of 500 and 600 MHz (June 1997). Has 9.3 million transistors.

▲ 21164PC: Lower-cost implementation intended to compete with Intel processors. 400, 466 and 533 MHz were announced in March 1997. Has 3.4 million transistors.

The following table lists the features of the Alpha processors.

Processor	Clock Speed (MHz)	Transistors (millions)	Bus Width (bits)		L1 Cache (kbytes)	Pins
			Internal Register and Address Bus	External Cache and DRAM Bus		
21066	33/166	2.2	64	64	16	287
21066A	33/233	2.4			32	
21064	150 166 200	1.6		128	16	431
21064A	233 275	1.8			32 [a]	431
21164	266 300 600	9.3		128 [b]	16 [c]	499

a. 16 kbytes for data, 16 kbytes for instruction.
b. The external address bus is 40-bits wide.
c. In addition to the 16 kbytes of write-through Level 1 data cache (8 kbytes for data, 8 kbytes for instruction), there are 96 kbytes of on-chip Level 2 3-way, set-associative, write-back, unified (data and instruction) cache.

As with most of what DEC has been doing lately, the Alpha processors are not very popular.

To promote acceptance of the processor, DEC will license the chip design (there are not many takers on this one, in 1996, Samsung Semiconductors was the first) and sell chips (rather than entire computers using the chips) to others (this is a bit more popular).

In October 1997, DEC sold its semiconductor manufacturing and most of its semiconductor development operations to Intel Corporation for $700 million, as part of a broad agreement to settle litigation (DEC sued Intel for using some of its technology in the Pentium), cross-license their patents, and get some money. Intel will continue to manufacture the Alpha processor as a foundry for DEC. DEC will develop and sell computer systems based on Intel's IA-64 architecture, and will port Digital UNIX to the IA-64 platform.

More information is available at *http://www.alphapowered.com*.

See **CACHE, INTEL, OPENVMS, OPERATING SYSTEM, PA-RISC, PC, PCI, POWERPC, RISC, SPEC, SUPERSCALAR,** and **VMS.**

AMI
Alternate Mark Inversion

See **ENCODING.**

AMPS
Advanced Mobile Phone Service

Standard analog cellular telephone service. Used in Canada, the U.S., Mexico, the Bahamas, Hong Kong, and Central and South America.

First implemented in Chicago in 1976 for a two-year test period.

Uses a 3-kHz (same bandwidth as a standard land-line telephone line) voice channel modulated onto 30 kHz FM carrier frequency pairs (one frequency for transmit, another for receive). The frequencies are spaced at 30 kHz. This method is therefore *frequency division multiple access* (FDMA).

The bandwidth for the initial 666 frequency pairs assigned to cellular telephone service was initially allocated for TV use (824 to 890 MHz, which was UHF channels 70 to 83). This was made available for cellular telephone use in the U.S. in 1981, and in Canada in 1984 (TV stations using those channels had to relocate to lower channels). In 1986 an additional 5 MHz (890 to 894 MHz) was made available (resulting in a total of 832 frequency pairs). The total of 50 MHz of bandwidth (there is an unallocated gap of 20 MHz from 849 to 869 MHz) is divided between two operators, each of which uses half of its bandwidth for the forward channel (from base station to mobile) and half for the reverse channel. The B *band* (or *block*) is assigned to the local telephone company (the "wire-line carrier"), and the A band is assigned to a non-wire-line carrier.

The following table lists the frequencies used by the A and B bands.

Band	Frequency Range (MHz)	Use
A	824 to 835 and 845 to 846.5	Transmit from mobile
	869 to 880 and 890 to 891.5	Receive at mobile
B	835 to 845 and 846.5 to 849	Transmit from mobile
	880 to 890 and 891.5 to 894	Receive at mobile

Each operator gets a total of 416 RF channel pairs. For each pair, the mobile's receive frequency is always 45 MHz higher than its transmit frequency. 7 to 21 of the 416 channel pairs are used for control purposes (at 10 kbits/s), leaving 395 to 409 available channel pairs for voice conversations, per operator (790 to 818 conversations total for both operators).

The entire "cellular" concept was created to solve the problem that there are not enough frequencies (a city needs more than 818 simultaneous conversations). By using lower-power transmitters (for the mobile telephone) and directional (often downward-pointing, to limit their distance) antennas, smaller cells of radio coverage are formed.

The radius of a cell is typically $\frac{1}{2}$ km (for an urban area that needs very high capacity) to 20 km (for a rural area that does not need high capacity).

Using a base station radio transmitter with an omnidirectional antenna (which provides 360°; of coverage), the adjacent cell radio base station sites would then (*very* roughly) form a pattern of hexagons, with a base station at the center of each.

The base station radio at the center would use frequency 1 and would use this to communicate reliably with any mobile within its coverage area (the hexagon around it). To ensure that the two conversations don't interfere, that same frequency cannot be reused for a conversation in any cell immediately adjacent to that one. This requires that the cells around the first cannot use the same frequency.

The accompanying figure shows a frequency reuse factor of 4. Adjacent cells never use the same frequency, and each cell can use $\frac{1}{4}$ of the available frequency channel pairs.

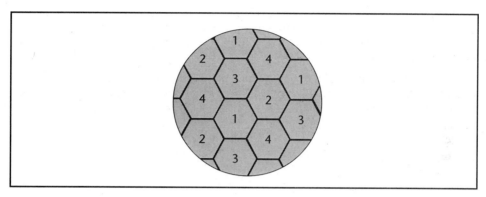

AMPS-1

By using antennas that cover less than 360°; (usually 120°; or 60°; and possibly positioned at the corners of the hexagons and pointing inward), smaller cells can be constructed (this is often called *sectorizing*). This permits a given frequency to be reused more often in a given geographic area. This increases the number of simultaneous conversations that can be supported. For example, 120°; antennas with a frequency reuse factor of seven could be as shown in the following figure.

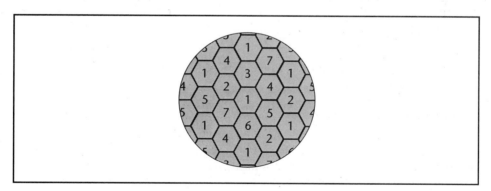

AMPS-2

The benefits of sectorizing and smaller cells are summarized in the following table.

Antenna Coverage	360°	120°	60°
Number of cells in frequency reuse pattern[a]	4	7	12
Frequency pairs (simultaneous conversations) per base station[b]	102	58	34
Relative capacity	1	22	140

a. Number of adjacent cells that cannot use the same frequency.
b. While sectorizing reduces the number of conversations per cell, the cells get smaller, so the total system capacity increases (as shown for the relative capacity).

As the cells get smaller, a lower transmit power must be used (so that the signal does not interfere with the same frequency being used in nearby cells). The mobile telephones have up to eight power levels (in 4-dB increments), from a minimum of 6 mW (which is the same as –22dBW—decibels referenced to 1 Watt) to a maximum of 0.6 W (–2.2 dBW) for handheld portables or 4.0 W (6 dBW) for car-mounted telephones. That is (for example), $10 \times \log_{10}(0.006/1) = -22$ dBW.

Base stations sense the received signal strength from mobiles and send commands back to them to adjust the mobile's transmit power so that the lowest necessary transmit power is always used.

Remarkably, the lower maximum transmit power of hand-held portables is not due to battery power limitations, but to the concern that having a transmit antenna that close to your head is not good for you—think of a nice steamy cauliflower coming out of a microwave oven (these operate at 2,450 MHz).

Base stations typically have:

▲ A much higher transmit power (100 W) so that the mobiles only need small antennas

▲ Tall antenna towers (often 100 m, or mounted on buildings about that high), and large antennas to accommodate the mobile's low transmit power (which is necessary both for health concerns, as mentioned above, and to extend the talk-time battery life)

▲ Antennas that point downwards, to give best coverage to ground-based users (so cellular telephones typically don't work very well in the upper floors of buildings—of course, the shielding effect of the building's reinforcing bars in the concrete, as well as any other metal used in the building's construction, also causes poor operation for all radios in buildings)

There are approximately 11,500 cellular telephone base station cell sites in the U.S.

Cellular telephones need to be programmed (usually by the dealer) with many numbers before use (these are usually set from a telephone's diagnostic and configuration mode, which is often entered by first pressing the "0" key 13 times), as shown in the following table.

Number	Length (bits)	Use
Mobile identification number (MIN)	34	The binary number corresponding to the telephone's 10-digit directory number (DN—area code plus 7-digit telephone number). This becomes the telephone's phone number. Binary is used because it is the most compact way to transmit the number).
Electronic serial number (ESN)[a]	32	Uniquely identifies the handset, and is factory-set—but sneaky people have figured out how to reprogram it (along with the MIN), to *clone* a handset (make it appear as another). Cloning is usually illegal, since it is one way to steal telecommunications service (air time and long distance calls are charged to the original handset's owner).
First paging channel	11	Identifies the lowest (such as 333) of the radio channel numbers used to track and signal the telephone. Commands on this channel switch the telephone to another of the control channels (to reduce the loading on the first paging channel).
Last paging channel	11	Identifies the highest radio channel number used to track and signal the telephone.
Home system identification	15	Identifies the telephone's cellular service provider. *Roaming* agreements (in which operators exchange billing information and revenue) enable other cellular service providers to provide service when a phone is used out of its home geographic area.

a. These are assigned by the TIA.

While there has been a dramatic increase in capacity due to sectorizing, the popularity of cellular has increased even faster. This, combined with the need for encryption and data transmission (throughput is typically only 2 to 3 kbits/s full-duplex, using modems optimized for cellular use), has resulted in other efforts. TDMA is the simplest expansion method and has been implemented and removed in many areas (the voice quality is too low). Expansion to PCS (CDMA and GSM—the European standard) is being implemented in many systems.

There are two enhancements to analog modems to support the (lousy) characteristics of cellular telephone channels, as summarized below:

▲ ETC (*enhanced throughput cellular*) was developed by AT&T Network Systems (now called Lucent Technologies Inc.).

▲ MNP10EC (*Microcom Networking Protocol Class 10 enhanced cellular*) was implemented by Rockwell International Corp.

AMPS is apparently a registered service mark of AT&T, as the technology was developed by their (at the time) Bell Laboratories. It is standardized in TIA/EIA-553.

See **CDMA, DN, EMF, ESMR, GSM, MNP, SST, TDMA, TIA1** (*Telecommunications Industry Association*) and **WIRELESS**.

Anik

Canada's geostationary communication satellites (Anik is the Inuit word for brother).

The first Anik satellite was Anik A1. It was the world's first geostationary communications satellite, and was launched on November 9, 1972 from Cape Canaveral (it began public service on January 11, 1973). It was retired in July 1982, which was 2.8 years past its 7-year design life.

The two other Anik A satellites (A2 and A3) were launched in April 1973 and May 1975. In 1981 these were both positioned in the same orbital slot (to increase capacity)—the first time that had been done.

Anik B was launched in 1978, and demonstrated the first direct to home TV broadcasting, using 1.2 to 1.8 m receiving antennas (larger antennas are required at higher latitudes, since the signal must travel farther, and must travel through more of the earth's atmosphere). Anik B was also the first dual-band (C and K_u) satellite.

Anik D1 was launched by a Delta rocket in 1982.

Anik C3 was launched in November 1982, and was the first commercial satellite launched from NASA's Space Shuttle Columbia. Anik C2 was launched from the Space Shuttle Challenger in 1983.

Anik D2 was launched by the Space Shuttle Discovery in 1984.

The Anik E satellites (E2 was launched in April 1991 by an Ariane rocket) are dual-band (C-band for voice and data communications, and K_u-band for television). They are about 21 m wide, most of which is the solar panels. On January 20 1994, a solar wind storm damaged some of Anik E2's (and to a lesser extent Anik E1's) position control electronics, and a more ground-based system had to be implemented. On March 26, 1996, a solar wind storm damaged one of Anik E1's power supplies (resulting in the satellite's power supply being reduced by 60%), so only 20 of the satellite's 56 transponders can now be used.

The first Canadian satellites were the Alouette I and II, which were launched September 29, 1962 and in 1965. Alouette I was the first satellite designed and built outside of the U.S. and Soviet Union. They assisted in studying the ionosphere's influence on high-frequency radio telecommunications and RADAR.

See **SATELLITE**.

ANS
ANS Communications Inc.

IBM and MCI together with Merit Inc. (a nonprofit consortium of Michigan schools) formed Advanced Network Services, Inc. (ANS), who was the original builder and operator of the National Science Foundation's backbone for the Internet (at least the part that was used for research and education). As the Internet became more commercially funded, they became just another major ISP, with both a high-speed backbone and a client base that includes commercial customers.

ANS was bought by America Online Inc. in November 1994, and then sold to WorldCom Inc. for $175 million in September 1997 as part of AOL's purchase of CompuServe's users and content (WorldCom got CompuServe's network along with ANS). Also as part of the deal, AOL will use WorldCom as the network provider for AOL's (and CompuServe's) network for at least 5 years.

ANS has an interesting WWW server at *http:/www.ans.net* and is located in Elmsford, New York.

See **CIX, INTERNET2, ISP, NAP**, and **T3**.

ANSI
American National Standards Institute

ANSI is a standards body, which has a membership of 1,400 companies, organizations and government agencies. It was created in 1918.

All U.S. national standards are created under ANSI's auspices. ANSI coordinates the U.S. voluntary standards system. ANSI recognizes several groups as *standards providers*, such as IEEE, EIA, and TIA.

ANSI is the sole U.S. member organization of the ISO (that is, ANSI represents the U.S.'s interests to the ISO). ANSI also does standards development work, such as FDDI.

ANSI has a WWW server at *http://www.ansi.org/*.

See **ARCNET, ATA, FDDI, ISO**, and **STANDARDS**.

API
Application Program Interface

The function *calls, subroutines* or *software interrupts* that comprise a documented interface so that a (usually) higher-level program such as an application program can make use of the (usually) lower-level services and functions of another application, operating system, network operating system, driver, or other lower-level software program.

The resulting library of functions provides a new capability, such as writing a file in an application program's proprietary format, communicating over a TCP/IP network, or accessing an SQL database. A very popular (and visible to the end user) API is the WinSock API, which gives your Microsoft Windows PC the capability to talk TCP/IP. This capability is required if you want to "surf the Internet."

The lower-level software may be integrated with the application program at compile/link time (using an `include` file or object library) or loaded (before the application program) as a driver, DOS TSR, Novell NLM, or Windows DLL (for example).

The accompanying figure shows an example API between an application program that needs the services of a protocol stack (such as a TCP/IP protocol stack) and the TCP/IP protocol stack (which itself has an interface to an Ethernet adapter).

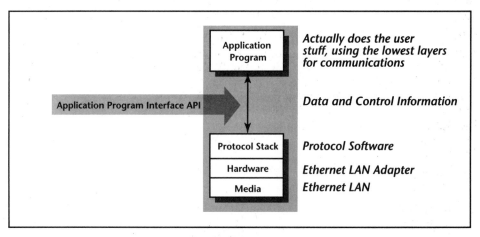

API-1

APIs are very popular now that open systems are popular and customers insist that systems and products work with those of other vendors.

See **APPC**, **CDE**, **CMC**, **CPIC**, **DDE**, **DMI**, **GDI**, **HLLAPI**, **MAPI**, **MESSAGING**, **MHS2** (*Message Handling System*), **MIDDLEWARE**, **MOTIF**, **OLE**, **OPENDOC**, **NAS**, **NDIS**, **NETBIOS**, **NLM**, **NSP**, **ODBC**, **ODI**, **PCMCIA**, **POSIX OSE**, **RPC**, **SAA**, **SDK**, **SOCKETS**, **SQL**, **TAPI**, **TSAPI**, **VIM**, **WABI**, **WINISDN**, **WINSOCK**, **WINX WINDOWS APIS**, **WOSA**, and **XAPIA**.

APM
Advanced Power Management

A method used by notebook PC manufacturers to gather and use information to monitor and conserve battery power. Information is shared between the PC's BIOS, operating system and application software—for example, whether the unit is currently running on battery power or from a 110V AC outlet, and the amount of charge left in the batteries.

Other capabilities include support for multiple battery packs and "waking" the PC upon an incoming call to its modem.

See **BATTERIES**, and **PC**.

APPC
Advanced Program to Program Communications

IBM's method (and APIs) for interprocess communication (that is, SNA's support for *distributed processing*). The API has about 32 *verbs* (commands), also called *procedures*, such as `ACTIVATE_DLC`, `ATTACH_LU`, and `SEND_DATA`, and over 1,000 error conditions. APPC uses the LU 6.2 protocol (and PU 2.1), so the term "APPC" is often used interchangeably with

"LU6.2." The following table shows (as a gross simplification) the component of the "new SNA" for each layer of the OSI 7-layer reference model.

OSI Layer Function	"New SNA" Name
7	CPI-C
6	APPC
5	LU6.2
4	
3	APPN or TCP/IP
2	Token Ring
1	

Communications can be between applications either on two workstations or on a workstation and a mainframe.

IBM's AS/400 uses APPC to enable PCs to access AS/400 resources, such as disk drives and printers, as if the resources were local to the PC. A separate APPC session on an AS/400 is required for each session from a PC running IBM's PC Support/400.

See **APPN**, **CPIC**, **LU 6.2**, **PU 2.1**, **SNA**, and **TOKEN RING**

APPI
Advanced Peer-to-Peer Internetworking

An SNA routing scheme proposed by Cisco that was to resolve some of APPN's weaknesses (an important one being IBM's multi-hundred-thousand-dollar licensing fee). It could also put SNA traffic over IP networks. The effort was abandoned when IBM became more open and reasonable about its APPN effort (and Cisco became worried that IBM would sue their pants off for patent infringement).

See **APPN** and **CISCO SYSTEMS**.

APPLE
Apple Computer, Inc.

The company that makes Macintosh computers (which were first released in 1984). It was started by Steven P. Jobs and Stephen Gary Wozniak (a.k.a Woz) on April 1, 1976, and the Apple II was the first product, announced in April 1977 (and shipped in 1978). It had 4 kbytes of RAM, and programs were stored on audio cassette tapes, using a standard audio cassette tape recorder. Actually, the Apple I was intended for hobbyists, who had to add their own power transformers, keyboard and TV monitor—and build their own case if they did not like the white cardboard one.

Usually, in the computer business, when you are first to market, you get the most market share, and Apple developed and successfully marketed many of the features that the PC industry took another 10 years to implement. For example, the Apple LaserWriter (available in 1984) was the first directly network-connected printer, and it supported PostScript years before this was available and popular in the PC industry.

Apple-IBM Alliance

Also, there are two options in designing and introducing a new product: you can have all of a very small market or a small part of a very large market. (There are lots of bankrupt companies with a small part of a small market and extremely few Microsofts with a large part of a large market.) Although Apple's first product (the Apple II) was being sold more than a year before the IBM PC was announced, Apple blew it. The company decided to limit the interfacing and expansion information that was available so that it kept the entire (and therefore very small) market to itself.

In contrast, IBM did not actively prevent third-party products from being developed and marketed (also, IBM was not litigious and even published some valuable information), so it got a small part of a very large market. (IBM's subsequent attempt to capture back market share through licensing and restricting the information available for its MCA bus was a complete failure.)

Realizing that it may not be a stable thing to have just 10% of a market (and also to be incompatible with 90% of the market), Apple is now trying new ways to compete with the "Wintel" (Microsoft Windows and Intel architecture) market:

▲ Offering to license its operating system (reportedly for about $45 per machine, though there are not many takers since Apple waited many years too long)

▲ Forming alliances with other companies (that used to be competitors) such as IBM and Motorola to try to compete

▲ Purchasing NeXT Software (for $400 million) in December 1996

Apple has a WWW server at *http://www.apple.com/*. A company that is big on Apple communications products is Farallon Computing, Inc., at *http://www.farallon.com/*.

See **A/UX**, **AFP**, **APPLE/IBM ALLIANCE**, **AURP**, **CHRP**, **MCA**, **NEXTSTEP**, **PC**, **POWERPC**, **QTC**, and **SMRP**.

Apple-IBM Alliance

An effort initiated in 1991 to make products to compete with Microsoft and Intel. *Kaleida*, *Somerset* (with Motorola), and *Taligent* are the joint ventures doing the work.

See **APPLE**, **CHRP**, **KALEIDA**, **SOMERSET**, and **TALIGENT**.

APPN
Advanced Peer-to-Peer Networking

IBM's peer-to-peer protocol developed to support computer-to-computer (that is, not to a 3270 terminal) communications. Derived from SNA. Runs over LANs and WANs (dedicated or switched links, load sharing supported).

A nonhierarchical (no FEPs required, either end can initiate a session), 1993 enhancement to PU 2.1 that supports SNA routing between two *end nodes* (where the applications are; they can be either clients or servers) through *network nodes* (which route data and find resources on the network by sending out broadcast messages).

A type of end node that supports a basic set of APPN functions is a *Low Entry Networking* (LEN) node.

Central directory servers are special VTAM hosts that can also be used to locate resources. The 3174 can run APPN network node software, which then queries a central directory server to find out where a CICS application resides and then communicates with that host using the most direct path.

The addressing scheme includes eight alphanumeric characters for LUs (nodes and resources) and eight alphanumeric characters for the subnet ID. Supports fair sharing of bandwidth among applications and congestion control by a prioritization based on *Class Of Service* (COS, which is something like ATM's QOS). Functions at the OSI network and transport layer.

Offers superior SNA integration, richer APIs, and better network management than TCP/IP (IBM would claim). Can (will be able to) carry NetBIOS and TCP/IP traffic by using IBM's MPTN.

The programmer interface is APPC or CPI-C.

APPN's very slow acceptance may result in it losing out to TCP/IP.

The APPN Implementors Workshop (AIW) has a WWW server at *http://www.networking.ibm.com/ app/aiwhome.htm.*

See **APPN, APPC, ATM** *(Asynchronous Transfer Mode),* **CPIC, CICS, DLSW, DLUR AND DLUS, FEP, LEN, LU 6.2, MPTN, PU 2.1, QOS, SNA,** and **VTAM.**

APPN+
APPN Plus

An enhancement to APPN (mainly to catch up to TCP/IP's features) that has better congestion control and dynamic rerouting around network problems (without dropping the session). Claimed to have 3 to 10 times the throughput of APPN through reducing the processing required by each intermediate network node.

Does not require hardware upgrades.

Also called APPN high performance routing (HPR).

See **APPN, APPN,** and **ATM** *(Asynchronous Transfer Mode).*

APPN++
APPN Plus Plus

A planned enhancement to APPN+ that will support ATM, Gbits/s line speeds, and multi-vendor protocols.

See **APPN.**

ARCNET
Attached Resource Computer Network

A LAN originally developed by the Datapoint Corporation. To promote its acceptance, Datapoint released technical specifications and supported development of complementary and competitive components (making it an industry standard).

Runs at 2.5 Mbits/s and is really low-cost. Was popular before Ethernet and while Ethernet was still expensive.

Ardis Company

For a while there was a faster version called ARCnetPlus. It ran at 20 Mbits/s and could share cable (and communicate at 2.5 Mbits/s) with ARCnet stations.

Then it became an ANSI standard (878.1). But, because of its late standardization, small size (maximum of 255 stations per LAN), small maximum frame size of 516 bytes, and limited WAN connectivity and trouble-shooting equipment support, it is not a good choice for new installations. Ethernet would be better (now there's an understatement).

A low-cost proprietary enhancement called TCNS (Thomas-Conrad Network System) runs at 100 Mbits/s over STP, RG-62 coaxial cable, and fiber-optic cable but is unlikely to be selected for newer installations because of the many other 100-Mbits/s schemes that are now available.

ARCnet was belatedly defined in ANSI 878.1.

See **S100BASET**, **S100VG ANYLAN**, **FDDI**, and **LAN**.

Ardis Company

Ardis provides a cellular packet-switched radio data service (which is called DataTAC) in the U.S. Now completely owned by Motorola (it used to be a joint venture with IBM). In Canada, the service is offered by Stentor's Mobility Canada.

Initially (1984), the network was designed by Motorola for IBM mainframe field service technicians so they could order spare parts without having to find a telephone (however, they were not allowed to use the hand-held units in computer rooms, as they can cause computers to hang or re-boot). The radio protocol is proprietary. The system has about 34,000 subscribers, about 10 times the number that the competing Mobitex system from RAM Mobile Data has.

Data transmission is at 4,800 bits/s (using 240-byte packets, resulting in about 2,000 to 3,000 bits/s of user-data throughput) or 19,200 bits/s (in larger U.S. and Canadian centers) using 512-byte packets, resulting in up to 8,000 bits/s of user-data throughput.

Usage charges are per kbyte of data transferred, rather than per minute of connect time.

Competes with RAM Mobile Data's Mobitex system (which is offered by Rogers Cantel Inc. in Canada) and CDPD.

Ardis has a WWW server at *http://www.ardis.com/*.

See **BELL ARDIS**, **CDPD**, **ESMR**, **GSM**, **MOBITEX**, **MOTOROLA**, **RAM MOBILE DATA**, and **WIRELESS**.

ARP
Address Resolution Protocol

A method of determining the 48-bit MAC (*Media Access Control*) address for a LAN-connected host running the TCP/IP protocol, as long as you already have the 32-bit IP address of the host (which you may have obtained by using the DNS).

The process is that you *multicast* (send to all LAN-connected hosts running the TCP/IP protocol) a message asking for the host having the specific MAC address of interest to reply. When it does, you typically store the results in an *ARP cache* so that you don't need to do this again.

Defined in RFC 826.

See **CACHE**, **DNS2** (*Domain Name System*), and **TCP/IP**.

ARPANET
Advanced Research Projects Agency Network

The predecessor to the Internet, officially phased out in 1990. Began in 1969, linking four computer sites (Stanford Research Institute, the University of Utah, the University of California at Los Angeles, and the University of California at Santa Barbara) that were doing research for the U.S. Department of Defense.

Later called DARPAnet, for the *Defense Advanced Research Projects Agency* (which is an agency of the U.S. Department of Defense), which issued the request for a proposal for the network's development.

Initially a computer science experiment, then developed to provide communications between government agencies, military facilities, defense contractors, and universities, with the goal that the network should be operational even when important parts were unavailable (that is, not vulnerable to "nuclear decapitation"). The first network to use TCP/IP.

Using 56 kbits/s *leased lines* for the connections between sites, grew to about 50 sites in the early 1970s and to a few hundred in the early 1980s. By 1987 the number of sites was several thousand, and the National Science Foundation sponsored a T1 (1.544 Mbits/s) *backbone* (rather than just linking all sites directly to each other), and the network began to be called NSFNet. By 1991 the backbone was upgraded to T3 (44.736 Mbits/s).

See **ANS**, **INTERNET2**, **MILNET**, **T1**, **T3**, and **WAN**.

ASCII
American Standard Code for Information Interchange

A specification for the 7-bit patterns used to represent *control* (such as *carriage return*) and *printable* characters (the letters, numbers, and punctuation marks) in computers and for data communications between them.

Used by most of North America (except, for example, for IBM mainframes, which use EBCDIC).

The following table shows the hexadecimal for each ASCII character. For example, a *line feed* is represented as $0A_{16}$ and "$" is 24_{16}.

Least Significant Digit	Most Significant Hexadecimal Digit							
	0	1	2	3	4	5	6	7
0	Null	Data link escape	Space	0	@	P	'	p
1	Start of heading	Device control 1 (and X-on)	!	1	A	Q	a	q
2	Start of text	Device control 2	"	2	B	R	b	r
3	End of text	Device control 3 (and X-off)	#	3	C	S	c	s

(table continued on next page)

Least Significant Digit	Most Significant Hexadecimal Digit							
	0	1	2	3	4	5	6	7
4	End of transmission	Device control 4	$	4	D	T	d	t
5	Enquiry	Negative acknowledgment	%	5	E	U	e	u
6	Acknowledge	Synchronization character	&	6	F	V	f	v
7	Bell	End of transmission block	'	7	G	W	g	w
8	Backspace	Cancel	(	8	H	X	h	x
9	Horizontal tab	End of medium	)	9	I	Y	i	y
A	Line feed	Substitute	*	:	J	Z	j	z
B	Vertical tab	Escape	+	;	K	[	k	{
C	Form feed	Field separator	,	<	L	\	l		
D	Carriage return	Group separator	–	=	M	]	m	}
E	Shift out	Record separator	.	>	N	^	n	~
F	Shift in	Unit separator	/	?	O	_	o	Delete

There are some reasons for some characteristics of ASCII:

▲ When mechanical *teletype* machines were used to send and receive messages, a paper tape punch/reader was often used to automate the process (you could type your message in advance, and then send it at full-speed—often a blazing 110 bits/s). The tape had a pattern of 7 holes across it, usually in ASCII—plus an even parity bit. A hole was a binary 1 (called a mark), and no hole was a binary 0 (called a space). If you made a mistake, you typed a delete over the pattern, this punched all the holes (all 1s), and such characters would be ignored by the receiving teletype machine. Hence, the ASCII DEL character is all 1s (and with the even parity used, it even has the correct parity).

▲ The SYNC character (0010110_2)was chosen so it would never look like a shifted copy of itself. Therefore, in *synchronous* data communications, several of them at the beginning of a message could be examined to determine where the byte-boundaries are (and from then on, take each 8 bits as the next byte).

▲ The numeric order of the characters is in the order often desired for sorting in alphabetical order. This reduces the complexity and CPU time of sorting.

With small changes (for example £ instead of $ or support for ¿ and é), used by most of the rest of the world, too.

ASCII was defined (initially in the mid-1960s, though there was an update in 1977) in ANSI X3.4 (which is officially called *American National Standard Code for Information Interchange*), which became one of the options (the others being for 10 other languages) in ISO 646, which defines 7-bit character encodings and graphical characters as well. International Alphabet 5 (IA5) is defined in ITU T.50, and is almost the same as ASCII (for example, the "$" can be a different character).

Since ASCII is a 7-bit code, it can represent only $2^7 = 128$ characters. Most computers support 8-bit bytes (which can represent $2^8 = 256$ characters), so many (unfortunately different) *extended character sets* have been defined (for example, by DEC, IBM, and Microsoft). These use the additional 128 codes for line-drawing characters (for example, ⌈ and ⌉) and other important things (☺).

256 characters are typically enough only for one country's characters (some countries need â, others need ä, and still others need å, for example). So *code pages* are usually defined (again, unfortunately, differently by each operating system), though ISO 8859 does define 8-bit character sets for many languages.

This whole mess is supposed to be cleared up by everyone adopting Unicode.

See **BAUD**, **BISYNC**, **EBCDIC**, **EIA/TIA232**, **INBAND**, **PARITY**, **SYNCHRONOUS**, and **UNICODE**.

ASPI
Advanced SCSI Programming Interface

Adaptec's interface to its SCSI disk controllers that permits multiple device drivers (for example, disk, tape, and CD-ROM) to share the disk controller. This is required when multiple devices are installed on a SCSI bus. Initially (in 1988, when it was first released) was called *Adaptec SCSI* Programming Interface, but Adaptec changed the name in the hope it would become an industry standard (and it has).

Competes with *Layered Device Driver Architecture* (LADDR, from Microsoft Corp.) and *Common Access Method* (CAM, from Future Domain and NCR Corporation), though ASPI is much more popular.

Adaptec has a WWW server at *http://www.adaptec.com/*.

See **ATASPI** and **SCSI1**.

ASTRAL
Alliance for Strategic Token Ring Advancement and Leadership

A group of Token Ring equipment manufacturers (including 3Com, IBM, Madge Networks, and Olicom USA and UB Networks) that have noticed that more people always have and, increasingly, still seem to be installing Ethernet rather than Token Ring LANs.

They hope to educate potential customers about the benefits of Token Ring.

See **LAN** and **TOKEN RING**

Asynchronous Data Transmission

The type of serial data transmission supported by a PC's COM port and usually the type used by PCs when using modems.

Literally, "not synchronous."

When used in low-speed data communications, it means that there is no predefined timing between the characters sent; typically, the characters are sent as they are typed by some human (and you know how unpredictable humans are). The method was designed to handle the expected case that the sender's and receiver's bit rates will never be *exactly* the same and only one character will be ready to be sent at a time.

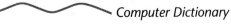

Asynchronous Data Transmission

The following description, and figure below, are for the polarities used on EIA-232 circuits.

While there are no data to send (idle), the data circuit is at a negative voltage.

When a character of data is to be sent, the UART first sends a *start bit* (a one bit-time duration positive voltage), which is of the opposite polarity of what *was* happening.

The transition from negative to positive voltage occurs exactly at the boundary between two bit-times, so the receiver now knows where the bit boundaries are (that is, *bit synchronization* and *character synchronization* have been achieved).

The receiver senses this transition, waits $\frac{1}{2}$-bit-time (the receiver must be preconfigured to nominally the sender's bit rate) to the center of the start bit, and *samples* (reads) the input again. If it is still a positive voltage, then the receiver can be somewhat sure that the initial edge was not just noise.

The receiver then begins assembling the first character of data (in this case, an ASCII d, by waiting a full bit-time, to the center of the first data bit (data are sent LSB first).

The input is then sampled, and the first data bit (a binary 0 in this case) is received. This is continued for (typically) 8 data bits total (the receiver must be preconfigured to the same number of data bits per character).

Then the receiver expects a stop bit. It is a one bit-time duration negative voltage, which is generated by the sender's UART. If one is not received (the line is still positive), then the receiving UART indicates a *framing error* (which may be interpreted as a *break signal*).

After the stop bit, either another character (beginning with a start bit) or an idle (a negative voltage of any duration) begins. Figure 1 illustrates this process.

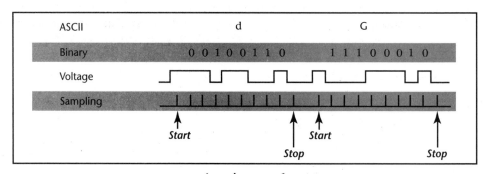

Asynchronous-1

Since the receiver samples at the center of each bit-time, it can be as much as $\frac{1}{2}$ bit-time off (too soon or too late) and still read the bit correctly. Since both the sending and receiving clock may be wrong, each could be up to $\frac{1}{4}$ bit-time off (allowing for the worst case, in which one is $\frac{1}{4}$ bit-time too fast and the other is $\frac{1}{4}$ bit-time too slow). Since the clocks get resynchronized at the start of each character (by the transition to the start bit), the clocks have to be matched only so that they drift by less than $\frac{1}{4}$ bit-time in the (approximately) 10 bits per character. This requires an accuracy of $\frac{1}{4}$ bit-time in 10 bits, which is ($\frac{1}{4}$/10 =) 2.5%, which is easily accomplished.

Because of asynchronous data communication's reliance on the addition of a start and stop bit to every character of data, it is usually less efficient than synchronous data communications (of every 10 bits sent, 2 are overhead). That is, 20% of the bandwidth is wasted on start and stop bits, so a 9,600-bits/s line provides only 7,680 bits/s of throughput. Some people call it *start/stop data communications* (IBM people say this in a derogatory way, as if the data lacked confidence and were prone to hesitation) in contrast to the *synchronous data communications* that are commonly used (for example) by IBM 3270-type equipment.

Asynchronous data communications equipment needs to be configured for the following:

▲ Bit rate (such as 9,600 bits/s)

▲ Number of data bits per character (such as 8)

▲ Parity type used (such as none)

▲ Number of stop bits (usually one, though stop bit durations of 1.5 and 2 bit-times are often settable, but these were needed only for ancient mechanical teletypewriters that needed more than one stop bit-time between characters)

Both ends of a link must have matching settings.

See **S3270**, **BAUD**, **EIA/TIA232**, **FLOW CONTROL**, **LSB**, **MODEM**, **PARITY**, **SYNCHRONOUS**, and **UART**.

Asynchronous Function Calls

Asynchronous process to process communication refers to function calls (typically between processes on the same computer, or on different computers) that return immediately, so the calling process can continue processing. If the reply can't be provided immediately (for example, a database query may require 20 ms to 2 s to process), then the calling function is informed when the reply is available by polling (periodically asking whether the answer is ready) or an asynchronous reply message.

See **SYNCHRONOUS FUNCTION**.

AT
Advanced Technology

IBM's name for its (now ancient) 80286-based PC, the PC/AT, which was introduced in 1984.

The IDE hard disk drive interface was first implemented on the PC/AT (though not when it was first announced). It used a disk drive controller developed by Western Digital.

See **BUS**, **DISK DRIVE**, **IDE**, **INTEL**, **ISA**, and **PC**.

AT Command Set

The command language developed by Hayes Microcomputer Products, Inc. to control auto-dial modems from a (usually EIA-232 connected) dumb asynchronous terminal or a PC emulating such a terminal.

All commands (except for "A/" which repeats the previous command, and "+++" which escapes from online data mode back to command mode), begin with AT (or at). Most

explanations are that these characters "get the modem's *AT*tention." While the letters AT do act as a command sequence delimiter, an important feature of those particular characters is that they have few transitions (an ASCII "A" is 1000001_2), and opposite parity. This enables the modem to automatically recognize and adjust to the terminal or PC's bit rate and parity. Also, while a few other letter combinations could have been used, AT suggested Atlanta to the founders, which is where they are from.

The original core command set was implemented for Hayes's first product, the Hayes Smartmodem 300 (a Bell 103 type modem), which was introduced in June 1981 (which was just before the IBM PC was announced, which created solid growth for the then-small company—though the company ran into tough times in 1996). The Smartmodem 300 had only about 15 commands, such as ATDT 555-1234 to dial using touch-tone and ATH to hang up the phone.

Modern modems, such as one supporting V.34 modulation, can have more than 250 commands. Commands include configuring features such as data compression, diagnostics, and flow control. Many modems support new features such as security, distinctive ringing and caller identification, and manufacturers often make up their own commands for these features. These commands are then specific to each manufacturer, so modem set-up strings need to be customized to the modem used.

Remarkably, though Hayes developed the command set, which has become a de facto standard, it is not patented. Virtually all modems and data sets that support switched connections and asynchronous communications use some subset or extension of the AT command set with no benefit to Hayes. This is because Hayes determined that the command set was not patentable.

What Hayes did patent is its method of escaping from online data mode. Since, once connected to a remote modem, a modem simply modulates everything sent from the terminal and sends it over the modem link to the remote modem, the problem is how to get the modem to escape back to command mode.

Hayes's patented solution (*Improved Escape Sequence with Guard Time*, or the *Heatherington method*, or the *'302 Patent*, which refers to U.S. Patent 4,549,302) was developed by Dale Heatherington and has been used by Hayes modems since 1981. The modem escapes from on-line data mode to command mode if it detects the following sequence in the data sent from the terminal:

▲ At least one second of no data, then

▲ Three ASCII plus signs ("+++"), then

▲ At least one second of no data.

The idle time before and after the plus signs is called the *guard time* (the modem can be configured for a different escape character, and a different guard time duration). When the modem is in command mode, commands such as ATH (to hang up) or ATO (to go back online) can be sent.

Hayes licenses this method to other modem manufacturers (see **TIES**). Actually, the modem IC manufacturer is usually licensed; this is most often Rockwell International.

Hayes Microcomputer Products was started by Dennis C. Hayes and Dale Heatherington in 1977, and their first product was a 300 bit/s modem board that plugged in to the MITS

Altair microcomputer's S-100 bus (this legendary computer was the first popular kit for the Intel 8080 processor). The modem was first sold in April 1977. The company's second product was the Micromodem II (also a plug-in printed circuit board), for the Apple II, and was the first modem that could be directly connected to the telephone network (that is, without an external *data access arrangement*—DAA—between it and the telephone network). These modems were controlled through software registers accessible on the modem boards, but each type of computer required a different modem. However, since all computers support an EIA-232 interface, the Smartmodem 300 could be used by any computer, and it quickly became very popular (especially after Hayes convinced communications software developers to support the AT command set).

Hayes has a WWW server at *http://www.hayes.com/.*

EIA-602 standardizes some AT commands.

See **ASYNCHRONOUS, ATT, BELL 103, DE FACTO, EIA, EIA/TIA232, FAX, MODEM, PARITY, PATENT, ROCKWELL INTERNATIONAL, SWATS, SWITCHED 56, TIES,** and **V.25BIS.**

ATA
AT Bus Attachment

The official name for what most people call IDE.

When ANSI standardized Western Digital's IDE disk interface, ANSI called it ATA. The "AT" refers to the 16-bit ISA bus, which was first implemented in IBM's PC/AT personal computer (which was based on the Intel 80286 microprocessor).

See **ANSI, AT, ATA-2, ATA-3, BUS, IDE,** and **ISA.**

ATA-2
AT Attachment 2

An enhancement to the IDE interface, sometimes called *advanced ATA*.

Also, ATA-2 is the name used by IBM and Toshiba for their implementation of ATA-2. That may sound strange (calling something what it is), but Western Digital calls their enhancement E-IDE, and Seagate calls their's Fast-ATA.

IBM and Toshiba use this interface for laptop PC 2.5" hard disk drives.

See **ATA, ATA-3, EIDE, FAST ATA,** and **IDE.**

ATA-3
AT Attachment 3

An enhancement to the IDE interface (actually, to the ATA-2 version of it) that has the following features.

▲ Data integrity features, such as CRC checking of the data transferred

▲ Security features, such as password protection

▲ Power features, such as power-down modes

ATA-PI

▲ Ultra DMA mode 2, which has a transfer rate of up to 33.3 Mbytes/s

▲ Single word DMA is no longer supported, and ATA-2's PIO mode 4 is still the fastest PIO mode supported

See **IDE**.

ATA-PI
AT Attachment Packet Interface

ANSI's name for Western Digital's enhancement to the IDE (also called ATA) hard disk drive interface.

ATAPI:

▲ Provides support for CD-ROM, tape, and other drives in addition to hard disk drives

▲ Supports features such as *Plug and Play* (see **PLUG AND PLAY**) and *Overlapped I/O*, in which one disk drive can be *seeking* (the read/write head moving to new data) while another is transferring data

▲ Is part of Western Digital's *Enhanced IDE* (E-IDE) specification (which was first released in 1994)

▲ Requires a software driver but otherwise simply requires that the CD-ROM drive (for example) be plugged into an available IDE connector in the PC

▲ ATA-PI is a superset of IDE, so standard IDE disk drives can be plugged in to an E-IDE ATAPI connector (though it only provides the original IDE features)

The term "packet interface" refers to the addition of transferring information between the adapter and peripheral using commands that are sent as *packets*. These have some number of bytes of data, in a defined format), rather than IDE's interface, which is reading from and writing to a set of *registers* (specific I/O addresses defined in the BIOS, that have special functions). The commands specified were derived from SCSI (which is a proven technology for accomplishing a similar task).

E-IDE (and the ATAPI specification included in it) competes with (though is less powerful than) SCSI, and with the more common (but decreasingly so) proprietary interfaces otherwise required by CD-ROMs.

See **AT**, **CDROM**, **EIDE**, **IDE**, **PLUG AND PLAY**, and **SCSI1**.

ATASPI
AT Attachment Software Programming Interface

A specification to provide a standard software interface to IDE (which is also called ATA) attached peripherals.

The goal is to support multiple devices and drivers on a single IDE interface.

Developed by Future Domain. ASPI is the similar specification for the SCSI interface.

See **ASPI**, **CDROM**, **EIDE**, **IDE**, and **SCSI1**.

Computer Dictionary

ATM
Adobe Type Manager

Adobe's program that enables Adobe PostScript Type 1 fonts (and now Windows TrueType too) to be printed on both non-PostScript printers and displayed on video monitors. Since the same fonts are used, this ensures the printed output to match the displayed output. It *rasterizes* the *outline fonts* (turns them into bitmaps at the required resolution).

It is a separate program for Windows and Macintosh, but is integrated into the OS/2 Presentation Manager.

Adobe Type 1 fonts and the scalable fonts built in to Hewlett-Packard LaserJet III and LaserJet 4 printers are resolution-independent (unlike Windows TrueType fonts), so a change in printer resolution will not affect a document's pagination.

The font files include those shown in the following table.

Font Filename Extension	Function	Comments
*.AFM		Used at installation time to create the *.PFM files. Can be deleted after installation.
*.INF		
*.PFB	Font outlines	Required to show fonts on-screen and to rasterize them for printing.
*.PFM	Font metrics	
*.WFA		Created by WordPerfect from the *.PFM files to speed up screen redraws and printing times of PostScript fonts under DOS. Can be deleted, as WordPerfect will recreate them as needed.
*.WFO		

The c:windowsATM.ini file shows the correlation between the DOS filename and the typeface name.

See **ADOBE, BITMAP FONT, FONT, MULTIPLE MASTER, OUTLINE FONT, POSTSCRIPT TYPE 1 FONTS, POSTSCRIPT TYPE 3 FONTS, RASTERIZE, SUPERATM, TRUETYPE,** and **TYPEFACE FAMILY.**

ATM
Asynchronous Transfer Mode

Voice and data communications is basically the sharing of expensive equipment—and ATM is the ultimate in cost, capability and complexity that has been dreamed-up (so far).

ATM is a very high-speed, full-duplex (simultaneous bi-directional), connection-oriented (only PVC initially, SVCs subsequently supported), fixed-length 48-byte (plus 5 bytes of overhead) cell-switching scheme that is suitable for data as well as digitized voice and video. A *switched* (rather than *shared* medium, as Ethernet typically is) technology, so each station gets its own connection to the ATM switch, and the full bandwidth of their link available for traffic (though *network* congestion is a complicated issue).

ATM networks consist of ATM switches, interconnected by point-to-point (that is, they only have two ends) links, typically running at DS-1 speeds and much faster.

ATM has been designed to be *scalable* (so very large ATM networks can be built without running into performance or architectural limitations) and to provide many levels of service (guaranteed throughput and network latency or not, for example).

Was initially to be used with SONet to be the basis for B-ISDN but is now considered a separate technology. "Asynchronous" because each cell can be independently addressed to allocate bandwidth between many virtual channels as needed.

ATM could eliminate the distinction between LAN and WAN, since ATM can be used for both. WANs will probably first be implemented as private ATM networks, then become a public offering.

ATM is based on segmenting user data into small, fixed-length cells, for the following reasons:

▲ So that it is easier to handle them in hardware (which can juggle cells faster than software)—since ATM typically runs at hundreds of megabits per second.

▲ So that networks can have predictable response times (since you know when the current cell will finish because you know its length). This *isochronous* capability is required to handle multimedia traffic (such as digitized voice and video).

▲ To provide short store-and-forward delays per switch (to reduce network delays, as required for interactive services such as video conferencing).

▲ To simplify memory management in ATM switches.

ATM is popular with carriers, as the *switching fabric* to support frame relay (which currently uses access speeds up to T1), voice traffic and other high-speed data services.

The Private Network to Node Interface (PNNI) specification describes how ATM switches within an organization interface and send signalling information to each other.

The *UNI* (User-to-Network Interface) specification defines the end user interface to an ATM switch, and includes the following transmission media:

▲ SONet; OC-3 (single-mode and multi-mode fiber (this uses a 1,300 nm light source and 8B/10 coding, so the actual line bit rate is 194.4 Mbits/s), as well as STP and Category 5 UTP copper

▲ 100 Mbits/s FDDI

▲ DS-3 (sometimes called T3)

▲ DS-1 (sometimes called T1)

▲ 25.6 Mbits/s (strongly pushed by IBM as an successor to Token Ring). Sometimes called ATM25, this is intended as a connection to desktop machines (rather than as a backbone or server technology), and can use STP and Category 3 UTP cabling. The weird rate is based on using a modification of IBM's 16 Mbit/s Token Ring encoding method. 4 user data bits are sent in 5 bits (this is called 4B/5B encoding), resulting in a raw bit rate of 32 Mbits/s (16 Mbit/s Token Ring uses differential manchester encoding, which also results in a raw bit rate of up to 32 Mbits/s, so this permitted IBM to re-use some of the same ICs and cabling rules). Many preferred a bit rate of 25 Mbit/s ($\frac{1}{4}$ of the 100 Mbits/s supported by many LAN technologies), or 25.92 Mbits/s ($\frac{1}{2}$ of the SONet OC-1 rate), but IBM won (of course the real test is whether anybody uses this rate at all, now that 100BASE-T is being rapidly accepted)—and the answer is that 25 Mbit/s ATM was never accepted by the market, so this is all just (interesting) historical trivia.

Other interface specifications include 100 Mbit/s *TAXI* and *DXI*.

Switched virtual connections (SVCs) are established using the signalling specified in Q.2931, and connectionless traffic is supported by the network quickly setting up and tearing down a virtual connection (without any involvement of the user).

The ATM model has four layers, as defined in the following table:

Layer	Defines
User	User-to-Network interface (UNI), where the network is an ATM switch, and the user is the end-user equipment
Adaptation	How *Segmentation And Reassembly* (SAR) are handled for each of the ATM adaptation layers.
Cell	Defines the handling of the 53-byte cells
Physical	Cables and connectors for DS-3, Transparent Asynchronous Transmitter/receiver (TAXI) for 100-Mbits/s multimode fiber (though this is seldom currently used), fibre channel for 155 Mbits/s, and SONet.

The *ATM adaptation layer* (AAL) exists only in end-stations, not in switches, and is responsible for segmenting the information into 53-byte cells (and at the receiving end, reassembles it back into its original form). That is, the AAL adapts the traffic to the ATM protocol layer. The following table describes the adaptation layers. AAL 5 and, to a lesser extent, AAL 1, are receiving the most interest from vendors and standards groups.

AAL	Use	Comments
0 or Null	When customer equipment does all AAL-related functions	Network AAL does not do anything in this case. The user equipment emits 53-byte ATM cells directly.
1	Isochronous traffic, such as digitized audio and video, which require *constant bit rate* (CBR) service	A 1-byte SAR (segmentation and reassembly) header is prepended to the 47-byte payload. This is used for a 3-bit sequence number, as well as error detection capability. AAL 1 is suitable for traffic that is sensitive to both cell loss and delay. Intended to replace fractional and full DS-1 and DS-3 services (using CES), as it can provide a far greater range of available speeds, and multiplex many such services together. AAL 1 is used for CBR service. While it is nice that this CBR traffic can share higher-speed connections with other traffic (providing economies of scale and other savings), ATM's 5-byte per cell overhead is less efficient than a leased-line overhead. Also, CBR traffic is allowed to be anything from 0 to the *peak cell rate* (PCR) negotiated at connection time. CBR bandwidth that is not used by the application (that is, when you send less than you have contracted for) is wasted (that is, it is not available for other users).

(table continued on next page)

AAL	Use	Comments
2	Isochronous variable bit-rate services, such as compressed video	
3/4	Variable bit-rate data, such as LAN file transfers	Originally intended as two AALs: AAL 3 for connection-oriented services (such as frame relay and X.25) and AAL 4 for connectionless services (such as IP and SMDS). It was later realized that only one AAL was needed for both capabilities, so they called it "AAL 3/4". Intended for traffic that can tolerate delay but not cell loss. Supports multiplexing of multiple conversations over a single ATM virtual circuit by utilizing 4 bytes from each 48-byte cell to identify the conversation and add information for error-checking, such as a sequence number. The computer industry then decided that this additional overhead is not worth the benefit, and AAL 5 was created (in AAL 5, applications get to use the full 48 bytes)—and is receiving most attention now.
5	Variable bit-rate data, carried in variable-length packets, such as that from bursty LANs	Similar to AAL 3/4 but with fewer features (for example, no cell multiplexing), so it is easier to implement. The payload data can be up to 64 kbytes, but usually a smaller maximum is used—such as the 9,180-byte maximum for Classical IP over ATM (RFC 1577). The payload data gets some padding bytes added, followed by a length field of the number of payload bytes, and followed by a CRC. The padding is added so that the entire *protocol data unit* (PDU) is an integral multiple of 48 bytes. The message is then segmented into the 48-byte cells, has the 5-byte ATM header added and is sent out whatever media is to carry the data. Note that unlike the other AALs, there are no overhead bytes in the cells; all 48 cell bytes are available for payload. Sometimes called the simple and efficient adaptation layer (SEAL). AAL 5 is used to carry the VBR, UBR and ABR service category traffic.

AAL2 was proposed in December 1990 to handle variable packet rate video. By Mid-1992 is was decided that this could be handled using the CBR service provided by AAL 1 (which has a payload size of 47 bytes per cell), so AAL 2 was abandoned (and AALs 1, 3/4 and 5 were approved). As it turned out, AAL 5's CBR and VBR services was later (by October 1994) proposed for MPEG-2 traffic. Since AAL 5 has a payload size of 48, rather than 47 bytes, so the MPEG-2 transport could have been defined to use 192- rather than 188-byte packets. Due to the specification of rt-VBR, by mid-1997 it was decided that only AAL 5's VBR service (and not CBR service) was needed for MPEG-2 traffic.

The accompanying figure illustrates the use of each bit of the 53-byte ATM cell.

Byte	Bit							
	8	7	6	5	4	3	2	1
1	Generic Flow Control				Virtual Path Identifier			
2	Virtual Path Identifier *(continued)*				Virtual Channel Identifier			
3	Virtual Channel Identifier *(continued)*							
4	Virtual Channel Identifier *(continued)*			Payload Type Identifier			Cell Loss Priority	
5	Header Error Control							
6–53	Payload Data							

ATM-1

The payload data is called the *service data unit* (SDU).

Two locations are connected by a *virtual path*, and there are 8 bits in the header to identify it (called the *virtual path connection identifier*—VPCI), allowing simultaneous connections to 256 locations.

Each virtual path can carry up to 65,536 *virtual channels* (simultaneous but separate connections between or through the same locations), each virtual circuit being identified by the 16-bit *virtual circuit identifier* (VCI—which uniquely identifies the connection, even through several cascaded virtual paths). The first 32 VCIs are generally reserved for control functions, such as signalling which uses VCI 5, and ABR flow-control, which uses VCI 6. These are called *well known virtual channels*, since their use is defined in the ATM standards.

That is, a virtual circuit joins a virtual path (with other virtual circuits), and splits off at the destination. The joining of a VC to a VP (and the splitting of a VC from a VP at the remote end) is handled by the *cell relaying function* (CRF).

Any bits that are set in the *generic flow control* field identify that some form of priority for the traffic is being requested (both the ATM switch and the end-station must support this, which is confirmed by the end-station echoing back the priority bits).

The list below describes the use of the three bits of the *payload type identifier* (PTI) field.

Note that the bits indicate the following:

▲ Whether the cell contains user data or control information.

▲ *Explicit Forward Congestion Indication* (EFCI), which is a mechanism in which any network element (typically an ATM switch) sets this bit in the ATM cell header to alert the receiver of impending network congestion (and that the cell (and others following it) may have been delayed by the network congestion). (the "Forward" in EFCI indicates that the congestion indication information travels in the same direction as the network congestion is occurring—from traffic source to destination.) It is up to higher-layer protocols to implement flow-control of the sender. While any service category can optionally implement and utilize EFCI for flow-control, the ABR service category builds on EFCI to create a much more complex bidirectional feedback (to the sender) based flow-control method which uses *resource management* (RM) cells.

▲ Whether the cell contains OAM: *Operations* (fault and performance management), *Administration* (addressing, data collection and usage monitoring), and *Maintenance* (analysis, diagnosis, and repair of network faults) information, as further described below.

▲ The SDU (*service data unit*) type. For AAL 5, the use of this bit is as follows: The data stream (such as a 9 kbyte IP packet) submitted to an AAL can generally be up to 64 kbytes (that is, much longer than 48 bytes). The SAR (*segmentation and reassembly*) process divides this into 48-byte SDUs, which are then sent through the ATM network, and the remote end reassembles the cells back into the original data stream. To indicate the last cell of the original (for example) 9 kbyte packet, the SAR process of the sender sends the last cell (which includes a packet length field and a CRC) as SDU-type=1 (that is, bit 2 of byte 4 of the cell header is set to a 1). The receiver then knows when it has the whole packet, and submits it to the higher-layer software (such as the TCP/IP stack) for further processing.

The *Cell Loss Priority* (CLP) bit in the cell header indicates that the cell can be discarded if necessary (for example, to reduce network congestion). Some networks carry this bit unchanged or examined as "data", and some networks can set (according to the GCRA, described below)—in which case the cell is referred to as a *tagged cell*—and act on this bit.

The *header error control* (HEC) field uses an 8-bit CRC-type code to detect errors in the previous 4 cell header bytes. The HEC can also be used to correct single-bit errors, but this is not done for some types of ATM interfaces. Multiple bit errors in the cell header always results in the cell being discarded by the receiver.

The *OAM* flow reference architecture (also called the *management plane reference architecture*) defines 5 layers (or *flows*) of an ATM point-to-point virtual circuit (VC), and the monitoring and diagnostics that can be performed using OAM cells, as summarized below (basically F1, F2 and F3 convey physical-level alarms, such as high bit error rates and line failures, and F4 and F5 are often used to enable loopback tests).

▲ The lowest level is F1, and this transmission would be traffic through a SONet repeater (so this level is also called the *regeneration section* level).

▲ F2 defines cell flow at the SONet *line* layer (also called the *digital section* level). SONet *terminal* equipment transmits data at this layer.

▲ F3 defines cell flow between a VC and the CRF (cell relaying function, from VC to virtual path), as well as between the 2 CRFs.

▲ F4 defines cell flow from an end station, through the VC, to the CRF, to the VP, to the remote end of the VP, and to the CRF at the remote end of the VP (which is called the VP CRF).

▲ F5 is the complete path, from end station across the VC to the VC CRF across the VP to the VP CRF, across the VC, to the destination.

Native ATM devices connecting to ATM switches use the *Interim Local Management Interface* (ILMI) for functions such as learning their ATM address from the switch (every ATM switch port has a unique address).

While ATM people would love everything to be ATM (and all PCs would have ATM cards in them), it is expected that at least for a very long time, Ethernet, and to a less extent, Token Ring and FDDI will be used to the desktop, and ATM may be used as a backbone technology. A means of supported existing LANs (for example, which are connectionless) over ATM (which is only connection-oriented, and which runs at different speeds than LANs) is required. There are at least two methods are defined to carry LAN traffic over ATM:

▲ Classical IP over ATM, which is defined in RFC 1577

▲ LAN Emulation (which is usually called *LANE*)

The WinSock 2.0 API specification is being supported by the ATM Forum as a method of supporting ATM adapters in end-user PCs, and allowing application programs to directly interact with ATM's features and benefits, such as specifying QOS.

ATM's *service-specific convergence sublayer* maps different services to ATM (and back).

The *convergence sublayer* compensates for different physical interfaces (T1 to E1, for example) that can be used to access an ATM network. As long as users utilize the same service class, communication between them will be possible even if they each use different interfaces.

Specific SSCSs and CSs need to be standardized for each interface. Frame relay is the farthest along so far.

ATM

The accompanying figure shows the relationship of the convergence sublayers to the types of traffic handled by ATM.

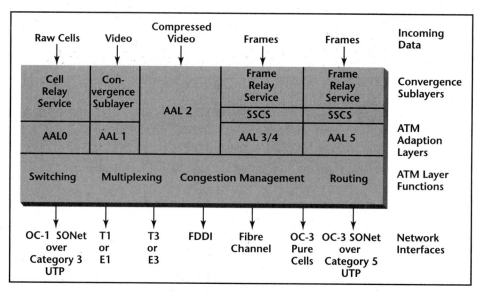

ATM-2

ATM supports four different addressing formats, as listed below:

▲ ITU E.164, which is basically an international format telephone number. This is the format used for ISDN telephone numbers, and can be up to 15 digits in length. It is the format recommended for public ATM networks.

▲ 3 types of *ATM* end-system addresses (AESAs), and are expected to be used for private ATM networks). These all use OSI's NSAP (*network service access point*) encoding format (which is specified in ISO 8348 and ITU X.213), and are distinguished by their *initial domain identifiers* (IDIs). These addresses have both an individual (to a single end system) and a group (to a group of end systems) format, as shown in the AFI table below.

▲ The NSAP domain specific part (DSP) is administered by the address authority (which is specified in the IDP (*initial domain part*). The DSP is typically hierarchical, and can be further subdivided by the addressing authority (for example, Cisco Systems uses part of the HO-DSP as a hierarchical address, and part as a switch address). The DSP format is specified in ISO 8348, RFC 1629 and in the ATM Forum UNI 4.0 specification. Note that the ESI field (*end-system address*—which is a fancy word for an ATM or other user device) is 6 bytes (48 bits), which is the same as the MAC address of Ethernet cards (for example). That is, the ESI address can simply be an Ethernet address. The Sel (*Selector*) field can be used for sub-addressing in the end-system. The format of the ESI and Sel fields is specified in ISO 10589.

▲ DCC uses a 2-byte *data country code* (these are given in ISO 3166) as the IDI. The 3-digit country code is in BCD, with a hexadecimal F to the right.

▲ ICD uses a 2-byte *international code designator* (which is specified in ISO 6523) in BCD as the IDI. ICD addresses are administered by the *British Standards Institute* (BSI), and are only assigned to international organizations. For example, Cisco Systems' ICD is 0091_{16}.

▲ E.164 uses the E.164 address, but in the 20-byte NSAP format. The E.164 address is represented in BCD (*binary coded decimal*), with leading zeros added to make 15 digits total (if necessary) and a hexadecimal F (binary 1111) added to the right end (to make 16 nibbles, which is 8 bytes).

The 3 NSAP address formats are shown in the following table.

The AFI byte is as shown in the table below (in hexadecimal), and depends on both the address format, and whether the address is an individual or group address:

AFI		ATM NSAP Address Format
Group	Individual	
BD	39	DCC
C5	47	ICD
C3	45	E.164

Along with one of the above ADDRESSES, establishing an SVC requires negotiating a *service contract*, which consists of specifying the service category, PCR and other traffic descriptor information, and QOS requirements (such as the maximum allowable CTD). The method of doing this is specified in the UNI signalling specifications.

Low-level addresses are determined by which port on the ATM switch you are connected to. User equipment does not have an address (just like telephone numbers; the telephone itself has no address—the central office switch determines what your telephone number will be, by deciding what telephone number causes your telephone to ring).

To support ATM, a router uses the selected ATM adaptation layer to add the appropriate convergence header to the variable-length packet or frame of data. The convergence sublayer then adds a CRC to the end of the end of the message and adds pad characters so that the message is an integral multiple of 48 bytes. This message could now be sent on a DXI interface. Alternatively, the message is segmented into 48-byte cells by the SAR sublayer, and the router adds the five-byte cell header from the ATM sublayer and sends the cell out on whatever physical interface is being used (a SONet OC-3, for example).

The ATM Forum's User-to-Network Interface (UNI) 3.0 specification was published in September 1993, and specified many important ATM features and interface characteristics and how ATM switches set up permanent and switched virtual circuits. This was followed by the 400-page UNI 3.1 (published in September 1994), which had substantial changes and additions. Then several aspects (such as physical interfaces and signalling) were split into different documents, and the Traffic Management Specification version 4.0 was published in April 1996, which further defined the four *service categories* (there are two types of VBR traffic, so there are sort of five service categories). These specify the *quality of service* (QOS—required bandwidth, allowable error rates, and other characteristics) requirements and traffic characteristics of voice, video, and data transmission.

The QOS and service categories apply to both virtual circuits (VCs) and virtual paths (VPs). The service categories are described in order of decreasing data priority in the following table.

Service Class	Flow Control Method	Service Characteristics
CBR	*Generic Cell Rate Algorithm* (GCRA).	*Constant Bit Rate*: At connection time, the user equipment specifies the *cell delay variation tolerance limit* (CDVT—maximum allowed jitter) and the *peak cell rate* (PCR—bandwidth required, in cells per second), which the network then reserves for the duration of the connection. The user can then transmit cells at or below the PCR at any time, and for any duration of time. The maximum *cell loss rate* (CLR, which is the lost cells divided by the total transmitted cells) is known. Intended for emulating T1 links (for example)—the ATM Forum calls this *circuit emulation service* (CES)—and for data such as uncompressed real-time digitized voice or video that need a guaranteed, fixed bandwidth—any more would be wasted, and any less would cause great problems. Also suitable for constant, high-volume data flows where response time guarantees are required. AAL 1 is used for this service category.

(table continued on next page)

Service Class	Flow Control Method	Service Characteristics
VBR	GCRA	*Variable Bit Rate*: At connection time, the user equipment specifies the PCR, CDVT, *sustainable cell rate* (SCR) and *maximum burst size* (MBS—as the maximum number of cells that can be transmitted at the PCR) required. User equipment can exceed the SCR (up to the PCR) as long as, over the averaging period, the SCR is not exceeded. Also, if the equipment bursts at the PCR for longer than the *burst tolerance* (BT), then the user equipment must send at a lower rate for a period of time (so that the network can carry any queued-up UBR and ABR traffic). Maximum cell loss rate is known. Intended for bursty traffic which cannot tolerate data loss. Two subcategories are defined: • *Real-Time* (rt-VBR), which guarantees network latency and jitter. This will be useful for compressed voice and video (such as MPEG-2) traffic, where due to the variable compression ratio, the data is bursty, but data loss cannot be tolerated. Good voice compression equipment will implement *silence suppression*, which stops digitizing when there is nobody talking (which usually happens about 50% of the time on normal conversations, since only one person talks at a time). Really good silence suppression implementations have a white-noise generator to keep the person talking believing that the line is still connected, since complete silence often indicates that the line has been disconnected (or the person at the other end fell asleep). AAL 5 is used for this service category. rt-VBR was first defined in the ATM Forum's Traffic Management version 4.0 specification, published in April 1996. • *Non-Real-Time* (nrt-VBR), which has an unknown amount of network jitter (the network does not guarantee the jitter). This is suitable for short, bursty data messages, such as mission-critical transaction processing where data loss is not acceptable (such as bank and airline transactions and process control) and some LAN interconnect applications (so long as the data bursts can be characterized adequately). Carrying frame relay traffic is another good application (since frame relay expects low data loss). nrt-VBR was first defined in the ATM FORUM'S UNI 3.1, which was published in September 1994.

(table continued on next page)

Service Class	Flow Control Method	Service Characteristics
UBR	No flow control. Applications keep on transmitting when network congestion occurs. Once ATM switch buffers over-flow, network discards cells (this is hopefully detected by the appli-cation, which will then reduce its trans-mission rate).	*Unspecified Bit Rate*: At connection time, no maximum jitter or bit rate is specified or enforced. The network offers no guarantee of whether or when the data will arrive at the destination. The user application and protocols does this if necessary.) LAN interconnec-tion, E-mail and ftp file transfers (that have no strict tim-ing requirements, and have their own error-detection and -correction protocols), and broadcast applications (such as news feeds) are expected to be applications for this service category.
ABR	In addition to the GCRA, uses *closed-loop, rate-based*[a] flow control, initiated by the network's ATM switches, to ensure that users do not send more data than the network can carry. That is, the flow-control algorithm con-tinuously specifies (and adjusts) the rate (in cells per second) at which each virtual cir-cuit can transmit cells. The network guaran-tees to carry traffic at least at the negotiated MCR.	*Available Bit Rate*: At connection time, user equipment specifies the PCR (which defaults to the access line rate) and the *minimum cell rate* (MCR—bandwidth, which defaults to zero cells per second). The network does not guarantee a maximum latency, jit-ter or a burst tolerance. Uses bandwidth available after CBR and VBR service classes have received the bandwidth they need (though this service class does provide a minimum bandwidth guarantee). Maximum cell loss rate is known, so long as the flow-control procedures are followed. This service category is best for non-real-time bursty traf-fic (such as LAN interconnection), since the flow control handles situations of network congestion without requiring cells to be discarded if a burst of traffic (on this connection, or elsewhere on the network), is unexpect-edly long. Due to the additional traffic guarantees and flow-control mechanism, this service category is getting much more interest and support than UBR.

a. This method was selected over a credit-based scheme (where end stations exchange information on the buffer space available on each link between them). The credit-based scheme would have resulted in lower-cost ATM adaptors in computers, and better performance in LAN environments. However, the rate-based scheme would result in less-expensive ATM switches (due to lower ATM switch buffer memory requirements, since each port would require dedicated buffer memory—and more memory for faster links), which the public carriers really liked. The ATM Forum voted that all ABR implementations had to use the same single flow-control method, and in 1995, rate-based ABR flow-control won.

The *Generic Cell Rate Algorithm* (GCRA) is used to determine, on a per cell basis, whether the traffic sent into the network conforms to the traffic contract (such as the peak cell rate). Cells exceeding the traffic contract have their CLP bit set, and these cells may be discarded in the network, if it gets congested. The algorithm may be implemented in any way—the Traffic Management specification only defines what the algorithm's inputs and outputs should be.

GCRA is also called a *continuous-state leaky bucket* algorithm, as an analogy to a bucket filled by random bursts of water (the incoming user traffic), but that empties through a hole in the bottom at a constant rate (the traffic over the ATM network to other switches). The size of the bursts that can be accommodated depend on how much time as passed since the previous burst, and the size of that burst.

GCRA is an *open-loop* flow control method, in that there is no feedback (according to the network congestion) on the traffic which may be sent into the network. Users are simply allowed to transmit data at their negotiated PCR, SCR, MBS, and so on. In contrast, ABR is the only service category where a feedback flow-control mechanism is specified.

The UBR and ABR service categories are considered *best effort*, since these service categories offer few QOS guarantees

Traffic shaping typically uses *buffering* (temporarily storing cells) or flow-control to reduce the size of traffic bursts, increase the time between bursts and otherwise make bursty traffic less disruptive to other network users. And to ensure that the traffic conforms to the commitments (such as maximum burst size) made by the user at connection time.

ATM connections always transmit cells constantly. Since many devices don't transmit constantly, or don't transmit as fast as the ATM links can carry cells, *idle cells* need to be inserted (using a separate virtual circuit reserved for that function) when the ATM connections would otherwise have nothing to transmit. This is called *cell rate decoupling*. The idle cells are automatically discarded by the destination ATM switch.

Frame discard is a feature of some ATM switches where an entire frame (such as a 1,500-byte Ethernet frame), rather than just some 53-byte cells, is discarded if necessary due to network congestion. Hopefully this reduces the number of frames that have one or more cells discarded (and which will need to be retransmitted by the error-correction in higher-layer software). This improves an ATM network's *goodput*—the amount of good traffic (no errors, and not retransmissions of earlier errored frames) carried. *Early packet discard* (EPD) is similar, but for packet-level traffic (such as *Classical IP* over ATM (RFC 1577) traffic).

CBR and rt-VBR are considered *real-time* service categories, since they have a maximum *cell transfer delay* (CTD) and peak-to-peak *cell delay variation* (CDV) specified in their QOS *traffic descriptor*. These, and other characteristics of the service categories are summarized in the figure below.

At connection time, the end-station requests the required quality of service (which stays the same for the duration of the connection), and the network will establish the connection only if it (including all switches along the path) can supply the resources that are necessary (these mechanisms are specified in the UNI Signalling version 4.0 and PNNI (private network to network interface) version 1.0 specifications. This is called *Connection Admission Control* (CAC). The QOS values can be different for each direction of traffic, for each connection. And they are considered longer term expectations, not short term guarantees (all network traffic planning is based on probabilities, and you never know when traffic will differ significantly for a short period from your expectations). *Usage Parameter Control* (UPC) discards cells that exceed the traffic commitments (such as PCR) made at connection time.

At connection time, the UNI signalling specifies the parameters (such as PCR, in cells per second) as 24-bit integers—which have a range of 0 to 16,777,215. RM cells use a 16-bit floating point notation which has a range of 0 to 4,290,772,992.

The *Available Bit Rate* (ABR) service category uses a feedback-based flow control mechanism. Implementations of ABR flow-control use at least one of the following methods, which all utilize resource management (RM) cells, which are identified by the PTI bit pattern 110 in the ATM cell header).

ABR Flow Control Method	Description
EFCI Marking	Basic *Explicit Forward Congestion Indication*: An end-to-end method (that is, the information is for use by the final destination), in which any ATM switch (along the path from source to destination) that detects network congestion sets the EFCI bit in the cell header. When the cell gets to the destination, the user equipment modifies the *Resource Management* (RM) cells (that it has been sending every *n* cells, with a maximum of 10 RM cells per second per connection) it sends back to the source (as a *backward congestion indication*), requesting the source to reduce its data rate. This method requires that both the source and destination implement this form of flow control. The longer the path from source to destination, the greater the time until the source reduces its data rate (so the network will require more buffering).
	If a source notes that some of the RM cells it should be receiving back from its destination are missing (presumably discarded because of network congestion), then the source must reduce its data rate.
	The source decides how to allocate its allowed bandwidth among its virtual circuits.
	The source also transmits RM cells (every *n* cells), which indicate the sending station's current transmission rate and the higher rate it would like to use.
RRM	*Relative Rate Marking*: Switches along the path can set the CI (*congestion indication*) bit (which requests the sender to reduce its allowed transmission rate (the *allowed cell rate—ACR*) by the factor specified in the RDF (*rate decrease field*), which has a range of 1 through 1/32,768. Or switches can set the NI (*no increase*) bit to prevent the sender from increasing its ACR. If neither the CI nor NI bits are set, then the transmitter can increase its ACR by the RIF (*rate increase factor*), which has a range of 1 through 32,768. Switches are not allowed to reset the CI or NI bits to a 0, so the bits stay set if any switch sets either one, until received by the destination.
ERM	*Explicit Rate Marking*: Switches along the path from destination to source can modify the RM cells (generated by the traffic's destination) to request the source to reduce its transmission rate to a specific rate (in cells per second), using the RM cell's ER (*explicit rate*) field. If the request is for a rate lower than the MCR, then the source can still send traffic at the MCR.
Segmented VS/VD	*Segmented Virtual Source/Virtual Destination*: Some of the network's ATM switches can generate the RM cells (as if they were a "virtual destination"), so there is no need to wait until the real Destination generates the cells (this is important for large networks). These switches can also respond to RM cells, thereby reducing the data rate they forward toward the congestion (and possibly discarding some of the traffic from the real source), therefore protecting the rest of the network from congestion.
Hop-by-hop VS/VD	*Hop-by-hop Virtual Source/Virtual Destination*: All of the network's ATM switches can generate and respond to the RM cells.

The Traffic Management version 4.0 specification requires that networks provide the at least the following 4 *Specified QOS* Classes of service, and define specific values of; peak-to-peak CDV, maxCTD and CLR (the QOS parameters) for each. In addition, networks can provide an *Unspecified QOS* Class, which has no parameters guaranteed.

QOS Class	Comments
Specified QOS Class 1	Provides performance equal to a digital private line, and provide *Service Class A*, which is intended to support circuit emulation and constant bit-rate video.
Specified QOS Class 2	Suitable for packetized audio, video and multimedia, and provide *Service Class B*, which is intended to support variable bit-rate audio and video.
Specified QOS Class 3	Suitable for frame relay traffic, and provide *Service Class C*, which is intended to support connection-oriented data transfer.
Specified QOS Class 4	Suitable for IP and SMDS, AND PROVIDE *SERVICE CLASS D*, which is intended to support connectionless data transfer. traffic
Unspecified QOS Class	Provides a "best effort" service (no traffic guarantees), such as that provided by the ATM UBR service category.

ATM *edge devices* are typically network devices that talk ATM on one side, and have legacy LAN interfaces and protocols on the other side. A router with an ATM interface, or a LAN switch with some routing and ATM capability are examples. Since one side of the device is part of the ATM network, and the other is not, the device is considered to be on the "edge" of the ATM network—hence the name. Some people say these devices "cellify" the data. Devices inside an ATM network don't do cellification, since the data are already in cells (switching of cells is the main thing that happens inside an ATM network).

PNNI and MPOA enable ATM networks to automatically learn and distribute routing information.

VTOA supports telephony over ATM connections.

IMA supports multiplexing ATM traffic over lower-speed circuits (such as T1).

Many of the basic concepts for ATM were first proposed and developed by CNET, which is the research group of France Telecom. They were looking for a digital network that could support real-time cable TV. To reduce store-and-forward delay (since greater delays allow greater echoes), those with a voice background wanted shorter cells (32 bytes of user data). To increase the protocol efficiency and provide lots of features, those with a data background wanted 64 byte cells, plus a 6-byte header. As we all know now, as a compromise, a cell format of 48 bytes of user data plus 5 bytes of cell header was selected (it turned out that the 32-byte cells still allowed enough echo that echo canceller circuits would be needed, so the larger cell size was no additional hardship).

The ATM Forum's specifications are available at *ftp://ftp.atmforum.com/pub/approved-specs*. Most are more conveniently available at *http://www.atmforum.com/atmforum/specs/approved.html*. In addition to the WWW references given in the entry for standards, ATM information is available from ATM equipment vendors, such as those listed in the following table.

3Com Corporation	http://www.3com.com/
General Datacomm, Inc.	http://www.gdc.com
Cisco Systems, Inc.	http://www.cisco.com
Fore Systems, Inc.	http://www.fore.com
Newbridge Networks Corporation	http://www.newbridge.com

See **ADAPTATION LAYER, ATM FORUM, B-ISDN, CARRIER, CELL, CES, CIF2** (*Cells in Frames*), **DXI, E.164, FUNI, IMA, ISOCHRONOUS, LANE, MAC, MULTIMEDIA, NNI, PNNI, RFC 1577, SMDS, SONET, STANDARDS, TAXI, UTP, VLAN, VTOA,** and **WINSOCK 2.**

ATM FORUM
Asynchronous Transfer Mode Forum

"A world-wide organization, aimed at promoting ATM within the industry and the end-user community."

Most ATM work is being done by the *ATM Forum*, which "develops implementors' agreements" (it has no authority to develop international standards). Since there always appears to be more work, it is difficult to know when the technology is ready for commercial use.

There are three types of members (and over 700 members in total):

▲ *Principal* members participate in committees and vote on specifications

▲ *Auditing* members do not participate in committees but do receive technical and marketing documents

▲ *User* members participate only in end–user roundtables, such as the *Enterprise Network Roundtable* (ENR), which consists of about 120 corporations and institutions

Formed in 1991 by Adaptive Corp., Cisco Systems, Northern Telecom, and Sprint Corp.

The ATM Forum has a WWW server at *http://www.atmforum.com/home.html/*.

See **ATM** (*Asynchronous Transfer Mode*).

AT&T CORP.
Previously American Telephone and Telegraph

They used to be called "the Bell System," "Ma Bell," or "the phone company." The first dramatic change came in 1968 when the FCC's "*Carterfone* decision" was made. A Carterfone was a device (invented by Tom Carter) which was electrically connected to a base station radio, and acoustically connected to a telephone handset (you simply placed a standard handset into the Carterphone's beige bakelite cradle—it had a microphone and speaker opposite the handset's earpiece and mouthpiece). The Carterfone enabled a mobile radio user to speak to someone on a telephone (which was manually dialed by the base station radio operator). This was the first non-telephone company device which could be connected to the telephone network (AT&T's network that is), and eventually led to other forms of interconnection, such as modems being directly connected (rather than acoustically coupled) to the telephone network (though a telephone company supplied *Data Access Arrangement* (DAA) was required to connect the equipment to the telephone network—to ensure the safety of both the network and technicians working on it. A second major event came in 1977, when the DAA could be incorporated into products, since it did not have to come from the phone company.

As people became more concerned about AT&T being a monopoly and that AT&T might therefore be restricting competition or not providing new technology and fair prices, in 1982 a U.S. federal court ordered AT&T to answer charges of anticompetitive behavior. Rather than face a full trial, AT&T agreed to give up ownership of the local phone companies (and couldn't even use the bell-inside-circle logo). This breakup (which occurred in 1984) was called *divestiture*.

AT&T was left with its long-distance business, manufacturing, and the research operations (Bell Laboratories).

As part of the divestiture, competition in the form of multiple IXCs was allowed.

AT&T later bought the following.

▲ NCR Corporation (previously National Cash Register) for $7.4 billion in 1991 and changed that group's name to Global Information Solutions (GIS). Then in late 1995 they changed the name back to NCR.

▲ McCaw Cellular Communications for $12.6 billion in 1994.

In 1995 AT&T decided that the synergy and integration of one big company was preventing parts of its organization from growing as fast as they could. For example, AT&T sold telephone switches to the RBOCs, and also competes with them for some long distance services—the RBOCs therefore may purposely not buy switching equipment from AT&T, though they may from the soon-to-be unrelated company. Also, AT&T will begin competing with RBOCs for local telephone services, some based on PCS.

In a "trivestiture" AT&T split itself into the following:

▲ The AT&T name will continue to be used for the core long distance and network business, the cellular telephone business, and the portion of Bell Laboratories (now called AT&T Labs) that provides communications research and development. This business has 1995 sales of about $53 billion.

▲ The Network Systems Division (which used to be called Western Electric) was renamed to Lucent Technologies. It makes the huge central office telephone switches (to which 60% of U.S. telephones connect), PBXs (which they now call Enterprise Communications Servers), telephones, answering machines, integrated circuits and other communication equipment. It also owns the rest of Bell Laboratories. They are allowed to use the AT&T logo for 5 years. This division has sales of about $24 billion, 40% of which was to the RBOCs.

▲ NCR, which used to be AT&T Global Information Solutions (after AT&T bought NCR). They had sales of about $8 billion.

AT&T has a WWW server at *http://www.att.com*, and GIS has a WWW server at *http://ncrinfo.attqis.com/*. Some unofficial AT&T information is at *http://www.nj.com/business/att/*.

See **BELLCORE, CARRIER, FCC, IXC OR IEC, LEC, RBOC OR RBHC,** and **TERADATA.**

ARCNET.

See **ATTACHED RESOURCE COMPUTER NETWORK**.

ATV
Advanced Television

The overall name for new television broadcasting standards, the main implementation being HDTV.

See **HDTV**.

AUP
Acceptable Use Policy

The U.S. National Science Foundation's one-page policy on what types of traffic the federally funded part of the Internet can carry.

Initially interpreted to mean that the Internet can be used to carry only research- and educational-oriented traffic (for example, the only advertising allowed was for new products and services for research and education), it is now generally accepted that this applies only to the part of U.S. backbone that is funded by the NSF.

Commercial providers of Internet access therefore usually charge commercial traffic users more, since the providers cannot route the traffic over the free part of the backbone and must use their own facilities or pay ANS (which runs the entire backbone) for access.

See **ANS**, **CIX**, **INTERNET2**, and **NSFNET**.

AURP
Apple Update-Based Routing Protocol

Apple's link-state replacement for its RTMP router-to-router protocol.

See **APPLE**, **LINK STATE**, and **RTMP**.

Authentication

Generally, a method to verify the source of a document and that the document has not been changed since it was sent (*message* or *data authentication*), or that a user logging on to a network is really who he or she claims to be (*user authentication*).

Data authentication is handled by encryption schemes, such as PGP. An authentication check can produce three results. The data can be:

▲ *Authentic* (it really is from the person it claims it is from, and has not been altered)

▲ *Forged* (it is not authentic)

▲ *Unverifiable* (since we don't have the sender's public key, we can't check whether it is authentic or not)

User authentication usually uses passwords, but better methods are needed and are being implemented. Passwords are too easy to guess (especially with the help of computers) or steal (for example, by monitoring data communication lines or reading others' electronic mail).

Two improved methods of user authentication are becoming popular: time synchronous intelligent tokens and challenge-response intelligent tokens. An *intelligent token* is a credit card–sized device that has an on-board processor and memory, and possibly a numeric LCD display and a keypad as well.

With time-synchronous intelligent tokens, each user gets a token. Using a preprogrammed 64-bit unique, imbedded, secret key, the token generates a new (usually) six-digit random number (usually) every minute, which is shown on its LCD display. Software or hardware at the central site knows the token's secret key and can calculate which number each user's token will be displaying at any time. Users logging in at a terminal's keyboard are prompted to enter a (usually) four-digit number identifying themselves and the number currently displayed on their token.

The central system adjusts its number-tracking algorithm for tokens that are found to be running slightly too fast or too slow.

The advantage of this scheme is that nothing needs to be plugged in to the remote user's communication line (this simplifies things and may be necessary if the remote device is LAN-connected or is a fax machine or voice-mail system).

Problems are that users need to type in numbers (within a short period of time), the method does not provide encryption for the subsequent data exchange, and there is a chance that someone monitoring a user's communication line could get the user's current random number and quickly (before the minute elapses and the number changes) log in elsewhere on the network.

With challenge-response intelligent tokens, a security device at the central site (and connected between the incoming communication line and the host to which access is being protected) sends a randomly generated number to the remote token. The remote token (which is connected between the incoming communication line and the remote PC) encrypts this number, usually using DES and an encryption key that was preprogrammed into the token (by a security administrator) by plugging it into a programmer before it was issued to the user.

The remote-token-encrypted number is then sent back to the security device (at the central site), which has a database of all valid encryption keys. If the remote Token's encryption key is found to be valid (that is, the returned encrypted number matches one that is generated at central by using the same random number), then the central security device allows communication with the host.

The intelligent token may then perform encryption/decryption for the subsequent data exchange.

The advantages of this method are that the user does not need to type anything and the data exchange can be encrypted.

Both of these methods are suitable for dial-up or Internet access as well as LANs and dedicated circuits.

Dial-back modems, in which you dial in and identify yourself, and the modem dials back to where that user is (securely) registered to be, are no longer considered secure. The problem is that some data burglar could use call-forwarding on your telephone line to redirect the call-back to any other location.

Authentication of data (*message authentication*) often includes ensuring the *integrity* of the data—that is, that the data has not been changed from that originally sent. A common method used is MD5 (*message digest 5*), which produces a 128-bit hash code, or fingerprint, of the data, using an algorithm which makes it extremely difficult to find a way to change the message so that the same hash code is produced.

Some vendors of authentication systems are at *http://www.axnet.com* and *http://www. securitydynamics.com*.

See **DES**, **ENCRYPTION**, **FIREWALL**, **IPSEC**, **KERBEROS**, **MD5**, **PGP**, **RADIUS**, **RSA**, **SESAME**, and **X.509**.

AVI

The filename extension for compressed video usually used under Microsoft Windows. *Key frames* are compressed by eliminating redundant information. Subsequent *delta frames* are constructed by recording only the differences from the immediately preceding frame (a process called *differencing*). The decompression is usually handled entirely in software.

Competes with MPEG-1, though MPEG-1 produces higher-quality video and requires specialized hardware for decompression.

See **MPEG** and **VIDEO**.

AYT
Are You There

Originally, a control sequence that could by sent from a UNIX computer telnet session (by first escaping to command mode, and then typing Control-] (holding the control key down, and typing the right square bracket character). If the remote telnet server was operational, it might reply [yes].

Now, people often type the letters AYT in a chat window, to see if anyone is there to "talk" to.

See **IRC**, and **TELNET**.

B

B8ZS
Bipolar, with 8-Zero Substitution

The method developed by AT&T to provide *clear channel* 64 kbits/s data communication service on a DS-0 (rather than the more common 56-kbits/s data communication service), while ensuring that T1's "1s density" rule is enforced.

The "bipolar" refers to the *Alternate Mark Inversion* (AMI) bit transmission used by T1. And the "8-zero substitution" refers to the replacement of 8 sequential zero bits with another pattern, as required by the 1s density rule. This rule requires that the average number of 1s in the data be at least 12.5% (one in eight) and that there be no more than 15 consecutive 0s in a T1 data stream (since 1s are required to keep the sender and the receiver in synchronization).

That is, the worst case allowed is as follows:

▲ Time slot 24 has 10000000

▲ Time slot 1 (the next time slot) has 00000001

▲ The framing bit (between those two time slots) is a 0

In summary, every time slot must contain at least one 1.

To back up a little bit, bits on a T1 line are sent as follows:

▲ A pulse indicates a binary 1, and each time a pulse needs to be sent, it is opposite in polarity to the previous one

▲ The absence of a pulse (that is, nothing) indicates a binary 0

This is called *Alternate Mark Inversion* (AMI). The purpose of the alternating polarity is to ensure that the average D.C. voltage is zero (since the signal spends an equal amount of time at each polarity), which is important in coupling the signal through a transformer (which would otherwise saturate and would therefore distort the signal).

To allow a transmitter to send any bit pattern, including eight consecutive 0s in a time slot, several methods are available:

▲ B7ZCS (*Bipolar 7, with Zero Code Suppression*) or another scheme that sets one of the eight 0 bits to a 1. Digitized speech listeners cannot perceive this messing around with the bits, but you can bet that a computer using the channel for data would. The method requires the full-time use of the eighth bit in each time slot, for use by the carrier (this bit is sometimes also used for line supervision). This leaves only seven of the eight bits for user data, which provide a (7 bits × 8,000 frames per second =) 56,000-bits/s data channel. This method is widely installed (historically, T1 circuits have been used for digitized voice, so there was no impact), but because of its inefficiency for T1 circuits that are used for data (8,000 bits/s of user data throughput is wasted), it is being replaced by other methods that can offer clear channel (full 64,000 bits/s) service.

▲ ZBTSI (*Zero Byte Time Slot Interchange*) is an ANSI standard (based on a slightly different and proprietary method developed by Verilink) that buffers four frames, switches time slots to avoid 1s density violations, and indicates which slots were interchanged using 2 kbits/s of the ESF framing supervisory data channel.

While ZBTSI can often be implemented more easily than B8ZS (which is described below), this method of providing clear channel service is not very popular, partially because of the expense (the electronics are expensive due to the buffering) and the requirement to use part of the supervisory data channel.

▲ B8ZS is becoming a very popular method of providing clear channel 64-kbits/s service for each T1 time slot. Time slots with all 0s are converted to a specific pair of *Bipolar Violations* (BPVs).

This is shown in the following diagram (which assumes that the last 1 in the previous time slot was a positive pulse—the opposite polarity pulses and bipolar violations would be used if the last 1 in the previous time slot were a negative pulse).

Note that the average DC voltage is still zero.

The conversion from the user's clear channel 64-kbits/s data to the B8ZS encoding is done by the CSUs. The CSUs at both ends of a link (typically one CSU at a customer site and the other in the nearest telephone company central office) must have B8ZS support. The B8ZS encoding is done for each point-to-point link and so may need to be done for each point-to-point link in a typical end-to-end connection. Usually, the CSUs will also support ESF.

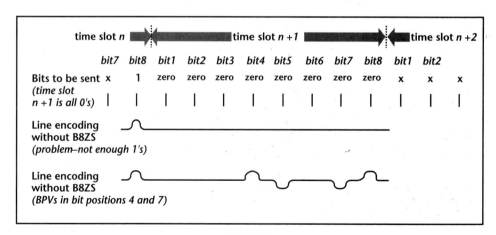

B8ZS-1

B8ZS is used on T1 lines that provide primary rate ISDN (so all 24 time slots can carry a full 64 kbits/s of user data).

Instead of AMI with B8ZS, E1 circuits (and therefore European ISDN PRI circuits) use *high-density bipolar 3* (HDB3), which inserts a bipolar violation instead of only 4 zeros.

See **CSU**, **DS0**, **ENCODING**, **ESF**, **ISDN**, **PRI**, and **T1**.

B-ISDN
Broadband ISDN

A very high-speed data communications service.

ISDN at more than T1 or E1 speeds (such as SONET OC-3). WAN-oriented. Will use ATM switching and support voice, video, and data. Usually simply called "ATM," since anything with "ISDN" in it doesn't sell well.

SMDS is a similar service and (in some places) is currently available, but not widely used nor being adopted.

See **ATM**, **E1**, **ISDN**, **NARROWBAND ISDN**, **OC-X**, **SMDS**, **SONET**, and **T1**.

Baby Bell

An RBOC.

See **IXC OR IEC**, **LEC**, and **RBOC OR RBHC**.

Backbone

The part of a network that carries traffic between areas or network access equipment. Typically, users do not connect directly to a backbone. For example, a backbone would be used to interconnect Ethernet concentrators (perhaps between buildings), and a backbone connects the Internet's NAPs.

Typically, there is less backbone cabling, but it has a higher capacity (analogous to a highway versus side-streets).

See **ETHERNET**, and **NAP**.

Bandwidth on Demand Interoperability Group

See **BONDING**.

Batteries

Correctly, a battery is two or more *cells* (a container with two *electrodes* in contact with an *electrolyte* that produces a voltage determined by the chemistry used) typically connected in *series* (to produce a higher voltage).

For example, a standard 12-volt automobile battery is six 2.2-volt cells connected in series (which produces a nominal 13.2 volts DC). However, people usually call a cell a battery (for example, a single "size D battery").

Batteries

There are two main categories of batteries:

▲ Primary batteries (which are not rechargeable, since the chemical reaction that produces the electricity is not reversible)

▲ Rechargeable batteries (also called secondary batteries)

Batteries have a rated capacity, abbreviated as "C" and stated in amp-hours (Ah). It is usually measured at a discharge rate of C/10 at 20°C (the capacity is very dependent on the discharge rate and temperature).

For example, a battery with a capacity of 1 Ah can supply 100 mA for 10 hours before dropping to below its rated voltage.

There are many types of primary batteries, as shown in the following table.

Type	Features
Standard zinc-carbon	Invented over 100 years ago (by someone named Leclanché). Advantages are mainly lowest cost. They have a nominal voltage of 1.5 V per cell. Problems include poor discharge characteristics (they become continuously weaker, rather than maintaining a high output and then quickly dropping) and unsuitability for high-current requirements (life shortens too much).
Heavy-duty zinc-carbon	Have only slightly better energy density (energy per unit volume) but are much better at high-current applications and wider-temperature operation than standard zinc-carbon batteries. They have the same nominal voltage of 1.5 V per cell.
Alkaline	Widely used (for example, Duracell). Good for low-current, long-life applications (such as clocks). Advantages include better energy density and shelf-life than zinc-carbon. Problems include the same poor discharge characteristic as, and only slightly better temperature range than, zinc-carbon. Slightly more expensive than zinc-carbon. They have a nominal voltage of 1.5 V per cell. Good for low-current, long-life applications (such as clocks).
Lithium	Several types (chemistries) available, but all have very high energy density, wide temperature range, very long shelf-life (more than 20 years at 70° C) and very good discharge characteristics. Problems include the potential fire hazard of the high energy density (high short-circuit current output) and the very toxic chemicals used. They have a nominal voltage of 3 V per cell, and are commonly used to supply backup power to memory.
Silver oxide	Commonly used in watches and cameras. Very good discharge characteristics but shorter shelf-life than lithium. They have a nominal voltage of 1.5 V per cell.
Zinc-air	Extremely high energy density. Starting to be used as a replacement for mercury batteries in hearing aids and pagers. They have a nominal voltage of 1.4 V per cell.

Some primary battery characteristics are shown in the following table.

Characteristic		Zinc-Carbon		Alkaline	Mercury	Lithium
		Standard	Heavy-Duty			
Capacity (Ah)	D	1.5		17		16
	C	1.0		7.8		6.0
	AA	0.18		2.6		2
	AAA	0.07		1.15		
	9V			0.57		
Energy density (Wh/in.^{3})		2	2.5	3.5	7	8
Temperature range (°C at 85% capacity)	Low	10	5	2	3	–30
	High	55	65	70	75	100
Cell voltage (volts)	Unloaded	1.5	1.5	1.5	1.4	3.8
	Loaded	1.0	1.0	1.15	1.3	3.0
	Discharged	0.45	0.7	0.8	1.0	2.0

Note: These numbers (especially the capacity-related ones) will change significantly with temperature (lower capacity at lower temperature) and discharge rate (lower capacity at higher discharge rate).

There are several types of rechargeable batteries as shown in the following table.

Type	Features
Nickel-cadmium (NiCd)	Low-cost, and well-suited to high current output applications. Widely used for consumer applications, such as power tools and video cameras.
	Good discharge characteristics (output voltage stays constant until almost discharged, then drops rapidly). But can overheat if overcharged (charged at too high a rate after already charged).
	Short shelf-life (loses about 2% of its charge per day, and completely discharges in about 3 to 4 months). Lasts about 500 recharges.
	A trickle-charge rate of C/16 is often used to maintain a rechargeable battery in a fully charged state. With suitable batteries and temperature monitoring, fast-charging (C/3 to 4C) can be used. Normal battery charging is at C/10 or less. The nominal voltage is 1.25 V per cell. The battery should not be used after the output voltage drops below 1.1V. At least 60% of the time, the batteries should be fully discharged (to 1.1 V) before charging (this erases the *memory effect* to which some say NiCd is still susceptible).
	A mature technology unlikely to have substantial further improvements.

(table continued on next page)

Batteries

Type	Features
Nickel-metal hydride (NiMH), also called Nickel hydride	Has 30% higher energy density than high-performance NiCd and 100% to 150% more energy density than standard NiCd. Conversely, NiMH supports fewer discharge recharge cycles than NiCd, and is not as well suited to high-current applications as NiCd. Generally though, NiMH is more desirable (and more expensive) for applications such as portable computers and cellular telephones.
	Similar charging as NiCd but heats up more during normal charging. Usually requires a different charger or special settings.
	Can be damaged (more easily than NiCd) by excessive charge or discharge rates.
	Has the same nominal voltage as NiCd, but has less memory effect.
	Self-discharges at about 30% per month.
	Lasts 300 to 500 recharges.
Lithium-ion	Better (and more expensive) than NiMH. Characteristics similar to those of primary lithium.
	Very high energy density—about 50% more than NiMH (by volume) and 80% more than NiMH (by weight); that is, lithium-ion is lighter than NiMH. Has a nominal voltage of 3.6V per cell.
	Self-discharges at about 10% per month (much better than NiCd and NiMH). Has no memory effect.
	Popular for small expensive devices, such as PCS portable telephones, small notebook computers and military applications.
	Lasts 500 to 800 recharges.
Sealed lead-acid (SLA)	Same chemistry as automobile lead-acid batteries.
	Advantages are high current output capability, low cost, long life (many discharge/charge cycles), good shelf-life and discharge characteristics, wide temperature range and no really toxic components, such as cadmium or mercury.
	Problems include low energy density (that is, SLA is good for applications requiring high-capacity batteries where weight is not a major concern).
	Has a nominal voltage of 2.2 V per cell. SLA batteries are usually charged at C/4 until the cell voltage reaches 2.4V. Then they are trickle-charged at C/10 to maintain a cell voltage of 2.25 to 2.3V.
	Widely used in UPS systems, wheelchairs and emergency lighting units.

(table continued on next page)

Type	Features
Rechargeable alkaline	A patented battery system developed by Battery Technologies Inc. in 1986, and sometimes called *rechargeable alkaline manganese* (RAM). Licensed to other companies, such as Rayovac Corp. (they call the product Renewal) and Pure Energy Battery Corp.
	Cells are sold fully-charged (unlike NiCd, which must be charged before use), and have a shelf life of up to 5 years (depending on the ambient temperature)—much longer than NiCd and NiMH (they lose about 10% of their capacity in the first year). They can also be charged at higher temperatures than NiCd or NiMH (so they can be used in solar charging systems). Also, they do not have the "memory effect of NiCd, and they don't have really toxic components, such as cadmium or mercury.
	Output voltage is 1.5 volts, so they can be used for applications that require more than NiCd's 1.2 V. An AA cell typically has a capacity of 0.6 to 1.5 Ah (amp-hours), and the discharged voltage is about 1.0 volts. They can be fully charged in 5 to 7 hours.
	A major limitation is that they can only be charged for about 25 cycles (depending on how much capacity loss you can tolerate), if they are fully discharged. If they are only discharged to about 70% of capacity, they last for 100 or more cycles. The total cumulative capacity is 8 to 50 times that of single-use alkalines, depending on the depth of discharge (full to very shallow, respectively). Rechargeable alkaline is therefore most cost-effective for applications that usually require only shallow discharges before recharging (in contrast, due to the *memory effect*, shallow discharges are not good for NiCd batteries).
	Rechargeable alkaline batteries' cost is only slightly more than single-use alkaline. NiCd cells typically cost two to three times as much as single-use alkaline. NiCd cells are therefore still usually more cost-effective than rechargeable alkaline (though you can bet they are working hard to change this).

(table continued on next page)

Batteries

Type	Features
Silver-zinc	Used for military and aerospace applications.
	Manufactured without their electrolyte (so they have a 5-year shelf life), which is added only when they are about to be used. They then have a 2-year life of up to 200 discharge/charge cycles.
	Advantages include light weight, high energy density, excellent capacity retention, and excellent discharge characteristics.
	Problems include being expensive and high-maintenance and their short life.
	Unlikely to be used in consumer equipment but may be found in surplus equipment.

Some rechargeable battery characteristics are shown in the following table.

Characteristic		NiCd		NiMH	Sealed Lead-Acid
Capacity (Ah)[a]	D	1.2 to 5		[b]	1.2 to 120
	C	1.1 to 2.8			
	AA	0.5 to 0.9			
	AAA	0.18 to 0.22			
	9V	0.1			
Energy density (Wh/in.^{3})		1.2		1.8	1
Temperature range (°C at 85% capacity)	Low	−15		−20	−50
	High	40		45	50
Cell voltage (volts)	Unloaded	1.35		1.4	2.1
	Loaded	1.2		1.25	2.0
	Discharged	1.0		1.0	1.75
Load Current		> 1C		0.5C	0.2C
Self-discharge rate (%/month)		25		30	5
Number of charge/discharge cycles		800		500	200 to 2000

a. The capacity of standard consumer NiCd batteries is at the lower end of the range. Specialty batteries (costing more and capable of faster charging or higher discharge rates) have higher capacity. That's why your camcorder battery pack costs so much more than the replacement cells you can buy at Radio Shack.
b. The capacity of NiMH and sealed lead-acid batteries depends on their physical size. A NiMH AAA cell has a capacity of up to 0.58 Ah. A AA cell has a capacity of about 1.2 Ah.

Battery rechargers initially charge at a *bulk charging rate* until a trigger *overcharge voltage* is reached. They then switch to a *trickle-charge rate* to maintain a cell's *float voltage* (this can be continued indefinitely without damage to the battery to keep it in a fully charged state).

The *memory effect* of NiCd batteries is a very controversial issue. That is, does repeatedly charging a NiCd battery before it is fully discharged (as is often necessary to ensure your portable phone is fully charged for the next day, or because your camcorder's automatic shutoff shuts down your camcorder before the battery is fully discharged—to ensure that the camcorder always works from fully charged batteries).

Generally, vendors say it used to be a problem, but is now solved. However, users generally feel it is still a problem. The answer seems to be that yes, improvements in the chemical formulations and construction of NiCd batteries have eliminated the *cyclic memory* effect (due to shallow discharges) which used to be a problem. However, a reduction in NiCd battery capacity due to *crystalline formation*—that is, the fine crystals of nickel and cadmium form into larger crystals (apparently as much as 150 times larger)—is still a problem (this is quite unrelated to Star Trek's crystalline entity). Since larger crystals have less surface area, there is less of a chemical reaction between the nickel and cadmium, hence the reduced capacity.

Also, the sharp edges of the larger crystals can pierce the cell's internal separator, causing a fast self-discharge. Crystalline formation is accelerated when cells are left charging for long periods of time (many days), or repeatedly charged without first being discharged (conversely, repeatedly discharging a cell just to charge it shortens its life, as there is a limit to the number of times NiCds can be charged).

Another type of "memory effect" that is often still a problem is the formation of a compound made of the nickel and cadmium that is not reversed by shallow discharges and recharges. With less cadmium for the chemical reaction, the capacity of the cell is reduced. Deep discharges (to 1 V per cell) and recharges typically can reverse this type of memory effect, and should generally be done once a month (this is called *exercising* a cell).

Reconditioning a cell to reverse crystalline formation involves slowly discharging it to 0.6 V. Pulse chargers (which use pulses of DC current, rather than a constant DC current) have also been shown to be effective in reversing crystalline formation.

This all amounts to the need for smarter battery chargers that can detect battery problems and automatically do whatever is needed to fix them, and these are becoming more common, and less expensive as new ICs customized to these applications become available.

Some battery manufacturer's information is at Yuasa-Exide Inc.'s web site at *http://www.yuasa-exide.com*, and Duracell Inc. New Products and Technology division is at *http://www.duracellnpt.com*. Benchmarq Microelectronics, Inc. makes ICs for monitoring batteries and controlling battery chargers. They are at *http://www.benchmarq.com*.

See **APM**, **EMPOWER**, **SBD**, and **SMBUS**.

Baud

The baud rate of a data communications system is the number of symbols per second transferred. A symbol may have more than two states, so it may represent more than one binary bit (a binary bit always represents exactly two states). Therefore the baud rate may not equal the bit rate, especially in the case of recent modems, which can have (for example) up to nine bits per symbol.

For example, a Bell 212A modem uses *Phase Shift Keying* (PSK) modulation, and each symbol has one of four phase shifts (of 0°, 90°, 180°, or 270°). Since it requires two bits to represent four states (00, 01, 10, and 11), the modem transmits 1,200 bits/s of information, using a symbol rate of 600 baud.

That is, the baud rate of a modem will not equal the bit rate and is of no interest to the end user. The end user only wants to know the bit rate (in bits per second) of the modem. The table below shows the baud rate and bit rate for popular dial-up type modems.

Modem Modulation Type	Baud rate (symbols/s)	Bit per symbol	Bit rate (bits/s)
Bell 103 V.21	300	1	300
Bell 212A V.22	600	2	1,200
V.22*bis*		4	2,400
V.32	2,400	4[a]	9,600
V.32*bis*		7[b]	14,400
V.34	3,200	9	28,800
V.34+	3,429		33,600

a. When using *trellis code modulation* (TCM), 5 bits per symbol are used, with the extra bit providing additional immunity to noise (this is a form of *forward error correction*—FEC).
b. Again, TCM is used. In this case there are 7 bits per symbol, and each symbol carries 6 bits of data.

Therefore in referring to the data rate of a modem, use bits/s (or kbits/s or Mbits/s), and not baud rate.

Named after J. Maurice-Emile Baudot.

See **ASCII, ASYNCHRONOUS, BAUDOT, BELL 212A, EIA-TIA232, ENCODING, MODEM, SYNCHRONOUS,** and **V.34.**

Baudot

J. Maurice-Emile Baudot's (1845–1903) last name. He was a French telegraph operator who worked out a five-level code (five bits per character) for telegraphs. It was standardized as *International Telegraph Alphabet Number 2*, and is commonly called Baudot (and is a predecessor to ASCII). Since 2^5 is only 32 and the uppercase letters, numbers, and a few punctuation characters add to more than that, Baudot uses *Shift In* and *Shift Out* characters (analogous to how the Caps Lock key on a PC keyboard reduces the number of keys needed by enabling each letter key to represent two characters).

Baudot is still used today for Telephone Devices for the Deaf (TDDs), initially because it became standard for hearing- or speech-impaired people to use surplus mechanical teletype machines (abandoned when the higher speeds of ASCII-based teletypes became standard in the business world). These older teletype machines used Baudot, and the small portable electronic ones also use Baudot, for compatibility.

In the U.K., TDDs are called *Ceephones*.

See **ASCII,** and **BAUD.**

BBS
Bulletin Board System

Software (usually implemented on PCs) that supports multiple simultaneous callers (usually running terminal-emulation software on PCs) to send and receive files and email. Most now provide Internet access as well. Common software packages include Mustang Software Inc.'s Wildcat! and Galacticomm's *The Major BBS*.

BBSs are often run by a company to provide software updates and technical support, though this function is often being replaced by the large service providers (such as CompuServe) and Internet access.

Galacticomm Inc. has an WWW site at *http://www.gcomm.com*, and Mustang is at *http://www.mustang.com*.

See **COMPUSERVE**, **INTERNET2**, **ISP**, **RIPSCRIP**, and **USENET**.

BCD
Binary Coded Decimal

A method of representing decimal numbers (that is, our *base 10* system, which has ten digits, 0 through 9). 4 binary bits (that is, base 2) are used for each digit.

Decimal Digit (in binary)	BCD Digit
0	0000
1	0001
2	0010
3	0011
4	0100
5	0101
6	0110
7	0111
8	1000
9	1001

The bit patterns 1010 through 1111 are not used in BCD, but are used for hexadecimal (and the digits those patterns represent are called A through F, and represent the decimal values 10 through 15.

Bell 103

An old, very low-speed modem modulation method used in North America.

A zero to 300 bits/s, full-duplex, two-wire *asynchronous* modem modulation standard for use on standard dial-up telephone lines. More than 20 years old but still widely used, for example, for retail store credit card authorization terminals.

Bell 202

The modulation method is called *frequency-shift keying* (FSK), since each bit of information is represented by a particular frequency, as shown in the table below. So that full-duplex operation over a single pair of wires, different frequency pairs are used by the modem which originates the call, and the modem that answers the call.

	Frequency (Hz)	
	Transmitted by Answerer	**Transmitted by Originator**
Binary 1 (mark)	1,270	2,225
Binary 0 (space)	1,070	2,025

Bell 103 is similar in technology to, but incompatible with, V.21 (which was popular in Europe, though it is also used by all Group III fax machines).

See **ASYNCHRONOUS**, **FAX**, **MODEM**, and **V.21**.

Bell 202

An old standard for modem modulation, usually only for asynchronous data. There are two types defined:

▲ *Bell 202S* supports half-duplex operation at up to 1,200 bits/s, over dial-up lines.

▲ *Bell 202T* supports full-duplex operation at up to 1,800 bits/s over two-pair leased lines. One-pair leased lines can support half-duplex operation. Conditioned lines are needed for operation over 1,200 bits/s.

The most popular implementation is the Bell 202T at 1,200 bits/s (both because 1,800 bits/s is a somewhat non-standard bit rate, and conditioned lines cost more money).

Frequency Shift Keying (FSK) is used. A binary 0 (called a *space*) is sent as a 2,200 Hz tone, and a binary 1 (*mark*) is sent as a 1,200 Hz tone (both with a tolerance of ±1%).

At 1,200 bits/s, a binary 1 is therefore 1 cycle of a 1,200 Hz sine wave, and a binary 0 is almost 2 cycles of a 2,200 Hz sine wave.

Typical amplitudes for the signal (for Caller-ID) are –13.5 dBm at the CO, and as low as –34.5 dBm by the time it reaches your house.

See **CALLER ID**, and **MODEM**.

Bell 212A

An old, low-speed modem modulation method used in North America.

A 1,200-bits/s, full-duplex, two-wire *synchronous* (*asynchronous* data is supported by a built-in converter) modem modulation standard for use on standard dial-up telephone lines.

Similar in technology to, but sometimes incompatible with, V.22 (which was popular in Europe).

See **ASYNCHRONOUS**, **BAUD**, **MODEM**, **SYNCHRONOUS**, and **V.22**.

Bell Ardis

BCE Mobile Communication's company (actually owned by their Mobility Canada) that offers the DataTac wireless digital data communications service in 28 cities (in 1996) across Canada. Initially, 40% of Bell-Ardis was owned by Motorola, but BCE bought their share in early 1997.

See **ARDIS**.

BELLCORE
Bell Communications Research Inc.

The common research and development organization (with 5,800 employees in 1996) that was required to be supported for 10 years after the (1984) AT&T divestiture, by the resulting seven U.S. Regional Bell Operating Companies (RBOCs). Its predecessor was mostly Bell Telephone Laboratories.

Bellcore initially worked on standards useful to all RBOCs (such as SMDS and T3). As the RBOCs are now offering much, much more than POTS and have now become competitive with each other, and want to fund their own proprietary research, they have agreed to sell Bellcore. Bellcore will continue to meet the national security and emergency preparedness obligations required by the 1984 AT&T divestiture, will retain some patent rights, and will continue to do some work for the RBOCs (such as administering ISDN IOCs).

Bellcore is located in Morristown, New Jersey, and was bought by Science Applications International Corp. in 1997. In 1996, SAIC also bought Network Solutions, who run the InterNIC.

Bellcore has a WWW Server at *http://www.bellcore.com/*.

See **ATT, CALLER ID, DN, RBOC OR RBHC, HDSL, INTERNIC, ISDN**, and **POTS**.

Berkeley Software Distribution UNIX

See **BSD UNIX**.

BERT
Bit Error Rate Test

A common test for data communication circuits. Test equipment is used to generate a bit pattern which is sent on the data communication circuit (which must be taken out of service for the test). At the other end of the circuit, either another tester is connected, or the data is looped back to the sender. The bit pattern is then examined for bits which are different than they were sent. The quality of the data communication circuit can then be quantified by one of many terms, such as:

▲ The number of bits in error (*bit errors*).

▲ Blocks (typically of 1,000 bits) of data that have at least one bit in error (*block errors*).

▲ Number of seconds during which no errors occurred (*error-free seconds*), or the opposite (*errored-seconds*).

Since some data communication circuits may have faults which appear when certain bit patterns are carried, there are standard *pseudo-random* bit patterns which cycle through

every possible bit pattern (of a given length). For example, the "BERT-511" pattern cycles through every combination of 9 bits—so-called, since the maximum number that can be represented in 9 bits is $2^9-1 = 511_{10}$). Longer bit patterns are typically used on faster circuits (they exercise the circuit better, and complete fast enough).

Depending on the type of transmission method and encoding used, different patterns stress the circuit in different ways. Therefore, many testers let you select other bit patterns, such as:

▲ Alternating binary 1s and 0s (also called *alternate mark-space*).

▲ All 0s.

▲ All 1s.

▲ The *fox* pattern, which is a message such as "the quick brown fox jumped over the lazy dogs back". This is a famous test message from a long time ago when mechanical tele-types were used, and these had different parts (solenoids, levers, linkages and hammers) for each letter. Since it would be possible for your "q" letter to be broken, a message which exercised every possible letter was a good one to remember. The fox message may be sent in ASCII or EBCDIC.

▲ A user-defined pattern.

Most data communication circuits will have so low an error rate, that you never see anything interesting happen—and you can't tell if the test equipment is actually set-up and configured properly. There is therefore usually an *insert error* button, which forces the transmitter to send a bit-error in the BERT pattern. The receiving tester should therefore see the appropriate counters increment as this is done.

See **ASCII**, **EBCDIC**, **EIA-TIA232**, and **ENCODING**.

BGP
Border Gateway Protocol

A router-to-router protocol.

A replacement for IP's *exterior gateway protocol* that provides *policy-based routing* (that is, including factors such as the traffic's importance in determining routing) between administrative domains.

See **RIP**.

Big Endian

A colorful way of describing the sequence in which multibyte numbers are stored in a computer's memory.

Storing the most significant byte in the lowest memory address, which is the address of the data. Since TCP defines the byte ordering for network data, end-nodes should call a processor-specific convert utility (which would do nothing if the machine's native byte-ordering is the same as TCP's) that acts on the TCP and IP header information only. This ensures the software will be portable. In a TCP/IP packet, the first transmitted data is the most significant byte. That is, *network byte order* is big-endian—most significant bytes gets transmitted first.

Most UNIXes (for example, all System V) and the Internet are Big Endian. Motorola 680x0 microprocessors (and therefore the VME bus and Macintoshes), Hewlett-Packard PA-RISC, and Sun SuperSPARC processors are Big Endian. The Silicon Graphics MIPS and IBM/Motorola PowerPC processors are both Little and Big Endian (bi-endian).

The term is used because of an analogy with the story *Gulliver's Travels*, in which Jonathan Swift imagined a never-ending fight between the kingdoms of the Big-Endians and the Little-Endians, whose only difference is in where they crack open a hard-boiled egg.

See **LITTLE ENDIAN**, **MS**, **OPERATING SYSTEM**, **PORTABILITY**, and **UNIX**.

Binary Synchronous Communications

See **BISYNC**.

BIOS
Basic Input/Output System

Low-level routines (programs) in a PC that provide standard program interfaces to perform hardware-oriented functions such as reading the keyboard, writing to the monitor's screen and accessing disk drives.

A PC can have more than one BIOS, such as a system BIOS (described below), video BIOS (provides a standard interface to vendor's unique display hardware, as well as additional display functions) and SCSI adapter BIOS (provides a standard interface to SCSI adapters, which may implement functions in different ways).

The system BIOS typically includes code (that is, a small program) to read an operating system from diskette or disk into memory (which is what your PC does when you power it on). The BIOS software itself is stored in (usually 64 kbytes of) nonvolatile EPROM so that it is available even after the PC has been powered off and on (normal PC memory is erased when the power is turned off).

The method of accessing the system BIOS functions (a *jump table* starting at a predefined location in RAM) makes it easy for software to replace or augment the PC's built-in BIOS functions. This is often how drivers loaded from `config.sys` (DOS disk drivers, for example) provide their functionality.

A typical BIOS call first loads specific CPU registers with values defined for that BIOS call. For example, to send a character out of a PC's `COM1` serial port, you would load register:

▲ `AL` with the character (for example, 31_{16} is an ASCII 1)

▲ `DX` with the port (0 for `COM1`, 1 for `COM2`, and so on)

▲ `AH` with 1 (this specifies that the interrupt 14_{16} *output character* service is to be used)

Then an `Int  14`$_{16}$ (software interrupt 14_{16}) instruction would be issued (normally, this would be done from a program, but you could do it interactively from the DOS' debugger `DEBUG` as well), and the character would be output. On return from the interrupt, Register `AH` has status information, such as whether the call was successful. Previously, another BIOS function (`Int  14`$_{16}$, service 0) would have been used to initialize the port (to set the bit rate, the number of data and stop bits per character, and the parity).

The BIOS reserves the first (that is, the lowest, starting at address $0000:0000$) $1,024_{10}$ bytes of memory (RAM) for the jump table. There is a possibility of 256 software interrupts (since the `Int` assembler instruction has a 1-byte field to specify the interrupt number). Each BIOS jump table entry is 4 bytes and specifies the *segment* and *offset* (a 20-bit linear address is formed by shifting the segment 4 bits to the left and adding it to the offset).

The BIOS jump table is therefore 256 4-byte entries, which requires 1,024 bytes total.

An `Int` 14_{16} (which is `Int` 20_{10}) looks in the 20th jump table entry, which is memory location 80_{10} (which is 50_{16}) for the address of the BIOS routine to be run to handle the `Int` 14_{16}. On my PC (and most others), location 50_{16} is storing the value $F000:E739$ (that is specified in the PC's segment:offset format, which is the same as $FE739_{16}$).

This BIOS routine is in the upper 64 kbytes (which is $F0000_{16}$ to $FFFFF_{16}$) of a PC's first 1 Mbyte of memory (which is 00000_{16} to $FFFFF_{16}$). This is as expected, since the entire BIOS is usually within this upper 64 kbytes. Note that running another operating system (such as OS/2) or loading COM drivers will likely change this *interrupt vector* to point to somewhere else in memory (wherever the entry point for that driver is).

The 256_{10} bytes of memory after the BIOS jump table (that is, from $0040:0000$ to $0040:00FF$, which is the same as 00400_{16} to $004FF_{16}$) is also reserved by the BIOS. It is used to store system information, such as disk drive and keyboard status. For example, to turn on your keyboard's Num Lock LED, run your debugger (for example, DEBUG from a `c:>` DOS prompt), and enter `E  0040:0017  20`. This writes ("enters") 00100000_2 into memory location 00417_{16} which is where (among other things) the keyboard's LED status is stored—and bit 5 is the Num Lock LED. `E 0040:0017 00` will turn off the Num Lock LED. The `Q` command quits out of DEBUG back to DOS.

Since this also writes other bits (such as whether `Insert` is active), you should be running DOS (not Windows) and reboot your PC afterward. Also, do be careful when playing in DEBUG. It is possible (though unlikely) to (for example) write over important parts of your disk drive.

See **ASCII**, **BOOTSTRAP**, **CMOS**, **DMI**, **FAT**, **IDE**, **NETBIOS**, **PC**, **PIO**, **RAM**, and **SHADOWED BIOS**.

BISYNC
Binary Synchronous Communications

The type of data communications used from older IBM terminals to mainframe computers.

A *character-oriented* (since specific characters such as the STX and ETX control characters have special meanings), synchronous, link layer protocol that provides simple error correction and flow control. There is some disagreement about exactly what BISYNC stands for. Some people say that it gets its name because there are two sync characters before the message (to establish bit, byte, and message synchronization); some say there are two devices involved in the communication; and some say it is because the data are binary. If I knew, I'd tell you. (Say, why do they call a baseball pitcher's warm-up area the bull pen?)

The ASCII and EBCDIC sync characters are different (00010110_2 and 00110010_2, respectively). Which is used depends on the data being carried (IBM uses the EBCDIC sync, everyone else uses the ASCII sync). Both have the same important characteristic that they never look like a shifted copy of themselves (as 00100010 would, for example).

Uses *synchronous* (rather than *asynchronous*) data communications.

Also called BSC.

Weaknesses of BISYNC include the following:

▲ The difficulty of carrying certain control characters (such as ETX) as data, since they indicate the end of the message

▲ Support for a window size of only 1 (so higher-speed and longer time-delay links and would provide lower throughput than necessary, since a second block of data cannot be sent until the acknowledgment to the first is received)

HDLC (and its many variations) solves these problems and is a much more powerful and widely implemented *bit-oriented* successor.

See **S3270**, **ASCII**, **ASYNCHRONOUS**, **DLC**, **EBCDIC**, **HDLC**, **MAINFRAME**, **SDLC**, **SYNCHRONOUS**, and **V.25BIS**.

Bitmap Font

A method of describing the shape of characters.

Also called an *image* or *raster* (as in a television raster, which scans horizontally across, then down a line to scan again) *font*. A nonscalable font (though lousy scaling can be done by duplicating or deleting raster rows).

Video display fonts are bitmap and can be produced on the fly from *outline fonts* by the Adobe Type Manager or TrueType.

Printers usually use outline fonts to provide high-quality scaling. The printers convert the outline fonts to raster while they are printing.

Bitmap fonts are less flexible than outline fonts but often look better, since they can be hand-tuned to produce the best quality output for that specific *point* size. Bitmap fonts will usually display and print faster, since rasterizing is not required.

See **ATM** (*Adobe Type Manager*), **FONT**, **SPEEDO**, **OUTLINE FONT**, **POINT**, **POSTSCRIPT TYPE 1 FONTS**, **POSTSCRIPT TYPE 3 FONTS**, **TRUETYPE**, and **TYPEFACE FAMILY**.

BITNET
Because It's There Network or Because It's Time Network

A UUCP-based, worldwide, store-and-forward, email-based, academic-use-oriented network that uses TCP/IP and has a limited connection to the Internet.

See **INTERNET2**.

BLOB
Binary Large Object

A large linear data type, such as a graphical image or multimedia object. That is, it does not have separate components, such as records or fields.

Blue Lightning

IBM's clock-tripled 25-MHz and 33-MHz 486 CPUs. They have 16 kbytes of Level One (internal) cache, a 386 (that is, slower than 486) type bus interface, and no math coprocessor.

See **INTEL** and **PC**.

BNC
Bayonet Nut Connector or Bayonet Neill Concelman

The type of connector that is often used for coaxial cables, such as those for ThinWire Ethernet or RGB video.

Some say that BNC stands for "Bayonet Nut Connector" (the push and turn action like that used for a Nikon camera lens is often referred to as a bayonet mount, probably because rifle bayonets are mounted that way).

Some say that it stands for "Bayonet Neill Concelman," for the people (person) who developed the thing (Mr. Bayonet taking the lead, no doubt).

I have also heard that it stands for "Bayonet N Connector," since it is like a quick-connect N connector (an N connector is the large CATV-like connector used on ThickWire Ethernet).

Still others say that the BNC connector was invented by the *Bently Nevada Corporation* (which makes vibration-monitoring equipment for rotating machinery so that you know the ball bearings on your 5,000-horsepower electric motor need replacing before they turn red-hot and seize). Well, Bently Nevada didn't invent the connector and it is not named after them (though they do use the connectors).

In any case, while the mating side of BNC connectors have always had the same dimensions, the side that connects to the cable has different diameters according to the type of coax (RG-58, RG-59, etc.) for which the connector is designed, and whether that coax is to be made of PVC (polyvinyl chloride)—the soft, flammable, plastic type of insulation—or Teflon (which is Dupont's trademarked name for polytetrafluoroethylene, which they call fluorinated ethylene propylene—FEP). Coax cables made of Teflon are nonflammable and have a smaller diameter than PVC coax.

So make sure you order the right kind. (Nothing is more frustrating than a bag of the wrong-size coax connectors—and a job that has to get done by morning.)

See **COAX**, **CONNECTOR**, **ETHERNET**, **LAN**, and **RGB**.

BONDING
Bandwidth on Demand Interoperability Group

A specification for combining switched digital circuits (such as switched 56 or ISDN) and resolving the timing differences between them. This provides a higher-speed switched service, often used for video-conferencing.

Initially developed by Ascend Communications Inc. and other companies in 1991 to be an interoperable (that is, standard) method of aggregating bandwidth. Unfortunately, they had such a descriptive name that the term is now often used to refer to any method of aggregating bandwidth (such as MLPPP), rather than the original one.

Such generic bonding is sometimes called *bundling*.

See **BRI**, **DS0**, **INVERSE MULTIPLEXER**, **ISDN**, **MLPPP**, and **T1**.

BOOTP
Bootstrap Protocol

A TCP/IP protocol that enables a diskless workstation (or other LAN-attached network device, such as an Ethernet switch or repeater) to learn its IP address (and some other information) from a centrally administered server.

Upon power-up, the network device broadcasts a request for a bootp server to respond (so the network device does not even need to be configured with the address of a bootp server). In addition, to the IP address, the bootp server can be configured with a *boot file* name which will be sent to the network device. The network device can then initiate a tftp session with a tftp server (likely the same host as the bootp server) to retrieve the program which the network will use to boot from (rather than from a local hard disk, for example).

bootp was standardized in 1985 as RFC 951.

DHCP is a more flexible and secure protocol, which is based on bootp. For example, `bootp` can only assign specific IP addresses to nodes with specific MAC addresses (typically, as configured in an ASCII text file).

See **DHCP**, **IP ADDRESS**, and **TFTP**.

Bootstrap

The term often used for starting a computer, especially one that loads its operating software from disk.

A conundrum: How do you read the operating system (which is basically bits on a disk) from a disk drive when the programs that know how to control and read the disk drive are only on the disk (and not yet in the computer's memory). Sounds impossible, like pulling yourself up off the ground by your own *bootstraps* (those are the straps on the top sides of the boots that help you pull them on).

Somehow, this analogy led the process of starting a computer (especially one with the operating system on disk) to be called bootstrapping and now simply *booting* (not to be confused with what you feel like doing to your computer when it is, shall we say, not exactly enhancing your productivity).

Many solutions to this problem (that is, the one about reading the disk on power-up) have been implemented, but all generally do the following:

▲ The computer has some nonvolatile memory (that is, it is programmed at the factory, and it never forgets, even after being powered off or the computer going loony) in which is stored a simple disk-reading program. (It usually only looks at a specific location on the disk, such as the very beginning.)

▲ On power-up, the CPU has been designed to start reading and executing at the location in nonvolatile memory where the disk-reading program is stored (possibly first doing some basic hardware checks). If the disk is *bootable*, then stored at the beginning of the disk is a program (sometimes called a *loader*) that is smarter (and larger).

▲ This loader is read into memory and, when executed, reads enough of the operating system into memory that the operating system can take care of itself (without so much as a "thank you" to the loader—in fact, the operating system simply writes over the now memory-resident copy of the loader).

Border Gateway Protocol

IBM calls this process *Initial Program Load* (IPL).

See **BIOS** and **OPERATING SYSTEM**.

Border Gateway Protocol

See **BGP**.

Branch Prediction

A technique for increasing the processing speed of computers.

A capability of most new processors with multistage execution units to predict which branch of a conditional jump or loop the processor will take (so it knows which instructions to read ahead and start executing).

Intel's Pentium's *dynamic branch prediction* maintains a table of jump history and assumes that if the processor encounters a jump it has seen before, it will take the same path as before, since most jumps are either almost never taken (for example, they test for error conditions) or taken many times (for example, looping to process some data).

See **INTEL** and **PENTIUM**.

BRI
Basic-Rate Interface

A digital, WAN-oriented data communications service.

An ISDN service that provides two B channels plus one D channel.

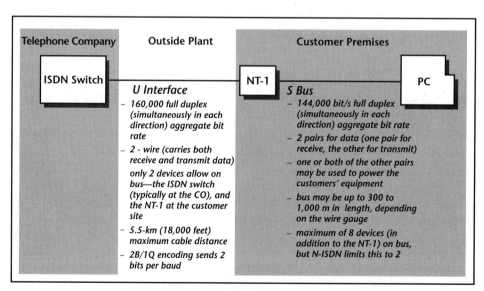

BRI-1

As shown in the above figure, the *S bus* (sometimes called the S/T interface) carries a total of 144 kbits/s ($2 \times 64,000 + 16,000$ bits/s), and the U interface (as standardized by ANSI for

North America) carries 160 kbits/s (all of this is full-duplex). In North America, the U interface uses an encoding method called *2B1Q*, where 2 bits of information are represented by a four-state ("quaternary") symbol, and data is sent full-duplex. The extra 16,000 bits/s on the U interface is used by framing (12 kbits/s) and maintenance (4 kbits/s) overhead. In Japan, the U interface uses a *ping-pong* method where it is sent half-duplex at 320 kbits/s, but changes direction so quickly that the service appears to be full-duplex.

The cable distance from the CO to the user's equipment can be a maximum of 5.5 km (18,000 feet). (Actually, the maximum attenuation for this cable run is specified to be 38.8 dB, but this is usually what you get after 5.5 km of 24 gauge cable.) If the distance is greater than that, the telephone company may install one or more repeaters (so each cable length is less than 5.5 km), or more likely, they'll tell you that ISDN is not available in your area.

If the PC does not have an ISDN interface, then a *terminal adapter* can be connected to the S bus. The terminal adapter's EIA-232 (for example) interface could then be connected to a PC's standard COM port. Some terminal adapters have built-in NT-1s.

Some *ISDN* adapters (a card in a PC that provides an ISDN S bus interface from the PC to the outside world) and terminal adapters can split their data over the two B channels so that the data rate is effectively 128 kbits/s. Since this is two telephone calls, double the normal long-distance charges would apply (for long-distance calls). Typically, long-distance charges are the same (per call) as standard analog telephone calls. A compatible device must be used at the other end of the call, as there are no widely accepted standards for such "bonding."

While ISDN can replace the need for modems, there will be a long time during which both ISDN (by some people) and modems (by other people) will be used. Manufacturers have therefore produced devices (sometimes called *ISDN* modems or *digital modems*) which enable communications with both ISDN devices and analog modems. A block diagram of these devices is shown in the following figure.

```
|<-ISDN       |<------------ ISDN Modem --------------------->|<-User
   Service->|                                                  Equipment->|

                                                        - Telephone
                                           ------------|
                                -----------  - CODEC -|          - Modem
 ISDN                          |          | |        |  Analog    - EIA-232
 BRI      ----- NT-1 -|        | |--|        - Modem -
 Interface                     |          | |        |  ISDN          |--|- Parallel
         ^         ^  |        |          |  - Terminal Adapter-|
         |         |  - V.42bis -    - Terminal Adapter-        - PC's Bus
         |         | Interface
         |        S/T Interface                                 - Ethernet
    U Interface
```

In all cases, the ISDN modem's only connection to the outside world is a 2B+D BRI ISDN connection.

The NT-1 may be internal or external to the ISDN modem. ISDN modems are therefore usually advertised as being available with either a U interface (if the NT-1 is internal to the ISDN modem), or an S/T Interface (when the NT-1 is external to the ISDN modem). In countries

where the NT-1 is provided by the phone company (this is usually the case in Europe, for example), then using an external NT-1 is the only choice.

Both the U interface and the S/T interface use an 8-pin modular jack (often called an RJ-45).

In countries where the NT-1 is usually provided by the customer (in North America) then either may be used. The internal NT-1 is usually more convenient. However, the U interface from the telephone company can connect to only one device, but up to 8 physical devices can connect to the S bus. This one reason why you may prefer an external NT-1.

The entire ISDN modem may be a stand-alone box (like an external modem), or may be a board that plugs directly in your PC (or whatever your computer is). For external ISDN modems, the connection to the PC will usually be through an EIA-232 connection. Since these connections are often limited to 115,200 bits/s, they are a "bottleneck" for ISDN calls that combine both B channels to produce 128,000 bits of capacity. Also, a PC's EIA-232 serial communications (COM) port uses asynchronous data communications. This reduces the COM port's throughput (due to the start and stop bits for every 8 bits of data) to about (8/10 x 115,200 =) 92,160 bits/s. Therefore, some manufacturers use parallel port connections to the PC instead of the serial port. Other manufacturers sell high-speed COM ports (230,400 or 460,800 bits/s) for PCs.

Internal ISDN modems may have built-in COM ports (so they have the same limitations as external ISDN modems), or may use a proprietary interface to the PC—similar to how a LAN adapter has a proprietary interface to the PC. The manufacturer then supplies a driver for the ISDN modem, and communications between the ISDN modem and PC can be at the full speed of the PC's bus. These have the highest performance, but are the most difficult to install.

Another way to access ISDN is using a router with an ISDN interface. In this case, the router would usually connect to your PC using Ethernet (usually 10BASE-T). The advantage of this is that multiple devices can connect to the ISDN router. Such ISDN routers usually would not support telephones or V.34 modem communication.

When the ISDN modem is used for a data call to another ISDN device, the ISDN acts as a *terminal adapter*, and converts the data from the PC to the ISDN protocol. The ISDN modem may implement data compression, such as V.42*bis*. The data compression would only be enabled if the called device supported the same type of data compression.

If the ISDN modem is used to call (or receive a call from) a standard analog modem, then the internal modem of the ISDN modem is automatically used (the D-channel signalling indicates whether the destination is an ISDN line or a analog). This is typically a V.34 modem, with its output digitized. The digitizing device is called a CODEC (though the actual implementation may do both the V.34 modem and the CODEC function in a single DSP integrated circuit). The digitized analog modem signal coming out of the CODEC is exactly the same as the digitized modem signal coming out of the CODEC in a telephone company central office switch, so the ISDN modem can call (or receive a call from) a remote standard V.34 modem (for example) on a standard POTS telephone line.

The analog side of the CODEC is also connected to at least one, and sometimes two 6-pin modular telephone jacks (often called RJ-11s). Standard telephones (or facsimile machines, external analog modems, answering machines, and so on) can be plugged-in to these jacks (the ISDN modem generates a fake dial tone, ringback, busy and so on—so all seems like a traditional telephone call to you). Therefore, these non-ISDN devices can be used to make (the ISDN modem changes the touch-tone dialling signals to ISDN signalling) and receive two separate telephone calls (one on each B channel). If the ISDN modem is internal to a PC, the PC usually must be powered-on if the telephones are to be used. Sometimes an external power supply can be used for these internal ISDN modems so the PC does not have to be powered-on at all times. Some ISDN modems require an external power supply to generate the 90 V AC signal required to ring a standard telephone. The ISDN modem or power supply will then specify a REN, to indicate how many telephones it can ring.

Many ISDN modems implement a really neat feature so that you can be "surfing the Internet" at 128 kbits/s (and even faster if data compression is used)—using both B channels of your ISDN connection. If someone telephones you, then the ISDN signalling on the D channel tells your ISDN modem that you have a call. If you have configured the ISDN modem to accept the call, then it terminates one of the B channel calls (while you are still surfing the Internet, but now at "only" 64 kbits/s) and accepts the telephone call (your telephone rings). When you complete the telephone call (you hang-up the phone), then the ISDN modem can automatically re-establish the B channel call to your ISP, and you are back to surfing at 128 kbits/s. Not all ISDN modems or service providers (telephone companies) support the signalling required to do this—but it is standard, and it does work if all the components are in place and configured.

Some ISDN providers offer a 0B+D service. This uses the 16 kbit/s of packet-switched bandwidth for access to X.25 networks (as well as for the call control purposes for which the D channel is always.

See **ASYNCHRONOUS**, **BUS**, **BONDING**, **CODEC**, **DSP**, **EIA-TIA232**, **ISDN**, **ISP**, **MODEM**, **NI1**, **NT1**, **PARALLEL PORT**, **POTS**, **PRI**, **REN**, **V.42BIS**, and **WAN**.

Bridge

See **ROUTER**.

Broadband
Broad Bandwidth

Now usually refers to data communications faster than T1 or E1 speeds (that is, more than about 2 Mbits/s).

It used to refer to communications using a broad range of frequencies, such as data communications using coaxial cable and radio frequency modems. These would usually be very high-performance (and high cost) networks. Examples include the 10BROAD-36 Ethernet specification and the 802.4 Manufacturing Automation Protocol. These were never widely implemented (only big installations with lots of money used them) and are seldom used now, due to the difficulty of maintaining and expanding the networks.

See **B-ISDN**, **E1**, and **T1**.

BSD UNIX
Berkeley Software Distribution UNIX

A type (flavor) of UNIX.

University of California at Berkeley's Computer Science Research Group's UNIX, the main competitor to USL's SVR4. The most recent version is 4.4BSD-lite, which is the first totally "unencumbered" (by copyright and licensing restrictions, as previous releases used source code from AT&T) version. BSD UNIX began as a collection of utilities to replace and augment those in AT&T's UNIX, but over time the Berkeley software distributions became a full stand-alone operating system. BSD originated important features such as vi, C shell, memory paging, good job control, and networking (TCP/IP and Ethernet).

See **OPERATING SYSTEM** and **UNIX**.

BTW
By the Way

A common email abbreviation.

Bugs

While most people are caught up with *software bugs* (things that don't work the way one would expect them to, probably because of a programming mistake), I was surprised to learn that current U.S. standards allow up to 75 insect fragments per 50-gram grain sample (really—check it out for yourself: *BusinessWeek*, September 5, 1994, page 83).

Bundling

See **BONDING**.

Bus

A bus is a data communications connection between two or more communicating devices.

Serial buses (which send 1 bit at a time) are typically used for longer distances and (perhaps) lower cost and lower performance. Examples are 10BASE-2 Ethernet LANs, ACCESS.bus, and USB.

Parallel buses send some number of data bits (such as 8 or 16), plus control and address signals, at the same time. Parallel buses are typically more limited in length because of the high cost of the multiconductor cable and connectors and for electrical reasons—the signals don't travel at the exact same speed in all conductors (*signal skew*), so the data rate must be reduced for longer cable runs (making the bus less desirable).

Some parallel buses are implemented by using cables and connectors (for example, IEEE-488 and SCSI). However, the rest of this description will discuss parallel buses that are internal to a PC and implemented on the motherboard of the computers.

A parallel bus is the collection of electrical connections, connectors and voltages, timing, and functionality defined for plug-in printed circuit boards (sometimes called *adapters*) in a computer to communicate with each other.

Each computer platform usually has a unique bus. Some examples are given in the following table.

Manufacturer	Equipment	Bus Used
Apple[a]	Macintosh	NuBus
Compaq and others	80386-based PCs	EISA
DEC	Alpha-based workstations	TurboChannel
IBM and compatible	PC and PC/XT	8-bit XT
IBM and compatible	PC/AT and later	16-bit ISA
IBM and compatible	486 PCs	VL-bus
IBM and compatible	Pentium	PCI
IBM	RS/6000 and PS/2 PCs	MCA
Sun	SPARC workstations	SBus

a. Many vendors, such as Apple, are now supporting PC-type buses (such as PCI) either exclusively, or in addition to their proprietary buses in the newer computers. This allows them to take advantage of lower-cost adapters (such as SCSI and LAN), to reduce costs.

Some characteristics of PC buses are shown in the following table.

Bus	Released	Bus Speed (MHz)	Data Path Width (bits)	Peak Throughput (Mbytes/s)
XT	1982	4.77	8	2
ISA	1984	8.33	16	8
MCA	1987	10	16	20
			32	40
EISA	1988	8.33	32	33
VL-bus v1.0	1992	33	32	132[a]
		40		148
VL-bus v2.0	1994	50	64	267
PCI v1.0	1992	33	32	132
PCI v2.0	1993	64	264	264
PCI v2.1	1995	66	32	264
			64	528

a. 132 Mbytes/s for reads, 66 Mbytes/s for writes.

Bus

Some additional comparisons are listed in the following table.

Bus	Address Bus Width (bits)	Interrupts	DMA Channels	Pins
XT	20[a]	6[b]	3[c]	62
ISA	24[d]	11	7	62 + 36[e]
EISA	32	15	7	100
MCA	32	11	0[f]	182
VL-bus v1.0	32	1	0[g]	116
VL-bus v2.0	64			
PCI v1.0	64[h]	4	0[g]	188[i]

a. This bus's 20 address lines support only 1 Mbyte of memory.
b. There are actually eight interrupts, but the highest-priority interrupts 0 and 1 are not brought out to the bus, as they are used for the timer and keyboard (which are implemented on the motherboard). The six remaining interrupts were required for the floppy and hard disk drive controllers, serial ports, and parallel printer port. This does not leave many spare for additional functions, such as LAN adapters and sound boards.
c. There are actually four DMA channels, but one is permanently assigned to the memory refresh function. Of the three remaining, two of these are required for the floppy and hard disk drive controllers.
d. This bus's 24 address lines support only 16 Mbytes of memory.
e. There are two connectors: the original 8-bit bus 62-pin connector and an additional 36-pin connector that provides the extra address, DMA, and interrupt lines.
f. Up to 16 bus masters are supported (each uses its own DMA controller).
g. Bus master DMA is supported, so every adapter can have as many DMA channels as is provided hardware for.
h. Address and data bus lines are multiplexed together.
i. Including keys to ensure that 3.3-V and 5-V cards cannot be plugged into the wrong voltage slots.

Finally, what they are typically used for is shown in the following table.

Bus	Suited to
XT	Obsolete, as XT (8088 and 80286) PCs are.
ISA	80386-based PCs (with either less than 16 Mbytes of memory or, more commonly, a proprietary bus for memory)
MCA	PS/2 PC and RS/6000 workstations.
EISA	High-end PCs, such as file servers.
VL-bus	The video adapters (and sometimes SCSI disk controllers or LAN adapters) in 486 PCs. ISA slots are used for other cards (such as serial ports and low-end disk and LAN adapters in these PCs)
PCI	Video adapters, disk controllers, and LAN adapters in Pentium PCs. ISA slots are used for low-end cards in these PCs.

See **ACCESS.BUS, BUS MASTER DMA, DMA, EISA, IRQ, ISA, LAN, LOCAL BUS, MCA, PCI, SCSI1, USB,** and **VLBUS OR VLB.**

Bus and Tag Channel

See **CHANNEL**.

BUS MASTER DMA
Bus Master Direct Memory Access

A method of transferring data between components of a computer system (such as a LAN adapter, the memory, and a disk controller).

A faster data transfer technique (at least for larger transfers) than standard CPU-based DMA, for the following reasons:

▲ The peripheral (a LAN adapter, for example) writes from its memory directly to the PC's memory in one bus cycle (reducing the load on the bus), rather than the two-step process of the CPU's DMA controller first reading the data (from the adapter) and then writing it to the PC's memory in a second bus cycle.

▲ Bus master DMA is therefore sometimes called *first-party DMA*, since the source or destination of the data is where the DMA controller resides (that is, on the disk controller or LAN adapter, for example).

▲ Often, the adapter will do its transfer as the data are received from the LAN, so no, or little, on-board LAN adapter memory is required (this saves money).

▲ Uses much less CPU time than other methods. For example, programmed input-output (PIO) requires the CPU to first check for the availability of the data, then read the data, and then write the data. This requires bus and CPU time for both fetching the CPU's instructions and for reading and writing the data. Also, bus master DMA is faster than standard DMA, since the CPU does not even need to load the DMA registers (for example, with the source and destination addresses) to set up each transfer.

Ungermann-Bass LAN boards use this technique.

Since the peripheral writes directly to the PC's RAM, the peripheral does not get the benefit of the CPU's memory mapping (for example, an 80386 processor's mapping of extended memory into the upper memory space between 640 kbytes and 1 Mbyte). Therefore bus mastering DMA controllers must usually write into conventional (below 640 kbytes) memory, since it is not memory-mapped (and the drivers may not work when loaded into high memory).

Also, the AT bus supports only one bus mastering controller (since there is no provision for arbitrating between two simultaneously requesting bus master devices).

Burst mode allows more than one data transfer cycle to take place without releasing the bus back to the CPU (though with a maximum time per burst, such as 15 ms for the MCA bus).

Streaming mode allows a block of sequential data (which most blocks are) to be transferred (perhaps in burst mode), sending only the starting address of the block at the beginning of the transfer. (Having to put the address on the bus only once per block of data speeds up the transfer.)

Butt Set

Data multiplexing (during a streaming mode transfer) allows the data and address lines to carry data (since they are needed only to carry address information once, at the beginning of the block), allowing more data to be transferred per cycle (perhaps 64 bits rather than 32 bits).

For smaller transfers, the time taken to set up all the DMA controller registers may be longer than the time saved by using DMA, so using programmed I/O (in which the CPU handles each byte) may be faster than DMA.

See **BUS**, **DMA**, **PIO**, and **PC**.

Butt Set

The rugged telephone worn (with pride) by telephone installers, on their tool belt. It typically has insulation-piercing clips in addition to a standard modular plug, to facilitate testing (the installer can connect the set to any pair of wires).

There are two stories on where the name comes from. Some say its because one wears it on their buttocks, others say it is because of what the phone enables an installer to do; listen-in (without being heard), and optionally butt-in, to conversations (telling the people the telephone company needs to test the line, because the installer doesn't want to find another pair of working wires on which to make his call).

See **POTS**.

C

CA*NET
Canadian Internet

The Canadian Internet backbone, which is owned by CA*net Networking Inc. CA*net grew out of the University of Toronto's link to the U.S. Internet, which was established in the 1970s. CA*net was established in 1989, and was initially managed by the University of Toronto Computing Services Department, and as of 1990, by CA*net Networking Inc.

CA*net links Canadian universities and (in 1997) 18 of Canada's largest ISPs (smaller ISPs connect get their Internet access through one of the larger ISPs). The actual communication circuits were provided by the Canadian network reseller Integrated Network Services (INSINC) as a result of competitive bidding in 1990 and again in 1994 (INSINC was bought by Sprint Canada in 1994).

As of September 30, 1995 (and until March 1999), Bell Advanced Communications (a subsidiary of Bell Canada) provides the communication services (which use ATM) and network management for both CA*net and CANARIE's requirements. Routing and switching equipment is provided by Cisco Systems and Newbridge Networks. As of March 31, 1997, CA*net Networking Inc. ceased operations, as Bell Advanced Communications new operates its network directly.

CA*NETII

CA*net has 10 regional hubs for the regional networks shown in the following table.

Regional Network	Switching equipment location
NLnet (Newfoundland and Labrador Network) and ACORN	St. John's
NSTN (Nova Scotia Technology Network) and ACORN	Halifax
PEInet	Prince Edward Island Network
nb*net (New Brunswick Network) and ACORN	Fredricton
RISQ (Réseau Interordinateurs Scientifique)	Québec and Montréal (Montreal has a link to the U.S.)
ONet (Ontario Network), OCRInet and LARG*net	Toronto, Ottawa, London, Sarnia, Sudbury and Windsor (Toronto has a link to the U.S.)
MBnet (Manitoba Network), FASTnet and MRnet	Winnipeg
SASK#net (Saskatchewan Network)	Regina
ARnet (Alberta Research Network), WURCnet	Calgary
BCnet (British Columbia Network), Rnet	Vancouver (which also has a link to the U.S.)

Each regional network is responsible for establishing its own acceptable use policy (there are significant differences between the various AUPs) and provides access for local School-nets, Free-Nets, community networks, universities, and other organizations. Used to use 56-kbits/s leased lines, but was upgraded to T1 lines by mid-1994, and to 100 Mbit/s ATM in 1996 (as part of the CANARIE initiative).

Growing at about 14% per month. Replaced NetNorth and CDNNet. CA*net is run by CA*net Networking Inc., which is part of CANARIE Inc.

They have a WWW Server at *http://www.canet.ca/*.

See **CANARIE**, **DNS2** (*Domain Name System*), **ISP**, and **INTERNET2**.

CA*NETII
Canadian Internet II

A high-capacity TCP/IP network linking universities and research institutions in Canada, to test new technologies such as QOS and other methods to ensure reliable multicast traffic (for example). Hopefully these new technologies will be the basis for new capabilities for the Internet, and for new products (the private companies hope) and new companies (the government hopes, especially ones that will export and make more jobs and make the government look good).

The first step is to create switching hubs (POPs) with the capacity to route traffic at gigabit per second speeds—sometimes called GigaPOPs.

Managed by CANARIE Inc.

See **CANARIE**, **CA*NET**, **INTERNET II**, **IP MULTICAST**, **POP1** (*Point of Presence*), and **QOS**.

Cable

A cable is typically two or more insulated *wires* (electrical conductors) held together and protected by an overall *jacket*.

Many types of cables are commonly used for data transmission, as summarized in the accompanying figure.

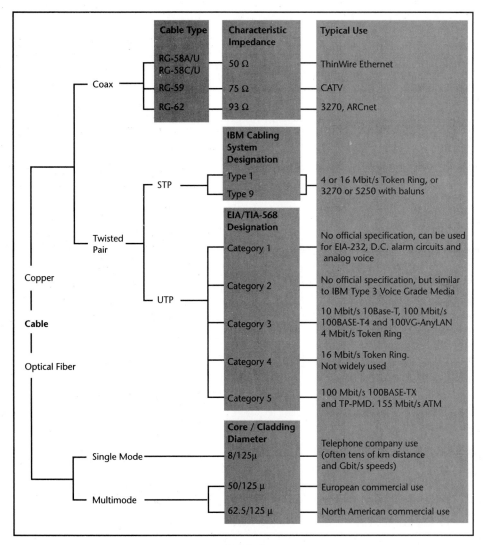

Cable-1

One characteristic of cable is the speed at which signals propagate along the cable. This has many implications, such as the size of Ethernet networks. The following table shows the velocity of propagation, relative to the speed of light in a vacuum (often called *c*)—which is the fastest anything can go), which is about 299,792,500 m/s (about 186,282 miles per second), or about 29.98 cm (11.80 inches) per nanosecond.

Type of Cable	Velocity of Propagation (relative to c)	Comments
Category 3 UTP	0.65	10BASE-T standard requires at least 0.585
Category 4 UTP	0.71	
Category 5 UTP	0.75	
RG-58 Coax	0.66	
RG-59 Coax	0.66	
RG-62 Coax	0.84	
10BASE-5 Coax	0.78	10BASE-5 standard requires at least 0.77
Twin-Ax	0.66	
STP	0.78	
Optical Fiber	0.66	

The use of cabling in buildings is covered by the following standards:

▲ EIA/TIA-568 *Commercial Building Telecommunications Wiring Standard.* Also EIA/TIA's TSB-36 Technical Service Bulletin *Additional Cable Specifications for Unshielded Twisted Pair Cables.* The similar Canadian standard is CAN/CSA-T529-M91 *Design Guidelines for Telecommunications Wiring Systems in Commercial Buildings.* These standards cover the technical requirements for cabling.

▲ EIA/TIA-569 *Commercial Building Standard for Telecommunications Pathways and Spaces.* The similar Canadian standard is CAN/CSA-T530-M90 *Building Facilities, Design Guidelines for Telecommunications.* These standards cover the building architectural requirements for cabling systems.

See **S10BASET, S100BASETX, ARCNET, CATV, COAX, CONNECTOR, EIA-TIA232, ETHERNET, FEP CABLE** (*Fluorinated Ethylene Propylene*), **FIBER, LATENCY, NEXT, STP, TIP AND RING, TOKEN RING, TSB,** and **UTP.**

Cache

Faster-access memory used to temporarily stored information provides a faster response time. There are many types of caches.

Disk caches are used to store data recently read from or written to a disk, to speed up writes and subsequent reads. There are several implementations. They all use RAM (usually $\frac{1}{4}$ to 16 Mbytes) to speed up disk accesses. The disk cache memory may be on the disk controller, part of the disk drive, or the main processor memory (and the caching done by the disk driver software or a TSR).

Write-behind or *write-back* disk caching initially writes data to RAM (freeing the application to continue immediately, as if the data had been written to disk). The data are later automatically written to disk (usually within a few seconds) either timed, or when the cache holds a preset percentage of unwritten data. This reduces the possibility that a problem (such as a power failure) will prevent the data from being successfully written to disk.

Write-through caching always writes directly to disk, ensuring that the application is never tricked into believing that the data are on disk when they may not be. This results in the highest data integrity, though with slightly reduced performance.

In both cases, cached data are read directly from the RAM.

Look-ahead caching (or *buffering*) reads disk sectors ahead of those requested, on the assumption that those will soon be requested. *Segmented look-ahead* can store several such look-aheads. This is important for multitasking computers, which may interrupt a long sequential disk read to service another task.

A common measure of a cache's effectiveness is the *hit rate*—the percentage of disk accesses that are served by RAM.

CPU memory caches are a small amount (typically 1 to 512 kbytes) of very high-speed RAM that the CPU can typically access at its full clock speed. Current processors are usually much faster than the main RAM, so *wait states* (in which the processor waits a few clock cycles) must be added to leave time for the slower main RAM to respond.

A *look-aside cache* design puts a request to both the cache and main memory at the same time so that if the cache does not contain the required data, the request to main memory is already in progress. The lower performance *look-through* design does not begin the main RAM access until it has been determined that the cache does not have the required data.

Write-through caches cache only reads from memory. Writes do not get written to the cache, so they are slow. This is a bigger problem on multiprocessor systems because of memory bus contention.

Write-into cache initially writes only to cache (and not to main memory). The cache is written to memory only when space in the cache is needed for newly-written cached data.

Posted write-through or *write-back caches* cache data both read from and written to memory. Written (and therefore cached) data are written (also called "flushed") to main memory later (depending on the cache design, perhaps when the memory bus is available, another bus master device tries to read that main memory location or when the data have been in the cache for too long). This type of cache design generally provides better performance than write-through.

A *direct-mapped cache* design maps each location in main memory to a cache location. If two main memory locations compete for the same cache location, then only one main memory location gets cached.

A *two-way set-associative cache* has two locations in cache for each main memory location. If both main memory locations are to be cached, then one goes into the alternative cache location.

Four-way set-associative designs extend this to four possible cache locations for each main memory location, increasing the possibility that data will be available in the cache but increasing the time needed to search the cache.

Fully-associative cache lets any block of memory be cached anywhere in the cache. This is usually not implemented for Level 1 (L1) cache, since it takes too long to search the cache.

The control logic for caches is substantial. To reduce this, earlier processors (such as the 486) have a Level 1 *unified cache*, where a single (for example, 8 kbytes) cache holds both instructions and data. Newer processors, such as the Pentium, usually have 8 kbytes of cache dedicated to instructions and a separate 8 kbytes dedicated to data.

Data stored in cache is usually as many blocks of sequential memory locations (partially because memory accesses are usually for sequential memory locations, and partially because storing the 32-bit memory address for each 8-bit cached byte would be very inefficient). For example, the 486's 8-kbyte cache is comprised of 128 sets of 4 (since it is 4-way set-associative) 16-byte *cache lines*. When a *cache miss* occurs, all 16 bytes for a cache line are read from Level 2 cache or (failing that) main memory.

A problem with all CPU memory caches and (especially preemptive) multitasking operating systems is that when the processor switches tasks, the entire cache becomes mostly useless, reducing the benefit of caching. Larger or switchable caches may solve this problem.

Recent CPUs typically have 1 to 32 kbytes of cache built-in to the same integrated circuit chippy as the processor itself. This is called *Level 1 cache* (or *L1 cache* or *primary cache*). This cache is typically accessed at the full processor internal clock speed, with *zero-wait-states*— that is, it runs as fast as the processor, so the processor never has to wait any clock cycles for the memory access to complete.

Tests show that there is a substantial performance improvement if there is more cache, but it is too expensive to make Level 1 cache larger (since this also increases the chance of a bad memory cell, making the whole IC useless—also, larger caches have a longer access time), so external but very fast memory is added. This *Level 2 cache* (also called *L2 cache, external cache* or *secondary cache*) is usually 128 kbytes to 1 Mbyte in size (512 kbytes for multiuser systems and 256 bytes for single-users systems is often used). L2 cache is typically accessed at a slower speed than the processor's internal clock (such as half the processor's clock speed for a Pentium II, or at 66 MHz for the Pentium). L2 cache timing is sometimes written as 3-1-1-1 (a typical fast rating), which means that 3 clock cycles are needed for the first memory access of a burst, and subsequent ones need a single memory cycle. Another important parameter is how fast the memory bus runs. 66 MHz is a typical speed. Laptop computers often do not have L2 cache, due to its power requirements.

Intel first implemented L1 cache in their 486 family of processors (as 8 kbytes of unified cache). L2 cache was first implemented (typically as 32 kbytes of 25 ns SRAM) in computers based on the Intel 80386DX processor.

Many other types of caching are done by application programs and protocol software, such as the following:

▲ An *ARP* cache remembers the mapping of IP addresses to MAC addresses, so the ARP process does not need to be repeated

▲ *Name caching* remembers which network names (such as NetBIOS names) are at which locations, so broadcasts need not be sent over WAN links every time a new station starts up and picks a name (to ensure the name is not already taken)

▲ *Route caching* remembers which path (through which bridges) Token Ring frames should be sent, so the route discovery process does not need to be repeated

See **ALPHA AXP**, **ARP**, **DLSW**, **NETBIOS**, **PC**, **POWERPC**, **RAM**, **SRAM**, and **TOKEN RING**.

Cairo

Microsoft's interim name for its major upgrade to Windows NT. Will be object-oriented. Will support symmetric multiprocessing, X.500 directory services, and Intel, MIPS, and PowerPC platforms.

May be released in 1997.

See **INTEL**, **OPERATING SYSTEM**, **POWERPC**, **SMP2**, **WINDOWS NT**, and **X.500**.

CALLER ID
Calling Number Identification or Caller ID

The telephone feature where you get to see the telephone number and (usually if you pay even more) name of the person calling you—before you answer the telephone. For residential single-line telephones, the information is sent at 1,200 bit/s, immediately after the first ring (and is all sent before the second ring starts) (this is called *on-hook delivery*). If you or your answering machine answers before all the bits come in, then you may not get the information. Therefore, recent answering machines can be set to wait until the second ring before answering.

Most telephone companies now also support *off-hook delivery*, so you can see who is calling while you are already on the telephone (this is sometimes called *spontaneous call waiting with caller ID* or *caller ID* with call waiting or *visual call waiting*).

In North America, the method used was developed by Bellcore. It sends the data using asynchronous data communications, as 8-bit characters with 1 start bit, 1 stop bit and no parity. Bell 202 modem modulation is used. There are two formats for the data, *fixed* (sometimes called *single data message format*—SMDF) and *variable* (sometimes called *multiple data message format*—MDMF).

All messages have the following components:

▲ Telephone rings are typically 2 seconds in duration, with a 4 second pause between rings. The CO starts sending the message 500 ms after the first ring. The message begins with a *channel seizure*, which is 30 characters of AA_{16} (this is 250 ms total). The channel seizure is not sent for off-hook delivery.

▲ Next is 70 to 150 ms of binary 1s (called a *mark signal*)

▲ Then there is 1 character called the message type. Several are defined, including: 0416 for the SMDF format, 0A16 for a message waiting indicator, 8016 for the MDMF format and 8116 for a test mode.

▲ Next is a *message length* byte which is the number (in binary) of bytes following in the entire message, excluding the trailing CHECKSUM byte.

▲ Next is the actual message. The format of this differs for the SDMF and MDMF messages, so will be presented separately below. Up to 10 mark bits (which are the same as stop bits) can be inserted between each character of the message.

▲ The last byte is the 2's complement checksum of the entire message, including the message type and length, but not the channel seizure or mark signal.

The fixed format is generally not used, now that most telephone companies offer the caller's name (usually as an extra cost service) as well as telephone number. The fixed format is as follows:

▲ After the message type and length fields will be 8 ASCII characters, providing the; month (without leading-zero blanking, so the ASCII characters 0 and 2 mean February), date, hour (in 24-hour format) and minute when the call was received (in local time).

▲ After the date and time field will be 10 ASCII characters giving the caller's telephone number, including area code.

▲ The checksum byte follows.

The *variable-format* is standard in North America. The entire Caller ID message is called a *package*, and it is comprised of *subpackages*. Or you could say that the entire message consists of one or more parameters (specified with a parameter identifier byte), and each parameter byte is followed by a length byte—expressed in binary, and is the number of bytes in the next field, which is the variable-length value for the parameter. Some common parameter identifier bytes used and the format of the value, are described in the following table.

Parameter Identifier (hexadecimal)	Parameter Value	Comments
01	Date and time	Typically as a total of 8 ASCII characters, in the format MMDDHHMM (month, date, hour and minute)
02	Calling number	Typically as a total of 10 ASCII characters (area code plus 7-digit local telephone number). The "calling number" may also be an ASCII "P" or "B", to indicate a private or blocked number, respectively)
04	Reason for absence of caller's number	B indicates it was blocked, typically because the caller pressed *67 before dialing your telephone number. O indicates out-of-area, that is, the call is likely a long distance call from a telephone company that does not support this feature. P means the number is unlisted (private).
06	Reason for absence of caller's name	
07	Caller's name	A maximum of 15 characters is allowed

These

A sample message (all in hexadecimal, and excluding the channel seizure and mark signal) would be:

```
80 1B 01 08 30 31 31 37 31 34 33 32 02 0A 34 31 36 35 35 35 31 34 33 30 07
03 41 42 43 15
```

The interpretation of this message is:

- ▲ 80 indicates that the rest of the message is the MDMF format. And the 1B (which is 27 in decimal) indicates that there are 27 message bytes following (but before the checksum)

- ▲ 01 08 means that the following 8 bytes are the date and time in ASCII (January 17, at 2:32 PM).

- ▲ 02 0A means that the telephone number follows, as 10 ASCII characters (and the number is 4165551430)

- ▲ 07 03 means that the caller's name follows, as 3 ASCII characters (their name is ABC in this example)

This is followed by the checksum (of 15 in this fictitious example). The order of the parameters and which are included will be different for different telephone companies.

Caller ID is sometimes abbreviated CID. Also, sometimes it is called *calling line identification service*.

In Europe, the equivalent service (Calling Line Identify Presentation—CLIP) uses V.23 modem modulation, and a method developed by British Telecom.

On ISDN circuits, the information is sent from the network to the customer's telephone equipment on the D channel, and is often called *Calling Number Identification*, *Calling Line Identification* (CLID) or *Automatic Number Identification* (ANI).

See **BELL 202**, **BELLCORE**, **CTI**, **ISDN**, **POTS**, and **TAPI**.

CANARIE
Canadian Network for the Advancement of Research, Industry, and Education

An initiative first proposed in 1988 to link Canadian universities and research organizations. Now an industry-led, private, federally incorporated nonprofit organization with the mandate to support the development of the information highway and to provide collaboration between the Canadian information technology industry and the federal government.

Established in March 1993 with support from Industry Canada, and run by a 21-person board, has more than 140 fee-paying members ($2,500 to $20,000, depending on the size and type of organization). Members include:

- ▲ Industry (carriers and information technology and content providers)

- ▲ Institutions (universities, nonprofit corporations, provincial and federal government departments)

- ▲ Nonvoting associate members (suppliers, consultants, etc.)

CA*net provides the actual data communication circuits.

Several phases of the upgrading of CA*net have been defined (and some have been completed), as shown in the following table.

Phase	Objectives
I	Upgraded CA*net's leased backbone network, which connects to 10 regional network nodes, to T1 (1.544 Mbits/s). This was completed in 1994. Funded partly by user fees paid by the regional networks, partly by federal government funding through CANARIE.
	Development of new user-friendly products, applications, and services for regional network users.
	Technology Development and Diffusion, a matching-funds program to support industry development of innovative high-speed networking products, such as advanced networking technologies, applications software, and services.
	Establishment of a high-speed experimental test bed network to act as laboratories in high-speed networking (such as ATM). Stentor and Unitel provided T3 circuits starting in 1994 to link OCRInet (in Ottawa) and Rnet (British Columbia). Other projects elsewhere in Canada may be connected later.
II	Upgrade CA*net's leased backbone network to T3.
	Stimulation of the development and use of new networking technologies, products, applications, software, and services that will either use or support a national communication network.
	Operation of the experimental test networks.
	Prepare detailed plans for Phase III.
III	Upgrade CA*net to Gbits/s speeds.
	Migrating technologies developed during earlier phases to commercial use.

The Phase I projects were funded by a $26 million contribution from the federal government plus anticipated contributions of $87 million from CANARIE members, clients, and project participants.

Phase II was funded by an $80 million contribution from the Department of Industry (announced in December 1994). Phase II is planned to end in 1999.

CANARIE has the features shown in the following table.

An operational network	Interconnecting the 10 regional hubs and the Internet (with connections to the U.S. from Vancouver, Toronto, and Montréal). Also, 13 Internet service providers are directly connected to CA*net.
A high-speed ("broadband") test network	A national (NTN) and regional test network (spanning 6,000 km) for the collaboration of public and private organizations in exploring new hardware and software. 12 provincial and municipal broadband research networks are supported. This National Test Network uses T3 links, and ATM switches (from Cisco Systems and Newbridge Networks). It was officially opened in late 1995.
A funding program	From both public and private sources, for research and development.

In early 1996, the Technology and Applications Development program announced a total of $18.5 million of funding for 50 information highway research and development projects selected from over 300 applications received during 1995. The program's emphasis is on business, research, health care and quality of life, and education and life-long learning.

CANARIE maintains a WWW site at *http://www.canarie.ca/*.

See **CA*NET**, **INTERNET2**, **T1**, and **T3**.

CardBus

The new name for the higher-speed PCMCIA (or PC Card) interface.

See **PCMCIA**.

Carrier

A public communications service provider, such as a telephone company. Many have WWW servers (some with excellent data communications information or pointers). Examples are listed in the following table.

Telephone Company	WWW Server URL
Ameritech	*http://www.ameritech.com*
AT&T	*http://www.att.com*
BCTel	*http://www.bctel.com*
Bell Atlantic Corp.	*http://www.bell-atl.com*
Bell Canada	*http://www.bell.ca*
Bellcore	*http://www.bellcore.com*
Bellsouth Corp.	*http://www.bellsouth.com*
McCaw Cellular	*http://www.airdata.com*
MCI Communications Corp.	*http://www.mci.com*
NYNEX CORP.[a]	*http://www.nynex.com*
Pacific Bell (owned by Pacific Telesis Group—PacTel)[b]	*http://www.pacbell.com* and *http://www.pacbell.com/Products/fastrak.htm*
All RBOCs	*http://www.bell.com/bells.html*
SaskTel	*http://www.sasknet.sk.ca*
SBC Communications Corp. (formerly Southwestern Bell)	*http://www.swbell.com*
Southern New England Telephone	*http://www.snet.com*
Sprint Corp.	*http://www.sprint.com*
Stentor Alliance	*http://www.stentor.ca*
Teleglobe Canada	*http://www.teleglobe.ca*
AT&T Canada Long Distance Services Co.[c]	*http://www.unitel.com*
US West Inc.	*http://www.uswest.com*
WilTel	*http://www.wiltel.com*

a. Bought by Bell Atlantic Corp. in April 1996.
b. Bought by SBC Communications Corp. in April 1996.
c. Was called Unitel Communications until September 9, 1996.

CAS

See **ATT**, **CPE**, **IXC OR IEC**, **LEC**, **POP1**, **POTS**, **RBOC OR RBHC**, **STENTOR**, **TELEGLOBE INC**, **TELEPHONE COMPANIES**, and **TELESAT CANADA**.

CAS
Communicating Applications Specification

The software interface to a fax board.

An API specification developed by Intel and Digital Communications Associates to provide support for programs sending data to other devices and computers. The initial (and likely only) versions of the specification only describe functions for a program to interact with a fax modem board.

Supported by Intel's Satisfaxtion boards (cute name, not a very popular standard though).

Competes with Class 1, 2, and 2.0.

A copy of the specification is at *ftp://ftp.faximum.com/pub/documents/cas.txt*.

See **API** and **FAX**.

CATV
Community Antenna Television

Standard cable TV, which currently brings lots of entertainment (!) to your home television. Maybe someday it will bring Internet access and telephone service too.

In the beginning, CATV was just a big antenna shared by a community, with a coaxial cable bringing the signal to everyone's house (hence the name). Now, with pressure to cram more channels into the cable, it gets more complicated (cable converters, pay-TV decoders).

It all starts with standard broadcast television, which has two main frequency bands:

▲ VHF (very high frequency), which provides channels 2 through 13 in the frequency range 54 to 216 MHz

▲ UHF (ultra high frequency), which provides channels 14 through 69, in the range 470 to 806 MHz. (It used to go up to channel 83, 890 MHz, but the top 14 channels were reallocated in 1974 to make spectrum available for analog cellular telephone service, which is officially called AMPS.)

As is shown in the table below, the radio frequency spectrum assigned to broadcast channels 2 through 69 is not contiguous. There are several reasons for this:

▲ Frequencies are usually assigned lowest first (these are the most desirable, since electronic equipment is easier to design for lower frequencies and lower frequencies usually travel the farthest). By the time television needed more channels, other services (such as amateur radio and the police) had been assigned frequencies.

▲ Even the original television broadcast band had gaps to ensure that no television channels existed at the second harmonic (double the frequency) of other channels (this simplifies the design of television tuners—which reduces their cost).

▲ Some frequencies have physical significance for studies such as radio astronomy and so are not available for assignment.

Since cable TV providers want to provide as many television channels as possible (and each channel requires 6 MHz of bandwidth), and since it is expensive to provide a greater range of frequencies (the cable attenuates higher frequencies more, and higher-frequency amplifiers are more expensive), cable TV services move channels to different frequencies.

For example, on cable, channels 14 through 22 are shifted down into the space between channels 6 and 7. For televisions with a built-in cable TV converter, you must tell the television whether it is receiving its signal from cable TV or not so that it knows which frequency to tune to. For example, as is shown in the table, channel 14 uses 470 to 476 MHz when broadcast but is moved to 120 to 126 MHz when on cable. So if there is a power failure, your television or VCR forgets that you are on cable, and that's why you don't get what you expected (except for channels 2 through 13, which don't get moved).

CATV uses 75 Ω impedance coaxial cable. For residential installations, RG-59 cable and Type F connectors are used (that's the official name for the coaxial cable connector on the back of your TV). Distribution systems (which bring the signal along the street, to your house) require amplifiers. These are mounted in aluminum enclosures that are $\frac{1}{2}$-meter wide × 20 cm high × 10 cm thick and either hang from an aerial CATV cable or are placed in a (usually green cylindrical or brown rectangular) *pedestal* (the meter-high enclosures sprouting from people's lawns, near the street). They are typically powered by 60-V, 60-Hz power sent along the coaxial cable from battery backed-up power supplies (you often see these small-suitcase-sized enclosures mounted on hydro poles, where they get their power), with a 2-cm diameter coaxial cable running out (bringing the power to a three-port coupler that connects to the distribution cable).

For a CATV system to carry more channels, it must support higher frequencies, and this requires higher-quality (lower attenuation) cable, and amplifiers spaced more closely. For example, a 1 GHz system can carry more than 150 channels, but requires amplifiers (sometimes called *extenders*) every 100 m. Since a defective amplifier causes all downstream homes to loose their signal, amplifiers usually automatically bypass themselves if they have a problem.

Some CATV systems carry a *reverse channel*. This uses the HF (high frequency) band from 5 to 42 MHz (which is comprised of the *low band* from 5 to 20 MHz, and the *high band* from 21 to 42 MHz). The reverse channel is used to bring signals back from customers to the CATV head-end (perhaps for interactive TV, or to support Internet access). This requires separate amplifiers, which are mounted in the same enclosures as the forward channel amplifiers. Therefore it costs money to provide this capability.

The reverse channel gets the cumulative noise added by every home, so it often a maintenance problem (any home with defective equipment can make the reverse channel useless for everybody). Remotely-controlled and separately addressed attenuators in each amplifier assist with isolating the location of problems.

Some CATV people say that future systems will put 6 to 12 digitized, compressed television channels in the 6-MHz bandwidth that is currently occupied by a single television channel. This way, CATV systems could offer hundreds of channels, and compete with the 500-channel satellite dishes that threaten to put cable TV out of business.

The cost of such compression equipment (and especially of decompression, since every television would need it), development and deployment of HDTV, quality of picture

required, and many other factors will all affect what eventually happens with compressed video CATV systems.

Cable modems convert digital data for transmission over CATV cables—at speeds up to 10 Mbit/s to 30 Mbits/s (the vendors and CATV system operators will quickly tell you). What they don't tell you is that you are sharing that 10 Mbits/s with a large number of other users (and they don't tell you what that large number is). So what you really get is 10 Mbit/s divided by some large number—which may work out to a speed that is greater *or* less than you could get with ISDN or even a standard POTS telephone line.

Typical systems have speeds of 4 or 5 Mbits/s, and share this between a few thousand houses. Typical download speeds (when the network is lightly loaded) are often only 1.5 Mbits/s (due to limitations of PCs and the protocol), and upload speeds (from the users to the network) of 300 kbits/s are common. Older systems share a 500 kbit/s bidirectional channel (similar in operation to Ethernet).

Often, you are only allowed a single PC at your location, since that would make their addressing more complicated, and they want to ensure that traffic between your PCs does not clog the coax.

Since there are huge costs and maintenance problems with providing an uplink (for example, noise from each user is cumulative, so isolating problems is very difficult), some systems use *telco return* where there is no upload channel through the CATV system. Instead, the uplink is through a standard telephone line, which is a lousy solution—you need to get two systems working (CATV and telephone), rather than one. Another problem with having your CATV provider be your ISP is that they typically only support access through the coaxial cable. If you are at another location (at work, or on a trip), there is no way to dial-in to check your e-mail.

Typically, the cable modem is provided by your cable company (since there are no standards, so all are proprietary, you can't buy them yourself anyway). The connection to your PC uses a standard 10BASE-T Ethernet connection (so you need an Ethernet board in your PC).

Cable Television Laboratories, Inc. ("CableLabs") was established in May 1988 as a research and development consortium of cable television system operators. It has a WWW server at *http://www.cablelabs.com/*.

Broadcast		Frequency (MHz)		CATV Channel	Comments
Use	TV Channel	From	To		
VHF					
TV	2	54	60	2	Channels 2 through 13 use the same frequencies and channel numbers for both broadcast and CATV use
	3	60	66	3	
	4	66	72	4	
Private radio	Not used for broadcast TV	72	76	1	This 4-MHz chunk is too small for an entire CATV channel and so is not used
VHF TV	5	76	82	5	
	6	82	88	6	

(table continued on next page)

Broadcast		Frequency (MHz)		CATV	
Use	TV Channel	From	To	Channel	Comments
FM radio	Not used for broadcast TV	88.1		FM Radio	Most CATV systems carry FM radio stations instead of CATV television channels 95, 96, and 97
		88.3			
		88.5			
		and so on, through to 107.7			
		107.9			
		90	96	95	Not usually used for CATV (see above)
		96	102	96	
		102	108	97	
Private radio		108	114	98	Not usually used for CATV
		114	120	▲ 99	
		120	126	14	With a cable TV converter (which can tune to these channels and convert them to one that a standard television tuner can receive, usually channel 3 or 4), these channels are also available. A 21-channel system therefore also requires a 216-MHz CATV system (see below).
		126	132	15	
		132	138	16	
		138	144	17	
		144	150	18	
		150	156	19	
		156	162	20	
		162	168	21	
		168	174	22	
VHF TV	7	174	180	7	12-channel CATV systems require a bandwidth of 216 MHz to carry channels 2 through 13
	8	180	186	8	
	9	186	192	9	
	10	192	198	10	
	11	198	204	11	
	12	204	210	12	
	13	210	216	13	

(table continued on next page)

Broadcast		Frequency (MHz)		CATV	
Use	TV Channel	From	To	Channel	Comments
Private radio	Not used for broadcast TV	216	222	23	A 35-channel system requires a bandwidth of 300 MHz
		222	228	24	
		228	234	25	
	and so on, up to				
		288	294	35	
		294	300	36	
		300	306	37	A 60-channel CATV system requires a bandwidth of 450 MHz
	and so on, up to				
		438	444	60	
		444	450	61	
		450	456	62	
UHF TV	14	470	476		The UHF broadcast channels start at 470 MHz
	15	476	480		
	16	480	486		
	and so on, up to channel 69				
		534	540	76	A 75-channel CATV system requires a bandwidth of 540 MHz
		618	624	90	A 90-channel CATV system requires a bandwidth of 625 MHz
		744	750	111	A 110-channel CATV system requires a bandwidth of 750 MHz
	68	794	800		
	69	800	806		Highest broadcast UHF channel. Since lower frequencies travel farther, most UHF stations choose low frequencies
Cellular telephone		824			
	82	878	884		
	83	884	890		UHF used to go up to channel 83, but cellular telephones were assigned those frequencies (824 to 894 MHz)
Private radio	Not used for TV	996	1,002	153	A 1-GHz CATV system can carry about 152 channels (numbering starts at 2)

See **S802.A14, AMPS, COAX, CONNECTOR, FCC, HDTV, ISDN, LMDS, MODEM, NTSC, POTS, PPM,** and **TDM.**

CCD
Charge-coupled Device

An integrated circuit that is sensitive to light. Often used in digital cameras.

The charging of each of the pixels, and the serial shifting out of the remaining charge on each pixel (that is, getting the image transferred out of the IC) is relatively slow. As a result, typical cameras can usually take a maximum of a picture every $\frac{1}{2}$-second to every 4 seconds.

Typical still-camera CCDs have an equivalent speed of ASA 800 to 1,600, and "shutter speed" of 1/30 to 1/4,000 second and a resolution of 500 to 1000 × 300 to 700 pixels.

A technology based on CMOS (complementary metal-oxide semiconductor) is being refined to make lower-cost and -power (than CCD) digital imaging ICs for cameras.

See **CMOS**, and **DRAM**.

CCIR
Comité Consultatif International Radio

The previous name for the ITU-R. Also called the *International Radio Consultative Committee*.

The CCIR 601 standard is the most common video digitizing method used for broadcast television. The 8-bit (per sample) version requires a data rate of 216 Mbits/s, and the 10-bit version (the most common) uses 270 Mbits/s. It provides a picture size of 720 × 486 pixels (for NTSC video).

See **ITU**, **NTSC**, and **VIDEO**.

CCITT
Comité Consultatif International Télégraphique et Téléphonique

The previous name for the ITU-T.

Also called the *International Telegraphy and Telephony Consultative Committee*.

See **ITU** and **ITUT**.

CCP
Compression Control Protocol

A method for negotiating data compression over PPP links so that multiple data compression algorithms (including open methods, such as V.42*bis*, and proprietary methods, such as that from Stac Electronics, both of which have a typical maximum compression ratio of 4:1) can be supported.

Both switched and dedicated (leased line) circuits are supported. The negotiation includes the type of compression and the dictionary size. Part of the negotiation process is that if one end of a link does not support data compression, then the connection will work, it just won't get any data compression (earlier compression technology required both ends to be from the same manufacturer, and if the equipment on only one side has compression enabled, it looks like your data link is broken).

For example, a router with built-in data compression could communicate over a WAN link with another router that has external data compression (by a V.42*bis* modem or a DSU with built-in LZS). Or two routers from different manufacturers could communicate over a WAN, while using their built-in data compression.

See **DATA COMPRESSION**, **DSU**, **LZS**, **PPP**, **STAC**, **V.42BIS**, and **WAN**.

CDE
Common Desktop Environment

A common UNIX graphical desktop environment approved by X/Open. The intent is to define a standard UNIX platform so that the UNIX industry can compete with Microsoft (especially Windows NT, which competes with UNIX most directly). The hope is that on the basis of CDE, *shrink-wrapped* (binary compatible) UNIX software will be possible, just like the PC industry has.

As it is, there are so many flavors of UNIX that shrink-wrapped software is not currently possible.

The effort includes the following:

▲ The X Window System functionality (the X11R5 version) and window management

▲ A single set of APIs (including messaging and drag-and-drop support)

▲ A visual-oriented scripting language

▲ A single graphical user interface (based on Motif version 1.2.3)

▲ A common look and feel (file management, online help, internationalization)

As of Fall 1995, no complete implementations were commercially available.

It is based on the following (these companies are the main proponents—I sure hope this stuff glues together cleanly):

▲ HP's *Visual User Environment*

▲ IBM's *Common User Access* model

▲ Novell's *UnixWare client tools*

▲ Sunsoft's (part of Sun Microsystems) *Deskset tools*

Some further information can be found at *http://www.austin.ibm.com/powerteam/tech/aixpert/aug94/aixpert_aug94_CDE.html* and *http://www.lib.ox.ac.uk/internet/news/faq/archive/cde-cose-faq.html/*.

The CDE effort is the main product of COSE.

See **API**, **COSE**, **DEC**, **MOTIF**, **PORTABILITY**, **UNIX**, **X OPEN**, and **X WINDOW SYSTEM**.

CDMA
Code Division Multiple Access

An improvement on AMPS analog and TDMA digital cellular telephone, and is one of the technologies used for PCS. CDMA, as implemented for PCS cellular telephones, uses direct sequence *spread spectrum transmission* (SST) to support more conversations in a given frequency bandwidth. Since it is a digital technology, it is well-suited to carrying data as well (for short messages, receiving e-mail, and the like).

All base station cell sites (even adjacent ones) use the same frequency bandwidth—this is a big increase in frequency utilization efficiency over traditional cellular telephone CDMA which can only use (for example) 1/7th of the frequencies in each cell. Initial CDMA development indicated that each cell had to have a carefully selected orthogonal pseudo-random *spreading code* to allow it to share the same bandwidth as an adjacent cell without interference; hence the name (perhaps CDMA should be called spread spectrum multiple access).

It was then determined that all users could use the same spreading code (called *pseudo-noise*), so long as each cell used a different starting point (called the *PN* offset). 512 such offsets are available, and adjacent or potentially interfering cells cannot use the same PN offset.

CDMA is therefore implemented using a standardized 2^{42}–1 bit-long *PN* code. This bit-pattern is so long, it takes 41 days before it repeats. Within a cell, each handset that is transmitting is dynamically assigned a 64-bit spreading code. This 64-bit code has special properties, and is called a *Walsh code* (there are a total of 64 of these, and the same 64 are used in every cell). Each bit is therefore transmitted as 64 *chips*.

Transmissions in a CDMA system must be precisely synchronized, and two methods are used. Cell sites each have a GPS receiver, and this provides timing to better than 1 µs accuracy. To get the synchronization to within the 0.8 µs required by CDMA, one of the forward channels (called a *pilot channel*) is reserved for carrying a synchronization code (at 1,200 bits/s). Another channel (the *Sync channel*) also runs at 1,200 bits/s and is used to identify the current PN offset, the time, and the channels used for *paging*. There are 1 to 7 paging channels per cell, and these run at 4,800 or 9,600 bits/s. They are used to send configuration information to the handsets and to indicate incoming calls to handsets.

Reverse channels (from the handset to the base station) can be one of the following:

▲ *Traffic channels*, which carry user digitized voice, or data. Data can be at 1,200, 2,400, 4,800 or 9,600 bits/s (lower bit-rates require lower power and cause less interference to other users, so are used when acceptable).

▲ An *access channel*, which is a 4,800 bit/s control channel used to carry control information from the handsets, such as registering with the cell site when the handset is powered on, acknowledging commands from the (forward) paging channels, and requesting the initiation, or indicating the termination of calls.

A power control bit sent from the base station to each handset, every 1.25 ms adjusts the handset's transmit power (in 1 dB steps, between 0.01 µW and 300 mW, which is –80 dBW to –5.2 dBW) to ensure that the handset is always using the optimal transmit power (too much power interferes with other users and wastes battery power, too low power provide poor voice quality)—and is quickly adjusted to allow for changing signal propagation characteristics—such as driving under a bridge.

The initial CDMA specification used a voice digitization rate of 8,000 bits/s. With overhead, this requires a raw data rate of 9,600 bits/s per mobile. Due to concern that the voice quality is too low (especially compared to GSM, an optional 13,000 bit/s voice digitization rate has recently been added to the specification (which uses a raw bit rate 14,400 bits/s—which can also be used for data transmission). These higher speeds are called *rate set 2*.

The actual frequencies used in North America for PCS are 1,851.25 to 1,908.75 MHz from handset to base station, and 1,931.25 to 1,988.75 MHz from base station to handset.

Theoretically, CDMA can fit about 90 to 130 conversations (assuming, for example, that because of the speaking gaps in an individual conversation and their half-duplex nature, a conversation is active less than 40% of the time) into 1.25 MHz of bandwidth.

CDMA (as used in PCS) provides 64 channels (in the forward direction, which is transmitted from base station to mobile)—as limited by the available Walsh codes. This can support a theoretical maximum of 61 simultaneous users (since 3 to 9 channels are used for control purposes), per 1.25-MHz frequency band (if taken from the standard AMPS allocation, this would be 42 standard AMPS channels, which is 10% of an operator's 12.5-MHz bandwidth). Actual systems usually support only 20 to 25 simultaneous users per 1.25 MHz band, due to many real-world limitations.

Standard AMPS would support 6 simultaneous conversations (per cell) from this (assuming a 1 in 7 frequency reuse), and TDMA supports 18 simultaneous conversations in this same bandwidth.

CDMA therefore provides an improvement by a factor of almost 22 times (quick—buy some of that company's stock). In actual implementation (due to fading, etc.), the improvement may only be 10 (some say 15) times (oops, this technology stuff is so risky). This will be reduced further in systems that use the higher-speed voice digitization (which is expected to be most systems).

Mobiles can simultaneously use two Walsh codes, so during a handoff, they can communicate with both base stations (the new one and the soon-to-be-previous one). By constantly receiving whichever signal is stronger, a *soft handoff* (no audio gap) is therefore possible (unlike the break-before-make nature of an AMPS' handoff).

While *multipath interference* (signals bouncing off buildings arriving slightly later than a direct signal) causes great problems for traditional radio (such as AMPS), CDMA uses multiple *correlators* (3 in mobiles, and 4 in base stations) to sum such signals and produce a better output. Also, traditional radio has small geographic areas (the location of which is related to the wavelength of the signal) where interfering signals at a particular frequency cancel each other out (so you can't talk or hear there). Since CDMA uses a range of frequencies, it has less of a problem with this type of signal fading.

Developed and promoted by Qualcomm Incorporated (which has a WWW server at *http://www.qualcomm.com/cdma*).

Defined in TIA/EIA IS-95 (Interim Standard 95). Data transmission capability has not yet been developed.

Competes with GSM.

See **AMPS**, **CDPD**, **ESMR**, **GPS**, **GSM**, **PCS1** (*Personal Communications Service*), **SST**, and **TDMA**.

CDPD
Cellular Digital Packet Data

A method first proposed and developed by IBM and McCaw Cellular Communications, Inc. (now owned by AT&T) to more efficiently carry data on existing analog (AMPS) cellular radio systems. First available in 1993, and now installed in the U.S., Canada (by Bell Mobility) and Mexico.

138-byte packets of data are sent, full-duplex, at 19,200 bits/s during gaps in conversations or on unused (no voice conversation established at that time) channels, using the full 30-kHz bandwidth of the channel (though the bandwidth available to users is typically about

13 kbits/s, due to protocol overhead, error-correction and other factors). Also, voice traffic always has priority over the data.

Actual air traffic consists of blocks of 63 (47 are information, 16 are *forward error correction* information) six-bit symbols, resulting in a user data rate of about 9,000 to 14,400 bits/s. The forward error correction can correct up to eight six-bit symbol errors.

Similar to Ardis and Mobitex in that charging is by the amount of data sent, rather than the connect time, however differences include the following:

▲ Use of the existing cellular radio infrastructure (CDPD overlays it), resulting in lower usage charges

▲ Built-in encryption and authentication

▲ The *land-line* interface is TCP/IP

▲ Security, since the data for a conversation are carried over many cellular radio channels (according to whichever has spare capacity), so it would be difficult to monitor the communication

▲ V.42*bis* data compression

▲ Multicasting to subsets of users (this is supported in version 1.1 of the specification, which was released in 1995)

▲ A full-duplex option

CDPD is an open specification that competes with the proprietary systems from Ardis and RAM. Since it is a packet-oriented service, the call setup time is fast (much faster than circuit-switched), charging is by the kilobyte of traffic carried, and it is best-suited to smaller transactions (up to 5 kbytes of data—larger transfers are better handled by circuit-switched methods, such as analog cellular with modems). While CDPD is available in most U.S. cities, it is not available in Los Angeles, perhaps because the cellular system is so heavily used there is not enough free airtime (that is, gaps between conversations) for CDPD to provide adequate bandwidth.

Promoted by five of the seven U.S. RBOCs and Motorola, Microcom, and some cable TV companies.

More information is available at *http://www.cdpd.org*.

See **AMPS**, **ARDIS**, **AUTHENTICATION**, **CDMA**, **ENCRYPTION**, **ESMR**, **GSM**, **IP MULTICAST**, **MOBITEX**, **RAM MOBILE DATA**, **TDMA**, and **WIRELESS**.

CD-ROM
Compact Disc, Read-Only Memory

One of many formats based on the same technology that is used for standard audio compact discs.

A 120-mm (4.72") diameter, 1.2-mm-thick polycarbonate plastic disk coated with reflective aluminum (so that the *pits* and *lands* can be read by a *laser diode*). The table at the end of this definition shows the many formats.

A standard *Mode 1* CD-ROM stores up to 74 minutes of audio (depending on whether the spiral track with the bits goes right to the 2 mm margin from the edge of the CD-ROM—manufacturing is more difficult if the spiral is too close to the edge). This format holds up to 333,000 2,048-byte *sectors* of data. This is 681,984,000 bytes (650 Mbytes, where 1 Mbyte is 1,024 × 1,024 bytes), plus a whole lot of error detection and correction, directory, and other "overhead" bits.

Mode 2 CD-ROMs don't store error detection and correction bits and can therefore store more data (333,000 2,336-byte sectors, which is 741 Mbytes). This would be done only for audio or video, for which bit-errors would not be a problem, or when there is another error detection scheme.

Other than capacity, another significant specification for a CD-ROM drive is the *access time*, which is the sum of the *seek time* (time for the drive's read/write head to move from its current position to the track to be read next) plus the *rotational latency* (time for the disk to rotate to the starting position for the next data).

Higher *data transfer rates* are obtained by spinning the CD-ROM faster (this also improves the access time). The rotational latency is usually specified as half the time for a full rotation of the disk (since this is the average needed to access data located at a random location on a given track).

The seek time may be given as the time for:

▲ *Full-stroke*: the time to move the read/write head over the entire disk surface, for example, the most inside track to the very outside track

▲ $\frac{1}{2}$-*stroke* or $\frac{1}{3}$-*stroke*: the time to move the read/write head over one-half or one-third of the disk surface

▲ *Track-to-track*: the time to move a single track

▲ *Random seeks*: the average time to move to access data at random locations on the disk.

The relevant specification depends on where the data are. For example:

▲ If large amounts of contiguous data are to be read, then track-to-track may be most relevant

▲ If data at a random location on the disk are to be read, then $\frac{1}{2}$-stroke may be most relevant

▲ If the disk's directory information is located near the disk's middle track (a smart thing to do to minimize the average seek distances) and the directory needs to be read before almost every seek, then $\frac{1}{3}$-stroke may be best

Most drive specifications in published product literature (and on the box) exclude the rotational latency when quoting "access times" (they should then be calling it the seek time, since it is only the time to get the read head to the right place, not the full time to seek, wait for the read head to settle in the exact right place, plus wait for the disk to rotate a half-turn, plus transfer some data). Also, these times don't usually state whether full-, $\frac{1}{2}$-, or $\frac{1}{3}$-stroke seek times are being provided (but given that a $\frac{1}{3}$-stroke is the shortest, it will have take the shortest time, so there's quite an incentive to quote this specification).

So have fun comparing disk drive specifications, and good luck. For the record, a typical fast CD-ROM will have a full-stroke seek time of 250 ms and a $\frac{1}{3}$-stroke seek time of 125 ms.

Data are stored on a CD-ROM starting at the center (actually, 23 mm from the very center), and spiraling out—around and around up to 20,625 times, with only 1.6 µm between spirals (the spiral is over 5 km long—I'm getting dizzy thinking about it). In contrast, a standard magnetic hard disk stores data in concentric rings, called *tracks*.

The bits on a CD-ROM are recorded as *pits*, which are each:

▲ 0.5 µm × 0.833 to 3.054 µm long (much smaller than an eensy-weensy spider)

▲ $\frac{1}{4}$-wavelength deep, so even if light does reflect off the bottom of the pit, the reflected light produces destructive interference (since it will differ in phase by $\frac{1}{2}$-wavelength), so very little light will reflect back

These pits are read by using a 780-nm laser diode (this is infrared light and therefore invisible, as is the light from your TV remote control's infrared LED).

The construction of the CD-ROM is that the clear plastic disk is formed by pressing it against a master. That side is then coated with aluminum (the shiny stuff). The aluminum is then covered with lacquer, which is then printed with the CD-ROM label. The CD-ROM is read through the clear side. You should therefore be a bit careful about both sides of the CD-ROM. The CD-ROM is read through the clear side, and scratches or dust could affect this. The label side though is very close to the aluminum, so a scratch could remove some of the aluminum, also likely ruining the CD-ROM.

Original CD-ROM drives (which were introduced about 1991) read 75 sectors per second (same as for audio CDs). Since CD-ROMs store 2,048 bytes of user data per sector, this is 153,600 bytes/s, which is 150 kbytes/s (where a kbyte is 1,024 bytes). Audio CDs have less error-correction data added to each sector, so they can store 2,352 bytes per sector, so reading at 75 sectors per second (called 1×) provides 176,400 bytes/s (which is the rate needed to provide 44,100 16-bit PCM samples per second of stereo audio). Double-speed CD-ROM drives were introduced in 1993, and read at twice this speed (so were called 2×). This is 150 kbytes/s, which is 307,200 bytes/s. 4× drives were introduced in 1994, 6× in 1995, 8×, 10× and 12× in 1996 and 16× in 1997.

CD-ROM

Unlike standard magnetic hard disks, traditional CD-ROM drives (such as those with speeds up to 12×) use *constant linear velocity* (CLV)—this means that the speed of the media relative to the read head is always the same, whether the read head is near the inside or outside of the disk. Therefore, so the CD-ROM must spin faster (about 1,000 revolutions per minute) when reading near the center of the CD-ROM and slower (about 400 RPM) when reading near the outside of the CD-ROM (these values are for a double-speed drive). This provides the maximum possible capacity, but the requirement to change the speed of the disk rotation when seeking to different tracks increases a CD-ROM's seek time (this is not a problem for audio CD-ROMs, which usually play an entire song at a time—one long spiral, with no sudden track changes).

In 1997, CLV and combination CLV/CAV drives became popular, so a CAV drive might be 12× when reading from the beginning of the disk (those tracks are at the inside tracks), and 20× when reading from the outside tracks. That is, for higher-speed drives, as the rotational speed of the drive changes to accommodate the current read position, there is a greater chance that at some speeds there will be a vibration problem. Also, designations such as 20× become less meaningful—especially since a CD-ROM is written from the inside towards the outside of a disk. If your (or the only) data is on the inside, then you don't get the benefit of the 20× speed (responsible vendors will label such drives as having a *maximum* speed of 20×).

Standard magnetic disk drives use *constant angular velocity* (CAV) —for example, they always spin at 5,400 revolutions per minute (unless they are powered off, of course—but who knows what your computer is doing or thinking when there's no one in the room). Since CAV drives do not need to change speed with the read position, and the drive can be designed to not vibrate at the rotational speed, CAV CD-ROM drives are becoming more popular for higher-speed operation. Some vendors mix both approaches, using CAV for the inner tracks and CLV for the outer tracks.

ISO's IS-9660 standard is the most common CD-ROM disk format—for example, for PCs and Unix computers (Macintosh CD-ROMs often use the *Hierarchical File System* format—HFS). IS-9660 is based on the previous *High Sierra* format, and has two implementation levels.

ISO IS-9660 *Level One* specifies the following:

▲ Directory names and filenames can use only uppercase letters, the numbers, and "_" (no special characters such as $, –, +, =, ~, !, @, #, or a space)

▲ Filenames are a "lowest-common denominator" (that is, the good news they can be read on any DOS, Windows, Macintosh or Unix computer, but the bad news is you can't use longer and more readable filenames) MS-DOS-style "8.3"—either the filename or the extension (but not both) can be empty (but usually neither is empty)

▲ Directory names are eight characters only (no extension)

▲ Filenames include a 15-bit *file version number* (from 1 to 32,767), using the DEC-VAX-style of separating the filename and version with a semicolon—for example, `file-name.txt;15` (most file systems do not support this feature)

▲ Up to seven levels of subdirectories plus the root- (or top-) level directory (to make eight levels total)

ISO IS-9660 Level Two supports:

▲ More than one period in a filename

▲ Up to 32 characters per filename

Level Two CD-ROMs are not supported by MS-DOS.

Microsoft's `mscdex` (*Microsoft CD*-ROM extension) provides CD-ROM support for MS-DOS.

Multisession capability means that data can be added (as long as there is room) to the disk incrementally (for example, new pictures added to a Photo-CD that already has some pictures on it). In June 1996, the Optical Storage Technology Association (OSTA) ratified a standard method called CD-UDF which uses *packet writing*. This method has lower overhead (that is, less disk capacity wasted) than standard multisession recording each time addition information is added to a CD-R.

Audio CD-ROMs (developed in 1981) and the initial extensions for computer data storage were developed by Sony Corp. and Philips Electronics NV.

Some additional information is in *ftp://ftp.cdrom.com/README, ftp://ftp.cdrom.com/pub/cdrom/readme.txt, http://www.cd-info.com/cd-info/CDInfoCenter.html, ftp://cs.uwp.edu/pub/cdrom*, and *ftp://ftp.apple.com/cdrom/README*.

The CD-ROM FAQ is in *ftp://ftp.cdrom.com/pub/cdrom/faq/faq1* (or another file with a name similar to that, in that directory) or *http://saturn.uaamath.alaska.edu/~gibbsg/cdromlan_FAQ.html/*.

The following table lists CD formats and their uses.

Format	Use
3DO	A new game format that has better colors, resolution, and sound than Sega CD or CD-I.
CD Audio or CD-DA	The first application for *Compact Discs*. Standard digital audio CDs (often called *Red Book*—guess what color the binders used for the standard was), these usually have "Digital Audio" printed below the disk logo. Each sector stores 2,352 bytes of user data, as two channels (which provides stereo) of PCM-digitized audio, each channel at 44,100 16-bit samples per second. The playback rate is therefore (44,100 samples/s × 16 bits/s × 2 channels =) 176,400 bytes/s, which is exactly 75 sectors/s. A total of about 74 minutes of audio can be stored on a single CD. Developed by Sony and Philips (in 1981) and standardized in IEC 908, which is called *Compact Disc Digital Audio Standard*. Provides low-resolution still images on a conventional audio CD useful for karaoke sing-alongs. Not widely used.

(table continued on next page)

Format	Use
CD-I	CD-interactive (also called *Green Book*) disks that store interleaved text, stereo sound and video (and software) and currently run only on Philips (who developed this) and Magnavox CD-I players. Intended for consumer multimedia and home entertainment systems. Uses Mode 2, so stored data can have either 2,048 or 2,336 bytes of user data per sector (depending on how much error-detection and -correction is needed). Uses MPEG-1 and requires an MPEG decoder IC to handle the decompression of the video. Standardized by the American CD-I Association, 213-444-6619. Philips has information at 800-845-7301. Further information is at *ftp://ftp.cdrom.com/pub/cdrom/cdi*. The *White Book* standard enables CD-I recordings to also be played in CD-ROM XA players. This is intended to support full-motion MPEG video.
CD+MIDI	Can play through MIDI synthesizers. Not widely used.
CD-Plus or E-CD or CD-Extra or Enhanced CD	An update to CD-ROM/XA. Since it also can mix Red Book audio and standard data sectors, these are sometimes called *mixed mode* or hybrid. The intent to provide data (such as playlists, the music score and lyrics, even interactive games and WWW links to the performer's web site), video (such as music videos and interviews) and graphics (such as album cover art) on an otherwise conventional audio CD (and a conventional audio CD player will simply play the audio tracks). There are two methods used to store the non-audio information on these Enhanced CDs. The *pre-gap* method stores it before the first track (so standard audio CD players skip it, since they start playing at the first track). The *Blue Book* method (sometimes specifically called CD Extra) was developed by Apple, Microsoft, Sony and Philips. It stores the non-audio information after the audio tracks. The Recording Industry Association of America (RIAA) has a certification program for both pre-gap and Blue Book Enhanced CDs.

(table continued on next page)

Format	Use
CD-R, CD-MO, or CD-WO	CD-recordable. A CD-ROM that is *recordable* using a $1,000 to $10,000 recorder attached to a standard PC. So that a low-powered laser diode can record on it, an organic dye (which is greenish, and is melted by the laser) is used along with a gold (rather than aluminum) reflective surface. CD-R disks are therefore gold-rather than silver-colored.
	There are two types: *magneto-optical* ("Part I," which are rewritable but not currently widely available) and *write-once* ("Part II," or hybrid disk, which can be written once only—these are by far the most common). Kodak's Photo-CD uses the write-once CD-R format.
	So long as the recorder and software support *multisession* (such support is called *Orange Book*), write-once CD-Rs can be written incrementally (each writing is called a session, and these can be done at any time). Each session writes a single *track* (after which the write laser is turned-off, requiring that 2 run-out blocks be left after the track, and 2 link block, and 4 run-in blocks are needed before the next track), so this is sometimes called *track-at-once* recording. For each session, there is a complete TOC (table of contents) and some other required indices and overhead generated. These require 13 to 16 Mbytes of storage, so you get the most capacity per CD-R when the number of sessio22ns is kept to a minimum. The CD-ROM player requires *multisession* capability to read recording sessions after the first. CD-Rs can have an area permanently written (using the Red, Yellow, or Green Book CD-ROM standards) when the disk is manufactured.
	Disk-at-once recording (sometimes called *single-session* recording) is the opposite of *track-at-once* multisession recording. It records the entire disk in one recording pass. This method must usually be used if the CD being written will be sent to a CD manufacturing facility for mass-production (also, audio CD players usually produce a click sound when they encounter the run-in blocks).
	Burning (that is, recording) a CD-R is a continuous process. A buffer in the recorder stores data yet to be written. If the PC does not send data fast enough, and the *buffer underruns*), then the CD-R won't work (this is often called "making frisbees", since the satisfaction of flinging them across the room is a small reward for the frustration and cost incurred). To reduce the chance of this happening, some recording software supports building a 680 Mbyte *physical image file* on your hard disk. This contains all of the files to be burned, in the exact same order, so that there will be no processing or disk access delays during the recording process. Other software does *on-the-fly recording*, which usually uses a *virtual image file*. This is simply all the pointers needed to find the files (elsewhere on your hard disk or network) during the recording session.
	Two CD-R capacities are available: a 63-minute disk (550 Mbytes) and a 74-minute disk (650 Mbytes—the most common size). They can both be read by standard CD audio and CD-ROM drives. Kodak's Photo-CD is an example of CD-WO technology.
	Sometimes called WORM: "Write once, read mostly" (or "many"). Developed by Philips and Sony, with specifications available only to their licensees.

(table continued on next page)

Format	Use
CD-RW or CD-E or CD-Erasable	*Compact Disc - rewritable* (or *erasable*). Better than CD-R since CD-RW can be erased and rewritten up to 1,000 times, but standard CD-ROM drives can't read CD-RW disks. But CD-RW drives can read *and write* CD-R disks (but not rewrite them). And to complete this complexity, CD-RW disks can be read in DVD drives, but CD-R disks cannot be read by DVD drives. The Optical Storage Technology Association's *Universal Disk Format* (UDF) version 1.5 specifies a *packet writing* method which allows writing to continue after a buffer underrun (marking that sector as bad, but not requiring the entire disk to be discarded or recording to be restarted from the beginning). Phase-change technology is used, and disk defragmenting is supported.
CD-ROM	Standard computer CD-ROMs (often called *Yellow Book*). This built on Red Book audio CDs by splitting the 2,352-byte sectors into a 2,048-byte data area, and the rest for error-detection and -correction and synchronization and header bytes. This is called *Mode 1*, and it loses substantial storage capacity to overhead. For "single-speed" CD-ROM drives, the playback data rate is therefore (75 sectors/s $\times$ 2,048 bytes/sector =) 153,600 bytes/s, which is 150 kbytes/s (where a "kbyte" is 1,024 bytes). Developed by Sony and Philips, and standardized in ISO 10149.
CD-ROM XA	*CD*-ROM extended architecture. A standard for interleaving data, audio and video while maintaining synchronization between them ("lip-sync"). As does CD-I, CD-ROM XA uses *Mode 2* sectors (that is, sectors without error-detection and -correction). These can be *Form 1* (which are like *Mode 1* sectors, in that they have 2,048 bytes of data plus 288 bytes of error-detection and -correction bytes)—Kodak's Photo-CD uses this format. Or, they can be *Form 2*, which each have 2,336 bytes of data (usually digitized audio, video or images where a few undetected and uncorrected bit errors are not a problem). These Form 1 (typically used for data) and Form 2 (typically used for audio) sectors can be interleaved, on the same CD-ROM. The CD-ROM drive usually plays the audio directly and passes the other information to the computer. CD-ROM XA is widely accepted (it is required for MPC Level 2), and is an extension to (and has largely replaced) the original CD-ROM (Yellow Book) standard. It is a subset of CD-I. Requires support in the CD-ROM drive (and most now do).
CD-V	Provides short music videos for a laser-disk player that can also play standard audio CDs. Not widely used.

(table continued on next page)

Computer Dictionary

Format	Use
Photo-CD	Developed by Kodak, who developed the Orange Book multisession standard as part of Photo-CD, to support incremental writing of pictures (using CD-R). Orange book allows mixing of audio and data sectors (sort of like a mixture of Red Book and Yellow Book audio—and that makes orange—somebody there had a "colorful imagination" in dreaming up the name). Can store about 100 very high-quality photographic images digitized from standard slides or prints. Pictures—and the table of contents (ToC) to find them—can be added incrementally (you don't need to record all pictures at the same time, and the additions to the ToC have pointers to previous ToCs, rather than having to rewrite the whole ToC). Each picture is stored in five 24-bit color resolutions: 3,072 × 2,048 (16Base) 1,536 × 1,024 (4Base) 768 × 512 (Base) 384 × 256 (Base/4) 192 × 128 (Base/16) The three lower-resolution resolutions are stored as bitmaps (not compressed) for fast searching. The two higher-resolutions are stored as the *Huffman-encoded* difference (*lossless compression*) from the middle-resolution image. Typical images require 6 Mbytes of storage. Photo-CD images typically have a filename extension of .PCD. Any CD-ROM XA player can read Photo-CD disks. More information is in *ftp:// ftp.kodak.com/pub/photo-cd/*.
Sega CD	A new format for game software for Sega and JVC machines. Will offer better resolution and motion.
Video-CD	A format to support interactive video. For example, it supports "hot-spots" on the display, which can be pressed (or clicked-on—whatever the hardware supports). This is used for interactive games and for self-service kiosks. The Video-CD 2.0 format can be played in both dedicated Video-CD players, as well as CD-I players that have a Digital Video cartridge. A player that can read CD-ROM XA disks can also be used (so long as there is also hardware or software support for MPEG-1 decoding). The Video-CD format begins with a track that has the CD-I player program, the table of contents and MPEG still and motion pictures and MPEG audio. The rest of the tracks have additional MPEG audio and video, and the last tracks have Red Book audio.

See **ATAPI, ATASPI, COMPACTFLASH, DISK DRIVE, DVD, LOSSY DATA COMPRESSION, MINI-DISK, MPC, MPEG, PCM, PD, SD,** and **WORM**.

Cell

Typically, the 53-byte unit of data carried by ATM switches.

A fixed-length, usually small unit of data. The advantage of being small is that it reduces the store-and-forward delays of network switches, and short network latencies are important for voice and other interactive traffic. A user's (variable-length) packet of data would likely need to be split into many cells. Fixed-length has the advantages of more hardware-oriented switching (therefore higher speeds) and deterministic delays (so isochronous services for video can be handled).

48 bytes (plus a 5-byte header) is a common size (used in SMDS, B-ISDN, and ATM). It has a 6.6 ms store-and-forward delay (at 64 kbits/s), and is a compromise between 32 bytes (best for voice—less store-and-forward delay, but greater protocol overhead) and 64 bytes (best for data—more efficient).

See **ATM** (*Asynchronous Transfer Mode*), **ISOCHRONOUS**, **LATENCY**, and **MULTIMEDIA**.

Cellular Telephone

See **AMPS**.

CELP
Code Excited Linear Prediction

See **G.728**, and **G.729**.

CERT
Computer Emergency Response Team Coordination Center

A group responsible for monitoring and advising about security on the Internet.

A U.S. government–funded organization with its *coordination center* located in Pittsburgh, at Carnegie-Mellon University, as part of the Software Engineering Institute. The *Incident Analysis Group* tracks and reports security problems on the Internet and recommends actions to be taken.

Founded a few weeks after November 3, 1988, which was when Robert Morris released a *worm* (a program that attempts to propagate itself to all machines on a network and can cause security or data integrity problems) into the Internet.

Information is available as shown in the following table.

email	*cert@cert.org*
Fax	412-268-6989
ftp	*ftp://info.cert.org*
List server	*mailto://cert-advisory-request@cert.org*
Phone	412-268-7090 (hotline for system administrators to report potential problems)
Usenet	*news://comp.security.announce* (announcements from CERT) *news://comp.security.misc* *news://alt.security* *news://comp.risks* *news://comp.virus*
WWW	*http://www.sci.cmu.edu/technology/cert.cc.html*

The SANS (System Administration Network and Security) Institute summarizes the biggest security threats, and has information at *http://www.sans.org*.

See **INTERNET2**, and **VIRUS**.

CES
Circuit Emulation Service

The circuit emulation service was defined to enable ATM to replace dedicated leased lines (such as DS-1 connections between PBXs). CES uses ATM AAL 1 which allows 47 bytes for payload, and 1 byte for synchronization (for a total of 48 bytes per cell. There are two CES services which may be implemented, as listed below:

▲ *Structured DS*-1/E1 Nx64 (also called *structured data transfer*—SDT). This is intended to replace fractional T1 (FT-1) lines, and only uses as much ATM bandwidth as there are timeslots used. Also, it can maintain the timeslots (any number, and they do not need to be contiguous) in the same order as sent, or timeslots can be reassigned before output at the remote end. Two services are available, as listed below:

▲ *Basic Service* carries each timeslot as a 64 kbit/s data stream.

▲ CAS (*channel associated signalling*) carries *robbed-bit signalling* (RBS) information, as is used on many DS-1 links to indicate on-hook, off-hook and other line signalling and supervision functions.

ESF (and optionally SF) framing is supported, as well as the *facility data link* (FDL). The FDL is terminated at the interface between the DS-1 link and the ATM CES, so it will monitor only the real DS-1 portion, and not the ATM portion of the connection.

The AAL 1 synchronization byte is used as a pointer to indicate to the remote ATM switch which timeslots are where.

The timing information (clocking) is generated by the ATM switch, though some ATM switches may be able to receive clock from an external source.

▲ *Unstructured DS*-1/E1. This is intended to replace entire DS-1 (or E1) circuits. The DS-1 data is carried as a stream of bits, without regard for maintaining any synchronization of the ATM cells with the DS-1 frames (so long as the bits come out of the far end of the ATM network in the same order that they went in). The full T1 of bandwidth is used, regardless of the number of timeslots that are actually active. If FDL information is present in the data stream, it is passed through the ATM network unchanged. There are two modes for handling the clocking.

▲ *Synchronous mode* generates the clock in the ATM switch, and the external equipment must use this clock.

▲ *Asynchronous mode* uses an external clock source, and there are two ways of doing this. *Adaptive clock recovery* adjusts the ATM switches clock speed to match that of the external clock source. A suggestion (but not requirement) is that the ATM switch monitors its output buffer (to the DS-1 circuit. If data is building-up, then the ATM switch should increase its clock speed (and vice versa). In *synchronous residual time stamp* (SRTS) clock recovery (which is the preferred method), a network-wide clock source is required. The ATM switch monitors the difference in the clock speeds of the external DS-1 clock source and the network-wide clock, and periodically transmits this difference—differences of up to 200 parts per million (PPM), which is 0.02% can be accommodated. The remote ATM switch then adjusts its clock accordingly, so that it stays synchronized with the original DS-1 clock.

▲ The AAL 1 synchronization byte is used to send the SRTS information.

The additional cell overhead causes each 1.544 Mbit/s DS-1 to use 1.74 Mbit/s of ATM bandwidth, and each 64 kbit/s channel to use 72 kbit/s of ATM bandwidth.

CES is expected to be a temporary solution for utilizing ATM with legacy-type equipment (such as PBXs) that do not have native ATM interfaces. The hope is that someday PBXs will have ATM connections, so CES will not be required.

CES is defined in the ATM Forum's Circuit Emulation Service Interoperability Specification (called CES-IS), which was published in September 1995.

See **ATM** (*Asynchronous Transfer Mode*), **ESF**, **FT1**, and **T1**.

CF
CompactFlash

See **COMPACTFLASH**.

CGI
Common Gateway Interface

A standardized method of sending information (such as a request or a response) to a WWW server.

A standard for interfacing (that is, providing a *gateway* to) an external application (such as a database server or an order-entry system) with a WWW server (a machine that runs an *HTTP daemon*). Can provide information to, and accept information from, people running WWW browsers (such as Netscape) elsewhere (anywhere) on the Internet.

Standard HTML documents retrieved from WWW servers are *static* (the exact same text is retrieved every time). In contrast, CGI enables a program (a *CGI* program, sometimes called a *gateway program*, running on the WWW server) to communicate with another computer to generate "*dynamic*" HTML documents in response to user-entered information (entered through a form on the user's WWW browser).

CGI programs have the following features:

▲ Are executables, located in a /cgi-bin subdirectory on a WWW server (this restriction is a security feature, to limit which programs can be run by users from cyberspace)

▲ Have URLs and are run when a user executes them (by clicking on a reference to them)

▲ Can be a *compiled* program (for example, written in C or C++) or be *interpreted* (for example, a PERL, Tcl, or UNIX shell script or a Microsoft Visual Basic program)

▲ Receive input as the string of characters (for example, as a comma-separated sequence of variable and value pairs) that appear after the first "?" in the URL (as constructed by the browser), or as environment variables (if forms are used). If the string of characters are a sequence of terms for a search, then the following characters have special meaning:

    – + used to represent a space or as a data separator character

    – = connects a parameter name with its value (which together are called an ordered pair)

    – & combines ordered pairs

    – % the one or two following characters are hexadecimal digits (such as %A8)

Output back to the user (in one of many formats, such as HTML, ASCII text, or another format, such as audio or video)

That is, CGI programs (typically stored in a subdirectory called cgi-bin) parse the input from the user, get the requested information, format a (usually HTML) response, and send the response back to the user.

For example, the URL http://www.temp.com/cgi-bin/test?query=noodle would be specifying that the browser should use the http protocol to contact the host with a DNS name of www.tmp.com. That host should find the program test in its cgi-bin subdirectory, and this program should be run, passing the command-line parameter query=noodle which presumably means something to that program (for example, that the variable query should be assigned the value noodle).

One weakness is that while CGI (as for all WWW exchanges) is connection-oriented, the connection is terminated after every URL access. A web server does not have any *state information*, such as where you've been, or whether you are new to the site or a regular visitor. That's why URLs get so long (for example, when you are examining search engine replies; they need to have all the information embedded in them about exactly what the next transaction is all about (either as a summary of your actions so far, or as an identifier for a file where the server stores information on your actions).

CGI is relatively easy to use, but provides slow performance—partially because of the way parameters are passed between the WWW server and CGI program (that is, as command-line or environment variables). Faster and more powerful (but, unfortunately, proprietary) types of web server programming interfaces include the API offered by Netscape Communications' (Netscape Server API—NSAPI) and Microsoft's Internet Database Connector (IDC), which is part of their Internet Server API (ISAPI). Another reason CGI is so slow is that every request requires a subprocess to be spawned (starting processes is usually a slow process) to run the CGI program. In contrast, the proprietary API allow shared access to already-running programs.

For more information, see *http://hoohoo.ncsa.uiuc.edu/cgi/overview.html.*

See **HTML**, **HTTP**, **TCL-TK**, and **WWW**.

Channel

The 1.25-, 3.0- or 4.5-Mbyte/s, parallel, copper, 400-foot maximum connection from an IBM mainframe to its front end processor and other communications-related devices. Uses a scheme called *bus and tag* to address peripherals.

See **ESCON**, **FEP**, **MAINFRAME**, and **PARALLEL**.

CHAP
Challenge Handshake Authentication Protocol

An authentication protocol (to ensure a user is really who they claim to be) which can be used on data communication links which use the PPP link layer protocol. Authentication is achieved by ensuring that a user accessing a server has a secret password (that the server already knows).

The server sends a request (the "challenge") to the user, consisting of an identification code, a random number, and the server's hostname or the user's username. The user's equipment

Checksum

(as a result of soliciting the password from the user) then replies with an encrypted (using a one-way hash algorithm, most commonly using MD5) version of the following:

▲ the received identification code

▲ the random number

▲ the user's secret password

The server's host name or the user's username is also returned (unencrypted) in the user's reply.

The server then encrypts its own copy of the user's secret password, and verifies that it matches that received from the user (note that the unencrypted password is never sent over the communication link—this is a good thing, since snoops can't learn the password from trapping data on the communication line, and they can't replay the encrypted session, since the next session will have a different random number).

PCS handsets use a similar technique to ensure that a handset's *electronic serial number* cannot be learned by receiving its transmission. AMPS cellular telephones send their ESN unencrypted over the air, and *cloning* is a major problem (where thieving varmints can make their handset act like yours, and therefore you pay for their calls).

CHAP also supports repeating the authentication process during a session—just to make sure the user is still who they were at the beginning of the session (a new random number is used in the challenge).

CHAP is defined in RFC 1334 as an optional authentication phase.

See **AUTHENTICATION, L2TP, PAP, PCS**, and **PPP**.

Checksum

A method of detecting errors in received data.

A type of *block check character* that is easier to compute in software than a CRC but provides less protection than a CRC. Is usually 8-bits, generated by the binary addition (or sometimes `exclusive-OR` ing) of each of the bytes in the block of data.

The weakness is that if (for example) the same bit in two different bytes is corrupted, then the checksum will not detect the error.

Was popular when messages were small, error detection was done in software, and computers were slow. Not used in new protocols, as the messages are too long and there is specialized hardware available that can do a better job of detecting errors.

See **CRC, ECC, FCS, PARITY**, and **XMODEM**.

Chicago

Microsoft's widely-publicized development code name for the successor to Windows 3.1. Initially it was expected to be called Windows 4.0, but Microsoft decided to call it Windows 95.

See **OPERATING SYSTEM**.

CHRP
Common Hardware Reference Platform

A specification for a hardware platform to compete with Intel PCs.

A PowerPC-based hardware platform specified by Apple and IBM that can run any of the Apple Macintosh Mac OS, Microsoft Windows NT, Sun Solaris, IBM OS/2 Warp, and IBM AIX operating systems and applications (or so they hope).

The intent is to encourage other manufacturers to make this platform so that PCs have some competition and these vendors can sell operating systems and PowerPC CPUs.

One requirement of CHRP is support for the IEEE *open firmware* standard (IEEE 1275), which includes the ability to boot multiple operating systems, and support for processor-independent plug-and-play add-in boards.

Apple and IBM could never agree on a single hardware platform (for example, Apple likes SCSI and IBM likes IDE), so yet another attempt at battling the Intel architecture failed because their competitors could not get together.

Intended to compete with PCs. Uses PCI. Replaces the PREP effort (and perhaps the ACE effort before that).

Pronounced "chirp."

See **ACE, OPERATING SYSTEM, PCI, PLUG AND PLAY, POWERPC,** and **PREP.**

CIAC
Computer Incident Advisory Capability

An organization sponsored by the U.S. government to investigate viruses and reports of them.

They have a web site at *http://ciac.llnl.gov:80/ciac/CIACWelcome.html.*

See **CERT,** and **VIRUS.**

CICS
Customer Information Control System

An IBM mainframe user interface providing a transaction-oriented communications service (application driver) that supports hosts at several sites. Runs under MVS. Well suited to systems with frequently run applications. An alternative is TSO.

See **MVS** and **TSO.**

CLASS A
FCC Class A Radiated EMI Limits

See **EMI,** and **FCC-PART15.**

CLASS B
FCC Class B Radiated EMI Limits

See **EMI,** and **FCC-PART15.**

CIDR
Classless Inter-Domain Routing

A method for dealing with the problem that there are no more worldwide unique Class A IP addresses and very few Class B addresses available for new networks. Also (for ISPs), a method of reducing the number of routing table entries (and also very importantly—reducing the routing advertisement messages between routers), by combining contiguous blocks of IP addresses (called *summarization*).

For example, 4 "Class C" address blocks (of 256 host addresses each) is assigned to one organization (perhaps 205.207.128.0 through 205.207.131.0), another 4 to another organization (205.207.132.0 through 205.207.135.0), and a block of 8 Class C addresses to another organization (205.207.136.0 through 205.207.143.0). This is a total of 16 blocks of 256 addresses, which is 4,096 hosts. Since 2^{12} is 4,096, it requires 12 bits of IP addresses for the host addresses. Using the standard Class C network numbering, this would require advertising 16 networks to other routers. But with CIDR, the ISP would only need to advertise the single network IP address of 205.207.128.0 with a subnet bit mask (in binary) of 11111111.11111111.11110000.00000000 (note that the lower 12 bits are all zeros—indicating this is the host—not network—part of the address). The subnet bit mask is more commonly written (in dotted decimal notation) as 255.255.240.0. In CIDR notation, this address and subnet bit mask are written as 205.207.120.0/20—since the top 20 bits are set to 1s.

A problem with this method is that the InterNIC did not want to administer these addresses, so they assigned large blocks of them to the Internet service providers, which then charge per address and assign the addresses only in quantities that are powers of 2 (1,024, 2,048, etc.), so you will probably have to pay for many more addresses than you need.

That is, its "classless" since there is no Class C (and Class B and Class A) anymore—where the dividing line between the network and host portion of the address had to be only at 8, 16 or 24 bits of the 32-bit address. With CIDR, the dividing line between network and host portion of the address can be at any number of bits of the 32-bit address.

With CIDR, blocks of addresses need to be assigned by ISP (rather than by end user), so users don't control their own IP addresses any more (and if they change ISP, they likely need to change their IP address block). And if they outgrow their block of addresses, they need to buy more from the ISP, and their new block will not likely be contiguous with the first.

CIDR is pronounced like that strong apple juice stuff ("cider"). It is described in RFCs 1517 through 1520 (CIDR that is, not cider—you'd have to drink some to actually describe the latter, but instead of trying to describe a ladder, I suggest visiting a hardware store).

Another method of dealing with the IP address shortage is described in RFC 1918.

See **INTERNIC**, **IP ADDRESS**, and **RFC-1918**.

CIF
Common Intermediate Format

See **H.261**.

CIF
Cells in Frames

A method of sending ATM cells in Ethernet or Token Ring frames. Some benefits are listed below:

▲ Standard Ethernet and Token Ring adapters can be used in PCs, and standard routers can be used for WAN links.

▲ Frames have less overhead than cells, since the entire frame gets a single 4-byte ATM header, followed by just the 48-byte payload for up to 31 ATM cells—so long as the ATM cells are all from the same virtual circuit (ATM VC). A modified LAN adapter driver, or a software *shim* (that fits between the existing driver and the NDIS interface) adds a 4-byte CIF header to the frame. This all fits into a 1,500-byte Ethernet frame. The shim also handles prioritization to support QOS and ATM ABR *explicit rate* flow control.

▲ Allows ATMs benefits, such as flow-control, QOS, and integration of voice, video and data traffic, to be extended to desktop PCs

A *CIF* edge switch switches these frames to other LAN segments, or connects to a standard ATM network, and repackages the cells each with their own 5-byte ATM header.

The *CIF* Alliance is at *http://www.cif.cornell.edu*, and further information is at *http://www.ziplink.net/~lroberts/Atmf-961104.html*.

See **ATM** (*Asynchronous Transfer Mode*), **NDIS**, and **QOS**.

CIPO
Canadian Intellectual Property Office

The Canadian federal government organization that administers legislation on the following:

▲ *Copyrights* for literary, artistic, dramatic, and musical works and computer software

▲ *Patents* for inventions (new kinds of technology)

▲ *Industrial designs* for the shape, pattern, or ornamentation of an industrially produced useful object

▲ *Trademarks*: words, symbols, or designs (or combinations of these) that are used to distinguish the goods or services of one person (or entity) from those of another

▲ *Integrated circuit topographies*: the three-dimensional configurations of electronic circuits embodied in integrated circuit products

Part of Industry Canada.

CIPO has a WWW home page at *http://info.ic.gc.ca/opengov/cipo/*, and further information is available at *http://info.ic.gc.ca/ic-data/marketplace/cipo/*.

See **COPYRIGHT**, **DESIGN PATENT**, **INDUSTRY CANADA**, **INTELLECTUAL PROPERTY PROTECTION**, **PATENT**, and **TRADEMARK**.

CID
Caller ID

See **CALLER ID**.

Cisco Systems

A company based in California that makes multiprotocol routers and has over 60% (by units shipped) of that market. The next largest competitor (Bay Networks, which was called Wellfleet before merging with SynOptics) has under 10%.

The products communicate over LANs with DEC, Novell, UNIX (TCP/IP), and many other computers using those protocols' native routing methods. For IP routing information, the Cisco routers can also communicate among themselves, using their proprietary IGRP, or many standard protocols.

Cisco buys many companies every year, such as:

▲ Kalpana, for its Ethernet switching technology

▲ Newport Systems, for its PC-based routers

▲ Cresendo, for its FDDI switching technology

▲ LightStream Corp., for its ATM technology

Cisco was started in 1984 by Leonard Bosack and Sandy Lerner, who were married (to each other) and professors at Stanford University—but could not send messages to each other due to the school's incompatible networks. When the company became wildly successful by 1990, they left the company. The company's name is a contraction of "San Francisco".

Cisco Systems has a WWW server at *http://www.cisco.com/*.

See **DLSW**, **IGRP**, **LINK STATE**, **RIP**, and **SWITCHED LAN**.

CIX
Commercial Information Exchange

When the Internet started to become available for commercial purposes, there was a need for the big commercial Internet Service Providers to be able to exchange traffic, with no restrictions (that is, an AUP) on the content of the traffic. And this was the reason CIX was formed in the early 1990s. For a while, the CIX was the part of the Internet's U.S. backbone that was funded by the companies providing commercial access to the Internet, such as Performance Systems International (PSInet), BARRnet, CERFnet, NEARnet, Sprint Corporation, Uunet Technologies, and NYSERnet, either by directly connecting their networks either to each other, or to a CIX router which was (and is) located in California.

CIX is mostly just another NAP now.

CIX has a WWW server at *http://www.cix.org/*.

See **AUP**, **INTERNET2**, **ISP**, and **NAP**.

Client/Server

The currently usually-desirable computer system architecture in which *clients* request a service and a *server* provides that service. Each machine can then be optimized for the task.

A common example would be a client using a database server. In this case the entry and display of users' data are separated (often on separate machines) from the storage and retrieval of the data. The client may have a large color display with a graphical user interface. The server may have dual power supplies (in case one fails), fast duplicated hard disks (in case one fails and to increase the number of disk requests that can be serviced per second), and a built-in tape drive for fast backup.

This provides a more flexible and open environment than the traditional "dumb-terminal and mini/mainframe computer" method, in which the program on the computer determines the user interface and the types of terminals that may be used.

The test of time has shown that client/server architectures are often more difficult to design and implement, and require more administration. The end result is that when (and if) the project gets completed, it costs more than anticipated. Some wonder whether the "bad old mainframe days" were really that bad.

Nonetheless, some think what we really need is to do less at the desktop, and more at the server. And some call this a thin client. The *network computer* (NC) is an example of this. Some think that we need distributed servers, and CORBA facilitates this.

Major client/server architectures are DEC's NAS, IBM's SAA, and OSF's DCE.

See **CORBA**, **DCE2** (*Distributed Computing Environment*), **FTP**, **HEADLESS**, **JAVA**, **MAINFRAME**, **NC**, **OSF**, **SAA**, **SQL**, and **X WINDOW SYSTEM**.

CLNP
Connectionless Network Protocol

An OSI network layer protocol. It may replace IP on the Internet someday (but you seem to hear less and less about OSI every day). The other OSI network layer protocol is CONP.

See **CONNECTIONLESS**, **CONP**, and **OSI**.

CMC
Common Mail Calls

An API developed by the XAPIA for application program messaging. Used mostly for cross-platform messaging. Supported by Microsoft and Lotus.

See **MAPI**, **VIM**, and **XAPIA**.

CMIP
Common Management Information Protocol

The OSI method of doing what SNMP does. But CMIP is *object-oriented* (another one of those trendy things, like user friendly, GUI, and client/server) and much more powerful. While OSI never became popular (especially in North America), CMIP is one of the few parts of OSI which is occasionally implemented. An example application is one where SNMP is the right kind of capability, but does not have enough functionality. Some carriers (such as US West) have CMIP projects.

See **GUI**, **OSI**, and **SNMP**.

CMOS
Complementary Metal-Oxide Semiconductor

A very low-power technology for making (among other things) battery-backed-up memory for PCs to store configuration information.

The battery provides power so the otherwise-volatile CMOS memory does not forget everything when you turn off your PC. The battery is typically a rechargeable NiCd type (charged when the PC is powered-on), so it never runs down.

PCs typically have 64 bytes of CMOS RAM, and this is used to store configuration information, such as the number and types of diskette drives and COM ports which are installed. The information is modified using a utility

Pronounced *SEA-moss*.

See **BATTERIES**, **BIOS**, **CCD**, **DRAM**, and **PC**.

CMS
Conversational Monitor System

An IBM mainframe editor and foreground driver for native application development under VM.

See **VM**.

CO
Central Office

The building at the other end of the telephone cable that comes to your house (the cable, not the building, comes to your house).

A usually nondescript, well-kept, one- or two-story, windowless building owned by the local phone company. Since analog voice signals from a telephone can travel about 5 km through copper cabling before they get too quiet or noisy, a CO. will typically serve all the customers within a 5-km radius from the CO.

Therefore COs are located so that all customers will be within about 5 km of their serving CO—all together, the RBOCs own about 13,000 COs.

From a CO, one pair of wires goes to each house, apartment, and business (and additional pairs for each additional phone line they may have). Higher-capacity lines (such as fiber-optic cables) go to adjacent COs.

Inside a CO will be the switching equipment—such as a Northern Telecom DMS-100 or a Lucent Technologies (formerly AT&T) 5ESS—and power supplies to run the telephone system.

Lucent Technologies has some information on call switching at *http://www.lucent.com/netsys/5ESS/index.html*.

See **CARRIER**, **DMS**, **LEC**, **PBX**, **RBOC OR RBHC**, and **TIP AND RING**.

COAX
Coaxial Cable

The type of cable that is used by cable TV and that used to be common for data communications (such as for Ethernet and 3270 terminals).

A round cross-section, two-conductor cable consisting of a single center solid wire (or stranded conductor) symmetrically surrounded by a braided or foil (or one or more of each) conductor (which is usually grounded).

Both conductors share the same axis (so they are *coaxial!*).

Coaxial cables have a *characteristic impedance* (expressed in ohms, just as D.C. resistance is— even though the two are not related), which is determined by the relative diameters of the two conductors and the material used for the insulator between the two conductors (which is officially called a *dielectric*).

The popular (in office and residential applications) types of coaxial cable are listed in the following table.

Cable Type	Characteristic Impedance (Ω)	Use
RG-58/U	53.5	Often used for Ethernet (is cheaper, and the connectors are easier to install) but should not be, as it is the wrong impedance and usually has a shield with too little coverage (too much space between the braiding)
RG-58A/U or RG-58C/U	50	10BASE-2 CSMA/CD (ThinWire Ethernet)
RG-59/U	75	CATV (cable TV)
RG-62/U	93	IBM 3270 terminals, ARCnet

RG stands for "radio guide," as the cable is guiding radio frequency signals. The "/U" means "general utility."

Coaxial cables are generally falling out of favor for the following reasons:

▲ They are too single-purpose; you need a different type for each application, and you can't use any of them for Token Ring, FDDI, RS-232, telephone, or ISDN.

▲ For the same length of cable, coaxial cable can have 5 to 500 times more attenuation (depending on many factors, such as the type of coax and the frequencies used) than fiber-optic cable.

▲ Running coaxial cable between buildings creates problems of ground-potential difference (the building grounds will be at different voltages), so the coax shield must be insulated from building ground in at least one of the buildings.

▲ Outdoor runs need lightning protection.

For the last two points, fiber-optic cable is a better choice, as it is an insulator (sometimes called a dielectric), so it does not need lightning protection.

See **S3270**, **BNC**, **CABLE**, **CATV**, **CONNECTOR**, **ETHERNET**, **STP**, and **UTP**.

Code Division Multiple Access

See **CDMA**.

CODEC
Coder/Decoder

The device that digitizes voice or video signals for transmission over digital data services and undigitizes it at the other end.

An analog-to-digital (A/D) converter optimized for audio signals.

See **ADPCM**, **BRI**, and **PCM**.

Color

Computers and data communications handling color rather than monochrome information are becoming more popular. So here is some background information on color and the methods of representing it.

People perceive colors, based on the primary wavelength of the light, as shown in the following table.

Wavelength (nm[a])	Color
380	Bluish purple[b]
460	Purplish blue
475	Blue
485	Greenish blue
490	Blue green
496	Bluish green
510	Green
545	Yellowish green
564	Yellow green
572	Greenish yellow
578	Yellow
584	Yellowish orange
590	Orange
610	Reddish orange
770	Red

a. 1 nm (nanometer) is 1,000 microns (1,000 μ), and 1 nm is also 10 angstroms (10 Å). So 380 nm is 0.38 μ, which is 3800 Å.
b. Purple is a combination of blue and red, rather than a single wavelength.

That is, visible light ranges in color from purple (about 380-nm wavelength) to red (about 770-nm)—these wavelengths correspond to frequencies of about 780 to 390 THz. Using retinal sensors, called *rods* and *cones*, our eyeballs sense color.

Rods basically detect the intensity of light. They are located mostly at the periphery of the retina, are most sensitive to low light levels, are most sensitive to green light (about 500 nm), and are used mostly to detect overall brightness and fast light changes (presumably to see dangerous animals out of the "corner of your eye," now mostly where you see CRT flicker).

Cones basically detect color. There are three kinds of cones (L, M, and H), which are sensitive to low, medium, and high frequencies, so called because they are most sensitive to the 570-, 550- and 440-nm wavelengths (near red, green, and blue light, respectively). Cones are mostly concentrated near the center of the retina (so you need to look directly at something to determine its color).

The luminosity and hue is determined in the retina, but saturation is developed in the brain.

Color is displayed or represented by using several different methods, as shown in the following figure.

See **COMPOSITE VIDEO SIGNAL**, **CRT**, **IRDA**, **MPEG**, **NTSC**, **RAMDAC**, **RGB**, and **VIDEO**.

Compact Disc

See **CDROM**.

CompactFlash

An industry-standard type of miniature (about $\frac{1}{4}$ the size of a PCMCIA card) removable storage device for consumer electronics devices, such as digital cameras and PDAs. Intended to store digital pictures, audio and data—with the goal of facilitating transfer of this information between cameras, cellular telephones, computers and other electronic devices.

The CompactFlash cartridge is about one quarter the size of a PCMCIA card, and initial versions hold 2 Mbytes to 15 Mbytes. Later versions are expected to hold up to 500 Mbytes.

The cartridge has 50 electrical contacts using a PCMCIA-type pin and socket connector. The card is 1.4" long × 1.7" × 0.1" thick— ("matchbook-sized") which is one quarter the size of a PCMCIA card. It is rated for at least 10,000 insertion/withdrawal cycles. Interfaces supporting both 8-bit-wide and 16-bit-wide data transfers are defined. The cards can support 5v, 3.3v and (in the future) lower interface voltages. The specification requires that the cards can handle at least 300,000 write/erase cycles.

CompactFlash cards have an on-board processor. This increases their cost, but allows several operating modes to be selected. For example, the card can appear as a block of memory, or it can emulate an ATA (also known as IDE) disk drive (presenting a standard set of IDE control registers, and reading and writing data in 512-byte blocks—just like disk sectors). This simplifies software development, and facilitates data transfer between different devices).

FlashPix is a standard file format which, among other things, stores digital photographs in multiple resolutions (as the Photo-CD CD-ROM format does). These can be used for fast viewing over the web, high-quality printing and other requirements.

Using a small *transition card*, CompactFlash cards can be inserted in Type II PCMCIA slots (facilitating data transfer to laptop PCs).

Initially developed by SanDisk (which used to be called SunDisk), and first introduced in 1994. The integrated circuits in the cartridges are designed and made by SanDisk, though a cross-licensing agreement permits Intel to make them as well. The standard is now promoted by the CompactFlash Association (CFA), which includes Apple Computer, Canon,

Method	Specifies	Comments
CMYK	Cyan, magenta yellow, and black	These (with the exception of black) are often referred to as the *subtractive primary colors,* as subtracting these colors from white can produce any color. Black is added to provide a better black and to save money (it is less expensive than an equal amount of the other three. Used when the light reflects off the image (*reflective*), such as in the printing industry (sometimes called a *four-color process*), and by ink jet printers. Combinations of these color inks are used to create (almost) any color.
HSV or HSI or HSL	Hue, saturation, and value (or intensity or luminance)	• *Hue* specifies the color (not including white, gray, or black, which are specified by having equal portions of the three primary colors at different brightness). Picture specifying a color in a rainbow. • *Saturation* is how intense or washed-out a specific color is (that is, how much white light is added to "dilute" the color). • *Value* (also called *intensity* or *luminosity*) is how light or dark the color is (imagine adjusting the brightness of the room lights while viewing a page with a color of a specific hue and saturation). These methods are closest to how people think of color.
RGB	Red, green, blue	Specifies how much of these three *additive primary colors* to combine to create the desired color. This method of representing color can be envisioned as a three-dimensional orthogonal axis, with a primary color along each. Used when the light is transmitted through the image (*transmissive*), such as an overhead projector transparency. Since specifying the value of each of the three colors separately is how electronic equipment usually works (for example, color monitors and televisions generate the three primary colors), it is most accurate and is often used by high-end video monitors (which therefore require three separate color signals).
YUV or Y/C	Luminance, Chrominance	• *Y-signal*—the luminance (or brightness) of a signal, which is the equivalent of a monochrome signals (as if the signals were shown on a black-and white television). Contributes the fine details and brightness to a color television signal. Made up 30% red, 59% green, and 11% blue (which matches human color perception). • *Chrominance*—the color of a signal, which has two components. The hue (also called tint) specifies what the color is. The saturation specifies how much white light is in the signal (making the color look washed out)—or conversely, how intense the color is. The chrominance is expressed as a two-dimensional value: • *Phase angle* (which determines the hue) • *Magnitude* (which determines the saturation) This two-dimensional polar-coordinate value can be resolved into rectangular components, and those (orthogonal) axis are called U and V. Used by color television broadcasting.

Color-1

Eastman Kodak, Hewlett-Packard, Matsushita, Motorola, NEC, Polaroid, SanDisk, Seagate Technology and Seiko Epson.

Competes with Miniature Card, though Miniature Cards require software drivers in order to act as a disk drive.

SanDisk has information at *http://www.sandisk.com/sd/product/compactflash_specs.htm.*

See **ATA**, **CDROM**, **FLASH**, **IDE**, **MINICARD**, **PCMCIA**, and **PDA**.

Compatible

A term that indicates that a product meets *some* parts (a subset, not all) of a specification. For example, only some modes of operation may be supported.

Two devices that are *compatible* with a specification may not be interoperable (that is, they may not work when connected to each other) because each implements a different (and incompatible) subset of features. It is therefore better to have *compliant* devices than *compatible* devices. Another choice is to define standard subsets of features.

See **COMPLIANT**, **PORTABILITY**, and **STANDARDS**.

Compliant

A term that indicates that a product fully meets a specification or standard. For example, all modes of operation are supported.

Two devices that are compliant with a specification should be interoperable (that is, they should work when connected to each other).

See **COMPATIBLE** and **STANDARDS**.

Composite Video Signal

The signal that specifies everything a television needs to display monochrome (called RS-170A) or color (called NTSC) pictures. Called "composite" because the signal (which can be carried by a single coaxial cable) is a *composite* of the following:

▲ *Luminance* information: the brightness of the electron beam as it scans across the television screen assuming that you have a *cathode-ray tube* (CRT) type of screen; produces a monochrome (black and white) picture. For color pictures, the luminance signal is a (not equally weighted, in order to match our eye's differing sensitivity to differing wavelengths of light) addition of the red, green and blue components of the picture.

▲ *Blanking* information: turns off the electron beam that creates the picture while the raster scan returns to start the next line (*horizontal blanking*) or field (*vertical blanking*)

▲ *Synchronizing* information, so that the beam knows when to start the next horizontal (*horizontal sync*) or vertical scan (*vertical sync*)

▲ *Audio* information, *frequency modulated* (FM) 4.5 MHz above the *video* (also called *picture*) *carrier.*

These three signals are combined into one, in which the *amplitude* indicates the luminance, with zero brightness blanking the signal and pulses of less than zero brightness indicating the synchronization pulses (the pulse width determines whether it is a horizontal or vertical sync pulse).

Compression

A *color composite video signal* will also include the *chrominance* (or *chroma*) information, which is made up of the *hue* (which color) and *saturation* (how intense the color is—for example, red to pink toward white).

(In contrast, RGB is not a composite signal, since it does not combine all the information into a single signal.)

To carry this chrominance information, an NTSC composite video signal modulates the monochrome (luminance) signal with a *color burst* reference signal, which has a frequency of 3.579545 MHz (±10 Hz). This produces a *color subcarrier* 3.579545 MHz (often called 3.58 MHz) above the luminance signal. At the beginning of each horizontal raster scan, 8 cycles of this 3.58 MHz signal (which is called the *color burst*) are sent to act as a reference for detecting the difference in the phase of the color subcarrier sent for the rest of the raster scan. This phase difference represents what color (hue) is being sent, and the *amplitude* of the color subcarrier represents the saturation.

This composite video signal (whether monochrome or color) is then used to *amplitude modulate* (AM) the *video* (or *picture*) *carrier's* frequency for whichever channel is being used. This video carrier frequency is always 1.25 MHz above the lower boundary for the 6-MHz bandwidth being used for that channel. For example, channel 2 uses 54 to 60 MHz, so the video carrier is at 55.25 MHz, and the color subcarrier will be 3.579545 MHz above that (58.829545 MHz).

The actual weighting of the red, green and blue components of the luminance (often called *Y*) is $Y = 0.59G + 0.30R + 0.11B$. Another way of visualizing the color (*chroma* or *chrominance*) information is to consider the phase difference from the color-burst reference as a two-dimensional value called *UV* or simply *C* (so this method is often called Y/UV or Y/C). The two dimensions are the red minus luminance, calculated as $R - Y = 0.70R - 0.59G - 0.11B$, and the blue minus luminance, calculated as $B - Y = 0.89B - 0.59G - 0.30R$.

These three signals (Y, R − Y and B − Y) are the three separate video signals carried by the three coaxial cables in an S-Video cable and connector. By separating them, they don't interfere with each other, nor require additional processing (which could create a lower-quality picture).

Video signals generally have an amplitude of 1 volt, measured peak to peak ($1 V_{p-p}$).

See **COLOUR**, **CRT**, **INTERLACED**, **NTSC**, **RGB**, and **VIDEO**.

Compression

See **DATA COMPRESSION**.

CompuServe

A company that was 80% owned by H&R Block (the tax people), but was bought by America Online in September 1997. To sound more cool, they changed their name to CompuServe Interactive, and refer to themselves as CSi. They operate a large (2.6 million of subscribers in 1997, a total of 42,000 dial-in lines in about 460 cities all over the world) information service and private data communications network. Provides Internet access too.

In 1997 WorldCom Inc. bought H&R Block's 80% interest in CompuServe for $1.2 billion. WorldCom then traded CompuServe's subscriber base and content (but keeping CompuServe's communications network) along with $175 million to America Online, in return for AOL's communications network and ANS and a commitment that AOL will use WorldCom for the AOL and CompuServe networks for at least 5 years.

CompuServe began in 1977, and operates a WWW server at *http://www.compuserve.com/*.

See **BBS**, **GIF**, and **ISP**.

Connectionless

Data communications that does not require that a connection be established before data can be sent or exchanged. Analogous to mailing a letter (you may have addressed the letter incorrectly, but you don't find out about the problem until after the network has received the message). Usually requires that the higher-layer protocols provide more robust error detection and correction than connection-oriented protocols or networks.

Ethernet and the UDP protocol are connectionless.

See **CLNP**, **CONNECTIONORIENTED**, **ETHERNET**, and **UDP**.

Connection-oriented

Data communications that requires that a connection first be established (*caller* calls and requests a connection, *callee* accepts the connection) before data can be exchanged. Analogous to a telephone call; you can't just pick up the phone and start talking (well you can, but you would be wasting your time talking to the dial tone).

Since it is known that the callee is "listening" (that is, you dialed the right number, the callee was available, and you have their attention), usually provides more reliable communication than connectionless protocols or networks.

X.25 networks and the TCP protocol are connection-oriented.

See **CONNECTIONLESS**, **CONP**, **TCP**, **WAN**, and **X.25**.

Connector

The electro-mechanical devices on the ends of cables that permit them to be mated with, and disconnected from, other cables.

The type of cable used usually determines the type of connector used, as shown in the following table.

Cable	Connector	Comments
Coax (ThickNet)	Type N	Like a larger Type F, in which a threaded coupling nut on the plug keeps it mated with the receptacle.
Coax (RG-58, and RG-62)	BNC	While all BNC connectors mate, the cable end must be sized according to the type of coaxial cable.

(table continued on next page)

Cable	Connector	Comments
Coax (RG-59)	Type F	Used for standard residential cable TV (CATV) coaxial cable.
Fiber-optic cable	ST	Stands for *straight tip* (as opposed to a conical type that is seldom used now). Each connector pair (male and female) connects one strand, so two connector pairs are usually required (one strand for the transmit, the other for the receive data).
	SC	Stands for *subscriber connector*. A newer, and push-on, pull-off type. Preferable to the ST type, as SCs can be spaced closer together (since room to grasp and twist the connector is not required), and the connectors can be keyed to ensure that a pair of them they are plugged-in to a pair of receptacles the right way around. A *duplex* type (two connectors—one for the transmit, and one for the receive) is usually used for ATM.
	Mini--MT	Even newer than SC, is a duplex connector (2 strands of fiber) for either single or multimode optical fiber. Like the SC, it is a rectangular push-on and pull-off type. The connector can be mounted using the same spacing as 8-pin modular jacks (0.55"), so fibre optic hubs can have the same port density as for UTP connections.
STP	DB-9	The DB-9 is used to connect STP cable to LAN adapters in PCs (since the IBM universal data connector is too wide for the slot available at the back of a PC) and for non-IBM uses (such as FDDI over STP).
	IBM universal data connector	For IBM cabling system uses, such as Token Ring wall plates and *multistation access units*.
UTP	8-pin modular *plug* (male) and *jack* (female, socket or receptacle)	Some people call these RJ-45 connectors, which is a misnomer, since that refers to the use of an 8-pin modular connector *wired for use with an AT&T* Definity PBX.
	TelCo, Amphenol, or RJ-21	Since this connector is often used by the telephone company, it is often called a TelCo, and since the connector is often made by the Amphenol Corporation, it is called an Amphenol. It has 25 pairs of electrical contacts, so is often used for 12 10Base-T Ethernet connections.
EIA-232	DB-25	The 25-pin D-subminiature (because it is shaped like a letter "D") connector is used for modems (female connector) and many other EIA-232 applications. The connector is defined in ISO 2110.
	DB-9	The 9-pin D-subminiature connector is often used for the EIA-232 COM port on PCs, since only *asynchronous data communication* is used, and 9 signal pins are therefore enough. Also, the DB-9 requires less space than a DB-25 (especially important for laptop PCs) and costs less.
	RJ-45	This type of connector is often used on Cisco routers, probably because it is even more compact, and lower cost than a DB-9.

AMP Incorporated is a major and huge manufacturer of all types of connectors. AMP has a WWW server at *http://www.amp.com/*. Some other component suppliers with WWW servers include Hamilton Hallmark (*http://www.tsc.hh.avnet.com*) and Anixter (*http://www.anixter.com/*).

See **BNC**, **CABLE**, **CATV**, **COAX**, **DB25**, **EIA-TIA232**, **FIBER**, **LAN**, **RJ45**, **SIMM**, **TIP AND RING**, **TOKEN RING**, and **WAN**.

CONP
Connection-Oriented Network Protocol

An OSI network layer protocol, suitable for use over X.25, point-to-point WAN links and Ethernet, Token Ring, and FDDI LANs. The connectionless OSI network layer protocol is CLNP.

See **CLNP**, **CONNECTIONORIENTED**, and **OSI**.

Cookie

Often called a magic cookie, since it does something known and understood only by the cookie's creator (this is a common term in role-playing games, where the cookies may have mystical powers).

The cookie itself (in the context of the world wide web, and browsers such as Netscape) is some ASCII text, initially sent to you from a server site you surfed to, as part of the page sent back to your PC. The cookie gets stored on your hard disk, for later retrieval by that same site.

For example, when you access a WWW server, you may be asked about your interests (so only information of interest to you is presented to you). The server could solicit this information from you each time you access it (but this would be an irritation), or the server could store your interests (but you would still need to identify yourself each time you accessed the server, so the server could look up your stored interests). Or the server could write all your interests into a small message (in any format or encoding it chooses), and send this to your computer—this is the cookie. Your computer then stores this cookie on your hard disk. The next time you access that same web server (and optionally, a specific page there), it asks your browser for the cookie. Now the server you're visiting knows your interests—automagically. Part of the cookie specification is that the web server can only access the same cookie (or cookies) it sent to you—it cannot access the rest of your cookie file (that is, it cannot receive cookies put there by other web servers).

Since all of this typically happens without any user involvement, some browsers have an option to warn of this (since the server is storing something on your computer without your knowledge—and this could be a security concern), or to refuse to store cookies.

Other common uses for cookies include your shopping basket (so you don't loose your selected items if the phone gets hung-up or you need to leave a site before making your purchase on-line) and maintaining interest profiles (what pages a user visited at a site) so that advertising displayed by the site to the user can be customized (and the vendors hope—more profitable for them).

To write a cookie to your PC's hard disk (Netscape's cookie file is called cookies.txt, and Internet Explorer's is `cookies`), the server embeds certain keyword/parameter responses along with the other HTML information it sends you.

The size of the cookie file is limited to 300 cookies, with a maximum of 20 from any single site (domain name). When these limits are reached, the oldest are automatically deleted to make room for the new ones. Each cookie can be a maximum of 4,096 bytes, with additional bytes truncated.

The actual text of the cookie as sent from a server (the users had visited site *http://www.noodle.com* in this example) is described below (there is some extra HTML angle bracket mumbo jumbo wrapped around it, but here is the interesting part that describes the capabilities and limitations of cookies).

The keyword `Set-Cookie:` precedes the cookie information sent from the server. This is followed by the following keywords and parameters:

▲ `name_of_stuff=stuff_to_be_stored;`, this is the actual information. For example, it may be `pref=barking`, which would mean that the variable name `pref` is set to the value `barking`, which might mean that the site determined (maybe from questions you answered, or specific pages you visited) that your preference is to bark, so next time you visit they may send you advertisements for dog food and doggie dating services.

▲ `expires=date_and_time;` specifies the date and time when the cookie expires (after that, the cookie will no longer be sent back to the server). If this is omitted, then the cookie expires when you leave the site.

▲ `domain=turkey.noodle.com;` specifies that a visitor to `www.noodle.com` will not receive the cookie—the cookie will only be sent if the visitor goes to `turkey.noodle.com`. The `domain` specified must have at least 2 periods (such as `.noodle.com`, specifying any site in the `noodle.com` second-level domain), and this is how servers are restricted to retrieving only the cookies they sent to your cookie file.

▲ `path=/canines;` specifies that the cookie will be sent from the server to the browser only if the user visits that subdirectory on the server. In this example, this would be a URL of *http://turkey.noodle.com/canines*. If this is not specified, it defaults to `path=/;`, so that visitors to any subdirectory under the domain will receive a cookie.

▲ `secure` specifies that the cookie will only be sent if SSL is used.

When the cookie is retrieved from your PC by a server, then the keyword `Cookie:` (and not `Set-Cookie:`) would have preceded it. For example `Cookie:  pref=barking` would be returned to the server.

Some more information on cookies is at *http://www.illuminatus.com/cookie.fcgi*, and the cookie recipe (ok, *specification*, humor isn't supposed to work in print) itself is at *http://home.netscape.com/newsref/std/cookie_spec.html*.

See **SSL**, and **WWW**.

Copyright

Literally, "the right to copy," and everyone else not having the right to copy.

Protection against others copying and selling the *expression* of ideas "verbatim"—not the ideas, concepts, principles and discoveries, processes, methods of operation, procedures, or systems themselves. Copyrights therefore will not protect the techniques used in a program or anything about the content of the program itself.

Copyrights *do not* cover the following:

▲ Song titles (unless the title is original and distinctive, in which case it may be protected as part of the work to which it relates)

▲ Names (and other short-word combinations and catch-phrases, though some short-word combinations, such as "business reengineering" and "change management" may be trademarked)

▲ The idea for a story's plot (only the *expression* of that plot, for example, as a play or movie, can be copyrighted)

▲ Facts in an article

▲ Computer program names (though these could be trademarked)

Copyrights *do* cover the following:

▲ Literary works: books, magazine articles, pamphlets, poems, and other works consisting of text, including computer programs

▲ Dramatic works: films, movies, videos, plays, screenplays, and scripts

▲ Musical works: compositions that consist of both words and music or music only (lyrics only are considered literary works)

▲ Artistic works: paintings, drawings, maps, game board surfaces, photographs, sculptures, and architectural works

Copyrights also apply to all kinds of recordings, such as records, cassettes, and compact discs (which are called *mechanical contrivances*). These are copyrighted separately from the creative works themselves.

Without the copyright holder's permission, the copyright laws also prohibit others from copying substantial parts of the work, including translations.

A copyright owner has the exclusive right to:

▲ Do or authorize the publishing, reproduction, and distribution of copies of the work

▲ Prepare derivative works

▲ Perform, deliver, transmit, or display the work

Contravening any of these is called *infringement*, which can result in requiring that the copies be destroyed and other legal remedies (not to mention having to deal with lawyers).

Proving infringement requires showing that the infringer had (or must have had) access to and saw the material and that the material must have been copied (for example, it is just not likely that two people could write a word-for-word identical article for a magazine).

Fair use (also called *fair dealing*) allows brief passages to be quoted for purposes of (for example) research, teaching, journalism (such as article reviews or newspaper summaries), criticism, parody and library activities. provided that the source and the author's name are included.

Copyright

The Canadian Copyright Act provides that:

▲ The author normally owns the copyright

▲ If the work is done as an employee, then the employer owns the copyright

▲ The copyright for works done for commission is owned by the person paying, unless a written agreement says otherwise

▲ When doing work on a contract basis (that is, not as an employee), the author of the work owns the copyright, unless a written agreement states otherwise

I bet the lawyers had a good time arguing those last two. I would do an agreement to clarify the copyright issue regardless of which side I was on and whether I thought it was commission or contract work.

Owners of copyrights can *assign* their copyrights to others, but the author still retains *moral rights* (though the author can waive these). Moral rights require that the work cannot be changed (the *right of integrity*) or associated with a product or service that damages the author's reputation or honor and also that the author's name must still be associated with the work.

If the original author's moral rights are violated, remedies can be the same as if there was an infringement.

Assignments can be for all or only some rights, for a specific time period or until the copyright expires, and for everywhere or only specified geographic areas.

A *license* gives someone permission to use a work for certain purposes and under certain conditions, but does not assign the copyright; the owner still owns the copyright. Licensing agreements often require that royalties or fees be payable to a copyright owner each time a work is performed or played.

The *Universal Copyright Convention* provides that copyrighted works have a *mark* such as: "©Mitchell Shnier, 1996," but there is no requirement in Canada for copyrighted works to be marked in any way. They are automatically covered. However, the mark does serve to remind potential infringers that the work is copyrighted. Some countries that are members of the Universal Copyright Convention but not of the *Berne Convention for the Protection of Literary and Artistic Works* (which was initially created in 1886) require such a mark.

Works can be *registered* as well (in which case you get a certificate which helps when asserting your ownership of the copyright). The mark can be used whether the work is registered or not.

Registration:

▲ Requires that you fill out a form and send in a fee (but not the work—the copyright office does not assess the work or want to store it, though the National Library requires two copies of every book published in Canada, as required under the *National Library Act*)

▲ Still requires that the owner of a copyright initiate legal action if necessary (the government won't do it)

▲ Does not prove that the work is original (if this is contested, only a court of law can confirm this)

Countries that are members of the Berne Copyright Convention or Universal Copyright Convention recognize each other's citizens' copyright claims (though these Conventions do not cover sound recordings).

A copyright lasts for the lifetime of the author plus 50 years (though there are exceptions, such as for photographs and sound recordings, for which the protection lasts 50 years after they were made).

To prove copyright infringement, it must be shown that the work was copied and not independently created.

The Canadian Copyright Office is part of the Canadian Intellectual Property Office. The Canadian Copyright Guide and Patent Guide is at *http://info.ic.gc.ca/ic-data/marketplace/cipo/contact/co nt_e.html*.

The U.S. Copyright office has some information at *http://lcweb.loc.gov/copyright*.

The Internet presents many new difficulties and challenges in interpreting copyright law. The Copyright Clearance Center (*http://www.openmarket.com/copyright* or *http://www.copyright.com/*) and the Center for Democracy and Technology (*http://www.cdt.org*) provide some assistance and information. Some explanation of the legal implications of publishing on the Internet is at *http://www.law.ubc.ca/papers/franson.html*.

A hypertext version of the U.S. copyright law is at *http://www.law.cornell.edu/usc/17/overview.html*, and some interpretation of this is at *http://www.benedict.com/fund.htm*. Current information on copyright law is at *http://www.library.yale.edu/~okerson/copyproj.html*.

See **CIPO**, **COPYRIGHT**, **INTELLECTUAL PROPERTY PROTECTION**, and **TRADEMARK**.

CORBA
Common Object Request Broker Architecture

Well, everything used to be mainframe-centric. That is, the mainframe computer did most everything. It stored your data, processed it, printed it and decided how to display it on your terminal. Minicomputers were pretty much the same, though most organizations had more than one of them.

Then the client/server architecture allowed more processing to be done at the desktop (perhaps deciding how to process or display the data), though the data typically was stored on a central server (likely running SQL).

The next step is to have information stored as objects, and those objects can be distributed all over your organization (or even the entire Internet). This is the goal of CORBA—systems which are comprised of computers from any manufacturer, located anywhere, running any operating system, and running programs created with any programming language.

CORBA specifies the architecture for communications between distributed objects. The Internet Inter-ORB Protocol (IIOP) is part of CORBA, and standardizes the communications between different vendor's CORBA implementations.

CORBA is an example of *middleware*—that is, software between the application programs (those that are written specifically for your company or industry) and the communications protocol (such as TCP/IP) that provides interoperability (so the application programs can understand each other's data).

CORBA competes with Microsoft's *Distributed Computing Object Model* (DCOM).

The first version of CORBA was released in 1991. IIOP was specified in CORBA 2.0, which was released in December 1994.

CORBA was created by the *Object Management Group* (OMG), which has the goal of specifying (and its members providing and using) a common framework for application development using object-oriented techniques.

The OMG has a web site at *http://www.omg.org*. CORBA information is also at *http://www.acl.lanl.gov/CORBA/*.

See **CLIENT/SERVER, MAINFRAME, OLE, OPENDOC,** and **SQL.**

COS
Corporation for Open Systems

An organization sponsored by OSI software vendors to provide conformance testing. Does not do interoperability testing. As with other OSI efforts, you don't hear much about this one any more (except for ISDN IOCs).

See **ISDN,** and **OSI.**

COS
Class of Service

A method of providing prioritization of traffic for easily identified types of traffic—such as that from specific switch ports or IP addresses. Such prioritization *policies* would be set by a network administrator.

Most current routers can provide this service, but the additional processing required significantly slows their packet-handling capacity. COS is therefore usually used to refer to more hardware-based implementations, such as those for ATM networks.

QOS includes the features of COS plus guarantees on minimum bandwidth, and maximum network latency and jitter, as requested when specific connections are established.

The IEEE 802.1p standard uses 3 bits in the 4-byte 802.1Q VLAN header to specify one of 8 traffic classes (that is, the priority) of Ethernet and Token Ring frames. Network equipment, such as switches, can then use this priority information to decide which frames are sent out first when traffic destined for a port arrives faster than the port will accept it.

Another way COS can be implemented is based on the *precedence bits* in the IP header. These are the 3 least significant bits in the 8-bit *Service Type* field (which is bits 8 through 16 of the first word) of the IP header. These bits have always been defined, but currently are seldom used. A higher number indicates higher priority.

See **ATM, PACE, QOS, ROUTER, SWITCHED LAN,** and **VLAN.**

COSAC
Canadian Open Systems Application Criteria

A Canadian government specification of which OSI standards to use and which options available in each standard to use to implement various computer communications functions.

The problem is that there are too many OSI standard ways of implementing systems, and the intent is to narrow these choices so that OSI-based systems will interoperate. GOSIP is the name of the U.S. and U.K. equivalent efforts (though all three specify different options).

See **GOSIP** and **OSI**.

COSE
Common Open Software Environment

OSF's "process" started in March 1993 by Hewlett-Packard (HP), IBM, Santa Cruz Operation (SCO), Sunsoft (Sun Microsystems), Univel (Novell), and USL (which was part of Novell) to standardize the UNIX desktop and application development environment (so that they can better compete with Microsoft). The main product of this work is CDE, which uses each vendors' technologies.

Other COSE work includes standards for graphics, multimedia, system management, objects, distributed computing, and a Windows-type interface that is compatible with Microsoft Windows.

Not very active lately (these coalitions all have enthusiastic announcements, but then everyone has other work to do, and you don't hear much from them).

Pronounced "cozy."

See **CDE**, **HP**, **IBM**, **OSF**, **SCO**, **SUN**, **UNIVEL**, and **USL**.

CPE
Customer Premises Equipment

In the old days (before 1984 or so), all voice and data communications equipment was owned by the telephone company (because *interconnect* was illegal). The telephone company had three kinds of equipment (according to where it was located):

▲ Central office; the switching, power supply, cross-patching (on the *main distribution frame*—MDF) and test equipment

▲ Outside plant; the underground (with splices in those green *pedestals* beside the road) and overhead (on utility poles) cabling between C.O.s, or between C.O.s and customer locations.

▲ Customer premises equipment; the telephones, cabling and jacks, and lightning arrestor(s) in the customer buildings.

Now that customers usually own the equipment within their own buildings (and the connection at the demarcation between the two cabling systems is called the *demarc*), some now say that CPE is an acronym for *customer provided equipment*.

See **CARRIER**.

CPI-C
Common Programming Interface for Communications

IBM's APIs, available for all of their platforms (and, they hope, third-party platforms as well), that facilitates cross-platform communications by providing a common programming interface.

CPU

Can run over MPTN, so can use APPN, TCP/IP, or other network layer protocols.

Pronounced "*c*-pick."

See **API**, **APPN**, **LU-6.2**, **MPTN**, and **TCP/IP**.

CPU
Central Processing Unit

The (usually) single integrated circuit (IC) that does the actual interpreting of program instructions and processing of data in a computer. Other parts of a computer are the memory, disk drive controller, and video adapter.

See **ALPHA AXP**, **INTEL**, **MPP**, **PA-RISC**, **PC**, **PIO**, **POWERPC**, **RISC**, and **SMP2**.

CRC
Cyclic Redundancy Code

A key component in the error-detecting capabilities of many protocols.

A number of bits (usually 16 or 32) generated from, and appended to the end of, a block of data to provide error detection. The message receiver also generates a CRC from the block of data and compares it to the one appended to the received message. If the two match, then there is a high probability that the received message has not been corrupted.

There are two commonly used 16-bit CRC *generator polynomials*. The ITU-T (CCITT) standard 16-bit generator polynomial (used on X.25 networks, and by the Kermit, YModem, and ZModem file transfer protocols, for example) is represented by $x^{16} + x^{12} + x^5 + 1$. This is called CRC-CCITT and represents the binary number 10001000000100001 (note that there is a one in bit positions 16, 12, 5, and 0).

IBM protocols such as SDLC use CRC-16, which is represented by $x^{16} + x^{15} + x^2 + 1$.

In either case, the CRC is the remainder after binary division of the message (taken as a long string of ones and zeros, regardless of byte boundaries) by the generator polynomial.

$$\text{generated CRC} = \text{the remainder of } \frac{\text{message received}}{x^{16} + x^{12} + x^5 + x + 1}$$

CRC-CCITT CRCs detect:

▲ All single- and double-bit errors

▲ All errors of an odd number of bits

▲ All error bursts of 16 bits or less (the length of an error burst is the number of bits between and including the first errored bit and the last errored bit—any number of bits between may be errored)

▲ In summary, 99.998% of all errors (that is   )

Because of these error-detection capabilities, 16-bit CRCs are usually limited to use with message of less than 4 kbytes (there are enough ways to corrupt messages larger than 4 kbytes that catching "only" 99.998% of them is considered inadequate).

32-bit CRCs are used for messages up to 64 kbytes in length. Such CRCs detect 99.999999977% (that is,   ) of all errors. The generator polynomial for the 32-bit CRCs used for both Ethernet and Token Ring is $x^{32} + x^{26} + x^{23} + x^{22} + x^{16} + x^{12} + x^{11} + x^{10} + x^8 + x^7 + x^5 + x^4 + x^2 + x + 1$.

See **CHECKSUM, PARITY, HDLC, KERMIT, MNP, V.42,** and **XMODEM.**

CRT
Cathode Ray Tube

The type of display commonly used for computer monitors, televisions and oscilloscopes. Often called a *video display terminal* (VDT), though a VDT would be an entire computer monitor, and a CRT is actually the just the glass display tube itself (without the plastic enclosure, driving electronics and controls, power supply and other stuff).

The CRT is made of glass, and it tapers towards the back. The inside front surface is coated with phosphors, and the back has a *cathode* (which simply means it is connected to a negative D.C. voltage). The cathode is heated, so that electrons will be emitted from it, and there is a vacuum in the enclosure so the electrons won't get stopped by air molecules. The face on most CRTs is convex rather than flat (which would be easier to read), as a curved surface is a stronger shape—just check out the bottom of a champagne bottle. Power supplies drive coils placed around the CRT, so that they focus the electron beam to a point, and also cause it to scan across the front of the CRT.

Color CRTs produce colors using three electron sources (sometimes called *guns*) that is sweep over three types of phosphors (that glow red, green or blue). So that each electron gun only illuminates its corresponding color phosphors, a *shadow mask* is used. This is a thin sheet of metal with holes exactly aligned with the phosphor dots. As it is bombarded by electrons, this metal gets quite hot and it is important that it not expand or otherwise distort its shape as it changes temperature (so that it continues to be exactly aligned with the phosphor dots). It turns out that an alloy that contains 63.8% Iron, 36% Nickel and 0.2% Carbon (C) has an extremely small coefficient of expansion. The trademarked name for this allow is Invar (*I* and *N* as in Iron and Nickel, and otherwise as in in*var*iable), and you may have seen this advertised as a high-end feature for color television picture tubes or the balance springs of mechanical watches.

The spacing of the holes for adjacent phosphor dots of the same color is called the *dot pitch*, and the smaller the dot pitch, the better the image produced. Typical good monitors will have a dot pitch of 0.25 mm to 0.28 mm. So that things are not too easy to compare, Sony and Mitsubishi use an *aperture grille* (made of an array of vertical wires, with horizontal *damping* or *stabilizer wires* to keep the vertical ones from vibrating), which creates a *slotted shadow mask*. So this type of monitor instead has a characteristic *stripe pitch*. Stripe pitches are typically the same 0.25 mm to 0.28 mm. Some say these monitors have brighter and crisper images, some say the damping wires are visible, and reduce the image quality.

Since the size (typically measured diagonally) of the largest viewable image on a CRT is less (due to rounding of the corners of the face of the tube, non-linearities when displaying near the edge of the tube, and other factors) than the size of the glass tube for the CRT, it is most useful for vendors to describe the size of the largest image that can be displayed. VIS (*viewable* or *visual image size*), viewable and DVI (*diagonal viewable image*) are common descriptions of the more meaningful measurement.

CRTC

See **EMF**, **LCD**, and **VFD**.

CRTC
Canadian Radio-Television and Telecommunications Commission

The federal agency that regulates Canada's broadcasting and telecommunications industries.

The CRTC's WWW site is *http://www.crtc.gc.ca/*.

The equivalent U.S. organization would be a combination of the FCC and the *Public Utilities Commissions*.

See **INDUSTRY CANADA**, **FCC**, and **PUC**.

CSLIP
Compressed SLIP

A more efficient version of SLIP, intended for use on (slow) dial-up connections. Both ends of the link must support CSLIP if it is to be used.

The IP packet header is 20 bytes. The TCP packet header is also 20 bytes. Most of the fields in these 40 bytes do not change (though some increment) during a TCP/IP session, so CSLIP compresses these 40 bytes to just 3 or 5, and allows up to 16 simultaneous TCP connections.

Defined in RFC 1144. Sometimes called Van Jacobsen compression.

See **PPP**, **TCP**, **SLIP**, and **VJ**.

CSMA/CA
Carrier Sense, Multiple Access with Collision Avoidance

A popular type of *access method* (the way a networked device decides if it can transmit) for wireless networks, and also for cabled networks that operate slower than a few megabits/s—such as Apple's LocalTalk which operates at 230,400 bits/s. Retransmitting on these networks will take a relatively long time, and messages are typically of much longer duration than the round-trip time-delay of the network.

Wired CSMA/CA systems, after "listening" and deciding that there are no other stations already transmitting, sends a "reservation tone" (or other indication that it is about to transmit data). The duration of this tone must be at least the one-way delay of the network; this ensures that no other stations are also about to transmit.

CSMA/CA is not used for high-speed networks (such as Ethernet) since a high-speed network could send the entire message in the time CSMA/CA sends only the reservation tone, so why not just send the message and get two jobs done (reserving the network, and sending the message) at the same time (which is what CSMA/CD does.

Collisions often occur because two or more stations sense that a network is available at the same instant (and then both transmit, causing a collision). Therefore, for wireless systems, CSMA/CA systems wait a random period after they sense that other stations are not transmitting and then check again.

CSMA/CA is used (instead of CSMA/CD) for wireless networks, since radios usually cannot "listen" while they are transmitting, so the "CD" (collision detection) of CSMA/CD cannot be used. Radios cannot listen while they are transmitting because their own transmitted signal swamps-out any received signal, and many radios are inherently half-duplex—they share some of the transmitting and receiving electronics to save money and size.

See **S802.A11**, and **CSMACD**.

CSMA/CD
Carrier Sense, Multiple Access with Collision Detection

The "access method" used by 802.3 and Ethernet LANs. It basically says "first come, first served" when it comes to getting permission to transmit. It has the following characteristics:

▲ Carrier Sense—stations (actually, the adapter cards in them) listen to see whether other stations are already transmitting, before they attempt to transmit. If the network is already busy, then the stations wait a random amount of time, and test the network again.

▲ Multiple Access—the stations all have the capability to transmit.

▲ Collision Detection—stations can detect if they are part of a "collision" (in which two or more stations transmit simultaneously). If so, they stop transmitting, wait a random amount of time, and try transmitting again (after first ensuring the LAN is not again busy).

CSMA/CD was invented by Robert Metcalf and was his Ph.D. thesis topic, as an improvement on the Aloha network (which he read about in a paper in the June 1970 issue of the American Federation of Information Processing Societies, by Norm Abramson). Aloha was a radio-based system, which did not do collision detection (which requires full-duplex radios, which are not common) or retransmission, so could not handle congested channels as well.

See **S802.3**, **CSMACA**, **ETHERNET**, **GIGABIT ETHERNET**, and **MAC**.

CSU
Channel Service Unit

A device usually required on a T1 (or FT1 or T3) line that performs several protective and diagnostic functions, such as the following:

▲ Lightning protection (protect the user's equipment from damage)

▲ "Ones density" enforcement (if the user equipment transmits more than 15 consecutive zeros, then the CSU either alarms and stuffs some ones in or implements some trick, such as B8ZS)

▲ Loopback (for diagnostic testing)

Both inputs and outputs to and from a CSU are raw T1:

▲ ±3-V signaling (±20%)

▲ *Alternate mark inversion* encoding (a binary zero is no pulse, a binary one is one +3V or −3V pulse), each pulse being the opposite polarity of the previous one

▲ Two twisted pairs (using a terminal strip or DB-15 connector for connection to the lines from the phone company)

CT2

For data applications, the CSU is often integrated with the DSU, so the resulting unit is then called a DSU/CSU.

In the U.S. and Canada, customers are allowed to, so usually do provide their own CSU/DSU. Therefore, some equipment (such as routers) have optional integral CSU/DSUs). In most other countries, the CSU must be provided by the local telephone company, so is a stand-alone external device.

See **B8ZS**, **DSU**, **CSU/DSU**, **DSX**, **FT1**, **T1**, **T3**, **V.25BIS**, and **V.54**.

CT2
Cordless Communications 2

A digital wireless communications standard that supports digitized voice and data at up to 32,000 bits/s.

See **PCTS** and **PCS**.

CTI
Computer Telephony Integration

Providing a link between telephone systems and computers to facilitate incoming and outgoing call handling and control.

Common CTI capabilities include the following:

▲ *Interactive voice response* (IVR), where you use your touch-tone telephone to provide or gather information

▲ *Screen pops*, where your telephone number is provided to an information operator at a call center, using the *automatic number information* (ANI) provided over a telephone company's ISDN line to the call center's automatic call distributor (ACD), which distributes the incoming calls to the operators, according to some criteria such as availability, capability and number of people on hold. The telephone number is usually used to display information about you or your recent dealings with the company, to speed your call handling.

▲ *Predictive dialing*, which speeds outbound dialing by automatically dialing telephone numbers for the telephone operators, and calling faster than they can handle the calls, on the (always correct) assumption that a high percentage of the calls will be ring-no-answer or busy. You know you have been called by such a system when you answer the phone, and need to say hello a few times before the operator responds—because they have not yet been connected to you (they are still handling the previous call).

The two main APIs to control the telephone systems are TAPI and TSAPI.

The physical link between a telephone or server, and the PBX may be an EIA-232, ISDN, LAN or proprietary link.

Other acronyms popular in telephony include the following:

▲ ACD (automatic call distributor) which is a souped-up PBX that can maintain multiple call queues, announce to callers the expected waiting time or the number of callers ahead of them in their queue, prioritize calls according to what number they dialed or touch-tone keys they pressed, and assign calls to operators according to criteria such as the operator's skill set.

▲ IVR (interactive voice response) is the traditional system which prompts callers to press touch-tone buttons to hear information, or enter numbers (such as their account number). The device that produces the speech is sometimes called a VRU (voice response unit)

▲ ANI (automatic number identification) displays the telephone number of the caller

▲ DNIS (dialed number identification service) provides the telephone number that callers dialed. ACDs (for example) use these numbers to route incoming calls to a call center that handles calls for many telephone numbers, to the desired group of people

Some CTI information is at *http://www.fbcs.fujitsu.com*. Dialogic Corp. has long been a leader in voice response hardware and software for PC platforms. They have a WWW server at *http://www.dialogic.com*.

See **CTI**, **DTMF2** (*Dual Tone Multi-Frequency*), **ECTF**, **POTS**, **SCREEN POP**, **TAPI**, and **TSAPI**.

CUT
Control Unit Terminal

The mode of operation of 3270-series terminals in which the controller (3274 or 3174) has most of the intelligence and the 3270 terminal has little. The other mode of operation is the newer DFT.

See **S3174 AND 3274**, **S3270**, and **DFT**.

D

DAB
Digital Audio Broadcast

A method of broadcasting audio as digital signals, instead of the analog method currently used for standard AM (amplitude modulation) and FM (frequency modulation) radio. It is expected to support the following features.

▲ Audio signals have compact-disc quality sound, with 5 channels (for surround-sound) per signal.

▲ Broadcasters can have several transmitters in a geographic area to seamlessly extend coverage, or to provide better coverage —with current technology, only a single transmitter can be used, and this can have areas of weak coverage (for example, behind a hill or in a valley). Receivers can dynamically switch to the best transmitter, taking advantage of signal reflections (which would normally interfere with the main signal).

▲ These frequencies penetrate buildings better.

▲ Other information can be carried as binary data, such as the name of songs and station, the type of music played, and weather and traffic reports.

▲ Pay-per-listen radio programs are supported.

To implement DAB, a standard called *Eureka 147* has been adopted by Europe and the U.K. (the U.S. is still evaluating which system to use). Eureka 147 was adopted by Canada in 1995. Some features of the Eureka 147 system are as follows.

▲ The frequency band from 1.452 GHz to 1.492 GHz (40 MHz in the L band—and generally called "1.5 GHz") was allocated for this use by the 1992 World Administrative Radio Conference (WARC), which was held in Torremolinos, Spain.

▲ It can operate at up to 3 GHz, from satellite (likely the primary method) or terrestrial antennas (likely to provide "fill-in" coverage), or over cable (along with cable TV signals).

▲ The audio compression scheme is called *Musicam*. It uses a bit rate of 224 kbits/s, and is the same as is used for MPEG-2 audio. In the 40 MHz of bandwidth, it supports 23 channels, each of 5 audio signals (to provide *surround sound*).

In some countries, 1.5 GHz was not available, or was planned to be used for other services. For example, since the U.S. military has 1.5 GHz reserved, the U.S. selected 2.3 GHz instead (specifically 2.310 to 2.360 GHz)—though the National Association of Broadcasters would prefer a method that uses the same frequencies as are already used for AM and FM radio. Many countries selected 2.5 GHz.

In Canada, the effort is being coordinated by Digital Radio Research Inc., which was established in 1993 to own, operate and evaluate the performance of experimental transmitters. DRRI is a joint venture of the Canadian Association of Broadcasters (private radio stations) and the Canadian Broadcasting Corporation (the national public radio station). It is expected that Eureka 147 will replace current conventional AM and FM broadcasting.

In the U.S. American Mobile Radio Corp. (a unit of American Mobile Satellite Corp.) and CD Radio Inc. will provide nationwide service, perhaps by late 1999.

Sometimes called *digital radio*, *digital audio radio* (DAR), and *digital sound broadcasting*.

Additional information is available at *http://www.kp.dlr.de/DAB/* and from the Canadian Association of Broadcasters at *http://www.ottawa.net/~cab/digital.htm*.

See **RDS**, and **WIRELESS**.

DASD
Direct Access Storage Device

The disk drive subsystem of an IBM mainframe.

See **DISK DRIVE**, **IBM**, and **MAINFRAME**.

Data Circuit–terminating Equipment

See **DCE1**.

Data Communications

Now there's a broad topic. I bet somebody could write a book on that!

One way of categorizing data communications is shown in the figure below.

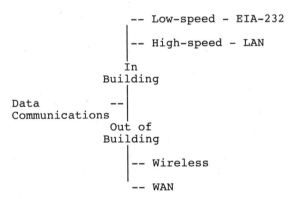

```
                         -- Low-speed - EIA-232
                        |
                        |-- High-speed - LAN
                        |
                     In
                  Building
                        |
     Data         --    |
     Communications     |
                   Out of
                  Building
                        |
                        |-- Wireless
                        |
                         -- WAN
```

For further information (and a more detailed tree), see the following entries.

See **EIA-TIA232**, **LAN**, **WIRELESS**, and **WAN**.

Data Compression

A process of reducing the number of bits required to represent some information, usually to reduce the time or cost of storing or transmitting it.

Some methods can be reversed to reconstruct the original data exactly (*lossless data compression*); these are used for faxes, programs and most computer data.

Other methods (*lossy data compression*) do not exactly reproduce the original data, but this may be acceptable (for example, it is probably good enough for a video conference, and not having to travel is appreciated). In addition, the reduction in image quality may be imperceptible; many voice and video compression schemes eliminate parts of the signal (for example, the phase relationship between frequencies) that are not discernible to people.

More than you ever wanted to know about data compression is in the FAQs at *http:// www.faqs.org/faqs/compression-faq/*.

See **CSLIP**, **CCP**, **CSU/DSU**, **LOSSY DATA COMPRESSION**, **FAX**, **LZS**, **LZW**, **MNP**, **RLE**, **STAC**, **V.42BIS**, and **VIDEO**.

Database Administrator

See **DBA**.

Dataroute

The Stentor (Canadian) name for a longer-distance (between cities, for example) digital *leased line* (also called a digital *dedicated circuit*)—shorter circuits are often called DCS. Available data rates are 1,200- to 56,000-bits/s, asynchronous or synchronous data communications.

The equivalent U.S. service is often called DDS.

See **ASYNCHRONOUS**, **DCS**, **DDS**, **STENTOR**, **SYNCHRONOUS**, and **WAN**.

DataTac

See **ARDIS**, and **BELL ARDIS**.

Daylight Savings Time

Setting clocks one hour ahead at 2:00 a.m. on the first Sunday in April (at least in the U.S. and Canada) to provide more sunlight in the evening (though many would argue that it provides more darkness in the morning so that the children don't get up at 5:00 a.m.).

When *Daylight Savings Time* is in effect, the time zone is, for example, *Eastern Daylight Time* (EDT) rather than Eastern Standard Time (EST).

Daylight savings time ends at 2:00 a.m. on the last Sunday in October, when clocks are set back one hour. There is therefore no net effect (wouldn't it be a hoot if we didn't do this?).

See **UTC**, and **VBI**.

DB-25

A 25-pin connector. This is often used for EIA-232 (formerly RS-232-C).

Also called a D-Subminiature connector (because the shroud around the pins is shaped like a "D", so you can't plug it in upside-down.

The *plug* (the male connector) is sometimes called a DB-25P. The *socket* (also called the receptacle, is the female connector) is sometimes called a DB-25S.

For EIA-232 a female connector is used on the DCE (*Data Circuit-terminating Equipment*, such as modems), and a male connector is usually used on the DTE (*Data Terminal Equipment*, such as PC COM ports).

Also a female DB-25 is used on computers for parallel printer ports (on PCs) and Macintosh SCSI ports.

The DB-25 connector is defined in ISO 2110.

The 9-pin version of the connector (often used for PC COM ports) is sometimes called a DB-9, and sometimes a DE-9 (with the DE-9P—the male or plug—on the PC). The 37-pin version (often used for EIA-449) is sometimes called a DB-37, and is defined in ISO 4902.

See **S1284**, **CONNECTOR**, **DCE1**, **DTE**, **EIA-TIA232**, **PARALLEL PORT**, and **SCSI1**.

DBA
Database Administrator

A person who is responsible for maintaining, designing, and implementing changes to, tuning, and expanding a database.

See **SQL**.

DBS
Digital Broadcast Service

Digitized and compressed traditional television signals broadcast from satellites to compete with local cable TV (CATV) service.

The first North American provider began service in 1994, and was DirecTV, which is a service from Hughes Satellite, of Hughes Electronics (which is a subsidiary of General Motors). It provides 150 to 175 digitally-compressed channels to 18" dish antennas. Other providers include USSB and Primestar. These services are sometimes called *direct-to-the-home* (DTH), as they don't first go to the headend of the local CATV company for wired delivery to people's homes.

See **CATV**, **HDTV**, **SATELLITE**, and **VIDEO**.

DCE
Data Circuit–Terminating Equipment

Usually a modem, though it may be a data set, DSU, or other device that is used to connect a computer to a data communications service.

For example, the typical use of modems is to connect two DTEs (*Data Terminal Equipment*), such as a terminal and a computer, over a network (such as an analog leased line data circuit).

That is, the modems are *Data Circuit-terminating Equipment* (DCE), since they terminate the data circuit. In the RS-232-C standard, modems were referred to as data communications equipment, since that is what they did. (I suppose they still do that, but someone thought you could look at it another way.)

The accompanying diagram shows the classic setup. Starting at the left, we have a DTE, which is a terminal (or a PC emulating one, for example), to an EIA-232 connection from the terminal to a modem, to a switched telephone network or a leased line, to another modem, which is connected to a computer, using another EIA-232 connection.

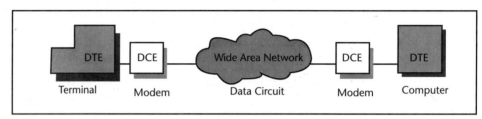

DCE-1

See **DSU**, **DTE**, **EIA-TIA232**, **MODEM**, **V.54**, and **WAN**.

DCE
Distributed Computing Environment

OSF's specification for the core services (sometimes called *middleware*) needed for cross-platform (that is, computers with different hardware and operating systems) *distributed computing* (which is more trendily called a *client/server* environment).

Since the function of, and communication between, these services is standardized, services can be provided by different suppliers and still be interoperable.

Includes specifications for the following:

▲ Threads, which are single processes that can have more than one section of code executing simultaneously

▲ *Remote Procedure Calls* (RPCs), which are used for communications between services

Directory Services, which are used to locate services, are called *cell directories*, and use X.500

Time service to have all computers' time-of-day clocks synchronized (with allowance for time-zone differences and Daylight Savings Time)

▲ Security, using *Kerberos*

Distributed file and print services, similar to NetWare file servers or NFS mounts

Version 1.1 of the specification was released in September 1994.

The OSF has some DCE information at *http://www.osf.org/dce/index.html*.

See **CLIENT/SERVER**, **KERBEROS**, **MESSAGING**, **NFS**, **OSF**, **UTC**, **RPC**, and **X.500**.

DCI
Display Control Interface

Intel's 1993 specification (now supported by Microsoft) to allow Windows software to directly access a video adapter's control registers and frame-buffer—with the goal to speed-

decipher. Governments usually feel that, for security purposes (catching crooks, eavesdropping on interesting conversations), they must be able to know what people are saying to each other.

This perceived weakness plus these points have limited the popularity of DES:

▲ DES-based cryptography equipment that uses keys 56 bits in length or longer cannot be exported outside of Canada or the U.S. (this limits the potential market size).

▲ Low cost DES integrated circuits are available, and hundreds or thousands of them could be (or maybe already have been) built into machines which would be able to apply all the DES ICs in parallel—to more quickly decipher messages (this limits the perceived strength of the security).

Therefore, DES is not widely adopted outside of situations which are required to use it (such as transactions between financial institutions).

To help keep DES a secure method of data encryption, the algorithm it uses was designed to be difficult to implement in software (and it therefore runs slowly in software). This makes software-only methods of breaking DES codes undesirable. Also, the U.S. government restricts sales of DES hardware, so obtaining DES hardware for the purposes of breaking codes would also be difficult.

DES was developed by IBM in the early 1970s, adopted by the U.S. government in 1977, and standardized as ANSI X3.92 and FIPS Pub 81 in 1981, and in 1988 as FIPS Pub 46-1.

Due to well-founded concerns that computers are now fast enough to decrypt messages encrypted with 56-bit key DES (that is, to figure-out the secret key), some companies are implementing *triple DES*. This encrypts the data 3 times, resulting in an effective key length of 112 bits (though some incorrectly say 168 bits, by simply multiplying 56×3—but this encryption stuff is more complicated than that, so don't believe them).

See **AUTHENTICATION**, **ENCRYPTION**, **IDEA**, **PGP**, and **RSA**.

Design Patent

The type of *intellectual property protection* in the U.S. that is similar to a registered Canadian *industrial design*. Protection lasts for 14 years.

See **INDUSTRIAL DESIGN**, **INTELLECTUAL PROPERTY PROTECTION**, and **PATENT**.

DFT
Distributed Function Terminal

The newer mode of operation supported by 3174s and required by the 3290. Supports up to five logical sessions per physical connection, though the 3290 supports only four simultaneously.

See **S3174 AND 3274**, **S3270**, and **CUT**.

DHCP
Dynamic Host Configuration Protocol

A TCP/IP protocol that enables hosts (for example, diskless workstations or mobile users) to obtain temporary IP addresses (out of a pool) from centrally-administered servers. The host runs the DHCP server, and the workstation runs the DHCP client.

Clients *broadcast* a request for a DHCP server, which then responds with the following (or more or fewer parameters, depending on how the server has been configured):

▲ Assigned IP address, which is valid for an administrator-configured time period (hosts can request an extension to this time period)

▲ Subnet Bit Mask

▲ Default router(s)

Duration for which the IP address assignment (called a *lease*) is valid

If more than one server replies, the client can choose which it prefers. This allows backup DHCP servers to be configured, though the servers cannot have overlapping pools of addresses.

DHCP is flexible so that other information can also be stored and retrieved. DHCP can usually be configured to assign specific IP addresses to machines with specific MAC addresses (this is called a *reservation* or *static IP* address. This is required for the DHCP server itself, and usually other servers as well since there is no standard way for DHCP servers to update DNS servers (to update the mapping of the server's DNS name to its new IP ADDRESS). However, for user workstations, it is more common to assign IP addresses from a pool.

A shortcoming is that there is currently no standard way to update *Domain Name Servers* with the new IP address for a user's DNS name (DNS names remain permanently assigned to hosts). Since important destination machines (such as servers) would use permanently assigned IP addresses, this should not be a big problem (in addition, there are many products that use non-standardized methods to update the DNS servers with updates from DHCP servers.

Another shortcoming is that there is no standard way to implement a back-up DHCP server, as there is no server-to-server protocol defined.

DHCP can download more types of information than `bootp`, so will likely replace it.

DHCP was developed in 1993, and is defined in RFCs 1533, 1534, 1541 and 1542.

See **BOOTP**, **DNS2** (*Domain Name System*), **IP ADDRESS**, **SUBNET BIT MASK**, and **TCP/IP**.

DID
Direct Inward Dialing Trunk

A type of telephone trunk in which the last few (typically three or four) digits dialed by the caller are forwarded to the callee on a special *DID* trunk, usually by *dial pulse* (just as if the caller had a rotary phone) or by *Multifrequency Tones* (MF—these are different from the DTMF tones and are usually used only within telephone networks). Some telephone networks can also use DTMF tones for trunk signalling.

For example, all the phone numbers from 555-1000 to 555-1999 could be assigned to a customer with 20 DID trunks. When a caller dials any number in this range, the call is forwarded on any available trunk of the 20 (that is, the trunks are *equivalent*, which is also called being in a *hunt group* or a *rotary*). If the caller dialed 555-1234, then the digits 2, 3, and 4 (assuming three-digit outpulsing was used) will be forwarded. These DID trunks could be *terminated* on (for example):

▲ A *Private Branch Exchange* (PBX), so it knows which number was called and rings that phone extension. This makes it look as though 555-1234 and the other 999 lines all have direct outside lines, while only requiring 20 trunks to service the 1,000 telephone extensions.

▲ A *fax server*, so it can provide routing for inbound faxes. Each fax user is assigned a unique telephone number. When the fax server gets the number dialed (from the DID trunk), it forwards the subsequent fax to the specified (according to the phone number dialed) person's PC (where it can be viewed, printed, or stored).

See **DN**, **DTMF2**, **FAX**, **POTS**, and **TRUNK**.

Differential Manchester Encoding

See **ENCODING**.

Digital 800

A digital, toll-free, circuit-switched dial-up WAN connection. Any number of DS-0 channels (providing any speed from 64 kbits/s to a full T1) can be used.

Standard "1-800-" type telephone numbers are used. The same number can often be used for both standard voice 1-800 calls, and digital 1-800 calls (the network knows whether the call is analog or digital (from where it originated) and routes the call to the destination equipment accordingly.

At the calling-end, access to the service is typically from a switched 56 or ISDN service. An *inverse multiplexer* can be used to provide this high-speed switched service—it makes as many simultaneous 56 (or 64) kbits/s calls as needed to supply the speed of service requested.

At the receiving (that is, the *called*) end, the calls may arrive on switched 56 or ISDN BRI line, in which case an inverse multiplexer will be required. Or, the carrier may provide an ISDN PRI (with any number of B channels, up to 23)—that is, the carrier does the inverse multiplexing. As many simultaneous calls as there are B channels can be accepted.

Because the calls themselves are standard 64 kbit/s time slots with standard telephone numbers, the calls can traverse other networks even if those networks don't support this service.

Charges are similar to those for standard 1-800 type calls.

AT&T calls its service *Worldworx 800* or *800 Multimedia* and MCI's is called *800 Digital Service*.

See **BRI**, **DS0**, **INVERSE MULTIPLEXER**, **ISDN**, **SWITCHED 56**, **PRI**, **T1**, and **WAN**.

DIMM
Dual In-line Memory Module

A higher-performance (than SIMM—because they handle 64-bits per memory operation rather than SIMM's 32-bits) type of memory module used in newer devices. DIMM modules

typically house Fast Page Mode, EDO-DRAM or SDRAM, and support Plug and Play. Two physical sizes (dimensions) of DIMMs are popular:

▲ 168-pin modules support 64-bit memory accesses, and are typically available in densities of 8 to 64 Mbytes per module. Modules are also available with 9 bits stored per byte (72 bits per 64-bit memory access) to support parity memory.

▲ 200-pin modules are typically used in higher-end PCs and workstations, and support ECC memory operations, by providing 8 bits of ECC per 64-bits of user data (again, a total of 72 bits per memory access).

A typical DIMM might be described as "4x64/72". This means that the module has 4 Mlocations of 64 bits (8 bytes) of storage, and outputs 64 bits of data per read or write (for a total module capacity of 4 M $\times$ 8 bytes =) 32 Mbytes). And it stores a total of 72 bits per 64 bits of data, to support ECC.

Typically, pairs of DIMMs interleave (work alternately) their output to deliver data at 128 bits per memory access.

The dimensions of DIMMs are specified by the Joint Electron Device Engineering Council (JEDEC). For example, the spacing between the electrical contacts is 0.05".

JEDEC has a web site at *http://www.eia.org/jedec.*

See **DRAM**, **ECC**, **PLUG AND PLAY**, and **SIMM**.

DirectDraw

Microsoft's replacement for their earlier DCI APIs, first supported in Windows 95 (everybody found out the hard way that DCI did not handle all the functions game developers required to provide fast-as-DOS video performance). DirectDraw handles additional functions (so they can then be off-loaded to the video adapter, for faster processing, or at least processing by the video adapter while the computer's main CPU does other things). Examples are BitBlt (also called *blit*—for *bit-block transfer*), transparent blits (where pixels of a specified color are not moved), color filling (filling a specified region with a specific color), page flipping (where the next image to be displayed is built in memory that is not yet displayed, so the relatively slow building process is not visible to the user), bit-map stretching, interpolation, color-keying, texture mapping, overlaying, rotating and mirroring.

Applications using DirectDraw interface to the video adapter using a single set of APIs, even though some functions may actually be executed directly on the video adapter—depending on whether that particular adapter has hardware support for those particular functions.

DirectDraw is part Microsoft's DirectX software development kit (SDK).

See **DCI**, and **DIRECTX**.

DirectX

Microsoft's DirectX software development kit, which provides features to enable Windows programs to offer better performance (typically for multimedia game support). There are three components.

DirectDraw provides faster video performance, by enabling programs to directly access video adapters and any special features they may have. DirectSound provides direct access to audio hardware, to support features like mixing of multiple audio sources. DirectInput is the third component, handling user input devices.

First released in October 1995.

See **DCI**.

Disk Drive

Usually refers to the sealed electromechanical device which is comprised of a motorized stack of platters, each coated with iron oxide, and the read-write heads and the controllers needed to move them to different positions over the platters. Since the platters are made of aluminum, often called a *hard disk drive, hard drive* or *fixed disk drive* (since the platters are not removable from the drive). Hard disk drives still have the best combination of lowest access time and cost of storage and the highest storage capacity for read/write digital storage. It is therefore the main method of storing data on computers.

The speed of many (if not most) file servers and user applications is limited by the number of disk drive operations (reads and writes) that can be performed per second.

The following table shows the times required for a typical disk operation (based on estimates by Western Digital).

Operation	Percentage of time spent	Comments
Head seek to required cylinder	35	Typical high-performance disk drives can move the read/write head over half the disk surface (an average seek) in 8 to 12 ms. Newer (and therefore higher capacity) disks are typically closer to 8 ms.
Rotational latency (wait for disk to spin to correct location)	25	At 5,400 revolutions per minute (a typical high-performance E-IDE drive), the disk does a half-revolution in 5.55 ms. Older disks (such as those less than 540 Mbytes) typically spin at 3,600 RPM. Drives larger than 1 Gbyte (which usually have a SCSI interface) are often 7,200 RPM (or faster), and usually have a SCSI interface.
Data transfer from disk to controller	25	While an IDE interface transfers data at a burst rate of about 2 Mbytes/s and SCSI typically transfers data at 10 Mbytes/s, the data is read from the actual disk drive at 5 Mbits/s to 48 Mbits/s. A 4,096 byte transfer (a typical cluster size) would transfer in 0.5 to 2 ms.
Disk driver software handling	10	Depends on the speed of the PC's CPU.
Data transfer from controller to memory	5	Depends on the type of bus used in the PC. ISA transfers at about 2 Mbytes/s, and PCI transfers at up to 132 Mbytes/s.

Disk Formatting

Hard disk drive capacity seems to increase linearly, as shown below, which shows the capacity of the disk drives most commonly shipped on PCs.

Year	1982	1983	1984	1985	1986	1987	1988	1989	1990	1991	1992	1993	1994	1995	1996	1997
Hard disk drive capacity (in megabytes)	5	5	10	20	20	40	80	100	120	150	200	340	500	850	1600	2200

A long time ago (about 1978) when disk drives were huge bar-regrigerator sized devices, IBM created a disk drive were the media was both removable from the drive, and flexible (it used a plastic called *mylar*). IBM called it a *diskette*, since it was so much smaller (8" diameter) than the disk of the day, and everybody else called it a *floppy*. 8" diskettes were superseded by $5\frac{1}{4}$" diskettes, and later by $3\frac{1}{2}$" diskettes that has a harder shell (so a protective sleeve is not needed when storing them), which remain popular to this day.

$3\frac{1}{2}$" diskettes and drives were standardized in July 1987 by ISO 8860-1 (media, liner material and temperature range) and ISO 8860-2 (covering the media's magnetic characteristics, formatting and recording details). In January 1988, ANSI X3.137 standardized diskette physical characteristics, such as the size and the positions of the door, write-protect tab and locating surfaces.

Some technical information on hard disk drives is available at the major disk drive manufacturer sites, as shown in the following table.

Maxtor Corporation	*http://www.maxtor.com*
Seagate Technology Inc.	*http://www.seagate.com*
Western Digital Inc.	*http://www.wdc.com*

See **ATA, ATAPI, ATASPI, BUS, CACHE, CDROM, DASD, DISK FORMATTING, EIDE, FAST ATA, FAT, IDE, MOORES, RAID, SCSI1, SLED, SMALL FORM FACTOR COMMITTEE,** and **WINCHESTER.**

Disk Formatting

There are three steps required to make a newly-manufactured disk drive usable for data storage:

▲ *Physical* or *low-level formatting*. This is usually done by the manufacturer, though really old disk drives, and SCSI drives typically come with utilities that allow you to repeat this low-level formatting process (IDE drives are typically only formattable by the manufacturer).

▲ This process writes the sector, track and cylinder information to the platters of the drive.

Partitioning a drive is typically done with the DOS FDISK utility (or something that works like it). A partition is a group of contiguous cylinders, and a physical disk drive is partitioned into 1 or more partitions. De facto standards (developed by disk drive manufacturers and BIOS developers) for partitions usually allow the partition program from one operating system, and the partitions they create, to be used by other operating systems.

A drive can have up to 4 *primary partitions* (a limitation created when the de facto standards were established). And DOS can only directly recognize a single primary DOS partition at a time—the one designated as *active* (and this is designated drive C:). In addition, an *extended partition* can be created, which can contain up to 23 *logical partitions* (sounds like an alphabet limitation to me). Some operating systems (such as DOS) cannot boot from logical partitions, but others (such as OS/2) can. The one partition set to be *active* is the one that is used when the computer is next booted. *Boot managers* are programs that make changing the active partition convenient.

Drive letters are typically assigned as follows: first the primary partitions (one per drive) on each drive, then the logical partitions on the first disk each get the next available drive letters, then the logical partitions on each subsequent drive, and finally any CD-ROM drives.

Logical or *high-level formatting* is done do each partition (primary or logical) on a physical disk drive, using a program specific to each operating system. Usually every operating system has its own high-level format—or *file system* (often along with supporting the DOS file system). High-level formatting creates the directory structure, including the cluster size, method of dealing with bad sections of the disk, and the file naming rules. A high-level formatted partition is often called a *volume* (though some operating systems allow a volume to span several partitions, either for better throughput or capacity, or for improved reliability).

For example, under DOS a hard disk is formatted to combine 2^n 512-byte *sectors* (where n is some integer) into *clusters* (the smallest unit of disk space that can be allocated to a file).

Some popular high-level disk formats are shown below.

File System		Comments
Acronym	**Name**	
FAT or FAT16	File Allocation Table	Used by DOS, Windows 3.1 (and earlier), and for diskettes in all versions of Windows
HPFS	High Performance File System	Used by OS/2
NTFS	NT File System	Used by Windows NT
VFAT	Virtual File Allocation Table	Used by Windows 95, and has support for longer file names
FAT32	32-bit File Allocation Table	Supported by newer versions of Windows 95

See **DISK DRIVE**, **FAT**, and **IDE**.

DLC
Data Link Control Layer Protocol

The link layer protocols used by IBM's SNA. The most common protocols are the following:

▲ LLC2 (*Logical Link Control*, Level 2), which is used on Token Ring LANs

▲ SDLC (*Synchronous Data Link Control*), which is used on recent EIA-232 and WAN links

▲ BISYNC (Binary Synchronous Communications), which is used on old EIA-232 and WAN links

DLL

Functions performed by these link layer protocols include error detection (through the use of a check character), error correction (through time-outs and retransmissions), flow control (through delayed acknowledgments and *receiver not ready* response frames), and multiple devices on the same media (through polling and acknowledgments).

See **BISYNC**, **CHECKSUM**, **CRC**, **DLSW**, **EIA-TIA232**, **FCS**, **LLC2**, **SDLC**, **SPOOFING**, **QLLC**, and **WAN**.

DLL
Dynamic Link Library

The name for software and resources (such as executable code, or data such as icons or fonts) used by Microsoft's Windows and IBM's OS/2 to provide services (such as a LAN driver or a TCP/IP protocol stack) to applications.

One memory-resident copy of the DLL can be simultaneously shared by all applications, which link to the DLL at runtime (hence the term *dynamic*), rather than when the program is compiled.

DLLs with only data are called resource-only DLLs.

DLLs may have (for example) a .exe, .dll, .drv, or .fon extension. They may have no extension. Some DLLs can be automatically loaded when needed by a program, and others (usually drivers) must be loaded at system startup.

See **WINSOCK**.

DLSW
Data Link Switching

IBM's widely waited-for, and now widely-accepted method for integrating SNA (both SDLC and LLC2) traffic and standard LAN traffic onto a single internet (WAN link).

For example, it handles SNA (from SDLC links) and NetBIOS (which are both nonroutable) and APPN traffic (on Token Ring links) over (at least initially) TCP/IP networks.

Typically, DLSw is implemented in a router. It uses *encapsulation* (the frames are carried in TCP/IP packets) so that *routing* can be used instead of *bridging*, therefore providing all the advantages of routed networks, such as more efficient WAN utilization. DLSw can put more than one SNA frame into a single TCP/IP packet—and all DLSw traffic to a location shares a single TCP connection. This reduces router and WAN loading.

Also intended to replace Token Ring's *source route bridging*, which has problems such as the following:

▲ The maximum hop count is seven (only seven bridge-to-bridge hops are allowed between any two communicating stations)

▲ There is substantial broadcast traffic (from *source route discovery* frames and *NetBIOS* name queries) which wastes WAN capacity

▲ *Keep-alive* and *acknowledgment* frames are sent end-to-end, which also wastes WAN capacity

▲ There is a lack of flow control and prioritization

DLSw supports *name caching* (to reduce broadcasts) and specifies how to convert SDLC (from low-speed synchronous links) to LLC2 frames (which are used on Token Ring LANs).

DLSw supports both LLC2 (used on Token Ring LANs) and SDLC (used on synchronous links up to 56 kbit/s) sessions. These are IBM's most popular DLC (Data Link Control) protocols. To provide more efficient WAN utilization, DLSw supports *local termination* (which is an example of *spoofing*), as shown in the examples below:

▲ For SDLC (on EIA-232 links), DLSw responds locally with a fake poll reply (so polls and their acknowledgments do not travel over the WAN). At the remote end of the link, DLSw generates the necessary polls.

▲ For LLC2 (on Token Ring LANs), DLSw responds locally with keep-alive messages (so these periodically-generated messages do not load the WAN) and LLC2 acknowledgments.

DLSw encapsulates WAN traffic into TCP/IP packets, so the WAN link will be error-free (due to TCP/IP's error detection and correction), and routers will be easier to configure (since most sites already use TCP/IP).

Local termination both reduces WAN bandwidth requirements (no polls or acknowledgments on the WAN) and ensures that WAN time delays don't cause DLC protocol time-outs. (Polling doesn't wait long for a response, so putting the polling on a WAN link that occasionally gets congested with other traffic would be a problem.)

A significant benefit of DLSw should be multivendor interoperability of SNA traffic encapsulated in TCP/IP. (Each vendor has developed its own proprietary methods in the absence of a standard.)

First used in IBM's 6611 multi-protocol router, and later released as an open standard, with further work being done by the *DLSw Working Group* of the *APPN Implementor's Workshop*. IBM defined the first version in RFC 1434, but this had significant shortcomings such as lack of support for:

▲ Flow control (currently, overloads are handled by discarding frames)

▲ SNMP

▲ Prioritization

▲ Standard subsets of features (therefore interoperability could not be guaranteed—a significant problem)

IBM, Cisco, and other router vendors have since defined a new draft standard that includes flow control and an optional SNMP MIB, as shown in the following table.

Category	Feature	RFC 1434	DLSw	DLSw+
Transport	TCP	✓	✓	✓
	Direct connection			✓
Media Conversion	SDLC → LLC2	✓	✓	✓
	LLC2 → SDLC			✓
	QLLC → LLC2			✓
	QLLC ↔ SDLC			✓
Performance	Flow control		✓	✓
	Custom queueing			✓
	Prioritization		✓	✓
	Load balancing		–	✓
Scalability	Caching			✓
	RIF reduction	✓	✓	✓
	Peer groups			✓
	On-demand peers			✓
Availability	Backup peers			✓
Management	Standard MIB		✓	✓
Interoperability	Standard-based		✓	✓

Token Ring frames have a *Route Information Field* (RIF), which has room for a maximum of eight ring number/bridge number entries. Since these entries (which are read by Token Ring bridges so that they can determine whether to pass a frame) specify the exact end-to-end path, this limit restricts the size and configuration of Token Ring bridged networks.

DLSw solves this by *terminating* the link. That is, the RIF need only describe how to get the frame from its source to a DLSw router (and not all the way to the destination). At the remote end, the DLSw router nearest the destination builds the RIF with only the entries to get the frame from that remote DLSw router to the final destination.

DLSw is defined in RFCs 1434 and 1795.

The APPN Implementors Workshop (AIW) has a WWW server at *http://www.raleigh.ibm.com/ app/aiwhome.htm.*

See **APPN, COMPATIBLE, CACHE, DLC, DLUR AND DLUS, ENCAPSULATION, LAN, LLC2, PRIORITIZATION, RFC, SDLC, SNMP, SPOOFING, TOKEN RING,** and **WAN.**

DLSW+
Data Link Switching Plus

An enhancement to DLSw, developed by Cisco (which is compatible with DLSw). Addresses issues such as the following:

▲ Availability (by storing alternative paths to destination so that if a link is lost, an alternative path can be used immediately without dropping the user's session)

▲ Any-to-any connectivity in very large networks (using name caching and other methods to reduce the need for broadcasting discovery frames)

▲ Simplified configuration (reducing the number of routers that need to be configured)

▲ Load balancing (by using all available paths)

▲ Supporting other transport methods, such as using only HDLC between directly connected DLSw+ routers (which avoids the extra overhead of TCP/IP)

Can also automatically detect and interoperate with other Routers that support:

▲ Cisco's previous Token Ring support—*Remote Source Route Bridging* and *SDLC*-to-LLC 2 *conversion* (SDLLC)

▲ DLSw

▲ DLSw+

Another feature is that it can automatically learn which destinations are on a local LAN before (needlessly) broadcasting over the WAN to find them.

See **DLSW**.

DLUR AND DLUS
Dependent LU Requester and Server

One of IBM's methods (another is DLSw) of carrying SNA traffic on routed WANs. APPN is used as the WAN protocol.

Typically, 3174s or routers would be configured to support DLUr, and VTAM hosts would be configured to support DLUs. LLC2 acknowledgments and keep-alive messages are responded to locally, so this traffic does not load the WAN.

Since this method works at the LU level, traffic does not need to be routed through mainframes along the path (which would needlessly waste their CPU time and slow the response time).

See **S3174 AND 3274, APPC, APPN, DLSW, SDLC, SNA, SPOOFING**, and **VTAM**.

DMA
Direct Memory Access

A fast way of transferring data within (and sometimes between) computers.

For example, DMA is often used to read data from a LAN adapter board and write it into a PC's memory (and vice versa). A DMA controller (often on a PC's motherboard) seizes the bus periodically (for example, once for every 16-bit transfer) to read data from the adapter, then seizes it again to write it to memory (therefore requiring two bus cycles per transfer).

DMA

This is sometimes called *non-bus master DMA* or *third-party DMA*, since the DMA controller is not part of the source or destination of the data (that is, it is not on a disk controller for example).

DMA is most useful in multi-tasking operating systems, which likely have something else to do while waiting for the data to be transferred (sometimes DMA is useful because the CPU is not fast enough to transfer the data, using PIO).

A *DMA* channel is the combination of bus signals (to request use of the channel and to receive acknowledgment that use of the channel has been granted) and the counters that provide the addresses for the source and destination of the transfers. 16-bit ISA bus PCs have eight DMA channels, though not all are available for use by add-on peripherals.

Most devices require a dedicated DMA channel (so the number of DMA channels that are available may limit the number of peripherals that can be installed).

A limitation of DMA on older computers running DOS or Windows 3.1 is that the DMA writes must typically be to conventional PC memory since extended memory that is mapped to upper memory blocks is mapped only for CPU accesses (for example, 80386 memory mapping is on-chip, not on the motherboard). Therefore device drivers that use DMA usually cannot be loaded into upper memory (unless the data buffers are in conventional memory or there is hardware support for *scatter/gather* to provide the memory mapping for the DMA controller). The following table summarizes the DMA channel assignments in an ISA bus PC.

ISA DMA Channel	Use	Comments
0	Was used for memory refresh on early PCs and is therefore not on the 8-bit ISA bus. Current PC dynamic memory (DRAM) is refreshed by a refresh circuit that does not use a DMA channel, and DMA channel 0 is on the 16-bit ISA bus.	
	Performs 8-bit transfers only.	
	Maximum 64 kbytes per transfer.	
	Only these four channels were supported by the original PC and PC/XT.	
1	Available, but often used by sound boards and ECP-mode parallel ports (if your PC has both, ensure that only one is set to DMA channel 1)	
2	Floppy and hard drive controller.	
3	Hard disk controller in (now-ancient) XTs only. Usually available in current PCs.	
4	Cascade line to link controller for DMA channels 4 through 7 to controller for DMA channels 0 through 3. Not available for use.	Can perform 16-bit transfers. Maximum of 128 kbytes per transfer. These four channels were added when the 16-bit PC/AT bus was introduced.
5	Hard disk controller (in PS/2s only). Usually available on other current PCs.	
6	Available	
7	Available	

DMA channels 2 and 4 are not available for add-on peripherals (such as LAN adapters or sound boards), and the first four DMA channels are capable of transferring only 8 bits at a time (since these channels are compatible with the original PC's 8-bit bus). Therefore the best DMA channels to choose for add-on peripherals are 5, 6, or 7.

See **BUS**, **BUS MASTER DMA**, **PIO**, **PC**, and **SHARED MEMORY**.

DME
Distributed Management Environment

OSF's multivendor distributed database support. Includes management of hubs, bridges, and routers.

See **OSF**.

Desktop Management Interface

DMI

The API defined by the *Desktop Management Task Force* (DMTF). Version 1.1 provides a standard software interface to let users (and management software) gather information, by providing the information interfaces needed to perform an inventory of system's components (such as the application software, bus slots used, and which boards are installed, and peripherals) and settings—without opening the computer.

The specification has the following features:

▲ Bi-directional—data can be read and written, and communication can be initiated by either a management station or a PC (when it has a problem, for example)

▲ Platform-independent—PC, Macintosh, and so on

▲ Operating system–independent (DOS, NetWare, OS/2, UNIX, Windows, and so on

▲ Protocol-independent—TCP/IP, IPX, and so on (also, while SNMP could be used to specify and retrieve the information, other mechanisms could be used as well)

There are three components to the specification—the management interface (MI), service layer (SL) and the component interface (CI). The relationship of these is shown in the diagram below.

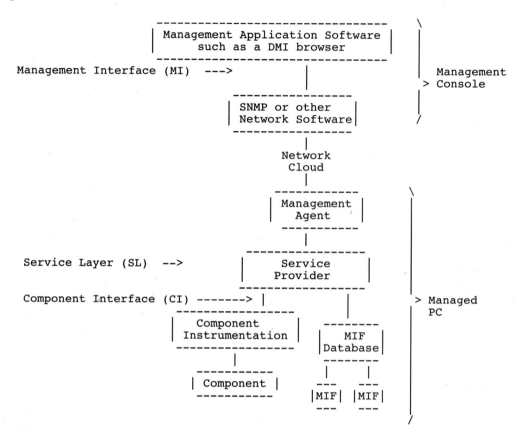

The component instrumentation software is customized (like a driver, to gather the information from whatever weirdo hardware is in your PC), which has a standard software interface (that is, the component interface), to provide information to the service layer. The service layer then stores the information in a MIF, for later retrieval by the management application, running on some management station elsewhere on the network. The service layer and component instrumentation are typically implemented as Windows DLLs. Intel's LANDesk Client Manager is a popular implementation. It allows MIF information to be viewed either locally or remotely, using either their own GUI, or a standard WWW browser.

Information gathered could include the following:

▲ Details of the computer system configuration, as gathered by the component instrumentation software (such as the amount of memory and the CPU type)

▲ Computer hardware status information, such as whether the PC is too hot internally, or a cooling fan has failed, whether power supply voltages are outside of the normal range, or the chassis has been opened. This requires specialized hardware and sensors to be built-in to the PC. Sometimes these are referred to as ASICs (*application specific integrated circuits*), as they are designed specifically to support DMI's requirements.

Data stored in the ASCII *management information files* (for peripherals, such as hard disks, CD-ROMs, and fax boards)—these are typically supplied by manufacturers with their products (a potentially big problem).

In their MIF, vendors could include any information, such as the following:

▲ Model number, serial number, warranty information, and the installation date

▲ Firmware version number and speed

▲ User-settable characteristics such as I/O addresses and screen resolutions available

When each peripheral is installed, its MIF is stored in a database on the PC's hard disk, or access by the service layer.

Typically, PCs supporting DMI have a DM (*desktop management*) compliant BIOS. The *Wake-on-LAN* feature requires special support in the LAN adapter. Operating system support allows low-memory and -disk space problems to be automatically reported, and peripherals (such as the diskette drive or keyboard) to be remotely disabled. Disk drives implementing SMART can provide alarms in advance of major failures. And alarms can be provided if ECC memory detects too many errors.

DMI version 2.0 was released in April 1996, with first implementations in late 1997. It specifies the remote procedure calls (RPCs) to interface to managed PCs, so this interface is no longer proprietary (previously, management applications had to use the each agent's own APIs). Version 2.0 also provides remote management capabilities, so the computers on a network can be managed and configured from a central location. For example, PCs can be shut down remotely, and a command can be sent to wake-up a PC from power saving mode.

Supported by Microsoft and Intel.

See **BIOS**, **DMTF**, **ECC**, **PLUG AND PLAY**, **RPC**, **SMART**, and **SNMP**.

DMS
Digital Multiplex Switching

Northern Telecom's line of usually huge, and central office–oriented, voice and high-speed data switches. A DMS switch typically provides telephone service for 10,000 or more customers—with less than two hours of down-time in 40 years.

See **C.O.** and **PBX**.

DMTF
Desktop Management Task Force, Inc.

A group of hardware vendors who are having trouble establishing a standardized way to report the software installed, and hardware components in a workstation ("desktop computer"). The resulting programming interface is called DMI. This effort won't result in an *SNMP* agent but would make developing an SNMP agent easier (since there would be a standardized way for it to gather the information it needs).

The DMTF was formed in 1992 by Intel, Microsoft and Novell. Progress has been very slow (they are trying to include support for many combinations of platforms and operating systems), though some would call Microsoft's Plug and Play a result of this work. Also, Plug and Play's .INF registry contains most of the information that the DMI's MIF needs, which should facilitate the implementation of the DMI.

The DMTF has a WWW server at *http://www.dmtf.org/*.

See **DMI**, **MIF**, **PLUG AND PLAY**, and **SNMP**.

DN
Directory Number

A standard telephone number, in the form 555-1234 (plus an optional area code). Standardized in ITU-T E.163.

As a side point, the "555" exchange is used for most sample telephone numbers (especially on television) since it is not assigned to anyone (other than 555-1212, which is for long-distance directory assistance).

North American telephone numbers are always a fixed 7 digits for local calls, plus a 3-digit area code for calls outside the local area code (which may or may not be a long-distance call). Other countries often have a variable-length local telephone number of 3 to 8 digits, plus a 1- to 5-digit *city code* (which is usually written in parentheses). This is sometimes called an *open numbering plan*. In some countries the total number of digits is fixed (for example, 8 in Mexico).

The official format for writing an international telephone number (as standardized in ITU's E.123 *Notation for National and International Telephone Numbers*) is as follows:

▲ A plus sign ("+"), which indicates that the caller is supposed to first dial whatever local prefix is required for international long-distance calls (for example, from North America, 011 is usually first dialed for a direct-dialed "overseas" call and 01 for a calling-card "overseas" call)

▲ The *country code*. For example, the country code is 1 for Canada, the U.S., Bermuda, the Bahamas and all the Caribbean except the Netherlands Antilles, Haiti, Aruba and Cuba. And the country code for the (for example) U.K. is 44.

▲ The *routing code* (more commonly called the *area code* in North America)

▲ The *local number* (in North America), this is 7 digits)

For example, +1 416 555 1430. This (including the "+" sign) is sometimes called *canonical form*.

The standard also specifies the notation for telephone extensions, spacing and other notations. Notably, it also provides a format for putting all this together, as shown in the following example:

```
                    within N. Amer. zone    416 555-1430
          Telephone  --------------------------------------
                    International +1 416 555 1430
```

Note the vertical alignment of the telephone numbers, to assist in seeing the correlation.

Outside of North America, "North America" would be replaced with "National". Also, "Telephone" and the other words would be in the local language.

The *North American Numbering Plan* (NANP) defines the now-familiar 10-digit domestic long distance telephone numbering scheme. The NANP was introduced in 1947, and used to be administered by Bellcore. It is now administered by the *Industry Numbering Committee*. The NANP defined two parts of the 10-digit telephone number:

▲ The 3-digit NPA (Numbering Plan Area), more commonly called the area code. Initially, all area codes did not use a 0 or 1 for the first digit, and only used a 0 or 1 for their middle digit. This allowed a total of 160 area codes, and these were all used by 1995. The rule was changed (as of January 1, 1995) to allow any digit for the middle digit (this allows 800 area codes).

The 7-digit telephone number. The first 3 digits are the NXX (so called since the first digit can be any number from 2 through 0, and the last two digits can be any number), and is often called the exchange (since all telephone numbers beginning with a given NXX are usually served by the same central office telephone switching exchange). The last four digits specify a particular telephone (it used to specify where the telephone was connected to the switch—such as the number 555-1430 being connected to the first bay of equipment, in the fourth shelf, on the third circuit card, on the last position).

The exchange used to be a "NNX", since the middle digit was never a 0 or 1. This is the opposite of the old restriction for area codes—perhaps to enable telephone switches to automatically tell the difference between local and long distance calls. Since most telephone companies require that long distance calls be prefaced by a 1 (before the area code), there is no advantage to this restriction. The rules were changed, and exchange codes can now have a 0 or 1 as the middle digit. This created another 160 exchange codes per area code, which is an additional 1,600,000 telephone numbers per area code (since there are 10,000 telephone numbers per exchange code).

Adding a new area code can be done by partitioning a previous one, in which case about half the existing people (in a defined geographic area) get a new (and different) area code (but keep their 7-digit directory number). Many people don't like this, as it requires much changing of PBX configurations, business stationary and address books—and is seen as favoring the group that did not need to change their area code.

Therefore, some new area codes are implemented as *overlays* where both area codes cover the same geographic area. Newly assigned numbers get the new area code, and existing customers all retain their area code and directory number. This method usually requires that even local calls to the same area code use 10-digit dialling—that is, with the overlay method the inconvenience is shared by all.

The NANP home page is at *http://www.belcore.com/NAMP/*. At *http://www.natltele.com/form.html* is a WWW server that has a database of all NPA/NXXs—with a search capability. Area codes are also listed at *ftp://gemini.tuc.noao.edu/pub/grandi/npa1995.txt* and *http://www.the-acr.com/codes/cntrycd.htm*.

See **S800**, **AMPS**, **BELCORE**, **DTMF2**, **E.163**, **E.164**, **FAX**, and **POTS**.

DNS
Digital Naming Service

DEC's network name service, soon to be X.500 based.

See **DEC** and **X.500**.

DNS
Domain Name System

The Internet's standard for host names (such as `ora.com`) and a hierarchical system of *domain name servers* to resolve them into IP addresses—so that a request to *http://www.ora.com* is translated to *http://198.112.208.23*). Other information, such as type of hardware, services supported, and how long to cache the entry can also be stored in the name server.

Before (or without) DNS, the translation of host names to IP addresses was done by the IP software doing a look-up in the file `/etc/hosts` or `/etc/inet/hosts` (on UNIX computers) or `hosts.txt` (on PCs). This becomes difficult to administer when there are more than a few stations on a network, and impossible for large networks (like the Internet).

Each name server has the IP address of a name server higher in the hierarchy to which it sends queries that it cannot resolve itself.

A full DNS name (for example) is *gateway.noodle.ajax.com*. In this case, *gateway* is the name of our host (though it need not be) in the subdomain, *noodle*. And *ajax* is the name of our network (called the second-level domain to DNS), all in the *commercial* "top-level domain."

Absolute names are complete. *Relative names* contain a smaller subset of the name (such as *gateway*). A specific user (with *username* on machine *gateway*) is often addressed as *username@gateway* (to send that user email from within the same network).

Every domain name can be translated to any IP address—even an address on a different network, or to the same address as another name. For example, the computer at *www.ora.com* may or may not be the same as the computer at *ora.com*. Usually, companies dedicate a computer to be a WWW server (at least for security reasons, if not performance reasons), so *http://www.ora.com* accesses a different computer than *http://ora.com*. The computer at *http://www.ora.com* may or may not have a hostname of *www*—likely not though.

The traditional top-level domain names are listed in the following table (these are defined in RFC 1591).

Domain Name	User
arpa	ARPAnet
com	Commercial organizations
edu	Educational institutions
gov	Government organizations
mil	U.S.-based military
net	Internet access providers
org	Nonprofit organizations
other	Countries outside the U.S., such as *uk* for the United Kingdom and *on.ca* for Ontario, Canada

A recent change is shown in the last row: top-level domain names are now often geographically related. ISO 3166 specifies the two-letter country codes (along with three-letter country codes, and three-digit country numbers), which are used. A similar list of two-letter country codes is provided at the end of this entry, sorted by country code. Some countries use a two-letter code before their two-letter country code to indicate whether a DNS name is commercial (*noodle.co.uk* for example) or an educational (academic) institution (such as *lansing.ac.uk*).

The *International Ad Hoc Committee* (IAHC) proposed that 7 new top-level domain names be added (such as *.info*, *.store* and *.web* but this group was disbanded as of May 1, 1997. The IAHC was replaced by the *generic top-level domain memorandum of understanding*, which is continuing that work.

Limitations on the names are as follows:

▲ DNS limits each name (*noodle*) to a maximum of 63 characters, and the entire name (*gateway.noodle.ajax.com*) cannot exceed 256 characters

▲ The InterNIC requires that for the Internet, the entire name be a maximum of 24 characters (plus the top-level domain name).

DNS is distributed in that name servers keep track of hosts that are below them in the hierarchy. If a name server does not directly know the IP address for a requested host name (such as `ora.com`), then the name server passes the query on to a name server farther up the hierarchy (such servers are called *authoritative servers*). Usually, each site (or their Internet Service Provider) has a name server—and a backup for it, since a failure of a DNS server could otherwise result in all the site's machines becoming unreachable).

A popular implementation of DNS is the *Berkeley Internet Name Daemon* (`bind`), it is usually just another process on a UNIX host. BIND was initially developed by the University of California at Berkeley, but is now sponsored by the Internet Software Consortium (and a Windows NT version is also available).

Name servers can be:

▲ *Primary Master*—these have the master copies of the file. For the entire Internet, a root name server is at the InterNIC, which is physically at Network Solutions, in Herndon, Virginia. In cyberspace, it is at *ftp://nic.ddn.mil/netinfo/hosts.txt* (there are 8 other global root servers elsewhere on the Internet). The file is over 500 kbytes, and if it does not know the IP address, or where to find it, then there is no Internet-registered IP address for that name. In late 1995 it handled about 250 queries per second.

▲ *Secondary Master*—these periodically check the primary to see whether anything has changed and requests an updated copy if so. Also, these machines provide backup for the primary.

▲ *Caching-only*—these temporarily store responses, and respond on behalf of a master when they can. The DNS administrator sets how long to cache entries, to ensure that if the translation is changed (on its master), it will be available to all. Caching-only servers are not authoritative, so will usually provide name service for the local network only.

Name servers usually have IP addresses only for names up to two levels below them. Resolving longer names therefore may involve a higher-level name server querying a lower-level name server to respond to a request.

End-user stations have a *name resolver* that caches frequent DNS queries. Their name resolver configuration file has IP addresses of a few nearby name servers, which are contacted when a name cannot be resolved locally.

The process for *registering* for a (guaranteed worldwide unique and known) domain name (and IP address) involves filling out a form. Other than checking that no one else has the domain name you request (and you have legal right to the name—typically by requiring that the name be a registered corporate name), the other requirement is that two currently-existing Internet name servers will get an entry for your name. Since you probably don't have any currently-existing name servers that will agree add your name to their hosts table, your Internet service provider will usually register the name for you (and add your name to their name servers). The InterNIC will then add your name to the Internet's root name servers, as pointers to your two name servers.

The administrator for your two name servers then manually enters an NS (name server) record for every machine in your network. Whenever any queries from the Internet want to access one of your machines, the Internet's root name server queries replies with the address of one of your name servers. The query then goes to your name server, to access the NS record to get the IP address for the particular machine requested.

Where the domain name registration form comes from (and to whom you return it, and how much money this all costs) depends on the type of name desired. Some examples are listed below:

▲ Names in the (for example) *.com* and *.net* top-level domains are administered by the InterNIC, which can be contacted at *http://internic.net/*. They sub-contract this work to Network Solutions Inc., and the database of domain names can be searched at *http://rs.internic.net/cgi-bin/whois*.

▲ Second-level names in the *.ca* top-level domain are administered by the CA domain registrar, which is at *ftp://ftp.cdnnet.ca/ca-domain/index*, with some information at *ftp://ftp.cdnnet.ca/ca-domain/introduction*. The database of names can be searched at *gopher://nstn.ns.ca:7006/7*.

▲ Similarly, names in other countries are administered by an organization in that country. The .uk domain names are administered by the department of computer science at University College London.

More information on DNS is available at *http://rs.internic.net/help/domain/dns.html*. DNS is defined in RFCs 882, 883, 973 and 1034. The operation of DNS servers is specified in RFC 1035 (which is available at *http://www.crynwr.com:80/crynwr/rfc1035/*). A less-than-serious discussion of the difficulty of choosing host names is in RFC 2100.

The IAHC is (was) at *http://www.iahc.org*, and gTLD-MOU (now that's a nice acronym) is at *http://www.gtld-mou.org*.

On-line listings of country codes are available at *http://www.ee.ic.ac.uk/misc/country-codes.html* and *ftp://ftp.isi.edu/in-notes/iana/assignments/country-codes*. Clickable maps are at *http://www.ee.ic.ac.uk/misc/bymap/world.html*.

See **CACHE**, **CA*NET**, **DHCP**, **INTERNET2**, **INTERNIC**, **IP ADDRESS**, **ISP**, and **TCP/IP**.

```
AD  Andorra
AE  United Arab Emirates
AF  Afghanistan
AG  Antigua and Barbuda
AI  Anguilla
AL  Albania
AM  Armenia
AN  Netherlands Antilles
AO  Angola
AQ  Antarctica
AR  Argentina
AS  American Samoa
AT  Austria
AU  Australia
AW  Aruba
AZ  Azerbaijan
BA  Bosnia and Herzegowina
BB  Barbados
BD  Bangladesh
BE  Belgium
BF  Burkina Faso
BG  Bulgaria
BH  Bahrain
BI  Burundi
BJ  Benin
BM  Bermuda
BN  Brunei Darussalam
BO  Bolivia
BR  Brazil
BS  Bahamas
BT  Bhutan
BV  Bouvet Island
BW  Botswana
BY  Belarus
BZ  Belize
CA  Canada
CC  Cocos (Keeling) Islands
CF  Central African Republic
CG  Congo
CH  Switzerland
CI  Cote D'ivoire
CK  Cook Islands
CL  Chile
CM  Cameroon
CN  China
CO  Colombia
CR  Costa Rica
CU  Cuba
CV  Cape Verde
CX  Christmas Island
CY  Cyprus
CZ  Czech Republic
DE  Germany
DJ  Djibouti
DK  Denmark
DM  Dominica
DO  Dominican Republic
```

```
DZ Algeria
EC Ecuador
EE Estonia
EG Egypt
EH Western Sahara
ER Eritrea
ES Spain
ET Ethiopia
FI Finland
FJ Fiji
FK Falkland Islands (Malvinas)
FM Micronesia (Federated States of)
FO Faroe Islands
FR France
FX France, Metropolitan
GA Gabon
GB United Kingdom
GD Grenada
GE Georgia
GF French Guiana
GH Ghana
GI Gibraltar
GL Greenland
GM Gambia
GN Guinea
GP Guadeloupe
GQ Equatorial Guinea
GR Greece
GS South Georgia and the South Sandwich Islands
GT Guatemala
GU Guam
GW Guinea-bissau
GY Guyana
HK Hong Kong
HM Heard and McDonald Islands
HN Honduras
HR Croatia (Hrvatska)
HT Haiti
HU Hungary
ID Indonesia
IE Ireland
IL Israel
IN India
IO British Indian Ocean Territory
IQ Iraq
IR Iran (Islamic Republic of)
IS Iceland
IT Italy
JM Jamaica
JO Jordan
JP Japan
KE Kenya
KG Kyrgyzstan
KH Cambodia
KI Kiribati
KM Comoros
KN Saint Kitts and Nevis
KP Korea (Democratic People's Republic of)
KR Korea (Republic of)
KW Kuwait
KY Cayman Islands
```

```
KZ  Kazakhstan
LA  Lao People's Democratic Republic
LB  Lebanon
LC  Saint Lucia
LI  Liechtenstein
LK  Sri Lanka
LR  Liberia
LS  Lesotho
LT  Lithuania
LU  Luxembourg
LV  Latvia
LY  Libyan Arab Jamahiriya
MA  Morocco
MC  Monaco
MD  Moldova, Republic of
MG  Madagascar
MH  Marshall Islands
MK  Macedonia (the former Yugoslav Republic of)
ML  Mali
MM  Myanmar
MN  Mongolia
MO  Macau
MP  Northern Mariana Islands
MQ  Martinique
MR  Mauritania
MS  Montserrat
MT  Malta
MU  Mauritius
MV  Maldives
MW  Malawi
MX  Mexico
MY  Malaysia
MZ  Mozambique
NA  Namibia
NC  New Caledonia
NE  Niger
NF  Norfolk Island
NG  Nigeria
NI  Nicaragua
NL  Netherlands
NO  Norway
NP  Nepal
NR  Nauru
NU  Niue
NZ  New Zealand
OM  Oman
PA  Panama
PE  Peru
PF  French Polynesia
PG  Papua New Guinea
PH  Philippines
PK  Pakistan
PL  Poland
PM  St. Pierre and Miquelon
PN  Pitcairn
PR  Puerto Rico
PT  Portugal
PW  Palau
PY  Paraguay
QA  Qatar
RE  Reunion
```

```
RO  Romania
RU  Russian Federation
RW  Rwanda
SA  Saudi Arabia
SB  Solomon Islands
SC  Seychelles
SD  Sudan
SE  Sweden
SG  Singapore
SH  St. Helena
SI  Slovenia
SJ  Svalbard and Jan Mayen Islands
SK  Slovakia (Slovak Republic)
SL  Sierra Leone
SM  San Marino
SN  Senegal
SO  Somalia
SR  Suriname
ST  Sao Tome and Principe
SV  El Salvador
SY  Syrian Arab Republic
SZ  Swaziland
TC  Turks and Caicos Islands
TD  Chad
TF  French Southern Territories
TG  Togo
TH  Thailand
TJ  Tajikistan
TK  Tokelau
TM  Turkmenistan
TN  Tunisia
TO  Tonga
TP  East Timor
TR  Turkey
TT  Trinidad and Tobago
TV  Tuvalu
TW  Taiwan, Province of China
TZ  Tanzania, United Republic of
UA  Ukraine
UG  Uganda
UM  United States minor outlying Islands
US  United States
UY  Uruguay
UZ  Uzbekistan
VA  Holy See (Vatican City State)
VC  Saint Vincent and the Grenadines
VE  Venezuela
VG  Virgin Islands (British)
VI  Virgin Islands (U.S.)
VN  Viet Nam
VU  Vanuatu
WF  Wallis and Futuna Islands
WS  Samoa
YE  Yemen
YT  Mayotte
YU  Yugoslavia
ZA  South Africa
ZM  Zambia
ZR  Zaire
ZW  Zimbabwe
```

DPI
Dots Per Inch

The measurement used for dot-matrix and laser printers for (you guessed it) how many dots can be printed per inch. For vertical resolution, a dot-matrix printer usually specifies how many *lines per inch* (LPI) it can print. For a laser printer, the resolution is usually give for both dimensions (for example, 600 × 600 DPI).

DPMS
Display Power Management Signaling

A specification from the Video Electronics Standards Association defining how any computer's video adapter can request the monitor to go to one of several power-saving modes (so that the monitor can be *Energy Star* compliant).

DPMS Level	Mode	Description
0	Screen Saver	This mode is not actually part of DPMS. But some non-DPMS monitors can detect when they are "displaying" a screen saver, and then the monitor goes into a power-down mode.
1	Standby	This optional mode saves about 30% of the power required for normal running mode and allows for instant-on as soon as needed
2	Suspend	Saves more power (by powering-off the CRT's main heater) but requires up to 5 seconds to turn back on
3	Off	Saves more power by turning power off to everything except the monitor's microprocessor

Typically, the display is fully powered-on when any keyboard key is pressed.

See **DDC, ENERGY STAR, TCO,** and **VESA**.

DQDB
Distributed Queue Dual Bus

The *access mechanism* (method to obtain permission to transmit) for a metropolitan area network that never became popular.

A protocol defined in the IEEE's 802.6 MAN specification that provides an access mechanism to a network. Two one-directional buses are used: a station with data to transmit puts a request to transmit on one bus and later transmits on the other bus.

See **MAN** and **SMDS**.

DRAM
Dynamic Random Access Memory

The type of memory usually used in PCs (and most other computers too) for the main memory (such as your "16 Mbytes of RAM"), since it is lower-cost (albeit slower) than other types (such as *Static Random Access Memory*— **SRAM**).

"*Dynamic*" refers to the memory's method of storage—basically storing the charge on a capacitor. Like all capacitors, the memory cells of a DRAM integrated circuit self-discharge over time (in this case, within about a millisecond) and need to be *refreshed*. This is done by circuitry (which cycles through memory addresses) that is part of the computer's memory subsystem.

It is worth the extra cost of the memory refresh circuitry because a DRAM requires only a single transistor (plus a capacitor) per bit of storage, whereas a SRAM requires six transistors per bit of storage (the transistors make a circuit called a *flip-flop*, in that it has two states, so it can store one binary bit. SRAM typically has much faster access time (typically 5 to 15 ns), and does not need to be refreshed—once you write a bit, it remembers it (hence the "static").

DRAMs of 16 Mbits (which is 2 Mbytes) per IC are currently common, as are 64 Mbit (8 Mbyte) ICs.

Both DRAM and SRAM are *volatile*, in that they loose the stored data if the power is turned off. There are many types of *non-volatile* memory, such as:

▲ CMOS (complementary metal-oxide semiconductor RAM), which uses so little power that a small battery can ensure that the memory is retained for years. It is typically used where individual bytes need to be modified, and less than a few hundred bytes of storage are needed (such as for the CMOS settings of your PC where details of your hardware configuration are stored, such as the type of disk drive, or which serial ports and diskette drives are installed).

▲ A programmable, in-circuit-erasable, non-volatile memory. Popular for storing the programs for devices that may need to be updated (such as the firmware for a modem, or the BIOS a for PC).

EPROM (erasable, programmable, read only memory) usually cannot be programmed when installed in the user equipment, so the integrated circuits must be plugged into an *EPROM* programmer, usually at the factory where the equipment is manufactured. No battery is required to maintain the memory's contents (that is, it is a *non-volatile* memory device), but erasing requires an ultra-violet light to illuminate the IC through the quartz glass window (regular glass blocks the ultra-violet light—which is why you can't get a sunburn inside your house) for 5 to 20 minutes. Nobody's too sure how long EPROMs will retain data (its at least 10 years though), but many feel that a sticker should be placed over the window just to be extra sure that stray light does not contribute to shortening the little bits' lives.

OTP (one-time programmable) EPROMs don't have a quartz window (so they cannot be erased), but are much less expensive than regular EPROMs since they can don't need the expensive ceramic package that the quartz window requires. Also, they are easy to program (using the same equipment as for regular EPROMs), so manufacturers can quickly change programs as assembly time.

Early DRAMs (when the original IBM PC ran at 4.77 MHz) had an access time of 250 ns. Current DRAMs are much faster (typically 50 to 70 ns access time), but current processors are much faster still. Therefore, the processor runs at some multiple (such as 3:1 or 4:1) of the memory bus speed. Standard DRAMs support memory bus speeds of up to about 40 MHz. Specialized types of DRAM (such as FPM, EDO, DRAM and VRAM) have therefore been developed. However, even a 133 MHz Pentium requires instructions and data every 7 ns, so *caching* is also used.

FPM-DRAM is a faster implementation of standard DRAM.

See **BIOS**, **CACHE**, **CMOS**, **COMPACT FLASH**, **EDO RAM**, **FPM**, **FLASH**, **MINICARD**, **PC**, **PENTIUM**, **PENTIUM PRO**, **RAM**, **RDRAM**, **SDRAM**, **SGRAM**, **SRAM**, and **VRAM**.

DS-0
Digital Signal Level 0

One of the 24 64,000-bits/s channels in a DS-1 data communications link.

Users likely have access only to 56,000 bits/s of this 64,000 bits/s (unless B8ZS is used).

See **B8ZS**, **FT1**, **PCM**, **SUBRATE**, and **T1**.

DS-1
Digital Signal Level 1

The bit format used for transmission on a T1 data communications link. A T1 provides 1.544 Mbits/s transmission over copper, fiber, or radio links (for example).

The term "DS-1" is usually used interchangeably with "T1," though T1 refers to a DS-1 implemented on a copper transmission media (that is, 2 pairs of copper conductors).

See **T1**.

DS-3
Digital Signal Level 3

The bit format used for transmission on a T3 data communications link. A T3 provides 44.736 Mbits/s transmission over copper, fiber, or radio links (for example).

The term "DS-3" is usually used interchangeably with "T3."

See **T3**.

DSP
Digital Signal Processing

The amazing technology that enables high-speed modems, digital cellular telephones, speech recognition and compression, echo cancellation and many other (usually) audio-frequency signal processing functions to be implemented at relatively low cost and with very few electronic components.

Usually, implemented as a single special-purpose processor IC, optimized for the mathematical functions required—as well as other operations, such as interfacing with analog to digital, and digital to analog converters. The MMX capability built-in to recent Pentium processors was designed to efficiently handle DSP functions.

The processors perform complicated real-time (that is, as fast as the voice is digitized, or the echoes occur) mathematical operations, that are typically very repetitive and calculation-intensive. For example, multiply and add operations are usually the most common calculation, as they are needed to implement digital filtering and many other common functions.

See **BRI**, **DSP**, and **MODEM**.

DSU
Data Service Unit

The device required to convert the digital data from (for example) the V.35 interface on a router's WAN port to the T1 voltages and encoding required for a T1 WAN connection to a public carrier.

An option (which must match the setting on the remote DSU) is often to invert the customer's data, so that the automatically stuffed zeros of HDLC data are 1s, and ensure that T1's *ones density rule* is not violated (so that non-clear channel T1, nor B8ZS needs to be used).

The DSU is often integrated with a CSU, so the resulting unit is then called a DSU/CSU.

See **B8ZS**, **CCP**, **CSU**, **CSU/DSU**, **ENCODING**, **T1**, **V.35**, and **WAN**.

DSU/CSU
Data Service Unit / Channel Service Unit

A device that has both DSU and CSU functionality in one enclosure. It is used to connect data equipment (such as a router) to a fractional T1 or T1 service (for example). The connection to the data equipment is typically a V.35 M34 or EIA-449 DB-37 connector, and the connection to the network is usually a DB-15 or 8-pin modular jack (RJ-45).

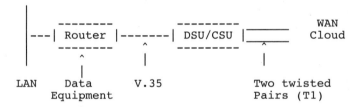

As for modems, DSU/CSUs have diagnostic LEDs. Also as for modems, the LEDs typically have cryptic 2-letter abbreviations for their function. In addition to the signal names described in the entry for EIA-232, there may be LEDs labelled as follows.

▲ NS (No Signal)—this indicates that the received (from the central office) signal level is too low.

▲ OS (Out of Service)—this indicates that the DSU/CSU is receiving a signal, but it is an out-of-service message from the central office.

Some DSU/CSUs have more than one port, and can be configured as multiplexers to assign each port's data to any (and any number of) DS-0 time slots. These are sometimes called *drop-and-insert* DSU/CSUs. The more traditional way of doing this is using a stand-alone box that can assign different data streams to different time slots—this is called a *digital cross-connect system* (DCS).

Some DSU/CSUs support remote configuration and diagnostics (using a proprietary protocol, typically using an ESF T1 circuit's *facility data link*). Because of such proprietary extra features, units from the same manufacturer must usually be used at both ends of a link.

Some CSU/DSUs have built-in *data compression*. TIA/EIA-655 specifies a standard way of doing this. It provides up to 4:1 data compression.

Major manufacturers of CSU/DSUs are Digital Link Corporation, which has a WWW server at *http://www.dl.com/*, and Adtran, Inc. at *http://www.adtran.com*.

See **CSU**, **DSU**, **DSX**, **EIA-TIA232**, and **ESF**.

DSVD
Digital Simultaneous Voice and Data

A standard for multiplexing voice and data over a single, standard telephone line (and modem). The voice is digitized by the modem, and sent along with the data.

Supporters include U.S. Robotics, AT&T, Hayes Microcomputer Products and Multi-Tech Systems. Standardized in ITU V.64. An enhancement is standardized in V.70.

See **SVD**, and **V.70**.

DSX-1
Digital Signal Cross-connect Level 1

A DS-1 signal which allows a maximum cable length of 655' (200 m). DSX-1 is usually used within a building to connect T1 devices together (such as connecting a T1 interface of a PBX to a multiplexer which has many DSX-1 inputs, and a T3 output).

The name comes from the patch-panels that used to be used to manually cross-connect T1 and T3 signals at telephone company central offices.

See **CSU/DSU**, and **T1**.

DTE
Data Terminal Equipment

Usually a computer terminal or a PC emulating one. Or a computer.

That is, equipment that sources or sinks data, as shown in the accompanying figure (so it is the *terminus*).

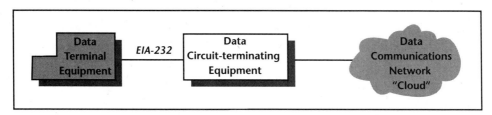

DTE-1

See **DCE1** (Data Circuit-Terminating Equipment), **EIA-TIA232**, **MODEM**, **V.54**, and **WAN**.

DTMF
Dual-Tone Multi-Frequency

The *in-band* signaling method used by touch-tone telephones for *station loop signalling* (that is between the telephone and the PBX or central office). DTMF was developed by AT&T Bell

Laboratories, and first available to the public in 1963 (as part of the 1500-type telephone set, which looked like the later and much more popular 2500-type set, but the 1500 did not have the * and # keys). Pairs of frequencies are assigned to each of 16 buttons, though most current telephones only have (some military phones have the full 16 buttons, the extra ones being used for cut through to a busy number, clearing the existing call—you better be sure you have authority to use that feature though). DTMF enables faster dialing, as well as end-to-end signalling (dial pulses only get as far as the first CO).

The following table shows the frequencies that are used (the buttons we are not used to are labelled A through D here).

		High Group Frequencies (Hz)			
		1,209	1,336	1,477	1,633
Low Group Frequencies (Hz)	697	1	2	3	A
	770	4	5	6	B
	852	7	8	9	C
	941	*	0	#[a]	D

a. AT&T calls this an *octothorpe*, though Bellcore and Northern Telecom call it a "number sign". Some call it a "pound sign" (which is the fastest to say), but this has less meaning, now that SI is becoming more widely used (and kilograms are used instead).

Many considerations went into the selection of the specific frequencies, for example the following:

▲ None of the frequencies are integral multiples of others (for example, the "column" frequencies are in the ratio 21:19—same for the row frequencies). This simplifies the design of the filters required for the DTMF receivers.

▲ The frequencies are mid-range in the 300 to 3,400 Hz bandwidth of standard telephone circuits, to ensure that they are carried reliably.

▲ The frequencies are separated enough to allow for tolerances in the frequency generating and detecting equipment, and to allow for frequency shifts caused by transmission equipment within the network.

Telephone companies typically require that the tones be present for at least 40 ms (a silence of less than 5 ms is ignored—that is, it is assumed that the tone was continuous), and that there is at least a 35 ms gap between successive tones. Most modems default to much longer tones and gaps (80 or 95 ms for example), but this can be reduced (so your modem dials faster) by setting status register 11 to a smaller value.

Standardized in ITU V.19.

See **DID**, **DN**, **INBAND**, **POTS**, and **SIT**.

DV
Digital Video

The industry standard method for recording digitized video information onto small magnetic tape cartridges, using digital camcorders. Typically an IEEE 1394 port is provided for uploading the digitized video to editing equipment.

See **S1394**, and **VIDEO**.

DVD
Previously Digital Versatile Disc

A technology to put video (such as movies) on things that look like CD-ROMs—and the DVD players can play standard CDs and CD-ROMs (and later, CD-R and CD-RW disks) also. DVD was initially an acronym for *digital video disk*, as this was the main intended use. As there is nothing in the technology that limits them to video, somebody thought of the new name (*digital versatile disc*) that still had the same acronym. Then someone decided that DVD wasn't an acronym for anything, it was simply the name of the technology (likely for some confusing trademark-related reason).

Here are some details on the DVD:

▲ One-sided, single-density disks, factory-recorded disks have a capacity of 4.7 Gbytes—which is enough to hold about 133 minutes of video (once it has been compressed)—this is enough for 95% of all new movies. These can be made 2-sided, and by manually flipping over the disk you get another 4.7 Mbytes of content (these may be called *flippy disks*).

▲ Disks with two layers, where the gold upper layer is semi-transparent will have a capacity of 8.5 Gbytes. By adjusting the output power, the laser will be able to read the upper or lower reflective silver layer. This disk has slightly less than double the capacity to accommodate the reduced quality of the signal. Double-sided, double-layer disks will have a capacity of 17 Gbytes (enough for an 8-hour movie).

The audio can use either Dolby Laboratories AC-3 multichannel (5.1) compressed audio (which is also called *Dolby Digital Surround sound*), PCM (not likely to be used) or MPEG-2 compressed audio.

The Dolby Digital Sound uses a bit rate of 384,000 to 448,000 bits/s (depending on how many additional 10 kbit/s language tracks are needed). The "5.1" refers to the 5 audio channels (front: left, right and center, and rear left and right for sound effects), plus one sub-woofer (low frequency speaker—it turns out that low frequency sounds are very non-directional, so it doesn't matter where you place this speaker) supported. Additional language tracks are typically provided for the center channel only, and the other channels—except for removing the speed from the front left and right channels—stay the same.

It is likely that North American releases will use the Dolby audio, and European releases will use the MPEG audio. The movie industry is pushing for this incompatibility, so they can release movies and DVDs at different times in North America and Europe, without ruining their own launches and sales.

▲ There is room for up to 8 digitized audio (speech) tracks (for example, English, French, Spanish, and so on), and 32 subtitle (text) tracks.

▲ The digitized video format is used called CCIR 656.

▲ MPEG-2 compressed video decoding.

▲ Movie sections can be rated (G, PG, and so on), and the player set so that it only plays certain versions of the same movie.

▲ Initial computer units play at 1,350 kbytes/s (about 11 Mbits/s), which is equivalent to an 8× or 9× CD-ROM drive (later units will be much faster). Stand-alone *entertainment units* (that plug into your television, as your VCR does) play at about 600 kbytes/s, which is equivalent to a 4× CD-ROM player. Entertainment units will need built-in MPEG-2 decompression hardware, so may actually cost more than computer units, which may do the decompression in software (though initial units require an *MPEG-2* video decoder board (this would only be needed if you wanted to watch movies on your PC).

▲ The error correction code method used can correct error bursts (due to dust or scratches for example) of up to 2,000 bytes (which corresponds to about a 4 mm length of track).

▲ As can be seen in the table below, DVD uses a smaller "pits" to record the bits, a closer spacing of the spiral track of pits (so more bits fit on a disk), and a shorter wavelength semiconductor laser diode (to read the smaller pits). The laser diode has a life of about 5,000 hours.

▲ Standard audio CDs and CD-ROMs can be read by DVD players (using a different lens in the pick-up assembly).

Integrating the output of DVD players with computer video monitors (for example, in a desktop window on the screen) initially uses the *analog-overlay* method where the computer leaves a black rectangle, into which the DVD output is merged (the computer's video adapter board's output passes through the DVD playback board to do this). This requires synchronization (usually manually, when the DVD drive is installed) of the timing and scanning frequencies of the two boards. As DVD becomes more accepted, the DVD output will be merged into the video frame buffer memory, by the computer's video board.

The video display formats supported are as follows:

▲ *standard NTSC* TV video (which has a 4:3 aspect ratio video)

▲ *letter-box* to show standard movie 16:9 aspect ratio video on a standard 4:3 aspect ratio TV—by leaving a black band at the top and bottom of the screen

▲ *pan-and-scan*, to show standard movie 16:9 aspect ratio video on a standard 4:3 aspect ratio TV—by not showing the sides of the picture

▲ *wide-screen* (for HDTV-type monitors (these have a 16:9 aspect ratio)

The following table compares CD-ROMs and DVDs.

Characteristic	CD-ROM	DVD[a]
Diameter of smaller pits (µm)	0.833	0.4
Spacing of tracks (µm)	1.6	0.74
Track density (tracks per inch)	16,000	34,000
Bit density (bits per inch)	43,000	96,000
Length of spiral (km)	Over 5	Almost 11
Wavelength of laser diode (nm)	780 to 820	635 to 650
User data capacity (Mbytes)	650 to 741	4,700
Error correction code bits (percent of entire disk)	33	13

a. For the initial single-layer, single density format.

Initial DVD drives can read CD-RW disks, but usually cannot read CD-R disks.

Unfortunately, several recordable technologies (all of which should be readable by standard read-only DVD drives—sometimes called DVD-ROM) have been proposed (or marketed), as listed below:

▲ DVD-R (*recordable*), which are consumer-recordable, write-once disks. The single-sided and single-density version will have a capacity 3.8 Gbytes.

▲ DVD-RAM (*random access memory*), which are consumer-erasable and re-recordable (also called write-many) disks. The single-sided, single-density technology will have a capacity of 2.6 Gbytes per disk. Double-sided disks (which have a protective cartridge) support 5.1 Gbytes each. DVD-RAM players will be compatible with all CD formats and CD-ROMs. DVD-RAMs will likely use *phase-change* materials, which (depending how quickly they cool) can be either ultrafine-grained polycrystalline (if it cools relatively slowly), or a disordered amorphous (non-crystalline) phase if it cools quickly (in which case it does not reflect light as much). This changes the reflectivity of the spot, and reading then uses a lower-intensity beam (so the material is not melted). This is supported by the DVD Forum—mainly Hitachi, Matsushita Electric and Toshiba.

▲ DVD+RW (read and write), which are consumer-erasable and re-recordable. They are expected to have a capacity of 3 Gbytes for single-sided, single-density disks. They use a phase-change technology, and are supported by HP, Mitsubishi, Philips Electronics, Ricoh, Sony and Yamaha.

▲ MMVF (*Multimedia Video File*), proposed by NEC. It has a capacity of 5.2 Gbytes per side.

There were initially two competing technologies (as listed below). Realizing that this would confuse and frustrate potential customers, the Hollywood Video Disc Advisory Group and the Computer Industry Technical Working Group (consisting of Apple, Compaq, Hewlett-Packard, IBM and Microsoft) forced (by refusing to endorse either competing technology) the two groups to work together on a single standard. This was completed in mid-1995.

Philips Electronics NV and Sony Corp. own the DVD patents, and Sony authorized Philips to handle the licensing of those to other manufacturers.

▲ Toshiba Corp. and Time-Warner Inc.'s SD (Super-Density). Most of the DVD's design, such as the physical characteristics, are based on this technology.

▲ Sony Corp. and Philips Electronics NV's (with backing from 3M Co.) MMCD (Multimedia CD), also called video-CD. The encoding used by DVD is based on this technology.

Both systems were to have supported at least 270 minutes of MPEG-2 compressed audio and video (that is, a full-length movie) on a single disk.

Customizations of the DVD technology are planned by several groups of vendors. These threaten to fragment the market, and ruin a potentially fantastic medium. Some of these are listed below:

▲ *Divx*. A pay-per-use system developed by Digital Video Express LP, a partnership of Circuit City Stores and the Hollywood law firm of Ziffren, Brittenham, Branca & Fischer. It is supported by Matsushita Electric Industrial Co., Zenith Electronics, Thomson Multimedia (who own RCA) and many other important companies. It allows movies to be purchased on DVD/Divx disks, and they can only be viewed for a 48-hour period beginning when the movie is first viewed. A modem in your DVD/Divx player then dials-up to a billing center about once a month to provide information on further viewings of the DVDs. This reduces the overhead of having to restock returned video-tapes, so movie rentals can be considered purchases, which is more attractive to a wider range of stores. Also, since you never return the disks (they apparently cost about 35¢ to make), there are no late fees. And you can give the DVD/Divx disks to your friends, and they pay for their own viewings (on their own DVD/Divx players).

▲ Recordable DVD, as described above.

Further information is at *http://www.ima.org/forums/imf/dvd/faq.html* and *http://www.sel.sony.com/ SEL/consumer/dvd/index.html*. Also try *http://www.mpeg.org/~tristan/MPEG/dvd.html*.

See **CDROM** (*Video CD*), **HDTV**, **SD**, and **VIDEO**.

DX4

Intel's central processing unit, which was popular from about 1993 to 1995.

A 3.3-volt 486DX (earlier 486s were 5-volt) with a built-in math coprocessor. They are usually clock-tripled, but can also run at 2, 2.5, or 3 times their external speed, as shown in the accompanying table. For example, a 100-MHz DX4 runs at 33 MHz externally and 100 MHz internally.

Has a 16-kbyte (which is double that of earlier 486s and the same size as a Pentium) internal (also called *Level 1*) RAM *unified* (not divided into separate sections for code and data) cache.

In contrast, the Pentium processor has separate sections for code and data. DX4-based PCs will typically have at least 256 kbytes of external (also called *Level 2*) cache.

The "4" in DX4 is supposed to remind you of 486. Intel is dropping the "486" part of the name, since it cannot be copyrighted.

DX4 Internal Speed (MHz)	External Speed (MHz)	Clock Multiple	Comments
75	25	3	Intended for laptop PCs
83	33	2.5	
100	33	3	

See **S486DX**, **CACHE**, **COPYRIGHT**, **INTEL**, and **PC**.

DXI
Data Exchange Interface

An interface between routers and CSU/DSUs that enables existing routers (that don't have the hardware capability to support ATM's cells) to support ATM—with only a software upgrade (but only at sub-SONet access speeds).

The trick is to have the CSU/DSU provide the *Segmentation and Reassembly* (SAR) functions (splitting the router's frames to ATM cells) at T1 or fractional T1 speeds. The router sends variable-length frames to the CSU/DSU, making it look (to the router) as though the ATM network accepts variable-length frames.

The router outputs CSPDUs (*Convergence Sublayer Protocol Data Units*) from ATM *adaptation layers* 3/4 and 5 (up to 4,090 bytes per frame).

Specifications include how LAN packets are segmented into ATM cells, the electrical interface (V.35, or HSSI at up to 45 Mbits/s), and the exchange of *local management information*.

Two modes of operation are defined:

▲ *Mode 1* handles up to 1,024 virtual circuits, supports AAL 5, uses a 16-bit CRC, and has a maximum packet size of 8 kbytes (limited by the CRC)

▲ *Mode 2* devices handle up to 16 million virtual circuits, support AAL 3/4 and 5, use 32-bit CRCs, and have a maximum packet size of 64 kbytes (again, limited by the CRC)

Based on the SMDS DXI. Frames use a 2-byte header with a 10-bit address (as does frame relay). *Quality of Service* (QOS) for each virtual circuit (including minimum throughput rate and maximum delay) can be specified.

Carriers may offer this service, making the link from the customer site to the C.O. switch more efficient—ATM's 53-byte cells are at least (5/53 =) 9.4% overhead. At this "low speed," competes with frame relay.

For a while DXI was called DX-UNI, but this is all obsolete now, replaced with the *Frame User to Network Interface* (FUNI). This supports all of the *User Network Interface* (UNI) functionality, including end-to-end signaling, traffic management, and network management, but does the SAR functions at the carrier's site, not the customer's. (The expectation is that it will be more cost-effective to do the SAR at a centralized location, for many customers.)

See **ATM** (*Asynchronous Transfer Mode*), **CRC**, **CSU**, **DSU**, **FUNI**, **HSSI**, **SMDS**, **T1**, and **V.35**.

E

E.163

The ITU-T standard that specifies the format for international telephone numbers. These *directory numbers* can be a maximum of 12 digits in length, and are comprised of two sections:

▲ The *country code* is 1 to 3 digits in length. For example, the country code for Canada and the U.S. is 1, and the country code for the U.K. is 44. A longer list is usually in the front of your local telephone book.

▲ The *national significant number* is up to 11 digits in length, and includes your area code (or whatever it is called in each country). In Canada and the U.S., this is typically 10 digits in length.

See **DN** and **E.164**.

E.164

The ITU-T standard that was designed as the international telephone number format for ISDN, SMDS and ATM, and as of 1997, replaces E.163 as the format for regular telephone numbers too. Basically, E.164 is simply E.163, but the national significant number can be up to 13 digits, and the entire telephone number can be up to 15 digits. The country code portion is unchanged from E.163.

As for E.163, addresses have a geographically hierarchical structure (which is well-suited to worldwide routing). In contrast, other addressing schemes (such as for the IP addresses for the Internet) are organizationally oriented.

E.164 addresses have the following components:

▲ *Subscriber Number* (SN)—For example, the local 7-digit telephone number used for an individual subscriber. It is assigned by the local carrier.

▲ *National Destination Code* (NDC)—For example, the area code. The combination of the NDC and the SN is called the *National Significance Number* (NSN), and can be up to 13 digits in length.

▲ *National Prefix* (P_N)—For example, dialing "1" before a long distance call.

▲ *Country Code* (CC)—For example, dialing 44 for the U.K. These codes are specified in ISO 3166.

▲ *International Prefix* (P_I)—For example, dialing "1"011 before an overseas long distance call. In this case, the National Prefix is not dialed.

ITU-T standard E.164 (*Numbering Plan for the ISDN* Era) is the same as ITU-T standard I.331.

See **ATM** (*Asynchronous Transfer Mode*), **CARRIER**, **DN**, **DNS2** (*Domain Name System*), **IP ADDRESS**, and **SMDS**.

E-SMR
Enhanced Specialized Mobile Radio

Another way to abbreviate ESMR.

See **ESMR**.

E1

The European equivalent of North America's T1. A point-to-point, dedicated, 2.048-Mbits/s digital communications circuit that carries 32 64,000-bits/s channels:

▲ 30 user-data 64,000-bits/s channels (unlike DS-1, E1 always provides clear channel 64 kbit/s channels).

▲ A 64,000-bits/s voice circuit signalling channel. This carries line supervision, such as whether the telephones are on-hook or off-hook, and uses timeslot 16.

▲ A 64,000-bits/s channel for synchronization, channel control and framing channel. This enables the receiving end to determine which timeslot is which, and uses timeslot 0.

Because of the higher speed (than T1), repeaters on copper links are required more often than every 6,000 feet.

There are 2 options for the physical media:

▲ 120 Ω twisted pair cabling (typically foil shielded, but it may be twin-axial). This is called a *balanced interface*, and uses a DB-15 or a 8-pin modular connector.

▲ 75 Ω coaxial cable. This is called an unbalanced interface (because the two conductors do not have an equal impedance to ground), and uses a BNC connector.

E1 is also used in Australia, Mexico and New Zealand.

While North American's like to call this E1, in Europe (where it is typically used), it is more commonly called CEPT-30 (*Conférence Européenne des Administrations des Postes et des Télécommunications–30*).

The E1 (and the higher-speed circuits in the hierarchy) are called PDH (*plesiochronous digital hierarchy*), but for really high-speeds, the newer SDH is used instead.

E1 is also used to carry ISDN PRI service in countries that use E1s instead of T1s.

Some E1 characteristics are specified in G.732. Also, G.703 specifies the electrical interface and G.704 defines the framing format.

See **DS1**, **E3**, **ESF**, **PCM**, **SDH**, **T1**, **TDM**, and **WAN**.

E2

A communications circuit that supports four E1s. The actual bit rate is 8.448 Mbits/s.

Rarely implemented.

See **E1** and **E3**.

E3

The European equivalent of North America's T3. Carries 16 E1 circuits on a 34.368-Mbits/s channel. This is 480 conversations (and each conversation is the same as a 64,000 bits/s circuit).

Also called CEPT-3.

The frame format typically used is that specified in G.703, and for copper connections, 75 Ω coaxial cable with BNC connectors is used.

See **E1**, **SDH**, **SONET**, **T1**, and **WAN**.

E4

The European point-to-point digital circuit with a speed greater than E3: 139.264 Mbits/s. Carries four E3 circuits, which are 64 E1 circuits. This is 1,920 conversations (and a conversation requires the same bit rate as a 64,000-bits/s circuit).

See **E3**, **SDH**, **SONET**, **T3**, and **WAN**.

E5

A communications circuit that supports four E4s (a total of 7,680 conversations).

The actual bit rate is 565.148 Mbits/s.

See **E3** and **E4**.

Easter Egg

A little surprise hidden in many commercial application programs, typically for the purpose of giving credit to the programmers that created the program.

They are at least a listing of the programmers' names, but often have sound and interesting pictures as well.

The Easter Egg Archive Page is at *http://weber.u.washington.edu/~davidnf/eggframe.html*.

EBCDIC
Extended Binary Coded Decimal Interchange Code

The 8-bit character coding scheme used by IBM mainframes and minicomputers (such as the AS/400—*Application Server 400*). Alphabetic characters are not represented by consecutive codes, because of EBCDIC's origin as the coding used for IBM Hollerith punch cards. The rest of the world (even the PC, which was designed by IBM) uses ASCII and maybe someday, Unicode.

The following tables show the hexadecimal for each EBCDIC character, for EBCDIC code page 37, which is for U.S. and Canada use (there are many code pages, each with characters for other languages, and for technical use). For example, a *line feed* is represented as 25_{16}, and "$" is $5B_{16}$.

Pronounced "*EB*-sa-dik."

See **ASCII**, **BAUD**, **MAINFRAME**, and **UNICODE**.

Least Significant Digit	Most Significant Hexadecimal Digit							
	0	1	2	3	4	5	6	7
0	Null		Data link escape	Digit select		Space	&	–
1	Start of heading	Device control 1	Start of significance				/	
2	Start of text	Device control 2	Field separator	Synchronization character				
3	End of text	Tape mark						
4	Punch off	Restore	Bypass	PN				
5	Horizontal tab	New line	Line feed	Record separator				
6	Lowercase	Backspace	End of transmission block	Uppercase				
7	Delete	Idle	Escape	End of transmission				
8		Cancel						
9	RLF	End of medium						\
A	Start of manual message	Cursor control	Set mode		¢	!	|	:
B	Vertical tab	Customer use 1	Customer use 2	Customer use 3	.	$	,	#
C	Form feed	Interchange file separator		Device control 4	<	*	%	@
D	Carriage return	Interchange group separator	Enquiry	Negative acknowledgment	(	)	_	'
E	Shift out	Interchange record separator	Acknowledge		+	;	>	=
F	Shift in	Interchange unit separator	Bell	Start of special sequence	| or [	⌐ or]	?	"

Least Significant Digit	Most Significant Hexadecimal Digit							
	8	**9**	**A**	**B**	**C**	**D**	**E**	**F**
0					{	}	'	0
1	a	j			A	J		1
2	b	k	s		B	K	S	2
3	c	l	t		C	L	T	3
4	d	m	u		D	M	U	4
5	e	n	v		E	N	V	5
6	f	o	w		F	O	W	6
7	g	p	x		G	P	X	7
8	h	q	y		H	Q	Y	8
9	i	r	z		I	R	Z	9
A								
B								
C								
D								
E								
F								

ECC
Error-Correction Code

A memory system that has extra (usually called "redundant" or "check") bits per word so that most memory errors can be detected and corrected. This is more important for computers which have tens or hundreds of megabytes of RAM, as is common on modern servers. For example, the Pentium Pro has built-in support for ECC memory, and the data bus is actually 72 bits wide—64 bits for data plus 8 bits for the ECC.

To calculate the fewest number of redundant (r) bits necessary to detect and correct single-bit errors in a message of length m use the following equation:

$$(m + r + 1) \leq 2^r$$

Therefore, for a 32-bit word, at least 6 ECC bits must be added, since $(32 + 6 + 1) \leq 2^6$. Each memory location would then need to store 38 bits. Errors in the check bits are handled in the same way as errors in the data bits.

A typical actual implementation requires seven check bits for every 32 data bits stored. This ensures that all single-bit errors are detected and corrected, all occurrences of 2 bits in error (per 32-bit word) are detected, and some occurrences of 3 and more bits in error are detected.

In 1950, a smart guy named Richard W. Hamming figured out a method of implementing ECC memory using the theoretical minimum number of redundant bits (this is called the *Hamming Code*).

Sometimes called *Error Detection and Correction* (EDAC).

The *parity* memory scheme used in many PCs adds only a single bit of memory per byte, and can only reliably detect single-bit (per byte of memory) errors.

See **DIMM**, **FCS**, **PARITY**, **PENTIUM PRO**, **RAM**, and **SIMM**.

ECP
Extended Capabilities Port

An enhancement to the original parallel port on a PC, which provides the following:

▲ Data transfer rates of more than 2 Mbytes/s

▲ Bidirectional 8-bit operation (a standard parallel port only has 4 input bits)

▲ Ability to specify bytes sent between the PC and peripheral (by the sender raising a signal line) to be either data or commands

▲ Support for CD-ROM and scanner connections to PCs

▲ Hardware strobe generation (the PC software does not need to raise and drop the strobe line to the printer for each byte transferred)

▲ 16-byte (or more) FIFO buffer to speed data transmission

▲ Support for *run length encoding* data compression, in which rather than sending many repetitive bytes (which, for example, is common from scanners), a single byte and a count of the number of times that the receiving driver should repeat it, are sent

▲ DMA support to increase transfer speed and reduce processor overhead

Developed by Hewlett-Packard and Microsoft (which have a big interest in faster and better communications to printers). Windows 95 supports ECP. Current ECP development work is being done within the IEEE 1284 group.

See **S1284**, **EPP**, **HP**, **MICROSOFT**, **PARALLEL PORT**, **PC**, and **RLE**.

ECTF
Enterprise Computer Telephony Forum

Formed on Northern Telecom's initiative, and comprising also of Dialogic Corporation, DEC, L.M. Ericsson AB, and Hewlett-Packard Co. to encourage industry-wide consensus and interoperability in standards implementations for *computer telephony integration*. In 1995, the rival Versit consortium (comprised of Apple Computer, AT&T, IBM, Novell and Siemens) joined, realizing that two standards are worse than none.

ECTF is now the owner of the following:

▲ The widely-supported *Signal Computing System Architecture* (SCSA)—developed by Dialogic as an open hardware and software specification to support TAPI, TSAPI and other CTI APIs.

▲ T*map*, which is an API (first released in 1994) that maps TAPI function calls to the TSAPI client library. Therefore, a TAPI application can work with a TSAPI PBX. The software was developed by Northern Telecom, and is available for free.

Dialogic and Northern Telecom have WWW servers at *http://www.dialogic.com/* and *http://www.nt.com/*, respectively.

See **CTI**, **TAPI**, and **TSAPI**.

EDAC
Error Detection and Correction

See **ECC**.

EDI
Electronic Data Interchange

There are estimates that 80% of what is printed by one computer is manually entered into another. In the process of doing business, companies will send and receive price lists, product orders, waybills, invoices, statements, and many more standard (for their industry) documents. The retyping of this information into other computer systems introduces unnecessary expense, delays, and errors.

EDI enables computers of different types to send and receive information directly.

Even once protocols and standards are worked out so that two computers could directly communicate, there are several potential problems. What if:

▲ The receiver's computer was down because of communication line problems, scheduled maintenance, or a hardware problem when the sender wanted to send the file?

▲ The receiver accidentally deleted the received file before processing it?

▲ The sender claims to have sent a file that the receiver has no record of receiving?

To avoid these problems, an EDI sender and receiver usually do not communicate directly. Instead, a trusted third-party service provider acts as a store-and-forward mailbox. Many companies offer this service, such as General Electric Information Services (GEIS), IBM Information Exchange, and Stentor TradeRoute. The third party:

▲ Guarantees to be up all the time

▲ Retains all transferred files for a few days, in case the receiver wants to re-receive it

▲ Keeps a log of all activities

In addition, the third party can do edit-checks on the data to ensure that the files are in a valid format.

Typically, the third party charges per line item transferred and uses the X.25 protocol to establish connections to the companies.

The Premenos Electronic Commerce Resource Guide is at *http://www.premenos.com/*. The Data Interchange Standards Association has a WWW server at *http://www.disa.org*. The EDI World Institute has a WWW server at *http://www.ediwi.ca:6900/*. GEIS has a relevant WWW home page at *http://www.geis.com*. The Electronic Data Interchange Council of Canada has a WWW server at *http://www.edicc.ca/edicc*.

See **ISBN**, **PGP**, **UPC**, **VAN**, and **X.25**

EDO DRAM
Extended Data Out Dynamic Random Access Memory

A slightly faster type of *Dynamic Random Access Memory*—as compared to Fast-Page Mode DRAM (which is sometimes called FPM). In turn, fast-page mode DRAM is faster than conventional DRAM).

EDO DRAM is based on fast-page mode DRAM, but adds latches so it can continue to output the accessed memory location's contents (so the computer has time to read it) even after the computer starts specifying the address of the next location to be read (specifically, the output remains active and valid while the first part of the next address—the *column address*—is presented to the memory IC). That is, a new memory cycle is started before the previous one has been completed. This "overlapping" enables the memory cycle time to be faster, as is required for faster CPUs such as the 120-MHz Pentium.

EDO DRAM memory accesses are often written as 6-2-2-2 (for example). This means that the first memory access in a burst requires 6 clock cycles (since the entire memory address needs to be specified), but the next three accesses only require 2 clock cycles each (since only the column address needs to be specified).

Like standard DRAM, EDO DRAM has a typical access time of 60 or 70 ns, however, due to the overlapped nature of the memory accesses, the cycle times (sequential input/out operations) can handle 66, 70 and even 83 MHz bus clock speeds (compared to a maximum of about 33 MHz for FPM and 25 MHz for conventional DRAM). If the memory is 64 bits (which is 8 bytes) wide, then (roughly), the memory could handle I/O operations at (8 × 70 =) 560 Mbytes/s, which is more than enough for a 33 MHz bus PCI-based computer.

Burst EDO DRAM (BEDO) is faster than EDO-DRAM. It supports a burst mode, where the full row and column address only needs to be specified for the first access, and a counter in the IC increments automatically for the next three accesses (so the column address does not need to be specified for those three accesses). This speeds the memory cycle time further, allowing burst accesses of 5-1-1-1 (for 52 ns BEDO DRAM on a 66 MHz memory bus—these can typically access the subsequent memory locations every 10 ns).

Memory access bursts of four 32-bit accesses are popular, since that is the typical width of an L2 cache line (which is 128 bits).

EDO-DRAM was popular in PCs in early 1996, and quickly replaced the use of FPM, since EDO DRAM did not cost any more, but was faster.

SDRAM is a still-faster DRAM technology.

See **CACHE**, **DRAM**, **FPM**, **PCI**, **PENTIUM**, **RAM**, **SDRAM**, **SIMM**, and **VRAM**.

EIA
Electronic Industries Association

A trade association that (among many other activities) produces many electrical and electronics-oriented standards. They were accredited by the American National Standards Institute (ANSI) in 1984, and prior to this, EIA's "standards" were *recommended standards* ("RS"), representing "the best practices at the time", rather than being official, recognized by ANSI standards. So prior to 1984 EIA's standards were designated (for example) RS-232 (or more fully, EIA RS-232-C, which is the third revision of the original standard). After EIA's accreditation in 1984, the EIA omitted the RS, so (for example), the successor to EIA RS-232-C was ANSI/EIA-232-D.

For a while, EIA said that standards which existed before 1984 would get the new name (without RS) when the standard was revised. However, now even standards that have not been revised since then (and that therefore still say RS-485 on their cover) are referred to in EIAs standards catalog's and Global Engineering's web site as EIA-485.

Also, at about that time, the many standards which were produced by the TIA (which was a section of the EIA, and did not yet have its own ANSI accreditation, so could not have its name first) were called EIA/TIA (for example, EIA/TIA-530) to show that the work was done by the TIA.

Current standards that are produced only by the EIA are simply called EIA (or ANSI/EIA, since EIA standards are recognized by ANSI).

The EIA's web site is at *http://www.eia.org*.

See **EIA449**, **EIA485**, **EIA-TIA232**, **EIA-TIA530**, **STANDARDS**, **TIA1** (*Telecommunications Industry Association*), **TIA-EIA422**, **TIA-EIA423**, **TSB**.

EIA-422

See **EIA**, **TIA1** (*Telecommunications Industry Association*), and **TIA-EIA422**.

EIA-423

See **EIA**, **TIA1** (*Telecommunications Industry Association*), and **TIA-EIA423**.

EIA-449

A digital interface used for connecting higher-speed data communications equipment. A typical use is for the 56 kbit/s to 1.544 Mbit/s ports on routers and video CODECs to connect to DSU/CSUs. The interface can be used with either asynchronous or synchronous data communications—though synchronous is far more common since EIA-449 is more expensive (than EIA/TIA-232), and generally only used for higher-speed communication, where efficient communications is important (no wasting time on start and stop bits) which is usually only necessary for shared-use devices such as routers, and these employ protocols (such as HDLC) that typically require synchronous communications (now that was long-winded, but better to explain it than just state the fact).

EIA-449 uses a DB-37 connector (which has 37 pins, and looks like a wider 2-row connector than the DB-25 often used for EIA-232). An optional 9-pin connector (using a DB-9) provides a secondary communications path (so you could have two separate simultaneous full-duplex conversations), though this is rarely implemented.

For the higher-speed signals (those more than 20 kbits/s, such as the transmit and receive data, and the clocking signals), it uses *differential* (also called balanced) signals. These are defined in TIA/EIA-422. For signals that do not change state often (such as call indication and loopback control) *single-ended* (also called unbalanced) signals are used. These are defined in TIA/EIA-423. The standard specifies that the waveshaping (rise time) of the TIA/EIA-423 signals be adequate for a 60 m (200 foot) cable length, and that the maximum cable length is 60 m.

The standard specifies that the interface can be used for data transfer rates up to 2 Mbits/s.

For most data applications (such as routers) in North America, V.35 is usually used instead of EIA-449. In Europe, EIA-449 (and X.21) are more popular than V.35, and are widely used for communications at up to E1 speeds.

The EIA-449 standard is officially called *General Purpose 37-position and 9-position Interface for Data Terminal Equipment and Data Circuit-terminating Equipment Employing Serial Binary Data Interchange*. The most recent revision of was produced in 1985, and the standard was rescinded in September 1992, with the expectation that EIA/TIA-530 would be used instead.

See **CSU/DSU**, **EIA**, **TIA-EIA422**, **TIA-EIA423**, **EIA-TIA530**, **UTP**, and **V.35**.

EIA-485

A physical-layer standard for interfacing multiple devices to a shared bus, consisting of a twisted pair of (typically) unshielded 24 gauge copper conductors. The standard is officially called *Electrical Characteristics of Generators and Receivers for use in Balanced Digital Multipoint Systems*.

Half-duplex, any to any communication is possible with a single twisted pair. Full-duplex communication is possible if two twisted pairs are used, and one host (often called the master) controls all communication with the secondaries (that can only directly talk to the master, not among themselves).

Usually, *transceivers* are used. These can both transmit and receive, and the standard defines the load presented by these. For example, each must have a resistance of at least 10.6 kΩ and draw a maximum of 1.8 mA (across its differential pair) at the maximum differential and common-mode voltages allowed. This is referred to as a *unit load*, and up to 32 are allowed on the bus. The actual transceiver is typically a single integrated circuit, and newer devices each often present less than a unit load—such as unit load), so (for example) 64 devices can be on a bus.

EIA-485 drivers must provide at least 1.5 V (differential) to a fully-loaded bus (32 unit loads, with a 120 Ω terminating resistor at each end of the bus), and output no more than 6 V (differential) *open circuit* (that is, with no load). When short circuited, or connected to ground, a driver cannot generate more than 250 mA.

Receivers can detect differential voltages as low as 200 mV. This allows for noise and signal attenuation of up to 1.3 V (since the minimum signal starts out at 1.5 V).

While the standard states that the maximum bit rate is 10 Mbits/s, it does not state the maximum cable distances at more typical bit rates—since this depends on many factors such as the number of unit loads, the type of cable (for example, its mutual capacitance) and the diameter (gauge) of the conductors, the ambient electrical noise and the quality of the transceivers (such as their leakage current and impedance).

However, commonly used maximums are 1.2 km (4,000 feet) at 38.4 kbits/s (with 32 unit loads). Other values are 1.8 km at 19.2 kbits/s and 5.5 km at 9,600 bits/s and less. Sometimes you see 10 Mbits/s at up to 12 m, and 1.2 km at up to 100 kbits/s.

Performance is best if each end of the twisted pair is terminated with a 120 Ω termination resistor (this matches the impedance of most twisted pair cabling.

The standard was first released in 1983, though TIA/EIA-485-A (the first revision) is expected by early 1998.

In 1994, EIA-485 was made into an international standard, as ISO 8482.

EIA-485 ICs are manufactured by many companies, including National Semiconductor and Texas Instruments. Application notes and data sheets are available at *http://www.national.com* and *http://www.ti.com*.

See **EIA**, **TIA-EIA422**, and **SCADA**.

EIA/TIA-232
Electronic Industries Association/
Telecommunications Industry Association Recommended Standard 232

A standard specifying the interface between (for example) a modem and a computer so that they can exchange data. The computer can then send data to the modem (which somehow sends them over a telephone line), and the data that the modem receives from the telephone line can then be sent to the computer.

Officially called *Interface Between Data Terminal Equipment and Data Circuit-Terminating Equipment Employing Serial Binary Data Interchange*. It specifies the connector, pin functions, and voltages used to connect two devices together so that they can send data to each other.

One device is the *data terminal equipment* (such as the COM1 serial port of a PC), and the other is the *data circuit-terminating equipment*, previously called *data communications equipment* (such as a modem).

PCs use a male DB-9 (sometimes called a DE-9, and the pin-out is standardized in EIA/TIA-574) or DB-25 (standardized in EIA/TIA-232) connector. Some devices use an 8-pin modular connector. A standard pin-out is specified in EIA/TIA 561, however, there are many non-standard pin-outs used, such as for the console port on Cisco routers.

A "binary" interface is used, with the following two states:

▲ A "high" signal is a positive voltage (anywhere between +3 and +25 volts DC). It has the following characteristics:

▲ It is considered on ("RTS is *high*"—or *on* or *true* or *asserted*)

▲ It is a space (the line is in a "spacing condition," or the bit is a "space parity" bit)

▲ It represents a binary 0 (the datum is a zero bit)

A "low" signal is a negative voltage (anywhere between –3 and –25 volts D.C.). It has the following characteristics:

▲ It is considered off ("CTS is *low*"—or *off* or *false* or *deasserted*)

▲ It is a mark (the line is in a "marking condition," or the bit is a "mark parity" bit)

▲ It represents a binary 1 (the datum is a one bit)

The following table shows the interface signals (or *pin-out*) for 9-pin and 25-pin connectors (when used for *asynchronous* data). Signal names are relative to the DTE (for example, the *transmit data* signal is data *from* the DTE).

Pin Number					Direction		
DB-25	DB-9	Standard 8-pin	Cisco 8-pin[a]	Pin Name	DTE	DCE	Pin Function
2	3	6	3	TxD	→		Data transmitted from DTE to DCE (for example, from PC to modem)
3	2	5	6	RxD	←		Data received from DCE to DTE (from modem to PC)
4	7	8	1	RTS	→		DTE requests permission to send data to modem
5	8	7	8	CTS		←	DCE grants permission to send
6	6	1	7	DSR		←	DCE indicates that it is operational (the modem is powered on)
7	5	4	4&5	Signal ground	↔	↔	Common ground reference
8	1[b]	2		DCD		←	DCE indicates that it is receiving carrier from remote modem
20	4	3	2	DTR	→		DTE indicates that it is operational (powered on)
22	9[b]			RI		←	DCE indicates that the phone is ringing

a. While Cisco's pinout is non-standard, it does have the advantage that it is symmetric, so reversing the order pins changes an interface cable from presenting a a DTE interface to a DCE interface. This is done by flipping over (at one end) the 8-wire flat cable typically used for the 8-pin modular jacks, before attaching the connectors.
b. Some DB-9 to DB-25 adapters do not connect these signals, thus providing hours of rewarding troubleshooting practice for lucky people.

For *synchronous* communications, *clock* signals are also required. A clock is a square-wave signal, at the same rate as the data. The falling edge of the clock (positive to negative voltage transition) indicates the center of the data bit.

Usually, *external clock* is used—the modem (which is "external" to the DTE) generates the signal (either internally or derived from the data received from the remote modem). The *transmit clock* signal (which is on pin 15) determines the rate at which the DTE transmits data. The receive clock (on pin 17) specifies the rate at which the modem is sending data to the DTE.

Sometimes, the *internal clock* is used (for example, when there is no modem). The DTE then generates the clock signal (on pin 24), and this specifies the data rate at which the DTE is transmitting data.

The previous table showed the signals commonly used for asynchronous communications. Some common functions of other pins are shown in the table below.

DB-25 Pin Number	Pin Name	Direction		Pin Function
		DTE	DCE	
1		↔		Protective ground
9	+12 volts[a]	←		Can be used for testing purposes
10	-12 volts[b]	←		
11	Local Digital Loopback	→		The DTE requests that the modem loops data from the network, back to the network
13	No Signal	←		Some data sets use this pin to indicate that they are not receiving a signal from the central office
15	TxC	←		The modem-generated clock signal of the bit rate at which the DTE must send data to the modem (which reads the data at each space to mark transition)
17	RxC	←		The modem-generated clock signal of the bit rate at which the modem sends data to the DTE (which must read the data at the clock's space to mark transition)
18	Local Analog Loopback	→		The modem loops data from the DTE back to the DTE, and data from the network back to the network
21	Remote Loopback	→		The modem sends a signal to the remote modem, so the remote modem goes into loopback mode
24	External TxC	→		If the DTE generates its own transmit clock signal, it is sent to the modem on this pin
25	Test Mode	←		Indicates that the modem is in a test mode (such as loopback)

a. The standard only reserves pins 9 and 10 for testing, but many manufacturers use them for these test voltages.
b. The standard does not assign a function to this pin, but some products use it for this function—which may be called RT (*Remote Terminal* Loopback).

There are no standard abbreviations for the signals, but some that are commonly used to label external modem LEDs are shown in the following table.

DB-25 Pin Number	Abbreviation	Meaning (when on)
2	SD or TD or TxD	The PC is sending (transmitting) data to the modem
3	RD or RxD	The PC is receiving data from the modem
4	RTS[a]	The PC will accept data from the modem
5	CTS[a]	The modem will accept data from the PC
6	MR or DSR	Data Set (or Modem) Ready—the modem is powered on
8	CD, DCD, RLSD, or CS	(Data) Carrier Detect, or Received Line Signal Detect or Carrier Sense
20	TR or DTR	Data Terminal Ready—the PC is powered on and ready to accept an incoming call
22	RI or AA	Ring Indicator or Auto-Answer—the phone is ringing (when flashing), or the modem is set to automatically answer incoming calls (when on constantly)
[b]	HS	High Speed—the modem is communicating with another modem and has negotiated a modulation with a data rate (for example) of: 2,400 bits/s or less (flashing), 4,800 to 14,400 bits/s (OFF), or 16,600 bits/s or faster (ON)
[b]	OH	The modem has the telephone line Off-Hook (a phone call has been or is being, made or answered)
[b]	TM	The modem is in a Test Mode

a. As described in the table, these signals are now usually used for *hardware flow control* (rather than their original intent for controlling half-duplex modems). For example, the modem puts a negative voltage on pin 5 while it cannot accept more data from the PC (because the PC has been sending data faster than the modem can transmit it to the remote modem). The modem will put a positive voltage on pin 5 when it has transmitted most of its buffered data to the remote modem and is ready to receive more from the PC.
b. These are not EIA/TIA-232 signals but are usually shown on modem status displays along with the other EIA/TIA-232 signals.

The combination of ITU's V.24 and V.28 (which is basically what EIA/TIA-232 is called outside of North America) are equivalent to EIA/TIA-232. So why does it take the ITU two standards to say what EIA/TIA says in one? Well, it's because ITU is being more modular, and separately specifies signal names, and their functions in V.24, and the electrical characteristics (voltage and current limits) and the pin assignments in V.28.

A previous version of the standard was RS-232-C (it was commonly called "RS-232"). It was released in 1969 and was the current version when most existing computer equipment was designed. At that time, the EIA referred to all of its standards as *recommended standards* and prefaced the number with "RS".

RS-232 allows up to 2,500 picofarads (pF) of mutual capacitance between ground and the signal, measured at the receiver, and including the cable between the DTE and DCE, and the capacitance of the receiver itself (typically 100 pF). Therefore the cable can have up to about 2,400 pF of capacitance. The length of cable allowed therefore depends on the amount of capacitance per meter (or whatever), and the standard suggests 15 m (50 feet). However, if a lower capacitance cable is used, then it can be longer. Also, the standard suggests a maximum speed of 20,000 bits/s. However, if the cable is much shorter than 15 m, it works satisfactorily at much faster speeds (115,200 bits/s is common).

In 1987, RS-232-D was released with the following changes:

▲ The EIA decided that it could raise its profile by getting rid of the somewhat meaningless "RS" and putting its own name there instead, so EIA-232-D is simply the successor to RS-232-C.

▲ The connector is defined (the DB-25, which was already being used).

▲ A *local loopback* function is defined, in which the DTE can put a positive voltage on pin 18 (which was previously unassigned) and the DCE will perform a local analog loopback (V.54 loop 3) until the signal on pin 18 is deasserted.

▲ A *remote loopback* function is defined, in which the DTE can put a positive voltage on pin 21 (which was previously used as a signal quality indicator from the DCE but seldom used) and the DCE will signal the remote DCE that it should go into *remote digital loopback* (V.54 loop 2) until the signal on pin 21 is deasserted.

▲ An indicator that the DCE is in either of these *test modes* is defined. Pin 25 is asserted (pin 25 was previously unassigned).

In 1991, EIA/TIA-232-E was released, with the following changes:

▲ The EIA began to work with the TIA on standards that concern telecommunications, so TIA gets its name in the standard too.

▲ Rather than the modem's *ringing indicator* (pin 22) always being asserted at about the same time as the phone rings, the DCE can be sensitive to telephone company *distinctive ringing* and assert pin 22 only if certain distinctive ring cadences occur.

▲ To support hardware flow control, pin 4 (previously *request to send*) can instead be used as *ready for receiving*, to indicate that the DTE can accept data. The use of request to send is necessary only for half-duplex operation, which is seldom used now, since modems are typically full-duplex. (Request to send is considered constantly asserted when pin 4 is used for flow control.)

▲ Also to support hardware flow control, the DCE can deassert pin 5 (*clear to send*) to signal to the DTE that the DTE should temporarily stop transmitting data to the DCE (for example, because the DCE is performing a retrain/entrain or error correction or is not able to compress the DTE's data enough to send it over the communications channel as fast as the DTE is sending it). Previously, pin 5 was used only for half-duplex operation.

▲ An alternative 26-pin (though the 26th pin is left unconnected) connector "Alt A" is defined. It is smaller than a DB-25 (about 20 mm wide, versus 40 mm) and uses square pins. The female of this connector is used on both DTE and DCE, and cables with male connectors on both ends are then used (unlike the DB-25, in which the DCE has a female connector and the DTE usually has a male connector).

▲ Pin 1 is redefined to be *shield* (for shielded cables) rather than *protective ground*. If the shield connection is used, then the cable's shield can be connected at the DTE only. If frame ground bonding of the DTE and DCE is required, then a separate conductor should be used (meeting local electrical codes).

As shown in the figure below, there are alternatives to using EIA-232 for in-building digital data communications.

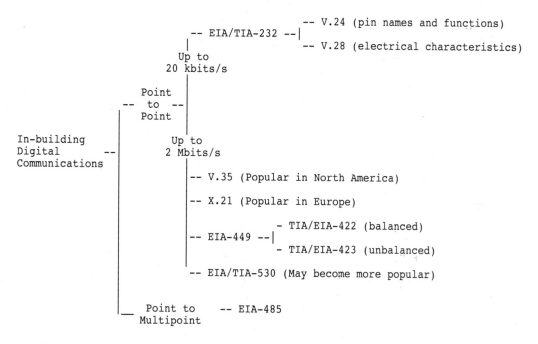

```
                                          -- V.24 (pin names and functions)
                         -- EIA/TIA-232 --|
                         |                 -- V.28 (electrical characteristics)
                       Up to
                       20 kbits/s

                 Point
        --  to  --
        |        Point
        |
In-building      Up to
Digital     --|  2 Mbits/s
Communications   |
        |        -- V.35 (Popular in North America)
        |
        |        -- X.21 (Popular in Europe)
        |
        |                      - TIA/EIA-422 (balanced)
        |        -- EIA-449 --|
        |                      - TIA/EIA-423 (unbalanced)
        |
        |        -- EIA/TIA-530 (May become more popular)
        |
        |__  Point to     -- EIA-485
             Multipoint
```

See **S16550A, ASYNCHRONOUS, DB25, DCE1, DTE, EIA, EIA-485, EIA/TIA-530, ENCODING, ESP, FLOW CONTROL, FULLDUPLEX, HALFDUPLEX, INBAND, MODEM, OUTOFBAND, STANDARDS, SYNCHRONOUS, TIA-EIA422, TIA-EIA423, UART, V.34, V.35, V.42BIS,** and **V.54.**

EIA/TIA-530

A standard developed in 1992 for higher-speed (than EIA-232) short-distance, point-to-point digital communications. It is officially called *High Speed 25-position Interface for Data Terminal Equipment and Data Circuit-terminating Equipment, Including Alternative 26-position Connector.*

It uses the same 25-pin DB-25 connector usually used by EIA-232, but the voltages and pin-out are not compatible with EIA-232.

EIA/TIA TSB-37a

EIA/TIA has never been widely accepted. In North America, V.35 remains the most popular alternative.

See **EIA**, and **V.35**.

EIA/TIA TSB-37a

The interim name for a standard ("Telephone Network Transmission Model for Evaluating Modem Performance") specifying types of analog communication line impairments (such as time delays, noise, and frequency, nonlinear and phase distortions) that are useful for simulating, to test modem performance.

Twenty-four types of CO trunks and seven types of lines are defined.

See **EIA**, **MODEM**, **PCM**, and **V.56BIS**.

E-IDE
Enhanced IDE

A popular interface that is used to connect a computer to its hard disk drive and other peripherals.

Sometimes called Fast IDE. E-IDE is based on ANSI's ATA-2 and ATA-PI. Enhancements over IDE include the following:

▲ *Multiple read* and *multiple write* (sometimes called *block mode*), where 2 to 128 sectors are read or written before the CPU is signalled (using a hardware interrupt) that the operation is completed (so it can set-up the next read or write). This reduces the CPU time that needs to be spent servicing the disk. Without this feature, the CPU is interrupted for every sector of data read or written. As for DMA, this is most useful for multitasking operating systems that likely have other things to do while waiting for disk I/O operations to complete.

▲ Logical block addressing, where the disk drive appears to be a long sequence of disk sectors, simply addressed by a 28-bit LBA, with LBA referring to cylinder 0 (which is at the outside edge of the disk platter), head 0, and sector 1. The actual location of the blocks of data on the actual disk drive (cylinder, head and sector) is hidden from the computer.

▲ Translation, where the cylinders, heads and sectors are remapped between the BIOS and the IDE interfaces, to increase the maximum disk size supported. An enhanced *BIOS* (E-BIOS), TSR or driver (such as is built-in to OS/2) is needed to accomplish this (or support may be built-in to the E-IDE interface). If support is built-in to the BIOS, then there will be 4 sets of hard disk drive parameters that can be set in the CMOS set-up screen.

▲ A secondary IDE port, as described below.

▲ Support for ATA-PI CD-ROM and tape drives

The specification was developed by Western Digital, as was most of the original IDE specification). A comparison of the two is shown in the table below.

	IDE	E-IDE
Disk drive capacity (Mbytes)	504	8,033
Data transfer rate (Mbytes/s)	1 to 3	Up to 16.6
Drives per adapter	2	4[a]
Types of drives supported	Hard disk	Hard disk, tape, CD-ROM, and more

a. Assuming two interfaces (primary and secondary) on the E-IDE adapter.

IDE's cable limitation of 0.5 m (18") total cable length still applies, so drives remain restricted to being internal to the PC.

The following table shows a PC's disk drive capacity limitations.

		BIOS Maximum	IDE Maximum
Cylinders		1,024	65,536
Heads per drive		255	16
Sectors per track[a]		63	255
Maximum drive capacity (assuming DOS's 512 bytes per sector)	bytes	8,422,686,720	136,902,082,560
	Gbytes	7.8	127.5

a. A track is a cylinder's data on one disk surface (that is, all the data that a single read/write head can see without *seeking*.)

The storage capacity of a PC's IDE drive is limited by the smaller of the BIOS's interrupt 13_{16} disk functions, and the IDE register limitations. The standard IDE maximum storage capacity can be calculated as follows:

▲ 1,024 cylinders (BIOS maximum)

▲ 16 read/write heads (disk surfaces) per drive (IDE maximum)

▲ 63 sectors (DOS uses 512-byte sectors) per track (BIOS maximum)

So the maximum IDE disk drive capacity is ($1,024 \times 16 \times 63 \times 512 =$) 504 Mbytes, where 1 Mbyte is ($1,024 \times 1,024$ bytes =) 1,048,576 bytes.

Enhanced IDE can remap blocks of data so that the BIOS sees more heads (but the enhanced IDE drive sees more cylinders) so that the BIOS maximum of 7.8 Gbytes becomes the maximum capacity of an enhanced IDE drive. The remapping converts all requests to a 28-bit *Logical Block Address*—LBA. The last block of a standard IDE drive is LBA 1,032,191, which corresponds to cylinder 1,024, head 16 and sector 63.

Standard IDE controllers typically use *Programmed I/O* (PIO) to transfer data to and from the processor (and do not require disk driver software—since the PC's BIOS handles IDE disk controllers). However, Enhanced IDE can use PIO—which is slower but simpler (since a PC's BIOS will typically already support PIO, so no drivers need to be loaded), and DMA (which provides faster data transfers, but additional disk driver software or an enhanced BIOS is required).

Using programmed I/O, maximum transfer rates are as follows:

▲ 2 to 3 Mbytes/s (on ISA bus systems)

▲ 11.1 Mbytes/s (when using *mode 3 PIO*)

▲ 16.6 Mbytes/s (when using *mode 4 PIO*). This is a faster transfer rate than many disk drives (such as those in laptop PCs) can provide (due to their rotational speed), so is only needed for high-end disk drives.

Using DMA, maximum transfer rates are as follows:

▲ 4 Mbytes/s transfers (when using Type B DMA, which is used for EISA bus adapters)

▲ 6.67 Mbytes/s or 8.33 Mbytes/s—both are defined, and either speed can be implemented by a manufacturer, depending on which PCI/ISA chip set is used (when using Type F DMA, which is used on a local bus, which will usually be PCI)

▲ 13.3 Mbytes/s, which is double the 6.67-Mbytes/s speed above, since multiple words are transferred during each DMA (when using *Mode 1 Multiword DMA*)

▲ 16.6 Mbytes/s, which is double the 8.33-Mbytes/s rate above, since multiple words are transferred during each DMA (when using *Mode 2 Multiword DMA*)

▲ 33 Mbytes/s, by reducing the time tolerances allowed for the DMA transfers.

These transfer rates and timings are specified by the *Small Form Factor Committee* and ANSI.

Products can support any subset of these transfer modes and still be called Enhanced IDE. (Makes it a bit difficult to compare products, doesn't it?)

IDE PIO data transfers are sometimes called *blind PIO*, since the PC reads data with no feedback about whether it is reading faster than the disk drive can supply the data. (This concern was never a problem when PCs were slow.) The IDE interface was designed to be slow enough to prevent a fast PC from reading too fast. Unfortunately, this needlessly reduces the performance of fast disk drives, such as those with high disk rotation speeds (5,400 RPM is considered fast) or built-in caches.

E-IDE supports feedback (that is, *flow control*) for PIO modes 3 and 4. The PC tries to transfer data as fast as it can. The disk drive can slow the transfer if it cannot provide the data as fast as the PC is requesting it, by using the PC bus's *IO* channel ready signal (IORDY).

To ensure that both PC and disk drive support flow control, the PC sends a command to the disk drive to enable the feature.

Support for four IDE devices per PC is provided by putting two IDE interfaces (each interface can support two devices) on the same printed circuit board. The *primary IDE* interface uses the standard IDE base I/O address (the address at which its registers start) of $01F0_{16}$ and interrupt 14. The secondary interface usually uses the reserved address of 0170_{16} and interrupt 15. Each of the two controllers has its own standard IDE 40-conductor flat ribbon cable (and each cable has two connectors for the peripherals, one for the master, the other for the slave). Usually, the primary IDE interface (or *channel* or *connector*) is PCI bus-based, and the secondary uses only the ISA bus signals. This reduces the cost, as the secondary channel is intended for slower devices (such as CD-ROM and tape drives).

Since MS-DOS 3.0, DOS has had support for up to seven disk drives, so only a BIOS change is needed for E-IDE support under DOS or Windows. The disk drivers for other operating systems, such as OS/2, NetWare, and Windows NT have support for both the primary and secondary IDE controllers.

IDE support for CD-ROMs (and soon, tape drives, CD-R, and other types of drives) has been defined by Western Digital using the *AT Attachment Packet Interface* (ATA-PI), which specifies the new commands (which are based on the SCSI-2 commands) and controller registers required. BIOS support will be required for ATA-PI. This will substantially lower the cost of CD-ROM drives, since a SCSI or additional (proprietary) interface will not be required (since most PCs already have an IDE interface for the hard disk drive).

Mixing fast and slow devices (for example, hard disk and CD-ROM drives) on the primary controller may cause slower data transfer for the hard disk (all transfers may go at the speed of the slower device). Put only hard disks on the primary controller.

Even with all these enhancements, hard disks with SCSI interfaces typically have better performance than EIDE disks. One reason is that vendors seem to announce disks with faster rotational speeds with a SCSI interface first.

EIDE competes with Seagate Technology's *Fast ATA* and *Fast ATA-2*. Also competes with IBM's and Toshiba's ATA-2.

Western Digital has a WWW site at *http://www.wdc.com/*.

See **ATA**, **ATA-2**, **ATAPI**, **ATASPI**, **BIOS**, **CACHE**, **CDROM**, **DISK DRIVE**, **DMA**, **FAST ATA**, **FAST ATA2**, **IDE**, **ISA**, **PC**, **PCI**, **PIO**, **SCSI1**, and **SMALL FORM FACTOR COMMITTEE**.

EISA
Extended Industry Standard Architecture

A 32-bit bus used in some (but not many) higher performance PCs. The newer PCI bus is better.

Supports many more features than ISA (for example, more than two bus masters and *switchless configuration*). A burst mode provides double the transfer rate (the address is supplied only at the start of the burst, and all subsequent data are assumed to go to sequential memory locations).

Runs at 8.33 MHz. The theoretical maximum transfer speed is 33 Mbytes/s. Competed with MCA. A main advantage over MCA is that ISA boards can be plugged into the EISA bus (though with no additional benefits or capabilities) but not into the MCA bus.

MCA was never widely accepted. (IBM was the main source of MCA PCs.) EISA is (was) more widely accepted, but was still usually found only in (expensive) servers. PCI is the current high-performance PC (and other platform) bus.

EISA was developed by the "Gang of Nine" (nine non-IBM manufacturers of IBM-compatible PCs, led by Compaq) when a 32-bit PC bus standard was needed and IBM wanted high royalties for its MCA bus.

See **BUS**, **ISA**, **MCA**, and **PCI**.

Electronic Data Interchange

See **EDI**.

Electronic Industries Association

See **EIA**.

Electronic Mail Broadcast to a Roaming Computer

See **EMBARC**.

Electromagnetic Field

See **EMF**.

ELF
Extremely Low Frequency

Frequencies of 300 Hz and less. For *electromagnetic fields* (and the MPR II standard), frequencies of 60 Hz (which are generated by power lines) and multiples of this are usually of most interest.

See **EMF**, **MPR II**, and **VLF**.

EMBARC
Electronic Mail Broadcast to a Roaming Computer

A pager-oriented broadcast (one-way only) data service for sending and receiving wireless electronic mail. Small devices receive the messages (for example, PCMCIA cards plugged into PCs that have their own RAM to store messages when the PC is powered off).

See **PCMCIA**.

EMC
Electromagnetic Compatibility

Generally means ensuring that electrical and electronic equipment can co-exist near each other, without the electromagnetic interference from one disrupting the proper operation of the other.

Now often refers to the Commission of the European Communities' (CEC's) *EMC* Directive, which supersedes any European country's national EMI regulations. It applies to all electrical and electronic products (including the cabling) bought or installed after January 1, 1996, and intended for potential international marketing and sale. Obviously, this is of great interest to manufacturers, as it ensures that countries can't use unique electromagnetic emission regulations to create arbitrary barriers to trade.

Manufacturers can *self-declare* compliance (that is, they can perform their own tests, according to the many (and still being developed) standards specified by the directive). Tests cover power-line disruptions, high and low frequency electric and magnetic fields emitted, static discharges and more. It even covers design steps required to enhance immunity to EMP (nuclear electromagnetic pulse), which is the brief, but huge electromagnetic field produced by a nuclear explosions, and which can damage and even destroy electrical and electronic equipment far away from the actual explosion.

Manufacturers of compliant products can affix the "CE" (Communauté Européene) mark. Regulators can shut down networks which exceed the EMI (electromagnetic interference) limits.

See **COMPLIANT**, **EMF**, and **FCC PART15**.

EMF
Electromagnetic Field

The *electric* and *magnetic field* radiated by an electrical conductor.

EMFs are increasingly prevalent (and proximate), as they are generated by computers, cellular telephones, and other electronic devices. The EMFs generated have different frequencies (measured in hertz) and field strengths (measured in *teslas*, and are very dependent on the distance to, and configuration of, the source of the EMF). A hot topic these days, since there are some studies that almost link some of these emissions with harmful health effects.

Since the electromagnetic field may interfere with the operation of other equipment (one person's music is another's noise), the EMF is often referred to as *Electromagnetic Interference.* EMI) is usually a concern only for higher frequencies, and the radiated signal strengths allowed for these (that is, above 10 kHz) are regulated by the FCC (in the U.S.) and the DOC (in Canada).

There are no North American standards for low-frequency EMFs from electronic equipment, but compliance with the Swedish MPR II standard for computer monitors is widespread (those monitor manufacturers will do anything to sell more monitors). In 1995, the U.S. National Council on Radiation Protection and Measurements recommended that schools and playgrounds not be built where ambient 60 Hz magnetic fields exceed 200 nT.

Magnetic fields are produced by electrical conductors carrying currents. This higher the current, the greater the magnetic field. Electric fields are produced by high voltages (whether there is current or not). The higher the voltage, the greater the field. These fields are separately measurable only when close (less than a few wavelengths of the frequencies of interest) to the source. At greater distances, typically 3 to 10 m, the two fields are best measured as a single electromagnetic field.

EMFs are *non-ionizing radiation*, in that they do not have high enough energy (that is, they are not a high-enough frequency) to actually temporarily remove an electron from atoms (which would change the number of electrons per atom—this would *ionize* the atom, since it will then have a net charge). In contrast, the *microwaves* (so-called, since they are a high-enough frequency that their wavelength is less than a meter—officially 1 mm to 300 mm), such as those inside your microwave oven, and X-rays are ionizing radiation.

A WWW server with lots of EMF-related information is at the site *http://www.infoventures. microserve.com/emf/*. More information on this controversial topic is at *http:// www.ncf.carleton.ca/bridlewood-emfinfo/* and *http://www.milligauss.com/info.html*.

See **AMPS**, **ELF**, **EMC**, **EMI**, **ENCODING**, **FCC**, **FCC PART15**, **MPR II**, **T**, **TCO**, and **VLF**.

EMI
Electromagnetic Interference

The electromagnetic fields from one device that are interfering with the operation of some other device are called electromagnetic interference.

See **EMF**.

EmPower

A system to provide power at airplane seat positions, so passengers can power their notebook computers and other small electronic devices from the airplane's power system.

15 V DC is provided to a connector at each seat position. Users then require an adapter to convert this to the voltage (typically 6 to 30 volts) and connector style required by their computer.

A vendor of such adapters is at *http://www.xmpi.com*.

See **BATTERIES**.

Encapsulated PostScript

See **EPS**.

Encapsulation

Carrying frames of one protocol as the data in another, usually for one of the following reasons:

▲ The first protocol is not routable (such as LAT, NetBIOS, SDLC)—and many networks will not carry nonroutable protocols (since these networks are built using routers). Even for networks that can carry nonroutable protocols (using the bridging capability built in to most routers), it is usually not desirable since bridged networks do not scale well (bridging usually makes inefficient use of WAN links, and service interruptions often occur when network connectivity changes).

▲ So that only one protocol needs to be carried by the network—hopefully simplifying the WAN administration and router configuration.

▲ To encrypt the encapsulated protocol, for security purposes, while leaving the "wrapper" unencrypted so standard routers and networks can be used. This allows both the data being transferred, and the source and destination addresses (an important part of security) to be hidden from snoops.

Usually, the encapsulating protocol will be TCP/IP (it's so popular these days).

Unfortunately, encapsulation is usually undesirable, since it is inefficient. Each protocol (the encapsulator and the encapsulatee) has its own error detection and acknowledgments (wasting CPU time and WAN and router capacity), and the packets get needlessly larger (wasting more WAN capacity).

Also, handling broadcasts is difficult (the simplest option is to establish links to every possible broadcast destination and send the encapsulated broadcasts along each of them), so the number of broadcast destinations is usually limited—for example, to 10. Not a very scalable solution.

However, there *are* benefits, such as providing rerouting around network failures (this is part of what TCP/IP routing does) without dropping sessions. Without this rerouting, SNA traffic and users of Token Ring *source route bridging* get unceremoniously disconnected if the part of the network they are using goes down—even if other parts of the network that provide the connectivity they need are still up.

Also called *Tunneling*.

See **DLSW**, **MPTN**, **PPTP**, **SCALABLE ARCHITECTURE**, and **SPOOFING**.

Encoding

Encoding can mean many things, but a common use of the term in *synchronous data communications* combines the clock and data into a single signal. This is necessary since LAN and WAN links are typically only a single signal (in each direction), and both clock and data are needed to send synchronous data. The receiver uses the clock so that it can "lock on" to the exact data rate of the received data (by using a *digital phase locked loop circuit*, which adjusts its frequency according to the transitions received).

Encoding schemes are designed for specific features, such as the following:

▲ Self-clocking (at least one transition will occur during each bit-time, regardless of the data)

▲ No DC voltage (that is, the average voltage is zero—important for transformer-coupled circuits to prevent the transformers from saturating or over-heating)

▲ Lowest possible bandwidth (reducing the number of transitions to reduce radiated *Electromagnetic Interference*—EMI)

Since there are often conflicting requirements (most commonly self-clocking with low bandwidth), there are many encoding schemes, each optimized differently.

Some common encoding methods used are described in the following table and illustrated in the accompanying figure.

Encoding Method	Commonly used for	Description
Alternate Mark Inversion	T1	A pulse indicates a 1. No pulse indicates a 0. Each pulse is the opposite polarity of the previous.
Differential Manchester	Token Ring LANs	A transition at the start of each bit-time indicates a 0. No transition at the start of a bit-time indicates a 1. A transition at the center of each bit-time is used for the clock.

(table continued on next page)

Encoding Method	Commonly used for	Description
Manchester	Ethernet, IBM 3270 and AS/400 5250 terminals	The complement of the data is sent during the first half of each bit-time, followed by a transition to the opposite polarity (un-complemented data) at the center of each bit-time. This transition is used for the clock. Another way of saying this is that the direction of the transition at the center of the bit-time indicates the data (a rising edge is a 1, a falling edge is a 0). Another transition will be needed at the start of each bit-time if two consecutive bits are the same.
NRZ (Non Return to Zero)	Some IBM BISYNC environments	Actually, is not encoded. Just a confusing way of saying the binary data are sent as is.
NRZI (Non Return to Zero Inverted)	Most IBM BISYNC environments.	A transition at the start of each bit-time indicates a 0. No transition at the start of a bit-time indicates a 1. The data must have enough 0s to keep synchronization (for example, HDLC's *zero-bit stuffing* ensures this).
RZ (Return to Zero)	IrDA	Voltage goes high at beginning of bit time (and returns to zero at the center of the bit time) for a 1. Voltage stays at zero for a 0.

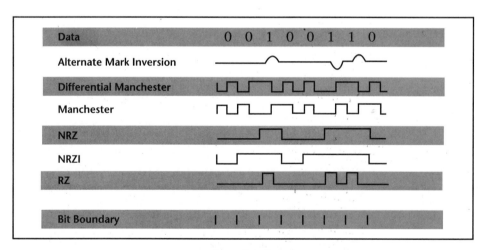

Encoding-1

See **S100BASET4, S100BASETX, S8B-10B, B8ZS, BAUD, BISYNC, EMF, ETHERNET, FDDI, HDSL, PPM, SYNCHRONOUS, T1,** and **TOKEN RING.**

Encryption

The process of changing a digital message (from *plaintext* to *ciphertext*) so that it can be read only by intended parties (also called *enciphering*), or to verify the identity of the sender (*authentication*), or to be assured that the sender really did send that message (*nonrepudiation*).

Some encryption schemes are described in the table below.

A *private key* (also called *secret key*, or *symmetric*) method has one key that is used to both encrypt and decrypt the message. Therefore the key must be kept secret (sometimes this is referred to as *closely held*). This makes the system more difficult to use, since the keys must be regularly changed, which requires secure distribution.

Public key encryption—PKE (or *asymmetric*) systems use two keys. One of the keys (called the *public, nonsecret* or *widely distributed* key) is used to encrypt messages, which can be decrypted only by using the secret corresponding decryption key (which only the intended recipient has). Or the secret key can be used to encrypt the message, and if it can be decrypted by using the public key, then the identity of the sender is assured. This brilliant concept was invented by Whitfield Diffie and Martin Hellman in 1976, when they were at Stanford University.

Some schemes provide authentication, to ensure that the message has not been modified without the sender's knowledge. Authentication can be added with a separate algorithm, such as the proposed digital signature standard.

Some schemes provide nonrepudiation, which provides the receiver with proof of who the sender is, so the sender cannot later deny sending the message ("*Hey, I'd never subscribe to a magazine like that!*").

Encryption Method	Key	Authentication	Comments
Clipper	Private	No	Uses an encryption algorithm called *Skipjack*. Developed by the U.S. National Security Agency. Proposed that the U.S. government keeps a copy of the decryption key for all encryption equipment produced.
DES (Data Encryption Standard)	Private	No	Currently very popular in the financial industry.
RSA (Rivest, Shamir, Adleman)	Public	Yes	The basis for the security in Netscape.

Many types of encryption technology (hardware units, or software) developed in Canada and the U.S. are restricted from being exported. For example, as of 1992 symmetric encryption keys larger than 40 bits (typically 56 bits and longer, or asymmetric keys larger than 512 bits—though there are some exceptions for small well-defined types of data, such as account numbers (and 56-bit key DES-encrypted financial data can be freely used worldwide for banking and financial transactions). The idea is that the U.S. should not be helping other countries to keep secrets from the U.S. Apparently, the U.S. government has computers that can decrypt messages encrypted with keys of 40 bits in less than a few days.

Energy Star

These regulations are made by the Offices of Defense Trade Controls and Munitions Control, U.S. Department of State. The actual Act (part of the U.S. Arms Export Control Act) is at *ftp://ftp.cygnus.com/pub/export/aeca.in.full*). Also, the International Traffic in Arms Regulation is at *ftp://ftp.cygnus.com/pub/export/itar.in.full*, and some of Cisco System's information on export and encryption is at *http://www.cisco.com/wwl/export/encrypt.html*.

For a good FAQ, call *http://www.rsa.com/pub/faq/faq.asc*. Many sources of encryption software and systems are listed at *http://www.tis.com*.

The Electronic Frontier Foundation has a great deal to say about the social impact of encryption. The Foundation has a WWW Server at *http://www.eff.org/*. Also, there is a good pointer page at *http://draco.centerline.com:8080/~franl/crypto.html*, and some information at *http://www.cryptography.com*.

See **AUTHENTICATION**, **DES**, **FAQ**, **IDEA**, **JAVA**, **KERBEROS**, **PGP**, **RSA**, **SSL**, and **WWW**.

Energy Star

A program of the Global Change Division of the U.S. Environmental Protection Agency to reduce the power requirements of PCs and their peripherals.

To receive certification (and be allowed to put the logo on the product), PCs and monitors must draw less than 30 watts each when in *low power state* (sometimes called *power save mode* or *suspend mode*). Some printers have an intermediate *stand-by mode* which has a faster turn-on time. Typically, the time before the printer switches to each mode is user-adjustable. Printers have the following requirements.

Printer Speed (pages per minute)	Default idle time until low power state (minutes)	Low power state power (Watts)
1 to 7	14	30
8 to 14	30	30
More than 15, and all color printers	60	45

Typical non–Energy Star PCs draw 150 watts (including the monitor).

In idle mode, Energy Star PCs shut off power to add-in boards (such as Ethernet cards). Therefore network connections (for example, to a file server) will be lost unless the board has been specifically designed for Energy Star PCs.

A list of Energy Star–compliant products is available by phoning 202-775-6650. Information is also available at the sites *http://www.epa.gov* and *http://www.epa.gov/ docs/energy_star*.

See **PC**.

EPP
Enhanced Parallel Port

An effort by Intel, Xircom, and Zenith Data Systems to define faster and bidirectional data transfer through a PC's parallel port.

Features include the following:

▲ Data transfer at up to 2 Mbytes/s

▲ Bidirectional 8-bit operation (a standard parallel port only has 4 input bits)

▲ Addressing to support multiple (daisy-chained) peripherals on a single PC parallel port

▲ Hardware strobe generation, so the PC software does not need to raise and drop the strobe line to the printer for each byte transferred; the PC's CPU can therefore use the very fast `rep outsb` instruction (repeat output string of bytes in sequential memory locations to the I/O port)

DMA is not supported (programmed or interrupt-based I/O is used).

Originally defined by its implementation by the Intel 360SL I/O integrated circuit (and called EPP v1.7). When the EPP group was merged into the IEEE 1284 multimodal port effort, the resulting IEEE 1284 EPP mode differed from EPP v1.7 enough that original EPP v1.7 peripherals are incompatible with the IEEE 1284 EPP parallel port. Newer EPP peripherals can be designed to be compatible with both the original EPP v1.7 and the IEEE 1284 EPP mode.

See **S1284**, **ECP**, **PARALLEL PORT**, and **PIO**.

EPS
Encapsulated PostScript

A PostScript file intended to be embedded in another document rather than printed directly (the "unencapsulated Postscript" format is used to print directly).

To elaborate, Adobe's *PostScript Page Description Language* is used for two purposes:

▲ As PostScript commands to be sent to a printer to print text, an image, or a combination of these. In this case these commands can be directly sent to a PostScript printer or stored on disk in a file (usually to be later sent to a printer). These files are called *PostScript* (PS) files.

▲ As PostScript commands (usually a file of commands that describe a graphic image) that are (or are to be) embedded in another document—for example, placing clip art (an image from a collection or created by using a different drawing program) into a word processing document. These files of commands are called *Encapsulated PostScript* (EPS) files.

That is, from your drawing program, you save your work in PostScript format if you will be printing the file. Save your work in encapsulated PostScript format if you will be embedding that file into another one.

EPS files consist of two parts:

▲ A preview image (often in TIFF or Macintosh PICT format) so that the image can be displayed and positioned when editing the document

▲ The actual PostScript commands that are required to generate the image (and that typically omit the PostScript `showpage` command which actually causes the image to be printed—since the entire document will be printed by using the document's word processing program)

Error-Correcting Code

Some notes on EPS files:

▲ EPS files are usually created by saving to that format; the original file (in Corel Draw or Adobe Illustrator format, for example) is usually the only one that can be subsequently edited.

▲ EPS files can be saved as ASCII or binary. ASCII files are stored as readable (by humans) PostScript, but are typically twice the size of the corresponding binary files—which use 8-bit codes that are not readable (by us).

At the beginning of the file, it will usually have EPSF 3.0, to identify the file's format to the document into which the file will be embedded.

▲ EPS files must produce an image that prints on a single page.

▲ EPS files usually cannot be edited from a word processing program.

▲ Usually, EPS files will not print if sent to a PostScript printer.

See **ADOBE, POSTSCRIPT TYPE 1 FONTS, POSTSCRIPT TYPE 3 FONTS**, and **TIFF**.

Error-Correcting Code

See **ECC**.

Error Detection and Correction

See **ECC**.

ES
End System

A host computer on an OSI network.

See **HOST, IS**, and **OSI**.

ESCON
Enterprise Systems Connection

A high-speed fiber-optic LAN for linking IBM mainframes to disk drives (DASD) or other mainframes. Links up to 3 km (and up to 15 miles with repeaters) are supported. Intended to replace the traditional IBM mainframe copper *Bus-and-Tag channel*, and compete with DEC's VAXcluster technology.

The original ESCON carried data at 10-Mbytes/s, and used multimode fiber optic cable and an LED light source. As part of ESCON II (which was introduced in 1991), 17-Mbyte/s transfer rates are now supported (though this requires a laser light source).

ESCON may support 27 Mbytes/s in the future.

ESCON never became as popular as (IBM) hoped, especially among smaller- and medium-sized shops.

See **CHANNEL, DASD, FEP, FIBER**, and **MAINFRAME**.

ESF
Extended Superframe

A framing standard for T1 that provides many useful benefits.

T1 uses a 193-bit frame (which is sent 8,000 times per second, which is every 125 μs). In each frame there are 24 channels, each carrying 8 bits of information, plus a framing bit.

In *Basic Superframe* (SF, also called D4 framing), 12 consecutive 193-bit frames comprise a *superframe*. (D3 framing had only 2 193-bit frames.) The 12 framing bits in this 12-frame superframe (one framing bit per 193-bit frame) goes through the 12-bit pattern 100011011100. That is, the framing bit is a 1 in the first frame, then 0 for each of the next three frames, then a 1 for the next two frames, and so on. By looking for this specific pattern in every 193rd bit, the receiver can establish *frame synchronization*—and then identify which 8 bits are for which of the 24 channels.

Extended Superframe extends this to not only provide frame synchronization, but also error detection and a data channel, all using the framing bit. In this case, 24 consecutive 193-bit frames make up an *Extended Superframe*, and the framing bit goes through a 24-bit cycle:

▲ Every fourth bit of this 24-bit cycle (that is, the framing bits for frames 4, 8, 12, 16, 20, and 24) goes through the pattern 001011 (note that this pattern never looks like a shifted copy of itself). This provides the frame synchronization.

▲ The framing bits for frames 2, 6, 10 (and so on) are used to send a 6-bit CRC, generated from the data in the previous 24 frames. This provides error detection. The receiving CSU can then track the error rate and generate an alarm if it gets too high. (This error checking is done constantly while the link is in service and for any type of data—neat, huh?)

▲ The remaining framing bits (for frames 1, 3, 5, 7, and so on) provide a 4,000-bits/s supervisory data channel that is used for other functions such as remote configuration and monitoring of CSUs. This data channel is usually called a *facility data link* (FDL).

See **B8ZS**, **CRC**, **CSU/DSU**, **E1**, **PCM**, and **T1**.

ESMR
Enhanced Specialized Mobile Radio

A two-way radio technology developed by Motorola and implemented in its *Motorola Integrated Radio System* (MIRS, announced in 1991). It was first implemented in Los Angeles in 1994. Motorola calls the current implementation of their technology *Integrated Dispatch Enhanced Network* (iDEN).

Uses TDMA technology to put six simultaneous conversations into one traditional 25-kHz UHF radio channel (in the 806- to 821-MHz band traditionally used by SMR).

Is overlapping-cell-based (like traditional AMPS cellular telephone), but cells are larger. Can do seamless hand-off (also like traditional cellular telephone) but is more complex.

In one handset, provides simultaneous:

▲ Cellular Telephone; to compete with traditional AMPS service as well as PCS

▲ Mobile Dispatch; the traditional use for the SMR service but with a wider range, and easy-to-use support for conference calls to selected groups (such as all your sales staff)

▲ Radio Paging; to compete with traditional alphanumeric pagers (but the pager can be an integrated part of your handset)

▲ Mobile messaging. Typically 140-character messages can be received to your handset, and sent (using sequences of numeric keypad presses to generate the letters).

Mobile data; at 4,800 bits/s. This competes with Ardis and Mobitex, and maybe CDPD and maybe GSM (what an alphabet soup!)—though it isn't yet available for many systems.

Has had a rough (perhaps ongoing) time becoming a reliable system with acceptable voice quality.

The hope is that the more efficient channel usage for dispatch will justify the technology and that the additional capabilities (such as paging integrated with a cellular telephone) will make it more desirable than other technologies. Expected to be most competitive for users who need more than one service (cellular telephone with mobile dispatch or radio paging, for example).

Some people try to pronounce this as *E-smur*.

Clearnet Communications Inc. offers ESMR service in Canada, and Nextel Communications offers the service in the U.S. (and there is a roaming agreement between the two service providers).

See **AMPS**, **ARDIS**, **CDPD**, **GSM**, **MOBITEX**, **MOTOROLA**, **SMR**, **PCS**, **PCTS**, **TDMA**, and **WIRELESS**.

ESP
Enhanced Serial Port

A PC serial port technology intended to handle bit rates faster than 38,400 bits/s.

Developed by Hayes Microcomputer products to handle higher-speed serial communications. It uses a standard 16550 buffered UART (and powers on to act as a standard 16550 serial port), but has an on-board processor and includes the following features:

▲ 1 kbyte receive and transmit buffers each. This reduces the number of times the PC's CPU must get involved with the data communications (this reduces processor loading)

▲ Support for DMA transfers between the ESP and PC's memory (this reduces the CPU time and the bus loading required to transfer the data)

Requires special communications drives (which are available for both OS/2 and Windows).

Not widely implemented.

More information is at *http://www.hayes.com/esp.htm*.

See **S16550A**, **DMA**, **EIA-TIA232**, and **UART**.

Ethernet

The predecessor to the IEEE's 802.3 CSMA/CD local area network standard (although the terms Ethernet and 802.3 are usually used interchangeably now).

Ethernet differs in many minor (but often—for network administrators—crucial) ways from 802.3. For example, the type of grounding for the transceiver cable and the use of the type/length field of the frame (that is, the frame format is different).

Named after the "ether" which was thought to be the medium through which electromagnetic waves propagated. The story goes that in the 1800's, learned people figured out that sound couldn't go through a vacuum; some medium such as air or water was needed. They then wondered what medium the light and heat from the sun needed. While they knew that there was no air in space, they drew an analogy and decided that there had to be *something* up there and called it the ether. Learned people now know that electromagnetic waves *can* propagate through a complete vacuum, and there is no "ether." As a play on this concept, the name Ethernet was chosen for the LAN. The medium was initially a thick (about 1 cm in diameter) coaxial cable, usually yellow (the specification actually required any color other than black, to distinguish it from power cables), and specially designed for the purpose (for example, it had 4 layers of shielding).

Ethernet LAN drivers can often report the following statistics.

▲ *Runts*—illegally-short (less than 64 bytes, including the frame overhead, but not the preamble) frames. These will also have a CRC error, since Ethernet requires frames to be at least 64 bytes in length (shorter frames are padded-up automatically by the Ethernet adapter or driver). Runts are typically generated during a collision, when two or more stations transmit simultaneously, and they stop as soon as they detect they are part of a collision.

▲ *Alignment errors*; frames which are not an exact multiple of 8 bits in length. These will also have a CRC error, since Ethernet requires frames to have 46 to 1,500 bytes (of exactly 8 bits each) of user data in them (the 18 bytes of frame overhead results in a frame size of 64 to 1,518 bytes).

▲ *CRC* (or *FCS*) *errors*; frames which have been corrupted (some of the 1 bits were changed to 0s, and/or vice versa), due to noise or a collision.

▲ *Jabber errors*; illegally-long (more than 1,518 bytes) frames.

Ethernet is installed on about 100 million network connections world-wide (in 1997), and is used for over 80% of all desktop network connections. For a while Token Ring was being installed at a greater rate (and there were predictions that Token Ring would overtake Ethernet by about 1992, but this never happened). Token Ring has always, and continues to generally cost more, and have less test and networking equipment available. Most new technologies (such as switching, 100 Mbit/s operation and RMON) are developed for Ethernet first, making Ethernet more desirable (and further enticing development of new things for Ethernet before Token Ring).

Ethernet was invented by Robert Metcalfe, with some aspects based on the Alohanet radio-based network, which was developed by Norman Abramson and Franklin Kuo at the University of Hawaii for communication between the islands and the University. It ran at 4,800 bits/s, and data was sent in packets. The idea was that when one station transmitted, all other stations received the message—but only kept the data if the message was addressed to them. As in any conversation, if two or more stations transmitted at the same time, then the transmitters would pause, and retransmit later.

Some substantial differences from Alohanet are that Ethernet has;

▲ no central controller (all stations directly transmit to destination stations)

▲ a single transmission channel and messages have both the source and destination address (Alohanet used one frequency to send to the central controller, and a second to listen to it)

▲ the capability to sense other stations transmitting (Alohanet could not do this because only the central controller received on the frequency on which the other stations transmitted)

▲ back-off (and an exponential one at that), where after stations detect that they were part of a collision, they wait a random amount of time (in multiples of 51.2 µs—the minimum message duration) before retransmitting (and each successive collision causes them to choose a random wait from a range of times that are double the previous range)

▲ a transmission speed of 10 Mbits/s (compared to Ahohanet's thousands of bits/s)

Ethernet was first implemented in 1973 on the Xerox Alto computer, which was developed at Xerox's Palo Alto Research Center (PARC), by Metcalf and David Boggs. Due to the clock speed of the Alto, Ethernet was first implemented at 2.944 Mbits/s.

Xerox patented Ethernet in 1975. The work was first publicly described in a paper Metcalf co-authored, which was published in the July 1976 *Communications of the Association of Computing Machinery*, titled *Ethernet: Distributed Packet Switching for Local Computer Networks*. In 1979 Metcalfe was working at DEC, and suggested DEC work with Xerox on implementing Ethernet for DEC minicomputers. In 1980, DEC, Intel and Xerox proposed the DIX standard to the IEEE, to become a de jure standard.

Some Ethernet references are at *http://www.ots.utexas.rdu/ethernet/*.

See **S10BASET**, **S100BASET**, **S3COM**, **S802.3**, **CABLE**, **COS2** (*Class of Service*), **CSMACD**, **ENCODING**, **GIGABIT ETHERNET**, **LAN**, **SWITCHED LAN**, and **TOKEN RING**.

Ethernet II

The frame format usually used by DEC's DECnet and LAT, and by Apple's AppleTalk Phase 1 on 802.3 LANs.

See **S802.3** and **LAT**.

ETSI
European Telecommunications Standards Institute

Used to be called CEPT.

See **E1**.

EVC
Enhanced Video Connector

The new and improved connector to replace the 15-pin D-subminiature connector used on video adapters, to connect to VGA (and higher resolution) video monitors (the VGA connector can handle a maximum frequency of about 150 to 180 MHz, which is not enough for the higher resolutions and vertical refresh frequencies planned for future video monitors).

The connector itself looks like a more dense D-subminiature type, as it has 30 pins (arranged as 3 rows of 10 pins) for the "lower-speed" analog and digital signals, plus a four pins in a square matrix pattern, with a ground plane in a cross shape between them (the horizontal part of the cross is part of the male connector on the cable, the vertical part is in the female connector which is part of the monitor). The connector manufacturer (Molex Electronics) therefore calls the connector *MicroCross*. The ground plane blades are longer than the signal pins, so the ground is established before the signals—this ensures that the connector can be *hot-plugged* (connected while the equipment is powered on) with no damage. The connector is rated for 5,000 mating and unmating cycles.

The 4 matrix pins and ground plane becomes a low-cost 75 Ω 4-signal coaxial cable connector, and these are the high-speed pins which are used for the separate red, green and blue (RGB) analog video signals, and a pixel clock signal (the horizontal and vertical synchronization signals are the low-speed pins).

The enhanced capabilities of EVC include support for the following:

▲ Higher display resolutions, horizontal scan frequencies and refresh rates, since it is capable of handling signals of 2 to 4 GHz on the "coaxial" high-speed pins.

▲ DDC, for *plug and play* support. This uses 3 pins, for the serial clock and data signals, and the ground pin.

▲ USB, so the monitor can be a USB hub, and provide a convenient connection point for a keyboard, mouse and other devices. This uses 2 pins for the bidirectional data pair of conductors, and shares power pins with other optional uses on the EVC connector.

▲ IEEE 1394 (FireWire), so video cameras can be connected. This uses 7 pins.

▲ Y/C video signal (separate and in addition to the RGB signal on the coax pins. These support standard NTSC or PAL color television monitors. This requires 3 pins, for the Y, C and ground pins.

▲ Stereo analog input and output. For example, to support speakers and microphones. This uses 6 pins (including the ground return for each of the input and output).

▲ +5 V DC power, for example to charge batteries in portable devices attached to the monitor.

In addition, two pins on the connector are undefined and reserved for future use.

Supporting any or all of the 3 popular types of serial buses (DDC, USB and IEEE 1394 enbles the monitor to become a hub for the connection of peripherals (since the monitor is usually more accessible than a PC's system unit).

Extranet

It is expected that subsets of these above capabilities will be implemented on actual monitors. The basic set of signals include the video and DDC signals. For multimedia support, the audio signals are added. For a full configuration, the remainder of the signals are added.

EVC was developed by VESA.

See **S1394, COLOUR, DDC, PLUG AND PLAY, USB, VESA**, and **VGA**.

Extranet

An IP-based network that facilitates information flow between a company and its trading partners.

Just as an *intranet* uses WWW servers for a company's internal staff, an extranet does this for a company's vendors, customers, and suppliers. Firewalls and other security measures provide access only to specific company resources.

See **INTERNET2**, and **INTRANET**.

F

Fab
Fabrication Plant

The integrated circuit manufacturing industry's name for the facility used to manufacture integrated circuits. Modern plants, capable of building high-end microprocessors, cost at least 1 billion dollars (that's $1,000,000,000.00—too big a number for the MICR-coding on a single check—I guess these things are paid for using a charge card). While ultra-clean on the inside, they use many very nasty chemicals, and environmental issues are often an issue.

The Integrated Circuits are chemically etched and deposited onto *wafers*. These are flat, round crystalline silicon slices, cut (like a salami) from a long cylinder of silicon which is slowly grown in extremely controlled conditioned). Each *die* (individual little square or rectangle) is then cut from the wafer, and usually packaged in an plastic epoxy or ceramic package. For example, the Pentium uses a *pin grid array* (PGA) package, which can be inserted into a socket. To reduce package size (crucial for laptop computers) a *tape carrier package* (TCP) can be used. It mounts the die on flexible tape (about the size of a dime for a Pentium), and this is soldered directly to the main motherboard (the printed circuit board).

The table below shows (very approximately) the following:

▲ When each size of wafer began being manufactured; larger wafers allow more ICs to be made per wafer, but the equipment is much more expensive.

▲ The line width (in microns, which are millionths of a meter) of the IC conductors; the smaller the lines, the more transistors can be stuffed into a smaller IC die (the actual chip that has the circuitry on it), and (usually) the faster it runs. For example, Intel's Pentium and Pentium Pro processors initially used a 0.35µ process, and current laboratory work is working on 0.18µ. As a side point, the Pentium has a die size of 91 mm^2, the Pentium Pro is 196 mm^2 and the Pentium II is 203 mm^2.

▲ The cost of a typical fabrication plant.

See **GAAS**, **INTEL**, **MICR**, **MOORES**, **SI**, and **ZIF**.

Facsimile

Year	Wafer Diameter (")	Line Width (μ)	Plant Cost ($ millions)
1968	2	10	5
1970		8	25
1973	3	5	50
1978	4	2	75
1982		1.5	100
1986	6	1.0	300
1991		0.8	400
1993	8[a]	0.5	900
1996		0.35 [b]	1,100
2000		0.25	1,300

a. Also called 200 mm.
b. For example, the initial 200 MHz Pentium Pro processors use a 0.35μ process.

Facsimile

See **FAX**.

FAQ
Frequently Asked Questions

A file on an online service of the most frequently asked questions and their answers. It is good etiquette to read this before posting questions (which may have already been frequently asked—and patiently and expertly answered).

Many Internet Usenet FAQs are on the ftp site *ftp://rtfm.mit.edu/pub/usenet-by-group/* which is often too busy; a mirror of it is at *ftp://ftp.uu.net/usenet/news.answers/*.

The uu.net site compresses such text files using a UNIX program called compress, and such compressed files have the filename extension .z (for example, noodle.z). To view these files from a PC, you need an uncompress program. Many such freeware and shareware programs are available, such as decomp2.zip at *ftp://ftp.uu.net/pub/OS/msdos/simtel/compress/*. Unfortunately, this file itself is compressed using pkzip (you need pkunzip or a work-alike). After you finally get the file uncompressed, you find that each line of a UNIX text file is terminated by a line feed only (which they call an end of line), not by carriage return *and* line feed (which is what PCs typically expect). Either import the ASCII file into a word processor (which usually fixes the line feed problem), or use a utility like crlf.com (you can search for the pkunzip and crlf utilities on CompuServe, using the GO IBMFF forum).

Of course, you can avoid this entire headache and get the FAQs from *http://www.cis.ohio-state.edu/hypertext/faq/usenet/FAQ-List.html*, where they are uncompressed and don't have the line feed problem. BUT the best place I've found for FAQs is definitely *http://www.faqs.org/faqs* (which is the same as *http://www.landfield.com/faqs*).

FAQs are very highly recommended reading (if there is one there for your topic).

See **RTFM**.

Fast-20

See **SCSI2**, and **SCSI3**.

Fast ATA

An interface that is used to connect a computer to a hard disk drive.

A faster IDE-type hard disk interface developed and promoted by Seagate Technology. It supports Mode 3 PIO), so can transfer data at 11.1 Mbytes/s. Using DMA, it can transfer data at 13.3 Mbytes/s (using *Mode 1 Multiword DMA*).

These rates are specified by the *Small Form Factor Committee*.

Supports drives larger than the IDE limitation of 504 Mbytes.

Competes with Western Digital's Enhanced IDE (E-IDE), and IBM and Toshiba's ATA-2.

Seagate has a WWW server at *http://www.seagate.com*.

See **ATA 2**, **DISK DRIVE**, **DMA**, **EIDE**, **IDE**, **FAST ATA2**, **PIO**, **SCSI1**, and **SMALL FORM FACTOR COMMITTEE**.

Fast ATA-2

Seagate Technology's enhancement to their Fast ATA. Fast ATA-2 supports Mode 4 PIO and also Mode 2 Multiword DMA, both of which transfer data at a burst rate of 16.6 Mbytes/s.

Competes with Western Digital's E-IDE.

See **FAST ATA**.

Fast IDE

Same as Enhanced IDE.

See **EIDE**.

Fast Ethernet

See **S100BASET**.

FAT
File Allocation Table

DOS's disk-based file system.

By using DOS's `fdisk` utility, a physical disk can be divided in one or more *partitions* (or *volumes*). DOS supports up to four partitions per physical disk.

A partition is represented by a single drive letter and has a *file allocation table* (in fact there is usually also a backup copy of the FAT), which is a sequence of up to 65,536 16-bit pointers (or *entries*).

A DOS disk is formatted into 512-byte *sectors*, and 2^n (4, 8, 16, 32, etc.) sequential and contiguous sectors are grouped into a *cluster* (which is sometimes called an *allocation unit*). A cluster is the smallest amount of disk space that can be allocated to a file.

Each of the FAT entries (the first of the sequence through to the last, up to number 65,535) corresponds to the first through to the last of the clusters in the partition. The 16-bit value stored in each of the FAT entries points to the cluster that is the next part of the file.

Some FAT entries are reserved for other uses:

▲ All zeros mean that the cluster is unallocated

▲ All ones (except for the last 4 bits) means it is the last cluster of the file

Because a partition can be a maximum of (only) 65,536 clusters, the larger the partition, the larger the cluster size must be.

For example, a disk with a cluster size of 8,192 bytes (that is, each cluster is 16 sequential 512-byte sectors) can have up to (8,192 bytes per cluster × 65,636 clusters per partition =) 536,870,912 bytes (which is 512 Mbytes) per partition.

On average, each file will waste half a cluster (since, depending on the exact file size, the last cluster in a file could have anywhere from 1 byte to a full cluster of data). Therefore, a smaller cluster size is usually desirable. As the partition size increases, the amount of disk space wasted per file also increases. If the files stay the same average size, then the percentage of larger-partition disks that is wasted increases at the same rate that the partition size increases.

This means that partitioning a large disk into several smaller partitions (so that DOS can use smaller clusters) is usually desirable (though many disk compression programs can use this otherwise-wasted space, providing better disk utilization).

Other reasons for partitioning a disk into more than one partition include using a different type of file system for some partitions (to support a different operating system that can be booted) and reducing the area over which the disk's read/write head must seek for files on a partition, which speeds access time.

A reason for not wanting a small partition size is that the smaller the partition, the smaller the cluster size and therefore the more pieces a file will be stored in—and each piece can be stored in a different part of the partition (rather than all sequentially), slowing file access. This is called disk or file fragmentation.

A file's *directory entry* is a 32-byte data structure that has the file's:

▲ 11-character (which is displayed in 8.3 format) name

▲ Pointer to the first cluster of the file

▲ Size (in bytes)

▲ Date and time of creation (or last modification)

▲ Attribute byte (starting at bit 0, the six attribute bits are read-only, hidden, system, volume label, subdirectory, and archive).

A partition's root directory (files in D:*.*, for example) is usually a fixed size of 16 kbytes (which allows for 512 file and subdirectory entries in the partition's root directory).

Subdirectories (D:\WP60*.*, for example) are like normal files and can be extended in size (as more files or subdirectories are created), one cluster at a time.

DOS (and Windows 3.1 and Windows 95—see below) 16-bit FAT cluster sizes are listed in the following table.

Partition Size[a] (Mbytes)		Cluster Size	Average Wasted per File
From	To	(bytes)	
1.44 (diskettes)		512	256
	<16[b]	4,096	2,048
16	<128	2,048	1,024
128	<256	4,096	2,048
256	<512	8,192	4,096
512	<1,024	16,384	8,192
1,024	<2,048[c]	32,768	16,384
2,048	<4,096	65,536	32,768

a. Including the space used by directories.
b. Before DOS 3.0, the FAT had only 12 bits per entry, allowing for a maximum of 2^{12} clusters (though actually only 4,078 clusters could be used, as 18 of the 4,096 cluster values are reserved for other uses—such as $FFF7_{16}$ for marking clusters with sectors that can reliably store data) per volume. Even for current DOS versions, floppy diskettes and hard disk volumes smaller than 16 Mbytes use a 12-bit FAT. 12-bit FAT hard disks usually use 4,096-byte clusters. A 16-bit FAT also reserves 18 cluster entries, leaving $2^{16} - 18 = 65,518$ clusters for data storage.
c. The maximum DOS and Windows 95 partition size is 65,518 x 32,768 = 2,146,893,824 bytes (which is about 2 Gbytes).

Therefore it is best to use a partition size of just under 512 or 256 Mbytes (that is, 511 Mbytes or 255 Mbytes):

▲ Equaling those sizes exactly would double the space wasted per file

▲ Sizes smaller than those would be inconveniently small (except, perhaps, for a partition that will store only smaller user data files, not application or operating system software)

▲ Sizes larger than those would waste too much space per partition

Windows 95 uses a *Virtual File Allocation Table* (VFAT) as its file system (also called FAT32). So that it can be DOS- and Windows 3.1-compatible, it is still limited to about 65,000 entries, so it has the same wasted cluster size problem as the 16-bit FAT system It uses 4 kbyte cluster sizes for disk partitions up to 8 Gbytes, 8 kbyte clusters for disks up to 16 Gbytes, 16 kbyte clusters for disks up to 32 Gbytes, and 32 kbyte clusters for disks equal to or greater than 32 Gbytes. Some other features of the VFAT system are the following:

▲ 255-character filenames (including both upper-case and lower-case characters and multiple periods)

▲ A maximum disk size of 2 Tbytes (2,199,023,255,552 bytes)

▲ FAT-compatibility (by storing an 8.3-style filename for each file, which is used for DOS access)

▲ A smarter disk space allocation algorithm, which reduces disk fragmentation (a file being stored in noncontiguous clusters, which results in longer file access times)

Newer hard disk formats, such as IBM's OS/2 *High Performance File System* (HPFS), Microsoft Windows' NT *NT File System* (NTFS—which cannot be read by Windows 95), and Novell NetWare's have the following:

▲ Filenames that are up to 254 characters and can contain lowercase letters (and even spaces and multiple periods)

▲ Smaller clusters (OS/2 always uses 512-byte clusters, Windows NT limits the maximum cluster size to 4 kbytes), regardless of the disk size

▲ *Lazy Writes* (also called *Write-behind* or *Write-back Caching*), which accept the data from an application immediately (making it believe that the disk write has been completed) and later write them to disk (if the disk write later fails, the file system writes to a different location on the disk, marking the first one so that the file system does not attempt to use it again)

▲ A smarter disk-space allocation algorithm, to reduce disk fragmentation

Note, however, that these operating systems file systems' support for floppy diskette drives always uses the DOS FAT system (8.3-style filenames, etc.).

Therefore (for hard disks), the average disk space wasted per file, for HPFS and NTFS, is only 256 bytes. NTFS supports clusters of up to 4,096 bytes (which are more efficient than 512-byte clusters but are used only for full clusters).

Disk data compression programs, such as DoubleSpace, DriveSpace and Stacker make use of all the storage space in clusters, so none is wasted. As a side point, PowerQuest Corp. sells a utility that can change partition sizes without reformatting your hard disk. They are at *http://www.powerquest.com*.

Microsoft's newer file system, called FAT32, supports disks up to 2 Tbytes, and more clusters per partition (so large partitions no longer have huge cluster sizes).

See **CACHE**, **DISK DRIVE**, **DISK FORMATTING**, **STAC**, and **TIMESTAMP**.

FAX
Facsimile

Those amazing machines (or boards in PCs) that can send and receive images of letters and drawings over a telephone line. Now so popular that many surveys show that fax traffic accounts for about 40% of the long distance telephone costs for larger companies, and about 35% of all U.S. long distance traffic.

Currently, Group III machines are the most common (though other types of machines are standardized). The *group* specifies the digitization and compression scheme, as shown in the following table.

Group	CCITT Standard	Year Released	Transmission Time per Page[a] Many nonstandard systems were used before Group I, primarily by the newspaper industry.
I	T.2	1968	4 to 6 minutes (depending on the length of the page), plus 30 seconds between pages (to change the page); sends 180 lines per minute, since the drum (on which the page to be sent was mounted) rotated 180 times per minute; scans at 98 lines per inch.
II		1976	2 to 3 minutes, plus 30 seconds between pages; sends 360 lines per minute and scans at 100 lines per inch.
III	T.4 and T.30	1980	9 to 50 seconds (at 9,600 bits/s), plus 15 seconds negotiation before first page.
IV	T.6	1984	3 to 12 seconds (at 64,000 bits/s).

a. Depends on resolution selected and the image sent.

Group III machines use the following modem modulations:

▲ V.29, at 9,600 (with fallback to 7,200) bits/s. This is by far the most common supported and used for the actual transmission of the fax image.

▲ V.27*ter*, at 4,800 (with fallback to 2,400) bits/s. This is automatically used on poor phone lines (or those with voice data compression or perhaps on cellular telephone connections).

▲ Sometimes V.17, at 14,400 (with fallback to 12,000) bits/s. This capability is built-in to most fax modems and boards, but only in higher-performance fax machines (perhaps because faster and more expensive mechanical components are needed).

Also, half-duplex V.21 modem modulation at 300 bits/s is used for the initial negotiation phase. This is specified in T.30 and described below.

The basic Group III resolutions are as follows:

▲ 1,728 pels in a scan width of 215 mm (this is about 8.5 inches and so is about 203 pels per inch)

▲ 3.85 or optionally 7.7 scan lines per mm (this is about 98 or 196 per inch)

These are summarized in the table below.

	Resolution		Bits per Square Inch	Relative Size of Image Data
	Horizontal (pels/inch)	Vertical (lines/inch)		
Standard	203	98	19,894	1
Fine	203	196	39,788	2
Super Fine[a]	203	392	79,576	4
Ultra Fine[b]	406	392	159,152	8

a. This remains a proprietary feature, only working between machines from the same manufacturer.
b. Standardized only for smaller page sizes, such as A6, and rarely implemented.

A scan width of 2,560 pels is optional. This would support a width of up to 12.6 inches (for example, to fax a B size 11" × 17" page).

Here is a summary of the sequence of a fax call:

▲ After dialing the called fax machine's telephone number (and before it answers), the calling Group III fax machine (optionally) begins sending a *calling tone* (CNG). This is a repeated $\frac{1}{2}$-second duration 1,100-Hz tone, with a 3-second pause between tones, which can be used by an automatic Voice/Data/Fax switch to connect the call as required.

▲ When the called fax machine answers, it replies with a 3-second 2,100-Hz tone, the *Called Station Identification* (CED).

▲ The two fax machines then communicate using 300-bits/s, V.21 modulation. This is an old, slow, reliable, full-duplex (though the fax machines interact half-duplex) modem modulation that uses *Frequency Shift Keying* (FSK). FSK which uses one tone to send a "1" and another for a "0"—this produces a distinctive warbly sound when carrying data. HDLC framing is used, with a 16-bit CRC and 256 (the default) or (optionally) 64-byte frames.

▲ The communication begins with the called (answering) fax machine sending the calling fax a 20-character identifying message. The standard allows this message to carry only the numbers, "+", and a space, but some fax machines support letters as well. This message is called the *Called Subscriber Identification* (CSI). It is manually programmed into each fax machine and is supposed to be the answering fax machine's telephone number in international format (for example +1-416-555-0641). The calling fax machine usually shows this on its LCD display.

The called fax machine then sends a 32-bit *Digital Identification Signal* (DIS), which requests the following:

▲ Bit rate to be used for fax transmission

▲ Time required to print a scan line (defaults to 20 ms but can also be specified as 0, 5, 10, or 40 ms; 0 ms is specified if the receiving fax machine can receive into buffer memory, to speed up the fax transmission)

Computer Dictionary

▲ Fax resolution

▲ Maximum paper size; support for specifying the A5 and A6 paper size is included in a larger (40-bit instead of 32-bit) DIS

The calling (transmitting) fax machine sends the called fax a *Calling Subscriber Identification* (CIG, though sometimes people make up new acronyms, and call this a *Transmit Station Identification*, or TSI). It is (typically) a 25-character (maximum) company or user name (as configured in advance through cryptic button-pushes on the calling fax). The receiving fax may show this information on its LCD display and include it in a log that can later be printed. Along with other information, such as time, date, and page count, the calling fax usually includes the CIG in the fax image sent to the called fax; this is called the TTI (Terminal Transmission Identifier). The U.S. telephone Consumer Protection Act of 1991 requires that the date and time sent and the sending organization's or individual's name and telephone number be at the top of at least the first fax page sent (though the significance of this with portable PCs with fax modems is questionable).

The calling fax then sends the called fax machine a *Digital Command Signal* (DCS), which confirms which options requested in the DIS will be used for the call; that is, the called and calling fax machines do a one-round-trip negotiation to agree on the options. These options are based on those requested and the capabilities of the called fax machine.

A test data transmission is then done at the agreed bit rate, and the fax machines switch back to 300-bits/s mode to confirm that the transmission was successful. If not, then a lower speed is used. Otherwise, page transmission begins.

After each page, the fax machines switch back to 300-bits/s mode to determine whether there are more pages to be sent.

Group III fax machines usually negotiate a scan width of 1,728 pels per row, which is used for a scan width of 215 mm (this is about 8.46"). This is used for both North American standard A-size $8\frac{1}{2}$" × 11" paper and Metric A4 (210 mm × 297 mm) paper.

These 1,728 pels are compressed using a data compression scheme that first looks for sequences of pels set to the same value in the horizontal raster scans of the source document and produces a count of the number of repetitions of that value (this is called *Run Length Encoding*—RLE).

Then a lookup table is used that produces bit patterns that are shorter to represent the more commonly expected counts. This form of data compression is called *Modified Huffman Encoding* and is often called MH in fax machine specifications. Almost all fax machines support this.

The table is designed to compresses long sequences of white space better than black (since this is what documents typically have). For example, an all-white row requires only nine bits. This is called *one-dimensional* compression. At *fine* Group III resolution, a single page is about 3,800,000 bits (464 kbytes). By using only one-dimensional compression, this can be compressed to 20 to 50 kbytes, depending on the image.

Group III fax machines can also use *two-dimensional* compression (though not all machines implement it), in which only the difference between the current and the previous (one-dimensional compressed) scan row is sent. This is called *Modified Read* (MR), and allows a typical fax page to be sent in 15% less time than MH-only encoding. To reduce the impact of scan rows lost due to line noise, this is limited to two rows for standard resolution and four rows for fine resolution (following a one-dimensionally compressed row). *Modified Modified Read* (MMR) encoding allows a fax page to be sent in 10% less time than MR-only encoding.

For example, at *standard* Group III resolution, a single page is about 250 kbytes; by using two-dimensional compression, this can be compressed to about 25 to 80 kbytes (10:1 to 3:1 compression).

Since Group IV fax machines always use error correction, there is no limit to the number of rows that can be two-dimensionally compressed (this is specified in T.6). Group IV machines typically have 50% better data compression than Group III.

Both one-dimensional and two-dimensional compression are examples of *lossless data compression*.

At the receiving end, if after decompressing each row of received data, the receiver does not get exactly 1,728 pels, then it knows that a data transmission error occurred. The corrupted row is ignored, and in its place, either the previous (good) row is repeated or a blank (white) row is used.

Some fax machines will request a retransmission of the entire page if that page had more than 32 or 64 (depending on the implementation) corrupted rows. Most transmitting fax machines ignore these requests (since the paper has already been scanned and the fax did not keep a copy to retransmit).

The T.30 standard also specifies an optional *Error-Correcting Mode* (ECM), which supports retransmitting corrupted rows (rather than the entire page).

Since ECM slightly increases fax transmission time and most fax calls have very few errors, most fax machines with ECM can be set to disable the feature.

Group IV machines require 56,000- or 64,000-bits/s communications (a switched 56 or ISDN B channel), and have selectable resolutions of 200×200, 300×300, and 400×400 dots per inch.

Work on the Group V standard shows that it may support color, and higher transmission speeds such as ISDN's H_{11} (1.544 Mbits/s).

A fax board's *service class* specifies how much of the work is done by a Group III fax board (the rest being done by the PC) and is also an extension to the *Hayes AT* command set, since it describes the commands supported by a fax modem.

Class 1 fax boards are defined in EIA/TIA-578 (*Service Class 1 Asynchronous Facsimile DCE Control Standard*) and the subsequent EIA Technical Systems Bulletin 43 (TSB-43). ITU-T's T.31 is an international version of the standard but includes some extra functions. Class 1 fax boards perform only the simplest functions such as:

▲ Converting the *asynchronous* data from the PC to *synchronous* HDLC data

▲ Generating and detecting the handshaking tones before a fax transmission

▲ Generating and checking for HDLC flags and performing HDLC zero-bit stuffing and deletion

The PC does everything else, such as the image rasterization and data compression. Many fax protocol functions are very timing-sensitive, which can be a problem for PCs with multi-tasking operating systems—especially UNIX, which is usually not good at meeting such *real-time* requirements.

However, Class 1 fax boards are the most flexible, since almost all functions are done in software on the PC, such as the following:

▲ Error-correcting mode (which is specified in T.30)

▲ *Adaptive answering*, in which the fax board (which also has a data modem) decides whether an incoming call is a fax or data call and handles it accordingly (this function usually can be performed only by a Class 1 fax board)

In addition to the Class 1 functions, *Class 2*–based fax boards perform the following functions (so the PC does not need to):

▲ *Line supervision* (that is, establishing and clearing the call)

▲ Support of error-correcting mode (though this is not widely implemented)

Note that not all Class 2 fax boards provide a Class 1 software interface (that is, they do the Class 1 functions, but this is built-in to the fax board, with no Class 1 software interface provided to external programs).

Because of the long time between the availability of the first drafts of the Class 2 standard (SP-2388, document TR-29/89-21R8, dated March 21, 1990, and a later version released August 1990) and the final approved standard (EIA/TIA/ANSI –592, released November 1992, with first products available in 1994), many fax boards (still) support only the draft. To distinguish these (there were changes made to the final standard), conformance with the draft standard is indicated by "*Class 2*" (there are many undocumented variations of the implementation of this *de facto* Standard), and conformance with the final standard is indicated by "*Class 2.0*" (this is not widely supported, with the significant exception of USRobotics and ZyXEL).

The ITU-T's international version of Class 2.0 is called T.32. It includes more functions, though, such as the data link functions described in TIA/EIA-602.

In addition to the Class 2 functions, *Class 3* boards were expected do the rasterization, based on higher-level information from the PC (such as text in ASCII and graphics data in TIFF format).

Initially, it was expected that offloading more functions to the fax board would result in Class 2 (and greater) fax boards making Class 1 boards obsolete. However, today's faster PCs can easily handle all the tasks necessary for faxing, even when using a "dumb" Class 1 fax board. Since the PC has the necessary processing power anyway, why waste money building more power into the fax board? It is likely that the Class 3 standard will never be approved.

There are three incompatible specifications to support *Binary File Transfer* (BFT) between fax boards, so that they can send the original file (in the original file format), not a rasterized version of it:

▲ CCITT's T.434 (and the similar TIA/EIA-614)

▲ Microsoft's *At Work Fax* (which also supports *public key encryption*, which provides *authentication* and *encryption*)

▲ Intel's not-very-popular CAS, which includes a BFT capability (which works only with CAS)

Only Class 1 (and not Class 2 or 2.0) fax boards can implement BFT or ECM.

A summary of fax options is shown in the figure below.

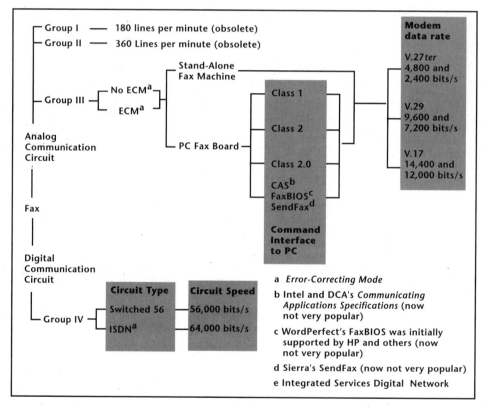

Fax-1

The Group III fax capabilities are specified in the following:

▲ ITU-T T.4 (which is the same as EIA/TIA-465). This describes the page widths, scan resolutions, transmission times per line, and one-dimensional compression scheme that are supported.

▲ ITU-T T.30 (which is the same as EIA/TIA-466). This covers the negotiation method and options that are negotiated at connection time and the protocol that is used to manage the session.

A pointer page to fax information on the Internet is at the site *http://www.faximum.com/FAQs/fax*.

A copy of the T.4 Standard is at *gopher://wiretap.spies.com:70/00/Library/Techdoc/Standard/ccitt.t4*.

A copy of the test pages used for fax transmission speed testing is at *http://www.cs.waikato.ac.nz/~singlis/ccitt.html*. The series of standards that contain these charts is IEEE 167A (167A.1 for black and white, 167A.2 for gray scale and 167A.3 for color).

Some additional information is at *http://www.grayfax.com/faxsminar.html* (they make fax test equipment) and in the Usenet newsgroup *comp.dcom.fax*.

Group III fax transmission over 64,000 bit/s ISDN circuits is defined in an ITU-T standard called 3-64. Its advantages over Group IV include universal compatibility, lower equipment costs and higher throughput rates.

See **ASYNCHRONOUS, AT COMMAND SET, AUTHENTICATION, CAS, DATA COMPRESSION, DID, DN, ENCRYPTION, HDLC, ISDN, MODEM, PAPER, PIXEL, RLE, SYNCHRONOUS**, and **USENET**.

FCC
Federal Communications Commission

The U.S. regulatory body that is responsible for the use of radio frequency transmissions and allocating frequency spectrum.

Having realized that the government was losing a revenue opportunity by giving away frequencies (initially by first-come, first-served, then by lottery), the FCC now auctions some services. The recent notable auction resulted in a total of $7 billion being bid for 99 licenses by 18 companies for PCS frequencies Blocks A and B to cover the 51 largest cities ("major trading areas"). Details are on the FCC's ftp server at *ftp://ftp.FCC.gov/pub/Auctions/PCS*.

The FCC has an ftp server at *ftp.fcc.gov* and a WWW site at *http://www.fcc.gov*.

See **ATT, CATV, CRTC, FCC PART15, ISM, PCS, PUC, SATELLITE**, and **V.21**.

FCC PART 15
FCC Code of Federal Regulations Title 47 (CFR 47), Part 15 (Radio Frequency Devices), Class A and Class B Radiated and Conducted EMI Limits

Initially to prevent interference to televisions, the FCC created limits on the allowable radiated electromagnetic interference (EMI) from commercially-available equipment, such as would be used in a business or home environment.

There are several subparts to Part 15, each covering a different subject. Subpart A covers general topics and definitions. Subpart B covers unintentional radiators, where signals greater than 9,000 Hz are required within the circuit (such as a computer's high-speed clock signal), but this is not intended to radiate from the device. Subpart C covers intentional radiators, such as a cellular telephone. Subpart D covers unlicensed PCS devices, which use transmit and receive frequencies of 1,910 to 1,930 MHz and 2,390 to 2,400 MHz. Subpart J concerns emissions radiated from "computing devices"—which includes most electronic devices which generate or use signals greater than 10 kHz. There are exemptions—for example digital devices in household appliances or transportation vehicles, and battery-operated devices that generate frequencies less than 1.705 MHz.

There are two groups of such devices.

▲ Class A computing devices are those that are "marketed for use in a commercial, industrial or business environment, exclusive of a device which is marketed for use by the general public or is intended to be used in the home". For example, a mainframe computer, oscilloscope or a central office telephone switch would be a Class A device. These devices need only be "verified"—which means that the manufacturer tests (or perhaps contracts some other organization to test) and labels the product as meeting the requirements.

▲ Class B computing devices are "marketed for use in a residential environment notwithstanding use in commercial, business and industrial environments". These would include personal computers (and their peripherals), electronic games, and facsimile machines. These devices must be "certified"—which means that the following must be submitted to the FCC; a detailed report of the measurements taken, a block diagram of the system, a description of the product's operation, a user manual, photographs of the inside and outside of the product, engineering drawings and schematics, the proposed FCC certification label—and the application fee. If all is well, the FCC sends you a Grant of Equipment Authorization.

The measurements are made using a device called a *spectrum analyzer*, and the units measured are microvolts per meter ($\mu V/m$). The spectrum analyses shows a graph of the signal strengths at a range of frequencies, and the maximum signal strength at any frequency in the measurement range is taken as the measurement. The maximum allowed signal strengths are shown in the table below.

To measure the *radiated EMI* (that is, signals that are transmitted through the air), measurements are made from an antenna located 3 m from the computing device (which is rotated to ensure that signals from all sides of the device are measured). The FCC requires that the emissions at all frequencies between 30 MHz and 1 GHz are checked.

The spectrum analyses then used to measure the *conducted EMI* (that is, signals transmitted out the device's power cord). These signals are measured between 450 kHz and 30 MHz.

Other "parts" of the FCC's rules specify other things. For example, Part 68 set out the requirements for connections to the public telephone network (to ensure that devices cannot harm the network).

Measurement	Frequency Range (MHz)	Class A Maximum (µV/m)	Class B Maximum (µV/m)
Conducted EMI	0.45 to 1.6	1,000	250
	1.6 to 30	3,000	250
Radiated EMI	30 to 88	300	100
	88 to 216	500	150
	216 to 1,000	700	200

As shown in the table (and the certification procedure), the Class B requirements are much more stringent. This means that devices for home use must be much "quieter" electrically, as there are more sensitive electronic components there (your television), in closer proximity.

Until 1996, each model of computer system sold by a manufacturer had to be tested by a certified laboratory. Subsequently sold systems would each get a label with an FCC ID number. This typically required 4 to 8 weeks. In response to industry pressure to streamline this process, the FCC now permits vendors to sell "self-declared" systems. That is, for systems which use components (such as disk and tape drives) that each have their own FCC labels, the computer system vendor need only include a "Declaration of Conformity" with the product, and put an FCC compliance label (which has no ID number) on the main chassis.

In the U.S., industrial, scientific and medical (ISM) devices are subject to the FCC's part 18 instead of part 15.

The equivalent European specification is the EU's EMC Directive. It generally requires lower emissions than the FCC limits, and in some cases, requires tests over a wider range of frequencies. The International Electrotechnical Commission (IEC standards 1000-4-*x*) and the Comité; Internationale Speciale des Perturbations Radioéctriques (CISPR standards 11, 16 and 22) also have regulations relevant to products sold to European countries.

See **EMC**, and **EMF**.

FCS
Frame Check Sequence

A generic term for the extra bits (usually a multiple of 8, such as 8 or 16 bits) added to a frame of data to assist in detecting errors (frames that had one or more bits changed because of noise on a data link, for example).

Several types are popular; they are listed in the following table.

Type of FCS	Generation	Length (bits)
BCC (Block Check Character)	Another generic term, like FCS. Is likely a check-sum or CRC. Usually refers to use on a low-speed (such as 9,600 bits/s), synchronous data communications circuit.	8 or 16
Checksum	Least significant 8 bits of the binary addition of the message. Usually generated in software, and refers to use on a low-speed (such as 9,600 bits/s) asynchronous data communications circuit.	8
CRC (Cyclic Redundancy Code)	Remainder of binary division of message by the generator polynomial. Usually generated in hardware, and used on LANs and serial data communication links (such as the WAN link between routers).	Usually 16 or 32
Hamming Code	Usually generated in hardware for ECC memory in a computer.	Depends on message length

See **CHECKSUM**, **CRC**, **ECC**, **FEC**, and **PARITY**.

FDDI
Fiber Distributed Data Interface

A higher-speed (and usually local) networking technology.

Supports 100 Mbit/s user data rate, dual ring (for redundancy), various topologies (ring, star, ring of stars), dual-homing (for reliability) and longer distances.

The fiber-PMD option supports up to 2 km (single-attached multimode fiber with 1,300-nm LED source), or 60 km (single-attached, single-mode fiber with high-power laser diode light source) between concentrator and workstation.

Each ring can have up to 500 nodes (or 1,000 if repeaters are used) and up to 200 km total fiber length (circumference)—though to allow for wrap-around during failure recovery, ring circumference is limited to 100 km.

Dual-attached stations on the main ring can be up to 2 km apart (62.5/125 μm or 50/125 μm multimode fiber) or 30 km (single-mode fiber).

With these great distances, some would say that this is also a MAN technology.

The TP-PMD (*Twisted Pair Physical Medium Dependent*) option supports up to 100 m over category 5 UTP.

Future media options may include 850-nm multimode fiber and STP (sometimes called SDDI—an informal *de facto* standard for this is called *Green Book*).

Frame size is a maximum of 4,500 bytes (4,478 bytes for the information field, plus the frame header and trailer).

The type of fiber-optic cable connector that is used is called a *Media Interface Connector* (MIC).

The main ring requires *Dual Attachment Stations* (DAS) to support the secondary ring which is used to provide a wrap-around for a cable break or failed station. Through a concentrator, *Single Attachment Stations* (SAS)—which are less expensive but have no redundancy—can be attached to the network. Each DAS port is either an A or a B port, as shown in the accompanying figure.

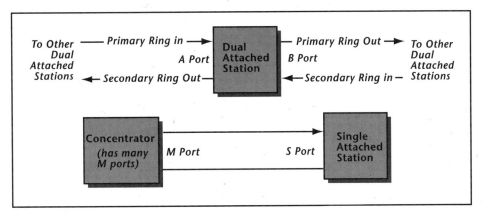

FDDI-1

SAS (and, optionally, DAS) stations are connected to the main ring through *concentrators*. The concentrator ports are designated the M (Master) ports, and the station ports are S (slave) ports. Therefore A ports connect to B ports, and M ports connect to S ports. Connectors are keyed to ensure that these requirements are met.

DAS stations (or concentrators) connected to two different SAS concentrators (one pair of fibers to each) provide *Dual-homing* redundancy (if either SAS connection fails, the other provides connectivity).

Most FDDI networks will have few DAS on the main ring (mostly concentrators), most devices being connected to the main ring concentrators or on second-level concentrators (which are connected to the main ring concentrators). This is called a *dual ring-of-trees* architecture. Smaller LANs would often have a collapsed backbone (*ring-in-a-box*) architecture, in which all stations connect to a single concentrator or all stations would be directly on the main ring (*dual-ring*).

The cable bit rate is actually 125 Mbits/s, since each 4 bits of information are *encoded* as 5 NRZI bits (called a *symbol*) to provide features such as:

▲ Data transparency

▲ Frame delimiting

▲ Clock recovery

Target Token Rotation Time (TTRT) is usually set to 8 ms. To ensure fair access, stations can transmit only for their *Token Holding Time* (THT, which is derived from the TTRT).

There has been some experimentation with a synchronous option that provides less network latency (8 to 16 ms, rather than standard FDDI's 10 to 200 ms). It is designed to support multimedia and to be compatible with standard asynchronous FDDI. Bandwidth is preallocated to stations with time-sensitive requirements. Bandwidth that they don't require is available to the asynchronous FDDI stations.

The *Station Management Layer* (SMT) provides features such as the following:

▲ Neighbor identification

▲ Fault detection and reconfiguration

▲ Insertion in, and deinsertion from, the ring

▲ Traffic statistics monitoring

The parts of the FDDI standard are shown in the following table.

OSI Reference Model Standard			FDDI		
Layer	Name				
2	Data Link	LLC[a]			
		MAC	MAC	SMT	
1	Physical		PHY		
			PMD		

a. Logical Link Control.

Each FDDI standard covers the features shown in the following table.

	FDDI Standard	Covers
MAC	Media Access Control	Controls access to fiber or cable Token handling Frames the data, generates the CRC Recognizes addresses
PHY	Physical Layer	Encodes and decodes Converts serial to parallel Clock recovery
PMD	Physical Medium Dependent	Specifies cable and connectors Specifies transceivers and optical bypass switch
SMT	Station Management	Controls all layers of the FDDI model Ring monitoring and management Connection management Generates and responds to SMT frames

Some people try to pronounce it as *FIH*dee.

SMT is standardized in ANSI X3T9.5 (released in 1989). The physical (PHY) layer is standardized in ISO 9314. A (patented) full-duplex version is called FFDT.

See **ANSI**, **BAUD**, **ENCODING**, **FDDI II**, **FFDT**, **FFOL**, **LAN**, and **MAN**.

FDDI-II
Fiber Distributed Data Interface II

An incompatible superset of the original FDDI that better supports multimedia, video, and voice, since bandwidth can be reserved for *isochronous* (regularly occurring, delay-sensitive) traffic. Divides the 100 Mbits/s into 16 6.144-Mbits/s circuits that can be allocated to carry asynchronous or isochronous traffic. Each of the 16 circuits can be subdivided into 96 separate 64-kbits/s channels.

A *synchronous bandwidth allocation* scheme uses a time-slicing algorithm to allow end-stations to reserve bandwidth.

Was never widely implemented (only one vendor every shipped product), as it was too slow for broadcast-quality video, and compressed video is bursty anyway (so isochronous service is of little use). ATM is faster and more flexible.

See **FDDI** and **ISOCHRONOUS**.

FDDI Follow-On LAN

See **FFOL**.

FDDI Full-Duplex Technology

See **FFDT**.

FEC
Forward Error Correction

A type of error correction often used either when errors occur often, or are difficult to get corrected by the usually error-correcting method—asking the sender for a retransmission.

Errors occur often in mobile data communications. For example, when the receiver is moving, it encounters *Rayleigh fading* which results in no bits being received every 5 feet of travel or so (depending on the frequency used)—due to the *destructive interference* between the many reflections of the signal (from buildings and other structures). The traditional retransmissions would encounter the same errors, so would not be of any use.

Satellite data transmission is usually to large numbers of receivers that often do not have transmission capability, or would collectively encounter so many errors on their individual reception paths, that too much time would be spent retransmitting.

The solution to both these problems is to send enough (carefully-calculated) redundant bits in the original message so that the receiver can reconstruct a correct message from the corrupted message. There are lots of such *Forward Error Correction* methods, each one optimized for the size of message and types of bit-errors encountered.

Trellis Code Modulation (TCM) is a form of FEC. Using TCM's implementation in V.34 as an example, every 4 data bits is encoded into 5 bit symbols—which are sent as a particular carrier frequency phase and amplitude combination. Since only particular transitions between symbols are allowed, some circuit noise can be ignored, making the data transmission more immune to some types of circuit impairments.

A graph of a symbol's phase (as a polar angle) and amplitude (as the distance from the origin) can be made in real time, and this display is called a constellation. V.34 modems have a total of 960 possible points on the constellation, and V.34+ modems have 1,664.

See **FCS**, **PARITY**, **SATELLITE**, and **V.34**.

FED
Field Emission Display

A type of electronic display expected to compete with other flat-panel display technologies, such as LCD and VFD.

They are like CRTs in that phosphors (excited by electrons) are used to generate the image (so they have a similarly wide viewing angle), but like LCDs in that a semiconductor-type process is used to manufacture them, and they are less than a few cm deep.

See **CRT**, **LCD**, and **VFD**.

FEP
Fluorinated Ethylene Propylene

The type of plastic used for insulating cables (especially datagrade UTP cable which has the following important characteristics:

▲ Fireproof (and non-smoking—always a desirable trait) enough to be plenum-rated. That is, it can be installed in the air-handling plenums above most commercial suspended ceiling systems. To provide this characteristic, a form of the halogen *fluorine* is added to the formulation of the plastic (the plastic is then called a fluoropolymer). As a result, if *other* things are burning enough to get the FEP above 800°, then the FEP gives off terribly poisonous gases (such as hydrogen fluoride and carbon monoxide). Strangely enough, while FEP cable *must* be used in North America (because of its low smoke release, and high ignition temperature), FEP (nor any other plastic made with a halogen) *cannot* be used in Europe, because of the fumes it releases when it does ignite.

▲ Low dielectric constant, which means the cable made from it has a low capacitance, which means that the cable can handle high-speed signals with low attenuation.

▲ High strength and low friction (so cable installations are easier).

DuPont Corporation makes more than 90% of the FEP sold, and their trademarked name for FEP is *Teflon* (same stuff that's used for your pots and pans). It is also called polytetra-fluoroethylene (PTFE).

The most common type of insulation used for non-plenum installations is polyvinylchloride (PVC). It is the soft, plastic (often grey or black) which is used for most of the telephone, computer and power cables you can see at your feet today. PVC is classed as a polyolefin.

For more information, see *http://www.dupont.com/teflon/datacomm*.

See **CABLE**, and **UTP**.

FEP
Front End Processor

A $20K to $400K box that provides communication services for IBM mainframes.

Sometimes called a *communications controller*, but now IBM calls some of them a *Network Node* or even an *Nways Multinetwork Controller*. This is all in keeping with IBM calling a Mainframe a server, because FEPs and Mainframe remind too many people of dinosaurs and the olden days of computing.

FEP services include data link activation, polling, and error detection and correction. The physical links to users include EIA-232, V.35 (which then goes to a 3274 to the users), and Token Ring. The link to the mainframe is either the IBM *bus and tag channel* or *ESCON*.

In increasing order of size and newness, IBM FEP model numbers are as follows:

▲ 3704 and 3705 (really old, no longer manufactured)

▲ 3720 and 3725 (old)

▲ 3745 and 3746 (the most common). Big ones cost $80,000 to $300,000 (plus thousands of dollars per month in software licensing fees), though small ones cost under $50,000. Can handle multiple mainframe channel connections, EIA-232, V.35, T1, Ethernet and Token ring connections. Depending on the software used, supports SNA, APPN, frame relay, X.25 (NPSI software is needed) and IP.

Runs NCP (network control program).

See **S3174 AND 3274**, **CHANNEL**, **ESCON**, **MAINFRAME**, **NCP2** (*Network Control Program*), **NPSI**, **PU-2**, **PU-4**, and **WAN**.

FFDT
FDDI Full-Duplex Technology

A method (developed and patented by Digital Equipment Corporation, they license it to others), to enable two FDDI devices (typically two switches, or a switch and a computer) to communicate full-duplex (which some people say then has 200 Mbits/s of capacity—and it does, but only if exactly half of that traffic needs to go in each direction at the same time).

Basically, they disable the token, and allow the stations to transmit whenever they want (rather than requiring them to wait for the single token before transmitting).

DEC expects applications will include connecting disk subsystems to high-performance workstations.

Competes (or at least it could compete, if FFDT were standardized and available) with fibre channel.

See **DEC**, **FDDI**, **FIBRE CHANNEL**, **FULL-DUPLEX**, and **HIPPI**.

FFOL
FDDI Follow-On LAN

The proposed name of a standard that was to replace FDDI. Was to operate at up to 2.4 Gbits/s, but all that was ever produced was some marketing literature.

See **FDDI**.

Fibre Channel

A very high-speed (up to more than 1 Gbits/s), low-latency (10 to 30 µs—which is better than ATM), full-duplex data communications scheme that is optimized to carry large blocks of data, with very low latency (about 500 µs) for both channel- and LAN-type connections (simultaneously, on the same medium).

Supports both:

▲ *Dedicated* media (also called *switched,* since each device gets its own switch port and does not share the media's bandwidth with other devices)

▲ *Shared* media

Three potential uses are:

▲ I/O device connections, for example, channels to disk drives, such as the SCSI interface and IBM's Escon

▲ Clusters of workstations

▲ Switched LANs, supporting computers from many vendors, using multiple protocols and interfaces, such as TCP/IP and ATM

Six speeds are defined (because of protocol overhead, the payload data rate is lower than the bit rate on the cable), as shown in the following table.

Cable Bit Rate (Mbits/s)	Payload Data Rate	
	Mbytes/s	Mbits/s
132.8125	12.5	100
265.625	25	200
531.25	50	400
1,062.5	100	800
2,125	200	1,600
4,250	400	3,200

The specified distances for the various media and data rates are given in the following table.

Media	Speed (Mbytes/s)			
	12.5	25	50	100
Single-mode fiber (long-wave laser)	10 km			
50/125 µm multimode fiber (short-wave laser)	[a]	2 km	1 km	[a]
62.5/125-µm fiber (long-wave LED)	500 m	1 km	[a]	[a]
Video coax	100 m	75 m	50 m	25 m
Miniature coax	40 m	30 m	20 m	10 m
Shielded twisted pair	100 m	50 m	[a]	[a]

a. Not defined in the standard.

The connector types are listed in the following table.

Media	Connector	Requires
Fiber	Duplex, polarized SC	One strand for transmitting, one for receiving
Coax	TNC (receiver) and BNC (transmitter)	One coax for transmitting, one for receiving
STP	9-pin D-subminiature	One pair for transmitting, one for receiving

Note that UTP is not a supported medium.

Frame size is up to 2,148 bytes, as shown in the following table.

Bytes	Function
4	Start of frame delimiter
24	Frame header, including 24-bit source and destination addresses and sequence numbers to support windowing and flow control
0 to 2,112	Higher-layer data (payload), may include a 64-byte optional header, reducing payload to 2,048 bytes
4	CRC
4	End of frame delimiter

Higher-level addresses are assigned to switch ports (stations then inherit these) and have a three-level hierarchy (domain, area, and port number).

Fibre channel has five layers (which are expected to be implemented as physically separate components), as shown in the accompanying figure.

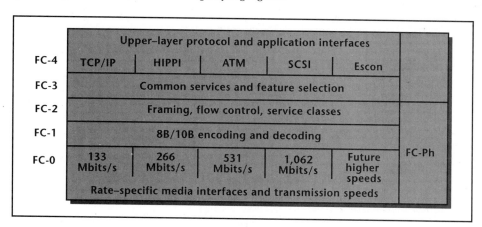

Fibre Channel-1

The lower three layers are called the *fibre channel physical* standard and define all the physical transmission characteristics.

FC-1 is the transmission encoding and decoding layer and uses IBM's patented Escon 8B/10B coding.

FC-2 is where most fibre channel functions take place. The FC-2 layer performs the following functions:

▲ Signaling—that is, establishing connections between originators and responders. The originator specifies the destination address (IEEE Ethernet-type addresses are used—these are 48 bits in length). The responder receives messages and sends back responses.

▲ Frame segmentation, reassembly, and sequencing functions. Fibre channel frame sizes are negotiated between each pair of communicating stations, and are from 36 bytes to 2 kbytes in length.

▲ Flow control (using a sliding window scheme), error detection (using a 32-bit CRC), and correction.

▲ The implementation of the four service classes (see below).

FC-3 provides features for special situations (which are expected to be important in the future), such as how data written to disk drives will be "striped" (split, with each part written to a different drive, to speed up the reading and writing), and multicast functions to deal with a video server (a device storing digitized video).

FC-4 (also called *multiple service interconnect*) handles interfaces with other (legacy) network protocols and applications, such as ATM AAL5, ESCON, HIPPI, IPI, SCSI, and TCP/IP.

The *Fibre Channel Systems Initiative* (consisting of Hewlett-Packard, IBM, and Sun Microsystems) promotes fibre channel interoperability. They have defined three *profiles* to ensure interoperability for specific uses, as listed in the following table.

Profile	Use
Storage	Point-to-point connections to data storage subsystems (based on SCSI or IPI) for use such as backing up data
Networking	How to encapsulate IP packets over fibre channel and the design of switches
Internetworking	Interfaces between fibre channel and Ethernet, Token Ring, and FDDI networks, as well as LAN and WAN versions of ATM

Four *service classes* are defined, as shown in the following table.

Class	Configuration
1	Configures switches so that a dedicated, circuit-switched, connection-oriented, guaranteed delivery (through the use of acknowledgments) channel is set up between source and destination. No other devices can connect to the source or destination ports. Best for sustained, high-throughput, time-critical, nonbursty transactions such as real-time graphics, mass storage, and links between supercomputers.
2	A connectionless (with guaranteed delivery through the use of acknowledgments), frame-switched service that supports multiplexing to share bandwidth from many ports into others. Best for bursty and interactive traffic. Does not guarantee that the data will be delivered in the original sequence (as each frame can be delivered over any available route—even a single fibre channel switch can have multiple paths), but sequence numbers in the frames permit the receiving station to present the frames in the correct sequence to the upper layers. Frames lost due to congestion or port contention are replied to with a *busy signal* and are retransmitted until they successfully get through the network and are acknowledged.

(table continued on next page)

Class	Configuration
3	Same as Class 2, but no guaranteed delivery (since there is no frame acknowledgment). Good for sending messages rapidly from one source to many destinations (emulating a broadcast) or when the round-trip delay is large. Has higher throughput (again, since there is no waiting for frame acknowledgments).
4	Isochronous (also called constant bit rate, or guaranteed fractional bandwidth) and guaranteed latency and original sequence of frames service for digitized voice and video. Will be specified in an addendum to the standard (*fibre channel enhanced physical*).

A fifth class—*Intermix*—is a mix of Class 1 and Class 2. The Class 1 frames get priority access to the full fibre channel bandwidth, and Class 2 frames are carried when capacity is available.

Three topologies (or types of *fabric*) have been defined, as shown in the following table.

Topology	Characteristics
Switched fabric	This will likely be the most common and requires that users (either a small workgroup or a campus-wide network) be connected to others through a switch. The switch can provide different speed accesses on different ports, and the communicating devices negotiate to ensure that the faster device does not send data faster than the receiver can accept it. This is called *dynamic rate conversion*.
Point-to-point	Two users are directly connected by a fibre channel connection. Both devices must be at the same speed.
Arbitrated loop (FC-AL)	A method of connecting more than two (and up to 127) users without requiring a switch (therefore reducing the cost). For this topology, only coaxial cable can be used for the media. Disadvantages are that bandwidth is shared and that coaxial cable distances are much less than distances for fiber-optic cable. All devices must be at the same speed. The loop can handle only a single connection (between two stations) at a time. That connection must be cleared before another connection can be established. A loop can be connected to a port on a switch. If multiple devices are contending for use of the loop, then the device with the lowest address wins.

Some topology notes:

▲ All stations support all three topologies (they look the same to the stations)

▲ Devices on one topology can communicate with devices on the other topologies

▲ Station capabilities are the same regardless of the topology used (for example, all service classes are available to all topologies)

▲ Topologies can be mixed in a single fibre channel network

Fiber Optic Cable

Fibre channel defines many types of ports, as shown in the following table.

Port	Used on	IEEE Addresses Assigned[a]
Fabric port or F port	Fibre channel switch (connects to N Port)	
Node port or N port	End-station (disk array, computer, etc.) directly connected to a Switched F Port	Highest addresses
FL port	Fibre channel switch (connects to a Loop)	Middle addresses
NL port	End station (connects to a loop)	Lowest addresses

a. When contending for control of a loop, the device with the lowest address wins. Therefore loop-connected end-stations have the highest priority.

The mapping of LAN and higher-layer protocols (including Ethernet and Token Ring, SCSI, TCP/IP, ATM AAL5, and 802.2) to Fibre Channel will be included as part of the specification.

Still under development, much of it by Hewlett-Packard (which bought the technology from Canstar). Standardized as ANSI X3T11.

The Fibre Channel Association's web site is at *http://www.Amdahl.com/ext/CARP/FCA/FCA.html*. The Fibre Channel Loop Community is at *http://www.symbios.com/fclc*. Ancot Corp. manufactures Fibre Channel test equipment, and has some information on the technology at the web site at *http://www.ancot.com*. Ancor Communications is also an equipment manufacturer, and they are at *http://www.ancor.com*.

See **S8B-10B**, **ATM**, **ESCON**, **FFDT**, **HIPPI**, **HP**, **ISOCHRONOUS**, **LAN**, **FIBER**, and **SCSI1**.

Fiber Optic Cable

A type of physical transmission medium that uses light (rather than the voltages used for copper media). Infrared light (which has a longer wavelength than red light, and is therefore invisible to humans) is typically used, since fiber optic cable has less attenuation at these wavelengths.

Usually silica glass optical fiber is used for serious data transmission work, though plastic optical fiber (POF) is used for some low-cost, limited-distance (less than 100 m) applications (especially illuminating hard-to-reach places, like instrument panels of automobiles—some kinds of doctors like the stuff too, but don't ask where they put it).

The most common type of fiber optic cable used in commercial data communications applications in North America is called *graded index, multimode 62.5/125 µ* (as further explained below). This type typically has a maximum distance between repeaters of 2 km and is specified in the EIA/TIA-568 *Commercial Building Telecommunications Wiring Standard* and also in ISO/IEC 11801.

▲ *Multimode fiber* (MMF) means that the glass core of the fiber has a large enough diameter that there are many ways that light can bounce down the inner core of the fiber. This large core means that more light can be carried down the fiber (so the receivers don't have to be as sensitive), and that the connectors don't have to be super-precise (since a misalignment of a few microns doesn't reduce the light by too much). Usually a light source (*light emitting diode*—LED) with a wavelength of 850 nm is used for multimode fiber as it provides a good trade-off between the lower attenuation (which is not too important for the relatively short fiber runs usually used for commercial installations) of longer wavelength light, and the higher cost of even longer wavelength light sources.

▲ *Graded index* means that the index of refraction (which is the ratio of the velocity of light propagation in a vacuum to velocity in the glass) increases towards the center of the glass core. This reduces the *modal dispersion* (where the modes of signal propagation have different travel times through the fiber, since they travel different distances). For example, the modes that mostly travel straight through the glass core have less distance to travel than the modes that bounce off the outer edge of the core. Since the glass has its greatest index of refraction at the core, the straight-through modes spend most of their time in the "slower glass", so they end up at the end of the fiber at about the same time as the other modes (which had farther to travel, but much of that trip was in faster glass). This reduces the *intersymbol interference*, so the bits (or "symbols") can be sent faster. This increases the bandwidth of the fiber. The *non-graded index* optical fibre is called step-index, and has a maximum bandwidth of about 2.5 Gbits/s.

62.5/125 μ refers to the diameter (in *microns*, which are millionths of a meter—and are abbreviated as μm or simply μ) of the inner core, and the outer glass *cladding*, respectively. A micron is about 1/100 of the diameter of a human hair—of course some people have thinner hair than others, and some people have hair that is thinning more than others, but that's quite a different topic.

The cladding has a lower index of refraction than the outer edge of the core, and the light travelling down the core experiences *total internal reflection* (sounds much more spiritual than I imagine it really is), where all of the light bounces off the boundary between the cladding and core. The cladding is formed by infusing impurities into the fiber, by immersing it in a bath during manufacture (and the impurities only move in from the outside surface a controlled amount).

In Europe, 50/125 μm fiber is most common for commercial applications.

Telephone companies typically use *single mode* fiber optic cable (SMF). This typically still has a 125 μm outside diameter (so it is easier to work with, and provides some level of standardization of connectors), but has a core diameter of (usually) 8 to 10 μm. This approaches the wavelength of the light itself, and therefore only supports a single mode of propagation down the fiber—straight through the center. Since there is only one mode ("single mode"), there is no modal dispersion, so the bandwidth of this type of fiber is very high (typically gigabits/s, over tens of kilometers of fiber). Since the core does not need to be graded index, single mode fiber is less expensive to manufacture, which is more important for the longer cable runs (as compared to the relatively short in-building runs used commercially) used by telephone companies.

Fiber optic cable has a generally decreasing attenuation with increasing wavelength—from about 6 dB/km at 600 nm (a greenish color) to less than 1 dB/km at 1,600 nm (infrared). However, there are small ranges of wavelengths which have much greater attenuation due to the absorption of the light by hydroxide ions (which are written as OH⁻). These impurities (which the manufacturers try very hard to eliminate) cause an extra 3 dB/km attenuation around 1,390 nm and about 0.4 dB/km around 1,250 and around 940 nm. Therefore it is generally best to use a light source which is just below one of these peaks in attenuation (since shorter wavelength light sources are generally less expensive). It is therefore considered that there is a *transmission window* of best optical properties at about 850, 1,310 and 1,550 nm, and these are the three most common wavelengths for optical fiber light sources.

Usually a wavelength of about 1,310 or 1,550 nm (which costs more, but typically results in a cable attenuation of as low as 0.2 dB/km) is used for single mode fiber, as fiber has a lower attenuation at these wavelengths than at 850 nm (in contrast, coaxial cable can have an attenuation of 2.5 dB/km for 1 MHz signals, and 50 dB/km or more for 1 GHz signals). The higher cost (compared to an 850 nm light source) of the light source (which may be an LED or a LASER—*light amplification by stimulated emission of radiation*) is usually preferred, due to the advantage of no repeaters required for the longer fiber runs (usually 2 km to 50 km) typically encountered.

LASER light sources are much more expensive than LED, but LASERs have much greater power output (perhaps –15 dBm, compared to only –50 dBm for LED) and concentrate their light output over a much narrower range of wavelengths—so their output falls mostly in a transmission window (rather than wasting light output on wavelengths which encounter greater attenuation at one of those nasty OH⁻ peaks). Using commercial equipment, single mode fiber optic cable runs using 1,550 nm LASER light sources can often be 120 km before needing a repeater.

While fiber optic cable can be used for analog transmission (this is common for video signals), for data communications, digital transmission is most common. That is, the light source is turned on or off (the exact method depends on the *encoding* used). For laser light sources, the light is not turned off completely, as it takes too long for the light to turn back on (at least too long for gigabit/s data rates). The light output is therefore only reduced from it maximum to indicate the other digital state. A typical *extinction ratio* (between the maximum and reduced output levels used to indicate the two binary states) is 9 dB or greater (in this case for Gigabit Ethernet).

Public carriers typically charge more for higher-speed data links, and they get to set the speed of a link, since they run the network (that is, carriers prefer to offer *services*, rather than raw transmission capacity). However, customers often request *dark fiber*, which is a direct run of fiber optic cable, with no electronic equipment provided by the carrier (which would "light" the fiber). The customer then puts their own equipment at the ends of the fiber, and run it at whatever speed they wish. The carrier then does not know (and cannot limit) the speed of data transmission. Most carriers (especially telephone companies) don't like offering dark fiber, since the carrier can't charge exorbitant tariffs for super-high data rates (since the carrier is not doing any more for the customer than if the carrier only provided a lower-speed link).

Rather than higher bit rates (such as OC-192, which is almost 10 Gbits/s), some feel that the way to get more capacity from fiber optic cable is to use *wavelength division multiplexing* (WDM). Basically, this uses different "colors" (better described as different wavelengths, since they are all invisible to us humans) of light simultaneously down the same strand of glass. A prism at the receiving end splits the colors, so that each illuminates a different receiver. For example, by using 16 different wavelengths, the capacity of a fiber can be increased by a factor of 16, without using super duper fast and expensive end electronics.

Another development is using analog signalling techniques for digital data transmission. Using multiple light levels per symbol, such as 8 light levels (rather than the current 2), 3 bits of information can be encoded into a symbol (rather than just 1).

A technology called *air blown fiber* uses small-diameter flexible plastic tubes to hold the fibers. It was developed by British Telecommunications PLC, and is manufactured by Sumitomo Electric. The fibers can be blown, using compressed air, into the tubes after the tubes have been installed. This ensures that the fibers will not be damaged when the tubes are installed, allows the fiber to be upgraded after installation, allows longer fiber runs without splices to be installed, and allows damaged fibers to be replaced.

Interestingly, glass turns brown in high radiation, so fiber optic cables (and monitoring cameras, because of their glass lenses) cannot be used really close to nuclear reactors.

After many years of development (to get attenuation down to an acceptable level), the first commercial fiber optic cable trial was in 1977. 62.5/125 μ optical fiber was first available in 1981, and single mode optical fiber was first available in 1982.

Corning Incorporated (which is a parent company of Siecor) is really big on optical fiber. The Corning Optical Fiber Information Center is at *http://www.corningfiber.com/*. Sumitomo Electric Lightwave Corp. has a web site at *http://www.sel-rtp.com*.

See **CABLE**, **CONNECTOR**, **ENCODING**, **FDDI**, **FIBRE CHANNEL**, **GIGABIT ETHERNET**, **LATENCY**, **OC-X**, and **STP**.

Field

See **INTERLACED** and **NTSC**.

Finger

A utility available on UNIX computers and included with many TCP/IP protocol suites (for other operating systems) that provides information about users with accounts on the local computer or a remote computer. Most of the information comes from the `/etc/passwd` file. Finger commands are listed in the following table.

Command	Displays
`finger user@host`	If user is a valid `login name` (exactly matching, including the case) or a complete first or last name (exactly matching one but the case need not match), as entered in the user's `given name` entry, then the following will be displayed: `Login name:` (the username the user logs in to `host` with) `In real life:` the user's given name `Directory:` the user's home directory `Shell:` the user's default shell `Last login` (if the user is not currently logged in) or `On since` (if the user is currently logged in): the time and date when the user last logged in to `host` and the port from which the user logged in `Project`[a]: the contents of the file `.project` in the user's home directory `Plan:` the contents of the file `.plan` in the user's home directory
`finger user`	As above, but for user on the local host
`finger @host`	The `login name`, `given name`, `port`, `idle time`, `login time` and `date`, and other information from the `passwd` file for each `user` currently logged in to `host`
`finger`	As above, but for the local host

a. For these files to be displayed, they must have `world read` and `execute` permissions.

Firewall

The destination host must be running a `finger` server, usually called `fingerd` (finger daemon) for the `finger` utility to display information for a given host.

Called "finger" because it is like putting your finger on someone to get information.

Specified in RFC 742.

See **RFC** and **UNIX**.

Firewall

A perimeter security device, in that it is deployed at the boundaries of networks, to protect them from external access.

A firewall is a device that links an organization's internal TCP/IP network to the Internet and restricts the types of traffic that it will pass, to provide security. The first firewalls were typically based on UNIX, since UNIX has a robust TCP/IP implementation, and is a good platform for customization of the operating system for additional features, such as security. However, Microsoft Windows NT is now becoming very popular as a firewall platform.

Simpler firewalls can be implemented by advanced commands in some routers. These are often called *packet-filtering* firewalls, in that they only pass or block some packets, based on relatively simple criteria, such as the following:

▲ Type of access (such as email, telnet, ftp, as determined by the TCP port number)

▲ Direction (whether the exchange is initiated by someone inside, or outside of the firewall)

▲ Source or destination IP address (host)

▲ Time of day

More complex firewalls (which are sometimes called *application-level gateways*) can also perform functions, such as the following:

▲ Filter based on the contents of the data accessed (for example, that files transferred to not contain the word "confidential").

▲ Create log files and audit trails of which users accessed which machines, at what times, and doing what actions.

▲ Check for viruses in transferred files.

▲ Provide *Network Address Translation* NAT, which converts internal IP addresses used by an organization to the registered IP addresses they use on the Internet. These registered addresses are typically from a smaller pool of shared addresses, so the organization does not need a world-wide unique IP address for every computer in their network. Also, the internal addressing structure (and the IP addresses of important internal computers) used by the organization will not be visible to the public, and this an important security benefit. NAT is defined in RFC 1631.

▲ Authenticate external users, often by using *tokens* (a small portable electronic device carried by authorized users).

Computer Dictionary

▲ Perform encryption of the data, and create links to other firewalls elsewhere on the Internet so users behind their own firewalls can securely exchange data over the Internet (that is, encrypted sessions to other firewalls are created). Such networks are sometimes called VPNs.

▲ Page, fax or e-mail somebody when a security problem has been detected.

These firewalls will be slower than simple packet-filtering firewalls.

Older firewalls require you first to log in to them (usually using telnet) and then to request a service (such as an ftp session) to the intended destination.

Newer application firewalls do this in one step, often using a facility called *quoting*, which passes command-line parameters, such as a username, password and service required, to the firewall, which then acts as your *proxy* (doing your work on your behalf). The proxy firewall is then both a server (to your desktop PC) and a client (since it makes requests of some other server—on your behalf). This is sometimes called an *application proxy*, since it needs to have a proxy agent for every application (ftp, http, and so on) that users require (and this can be a problem, if your firewall does not have a proxy agent for your particular application). Since proxy servers become the initiator of the ftp session (or whatever) to the remote server, they can know exactly what is going on, and therefore are considered more secure than packet-filtering firewalls. A popular client API toolkit for transparently using a proxy server (and providing authentication to it) is called *Socks*.

Firewalls with a proxy function replace the source address of transactions with their own IP address, so resources on the Internet only see the address of the firewall, and cannot learn anything about the IP addressing structure on the secure side of the firewall (a similar benefit to that of NAT, though NAT replaces the source address with one from a pool that remains assigned to that user at least for the duration of the surfing session).

Between the simplicity of implementation simple packet filters, and the complexity of application-level proxy firewalls, *stateful inspection* tracks what users are doing, and enforces additional rules, such as ensuring that no more communication occurs to a TCP port (such as that providing telnet service) when a user is finished with it, or that a *response* is only accepted if there was an outstanding *request*.

By default, firewalls typically do not allow UDP packets through, since UDP is connectionless, so it not possible to confirm who the sender is. Some audio applications use UDP, so would require special configuration of a firewall to pass through it.

Firewalls (and other security measures) are an excellent technical solution to security. Security problems which are more of a human issue include the following:

▲ People who use the same password on multiple systems, including systems that don't encrypt passwords. Passwords can then be learned, and used to get access to systems that do encrypt them.

▲ People that use easy-to-guess passwords—there are lists of these, and they include family member's names, sports teams and the word "secret" (and you can bet that hackers know about these lists).

▲ Companies that make products that have default passwords (for example, Newbridge Networks Corporation's Mainstreet multiplexer products all have the password "mainstreet" for the configuration and diagnostic interface. Company technicians do not change these passwords when the product is installed, and these products are widely used by telephone companies.

▲ *Social engineering* is the polite term used for people who lie, impersonate and otherwise attempt to trick unsuspecting employees into revealing passwords ("hi, I'm here from your branch office trouble-shooting a problem, can you give me your password so I can ensure that you can still log-in"—you need to be good at saying that in a rushed, nonchalant and insider's kind of a voice).

The National Computer Security Association has a certification program for firewalls. They have information on firewalls at *http://www.ncsa.com*. In addition to that, there's tons of security information available on the Internet. Some is at *http://www.cis.ohio-state.edu/hypertext/faq/usenet/security-faq/faq.html*, *http://www.v-one.com/pubs/fw-faq/faq.html*, and *http://www-genome.wi.mit.edu/WWW/faqs/www-security-faq.html*.

See **ANS**, **AUTHENTICATION**, **CERT**, **ENCRYPTION**, **INTERNET2**, **INTRANET**, **RFC-1918**, and **VPN**.

FireWire

Apple Computer's trademarked name for IEEE 1394.

See **S1394**.

Flame

The email equivalent of raising your voice and criticizing or insulting someone. Most people think that flaming someone is seldom a mature thing to do.

Called "flame" because it is like blasting someone as an angry fire-breathing dragon might. (Of course, I've never actually seen a dragon toasting someone, but I don't expect it would be a pretty sight.)

Flash Memory

A non-volatile, in-circuit-erasable and -programmable solid-state memory—that does not need a backup battery. Sometimes it is called an *electrically erasable, programmable read only memory* (EEPROM). Invented by Fujio Masuoka at Toshiba Corp. between 1984 and 1987, but Intel Corporation currently sells the most flash memory ICs.

Very popular for firmware (software that is immediately available when a device is powered-on), such as that for a modem or a PC's BIOS—that may need to be updated in the field. Also becoming popular in consumer electronics equipment enclosed in small modules. There are two competing implementations: SanDisk's *CompactFlash* and Intel's *Miniature Card*.

Initial devices required special voltages (+12 V), guaranteed only 10,000 write-erase cycles, and the entire IC had to be erased to change any memory locations. Current devices use the (now) far more standard voltages of 5 or 3 V, guarantee 100,000 write-erase cycles (and typically work for 1,000,000 and more), and require only the changed memory location's sector(s) (which are typically blocks of 256 to 512 bytes) to be erased. Capacities typically range from 32 kbytes to 1 Mbyte and more per IC.

Flash memory does not require a battery, but usually must be written in blocks of many bytes, and can store many thousands of bytes. It is therefore most often used to store the complete program (perhaps except for a small loader program) for devices which may need their software updated periodically (such as modems and a PC's BIOS).

In September 1997, Intel Corp. announced the development of flash memory that could store 2 bits per memory cell. They call their implementation StrataFlash, and first devices could store 64 Mbits (8 Mbytes) per IC. SanDisk (developers of CompactFlash) call their implementation *DoubleDensity*. Previously, all commercial digital storage devices stored a single bit per cell.

In March 1996, a standard file format for data stored on in flash memory in PC Cards was adopted by the PCMCIA. The format is called the *flash translation layer* (FTL), and enables PC Cards (and possibly MiniCards as well) to appear as a standard disk drive (that is, you can create and delete subdirectories, read and write files, and so on). Much fancy work is done by the FTL driver to shield the operating system from the idiosyncrasies of the flash memory (such as needing to erase old data before writing new data, and only being able to erase data in 64 kbyte blocks). Other FTL functions include: ensuring that data is not corrupted or lost if a card is removed while data is being written to it, equalizing where data is stored in the flash memory, so some memory locations don't wear out sooner than others, and remapping bad memory locations, using programming algorithms appropriate for each type of flash memory used.

Intel has flash memory information at *http://developer.intel.com/design/flcomp*. Further information on FTL is at *http://www.m-sys.com*, the developer of FTL.

See **COMPACT FLASH**, **DRAM**, **MINICARD**, and **PCMCIA**.

FLOP
Floating Point Operation Per Second

A measure of computing speed often used for supercomputers—which some define as a computer that can complete an infinite loop in less than 3 seconds (that's was supposed to be a joke). Now that you've finished laughing, supercomputers are really fast, and typically very good at doing floating point math (as opposed to integer math).

As of 1995, the world speed record was set at Sandia National Laboratories, by a linked pair of supercomputers made by Intel. Together, the supercomputers had 6,768 Pentium processors and could process 281 gigaflops. Traditional supercomputers have one, or just a few really fast processors.

See **MIPS**, **MPP**, and **SPEC**.

Flow Control

Whenever two computers (or people) communicate, there is always the chance that the transmitter will transmit faster than the receiver is able to accept the information (for example, because it is busy doing something else, cannot process the information fast enough, or does not have enough buffer space).

A solution to this is to have the receiver control the flow of information (by requesting it to temporarily stop sending).

For EIA-232 asynchronous communication links (such as your PC's COM port connecting to an external modem), there are two common flow control methods:

▲ x-on/x-off (as in transmit-on/transmit-off); the receiver sends the ASCII x-off character (which is 13_{16}, and can often by generated from a keyboard by typing Ctrl-S) to stop the transmitter. When the receiver is again ready to receive, it sends the x-on character (which is 11_{16}), which is the Ctrl-Q character).

▲ This is an *in-band* method (since the flow control is sent using the same method as the data), and is usually undesirable since the x-on and x-off characters cannot also be part of the data (which may not be possible to ensure). Also, this method requires the transmitter to check every character received to see if it is a flow control character. The advantage of this method is that it does not require any additional wires on the EIA-232 interface.

RTS/CTS (also called hardware flow control); the DCE (such as the modem) puts a negative voltage on the CTS line when it wants the DTE (such as your PC) to stop transmitting. When the DCE is ready to accept more data, it puts a positive voltage on the CTS line. Similarly, the DTE puts a negative or positive voltage on the RTS line to stop and resume the data flow from the DCE.

This out-of-band method is usually faster (the transmitter can act on it even if it is buffering received characters, and has not yet checked to see if one is an x-off character), and more importantly, allows any character to be transmitted as data.

Synchronous data communications usually performs flow control on a per-frame (rather than per-character) basis, using the following methods:

▲ The protocol allows the transmitter to have only a certain number of frames outstanding (that is, those which have been sent, but not yet acknowledged by the receiver). As an example, protocols based on HDLC usually use a window size of 2 or 7. This ensures that the transmitter cannot send more than a window-size of frames.

▲ HDLC supports a *Receiver Not Ready* (RNR) acknowledgment, which requests the transmitter to not send any more frames (even if the window is not yet full)—the transmitter will continue to send the remainder of the frame if one is being transmitted at that time. The receiver sends a *Receiver Ready* (RR) frame to request the transmitter to resume sending.

See **ASCII, ASYNCHRONOUS, EIA/TIA-232, HDLC, IN-BAND, MODEM, SYNCHRONOUS,** and **V.42BIS.**

FOIRL
Fiber-Optic Inter Repeater Link

An 802.3 option for linking repeaters over fiber-optic cable.

See **S10BASEF.**

Folders

The Apple Macintosh and Windows 95 operating systems' name for disk subdirectories. Also used to refer to the subdirectory-like method used for filing electronic mail messages in many email programs.

Computer Dictionary

Font

Usually refers to a particular *typeface* (or more simply, *face*)—which is the set of characters (including letters, numbers and punctuation) of a particular shape or design (such as Times or Helvetica).

There are two broad categories of how fonts are stored and displayed:

▲ *Bitmap* or *raster fonts*

▲ *Scalable* or *outline fonts*

While scalable fonts are usually more desirable (because you can adjust the size while maintaining the proportions and smooth edges), bitmap fonts are required for raster devices, such as computer monitors and dot matrix printers.

Software such as *Adobe Type Manager* (ATM, for *PostScript Type 1 Fonts*) and Microsoft's *True-Type* (for its *TrueType Fonts*) can convert scalable fonts to bitmap fonts. The accompanying figure shows the common types of fonts currently available.

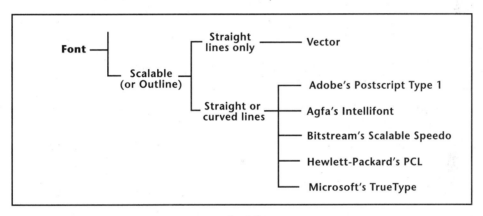

Font-1

See **ATM** (*Adobe Type Manager*), **BITMAP FONT**, **OUTLINE FONT**, **PCL**, **POINT**, and **TYPEFACE FAMILY**.

FOO.BAR

F _ _ _ _ _ Up Beyond All Recognition

During the Second World War, the term "fubar" was used in status reports and on repair tags to indicate (likely unrepairable) defective machinery and equipment.

The (to many people) meaningless two-syllable word somehow came to people who need an example filename when producing program manuals and documentation. The spelling changed, and the two syllables were used as the separate file name and file extension.

See **NFG**, **RTFM**, and **SNAFU**.

FPM
Fast-Page Mode DRAM

A type dynamic random access memory which provides faster throughput than conventional DRAM.

As with all memory, the bits are stored in memory cells, arranged as a matrix of rows and columns. As for all DRAM, the memory IC has only half the number of pins needed to specify the address to be read or written. A memory cycle begins by the CPU first specifying the row (this requires half the address bits), and then the column (this is the other half of the address) address of the data. The data is then read or written.

Fast-page mode allows the next column (which corresponds to the next sequential memory address) to be addressed next without specifying the row again. This reduces the time for the next few subsequent memory accesses (so long as you haven't got to the end of the row yet), increasing throughput.

FPM DRAM has a memory cycle time as fast as 50 ns, which can support memory accesses at the rate of about 30 million per second (30 MHz). This is not fast enough for the 60 or 66 MHz memory bus of a typical Pentium processor. Therefore, memory accesses require more than one memory cycle, and are performed in bursts, so the memory address does not need to be specified for every access (this is possible because memory accesses are usually to sequential memory locations—if not, then the extra accesses are not used, or the data is ignored). The memory access burst is often written as 6-3-3-3, which means that the first memory cycle requires 6 clock cycles (since the full address needs to be specified), and the next three accesses require only 3 clock cycles each. The clock cycles are typically at the processor's memory bus speed. This is often 60 or 66.6 MHz for a 120 or 133 MHz (internal clock speed) processor (respectively).

FPM was popular in PC in 1995. EDO-RAM is a faster type.

See **EDO RAM**.

Frame

A unit of data exchanged within a network or subnetwork. An ISO/OSI Layer 2 (link layer) protocol data unit.

See **S802.3**, **FRAME RELAY HDLC**, **PACKET**, and **PDU**.

Frame

See **INTERLACED** and **NTSC**.

Frame Relay

A variable-length (up to 8,189 bytes, including the frame header but not the CRC, but more commonly implemented as up to 4,096 bytes), shared-bandwidth WAN. Uses a subset of HDLC called LAPD.

Frame relay is optimized for use over higher-speed (such as T1) and very low error-rate data circuits. For example, many carriers now use ATM to carry frame relay traffic, and ATM networks require circuits with *bit error rates* (BERs) of less than 10^{-10} (which means that less than 1 bit in 10,000,000,000 will be corrupted in transit). For example, to reduce the processing load on, and latency through, frame relay networks, the switches do not perform any error correction (other than discarding corrupted frames) nor flow control—other than setting the *Forward Explicit Congestion Notification* (FECN) and *Backward Explicit Congestion Notification* (BECN) bits in the frame header. If the user equipment does not react fast enough (or at all) to the flow control, then the network discards frames when it gets congested. Whether due to corrupted frames or a congested network, discarded frames must be retransmitted by the end users' equipment (such as the TCP protocol software running in your PC).

Since frames can take different paths through a network, the receiving equipment (for example, the TCP protocol in the destination computer) also must perform frame reordering at the receiving end.

The first frame relay networks only offered PVC (Permanent Virtual Circuit)-based connections—you choose where each virtual circuit is connected, when the service is set up (that is, at *subscription time*). Frame relay networks supporting SVC (*switched virtual calls or circuits*) began being offered by public carriers in 1997 and 1998. This allows users to specify where calls are made just before a call is established—just like you do when you dial a telephone, and just as X.25 has always supported.

Port speeds (the speed of the physical data circuit *access line* from the user to the service provider's frame relay switch and the speed of the switch port) are typically between DS-0 and T1, though there are usually only two choices:

▲ 56,000 or 64,000 bits/s (whichever is offered)

▲ T1 (1.544 Mbits/s)

Some service providers offer a fractional T1 option (that is higher multiples of 56 or 64 kbit/s).

As was stated above, the network does not use conventional window-based flow control (which only lets end-stations transmit a predetermined number of messages before they are acknowledged). Instead, carriers commit to being able to carry a prespecified data rate (the *committed information rate*) for each PVC. The CIR (which will usually be up to one-half of, but could be equal to, the speed of the access line) is specified as a bit rate averaged over a 1-second period. Carriers charge more for higher CIRs.

Each PVC will also have an *excess information rate* (sometimes called the *burst excess bandwidth*), which is the maximum bit rate at which a user can send data for that PVC. Most networks allow bursts up to the speed of the physical access line (such as 56 kbit/s or T1). If the network has capacity at that moment, then it will carry (and charge) this excess data. If the network cannot handle the excess burst of data, then it can discard it (and not charge for carrying it). Such discarded data is retransmitted by the higher-layer protocols, such as the TCP running on the end-user computers (usually, only the one lost 1,500-byte TCP segment needs to be retransmitted). The CIR and EIR is configured into both the user equipment (typically a router) and the network switch as part of bringing up the service.

Most frame relay providers charge a flat rate per month (regardless of distance or traffic), though some charge according to the number of megabytes of traffic sent.

Due to queueing and store-and-forward delays, frame relay has a greater latency than (for example) a dedicated 56 kbit/s point-to-point link. Typical frame relay network round-trip latencies within North America are 30 to 70 ms, and 250 to 300 ms internationally.

The frame relay frame header includes a *discard eligibility* (DE) bit (usually set by the transmitting router when it knows it is sending data faster than the CIR). This indicates to the network which frames the network should choose first when frames must be discarded. Part of some router's configuration is which traffic is lower priority (such as a file transfer) and which is higher-priority (perhaps interactive terminal users data, or digitized voice), so the router can set this bit to cause the least disruption to time-sensitive applications.

Some carriers offer PVCs with zero CIR (at a cost savings to the user). Users typically find that these services drop less than 0.01% of traffic and so are often a cost-effective choice.

When networks determine that they are getting congested (and will soon have to drop frames), they signal this by setting the BECN (backward explicit congestion notification) and FECN (forward explicit congestion notification) bits in the frame relay frame header. The FECN bit indicates that there is network congestion somewhere along that PVC's path in the direction of that frame. The BECN bit indicates that there is network congestion in the opposite direction of that frame. The correct action then is to temporarily reduce the data transmission rate to the CIR.

What a router does with the FECN and BECN bits is not specified (mostly because there is no assurance that a router *could* do anything—since flow control is often handled in higher-layer protocols than routers get involved in. For example, for Novell NetWare's IPX protocol, the NCP (NetWare Core Protocol) layer does flow control, and routers have no control over this.

The most common application for frame relay is to connect many branch offices to a head office. A single (higher-capacity) line (with many PVCs (logical connections to different locations—typically one for each remote location) goes from the head office to the public frame relay network. Then each branch office has a lower-capacity frame relay line from the network to their location. Each PVC is assigned a *Data Link Connection Identifier* (DLCI) by the people configuring the frame relay switch. This also must be configured into the user's router.

A single access line can have many PVCs (logical connections to different locations), and the CIRs for those PVCs can be configured to exceed the speed of the access line; this is called *oversubscribing*.

Oversubscribing is usually in the user's interest, since the user's data are likely to be very bursty (that is, the user won't be sending at the full CIR on all PVCs simultaneously). Oversubscribing ensures a high data rate to each PVC's destination when needed, while reducing the cost of the access line. Carriers typically allow oversubscribing of 200% to 400%. For example, a 64-kbits/s access line carrying four PVCs with CIRs of 32 kbits/s each would be oversubscribed 200%.

Some carriers offer a *simplex* service, where the data go only in one direction. This is useful for broadcasting, such as a stock price feed. Or, two simplex circuits (in opposite directions) could be used, each with a different CIR. This would be useful for data communications where a high volume of data go in one direction (such as large file transfers), but very little in the other direction (the protocol's acknowledgments). In contrast, standard duplex frame relay circuits require the same CIR in both directions.

Other types of access circuits, such as asynchronous dial-up (perhaps using SLIP), switched 56, and ISDN BRI (useful for disaster recovery sites), are becoming available from some service providers.

There are two optional methods for user equipment (such as a router) to periodically query the network for a list of the defined DLCIs and their status. The de facto *Local Management Interface* (LMI) was the first method. When it was submitted to ANSI to be a *de jure* standard, ANSI changed the following:

▲ The DLCI used for the status query from 1,023 to 0, and added the capability for the network to query the user equipment as well. This ANSI method is more common, and is Annex D of ANSI T1.167—more commonly simply called "Annex D".

▲ ANSI abbreviates *Local Management* as LMT (rather than LMI).

MCI Communications Corp. and Stentor call their service *Hyperstream*. AT&T calls its service *Interspan*. AT&T Canada calls its service *DataVPN* Interspan.

A problem with frame relay service is that carriers are just beginning to establish connections between each other. While a technical specification exists (*Network-Network Interface—NNI*—which covers the signaling aspects), it does not address *operational issues* such as billing and troubleshooting. Other aspects, such as harmonizing billing rates and policies, how retransmissions are billed, performance guarantees, and troubleshooting procedures will need to be negotiated between all interconnected carriers.

The *Frame Relay Forum* "is an association of Corporate members comprised of Vendors, Carriers, Users and Consultants committed to the implementation of Frame relay in accordance with National and International Standards." It was formed in 1991, and maintains chapters in North America, Europe, Australia/New Zealand, and Japan. It promotes and develops standards for frame relay (such as *voice over frame relay*, VoFR, which is specified in FRF.11), and has a WWW server at *http://frame-relay.indiana.edu/*. Archives of the newsgroup *news://comp.dcom.frame-relay* are at *http://frame-relay.indiana.edu/archives/archives.html*.

Encapsulation of other protocols (such as SDLC, LLC2, IP and IPX) is defined in RFC 1490.

The Frame Relay Forum is at *http://www.frforum.com*.

In addition to the WWW references in the entry for standards, there is a good frame relay pointer page at *http://www.mot.com/MIMS/ISG/tech/frame-relay/resources.html*.

Also, additional information is available from equipment vendors, a major one being StrataCom Inc. at *http://www.stratacom.com* (they were bought by Cisco Systems for $4.1. billion in April 1996).

See **BRI, DS0, ENCAPSULATION, FT1, FUNI, HDLC, LATENCY, NCP1** (*NetWare Core Protocol*), **NNI, PRIORITIZATION, STANDARDS, SWITCHED 56, T1, WAN,** and **XMODEM**.

Frequently Asked Questions

See **FAQ**.

FT1
Fractional T1

A (usually) 128-, 256-, 384-, 512-, or 768-kbits/s point-to-point digital data communications channel (which corresponds to 2, 4, 6, 8, or 12 channels of a T1). The physical circuit is a full 1.544 Mbits/s T1 line with CSU/DSUs, but only some (that is, a *fraction*) of the 24 slots are used.

Some telephone companies will allow individual DS-0 channels to be switched to different locations. The central office switch that splits out, and redirects these DS-0 channels is called a *Digital Access Cross-connect Switch* (DACS).

In Europe, the equivalent service (for their E1 circuits) is called N×64.

See **CSU**, **DSU**, **HDSL**, **T1**, and **WAN**.

FTAM
File Transfer, Access, and Management

An OSI-compliant standard for file transfer, remote creation and deletion, and setting and reading attributes. The standard also describes the format of files to be transferred (for example, it supports stream, flat records, binary/text, indexed, and disk directory formats).

The analogous TCP/IP service is ftp.

See **FTP** and **OSI**.

FTP
File Transfer Protocol

An interactive file transfer capability that is often used on TCP/IP networks. Requires users to log in to (have an account on) the remote computer.

Anonymous ftp allows users to log in using the *username* anonymous. It is then polite to use your email address as your *password* so that the administrators of the remote computer can keep a record of who accessed their computer.

The computer initiating the ftp session requires client software, and the server which will respond to the client's request must be running an ftp *daemon* program which is listening (awaiting a connection request) on TCP port 21. When a connection is established, port 21 is used for login and control functions (using a telnet-type protocol), and the actual data is transferred over a separate connection (which the client initiates) to TCP port 20 on the server.

ftp is defined in RFC 959.

See **CLIENT SERVER**, **TCP**, **TCP/IP**, and **TFTP**.

FUD
Fear, Uncertainty, and Doubt

A marketing tactic (which many used to accuse IBM of using, now more often Microsoft is the target of such accusations) to discourage buying from the competition.

The allegation is that starting (possibly exaggerated) rumors of products or features that don't yet exist (usually because they are not yet ready) would scare potential purchasers into delaying purchasing decisions (or deciding not to buy from the competition at all) for fear that they will purchase the wrong product (that is, one that won't have the compatibility or features desired).

See **IBM**, **MARKETECTURE**, and **MICROSOFT**.

Full-duplex

Communications in which both sender and receiver can send at the same time. Communications on a point-to-point WAN link between two routers is full-duplex (since the routers are likely connecting two buildings full of people, each of whom will be sending or receiving simultaneously).

See **SIMPLEX** and **HALFDUPLEX**.

FUNI
Frame-based User to Network Interface

An ATM Forum specification, which, along with specifications from the Frame Relay Forum permit frame relay and ATM networks to be interconnected. The frame relay traffic is carried over ATM PVCs (using the ATM VBR service category).

User equipment on the frame relay network use the FUNI interface. User equipment on the ATM network use the DXI interface.

See **ATM** (*Asynchronous Transfer Mode*), and **DXI**.

FWIW
For What It's Worth

A common email abbreviation.

G

\<G\> OR \<GRIN\>

Grin

A common email expression that is used when something is stated with a smile (for example, to indicate a joke).

G.703

See **E1**.

G.711

The *pulse code modulation* (PCM, which may be μ-law or A-law) audio digitizing scheme used by carriers, such as your local telephone company. The same method is often used for video-conferencing systems. For example, it is an option in H.320.

The audio uses a full 64 kbits/s data channel, and this provides 3 kHz bandwidth "telephone-quality" audio.

Transcoding is the term given to the process of changing received compressed audio (such as that from G.723, G.728 or G.729) to standard 64 kbit/s PCM.

See **ADPCM**, **H.320**, and **PCM**.

G.721

An audio digitizing scheme that uses ADPCM.

Every 125 μs, a 4-bit difference (from the previous value) is produced, resulting in a bit rate of 32,000 bits/s. This method produces voice at the same perceived quality as 64,000 bit/s PCM (such as G.711), but typically does not work well for modem traffic at greater than 2,400 bits/s.

This method is popular for residential digital cordless telephones.

See **ADPCM**, and **PCM**.

G.722

An audio digitizing scheme often used for video-conferencing systems. For example, it is an option in H.320.

Mode 1 of the method divides the frequencies to be digitized into two sub-bands of 50 Hz to 4 kHz and 4 kHz to 7 kHz. The lower sub-band is then digitized at 48 kbits/s and the upper sub-band at 16 kbit/s (both using ADPCM).

Mode 2 uses a total of 56 kbit/s for the digitized voice, and uses the remaining 8 kbit/s as an auxiliary data channel (for example, for video-conference system remote camera control). Mode 3 uses only 48 kbit/s for the voice, and reserved 16 kbit/s for data.

The total bit rate is therefore 64 kbits/s. This method is also called *sub-band ADPCM*.

See **ADPCM**, **G.711**, and **H.320**.

G.723

Also called MP-MLQ and TrueSpeechII (now guess which name the technical people thought up, and which is from the marketing people).

The full designation for the standard is actually G.723.1.

See **H.320**, and **MPMLQ**.

G.726

An ITU-T standard for 16, 24, 32 and 40 kbit/s ADPCM-encoded digitized speech.

Popular for providing more voice channels on a T1 (or E1), in which case it is called *transcoding*, since the 64 kbits/s PCM digitized speech is converted directly to a different bit-rate (without first being converted to analog—which would reduce the voice quality, and increase the cost).

The 32 kbit/s G.726 method is very similar to ANSI's T1.301 method.

See **ADPCM**, and **ITUT**.

G.727

A method of digitized voice compression using ADPCM at 32 kbits/s.

See **ADPCM**, and **ITUT**.

G.728

An audio digitizing scheme often used for video-conferencing systems. For example, it is an option in H.320. Provides near telephone-quality audio at a data rate of 16 kbits/s.

The method is sometimes called *low-delay code-excited linear prediction* (LD-CELP). *Linear prediction coding* (LPC) is a speech compression scheme that mathematically models the human voice, and sends audio by sending the filter co-efficients representing the changing shape of the vocal tract. This turns out to have a lower bit-rate, and higher quality than *brute force* compression schemes (that don't understand the characteristics of what they are compressing), such as ADPCM. The input to LPC algorithms is typically 64 kbit/s PCM.

RTP is expected to be used to facilitate playing back compressed digitized speech at a constant rate, even though the packets may have encountered varying delays in the network.

G.729

Since newer methods such as G.729 provide almost the same speech quality, but with much lower bit rates, G.728 is no longer very popular for new installations.

See **G.729**, **H.320**, **PCM**, and **RTP**.

G.729

A newer method for digitizing and compressing speech. G.729 provides speech quality near that of ADPCM at 24 kbit/s (this is standardized in G.726) and LD CELP at 16 kbits/s (this is standardized in G.728). The algorithm G.729 uses is called *conjugate-structure algebraic-code-excited linear prediction*—CS ACELP, though this is often called simply (well, almost simply) A-CELP.

Two methods are actually defined, G.729 and G.729a. Both require 8 kbits/s, and provide similar quality speech.

See **G.728**.

G.732

A specification for some of the characteristics for E1.

See **E1**.

G.733

A specification for some of the characteristics for T1.

See **T1**.

GAAS
Gallium Arsenide

The main two types of elements (the chemical symbols for them are Ga and As) used to make semiconductors—such as transistors and integrated circuits (ICs—that are faster and lower-power that those made from Silicon.

Silicon (chemical symbol Si), is the main component of the semiconducting crystals currently used to make ICs. It can switch at a maximum frequency of about 1 GHz. But newer technologies such as PCS at 1.9 GHz, CATV with more channels and digital TV signal decoding and decompression all require GaAs.

See **CATV**, **DBS**, and **PCS**.

Game Port

To support joysticks for game playing, PCs often have a 15-pin connector which can support two joysticks (this is usually a DB-15 female connector on the sound card).

By reading the voltages which vary with the two-dimensional position (in an *x-y* plane) of the joysticks, the PC can track the position of the joystick (the voltages vary between 0 V and +5 V). Each joystick also has two momentary-contact buttons (*Fire 1* and *Fire 2*).

The pin-out of the connector is shown in the table below.

Pin Number	Function
1	+5 V DC
2	Joystick 1, Fire 1
3	Joystick 1, x-axis
4	Ground
5	Ground
6	Joystick 1, y-axis
7	Joystick 1, Fire 2
8	+5 V DC
9	+5 V DC
10	Joystick 2, Fire 1
11	Joystick 2, x-axis
12	Ground
13	Joystick 2, y-axis
14	Joystick 2, Fire 2
15	+5 V DC

The game port (also called joystick connector) on PCs is also used for MIDI.

See **MIDI**, and **MPC**.

GDI
Graphical Device Interface

The software interface (that is, a set of APIs) between a Microsoft Windows program and computer's output devices, such as the video adapter and printer. GDI provides hundreds of functions for drawing geometric shapes (such as lines and boxes) and font rendering. The video driver then generates the actual pixels required, at whatever resolution the video system supports, and for which it has been configured.

A great idea, in that it provides the same interface (APIs) for programmers—regardless of the actual video hardware. Unfortunately, this means that unique hardware-accelerated features of a particular video adapter (such as support for 3-dimensional objects) are not accessible to the programmers.

Games and other multimedia applications therefore often run slower under Windows that under DOS (not exactly progress!). DCI was the first step in remedying this.

See **API**, and **DCI**.

GeoPort

A serial bus, developed and available for license from Apple Computer, Inc. Intended to support telephony, so the bus supports a TDM mode (as well as packet-transfer for non-delay sensitive traffic).

Ghostscript

Transfer rates are up to 2 Mbits/s, and cable lengths up to 4 feet (radiating from a central hub). EIA-422 signal voltages are used, and a 9-pin connector (for 8 signal wires, plus an optional power wire).

See **S1394**, **ADB**, **EIA422**, and **SERIAL BUS**.

Ghostscript

A utility available for computers running the UNIX operating system which print PostScript files on non-PostScript printers.

See **POSTSCRIPT PAGE DESCRIPTION LANGUAGE**.

GIF
Graphics Interchange Format

A file format developed by CompuServe Information Service (in 1987) for storing 256 color (maximum—that is, a maximum of 8 bits is allocated to represent each pixel), raster (as opposed to vector) graphical images. Maximum image size is $65,535 \times 65,535$ pixels. Images are compressed using LZW data compression algorithm, which is *lossless*. The GIF89 format is widely used in WWW documents.

When stored in a file, GIF images typically have a filename extension of `.GIF`.

One of GIF's features is *interlacing* (also called *progressive display*)—images can be initially sent as just every other line (with the lines between those sent afterwards). This permits a (somewhat blurry) image to be displayed sooner, which people usually prefer.

Another feature of GIF is that pixels can be either transparent (so the color under the bit-map shows through) or opaque (so the color under the bit-map is over-written).

Because of the licensing requirement for LZW, in 1995 CompuServe developed the *Portable Network Graphic* (PNG) format to replace GIF.

Pronounced *jiff*.

Two versions of GIF are called GIF87a and GIF89a. GIF89a supports additional features such as supporting ASCII text and comments, and whether it completely replaces, or transparently covers an image below it.

See **COMPUSERVE**, **LOSSY DATA COMPRESSION**, **LZW**, and **PNG**.

Gigabit Ethernet

An even faster version of Ethernet that is faster than fast Ethernet (fast Ethernet is also called 100BASE-T)—1 Gbit/s of user data to be specific (as if you needed a book to tell you that—although the actual raw bit rate on the cable will be 1.25 Gbit/s for most media). As for 100BASE-T, Gigabit Ethernet will use the access method (CSMA/CD) and the same frame format and allowable frame sizes as 10 Mbit/s Ethernet (otherwise they wouldn't be allowed to call it Ethernet—which would make the marketing of the thing much more difficult). This also facilitates interconnecting the different speed Ethernets, since no changes are required to the frames, just a change in speed. When Gigabit Ethernet is used in full-duplex mode (this can be done when the connection is between a server and a switch, but not to a concentrator), some say it operates at 2 Gbits/s (1 Gbit/s in each direction).

Keeping as much of the frame format and access method the same as traditional Ethernet facilitates the development of switches and other Gigabit Ethernet networking devices, hopefully ensuring its acceptance over other potentially competing technologies, such as the occasional rumbling of a faster Token Ring.

Gigabit Ethernet uses same bit-encoding and other physical-layer transmission methods are used as for Fibre Channel. This reduces the risk and development costs, and speeds the standards process, as well as the development and commercial availability of products. There are some changes however. For example, while the bit rate for Fibre Channel is 1.0625 Gbit/s, Gigabit Ethernet on fibre optic cable requires a bit rate of 1.25 Gbit/s which provides a user data rate of 1.0 Gbit/s due to the *8B/10B encoding* used (8 user data bits are sent as 10 bits on the fiber).

Gigabit Ethernet has the right expected price-performance advantages to ensure it is quickly adopted for many applications. It offers 10 times the performance for perhaps a cost 2 to 3 times greater than fast Ethernet.

As Gigabit Ethernet will be much less expensive and simpler (and in some cases, faster) than ATM, some feel that it will replace ATM. This is unlikely, since ATM has many important features such as flow-control and QOS that are required for many applications (and providing QOS assurances for Ethernet's variable-length frames and connectionless operation will be difficult). However, it is likely that Gigabit Ethernet get some of these features through 802.p, 802.Q, RSVP and other efforts. Gigabit Ethernet will likely be a better choice than ATM to link fast Ethernet switches together, and as a lower-cost, high-performance way to connect to servers (though these servers will need a faster bus than PCI at a 33 MHz bus speed and 32-bit transfers).

802.3x is being developed to provide a flow-control mechanism for Gigabit Ethernet.

The maximum cable distances are expected to be as follows:

▲ 1000BASE-SX (shortwave laser of 770 to 860 nm—typically 780 or 850 nm; these are less expensive than longer-wavelength lasers, but fiber has greater attenuation at these wavelengths): 260 m over 62.5/125 μ multimode optical fiber, and 550 m over 50/125 μ fiber (which is common in Europe)

▲ 1000BASE-LX (longwave laser of 1,270 to 1,335 nm—typically 1,310 nm): 440 m over 62.5/125 μ multimode optical fiber, 550 m over 50/125 μ optical fiber, and 3 km over single mode optical fiber.

▲ 1000BASE-CX (dual twin-ax type coaxial cable): 25 m. This is expected to be used for jumper cables in wiring closets.

▲ 1000BASE-T (Category 5 UTP); 100 m. Just to make those people who listened to IBM and installed STP for its future look silly, STP is not expected to be an option (Ethernet people never did like that stuff anyway).

Due to the CSMA/CD access method used by all shared Ethernet implementations, the network diameter needs to be $\frac{1}{10}$ that allowed for fast Ethernet (which in turn is about $\frac{1}{10}$ that allowed for 10 Mbit/s Ethernet). Since a 20 m network diameter (the distance between the

farthest two stations) is somewhat useless, some tricks are required to maintain a 200 m maximum network diameter), as listed below:

▲ The easiest method (and that used by the initial implementations of Gigabit Ethernet) is to make all network ports switched full-duplex ports, rather than shared concentrator (repeater) ports. Therefore, any station can transmit at any time, since there is no chance of a collision—since the full-duplex switch allows sending and receiving simultaneously so there will be no collisions with frames already being sent to us, and the switch can temporarily store frames, so we won't collide with frames already being sent from elsewhere on the network. The same Ethernet minimum interframe gap (IFG) of 96 bits is used as for lower speed Ethernets.

▲ The problem with this is the greater cost of providing full-duplex switched ports for all users, as compared to the lower cost of a shared half-duplex hub port for each user.

▲ The lower-cost approach is to keep Ethernet half-duplex, but modify the Ethernet MAC layer using *carrier extension*. This extends the minimum size of an Ethernet frame from 512 bits (which is 64 bytes) to 4,096 bites (512 bytes). And collisions occurring while these extra bytes of carrier are sent count as a regular collision, and the stations stop transmitting, send the jam signal and backoff and retransmit, just like the original Ethernet. The *slot time* (a random multiple of which colliding stations wait before attempting to retransmit) has also been extended to 512 byte times. The minimum frame size would have to have been 5,120 bits (640 bytes), but rather than waste this much bandwidth for short frames (further reducing the protocol efficiency), it was found that by reducing the number of repeaters allowed between stations from fast Ethernet's 2 to only 1, and by eliminating some timing tolerances that manufacturers can do without, the minimum frame (plus carrier extension) size only had to be increased by a factor of 8. Nonetheless, for the ridiculous case of sending a 1-byte message, 512 bytes would need to be sent—resulting in a protocol efficiency of about 0.2%, and a throughput of about 2 Mbits/s (about the same throughput as you'd get for fast Ethernet). So Gigabit Ethernet is most efficient for larger frame sizes (which is certainly more typical).

▲ To increase the protocol efficiency of half-duplex Gigabit Ethernet *packet bursting* is allowed, instead of (or as part of) the carrier extension used for half-duplex Gigabit Ethernet. Servers, switches and other devices can send a sequence of smaller packets (adding to at least 512 byte times), since this time would have been wasted by the carrier extension, they can now send packets instead.

▲ Another option half-way between full-duplex and half-duplex is a *buffered distributor*. This has the store-and-forward and full-duplex features of a switch or bridge (to allow the network diameter to be increased, since you don't need to worry about collisions on the far side of it). In addition to the full-duplex features specified in 802.3x, a buffered distributor supports 802.3x's flow-control to ensure its buffer memory does not overflow while waiting for a break in the network activity to send its stored frames. But unlike a switch or bridge, it does not learn addresses, so in that respect, it is like a concentrator (Ethernet concentrators are also called hubs and multi-port repeaters). These simply boost the signal and send it out all other ports. Buffered distributors are sometimes called *full-duplex repeaters* or *buffered repeaters*.

The main (such as the changes to the MAC layer) and optical parts of Gigabit Ethernet are being standardized by 802.3z. Initial applications will be full-duplex fiber optic cable links between switches. Since it is expected that development of the transmission method for Category 5 UTP will take longer, this work is under 802.3ab (they used up all the letters a through z for additions to 802.3, so they now go to aa, ab and so on).

Gigabit Ethernet is promoted by the Gigabit Ethernet Alliance, that includes 3Com Corporation, Bay Networks, Cisco Systems Inc., Hewlett-Packard Co., Intel Corporation, Packet Engines Inc. and Sun Microsystems.

The Gigabit Ethernet Alliance has a web server at *http://www.gigabit-ethernet.org/*, and some standards development documents are at *ftp://stdbbs.ieee.org/pub/802main/802.3/gigabit*. Information on interoperability testing is at *http://www.iol.unh.ed/consortiums/ge/index.html*. Some information on the protocol is at *http://www.ots.utexas.edu:8080/ethernet/gigabit.html*. Packet Engines (an equipment manufacturer) has a web server at *http://www.packetengines.com*.

See **S100BASET**, **S802.3X**, **S8B-10B**, **CSMACD**, **ETHERNET**, and **FIBER**.

GMT
Greenwich Mean Time

The time in Greenwich, England, the location of which defines where the *prime meridian* (that is, 0° longitude) is. The rest of the world's time zones (and longitude) are referenced to this meridian.

No longer used as a time reference, since time is no longer referenced to the stars (the world doesn't rotate consistently enough for this, it apparently wobbles and slows too much).

See **SATELLITE** and **UTC**.

Gopher

A method of snooping through the Internet for files and retrieving them. Easier to use than the `ftp` utility (though gopher actually retrieves files using `ftp`), but not nearly as much fun, and not as powerful as the WWW.

A series of menus (on destination machines) provide pointers to resources, which the gopher client software (running on your local machine) displays, or uses as a trigger to launch other applications, such as telnet or WAIS.

Many WWW browsers can also be gopher clients (for example, enter *gopher://internic.net/* into Netscape).

The name comes from the system's function: to "go fer" things. Also, it was developed at the University of Minnesota, and its Twin Cities campus athletic teams are called the Gophers.

The gopher FAQ is at *ftp://rtfm.mit.edu/pub/usenet/news.answers/gopher-faq*.

See **FTP**, **WAIS**, and **WWW**.

GOSIP
Government OSI Profile

Government specifications of the OSI standards and options to use to implement various computer communications functions. The U.S. and U.K. both have a GOSIP with the same intent, but the specifications are different. COSAC is the Canadian equivalent specification.

See **COSAC** and **OSI**.

GPS
Global Positioning System

A system of 24 satellites, each of which orbits the earth every 12 hours at a height of 20,200 km. Four satellites are located in each of six planes inclined at 55° to the plane of the earth's equator. The orbits were designed so that there would always be at least 4 satellites in view (that is, over the horizon from any location on the surface of the earth, at any time). Usually there are 5 to 11 GPS satellites that can be tracked.

Given that all a GPS receiver can determine is the time it takes for it to communicate with a GPS satellite, and that the position of the satellite is accurately known, when in communication with a single GPS satellite, your distance from that one satellite can be determined. That is, you are somewhere on a sphere (which has a radius equal to your distance from the satellite) which is centered on the satellite. If you can simultaneously communicate with 2 GPS satellites, then your location is somewhere on the intersection (which turns out to be a circle) of the spheres centered on each of the satellites. When 3 satellites are in view (think of a circle intersecting with a sphere), then your position is at one of 2 points on the circle. When 4 satellites are in view, then your position can be accurately determined, subject to timing and other errors in measuring your distance to the satellites.

When receivers "see" three satellites simultaneously, they can calculate the following:

▲ *latitude* and *longitude*, with an accuracy of 100 m (95% of the time) horizontally for public use and 16 m for military use

▲ *velocity*, with an accuracy to 0.1 m/s

▲ *time* information is provided, allowing the time to be calculated with an accuracy of about 150 ns (the atomic clocks on the satellites run at 10,229,999.99543 Hz., which appears to us earthlings as 10,230,000 Hz—due to the effects of relativity!).

Having only 3 satellites in view is usually only useful if you already know your altitude (for example, sea-level, because you are in a boat on the ocean).

When a fourth satellite is simultaneously in view, *altitude* information is also available (to an accuracy of 156 m for public use).

Most GPS receivers track 6 or more satellites, choose those with the best signal reception, and average the results to reduce timing and other errors. Since GPS receivers may be moving while they are tracking the satellites, good ones will have 4 or more *demodulators* (also called *channels*) so they can simultaneously track the multiple satellites (otherwise, the GPS receiver will need to sequentially receive from each satellite, and the GPS receiver's movement after receiving from each satellite will reduce the accuracy of the final position determined).

It can take many minutes for a GPS receiver to determine which satellites are in view, and calculate position information. Since this *time-to-first-fix* (TTFF) is of interest to many frantic and lost people, GPS receivers often stay in a standby mode (rather than completely powering-off) in which they estimate the expected position of satellites, so they can more quickly calculate position information after being powered-on from such a standby state. Tracking more than the minimum number of satellites also helps reduce the TTFF.

From a "coldstart" (not having any idea of where it is), a GPS receiver requires about 5 to 15 minutes to figure out where it is. So long as it stores this last known position (and can determine the time elapsed), subsequent "warmstarts" require less than 2 minutes after powering on to determine their location. While powered-on, location updates are typically provided every $\frac{1}{2}$ or 1 second.

GPS satellites transmit on two frequencies. L1 (the *coarse acquisition* code, or *C/A* code) uses a center frequency of 1,575.42 MHz with a bandwidth of 2 MHz. L2 is at 1,227.6 MHz, and is the *precision code* (*P-code*), and is used for the Precise Positioning Service (PPS), which enables receivers to determine their location with an accuracy of about 1 m.

The satellites all transmit at the same frequencies, and using SST-type methods, receivers can isolate the signals from individual satellites.

Fearing that enemies could use GPS's positional information to help target bombs, the P-code is encrypted, so it is fully available only to the U.S. military. (The other reason for encrypting the GPS PPS is that it is therefore more difficult to jam the signal for the purposes of disruption or deception.)

Without being able to decrypt the P-code—that is, the positioning information available to the general public—has random errors of up to 200 ns added to the signal, providing location information with an accuracy of about 100 m (consumer GPS receivers are typically accurate to 15 m themselves, but the selective availability timing errors added by the satellites reduce this accuracy to 100 m). This public service is officially called the *Standard Positioning Service* or *Selective Availability* (SA or S/A).

Now that there are many economic benefits to providing more precise location and time information (aircraft guidance systems and mobile telephone systems use GPS), the adding of errors to the positioning information may be terminated in 1998. In any case, the errors can be cancelled-out by averaging them over an 18-hour periodμso fixed or very slow-moving equipment can be accurately tracked. In 1993, the U.S. government offered the GPS system would be available for worldwide civil aviation use for a period of 10 years. In 1993, the U.S. Federal Aviation Administration approved use of GPS as a supplementary aid to navigation for enroute, non-precision approach, and terminal flights.

Some points on accuracy:

▲ GPS location accuracies are measured as *Spherical Error Probable* (SER); that is, 95% of all location fixes will be within (for example) a sphere of 16 m radius.

▲ If only the horizontal accuracy is of concern (usually the case for things that don't fly), then the accuracy is stated as "*2DRMS*" (twice the distance, *root mean square*), which produces a slightly different number (21 m for this example, but typically 100 m, 70% of the time for consumer GPS receivers).

Differential GPS (DGPS) uses a second GPS receiver (for example, at an airport or harbor) that has a precisely known location. It calculates its location (according to the GPS information), and determines the error (since it knows its location, and it never moves). The differential GPS receiver then transmits this error information to mobile GPS receivers, that use this information to reduce the errors of their own GPS location calculation. Typically, the differential GPS receiver must be within about 10 km of the moving one, so that they both receive signals from the same satellites, and are subject to the same conditions that cause errors (such as atmospheric refraction, satellite location and clock speed). Differential GPS is method is required for aircraft navigation use, and can provide positional information (for the first receiver) as follows:

▲ For S/A, the accuracy is 1 to 5 m (depending on the quality of the receiver)—if the receiver is stationary or only moving slowly—and by tracking the difference in phase of the received carrier frequency (between the two receivers), location accuracy of about 25 cm can be achieved. The accuracy may be reduced to 15 m for faster-moving objects, such as airplanes.

▲ For PPS (that is, for the military), the accuracy is a few centimeters.

While a minimum of 18 satellites are needed for basic service, 24 are needed for a reliable system with full coverage. On December 8, 1993, 24 satellites were first available (though some were the initial 11 experimental satellites). The system was to have been completed by 1987, but Challenger disaster delayed satellite launches.

The satellites have a service life of about $7\frac{1}{2}$ years, then must be replaced (this began in 1996). Since the service is so important (and becomes more so as cellular telephone and aircraft landing systems use the service), there are a few spare satellites kept in orbit (for example, there were 35 GPS satellites launched between February 1978 and March 1994). The U.S. Department of Defence budgeted $10 billion for the system in the 1970s.

There are 5 surveillance and tracking stations around the world, and all satellites are continuously monitored by at least one station. The overall control center is in Colorado.

The GPS system is officially called *Navstar*.

A similar Russian system is called the *Global Navigation Satellite System* (GLONASS). It also uses 24 satellites. Receivers that use satellites from both systems simultaneously can provide location information with an accuracy of 10 to 15 m, at a 95% probability. Differential receivers provide location information with an accuracy of about 90 cm.

The last of the satellites required for its operation became operational in late 1995. The system offers accuracy of about 100 to 150 m, about the same as GPS's public capability.

To provide better accuracy for aviation (to within 7.6 m) a system of 24 ground stations in the continental U.S. are being installed (for first commercial use in 1999, and nationwide use in 2001) to be the fixed side of a differential GPS system for commercial aircraft. The system is called WAAS (wide-area augmentation system).

The GPS Joint Program Office is at *http://www.laafb.af.mil/CZ/homepage/*, the U.S. Naval Observatory has GPS information at *http://tycho.usno.navy.mil/gps.html*, and the coast guard has some information at *http://www.navcen.uscg.mil/*. Trimble Navigation is a major manufacturer of GPS receivers, they have a web site at *http://www.trimble.com/gps/*. Paul Tarr's GPS web page is at *http://www.inmet.com/~pwt/gps_gen.htm*.

See **CDMA**, **NAVSTAR**, **SATELLITE**, **SST**, and **UTC**.

GREP
Global Regular Expression Print

A popular UNIX utility (and the basis for many other utilities with slightly different capabilities). It is used for searching through all the lines of a file, or many files (hence the "global") for patterns of characters (which are described—using a syntax called a "regular expression"), and to print (or more commonly, display on your monitor) the lines which contain a match.

See **UNIX**.

GSS-API
Generic Security Service—Application Program Interface

An IETF-approved API for securely passing *authentication* information (determining who can run which programs) between application programs in a distributed computing environment.

Specified in RFCs 1508 and 1509.

See **API**, **AUTHENTICATION**, and **IETF**.

GSM
Global System for Mobile Communication (previously Groupe Spécial Mobile)

A widely deployed digital cellular telephone standard (partially because the European Union gave away radio spectrum for free to network operators that adopted GSM). Public service was first available in 1991, and it is now used in over 200 networks in more than 108 countries (from Albania to Zimbabwe) including; all of Europe and Asia (such as China, but not Japan or South Korea), South Africa, South America, some countries in the Middle East (such as Lebanon) and other Persian Gulf states, and parts of the former Soviet Union and of Australia. The frequency band is typically between 890 and 915 MHz.

The initial work (largely to get a single pan-European cellular telephone standard) was begun in 1980 by the *Groupe Spécial Mobile*. Since 1989, development work has been done by the European Telecommunications Standards Institute (ETSI).

The frequencies allocated to the service are divided into 200-kHz blocks. The raw data rate is 270,833 bits/s, and this supports 8 simultaneous users. Each user gets a 577 µs time slot in the 8-timeslot frame of data, which is sent 216.68 times per second. That is, TDMA is used, and handsets must have precisely-controlled transmitter power-up and -down characteristics (or else they will adversely affect adjacent time-slot users). Each user's time slot carries 114 bits (which includes signalling and error-protection bits), the remainder of the 32.25 bit-times being used for synchronization, doppler-shift allowance, equalization, guard time between each handset's transmission, and other protocol overhead uses. 16 simultaneous conversations per 200 kHz channel may be supported in the future, if lower bit-rate voice digitizers (with intelligible voice quality!) become economically available.

For actual user data (or digitized voice) transmission, 13-kbits/s per user is available (including signalling and error-correction information, each user uses 24,700 bits/s, and including timing and protocol overhead bits, each user uses 33,850 bits/s). This is divided into two channels:

▲ The main channel (the *Bm* channel), which can be used for 9,600-bits/s asynchronous or synchronous data, or digitized voice (which uses most of the 13 kbits/s). This channel is circuit-switched, taking 20 to 30 seconds for a call setup.

▲ A 382-bits/s channel (the *Dm* channel), which is used for signaling (setting up and clearing the Bm channel's calls).

▲ Since the Dm channel can carry messages of up to 160 characters, it can also be used for *Short Message Services* (SMS), such as providing caller identification, notifying users of waiting voice mail messages or received (and stored on a server for later retrieval) faxes, stock price changes, and weather reports for cities keyed in by the caller.

Supports encryption of voice and data. Less frequency-efficient than the North American TDMA (IS-54) method, but very robust.

GSM is similar to North American (analog) AMPS Cellular, in that they both use cells and handoffs—though not all operators track users, so some GSM operators only offer outgoing service (originated from the mobile phones).

Advantages over North American analog cellular is that GSM can carry 3 to 6 times more traffic in a given amount of bandwidth, and GSM is a digital system, and was designed to handle data communications.

GSM supports two data modes:

▲ *Transparent* provides a raw data channel, complete with whatever errors occur.

▲ *Nontransparent* uses a GSM-specific error-correcting protocol, which usually provides better throughput than end-user error correcting protocols, though some say that the GSM error-correction is not robust enough.

GSM handsets accept a standardized credit-card sized *subscriber identity module* (SIM) or the smaller microSIM (which can be inserted into a SIM). Sometimes called *Smart Cards* (specified in ISO 786), these provide identification of the user (for billing purposes), while encrypting this information before sending it over the air. This is a major advantage over standard North American AMPS handsets that can be *cloned* by stealing the telephone or even by monitoring (with special test equipment) the handset's transmissions—so that the handset can be duplicated, with all charges going to the original owner. Borrowing someone else's handset, and inserting your own SIM results in you paying all charges (GSM operators are quickly establishing *roaming* agreements to work out the billing amongst themselves to support this).

The GSM protocol's timing design allows cell sizes of up to 33.2 km radius, though actual installations will typically use much smaller cells to increase capacity (through frequency reuse) or due to the local terrain and antenna limitations.

Support for fax, ISDN, and X.25 access is either available or in development. Some operators assign multiple phone numbers to a phone to differentiate in-coming calls to the phone as voice, data, or fax.

While all GSM services and telephones are compatible, much work remains to be done before users will be able to use their telephones anywhere and receive the same services. For example:

▲ Roaming agreements between operators (for billing purposes) are required before operators will provide services to other operators' customers.

▲ Many operators are just beginning to offer data services (which require the addition of modem connections to land-line services).

▲ Network design may need to be modified to offer all services. For example, voice traffic requires low delay but can tolerate brief communication problems (such as noise), whereas data service can tolerate delays but brief transmission problems are often unacceptable.

The initial GSM installations all used the 900-MHz frequency band. The specific frequencies are typically 890 to 915 MHz—in some installations this has been extended to 880 to 915 MHz to provide more capacity). The mobile's transmit frequency is 45 MHz below its receive frequency.

In some countries, GSM is being expanded to *Digital Communication System*. This is usually called (DCS 1800, as it uses frequencies from 1,710 to 1,785 MHz (and the spacing between the transmit and receive frequencies of a conversation is 95 MHz). It is sometimes called *Personal Communications Network* (PCN). DCS 1800 supports more users, and has smaller cells (so more base stations are needed to cover a given area). The smaller cells allow the telephones to use lower transmit power, so they can have smaller batteries and therefore be lighter and/or last longer between recharging.

GPRS (General Packet Radio Service) is a new standard to be used to enhance existing voice-only GSM systems to provide a packet-based system with faster call set-up times to handle bursty data (such as short transactions). It is expected to be in commercial service by 1999.

A version of GSM designed for the 1.9 GHz North American PCS frequency band is called PCS 1900. As for all PCS services, the mobile's transmit frequency is 80 MHz below its transmit frequency. The first systems implemented were in commercial service in November 1995 (in Washington DC).

PCS 1900 is also used by Microcell Telecommunications in Canada, and by BellSouth and PacTel in the U.S. Since different frequencies are used in North America than in Europe, it will not be possible to use a North American GSM handset in Europe. But, you can use your SIM.

UMTS is an attempt to define the next generation of GSM-type services.

Prior to GSM, most European countries developed their own incompatible (that is, country-specific) analog systems, which used technology similar to North America's AMPS. For example, England has a system called TACS, and the Scandinavian countries have a system called NMT.

Ericsson Radio Systems (Stockholm, Sweden) is a huge manufacturer of GSM equipment. They have a web site at *http://www.ericsson.se*. They have GSM information at *http://www. ericsson.com/systems/gsm*.

See **AMPS**, **ARDIS**, **CDMA**, **ESMR**, **MOBITEX**, **PCS1** (*Personal Communications Service*), **RBOC OR RBHC**, **RDS**, **SMARTCARD**, **TDMA**, **UMTS**, and **WIRELESS**.

GUI
Graphical User Interface

Sometimes called a WIMP interface; windows, icons, multitasking (or mice) and pointing device (such as a mouse or track-ball)—or pull-down. Also sometimes called a mousey-clicky interface. All this, since you get to do most things by clicking on different parts of the screen.

GUIs are supposed to be easier to use, and require less training. The first implementations were done at Xerox Corporation's Palo Alto Research Center (PARC) in the 1970s. Apple Corporation enthusiastically used their concepts in their Macintosh OS, and Microsoft began implementing it for the PC world in their Windows product. The UNIX world also decided it was a better way to go, and they implemented it in their *OPENLOOK* and *Motif* user interfaces.

The old way of doing things is often called *command-line*, where you type all commands on a single line (such as `c:> dir /w /p`). All early computer operating systems (those for mainframes and minicomputers) and the operating systems for the first microcomputers (CP/M and DOS) also used command-line interfaces.

See **S3COM, MOTIF,** and **OPENLOOK.**

H

H.245

A standard for call control, typically used for video conferencing systems.

For example, H.245 specifies the following:

▲ how a connection should be established and terminated

▲ how mutual capabilities will be negotiated, such as; whether both ends support full-duplex audio transmission, the audio compression method (or CODEC) used, data encryption and method, preferred bit resolutions for images, maximum data rates, and end-point capabilities, such as facsimile support

▲ the exchange of *bit-rate allocation signal* codes to apportion the bandwidth among the services to be provided for the communication

▲ how to monitor jitter (short term variations in the network latency)

A reliable protocol, such as TCP/IP must be used (though an unreliable protocol, such as UDP can be used to carry the actual digitized audio or video for the users' communication).

See **FULL-DUPLEX**, **H.320**, and **LATENCY**.

H.261

A video digitization and lossy compression scheme which uses MPEG for analog video, typically used for video conferencing (such as is defined in H.320).

Two video formats are specified:

▲ The full screen *Common Intermediate Format* (CIF, sometimes called *Full Common Intermediate Format*—FCIF) is 352 horizontal × 288 vertical pixels

▲ The *Quarter CIF* (QCIF) option is 176 × 144 pixels. This is $\frac{1}{4}$ the size, and requires $\frac{1}{4}$ the bandwidth of CIF

Both are at 30 frames per second.

One or two 64-kbits/s channels are usually adequate for QCIF. This shows the power of data compression—uncompressed CIF would require 73 Mbits/s at 30 frames per second.

See **H.263**, **H.320**, **MPEG**, and **VIDEO**.

H.263

A video digitization and compression scheme which is more efficient than H.261. It includes a Sub-QCIF format (SQCIF) which is 128×96 pixels.

See **H.261**, and **H.320**.

H.310

A suite of videoconferencing standards, intended for use over ATM and Broadband ISDN connections. MPEG-2 video compression is specified.

See **H.320**.

H.320

A suite of standards (for example, H.261 is the video digitizing and compression scheme) that describe how video-conferencing systems communicate over leased-line or circuit-switched WANs, such as fractional T1, switched 56 and (most commonly) ISDN. In addition to integrating voice and digitized video on the WAN, control messages are also defined. Typically, one or more 64-kbits/s channels are used (so it is sometimes called $P \times 64$ ("P times 64").

The input could be a video camera or a portion of a PC's screen (so that everyone can see what is being displayed).

Three types of digitized audio are defined:

▲ G.711—which uses a full 64 kbit/s channel to provide 3.4 kHz bandwidth audio using A-law or μ-law CODECs. Support for this is required in H.323.

▲ G.722—a more intelligent algorithm than G.711, which uses up to 64 kbit/s of bandwidth to provide 7.5 kHz bandwidth audio. Support for this is optional.

▲ G.728—provides slightly less quality audio than G.711, but uses only 16 kbits/s of bandwidth to do this. Support for this is optional.

Other standards specified by H.320 include the following:

▲ H.321 defines how ATM and Broadband-ISDN would be used instead of 56 or 64 kbit/s circuits.

▲ H.322 defines how networks (typically LANs) that can guarantee a *Quality of Service* ("QoS"), such as 802.9A iso-Ethernet, can be used for video-conferencing.

▲ H.323 describes how any packet switched network (such as an Ethernet or Token Ring LAN running IP, the Internet, or IPX) that do not support a guaranteed QOS can be used for audio (the basic requirement) or video conferencing (this support, as well as for data, is optional). The same type of video compression as is used for H.320 is specified (H.261

and H.263), facilitating interoperability. Both point-to-point and point-to-multipoint networks are defined. Support for G.711 is required, and G.723 or MPEG-1 audio can optionally be supported. The video and audio data can be sent using an unreliable protocol, such as UDP. A *gateway* function is also defined that allows interoperation with H.321 (ISDN) and H.324 (POTS) videoconferencing units. H.245 is specified for system and call control, and to negotiate facilities (optional features) between the participants, as well as with network devices.

▲ H.324 (which was called H.32P during development) defines how POTS (that is, the standard voice telephone network and analog modems) can be used instead of 56 and 64 kbit/s digital channels for desktop videoconferencing. A 28.8 kbit/s modem can usually provide video at only about 2 frames per second.

▲ H.324/M is a superset of H.324, and has support for wireless (mobile) videoconferencing (now that's a good one, now people are going to be driving while videoconferencing, in case driving while just talking on the cellular telephone was not enough).

RTP is specified to be used to timestamp UDP packets, so the receiver can play them back at a constant rate, regardless of variable delays in the network (so long as the receiver buffers as much data as a the maximum expected network delay).

An MCU (*multipoint control unit*) allows more than 2 end-points to partake in an audio or video conference, by *bridging* everybody together.

Typically, 5 to 20 seconds is required for the initial connection negotiation and synchronization before audio and video begin to be exchanged. The initial update of the entire video screen may require up to another 20 seconds.

H.320 was first released in 1990, but additional work has been done since then.

The International Multimedia Teleconferencing Consortium has further information at *http://www.imtc.org*.

See **ATM**, **S802.9A**, **CODEC**, **G.711**, **G.722**, **G.723**, **H.245**, **H.261**, **H.263**, **H.310**, **ISDN**, **FT1**, **MPEG**, **MPMLQ**, **PCS** (*Personal Conferencing Specification*), **POTS**, **QOS**, **RTP**, **SWITCHED 56**, **T.120**, **VIDEO**, and **WAN**.

Hacker

For some reason, hacker is now considered to be a complementary term for someone who really understands some aspect of computers (though perhaps just for the purposes of circumventing security systems to gain unauthorized access them).

However, a hacker used to be a derogatory term for someone who makes things using poor workmanship. For example, a set of bookshelves that look as if they were made by hacking them out of wood with a machete would have been made by a hacker.

See **VIRUS**.

Half-Duplex

Communications that can go both to and from all parties but in only one direction at a time.

The classic analogy is a narrow country bridge. Cars can cross in either direction, but only one direction at a time.

Spoken communications between two (polite) people and data communications on traditional Token Ring and Ethernet LANs are half-duplex (though full-duplex versions have been implemented—of LANs, that is).

See **S10BASET**, **SIMPLEX**, and **FULL-DUPLEX**.

HDLC
High-Level Data Link Control

A *bit-oriented*, synchronous, link layer, data-framing, flow control, and error detection and correction protocol.

Uses a header with control information and a trailing *cyclic redundancy check* character (which is usually 16, but may be 32 bits in length).

Flag characters (which are the bit pattern 01111110—that is, 6 contiguous 1s) delimit frames of data (that is, flag characters are sent when there is no data to send). To ensure that users can send any bit pattern (including 6 1s in a row), the UART does *zero-bit-stuffing*, where a 0 bit is inserted after 5 contiguous 1s of user data (the receiving UART removes these stuffed 0s).

Implementations are both standard subsets (see below) or vendor-specific (such as that used for the 56,000-bits/s interfaces on a vendor's remote bridge or router). IBM calls HDLC *SDLC*.

Some standard subsets are listed in the following table.

	HDLC Subset	Used for
802.2	Logical link control	FDDI, Token Ring, and some Ethernet LANs
LAP	Link Access Procedure	Early X.25 implementations
LAPB	Link Access Procedure, Balanced	Current X.25 implementations
LAPD	Link Access Procedure for the ISDN D channel	ISDN D channel and frame relay
LAPM	Link Access Procedure for Modems	Error-correcting modems (specified as part of V.42)

BISYNC is (was) an older method of synchronous data communications.

See **S802.2**, **BISYNC**, **CRC**, **DLC**, **DSU**, **FRAME RELAY**, **ISDN**, **MNP**, **PPP**, **SDLC**, **SYNCHRONOUS**, **UART**, **V.42**, and **XMODEM**.

HDSL
High-Bit-Rate Digital Subscriber Line

A technology developed by Bellcore that provides full-duplex T1 service (using two twisted pairs of cable) over greater distances than the *alternate mark inversion* encoding that is traditionally used by T1.

Also, full-duplex *fractional T1* service can be provided over a single pair of wires.

Uses:

▲ Two copper twisted pairs (same as T1) but runs each full-duplex at 784 kbits/s on each (the lower bit rate reduces cross-talk). The 784 kbits/s includes 768 kbits/s of time-slot information (12 standard 64 kbit/s DS-0 channels) plus 8 kbits/s of T1 framing-bit overhead plus 8 kbit/s of HDSL overhead. (Other implementations can provide speeds from 384 kbits/s to 2.048 Mbit/s—though 2.048 Mbit/s requires 3 pairs of cable.)

▲ ISDN's 2B1Q line coding—2 binary (two-state) bits encoded into a four-state (*quaternary*) symbol

▲ *Echo cancellation*, which permits use on lines with *bridge taps* (splits to multiple locations), changes in the wire gauge and twisted pairs in a cable that are not in their own binder group (a *binder* is a colored thread wrapped around some of the pairs in a cable, to keep them together when the cable is manufactured, and to help identify the pairs after installation)

▲ *Adaptive Equalization* (automatically adjusts to permit operation over changing- and poorer-quality lines)

Maximum repeaterless cable distances are approximately (the exact distances depend on the desired bit error rate and the noise on the pairs):

▲ 12,000 feet for 24-gauge cable

▲ 9,000 feet for 26-gauge cable

Since more than 80% of all T1 customer loops are less than 12,000 feet in length, and T1 links over 6,000 feet require a repeater, HDSL, it is expected that HDSL will be popular someday (but for now, it is available, but too expensive for wide deployment).

ADSL provides a somewhat similar service.

HDSL2 is to provide full-duplex T1 over a single 26-gauge twisted pair of copper conductors, up to 3,650 m (12,000 feet) in length. Very high-speed digital subscriber line (VHDSL) is expected to provide 13 to 52 Mbits/s (which is the, SONet OC-1 rate)) downstream (from the CO), and 1.544 to 2.3 Mbits/s upstream, over a single pair of copper cabling, up to 1.4 km in length.

HDSL is standardized in ANSI T1E1.4/94-006 and Bellcore TA-NWT-001210.

See **ADSL, B8ZS, BELLCORE, ENCODING, FT1, FULL-DUPLEX, SEALING CURRENT, SONET**, and **T1**.

HDTV
High-Definition Television

A digital television (and more) broadcasting method to be an enhancement to the current standard NTSC broadcast and cable TV television signals used today.

Some features are the following:

▲ Provides a 16:9 (horizontal:vertical) aspect ratio, like a movie screen that is showing a standard 35-mm (called *Academy format*) or 70-mm movie film. This is wider than the 4:3 ratio of current standard televisions.

▲ Provides up to a 60-frames/s screen writing rate.

▲ Uses a subset of MPEG-2 data compression (and the *discrete cosine transformation* method that it specifies) to compress the source information (which has a data rate of about 900 Mbits/s to 1.2 Gbits/s, depending on the digitizing method used) by a factor of more than 60:1, to a broadcast data rate of 19.39 Mbits/s per TV channel.

▲ Using AC-3 digitized audio, which provides 5-channel (plus a low frequency enhancement channel) sound.

▲ Using something called 8-VSB—*8-level digital vestigial sideband*—modulation (wow, now if that doesn't impress you, they hope the picture quality will), this still fits into the current standard 6-MHz bandwidth broadcast television channels.

▲ In fact, for cable TV broadcasting, a single 6-MHz channel can carry two HDTV signals, since the HDTV signal can be simplified because the CATV environment is very (electrically) quiet.

▲ For broadcast, HDTV will initially (for at least 15 years, beginning in 1998) use either the 6 MHz channels that were left unassigned (to reduce interference) between currently assigned TV broadcast channels (that is, if channels 3 and 5 are assigned and used in a coverage area for standard NTSC broadcast television, then channel 4 will be available and will be used for HDTV). Or a UHF channel will be assigned. Each of the U.S.'s 1,500 to 1,600 television stations get the use of a second frequency. It is not clear whether the second frequency will ever be returned, and if so, which of the two will be returned (generally, lower frequencies are more desirable, as they propagate farther). The FCC decided this in April 1997, after some controversy (and a huge amount of lobbying of the FCC and the government) about whether TV stations should pay for the use of this spectrum (the stations get the use of the second channel for free). Current requirements are that by May 1999 the top 4 networks in the top 10 U.S. markets must have begun broadcasting HDTV signals. By November 1999 the top 4 networks in the top 30 markets must have started HDTV broadcasts. By 2002 all commercial, and by 2003 all public television broadcasting stations must be using HDTV.

▲ The government's expectation is that the rollout of this digital television would be completed by the year 2006, and the extra frequencies for the transition would no longer be needed soon after this, as television stations are supposed to stop broadcasting the now-standard analog television signals after 2006 (so your current televisions, VCRs and camcorders are obsolete by then). It is expected that stations may use the extra channel to carry several channels of digitally-compressed standard and pay television—instead of for a transition to HDTV.

Several frame rates and formats are defined, as shown in the following table. Most yield "square pixels—that is, the number of pixels per inch is the same horizontally and vertically. This facilitates conversions between HDTV formats and also to common PC monitor resolutions.

Formats, in number of...		Aspect Ratios supported		Frame Rates Supported (Hz), by type of scanning[a]	
Active[b] samples[c] (horizontal pixels)	Active lines (vertical pixels)	4:3 (NTSC)	16:9 (HDTV)	Interlaced	Progressive
1,920	1080[d]		✓	29.97, 30	23.976,24, 29.97, 30
1,280	720		✓	None	23.976,24
704[e]	480[f]	✓	✓	29.97, 30	29.97, 30
640[g]	✓		59.94, 60		

a. The wide range of scanning rates is supported to allow for the various sources of program material; movies are 24 frames per second, NTSC television is 29.97 fields per second and 59.94 frames per second, and PC video is typically 30 frames per second. 60 frames per second is best-suited to sports and other fast-action scenes.

b. *Active* means that they are visible. For example, NTSC has 481 active lines out of the total of 525 horizontal lines. The remaining 44 lines occur while the scanning beam is *blanked* during its *vertical retrace* back to the top-left corner of the screen.

c. Note that the numbers of horizontal pixels for the formats are usually related, to simplify converting formats. For example, there is a 3:2 ration between the 1,920 and 1,280 horizontal pixels of the top two formats. And there is a 2:1 ration between the 1,280 and 640 horizontal pixels the second and fourth formats.

d. MPEG-2 requires that the number of lines for all formats be an integer multiple of 16 (since the macroblocks are 16 pixels horizontally and vertically). Therefore, this format actually encodes 1,088 lines, and the last 8 lines are ignored.

e. This format is the only one that does not have square pixels. It is provided since it closely matches the 720 line × 483 pixel ITU-601 format which is popular in television studio production environments. (When encoded, 3 of the 483 horizontal pixels are ignored, and the top 8 and bottom 8 lines of the 720 are also ignored.)

Similarly, the 1,280 × 720 and 640 × 1,080 formats were chosen because they are also popular television production standards.

f. The 704 × 480 and 640 × 480 formats are called standard-definition STDV, as they are compatible with current NTSC television production and display equipment.

g. This format matches PC VGA resolution.

The specification recommends that receivers "seamlessly" (without loss of video or synchronization) switch between these video formats, as it is expected that changes will frequently occur (for example at commercial breaks, between programs and during news reports).

HDTV uses Dolby Laboratories AC-3 multichannel digital sound system, which provides the following audio channels (which is sometimes called 5.1—5 channels plus the bass enhancement):

▲ Left

▲ Center

▲ Right

▲ Left-surround

▲ Right-surround

▲ Low-frequency enhancement (for frequencies up to 120 Hz)

All this audio is first digitized at 48 ksamples per second (typically at 16 bits per sample), and compressed into a 384-kbits/s bit stream to provide compact-disc-quality audio. Other audio features are provided, such as the following:

▲ A constant volume level when switching channels

▲ Using the multiple audio channels for different languages or for services for the visually or hearing impaired

The digitized video, audio, and auxiliary information are packaged in 188-byte packets (only one type of information per packet). A 4-byte header in the packet:

▲ Includes an 8-bit synchronization byte

▲ Identifies (using 13 bits) what type of information the 184-byte packet payload carries

▲ Provides encryption (scrambling) control (to support pay-per-view and other premium services)

Information that is sent periodically in the payload provides synchronization between the different data streams, for example, to ensure lip-sync between the voice and video.

Added to each 188-byte packet are 20 bytes of Reed-Solomon *forward error correction* bytes to enable many (hopefully most) errored packets to be corrected by the receiver. (Packets that are too corrupted to be corrected are ignored.)

HDTV televisions will likely be sold only in very large sizes (and therefore be expensive) so that viewers will be able to see the benefit of the improved picture resolution.

Current standards efforts are promoted by the Advanced Television Systems Committee (ATSC). Prior to this group, the development work was done by the Digital HDTV Grand Alliance, which was formed in 1993. The members started out as competitors, each proposing its own system to be accepted by the FCC, but the huge development expense, need to share technology (none had the best system overall), and threat of "winner-take-all—and the rest lose all" were too great to continue competing.

The members (and their contributions) are the following:

▲ AT&T and General Instrument (video encoder)

▲ The Massachusetts Institute of Technology

▲ Philips Electronics North America (video decoder)

▲ The David Sarnoff Research Center and Thomson Consumer Electronics (transport subsystem and system integration)

▲ Zenith (modulation subsystem)

All initial HDTV work used analog technologies. Early work (1968 to 1987) developed a system called MUSE (*Multiple Sub-Nyquist Encoding*), but it:

▲ Required two standard 6-MHz channels per HDTV channel

▲ Was susceptible to ghosting and other interference

▲ Was developed in Japan, and many in the United States thought HDTV was an important technology to keep the United States competitive in both technology and manufacturing

Then, in 1990, General Instrument proposed a digital system. This was a dramatic surprise. It was previously thought that digital would be too expensive and would not offer any user-perceived benefits, given the bandwidth restrictions. Digital's feasibility and advantages were demonstrated, and all analog development work was abandoned.

May be called *Digital Television* (DTV) in the future, to emphasize the flexibility of the technology to simply be a high-speed wireless data transport—possibly used (also) for broadcasting electronic newspapers, stock prices, or even an ATM data feed.

The ATSC Digital Television Standard (document A/53) itself, as adopted by the FCC, is at *ftp://ftp.atsc.org/pub/Standards/A53*. Many other related documents (such as the AC-3 audio standard) are at *http://www.atsc.org/stan&rps.html*.

See **ATV**, **CDROM**, **DBS**, **FCC**, **INTERLACED**, **MPEG**, **NTSC**, **PAL**, **SDTV**, **SECAM**, **VGA**, and **VIDEO**.

Headless

A computer with no monitor.

As PCs and UNIX workstations become less expensive, they are more often used for server and processing functions in remote locations and are managed over a network from a more convenient location (using telnet or the X Window system, for example). To save money, reduce the size and enhance security, the display (CRT, monitor—whatever you want to call it) is removed, so the computer looks "headless".

See **CLIENT/SERVER**.

High-Bit-Rate Digital Subscriber Line

See **HDSL**.

High-Level Data Link Control

See **HDLC**.

HIPPI
High-Performance Parallel Interface

A connection-oriented (you have to establish a call before you can send data), circuit-switched (the entire link is dedicated to the connection for the duration of the connection), point-to-point (only two connections can be on a link, one at each end), somewhat expensive, and really high-speed networking technology.

Some characteristics are the following:

▲ Speed:

▲ 800 Mbits/s or 1.6 Gbits/s (either implementation can be Simplex or Full-duplex)

Distance:

▲ 25 m over copper cable (either directly between two end-stations or from an end-station to a switch—switches can be cascaded to provide a total distance of up to 200 m)

▲ 300 m on multimode fiber-optic cable

▲ HiPPI-serial can go 10 km over single-mode fiber-optic cable (using SONet)

Cable:

▲ 62.5/125 multimode fiber-optic cable

▲ A 50-pair STP copper cable (using 100-pin connectors) provides a simplex, 800-Mbits/s (total throughput), 32-bit-wide data link. A second cable can be used to provide either a 1.6-Gbits/s capacity or a full-duplex link. An additional two cables (four total) can be used to provide a 1.6 Gbits/s, full-duplex data link (sounds a bit expensive and bulky to me).

Delays:

▲ Connections established in less than 1 μs.

▲ Latency averages 160 ns

Protocols:

▲ HiPPI specifies a frame format, which can be used directly

▲ The HiPPI frames can carry TCP/IP or IPI-3 (*Intelligent Peripheral Interface*, a protocol used to communicate to RAID disk subsystems)

Switching:

▲ HiPPI uses 24-bit addresses, and each switch's ports each require a unique address

▲ The number of cascaded switches is limited by the addressing (for example, up to six 16-port-in/16-port-out switches can be cascaded, since each switch port requires a 4-bit address, so six switches would use up all 24 address bits)

Initially developed for connections between mainframes, supercomputers, disk drives, and tape drives.

Standards for interconnecting with ATM, SONet, and fibre channel (which is similar in goal and is also an ANSI standard but has many more implementation options) are in development.

Standardized by ANSI and promoted by the *HiPPI* Networking Forum (HNF). RFC 1347 covers HiPPI and IP.

Further information is at *http:www.cern.ch/HSI/hippi/hippi.html* and *http://www.esscom.com/hnf/*.

See **ATM** (*Asynchronous Transfer Mode*), **FDDI**, **FFDT**, **FIBRE CHANNEL**, **FULL-DUPLEX**, **RAID**, **SIMPLEX**, and **SONET**.

HLLAPI
High-Level Language Application Programming Interface

IBM's PC-based API for communication between a program and 3270 terminal-emulation software.

Enables an application program running on a PC to communicate with a mainframe, though in a very awkward way—by reading and writing characters on a computer terminal's screen at specific locations, searching for text strings, transmitting the screen, waiting for a reply—just like real people do. This is often called "screen scraping," and is the only way to get a PC to communicate with a (typically old and unchangeable) mainframe program that was written to only talk to computer terminals.

LU 6.2 is a much better way of doing this. It is a peer-to-peer-oriented successor that (don't things always go this way?) requires much more RAM on the PC (possibly leaving less for the PC's application program).

See **S3270**, **API**, and **LU-6.2**.

Home Page

An ASCII file (which is in HTML format) typically accessed over the Internet from client computers running Web browser programs such as Netscape. The file is called a home page since it is typically a starting point, as the home page usually has references to other HTML pages on the same computer, or computers connected to that one (typically over the Internet).

The address of the home page file is called a URL, for example, *http://ourworld.compuserve.com/ homepages/Mitchell_Shnier*. This specifies that on the host ourworld.compuserve.com, in the directory /homepages/Mitchell_Shnier there is a file (the name typically defaults to something like HOMEPAGE.HTM, Welcome.html) or index.html, which is accessed using the HTTP protocol. The host computer runs a program called an http daemon (typically called httpd), and the host is then called a Web Server, since the cross-links to other home pages built in to this home page creates a Web (like a spider's web) of interconnections, between the Web servers interconnected through the Internet.

The Web server listens (usually on TCP port 80) for page requests from clients, and replies with the contents of the requested page.

See **ASCII**, **CLIENT/SERVER**, **HTML**, **HTTP**, **INTERNET2**, **TCP**, **URL**, and **WWW**.

Host

The name for any device on a TCP/IP network that has an IP address. Also any network-addressable device on any network.

A file on computers running TCP/IP is typically called hosts or hosts.txt, and provides the translation between host names (and optionally multiple aliases for each), and the corresponding IP address. The typical format for such a file is below.

```
11.54.177.1    33Yonge Main
159.231.165.200 200King
```

See **DNS2**.

Hot Plug

Hot plugging refers to inserting a printed circuit board (PCB) into its motherboard while the motherboard is powered up. This enables parts of systems to be swapped or upgraded without having to turn off the system (which would inconvenience others using the rest of the system).

This capability typically requires special mechanical or electronic design.

You may, as I did, wonder why plugging-in a PCB to a powered-on system is any different from simply powering-on the entire system (including the PCB)—why is special support required.

As I found out, the problem is capacitors. If you don't know or care what a capacitor is, then you can go continue on with your day, as you might not be as captivated with the explanation as I was.

But if you're still here, here's the story (or at least, an example answer). Many electronic circuits require both positive and negative power supplies (sometimes called *bipolar*). For example, +5 V (volts) and –5 V (these are all measured relative to the power supply *ground*). Some electronic components need +5 V, and some need –5 V. As parts of the circuits switch on and off, they require greater or less current, which can temporarily reduce and increase the power supply voltage (until the power supply senses this, and reacts by adjusting its output). To smooth the power supply voltages, capacitors are used (actually, these are often called *bypass capacitors*, since they bypass voltage spikes to ground, where they do no harm). They connect across the power supplies (one lead of the capacitor to the +5 V, the other to ground, for example), and act like miniature batteries by storing electrical charge. Capacitors come in different sizes (measured in *farads*, though the size for this purpose are typically measured in microfarads (μF). And the total capacitance of two capacitors connected in parallel (for example, those that located in different places on the PCB) is the addition of their individual values. Also, capacitors discharge (to zero volts) when the power is turned off. So, here we are, plugging-in a PCB to a powered-on motherboard (which provides all electrical connections for the PCB—both power and signal), and perhaps the two power contacts (for the +5 V and –5 V power) get connected first, by a few milliseconds (because we insert the board on a slight angle, and the power pins are at that end of the connector). And perhaps there happens to be more bypass capacitors (therefore having a greater total capacitance) on the +5 V than on the –5 V power supply. So the +5 V capacitors take longer to charge (they stay at zero volts for a few milliseconds while the –5 V capacitors start charging).

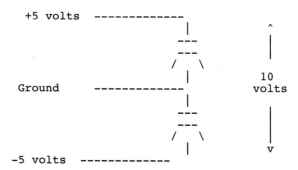

Computer Dictionary

Now, if the ground is not yet connected, a –nd since there is 10 V across the two power supplies, and since the +5 V capacitor has zero volts across it, then the full 10 V is across the electronic components for the negative power part of the circuit—which were only designed for 5 V. This can quickly damage many components (as they say, it lets the magic smoke out of them, so they won't work any more).

Another problem with hot plugging is that some devices (older CMOS ICs for example) require power before signals are applied to them. If the power pins happen to get connected after the signals, then the devices can "lock-up" (get stuck in some state, and not work as they are supposed to until power is removed and reapplied properly).

One technique for making devices hot pluggable is to ensure that the ground connection to the PCB is established before the power is applied. This might be done with a longer ground pin, so it touches before the others. This requires special connectors.

A simpler reason why hot plugging can be bad is simply that the capacitors on the PCB will draw a momentary heavy current while they charge, momentarily dropping the power supply voltage on the bus to all PCBs. And if this drop is too great, then the other boards may malfunction.

Some PCI implementations support hot plugging. Ethernet concentrators and central office switches typically support hot plugging.

See **C.O.**, and **PCI**.

HP
Hewlett-Packard Company

A humongous big company (sales of over $30 billion) started by two nice guys (guess what Bill and Dave's last names were) in 1939 to make electronic test equipment. William Hewlett and David W. Packard graduated from Stanford University engineering school in the 1930s. The garage in Palo Alto California where they began work is the designated birthplace of "Silicon Valley". The legendary culture of the company is called the "HP way"; a respect and concern for employees, with complete corporate integrity.

The first product was a relatively low-cost but high-quality audio sine-wave oscillator—the HP 100A. (The story goes that 8 of these were used to test the sound system developed to make the Walt Disney Studios movie *Fantasia*.)

In addition to laser printers (and test equipment), Hewlett-Packard makes over 10,000 other products, such as lots of really complicated medical equipment and scientific test equipment.

Hewlett-Packard has a WWW server at *http://www.hp.com*, and Interex (the International Association of Hewlett-Packard Computing Professionals) has a WWW server at *http://www.interex.org/*.

See **COSE**, **HPUX**, **IRDA**, **OSF**, **P7**, **PA-RISC**, **PCL**, and **SNMP**.

HPC
Handheld PC

A hardware specification for computers which are to support Windows CE. Requirements include the following:

▲ 640 × 240 or 480 × 240 pixel display

▲ IrDA port, with support for 115.2 kbits/s

▲ Serial (COM) port

▲ Either a PCMCIA or a MiniCard slot

▲ 4 Mbytes to 8 Mbytes of ROM (holds the operating system and the basic applications, such as word processing and spreadsheet) and 2 Mbytes to 4 Mbytes of RAM (typically)

See **IRDA, MINICARD, NC, NETPC, PCMCIA,** and **WINX WINDOWS APIS.**

HP-UX

Hewlett-Packard's older UNIX-like operating system.

See **HP** and **UNIX.**

HPR/APPN
High-Performance Routing/Advanced Program-to-Program Communications

A new version of APPN that supports a connectionless network-layer service.

See **APPN.**

HSSI
High-Speed Serial Interface

A 52-Mbits/s link used for connecting an ATM switch to a T3 DSU/CSU (for example).

Standardized in EIA/TIA-613, and pronounced *HISS-ee*.

See **ATM** (*Asynchronous Transfer Mode*), **CSU, DSU, FIBRE CHANNEL, HIPPI,** and **T3.**

HTML
Hypertext Markup Language

The language used to describe WWW pages so that font size and color, *hypertext* links, nice backgrounds, graphics, and positioning can be specified and maintained (though users can change how these are actually displayed by their own browsers).

A tag-based ASCII language that is used to specify the content and hypertext links to other documents on *World Wide Web* servers on the Internet. *Browsers* (such as Netscape and Mosaic, which can be made for any operating system, hardware platform, monitor resolution, etc.) can then be used to view the prepared documents and follow links to display other documents.

▲ Characters for languages other than English are supported, through support for ISO 10646 (of which Unicode is a subset), and RFC 2070 (which is called *Internationalization of the HyperText Markup Language*).

▲ Support for *Cascading Style Sheets Level 1* (CSS1) which allows common fonts, colors and other information to be specified for all the pages for an entire web site (for example), to permit a common look for all pages, while allowing this information to be changed easily (that is, it is all specified in one place, rather than being hard-coded into every page).

Recognizing that vendors will keep adding tags that are not yet standardized (in the hope that their new feature will make their produce more desirable than the competition's), HTML includes support for a new element called an *object*. This container specifies a program that should be run to handle the object (rather than your browser trying to guess this from the filename's extension), along with the data to be submitted to the program, and any additional parameters.

XML is a more ambitious and flexible way of extending HTML's capabilities.

Due to competition, vendors have always included features that are not yet in standards—hence the "Best viewed with *<whatever>*" box trying to get you to download that browser.

Further information is available at *http://www.w3.org/pub/WWW/*, and an HTML primer is at *http://www.ncsa.uiuc.edu/demoweb/html-primer.html*.

Tools are used to prepare the *home pages* and linked documents. For example, see *http://www.sq.com*.

Initially developed as a research project at the European Laboratory for Particle Physics (CERN—which is the acronym for the laboratory's name in french).

Modeled after, but much less powerful and not interchangeable with, SGML.

See **CGI**, **HOME PAGE**, **HTTP**, **INTERNET2**, **SGML**, **UNICODE**, **VRML**, **WWW**, and **XML**.

HTTP
Hypertext Transfer Protocol

The connection-oriented (it uses TCP, not UDP) protocol used to carry WWW traffic between a WWW browser computer and the WWW server being accessed.

The first version of HTTP was 0.9, but since 1995 most browsers have used version 1.0 of the protocol (which is defined in RFC 1945). A connection is established for each hypertext click of your mouse. The server sending the resulting HTML, GIF or whatever, then closes the connection when the page or graphic is received (or you close the connection sooner by clicking on stop or a different icon during the downloading). If a page contains several images, then a separate connection is opened and closed for the transfer of each one. Most browsers support opening more than one connection at a time (typically 4, though this can be configured from the pull-down preferences), and this speeds the downloading of the page (but usually makes for a confusing status display of how much of the page has been received).

The new version 1.1 of HTTP has several important improvements, as summarized below.

▲ Since repeatedly opening and closing TCP connections wastes time, network bandwidth and CPU time, *persistent connections* are supported. The browser specifies how many requests will be made during the current connection, and the server will not close the connection until all images have been sent.

▲ A browser can request an additional image, before a previous one has been fully received. This is called *pipelining*.

▲ While a maximum packet size of 576 bytes is often used on the Internet to ensure that all devices can handle the packets without having to fragment them into smaller pieces, communication is more efficient (since packets have a fixed number of overhead bytes regardless of the number of data bytes in them) with larger packet sizes. Since servers, clients and the Internet itself typically support larger packet sizes, HTTP 1.1 will also use larger packet sizes.

▲ The DNS translation from URLs to IP addresses will be locally cached by the browser, so that repeated DNS lookups will not need to be made.

▲ Support for splitting load across multiple web servers.

▲ A put command, which enables clients (browsers) to write files to a WWW server.

The HTTP 1.0 protocol is documented at *http://www.w3.org/pub/WWW/Protocols/HTTP/HTTP2.html*. HTTP 1.1 is defined in RFC 2068 (in which they use the word *idempotence*, not exactly everyday English), and is at *http://www.w3.org/WWW/Protocols/#ID1106*.

See **GIF**, **HOME PAGE**, **HTML**, **SHTTP**, **SSL**, **TCP**, **URL**, and **WWW**.

I

I₂0
Intelligent Input/Output

An open specification which defines a standard software interface for intelligent I/O cards (that is, they have a processor on-board, rather than just being a simple device that can input and output data). This enables some processing to be off-loaded to the card, and the same driver software to be used for multiple operating systems.

Developed by Compaq Corp., Hewlett-Packard Company, Intel Corp., Netframe Systems Inc. and Novell Inc.— all of the I₂0 vendor special interest group.

Further information is available at *http://developer.intel.com/design/IIO/i2osigit.htm*.

See **NIC2** (*Network Interface Card*).

IAB
Internet Architecture Board

The coordinating committee for Internet design, engineering, and management. Oversees the health and evolution of the Internet (in practice by withholding the approval of new standards) and approves new standards. Previously called the *Internet Activities Board*.

They are at *http://www.iab.org/iab*.

See **IETF** and **INTERNET2**.

IANA
Internet Assigned Numbers Authority

The central organization that assigns and maintains a registry for important numbers for Internet protocols. Or, in their words "the IANA is chartered by the Internet Society (ISOC) and the Federal Network Council (FNC) to act as the clearinghouse to assign and coordinate the use of numerous Internet protocol parameters."

The assignments include ensuring unique values are assigned for MIB object identifiers and private enterprise numbers, routing protocol autonomous system numbers (such as are required for *external gateway protocols*—EGPs), protocol and TCP well-known port numbers, and IP multicast addresses.

They also administer the *.us* top-level domain name, though most of the actual assignments are delegated to state-based organizations.

Some try to pronounce IANA as *I-anna*.

IANAL

They are located at and operated by the Information Sciences Institute (ISI) of the University of Southern California (USC), where Jon Postel, author of many of the fundamental RFCs works. IANA has a web site at *http://www.iana.org/iana/*. Many of these values are at *ftp://ftp.isi.edu/in-notes/iana/assignments*. ISOC is at *http://info.isoc.org/index.html*.

See **IETF**, **INTERNET2**, **IP MULTICAST**, and **TCP**.

IANAL
I am not a lawyer (but...)

A common email abbreviation.

See **IMHO**, **PMFJI**, and **ROFL**.

IAP
Internet Access Provider

Same as *Internet Service Provider*.

See **ISP**.

IBCS
Intel Binary Compatibility Standard

A standard for Intel-based implementations of UNIX to permit *binary portability*. That is, the same compiled and linked program executable can run on more than one UNIX—for example, SCO and Interactive UNIX.

A newer version of the standard is iBCS2.

See **PORTABILITY**, **SCO**, **SOLARIS**, and **UNIX**.

IBM
International Business Machines

A really big company.

IBM has (or had) more to do with current computing than most people realize:

▲ IBM developed the technology (called *selector channel*) on which SCSI is based (which is likely the original source for the acronym SCSI).

▲ IBM owns part of the company that runs the Internet backbone.

▲ IBM developed SQL.

▲ IBM invented the RISC concept.

▲ IBM designed the original PC and chose to license (and not ignore or buy outright) MS-DOS from Microsoft, thereby giving Microsoft a start.

▲ IBM developed HDLC (which it calls SDLC).

IBM operates a WWW Server at *http://www.ibm.com*.

See **ANS**, **COSE**, **INTERNET2**, **HDLC**, **MAINFRAME**, **OSF**, **PC**, **RISC**, **SCSI1**, **SDLC**, and **SQL**.

ICMP
Internet Control Message Protocol

An IP protocol that permits routers to inform other routers or hosts of IP routing problems or suggested better routes.

See **HOST**, **IP**, **PING**, **RIP**, and **TTL1** (*Time-To-Live*).

ICOMP
Intel Comparative Microprocessor Performance Index

A benchmark for comparing the relative power (that's processing power, not heat dissipation) of Intel processors.

Intended to highlight how fast the CPU executes instructions, because Intel thought that consumers were paying too much attention to the clock speed—which is measured in megahertz, or millions of cycles per second (MHz)—of processors. Intel knew that new processors would be much more powerful while possibly having a lower clock speed (for example, because of clock doubling, a math coprocessor, or *superscalar* design).

A 25-MHz 486SX is given the rating of 100, and all other ratings are relative to this.

A weighted average, based on the instruction mix that Intel expects to be representative for operating systems and applications for the next 3 to 5 years (which are, for example, expected to have a growing emphasis of 32-bit applications). This is an important distinction and assumption, as Intel's Pentium Pro (for example) is so optimized for 32-bit operations that it is only slightly faster (and can actually be slower) when executing 16-bit applications (which will continue to be widely used for years to come).

The current iComp rating is made up of four industry-standard benchmarks (which measure both 16-bit and 32-bit processor performance for integer, floating-point, graphics, and video performance), each weighted as shown in the following table.

Benchmark	Percentage Weighting	Benchmark Measures
SPECint92	25	Integer math performance
SPECfp92	5	Floating-point math performance
PCBench	68	Ziff-Davis' DOS CPU performance (only the *processor harmonic* measurement is used)
Whetstone	2	Floating-point math performance
Total	*100*	

The rating does not include tests of disk or video system performance, nor other important aspects of a system, such as the number of expansion slots or type and speed of the system bus.

That is, the iComp rating is only one of many important metrics in comparing computer systems. For example, throughput of a file server is usually limited mostly by the disk subsystem and the bus. Usually, CPU processing power is not the most important factor in determining capacity.

Intel says that it will revise the method of calculating the rating to keep it relevant to the current and expected applications and operating systems.

Some actual iComp ratings are listed in the following table.

Processor	Clock Speed (MHz) [a]	iComp Rating
486SX	20	78
486SX	25	100
486DX or SL	25	122
486SX	33	136
486DX or SL	33	166
486DX2	25/50	231
486DX2	33/66	297
DX4	25/75	319
DX4	33/100	435
Pentium P60	60	510
Pentium P66	66	567
Pentium P75	50/75	610
Pentium P90	60/90	735
Pentium P100	66/100	815
Pentium P120	60/120	1,000

a. If clock-multiplying technology is used (clock doubling, etc.), then the external/internal clock speeds are both shown.

See **INTEL**, **P RATING**, **PC**, **PENTIUM PRO**, **SPEC**, and **SUPERSCALAR**.

IDE
Integrated Drive Electronics

A very popular (even the Macintosh supports it now) industry-standard hard disk drive interface developed by Western Digital and Compaq (in 1986) as an improvement on IBM's ST-506 and ST-412 (which were the popular PC disk drive interfaces at the time).

Until IDE, disk drives had very low-level interfaces. For example, one wire would be pulsed to step the read/write head, and another wire would determine the direction of the step. The disk controller would provide these step pulses (after being programmed by the computer with the rate at which that particular drive can accept the pulses). The disk controller's interface to the computer would be several registers that would be written with (for example) the desired destination cylinder number. The disk drive controller would then provide the correct number of step pulses in the correct direction so the read/write head ends up at that cylinder number.

An IDE drive has these registers, and the disk controller logic integrated with the other electronics needed to control the disk drive—hence the name. That is, the IDE interface is the registers that used to be on the disk controller, but now that are part of the disk drive. The 40-pin IDE interface itself is basically a connection between an ISA bus and the IDE disk drive. The interface requires very little control logic.

The actual IDE programming interface consists of 9 8-bit control and status registers plus a 16-bit read/write register.

The IDE physical interface supports a maximum of two standard hard disk drives—the master and one slave (as selected on the drives).

The typical maximum sustained data transfer rate is 1 to 3 Mbytes/s

IDE uses the PC BIOS's interrupt 13_{16} to provide an interface to the computer's operating system.

Since the BIOS allows up to 1,024 cylinders and 63 sectors per track, and IDE allows up to 16 heads and DOS supports 512 bytes per sector, maximum IDE drive capacity is therefore 504 Mbytes ($512 \times 63 \times 1,024 \times 16 = 528,482,304$ bytes), where a Mbyte is ($1,024 \times 1,024$ bytes =) 1,048,576 bytes.

As shown in the family tree diagram below, IDE was first developed in 1986, mainly by Western Digital (and became a de facto standard). The *small form factor committee* then took control of the standard and submitted it to be an ANSI standard, which happened in 1989. ANSI's name for IDE is ATA (*AT* attachment). The SFFC then produced the following two enhancements.

▲ *ATA-2*—an enhancement to ATA (after all, what good is a standard if you can't have a second version of it). ATA-2, and its successors, are sometimes called *Advanced ATA*. ATA-2 provides the following enhancements over IDE:

▲ PIO modes 3 and 4 (which provide an 11.11 and 16.66 Mbyte/s transfer rate)

▲ Multiword DMA modes 1 and 2 (which provide a 13.33 and 16.66 Mbyte/s transfer rate)

▲ A more detailed `identify drive` response from drive, such as which PIO and DMA modes it supports, and information needed for Plug and Play support.

▲ Logical block disk sector addressing. This makes the disk drive look like a long sequence of 512-byte blocks of data. Their actual cylinder, head and sector are hidden from the computer (SCSI has always done this). This simplifies disk drive interfacing, since the computer does not need to know the physical geometry of the disk drive (so you don't need to set this information into your PC's CMOS), and speeds disk access for operating systems than internally use the LBA type of disk sector addressing. A PC's BIOS and DOS do not use LBA addressing, so they require additional translation software (and CPU) time to use LBA.

▲ *ATA-PI*, also written as *ATAPI* (ATA packet interface). It typically needs software drivers to be loaded, and has the following new features (compared to IDE):

▲ Support for CD-ROM drives, tape drive and other types of removable storage devices to be connected to the IDE connector.

▲ SCSI-like commands (rather than the IDE register type of interface)

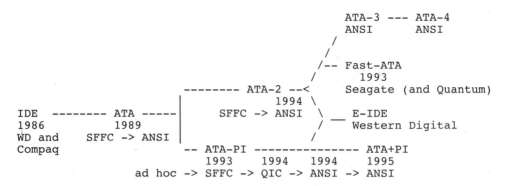

```
                                              ATA-3 --- ATA-4
                                              ANSI      ANSI
                                           /
                                          /
                                         /-- Fast-ATA
                                        /      1993
                       -------- ATA-2 --<      Seagate (and Quantum)
                                  1994  \
IDE  -------- ATA -----      SFFC -> ANSI  \ __  E-IDE
1986          1989       |                  /    Western Digital
WD and    SFFC -> ANSI   |                 /
Compaq                   -- ATA-PI --------------- ATA+PI
                            1993     1994   1994     1995
               ad hoc -> SFFC -> QIC -> ANSI -> ANSI
```

Note that all these interfaces use the original, standard IDE 40-pin connector and cable.

Fast-ATA is Seagate Technology Inc.'s name for their implementation of ATA-2. As shown in the diagram, Fast-ATA does not include ATA-PI functionality.

Western Digital's *Enhanced IDE* (E-IDE or EIDE) is their implementation of both ATA-PI and ATA-2. It consists of both hardware and software, as summarized below.

▲ Software. This is sometimes called an *Enhanced BIOS* (or E-BIOS), and provides translation of the maximum numbers of cylinders, heads and sectors that can be addressed by a standard BIOS and an IDE drive, so that more than 504 Mbytes can be addressed.

▲ Hardware. This includes the new features provided by both ATA-2 and ATA-PI. It therefore supports PIO modes 3 and 4, DMA mode 2 and several other features.

The table below shows the defined time between 16-bit transfers (and the resulting data transfer rate) for the ATA and ATA-2 PIO transfer modes (drives must support the *I/O* Channel Ready signal for flow control purposes).

PIO Mode	Time per 16-bit transfer (ns)	Transfer rate (Mbytes/s)	Defined in...
0	600	3.33	Original ATA
1	383	5.22	
2	240	8.33	
3	180	11.11	ATA-2
4	120	16.66	

The tables below show the defined time between 16-bit transfers (and the resulting data transfer rate) for the ATA and ATA-2 *Single word* (which is seldom used) and *Multiword* DMA (which is supported on EISA, VLB and PCI bus computers, and allows more than 1 16-bit word to be transferred before releasing the bus back to the main CPU) transfer modes. DMA transfers interrupt the CPU only once, at the completion of the entire transfer. They therefore require much less CPU time than PIO transfers (which interrupt after every 256 16-bit words are transferred, or less often if multi-block PIO is used).

Single word DMA Mode	Time per 16-bit transfer (ns)	Transfer rate (Mbytes/s)	Defined in...
0	960	2.08	Original ATA
1	480	4.16	
2	240	8.33	

Multiword DMA Mode	Time per 16-bit transfer (ns)	Transfer rate (Mbytes/s)	Defined in...
0	480	4.16	Original ATA
1	150	13.33	ATA-2
2	120	16.66	

ATA-4 defines a CRC check for each block of data transferred, to ensure that errors do not occur while data is being transferred between a disk controller and a disk drive interface (it was discovered that errors on these transfers were becoming problems for PIO mode 4 transfers). ATA-4 also defines a synchronous DMA mode with tighter timing tolerances, so less time needs to be allowed for each transfer. This is called Ultra DMA, Ultra DMA/33 and sometimes Ultra-ATA. It supports transfer rates of up to 33 Mbytes/s (though actual rates will vary with other factors, such as disk drive speed, errors and CPU processing times).

Ultra DMA Mode	Time per 16-bit transfer (ns)	Transfer rate (Mbytes/s)	Defined in...
0	235	16	ATA-4
1	160	24	
2	120	33	

Manufacturers can claim compliance with ATA-2 if they support at least PIO modes 0 and 3.

Now that IDE is used to interface to more than just disk drives, some say that it is now an acronym for *Integrated Device Electronics*.

Standard IDE disk drives can be connected to controllers that support ATA-2 (such as E-IDE and Fast-ATA), but only IDE features will be available. Some controllers will allow both IDE and ATA-2 drives to be connected at the same time, communicating at whatever the fastest speed each drive supports.

Similarly, E-IDE or Fast-ATA drives connected to standard IDE interfaces will work, but only provide standard IDE features.

Similarly, Ultra DMA 33 Mbyte/s drives and controllers are backward compatible with earlier drives and controllers (that is, they work fine, according to the earlier standard common to the drive and controller).

Western Digital's *Enhanced IDE* competes with Seagate's *Fast ATA*.

IDE is also an acronym for *integrated development environment*, and this refers to the programs and utilities required to develop (edit, compile and debug) new computer programs.

IDEA

This IDE has nothing to do with the disk drive interface IDE, and is just another example of running out of unique acronyms (see **TLA.**

Some good disk drive interface information is at *http://www.wi.leidenuniv.nl/ata/.*

Seagate Technology has a WWW server at *http://www.seagate.com*, and Western Digital is at *http://www.wdc.com.*

See **AT, ATA, ATA-2, ATA-3, ATASPI, BIOS, DISK DRIVE, FAST ATA, FAT, EIDE, IRQ, ISA, PC, PIO, SCSI1**, and **WINCHESTER.**

IDEA
International Data Encryption Algorithm

An algorithm for encrypting data, making it well-nigh impossible for others to read your message.

A *single-key* encryption algorithm (as is the much better-known DES). IDEA was selected (not DES or RSA) for use in certain parts of PGP because IDEA:

▲ Has a much longer key (128 bits, rather than 56 bits), making it much more secure

▲ Runs much faster than DES when implemented in software (DES was designed to run slowly in software, to make decrypting messages without the key more difficult)

▲ Runs about 4,000 times faster than RSA

▲ Is not export restricted from North America (as DES is)—in fact, IDEA was developed in Switzerland at ETH (Eidgenössische Technische Hochschule, which is the Swiss Federal Institute of Technology, at Zürich), by James Massey and Xuejia Lai.

▲ Is much more secure than RSA for a given key size (the 128-bit idea key is apparently as secure as a 3,100-bit RSA key—and 1,024 bits is the current maximum RSA key size)

Patented (by Ascom-Tech AG), but no license fee is required for noncommercial use of IDEA.

See **DES, ENCRYPTION, PGP**, and **RSA.**

IDEN
Integrated Dispatch Enhanced Network

Motorola's name for their ESMR system.

See **ESMR.**

IEC
Interexchange Carrier

Same as IXC.

See **IXC OR IEC.**

IEC
International Electrotechnical Commission

The first international standards-setting organization. It's standards mostly affect European products. The IEC was formed in 1906. Its standards are mostly oriented to electrical and electronic engineering.

They are at *http://www.iec.ch*.

See **STANDARDS**.

IEEE
Institute of Electrical and Electronics Engineers

A professional association of 320,000 individual members from 147 countries that was founded in 1884. Among many other things, the IEEE produced the standards for Ethernet and Token Ring (which is done by the 802 Committee, so-named because it was formed in February of 1980).

IEEE standards can be ordered from them at 1 800 678-4333. Their web site is at *http://www.ieee.org*, and the catalog of standards is at *http://stdsbbs.ieee.org/products/catalog/catalog.html*.

See **S10BASET, S10BASEF, S100BASE-FX, S100BASET, S100BASET2, S100BASET4, S100BASETX, S1284, S802.1H, S802.2, S802.3, S802.5, S802.6, S802.9A, S802.A10, S802.A11, S802.A12, S802.A14, LAN, POSIX-OSE**, and **STANDARDS**.

IETF
Internet Engineering Task Force

The group (formed in 1986) that determines new protocols and application requirements for the Internet, with the following characteristics:

▲ The protocol engineering and development arm of the Internet

▲ A large open international community of network designers, operators, vendors, and researchers who are concerned with the evolution of the Internet architecture and the smooth operation of the Internet

▲ Supervises the development of RFCs

▲ Reports to the IAB

While most of their work is done by e-mail and other communication over the Internet, they hold three 1-week meetings per year, and has an administrative secretariat provided by CNRI (Reston, Va).

The IETF has a WWW server at *http://www.ietf.org*.

See **IAB**, **INTERNIC**, and **RFC**.

IGP
Interior Gateway Protocol

A protocol (such as RIP or OSPF) that is used for routing within a TCP/IP *autonomous system*.

See **OSPF** and **RIP**.

IGRP
Interior Gateway Routing Protocol

A proprietary, router-to-router, intradomain protocol that was developed by Cisco Systems for routing TCP/IP and OSI CLNP.

One of the main functions of a router is to choose the "best" path between a source and a destination. Since each path might comprise many links, a method of comparing the links is required. Rather than characterizing each link along the path with only one metric (as does RIP—it counts only hops), IGRP uses five (count 'em, folks) metrics.

The metrics evaluated are the link's speed (or available bandwidth), delay, packet size, loading, and reliability.

In networks with diverse data link types, this can be an important improvement. Of course, then the problem is what you mean by "best"—the fastest or the most reliable. And what if sometimes you mean one (for example, for file transfers), and other times you mean another (for email)? Application programs and protocols usually have no way of communicating their individual requirements to the router.

Enhanced IGRP supports TCP/IP, IPX, and AppleTalk and provides many of the benefits of link-state router-to-router protocols, such as the following:

▲ Fast convergence (more quickly propagating updated routing information to the entire network)

▲ Variable-length subnet bit masks (that is, each subnet can have a different subnet bit mask)

▲ Updates sent as soon as connectivity changes take place

▲ No periodic router-to-router broadcasts

See **CISCO SYSTEMS, LINK STATE, QOS, RIP,** and **SUBNET BIT MASK.**

ILSR
IPX Link State Router

Novell's proprietary enhancement to its RIP distance-vector-based routing protocol.

See **LINK STATE.**

IMA
Inverse Multiplexing over ATM

A method of proving higher-speed WAN connections (including QOS guarantees) between ATM switches, over multiple lower-speed circuits (such as several T1s).

Expected to be popular for WAN links where (for example) a full T3 is too expensive (and more than needed), but a single T1 is not enough (in the descriptions below, T1s are assumed to be used for the WAN links).

IMA defines a *user to network interface* (UNI), where the "user" is the ATM switch, and the "network" is the public T1 (or whatever) circuits. A network to network (NNI) interface is also defined, for the ATM switches at each end of the T1s to communicate.

Each ATM cell header indicates the AAL type, and on a per T1 basis, the priority of those cells can be set. Typically, CBR traffic would be sent first, followed by VBR, UVR and ABR.

Cells to be transmitted are distributed, cell by cell, in a round-robin sequence among the available T1 circuits.

An *IMA* control protocol (ICP) is defined, using OAM cells. These carry information on the state of the link, number of T1s in the group, type of data being carried and differential delay statistics. T1s can also be dynamically dropped from or added to the *group* (without loosing cells), under control of ICP (typically when they become defective and are later repaired, or more capacity is needed).

Data sent on a T1 is formatted into IMA frames. The default size is 128 cells, and other sizes are 32, 64 and 256 cells (the trade-off is overhead versus faster notification of connection status changes). This means that an ICP cell is sent for every 127 data cells (on each link). The offset of the ICP cell within the frame, and the size of the IMA frame can be different on each T1, and is established before data is sent over each T1. When there is no data to send, empty cells are transmitted (to continuously monitor that the link remains operational).

Much of the specification concerns compensating for different transit delays across the T1s. Differential delays of up to 25 ms are allowed (though some vendors can compensate for longer delays—its mostly a matter of how much buffer memory is in the equipment).

See **ATM** (*Asynchronous Transfer Mode*), and **INVERSE MULTIPLEXER**.

IMAP
Internet Message Access Protocol

The newer protocol used to communicate from e-mail clients to mail servers—also called post offices, which store incoming mail (from the network, for later delivery to the client) for clients that are not always connected to the network. IMAP allows connected stations to do the following:

▲ view message headers and choose which, of the mail messages or attachments, they wish to receive (the others remain stored in the post office until deleted)

▲ retrieve mail messages according to size (so really huge attachments won't be retrieved over a slow dial-up link) or sender

▲ specify which retrieved mail messages should be marked as read

▲ manipulate mail folders (create, rename, and delete)

▲ search mail documents for specific text strings

▲ specify what types of capabilities the client has (such as playing audio

▲ retrieve Usenet news and other types of messages

▲ automatic encoding and decoding, as specified in MIME

Clients can have more than one mailbox (and mailboxes can be shared between clients). Clients interact with IMAP4 in one of three modes, as summarized below:

▲ *Off-line* mode requires that clients store their mailboxes on their own local disk drives. Mail messages are prepared and left in their local mailboxes, and received mail messages are downloaded (and typically deleted from the post office), and mail messages are read from the local mailbox (typically after disconnecting from the post office). This is the mode usually used by POP3, and is best-suited to clients that call in from different locations to quickly upload and download mail, and then disconnect.

▲ *On-line* mode has the mailboxes on the post office, and clients can manipulate these remotely. This is typically used by users who are LAN-connected (that is, by a high-speed connection) to their post offices, or for users that have very low-end terminals (that can't store mail messages). POP3 has some on-line capabilities. Since files are in a central location (the mail server), administrators can be assured that backups are being done.

▲ *Disconnected* mode is a mix of the above two. The client downloads a copy of the received mail (which remains stored on the post office), and disconnects from the post office. Work proceeds as in disconnected mode, but when a connection to the post office is re-established, synchronization automatically updates both the client's and the post office's copy of the mail messages.

IMAP4 is defined in RFCs 1730 (mainly, but also), 1731, 1732, 1733, 1176 and 1203. IMAP4, revision 1 has features to provide better performance over slower dial-up links, and is specified in RFC 2060. IMAP is an open standard, and is a superset of POP. IMAP post offices therefore support the older POP version 2 and POP version 3 protocol (POP2 and POP3), supporting only the POP functionality when using these older protocols.

IMAP was developed at Stanford University in 1986.

The Internet Message Support Protocol (IMSP) is an enhancement to IMAP, but will itself likely be replaced by the *Application Configuration Access Protocol* (ACAP) when it is approved.

For more information, see *http://www.imap.org* and *http://www.washington.edu/imap*, which are maintained by the University of Washington.

See **ACAP**, **INTERNET2**, **MIME**, **POP2** (*Post Office Protocol*), **SMTP**, and **USENET**.

IMHO
In My Humble Opinion

A common email abbreviation.

In-Band

As in *In-bandwidth*, that is, using the same bandwidth (wires or data channel) for *signaling* (sending control information) as for data transmission.

Examples of in-band signaling include the following:

▲ On an EIA-232 interface, sending and receiving the x-on and x-off flow control characters (11_{16} and 13_{16}) on pins 2 and 3—that is, as part of the sent and received data (this means that the data cannot have any x-on or x-off characters in them)

▲ On a standard touch-tone (DTMF) telephone or service type II switched 56 data set, sending the phone number dialed to the central office on the same pair of wires that the voice or data communications uses

While usually less expensive to implement than an out-of-band signaling method, in-band signaling is usually undesirable, since it restricts or disrupts the data that can be sent.

Also, in-band signaling leaves the possibility that users can inadvertently (or purposely) affect the signaling. For example, on standard telephone connections the telephone company uses a 2,600-Hz tone to indicate that a long-distance call is completed, and sending one at the right time can provide free long-distance calls. People who often call themselves *"phone phreaks"* make or buy *blue boxes*, which can generate this tone. Mind you, this is *theft of telecommunications services*, a bad thing to do. The Usenet newsgroup *news://alt.2600* has many people trying to fool others that they have done this, trying to entrap people that do this, and claiming that others are trying to entrap others.

Much of this "fun" changed with the advent of the *Common Channel Signaling System Number 7* (CCS #7 or more commonly SS7). This is an out-of-band signaling method (which uses a separate 56 kbits/s DS-0 link between CO switches) that prevents users from messing with the phone company's signaling and enables the phone company to offer (and charge for) new features, such as Caller ID and local number portability (LNP).

Another example of in-band signaling is that pay phones indicate how much money has been deposited by sending a 2,200-Hz tone to the central office for each 5¢ deposited; a nickel is a 60-MS tone pulse, a dime is two 60-MS tone pulses, separated by 60-MS, and a quarter is five 15-MS tone pulses.

Since the tones are sent on the same pair of wires as your voice is, what stops you (other than the law) from making a device that can generate these tones and holding it to the telephone mouthpiece?

While I never got my *red box* working, sometimes you get a pay phone that doesn't mute the earpiece when you drop in the money, and you can hear these tone pulses.

The hacker's magazine *2600* has a web site at *http://www.2600.com*.

See **ASCII**, **DTMF2**, **EIA-TIA232**, **FLOW CONTROL**, **ISDN**, **LEC**, **OUTOFBAND**, **SIT**, **SWITCHED 56**, **USENET**, and **VIRUS**.

IND$FILE

A program that runs on an IBM mainframe (which is running TSO, CICS, or VM/CMS) that provides the mainframe side of a file transfer capability from 3270-type terminals (or PCs emulating them). Many third-party PC-based terminal-emulation software packages provide the terminal side of this file transfer capability.

Also called *SEND/RECEIVE*.

See **S3270**, **CICS**, **MAINFRAME**, and **VM**.

Industrial Design

In Canada, a *registered industrial design* receives protection against others copying the aesthetics and appearance of the product.

Covers the shape, pattern, or ornamentation (either of the entire product or of a component part of it) of a useful mass-produced article, regardless of how the article is actually manufactured. That is, an infringement would look as though it (or an important part of it) came from the same mold (more than it looks as though it came from some other *prior art*).

In the United States, a *design patent* provides similar protection.

The design must have features that are specifically included for visual appeal (though their quality and merits are not judged). For example, users should be able to see the article when the product is used normally, and the article should be a substantial and important part of the product.

Products that are created as a work of art are automatically protected by *copyright* (no *registration* required), but if a product is used (or intended to be used) as a model or pattern to produce more than 50 single useful articles or sets of articles it becomes an *industrial design*, which can be protected only if it is registered as an industrial design.

Some products (a distinctive package, for example) can be covered by both an industrial design (initially) and later (after the product has been put on the market), a *trademark*.

An industrial design must be original and produced in quantity (or there must be an intention to do so).

The following cannot be registered as industrial designs:

▲ Designs for articles that serve no useful purpose, are utilitarian only (and are not intended to provide visual appeal), have no fixed appearance (they can change shape, such as a bean bag), or are normally hidden by other parts of the article

▲ A manufacturing process, an article's construction method, or the materials used in the construction

▲ An idea

▲ The function, useful purpose, or functional features of the article

▲ The particular colors used for an article

An *industrial design application* (for registration) must be filed within one year of publicizing the design or offering the product for sale (and preferably before the design has been so "published"). If you wait longer than one year, you cannot get industrial design protection. As for patents, some countries do not permit publicizing before applying for protection of an industrial design.

Registration is required (to get any protection), and it enables the owner to prevent others from making, using, renting, or selling the design in Canada for 10 years from the registration date.

The application must cover the distinctive, important and original visual features of the design (and not the functionality of the resulting article). If the description does not cover the details, then the resulting registration will not provide the coverage needed. Too broad a description will be impossible to enforce. Detail should be provided to differentiate the design from others that are known to exist.

The application must include drawings or photographs (showing how the industrial design will be used on the product to be manufactured) that correspond to the description.

In addition to the *examination fee* required for registration (and the fees for the *patent agent* who usually prosecutes the application), a one-time maintenance fee must be paid before five years have elapsed (if it is not paid, the registration expires, and others may freely use the design, just as if the 10-year period had expired).

The proprietor of an industrial design is usually the creator, but industrial designs done for an employer are the property of the employer. Designs done under contract (that is, not in an employer-employee relationship) are the property of the person who pays the contractor (it is the other way around for copyrights).

The ownership of industrial designs may be permanently transferred (*assigning* some or all of the rights), as that of any property can.

A proprietor of a registered industrial design can also *license* the use of the industrial design for a specific use, for a period of time, and for a specified geographic area.

Marking a registered industrial design with the name of the proprietor (for example, ® Mitchell Shnier Designs) on the article, its label, or packaging, is not required. However, if a court finds that someone has been infringing, and the article is not marked, the only remedy is an *injunction* preventing further infringement; if it is marked, a court can also award a remedy of financial compensation.

In Canada, industrial designs are administered by the Industrial Design Office, which is part if the CIPO.

Intellectual property protection documents are available from Micromedia Limited, at *http:// www.mmltd.com*.

See **CIPO**, **DESIGN PATENT**, **INTELLECTUAL PROPERTY PROTECTION**, and **PATENT**.

Industry Canada

The current name for the Canadian federal government agency that is responsible for licensing and managing the radio frequency spectrum.

Was previously called the Department of Communications, and before that, Communications Canada, and before that, the Department of Communications. (My, but they are busy over there.)

Industry Canada is also responsible for *intellectual property protection*.

They have a WWW server at *http://www.ic.gc.ca/ic-data/ic-eng.html*.

See **CATV**, **CIPO**, **CRTC**, **FCC**, and **INTELLECTUAL PROPERTY PROTECTION**.

Infrared Data Association

See **IRDA**.

Initial Program Load

See **IPL**.

Integrated Circuit Topography Act

The Canadian act that provides protection from others copying an integrated circuit (IC) design. It covers both the three-dimensional and per-layer design for up to ten years. The design must be original, but can be based on *reverse-engineering* other designs (obviously most everyone agreed that reverse engineering is a normal part of engineering design—incrementally improving on earlier work).

Registration is required.

Since protection of integrated circuit designs is dramatically different in different countries, international protection is difficult to obtain.

The U.S. act that provides similar protection is the *Semiconductor Chip Protection Act*. There is some information at *http://www.law.cornell.edu/topics/copyright.html*.

See **INTELLECTUAL PROPERTY PROTECTION**.

Integrated IS-IS

DEC's proprietary link-state, interdomain, *and* intradomain routing protocol based on OSI's IS-IS. One advantage of DEC's implementation is that it currently handles DECnet Phase IV, OSI CLNP, and IP. Also, IPX and AppleTalk are handled by encapsulating them into IP.

See **LINK STATE**.

INTEL
Intel Corporation

Initially a manufacturer of IC, such as DRAM (which it developed by 1969, and first sold commercially in 1970).

Also the inventor of the first microprocessors—starting with the 16-pin 4004, which was designed starting in 1969 as a flexible single-IC solution for a Japanese company called Busicom, for calculator innards (rather than 12 separate ICs, which was the conventional design at the time, and the 7 ICs planned by Busicom). The design was first proposed and detailed by Ted Hoff, and implemented by Federico Faggin and Stan Mazor, with help from Busicom's Masatoshi Shima. The processor supported 45 8-bit instructions, and had a 4-bit data bus (which is all that is needed for a BCD digit).

The Intel processor architecture remains the basis of all PCs (at least, as PCs are defined in this book—computers that have (Intel-architecture processors), though other companies have developed clones of it. Intel has about 85% of this market.

The following table lists some Intel processors and their features.

| Processor | Clock Speed (MHz)[a] | MIPS (thousands) | Transistors | Bus Width[b] (bits) | | | Introduced |
				Internal Data Bus/	External Data Bus/	Address Bus	
4004	0.108	0.06	2.25	4	4	12	1970
4040				4	4	12	1972
8008	0.3	0.06	3.3	8	8	14	1972
8080	2	0.1[c]	4	8	8	16	1974
8086	5	0.33[d]	29	16	16	20	1978
8088	5	0.33	29	16	8	20	1979
80286	8	1.2[e]	134	16	16	24	1982
80386DX	16	6[f]	275	32	32	32	1985
80386SX	16	2.5	275	32	16	24	1988
486DX	25	20	1,200	32	32	32	1989
486SX	20	16.5	1,185	32	32	32	1991
486DX2	50[g]	40	1,200	32	32	32	1992
	66[h]	54	1,200	32	32	32	1992
486DX4	100	112	1,600	32	32	32	1994
Pentium	66		3,100	32	64	32	1993
	100	170	3,300	32	64	32	1994
	166	219		32	64	32	1996
Pentium Pro	150	285[i]	5,500[j]	32	64[k]	32	1995
Pentium MMX	200		4,500	32	64	32	1997
Pentium II	300	750	7,500	32	64	32	1997
P7 (Merced)[l]	600	500	10,000	64			1999

a. For processors available for different clock speeds, a typical clock speed is given.
b. The external data bus width is (for example) the number of bits in each read from Level 2 cache.
c. Up to 0.64 MIPS for faster clock speeds.
d. Up to 0.75 MIPS for faster clock speeds.
e. Up to 2.66 MIPS for faster clock speeds.
f. Up to 11.4 MIPS for faster clock speeds.
g. This was the first Intel processor to use clock-multiplying (doubling in this case, since the external bus ran at 25 MHz, while the processor itself ran at 50 MHz).
h. Actually, most "66 MHz" processors run at 66.66 MHz (otherwise, your 100 MHz processor would only run at 99 MHz).
i. Up to 400 MIPS for faster clock speeds.
j. Not including the 15.5 million transistors for the 256-kbyte Level 2 cache (or the 31 million for the version with the 512 kbyte Level 2 cache) that is in the same IC package as the CPU.
k. The data bus is actually 64 data bits plus 8 bits for ECC.
l. This information is based on rumors.

Intellectual Property Protection

Because of competitive pressure, the development work for recent Intel processors has started before predecessor processors have been finished, as shown in the accompanying figure (yes, data for dates in the future have been estimated). This has accelerated the release of new processors to faster than every 4 years (as shown in the table).

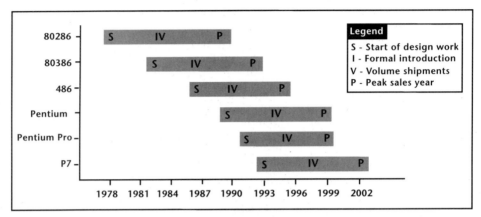

Intel-1

Intel maintains a WWW server at *http://www.intel.com*, with additional details on the evolution of their processors at *http://www.intel.com/product/tech-briefs/man_bnch.htm*. Their server at *http://www.cs-intel.com/oem_developer/motherbd/* has technical information about their motherboards. A very interesting web site with lots of critical (in at least two senses of the word) information on Intel and their products is at *http://www.x86.org*.

See **S486DX, S486DX2, S486DX4, S486SX, S486SX2, S80386DX, S80386SX, AGP, BCD, DX4, ECC, ICOMP, MIPS, MOORES, OVERDRIVE, PC, PENTIUM, PENTIUM PRO, P7,** and **VLIW.**

Intellectual Property Protection

The purpose of *intellectual property protection* is to protect owners of intellectual property while promoting creativity and the orderly exchange of ideas.

Many forms of protection are available, as shown in the following table

Protection	Protects	Requires	Lasts
Copyright	Artistic and creative works—the expression of an idea	Automatically covered, though a © serves as a reminder. Works can be registered as well.	The lifetime of the author, plus 50 years
Canadian Industrial Design	The shape, pattern, or ornamentation (aesthetics and appearance) of a useful manufactured article	Registration in each country	10 years from registration
U.S. Design Patent			14 years from registration

(table continued on next page)

Protection	Protects	Requires	Lasts
Patent	The idea itself (functionality, processes, and techniques)	Filing and granting of a patent in each country	20 years from the date of application
Integrated Circuit Topography	Integrated circuit designs	Registration	Up to 10 years from registration
Trademark	Distinguishing words and symbols	Can be covered automatically after a period of use, but registration is recommended	15 years after registration, renewable in 15-year periods thereafter

Ideas and concepts can be covered by *copyright* or *patent* protection only after being translated into a tangible form (such as a written description or a built unit).

The Geneva-based *World Intellectual Property Organization* (WIPO, which has about 120 member countries) promotes intellectual property protection through *international treaties* and technical assistance to developing countries. It administers several international treaties, such as the following.

▲ *Paris Convention for the Protection of Industrial Property*, which was developed in 1883, and covers patents, *trademarks*, and *industrial designs*. In 1995, there were 135 countries party to this convention.

▲ The Paris Convention provides for *national treatment*, which means that member countries grant the same level of intellectual property protection and remedies against infringement to each others' citizens as they grant to their own.

▲ The *Berne Convention for the Protection of Literary and Artistic Works* has 115 countries party to it. See the entry for **COPYRIGHT** for more information.

▲ The *Patent Cooperation Treaty* (PCT). In 1995, 81 countries were party to this treaty, which facilitates applying for patents in several countries. See the entry for *Patent* for more information. The CIPO is the contact for making use of the PCT in Canada.

Patent and copyright protection is more similar in different countries than are industrial design and (especially) integrated circuit design protection.

The Cornell Law School's Legal Information Institute has a WWW page with (among other things) intellectual property protection information at *http://www.law.cornell.edu/topics/topic2.html#intellectual property* (wow—there is space between intellectual and property; I've never seen that before). More intellectual property protection information is available at *http://www.patents.com*.

See **CIPO, COPYRIGHT, DESIGN PATENT, INDUSTRIAL DESIGN, INTEGRATED CIRCUIT TOPOGRAPHY ACT, PATENT, TRADEMARK,** and **TRADE SECRET**.

Interexchange Carrier

See **IXC OR IEC**.

Interlaced

A lower-cost way of producing high-resolution images on a video monitor while reducing *flicker.*

Flicker is an observation that the display is quickly turning on and off (which is more apparent when the displayed image has a light-colored background or when the room lighting is fluorescent, which itself flickers).

A monitor's *electron beam* scans across the screen (left to right), being turned on and off by the video adapter to illuminate dots (called *picture elements, pixels,* or *pels*). At the end of each horizontal *raster scan,* the beam is turned off, and it returns back to the left side of the screen (this is called *horizontal retrace*) and moves one row (or *line*) down. This continues until all rows are displayed, then the beam is returned back to the top of the screen (*vertical retrace*).

It can be less expensive, especially for televisions and higher-resolution computer displays, to use an *interlaced* display. In this case, during the first *display refresh cycle,* the odd-numbered (1, 3, 5, and so on) rows are scanned (illuminated). This is called a *field.* During the next cycle, the even-numbered rows (2, 4, 6, and so on, each of which is between the just-displayed odd-numbered rows) are scanned. This is the next *field.* The two fields comprise a *frame.*

A fast display cycle can then be used, which increases brightness, reduces flicker and permits faster-moving objects to be displayed, while reducing the cost of the monitor and adapter (since the electron beam has to write only half the pixels per display cycle).

Most modern computer monitors don't do this interlacing trick. They have a *noninterlaced* (or *progressively scanned*) display. The entire screen is rewritten each display cycle, which must occur at 70 Hz or more to eliminate flicker.

Standard broadcast television (NTSC) uses interlacing. It has a frame rate of 29.97 frames per second, and a field rate of 59.94 fields per second.

See **COLOUR, COMPOSITE VIDEO SIGNAL, NTSC, PIXEL, RASTERIZE,** and **VIDEO.**

International Organization for Standardization

See **ISO.**

internet

A (usually private) network of networks, such as a network interconnecting a company's many in-house networks. Often, TCP/IP is the one protocol common to all networks.

See **INTERNET2,** and **ROUTER.**

Internet

The largest network in the world.

A TCP/IP-based network linking more than 20 million users (160,000 new ones per month) and 1.5 million computers on more than 45,000 networks in 46 countries. These numbers are completely out of date (and were never very accurate), because each subnetwork is administered by its owner, and the number of hosts on the Internet doubles every 7 months (15% growth per month). 120 new commercial network IDs are registered per day.

In the 1970s and 1980s, major portions of the Internet were funded by the U.S. government, so they got to name it (they called it the *National Research and Education Network*), and state what types of traffic could be carried. This policy statement was called the *acceptable use policy* (AUP), and commercial traffic was not allowed on the Internet (as this would be government funding selected private organizations). As private funding supported more of the Internet, commercial traffic was allowed to be carried on those parts of the Internet. NSF funding of the Internet's backbone stopped in 1994.

A volunteer-based organization, the *Internet Society* (ISOC) has the ultimate authority for the future of the Internet. Anyone can join the ISOC, which has the purpose of promoting global information exchange through Internet technology. The ISOC appoints a council called the *Internet Architecture Board*, which regularly meets to sanction standards and allocate resources, such as addresses. The IAB decides when a standard is required, determines what the standard should be, and announces it.

Internet users provide input through the *Internet Engineering Task Force* (IETF, also a volunteer-based organization). It meets regularly to discuss operational and near-term technical problems of the Internet. IETF working groups are formed to address significant problems.

Countries other than the U.S. typically have their own Internet backbones, and connect (often directly) with the U.S. Internet backbone. For example, the Canadian Internet backbone is called CA*net, and it is connected to the U.S. Internet at 3 separate locations, for greater reliability and throughput).

The Internet's creation is generally attributed to Vinton Gray Cerf and Robert E. Kahn, and was a project to show that data communications networks could be based on *packet switching*, where data is divided into packets (of a few hundred bytes each), so that bandwidth can be shared by many users. Previously, connections between computers were dedicated to traffic for the computers on each end of the circuit. Much of the early development work was done by BBN Corp. (now owned by GTE and called GTE Internetworking), as they were awarded (in January 1969) a contract from the U.S. Pentagon's Advanced Research Projects Agency (ARPA) for the development of the packet switching nodes. These were called *Interface Message Processors* (IMPs), and such devices are now generally called *routers*). Earlier work had shown that such distributed switching networks had military advantages, as there would be no single switching points, which could be a single point of failure (or a good place to attack).

The first IMP was installed at the University of California at Los Angeles (UCLA) on Labor Day weekend, 1969, and the first messages were switched between computers directly connected to the IMP by the Tuesday. The second IMP was delivered to Stanford Research Institute (SRI) the next month, and connected with a communication line. Later in 1969, the University of California at Santa Barbara and the University of Utah were connected. The IMPs were Honeywell 516 minicomputers with 16 kbytes of memory (including 4 kbytes for packet buffers). They could handle packets of up to 1,000 bits of data, had a throughput of about 100 kbits/s. The connections between IMPs eventually ran at 50 kbits/s. These "high-speed" circuits were actually provided by using *inverse multiplexing* over 8 standard telephone circuits.

To facilitate the Internet being more civilian in use and benefit, the National Science Foundation (NSF) became the Internet's custodian in 1986 or so.

Internet 2

While the Internet used to have a single backbone for traffic, funded by the NSF, it now consists of nation-wide backbones (running at DS-3, OC-3 speeds or greater) from each of about 6 major ISP, which are interconnected at the NAPs. The 6 major ISPs are as follows:

▲ Apex Global Information Systems (AGIS)

▲ BBN Planet (BBN was one of the original developers of the Internet—designing its own routers to do so)

▲ MCI

▲ PSI (Performance Systems International)

▲ Sprint

▲ UUnet (purchased by MFS in 1996)

Internet backbone and background information is available all over the place, including *http://www.agis.net*, *http://www.ans.net*, *http://www.bbnplanet.com*, *http://www.mci.com*, *http://www.merit.edu*, *http://www.psi.net*, *http://www.ripe.net*, *http://www.sprint.com*, and *http://www.uu.net*.

Russ Haynal's superb ISP page is at *http://navigators.com/isp.html*.

Some estimates of the number of people using the Internet are at *http://www.cyberatlas.com*, *http://www.commerce.net,ftp://nic.merit.net/statistics/nsfnet*, *http://www.nordicity.com*, *http://www.npd.com*, *http://www.nw.com* and *http://www.survey.net*.

Some traffic statistics are available at *http://www.ra.net/statistics/*, and network latencies are at *http://www.netstat.net/*, *http://wwww.mids.org/index.html* and *http://www.internetweather.com*.

See **ANS**, **ARPANET**, **AUP**, **BITNET**, **CA*NET**, **CERT**, **CIX**, **DNS2** (*Domain Name System*), **EXTRANET**, **GOPHER**, **HOME PAGE**, **IAB**, **IANA**, **IETF**, **INTERNET II**, **INTERNIC**, **INVERSE MULTIPLEXER**, **IP ADDRESS**, **IMAP**, **INTRANET**, **IRC**, **ISP**, **HOST**, **NAP**, **NREN**, **NSFNET**, **PING**, **POP2** (*Post Office Protocol*), **ROUTER**, **SET**, **TCP/IP**, **UUCP**, **VPN**, **WAIS**, and **WWW**.

Internet 2

An experimental network connecting universities, to test and develop future communications protocols and equipment for higher-speed networks—such as those using OC-48 SONet connections (which run at about 2.4 Gbits/s). Supported by U.S. universities and private companies (that hope to benefit by learning how to make products needed for such future uses of the Internet).

The *Next Generation Internet* (NGI) is a similar effort funded by the U.S. government.

Further information is at *http://www.Internet2.edu*.

See **CA*NETII**, **INTERNET2**, and **POP1** (*Point of Presence*).

IAP
Internet Access Provider

See **ISP**.

INTERNIC
Internet Network Information Center

The National Science Foundation (NSF) created the InterNIC in 1993 through competitive bidding on the "three-part contract". These contracts were for a 5-year term (expiring in March 1998), and the parts were as follows:

▲ Registration services. This was won by Network Solutions, Inc. (NSI), which itself was founded in 1979 and is based in Herndon, Virginia. They handle domain name registrations for the *.com, .org, .edu, .gov* and *.net* top-level domains. They also handle the IP address assignments for North and South America. NSI also provides some technical support services for the research and education community, and provide some educational services as well. Initially, NSI received funding from the NSF for their registration services, but this is now funded by the fees charged for registrations. The change to charging for registrations has the side benefit of freeing-up names and addresses that are not being used.

▲ Information Services. This was won by General Atomics, but after a review this service was discontinued in February 1995.

▲ InterNIC directory and database services. This was won by AT&T.

The InterNIC's WWW server is at *http://www.internic.net*. NSI's web site is at *http://www.netsol.com*.

See **BELLCORE**, **CA*NET**, **DNS2** (*Domain Name System*), **IANA**, **INTERNET2**, **IP ADDRESS**, and **RFC**.

Interrupt Request

See **IRQ**.

Intranet

An organization's private, internal network which has; one or more web servers, routers, and LAN and WAN connections—that is, the same technology and equipment as the Internet. However, the Intranet is only available to internal company users (through the implementation of security systems such as firewalls). Intranets are used to disseminate information and forms throughout the organization, such as the employee telephone directory, internal job openings, procedure manuals, expense and requisition forms, newsletters, product information and training, costing calculators and so on.

It is expected that the market for intranet equipment will remain larger, and grow much faster than the market for Internet equipment. Many companies offer their services for free on the Internet (such as search engines) as advertising so companies will buy the equipment for their own intranets.

As for SNMP support, the network must typically support TCP/IP, so this is yet another reason why TCP/IP is becoming so common in organizations—especially for new applications.

An *Extranet* is an Intranet with access provided to selected external (to the company) users, such as clients and vendors. E-mail, product information and other information can then be securely exchanged and shared.

See **EXTRANET**, **FIREWALL**, **INTERNET2**, and **WWW**.

Inverse Multiplexer

Usually, a *multiplexer* is used to provide many users (typically low-speed asynchronous terminals, such as DEC VT100s, or PCs emulating them) with access to a single higher-speed connection (since it is less expensive to provide one higher-speed link than many lower-speed links).

An *inverse multiplexer* works the other way around. It solves the problem that high-speed (greater than 64 kbits/s), switched (you choose who you want to connect to, just before you send data) WAN services are not (yet) widely available.

The inverse multiplexer provides a high-speed switched service by establishing many (typically) 56- or 64-kbits/s switched connections simultaneously (and handling the splitting and combining of the data). For example, if you needed a 384-kbits/s service for a two-hour video conference, the inverse multiplexer would make six simultaneous 64-kbits/s calls (perhaps using several ISDN BRI connections). If the connection was long-distance, you would pay six times the rate for a single 64-kbits/s call.

Inverse multiplexers can be an external hardware box, or software (such as MLPPP). Hardware inverse multiplexers are an interim technology (they're a kludge), which will likely be replaced by *Multirate ISDN*, frame relay SVCs, ATM, and other cleaner solutions in the near future.

See **S800**, **ATM** (*Asynchronous Transfer Mode*), **BONDING**, **DIGITAL 800**, **FRAME RELAY**, **IMA**, **ISDN**, **MLPPP**, **SWITCHED 56**, **TDM**, and **WAN**.

IP
Internet Protocol

UNIX's internetworking protocol (OSI layer 3). Includes information for fragmentation/reassembly and Time-To-Live and identifies the encapsulated protocol (for example, TCP). Routers use this information.

IP routers drop packets to handle congestion (the sending router is supposed to detect the congestion by the high rate of retransmit requests from the receiver and slow down).

The currently used version is Version 4 (IPv4), and is defined in RFCs 791 and 1577.

See **CSLIP**, **DNS2** (*Domain Name System*), **ICMP**, **INTERNET2**, **INTERNIC**, **IP ADDRESS**, **IP MULTICAST**, **IPNG**, **LINK STATE**, **MOBILE IP**, **RIP**, **SLIP**, **TCP**, **TTL1** (*Time-To-Live*), and **UNIX**.

IP Address

All network-layer protocols have an address format, and for the 32-bit IP addresses of the TCP/IP protocol, addresses are of the form "`199.12.1.1`". This is called *dotted decimal*, and each of the four sections is a decimal number from 0 to 255, representing 8 bits of the IP address. Part of the address specifies a *network*, and the rest of the *address* specifies a specific host on that network.

Since there are only 32 bits to the entire IP address and some networks have many more hosts than others (and there are fewer larger networks), there are different *address classes*. These allocate different numbers of bits to the network and host portion of the address.

The address classes are summarized in the following table.

IP Address Class	Address Range[a]	Comments
	0.0.0.0	The local host[b] also used to signify the default router
A	0.x.x.x	Host x.x.x on the local network
	1.0.0.1 to 126.255.255.254	2^7–2 (126) Class A networks total, each with 2^{24}–2 (16,777,214 to be exact) hosts
	127.x.x.x	Used for internal host loopback
B	128.0.x.x	Reserved
	128.1.0.1 to 191.254.255.254	2^{14}–2 (16,382) Class B networks, each with up to 2^{16}–2 (65,534) hosts
	191.255.255.x	Reserved
C	192.0.0.x	Reserved
	192.0.1.1 to 223.255.254.254	2^{21}–2 (2,097,150) Class C networks, each with up to 2^8–2 (254) hosts
	223.255.255.x	Reserved
D	224.0.0.0 to 239.255.255.255	Reserved for multicast groups
E	240.0.0.0 to 254.255.255.254	Reserved for experimental and future use
	255.255.255.255	Broadcast to all hosts on the local network

a. The network number (or ID) part of the IP address is set in *bold* in this chart.
b. By convention, setting the network or host part of the address to zero refers to the *local* ("*this*") network or host (respectively). Setting the host part to all ones refers to *all* hosts on the specified network. Therefore, a network or host address of all ones or all zeros cannot be used as a specific network or host ID.

Because all Class A addresses have been used and there are very few Class B addresses left (to get a Class B you need to demonstrate that there is an immediate need for at least 25% of that address range, that 50% of the 65,534 addresses will be used within 1 year, and provide detailed deployment information), new addressing schemes are required for networks that have more than 254 hosts.

Efforts to handle this addressing problem include *Classless Inter-Domain Routing* (CIDR), IPng, and RFC 1918.

In Canada, the assignment of IP addresses used to handled by the University of Toronto, but is now handled by your Internet Service Provider (ISP).

In the U.S., the InterNIC handles (or subcontracts) the assignment of IP addresses.

A list of the assigned multicast addresses is at *ftp://ftp.isi.edu/in-notes/iana/assignments/multicast-addresses*

See **CIDR, DNS2** (*Domain Name System*), **HOST, INTERNIC, IP MULTICAST, IPNG, ISP, RFC-1918**, and **SUBNET BIT MASK**.

IP MULTICAST
Internet Protocol Multicast

Video conferencing, electronic whiteboards, software distribution and other anticipated multimedia uses for networks will need *one-to-many* and *many-to-many* communication capability (called *traffic flows*), which has substantially different requirements from the traditional *one-to-one* or *point-to-point* connections that most current LAN and WAN applications use. Other possible uses for multicasting capability include nonmultimedia applications, such as "ticker-tape" stock market feeds, weather information, and updating mail server databases.

In addition to being able to send a single message to many destinations at once (current technology would require the same message to be sent many times, once to each destination), requirements are as follows:

▲ Routers must be able to efficiently locate routes to many networks at once

▲ Only a single copy of each packet should be sent on any shared link

▲ Traffic should be sent only on links that have at least one recipient (this addresses both network loading and security concerns)

IP multicast supports these capabilities for the TCP/IP protocol (though only for UDP, since IP multicast only supports connectionless protocols).

IP multicast requires destination hosts wanting to receive a multicast to *subscribe* (also called "register"), using the *Internet group management protocol* (IGMP—which is specified in RFC 1112. IGMP specifies the following operations:

▲ Subscribing (requesting to participate in an IP multicast group) is done by the receiver specifying the Class D IP address used for the particular multicast (just like tuning to a particular television channel). Subscribing and leaving is *dynamic* (so can be done at any time).

▲ Class D addresses can also be permanently assigned (manually, by an administrator).

▲ Any number of hosts, in any location (for example, eventually, anywhere on the Internet) can be part of the multicast group. Hosts can be members of more than one multicast group. And a multicasting host does not need to subscribe (if it does not want to receive the multicast traffic).

▲ A multicasting host (that is, the server running the IP multicast application) sends the traffic to that Class D address. The scope of a multicast can be limited be reducing the time-to-live (TTL) count in the IP header.

All of this (that is, IGMP) is defined in RFC 1112.

Routers track such IGMP requests and build a *connectivity tree* for each possible sender to each registered receiver. When multicast traffic is received from a particular sender, the router then uses its tree for that sender to determine on which ports traffic needs to be forwarded.

The MBone is a network layered on top of parts of the Internet, to support IP multicast. It currently has three router-to-router protocols (so they can dynamically learn which multicast group's data need to be sent out which ports—that is, the building of the trees), as itemized below:

▲ *Protocol Independent Multicast* (PIM, supported by the IETF and Cisco), which works with more protocols than just TCP/IP

▲ *Distance Vector Multicast Routing Protocol* (DVMRP); this is specified in RFC 1075, is similar to RIP, and can only run on networks that use RIP between their routers. DVMRP is the most widely-implemented router-to-router protocol on the MBONE and is supported by 3Com and Bay Networks

▲ *Multicast Open Shortest Path First* (MOSPF); defined in RFC 1584, is an extension to OSPF (and requires OSPF to be the router to router protocol), and is supported by 3Com and Proteon

DVMRP and MOSPF are both dense-mode approaches, in that they flood the network (through paths that comprise a branching tree, with the base at the server) with the multicast traffic. However, DVMRP and MOSPF each work with only specific router to router protocols (unlike PIM).

The table below shows the Class D IP multicast addresses, as assigned by the IANA.

IP Address Class	Address Range	Comments
D	224.0.0.0	Reserved (cannot be assigned to any group)
	224.0.0.1 *to* 224.0.0.255	Reserved for use by routing, topology discovery and maintenance protocols[a]
	224.0.1.0 *to* 238.255.255.255	For assignment for specific multicast applications
	239.0.0.0 *to* 239.255.255.255	For local (not Internet-wide) applications

a. For example, 224.0.0.2 multicasts to all routers on the subnet, and 224.0.0.5 multicasts to all MOSPF routers on the subnet.

When multicast traffic arrives from the Internet at a router, there is still the job of getting it to the final (likely LAN-connected) computer. To facilitate this (and avoid having to use the ARP, and to instead take advantage of LAN adapter's built-in support for multicast addressing), the IEEE has reserved the block of MAC addresses beginning with 01-00-5E for this purpose. The least significant 23 bits of the IP multicast address are used to construct the MAC-layer address. If you count the bits, you see that the upper 5 bits of the IP multicast address are ignored, so that up to 32 IP multicast addresses get mapped to the same MAC multicast address. The IP software in the destination computer would then look at the full IP address in the IP header to determine whether to receive the multicast.

Apple's *Simple Multicast Routing Protocol* (SMRP) provides similar capabilities but currently only for AppleTalk traffic from applications such as QuickTime Conference.

More information is available from the IP Multicast Initiative (IPMI), at *http://www.ipmulticast.com*.

See **CDPD**, **CONNECTIONLESS**, **IANA**, **IP ADDRESS**, **MBONE**, **MULTIMEDIA**, **OSPF**, **PIM**, **PUSH**, **QTC**, **RIP**, **SMRP**, **TTL1** (*Time-To-Live*), and **UDP**.

Initial Program Load

See **BOOTSTRAP**.

IPNG
Internet Protocol, next generation 6

See **IPNG**.

IPSEC
IP Security

A suite of authentication and encryption protocols, for all types of IP traffic, to create VPNs (so that data can be securely sent (perhaps over the Internet) between the two end stations or networks). IPSec encrypts and encapsulates IP packets, so the true source and destinations cannot be observed by outsiders. Two *headers* (a few bytes before the actual data) are added to each packet, as described below:

▲ An *authentication header* (AH) uses MD5 to ensure message integrity.

▲ The *encapsulated security payload* (ESP) header describes how the packet was encrypted. Two options are *transport mode* where just the payload is encrypted, and *tunnel mode* where the entire packet is encrypted.

IPSec would typically be implemented on a firewall. Defined in RFCs 1826, 1827 and 1829.

Some IPSec information is at *http://www.ietf.org/html.charters/ipsec-charter.html*.

See **AUTHENTICATION**, **ENCRYPTION**, **FIREWALL**, and **VPN**.

IPV6
Internet Protocol version 6

It is anticipated that the current implementation of TCP/IP's *Internet Protocol* (which is IPv4) will run out of addresses within the next few years (though the increase in the rate that IP addresses are being assigned is decreasing now that most organizations have firewalls that map a small number of registered IP addresses to the organization's internal IP addressing scheme, and since there is now an annual charge for IP addresses). IPv6 is to be the next version of IP and is to support a larger address (for example, it may come to pass that every lightbulb and appliance in your house has a unique IP address).

A committee of the IETF is developing standards for the migration of IP to support this larger address field and other features required for the future. The address field will be increased from the current 4 bytes to 16 bytes (that is, 32 bits to 128 bits) and will allow users to use the same IP address even when they physically connect to a different place on the Internet (currently, your IP address usually has to be part of the range of addresses assigned to your ISP). Many people have played with calculators to decide whether this is a large-enough address space. For example, this is an increase from 4 billion to 3×10^{38} addresses. This allows 6×10^{28} addresses for every person on the earth. Another way of looking at a number that big is that it provides at least 1,564 addresses for every square meter of the earth's surface (even when allowing for an inefficient address allocation scheme). A more optimistic prognostication shows that there would be 10^{12} address per square meter.

Rather than just the *dotted decimal* notation commonly used for the 32-bit IPv4 addresses (such as 207.205.85.1, where each number—which can range from 0 to 255—represents an 8-bit value), IPv6 also uses *colon hexadecimal* notation. In this case, colons separate 32-bit groups of bits, and the address itself is in hexadecimal (so each 8-bit number can range from 0_{16} through FF_{16}). The hexadecimal numbers may be prefaced by 0x. Also, double colons (::) can be used to zero-fill a field—to the right, left or center (depending on where the double colons are). For example, and address of ::A8 indicates that the field is zero-filled to the left.

IPv6 (and the many ancillary protocols for managing traffic) will include support for:

▲ Encryption.

▲ User authentication (using a 32-bit *security association ID* and a variable-length field that carries authentication data in the header, hosts negotiate the type of encryption algorithm and the key size for each session).

▲ Automatic network configuration (automatically assigns IP addresses to hosts).

▲ The ability to handle real-time and delay-sensitive traffic (such as multimedia), by using a 24-bit *Flow ID* in the header that identifies delay-sensitive traffic to routers. There are also 16 priority classes. Therefore, routers can perform prioritization based on information in the address field.

Also, it is designed to run well on very high-speed networks (such as those using ATM, as well as slow networks (such as wireless networks).

IPv6 is a new protocol, not backward-compatible with IPv4 (which is the current version). Of course, that brings up the question of what happened to IPv5 (there has always been a 4-bit field in the IP header reserved to identify the version of IP). IPv5 was previously assigned to something called the *Stream Protocols*—ST and ST-II. A list of the IP version number assignments is at *ftp://ftp.isi.edu/in-notes/iana/assignments/version-numbers*. The first 4 bits of the IP header are the *Vers* field, and this is where the IP version number goes, so that networking devices can know how to interpret the remainder of the header.

Converting to IPv6 is expected to be a major difficulty, as it is basically a completely different protocol.

Also called IPng (*Internet Protocol, next generation*, sort of like *Star Trek: The Next Generation*).

See **S802.A11**, **AUTHENTICATION**, **DHCP**, **ENCRYPTION**, **IP ADDRESS**, **ISP**, **MULTIMEDIA**, and **PRIORITIZATION**.

IPX
Internet Packet Exchange

The network layer (OSI layer 3) datagram-based protocol usually used by Novell's NetWare network operating system.

Supports any window size—and packet sizes up to 64 kbytes. Novell's NCP and SPX both use IPX.

The higher-layer workstation shell (NCP, as implemented in NetX, for example) controls the *window* size, the number of frames that can be outstanding (sent but not yet acknowledged), and the *frame* size (the number of bytes per frame).

Since NetX was based on XNS, it has several of its limitations, such as a window size of 1 and a frame size up to only 576 bytes. These significantly reduce performance for longer-delay and lower-speed data links, such as most WAN links between routers.

Novell's newer shell software (VLMs) supports a window size of up to 16 and a frame size of up to 4,096 bytes.

The protocol includes several periodically sent packet types as shown in the following table.

Packet Type	Use
Router Information Protocol (RIP)	Multicasted every 60 seconds by routers (which may be stand-alone or built in to file servers) to keep other routers current about open paths.
Service Advertising Protocol (SAP)	Multicasted every 60 seconds by all servers (such as file servers, print servers, and communication servers) so that clients can learn the names, services, and MAC addresses of the servers. These messages are usually offset from a file server's RIPs by 30 seconds.
Watchdog Packets	Sent by servers (an ASCII "?" is sent at least every 4 minutes and 57 seconds) to confirm that clients (which respond with a "Y") are still up and connected.
Serialization Packets	Servers multicast their NetWare license number to confirm that the same copies of the servers' software are not (illegally) installed elsewhere on the network.

Has nothing to do with the Internet.

See **ILSR**, **NCP1**, **NOVELL**, **RIP**, **SAP**, **SPOOFING**, and **XNS**.

IRC
Internet Relay Chat

A multiuser chat system. That is, the messages that everybody types are displayed to everyone else connected to a server on the same IRC network, such as DALnet, EFnet and Undernet. Each IRC network typically consists of tens or hundreds of servers, each with perhaps tens or hundreds of users. It is often used on the Internet, was originally written by Jarkko Oikarinen in 1988, and was first used in Finland.

As on a citizens band radio, there are different *channels* to support simultaneous conversations and topics. However, you can also start your own channels—you then get to be the *channel operator* (or *op* or *chop*) and get a @ before your name—and control the name and access to the channel, and perhaps invite others to join you. Some client software allow direct communication with other clients—without needing a server.

IRC commands start with "/", so /help provides some local help. Once the user is on-line with IRC, on-line help is available on channel #irchelp (channel names are preceded with a "#"). /list provides a list of available channels, and to join a channel, type /join #channelname.

VRML is a graphical and visual method of doing what IRC does.

IRC client software (which runs on your PC) can be downloaded from *ftp://cs-ftp.bu.edu/irc/clients/pc/windows*, *http://www.mirc.co.uk* and *http://www.bcpl.lib.md.us/~frappa/pirch.html*.

Some IRC servers are *irc://irc.bu.edu*, *irc://irc.mcgill.ca* and *irc://mickey.cc.utexas.edu*. A list of IRC networks is at *http://home.sprynet.com/sprynet/saint*.

The IRC FAQ is at *http://www.kei.com/irc.html* and *ftp://cs-ftp.bu.edu/irc/support/alt-irc-faq*.

RFC 1459 describes IRC.

See **AYT**, **INTERNET2**, **RFC**, **UNIX**, and **VRML**.

IRDA
Infrared Data Association

An industry association of about 100 companies, first formed in 1993 to with the charter "to create an interoperable, low-cost infrared (that is, a longer wavelength of red light than humans can see) data interconnection standard that supports a walk-up, point-to-point user model that is adaptable to a broad range of appliance, computing and communicating devices."

Version 1.0 of the standard was released in 1994.

It supports two-way data transmission, and uses 880-nm infrared light. TV remote controls also use infrared light but usually use a different "color"—880 to 950 nm wavelength.

Realizing that if there is a problem, users may hold the devices directly together, the specification requires correct IrDA operation from a distance of 1 cm to 1 meter (though up to 3 meters are optionally allowed by the specification), and up to 15° from center for the transmitter, and up to 30° from center for the receiver. Typical maximum distances for actual products are 4 to 6 feet.

Eight-bit data are sent LSB first, half-duplex (so that transmitters can easily ignore their own reflections). The first version of the standard (1.0) has an initial default speed is 9,600 bits/s, but devices can negotiate to use 2,400, 19,200, 38,400, 57,600, or 115,200 bits/s (most support this speed).

Version 1.1 of the standard (released in late 1995) also supports a transfer rate of 1.152 Mbits/s (ten times faster than the previous maximum) and version 2.0 of the standard supports 4 Mbit/s (expected to be popular to transfer color-graphic documents to printers). Version 1.1 and 2.0 devices are interoperable with version 1.0 devices (they simply negotiate to use one of the lower speeds). Support for these faster speeds is sometimes called *Fast IR* or *FIR*.

Bits are sent as follows:

▲ A binary 0 is a pulse of infrared light, sent at the beginning of the bit-time. The pulse can be either a fixed-length 1.6 µs pulse (regardless of the bit rate) or a 3/16 bit-time pulse (this is a lower-cost implementation that unfortunately requires more power).

▲ A binary 1 is no pulse.

An HDLC-like protocol (called *IR* Link Access Procedure—IrLAP) is used, which guarantees that there will never be more than five sequential ones in the data stream. The protocol also allows the transmission to be interrupted for many seconds (up to 10 for example), and resume with no data loss (long interruptions require the transmission to be manually restarted).

The error rate is expected to be better than 10^{-9} (no more than one bit in error, out of 1,000,000,000 bits). IrDA is based on Hewlett-Packard's SIR (*Serial Infrared*) scheme (for example, the 3/16 bit-time pulse is from SIR), of which several parts are patented. Popular applications for IrDA include printing from laptop PCs and transferring data between PCs and PDAs.

IrDA is a point-to-point technology. *Diffuse IR* schemes are available (which basically cover an entire room with IR light, so many devices can communicate. These are not popular or widely available as they cost too much, and provide relatively low performance (less than 1 Mbit/s). IR has advantages over RF (radio frequency) wireless solutions in that IR is immune to external noise (so long as you're not in direct sunlight), and transmission is line-of-sight only, which has security benefits.

The Infrared Data Association is at *http://www.irda.org/*.

See **S1284**, **COLOUR**, **HDLC**, **HP**, **PDA**, and **PPM**.

Iridium

A system of *low earth orbiting* (LEO) satellites which will enable portable handsets to provide voice and data communications anywhere on the earth.

The $4 billion (some say $5 billion) system is being developed by a partnership of 17 organizations called Iridium LLC (the LLC part is for *limited liability company*). The company is based in Washington DC, and is headed by Motorola's Satellite Communications Division (Motorola owns 25% of the partnership, and they supply much of the electronics—Lockheed Martin Corp. makes much of the other parts of the satellites). The nice name comes from the element Iridium, which has an *atomic number* of 77 (which means that every atom has 77 electrons)—and 77 is the original number of satellites proposed for the system (design work began in 1987). To reduce costs, the system was redesigned to use 66 satellites (and 6 backup satellites), but either the name Iridium had some marketing mind-share by then, or the name Dysprosium (the element which has 66 electrons) didn't have the same *cachet*.

In any case, the satellites orbit at a height of 780 km, and it has been announced that service to the public will begin at 9:00 AM on September 23, 1998—to show they mean business. These satellites communicate directly with each other, with earth stations—and with your handset too. Handset to satellite communications use the frequencies of 1,616.0 to 1,626.5 MHz.

Services provided will be voice (just like a world-wide cellular telephone network), facsimile, paging and data services.

A neato and very complicated unique feature of Iridium is that all communication between satellites (when the caller and callee are closest to different Iridium satellites) will be done directly between those (and other) Iridium satellites. Competing satellite systems only use the satellites for communication to the users, and have downlinks to earth stations, which then use traditional terrestrial land-line links and ground-based switching systems to communicate with the earth station nearest the satellite which is nearest the destination user.

A total of 17 launches (from U.S., China and Russian sites) will be required (launch vehicles each carry more than one satellite, to reduce launch costs) to get all the birds in the air. The first 5 satellites were launched on May 5, 1997 and there were 17 up by August 1997 and 27 by October 1997 (7 were launched by a single Russian Proton-K rocket on September 14, 1997). Ground stations in 11 countries are needed to control the system.

Just to keep themselves busy, Motorola has already begun work on Celestri, which is to be a $13 billion system of 72 satellites to carry video and data.

See **SATELLITE**.

IRQ
Interrupt Request

The name of the hardware interrupt signals that PC peripherals (such as the serial or parallel ports) can use to get the processor's attention.

For example, interrupts are used to drag the processor away from whatever interruptible task it is currently doing and give it a byte of received data that just can't wait (otherwise another byte of data will overwrite that one, therefore losing data).

The original 8-bit IBM PC and PC/XT used a single *interrupt controller* IC, which supported eight hardware interrupts (of which two were used on the CPU motherboard and are not brought out to the bus). Other interrupts were reserved for controllers and ports.

The later IBM PC/AT 16-bit ISA bus extended this to another eight interrupts by cascading a second interrupt controller to the first interrupt controller's IRQ 2 input (making IRQ 2 unavailable for use), though the new interrupt 9 was mapped to appear as interrupt 2.

Other peripherals that use interrupts include LAN adapters, sound boards, scanner interfaces, and SCSI adapters. Interrupts usually cannot be shared (though interrupts can usually be shared on PCI buses), so on non-PCI buses, each card must be (usually manually) assigned a unique interrupt (sometimes called an interrupt vector).

The lower interrupt numbers have higher priority.

IRQ

The following table shows the ISA bus interrupt assignments (interrupt numbers are in decimal).

IRQ	Use
0	System timer (provides 18.21-MS ticks to the operating system). Since lower IRQs have higher priority (if two interrupts are signaled at the same time), this has the highest priority.
1	Keyboard.
2	Not available on the 16-bit ISA bus, since it is used to connect to the output of the interrupt controller for interrupts 8 through 15. The interrupt 2 pin on the 16-bit ISA bus is connected to the interrupt 9 input of the interrupt controller. The PC is configured to call the interrupt handler for interrupt 2 when interrupt 9 is activated.
3	Serial communications port 2 (COM2) and sometimes 4 (COM4), if installed.
4	Serial communications port 1 (COM1) and sometimes 3 (COM3), if installed
5	Initially used for the hard disk controller in the PC/XT (but not in later PCs). Then reserved for a second parallel printer port (LPT2) in the PC/AT. Since it is rare to have more than one parallel printer port in a PC (and the PC's BIOS usually does not use interrupts for printing anyway), IRQ is usually available for use. Often used by a sound board (for example, SoundBlaster often requires interrupt 5) or LAN adapter.
6	Floppy diskette controller.
7	First parallel printer port (LPT1). While WordPerfect (if using the `Print to Hardware Port` option for better performance) and Novell's `RPrinter` (and a few other programs) use interrupts for printer output, most programs (and DOS) do not. Therefore interrupt 7 may be available to use even if LPT1 is present (and used) in the PC. This is the lowest priority interrupt.
8	A PC's real-time clock IC (which contains both the battery-backed-up CMOS memory and the time-of-day clock, which is read when the PC is powered on) can be set to generate an interrupt 8, in binary multiples from two per second to 8,192 per second. Interrupt 8 has a lower priority than interrupt 1 but a higher priority than interrupt 9.
9	Used to handle boards that generate interrupt 2 (that is, interrupt 2 on the ISA bus is wired to the interrupt controller input for interrupt 9), since the real interrupt 2 is used for the cascade of interrupts 8 through 15. The ISA bus therefore has no interrupt 9 pin.
10	Available.
11	Available.
12	May be used by the IBM PS/2-style bus mouse, but usually is not, so it typically available.
13	Reserved for math coprocessor error indications. Not available on the ISA bus.
14	Used by the non-SCSI hard disk controller (usually IDE) in PC/AT (and later) PCs.
15	Often used by SCSI disk controllers, but there is no "standard" setting for a SCSI disk controller interrupt. Has a lower priority than interrupt 14 but a higher priority than interrupt 3.

See **BUS, DMA, INTEL, ISA, MOUSE, PC, PIO, PLUG AND PLAY**, and **SHARED MEMORY**.

IS
Intermediate System

A router on an OSI network.

See ES, IS-IS, and OSI.

IS-54

See TDMA.

IS-95

See CDMA, and PCS1 (*Personal Communications Service*).

IS-136

See TDMA, and PCS1 (*Personal Communications Service*).

IS-IS
Intermediate System to Intermediate System

The OSI router-to-router protocol. It is a link-state (as opposed to distance-vector) based algorithm that works only with OSI's network-layer protocol CLNP.

See CLNP, IS, LINK STATE, and OSI.

ISA
Industry Standard Architecture

The bus used in standard IBM-compatible PCs to provide power to add-in boards and communication between the add-in boards and to the motherboard (into which the boards plug).

Since IBM did not publish timing specifications, there were initially compatibility problems. This was resolved in 1987, when the IEEE produced a complete bus specification (including timing).

Since the Intel 8088 CPU (used in the first 4.77-MHz PCs introduced in 1982) had an 8-bit data bus, the bus in the original PC also had an 8-bit data bus (usually called the *8-bit PC* or *PC*/XT Bus), and data were transferred 8 bits at a time. This 62-pin bus supported the following:

▲ 8 data lines (allowing for 8 bits of data to be transferred at a time)

▲ 20 address lines (1 Mbyte of addressing, though the video adapter was assigned 128 kbytes, starting at address 640 kbytes, and this created the now-infamous DOS memory limitation)

▲ Interrupts 2 through 7 (separate signal for each interrupt)

▲ DMA channels 1, 2, and 3 (two signals for each channel, request and acknowledge). The original PC's motherboard used DMA channel 0 for memory refresh, and since the DMA controller and the memory were on the motherboard, the signals were not brought to the bus.

The other pins are used for power and timing signals.

The 80286 used in the IBM PC/AT (*"advanced technology,"* which it was when it was introduced in 1984) had a 16-bit data bus, so IBM (then still the sole standards-setter for PCs) added 36-pin connector which provided the following:

▲ Eight more data lines (allowing for 16-bit data transfers)

▲ Four more address lines (allowing 16 Mbytes of addressing)

▲ Interrupts 10, 11, 12, 14, and 15 (interrupt 13 is reserved for a math coprocessor, which would be on the motherboard, so interrupt 13 is not brought out to the bus)

▲ DMA channels 0, 5, 6, and 7 (DMA channel 4 is used to link the new DMA channels to the original ones). Unlike the original PC, the PC/AT uses a dedicated memory refresh circuit, so DMA Channel 0 is available for use, and it is brought out to the bus.

This is the *16-bit PC*/AT bus, or, more commonly (and simply), the *ISA* bus which is provided in most PCs (older PCs only support ISA; newer PCs typically support both ISA and PCI). The ISA bus is sometimes called an AT bus. For example, the IDE interface (which basically connects a disk drive directly to the ISA bus is called an ATA (AT bus attachment) interface.

8-bit ISA cards can usually be plugged-in to 16-bit ISA slots, so long as the board's "skirt" is high enough to clear the 16-bit ISA bus's additional connector.

The ISA bus has a *theoretical* maximum transfer speed of 16 Mbytes/s (more commonly stated as 8 Mbytes/s, since it usually requires one bus cycle for the address and another for the 16 bits of data). The *typical* maximum speed is 1 to 2.5 Mbytes/s (which is 8 to 20 Mbits/s). This speed is so variable because of bus contention with other devices (mainly memory) and buffering delays due to the asynchronous nature of the bus (the processor speed is different from the bus speed).

See **ATA**, **BUS**, **DMA**, **EISA**, **IEEE**, **IRQ**, **PC**, **PCI**, and **PIO**.

ISBN
International Standard Book Number

This is not a computer term, but there is one of these for this (and every) book, and an ISBN another one of those things that are seen everywhere, but seldom explained.

The ISBN is part of the Internationally-used *European Article Numbering* (EAN) system of numerical identification for everything. In this case, for published works to expedite their ordering, handling and inventorying by publishers, booksellers, librarians and others in the book industry. Initially, ISBNs were only for books (hardcover and softcover), but now are assigned to other published media, such as pamphlets, brochures, software and microfilms.

ISBNs are always a total of 10 digits (typically preceded by "ISBN"), and are comprised of 4 numbers, each separated by dashes (so there are always a total of 3 dashes). Beginning at the left, the numbers are as shown in the table below.

Field	Length (digits)	Description
Origin	1 to 4	Denotes the language in which the book was published (or sometimes the country). For example, a 0 or a 1 indicates that the book was published in an english-speaking country such as the U.S., Canada, England or Australia. A 2 indicates a french-speaking country, such as France, Canada or Belgium.
Publisher's Prefix	2 to 7	Identifies the publisher, as each is assigned their own prefix. The assigning agency chooses shorter prefixes for publishers that publish more titles (so that there will be more digits available for the next field).
		A publisher will be assigned additional Publisher's Prefix codes if they use up all the titles in their initially-allocated block.
Title	6 to 1	The title field will be a maximum of 6 digits when the origin field is 1 digit (which is usually the case). For ISBNs with a 2-digit origin, then the title field will be a maximum of 5 digits, and so on.
		Each title published by the publisher is assigned a unique title number (additional printings of the exact same work keep the original ISBN). If the same title is substantially changed in form, or has a second edition published (with the text changed), then a new ISBN is assigned.
Check digit	1	A digit generated from the other 9 digits, to assist in detecting mistakes in typing the number.

In the U.S. the ISBN-assigning agency is R.R. Bowker, at (908) 665-6770 and *http://www.bowker.com/main/home/standards/isbn.html*. They charge $175 for a publisher's prefix, and for that you get a logbook with your assigned ISBNs printed in it (complete with the check digits). If you are a small publisher, then you get a 7-digit publisher's prefix, and a block of 10 ISBNs. Larger publishers get a 6-digit prefix, and a block of 100 ISBNs, and so on. If you use up your block within 5 years, you get a new prefix for free. Each time you publish a title, a form is sent back to the agency, with information about the title.

In Canada, ISBNs are assigned by the *Canadian ISBN* Agency, which is part of the National Library of Canada. They are at (819) 994-6872. There is no charge for being assigned a publisher's prefix.

The *Publishers International Directory* (available in libraries) lists the origin codes and assigned publisher's prefixes.

ISBNs printed as bar codes on the back of books use the EAN-13 format, which has 13 digits. This is supposed to be the only barcode on the outside cover of books and other items for use in bookstores, schools and libraries (which is why you sometimes see another barcode inside a book, especially those often sold in grocery stores, so the barcode scanner does not get confused by the UPC barcode).

The first three digits of the EAN-13 are an identifier for the subsequent numbering system. The digits 978 are reserved for ISBNs (and 979 when they run out of those). A complete list of these leading digits is at *http://www.uc-council.org/d08-c.htm*.

After the 978, the EAN has the ISBN, with the ISBN check digit replaced by a new check digit that covers the entire EAN. On books, after the 13-digit EAN is a 5-digit price barcode. If the first digit is a 5, then the next 4 digits are the price is in U.S. dollars (if the price is greater than $99.99, then $99.99 is used as the price). If the number begins with a 6, then the price is in Canadian dollars. If the number begins with a 9, then there is no price, and the next four digits are zeros (though the price may be separately printed in digits above the barcode).

The Book Industry Study Group (at 212 929-1393) has more information. EAN International is at *http://www.ean.be*.

Items which do not require an ISBN include periodicals, magazines, and items with little text, such as posters, coloring books and greeting cards. "Serial" publications, such as newspapers and magazines (which are published in successive parts, hopefully indefinitely) have an 8-digit *International Standard Serial Number* (ISSN). This is printed as two groups of 4 digits (beginning with 977), separated by a hyphen, and prefaced by "ISSN."

See **EDI**, **FCS**, and **UPC**.

ISDN
Integrated Services Digital Network

A WAN-oriented data communication service provided by telephone companies. It is well-suited to switched connections requiring greater bandwidth than that provided by analog modems, for traffic that usually is of a fixed duration (of typically less than 4 hours per day). Such applications often include remote LAN access, video-conferencing and disaster recovery.

The most popular types of channels provided are the following:

- ▲ *B channels* (bearer):
- ▲ Circuit-switched (the whole connection is switched to one destination, as a telephone call is)
- ▲ 64,000 bits/s each
- ▲ Full-duplex (data can be sent and received simultaneously)
- ▲ Carry digitized voice or data (voice calls can be made to either ISDN or standard POTS telephones)
- ▲ *D channels* (delta)
- ▲ Packet-switched (each frame of data can go to a different destination, like on a LAN or X.25 network)
- ▲ 16,000 bits/s (for basic rate ISDN) or 64,000 bits/s (for primary rate ISDN) each
- ▲ Full-duplex (data can be sent and received simultaneously)
- ▲ Carry both signaling (dialed digits, incoming call's telephone number, ring the telephone, and so on) and data (typically, up to 9,600 bits/s on basic-rate ISDN, to leave capacity for the signalling information)

ISDN is unique among WAN services in that it provides access both to the circuit-switched *public switched telephone network* and to packet-switched services, such as X.25 and frame relay.

Basic-rate ISDN provides two B channels and one D channel.

Primary-rate ISDN provides 23 B channels and one D channel (in Europe, PRIs have 30 B channels plus one D channel), though by using *Nonfacility Associated Signaling* (NFAS), a single 64 kbits/s D channel can provide signaling for many primary rate ISDN lines, so the ISDN lines after the first typically provide 24 B channels and 0 D channels. The 64 kbit/s D channel typically has capacity to handle the signalling for up to about 20 PRI lines, but telephone companies typically recommend installing a backup D channel for every 8 PRI lines.

The common channel signalling system #7 now widely used in telephone networks (especially those that offer ISDN service) has a goal of call set-up times of a maximum of 250 ms within a country—and this is reflected by the corresponding very fast call set-up times for ISDN circuits—typically a half a second, though the subsequent PPP negotiation (for example) will extend this.

That is, because B channel calls are established digitally (by signaling the D channel), depending on the connection process, call set-up time is typically a maximum of 1 to 3 seconds—and often less than a second, since there is no need for the slow process of sending and decoding DTMF tones, and no need to wait for modem negotiations. In contrast, a typical analog modem call requires 30 to 60 seconds to establish. Another neat feature of ISDN D channel signaling is that if both your BRI B channels are being combined to provide faster access to your Internet service provider and an incoming voice call is signaled, one B channel can be hung up to accept the incoming call (slowing your Internet access to half-speed during your voice connection). When finished talking, the B channel can be automatically reconnected for your full-speed surfing pleasure (most ISP charge extra for connecting with 2 B channels simultaneously, since you are using more resources).

The ISDN protocols inherently support Caller ID.

ISDN ordering codes (IOCs) are sets of ISDN switch configuration parameters required for the correct operation of customer equipment. They were first developed by the *Corporation for Open Systems* (COS), but are now administered by Bellcore (they inform carriers of the configurations needed for each IOC), and developed by the ISDN Solutions Group (a consortium of vendors and telephone companies).

By defining and publicizing IOCs (or getting their equipment to work with those already defined) required for each product, customer equipment vendors can easily communicate their configuration requirements to ISDN service providers. *Intel Blue* and the four IOCs defined by Nynex, Bellsouth and Bellcore in their *ISDN* Easy definition are examples of these.

Three popular IOCs are summarized below:

ISDN Order Code	Description
B	Supports a single B channel provisioned for data only, and Calling Line ID
R	Supports two B channels, both provisioned for data only, and Calling Line ID
S	Supports two B channels, both provisioned for data and voice

Provisioning ISDN service for data only (and no voice) typically reduces the monthly cost substantially—so carriers often forget to mention this option—ask for it if it would serve your needs.

Multirate ISDN allows a specified number of B channels to be combined to provide higher-speed dial-up circuit-switched digital connections, using *Digital 800* service.

Multilink PPP ("MP") is a more popular standard for inverse multiplexing. For ISDN, it is specified in RFC 1618.

Telephone companies have always wanted to charge per minute for local calls, which is sometimes called *local measured service* (LMS)—like they do for long distance calls). But in areas where there has never been LMS, there is substantial customer resistance to this. ISDN has given telephone companies the opportunity to sneak in some LMS, since it is a new service, they just started off offering the service charging per minute, even for local calls. Typically, the usage charge is 1 or 2 cents per minute per B channel call established, usually with volume discounts and either a fixed price or monthly maximum plan. Some telephone companies also charge for call set-up attempts, whether the calls are answered or not—the phone companies don't like people being able to call long distance to their answering machines to check for messages, and hanging-up if it rings more than a few rings, which indicates that there are no messages (and yet the callers did not have to pay for the call).

Due to regulations, or customer resistance, some telephone companies charge per minute only for ISDN data calls, and (in the local calling area) do not charge per minute for ISDN voice calls. Some TAs can send data in a voice call (solely to avoid the per minute charge), and this capability is often called *data over circuit switched voice* (DOCSV). DOCSV calls can only be made if the remote TA (or other dial-in router) also supports DOCSV, and are limited to 56 kbits/s of throughput, whereas regular ISDN data calls carry data at 64 kbits/s.

Another problem with ISDN is the wide range in monthly costs for the service—both in different parts of the U.S., as well as in different countries. Whether it is economical therefore requires an analysis for each installation.

When used for video conferencing, the H.320 standard is usually used.

In late 1995, the *ISDN* Forum was founded by AT&T, 3Com, Ascend Communications and U.S. Robotics. It has the goal of making ISDN easier to use, for small businesses and consumers.

Bellcore operates a national ISDN hotline, and has the current ISDN pricing plans for all U.S. local and long-distance carriers. Call them at 1 800 992-4736.

The ISDN FAQ is at *ftp://rtfm.mit.edu/pub/usenet/news.answers/isdn-faq*, and Dan Kegel's ISDN page is at *http://alumni.caltech.edu/~dank/isdn*. The carriers would love you to understand more about ISDN, and their offerings. Bellcore has some ISDN information at *http://www.bellcore.com/demotoo/ISDN/ISDN.html*. Canada's Stentor has some Canadian ISDN information at *http://www.canisdn.net*.

Ascend Communications is a major vendor of ISDN networking equipment. They are at *http://www.ascend.com*.

While we are on the topic of ISDN people with WWW pages—Scott Adams (creator of Dilbert, Dogbert and their brethren) worked for 9 years for Pacific Telesis Group's Pacific Bell subsidiary (also known as PacTel), the last few in its ISDN Lab as an applications engineer. While employed there, he claimed that he didn't need the job but that it was a good source of material for his cartoon strip. He left somewhat voluntarily in 1995, after Dilbert became wildly popular. The Dilbert home page at *http://www.unitedmedia.com/ comics/dilbert/*.

See **B-ISDN**, **BELLCORE**, **BRI**, **BONDING**, **COS1** (*Corporation for Open Systems*), **DIGITAL 800**, **DTMF2**, **H.320**, **IETF**, **INBAND**, **INVERSE MULTIPLEXER**, **NARROWBAND ISDN**, **NI1**, **NI2**, **NI3**, **NT1**, **OUTOFBAND**, **PCM**, **PPP**, **PRI**, **SPID**, **SPOOFING**, **STAC**, **TA**, **V.25BIS**, **V.120**, **WAN**, and **WINISDN**.

ISM
Industrial, Scientific and Medical radio frequency bands

The three radio frequency bands (range of frequencies) allocated by the FCC that can be used in the U.S. without a license—so long as you comply with the FCC's rules (such as a maximum signal strength of 1 watt, and SST must be used). The frequency bands are:

▲ 902 to 928 MHz. This is usually called *900 MHz*, and is the most popular in the U.S. and Canada (lower frequencies usually provide better signal coverage, and building equipment for lower frequencies is always easier and less expensive than higher frequencies). It is commonly used for wireless LAN, and retail and factory mobile communications. Outside of the U.S., Canada and Mexico, this frequency band is either not available or requires a license (so this frequency band is not usually used for SST outside of these countries).

▲ 2.4000 to 2.4835 GHz (an 83.5-MHz bandwidth). This usually called *2.4 GHz*, and is becoming more popular now that the lower frequency band is becoming very busy. Also, 802.11-compliant devices that use this frequency band should be interoperable. This frequency band is available for use (without a license) in the U.S., Canada, Mexico and most other countries as well. Unfortunately, these higher frequencies do not propagate as far, and users may encounter interference from microwave ovens (which operate at 2.450 GHz).

▲ 5.725 to 5.850 GHz. This is not used much, mainly because there are not yet any inexpensive radio frequency integrated circuits that can operate at these awesomely high frequencies. One plan is to use this band (plus 5.15 to 5.35 GHz) for 25 Mbit/s ATM cell traffic as part of the U.S. *supernet/NII* (National Information Infrastructure). This would support wireless multimedia communications.

See **S802.A11**, **FCC**, and **SST**.

ISO
International Organization for Standardization (Organisation Internationale de Normalisation)

An international standards-setting organization. It is a federation of about 118 national standards bodies, one from each country—for example ANSI represents the U.S., and the SCC represents Canada. ISO was formed in 1947, with the mission to "promote the development of standardization and related activities in the world with a view to facilitating the international exchange of goods and services, and to developing cooperation in the spheres of intellectual, scientific, technological and economic activity" (that is, fostering trade between countries). ISO's work results in international agreements, which are documented in the published International Standards.

The ISO recognizes input only from official government-designated national, standards-setting organizations (and not vendor forums, such as the ATM Forum or the Frame Relay Forum). However, the national organizations may in turn, recognize other organizations (such as the IEEE and the IETF) for the development of standards for particular areas of expertise. But these would typically be standards-setting organizations, not vendor forums.

ISO is actually not an acronym, but a word derived from the Greek word for *equal*—which is "isos". It is an effort to get a name that both denotes equality (as standards are supposed to promote)—as in *isosceles triangle* (which has 2 equal-length sides), and is the same in ISO's 3 official languages—English, French and Russian (though standards are not typically published in Russian).

ISO standards include paper sizes, screw threads, film speeds, the SI units of measurement, automobile instrument panel symbols, country name and currency abbreviations and quality control systems.

The ISO has a WWW server at *http://www.iso.ch/welcome.html*. This site has lots of information and pointers available to all comers. But to see the full text of the ITU standards you need to subscribe (this cost $2,665 per year in 1996). Individual standards are priced per page.

See **ANSI**, **IEC2** (*International Electrotechnical Commission*), **IEEE**, **IETF**, **SCC**, **SI**, and **STANDARDS**.

ISO 900X
International Organization for Standardization 9000 Certification

ISO certifications (first introduced in 1987) of quality systems that help manufacturers and service providers develop a quality-conscious approach for their research, testing, manufacturing, and support operations.

Addresses how products and services are put together, not how well those products and services work (that is, the standards have nothing to do with the performance of the resulting products, only with the system that makes them, to ensure that the products and services meet the specifications—whether they are good specifications or not). Each standard applies to different types of processes, as shown in the following table.

ISO	Certifies Facilities That Handle...
9001	Research and development, product manufacturing, and product installation and maintenance
9002	Product manufacturing and installation only
9003	Product testing and final inspection of products

ISO 9000 (*"Guidelines for selection and use"*) itself is a guide to the concepts and philosophy of the other ISO standards, to assist in determining which are most applicable to a given organization.

ISO 9001 (*"Quality assurance in design, development, production, installation and servicing"*) is the most extensive of the three quality system standards, as it covers the entire business cycle (including design, development, development and support, for either a product or a service). It covers 20 basic elements that affect quality, such as customer service, engineering, and manufacturing.

ISO 9002 (*"Quality assurance in production, installation and servicing"*) does not include ISO 9001's design requirements, so is intended for organizations working with already-designed products or services.

ISO 9003 (*"Quality assurance in final inspection and test"*) is intended for organizations that are only concerned with assessing the quality of an already produced product or service. Includes requirements for contract review, control of customer-supplied product, corrective actions and internal quality audits.

ISO 9004 (*"Quality management and quality system elements"*) is a 4-part standard with guidelines for; the design and implementation of a quality system, the management of service activities, the ensuring of quality processed materials (for example, liquids, solids and wires), and the improvement of operational efficiency and effectiveness.

The above list includes changes made in the 1994 version of the standards.

Registration is granted by independent, third-party organizations, such as *Bureau Veritas Quality International* and *Det Norske Veritas*, and is valid for 3 years, subject to periodic audits.

Many European countries now require suppliers to have ISO certification.

While the ISO 9000 certifications emphasizes the management of process, the U.S. National Institute of Science and Technology's Baldridge Program emphasizes more organizational issues, such as management leadership, analysis of comparative quality measurements, and strategic quality planning.

ISO technical committee 176 is responsible for the ISO 9000 family of standards.

See **ISO** and **SIX QUALITY**.

Isochronous

Isochronous data is that which is periodic in creation, delivery and consumption (such as 8 bits every 125 µs). The most common examples of this data are digitized (and uncompressed) voice and video. Generally, all *multimedia* traffic is isochronous. Only some data channels can support this type of data (such as the B channels of an ISDN service). These can each carry the 8 bits of data every 125 µs produced by telephony PCM.

Higher-speed isochronous services can carry other traffic between the times that the isochronous traffic needs the communication channel. For example, ATM can carry isochronous traffic using the *constant bit rate* (CBR) service.

Packet-switched services (such as X.25) and standard Ethernet cannot support isochronous traffic, since other traffic may briefly prevent the isochronous traffic from being carried.

See **S802.9A**, **ATM** (*Asynchronous Transfer Mode*), **FIBRE CHANNEL**, and **MULTIMEDIA**.

Isochronous Ethernet Integrated Services

See S802.9A.

iso-Ethernet

See S802.9A.

Internet Service Provider

ISP

A company that provides end users (such as you, me, and big companies) access to the Internet.

As shown in the figure below, the computer equipment at an ISP will typically include the following:

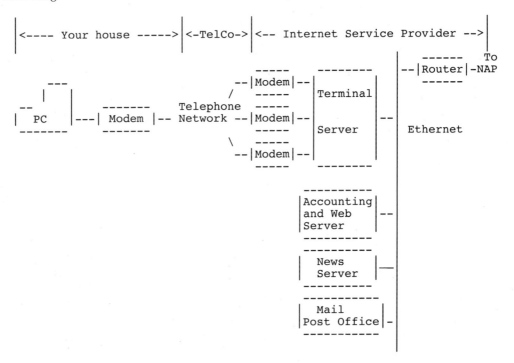

▲ The incoming telephone lines (typically 20 to a few hundred) each connect to a V.34 auto answer modem. There will typically be a ratio of about 1 telephone line for every 12 to 15 of the ISP's subscribers (though this ratio—and keeping-up with growth) is a business decision for the ISP (more lines mean few busy signals at peak times, but more costs to the ISP).

▲ Each modem's EIA-232 serial port runs at 115,200 bits/s and is connected to a cable to a terminal server (which is often made by Cisco).

Computer Dictionary

▲ A terminal server is a device with (usually) 8 to 32 EIA-232 ports and one Ethernet port. The terminal server (initially) converts the asynchronous data from the EIA-232 ports to the TCP/IP telnet protocol on the Ethernet.

▲ In addition to the above, there will usually be a router with incoming ISDN and dedicated 56-kbits/s circuits, which will also be connected to the Ethernet. These lines support users accessing the Internet service provider at higher speeds than analog telephone lines and V.34 modems can support.

▲ The connections from the router's ISDN lines and the terminal server's modems are configured to initially be established with a workstation (usually made by Sun Microsystems). The workstation handles the following functions (actually, there will often be two or more workstations for increased capacity and reliability):

▲ Security (storing and prompting for usernames and passwords)

▲ Billing (tracking and reporting on the duration of connections)

▲ Receiving, storing, and forwarding USENET news (usually dedicating a 1- or 2-Gbyte disk drive to that function)

▲ Receiving, storing, and forwarding email

▲ Storing WWW home pages (built by both the ISP themselves and by users)

▲ Being a Web and ftp server

If the dial-in users (after logging in) choose a menu item to run the SLIP or PPP protocol (as is usually the case), then the Sun workstation sends commands to the terminal server to have the terminal server run the SLIP or PPP protocol on the asynchronous port to the user.

▲ The dial-in user's WinSock (or whatever TCP/IP protocol stack they are using) TCP/IP packets are then encapsulated into SLIP or PPP frames by their PC's dialing program. When the terminal server receives these frames from the users, it strips off the SLIP or PPP frames from the TCP/IP packets, encapsulates them in Ethernet frames, and forwards them onto the Ethernet at the ISP.

▲ Connected to the ISP's Ethernet is a router (often made by Cisco Systems) which has a T1 (or faster, or slower, depending on the number of simultaneous users to be supported) connection to the Internet. The T1 will either go directly to an Internet backbone router (at a *Network Access Point*—NAP), or through a closer router—which then connects to a NAP (likely through a higher-speed link, such as a T3).

▲ The dial-in user is now a node on the Internet, and can run any program and TCP/IP protocol they wish (ftp, http, and so on). Packets are then forwarded directly from the terminal server's Ethernet port to the router to the Internet. They no longer go to the Sun workstation (unless the dial-in user specifically connects to the workstation, for example, by running their mail program).

The duration of an average voice telephone call is about 3 minutes, and the telephone network is built—and your telephone service's monthly cost is determined—based on this. The average *holding time* (the telephony industry's name for call duration) for a caller to their ISP is typically 20 to 30 minutes.

While typical business telephone lines are each busy about 16% of the time (and residential lines are about half this), at an ISP, their telephone lines are typically busy at least 75% of the time for most of the day. Telephone companies are therefore finding that they need to add capacity to their networks (more trunks interconnecting Central Offices are needed, for example), and somebody has to pay for this.

Since voice calls occupy bandwidth whether someone is talking (or a modem is transmitting) or not, some telephone companies are offering services optimized for ISP purposes. Noting that data is typically very bursty in nature, telephone companies have a bank of modems in their CO, and then send just the data over a data network (which is shared with other users' bursty data) to the ISP. Northern Telecom's system that performs this is called Internet Thruway.

Two large ISPs are Netcom On-Line Communication Services, Inc. (see *http://www.netcom.com*) and Performance Systems International (which has much more interesting stuff on its WWW server, which is at *http://www.psi.net*). BBN has been involved with the Internet since the beginning, and they are at *http://www.bbn.com*.

IBM and CompuServe provide Internet access from a local telephone call in hundreds of cities all over the world (*http://www.ibm.net* and *http://www.compuserve.com*). Big lists of ISPs are at *http://www.boardwatch.com*, *http://www.primus.com/providers/*, *http://www.tagsys.com/providers* and *http://www.thelist.com*. Performance ratings of ISPs are done by *http://www.inversenet.com*. Larger ISPs often participate in the North American Network Operators' Group, who are at *http://www.nanog.org*

See **ANS, C.O., CISCO SYSTEMS, CIX, EIA/TIA-232, ETHERNET, FT1, INTERNET2, ISDN, MODEM, NAP, PING, PPP, SLIP, SUN, T1, TELNET, TCP/IP, TRUNK, USENET, V.32BIS, V.34, WINSOCK,** and **WWW.**

ITU
International Telecommunication Union

A standards-setting organization which is now a specialized agency of the United Nations (and also the oldest organization in the United Nations). It facilitates the global development of telecommunications (including telephone and radio communications). The ITU's membership represents 187 governments (in 1997), and they set the budget and choose the goals of the organization. While private-sector companies (such as carriers and vendors) can also be members, they must be approved by their governments (there were about 400 private-sector members in 1997).

ITU's headquarters is in Geneva, Switzerland, and ITU has the following mandate (guess whether these are my words or not):

▲ To maintain and extend international cooperation for the improvement and rational use of telecommunication of all kinds

▲ To promote the development of technical facilities and their most efficient operation with a view to improving the efficiency of telecommunication services, increasing their usefulness, and making them, as far as possible, generally available to the public

▲ To harmonize the actions of nations in the attainment of those common ends

In 1993, the ITU was reorganized into three *sectors* (plus the coordinating *general secretariat* from the previous structure) as shown in the following table.

Sector	Abbreviation	Responsibilities
Telecommunication Standardization	ITU-T	All standards development activities of the previous CCITT and CCIR
Radiocommunication	ITU-R	Other activities of the previous CCIR and previous International Frequency Registration Board (IFRB), such as radio regulatory issues and frequency assignments
Telecommunication Development	ITU-D	Telecommunication support for developing countries, for example by offering technical cooperation and assistance

The ITU is the successor to the International Telegraph Union (formed on May 17, 1865) and the group of signatory countries to the International Radiotelegraphy Convention, which began in 1906.

The ITU has a WWW server at *http://www.itu.ch*.

See **CCIR**, **CCITT**, **ITUT**, and **STANDARDS**.

ITU-T
International Telecommunication Union, Telecommunication Standardization Sector

The new name for the CCITT—though some say that standards that were created before the name change (and not modified since) continue to be called CCITT standards. Along with the name change is a substantial change in the *standards approval* process. It can now be conducted by correspondence (typically within 3 months), provided that the study group is in consensus. Previously, this approval could be finalized only at the Plenipotentiary Conferences, which are held every 4 years.

Only *countries* are members (no companies or standards organizations, such as the IEEE).

However, a country can designate a standards organization to be its representative in certain areas. For example, the United States has designated ANSI to be its ITU-T representative for telecommunications matters.

The ITU-T's standards are produced by *study groups*. The standards approval process begins with a *recommendation* (standards are called recommendations before they are approved), which must pass three major steps:

▲ Determination—The study group's chairman declares that the recommendation is *Determined* when the study group has agreed that the "intent" of the recommendation's technical content is complete. That is, there may be some disagreement of the exact wording and technical details, but basically everyone agrees with the recommendation (which you might call a "draft of the standard").

▲ A *Decision to Put to Ballot* is then scheduled for the next ITU-T meeting. During the time before the next ITU-T meeting (perhaps 6 to 9 months), the exact wording and technical details are finalized.

▲ Decision to Put to Ballot—At that next ITU-T meeting, the final version of the recommendation is presented to the ITU-T membership (each representing a country). If there are no objections, then a formal vote is scheduled and the recommendation is considered *Decided*.

▲ Since the recommendation is almost sure to pass, manufacturers often begin developing and producing products at this point.

▲ Ballot—Ballots are sent to all of the ITU-T's general membership. If 70% of the respondents approve the recommendation, over the next 90 days, then it is officially published as an ITU-T standard.

See **G.726**, **H.261**, **H.320**, **ITU**, **STANDARDS**, **T.120**, **X.400**, and **X.500**.

IXC
Interexchange Carrier

A long-distance phone company, usually using its own long-distance facilities (rather than only *reselling* others'). Provides voice and data services between LECs (one or both of the LECs involved may be one of the RBOCs).

The three largest IXCs are listed in the following table.

IXC	Market Share (percentage)
AT&T Corp.	60
MCI Communications Corp.[a]	20
Sprint Corp.	10

a. In October 1996, British Telecom bought the 80% of MCI that they did not already own, and renamed the resulting merged company Concert PLC.

The remaining 10% is divided among more than 300 smaller providers. (No one knows exactly how many there are.)

For each long-distance call, IXCs pay the LEC that owns the cable to the destination telephone an *access fee* to route the call to its destination.

IXCs establish a *Point Of Presence* (POP) within each LEC's service area (physically a termination point in the LEC's central office, often caged-in to ensure that they don't fiddle with each other's equipment).

See **CARRIER**, **LATA**, **LEC**, **POP1** (*Point of Presence*), and **RBOC OR RBHC**.

J

JAVA
Java Programming Language

A programming language based on C++ (which in turn, is based on C). It was developed by Sun Microsystems in the early 1990s as a language for embedded controllers in consumer electronics (such as microwave ovens and televisions). Eventually it migrated into a platform-independent, object-oriented language that is expected to replace C++ for general programming, and be popular for applications to be run over the Internet as the applications can be downloaded and installed automatically as needed. Following Netscape's example of getting market (and mind) share by giving away the client software, Sun provided the client software, for free over, the Internet, in June 1995.

The background for Java is that in the 1960s and 1970s, the mainframe and minicomputers were basically huge servers, and the "clients" were the fixed-function terminals on people's desks. The terminals were not programmable, and could not add any value to the information. They could not change the way the information was displayed, and could not do any further processing or analysis of data. The administration (adding programs, authorizing new users, trouble-shooting problems) of these computers was easier that later methods, since the operating systems were very mature (the finally got around to adding the programs needed) and there were few computers. Everything was mainframe- or minicomputer-centric (some simply call this *server-centric*), in that the programming of those computers was a limitation for all computing in the organization. Users had long waits for programming changes required to match their changing business needs.

In the 1980s and early 1990s, file servers became popular. These were "thin servers", in that they had very little functionality—they basically provided entire program and data files. All processing was done by "fat clients", which were the PCs on people's desks. All value added to the information (running of programs, display and analysis of data) was done on the desktop. While users had complete control over their computing environment (they could write their own database-access programs and customize their PCs), the administration became a greater cost than the computers themselves. Also, the choice in computing platforms basically was reduced to none. Most business ran an Intel architecture processor and a Microsoft operating system.

The proposed next step in the evolution of computing is many servers, and thin clients. The clients can do processing, but the programs are all dynamically downloaded to the clients. Programs and data are administered centrally, but the desktop computing power is on the desktop. Clients all look the same, in that they can run the same programs, regardless of their actual operating system or hardware platform. Therefore, there is flexibility and diversity, but only one version of application programs is required for all clients. (A network-connected computer that only runs a web browser is sometimes called an *ultrathin client*, in that it can be used to display and enter information, but can't do much local processing of information.)

Java is to provide the basic support needed for this multiple server / thin client model of computing.

Some characteristics and advantages of Java are listed below.

▲ It is object-oriented. This is important (in all types of programming) as it supports good programming practices (such as reusing proven code, and isolating the definition and use of global information)

▲ The original Java program is compiled to *byte code* as part of the software development process. This portable bytecode file format is what gets distributed to user computers (the exact same bytecode to all computers). Java programs can be stand-alone (you run them by themselves), or they can imbedded in an HTML page, so they are automatically run when the page is viewed with a Java-compatible WWW browser—such as Netscape's or Microsoft's Explorer.

▲ When the Java program is run, the bytecode is *interpreted*, which means that it is converted to the actual native processor instructions on-the-fly—. Interpreters have been around for many years (BASIC is an example), and such programs run more slowly than a program pre-compiled for a specific processor (as most application programs currently are). The program is therefore processor-independent, since it can then be run on any computer that supports Java, since processor- and operating system-specific software (typically part of that computer's operating system) in the computer creates a *virtual Java machine* (or virtual machine—VM), which supports the Java standard instruction set, which is the same for all operating systems and hardware platforms (though experience has shown that testing on each platform is required to ensure operability).

▲ Rather than interpreting as the code is executed, some vendors are now support *just-in-time* (JIT) compiling, where the bytecode is compiled into native (for that specific processor) code before it is first run. This results in a slightly longer delay before the code first runs, but then code then runs much faster—the same as any compiled code.

▲ Viewers and other programs and support needed to make use of received data (such as digitized audio or a picture encoded in some new manner) are automatically received along with the data—and used without any installation or user-intervention required.

▲ The transmission of Java programs uses *public-key encryption*, to authenticate the source of the program. The language was created with security as a requirement, for example, that a problem with one program cannot adversely affect others.

▲ Unicode is supported, so special symbols (like ®) and languages other than english (with characters such as é and ö) can be used—and displayed the same everywhere

The programs produced by a Java compiler are called *applets*, since they are usually small application programs.

While the client-side software is free, to develop Java tools and server software requires a license from Sun, and they charge at least $125,000 per company for this.

Java was for a while called Oak, after the tree outside of James Gosling's office, who starting writing the language in 1990 (he also create EMACS, which is a complex and powerful text editor popular on Unix computers). But the name "Oak" was found to be too-commonly used to be trademarked. The language was intended as a basis for consumer electronic equipment to communicate with each other (TVs, VCRs, and so on). It was first expected it would be used in Microwave ovens, then TV set-top boxes, then video games and then on CD-ROMs.

Being web-oriented, there are lots of Java web sites, for example: *http://java.sun.com*, *http://www.javasoft.com*, *http://www.javaworld.com* and *www.gamelan.com*.

See **ENCRYPTION**, **INTERNET2**, **NC**, **SUN**, **UNICODE**, and **X WINDOW SYSTEM**.

Joystick

See **GAME PORT**.

JPEG
Joint Photographic Experts Group

The name of a standard developed in 1991, for *lossy data compression* of digitized still images (you get to choose a *quality factor* when the image is compressed, that determines how much compression versus how much loss in image detail is desired). A method called a *discrete cosine transform* (DCT) is used to eliminate the higher-frequency components of the signal.

JPEG supports up to 24 bits of color per pixel, and image sizes can be up to $65,535 \times 65,535$ pixels.

JPEG can also be used for compressing motion video, but there are no standards for this extension (vendors use their own proprietary methods). Some advantages of Motion JPEG (over MPEG) are listed below:

▲ Suitable for frame-by-frame editing, since *frame interpolation* is not used for compression

▲ Does not remove the information in the blanking intervals (which may be needed for synchronization)

▲ Digitizes the color information at the full rate

Progressive JPEG (PJPEG) supports *interlacing* (as GIF does), so that initially, every other raster line can be displayed (with the intermediate lines displayed afterwards). Given that they'll eventually see the exact same quality of image, people usually prefer seeing a blurry image of the whole picture, rather than a good image of only half the picture.

Pronounced *JAY-peg*.

See **DATA COMPRESSION**, **GIF**, **LOSSY DATA COMPRESSION**, **MPEG**, and **VIDEO**.

JTAG
Joint Test Access Group

A serial interface often designed-in to complex integrated circuits, which directly controls or reads each IC pin—usually for in-factory testing. It can also be used for other functions, such as programming flash memory.

The JTAG interface consists of the following 4 or 5 signals (plus a ground for each).

Pin Name	Function	Comments
TCK	Clock	Sets the bit rate for the serial data
TMS	Mode select	Sets whether data is being sent in or out of the IC
TDI	Serial data in	Data input to the IC
TDO	Serial data out	Data output from the IC
TRST	Reset	An optional signal to reset the interface

JTAG ICs can be daisy-chained, permitting a single JTAG bus to test or control many ICs.

Standardized in IEEE 1149.1 and also called *Background Debug Mode* (BDM) and *Boundary Scan*.

K

Kaleida Labs

The Apple-IBM joint venture created to develop multimedia software, technology, and standards—to compete with Microsoft. One of the few products developed was Script-X, a multimedia programming language (that never became popular).

Began in 1991, and officially cancelled in late 1995 (too bad—it had such a nice name).

See **APPLE–IBM ALLIANCE**.

Kerberos

A security system for client/server computing.

Entirely software-based and can have multiple secure areas (or *realms*, usually delimited by administrative boundaries) in an Enterprise network. Its uses are:

▲ Encryption to secure network transmissions

▲ A password-authentication service to verify a user's right to access a given host or server

Also supports time-based limits for accesses.

The *Kerberos server* (a "trusted third-party server") consists of two parts:

▲ An *authentication server*, which verifies identities (and has the user ID and password for all users)

▲ A *ticket-granting server*, which gives clients permission to access various servers and applications on the network

The Kerberos server is used to validate the verification procedures between all clients and servers. Clients must (and servers optionally) prove their identity for each service invoked.

All servers (file servers, database servers, etc.) must be registered in the authentication server's *database*, and share a secret key with the authentication server.

Users first log in to the authentication server (by providing their user ID), requesting a *ticket-granting ticket*. The authentication server then looks up the user's password and provides a ticket-granting ticket and a session key (valid for the current log-on only), both of which have been encrypted using the user's password. At the user's workstation, the user is then prompted for his or her password, which is then used to decrypt the received message (note that the user's password was never sent over the network).

Kermit

The decrypted ticket-granting ticket includes the following:

▲ The user's ID

▲ A time stamp

▲ Duration (specified by the network administrator, perhaps half an hour to 8 hours) for which the session is valid

▲ A ticket-granting server's ID

The ticket-granting ticket is DES-encrypted using a key that is known only by the authentication server and the ticket-granting server, so the workstation cannot tamper with the ticket-granting ticket, and only the specified ticket-granting server can use it.

For the allowed period of time (the duration), the workstation can use this ticket-granting ticket to request access to another server or device on the network (to actually get some work done—you gotta do that once in a while), using a similar process.

Kerberos version 4 has been in use for several years. MIT's Project Athena recently released version 5, which includes support for:

▲ Security algorithms other than DES

▲ One server to access another server on the user's behalf (for example, a print server getting a specified file from a file server)

Intended to be highly portable across operating systems and hardware platforms.

The name is from the three-headed dog that guards the gates of Hades in Greek mythology.

Specified in RFC 1510.

See **AUTHENTICATION**, **CLIENT/SERVER**, **DES**, **ENCRYPTION**, **RSA**, **PGP**, and **SESAME**.

Kermit

A project based at Columbia University that has produced interoperable data communications programs (primarily used for file transfer and terminal emulation) for hundreds of computer platforms (including PCs, UNIX computers, Macintoshes, VAXes, Data General minicomputers, Honeywell/Bull and IBM mainframes, Cray supercomputers, and on and on).

Initially (before the mid-1980s), the effort was financially supported by Columbia University (though much of the programming was done by volunteers) and the programs were completely free. The programs were distributed directly by Columbia, but more often you got them from your local bulletin board system, DECUS (the DEC user society magnetic tapes) or a friend.

Now, some versions (such as that for Windows 95) of Kermit are "shrinkwrap" and available commercially just like most other software. Other versions (such as my favorite—the MS-DOS version which is written in assembler) are distributed over the Internet, you are free to reproduce and share them—so long as you don't try to sell them. End users are encouraged (on the threat that the project won't be able to continue if no one pays for it) to pay for each copy used—usually by buying the documentation (they mail you a nice book)—this has the desired side-effect of reducing the support requirements.

Other than being an extremely flexible, customizable, and powerful data communications program, a major feature is that the source code is also available (including a C version), so it can be compiled for new machines or modified and enhanced. Currently, the most popular (and current) versions of Kermit are the following:

▲ Kermit 95, for Windows 95 and Windows NT

▲ MS-DOS Kermit, for MS-DOS and Windows 3.1

▲ C-Kermit, for UNIX, VMS, OS/2 and many other operating systems

▲ IBM Mainframe Kermit, for VM/CMS, MVS/TSO and CICS

The early versions of Kermit were somewhat like XModem in that the file transfer protocol had a small frame size (94 bytes) and a Window size of 1, resulting in slow transfer times. However, the protocol always supported robust error-detection and correction, and binary file transfer over communication links that only carried 7-bits of user data per character or reserved certain control characters for other functions. Also, the Kermit protocol was designed from the start to be extensible, so all versions of Kermit can communicate with each other (none of this XModem, YModem, ZModem stuff, where you have to manually select the protocol used by the remote end). Also, Kermit has always been available for a wide range of platforms, and XModem is primarily found on PC-based systems.

Newer versions of Kermit also support the following:

▲ Frame sizes up to 9,024 bytes

▲ Window sizes up to 31 frames

▲ TCP/IP (telnet), NetBIOS, and some others, such as Rlogin, DECnet, Named Pipes, X.25 and others.

▲ COM3 and COM4 at any interrupt and port address and support for LANs (Ethernet, Token Ring, etc.)

▲ A very powerful scripting language, which permits automation of data communication tasks

▲ Character set translation, languages which write from right to left, keyboard key re-mapping, emulation of many kinds of terminals and many more well-documented and -implemented functions.

▲ Server mode, in which a host machine can be left waiting (unattended) for a call and the calling machine can send and receive files and issue DOS commands to the server machine.

Many bulletin board systems and commercial data communication programs (such as Pro-Comm and SmartTerm) support the well-documented Kermit file transfer protocol (so they can transfer files to and from people using the Kermit program). However, these programs often implement older versions of the Kermit protocol that don't support the larger frame and window sizes (or the user has not configured the software to use the larger frame and window sizes). Many people therefore erroneously think that Kermit is a slow protocol.

Kermit is named after Jim Henson's Muppet *Kermit the Frog* (the idea was that the program would be easy to work with and fun, just like Kermit). The name is used with permission (from Henson Associates, not from Kermit the Frog).

Keyboard

The software is maintained and supported by staff at Columbia University in New York. Contacts are shown below.

email	mailto://kermit@columbia.edu
fax	212-663-8202
ftp	ftp://kermit.columbia.edu
Phone (ordering)	212-854-3703
Phone (technical)	900-555-5595 or 212-854-5126
Usenet	news://comp.protocols.kermit.announce news://comp.protocols.kermit.misc
WWW	http://www.columbia.edu/kermit

See **BBS**, **EIA-TIA232**, **NETBIOS**, **TCP/IP**, **TELNET**, and **XMODEM**.

Keyboard

The original PC used a larger, 5-pin round connector (often called a DIN connector, for *Deutsche Instustrie Normen*, that produced a standard for that connector).

The PS/2 used a smaller DIN-type connector (like the one always used for a bus-type mouse), so the newer smaller connector is often called a PS/2 style, or mini-DIN. It is common for newer PCs. The same voltages are used, so a simple adapter is all that is needed to match keyboards and PC connectors of different types.

Taking pin 1 as the right pin, looking into the female DIN connector (on your PC), with the locating notch at the top, and the pins as a semi-circle at the bottom, the pin functions are as follows.

Pin	Function	Comments
1	Clock	Sent by the keyboard, data is valid on falling edge
2	Ground	For both the power and the signals
3	Data	Bidirectional data
4	+5 V	PC supplies power to keyboard, which has both LEDs and a microcontroller
5	Not used	

Communications between the PC and its keyboard uses a form of bidirectional synchronous serial communications (the one data line carries data in both directions). Each keypress (or character from the PC to the keyboard) uses 1 start bit, 8 data bits (least significant bit first), an odd parity bit, and a stop bit. The clock signal is provided by the keyboard (though the PC can hold the clock signal low to flow-control the data from the keyboard), as a square wave with a period of typically 60 to 100 µs. The bit rate of the data is therefore 16,666 bit/s to 10,000 bits/s. The data is valid when the clock signal falls, and while it is low.

Typically, the keyboard provides key press and release (make and break) codes to the PC, though the PC can also send messages to the keyboard requesting it to restart (and runs its power-on self test), resend the last character or turn on or off the 3 LEDs on the keyboard (Num Lock, Caps Lock and Scroll Lock).

See **PARITY**, and **PC**.

L

LAN
Local Area Network

A limited-distance (typically under a few kilometers) high-speed network (typically 4 to 100 Mbits/s) that supports many computers (typically two to thousands).

The popular standard LANs are shown in the accompanying figure.

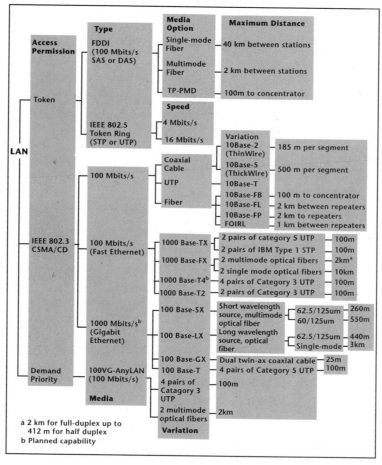

LAN-1

The table below shows four options for upgrading Ethernet and Token Rings (which would prove the old saying that the nice thing about standards is that there are so many to choose from).

Technology	Benefit
100Base-T (Fast Ethernet)	Easy upgrade from 10Base-T Ethernet (same drivers, hopefully using the same cabling) Low cost
100VG-AnyLAN	Uses existing cabling Has upgrade path for Ethernet *and* Token Ring Suitable for multimedia Low cost
FDDI	Most mature technology (wide vendor support, proven interoperability) Fault tolerance option (*dual homing*) Medium cost
ATM	Most future-proof (speeds from 25.6 Mbits/s to more than 2.4 Gbits/s—whatever you can afford) Is already a switched technology (dedicated bandwidth to each user) Suitable for multimedia Highest cost
802.9 (Isochronous Ethernet)	Easy upgrade from 10BASE-T (but not Token Ring) Supports multimedia and links to ISDN Uses existing cabling Low cost
Switched LAN	Easily added to existing Ethernet or Token Ring LANs Uses existing cabling and workstation LAN adapters Low cost

See **S100BASET, S100VG ANYLAN, S10BASEF, S10BASET, S802.3, S802.9A, ATM** (*Asynchronous Transfer Mode*), **CABLE, COAX, ETHERNET, FDDI, FIBRE CHANNEL, HIPPI, HSSI, MAN, STP, SWITCHED LAN, TOKEN RING,** and **UTP.**

L2TP
Layer 2 Tunnelling Protocol

A method of providing secure (encrypted and authenticated) connections through the Internet.

Based on PPP, and using CHAP or PAP for a small measure of authentication, it allows a secure link layer session to be established.

Based on the proprietary point-to-point tunnelling protocol (PPTP) from Microsoft and Layer 2 Forwarding (L2F) protocol from Cisco Systems. L2TP is defined in RFC 1661.

See **CHAP, PAP,** and **PPP.**

LANE
LAN Emulation

A method of enabling ATM to support the bridged interconnection of LANs, without requiring any modifications to the LAN-attached PCs, servers and other devices. LANE version 1 is a MAC-layer (it only knows about Ethernet addresses, not IP subnets, for example) specification, and provides support for existing LANs (Ethernet and Token Ring) and LAN protocols (such as TCP/IP, IPX and AppleTalk) through the creation of *virtual LANs* (which are called *emulated LANs*—ELANs by some vendors). LANE makes ATM's connection-oriented switching fabric to emulate the connectionless nature of a LAN, through quickly setting-up and clearing down connections as required for multicast and broadcast traffic. So the IP or IPX software in your PC thinks it is running over Ethernet, while lower-layer software in your PC (or elsewhere on the Ethernet) handles the conversion of the connection Ethernet traffic into connection-oriented ATM cells.

Among other requirements, *LAN* emulation involves the development (and standardization) of a method to support broadcasts (ATM is connection-oriented, yet many LAN protocols depend on broadcasts for some important functions). Using LAN emulation enables NDIS and ODI devices to access each other and native ATM devices.

A LAN-to-ATM converter adds an ID header to the Layer 2 (Ethernet or Token Ring) frame header, strips off the CRC, and emits ATM AAL 5 PDUs (cells). The LANE specification requires support for 1,500-byte LAN frames (called a *maximum transmission unit*—MTU) for Ethernet support, and also specifies 4,500, 9,000 and 18,000 byte frames for Token Ring support (devices do not need to support all sizes—for example, supporting only 1,500 and 9,000 byte MTUs is popular). If there are any Ethernet LANs in the network, then only 1,500-byte MTUs should be used, so all LANs can be bridged (routing can be used to split larger packets, but routers can be performance bottlenecks) together without any concern about frames that are too large being sent to Ethernet.

The requirements for LAN emulation are specified in the *LAN* emulation user-to-network interface (L-UNI, pronounced "loony").

LAN emulation requires LAN emulation client (LEC) software (either in the LAN-to-ATM converter or in the ATM device) and a LAN emulation server (LES).

The LEC establishes a connection with the LES, for example to request the LES to map the LEC's MAC addresses into an ATM addresses (this is called *address resolution*). This is done using the Integrated Layer Management Interface, which is an SNMP-like protocol which runs over the UNI, so that the ATM client can learn its ATM address automatically from its ATM switch. (Previous versions of ILMI were abbreviations for *Interim Local Management Interface*.)

The *LAN emulation service* (LES) provides these services:

▲ Supports unicast (point-to-point) data transfer

▲ Supports multicast (one-to-many) data transfer

▲ Responds to requests to resolve MAC addresses to ATM addresses

LANE 1.0 only supports a single LES, which is therefore a single point of potential failure (I've got it, lets just make a new version of the specification that addresses that problem—but it is exactly that kind of instability of the standards that frustrates manufacturers and users alike).

The LES requires three servers (which may all reside in an ATM switch or may be separate on other ATM-connected devices):

▲ *Configuration server* (provides configuration information about the ATM network, frame size allowed on LAN, and type of LAN and provides the address of the LES to the LEC).

▲ *LAN emulation server* (registers and resolves MAC addresses to ATM addresses).

▲ *Broadcast and unknown server* (BUS, supports multicasting, so the LEC has only to send a single message to the BUS, which then handles the multiple connections and transmissions to all ATM devices in the broadcast domain). The BUS is also used for *unicast* (station to station) traffic for the brief interval after it is sent, but before an ATM connection has been established.

LANE allows ATM networks to support "legacy LANs", without any changes being required to the LANs. This is good news and bad news. The good news is that you get many of the benefits of ATM (such as load sharing across redundant links). The bad news is that the applications don't have direct access to the ATM network, for example to specify QOS requirements. WinSock 2 is an API that will support such direct interaction, and may be the standard software interface used to support ATM cards in end-user PCs.

LANE version 1.0 was published by the ATM Forum in January 1995. One of its weaknesses is that only one LES can be active (secondary LESs are supported, but they are only used if the primary stops working). ATM networks that span more than one building therefore need to use a LES in a different building (which clogs the WAN, slows response time and makes local operation dependent on the WAN links being operational). What is needed is more complexity—that is *distributed LANE*. This is part of LANE 2.0.

ATM (*Asynchronous Transfer Mode*), **RFC-1577**, **ROUTER**, and **WINSOCK 2**.

LAPM
Link Access Procedure for Modems

One of the two error detection and correction protocols specified in V.42 to correct data communication errors occurring on the link between two modems.

Each frame of data holds up to 128 bytes of data and has a 16- or 32-bit CRC.

Up to 15 (which is also the default value) frames can be sent before an *acknowledgment* is required (that is, the *window size* defaults to 15). Therefore, 1,920 bytes of memory must be reserved for storing unacknowledged frames (since they may need to be retransmitted).

See **CRC**, **MNP**, and **V.42**.

LAST
Local Area Systems Technology

A simple and fast DEC protocol used by Pathworks for disk and printer access over a LAN from DOS PCs. Built on LAT.

See **LAT** and **PATHWORKS**.

LASTPORT
Local Area Storage Transport

Same as LAST.

See **LAST**.

LAT
Local Area Transport

A DEC protocol for interactive, asynchronous terminal traffic over a LAN (typically between a DECserver *terminal server* and a VAX minicomputer).

Operates at the transport layer. Does not have a network layer and so is not routable.

See **DEC**, **ENCAPSULATION**, **ETHERNET II**, and **VMS**.

LATA
Local-Access Transport Area

The geographic area within which telephone calls can be handled without going through a long-distance carrier.

Telephone calls between different LATAs must go through a long-distance carrier (that is, an IXC, such as AT&T or MCI).

Short-hop (or local) toll telephone calls (that is, calls within LATA) can be handled by a LEC (usually an RBOC) or (in most states) by an IXC (though extra digits must usually be dialed to select a carrier other than your LEC for these short-hop toll calls).

See **CARRIER**, **IXC OR IEC**, **LEC**, and **RBOC OR RBHC**.

Latency

The *time delay* of data traffic through a network or switch.

Interactive multimedia, database, and other applications usually require short round-trip delays. Since the traffic will likely pass through many networking components in the "big grey cloud" between the users and computers, each component must have a short (and often predictable) *latency*. That is, if there are three switches between a client and server, then there will be six switch delays in a round-trip message.

As the bit rates of networks get faster (so the time taken to shift the bits out of one computer and into another is shorter), the tolerable network delays get smaller (since the network's internal delays become more apparent). Also, new applications, such as MPEG-2 video compression, can be more adversely affected by variable delays.

Other metrics are still important, such as bits, frames, or packets per second, and lost data.

Some typical equipment and network latencies (first-bit-in to first-bit-out) are listed in the following table.

Component	Typical Latency (μs)
SCI	0.1
ATM switches	10 to 130
Ethernet switches	20 to 100
Ethernet bridges	250 to 500
Routers	1,200 to 5,000
Analog telephone line	50,000 to 80,000

A key component of the time-delay is the bit-serialization time for store-and-forward devices (such as gateways, routers, bridges and store-and-forward switches). That is, if you send a message to a device, then after it has received the entire message, it must shift it out, one bit at a time. This time depends on the speed of the link and the length of the message. For a 100 byte message at 64 kbits/s, this will be about 12.5 ms (one-way). One reason for the small size selected for ATM cells is to reduce the store-and-forward delay time.

In addition, real-world devices will have a processing delay, and possibly a queueing delay (if messages are queued waiting for processing or output).

In addition, WAN links will have delays due to the length of the connection. For example, signals in fiber optic cable typically propagate at about 66% of the speed of light in a vacuum (this ratio is called the *index of refraction*). Therefore, the round-trip delay of a signal through a 1,000 km run of fiber would be about 10.1 ms Including the delays due to amplifiers, and the fact that cables don't run "as the crow flies", but typically take a longer path—for example, along major highways or railway lines, results in a total round-trip delay of about 12 ms per 1,000 kilometers (which is 6μ per km, one-way). North America is about 4,000 to 5,000 km wide, depending where you measure (somehow this reminds me of ordering clothes by mail-order), so the round-trip propagation delay for terrestrial links across North America is 48 to 60 ms.

On voice circuits, one-way delays of more than 25 ms can result in echoes that are noticeable. Delays of more than 75 ms can be perceived in interactive conversations (typical telephone connections have 50 to 80 ms of round-trip delay), and one-way delays of more than 200 ms will result in circuits with perceived lower quality. This is one reason why ATM uses such small cells—the store-and-forward delay is shorter.

Some organizations consider that one-way delays of 150 ms are acceptable for normal business communications, delays of 150 to 400 ms are acceptable when the parties understand that the call is over a great distance (overseas, for example), and that delays greater than 400 ms may occur during (hopefully rare) network congestions situations.

See **FRAME RELAY, MULTIMEDIA, MPEG, QOS, RTP, SATELLITE, SCI**, and **SMP2** (*Symmetric Multiprocessing*).

LBX
Low Bandwidth X

An option in the X11R6 *X Window* specification that supports operation over low-speed (preferably 9,600 bits/s or faster) asynchronous (usually dial-up) communication lines. LBX would run over TCP/IP over PPP.

See **ASYNCHRONOUS**, **TCP/IP**, **PPP**, and **X WINDOW SYSTEM**.

LCD
Liquid Crystal Display

A popular type of display for laptop computers. There are many ways to categorize them.

A *reflective* display reflects the ambient light. This is difficult to read in low light conditions, so a *transmissive* type is often used, with a back-light. The back-light is often an *electroluminescent* module, which generates (usually) white light (and little heat) when powered by a 400Hz, 100-V to 160-V supply. Other back-light technologies include LED and cold-cathode fluorescent light (called a CCFL or CFL, or even CCFT for cold-cathode fluorescent tube).

The construction of an LCD module uses two flat, parallel sheets of glass, separated by about 10 µm. The inside surfaces of the glass have very fine parallel lines etched, and the two sheets of glass are rotated (*twisted*), so the lines are 90° relative to each other. A polarizing film (like your sunglasses have) is applied to the sheets of glass, in a direction which is parallel to their respective etched lines. Since the polarized films are not aligned, light will not be passed by the sheets of glass (so it appears dark). However, a type of chemical called a *liquid crystal* (so called because it retains some of the ordered properties of crystals even when slightly above their melting temperature—that is, at room temperature) fills the space between the sheets of glass. Depending on the type of liquid crystal and the temperature, some liquid crystals have a *nematic phase*, in which the molecules align themselves along the etched lines. Since the lines are twisted relative to each other, the molecules also twist (as a stack of paper does). The molecules twist the polarization of the light, so the light will pass through the glass (so the display appears light). The insides of the sheets of glass have a transparent pattern of parallel conductive lines deposited, also arranged 90° to each other. When a voltage (about 4-V to 15-V DC) is applied across the two plates, the liquid crystal's alignment with the etched lines changes (since the molecules are *polar*, they align themselves with the electric field), so that the molecules align with the applied electric field instead. Light no longer passes through this point (since the polarization of the light is not being twisted to match the polarizers any more), so that position (*pixel*) of the display is dark. More amazing still, is that all of this actually works.

A VGA display would need 640 vertical lines and 480 horizontal lines. The display is typically updated by scanning it quickly (it takes fewer connections and less electronics to do this). Therefore, rather than being on all the time, the display is only turned on part of the time (perhaps for one out of 128 time intervals), and it slowly reverts back to off during the rest of the scan. This creates a lower *contrast* (between an on and an off pixel) *ratio*, making the display more difficult to read.

The least-expensive step taken to improve the contrast is to split the screen into two separate scanning areas. These displays are called *dual-scan twisted nematic* (DSTN).

To improve the contrast ratio further, some displays twist the two parallel lines more than 90°—these are called *super twisted nematic* (STN). STN color displays are sometimes called CSTN, and have a filter between the light source and each pixel, so they are each illuminated by only one of the three primary additive colors (red, green or blue). Each "colored pixel" of a color display therefore consists of 3 pixels, so the display requires 3 times more actual pixels than a monochrome display.

To get an even better contrast ratio and faster response time (which is important for full-motion video, or so you don't see trails behind your mouse cursor), some displays use one or more transistors at each pixel position (at the crossing of each horizontal and vertical line). This keeps the pixel turned on until the scanning changes it (so it doesn't start to drift back to off during the time until the next scan). This type of LCD display is therefore sometimes called *active-matrix*—since a transistor is considered an active device (resistors, for example are considered passive devices, since they always do the same thing, and can't be controlled). The technology used to manufacture this transistor is called *thin-film*, since it is built using a thin film of chemicals. So this type of display is also called a *thin-film transistor* (TFT) LCD display. Again, since these are usually color displays, they may be called a CTFT. The viewing angle for this type of display is typically ±15° vertically, and ±40° horizontally.

The older *amorphous-silicon* type of transistor is relatively large, and so blocks some of the light from each pixel, reducing contrast (you see a black outline to the pixels). The newer *polysilicon* type of transistor is smaller, so allows for a brighter display (these are often used in LCD projectors, where they also permit smaller LCD panels to be made, reducing the size of the projector).

See **COLOUR**, **FED**, and **VFD**.

LDAP
Lightweight Directory Access Protocol

A simplified version (mostly a subset) of the directory access protocol of X.500 (which also describes a hierarchical directory structure for storing information). LDAP uses TCP/IP rather than the OSI transport (and lower) protocols.

It was developed in 1993 by some academic users at the University of Michigan.

Standardized in RFC 1777. LDAP information is available at *http://www.umich.edu/~rsug/ldap*.

See **X.500**.

Leap Year

There are several ways astronomers define a year, but the one of interest to us common folks is called the *tropical year*, which is 365.242199 days (which is 365 days, 5 hours, 48 minutes and about 45.99 seconds). A tropical year is the time between *vernal equinoxes*— that is, when the sun passes directly over the equator (which defines when spring officially begins). This definition of a year matches the changing of the seasons, so it ensures that the seasons occur in the same months each year. (The other definitions of a year are the *sidereal year*—which is 365.2564 days, and the *anomalistic year*—which is 365.2596 days. These are based on one full rotation of the earth around the sun—relative to the stars, and relative to the earth's *perihelion*—time when the earth is closest to the sun, respectively).

Since a year is not exactly 365 days, and a day must be exactly 24 hours, there needs to be some adjustment in the number of days in some years so that spring (for example) always arrives near March 21. Without these adjustments, the date when spring (and the other seasons) begins would cumulatively shift (which is what happened with previous calendar systems).

An early attempt to fix this problem was called the *Julian calendar*. It had a *leap year* (of 366 days) every fourth year (specifically, each year that is exactly divisible by 4). The other years are called *common years*, and have 365 days. A year would therefore be an average of 365.25 days, which still has an error of about 674 seconds per year, which adds up to about a full day every 128 years.

The improvement to this is our current calendar system is called the *Gregorian calendar*, after Pope Gregory XIII who noted that Easter (which is defined according to the date and the phase of the moon) was increasingly drifting away from where is was supposed to be (even with the Julian Calendar's leap years). When the Gregorian calendar was adopted, things had already drifted 10 days from where they were supposed to be. To fix this, by proclamation, the day following October 4, 1582 was declared to be October 15, 1582 (though England and the American colonies did not adopt this calendar until 1752, when a parliamentary decree declared that September 14 follow September 2). To keep such cumulative errors from happening again, the Gregorian calendar had a better system of *leap years*, so that adjustments would be a maximum of 1 day at a time (jumping so many days created problems for landlords collecting monthly rents, and the like).

The ideal fix needed would be that once every 128 years, one leap year would instead be a common year. The Gregorian calendar achieves this with the following rules:

▲ Begin by assuming that all years evenly divisible by 4 are leap years (this provides the basic average of 365.25 days per year, as provided by the Julian calendar). Therefore (for example), the years 1992 and 1996 are leap years. Then adjust this, with the following rules to eliminate one leap year every 128 years.

▲ Only century years (all of which the Julian calendar would make leap years) that are evenly divisible by 400 are leap years (the others are common years). Therefore, the years 2000 and 2400 are leap years, and the years 2100, 2200 and 2300 are common years. Therefore, the year 2000, in addition to being an "unexpected" leap year (so it does have a February 29) is expected to cause great problems for computer programs that do not correctly handle the new century.

▲ This calendar is accurate to about 1 year in 3,300 years. A subsequent modification makes the years that are exactly divisible by 4,000 common years. Therefore, the years 4,000, 8,000 and 12,000 (and so on) are common years. This makes the calendar accurate to about 1 day in 20,000 years (so make sure you get this all included in your programming—you never know how long your software will be used).

Most of the western world and parts of Asia use the Gregorian calendar. The Eastern Orthodox church uses a slightly different (and more accurate calendar). Since the first difference is in the year 2800, I'm not going to worry about it.

See **UTC**.

LEC
Local Exchange Carrier

In the U.S., the "local phone company." If it used to be part of the Bell System (that is, owned by AT&T), then the LEC is owned by one of the seven RBOCs. Otherwise, the LEC is one of the hundreds of rural telephone companies that were never part of the Bell System and typically have under a few thousand subscribers each (though some have 500,000 or more).

LECs own the central office(s) and the *local loop* (the cable from the CO to each of their subscribers) to provide communications services within a limited geographic area (called a LATA).

After the AT&T divestiture, LECs were restricted from providing long-distance services (and the IXCs were restricted from providing local service), though this is changing. LECs have always been allowed to charge (that is, the call is a *toll call*) for longer-distance calls within their own territories.

The traditional LECs are sometimes now called ILECs (*incumbent LECs*), to distinguish them from the newly certified Competitive LECs (CLECs).

A key part of being able to offer competitive local service is *local number portability* (LNP). That is, if a competitor to your local telephone company wants to offer you local service (that is, provide their own cable to your house, and their own central offices and switches), then most customers will want to keep their telephone number. Since telephone numbers have traditionally been associated with central office switches, new technology (such as signalling system 7—SS7) is required to offer this.

See **ATT**, **CARRIER**, **C.O.**, **INBAND**, **IXC OR IEC**, **LATA**, and **RBOC OR RBHC**.

Legacy System

A traditional (usually IBM) mainframe system.

This term has long been used by the TCP/IP and UNIX community as a polite reference to big old dinosaur IBM environments (FEPs, CICS, SNA, SDLC, 3270-type dumb terminals, and the like).

Now, "legacy" is also used to refer to anything users are migrating away from, such as Novell file servers and the IPX protocol and DEC VAX minicomputers and the DECnet protocol.

See **S3270**, **CICS**, **FEP**, **MAINFRAME**, **SDLC**, and **SNA**.

Lempel-Ziv-Stac

See **LZS**.

Lempel-Ziv-Welch

See **LZW**.

LEN
Low-Entry Networking

The most basic subset of APPN functionality for an *end node*.

See **APPN** and **PU-2.1**.

Computer Dictionary

Link Access Procedure for Modems

See **LAPM**.

Link-state

A method used by routers to determine the best path between two hosts that wish to communicate.

A type of *routing algorithm* (OSPF and IS-IS are example implementations) that improves on RIP methods by including more factors in the calculation of shortest path, according to the upper-layer *type of service* requested—for example, the path with the least delay, fastest throughput, and/or best reliability.

Communication between routers is more efficient than with RIP, since only changes in network connectivity are sent as they occur, rather than periodically exchanging entire routing tables. Another advantage of link-state is that routers will load-share over equally "short" links, whereas RIP will choose only one of the links.

A problem with link-state is that the router's CPU and memory requirements grow as the network size increases. If network changes occur too often (before new paths can be calculated), there will be routing problems.

Most protocols have a new link-state protocol, as shown in the table below, to (eventually) replace their RIP-based protocol.

Protocol	Link-state Router to Router Protocol	Acronym
AppleTalk	AppleTalk Update-based Routing Protocol	AURP
DECnet Phase V	Integrated IS-IS	Integrated IS-IS
IP	Open shortest path first	OSPF
IPX	NetWare Link Services Protocol (uses the IPX link state router)	NLSP
OSI	Intermediate System to Intermediate System	IS-IS

See **AURP, IGRP, ILSR, INTEGRATED IS-IS, IS, IS-IS, NLSP, OSPF, RIP**, and **SPF**.

Linux

A version of UNIX created by Linus Torvalds of Helsinki University in Finland (so he got to choose the name), in collaboration with people all over the Internet. Work began around 1991, and all source code is available for free (some are freeware utilities that have been around since before Linux, some were specifically written or modified for Linux). There are companies selling low-cost versions of Linux who have collected the code required all in one place, compiled for various machines, and provide some technical support.

Pronounced *LIH-nucks*.

NetBSD is another freeware UNIX-like operating system. It is based on the (you guessed it) very recent 4.4BSD-lite version of UNIX, and available for (ported to) many platforms.

See *http://www.linux.org* for Linux files, and *http://www.netbsd.org* for more on NetBSD.

See **OPENLOOK**, and **UNIX**.

Little Endian

Specifies that the *least significant byte* is stored in the lowest-memory address, which is the address of the data.

The Intel 80X86 and Pentium and DEC Alpha RISC processors are Little Endian (so therefore, the ISA and PCI buses are also Little Endian).

Windows NT and OSF/1 are Little Endian.

Little Endian is the less common UNIX implementation.

See **BIG ENDIAN**, **MS**, **OCTET**, and **UNIX**.

LLC2
Logical Link Control Type 2

The frame format used to carry 3270 and other types of traffic on Token Ring LANs.

A *connection-oriented* link layer protocol. It includes a sequence number for each frame and error-detection and -correction. Acknowledgments (called Receiver Ready—RR—frames) are typically required for each frame sent (and the timer may require this to be received within 1 second). Also, IBM implements *keep-alive* messages to ensure that both ends of a connection are still up.

When sending LLC2 frames over a WAN, these acknowledgments and keep-alive messages waste WAN bandwidth. Other technologies (such as DLSw) can spoof (produce the required responses locally) these messages to conserve WAN bandwidth.

Since LLC2 is a reliable link layer protocol, it can be (and is) used as a replacement for BISYNC and SDLC (which typically use 9,600 to 56 kbit/s connections). In contrast, LLC type 1 (which is used by Ethernet connections carrying TCP/IP, SPX/IPX and other protocols) is connectionless, and there is no link layer acknowledgments or error-correction. In this case the error correction is done by higher-layer protocols, such as TCP or SPX.

See **CONNECTION-ORIENTED**, **DLC**, **DLSW**, **FRAME RELAY**, **SNA**, and **SPOOFING**.

LMCS
Local Multipoint Communications System

The Canadian name for LMDS.

Industry Canada reserved 3 GHz in the "28 GHz" band for the service, but has initially (in late 1996) only licensed the first 1 GHz—as two 500 MHz frequency blocks. They are 27.35 MHz to 27.85 MHz and 27.85 GHz to 28.35 GHz.

Unlike cellular telephone licensees (where licensees requested national coverage), different companies requested specific rural areas, and others specific urban areas.

See **AMPS**, and **LMDS**.

LMDS
Local Multipoint Distribution Service

A new high-capacity (sometimes called "wideband") two-way, wireless, fixed (both transmitters and receivers are not mobile) voice and data communication service hoped (by its proponents) to be used to replace Cable TV coaxial cables (so often called *wireless cable*), fiber optic cables (so often called "virtual fiber") copper telephone cables, and to provide any types of communication service needed (such as telephone, digital television, video-conferencing, wireless debit card terminal support, interactive shopping, point-to-point data links and high-speed Internet access). Data transfer rates up to 30 Mbit/s (full-duplex) will be supported, but this depends on the amount of bandwidth allocated to each function (expected to be 30 MHz to 40 MHz each).

The hope is that the service is easy to install (no digging-up roads), new services can be added easily, services are mobile (your home telephone would be like a cellular telephone), and there would be competition for the local telephone service and for the Cable TV service (there is usually a monopoly for each of these services now). High-speed data services could be provided in areas, such as industrial subdivisions, where the distances and low density of customers (not very many along an individual street) make it uneconomical for service providers to use more traditional media, such as fiber. Other areas where cabling is difficult, or fast installation is a competitive advantage (such as shopping malls for credit card verification) may also be potential applications. Conversely, in urban areas where many buildings block radio signals, and buildings (each with many customers) are located close to each other, fiber will likely continue to be used, and LMDS won't be.

While the "last mile" to the subscribers is wireless (a 6" square or 12" parabolic antenna will likely be used), LMDS backbones (connecting the carrier's antennas near subscriber premises to the switching centers and signal sources) may be fiber, microwave and other more traditional media.

In the U.S., LMDS uses the 26 to 29 MHz frequency band—specifically 25.25 to 29.5 GHz, and also some in the 31 GHz band (awesomely high frequencies, dude). At these high frequencies, pizza-sized dish antennas are used, and signal propagation is a maximum of 3 to 5 km. These radio coverage areas are cellular-telephone-like, in that the frequencies can be reused, since the coverage area is relatively small (but handoffs to support mobile subscribers is not part of current designs or plans).

May compete with Direct Broadcast Satellites (DBSs—though these are one-way only) and MMDS for wireless services. Also competes with ADSL, CATV and other higher-capacity wired services.

See **MMDS**, **SATELLITE**, and **WIRELESS**.

Local Management Interface

A *de facto* standard for CPE (customer's equipment) to query a frame relay network for a list of the defined DLCIs and their status.

See **FRAME RELAY**.

LMWS
Licensed Millimeter Wave Service

A 28 GHz frequency band expected to be used for services similar to LMDS.

See **LMDS**.

LNM
LAN Network Manager

IBM's software for managing Token Ring LANs.

Polls stations for logged errors, such as bad CRCs.

See **CRC**, **TOKEN RING**, and **SNMP**.

Local Bridge

A bridge that is directly connected to the LANs it serves. (In contrast, a pair of remote bridges have a WAN link between them.)

See **REMOTE BRIDGE**.

Local Bus

A bus that provides full processor clock-speed and processor bus-width access directly to a 486 (or higher) PC's processor, rather than going through the 8- or 16-bit-wide ISA bus (which always runs at 8 MHz, even when the processor runs faster).

VESA's VL-bus and Intel's PCI are competing local bus standards (although there's not much competition left—VL-bus lost). PCs will usually also have an ISA, EISA, or MCA bus for lower-speed peripherals, such as sound boards.

See **BUS**, **MCA**, **PCI**, **VESA**, and **VLBUS OR VLB**.

Lossy Data Compression

A data compression scheme that loses some information (that is, the reconstructed data will have lower quality) in order to provide the most compression possible.

Used where the loss of information will not be a problem (such as video conferencing, where providing smooth motion and color is more important than very fine detail). In contrast, *lossless data compression* uses a method that enables the original data to be reconstructed exactly (for example, by calculating the difference between successive pictures).

See **CDROM**, **DATA COMPRESSION**, **GIF**, **H.261**, **MINIDISK**, **MPMLQ**, **PNG**, and **VIDEO**.

LSB
Least Significant Bit (or Byte)

The lowest-order bit. For example, the least significant bit of 01000111 is a 1 (er, that's the 1 on the very right). The *most significant bit* is a 0 (yep, that's the 0 on the very left).

See **BIG ENDIAN**, **MS**, and **OCTET**.

LU
Logical Unit

A subset of SNA, used for a specific upper-layer function, such as printing. An individual session between an IBM computer terminal (which may support more than one LU at a time— that is, the actual terminal can support more than one logical terminal) and a mainframe.

See **S3270**, **LU**, **LU-0**, **LU-1**, **LU-2**, **LU-3**, **LU-4**, **LU-6.1**, **LU-6.2**, **LU-7**, **MAINFRAME**, **PU**, **PU-2**, **PU-2.1**, **PU-4**, and **PU-5**.

LU 0
Logical Unit Type 0

A non-architected (you can interpret the data any way you want to), peer-to-peer (program-to-program) type of data communications and API that is more flexible but has fewer built-in capabilities than LU 6.2.

Used for applications, such as file transfers, in which the protocol is defined by the file transfer programs running at each end of the link, and all that is needed is a reliable transport.

See **LU-6.2**.

LU 1
Logical Unit Type 1

The LU type used for sending *SNA Character String* (SCS) data streams from host-based applications to remote terminals, such as 3270 printers and 3770 RJE terminals.

See **S3270** and **RJE**.

LU 2
Logical Unit Type 2

The LU type used for communications to 3270-type computer terminals.

See **S3270**.

LU 3
Logical Unit Type 3

The LU type used for communications with 3270-type printers.

See **S3270**.

LU 4
Logical Unit Type 4

A peer-to-peer communications method now made obsolete by LU 6.2.

See **LU-6.2**.

LU 6.1
Logical Unit Type 6.1

The LU type used for program-to-program communications, in which the program at one end is IBM's CICS or *Information Management System* (IMS).

See **CICS**.

LU 6.2
Logical Unit Type 6.2

IBM's recent (well, not that recent, but more recent than the original SNA), open networking standard and API enhancement to SNA. Supports peer-to-peer communication—for example, either side can initiate a connection, and both sides can be user workstations (typically PCs). Also supports program to program communications, in that the programs running on the peers can send binary data (that is, any 8-bit pattern per byte) directly between them. In contrast, the original SNA only supported sending printable EBCDIC characters (that is, screen images and print jobs) from a mainframe to a printer or fixed-function terminal (more commonly called a dumb terminal).

While (the much less popular) LU 6.1 also supports program-to-program communication, LU 6.1 is not peer-to-peer since one side must be a mainframe. A *logical unit* is a session on a terminal. Defines the operations and responses for one *half-session* (which may be a terminal or a program in a PC or mainframe) that communicates with another half-session elsewhere. Requires so much RAM that LU 6.2 is not feasible under DOS.

Sometimes called APPC. Is part of SAA.

HLLAPI is a simpler and terminal-emulation-based predecessor.

See **APPC, APPN, CPIC, HLLAPI, SAA,** and **SNA.**

LU 7
Logical Unit Type 7

The LU type used for communications between an application program and a 5250-type terminal.

See **S5250.**

Luminance (Y), Chrominance (UV)

See **YUV.**

LZS
Lempel-Ziv-Stac

A data compression algorithm developed by Stac Electronics and often used by routers, and some ISDN terminal adapters.

Multiple *compression dictionaries* can be maintained so that when a certain type of data is detected, the best dictionary can immediately be used without first building it and sending it to the receiver. A 2:1 compression ratio is typically attained.

See **CCP, DATA COMPRESSION, LZW, STAC,** and **TA.**

LZW
Lempel-Ziv-Welch

A data compression algorithm that builds a dictionary of frequently repeated groups of (8-bit) characters (such as ASCII "the") on a per-file basis and represents these frequent character-strings as shorter bit patterns. Before compressed data transfer, the sender's compression dictionary must be sent error-free to the receiver (so an error correcting protocol must already be established on the data link).

The method is therefore good at compressing text files but not as good at other types of files (such as graphics files, which may have repeating patterns at intervals that are not multiples of 8 bits). *RLE* is another type of compression.

In 1985, LZW was patented by Sperry Corp. (which is the predecessor company to Unisys Corp.), and Unisys later decided to enforce its patent rights and requires users of LZW to pay royalties. Since LZW is part of the GIF graphics file format developed by CompuServe, CompuServe paid a one-time licensing fee to Unisys (rumored to be $125,000), and now CompuServe charges a licensing fee for application software (per copy sold) that uses the GIF file format.

TIFF images can also be compressed using LZW.

Also, the V.42*bis* modem data compression standard uses a similar data compression method, and most V.42*bis* modem manufacturers pay a royalty to Unisys.

Based on the *Lempel-Ziv* (named after Abraham Lempel and Jacob Ziv) universal data compression algorithm, which is in the public domain.

See **COMPUSERVE, DATA COMPRESSION, GIF, LZS, RLE**, and **V.42BIS**.

M

MAC
Media Access Control

The part of the data link layer (which is layer 2 of the OSI 7-layer reference model) that includes the 6-byte (48 bit) address of the source and destination, and the method of getting permission to transmit (which is CSMA/CD, in the case of Ethernet).

A worldwide-unique address MAC address is permanently assigned to LAN adapter cards when they are manufactured. This is called the layer 2 address, hardware address and MAC layer address.

The IEEE assigns each manufacturer a 22-bit number, and the manufacturer is then responsible for programming each card with the 22-bit manufacturer ID and a unique (to the manufacturer) serial number.

The same format of address is used for Ethernet, Token Ring, FDDI and ATM ESIs, facilitating interoperation. The format is shown in the figure below.

```
 -----------------------------------------------------------------
|I/G|U/L|     Manufacturer ID     |        Unique Address        |
 -----------------------------------------------------------------
  |   |               |                           |
  |   |               |                           - 24-bit serial number
  |   |               |
  |   |               --------------------------- 22-bit manufacturer
  |   |                                           identification
  |   |
  |   0 --------------------------------------- Globally administered
  |   |                                         address
  |   1 --------------------------------------- Locally administered
  |                                             address
  0 --------------------------------------- Individual address
  1 --------------------------------------- Group address
```

The first bit specifies whether the destination is a single station (called a *unicast*) or a group of stations. If all 48 address bits are set to 1, then the message is *broadcast* to all stations. If the group address bit is set, but all the other address bits are not 1s, then the message is a *multicast*, and is sent to a group of stations. Multicasts are used for advertising services and other functions where a defined group (such as those running a particular protocol) needs to receive the message.

If the second bit is a 1, then (other than the unique case described above where all 48 bits are 1s) it indicates that the other 46 bits have been manually configured by the user (so the address is a *locally administered address*—LAA), not by the manufacturer (which is called a *universally administered address*—UAA). UAAs are commonly used on Token Ring and DECnet networks. They are typically set in some configuration file, and are typically selected to provide some geographic significance to the address. For example, a country code, city code, building code, floor number and floor grid position could be used as an address, to assist in locating workstations that are sending too much traffic.

The IEEE charges $1,000 for a manufacturer identification code.

For Ethernet, the MAC address is transmitted with the most significant byte first, and each byte is transmitted with the least significant bit first.

See **S802.3**, **CSMACD**, **ETHERNET**, **OSI**, **ROUTER**, and **SWITCHED LAN**.

Mach

Carnegie-Mellon University's extension of AT&T System V Release 2.2 UNIX.

See **OSF-1** and **UNIX**.

Magic Cookie

Another name for cookie.

See **COOKIE**.

Mainframe

The classic multimillion-dollar huge (and usually IBM) computer handling the accounting or inventory functions for a huge organization. Security and procedures surround it, as does an air-conditioned, raised-floor, power-conditioned computer room, staffed by 24-hour-per-day operators reading the local tabloid-sized daily newspaper.

Mainframes are often called "big iron." And IBM was often referred to as "big blue," because the company is so big, and its computers usually had blue dress panels (especially in the 1980s and earlier). But my friend Harvey told me that one could actually order the computers in other colors, but salesmen never told customers this for fear of flustering the customer with yet more decisions (can you imagine the heated high-level meetings on this topic), and delaying the order.

Common IBM mainframes (in increasing size) are System/370 (now that's an old family), 9370, 43xx (4361, 4381), 303x, 308x, 3090, and ES/9000. All recent IBM mainframes are part of the System/390 (write that as S/390 to be cool) family. IBM computers would typically talk to "dumb terminals" (which is not a politically correct thing to say—call them fixed-function terminals), such as the 3270 series.

Mainframes used to be IBM's stranglehold on the business community and government, but newer computing technologies are reducing most corporations' emphasis on mainframes:

▲ PCs: IBM invented these in 1981 but lost its commanding market share when IBM did not innovate or drop prices fast enough

▲ Microsoft DOS and Windows: IBM gave Microsoft its start by using Microsoft DOS and Basic for IBM PCs; now Microsoft dominates the PC software industry—something IBM would have preferred to have done themselves

▲ Apple Macintoshes: these used to be IBM's enemy; now IBM cooperates with Apple on the PowerPC to compete with Intel (and IBM made Intel famous by using Intel's CPUs in the PC)

▲ UNIX workstations: IBM has its own RS/6000, but these are not in first or second place

▲ Minicomputers: here IBM has a winner, the AS/400

Realizing that its just not cool to sell or have mainframes anymore (client/server is the trendy architecture of the decade—at least so far), IBM now calls their mainframes *servers*— for example, an *S/390 server* or *System/390 Parallel Enterprise Server*, instead of a *System/390 mainframe* (see for yourself at *http://www.s390.ibm.com*). IBM often ships these with red or even yellow stripes (more like vertical accents, than horizontal racing stripes), to make them look less like big fat mainframes.

IBM does have a point about their mainframes being a good idea. They have very mature, proven and widely accepted management and security utilities available both from IBM and third parties—something the PC and UNIX workstation server market is *still* working on. Their operating systems are more stable, and well-trained staff are all over the place.

See **S3270, AIX, CHANNEL, CICS, CLIENT/SERVER, DASD, DLC, EBCDIC, FEP, IBM, IND FILE, LEGACY SYSTEM, LU, LU-0, LU-1, LU-2, LU-3, LU-4, LU-6.1, LU-6.2, LU-7, MVS, PU, PU-2, PU-2.1, PU-4, RJE, SDLC, TSO, VM, VTAM,** and **X WINDOW SYSTEM.**

MAN
Metropolitan Area Network

A high-speed network that covers more than a few kilometers (that is, larger than a LAN) but less than any arbitrary distance (that is, smaller that a WAN).

The IEEE 802.6 standard was supposed to be a (the?) standard MAN, but you don't hear much about it anymore.

Although FDDI is usually considered a LAN technology, it could also be considered a MAN technology, since FDDI can have up to a 200-km circumference.

See **DQDB, FDDI, LAN, SMDS,** and **WAN.**

Manchester Encoding

See **ENCODING.**

MAPI
Messaging API

Microsoft Corporation's API for messaging. A standard way of providing communication services to applications (making them *mail-enabled*) so that they can send and receive "mail" (blocks of data, documents, files, etc.), directly from within applications. Part of WOSA.

The APIs are independent of platform, mail system, and transport protocol.

MAPI is the most popular messaging API for the PC environment. Backed by Microsoft, Novell/WordPerfect (Corel), and Lotus (IBM).

Two levels are defined:

▲ *Simple MAPI* does basic mail functions (such as sending and receiving messages).

▲ *Extended MAPI* has a *Service Provider Interface* (SPI), which will interface to software that provides an interface to other mail services, such as CompuServe—so that any application using the extended MAPI will be able to use CompuServe as a message carrier.

Competes with VIM (though VIM is used mostly for Lotus applications running under Windows or OS/2) and XAPIA's CMC (which is used more for cross-platform use).

See **CMC**, **MHS2** (Message Handling System), **VIM**, **WOSA**, and **XAPIA**.

Marketecture

A combination of the words *marketing* and *architecture*. Usually used derogatorily to indicate that technical-sounding words are being used for marketing and sales purposes (to make the competition look worse, or your own product look better), rather to clearly and without bias explain what is really (technically) going on.

See **FUD**.

MBONE
Internet Multicast Backbone

The parts of the Internet that support IP multicast traffic, comprise the MBone. These include the routers and (through them, the) subnetworks connected to (or are part of, depending on how you define it) the Internet.

The Mbone was created beginning in 1992 as a volunteer and experimental effort, to support multicast traffic over parts of the Internet that do not support IP, multicast (for example, it is used by about 1,000 receivers during IETF meetings). This is accomplished by encapsulating the multicast traffic into standard unicast IP packets, and sent to other parts of the MBone. The connections carrying the encapsulated packets are called *tunnels*, and are also part of the MBone. These routers and tunnels only carry a single copy of traffic destined for multiple locations on the far side of remote MBone routers—the remote MBone router splits the traffic as required.

IP multicast was designed to carry traffic intended to go simultaneously to more than one location—without having to send a copy separately (and sequentially) to each location (which would needlessly load the Internet). Multimedia applications, such as for video conferencing is expected to be a major use for the MBone.

The expectation is that some day, all routers will support IP multicast—but until then, the MBone is a semipermanent test bed (which is layered on top of the Internet) for the development of IP multicast.

For more information, see *http://www.best.com/~prince*.

See **IP MULTICAST**, **MULTIMEDIA**, and **PIM**.

MC
Miniature Card

See **MINICARD**.

MCA
Micro Channel Architecture

The 32-bit bus used in most IBM PS/2 PCs and the RS/6000 workstations. It is also used in IBM's Power Parallel SP2 high performance computer. A 256-processor version of this computer (which runs AIX) is Deep Blue, the chess-playing computer that played Garry Kasparov in May of 1997.

The MCA bus was introduced in 1987. Some characteristics of it are listed below:

- ▲ It runs at 10 MHz
- ▲ The theoretical maximum data transfer rate is 20 or 40 Mbytes/s (depending on the mode)
- ▲ The connector has 112 pins
- ▲ It supports up to 16 bus masters

Two types of slots are defined:

- ▲ 16-bit slots have a 16-bit data bus and a 24-bit address bus and support for video and audio
- ▲ 32-bit slots support separate 32-bit data and address buses.

Was never accepted as widely as expected, perhaps because IBM (at least initially) charged too high a royalty for its use, or because existing PC adapter cards could not be used (requiring that customers buy all new cards and that manufacturers design new cards).

See **BUS** and **BUS MASTER DMA**.

MD5
Message Digest 5

A method of ensuring message integrity.

MD5 is a message authentication method based on producing a 128-bit "signature" (also called a *fingerprint* or "hash code") from a message. The algorithm that produces the message digest is designed so that changing the message in any way is (almost 100%) sure to change the message digest, so a recipient can know that the message has been changed.

Defined in RFC 1321.

See **AUTHENTICATION**, **OSPF**, and **PGP**.

MDS
Multipoint Distribution Service

The Canadian name for MMDS.

See **MMDS**.

MD
Mini Disc

A re-writable 60-mm diameter "CD-ROM" (standard CD-ROMs are 120 mm in diameter) that uses *magneto-optical technology* to store up to 140 Mbytes per disk. This would only be about 14 minutes of standard CD-ROM audio (16-bits per sample, 44,100 samples per second, stereo), but a lossy form of data compression (which Sony calls *Adaptive Transform Acoustic Coding*—ATRAC) is used to provide about 74 minutes of stereo audio (the same as for standard compact discs).

Data can be directly overwritten, and a separate erase pass is not required. Can be used for both audio and data. Developed by Sony. Never became popular in North America for data or consumer audio use, but are more common for professional studio audio use.

Mini Discs were first available in 1982, there is now a proposed MD 2.0 version of the standard that supports 280 Mbytes per disk.

See **CDROM**, and **LOSSY DATA COMPRESSION**.

MINICARD
Miniature Card

A standardized, removable memory card which is 33 mm wide by 38 mm long (approximately $\frac{1}{4}$ the size of a "PCMCIA" PC Card). Intended to be used for data transfer between consumer electronic devices such as digital cameras, audio recorders, cellular telephones and PDAs.

The standard supports up to 64 Mbytes of storage per card, though initial cards typically support 2 Mbytes or 4 Mbytes.

A replaceable 60-contact elastomeric connector is used, rated for at least 5,000 insertion/withdrawal cycles. It gets squeezed between the card and the connecting equipment, making electrical contact through conductive rubber stripes.

Often lower-cost than the competing CompactFlash, since MiniCard has no on-board processor. However, Minicard is simply memory, so more software (that is, drivers and CPU time) is required for the connecting equipment (this is called the *flash translation layer*—FTL. MiniCard also supports *execute-in-place* (XIP), so that programs can be run directly from the MiniCard memory (in contrast, CompactFlash contents must first be read into a PC's main memory before the program can be executed).

The interface supports 8-bit-wide and 16-bit-wide data transfers, and has 25 address lines. Interface signals are provided to allow flash (the initial use), DRAM and ROM to be supported. Also, 5v, 3.3v and (in the future) a lower interface voltage is supported (a mechanical keying scheme is defined to ensure the wrong voltage card is not inserted into a wrong voltage slot).

An *attribute information structure* (AIS) at the beginning of the memory space defines the timing and power requirements for up to 4 different blocks of memory on the card. The AIS can optionally be stored on a small non-volatile memory IC, and accessed using the I²C bus, so the MiniCard main memory can be volatile (that is, it forgets its contents when you power it off).

Supported by AMD, Compaq, Fujitsu, Hewlett-Packard, Intel (now there's an important backer), Philips Electronics, SCM Microsystems, and Sharp.

Sometimes called MC.

The Miniature Card Implementors Forum is at *http://www.mcif.org*, and much information is at *http://www.intel.com*.

See **ACCESS.BUS**, **COMPACT FLASH**, **FLASH**, **PCMCIA**, **PDA**, and **SERIAL BUS**.

Messaging

A loosely coupled method of communication between platforms.

Uses *mailboxes* rather than RPCs. Mailboxes permit asynchronous interprocess communication.

The Message-Oriented Middleware Association (MOMA) has a WWW server at *http://www.sbexpos.com/sbexpos/associations/moma/home.html*.

See **API**, **MAPI**, **VIM**, and **RPC**.

MHS
Message Handling Service

An OSI-compliant standard for electronic mail, as described in the X.400 standard.

See **X.400**.

MHS
Message Handling System

Novell's support for electronic mail (and files and notifications) management, storage, exchange, forwarding, and routing.

The idea is that a third-party mail program (such as Microsoft Mail or cc:Mail) delivers mail to Novell's MHS, which then gets the message to the destination server. The destination server then delivers the message to the mail program for delivery to the destination user.

Based on Novell's *standard message format* messaging APIs.

Competed with Microsoft's MAPI, and MAPI won, so MHS was modified it could communicate with MAPI.

Unrelated to the X.400 MHS.

See **CMC**, **MAPI**, **NOVELL**, and **VIM**.

MIB
Management Information Base

The variables stored by an SNMP agent.

The basic set of MIB variables stored by most network devices supporting SNMP is defined as MIB II, and these are specified in RFC 1213. Extensions to MIB II support specific devices, such as LAN concentrators, bridges and routers.

The *Mobile MIB* Task Force is working on a MIB and MIF for wireless equipment (see *http:// www.epilogue.com/mmtf*).

See **DMI**, **DMTF**, **RMON**, **MIF**, and **SNMP**.

MICR
Magnetic Ink Character Recognition

The method that is used to print and read account numbers and bank transit numbers from checks. Ferromagnetic ink is used, so it can be read electromagnetically rather than optically. The very unique font for the magnetic character encoding is officially called the American Banker Association E-13B font. It was developed in 1958, and has the following characters.

▲ The digits 0 through 9, plus a space

▲ A *Federal Reserve District Transit Symbol*, (a vertical rectangle followed by two squares which are arranged vertically)

▲ An *amount* symbol (three squares in an upward diagonal)

▲ An *on-us* (own use) symbol, which is two short vertical bars followed by a square

▲ A *dash* symbol, which is two small vertical rectangles followed by a short vertical bar

The ANSI X3.2, X9.13, X9.7 and X9.18 standards specify the position, background, size and weight for the checks.

The standard specifies that up to 65 characters and symbols can be at the bottom of each check, arranged as four fields. The figure below shows the four fields, and the character positions in each.

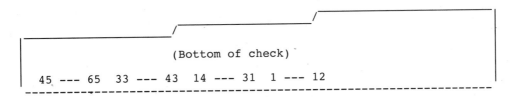

Beginning with the right-most field, the use of each character position is shown below.

▲ The field with character positions 1 through 12 is for the amount of the check (this field is not pre-printed on the check, but may be added after the check has been written). Position 1 has the *amount* symbol, positions 2 and 3 are the cents of the amount, positions 4 through 11 are the dollars of the amount (zero-left-filled to use all positions) and position 12 is the *amount* symbol again. The maximum check amount is therefore $99,999,999.99—just enough for my pay check!

▲ The next field is optional, and is usually used for the account number. If it is present, then position 31 has the *on-us* symbol, and the other (up to) 17 positions have the

account number, possibly including the *dash* symbol. In Canada, the Canadian Payments Association (CPA) determines the exact format of this field.

▲ The next field is for the financial institution's transit number. Position 33 is the *transit* symbol and position 34 is a check digit (to ensure the rest of this field is read correctly). Positions 35 through 38 are the Bank Identification code (the four-digit transit number). Position 39 is a dash and positions 40 through 42 are the bank's routing number. Position 43 is the transit symbol again.

▲ The left-most field is an auxiliary own-use field. It is usually used for the check's serial number (which is printed in a more human-readable font at the top-right of the check). Position 45 is the *on-us* symbol. The next (up to) 19 digits are the check number, followed by the *on-us* symbol again.

Pronounced *MY-ker.*

Micro Channel Architecture

See **MCA**.

Microsoft Corporation

What can be said? Microsoft is big, hires enthusiastic programmers who work around the clock, and has a WWW server at *http://www.microsoft.com.*

80% of all desktop computers run Microsoft operating systems.

Middleware

Software that facilitates cross-platform distributed computing (that is, getting computers from different vendors and running different operating systems to communicate).

APIs that shield developers from underlying transport protocols and operating systems, along with a mechanism (such as *message passing* or *remote procedure calls*) for cooperating applications to communicate (over a LAN or WAN or within the same machine).

See **API**, **MESSAGING**, and **RPC**.

MIDI
Musical Instrument Digital Interface

A standard for mixing computers and music, which was developed in 1983.

A daisy-chained (each component has a *MIDI* In and a *MIDI* Out connector), serial communications (at 31,250 bits/s), and messaging scheme to connect electronic musical instruments (usually *synthesizers* of some sort) to a *controller*. The controller may be an electronic keyboard, a *sequencer* (which stores sequences of keyboard commands), or a PC running a game.

The sequencer is usually a PC, and the game port can be used for the MIDI interface (with the right software, and a suitable adapter cable).

Messages are typically 1 to 3 bytes in length. A typical message would be as follows:

▲ Byte 1: *Message type* (such as Note On)

▲ Byte 2: *Key number* (which note, out of 128 possible notes)

▲ Byte 3: *Velocity value* (how fast the key was pressed)

Specifies *big endian* transmission and storage (most significant bytes first).

A five-pin DIN connector is used, but only three of the pins are used (current loop data out and return plus a shield).

The MIDI minimum requirement is to be able to create 128 pitched instruments, each able to produce 24 notes on 16 different channels.

The MIDI capability of PC sound cards producing musical instrument sounds can be provided by one of two methods:

▲ *FM* (Frequency Modulation) *synthesis* is an older and inexpensive method that uses combinations of (usually four) sine waves (as specified in the sound card's ROM or RAM) to imitate the instrument's sound.

▲ The better-sounding *wavetable lookup synthesizer* method uses actual prerecorded samples of instrument sounds, which are modified according to the MIDI commands.

▲ Yamaha Corp. is a major manufacturer of MIDI keyboards. They have a web site at *http://www.yamaha.com*. Much MIDI information is at *http://www.midifarm.com* and *http://www.midiweb.com*.

See **BIG ENDIAN**, **GAME PORT**, **MPC**, **POLYPHONY**, **SCALE**, and **SMPTE**.

MIF
Management Information Format

The data format of the file provided with, and automatically updated by DMI-manageable PCs (when the machine is powered on, or the system configuration changes—for example when a laptop is plugged-in to its docking station). The file contains system information, such as the model number and serial number, as well as some details of (hopefully) all installed software (such as which version is installed) and hardware (what the manufacturer and model number is).

Version 2.0 of the MIF (ratified in December 1995) adds the capability for application programs to pass more detailed information to desktop management applications (such as which software drivers an application needs, or what programs are needed to run the application).

The collection of the MIFs in a computer is the *MIF* database. It is stored by the *service layer* software in a proprietary format, to allow faster access.

See **DMI**, and **DMTF**.

Milnet

A government military network run by the U.S. Defense Communications Agency.

See **ARPANET**.

MIME
Multipurpose Internet Mail Extension

A standard method for sending and receiving attachments to Internet mail (usually called "email" or simply "mail") messages. Attachments are typically non-ASCII files, such as a spreadsheet or word processing document, or a graphical image that is appended to the end

of the mail message (that is, after any text). The attachment is usually either too large to be pasted into the sender's email message or is binary (which is not directly supported by Internet email).

MIME provides a structure for standard RFC 822 type mail messages, by using additional header fields (these are defined in RFC 1049).

The following steps describe how MIME mail messages are handled (from the users point of view):

▲ An option in the sender's email program allows the sender to specify the filename of the file to be attached to the mail message. The file may have graphical or multimedia (images, video, sound) information.

▲ The file's extension (.doc or .wri, for example) indicates what the file's format and content are.

▲ If the file is binary (that is, it has other than the printable ASCII characters in it), it is automatically converted to ASCII (prior to MIME, this required a separate step, often using the uuencode and uudecode programs). This file conversion increases the length of the attachment (not a surprise—even with marvellous computers, you can't get something for nothing).

▲ The mail message and attached file are mailed to the recipient.

▲ The recipient's mail program (which must support MIME) converts the file back to binary, and displays an icon (for WordPerfect or Word, for example) in the received mail message (according to the attached file's filename extension). Clicking on the icon starts the application (such as WordPerfect or Word), so the attached file can be viewed (or edited, printed, and so on).

MIME works across different computing platforms.

Here is what actually happens to the mail message.

All mail messages (as described in RFC 822) have message headers that identify the sender, destination, subject and other information needed to transfer the e-mail message. MIME defines five additional message headers. These are listed below.

▲ MIME-Version:—this is currently 1.0.

▲ Content-Type:—this is the *MIME type*, and is comprised of a *type* and *subtype*, separated by a /. For example Content-Type: image/gif. These are defined by the *Internet Assigned Numbers Authority* (IANA), and the table below lists the common MIME types. Users are allowed to define their own types, so long as they are prefaced by x-.

▲ Content-Transfer-Encoding:—specified any encoding used to ensure that the message uses only 7-bit characters. For example, Content-Transfer-Encoding: base64 indicates that the body of the message was encoded using the base64 method. The encoding methods defined are listed in the table below.

▲ Content-ID:—which is a world-wide unique identifier for the message (such as a current time and date stamp appended to the user's e-mail address). This could be used for referencing the message in another message.

▲ Content-Description:, which is like the subject field of an e-mail message—a human-readable helpful description.

Some common MIME types are listed in the table below.

Type	Subtype	Comment
application	octet-stream	Binary data
postscript	A postscript file	
audio	basic	8-bit ISDN μ-law digitized audio
midi	MIDI digitized audio	
wav	`.WAV` format digitized audio	
image	gif	Bitmapped image in `.GIF` format
jpeg	Bitmapped image in JPEG format	
message	rfc822	Mail message in the traditional RFC 822 format
partial	A fragment of a larger mail message	
text	html	Text in HTML format
plain	ASCII text (this may be further qualified by `charset=us-ascii` as a parameter)	
richtext	Text formatted according to RFC 1341	
video	mpeg	MPEG compressed video
quicktime	Video in Apple's Quicktime video format	

The MIME encoding methods are listed in the table below.

Content-Transfer-Encoding	Comment
7bit	Message is not encoded, and contains only 7-bit printable text (this is the default value)
8bit	Message is not encoded, and contains some 8-bit text. However, the line length (number of characters until a carriage return/line feed) is still short (perhaps under 1,000 characters—some mail gateways may not be able to handle arbitrarily long lines of text). This method can only be used if the rest of the e-mail system is known to be able to carry binary data (which is rare).
base64	Three 8-bit bytes of the original message are represented as four characters. The process is to take the 24 bits of the original three 8-bit bytes, and consider them to be four 6-bit values. The 6-bit values can therefore be any value from 0 to 63. A conversion table is then used which represents each of these 64 values as an ASCII character. Value 0 through 25 is ASCII A through Z. Value 26 through 51 is ASCII a through z. Value 52 through 61 is ASCII 0 through 9. Value 62 is ASCII +, and Value 63 is ASCII /.
	This is specified in RFC 1421.
binary	Message is in binary, and may include any number of characters before a carriage return/line feed. This can only be used if the rest of the e-mail system is known to be able to carry binary data (which is rare)
quoted-printable	Any 8-bit characters in the message are replaced by an equal sign (=) followed by the character's hexadecimal value in ASCII (so the 8-bit value 10000011_2 in the message would be converted to the three characters =83. This method is best when there are only a few 8-bit values in the e-mail message.

An extension called S/MIME (Secure MIME, developed by RSA Data Security Inc.) uses encryption to guard against unintended recipients reading, changing or forging email messages. This is done using a method similar to that used by PGP (though S/MIME is more CPU-intensive)—that is, a combination of public and private key encryption, hash codes and certificates. A major part of S/MIME is the negotiation of the encryption algorithm and key-length, as a wide variety of these are used.

MIME is defined in RFC 1521. RFC 1522 defines the handling of non-ASCII text in message headers.

See **ASCII, ENCRYPTION, IANA, IMAP, PGP, RSA, SMTP**, and **UUENCODE**.

MIPS
Millions of Instructions Per Second

A measure of CPU processing power that is often used to compare computer processing speed. Often called *"Mythical Instructions Per Second,"* as many consider the measure to be too simplistic to be meaningful (if nothing else, you have to specify which instructions are being executed).

The legendary DEC VAX-11/780 is used as a basis (it was popular in the late 1970s and early 1980s) and is defined to be a one-MIP machine.

Since VAXes (or, as VAX lovers like to pluralize them, VAXen) are fair to compare to each other (more so than to computers with other architectures), DEC uses the term VUP (VAX unit of processing power)—with one VUP equal to one MIP.

Because of the poor definition of what type of instructions to use to measure it, MIPS is seldom used today. Intel developed iComp, and workstation manufacturers use SPEC and other benchmarks, such as Dhrystone and Whetstone.

A processor's MIPS rating is typically somewhere between its SPECint92 rating and twice its SPECfp92 rating.

See **DEC, ICOMP, FLOP, INTEL PC**, and **SPEC**.

MIPS Technologies Inc.

A company (now owned by Silicon Graphics Inc.) that makes RISC processors (R3000 and R4000 and now newer ones) that are used mostly by SGI's workstations.

For a while, DEC, Silicon Graphics, Toshiba, NEC, Siemens and Sony were designing workstations using the processor. (The deal was that each vendor could design a chip for a specialized market—the main success of this is Integrated Device Technology that makes an R4000 with digital signal processing capability.)

Also, Microsoft (Windows NT), SCO (ODT), and USL (SVR4) were working (separately) to produce a *little endian* version of their operating systems for this processor.

There are many versions of MIPS processors, as listed below.

▲ MIPS R2000. The first product, shipped in 1986. It had 185,000 transistors.

▲ MIPS R4000. The 100 MHz version was announced in March 1992.

▲ MIPS R4400. The 150 MHz version was announced in June 1993, the 200 MHz version in June 1994, and the 250 MHz version in July 1995.

▲ MIPS R4600. The 100 MHz version was announced in March 1994, and the 133 MHz version in June 1994.

▲ MIPS R5000. The 200 MHz version was announced in February 1996.

▲ MIPS R8000. The 75 MHz version was announced in June 1994, and the 90 MHz version in May 1995.

▲ MIPS R10000. The 200 MHz version was announced in March 1996.

Silicon Graphics has a WWW server at *http://www.sgi.com*.

See **ACE**, **DSP**, **LITTLE ENDIAN**, and **RISC**.

MIRS
Motorola Integrated Radio System

See **ESMR**.

MLPPP
Multilink Point-to-point Protocol

An IETF standard for *inverse multiplexing*. Using synchronous PPP, it specifies how to split, recombine and sequence datagrams across lower-speed switched circuits to provide higher-speed connections. A popular use is to combine the two ISDN BRI B channels to provide a 128 kbit/s connection.

An enhancement to MLPPP supports *bandwidth on demand* (also called *rubber bandwidth*), in that additional switched circuits can be established and used for an existing connection, when throughput requirements increase, or when a circuit fails. Connections can also be automatically cleared when usage falls below a pre-set threshold. This capability is called the *Bandwidth Allocation Control Protocol* (BACP), and an early specification is at *ftp://ftp.shiva.com/outgoing/eng/bacp.txt*. It is based on Shiva's proprietary dynamic MLPPP.

Circuits can be SVCs (switched virtual circuits, such as X.25, ISDN or ATM) or PVCs (permanent virtual circuits, such as frame relay). A single logical connection can have one or more connections using one or a combination of these circuit types. For example, a frame relay circuit could be used for most data traffic, but if loading gets too heavy (perhaps due to month-end processing), then (more expensive) ISDN circuits can be established during the peak periods.

The group of connections comprising a higher-speed logical connection are called a *bundle* or *MLPPP* group. Prioritization can be implemented by assigning different protocols to different bundles is one way to ensure that one protocol does not hog all the bandwidth, causing another protocol to time-out.

Protocols supported are: DECnet, IP, IPX, NetBIOS and SNA. Protocol *spoofing* is supported, to reduce WAN bandwidth requirements. For example, keep-alive messages will be filtered from the WAN, and recreated at the remote end.

MLPPP is a layer of software above PPP (usually above several PPP sessions, one per connection), and below the network protocols—possibly several are sharing the PPP connection(s).

MLPPP therefore supports all of PPP's features. For example, MLPPP also supports a negotiation phase when a connection is first established, to automatically set configuration options. (In fact, the PPP LCP negotiation is extended to include an multilink option message in the negotiation.)

In operation, the MLPPP software receives *protocol data units* (PDUs) from the higher layer software, fragments these according to frame size negotiated by the LCP for each PPP connection, adds a header, and sends the packets over all established PPP connections. Some call this *packet-based inverse multiplexing* (as opposed to *circuit-based inverse multiplexing*, which requires that all connections be the same speed).

MLPPP was first released in November 1994, and is defined in RFC 1717.

Sometimes called MP or ML-PPP.

See **ATM**, **FRAME RELAY**, **INVERSE MULTIPLEXER**, **ISDN**, **PPP**, **PRIORITIZATION**, **RAS**, **SPOOFING**, and **X.25**.

MMDS
Multichannel Multipoint Distribution System

A U.S. system (the equivalent service in Canada is called *Multipoint Distribution Service—MDS*) sometimes called "wireless cable" (which some would call an oxymoron), since it offers a superset of the features of CATV, using radio (so no wires are needed). The service is one-way (broadcast) only, can provide data rates of up to 10 Mbits/s, and requires line-of-sight between the transmitting and receiving antennas (buildings and mountains cannot be in the way).

Uses the 2.1 and 2.7 GHz bands to provide a total of 33 analog 6 MHz channels, with a range of 30 to 50 km. These frequencies were allocated by the FCC in the 1970s for educational use (so most licenses are still held by schools—they can lease these to commercial companies). Using video compression, the 33 6-MHz channels could carry a total of 100 to 150 channels, which is enough to interest companies in offering services to compete with the local cable TV provider.

Important advantages over traditional cable TV include faster roll-out (no need for all that messy digging to bury cables or fiber) and possibly interactivity (two-way communication would be a major advantage, but initial installations will not have this capability).

Some communication providers use the MMDS for wireless Internet access. The MMDS band is used for high-speed downloading from the Internet (since it is broadcast-only, from the carrier to the users), and another band (such as 510 to 600 MHz in the UHF band) is used for receiving from the users.

Warp Drive Networks is a wireless ISP using MMDS. They are at *http://www.warp-drive.net*.

See **CATV**, **LMDS**, and **WIRELESS**.

MMS
Manufacturing Message Specification

An effort to use OSI protocols for industrial applications, such as electric utility equipment monitoring and control. Replaces the manufacturing automation (MAP) effort.

See **OSI**.

MMX
Matix Math Extensions

Intel's extension to their architecture to support multimedia, such as faster video (for image processing and video conferencing, for example) and 3-dimensional rendering (for games).

Specifications were first released in March 1996, and the first processor to get MMX support was an enhanced Pentium, released in January 1997, and simply called Pentium Processor with MMX Technology. That first processor ran at 166 MHz, and was called the P55C during development.

Intel says MMX is not an abbreviation for *Multimedia Extensions*—, even though it will provide substantial improvements in a Pentium (or other) processor's capability to handle multimedia. Some say MMX is actually for *Matrix Math Extensions*, since that is primarily what they are—extensions to the Pentium's architecture (57 new instructions, 8 new registers) to support processing matrices of numbers, as is required for real-time (that is, as fast as you need to hear and see it) audio and video compression and decompression and 3-dimensional graphics support (for example). Some say the reason why Intel denies MMX is an acronym for anything is because acronyms can't be trademarked.

Traditional 32-bit processors can add two 8-bit numbers by placing each of then at the lower-end of a 32-bit register. The upper 24 bits of the registers are not used, so a single ADD instruction (for example) adds two 8-bit numbers. In contrast, the 64-bit MMX registers are able to hold 8 separate 8-bit numbers (bytes), and these can be added to another 8 bytes in a single add operation. The 64-bit registers can also be used to simultaneously add 4 16-bit words or 2 32-bit longwords. These operations are called *single instruction, multiple data* (SIMD). Other MMX instructions include a multiply-accumulate function, which is a key operation in *digital signal processing* (DSP).

MMX also supports *masks* (processing only some of the data values in the 64-bit registers) and *saturating arithmetic* which ensures that the results of mathematical operations don't overflow the registers (for example, they just get set to the maximum non-overflow vale).

MMX only speeds processing for integer-math intensive programs, and only those that were written to take advantage of MMX.

For the initial MMX implementations, the 8 "new" MMX registers are actually the floating-point registers, so programmers have to ensure they don't try to use them for both functions simultaneously.

MMX should provide the hardware support that NSP needed.

MMX is implemented by some of Intel's competitors, however some don't mention is that some MMX implementations are different than others. For example, Intel's Pentium MMX and Pentium II can process two MMX instructions simultaneously (with some restrictions, such as only one multiply or shift or memory reference can be done at a time—that is Intel MMX can do two adds or subtracts simultaneously), but the AMD K6 and Cyrix 6x86MX can only process one MMX instruction at a time.

See **DSP**, **MULTIMEDIA**, **NSP**, **PC**, and **PENTIUM**.

MNP
Microcom Networking Protocol

A series of data communication–enhancing protocols developed by Microcom, Inc., that are usually embedded into modems (rather than being part of a PC's communication software). Because the newer protocols generally build on earlier ones, and offer more features, they are referred to as *levels* (or sometimes *classes*). All offer error-detection and -correction. Some are summarized below (and some don't exist).

MNP Level	Function
1	An asynchronous, character-oriented half-duplex protocol (like BISYNC) which provides error-detection and correction. Efficiency is about 70% (a 9,600 bit/s modem with MNP 1 will have a throughput of about 6,700 bits/s). Modems no longer support Class 1.
2	A full-duplex version of level 1. Has about 84% efficiency. Most modems support Class 2 as their simplest method of error correction.
3	A synchronous, bit-oriented version of level 2 (users still use asynchronous communications to the modem from their PC). Just as for HDLC, uses a 16-bit CRC for error-detection, and a flag character of 01111110_2 to delimit frames. Because start and stop bits do not need to be sent, the efficiency is greater than 100% (about 108%, so a 9,600 bit/s modem would have a throughput of about 10,300 bits/s).
4	An enhancement of level 3 that can dynamically adjust the frame size (to 32, 64, 128, 192 or 256 bytes) according to the detected error rate (they call this *Adaptive Packet Assembly*). Larger frames provide more efficiency (since there are more data bytes compared to the fixed number of protocol overhead bytes). But smaller frames are best when the error rate is high (so that fewer frames end up with at least one bit in error, and so that there is less to retransmit when an error does occur). The efficiency of this protocol is about 120%.
5	Adds adaptive data compression. The compression algorithm adjusts to the user's data, and the compression ratio achieved depends on the type of data. With very compressible files (such as word processing documents), data compression can be up to 2:1, providing a protocol efficiency of 200% (so two 9,600 bit/s MNP level 5 modems would have a throughput of 19,200 bits/s). However, the data compression algorithm can actually have an efficiency of less than 100% if the files are not compressible (such as executable program files), or have already been compressed by another program (such as pkzip). V.42*bis* is an ITU standard alternative to MNP level 5. V.42*bis*) has both a better compression algorithm (typically up to 4:1 compression), and it detects uncompressible files and disables its compression algorithm so it never has an efficiency less than 100%.

(table continued on next page)

MNP Level	Function
6	Automatically tries switching from V.22*bis* mode (which will also support Bell 212A and Bell 103) to V.27, V.29 and V.32), to provide the highest possible data transmission speed supported by both ends (they call this *universal link negotiation*). Half-duplex modems (such as V.27 and V.29 will be in this case, since only a one-pair dial-up circuit is used) require the terminals and host computers to raise their EIA-232 RTS line to transmit (and only one end can do this at a time). MNP level 6 simulates a full-duplex modem (they call this *statistical duplexing*) by allowing the EIA-232 devices to leave their RTS lines high all the time. The modems monitor which has more data to send, and automatically sets up the transmission in that direction until that data is sent. Nowadays, these are all quite useless features (the modem standards are completely full-duplex, and do all the speed negotiations too), but I suppose someone was quite proud of themselves once for getting all this to work. Also supports MNP level 5, and the lower levels too.
7	A data compression algorithm with an efficiency of up to 300% (that is, 3:1, as compared to MNP level 5's 2:1). The algorithm (which they describe as "an adapted Huffman encoding technique with a predictive Markov algorithm") tries to determine the type of data (word processing file, executable file, and so on) being sent, so it can set-up its compression tables sooner (rather than waiting to analyze streams of the data to build the tables). Still, V.42*bis* does 4:1, so who cares about this.
8	Adds the simulated full-duplex feature for V.29 modems to MNP level 7's enhanced data compression algorithm.
9	Piggybacks acknowledgments on user data, to reduce protocol overhead. Also, negative acknowledgment messages indicate which frames were lost, so retransmission is only of the corrupted and lost frames, rather than all frames since the first bad one. Also implements MNP level 7's enhanced data compression algorithm for V.32 modems and detects and works with V.27 and V.29 modems.
10	Adds features for poor and varying line qualities—such as would be encountered for data transmission using a modem connected to a cellular telephone (though this Class was initially developed for data transmission on overseas long distance calls). Will spend longer at initial connection time trying to establish the connection (in case the line is bad at that time), rather than giving up. Also, holds the connection open during the break in audio during a cell site hand-off. Link management idle packets are exchanged when there is no data to send to continuously monitor the line quality. Small frame sizes are used initially, and this is increased if the error rates permit. It quickly reduces the frame size when error rates increase (frame sizes of 8 to 256 bytes are supported). Speed, modulation method and transmit signal strength are changed during calls to accommodate changing line quality. They collectively call these *adverse channel enhancements* (ACE).

MNP levels 4 and 5 are by far the most common MNP levels implemented. They both use a block size of up to 256 characters.

The following points apply to data communication links using modems which use MNP 5 data compression:

▲ MNP 5 compresses data at up to a 2:1 ratio (so you can feed data at 19,200 bits/s into an MNP 5 9,600-bits/s modem), but the actual data compression ratio depends on the data—ASCII text (which is only 7-bit data, and has lots of "e"s, for example) will be much more compressible than an executable program file (which is 8-bit data and will likely have almost random bytes).

▲ You should set the PC's (or whatever is sending the data) ports (at both ends of the link) to at least twice the modem data-pump speed (the bit rate at which the modems actually are sending data). Otherwise, you don't get the full (or any) benefit of data compression.

▲ You must configure the PC's serial port for flow control (either x-on/x-off or RTS/CTS) so that the PC does not send data too fast when the data are not very compressible and to stop the data from the PCs while the modems retransmit during error correction. If the data are not compressible at all (for example, because they were already compressed with a program such as pkzip or lharc), then MNP 5 actually makes the data bigger. (V.42*bis* is smart enough to shut itself off if it detects that the data are not compressible.)

MNP 4 and 5 have been superseded by LAPM (which is part of the V.42 standard) and V.42*bis*. MNP 4 and 5 are only used if that is all the remote modem supports.

Microcom was bought by Compaq Computer Corporation in April 1997. They has an WWW server at *http://www.microcom.com*.

See **CRC**, **FLOW CONTROL**, **HDLC**, **LAPM**, **MODEM**, **V.42**, and **V.42BIS**.

MOBILE IP
Mobile Internet Protocol

An effort to enable a (likely wireless) TCP/IP device to roam (as cellular telephones do) across different subnets of an IP network.

This is handled by forwarding packets from the device's *home router* to its current (or *away*) *router*. As the mobile device finds it is in a different router's territory, it tells that router the address of the device's home router. The away router then sets up a connection to the device's home router and acknowledges to the device that the away router can forward packets between the device and its home router.

Changes to the standard TCP/IP protocol stacks in both the devices and the routers are required.

Developed by IBM.

See **IP**.

Mobitex

Ericsson's Eritel subsidiary's cellular land-radio-based packet-switched data communication system. Offered by RAM Mobile Data in the U.S., and Cantel AT&T in 8 cities (in 1996) Canada.

The raw data transmission bit rate was originally 8,000 bits/s (using 512-byte packets) for most installations (though some are as low as 1,200 bits/s), which provides a user data throughput of about 2.4 to 5 kbits/s, but this has been upgraded to 19,200 bits/s in some larger cities.

The required radio modem is called a *Mobidem*.

Usage charges are per kilobyte of data sent, rather than by minutes of connect time (as a circuit-switched service, such as GSM would charge).

More open that the competing Ardis system, since all specifications are developed by the *Mobitex Operators Association*. However, both Ardis and Mobitex are only popular for a few applications, such as tracking package deliveries. This is largely because the huge amount of custom software that must be written to interface to the radio network and terminals.

Was designed by L.M. Ericsson and Swedish Telecom. Uses 896 to 901 MHz and 935 to 940 MHz in North America.

Available in about 15 countries, but different frequencies are used in many countries, so roaming is complicated or not possible.

L.M. Ericsson has a WWW server at *http://www.ericsson.nl/*.

See **ARDIS**, **CDPD**, **ESMR**, **GSM**, **RAM MOBILE DATA**, and **WIRELESS**.

MODEM
Modulator/Demodulator

An electronic device that converts binary data (for example, the ±12 V EIA-232 signals from a PC's COM port) to analog tones and voltages that are suitable for transmission over an analog communications channel, such as standard dial-up or *leased line* telephone lines, or CATV cable.

Given the fixed 3,000-Hz bandwidth of typical POTS analog lines and the increasing power of *Digital Signal Processing* (DSP) ICs, newer modems use more complex types of modulation to provide faster data rates. The following table summarizes the types of dial-up (in contrast to leased line) modems.

Modulation	Data Rate (bits/s)	Comments
Bell 103	300	
Bell 212A	1,200	Usually compatible with V.22
V.22*bis*	2,400	
V.32	9,600	
V.32*bis*	14,400	Pre-V.34, nonstandard modulation, with fewer features than V.34
V.terbo	19,200	Pre-V.34, nonstandard modulation, with fewer features than V.34
V.FC	28,800	
V.34	28,800	Was called V.*fast* during development
V.34+	33,600	Also supports 31,200 bits/s
PCM	56,000	Standard V.34+ speeds are used for transmission from the user to the network

Current *external dial-up modems* (they are separate boxes that connect to your PC's serial COM port, through an EIA-232 cable) will usually handle both *synchronous* (as required by X.25 and IBM 3270 and 5250 protocols) and *asynchronous* (as used by standard PC serial COM ports and most bulletin board systems) data communications.

Internal modems (which are *printed circuit boards* that mount inside a PC and include a built-in serial COM port) are often asynchronous only.

Most current modems have both built-in V.42 error correction and V.42*bis* data compression.

Many current modems also have fax capability:

▲ Fax machines (and PC fax modems) use different types of modems than data modems; since a fax transmission is basically one-way during a call, half-duplex modems are used (they are less expensive).

▲ All current fax machines and modems that use standard telephone lines are *Group 3*. Most have an *Error Correction Mode* (ECM).

▲ Fax boards require a command interface for the PC to communicate with the fax modem. There are several such interfaces, but the most common is *Class 1*, which requires the host PC (and not the fax modem's on-board processor) to do most of the work (this provides the most flexibility and features, the lowest cost, and usually the best performance, since the PC's processor is far faster than any fax modem's dinky little single-chip controller).

At connection time, modems send tones to each other to negotiate the fastest mutually supported modulation method that will work over whatever quality line has been established for that call.

If you wanted the best modem on your block, you would want one with the following:

▲ *V.34+ modulation*, which sends data at up to 33,600 bits/s, depending on how good a phone connection you get and whether the other end has an equally fast modem (or maybe one of the 56 kbit/s modems once there is a standard).

▲ *V.42 error detection and correction*, which specifies both LAPM and MNP 4 so that you will be compatible with whatever the modem at the other end may support.

▲ *V.42 bis data compression* and maybe MNP 5 data compression too—in case that's all the modem at the other end has.

▲ *V.17 fax modulation*, which sends fax images at 14,400 bits/s (if the fax machine or modem at the other end has this modulation and the connection is good enough) or slower (most commonly V.29 9,600 bits/s).

▲ The fax modem or software should also implement ECM.

The "universe" of dial-up modems and features is shown in the accompanying figure.

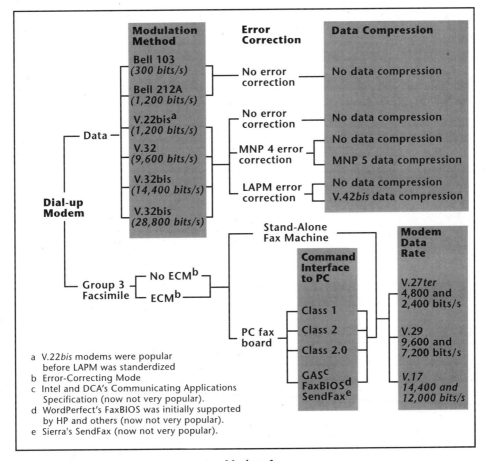

Modem-1

Most telephone line modems are based on ICs made by Rockwell International. U.S. Robotics is a major supplier of consumer-type modems (*http://www.usr.com*).

See **S56K MODEM, ASYNCHRONOUS, BAUD, CAS, CATV, DCE1, DTE, EIA/TIA-232, EIA/TIA--TSB37A, FAX, FULLDUPLEX, MNP, PCM, POTS, ROCKWELL INTERNATIONAL, RPI, SYNCHRO-NOUS, V.8** through **V.120**, and **WAN**.

Monitors

UNIX workstations often have 16- or 20-inch monitors, with a resolution of $1,152 \times 900$ or $1,280 \times 1,024$ (horizontal × vertical). For comparison, a PC's VGA is 640×480, Super VGA (SVGA) is 800×600 and XGA is $1,024 \times 768$.

Images to test the quality, and to help adjust your monitor, are available from Sonera Technologies at *http://www.displaymate.com*. Equipment to measure the quality of a monitor's display is available from *http://www.microvsn.com*.

See **CRT**, **HDTV**, **VGA**, and **VIDEO**.

Moore's Law

In 1965, Gordon E. Moore was the director of the research and development laboratories at Fairchild Semiconductor Corp—he was co-founder of Fairchild in 1957, and in 1968 he was a co-founder of Intel Corporation, along with Robert N. Noyce). And he was asked to write an article for the 35th anniversary issue (dated April 19, 1965) of the (then) key industry magazine *Electronics*. The article was to make predictions on the future of semiconductor components over the next 10 years. Moore titled the article "Cramming More Components Onto Integrated Circuits". Just to put things into perspective, transistors were invented in 1947 by several researchers at Bell Laboratories. But these were a type called *point contact*, and were not suitable for building as part of a monolithic integrated circuit, where the transistor (a contraction of the terms transfer and resistor) is built on a flat die of silicon, and can be connected to adjacent components through processes of masking and chemical etching and plating.

Starting in 1959, with the first IC transistor (it was a large type called a *planar transistor*), and seeing that in 1964 there were 32, and later in 1965 they expected their lab to have 60-component (adding up both the transistors and the resistors) integrated circuits ready for commercial production. Moore saw that the number of components for minimum component cost had doubled every year. He then predicted that this would continue for 10 years (which was the scope of the article, and a thousand-fold increase), and require a die about 6 mm square.

As it turned out, that prediction was very accurate, and soon after 1975 it came to be called Moore's Law. Some say that the prediction was actually self-fulfilling, since companies have begun to expect that this is almost a law of physics, and make product plans and designs assuming that the many aspects of technology that need to be advanced to realize the goal will be in place in time. While there have often been indications that some physical or cost constraint would affect this prediction. As it has turned out, as each predicted limit gets closer, some brilliant person or company finds a solution.

For example, for many years, there have been predictions that there will be some physical limit reached (such as the minimum width of the interconnections between the transistors), which will slow and eventually stop this predicted increase. Technology keeps advancing, and the year when this limit is be reached keeps getting pushed farther into the future (in 1996 Intel predicted that the limit for the standard Silicon-based IC process would be reached in the year 2017).

In 1975 (as IC component counts increased past 64,000 transistors), Moore noticed that the growth was slowing, and Moore revised his law to a doubling every 2 years. Analysis of the growth since 1959 shows that it has been very close to doubling a every 18 months. Also, it has turned out that microprocessor processing speed has doubled every 18 months or so (some would argue that depending on the components and data you choose, this period is somewhere between 18 and 25 months, which is a wide-enough range that the only "law" is that there is an exponential component to the increase).

Other IC-related characteristics that have exponentially increased for many generations include the following:

▲ The density of ICs (that is, the number of components per unit area). It has turned out that the line widths (the minimum dimension of IC conductors) has been reduced by a factor of 0.7 every 3 years. Since component density decreases to the square of this (which is 0.49), density has doubled (or the same number of components fit in half the space) every 3 years. Reducing the size of a given IC is an important process improvement, since it typically increases the yield (percentage of good *dies* per wafer), since there are typically a predictable number of defective spots on a wafer, and the smaller the die, the less chance it will have a defective spot on it. Typical yields for mature processes are about 90%.

▲ DRAM density has always been greater than microprocessors (due to the very regular nature of a memory IC, where a basic circuit is repeated, and designing to reduce interconnection and waste space is a high priority). However, the slope of DRAM density increases closely matches that for microprocessors (that is, DRAM density also doubles about every 18 months).

▲ The cost of a given amount of CPU power is halved every 18 months (or so). The produces new markets where processing can be used. Video games and electronic thermostats are examples of this.

▲ Some have noted that unfortunately, the size of computer programs has increased faster than Moore's law.

▲ The cost of IC fabrication plants has approximately matched the increase in IC density ($14 million in 1966 to 1.5 billion in 1995 to $3 billion in 1998.

As IC density has increased, speed increases (there is lower capacitance and shorter circuit distances), power is reduced (lower currents are needed to switch the smaller transistors) and reliability improves. That is, there has been little need for trade-offs, most things get better when IC sizes are reduced.

Interestingly, disk drive capacity seems to increase closer to linearly—and this has proved to be adequate. Also, Moore has observed that in 1997 the semiconductor industry produced about 1 quintillion transistors and he notes "that's at least as many as all the ants on earth".

See **DISK DRIVE, FAB, INTEL,** and **SI.**

MOTD
Message of the Day

A (hopefully) brief message displayed to users after they log in to a UNIX computer. The text is stored in the file /etc/motd and typically concerns system administration announcements such as new features or procedures.

See **UNIX**.

Motif

OSF's (which developed it) *graphical user interface* (therefore sometimes called OSF/Motif), which is sometimes called a *window manager*. Motif is widely licensed by OSF to others. It is both a standard API (and GUI) and a GUI alone (the "look-and-feel" to the end user), since there are other APIs, such as Tcl/Tk, that can provide a Motif-like user interface (almost the same appearance and behavior).

The Motif API is a standard tool kit for GUI applications that works at the level of menus and icons.

Motif is based on work by Hewlett-Packard and DEC and is also promoted by IBM. (These three companies are therefore major proponents of the technology.)

Motif uses the *X Window System* as its communication protocol and low-level (that is, drawing boxes and the like) display interface.

Competed with, and won out over, OPENLOOK, perhaps because Motif:

▲ Is not controlled by a single company

▲ Always had solid support (Sun initially supported something else called NeWS and then OPENLOOK)

▲ Looks more like Microsoft Windows

▲ Has always had a nicer, three-dimensional look

▲ Can have keyboard keys assigned to specific functions

▲ Had a single set of APIs (which was an advantage while it competed with OPENLOOK)

The OSF has some Motif information at *http://www.osf.org/motif/index.html*.

See **API**, **CDE**, **COSE**, **GUI**, **HP**, **OPENLOOK**, **OSF**, **TCL-TK**, **X-OPEN**, and **X WINDOW SYSTEM**.

Motorola, Inc.

A really big company. They were founded in Chicago, by Paul V. Galvin in 1928, as the Galvin Manufacturing Corporation. Their first product was a *battery eliminator*, that enabled home radios to be powered from the 110 V AC household power, rather than from batteries. In the 1930s, they began to sell the first mass-produced automobile radios under the brand name Motorola, as the name combined the concepts of motion and sound—"Victrola" was the common (and trademarked) name for a phonograph at the time. The company then began manufacturing home and police radios, and the name of the company was changed to Motorola, Inc. in 1947.

Motorola's web site is at *http://www.motorola.com*.

See **S88OPEN**, **AMPS**, **ARDIS**, **ESMR**, **POWERPC**, **SATELLITE**, and **SUN**.

Mouse

The mouse (so-called, likely because the shape, and the wire coming out of it reminded someone of a mouse) was invented in 1963 by Dr. Douglas Engelbart, while he was at Stanford Research Institute. His mouse was a wooden block with orthogonal wheels driving multi-turn potentiometers that created voltages proportional to the mouse's X and Y position. This mouse was patented in 1970, but Douglas gets no royalties, as the patent was assigned to his employer. At the Xerox Research Laboratories, the mouse was improved to what we now recognize—usually a rotating ball that drives shaft encoders which produce pulses as the mouse is moved.

Douglas Engelbart currently co-runs the Bootstrap Institute, at *http://www.boostrap.org*.

See **IRQ**.

MP
Multilink Point-to-point Protocol

Also called MLPPP.

See **MLPPP**.

MPEG-2 Audio Stream Layer-3 Compression

The type of digitized audio compression specified for use with MPEG-2.

See **MPEG**.

MPC
Multimedia PC

A certification from the *Multimedia PC* Marketing Council (an independent special interest group of the *Software Publishers Association*) that a PC meets minimum requirements suitable for multimedia. The initial specifications (*Level 1*, released in 1990) were often criticized as not being powerful enough, hence the *Level 2* MPC specification (released in 1993).

All levels require at least the following components:

- ▲ 2-button mouse
- ▲ 101-key keyboard
- ▲ 1 serial port, and 1 parallel port
- ▲ 1 MIDI I/O port and 1 joystick port
- ▲ headphones or speakers

The following table lists the minimum requirements for the other components required.

	MPC Level	
	1	**2**
CPU	16 MHz 80386SX	25 MHz 486SX minimum
RAM	2 Mbytes	4 Mbytes (8 Mbytes recommended)
Hard disk	30 Mbytes	160 Mbytes minimum (340 Mbytes recommended), and a $3\frac{1}{2}$" floppy diskette drive too
CD-ROM	150-kbytes/s transfer rate using less than 40% of CPU time, seek time under 1 second	300-kbytes/s (double-speed) transfer rate using no more than 60% of CPU time, 400-ms maximum access time, XA-ready, multisession-capable
Sound	8 bits per sample, output at 22,050 and 11,025 samples/s, input at 11,025 samples/s	16 bits per sample, output and input at 44,100, 22,050 and 11,025 samples/s stereo sound (.WAV digital audio) and MIDI recording and playback; also CD-ROM XA-audio recommended
Video	16- and 256-color VGA (640×480 pixels)	65,536-color VGA (640×480 pixels), 1.2-Mpixel/s writing speed with less than 40% CPU utilization recommended[a]

a. Provides 15 frames per second motion video at 320×240 pixel resolution and 256 colors.

Multisession-capable means that the CD-ROM can read files added incrementally, such as those produced by Kodak's Photo-CD system.

CD-ROM XA-ready (extended architecture) means that the CD-ROM drive can read XA CD-ROM files (a standardized way of playing back video clips synchronized with compressed audio).

The MPC Level 3 (sometimes called MPC-3) requirements are listed below.

▲ 75 MHz Pentium with hardware-assisted MPEG-1 and no level 2 cache, or a 100 MHz Pentium with 256 kbyte level 2 cache and only software MPEG-1. Equivalent performance processors of other types are also allowed (a test suite is specified to verify the performance).

▲ 8 Mbytes RAM and 540 Mbyte hard drive (with at least 500 Mbytes available). Laptop PCs don't require the $3\frac{1}{2}$" floppy diskette drive. Many performance specifications are given for the hard disk drive, such as greater than 4,000 RPM).

▲ 4x (600 kbytes/s) CD-ROM drive (many performance specifications are given, such as seek times less than 250 ms.

▲ In addition to the previous rates, sampling at 16 and 8 kbits/s. Also audio is recommended to be full-duplex. Speaker performance and connector details are detailed

▲ Video to support 352×240 pixel updates at 30 frames per second, with 15 bits per pixel.

▲ 16550AF UART, with support for 115,200 bits/s required for serial port.

▲ If a modem is provided, it must be at least V.34 and support for data and fax. The driver must support TAPI.

▲ USB is allowed for keyboard, mouse and joystick.

Further information and details are at *http://www.spa.org/mpc*.

See **CDROM**, **GAME PORT**, **MIDI**, **MPEG**, **MULTIMEDIA**, **PCM**, **TAPI**, **USB**, **VGA**, and **VIDEO**.

MPEG
Moving Picture Coding Experts Group

A committee of the ISO and IEC that has produced an international standard for *lossy data compression* and storage of full-motion video and audio. The standard only describes how the compressed data is represented, manufacturers are free to implement both the compression and decompression systems any way they want. MPEG tries to fit the best quality picture into a given bandwidth (knowing that when it comes down to implementing it, there will be a fixed bandwidth available to carry the bits—for example, from your cable TV company, or through your satellite dish).

Interpolating between frames is used to provide better compression than the JPEG method, but this prevents the MPEG method from being used in frame-by-frame applications, such as editing and switching (MPEG can only do moving pictures).

MPEG-1 (first released in 1991) is intended for computers, games, and set-top boxes (that is, a box that sits on top of your television, perhaps bringing video from the information highway—whatever that turns out to be). It only supports progressive (not interlaced) scanning, and the video was initially to be 30 frames per second, and have a resolution of 352 × 240 pixels (horizontal by vertical)—which is called the *small image format* (SIF). Using specialized hardware (an MPEG decompression IC), it would provide near VHS-quality desktop video (that is, it is almost as good as playing a rented videotape on a home VCR) at a data rate of 1.2 Mbits/s (which is 150 kbytes/s—the data rate from a standard single-speed CD-ROM player—which were common when MPEG-1 was released). When finally released (they worked on the standard for about 4 years), MPEG-1 supported higher resolutions and faster data rates.

MPEG-2 has the following characteristics:

▲ It was initially intended for use with broadcast-quality (that is, really expensive and very high-quality), interlaced (that is, supporting standard television) applications, requiring a compressed data rate of 4 to about 15 Mbits/s (the original uncompressed data often has a bit rate of 270 Mbits/s). However, recent rapid hardware advances have enabled MPEG-2 decompression to be provided on consumer electronic equipment.

▲ Is typically used to provide compression by a factor of 25 to 50 (the amount of compression largely depends on the CPU time of the compressor. A high-quality compressed video signal, as might be used on CATV systems typically requires 5 to 8 Mbit/s.

▲ Supports both progressive and interlaced scanning, and a maximum picture size of 4,096 × 4,096 pixels (though 352 × 352 is a common implementation for PC monitors)

▲ It defines a transport (protocol) for the compressed data. It supports functions such as adding closed-captioning and different language channels. The compressed data is sent in blocks of 188 bytes (that is, the transport uses a packet size of 188 bytes), which was selected partially because it is a nice multiple of the payload size (47 bytes) of ATM adaption layer 1 (AAL 1) which was expected to be used for such information (so 4 frames of 47 bytes would carry a 188-byte MPEG-2 data block). As it turned out, AAL 5 was later determined to be adequate for MPEG-2 traffic, and this has a payload size of 48 bytes per cell, but it was too late to change to 192-byte MPEG-2 packets.

▲ MPEG-1 is a subset of MPEG-2, and MPEG-2 decoders can decode MPEG-1 bit-streams.

MPEG compression is based on the same three components commonly used to represent color television—the luminance (Y) and chrominance (C_r and C_b components, which are the difference of the luminance from the red and the luminance from the blue, respectively). It turns out that the human eye is more sensitive to brightness changes over short distances than it is to color differences. MPEG compression takes advantage of this, by sampling the chrominance information at a lower frequency than the luminance information, as described below.

First, the image is digitized (typically into 8-bit samples of the luminance and the two chrominance components). Then the luminance information is divided into a matrix of 16 horizontal pixel by 16 line *macroblocks* (that is, a squares of 256 pixels).

Typically, "4:2:2" encoding is used (largely because that is what ITU Recommendation 601 specifies—since ITU 601 is popular in production environments it minimizes the loss in quality when multiple conversions are required). For MPEG-2, the "4" refers to 14.5 MHz, which was the original sampling frequency to be used for the luminance digitizing. However, this was changed to 13.5 MHz since it is related to both the 625 and 525 lines per frame of NTSC and PAL source material. The subsequent "2" indicates that the chrominance information is sampled horizontally at half the rate of the luminance information, and the last "2" means that the chrominance information for the next line is handled the same way as just described. This means that the complete 4:2:2 macroblock is comprised of 6 blocks of 64 pixels of information. 4 blocks are the 256 pixels of luminance (Y) information from the 16×16 original picture. And 2 blocks are each of the C_r and C_b 8×8 blocks from the original 16×16 pixels of chrominance information.

There are other encoding methods. For example, until January 1996 4:2:0 was specified. For progressively scanned frames, this interpolates chrominance values from two adjacent lines, therefore halving the number of lines of chrominance values output. The "0" in the encoding method notation refers to the eliminating of every second chrominance line.

MPEG video data is composed of *Groups of Pictures* (GOPs), which each begin with an I frame, followed by P and B frames—which are all described below:

▲ I (*intra*) key frames (so called, since they only use information within that frame, and do not reference any in the adjacent frames) are compressed by using JPEG methods, and used to support quickly scanning through a file and as reference points for the adjacent B and P frames. (I frames are descriptively, but incorrectly sometimes called independent frames. An I frame is sent at the beginning of each scene change (or switch to a commercial), and periodically after that. The standard only suggests an I frame at least every 1,024 frames, but I frames are usually sent much more often than that. For example, low-speed video conferencing typically sends one every second, and for HDTV an I frame is sent every 400 to 500 ms. For example, in broadcast television, an I frame would be sent every 13 frames (which is just less than a $\frac{1}{2}$-second)—otherwise people need to wait too long to see the picture when flipping channels, and excessive bit errors cause the picture to go away for too long.

▲ *P* (*forward predicted*) frames are generated based on the most recent previous P or I frame (and specifies the difference from that). It is generated by comparing redundancies in images that are up to several frames apart (for example, looking for blocks of video data that are the same as portions of previous I frames, because that part of the picture moved, but did not change shape).

▲ *B* (*bidirectional predicted* or *interpolated*) frames are generated by looking for redundancies in the immediately preceding and also succeeding (called *future*) P or I frames (P and I frames are therefore called *anchor frames*). This is sort of like taking an average of the adjacent P and I frames, and specifying the difference (*error term*) from that. To make the job of the MPEG decoder easier (that is, to reduce the cost of an HDTV television), the future P or I frames used to generate B frames are sent before those B frames. The decoder then temporarily stores the P and I frames until after the B frame is received, decoded and displayed. This out-of-order transmission requires that the transmission be delayed slightly.

While any number of B and P frames can be used, typical encoders for broadcast television will produce a sequence such as IBBPBBPBBPBBP, which is called a *group of pictures* (GOP). And each "BBP" frame sequence is called a sub-GOP. As described above, the GOP is typically sent as IPBBPBBPBBPBB. The GOP is what gets decoded as a unit. The GOP always starts with an I frame (since the decoding of I frames does not depend on any past or future frames).

Compression methods used include the following:

▲ Removing high-frequency components, using a methods based on *discrete cosine transforms* (DCTs) and other complex mathematical algorithms.

▲ *Motion vectors* where the movement of a previously-sent block of pixels (either because the camera panned, or because something in the picture moved) is described (rather resending all the pixels). In addition, an *error term* can be sent. This describes the difference between a simple movement of the referenced block of pixels and what actually happened.

Compression acts on the 8 × 8 pixel luminance and chrominance blocks. If there is no difference from the previous macroblock, then the macroblock does not need to be sent at all.

For HDTV, where there is a fixed maximum bit rate allowed, the quantization (number of levels used for the digitizing of the luminance and chrominance) is dynamically adjusted to ensure that the overall digitized bit rate stays near the maximum allowed. Therefore, slowly moving scenes will be encoded with slightly better resolution, and quickly moving scenes will be encoded with less resolution. A buffer (specified by the ATSC to be 7,995 kbytes) allows for the digitized bit rate to briefly exceed the 19 Mbits/s which the 6 MHz broadcast television channel can carry.

MPEG-1 competes with AVI video.

For normal home use, MPEG-2 encodes at 3 Mbits/s, so an average 2-hour movie would require 2.7 Gbytes of storage.

MPEG-1 supports only 2 audio channels—the traditional left and right stereo.

MPEG-2 audio is sometimes called MP3 (for MPEG-2 layer-3). It requires a bit rate of 384 kbits/s and supports 5.1 (sometimes written 5+1) channels, which is comprised of the following (this has similar capability, but is different than the Dolby AC-3 method used for HDTV):

▲ left and right, in front of you, as in traditional stereo

▲ center, also in front of you

▲ left and right surround, these speakers would be located behind you, and fill-in the sound beside and behind you

▲ low frequency enhancement, the location of the speaker does not matter much, and such frequencies are very non-directional (the fill the room)—the "+1" or ".1" refers to this channel

The Open MPEG-1 MCI (*Media Control Interface*) specification is promoted by the OM-1 Foundation, and is the API for playing back MPEG-1 video.

Pronounced *EM-peg*, and now somewhat more popular an acronym since it (and JPEG) won an Emmy from the U.S. Television Broadcasting Academy in 1996. MPEG began in 1988, and is officially called the Joint ISO/IEC Technical Committee on Information Technology (JTC 1), Subcommittee 29, Working Group 11 (wow, that's fancier than a person who has two middle names).

Most of MPEG's development happens at the Centro Studi e Laboratori Telecomunicazion SpA (CSELT), which was founded in the 1960s as part of Italy's national telecommunications company STET.

MPEG-1 is standardized in ISO/IEC 11172 (which was released in 1993). MPEG-2 is standardized in the ISO/IEC 13818 series of standards (which is the same as ITU H.222).

MPEG-3 was initially to work on coding standards for higher-quality video (such as HDTV), using a bit rate of 40 Mbits/s. However, this was found to be unnecessary, as HDTV could be compressed to fit a standard 6 MHz television channel. So MPEG-3's work was included in MPEG-2, and the next version of MPEG is MPEG-4.

MPEG-4 is to cover the transmission of motion video at lower bit-rates, as would be required over the Internet. It is also to support 3-dimensional images and include capabilities for the user to move around a scene, and to pan, mix, zoom and replay images. MPEG-7 is to cover support for multimedia.

A very good MPEG home page is at *http://www.mpeg.org/~tristan/MPEG/MPEG-content.html*. The MPEG FAQ is at *http://www.crs4.it/luigi/MPEG/mpegfaq.html*. There is also MPEG information at *http://bmrc.berkeley.edu/projects/mpeg*, *http://www.netvideo.com/technology/technology.html*, *http://www.cablelabs.com/PR/950327mpeg_ipr.html* and *http://www.sarnoff.com/mpeg/test/bitstreams*. The best MPEG home page is the one supported by the father of MPEG himself, Leonardo Chiariglione, at *http://drogo.cselt.stet.it/mpeg/*.

See **AVI**, **CCIR**, **CDROM**, **COLOUR**, **H.261**, **H.310**, **HDTV**, **JPEG**, **LOSSY DATA COMPRESSION**, **NTSC**, **VHS**, **VIDEO**, **VRML**, and **YUV**.

MP-MLQ
Multipulse Maximum Likelihood Quantization

A method of low bit-rate audio digitization and compression that is well-suited to multiple compression/decompression cycles (which is important for larger networks, where you can't always get everywhere in one digitization/compression hop). Compared to other speech compression methods, such as G.728 and G.729, MP-MLQ is also well-suited to compressing non-speech signals, such as music.

G.723 uses MP-MLQ at compressed speech bit rates of 5,300 and 6,300 bits/s. G.723 is the voice digitizing method specified for H.324, and is optional for H.320, H.321, H.322 and H.323.

Developed primarily by AudioCodes Ltd.

Further information is available at *http://www.audiocodes.com*.

See **LOSSY DATA COMPRESSION** and **PCM**.

MPOA
Multiprotocol Over ATM

MPOA provides a high-performance, low-latency (as required for ATM's high speeds, and as may not be possible from conventional router technology) way of routing multiple protocols (more than just IP) across ATM networks, or between different VLANs on the same network.

Using *LAN* emulation (and other methods), ATM networks can carry traffic from non-ATM devices (such as those on Ethernet LANs), and MPOA can provide routing between these LANs as well.

MPOA uses a *route server* architecture, in that a central machine (the MPOA server) tracks all network connectivity, and VLANs and ATM hosts (the MPOA clients) consult that machine to get a route. MPOA clients can either be *edge devices* (they interface to non-ATM networks and devices) or native ATM devices.

MPOA was written so that the MPOA clients could be inexpensively implemented—typically on an ATM adapter card or *ATM* edge device.

See **ATM** (*Asynchronous Transfer Mode*), **PNNI**, **ROUTER**, and **VLAN**.

MPP
Massively Parallel Processing

At least 64 processors (each with local memory) grouped together to work on a large computational problem.

For very specialized applications (such as searching databases or processing graphical images), this can produce huge performance gains. For applications that cannot be so easily split into separate tasks, the communications required between processors usually result in this not being the best computing technology choice.

See **FLOP**, and **SMP2** (*Symmetric Multiprocessing*).

MPR II

A standard limiting the electromagnetic emissions of computer equipment.

A voluntary (non-mandatory) standard first published as MPR I by SWEDAC (the Swedish Board for Technical Accreditation) and MPR (the Swedish National Board for Measurement and Testing) in 1987. It specifies the maximum levels of EMF emissions allowed for computer monitors (sometimes called CRTs or VDTs).

To pass MPR I, the EMFs in the range of 1 kHz to 400 kHz were measured at a distance of 50 cm at 16 equally-spaced intervals around the monitor (that is, every $22\frac{1}{2}°$). These measurements were then repeated for a total of 5 planes, and the maximum measurement could be 50 nT (peak). Since these frequencies mostly overlap the VLF (very low frequency) band (which is 300 Hz and up to 30 kHz), these measurements are often called the VLF measurements.

On July 1, 1991 the MPR II standard was released. It is much more comprehensive, as summarized below.

▲ In *band 2* (as they call it, which is 2 kHz to 400 kHz), the maximum emission is 25 nT (RMS). Again, magazines usually refer to this as the VLF measurement.

▲ In *band 1* (5 Hz to 2 kHz), the maximum emission allowed is 250 nT (RMS). This is usually referred to as the ELF measurement, even though ELF is usually defined as frequencies below 300 Hz.

▲ The measurements are again taken at 16 equally-spaced intervals around the monitor, but on a total of 3 planes, which are 25 cm apart.

▲ Guidelines are included for visual factors, such as the focus and character distortion.

▲ Maximum allowable electric fields are also specified. Meeting these typically requires a conductive surface on the CRT (which is grounded) and metal shielding for the CRT's high-voltage power supply (and usually a conductive coating on the inside of the plastic enclosure).

Since higher frequencies contain more energy, the allowed emissions are lower for the VLFs than the ELFs.

The RMS value of a signal is the square root of the average of the squares of the peak values of the signal (as it changes with time). It turns out that this measurement is a more meaningful representation of the energy in a signal which continuously changes (such as a sine wave). The physical analogy is that the RMS value of a signal equals the voltage of a DC (that is, constant) value that would produce the same amount of work (such as heat a resistor). The "110 V AC" from a standard wall receptacle is actually the RMS voltage (the actual peak voltage is 1.414 times this, so long as the voltage is a sine wave). It is not known whether the harmful effects (if there are any) of EMFs also follows this rule. The EMF limits allowed are mostly based on what is technically achievable for mass-produced electronic equipment, and what is measurable. The limits are not based on biological or other medically-determined values, since no one knows what these are.

Another standard (which requires lower EMF emissions) is often called TCO.

See **CRT**, **DPMS**, **ELF**, **EMF**, **TCO**, **T**, and **VLF**.

MPS
Multiprocessing Specification

Intel Corp.'s specification for the hardware support needed for SMP systems with up to 4 (initially Pentium Pro) processors.

MPS specifies that each of the processors will share the main memory. Therefore, only a single copy of the operating system is needed, and the system basically runs simply like a faster version of a single-processor system. MPS also specifies I/O symmetry, which means that any processor can receive and handle interrupts.

Processors may have separate L2 caches—but this requires the addition of hardware to ensure *cache coherency*. That is, if one processor writes to memory, but this is only cached in the L2 cache, and not yet written to main memory, if another processor reads that main memory location then the second processor would not read the updated information (because the first processor has not yet written its cache to main memory). The solution is that hardware detects this situation, stalls the second processor, and forces the first processor to write its cache to main memory. A method for handling this is called *MESI* (an abbreviation of the four possible states of cache's data—*modified*, *exclusive*, *shared* and *invalid*).

See **PENTIUM PRO**, and **SMP2** (*Symmetric Multiprocessing*).

MPTN
Multi-Protocol Transport Network

IBM's software that translates transport-layer software from one protocol to another transport protocol so that only one transport protocol need be supported on WANs.

Initial uses will be to translate (rather than the less-efficient *encapsulate*) TCP/IP to SNA and SNA to TCP/IP. The most common use will likely be to carry SNA packets over TCP/IP, so that WANs only need support TCP/IP.

Support for NetBIOS, AppleTalk, IPX, and DECnet IV is expected.

MPTN can be software on end-systems or on gateways. MPTN does not translate higher-level protocols (such as CPI-C or RPC), so end-systems must still be compatible at layers above the transport layer.

MPTN is supported under OS/2 and on IBM's 6611 multi-protocol router.

See **CPIC**, **ENCAPSULATION**, **RPC**, and **TCP/IP**.

MS
Most Significant

The upper bytes or digits. For example, the MS digit of the number 832 is 8.

See **BIG ENDIAN**, **LITTLE ENDIAN**, and **LSB**.

MSAT
Mobile Satellite

A Canadian-developed geosynchronous satellite offering circuit-switched data, paging, and voice communications anywhere in North America (including the Arctic, and the nearby coastal waters). Packet-switched data and dispatch services will be offered later. The service

is expected to be especially popular for its coverage of large, lightly-populated areas where other forms of wireless communications, such as cellular, are not available or economical to offer. Trucking companies and remote mining camps are expected to be a large part of the customer base. Other applications will include equipment monitoring and location tracking. Became operational in April 1996.

Has a capacity of 1,800 simultaneous telephone conversations, which will be charged per minute of usage. "Telephones" (which are the size of a small suitcase) require a small dish antenna, and both fixed and mobile units are available.

Since the satellite is geosynchronous (so that only a single satellite is required), it must be in a geosynchronous orbit, which means that there will be about a 480 ms delay for round-trip signals. This is undesirable for many interactive data applications, so *low earth orbiting* satellites may be more desirable for these applications.

Initially, paging will be done to truckers using a converter mounted in the truck which retransmit the satellite's transmit frequency at standard paging frequencies, so that standard pagers can be used.

TMI Communications (a subsidiary of BCE Inc.) runs the system, and service is available through Glentel Inc. and Mobility Satellite. Initially, the service used a satellite owned by American Mobile Satellite Corp. The service is now provided by the $220 million Canadian-owned MSat-1 satellite, which was placed into orbit on April 20, 1996 by an Ariane rocket. The satellites were built by Spar Aerospace Ltd. and Hughes Aircraft Co., and now provide backup services to each other.

Some further information is available at *http://www.bellmobility.ca*.

See **SATELLITE**.

MTA
Message Transfer Agent

A computer that transfers X.400 messages between mail systems.

See **UA**, **SMTP**, and **X.400**.

MTBF
Mean Time Between Failures

Roughly, the average time (typically measured in hours) before the equipment will fail.

More precisely, it is the time when half of the equipment has failed, and the other half has not yet failed (there is a difference between these two definitions if the equipment does not fail at a constant rate).

Nonetheless, the number can be somewhat meaningless in predicting how the equipment will behave for your installation, since other factors such as ambient temperature, whether the equipment is powered off frequently or for long periods of time, and whether lightning storms are common will dramatically affect equipment failure rate.

The term *Mean Time To Repair* (MTTR) is (roughly) the amount of time it takes to fix the equipment. Again, if you don't have the needed spare parts, or take a long time to identify which unit is defective, then this number is also a bit meaningless.

The numbers are useful for historical analysis, for example of equipment repair histories, or to compare potential designs.

See **SIX QUALITY**.

Multicast

Sending a message which is addressed so it will be received by a pre-defined group of recipients. Most LANs protocols support this.

For WANs to support conferencing, the routers require support for Multicasting if the WAN is to be used efficiently (otherwise, the same message must be sent as many times as there are remote users). Many networks (such as frame relay) and protocols (such as TCP/IP) are being augmented with the capability.

See **FRAME**, **IP MULTICAST**, **MBONE**, **MULTIMEDIA**, **PCS** (*Personal Conferencing Specification*), **PUSH**, and **T.120**.

MULTICAST IP
Internet Protocol Multicast

Another way of saying IP Multicast.

See **IP MULTICAST**.

Multicast Backbone

See **MBONE**.

Multimedia

Literally "many media," for example, using sound, pictures, and text to (hopefully) make a more effective, understandable, or memorable presentation or conference.

To support multimedia, networks must provide:

▲ *Scalable* bandwidth (as new users and applications require connectivity, the network must support ever-increasing traffic loads)

▲ Consistent *Quality of Service*; that is, the error rate (usually due to dropped packets), network latency (typically less than 400 ms, round-trip), and network throughput must be selectable (according to the needs of the application) and predictable

▲ *Multicast* routing, to efficiently support *one-to-many*-type traffic

While ATM is designed to provide these features, other technologies (such as IP multicast, routers with support for priority queuing, and RSVP) can (hopefully) support multimedia over existing networks and at lower cost.

Multimedia traffic has characteristics such as:

▲ *One-to-one* (point-to-point) or *one-to-many* (point-to-multipoint)

▲ Interactive (bidirectional) or playback (one-way)

Multimedia PC

Some example uses, and the quality of service required to provide the required data communications, are shown in the table below.

		Playback	Real-Time Interactive
Point-to-Point	Example use	Multimedia mail	Self-paced training
	Quality of service required	Available bit rate	Variable bit rate
Point-to-Multipoint	Example use	LAN TV	Desktop conferencing
	Quality of service required	Constant bit rate	Variable bit rate, low latency

Some further characteristics of the types of traffic are the following:

▲ *Constant bit rate*: traffic such as that from digitized audio and video that requires a certain minimum data rate (the digitization rate) and does not benefit from additional bandwidth

▲ *Variable bit rate*: traffic such as interactive terminal sessions (telnet traffic), which are very bursty in nature

▲ *Available bit rate*: file transfers, and other applications that simply run, and likely complete, faster as they get more bandwidth

See **S802.9A**, **S1394**, **ATM** (*Asynchronous Transfer Mode*), **IP MULTICAST**, **ISOCHRONOUS**, **FDDI**, **FDDI-II**, **LATENCY**, **MIME**, **MULTICAST**, **MPC**, **PACE**, **PCM**, **PRIORITIZATION**, **RSVP**, **RTP**, **QOS**, and **QTC**.

Multimedia PC

See **MPC**.

Multiple Master

Adobe Systems, Inc.'s extension to its *Type 1* font format that supports very flexible font modification (for example, reducing the serifs, compressing the text, making the stroke slightly bolder) while maintaining high quality.

The intent is to facilitate document distribution and maintain the look and paging of documentation without having to distribute all the fonts.

See **ACROBAT**, **OUTLINE FONT**, **POSTSCRIPT TYPE 1 FONTS**, and **SUPERATM**.

Multiprocessing

See **SMP2** (*Symmetric Multiprocessing*).

Multipulse-Maximum Likelihood Quantization

See **MPMLQ**.

Multitasking

See **WINX WINDOWS APIS**.

Multithreading

See **WINX WINDOWS APIS**.

MVIP
Multi-Vendor Integration Protocol

A 16 Mbit/s time-division multiplexed parallel bus used for connecting cards in a PC. For example, a card with V.34 modems could be connected to an ISDN PRI card, so that the PC's bus does not need to be loaded with this traffic. The bus uses ribbon cable.

See **CABLE**, and **PARALLEL**.

MVS
Multiple Virtual Storage

IBM's mainframe operating system for heavy-duty large-database and high-transaction-rate support.

Predecessors in this *OS* family of operating systems are (were) VS2, VS1, and DOS (not the PC kind).

Multiple MVS *virtual machines* can run under VM.

See **MAINFRAME**, **TPC**, and **VM**.

N

N-PCS
Narrowband PCS

See **NARROWBAND PCS**.

NAP
Network Access Point

Most Internet traffic between U.S. ISPs (and access for the major ISPs to other Internet back-bones) goes through a *network access point*.

In 1994, the NSF awarded 4 organizations the right to run NAPs. Initially, they each had a single switch (located in California, Chicago, New York and Washington DC), but this has grown since then (the first of each organizations' NAPs are sometimes called the primary NAPs). In 1997 there were about 80 NAPs world-wide. There are about 32 NAPs in the U.S., and some are listed below.

Operator	Location	Comments
Pacific Bell	San Francisco, California	There are 4 separate switches in San Francisco. Bellcore provides some assistance.
	Los Angeles, California	
Ameritech	Chicago, Illinois	Bellcore provides some assistance.
Sprint	Pennsauken, New Jersey	This is sometimes called the New York NAP
MFS[a] (Metropolitan Fiber Systems)	Washington DC (MAE[b] East)	
	San Jose, California (MAE West)	
	Chicago, Illinois (MAE Chicago)	
	Dallas, Texas (MAE Dallas)	
	Houston, Texas (MAE Houston)	
	Los Angeles, California (MAE Los Angeles)	
	New York, New York (MAE New York)	

a. MFS Communications Co. was bought by WorldCom Inc. for $12.5 billion in December 1996.
b. A MAE initially stood for *metropolitan area Ethernet*, which was a high speed data communications service provided by MFS (MFS Communications merged with WorldCom in August 1996). Now they say it is an abbreviation for *metropolitan area exchange*. MAE East is located in an underground parking garage in McLean Virginia. Some have a concern that this is not a good place for something that carries a third of the world's Internet traffic.

The MAE exchange points are actually places where vendors attach their routers, so that they can exchange data with each other. The other NAPs are often ATM switches, such as a Cisco Stratacom BPX Service Node ATM switch or FDDI ring.

The first Canadian NAP is run by BC Tel Advanced Communications and BCnet. It is located in Vancouver, Canada.

Unlike routers in commercial enterprises which only need to track all networks to which they are connected, and have a default router to which they send messages destined for addresses they know nothing about, the routers at NAPs do need to track all networks in the Internet.

In addition to NAPs (where participants bring their data to a a common point—which is the NAP), larger Internet Service Providers have direct links (typically T3 or faster) with each other to exchange traffic. This is called a *private peering point* or *transit arrangement* (depending on how it is done), and typically the same amount of traffic is exchanged in each direction (hence the "peer")—so only equally-huge ISPs (such as ANS, BBN, MCI, PSI-net and Sprint) typically have such arrangements. These typically have more capacity than the NAPs. Such peering points are in cities such as San Francisco, Dallas, Chicago and Boston, and are preferred by ISPs, since they get to keep their equipment in their own facilities.

The organizations' web pages describing their NAPs in more detail are at *http://www.pacbell.com/products/business/fastrak/networking/nap/index.html*, *http://www.sprintbiz.com/nap/*, *http://www.ameritech.com/products/data/teamdata/net/4011chnp.html*, and *http://www.mfs.net/MAE/doc/mae-info.html*.

There is also some information at *http://www.isi.edu/div7/ra/NAPs/naps_sa.html*.

See **ATM**, **CIX**, **INTERNET2**, **ISP**, **FDDI**, and **NSF**.

Narrowband ISDN

Basic rate 2B+D ISDN service and primary rate ISDN service (either 23B+D or 30B+D).

For a while, these services were criticized as "too little, too late." Too little, because of too slow a data rate and because B channels are only circuit-switched (requiring the full line to be used for one purpose, and the time required for call set up may be a problem for some applications). Too late, because that level of performance is available with more conventional services.

However, it now seems well suited to video conferencing, dialing-in to LANs and the Internet, and disaster recovery site connectivity.

Broadband ISDN (B-ISDN) service is (will be) based on ATM, and have speeds greater than 2.048 Mbits/s.

See **B-ISDN**, **H.261**, **ISDN**, and **WAN**.

NARROWBAND PCS
Narrowband Personal Communications Service

A nationwide, high data-rate, two-way paging service which uses 3 blocks of 1 MHz each, near 900 MHz. Expected uses include:

▲ Two-way paging (including acknowledgments, text messaging and receiving digitized voice)

▲ Telemetry (such as data collection from vending machines, utility meters and couriers)

▲ Interactive Internet and e-mail access (for example, from portable PCs)

There are two competing technologies and protocols:

▲ AT&T's is called *personal air communications technology* (PACT).

▲ Motorola Inc. actually has 2 technologies for narrowband PCS. Their *ReFLEX* is for digital messaging and *inFLEX*ion supports voice messaging as well.

It turns out that due to the low transmit power of two-way pagers, about 3 times as many base station receivers are needed than transmitters. This is expensive, but has the advantage that users can be tracked (two-way pagers periodically send out messages for this purpose) so nationwide paging can be offered without having to transmit the page messages everywhere (which wastes bandwidth).

The U.S. spectrum for the service was auctioned by the FCC in 1994. Six organizations paid a total of about $650 million for it.

See **PAGING**, **PCS1**, and **WIRELESS**.

NAS
Network Application Support

DEC's API (that is, the development environment) for its *Advantage Networks*. The set of functions that are available to application programs to use the network services.

See **ADVANTAGE NETWORKS** and **DEC**.

National ISDN

See **NI1**, **NI2**, and **NI3**.

NAVSTAR
Navigation Satellite Timing and Ranging

The U.S. Air Force's official name for GPS. (They run the system, so they get to choose the official name.)

Some information is at *http://www.laafb.af.mil/MC/CZ/homepage/segments*.

See **GPS**.

NC
Network Computer

Yet another attempt (as was ACE, COSE, OS/2, PREP and CHRP) by non-Wintel companies to make a widely-accepted alternative to your standard office PC running Windows.

The big draw this time is lower purchase and operating costs. There are lots of studies that show the annual cost of operating a PC (typically about $8,000 for configuration, software administration and trouble-shooting) is substantially more than the purchase price of the computer.

The idea is that if you don't have any floppy diskette, hard drive, CD-ROM drive or controllers, nor local printer, nor expansion slots then the machine will be much smaller and lower-cost. (Initially—in 1996—these computers were to cost $500, but the actual announced prices of all usable machines have been more than this.)

Then, if all software is loaded over the network (the machine would have a built-in LAN adapter), then all administration (software installation and updates) could be done centrally, rather than individually on each machine.

Then, if the software was all written in Java, then software would automatically be loaded over the network (both from the local LAN, as well as from the Internet), as needed. Different computing platforms could be used to run the exact same software, creating competition, new companies and innovation.

Lots of big companies, such as Apple Computer, Inc., Oracle Corp., IBM Corp., Netscape Communications, Sun Microsystems are very excited about this. In May 1996 they (through Oracle Corp.'s subsidiary Network Computer Inc.) announced the Network Computer Reference Profile (NCRP), which specifies the minimum requirements for an NC. These include the following:

▲ a monitor with at least VGA (640 × 480 pixel) resolution—this relatively low resolution can be provided by a television monitor

▲ audio output (and support for the .wav and .au audio file formats

▲ text input (perhaps by a keyboard, but handwriting or pointing is also allowable) and pointing (such as by a mouse)

▲ "persistent storage" (such as a disk drive) is not required (but is allowed)

▲ TCP/IP—and ftp, telnet, SNMP, SMTP (and POP3 and IMAP4), NFS (and UDP), HTTP and HTML (and GIF and JPEG graphic file formats) must be supported

▲ Bootp or DHCP, and being able to use the information from these protocols to boot from the network, using their IP address, the address of a boot server, and the name of a file to request as the boot program provided by these protocols

To keep things messy, the Open Group has announced that a Network Computer is defined by the Hardware Reference Design, which requires support for 4 to 64 Mbytes of memory, an 8 Mbyte ROM card, a Smart Card slot, infrared and LAN interfaces and parallel, mouse and keyboard ports.

Further information on NCRP is at *http://www.nc.ihost.com.*

Realizing that it is largely the administration cost that matters, the Wintel people have lots of white papers that discuss TCO (total cost of ownership), ZAW (zero administration workstation), Net PC and other acronyms to keep potential consumers completely confused, and compete with the NC people's *thin client* term (which means that the server does most of the work, unlike your standard PC running Microsoft Windows, where the server may only provide the raw data).

NCP

See **ACE, CHRP, CLIENT/SERVER, COSE, HPC, JAVA, NETPC, OS/2, PC, PREP, SMARTCARD,** and **WINTEL.**

NCP
NetWare Core Protocol

Novell's NetWare client/server protocol.

Runs on top of IPX. Traditionally has had a window size of 1, but Novell's recent *packet burst mode* shells (BNetX and the VLMs) support larger window sizes.

See **IPX** and **NOVELL.**

NCP
Network Control Program

The software running on an IBM FEP.

See **FEP** and **IBM.**

NDA
Non-Disclosure Agreement

A contract signed so that somebody will tell you something secret. This may be done so that a vendor will tell you some of their product plans, and they hope that in return you'll choose them as your supplier.

See **TRADE SECRET.**

NDIS
Network Device Interface Specification

A software interface between driver software supplied by a LAN adapter manufacturer and protocol stacks (such as DEC's PathWorks or Wollongong's TCP/IP) above it, as shown in the accompanying figure.

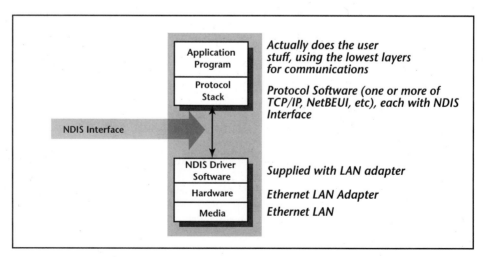

NDIS-1

Computer Dictionary

Also, simultaneously using more than one protocol stack usually requires an NDIS (or the competing ODI) interface.

Developed by Microsoft in 1990. Supported by 3Com, Banyan (in VINES), and DEC (for Pathworks). It is usually considered more open than the competing ODI, since ODI is controlled only by Novell.

See **API**, **NDIS**, and **ODI**.

NDS
NetWare Directory Services

Novell's method of distributing resource information to LAN clients (first released in 1993 as part of NetWare 4.0). In 1996, they changed the name to *Novell Directory Services* in an attempt to sell it as a stand-alone product.

The global (spans an entire enterprise), distributed (databases are kept close to users, rather than in a single, central location), replicated (for fault-tolerance) database that keeps track of users and resources and provides controlled (by system administrators) access to network resources (such as files and printers).

All network objects (users and resources) are grouped into *containers*, which are organized hierarchically (like a disk's subdirectory structure). The hierarchy may be geographic or organizational. Similar to the X.400 method of addressing, in that it has (in order, and for example) a: root, country, organization, organizational unit and user name.

Also stores the MHS database.

Replaces the *Bindery* of NetWare 3.*x*. All in all, a wonderful and powerful enhancement—but somewhat inconsequential since Windows NT is rapidly overtaking NetWare in market and mind share.

See **MHS2** (*Message Handling System*), **NETWARE 4.X**, and **X.500**.

NETBEUI
NetBIOS Extended User Interface

Microsoft's nonroutable LAN transport protocol that uses an extension to the NetBIOS API.

That is, NetBEUI is both an extension to NetBIOS, and a transport protocol for LANs. Since it has no network layer, it is nonroutable—a routable protocol requires two addresses—the *link layer* address specifies where the frame is going next (such as a router, to get to another network), and the *network layer* address specifies the final destination of the packet (packets are carried in frames).

NetBEUI is used for IBM's OS/2-based LAN Manager and Microsoft's LAN Manager and Windows for Workgroups.

NetBEUI (and NetBIOS, on which it is based) is old, and (for good reason) is nobody's favorite protocol (it has a small packet and window size, is nonroutable, and is proprietary), so Microsoft has selected WinSock as its choice for preferred communications API.

See **NETBIOS**, **WINSOCK**, and **WOSA**.

NETBIOS
Network Basic Input/Output System

An IBM-developed (initially for IBM's Sytek PC LAN program) standard software interface (API) to a network adapter. Has become a standard interface supported (either natively or with an additional layer of software) by most network operating systems to permit PC application programs to communicate directly with other PCs at the transport layer.

NetBIOS is now usually considered an intercomputer communication API, rather than a transport protocol, since current implementations use many different transport protocols (such as NetWare's NetBIOS emulator, which uses IPX, and the NetBIOS interface for TCP/IP).

When the NetBIOS software is loaded, it broadcasts its proposed (up to 15-character) name to all other stations to ensure that it will have a network-unique name.

NetBIOS:

▲ Does not support windowing (it has a Window size of 1)

▲ Has a small packet size (under 678 bytes)

▲ Does not have a network layer (so it is not routable)

These are among the reasons why NetBIOS is not a desirable protocol (especially for WAN links).

Now that TCP/IP is so widely available, it far more desirable (optimized for WANs, standard API, standard transport protocol, and on and on) has replaced NetBIOS as the choice for computer to computer communications.

See **BIOS**, **DLSW**, **NETBEUI**, and **WINSOCK**.

Net PC

An effort by Intel and Microsoft to fight back the NC effort from Oracle, Sun and others.

The hope is that by using something that is basically a PC (which people already know and love), but by eliminating some of the troublesome parts (such as diskette and CD-ROM drives, and ISA expansion slots) which are a source of configuration problems, viruses and games, the PC might be easier to administer.

The Net PC can have the following:

▲ a hard disk drive, though this is only supposed to be used to cache data, not store files or programs

▲ a boot ROM to boot from a network server (so all software can be stored and backed-up centrally)

▲ a PCI slot (for example, for a LAN adapter) other that whatever might be built-in to it

Net PCs are also called NetPCs and LANstations.

See **HPC**, **NC**, and **PC**.

Netscape

A WWW browser.

See **SSL** and **WWW**.

netstat

A UNIX program to confirm IP addresses and port numbers for a connection. The *-n* option leaves addresses in numerical (not name) form.

See **DNS2** (*Domain Name System*) and **IP ADDRESS**.

NetWare 4.*x*

A major enhancement over NetWare 3.*x* is the *NetWare Directory Services* (NDS, though they later changed to be an acronym for *Novell Directory Services*), which provides resources according to network-wide permissions, rather than file server–specific permissions. For example, to print a file on a printer, only the name of the printer (and permission to print on it) is required, rather than having to first log in to (and having a username and password for) the file server that controls that print server and then printing the file.

After Novell NetWare 4.11, Novell decided to change the name of their product to *Intranet-Ware*, since Intranets are so trendy.

See **INTRANET**, **NDS**, **NLM**, **NOVELL**, **OPERATING SYSTEM**, and **SPARC**.

Network Information Center

See **INTERNIC**.

NNTP
Network News Transfer Protocol

The TCP/IP-protocol used to transfer new postings to the Internet newsgroups (a subset of which is the usenet news).

It is defined in RFC 977.

See **TCP**, and **USENET**.

Newsgroups

See **USENET**.

NEXT
Near End Crosstalk

Data communications over twisted pair cabling (such as UTP) typically uses (at least) two pairs—one to transmit the data, and the other to receive the data. Due to electromagnetic coupling, some of the signal in the transmit pair is "picked-up" by the receive pair. Such *crosstalk* is worse when the transmitting signal is "louder", which is at the near end (relative to the transmitter) of the cable (before the signal is *attenuated* by the resistance, capacitance and inductance of the cable).

Therefore, a measurement of the NEXT is an important metric in specifying cabling. The measurement is how much "quieter" the crosstalk signal is, compared to the transmitted signal. Therefore, larger numbers are better. The measurement unit is dB (decibels), which is 10 times the *logarithm* (that's one of the buttons on a scientific calculator) of the ratio of the power of the signals on the two pairs (transmit versus receive). Since it is easier to measure the *voltage* of the signals (typically, using an oscilloscope), the measurement can be restated as:

$$NEXT = 20 \log (V_t/V_r)$$

Where V_t is the voltage on the transmitting pair, and V_r is the voltage on the receive pair.

See **CABLE**, **STP**, and **UTP**.

NeXTStep

The object-oriented operating system that originally only ran on NeXT workstations. NeXTStep 486 runs on Intel platforms as well.

Developed by NeXT Computers, Inc. as part of the NeXT computer (the company eventually gave up on the hardware side of the business). The company was started (and funded with $27 million) by Steven P. Jobs, co-founder of Apple Computer, after he left Apple Computer (not exactly voluntarily, in May 1985) because he didn't like how John "sugar water" Sculley was running it (and Apple's board lost confidence that Steve could run a company that size). In 1986, Jobs bought the Pixar animation studio for $10 million and in 1996 made lots of money on the movie *Toy Story* (after putting another $50 million in).

NeXT Computer Inc. has a WWW server at *http://www.next.com*.

See **APPLE**, **INTEL**, and **OPERATING SYSTEM**.

NFG
No F _ _ _ _ _ _ Good

An abbreviation that is often used to label defective (and probably not repairable) electronic equipment.

See **FOO.BAR**.

NFS
Network File System

A method of mapping (technically called "mounting") shared remote disk drives so that they appear to be local. Developed and licensed by Sun Microsystems.

Uses UDP, not TCP.

Defined in RFC 1094.

See **NIS**, **ONC**, **RFS**, **RFC**, **SUN**, and **UDP**.

NI-1
National ISDN-1

While ISDN is a great idea, the many incompatible implementations have adversely affected its acceptance. The national ISDN effort is a successful effort to have a common implementation standard.

A consistent North American implementation of basic rate ISDN, as specified by Bellcore. Features that must be included are the following:

▲ Call forwarding

▲ Automatic callback

▲ Call hold

▲ Calling number identification

Euro-ISDN is the homologous pan-European effort. It was developed by the European Telecommunications Standards Institute (ETSI).

Other common ISDN implementations are AT&T 5ESS (number 5 electronic switching system) and Northern Telecom DMS-100 (digital multiplex switching 100), named after the central office switches which implement the protocol. This information often needs to be entered into ISDN equipment when configuring it.

See **BELLCORE**, **BRI**, **ISDN**, **NI2**, **PRI**, and **SPID**.

NI-2
National ISDN-2

Extends NI-1 to include the following:

▲ Universal feature operations

▲ Some aspects of primary rate ISDN

However, NI-2 still does not include the plethora of features provided by the proprietary telephone sets and digital signalling used with typical Northern Telecom and AT&T (for example) PBXs. Therefore, you don't find standard ISDN BRI telephones connected to office telephones (or if you do, then you don't see them with fancy features, since the NI-2 protocols don't define many of these).

See **NI1** and **NI3**.

NI-3
National ISDN-3

Extends NI-2 to include the following:

▲ Further primary rate features

▲ Calling name delivery

▲ Music on hold

▲ Improved testing capabilities

See **NI2**.

NIC
Network Information Center

See **INTERNIC**.

NIC
Network Interface Card

A name for the LAN adapter (printed circuit board), installed in a PC, that enables it to communicate over a LAN. The term is used more often by IBM customers and Token Ring people.

See **TIC**.

NIS
Network Information Service

Along with NFS, results in a method of providing a distributed database system to centralize (storing one copy, each on a single computer) common configuration files, such as the password file (`/etc/passwd`) and the hosts file (`/etc/hosts`). The advantages of centralizing such files are:

▲ Files do not need to be replicated—which would invite administration problems in keeping the copies identical.

▲ Users in a (usually UNIX) distributed computing environment all see a familiar and consistent system (for example, network mounted file systems, application programs and development tools, host and file access rights, and so on) regardless of which machine they log in to.

NIS servers manage copies of the database files, and NIS clients request information from them, instead of using their own local copies (which would be an administrative impossibility to keep consistent and current). For example, when running NIS, the TCP port numbers (normally kept in `/etc/services`) are served over the network from a central machine.

NIS was developed by Sun Microsystems, and they have licensed it to about 300 companies and universities.

Since NIS was formerly called *Yellow Pages* (unfortunately, that name is trademarked—somebody else thought of it first), many commands and directory names still start with yp.

See **NFS**, **ONC**, **SUN**, **TCP**, **TRADEMARK**, and **UNIX**.

NIST ACTS
National Institute of Standards and Technology Automated Computer Telephone Service

NIST does lots of standards and research stuff. Until 1988, it was called the National Bureau of Standards (NBS), who were formed to be the official keeper of weights and measures.

NIST is at *http://www.nist.gov*, and there is lots of information on time at *http://www.boulder.nist.gov/timefreq*.

They have a dial-up service which displays super-duper accurate time on your screen at (303) 494-4774. Information on interpreting this information is at *http://www.bldrdoc.gov/timefreq/service/acts.htm*. The U.S. Naval Observatory provides a similar service at (202) 762-1594, with further information at *http://tycho.usno.navy.mil/modem_time.html*. These services report the date in both normal year-month-day format, and also *modified Julian date* (MJD) format, where the date is the number of days since January 1, 4713 BC (date calculations are often simpler if everything is in days, so your computer program doesn't have to bust its bits thinking about leap-years and "30 days has September" kind of stuff). The services also report the current difference between UTC and UT1 (see **UTC**).

Also, while you're cruising NIST, check out the requirements for operating systems to receive a C2 security rating, at *http://csrc.ncsl.nist.gov/secpubs/std001*.

See **GPS**, and **UTC**.

NLM
NetWare Loadable Module

The shared programs, drivers, and function libraries that a Novell NetWare 3.*x* file server runs to perform some of its functions (especially when it is for an optional feature or one that may require updates), as shown in the following table.

NLM Filename Extension	Use
.DSK	Disk drivers
.LAN	LAN adapter drivers
.NLM	All other programs (such as install) and libraries (such as clib.nlm, which are analogous to a Windows or OS/2 .DLL)

NLMs can be loaded and unloaded from the system console, while the server is running, with users logged in. NLMs are automatically loaded when one NLM references another that is not yet loaded into the file server's memory.

See **API** and **NOVELL**.

NLSP
NetWare Link Services Protocol

A link-state protocol based on OSI's IS-IS, and developed by Novell to do the following:

▲ Replace its use of RIP (a *distance-vector* router-to-router protocol that involves broadcasting routing tables every 60 seconds)

▲ Change the way SAP (server broadcasts every 60 seconds identifying their name, service, and address to potential clients) is used

Has lower network overhead and faster convergence—especially useful over slow (9,600-bits/s) WAN links.

Each NetWare router maintains two databases:

▲ The *Adjacency Database* tracks the router's direct network links and immediate neighbors

▲ The *Link State Database* is the connectivity map for the entire network, which will allow all NLSP devices to determine (or converge on) the same, best route for each possible source-to-destination pair of communicating nodes.

NNI

Costs (the metric used to determine the best path) can be manually changed for each link to direct traffic toward or away from particular links (for example, faster or more expensive WAN communications links).

As with all such *link-state* algorithms, rather than broadcasting every router's entire table every 60 seconds, NLSP sends only the changes.

NLSP routers will detect RIP/SAP routers and act as traditional RIP/SAP routers on those links.

See **IS-IS**, **LINK STATE**, **OSI**, **RIP**, **NOVELL**, and **WAN**.

NNI
Network-to-Network Interface

Frame relay's and ATM's (completely different, but similar in goal) specification for the interface between two networks (for example a public frame relay network and a company's private frame relay network, or between two public ATM networks, each run by a different carrier).

Similar in intent to X.75 for X.25 networks, in that it is an extension to the protocol to permit two networks (of the same type) to be interconnected.

See **ATM** (*Asynchronous Transfer Mode*) and **FRAME RELAY**.

NNTP
Network News Transfer Protocol

See **USENET**.

Novell

First introduced in 1983, Novell's NetWare had up to 65% (by nodes) of the network operating system market. The next largest competitors (Banyan, DEC, IBM, and Microsoft) had about 4% each. However, beginning in 1996, Microsoft's Windows NT began rapidly finding its way into many previously Novell-only companies.

In June 1993 Novell bought Unix System Laboratories for $320 million, and in March 1994 Novell bought WordPerfect Corp. for $855 million. Novell sold their UNIX business in September 1995 to SCO for $72 million.

Novell has a WWW server at *http://www.novell.com*.

See **IPX**, **MHS2** (*Message Handling System*), **NCP1** (*NetWare Core Protocol*), **NDS**, **NETWARE 4.X**, **NLM**, **NLSP**, **ODI**, **OPERATING SYSTEM**, **SCO**, **UNIVEL**, and **VLM**.

NPSI
Network Control Program Packet-Switching Interface

IBM's FEP software that supports X.25.

See **FEP**, **NCP2** (*Network Control Program*), **QLLC**, and **X.25**.

NREN
National Research and Education Network

For a while, the official name for the Internet, because the 1991 U.S. Congress act by this name says so. Intended to link research communities in government, industry, and higher education.

See **INTERNET2**.

NRZ
Non-Return to Zero

See **ENCODING**.

NRZI
Non-Return to Zero Inverted

See **ENCODING**.

NSF
National Science Foundation

The U.S. agency that provides some Internet funding—initially only for the backbone, now for routing support ($20 million over 5 years to Merit, Inc. and the University of Southern California Information Sciences Institute; this work used to be done by ANS).

See **ANS**, **NAP**, **NSFNET**, and **INTERNET2**.

NSFNET
National Science Foundation Network

The part of the Internet that used to be funded by the U.S. Government, but direct funding and the existence of NSFnet disappeared as of April 30, 1995.

Further information on the transition to the current commercial-based Internet is available at *http://nic.merit.edu/nsfnet/transition/index.html*.

See **ANS** and **INTERNET2**.

NSP
Native Signal Processing

Another effort by Intel to get the processor (which is likely made by Intel— and they would like to give you a reason to want a faster one) rather than specialized ICs, such as *digital signal processors* (that might not be made by Intel) to handle tasks such as simple sound playback and mixing.

The effort includes the PCI chip sets, software drivers, and APIs to encourage manufacturers and application developers to use the technology for (at least) the following:

▲ Sound (including special effects, sound mixing, and speech synthesis and recognition)

▲ Telephony

▲ Video (MPEG decoding and video conferencing)

▲ Handwriting recognition

Since Intel's original NSP specification (released in 1995) gave Intel control over the APIs, and could favor Intel processors, the effort was not supported by Microsoft (who would rather their DirectX APIs are used) and other major vendors (such as Cyrix). As of August 1995, NSP was put on hold (that is, it never happened, and it never will). Intel decided they would be best to provide the hardware capability, and let others do the software—hence MMX.

See **API**, **DIRECTX**, **MMX**, **PC**, **PCS** (*Personal Conferencing Specification*), and **PCI**.

NT-1
Network Termination Type 1

A device needed to connect an end user's ISDN equipment to the pair of wires from the phone company.

Specifically, and NT-1 is the device that connects the ISDN *U interface* (the single pair of copper conductors from the telephone company's central office) to a building's internal ISDN *S bus*. Often the NT-1 is used to directly connect to the S/T interface on ISDN equipment (such as a router or terminal adapter). The ISDN S bus is the four-pair cabling (with 8-pin modular jacks) used to interconnect ISDN devices, and may also be used to power them. An ISDN S bus has nothing whatsoever to do with Sun's "*SBus*." The U interface from the telephone company typically also uses an 8-pin modular jack (also called an RJ-45).

The NT-1 gets its power from a connection to the building's 110-V A.C. and usually also has a built-in rechargeable battery so that telephone service is available during power failures (unlike standard POTS telephones, ISDN telephones have active electronic devices in them and need power). Of the four pairs of wires of the *S bus*, two are for data, and the other two can be used to send power from the NT-1 to the ISDN telephones and other devices.

The NT-1 may be built in to a *terminal adapter*. The single "terminal adapter/NT-1" unit is then all that is needed to connect (for example) a PC's standard EIA-232 COM1 port to the *basic-rate* ISDN U interface from the telephone company.

Outside of the U.S. and Canada, the local telephone company usually must supply the NT-1, so the NT-1 is external to the terminal adapter (or the router's ISDN card).

When a (typically PRI) ISDN circuit terminates on a PBX, an NT-2 is used instead of an NT-1, since the PBX provides the higher-layer functions otherwise handled by an NT-1.

See **BRI**, **BUS**, **CONNECTOR**, **EIA/TIA-232**, **ISDN**, and **POTS**.

NTP
Network Time Protocol

A protocol for communicating the time from NTP time servers to other hosts on an IP network.

Using a calculation of the round-trip delay time between the host and the NTP server typically allows the host's time of day clock to be set to within 100 to 200 ms.

NTP is defined in RFCs 1119 and 1305. The *Simple Network Time Protocol* (SNTP) is a subset of NTP, and is defined in RFC 1361.

Some U.S. Naval Observatories allow public access over the Internet to their super-duper accurate NTP servers. Two of them are at IP address *128.102.18.31* and *130.113.64.9*.

See **TCP**, and **UTC**.

NTSC
National Television System Committee

The name for the method used to transmit television signals in North America, Japan and Korea.

Actually, the name of the group that sets the broadcast television standards in North America. Originally formed (in 1940) to standardize the method for color television broadcasting. Members included all U.S. companies and organizations interested in television. The monochrome television standard was developed by 1941. Between 1950 and 1953 work was done to select a method for color television broadcasting. The method chosen (augmenting the existing monochrome *composite video signal*) was standardized in 1953 (and approved by the FCC) and is still the standard for North America and Japan (not many electronics-related standards are still relevant after so many years).

The electron beam which excites the phosphors in on the inside surface of a cathode ray tube display scans each horizontal line every 63.5 µs (resulting in a 15.7 kHz horizontal scan frequency). As the lines are successively scanned from left to right, each line below the previous, a *field* is displayed.

Each *frame* is made up of two *fields* (field 1 and field 2), with the lines of field 2 being written between the lines of field 1. This provides more displayed lines per frame (the *persistence* of the CRT phosphor is long enough that the first field remains displayed while the second is being written). This display method is called *interlaced*. In contrast, when there is more bandwidth available (such as for computer monitors), *progressive* (also called *noninterlaced*) scanning (which simply displays every line during every frame) is typically used.

Each NTSC interlaced frame is made up of 481 horizontal lines (240.5 lines per field) that are visible (sometimes called "*active*") plus another 44 lines (22 per field) that are *blanked* (the electron beam is turned off), since they occur while the scanning beam returns to the upper-left corner of the screen. This makes a total of 525 lines per frame.

Interlaced scanning is necessary to obtain the screen resolution desired within the video bandwidth available—while reducing the flicker which would be noticeable if the screen was only updated 29.97 times per second.

Before the method of displaying color NTSC signals was developed, the frame rate (for monochrome television signals) was 30 frames per second—which requires a field rate of 60 fields per second. This was chosen so that the 60 Hz power line frequency (which would typically be the same for everybody within television broadcast range, since they'd be connected to the same power generators, or to generators synchronized to each other) used in North America could be used to provide synchronization between the field frequency used at the television station and at everybody's home televisions. When color NTSC was developed it was found that there was interference between the signals for the 30 frames per second and the color subcarrier, so the frame rate was reduced by 0.1% to 29.97 frames per second (which is 59.94 fields per second). This is close enough that existing monochrome televisions would still work, while eliminating the interference problem. By then crystal oscillators were common and low-cost enough that they could be used for the synchronization rather than the power line.

To reduce costs, and simplify the design of televisions, the same crystal oscillator is used for the color burst and for the horizontal and vertical scan oscillators. So, for example, the horizontal scan frequency (of approximately 15.7 kHz) is exactly 2/455 of the color burst frequency.

In contrast, computer video usually runs at exactly 30 (and not 29.97) frames per second, since it does not use (or have the problems of) the NTSC composite video color subcarrier method to carry the color information. Also, in Europe while the same 15.7 kHz horizontal scanning frequency is used, the number of lines per frame, and the frame rate are different so they also (once could) synchronize with the 50 Hz power line frequency used there.

The term "NTSC" is also used to refer to the standard video signal that is used (for example) between a *video cassette recorder* (a standard home VCR) and television (it uses what is often called an RCA connector).

When broadcasted, an NTSC signal requires a *6-MHz bandwidth*. That is, channel 2 is 54 to 60 MHz, channel 3 is 60 MHz to 66 MHz, and so on. To reduce interference, adjacent television channels (for example, channels 3 and 4) are not assigned in the same coverage area, and the transmitting antennas of transmitters that are assigned to the same frequency must be at least 155 miles apart.

For each 6-MHz channel:

▲ The main (sometimes called picture, or video) carrier frequency is 1.25 MHz above the channel's base frequency (of 54 MHz for channel 2, for example—so the video carrier is at 55.25 MHz).

▲ This carrier is *amplitude modulated* (AM) by the *composite video signal* (which has all of the picture and synchronization information).

▲ The (left+right) sound information is sent by *frequency modulating* (FM) a sound subcarrier that is 4.5 MHz above the video carrier frequency (so the sound for channel 6 is at 87.75 MHz—which explains why you can usually hear broadcast TV audio on a standard FM radio, since FM starts just above this, at 88 MHz).

▲ For stereo signals, an FM left–right audio signal is also sent, at a pilot frequency above the sound subcarrier.

Standard television has a 4:3 (horizontal:vertical) aspect ratio. One of the following methods is used to display the wider picture of the 16:9 aspect ratio used for motion pictures.

▲ *Pan and scan.* This displays the full height of the picture using the full height of the screen, but chops off the sides of the picture (usually an equal amount off each side, so you don't see things that happen at the very side). This is typically done for movies, so they display a message at the beginning that if was "formatted to fit your television," or some message like that.

▲ *Letterbox.* This presents the full width of the picture, but has black bars at the to and bottom of the screen.

▲ *Distorted.* This simply squishes the picture horizontally so you still see everything, but narrower than real life.

The latter two methods are often done at the beginning or end of movies when the credits span the full width of the screen. The less-noticeable first method is typically then used for the majority of the movie.

Regular *monochrome* (black-and-white) television broadcasts began in 1936 in Britain and in 1939 in the U.S.

NTSC video can produce the changes per horizontal line listed in the following table. These limitations are due to the modulation methods and frequencies chosen (which were selected to conserve transmission bandwidth, as human color perception has lower resolution for chrominance information than for intensity information).

Value	Changes per Line	Used for
Luminance (intensity)	267	Fine monochrome detail
Orange-blue color	96	Flesh tones and other colors
Purple-green color	35	Other colors

PAL and SECAM are similar-technology systems that are used outside of North America.

A higher-quality (than NTSC) standard is called *S-Video* and is supported by some VCRs and televisions. It uses three separate coaxial cables to provide a separate signal path for each of the main components of the video signal.

See **CATV, COLOUR, COMPOSITE VIDEO SIGNAL, CRT, HDTV, INTERLACED, PAL, PPM, SDTV, SECAM, VBI, VHS,** and **VIDEO.**

NWay

See **S100BASET.**

O

OC-*X*
Optical Carrier

The standard speeds used for high-speed data transmission (typically used for ATM) in North America.

The standard for SONet data transmission over optical fiber. Common speeds are OC-3 (155.52 Mbits/s) and OC-12 (622.08 Mbits/s). Equipment with speeds as fast as OC-192 (9,953.28 Mbits/s) are currently commercially available (each OC-192 can carry about 1,300 high-quality full-color, full-motion video signals, or 129,024 voice conversations).

A "c" indicates that the SONet signal is concatenated (that is, not channelized)—the entire payload bandwidth is used for a single high-speed signal. For example, and OC-12c carries one 622 Mbit/s signal (not 12 OC-1 signals). This could be used for a really high-speed data channel, super-quality video, or whatever.

Using multimode optical fiber, connections can typically be up to 2 km in length. Single mode optical fiber (which uses higher-power lasers for transmission) can typically go 15 km or more. SC connectors are typically used for both types of optical fiber.

See **ATM** (*Asynchronous Transfer Mode*), **FIBER**, **SONET**, and **STS**.

Octet

The term used in most standards documents to refer to a group of 8 bits. Most of us just call that a byte. Some say the difference is that while a byte is usually a related group of bits (such as those of an ASCII character), an octet is just 8 bits that may not have any relation to each other (for example, many protocols designate each bit in a packet header as each having a specific meaning).

A *character* usually refers to a group of bits (typically 7 or 8 of them) that represent something themselves (such as a printable character or a field delimiter).

A *byte* typically refers to something stored in a computer's memory or disk drive. It may be part of an executable program, data in a file or part of a binary number.

See **ASCII**, **LITTLE ENDIAN**, **LSB**, and **STANDARDS**.

ODBC
Open Database Connectivity

Microsoft's effort to provide a single API for database (called *data sources*) access, even though those databases were created by any of several different programs.

Data sources with ODBC interfaces include:

▲ XBase (*.DBF) files, such as those produced by dBASE.

▲ SQL databases

▲ Microsoft Access, Excel and FoxPro

▲ Oracle

▲ Paradox

▲ Novell Btrieve files

▲ IBM DB2

Since it is a general-purpose interface (not tailored to a specific database), it provides only a subset of most database vendors' capabilities.

ODBC is part of Microsoft's WOSA and an implementation of *CLI 1992* (*Call-Level Interface*), which was created in 1992 by the *X/Open Group* and the *SQL Access Group*.

The ODBC home page is at *http://www.roth.net/odbc/*, and a FAQ is at *http://www.roth.net/odbc/odbcfaq.htm*.

See **DBA**, **SQL**, **WOSA**, **XBASE**, and **X-OPEN**.

ODI
Open Data-Link Interface

A software interface between driver software supplied by a LAN (such as Ethernet) adapter manufacturer and protocol stacks (such as Novell's IPX or Wollongong's TCP/IP), as shown in the accompanying figure.

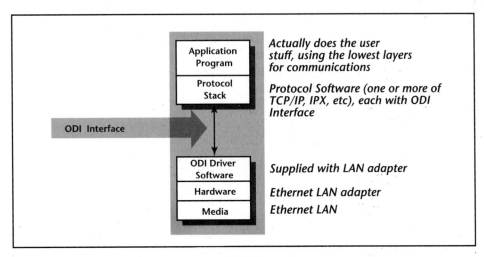

ODI-1

Using more than one protocol stack simultaneously usually requires an ODI (or the competing NDIS) interface.

Replaces the previous network-specific IPX drivers.

Developed by Novell. Also supported by Apple.

See **API**, **NDIS**, and **NOVELL**.

OLE
Previously Object Linking and Embedding

A method used by Microsoft's Windows products to integrate the output from one program as data into another (for example, a drawing or spreadsheet into a word processing document).

Documents that contain links to, or the actual embedded output from, other applications are called *compound documents*. An application that produces embedded objects, or links to them, is called an *OLE* server or *component*. An *OLE* client, or *container*, application produces compound documents. Embedded objects are stored in the OLE client's native file format. Linked objects have only links to separate files stored in the compound document.

Whether an object is linked or embedded, only the client application is needed to display or print the entire compound document. To edit the linked or embedded object requires the server application.

OLE 1.0 supported basic functions. For example, when you select the drawing with mouse clicks, the appropriate program (such as the drawing package) is automatically run (in a separate window—sometimes called *open editing*) so you can edit the drawing.

OLE 2.0 supports *in situ* editing (sometimes called *visual editing*), so that rather than opening or moving you to a new window, it lets you edit the embedded object without hiding the rest of the document (clicking starts the required application and changes only your menus and tools). (For linked objects, only open editing is supported.) OLE 2.0 supports many other new features, such as drag-and-drop.

Microsoft promises that all future enhancements to OLE will be supersets of the existing functions, and that incompatible versions and implementations of newer and older containers and servers will not be a problem. Therefore, there will be no version numbers for future enhancements, just new features. This capability is based on OLE's *Component Object Model* (COM).

COM defines a standard way for objects to communicate with each other—through an *interface*, which is a collection of related functions required to get the job done. To provide a standard way to access the parts of compound documents, a OLE defines a *structured storage* (SS) interface (which is a lot better than every application defining their own proprietary file format). For example, every OLE file has a *root storage* which points to other *storages* (analogous to a subdirectory) and *streams* (analogous to a file).

Some uses for OLE are listed below:

▲ Utility programs that won't be used by themselves but are very useful when integrated with other programs. The favorite example here is a spell checker. Everyone would like to use their own spell checker (with their own customizations) with all of their programs (email, database, spreadsheet, desktop publishing, etc.).

▲ Conversion utilities (for example, to convert a word processing or graphics file format to a different format—WordPerfect to Word or `.tif` to `.bmp`), accessed by mouse-clicking a selection from the file icon's properties. No need for a new user interface for the conversion program, as it uses the already-familiar properties-setting method built in to whatever operating system is being used.

Pronounced *o-LAY*.

Developed by Microsoft and generally a more powerful feature than its predecessor—DDE (which is used by OLE). Successors include VBX (Visual Basic Control) and OCX (OLE Control)—both of which are now merged into ActiveX. Also COM's superset is DCOM (Distributed COM).

Competes with Apple's *OpenDoc* and IBM's *System Object Model* (SOM).

See **CORBA**, **DDE**, and **OPENDOC**.

OLTP
On-line Transaction Processing

Handling real-time *transactions* such as those that stock exchanges and airline reservation systems require. Such systems require transaction management, extensive audit trails, routing, scheduling, and administration.

See **SQL** and **TPC**.

ONC
Open Networking Computing

Sun's networking protocols to support distributed computing. Includes NFS, NIS, and RPC.

A newer version (ONC+) is part of Sun's Solarix 2.*x* operating system and includes security and performance enhancements.

See **NFS**, **NIS**, **RPC**, **SOLARIS**, **SUN**, and **UNIX**.

Open Database Connectivity

See **ODBC**.

Open Data-Link Interface

See **ODI**.

OpenDoc

A method of integrating the outputs of more than one application program into a single document.

A vendor-neutral (unlike OLE), cross-platform (DOS, Windows, UNIX, OS/2, and Macintosh) open standard for the APIs to create and edit *compound documents* (which are documents that can be composed of tables, charts, text, video, sound, and graphics—all in one file). Different programs can be used to edit each component (or *part*) of the file.

OpenDoc is based on IBM's *System Object Model* (SOM), which is available for AIX, OS/2 and Windows. SOM complies with the *Common Object Request Broker Architecture* (CORBA) specification, which enables cross-platform interoperability between applications and objects. CORBA was developed by the *Object Management Group* (OMG), which is a consortium of more than 300 vendors and end-user companies. An *object request broker* (ORB) handles the interaction between applications and objects, and IBM's Distributed SOM (DSOM) is an implementation of a CORBA ORB.

OpenDoc competes with Microsoft's COM, and is promoted by Microsoft competitors such as Apple, Borland, IBM, Novell, Sun, and Taligent.

Originally developed by Apple but now owned and controlled by *Component Integration Laboratories*.

Competes with, but will also work with, OLE.

See **CORBA**, **DDE**, and **OLE**.

OPEN LOOK

The graphical user interface developed by Sun.

Uses the *X Window System*'s X11 communication protocol (as does the competing *Motif*) but presents a different user interface (look-and-feel) than Motif.

Even though OPEN LOOK has some neat features—for example, it has nicer scroll bars (they show how far through the document you are), and the toolkit (XView) is freely available with SunOS, Solaris and most Linux versions—Motif is now much more widely used for commercial X Window applications (even Sun now includes Motif support). OPEN LOOK is still used in Linux and some Sun environments.

A valuable archive of OPEN LOOK information and code is at Ian Darwin's site, at *http://www.darwinsys.com/olcd*. The OPEN LOOK FAQ is at *http://www.cis.ohio-state.edu/hypertext/faq/usenet/open-look/*.

See **CDE**, **GUI**, **LINUX**, **MOTIF**, **X WINDOW SYSTEM**, and **UNIX**.

OpenVMS

DEC's new name for their VMS operating system, now that they will license it to run on other platforms. (It's amazing what a little serious competition will do—Apple has done the same previously unimaginable thing with their Mac OS operating system).

See **ALPHA AXP**, **DEC**, **OPERATING SYSTEM**, and **VMS**.

Operating System

The hugely complicated software (Windows 95 reportedly has 11 million lines of code) that runs user applications and provides an interface to the hardware. Hardware that runs more than one operating system is becoming more popular (or perhaps it would be better to say that there are fewer hardware platforms now but more companies with operating systems). The following table shows which hardware platforms run what operating system(s).

Hardware Platform	Operating System					
	IBM		**Microsoft**			
	AIX	**OS/2**	**DOS**	**Windows NT**	**NeXTStep**	**Other**
DEC Alpha				✓		DEC OpenVMS, and UNIX
HP PA-RISC					✓	HP-UX
IBM/Apple/ Motorola PowerPC	✓	✓[a]		[b]		Apple Macintosh Mac OS, Sun Solaris
IBM RS/6000	✓					
Intel Pentium and compatible		✓	✓	✓	✓	Banyan VINES, Novell Net-Ware and UnixWare, Sun Solaris, SCO UNIX and OpenServer, Windows 3.1 and 95
Motorola 68000					✓	Apple Macintosh
Silicon Graphics MIPS R4x00				[b]		Silicon Graphics IRIX, SVR4
Sun SuperSPARC					✓	SunOS, Sun Solaris

a. While IBM sort of had OS/2 running on the PowerPC, on January 25, 1996 IBM announced that they were stopping development of OS/2 for PowerPC.

b. Windows NT version 4.0 (released in 1996) was the last to support the MIPS and PowerPC platforms

Optical Fiber

The following figure shows a family tree of operating systems one usually finds installed, and the platform on which they run.

```
                    -- Apple ---- MacOS (Macintosh PowerPC)

                   |-- DEC -- OpenVMS (VAX Minicomputer and Alpha Workstation)

                                -- OS/2 (PC)
                   |-- IBM ---|-- OS/400 (AS/400 minicomputer)
                                -- MVS (Mainframe)

                                   -- DOS (PC)
                                  |                    -- 3.1 (PC)
Operating__|-- Microsoft --|                          |
System                     |                          |-- for Workgroups 3.11 (PC)
                            -- Windows --|-- 95 (PC)
                                         |               -- Workstation
                                         |              |  (Desktop, PC)
                                          -- NT --|
                                                   -- Server (PC)

                                 -- 3.11 and 3.12 (PC)
                  |-- Novell NetWare --|
                                 -- 4.1 (PC)

                    -- DEC -- Digital UNIX (Alpha Workstation)

                   |-- HP -- HP-UX (PA-RISC Workstation)

                  |-- UNIX --|-- IBM -- AIX (PowerPC and RS/6000 Workstation)

                   |-- SCO -- Xenix, OpenServer and UnixWare (PC)

                   |-- SGI -- IRIX (Silicon Graphics Workstation)

                                 -- Solaris (Sun Workstation)
                    -- Sun --|
                                 -- SunOS (Sun Workstation)
```

See **ALPHA AXP, INTEL, NIST ACTS, PA-RISC, PC, POWERPC, RISC, SPARC,** and **UNIX.**

Optical Fiber

See **FIBER.**

OS/2
Operating System/2

IBM's *multithreading* and *preemptive multitasking* (tasks are interrupted when their time-slice has expired or when there is a more important task to do), PC GUI operating system that competes with Microsoft Windows.

Version 2.0 was released in March 1992. Version 3 (which was internally, and then externally, called Warp) was released in October 1994. Version 4 was released in late 1996.

By market share, OS/2 has lost to Windows for your standard home or office desktop operating system. Most would say that IBM had a chance, but just didn't make it. While IBM did eventually produce a version of OS/2 for the PowerPC, it is not generally available.

See **IBM, IBM WINX WINDOWS APIS, OPERATING SYSTEM,** and **POWERPC.**

OSF
Open Software Foundation

A nonprofit research and development organization that was formed in 1988 and devoted to open software (that is, software with standardized and publicized interface specifications).

DEC, HP, and IBM formed the OSF when Sun and AT&T (which then owned UNIX) formed a partnership (this caused more than a bit of concern to the rest of the UNIX industry), though many other companies are now members.

The goal is (was) to develop OSF/1 (which is a merging of System V, BSD, and Mach) as competition to UNIX International's SVR4 UNIX and to develop other standards, such as DCE and the X Window System, that facilitate multivendor, distributed computing.

DEC has implemented OSF/1 on their Alpha processor (they now call this Digital UNIX).

Initially, Sun felt that OSF's only purpose was to work against Sun (Scott McNealy termed it "Oppose Sun Forever"). However, OSF was reorganized in 1994 to Sun's satisfaction, and Sun joined.

OSF oversees COSE's work.

The OSF has a WWW server at *http://www.osf.org/*.

See **DCE2, DEC, DME, MACH, MOTIF, OSF-1, SUN, SVR4, X-OPEN,** and **X WINDOW SYSTEM.**

OSF/1

OSF's UNIX-like operating system. It was to have been based on AIX, but the Mach version 2.5 kernel was used instead (and is now based on Mach 3.0). Includes POSIX 1003.1 and XPG features. DEC's implementation for their Alpha AXP processor (which they now call Digital UNIX) is *binary compatible* with their Ultrix.

See **AIX, ALPHA AXP, MACH, OPERATING SYSTEM, OSF, PORTABILITY, POSIX-OSE, SVR4, UNIX,** and **XPG.**

OSI
Open Systems Interconnection

A suite of protocols and standards sponsored by the ISO for data communications between otherwise incompatible computer systems. These protocols were to be an open, standardized solution to all communication requirements. Unfortunately, the standards setting process allowed everybody to have their endless say, and the requirements and solutions became too complicated.

Unfortunately (for the many people and companies that spent so much time and money on the effort), the TCP/IP suite of protocols has eclipsed OSI, and you don't hear much about OSI anymore (except for a few applications, such as the X.500 directory service).

When work began (in the late 1970s) on providing a standard method for communications between different hardware platforms, TCP/IP was not considered an option for serious commercial applications, since TCP/IP:

▲ Required you to run UNIX (which, at the time, was not used for commercial applications and had only a command-line user interface)

▲ Had poor security and management features

▲ Had too small an address size

Therefore the ISO promoted development of OSI (how palindromic).

Although all major (and many minor) computer vendors now have OSI products, the OSI protocols were never widely implemented, and TCP/IP has become the first choice for multi-vendor networking, because of its:

▲ Lower-cost and more-efficient implementation (less CPU time required, smaller programs)

▲ Availability for most operating systems

▲ Fast standardization and development cycle (usually using the Internet to facilitate communications) when a new requirement is identified

▲ Familiarity among college graduates (universities use TCP/IP, so once out of school, a graduate's first choice when designing a system is to use TCP/IP)

▲ Easier-to-access (and zero-cost) documentation and standards (they are all available on the Internet)

The following table shows the OSI name for the protocol, standard, or function of the homologous TCP/IP-based networking component.

TCP/IP Name	OSI Equivalent	
FTP	FTAM	File Transfer, Access, and Management
Host	ES	End System
IP	IP	Internet Protocol
OSPF	IS-IS	Intermediate System to Intermediate System
Router	IS	Intermediate System
SMTP	X.400	ITU-T's Electronic Mail Standard
SNMP	CMIP	Common Management Information Protocol
TCP	CONP	Connection-oriented Protocol
TELNET	VTS	Virtual Terminal Service
UDP	CNLP	Connectionless Protocol

In addition to X.500 (and LDAP), and to a lesser extent, X.400, one of the few real-world OSI-based efforts is the Utility Communications Architecture (UCA), sponsored by the Electric Power Research Institute (ERPI). It is a series of efforts (including Database Access Integration SERVICE—DAIS) to define common protocols for electrical utilities.

See **COSAC, CLNP, CONP, COS1** (*Corporation for Open Systems*), **COSAC, ES, FTAM, FTP, GOSIP, IP, IS, IS-IS, ISO, MMS, OSINET, OSPF, RFC, SNMP, SPF, STANDARDS, TCP, TCP/IP, TELNET, UDP, X.400,** and **X.500.**

OSInet

A test network set up by a consortium of North American OSI software vendors and users that offers the *Network Registration Service* (NRS) database of successful interoperability testing.

OSPF
Open Shortest Path First

A newer protocol for the communication of network connectivity and status information between TCP/IP routers.

A link-state, intradomain routing algorithm that is becoming a replacement option for RIP. Handles only TCP/IP's IP. As shown in the following table, OSPF produces much less router to router network traffic, and provides faster connectivity updates too.

Method of Sending	RIP	OSPF
Changes in network connectivity table	Not supported	Multicasted (to routers only) as soon as they occur
Full network connectivity table	Broadcasted to all stations every 60 seconds	Multicasted (to routers only) every 30 minutes

Each router learns the status of all links within an *autonomous system* and calculates the shortest path (based on hops, link speed, and other factors) to the destination as a tree, with that router at the *root* and each possible path to the destination as a path on the tree. This calculation is done using something called *Dijkstra's algorithm* (he figured out the method, which is based on mathematical concepts such as *graphs* (not like those that first come to laymen's minds like ours) and *minimum length trees*).

The shortest path calculated may depend on the requested *type of service*.

The router then sends the packet the one hop to the next router, which then repeats the calculation to send the packet one hop closer to the final destination, again along the shortest calculated path for the tree built by that router, with that next router as the root.

In 1997, work completed on version 2 of OSPF. It includes support for using MD5 (*message digest 5*) authentication of propagated routing information.

OSPF is defined in RFC 1247, and OSPF version 2 is RFCs 1321 and 2178.

See **AUTHENTICATION, IP MULTICAST, LINK STATE,** and **RIP.**

OTOH
On the other hand

A common e-mail abbreviation.

Outline Font

A method of storing the definitions of font shape. Also called a *scalable* or *vector font* (though vector fonts are made of only straight line segments).

It is a scalable font because the *outline* of each character is described by lines that can be scaled (adjusted to any size). The curves between the end-points of the lines are usually specified by using a *Bézier spline* (which has a pleasing curve). Outline fonts can usually be rotated as well (you used to need a different font to print sideways, as required to print your spreadsheet in *landscape* format).

Outline fonts need to be *rasterized* (converted to a bitmap, at the required point size) before being displayed. This is done when a new display font is selected. The rasterized font is stored in a *font cache*, so it only needs to be rasterized once.

Outline fonts also need to be rasterized before use by raster-oriented printers (for example, dot matrix and laser). This can be done in the printer (for example, if the printer supports PostScript) or by the PC (for example, if it uses Adobe Type Manager).

Since the scaling process may produce asymmetric characters (because of rounding), *hinting* is often used to specify requirements (such as that both legs of an "M" be the same width).

The major formats of outline fonts are listed in the following table.

Font Format	Defined by	Used by
Intellifont	Agfa Division of Miles, Inc.	PCL 5 (HP LaserJet printers)
Speedo	Bitstream, Inc.	Many software packages
TrueType	Apple Computer, Inc., Microsoft Corporation	Microsoft Windows
Type 1	Adobe Systems, Inc.	PostScript printers and displays

An older technology is the bitmap font.

See **ATM** (*Adobe Type Manager*), **BITMAP FONT, FONT, POSTSCRIPT PAGE DESCRIPTION LANGUAGE, PCL, POSTSCRIPT TYPE 1 FONTS, POSTSCRIPT TYPE 3 FONTS, RASTERIZE,** and **TYPEFACE FAMILY**.

OUT-OF-BAND
Outside of bandwidth

Using a separate channel for signaling (than the voice or data channel).

The separate channel may be physically separate wires, or may be a time-multiplexed channel (such as an ISDN D channel). While this often costs more it ensures that the full bandwidth is available for the voice or data.

For example, an EIA-232 interface using RTS/CTS (*Request to Send/Clear to Send*) flow control is out-of-band flow control, since these signals (pins 4 and 5) are separate from the data.

See **EIA/TIA-232, INBAND,** and **ISDN**.

OverDrive

Intel's name for the upgrade CPUs that usually plug into an extra socket on a PC's motherboard, which is intended for that use (to add functionality), or that entirely replaces the existing CPU.

A 169-pin socket in most 486SX and 486DX-based PCs, which can accept a version of a 486 CPU that runs internally at double the system clock speed while running externally at the normal system clock speed. This permits a (for example) 33-MHz 486-based system to be upgraded by simply plugging an OverDrive chip into the socket. (This disables the original 486, and all processing is performed by the OverDrive chip.) The system will then run at 66 MHz when doing internal operations (such as math and register operations and processing out of its internal Level 1 cache), while having "normal" external timing, so no modifications are required to the standard 33 MHz 486 motherboard. Systems that are *initially designed* with speed-doubled processors use the similar 486DX2.

The 63 MHz OverDrive Pentium processor for a 486 motherboard is called a P54C. The P54T 83 MHz OverDrive Pentium processor for a 33 MHz 486DX or 66 MHz 486DX2 motherboard uses only 3.3 V internally, has most other features of a standard Pentium (such as superscalar architecture and branch prediction), but has only a 32-bit external data bus. In contrast to a standard Pentium's 16 kbytes, the P54T has 32 kbytes of L1 cache.

The clock-doubled 3.3-V Pentium processor upgrade for a Pentium motherboard is called a P54CT (a regulator on the chip converts the motherboard's 5 volts to the 3.3 volts).

A 120/133 MHz Pentium OverDrive processor is available for 60 and 66 MHz Pentium systems (it includes the necessary voltage regulator, since it uses a lower voltage). Also, a 150 MHz Pentium OverDrive processor is available for 75 or 90 MHz Pentium systems.

And a 125 MHz Pentium Overdrive processor with MMX can replace a 75 MHz Pentium (and 90 MHz and 100 MHz Pentiums can be replaced with 150 and 166 MHz Pentium Overdrive processors with MMX).

See **S486SX**, **S486SX2**, **INTEL**, **PC**, and **PENTIUM**.

P

PR Rating Specification

A system developed by Intel's competitors to easily show the speed of their Pentium-class processors compared to the Intel Pentium (instead of showing the actual clock speed of their processor, since this is seldom a meaningful comparison due to clock doubling, cache sizes and other factors). For example, if a Cyrix 6x86 processor based computer system running with a processor internal clock speed of 133 MHz performs within 1.5% of the speed of an otherwise identically-configured 166 MHz Intel Pentium based system, then the Cyrix 6x86 gets a PR (*performance rating*) rating of PR166. If the Cyrix runs faster than the 166 MHz Pentium, then the Cyrix gets a PR rating of PR166+ (the "+" is not part of the PR rating system, but vendors used to use it when their system is more than 1.5% faster than the Intel processor to which they want to compare their processor's—but not within 1.5% of the next faster Intel processor).

Since there are so many ways to test the performance of a processor, and different processor designs are faster in some areas than others (such as floating-point math, integer math, graphics handling, and so on), such rating systems are sure to be over-simplifications. However, independent tests do show that the PR ratings assigned are accurate.

The PR rating system was developed by Advanced Micro Devices (AMD), Cyrix, IBM Microelectronics and SGS-Thomson Microelectronics. It was first used by Cyrix for their 6x86.

The PR rating is assigned based on Ziff-Davis Publishing Company's Business Winstone 97 benchmarks tests, which run under Windows 95. The tests are performed by an independent testing organization (MDR Labs, which is part of MicroDesign Resources, which is a subsidiary of Ziff-Davis).

Initially, this was called the *P-rating system* (and was based on the Winstone 96 benchmark tests). It was likely changed to placate the lawyers that there was no attempt to confuse the public about whether "P" was for "Pentium" or "performance" (since Pentiums are often referred to by designations such as P55C during development, though lately Intel seems to be using names of rivers instead).

A current problem with this system is that now that there are many types of Pentium processors (Pentium, Pentium MMX, Pentium Pro, Pentium II), the PR rating does not indicate to which type of Pentium the rated processor is being equated.

PR rating test results are available at MicroDesign's web site, at *http://www.chipanalyst.com.* MDR is at *http://www.mdronline.com.*

See **ICOMP**, and **PENTIUM**.

P6

The sixth generation of Intel's microprocessors (after the 8086/8088, 80286, 80386, 486 and Pentium). The name Pentium is a nice trademarkable word that indicates the fifth generation. The first "P6" processor was the Pentium Pro, and the P6 series includes the Pentium II.

See **PENTIUM II**, and **PENTIUM PRO**.

P7

Intel's successor to the Pentium Pro and Pentium II.

This processor will include RISC capabilities developed as part of Intel's work (which began in 1994) with Hewlett-Packard, and their PA-RISC architecture. A compatibility mode enables the processor to be binary compatible with both the PA-RISC and Intel *x86* architecture (so it can run current programs). However, to get the full benefits of the new processor, programs will need to be recompiled for the new processor.

The big new feature is the new 64-bit-wide instruction set, which Intel calls IA-64 (the Pentium II and previous 32-bit wide instruction sets are a subset of IA-64, and are now called IA-32). Multiple instructions are encoded into 128-bit words, with extra bits to support additional registers, and to indicate which instructions can be executed in parallel (the compiler will know this, which is one reason why porgrams need to be recompiled to get the full benefit of the new architecture.

Intel has announced that this processor will be shipped in 1999, and initial versions may run at 600 MHz internally.

HP calls the P7 a *PA*-9000. Intel calls it *Merced*.

See **INTEL**, **HP**, **PENTIUM PRO**, **PA RISC**, **PORTABILITY**, **RISC**, and **VLIW**.

PA-RISC
Precision Architecture-RISC

Hewlett-Packard's RISC architecture, which is derived from the processors of the Apollo workstations (they bought Apollo in the 1980s). The PA-RISC processors were first introduced in 1986, and are now used in HP's HP 9000 servers and workstations.

PA-RISC processors have *bi-endian switching* (they can be either *little endian* or *big endian*).

The PA-RISC processors are the successor to the HP 3000 minicomputer architecture.

See **ALPHA AXP**, **BIG ENDIAN**, **HP**, **LITTLE ENDIAN**, **P7**, **RISC**, and **SPEC**.

PABX
Private Automatic Branch Exchange

Another name for Private Branch Exchange.

See **PBX**.

PACE
*Priority Access **Control** Enabled*

3Com Corporation's method of supporting multimedia over Ethernet, so that even under heavy load, time-sensitive traffic will have a maximum latency of 5 ms. Both 10- and 100-Mbits/s Ethernet are supported. Standard Ethernet adapters are used in the user workstations, but Ethernet switches replace conventional concentrators.

The switches use a technique called *interactive access*, which anticipates the behavior of the standard Ethernet adapters to provide different *classes of service* (time-sensitive and not time-sensitive) so that the Ethernet link can be shared between different types of traffic.

Standard Ethernet has an *interframe gap* of 9.6 µs. That is, no stations are allowed to transmit for 9.6 µs after the end of a frame. In PACE, for time-sensitive traffic, the switches begin transmitting sooner, so have guaranteed access to the LAN. Different MAC addresses are used for the different *Classes of Service* (COS). Applications must be written (using 3Com's proprietary methods) to take advantage of PACE.

3Com expects that ATM (which supports various classes of service, for the same reasons) will be a *backbone* technology, and 3Com's PACE technology will make it possible to use Ethernet to bring multimedia capability (cost-effectively) to the desktop.

Unfortunately, other vendors never got excited about PACE, and the standard (and widely accepted) method of providing this much-needed support for COS for Ethernet will likely be 802.1p (for prioritization) or some other technology.

See **S10BASET**, **S100BASET**, **S802.3**, **COS2** (*Class of Service*), **ETHERNET MULTIMEDIA**, and **SWITCHED LAN**.

Packet

A (OSI layer 3) unit of data exchanged between end systems (host computers).

See **FRAME**, **PDU**, and **ROUTER**.

Paging

Traditional pagers operate using one of three frequency ranges, as listed below:

▲ VHF, specifically 138 to 174 MHz

▲ UHF, 406 to 512 MHz

▲ 900 MHz, specifically 929 to 932 MHz

The paging protocol used is called POCSAG (Post Office Code Standardisation Advisory Group), and it is an international standard (CCIR Recommendation 584). It initially operated at only 512 bits/s, but 1,200 and 2,400 bit/s systems are currently in operation.

Motorola's one-way paging protocol is called FLEX, and it has improvements in capacity (1,600, 3,200 and 6,400 bit/s data rates are supported). Motorola's two-way paging protocol is called ReFLEX, and it offers further improvements in battery-saving and sharing frequencies between different speed, and one-way and two-way paging.

Further information is available at *http://village.ios.com/~braddye/protocol.html*, and CCIR 584 is at *http://village.ios.com/~braddye/rpc1.html*.

See **NARROWBAND PCS**, and **WIRELESS**.

PAL
Phase-Alternation Line

The broadcast color television standard used in Western Europe (including the U.K.), Asia, Australia and most everywhere else other than North America, Japan, Europe and Russia.

Compared to North America's NTSC, PAL:

▲ Is not as well standardized (many countries use slightly different implementations)

▲ Usually has better resolution (625 lines, compared to NTSC's 525 lines)

▲ Usually has a slower *frame rate* (25 rather than 29.97 frames per second—therefore often showing noticeable *flicker*)

▲ Uses a similar method of adding the color information (using a *sub-carrier*)—though the color (often called the *hue* or *tint*) is automatically calibrated and so does not need adjustment, as North American televisions do

▲ Has the same 4:3 aspect ratio, 2:1 interlacing and 1 V p-p signal as NTSC

Many countries have slightly different implementations of PAL, with names such as PAL-M (which is used in Brazil and is similar to NTSC in that it requires 6 MHz for each channel, has 626 lines per frame, and uses 60 Hz scanning) or PAL-I1 (which requires 8 MHz per channel, has 625 lines per frame, and uses 50 Hz scanning—and can provide a better picture because of it).

See **HDTV**, **NTSC**, **SECAM**, and **VIDEO**.

PAP
Password Authentication Protocol

A security protocol used on data communication links which use the PPP link layer protocol. An *Id* (that is, a user identifier such as a username) and a *Password* are sent over the link after the LCP is established, but before user data can be sent. Since the passwords sent are not encrypted (so snoops can capture and display them with diagnostic tools), CHAP is preferable.

CHAP is defined in RFC 1334 as an optional authentication phase.

See **AUTHENTICATION**, **CHAP**, and **PPP**.

Paper

Did you ever wonder:

▲ How big an E-size drawing is?

▲ What the dimensions of a "standard A4" piece of paper are?

▲ What "20-pound bond" paper is and why it is almost the same weight as 50-pound book or envelope paper?

▲ What "*long grain*" means on your laser printer paper?

Well I did, and here is what I found.

Paper

Nonmetric paper sizes are listed in the following table.

Size	Width	Height	Comments
	Inches		
A	8.5	11	Standard North American *letter size* paper.
Legal	8.5	14	Lawyers love this stuff.
B	11	17	Sometimes called *tabloid* or *ledger* (accountants love this stuff)
C	17	22	
D	22	34	
E	34	44	
F	28	40	
G	11	42	These sizes are intended to be stored rolled, rather than flat.
H	28	48	
J	34	48	
K	40	48	

Metric paper sizes (as standardized by the ISO) are listed in the following table.

Size	Width	Height	Width	Height
	mm		inches	
2A0	1,189	1,682	46.81	66.22
A0	841	1,189	33.11	46.81
A1	594	841	23.39	33.11
A2	420	594	16.54	23.39
A3	297	420	11.69	16.54
A4	210	297	8.27	11.69
A5	148	210	5.83	8.27
A6	105	148	4.13	5.83
A7	74	105	2.91	4.13
B0	1,028	1,456	40.48	57.32
B1	728	1,028	28.66	40.48
B2	514	728	20.24	28.66
B3	364	514	14.33	20.24
B4	257	364	10.12	14.33
B5	182	257	7.17	10.12
B6	128	182	5.04	7.17

Metric A4-size paper is the size that is supposed to replace standard $8\frac{1}{2}$" × 11" office paper (A4 is slightly narrower and taller).

Other than size, the most common distinguishing factor for paper is its weight (which actually refers to its *basis weight*—the paper's actual thickness (which is sometimes called the *caliper*) depends on many factors, such as whether the paper is *coated* to give it a shiny and smooth surface.) This weight is expressed as the number of pounds for 500 sheets (one *ream*) of paper in its *basis size*—and this size depends on the type of paper!

As a side point, this is similar to the way cloth weight is expressed—14 oz. denim (for example) is the number of ounces that 1 square yard of the material weighs. Even farther to the side, 210-denier nylon means that 9,000 m of the stuff weighs 210 g. Back on topic, the following table shows the different basis sizes for various types of paper.

Type of Paper	Basis Size (inches)	
	Width	Height
Bond	17	22.5
Book paper	25	38
Book cover	20	26
Vellum Bristol	22.5	28.5
Index	22.5	30.5
Tag	24	36

This explains why an $8\frac{1}{2}$" × 11" piece of 20-pound bond (sometimes written as *20#* or *20 lb.*) actually weighs a different amount than an $8\frac{1}{2}$" × 11" piece of 20-pound book paper—these papers have different basis sizes.

Perhaps the most common papers are standard *20-pound office bond* (the type you use in your photocopier and laser printer) and *60-pound book*, also called *offset* (the type used in softcover books). Since these papers have different basis sizes, the metric measurement (grams per square meter) is a better way to compare weights, as shown in the following table.

Paper Type	Common Paper Weights					
Bond	pounds	16	20	24	28	36
	g/m^2	60.2	75.2	90.2	105.3	135.4
Book (or offset)	pounds	40	50	60	70	90
	g/m^2	59.2	74.0	88.8	103.6	133.2

As shown, 20-pound bond paper is almost the same weight as 50-pound book paper (just another reason why metric is a good idea). The weights for other papers can be calculated by scaling these numbers linearly. For example, 32-pound bond would be (32/28 × 105.3 =) 120.3 g/m^2.

Paper is made of fibers (from a tree) and the direction of these fibers is called the grain (just like in wood). Paper is manufactured in huge rolls, and the grain runs lengthwise on these rolls. When the rolls are cut-up into sheets, the the grain may run along the length of the sheet ("long grain"), or accross the width ("short grain"). Since paper curls at the ends of of

Parallel Bus

the grain, and this curling can cause jamming, printer and photocopier manufacturers usually suggest that paper with the grain running the length of the page be used. The ream of paper for such use is therefore typically labelled "long grain", "grain: long" (or something like that). The other way to tell the grain direction is that the second paper size measurement is the grain direction. For example, $8\frac{1}{2}$" × 11" paper would be long grain, and 11" × $8\frac{1}{2}$" paper would be short grain.

Paper sizes are standardized internationally by ISO 216.

See **REAM** and **SI**.

Parallel Bus

A type of interconnection between computers or computers and peripherals where the data is transferred more than one bit at a time. PC parallel printer ports and the SCSI bus are examples, where 8-bits (or more) are transferred with each bus cycle.

While parallel buses transfer data faster than *serial buses* (which transfer only a single bit at a time), parallel buses are typically limited in length due to signal skew (the difference in the signal arrival times at the end of the cable, due to the different propagation speeds of each pair in the cable) and the cost of the cables and connectors (which must support more signals).

Most data communications (Ethernet, Token Ring, FDDI, EIA-232, and so on) uses bit-serial communications.

See **BUS**, **CHANNEL**, **MVIP**, **PARALLEL PORT**, and **SCSI1**.

Parallel Port

A PC's standard, traditional parallel printer port is a female DB-25 connector. The interface has 8 data bits to the printer, plus 5 control signals to the printer, and 5 control signals from the printer.

The pin-out is shown in the table below.

The interface uses TTL (*Transistor-Transistor Logic*) voltages which are *unbalanced* signals (all signals are referenced to a common ground and are therefore very susceptible to electrical noise). The interface can source about 2 mA per signal.

With standard printer cables, the maximum cable length is about 15 feet. With well-shielded cable, this can be extended to about 50 feet but is not recommended.

The interface and the 36-pin connector was first defined by the implementation by the Centronics Data Computer Corporation, on their printers (beginning in the mid-1960s). The interface is therefore sometimes called a *Centronics interface*.

Typical actual transfer rates are up to 100 kbytes/s.

There are two competing efforts (ECP and EPP, now both merged into the IEEE 1284 standard effort) to define higher-speed and better bidirectional capabilities.

The table below shows several details of PC parallel printer ports. Included are the pin numbers (for both the DB-25 on the back of a PC and the Centronics connector on the printer), and the signal name, function, and direction of the signal.

Pin Number			Direction		
DB-25	**Centronics**	**Pin Name**	**PC**	**Printer**	**Pin Function**
1	1	/Strobe[a]		→	The data to printer is valid when this signal is low (and for at least 0.5 µs before and after this). The printer should read the data on the signal's falling edge.
2	2	Data bit 0		→	
3	3	Data bit 1		→	
4	4	Data bit 2		→	
5	5	Data bit 3		→	Data to printer
6	6	Data bit 4		→	
7	7	Data bit 5		→	
8	8	Data bit 6		→	
9	9	Data bit 7		→	
10	10	/Ack		←	Acknowledge—the printer finished processing the byte of data and is ready for more when this signal goes high.
11	11	Busy		←	When this signal goes high, the printer has accepted the byte of data and is processing it (and will not accept another byte of data) until this signal goes low (and /Ack goes high).
12	12	PE		←	Paper Empty (the printer is out of paper when this signal is high), or maybe there is a paper jam—there is no single definition.
13	13	Slct		←	Select (or on-line)—when this signal is high, the printer confirms that it is selected and on-line.
14	14	/Auto Fd		→	Auto Line Feed—when this signal is low, the PC has requested that the printer insert a line feed after each line (carriage return) sent from the PC.
15	32	/Error or /Fault		←	The printer is saying that an error condition has occurred (when this signal is low).
16	31	/Init		→	Initialize Printer—when this signal goes low, the PC has requested the printer to do an internal reset (clear the input buffer, reset printer logic, and return the print head to the left margin) to initialize itself.
17	36	/Select In		→	Select Input—when this signal is low, the PC has selected the printer, which should then accept subsequent data from the PC.
18-25	16, 19-30, 33	Ground		↔	Signal ground.

a. Note that these signals are inverted between the PC's I/O port registers and the PC's parallel port. This table presents the information as it appears on the PC's parallel port.

Parity

In the preceding table, signals prefaced by a slash indicate that the signal is *negative logic*; that is, it is considered asserted when the signal is low.

See **S1284**, **ECP**, **EPP**, and **TTL2** (*Transistor-Transistor Logic*).

Parity

A weak method of error detection (but not correction) in which the sender generates extra data bits (that are appended to the data) so that the receiver can determine whether the data have been corrupted (with a somewhat low confidence, since an even number of bits in error in the same byte will not be detected).

In *serial data communications*, communications software can configure a PC's UART to add (for example) an odd parity bit to each transmitted character. The UART will then set the parity bit to either a binary 1 or 0, as required to ensure that the total number of ones (that is, bits that are set to binary 1) in the character (including the parity bit) is an odd number.

Other serial data communications parity settings are:

▲ *Even*—the total number of ones is an even number

▲ *Mark* or *1*—this is a silly setting, since the parity bit is always set to binary 1, which does not provide any error detection and just reduces the throughput of the communication line by about 10%

▲ *Space* or *0*—the parity bit is always set to a binary 0, also a silly thing to do

▲ *None*—no parity bit is sent

ANSI X3.16 defines that asynchronous data communications (and paper tape punches, such as those on the now ancient ASR (automatic send/receive) 33 teletype machines (that only really old people remember) uses even parity, and synchronous data communications uses odd parity. The document even goes on at some length on the difficulty they had in determining these choices.

For serial data communications, parity is generally not used (it is set to none), since for interactive use it is usually obvious when there is data corruption (junk characters are displayed on your screen) and file transfers use a protocol (such as `ZModem` or `Kermit`) that is much better at detecting errors, through the use of CRCs, and in both cases, error correcting modems are usually used.

A PC's memory usually uses parity. It stores 9 bits for each byte (8 bits) to be stored, the ninth bit being an even parity bit for the byte. When each byte of data is retrieved from memory, a hardware circuit checks the parity, and, if it is incorrect, generates a hardware interrupt (which requests the operating system to do something, such as display a message to the user).

Since memory is becoming more reliable and implementing parity is expensive—it requires $\frac{1}{8}$ (12.5%) more bits, costing 12.5% more—many newer PCs don't use parity RAM. Therefore memory errors would go undetected (perhaps causing the PC to hang the once every few years it is predicted memory errors would occur). Macintoshes have used nonparity memory for several years.

Rather than only detecting (some) errors, high-end servers (for which cost is less of a concern, relative to reliability) often use ECC (*Error Correcting Code*) memory, which can detect and correct some errors. The method requires adding several "redundant" bits to each (usually) 32-bits of memory. Typically, single-bit errors can be corrected, and 2- or 3-bit errors can be detected.

See **AT COMMAND SET**, **CHECKSUM**, **CRC**, **ECC**, **KEYBOARD**, **FCS**, **FEC**, **MNP**, **RPI**, **SIMM**, **UART**, and **V.42**.

Patent

A federally-administered legal protection against others manufacturing and selling your product.

Patents will be granted only if they are:

▲ *New*: first in the world—though the *Patent Cooperation Treaty* (PCT) allows some time for patents filed in one country to be filed in some other countries, and still be considered new

▲ *Novel*: show inventive ingenuity and not be "obvious to someone skilled in the technology"—they should be thinking "now why didn't I think of that?"

▲ *Useful*: passes the "utility test"—it has to really work and solve a real problem

Patents can be any of the following:

▲ *New technologies*: mechanical, electrical, or chemical inventions or discoveries

▲ *Techniques*: such as manufacturing processes or methods, and surgical techniques

▲ *Equipment*: mechanical or electrical products, devices, tools, or apparatus (which may in turn be used to make other products

▲ *Compositions*: chemical compounds

▲ An improvement on any of these (90% of patents are improvements to other existing patented inventions)—to use the new patent may require a license from the original patent holder.

Patents do not cover the artistic or aesthetic qualities of an article (though other forms of intellectual property protection may).

A patent is granted only for the *physical embodiment* of an idea (not the idea itself), for example, a description of a product's construction, or a process that produces something tangible or of value.

Patents will not be granted for a scientific principle, idea, abstract theorem, method of doing business, computer program, or medical treatment.

In the U.S. and Canada, a *patent application* must be made within one year of publicizing the patent (though preferably before publicizing it—especially since most other countries require that the patent application be made before any publicity or use anywhere—that is, it must have *absolute novelty*). The U.S. and Canada's one-year grace period enables you to go to a trade show or do some market research before committing the resources to the patent process.

While the actual filing fees are only about $400 and $150, for a U.S. and Canadian patent, respectively, a patent will cost at least $4,000 to $6,000 (mostly for a patent agent or lawyer's time in preparing the documentation) per product per country. A worldwide patent could cost as little as $12,000 if only major English-speaking countries need to be covered and the required legal work is small. More likely, it will cost up to $10,000 to prepare the patent application, and perhaps another $5,000 in after that for the agent's time to answer questions that arise. Many report costs of $50,000 and more (costs escalate rapidly if the patent application requires a great deal of legal assistance, research or refinement)—plus the annual maintenance fees (in the U.S. alone, there are 25,000 patents per year which expire because the maintenance fee is not paid).

It is up to the owner of a patent to find patent *infringers* and take legal action—if this is not done, then the strength of the patent against future infringers is substantially reduced. Prosecuting an infringer can cost $250,000 and more. It is worth patenting something only when there is real and lasting business value in having a patent. Devices that can be made in many ways or will be obsolete before the year or two (minimum) required to obtain a patent are not good candidates for patents.

The core and essence of a patent is the *claims* section that describes the uniqueness of the patent. It must be written by a person skilled in the art to make the patent of any value.

The purpose of a patent is to both protect the owner and "promote the creation and implementation of technological information, so that all can share in the benefit from the advance in technology and knowledge" (nice chunk of words). It tells your competitors exactly what they cannot make and sell.

A patent application consists of the following:

▲ *An abstract*—a brief summary of the contents of the specification.

▲ *A specification*, which has two parts: a clear and complete description of the invention and its usefulness (this cannot be expanded with *new matter* after the application has been filed), and the *claims*, which set out the *essential features* and define the *boundaries* of patent protection being sought. (Information provided in the patent that is not covered by the claims can be used by anyone immediately, but if the claims are too broad, then the patent will likely be refused for overlapping existing patents.)

▲ A test of the specification's clarity is that it should enable anyone with average skill in the technology to make or use the invention (after all, that's the deal; you describe the technology for the benefit of others, and the government gives you exclusive use of the technology for 20 years).

▲ *Drawings* (if the invention can be shown by one; possible exceptions include chemical compositions and processes) showing all features of the invention, as defined by the claims.

As most countries do, Canada uses "first to file," rather than "first to invent" to decide who gets a patent if there is more than one application for the same thing. But don't file too soon, or you might not yet have all of the important details for a working, useful invention worked out—and you will need to file a second patent (more fees, please). In the U.S., proof (such as laboratory notebooks) that an invention was made first (and not that a patent application was filed first) determines who gets the patent (until January 1, 1997 though, foreign inventions were dated by their U.S. patent filing date, not the invented date).

In the U.S., the Patent and Trademark Office keeps a patent application secret until the patent is issued or rejected, at which time it becomes public information.

In contrast, the Canadian Patent Office publishes (also called *opens*) patent applications 18 months after they are filed, which is most likely before the patent would be awarded (yet another reason why most people prefer to apply for a U.S. patent before applying for a Canadian patent). This publicizing would make it impossible to get patent protection in most other countries (such as Mexico, China and all of Europe) that require that the invention not be publicized before filing for their patent protection. In Canada, you cannot get a patent if you publish or publicly show (anywhere in the world) details of the invention more than a year before filing a patent application.

In the U.S. you cannot get a patent if you publicize the invention more than one year before filing a patent application. This *publicizing* includes publishing a description of the invention anywhere in the world, or offering the invention for sale or even using the invention in public in the U.S. An exception is that secret, non-commercial trials are not considered publicizing.

The information contained in patents may be used by anyone if the patent is later rejected (when they get around to examining it).

If the patent is formally *abandoned* before 18 months (in Canada) or before being awarded or rejected, then the information will be kept secret.

In Canada and the U.S., patent protection lasts 20 years from the date of application. (In the U.S., until 1995, this was 17 years from the date the patent was granted.)

While patent protection does not begin until a patent is granted, inventors may use the term *"Patent Pending"* once an application has been filed (even without requesting the patent be examined; this creates up to a 1-year *priority period*). This provides no legal protection, but gives the inventor time to assess the feasibility or marketability of the invention and may discourage potential infringers.

Among other things, examiners check for *prior art*; that is, whether something too similar has already been patented. While a new patent will not be awarded for something that is almost entirely based on one or more previous patents, combining such prior art in a new and novel way can be patentable. There is no requirement that patented products be *marked* "Patented," but it is certainly a good deterrent to potential infringers to let them know that a product is patented.

It is illegal to mark unpatented products as patented.

In addition to the *filing* and *examination fees* that are required to get a patent (not to mention the fees of a *patent agent*, which most inventors choose to use), an annual *maintenance fee* is required. (If you don't pay it, your patent lapses, and anyone can use it as if it were expired.) When a patent expires, anyone can freely make, use, or sell products based on the invention and the information in the patent.

Many standards (such as those for Ethernet and Token Ring) specify the use of patented technologies. Standards-setting organizations permit this only if the patent owner agrees to license the technology to any company requesting it, for a reasonable licensing fee.

The rules for the U.S. and Canadian patent process and protection are somewhat similar (that is, if you can get a U.S. patent, you will likely be able to get a Canadian one as well), except for coverage of life forms (for example, laboratory rats with special features) and computer programs.

To support improvements and next generation products, the U.S. patent system allows *continuation in part*, so that a patent that has already been applied for can be modified without being considered to be new matter.

As of July 1997, the U.S. provides an optional expedited review for patents for anti-terrorism, cancer and AIDS related inventions, and for other inventions from inventors that are more than 65 years old or in poor health.

The *Canadian Patent Act* provides that independent contractors own the patents for their inventions (even when the development work is paid for by the contractee) unless there is a written agreement otherwise. However, the *Integrated Circuit Topography Act* states the opposite (for integrated circuit topographies); the principal owns the work, not the contractor (unless there is a written agreement otherwise).

The *Canadian Patent Office* is part of the CIPO. In the U.S., the *Patent and Trademark Office* administers patents (they have about 5,100 employees, and issued about 100,000 patents in 1994).

In the U.S., the term *design patent* is roughly equivalent to the Canadian term *industrial patent*. And the U.S. term *utility patent* is roughly equivalent to the Canadian term *patent*.

The U.S. Patent and Trademark Office has a Web site at *http://www.uspto.gov*. Some of their patent database can be searched from there.

The Cornell Law School has some U.S. Patent Law information at *http://www.law.cornell.edu/topics/patent.html*.

See **CIPO**, **INTELLECTUAL PROPERTY PROTECTION**, and **TRADE SECRET**.

Pathworks

DEC's marketing name for their LAN data communications software.

DEC's implementation of Microsoft's LAN Manager for VMS.

But can also refer to DEC's LAN servers and protocols for VMS on Ethernet (LAST), VMS on Token Ring (DECnet or NetBEUI), Ultrix (DECnet or optional TCP/IP), SCO/UNIX (TCP/IP), DOS (NetBEUI or optional IPX), OS/2 (NetBEUI), and Macintosh. Also supports LAT and OSF's Motif GUI. Optional IPX support is available. Pathworks for DOS can be run out of high memory (DOS 5 or Windows).

See **DEC**, **LAST**, and **VMS**.

PBX
Private Branch Exchange

The telephone switch that is used at a (typically) small to medium-sized company. Has a separate pair of wires to each user's telephone (or possibly more than one pair per telephone if the phone has fancy features, such as an LCD display or a speaker-phone) and to the nearest central office, for each outside trunk.

Typical basic features include transferring (forwarding) and conferencing calls.

When you pick up your handset, the dial-tone that you hear is generated by the local PBX. If you dial "9," the PBX selects an outside line for you (connects your extension to an outside trunk that goes to the nearest central office), and you then hear the dial-tone from the CO.

Sometimes called a Private Automatic Branch Exchange (PABX).

See **C.O.**, **CTI**, **DMS**, **DSX**, **POTS**, and **TRUNK**.

PC
Personal Computer

A computer that is run by an Intel (or Intel-compatible) processor (at least, as I've defined it for this book—others can define a PC to be any computer largely used by one person at a time, such as a Macintosh or Unix-based workstation).

Some characteristics of recent such processors are listed in the following table, along with some non-PC processors (the DEC Alpha, Motorola PowerPC and Sun UltraSPARC).

Processor	Speeds (MHz)[a]	Voltage[b]	Internal (L1) Cache Size (kbytes)[c]	Type[d]	Math Coprocessor[e]
8080[f]	2, 2.5, 3.0	5.0	0	None	External
8088	4.77, 8, 10	5.0	0	None	External
80286	6, 8, 10, 12	5.0	0	None	External
80386SX	16, 20	5.0	0	None	External
80386DX	16, 20, 25, 33	5.0	0	None	External
Intel 486SX	16, 20, 25, 33	5.0	8	Write-through	External
Intel 486SX2	25/50, 33/66	5.0	8	Write-through	External
Intel 486DX	25, 33, 50	5.0	8	Write-through	Internal
Intel 486DX2	25/50, 33/66	5.0	8	Write-through	Internal
Intel DX4	25/75, 33/100, 50/100	3.3	16	Write-back	Internal
Intel 486SL	25, 33	5.0, 3.3[g]	8	Write-through	Internal
Intel Pentium OverDrive (P54T)	25/63, 33/83	5.0, 3.3[g]	16/16	Write-back	Internal

(table continued on next page)

| Processor | Speeds (MHz)[a] | Voltage[b] | Internal (L1) Cache | | Math Coprocessor[e] |
			Size (kbytes)[c]	Type[d]	
Intel Pentium (P54C)	60, 66	5.0	8/8	Write-back	Internal
	50/75, 60/90, 66/133, 66/166	3.3, 2.9[h]			
	66/100, 60/120, 66/166, 66/200	3.3			
	60/150	3.3, 3.1[h]			
Intel Pentium MMX (P55C)	60/150, 66/166	3.3, 2.45[h]	16/16	Write-back	Internal[j]
	66/200, 66/233[i] PCs	2.5, 1.8[h]			
	66/166, 66/200, 66/233[k]	3.3, 2.8[h]			
Intel Pentium Pro	60/150, 66/166, 60/180, 66/200	3.3, 2.9[h]	8/8	Write-back	Internal
Intel Pentium II	66/233, 66/266, 66/300	2.8	16/16	Write-back	Internal[j]
AMD Am486SX	33, 40	5.0, 3.3[g]	8	Write-through	External
AMD Am486SX2	25/50	5.0	8	Write-through	None
	33/66	3.0		Write-back	
AMD Am486SX4	33/100	3.0	8	Write-back	None
AMD Am486DX	33, 40	5.0, 3.3[g]	8	Write-through	Internal
AMD Am486DX2	25/50, 33/66	5.0	8	Write-through	Internal
	40/80	3.0	8	Write-back	Internal
AMD Am486DX4	33/100, 40/120	3.0	8 or 16	Write-back	Internal

(table continued on next page)

| Processor | Speeds (MHz)[a] | Voltage[b] | Internal (L1) Cache | | Math Coprocessor[e] |
			Size (kbytes)[c]	Type[d]	
AMD 5K86 (previously K5)	75, 90, 100, 116.7[l]	3.3	16/8[m]		Internal
AMD K6[n]	66/166, 66/200, 66/233	3.2	32/32	Write-back	Internal
Cyrix Cx486SLC2[o]	25/50	5.0	2	Write-through	External
Cyrix Cx486DX	33, 50	5.0, 3.3[g]	8	Write-back	Internal
Cyrix Cx486DX2	25/50, 33/66	5.0 or 3.45	8	Write-back	Internal
Cyrix Cx486DX2	40/80	3.45	8	Write-back	Internal
Cyrix Cx486DX4	33/100	3.45	8	Write-back	Internal
Cyrix Cx5x86 (previously "M1sc")	75, 100, 120	3.3	16	Write-back	Internal
Cyrix 6x86 (previously "M1")[p]	55/110, 66/133,[q] 75/150[s]	3.3, 2.8[h]	16		Internal
Cyrix 6x86MX (previously "M2")	66/150, 66/166, 75/187.5[t]	3.3, 2.8[h]	64	Write-back	Internal
Cyrix MediaGX[u]	120, 133, 150, 166, 180	3.3, 2.9[h]	16	Write-back	Internal
DEC Alpha 21164	266	3.3	16	Write-thru	Internal
IBM 486SLC2	25/50, 33/66	5.0, 3.3[g]	16	Write-through	External
IBM "Blue Lightning"	25/50, 25/75, 33/66, 33/100	5.0, 3.3[g]	16	Write-through	External
IBM 486DX2	33/66	3.3 or 3.45	8	Write-back	Internal
	40/80	3.45			

(table continued on next page)

Processor	Speeds (MHz)[a]	Voltage[b]	Internal (L1) Cache		Math Coprocessor[e]
			Size (kbytes)[c]	Type[d]	
IDT WinChip C6[v]	180	3.3	32/32		Internal[w]
	200	3.52			
NexGen Nx586	35/70, 37.5/75, 42/84, 46.5/93	4.0	16/16	Write-back	Optional
Sun UltraSPARC-1	167		16		Internal

a. The external main memory bus speed (sometimes called the system bus speed) and the internal CPU speed are shown separately (such as "25/50") for clock-doubled (and tripled, and so on) processors. Processors with memory bus speeds of 50 MHz or faster (for example, all of the Pentiums) typically run the expansion bus (typically ISA or PCI) at half the memory bus speed, so a 120 MHz Pentium runs the memory bus at 60 MHz and the I/O expansion bus (PCI or whatever) at 30 MHz (since PCI buses prior to PCI version 2.1 supported a maximum of 33.3 MHz PCI bus clock rate). For example, a 166 MHz Pentium runs the memory bus at 66.6 MHz, and the PCI bus at 33.3 MHz. Memory bus speeds of 66.6 MHz (usually called 66 MHz) were first used in 1993, for the 66 MHz original Pentium.

b. Recent versions of newer processors operate at lower voltages to reduce power consumption (for longer battery life or Energy Star compliance). This also reduces heat dissipation (so there is no need for a fan).

c. Rather than a single *unified* cache, some processors have separate code and data caches (indicated by a "16/8" for example).

d. Write-back caches store both reads and writes. Write-through caches store only reads (so they can be read quickly again), so write performance is slower (this is more reliable, since you can be sure that data was written through the cache before the processor continues processing). Some PC BIOSs allow write-through caching to be disabled.

e. Processors before the 486DX had no built-in math coprocessor.

f. Being an 8-bit processor, the 8080 could not run DOS (so could not be used in a PC)—it is included for comparison only.

g. 5 V is used for interfacing to external ICs, but 3.3 V is used internally, to reduce the heat dissipation and cooling and power requirements of the processor.

h. 3.3 V (and subsequent to that, 2.5 V) has become a standard (to replace 5 V) IC external interface voltage, and this processor interfaces with external components at this voltage. However, it uses the lower voltage (such as 3.1, 2.9, or more recently 1.8 V) internally (Intel calls their implementation *Voltage Reduction Technology*—VRT) to reduce power consumption and heat generation.

i. These versions are intended for portable laptop computers.

j. Processor also supports MMX.

k. These versions are intended for desktop PCs

l. The 100 and 116.7 MHz versions are rated PR133 and PR166 respectively.

m. 16 kbytes for instructions and 8 kbytes for data.

n. Was the NexGen 686 until AMD bought NexGen to help with the next generation of the AMD K5.

o. Cyrix Corporation was bought by National Semiconductor in 1997.

p. Also called the IBM 6x86, as IBM Microelectronics manufactures it

q. Cyrix rates these as PR133, PR166 and PR200, respectively. This performance rating is supposed to indicate the clock speed of Intel Pentium which this processor performs closest to.

r. This was the first PC processor to use an external system bus speed greater than 66 MHz.

s. These are rated at PR166, PR200 and PR233, respectively.

t. Includes an SVGA graphics controller (which uses system DRAM for memory), audio controller, DRAM controller and PCI bus interface, to be used to make low-cost, medium-performance PCs.

u. This is sold by Centaur Technology, which is a subsidiary of Integrated Device Technology. While these low-cost processors have fast clock speeds, they are not superscalar and don't have other advanced features such as branch prediction.

v. Also includes a basic implementation of MMX, for example, only a single instruction can be executed at a time.

w. A separate bus to the L2 Cache runs at the full CPU speed. But who really cares, because NexGen was not doing too well, and they got bought by AMD who already have a similar product, so this processor and the AMD name are history.

The table below shows the following:

▲ The internal clock speed (that's the one advertised as the speed of the computer—in MHz) of the (usually Pentium) processor. This is also the rate at which the L1 (primary) cache is accessed. The processor does internal operations (such as adding and moving numbers between internal registers and L1 cache) at this rate.

▲ The bus speed for the L2 (secondary) cache and also of the main memory—such as the 32 Mbytes of RAM (this is also called the *motherboard speed*, the *system bus* speed and the *memory bus* speed). Main memory also uses this bus, but since it is slower, it uses more wait-states than the L2 cache.

▲ The "clock multiplier" (ratio of internal to external memory bus speed).

▲ The speed of the I/O expansion bus (typically PCI for recent processors, which for PCI version 2.0 and earlier is 33 MHz maximum).

Processor Internal Speed (MHz)	L2 Cache and Memory Bus Speed (MHz)	Processor Clock Multiplier	PCI Bus Speed (MHz)
60	60	1	30
66	66	1	33
75	50	1.5	25
90	60	1.5	30
100	66	1.5	33
120	60	2	30
133	66	2	33
150	60	2.5	30
166	66	2.5	33
200	66	3	33

The table below presents some comparative processing speeds.

Processor	Clock Speed (MHz)	MIPS (Drystones v1.1)	PC Magazine PC Bench 8.0 Processor Score	Relative Speed
80486SX	25		18	1.0
80486DX	25	20		
80486SX	33	27.2	24.5	1.2
80486DX	33		29	1.3
80486DX2	25/50	41	27.7	1.8
80486	50		35	1.9
80486DX2	33/66	53.9	46.7	2.2
DX4	33/100	70.7	64.3	3.5
Pentium	60	100.0	72.7	4.0
Pentium	66	112	78	4.3
Pentium	60/90	150	102	5.7
Pentium	66/100	166	120.2	6.7
Pentium Pro	66/133	250		

A main reason for the PC being so popular (especially as compared to Apple's Macintosh) has been the documentation and standardization of the PC's bus—so *printed circuit boards* (or *cards*) could be added to provide new capabilities. These boards plug into the PC's *bus*. So that the processor can individually address each board, each board must be configured to have unique settings for the items in the table below. (Most boards don't use all of these communication methods, so they don't require all these settings.)

Setting	Typical Settings	Function
DMA Channel	0 through 7	DMA is used for high-speed data transfers between peripherals and memory. See *DMA*.
I/O Address	$02E8_{16}$	Input/output ports are the addresses at which peripherals exchange data with the CPU. See *PIO*.
IRQ	2_{10} through 15_{10}	Interrupts interrupt whatever the CPU is doing so that time-critical information can be transferred when needed. (For example, data from a modem will be read before another character comes in and overwrites the first.) See *IRQ*.
Memory Address	$D000_{16}$	Each byte of a PC's 640 kbytes of RAM has a unique memory address. Some peripherals communicate with the PC's CPU by using a block of memory addresses (the memory is actually on the peripheral). PC RAM and other peripherals must not be configured to have memory at the same addresses. See *Shared Memory*.

The original IBM PC was announced as the *IBM* Personal Computer, at an IBM press conference in New York on August 12, 1981 (though the first units did not ship until October 1981). It had a single-sided (that is, the bits were stored on only one side of the diskette), 160 kbyte capacity, $5\frac{1}{4}$" diskette drive, 64 kbytes of DRAM, a 12" monochrome display (monitor) and ran PC-DOS version 1.0 (all this, for a list price of $2,880). It also had the capability to use a standard color television as a display, and it therefore had to have a 3.579545 MHz (see **NTSC**) quartz crystal oscillator (so-called, since it is based on a little crystal of the mineral quartz, which has been precisely-ground and -shaped to vibrate at that frequency when excited by a small voltage). The PC designers decided to put an oscillator of four times this frequency (14.31818 MHz) into the PC, since this frequency could be divided by 4 for the color television signal and by 3 (producing approximately 4.7727267 MHz) to produce a clock signal for the 8088 processor (which had a maximum clock speed of 5 MHz). While this resulted in the processor being run at slightly less (4.5%) than its maximum speed, it was close enough that the cost savings (of not having to use a second oscillator) were apparently considered worth the performance loss.

A hardware counter IC in the PC used the 4.7727267 MHz processor clock signal divided by 4 (which is 1.19318167 MHz) to drive a 16-bit counter, which divided this by 65,536 to produce a hardware interrupt (IRQ 0) at approximately 18.2065 Hz. DOS uses this 54.925 Hz "tick" to keep track of the time of day (as ticks since midnight) *once the PC has been told what the current time is*.

Since the PC's ticks only enable the PC to track the accumulated time since the PC was powered on, starting with the PC/AT, PCs have had a battery-backed-up *Real-Time Clock* (RTC) IC, which keeps track of the time and date even when the PC's power is off (this clock typically drifts from the actual time by 1 to 2 seconds per day). The RTC is read when the PC is (re)started to set the operating system time. The RTC IC also has 64 bytes of battery-backed-up CMOS RAM (*Complementary-symmetry Metal-Oxide-Semiconductor Random Access Memory*) to store:

▲ The time and date (10 bytes)

▲ RTC control and status (4 bytes)

▲ System settings (50 bytes), such as the type of diskette drives installed

The PC's BIOS has a program (usually started by pressing Ctrl-Alt-Esc or Ctrl-Alt-Ins—or perhaps the Del or F1 key during the short period when prompted, soon after the PC is first powered on) to examine and change these CMOS settings.

The RTC IC uses a 32,768-Hz oscillator, which easily divides to exactly 1 second. The oscillator is typically accurate to 0.005%, which is about ±2 minutes per month—which explains why your PC's clock needs to be corrected periodically (unless it gets set automatically by an accurate server elsewhere on your network).

An idiosyncracy of having two clocks is that the PC BIOS and RTC may not support the year 2000 and beyond, but the operating system software clock will. The PC may be able to be set to the current time and date (after the year 2000 for example), and will maintain the correct time and date—until the PC is powered off. It will then power on to an incorrect date, and require the date to be manually corrected.

A recent trend is to reduce the cost of providing new PC functions by using the main CPU for functions that used to be off-loaded to smaller processors on other add-in boards, such as those in the following table.

Effort	PC's Resources Used for	Instead of
Class 1 fax modem	Fax image rasterizing	Class 2 fax modem
Controllerless modem	Interpreting the AT command set	Modems with controllers (processors)
DCI and GDI	Video processing	Video adapter
LAN adapter PIO	Replacing DMA	LAN adapters with DMA and bus master DMA.
NSP	Audio processing	Sound boards with dedicated DSP ICs (Digital Signal Processing Integrated Circuits)
PCS	Desktop video conferencing image compression	Video boards with dedicated compression hardware
RPI	Serial data communications error correction and data compression	Modems with processors that handle V.42 and V.42*bis* onboard
USDA	Video memory	Dedicated memory on video adapter

Advanced Micro Devices, Inc. (AMD), Cyrix Corporation and Intel have WWW servers at *http://www.amd.com*, *http://www.cyrix.com* and *http://www.intel.com*, respectively. Further details are available from MDR Labs, at *http://www.mdronline.com/pc_processors* and *http://www.mdronline.com/mpf*.

See **APM, AT, BIOS, BUS, CACHE, CMOS, DCI, DMA, EDO RAM, ENERGY STAR, FAX, ICOMP, INTEL, IRQ, KEYBOARD, MIPS, NC, NSP, NTSC, P RATING, P6, PENTIUM, PLUG AND PLAY, PCS** (*Personal Conferencing Specification*), **PIO, RPI, RAM, SHADOWED BIOS, SHARED MEMORY, SPEC, SUPERSCALAR, TICK, USDA**, and **UTC**.

PC95

A designation Microsoft dreamed up to define the minimum requirements for a PC to run Microsoft's Windows 95 operating system (and therefore get a Windows certification logo):

▲ 80386 or better CPU

▲ 4 Mbytes or more RAM

▲ 640 × 480 display (standard VGA) with 256 colors (or more)

▲ Dedicated mouse (or other pointing device) port (that is, don't use up a serial port for it) or an integrated pointing device

▲ One serial port

▲ One parallel port

Microsoft's PC97 specification is almost 400 pages in length, adds a requirement for USB support and includes motherboard form factors (the layout of motherboards).

Microsoft, Intel and Compaq collaborated on the development of the PC98 specification, which specifies AGP and faster system buses (66 and 100 MHz). It is expected that PC99 will no longer specify ISA bus slots.

See **OPERATING SYSTEM**, **PLUG AND PLAY**, **PC**, **USB**, and **WINDOWS 95**.

PC Cards

The new name for PCMCIA cards. The organization that defines the standard is still the PCMCIA.

See **PCMCIA**.

PCCA
Portable Computer and Communications Association

A group that is developing extensions for NDIS and ODI so that these interfaces (which previously supported only wired media) can also be used between protocol stacks and hardware that supports wireless transmission.

The same group has also developed an extension to the *AT* command set called SWATS.

See **S802.A11**, **MOBILE IP**, **NDIS**, **ODI**, **SWATS**, and **WINSOCK**.

PCI
Peripheral Component Interconnect

Intel's *local bus* standard.

Introduced in June 1992 (the first version) and 1993 (Release 2.0). Supports up to 16 physical slots (an addressing limitation), which won't be reached because of the electrical limitation of 10 *electrical loads* (which typically is used up by three or (rarely) four plug-in PCI cards) per PCI bus.

PCs can have two or more PCI buses (each driven by a *PCI* bridge IC, so there can be six or more PCI cards per PC. If the second PCI bus is driven from the first, then it is called a *cascade* or *hierarchical* design. This is usually undesirable, since the first bus must carry the second bus's load. If the PCI buses are each driven directly from the processor's bus, then it is called a *peer* design.

32- and 64-bit-wide bus implementations are defined. 64-bit support uses an additional in-line connector (similar to the AT bus's extra connector).

32- and 64-bit cards can be installed in 64- and 32-bit slots (and the other way around too—the cards and buses detect this and work properly). When a 64-bit card is installed in a 32-bit slot, the extra pins just overhang, without plugging into anything.

Implementations have a separate (from the processor's) clock, running at DC to 33 MHz (though usually at 33 MHz). Slowing the bus's clock speed is needed to reduce PC power consumption when the PC is not being used.

Since the bus is *multiplexed* (the same pins carry address and data), two *bus cycles* (one to send the address, the next to send the data) are required per 32- or 64-bit transfer.

However, a *burst mode* is defined for reads and writes (though a PCI bus with a 486 processor can only support read bursts), which allows any number of data cycles to follow a single address cycle. This substantially increases the transfer capacity.

A 32-bit, 33 MHz PCI bus implementation therefore has a nonburst peak transfer rate of 66 Mbytes/s (two bus cycles to transfer 4 bytes) and a burst peak transfer rate of up to 132 Mbytes/s (once the address cycle finishes). However, these bursts are typically limited to 4 long-words (which are 4 bytes each), which is 16 bytes total. After this, the requesting device has to request and be granted control of the bus again (and do an address cycle). Therefore, a 32-bit PCI bus has a typical sustained burst transfer rate of 80 Mbytes/s—which is still enough to handle 24-bit color at 30 frames per second (full-color, full-motion video).

PCI supports bus mastering DMA, though some PCI implementations may not support bus mastering DMA for all PCI slots. The CPU can run concurrently with bus mastering peripherals.

Sometimes PCI is called a *mezzanine* (or *intermediate*) bus, since it is not the processor's bus. This is good, since processor buses tend to match (and be limited to) that particular processor. (Witness the fast decline of VL-bus when the 486 became old news.)

ISA, EISA, and MCA buses can be driven by a PCI bus (using the appropriate type of *bridge* chip set), so non-PCI peripherals can be used in the same PC.

Since PCI is not processor-specific (VL-bus is 486-specific), it can be used for other processors, such as DEC's Alpha and the PowerPC (so Macintoshes can use PCI peripherals).

PCI is the first bus to support both 3.3- and 5-V cards. Keys in the connector ensure that the (single-voltage and non-interchangeable) cards are not plugged into the wrong voltage slot (smokers!).

Dual-voltage cards and slots can be made—these automatically try 3.3-V operation first and then try 5-V if that is not supported.

The actual PCI signals are produced by an IC which typically also is the level-2 cache controller, runs the memory bus and interfaces to the processor.

PCI competes with (but is generally faster than and better suited to processors better than the 486) VESA's VL-bus.

PCI boards support:

▲ Automatic configuration (they don't require manual assignment of BIOS extension addresses)—that is, they support plug-and-play very well

▲ Sharing of interrupts (the same interrupt number can be used by more than one device)

▲ Parity checking of the data and address bus signals

▲ *Scatter/gather DMA* (up to four 4-kbyte blocks of data that are scattered because of virtual memory management schemes can be transferred with a single DMA operation)

PCI cards have from 64 (the mandatory *base set*) to 256 bytes (recommended) of configuration memory, which provide the following information:

▲ 16 bits are reserved for a vendor identification code (each vendor gets a unique number)

▲ 16 bits are reserved for a device identification (vendors assign a unique number to each of their products)

▲ 8 bits are reserved for a revision identification

▲ 24 bits are for a Class Code, which describes a board's basic function (LAN adapter, video controller, and so on)

▲ The remainder of the first 64 bytes are reserved for future use

The rest of the memory is available for vendor-specific use.

Competes with EISA, but PCI:

▲ Has a much faster transfer rate (both providing faster operation and leaving more bus time for other peripherals)

▲ Has lower-cost cards (for example, because PCI is fast enough to transfer data from a LAN—and LAN adapter—to a PC's memory at full LAN speed, less buffer memory is needed on the LAN adapter)

▲ Supports *Plug and Play*

▲ Is faster to install (EISA's irritatingly slow configuration procedure is not needed)

A limitatation of PCI 2.0 is that it only supports chip-specific identification codes. If (for example) two vendors implement the same integrated circuit differently, then Plug and Play may load the wrong device driver. PCI 2.1 was released in 1995, and supports the following:

▲ 66 MHz bus speeds, so the maximum data transfer rate is 528 Mbytes/s

▲ *Subsystem IDs* so Plug and Play can identify the specific driver required for a board

An extension to PCI 2.1 is called *concurrent PCI*. It is intended to provide better multimedia support, and has the following enhancements.

▲ *Multi-transaction timer* (MTT). This allows PCI bus master DMA boards to hold the bus for short bursts, without having to re-arbitrate to get control of the bus each time. This is intended to allow higher throughput for video.

▲ *Passive release*. This allows a PCI bus master DMA board to transfer (likely video) data on the PCI bus while an ISA bus transfer (likely of audio) is in progress (this normally blocks PCI transfers, since the PCI bus is used to connect the CPU to the ISA bus).

▲ *PCI* delayed transaction. This allows a PCI bus master transfer to get priority over a queued (in the PCI chip set) PCI to ISA transfer (which then gets completed later).

▲ *Enhanced write performance*. The PCI chip set has larger buffers (so when the PCI bus is busy, transactions can be queued until later), performs write merging (which collects byte, word and double-words that can be written in a single 8-byte write operation, into a single write operation).

PCI has been adapted for non-Intel processors, such as the Alpha, MIPS, PowerPC, and SPARC.

PCL

The PCI standard is developed by the PCI Special Interest Group, they have a web server at *http://www.pcisig.com*.

See **ALPHA AXP, BUS, BUS MASTER DMA, DMA, ENERGY STAR, LOCAL BUS, PLUG AND PLAY, POWERPC, SPCI, VIDEO,** and **VLBUS OR VLB.**

PCL
Printer Command Language

Hewlett-Packard's language for controlling their printers (though many competitor's printers are compatible with it).

Competes with Adobe's PostScript *Page Description Language* (in the sense that the commands sent to a printer are usually one or the other—but PostScript is a more powerful language).

PCL commands are *escape sequences* (a few characters starting with the ASCII escape character—which is $1B_{16}$ or 27_{10}). For example, PCL 5 includes commands for specifying the following:

▲ Number of copies, page size, source paper tray, and output bin

▲ Print resolution

▲ Page margin and orientation

▲ Cursor positioning

▲ Font, line spacing, character spacing and height, stroke weight

▲ Downloadable font and pattern data

▲ Rectangle draw and fill commands

▲ Switch to HP-GL/2 mode (HP Graphics Language, originally developed for HP plotters, which are vector-oriented—they draw with pens)

For example, the command `<Esc>&16D` (it is conventional to represent the Escape character as <Esc>) specifies printing at 6 lines per inch. Along with their LaserJet printers (which were first shipped in 1984), PCL has evolved over time, and each new version supports all previous features, plus the new features, as shown in the following table.

PCL Version	Used for	Example New Features
1		Basic printing and spacing functions for dot-matrix and ink jet printers, suitable for single-user printers
2		Adds multiuser printing tools
3	LaserJet[a]	Adds high-quality office printing support
4	LaserJet Series II	Page formatting functions
5	LaserJet III and 4	Scalable fonts and HP-GL/2 support
5e[b]	LaserJet 4L	Power-down modes
6	LaserJet 5M	Additional drawing primitives, such as rounded-corner boxes, rotations, and bezier curves

a. This is the first LaserJet, and was introduced in 1984.
b. The "e" is for "enhanced."

PCL 6 is a major enhancment to PCL. It supports complex drawing commands, just as Post-Script has for years, and has a font-synthesis capability, so printed output more closely matches that displayed on your PC's screen. PCL 6's commands are similar to those supported by Windows' GDI so less translation work is required by the print driver. This reduces the size of the print commands (reducing LAN loading and transfer times), and speeds printing, and control returns to the user's application software sooner. Also, PCL 6 supports other types of graphics hardware, such as fax machines and scanners.

See **ASCII**, **HP**, **POSTSCRIPT PAGE DESCRIPTION LANGUAGE**, and **TRUETYPE**.

PCM
Pulse Code Modulation

A method of digitizing audio (turning it into those ones and zeros that computers love so much).

Periodically (8,000 times a second for telephone systems, 44,100 times a second per right and left channel for audio CDs) samples the input and produces (for example) an 8-bit (for telephone systems) or 16-bit (for audio CDs) value representing the amplitude of the audio input at that instant in time.

Since digitizing assigns a specific (binary) number for any input amplitude, and only a given number of amplitudes are available (for example, 256 for 8-bit digitizing), chances are that the assigned number will be a little bit too high or a little bit too low compared to the actual input. This error is called *quantization error* and produces *quantization noise* at the output.

Since better accuracy is required for lower signal levels (since the quantization error is more significant compared to the signal), digitization values are assigned closer together for lower signal levels. This is called *companding* (compressing/expanding). This type of nonlinear quantization is done by an *Analog-to-Digital converter* (or A/D) which is called a CODEC (*Coder/Decoder*).

8-bit companded audio sounds about the same as 12- to 14-bit (depending how you measure it) non-companded audio (that is, you can use 50% fewer bits and get the same sound quality), so is very popular. Specifically, 8-bit unsigned PCM has a dynamic range of 48 dB (that is, the ratio of the voltage level of the quietest signal to the loudest signal is 256:1, which expressed in decibels is $20 \times \log_{10} 256/1$, which is 48 dB). Unfortunately, there are two such nonlinearities standardized (in ITU G.711):

- ▲ *μ-law* (pronounced "moo law" or "mew law"), used in North America, Japan, and South Korea

- ▲ *A-law*, used in the rest of the world

The dynamic range of these methods are 72 dB and 64 dB, respectively, which is equivalent to 14- and 13-bit PCM.

Converters are therefore required to interconnect these two types of PCM-digitized voice channels.

The digitized audio can be carried by ISDN B channels or E1 or T1 channels.

PCMCIA

Analog signals passing through one or more PCM digitizations will have some level of *non-linear signal distortion*, which may affect the maximum data rate that modems using the channel can achieve.

See **S56K MODEM**, **ADPCM**, **CDROM**, **CODEC**, **E1**, **G.711**, **ISDN**, **MPMLQ**, **MULTIMEDIA**, and **T1**.

PCMCIA
Personal Computer Memory Card International Association

The name of the group that produced the specification for the credit card–sized plug-in boards (initially) for laptop computers.

Initially, the cards were called that too, but it was decided that nonpronounceable six-letter acronyms just don't cut it. So the cards are now called *PC Cards* (which is an ambiguous but nonintimidating name).

The PC (that is, *Personal Computer*, not *Printed Circuit*) cards are 85.6 mm deep × 54 mm wide and have a 68-pin connector (two rows of 34 pins on 1-mm centers).

The predecessor cards were developed by the *Japan Electronics Industry Development Association* (JEIDA) to store keyboard parameter sets for music synthesizers and sampling keyboards and were therefore only memory cards.

Several different height PC cards are defined, as shown in the table below.

Type	Height (mm)	Common Use
I	3.3	Memory (RAM or Flash ROM)
II	5	LAN adapters and modems
III	10.5	Hard disks
IV[a]	15.5	Hard disks

a. Not standardized

Although JEIDA had specified a Type IV card slot, PCMCIA rejected it as part of the PCMCIA standard, and only a few manufacturers (for example, Toshiba) use this type of slot.

Thinner cards can be plugged into thicker slots (for example, a Type II slot will accept a Type I or Type II card).

The cards can provide up to 64 Mbytes of memory or be I/O (Input/Output)- or file-transfer-oriented devices. The cards are specified to operate over a range of 0°C to 55°C.

The original 16-bit interface version (sometimes called PC Card-16) interface supports only one interrupt (which can be a limitation for multiple-function cards, such as LAN adapters and modems), and does not support bus mastering DMA (so data transfers have relatively high CPU processing demands).

There are several versions of the specification:

Release 1.0 (the standard was released in September 1989, first products appeared in 1990) of the standard defined only Type I cards and did not define I/O capability or software drivers (as the cards only had some form of memory and so did not need drivers).

Release 2.0 (September 1991) defined I/O, but standard software drivers were still not available (vendors provided proprietary drivers with their cards). The interface to the PC is an 8- or 16-bit data path with a bus speed of 8 MHz (basically, the same as a PC's ISA bus).

Release 2.1 (November 1992) was mainly typographical corrections to release 2.0, and the standard was finally broadly accepted as it provided a good level of standardization and features. For example, v2.1 PCMCIA cards provide the following:

▲ *Host Independence*—they work in any type of computer with a PCMCIA slot

▲ *Plug and Play*—no manual configuration is required

▲ *Hot Swapping*—no need to power off or reboot the computer (the connector pins at the outside edges are the power pins and are longer than the rest—ensuring that the card gets power before data, so it can power up in an orderly way)

▲ *Execute in Place* (XIP)—programs run directly from the ROM in the PCMCIA card, so there is no need to transfer the memory contents to the computer's RAM first

Also, v2.1 defined:

▲ Software drivers called *card services*, which is a higher-level Application Program Interface (API). It assigns the base I/O address, interrupt and memory address (if these are used) to the *PC* Card.

▲ *Socket services*, which is a BIOS-level interface which has standard calls regardless of how a vendor implements the function

The card services can be either:

▲ Separate drivers, which are loaded by `config.sys` (for MS-DOS and OS/2 v2.1)

▲ Built in to newer operating systems, such as OS/2 Warp version 3 and Windows 95, as part of their Plug and Play support

These standard software interfaces have made the PCMCIA much simpler and more useful.

The next version of the standard ("3.0") is called the *PC* Card Standard (that is, it is not called PCMCIA anymore—no one liked that abbreviation), *February 1995 Release* (in their wisdom, they stopped using version numbers—they felt it was causing consumer confusion by letter us know what we are really buying) and refers to the cards as *PC* Cards.

This PC Card Standard now includes specifications for the following:

▲ Non-bus mastering DMA support (sometimes called third-part DMA) for the PC Card-16 interface.

▲ *CardBus*, which is 32-bit *bus mastering DMA*, at a bus speed of 20 to 33 MHz—the peak bus transfer rate is therefore up to 132 Mbytes/s. This provides performance similar to EISA or PCI buses, and this is needed for Fast Ethernet, recent SCSI speeds and other faster functions. In fact, CardBus is basically the PCI bus implemented on a PCMCIA-style connector (the address and data lines are multiplexed, so that the 68 pins on the connector are enough). Since CardBus is basically the PCI bus on a tiny connector, it is only offered on computers that have PCI support (that is, computers with a Pentium-type processor).

▲ Multifunction adapters (for example, a combination Ethernet/Modem adapter)

▲ 3.3-V (instead of 5-V) operation (this reduces the power requirements—important for battery-operated laptop PCs)

Each card has a *Card Information Structure* (CIS), which specifies the card's:

▲ Manufacturer and model number

▲ Voltage and current requirements

▲ I/O configuration information (for example)

It is a linked-list (resident in the *attribute memory* of the card) of information stored in *tuples*, which are three-part data structures (information type, link to next tuple, and information).

A related feature for PC Cards (developed by Toshiba) is called Zoomed Port Video (ZPV). This is an additional connector to a PC's (typically a notebook PC) display and audio systems, so that full-motion video information (typically video-conferencing, television or MPEG) from the PC Card can bypass the PC's system bus.

Other than ZPV (which is not actually part of the PC Card standard anyways), other connectors (for user equipment) are not defined by PC Card (such as for the cable to a telephone line or LAN)—only the interface to the PC's bus.

The PCMCIA is at *http://www.pc-card.com*. Some additional information resources are listed at *http://www.sycard.com/cardlink.html*.

See **BUS MASTER DMA, COMPACT FLASH, DMA, EISA, FLASH, IRQ, MINICARD, PCI, PLUG AND PLAY,** and **SPCI.**

PCS
Personal Communications Service

The second generation cellular telephone service, with the following advantages over the traditional analog cellular telephone service (which is officially called AMPS):

▲ Is inherently digital, so can offer more noise-free voice, as well as faster digital transmission.

▲ Voice and data encryption can ensure secure conversations.

▲ Handsets are lighter, and batteries last longer.

▲ The antenna is smaller (both on the handset, and at the base station site—which is becoming a major issue—people are noticing the antennas cluttering-up the landscape).

▲ Digital services, such as Internet access, stock quotes and paging can be made part of the service.

▲ Operation within (and outside too—using the same handset) buildings.

▲ Frequency use is more efficient, permitting more conversations for a given amount of bandwidth.

PCS uses lower transmit power (than standard AMPS cellular telephones), so the telephones can be smaller and lower-cost (since smaller batteries and less-powerful components are needed). Cell sizes are only up to several hundred meters in diameter, compared to a kilometer and more for traditional AMPS cellular service.

Also, one of the original intents was to provide one phone number per person, which would be used for home (personal), office (indoors, for business), paging (anywhere), and mobile communications (outdoors, and in public places). It would be able to provide a "follow-me" service, in which the one phone number always finds you—regardless of where you are.

An initial expectation was that *personal agent* (software) would be programmed to (for example) pass business calls home only if they were urgent and to forward them to your voice mail if not. This and many other features (such as Caller ID) are now second priority to what the providers have more recently learned is the main desire of (potential) users— less expensive talk time. While initial analog AMPS had only 2 suppliers per geographic area (and they had no incentive to compete on price, since the other would simply match it), there are typically 2 to 6 PCS licensees per geographic are, resulting in much more consumer choice, and hopefully, incentive for the network operators to compete on price.

Three technologies were considered, and unfortunately, rather than one being selected (which would simplify everyone's life), all 3 are deployed in different parts of the country, and by different network operators.

- ▲ GSM—This is the widely accepted European standard for Cellular telephone service. The technology is therefore proven, with established suppliers. Also, using this technology for North America as well could facilitate roaming (except for the fact that different frequencies are used in Europe and North America, so the most you can do is take your subscriber ID module with you). Also, it is a proven technology with many manufacturers and a high transmission rate. However, it has a relatively high cost, and is not as secure as CDMA. About 25% of U.S. system operators selected GSM for their PCS technology.

- ▲ Canada's Microcell Telecommunications Inc. selected GSM-1900 (which is sometimes called PCS1900) for their 30 MHz of PCS bandwidth. It is a version of GSM that operates at the 1,900 MHz PCS frequencies. They offered the first PCS service in Canada, in late 1996 in Monteal. As for standard GSM, channels are spaced at 200 kHz, and each support 8 simultaneous conversations.

- ▲ CDMA—This is standardized in TIA/EIA IS-95 (Interim Standard) and supports the most simultaneous users for a given amount of bandwidth, offers the most secure transmission, has "soft-handoffs" (there is no break in the transmission when the handset moves from one cell to another—this is only needed during voice calls) and has a lower cost per cell site. However (there's always one of those), it is a newer, less-proven technology, and (at least initially) had a slower transmission rate. Different users can be allocated different bit-rates (for example, for data transfer), within the same 1.25 MHz shared bandwidth. This could be used for more efficient bandwidth utilization—low bit-rate for paging and low cost, and a higher bit-rate and higher cost for mobile faxing.

▲ CDMA was selected by about 60% of system operators, such as Sprint, PrimeCo (an alliance of 3 RBOCs) and AirTouch Communications (previously Pacific Telesis). In Canada, Clearnet offers PCS services using CDMA (using the 30 MHz of bandwidth they were awarded in December 1995), as does Bell Mobility (due to the voice compression possible with CDMA, the 10 MHz of PCS bandwidth awarded to Bell Mobility provides about 4 times the capacity of the 25 MHz used for traditional analog AMPS).

▲ Up-banded TDMA (also called D-AMPS 1900, and is standardized in IS-136). This technology the simplest, and is based on TDMA (which is sometimes called *North American Digital Cellular* or D-AMPS, and is standardized in IS-54B). TDMA is mature and widely deployed in North America. However, it offers the least security, supports fewer users for a given amount of bandwidth (compared to GSM and CDMA), and offers relatively poor voice quality. As is the same for standard TDMA, IS-136 channels are spaced at 30 kHz, and each channel supports 3 simultaneous conversations.

▲ TDMA was selected by about 40% of U.S. system operators, notably AT&T. In Canada, Cantel offers PCS using D-AMPS (which means roaming is technically possible, and indeed there is a roaming agreement in place). Initial offerings use the standard AMPS 800 MHz frequency band, but use advanced signalling to provide PCS features such as Caller ID and text messaging. Later, they will use their 10 MHz of PCS bandwidth to offer additional capacity.

As with all digital systems, PCS will provide higher-quality voice so long as the signal strength is adequate. At weaker signal strengths the voice quality is worse than analog cellular service.

Most PCS handsets are *dual-mode* in that they can use both one of the new digital methods (GSM, CDMA or TDMA) as well as standard analog AMPS. This permits users to roam to (that is, get service in) other areas that do not yet have coverage for that type of PCS technology, or do not have PCS roaming agreements with the user's home service provider in place.

Each PCS handset uses a *Subscriber Information Module* (SIM) that must be inserted in the handset before it will operate. It has information, such as the user's name and billing address, as well as your saved favorite telephone numbers and received text messages. GSM handsets have used these since their inception, and the hope is that PCS SIMs will be compatible with GSM's.

Putting your own SIM into someone else's handset results in you paying for the airtime and other charges incurred. An encryption algorithm in the SIM prevents others from reading your confidential information "over the air"—a crucial improvement over AMPS *electronic serial number* which can now easily be read by others and programmed into other handsets. This is called *cloning*), since this handset appears to cellular telephone operators exactly like the original handset, so airtime gets charged to the first user.

140 MHz (120 MHz for licensed use, 20 MHz for unlicensed use) in the "2-GHz" band has been reserved for PCS in North America. The licensed bands are divided into three 30-MHz blocks (called A, B and C) and 3 10-MHz blocks (D, E and F). In the U.S., each block was auctioned off (by the FCC) for each geographic area, and the winners then get exclusive use of their frequencies in their area(s)—and can use any technology they want. Blocks A and B were auctioned in 1995 (and the geographic areas that were auctioned included more than

one state—called *major trading areas*—so only really big companies and consortiums bid on these). Block C was auctioned in 1996 (and was auctioned as *basic trading areas*—typically as a single metropolitan area each, so smaller companies could participate). In total, about $7.6 billion was bid. Both the FCC and bidders hired gaming and gambling consultants to devise strategies (the FCC on how to structure the rules to get the most money, the bidders on how to win at the lowest cost).

In Canada, the CRTC evaluated proposals from prospective carriers, and awarded licenses (in December 1995) based on details such as the timing of implementation and the commitments for funding research and development, manufacturing and other economic investments.

The unlicenced blocks are divided into two 10-MHz blocks (*unlicensed use* means that you can use the frequencies without getting a license to use them, but you will be sharing the frequencies with other unlicensed users—and there are rules to ensure fair sharing). An example of equipment which uses the unlicenced frequencies is the Northern Telecom Companion in-building wireless handsets (where the handset of your desk telephone is wireless, so you can roam your office and building).

The exact PCS frequencies are shown in the table below.

Frequency Block	Frequency (MHz)	
	From handset [a]	To handset[b]
A	1,850 to 1,865	1,930 to 1,945
B	1,870 to 1,885	1,950 to 1,965
C	1,895 to 1,910	1,975 to 1,990
D	1,865 to 1,870	1,945 to 1,950
E	1,885 to 1,890	1,965 to 1,970
F	1,890 to 1,895	1,970 to 1,975
	Unlicensed (asynchronous)	1,910 to 1,920
	Unlicensed (isosynchronous)	1,920 to 1,930

a. The transmit frequency from the handset (mobile) to the base station is also called the *reverse channel*.
b. The transmit frequency from the base station to the handset (mobile) is also called the *forward channel*.

The transmit and receive frequencies of a conversation are always 80 MHz apart, with the mobile transmitting at the lower frequency (it costs less to build lower-frequency transmitters, and there ae more mobiles than base stations, so the overall cost of the service will be lower this way). Also, less transmit power is required for a given quality of signal at lower frequencies, which is more important for the usually battery-operated mobile.

All PCS systems sold into the U.S. must not power-up until it has been confirmed that previous users (such as terrestrial microwave) of the frequency spectrum have been relocated (typically to the 7 or 23 GHz band). The FCC has designated UTAM Inc. (*Unlicensed Ad Hoc Committee for 2 GHz Personal Communications Services Transition and Management*), which is a non-profit consortium of manufacturers) as the frequency coordinator for the unlicenced 20 MHz. Once UTAM has verified that the frequency spectrum is clear of the previous users, they issue a password which enables the PCS system. The PCS system records information about the frequency band, and if it is sensed that the system has been moved (because newly-detected, non-PCS frequency use is sensed), then the PCS system shuts down until a new password is entered.

There are rules for use of the frequencies. For example, while both FDMA (which uses frequencies continuously) and TDMA can be used, FDMA should attempt to use only the lower 3.75 MHz of the allocated spectrum. TDMA systems should attempt to use only the upper 3.75 MHz of spectrum.

In Canada, national 30 MHz licenses were awarded to each of Clearnet Communications Inc. and Microcell Telecommunications Inc. in December 1995. The two existing national Cellular providers (Rogers Cantel Mobile Communications Inc. and Mobility Personacom Canada Ltd.) were awarded national 10 MHz PCS licenses. The remaining 40 MHz of PCS bandwidth is being held by Industry Canada for future allocation (perhaps as a third 30 MHz license and a third 10 MHz license). The 20 MHz that does not require a licence ("license-exempt PCS") has been designated as being 10 MHz for voice and 10 MHz for data applications.

Other services are already using these frequencies—these include electrical utilities, police, and others, but mostly telephone company terrestrial microwave links (the huge four-legged towers offering long-distance telephone service for thousands of simultaneous conversations). In Canada alone, there are 1,400 such links, which must be relocated to other frequencies before PCS can be offered in those areas. After an initial period of time (which, in Canada, expires in July 1997), the existing frequency users must relocate to other frequencies whenever the PCS companies are ready to use the PCS frequencies (with the cost paid by the PCS companies—for example, about $70 to $100 million to relocate Canada's OPP microwave system to other frequencies).

To distinguish PCS from narrowband PCS, PCS at 1.9 GHz is sometimes called *broadband PCS*.

Other similar (to PCS) efforts include the following.

- ▲ PCTS (Public Cordless Telephone Service) in Canada, though it is now called PCS).

- ▲ PHS (Personal Handyphone Service) in Japan. This system officially was available as of July 1, 1995 and is very popular. It has very small handsets which function as both a cordless private telephone in the home and office, and a public mobile telephone in public places. They also handle voice, fax and even video and data traffic (at up to 32 kbits/s). The very small size of the radio coverage cells results in the system not handling hand-off well, so it is not suited to use in travelling automobiles.

- ▲ DECT (Digital European Cordless Telephone) in Europe.

The next generation of public mobile personal communication services is the subject of UMTS.

Some information on PCS in Canada is at *http://www.wirelessinc.ca*. Ericsson Radio Systems AB, at *http://www.ericsson.se*, is big on D-AMPS and GSM.

See **AMPS**, **CALLER ID**, **CDMA**, **CHAP**, **CT2**, **DECT**, **FCC**, **GAAS**, **GSM**, **NARROWBAND PCS**, **PCTS**, **TDMA**, and **UMTS**.

PCS
Personal Conferencing Specification

A cross-platform (Windows, OS/2, Macintosh, and UNIX) desktop (that is, to the PC, not a conference room) conferencing communications standard intended to facilitate global workgroups sharing video, voice, text, and graphics over LANs, ISDN, and analog phone lines.

Version 1.0 (released in December 1994) supports mixed audio (digitized voice), video (from cameras), and document (shared PC monitor screens, for example, showing a spreadsheet in real-time) conferencing over LANs and over ISDN and switched 56 WANs.

Version 2.0 is to add specifications for multimedia (LANs only), network administration, LAN/WAN gateways, and video conferencing over analog phone lines.

Builds on Microsoft's TAPI and Novell's TSAPI.

Promoted by Intel (it is based on their Indeo algorithm) and AT&T. Some would say that Intel is big on video technology because it requires faster processors (likely from Intel—what a surprise!).

Initially competed with H.320 (though H.320 initially defines only WAN-connected users) and T.120 (for document conferencing). But in 1995 they added the H.320 videoconferencing and T.120 data conferencing specifications to their standard.

The standards are being developed by the Personal Conferencing Work Group. For more information, see *http://www.gopcwg.org/pcwg*.

See **H.320**, **ISDN**, **NSP**, **PC**, **PCWG**, **T.120**, **TAPI**, and **TSAPI**.

PCTS
Public Cordless Telephone Service

The original intent of the system which followed analog cellular telephone (AMPS) was that from its inception, the handsets would offer public "cellular-like" service in public places, and function as cordless telephones at home (and in your office). The name for this Canadian "digital cordless telephone service" was PCTS, and for a while it was on a fast track (that is, ahead of the U.S. PCS effort) so it would become the *de facto* standard for PCS. Unfortunately, manufactuers had no interested in making equipment for Canada only, so the effort stalled, and was completely replaced by what is generally today called PCS.

PCTS was to be as described below.

It would use very low power base stations (10 mW transmit power). This would result in very small cells, so it would have high capacity (the frequencies could be reused many times in a large area), and very small handsets (since they would use small batteries, and be low power, since the base stations would be within a few hundred meters). Private base stations would provide service for private use (at your house, and at your own office), and public base stations would communicate with the same handsets when they are in serviced public areas, such as shopping malls and restaurants.

Digital technology would be used, as it offers many advantages, including noise-free and secure (encrypted digitized voice) communications, calling number identification, and numeric paging.

Wireless services are usually standardized by what is sent and received over the air, so the standard is called a *common air interface*. There are several generations and varieties of this type of cordless service, as shown in the following table.

Name	Capability	Comments
CT1	Standard residential-type analog cordless phones. Uses separate frequencies for transmit and receive. Uses *Frequency Division, Multiple Access* (FDMA), and only 10 frequency pairs are assigned in North America, so interference with neighbors is common. Maximum range is about 50 m.	Very noisy service because of analog technology
CT2	Uses FDMA—each channel uses a 100-kHz bandwidth, out of a total bandwidth of 4 MHz. Speech is digitized at 32 kbits/s, and "full-duplex" conversations are supported over a single channel using *time division duplexing* (also called "*ping-ponging*," since the direction of transmission is changed 500 times per second). There is no location tracking, so mobiles cannot receive calls, only generate them.	Developed for use in Britain; is currently also in use in parts of Europe and Asia. Usualy uses 864 to 868 MHz.
CT2Plus	CT2 (using FDMA) with the addition of common-channel signaling for faster call delivery, automatic location registration to provide both incoming and outgoing service, and up to 40 MHz of total bandwidth for greater call-handling capacity. Cell sizes are from 30 m to 200 m in diameter and so are called *pico-cells*—these can be linked to form *zones*, which support handoffs between pico-cells for uninterrupted service while moving. CT2Plus systems can operate in CT2 environments.	The *CT2Plus Class 2* technology has been approved for use in Canada, for *enterprise wireless transmission* (cordless telephones for use within companies). The 944 to 948.5 MHz band has been allocated. This provides 40 full-duplex 100-kHz speech channels and 60 signaling channels. 948.5 to 952 MHz is being held for possible future allocation.
CT3	Similar to DECT	Developed by L.M. Ericsson for high-capacity wireless-handset PBXs
DECT	*Digital European Cordless Telecommunication* standard was created by the Council of European PTTs for both public and private use. Uses *time division multiple access* which is more efficient than FDMA (*Frequency Division Multiple Access*, where the frequencies available are divided among the simultaneous users). Uses the 1.88 to 1.90 GHz band and supports up to 10 times more traffic in this 20 MHz than CT2Plus handles in 8 MHz.	

While CT2Plus (for which the Canadian DOC allocated a total of 30 MHz of bandwidth in the 944-MHz band) was selected by Canada, the U.S. later selected the "2-GHz band" (the frequencies are actually just above 1.9 GHz) for their PCS service, and Canada realized that to get economies of scale in manufacturing equipment and to support roaming, the Canadian PCTS service had to be compatible with the U.S. service. Therefore rather than leading and defining PCS, the Canadian public effort is being developed in parallel with the U.S. effort (Northern Telecom still uses CT2Plus for its office cordless telephone service—which they call Companion).

One anticipated difference between PCS and cellular is that all PCS handsets will work with all base stations (so long as they use the same technology)—whichever service provider's is closest. In cellular, your handset communicates only with base stations from your own service provider (either the local wire-line or the non-wire-line carrier).

Under huge timing pressure (everyone wanted to be first, but noone wanted to make the wrong choice), several technologies were evaluated for PCS, including CDMA (which has the potential for the most conversations within a given frequency bandwidth), GSM (which has the advantage that it is the European standard, so handsets could be used in Europe) and TDMA (which is proven, but has relatively low bandwidth efficiency and poor audio quality).

See **AMPS**, **CARRIER**, **GSM**, and **PCS** (*Personal Communications Service*).

PCWG
Personal Conferencing Work Group

A group promoted by Intel (and consisting of over 150 vendors) to develop a desktop video conferencing standard called PCS.

See **PCS** (*Personal Conferencing Specification*).

PD
Phase-Change, Dual-Technology

An optical disk technology supports recording and (unlike most CD-R disks)—erasing as well.

A laser heats the disk surface, and lets it cool in either a crystalline state (which is more reflective) or an amorphous state (which is less reflective).

Disks have a capacity of 650 Mbytes, and drives can also be used for reading standard CD-ROMs. Like standard magnetic hard disks (and unlike CD-ROMs), PD disks spin at a constant angular speed, and have their data arranged in concentric rings.

See **CDROM**, and **DISK DRIVE**.

PDA
Personal Digital Assistant

A small, hand-held, battery-operated, microprocessor-based device that is expected to do things such as:

▲ Store telephone numbers, addresses, and reminders

▲ Send and receive email and faxes (wirelessly) .

▲ Receive pages (just like an alphanumeric pager)

▲ Recognize handwriting

Since some initial PDAs were far below users' expectations, some marketing types now refer to these devices as HPCs (hand-held PCs).

See **S802.A11**, **COMPACT FLASH**, **MINICARD**, and **POWERPC**.

PDH
Plesiochronous Digital Hierarchy

See **TDM**.

PDU
Protocol Data Unit

A generic term for a unit of data exchanged as part of a data communications protocol.

At the network layer, the PDU is called a *packet*, and at the link layer the PDU is called a *frame*. There are no more nice names like that, but there are more layers, so the term PDU can be used at any layer (a transport layer PDU, and so on).

See **FRAME**, and **PACKET**.

PEL
Picture Element

The term used for *pixel* by many IBM people and in fax documentation.

See **FAX** and **PIXEL**.

Pentium

Intel's name for their *superscalar* (it can execute more than one instruction per clock cycle) successor to their 486 processor.

Was not called "586" because Intel found out (the hard way) that numbers cannot be trade-marked.

Pentiums have the following:

▲ 64-bit data bus, though internal registers and the address bus are both 32 bits wide

▲ Two instruction execution units so that up to two instructions per clock cycle can be handled—however, there are many restrictions to both units munching instructions simultaneously, so code should be compiled for the Pentium (the compiler tries to work around these as restrictions as much as possible)

- ▲ A built-in floating-point unit

- ▲ Separate (nonunified) 8-kbyte (each) write-back data and instruction caches

- ▲ A programmable clock generator, which supports internal-to-external frequency ratios such as 3:1, 2.5:1, 2:1, 1.5:1, and 1:1. This enables the external memory bus for the 100-, 133- and 166-MHz processors to run at 66 MHz, and at 60 MHz for the 90-, 120- and 150-MHz processors. The PCI bus would then run at 33 MHz or 30 MHz, respectively.

- ▲ 273 pins, using a pin-out called *Socket 7*

Initial versions (called P5):

- ▲ Ran at 60 and 66 MHz (some say that the 60-MHz versions were simply 66-MHz chips that couldn't run at full speed)

- ▲ Were first shipped in March 1993

- ▲ Have no clock doubling

- ▲ Use 5 volts

The standard desktop PC 90- and 100-MHz versions (called the P54C):

- ▲ Run at 60 and 66 MHz externally (therefore using a clock multiplier of 1.5)

- ▲ Were first shipped in March 1994

- ▲ Use 3.3 volts (rather than the 60-MHz Pentium's 5 volts)—therefore using about $\frac{1}{4}$ of the power of the 60-MHz Pentiums

The Pentium version for the 237- or 238-pin *OverDrive* socket of 25- and 33-MHz 486 systems is called the P24T. Such upgraded 486 Pentiums:

- ▲ Are slower than same-clock-speed native Pentium systems because of the narrower bus (486 systems have only a 32-bit external data bus)

- ▲ May not support other Pentium features such as *burst-mode* reads and writes (depends on the existing PC's bus)

- ▲ Have a nifty built-in fan, and you run a TSR that monitors the fan's speed. If the fan doesn't run fast enough or the chip detects a heat problem, then a message pops up, and the CPU is slowed to the 25- or 33-MHz system clock speed. A slower clock speed dissipates less heat, since most heat is generated when the clock signal changes state—from high to low or from low to high (funny things are everywhere).

- ▲ Almost triples the processing power of a 25-MHz 486 and almost doubles the processing power of a clock-doubled 486DX2/50. Uses a 2.5:1 internal-to-external clock speed.

A 75-MHz version (which runs at 50 MHz externally) uses Intel's SL technology, which enables the processor to be stopped when it is not needed, to save power. It was first shipped in October 1994. The actual integrated circuit die (the unencapsulated chip, which is directly bonded to a portable PC's printed circuit board) weighs less than 1 gram.

Pentium support for *dual processing* (two Pentium processors sharing system RAM and *Level 2* cache) requires adding a P54CM Pentium to a P54C-based system. The P54CM is identical to the P54C but has a pin that ensures that the system starts in single-processor mode, letting the operating system enable the second processor when it is ready.

Pentium II

The Pentium communicates with level 2 (L2) cache at system bus speed—typically 60 or 66 MHz.

Both the 75- and 90-MHz versions support a *Voltage Reduction Technology* (VRT) that provides a 3.3-V (which is the new lower standard voltage—than the 5 V previously set by TTL) external interface (to the CPU's input and output pins) while operating the innards of the CPU at 2.9 V. This substantially reduces the power required (important for battery-operated portable PCs), and the heat dissipation (reducing or eliminating the need for cooling fans (an important reliability, noise, and power consideration).

The 120 MHz version first shipped in March 1995, the 133 MHz version in June 1995, the 150 and 166 MHz version in January 1996, and the 200 MHz version in June 1996.

The first Pentium to support Intel's MMX was the P55C. It was shipped in late 1996, and has a 32 kbyte L1 cache (16 kbytes for data and 16 kbytes for instructions), which is double that of previous Pentium processors. It uses a 2.5 V supply voltage.

Pentium processors are often referred to as P*xxx*, where *xxx* is the internal clock speed—for example, a P100 would be a 33-MHz (externally)/100-MHz (internally) Pentium processor.

See **BRANCH PREDICTION**, **CACHE**, **EDO RAM**, **ICOMP**, **INTEL**, **MMX**, **OVERDRIVE**, **P6**, **PC**, **PENTIUM II**, **PENTIUM PRO**, **SMP2** (*Symmetric Multiprocessing*), **SUPERSCALAR**, **TRADEMARK**, and **TTL2** (*Transistor-Transistor Logic*).

Pentium II

The successor to the Pentium Pro, but has MMX support. Called Klamath during development.

Instead of the traditional large flat IC package with pins (as was used for the predessor Pentiums, which use a pin-out called *Socket 7*), Intel mounts the Pentium II processor IC itself onto a small circuit board—complete with level 2 (L2) cache (and the associated TagRAM which stores what blocks of memory are in the L2 cache)—and puts a black plastic cover (with a neat-looking hologram sticker with a picture of the Pentium II's die) and an aluminum cooling plate on the other side of the board (pressing against the top of the ICs). The board mounts vertically, and has a row of electrical contacts along its bottom edge, so it is sometimes called a single edge contact (SEC) cartridge. One reason for the new electrical contact layout is to reduce EMI emmissions (which becomes even more important at the increasing clock speeds used in these new processors.

The L2 cache is 512 kbytes of four-way, set-associative, nonblocking, synchronous-burst SRAM. The Pentium II communicates with the L2 cache at half the processor speed, rather than the 66 MHz maximum of previous Pentium processors (except for the Pentium Pro which communicated with its L2 cache at full processor speed, due to the dual-cavity design of its processor module).

Two major enhancements from the Pentium Pro are faster segment writes (so the Pentium II runs 16-bit code, such as Windows 3.1 and Window 95), and the addition of MMX support (and it can execute two MMX instructions simultaneously). Since an update to a segment register (which specifies the upper portion of the address of an operand) means that subsequent half-executed instructions in the execution pipeline may be wrong, the Pentium Pro had to flush its pipeline. The Pentium II supports *register renaming* and *speculative writes*, so that the half-executed instructions (and the registers they update) are not flushed, but rather are kept in temporary registers. If it is found that the segment write does not affect those temporary results, they are kept, rather than being flushed.

Two-way glueless SMP is supported, which means that the processors have the logic required for a second processor to be added without needing any additional logic to arbitrate bus access and other interactions between the processors and their shared resources. In contrast, the Pentium Pro supported glueless four-processor SMP.

The Pentium II processor IC itself has 528 leads, and uses a package called a *plastic land-grid array* (PLGA). The bus interface is called *Slot 1*, which is equivalent to the Socket 8 interface of the Pentium Pro. It supports multiple buses, one of which is within the SEC cartridge, and is used for the half-processor speed communications with the Level 2 cache SRAM.

The Pentium II processors (233, 266 and 300 MHz versions) were first announced in May 1997.

See **CACHE**, **MMX**, **PENTIUM**, **PENTIUM PRO**, **SMP2** (*Symmetric Multiprocessing*), and **SRAM**.

Pentium Pro

Was called the P6 during development, and is Intel's successor to its Pentium processor. The 133 MHz version was shipped, and the 150 MHz version was announced in November 1995. The 166, 180 and 200 MHz versions were announced in February 1996.

Has 5.5 million transistors (not including those required for the integrated L2 cache). The first versions of the Pentium Pro processors ran at 133 MHz internally and 66.5 MHz externally, and provide almost twice the performance of a 100-MHz Pentium—but only for 32-bit operating systems and applications, such as Windows NT and UNIX). For Windows 95 the Pentium Pro performs about the same as a same clock speed Pentium. For Windows 3.1, the Pentium is sometimes slower than the Pentium (depending on what the application is doing—for example, segment register loads and also when 8-bits of a 16-bit register are written, and then the full 16-bits of the register are read—these cause a *pipeline stall*, which substantially slows the processor).

Intel's market projections showed that by the time the Pentium Pro would be available, 32-bit operating systems (such as UNIX, Windows NTand OS/2) and applications would be popular, so they optimized the design of the Pentium Pro for 32-bit software. As it turned out, the software was late (not exactly the first time that has happened), and Windows 3.1 and 95 was more popular when the Pentium Pro was released. Therefore, Intel initially marketed the Pentium Pro as the best choice for servers and power users (which typically run 32-bit software). When Pentium competitors (such as AMD and Cyrix) arrived, Intel dramatically dropped the price of the Pentium Pro.

The Pentium can process two instructions at once; however, if the processing of one instruction must wait (for example, if a branch took an unexpected path so the next instruction has not yet been fetched), then the processing of the other instruction is also stopped. This avoids the complicated situation of instructions being executed out of the original order.

In contrast, the Pentium Pro can process three instructions (so the processor is called *super-pipelined*) at once (and three instructions per clock cycle—wowzers!). If the processing of one instruction must wait, then the other instructions can continue being processed. (I guess that's what uses up the additional 2.2 million transistors.) Intel calls this *dynamic execution*. This out-of-order instruction execution cannot be used when certain instruction occur (such as loading an new value into a segment register—segment registers point other registers to 64

kbyte blocks of memory; or writing only 8 bits of a 32-bit register, then reading all 32 bits). All the execution units of the processor must wait until these instructions are executed—briefly losing the benefit of the superpipelined architecture, and lowering performance.

Runs at a new lower voltage of 2.9 V and (still) dissipates 15 to 20 watts (hot). Has built-in multiprocessor support for up to four processors per computer; the four processors can be directly connected without any additional logic components, greatly facilitating designing symmetric multiprocessing ("SMP") computers. The hardware support needed for this is described in Intel's MPS.

Can use a clock multiplier (the ratio of internal to external clock speed) of 2:1 (which is used by the initial version of the processor), 3:1, or 4:1 (which will be used later, when they figure out how to get the innards running lots faster). The different dividers are used to run the processor at full-speed internally, while keeping the external bus running at a maximum of about 66 MHz (typically 66.5 or 66.66 MHz), since standard DRAM cannot support faster speeds, and motherboard designs to support bus speeds greater than this are really expensive (faster DRAM technologies include EDO-RAM and SDRAM).

Has the same size on-chip *Level 1* cache as the Pentium (8 kbytes for instructions, 8 kbytes for data).

The Pentium Pro is available with either a 256 kbyte or a 512 kbyte *Level 2* (or "L2") cache. The larger cache is necessary for multitasking and multiuser servers, where the frequent task switches would make most of the cache information of a small cache useless (since it would be cached information for the previous task).

The four-way, set-associative L2 cache (which has 15.5 million transistors for the 256 kbyte size, and 31 million for the 512 kbyte size) is on a separate die (the actual eeny-weeny little chippy) but is mounted in the same package (called a dual-cavity design or a multichip module) as the processor die. This design enables the processor to communicate with the L2 cache at the full processor speed (such as 133 MHz and faster)—since the high-speed connections are so short. Earlier processors with external L2 cache were typically limited to communicating with their L2 cache at half (or some other fraction) of the processor speed—since all communications outside the processor are at the memory bus (also called the system bus) speed which is often 66 MHz, which is designed around the access time limitations of the L2 cache memory devices used.

The Pentium Pro's 64-bit-wide data bus has an additional 8 bits for ECC support. This is an important feature when huge amounts of RAM are used (which is typical for important servers). The processor is packaged in a ceramic *pin grid array* (PGA) package (basically an array of gold-plated pins sticking out the bottom), and has 387 pins. The pin-out is called *Socket 8*, which is equivalent to the Pentium II's *Slot 1*. It supports multiple outstanding bus transactions that can complete in a different order than they started (this facilitates multiple processor systems). (Intel Pentium and Pentium MMX processors used a processor interface called *Socket 7*.)

While earlier Intel processors used TTL-style 5 volt interfaces, the Pentium Pro supports interfaces of 2.4 V to 3.4 V (using an extension of *Gunning Transistor Logic* called GTL+). The first Pentium Pro processors used 2.9 V.

See **CACHE, DRAM, ECC, ICOMP, INTEL, MPS, PENTIUM, PC, SMP2** (*Symmetric Multiprocessing*), **SUPERSCALAR**, and **TTL2** (*Transistor-Transistor Logic*).

PEP
Packet Ensemble Protocol

A previously popular (especially in the UNIX community) proprietary high-speed (23,000 bits/s, half-duplex) modulation method used by dial-up modems from Telebit Corporation.

Obsolete now that standard high-speed modem modulation methods are available (such as V.32*bis* and V.34).

See **MODEM** and **V.8** through **V.34**.

PERL
Practical Extraction and Report Language

A popular scripting language that is used under UNIX (and more recently, under Windows NT too).

It provides access to all operating system calls but was initially created to (and is very powerful for) string and text processing. Perl is an *interpreted* (not *compiled*) language, so it is faster to code and easier to debug than writing in C (for example) but runs more slowly (this is usually not a concern for the type of work for which scripts are usually used).

Scripts typically have a `.pl` extension to the filename.

The Perl Language Home Page is at *http://www.perl.com/perl*.

See **TCL-TK**, and **UNIX**.

Personal Communications Service

See **PCS1**.

Personal Computer

See **PC**.

Personal Computer Memory Card International Association

See **PCMCIA**.

Personal Conferencing Specification

See **PCS**.

Personal Conferencing Work Group

See **PCWG**.

Personal Digital Assistant

See **PDA**.

PHIGS
Programmers' Hierarchical Graphics Standard

An ANSI three-dimensional graphics description and manipulation standard that is well suited to hierarchical structures (something made up of parts, each of which is made up of other parts). Each level of detail can be described separately.

PGP
Pretty Good Privacy

A freeware, *public-key* authentication and encryption method based on the *IDEA single-key* and RSA public-key encryption algorithms.

Well suited to electronic-mail communications (email), *Electronic Data Interchange* (EDI), and *Electronic Funds Transfer* (EFT). It does not require the secure exchange of encryption keys (even initially), yet messages that are exchanged will be authenticated (so both the sender and receiver can be assured that the message was not changed) and encrypted (so only the intended receiver can read the message), and the receiver can be assured that the sender really did send the message. Neat, huh?

Has other features too, such as:

▲ Key management and distribution

▲ Data compression (using an algorithm compatible with `pkzip`)

Here is how the method works:

▲ Each sender and receiver needs a copy of the PGP software. Versions for PCs (DOS, Windows, and OS/2), Macintoshes, VAXes, Amigas, and most UNIX workstations are available.

▲ Using the software, each user generates a pair of long, binary numbers (each up to 1,024 bits); one is the public key, and the other is the *private* (or *secret*) key. The numbers are stored in a file called a *key ring*, but to distribute the public key, it can be written to an (optionally) ASCII file (so that the keys can be sent through email systems that cannot handle binary files).

▲ The public key file includes the owner's name (and usually email address) and can be viewed with the PGP software. The public key file (when typed directly to your screen) with only one entry might look like this:

```
-----BEGIN PGP PUBLIC KEY BLOCK-----
Version: 2.6.2i
iQCVAwUAL6KYxbCfd7bM70R9AQFfrgP/ZnxreHTVXc
zO69bJav3FGjfTiVxGEOqbE4EgbYvKgfc60=
=Qmmk
-----END PGP PUBLIC KEY BLOCK-----
```

There—now you can say you've seen a key.

The secret key is kept secret. You don't give it to anyone. You keep it on your own key ring file. In fact, it is encrypted before you store it in your own key ring file (in case anyone snoops through your files or steals your computer).

▲ Everyone who wants to exchange messages sends a copy of their public key to everyone else who may want to exchange messages with them. This exchange can be done by diskette, by email, or using Internet-accessible *public keyservers*. There is no need to keep your public key secret, since all it is good for is encrypting messages (that only you can decrypt—because only you have the secret key) and authenticating messages from you. It is of no help in attempting to decrypt messages from you.

▲ There are now two ways to use the PGP software to send messages:

▲ *Authentication* (so that the receiver can be sure the message was from you and that it has not been tampered with). Using your secret key, PGP can be used to encrypt your message. While everyone can decrypt the message (using their copy of your public key), they can be sure it was sent by you (since your public key is the only way to decrypt your message, they know that that message could only have been encrypted by using your secret key—and only you have your secret key). This provides authentication (a "digital signature"), nonrepudiation (it *had* to be from you, and you can't deny that you sent it—unless you let someone else have your secret key), and assurance that the message was not tampered with (nobody changed it).

▲ *Encryption* (so that only the intended recipient can read the message). Using the intended recipient's public key, you can encrypt your message so that only the intended recipient can read the message (only the recipient's secret key can decrypt it). This provides encryption so that no one else can read your message.

One, the other, or both of these can be used for every message—depending on what you want: authentication, encryption, or both.

That is basically the story, but here are some implementation notes that show why things need to be just a little bit more complicated. (Isn't software always like that?)

▲ The secret key is an impossible-to-remember (up to) 1,024-bit number. Even if it is coded into ASCII, it will still be impossible to remember. (Could you remember the public key shown above?) How do you keep a copy of something that is too long to be remembered and too secret to be written down or stored on a computer? What happens is the following:

▲ PGP prompts you for a *pass phrase* (as opposed to a pass*word*), that is, for *many* words (including punctuation and numbers), perhaps a short meaningless sentence that you can remember and not write down anywhere.

▲ The pass phrase is used in a single key encryption of the secret key, and only the encrypted secret key is stored on your key ring.

▲ When the secret key is needed (to decrypt a received message, for example), PGP prompts you for your pass phrase, uses it to decrypt your secret key, and then uses the secret key to decrypt the received message.

▲ The RSA public key encryption method runs too slowly to be used to encrypt or decrypt messages longer than a few words. To encrypt a message using the public key, here is what actually happens:

▲ For each message to be sent, the PGP software creates a random one-time 128-bit-long number called a *session key* (which has nothing to do with the RSA public and secret keys discussed already). This session key is used to encrypt the message, using the IDEA single key algorithm (which encrypts messages 4,000 times faster than the RSA public key method). That is, your message is actually encrypted by using a conventional single key algorithm, *not* RSA.

▲ The public key actually is used only to RSA-encrypt the one-time session key (since this session key is only 128 bits, it RSA-encrypts fast enough).

▲ The IDEA-encrypted message is sent to the recipient, along with the RSA public-key-encrypted one-time session key.

▲ The receiver uses its RSA secret key to RSA-decrypt the session key, which is then used to IDEA-decrypt the message.

The PGP software does all this stuff for you, and users don't normally know (or care) that their messages are not actually encrypted by using RSA.

That is, because it runs so much faster, conventional single key encryption is used for the actual message. The RSA public key encryption is used only to get the conventional single key securely to the other end.

▲ For authentication, using the RSA secret key to encrypt a message would take too long (as above, the RSA algorithm runs too slowly) and would require the receiver to have the PGP software to decrypt the message, even if the receiver doesn't happen to need authentication.

▲ Therefore the following is what is actually done to digitally sign a message (that is, for authentication):

▲ A one-way hashing algorithm (currently one called MD5, which was developed by Ron Rivest, of RSA Data Security, the same company that developed the RSA algorithm itself) is used to produce a 128-bit *message digest* of the message that requires authentication.

▲ The MD5 hashing algorithm is designed so that if the message is changed in any way, the message digest will also change (and it would be extremely difficult to find a way to change the message while still producing the same message digest). Also, you cannot reconstruct the message from the message digest.

▲ The message sender's RSA secret key is used to RSA-encrypt the message digest, which is then converted to ASCII and called a *PGP signature*. This "digital signature" is placed at the end of the *plaintext* (unencrypted) message that requires authentication. For example:

```
-----BEGIN PGP SIGNED MESSAGE-----
This is the plaintext ASCII message we want to
ensure is authentic.
-----BEGIN PGP SIGNATURE-----
Version: 2.6.2
iQCVRonqMX0UleysqYqjcUtm0rvbrXoYUy8a9vJzj4
WuyfGtoLVxsfTjNNTrY0810SXx/yOMYtBW7mq+zNmq
EykGFZTdfsVKFEyFw6AJ//BAh+LQNb01Xo=
=aW2m
-----END PGP SIGNATURE-----
```

▲ In addition, if desired, the message can now be encrypted by using the intended receiver's public key (this ensures that no one else can read the message). The recipient will then decrypt the received message, using his or her secret key, with the comfort of knowing that no one else has been able to read it.

▲ If it was decided not to encrypt the message, then all recipients of the message can simply read the actual plaintext message (which will be above the line -----BEGIN PGP SIGNATURE-----).

▲ If desired, any recipient of the message can authenticate it, using the PGP software. The software will prompt for the sender's public key, which will be used to decrypt the received message digest, and compare this with a message digest calculated from the received plaintext message.

▲ If you can't trust the method through which you received someone's public key (for example, you did not get it directly from a trusted keyserver), you might want to verify that your copy of someone's public key is authentic. Use the PGP software to generate a *key digest*—a shorter (16-byte), hashed version of a public key—and phone the key's owner and compare key digests (reading the ASCII hex digits to each other).

PGP was designed, and the first version written (and first released as freeware in 1991), by Philip Zimmermann, a Colorado-based consultant who for a while was in big heckers with the U.S. government, which claimed he might have exported munitions (in this case, the encryption algorithms embedded in the PGP software, which someone else posted on some bulletin board systems and eventually were posted on Internet-accessible computers).

For personal, noncommercial use, the software (source code, documentation, and compiled executables) are freeware, and the primary source is the Massachusetts Institute of Technology's ftp site net-dist.mit.edu, in the /pub/PGP subdirectory.

For PCs the file has a name like p262i.zip, which means version 2.6.2.i, where the "i" means *international version*. The only difference between this and the U.S. noninternational version is that some parts of the international version use code that may be patented in the United States, so the U.S. version was written with the same functionality (and both versions can read files encrypted by the other version), but avoids infringing the patent.

For commercial or government use in Canada or the U.S., a version (which is completely compatible with the freeware version) is also available. PGP Inc. is at *http://www.pgp.com* (Philip Zimmermann gets to be chairman).

One problem with PGP is that it usually has a command-line interface, so it is somewhat difficult to learn to use.

An international version of PGP is available from *http://www.ifi.uio.no/pgp/*. Additional PGP information is at *http://web.mit.edu/network/pgp.html* and *http://www.mantis.co.uk/pgp/pgp.html*.

See **AUTHENTICATION, DES, EDI, ENCRYPTION, IDEA, MD5**, and **RSA**.

Picture Element

See **PEL** and **PIXEL**.

PIM
Protocol-Independent Multicast

A router-to-router protocol that supports multicast traffic over existing unicast routing protocols, such as IGRP, IS-IS, OSPF, and RIP.

Two modes have been defined:

▲ Dense-mode PIM:

▲ Intended for networks in which most LANs need to receive the multicast (such as LAN TV and corporate and financial information broadcasts).

▲ Uses *reverse-path forwarding*, in which the traffic is initially *flooded* (sent to) all router interfaces (except the one on which it arrived), through a branching tree (with each sender at the base of its own tree) of paths that cover each possible recipient. Downstream routers that do not need a traffic feed (either because they have no receivers on their interfaces or because they are already receiving the feed from another port) reply with a *prune* message, asking to be removed from the forwarding list (*tree*).

▲ Sparse-mode PIM:

▲ Intended for networks in which several different multicasts (each going to a small number of receivers) are typically in progress simultaneously (such as desktop video conferencing and *collaborative computing*). Also when there are a relatively small number of multicast receivers, spread over a relatively large network. And also when the bandwidth between receivers is relatively limited.

▲ Senders and receivers first *register* with a single router, which is designated the *rendezvous point*.

▲ Traffic is sent by the sender to the rendezvous point, which then forwards it to the registered receivers.

▲ As intermediate routers see the source and destination of the multicast traffic (it is unlikely that the best path from source to destination goes through the rendezvous point), they optimize the paths so that the traffic takes a more direct route (likely bypassing the rendezvous point). The same paths are used for all multicasts, regardless of source.

▲ Traffic is still sent to the rendezvous point, in anticipation of new receivers registering.

Supported by Cisco.

See **IGRP**, **IP MULTICAST**, **IS-IS**, **OSPF**, and **RIP**.

PING
Packet Internet Groper

A TCP/IP diagnostic program that sends one or a series of *ICMP* (*Internet Control Message Protocol*) echo packets to a user-specified IP address. The echo packet requests the receiver to reply with an echo reply packet. The ping program typically measures and displays the round-trip time and percentage of returned packets.

Very useful to confirm:

- ▲ Network connectivity (whether the address is considered valid)
- ▲ That the destination host is operational
- ▲ Network loading and speed (how long it takes the replies to return)
- ▲ Network errors (percentage of packets that are lost)

Good `ping` utilities will let the user specify the size of the `ping` packets (number of bytes), number of packets sent, time to wait between each packet sent, and time to wait for a reply (before giving up and sending the next) and will display the minimum, average, and maximum response times and the number (and preferably percentage) of responses not received (presumably because the outgoing `ping` or the corresponding response was lost by the network or the destination host).

The maximum size of a ping packet is 65,507 bytes—as this is the largest payload size supported by IP. Sending a larger ping packet (most utilities allow this) results in corrupting the TCP/IP protocol software of the receiving computer, often halting the protocol, and possibly operating system software. This is called a *ping of death*. A list of TCP/IP protocol stacks that are not vulnerable to this problem is at *http://prospect.epresence.com/ping*.

Like other acronyms that are memorable, meaningful, and pronounceable ("PCMCIA"— not!), this one was likely made up after the term was in common use. The idea is that you are "bouncing a packet off of some computer" and listening for (and timing) its return— just like radar and sonar (which stand for *Radio Detecting and Ranging* and *Sound Navigation and Ranging*).

See **ICMP**, **IP**, **PCMCIA**, **SPOOL**, and **UDP**.

Pink

A new object-oriented operating system that is being developed by Taligent.

See **TALIGENT**.

PIO
Programmed Input/Output

A (usually) slower-response-time (but lower-cost and lower-CPU-overhead) method of transferring data from, or to, a peripheral (such as a disk drive controller or LAN adapter).

The PC's CPU does an input or output operation for each byte or word of data either:

- ▲ After the CPU has determined that data are available, by polling (checking periodically) the hardware to determine its status
- ▲ During a hardware interrupt (which was triggered by the availability of data)

Since the CPU must perform several instructions (many bus accesses) for each transfer, this method is usually slower than the *shared memory, DMA,* or *bus master DMA* methods.

An advantage is that neither a DMA channel nor upper memory space is required (maybe no interrupt either). This simplifies installation and reduces conflicts with other peripherals. Also, PIO is the only method supported by the BIOS routines (which are also called `Int` 13, as these routines are accessed by using a call to software interrupt 13_{16}) built in to PCs.

For a PC to use DMA, *drivers* (which are typically DOS TSRs or Windows VxDs) must be loaded (which is a headache).

First introduced with their 3C509, 3Com uses a very fast implementation of PIO (which they call *parallel tasking*—the data are transferred to the PC while the Ethernet frame is being received). Since the Ethernet bytes arrive (Ethernet cable to Ethernet adapter) slower than the PIO transfers data (Ethernet adapter to PC memory), this implementation of PIO is no slower than DMA—and can be faster, since the transfer starts when the Ethernet frame begins to arrive, not after it has completely arrived (as a DMA transfer would typically require).

See **BIOS, BUS, BUS MASTER DMA, DMA, EIDE, IDE, IRQ, PC, PIO**, and **SHARED MEMORY**.

PIXEL
Picture Element

The smallest unit of resolution, usually measured separately for horizontal (the number of dots across) and vertical (the number of rows).

For monochrome display or output, a pixel requires 1 bit of storage. For color displays, a pixel will represent many bits of storage. For example, 24-bit color (8 bits each for red, green, and blue) requires 3 bytes of storage.

Also called *pel* (especially by IBM people and in fax specifications).

See **FAX, INTERLACED**, and **VIDEO**.

PMFJI
Pardon Me for Jutting in

A common email abbreviation, used by a person adding a message to an ongoing conversation (that is, a series of messages on a particular topic, which is called a *thread*).

Sometimes you see PMFBI—pardon me for butting in.

PNG
Portable Network Graphic

A method of representing graphic images which renders images faster (over slow Internet links) than GIF (which also has some licensing restrictions) and JPEG (which is a lossy compression method, so provides a lower quality image).

PNG offers 24-bit colour, sometimes called *True Color*, which stores 8 bits for each of the red, green and blue value for each pixel. In addition, each pixel can be assigned an *alpha* value, which specifies how transparent or opaqe it is (that is, how much of the color under the PNG image shows through).

The LZ77 method of lossless data compression is used, and images are rendered initially at a very coarse resolution (the pixels are 64 times larger), and as more of the image is received, the resolution is improved. This method provides graphics and text that can be understood in a half or a quarter of the time as for GIF. The maximum image size is $2^{31}-1 \times 2^{31}-1$ pixels

See **GIF**, and **LOSSY DATA COMPRESSION**.

Plug and Play

See **PNP**.

PNNI
Private Network Node Interface

PNNI defines the communication required between ATM switches—that is, the interface between ATM networks. It enables switches to determine the best path over which to establish an ATM connection, according to the requirements of the connection, and the state of the network.

The ATM Forum's method for providing some router-like functions for ATM networks. Just as RIP is a router to router protocol for IP traffic, PNNI is an ATM switch to ATM switch protocol to distribute network connectivity information such as link metrics and attributes (including the speed of links).

Areas of the ATM network are configured as *peer groups*, so that their information can be summarized for higher level peer groups. This hierarchical distribution enables very large ATM networks to be supported (that is, it is PNNI was designed to be very *scalable*).

PNNI is a link-state router protocol (as is OSPF), but adds many features to the exchanged routing metrics as required for ATM. For example, link metrics include tracking established connections and their QOS requirements, to know what resources remain available for new connections requests. Using PNNI, the source node gathers network information, calculates the best path through the network (based on the service category and other requirements for the traffic), and specifies the path (this is called *source routing*) to the ATM switches, using enhanced UNI signalling, to establish the connections.

PNNI replaced the *Interim Inter-switch Signalling Protocol* (IISP).

The early versions of PNNI were called Private Network-to-Network Interface, and were abbreviated as P-NNI.

Integrated PNNI (IPNNI) is an extension that distributes network connectivity information between ATM route servers, ATM switches and *ATM* edge devices—but not to hosts with ATM interfaces (that what MPOA does).

See **ATM** (*Asynchronous Transfer Mode*), **MPOA**, and **OSPF**.

PNP
Plug and Play

An effort initiated by Microsoft (first supported in Windows 95) and Intel to make adding adapter boards to PCs simpler (another case of playing catch-up with Apple's Macintosh).

The result is that once a new adapter board is plugged in and the PC is powered on (or a notebook computer is plugged into its docking station or a wireless PC comes into range of its network), the boards would be automatically configured (DMA channel, interrupt, memory, and I/O port addresses are all set to valid, unique values)—no need to manually set jumpers or switches on the boards—and the necessary and correct drivers would be automatically loaded (no need to manually enter commands into `config.sys` or `autoexec.bat`).

Plug and Play device drivers support *dynamic reconfiguration*, so they can be loaded and unloaded while a system is running. Therefore a Plug and Play laptop PC could be removed from, or inserted into, a docking station, and PCMCIA boards can be inserted and removed without powering down the system.

On power-up, a *configuration manager* calls software components called *enumerators* (one for each type of bus, for example, ISA, PCI, and PCMCIA) to identify the installed devices (*enumeration*).

The enumerators request the identification codes from the boards and then the board's `.INF` file is read to determine its requirements and setting options. The `.INF` files are collectively called the `.INF` registry. Software called a *resource arbitrator* then determines a non-conflicting configuration of resources, which is then recorded in (for example) Windows 95's registry. The configuration manager then loads the required device drivers, which then configure the devices as required (for example, the interrupt and input/output address settings).

For new boards (so that there is a better chance that systems can be configured with no conflicts), Microsoft strongly recommends that they can be automatically set to any of:

▲ Eight IRQ lines

▲ Three DMA channels

▲ Eight I/O port base addresses

▲ Eight memory addresses

To get completely automatic operation, support must be built in to the adapter boards, PC's BIOS, and operating system.

For systems that don't have all of this support:

▲ For existing (non–Plug and Play) ISA boards, and using a Configuration Utility, a Plug and Play PC will provide *plug and tell* capability to specify how the board should be manually configured.

▲ For existing operating systems (DOS and Windows 3.1), a Plug and Play utility (ISA configuration utility—icu) is used to gather information from Plug and Play boards, keep track of available resources, and manually reserve resources for non-Plug and Play boards.

▲ For existing PCs (with no Plug and Play BIOS), a utility (configuration assist—cassist) tries to determine what resources are already used by non-Plug and Play boards and writes this information to a file (which icu can read).

SCAM provides Plug and Play support (and other features as well) for SCSI devices.

Support for VESA's DDC is required for monitor Plug and Play support.

Intel's Plug and Play page is at *http://www.intel.com/IAL/plugplay/index.htm*, and Microsoft's is at *http://www.microsoft.com/win32dev/base/pnp.htm*.

See **BIOS, DDC, DMA, DMTF, EVC, IRQ, ISA, PC, PC-95, PCI, PCMCIA,** and **SCAM.**

Point

In computer-based typesetting, $\frac{1}{72}$ of an inch. In traditional typesetting, one point is slightly less than this ($\frac{1}{72.27}$", to be exact—which is about 0.351 mm).

A *pica* is 12 points.

To describe the size of type, the point size is measured from the top of the font's highest *ascender* (the top of a lower-case f or h, for example) to the bottom of the font's lowest *descender* (the bottom of a lower-case g or p). Fonts sizes of 10 to 12 points are usually used in books and business correspondence.

See **FONT** and **TYPEFACE FAMILY**.

Point-to-Point Protocol

See **PPP**.

Polyphony

The number (or capability) of simultaneous sounds or notes (typically at least 24 or 32) that can be produced by a sound board or MIDI synthesizer.

See **MIDI**.

POP
Point of Presence

The communications equipment located in (for example) a multi-tenant building that provides an alternative communications service. Connection to this point of presence could then provide communication service using (for example) the local cable TV provider's coaxial cable or fiber-optic cable (presumably at lower cost), rather than the local telephone company's facilities.

A POP can also refer to the locations where an Internet Service Provider offers access to its network. A gigaPOP is an access point for really fast Internet backbone connections (at gigabit per second data rates), such as for Internet 2.

See **CA*NETII**, **CARRIER**, **CATV**, **COAX**, **INTERNET II**, **ISP**, and **IXC OR IEC**.

POP
Post Office Protocol

The older (but still widely used) protocol to communicate with e-mail post offices. POP clients periodically make a TCP connection to a POP server to check for mail. Very few commands are supported, as listed below:

▲ The only information which all POP3 servers must be able to provide about individual mail messages (that is, without actually retrieving the messages) is their size (in bytes).

▲ All, selected (for example, a client can only retrieve files smaller than a certain size) or none of the mail messages can be retrieved from the post office.

▲ All, selected (for example, a client can decide to delete only messages that have been retrieved) or none of the messages can be deleted from the post office.

Port Number

The RFC defines an optional command which requests the post office to send a specified number of lines from the start of a selected message. This is not widely supported. POP3 does not support sending mail (from a client to the network), so SMTP is used instead.

POP3 is defined in RFCs 1082, 1725 and 1734. POP3 superceeded POP version 2 (POP2), which was developed in the mid-1980s.

Most new post offices (and clients) use the newer IMAP protocol instead.

See **IMAP** and **SMTP**.

Port Number

See **TCP**.

Portability

The capability of running software that (usually) was designed and developed on one platform (type of CPU, hardware, and operating system) on another platform (for example) to standardize on the software across an enterprise or to have a larger market for the software.

Some people make a verb from the word: "to port the software to another platform" or "ported from the Sun environment."

▲ *Source-code portability* means that recompilation is necessary. For example, you get the C language source code and compile it using the compiler for the *target system* (new computer platform). Ideally, the software can now be run on that target system. Usually, small problems are encountered (often because operating system functions work slightly differently) that need to be isolated, and the source code needs to be changed.

▲ *Object-code portability* means that the software needs to be relinked (but not compiled).

▲ *Binary portability* implies that the executable code is ready to run on any compatible machine. The most common example of this is PC programs that can be run on any processor from the 8088 to the Pentium and clone processors as well (such as Cyrix, AMD, etc.).

See **CDE**, **COMPATIBLE**, **IBCS**, **PC**, **POSIX OSE**, **POWERPC**, and **RISC**.

POS
Point-to-point Protocol Over SONet

An implementation of PPP to connect really fast routers over really fast (SONet) WAN links.

ATM (*Asynchronous Transfer Mode*), **PPP**, and **SONET**.

POSIX OSE
Portable Operating System Interface (UNIX-like) Open Systems Environment

IEEE-sponsored work to define standard interfaces for APIs and many other functions so that applications will be source-code (but not object-code) portable between different hardware/software platforms. There are several efforts, as shown in the following table.

POSIX-related standard	Covers
1003.1	Basic file and I/O APIs (kernel), now includes 1003.4
1003.2	Shell and utilities
1003.2a	Extension utilities for time-sharing systems
1003.4	Threads extension to support real-time features, such as timers, priority scheduling asynchronous event notifications, and I/O (now included as part of 1003.1)
1003.5	1003.1 APIs for Ada
1003.6	Security extensions such as access control lists
1003.7	System administration support, such as adding users and checking device status
1003.8	Transparent network file access (NFS-like features)
1003.9	1003.1 APIs for FORTRAN
1003.12	Protocol-independent communication services
1003.15	Batch (noninteractive) support
1003.17	Distributed name space and directory service
1201.1	Window GUI
1224	X.400 message-handling interface
1238.0	Lower-layer OSI support
1238.1	OSI file transfer access method

Both SVID and BSD4.3 UNIX proponents are working on POSIX compliance for their systems (though POSIX is more similar to SVID). System administration will likely continue to be very product-specific.

Many non-UNIX systems (such as Windows NT) are POSIX-compliant, especially for non-user-interface efforts, such as 1003.1.

IEEE POSIX standards are made into ISO standards, such as ISO IS 9945.

The ISO has a WWW server with POSIX information at *http://www.dkuug.dk/ JTC1/SC22/ WG15,* and the IEEE has some POSIX information at *http://stdsbbs.ieee.org:70/1/pub/PASC/*

See **IEEE, ISO, PORTABILITY, SVVS, UNIFORM,** and **UNIX.**

PostScript Page Description Language

Adobe Systems, Inc.'s device-independent, ASCII language sent to a printer (which has a PostScript interpreter) to describe where to draw lines, circles, and other graphics. The printer then prints these at whatever its resolution is. Includes font selection and scaling commands.

PostScript *Level 2* interpreters (the software in the printer that converts the PostScript language into printer commands) are more advanced than *Level 1*. For example, Level 2 supports the following:

▲ *Dynamic memory allocation*, which can usually avoid *limitcheck* memory errors, which Level 1 interpreters encounter when a path has more than 1,500 points

▲ Color

▲ Compressed images, which reduces the amount of time needed to send the image to a printer

PostScript Type 1 Fonts

TrueImage was Microsoft's abandoned attempt to compete with PostScript.

Adobe receives about 3% of the price of any PostScript printer as a royalty.

There are "clone" PostScript interpreters available, presumably because the suppliers charge less than Adobe does. These would be used by printer manufacturers and built in to their printers (so the printers can be controlled by the PostScript output of application programs). For example, Phoenix Technologies (famous for IBM PC-clone BIOSes and now owned by Xionics Document Technologies) has a clone PostScript interpreter called PhoenixPage.

The PostScript FAQ is at *http://www.cis.ohio-state.edu/hypertext/faq/usenet/postscript/faq/top.html*.

See **ATM** (*Adobe Type Manager*), **EPS, GHOSTSCRIPT, MULTIPLE MASTER, OUTLINE FONT, PCL, POSTSCRIPT TYPE 1 FONTS, POSTSCRIPT TYPE 3 FONTS, SPEEDO**, and **TRUETYPE**.

PostScript Type 1 Fonts

Adobe and several other *Type Foundries* produce *Type 1* fonts, which are described by a subset of the *PostScript Page Description Language*.

Type 1 fonts were the first *hinted* outline fonts—that is, the font descriptions include information on how to print on lower-resolution devices while maintaining print quality (such as character symmetry and shape). PostScript is widely supported, especially for professional typesetting work.

Competes with TrueType (which is oriented to the mass market and Microsoft's Windows).

See **ATM** (*Adobe Type Manager*), **FONT, OUTLINE FONT, POSTSCRIPT PAGE DESCRIPTION LANGUAGE**, and **POSTSCRIPT TYPE 3 FONTS**.

PostScript Type 3 Fonts

Unhinted fonts that can be printed on PostScript printers but cannot be used by *Adobe Type Manager* (to be displayed or printed on non-PostScript monitors or printers).

See **ATM** (*Adobe Type Manager*), **FONT, POSTSCRIPT PAGE DESCRIPTION LANGUAGE**, and **POSTSCRIPT TYPE 1 FONTS**.

POTS
Plain Old Telephone Service

The only type of telephone service you could get 20 years ago. A simple analog telephone (and the corresponding service from the phone company) on which you can dial and receive calls.

The lowest common telephone service available everywhere. While there were many earlier models, the most popular standard dial telephone was called a *500-type* telephone set, and was first introduced in 1949 (in black only, other colors were first introduced in 1954). The "newer" touch-tone telephone design (that still had the classic design of the 500 set) was called a *2500 set*.

For this standard analog POTS, a pair of copper conductors (a *twisted pair* of wires, called the *local loop*) connects your telephone to the nearest *central office*. It is estimated that there are about 560 million such local loops in the world, so there is a substantial effort to provide higher speed services (such as ADSL, ISDN, and switched 56) to work over these existing local loops.

The telephone company puts a nominal –48 V DC across the two conductors, which powers the microphone (mouthpiece) in your telephone. The two conductors are typically called *tip* (which is the green wire, and has 0 V on it) and *ring* (which is the red wire, and has the –48 V DC). To ring your telephone, they apply a 90 V (nominal) 20 Hz AC signal.

All signaling is done through *inband* tones (that is, tones that are between 300 and 3,000 Hz, and carried just as the voice is). Most *call progress* tones you hear are actually combinations of two frequencies, as shown in the following table.

Indication Tone	Frequencies (Hz)	Seconds On	Seconds Off
Dial; The telephone network is ready for your dialling	350 + 440	Continuous	
Busy; The called party's telephone is off-hook	480 + 620	0.5	0.5
Ringback (normal); Central Office-generated "ringing" signal to indicate to the caller that the called party's phone should be ringing (this is supposed to sound like the actual telephone's ringing sound)	440 + 480	2	4
Ringback (PBX); PBX-generated "ringing" signal to indicate that the called party's phone should be ringing	440 + 480	1	3
Congestion (Toll—also called a *Fast Busy*, or 120 IPM, since there are 120 interruptions per minute of this tone); The call could not be completed because there were no long-distance circuits available, internal to the telephone network	480 + 620	0.2	0.3
Reorder (Local—also called a *Fast Busy*, or 120 IPM, since there are 120 interruptions per minute of this tone); The call could not be completed because there were no local circuits available, internal to the telephone network (that is, between central offices)	480 + 620	0.3	0.2
Receiver Off-hook; A very loud (0 dBm[a]) and annoying signal to alert you that your handset has been left off-hook, without a call being established	1,400 + 2,060 + 2,450 + 2,600	0.1	0.1
No such number; The number dialed does not exist	200 to 400	Continuously varies at 1 Hz rate	

a. 0 dBm is defined as a 1 mW signal into a 600 Ω impedance. This is the same as a 0.775 V signal into 600 Ω;. A more typical signal level is –20 dBm, which is a 0.01 mW signal (one-hundredth of the power of the 0 dBm signal).

When you talk into a telephone handset, a circuit in the telephone reproduces your own voice in your earpiece (so you hear yourself talk). This is called *sidetone*. The circuit automatically makes this sidetone quieter when the connection from the telephone to the central office is longer (this is sensed by the reduced loop current, due to the greater line length). This makes people talk louder, as required to accomodate the greater loss on the longer connection.

PowerOpen

The standard telephone network is often called the PSTN—*public switched telephone network*. In many standards documents, it is called the GSTN—*general switched telephone network*.

Newer telephone services include Caller ID, distinctive ringing, ISDN, and on and on—which some people call *Pretty Amazing New Stuff*—that is, a change from POTS to PANS. (Har har har, ho ho ho, he he—look at that—those telephone guys can make better acronyms than the computer guys.)

To demonstrate how the telephone network has changed from the good old POTS days, Northern Telecom (who now like to be called Nortel) has figures that show that by October 1996, their telecom equipment was handling more data traffic than voice traffic—all measured in bytes.

For many telecommunications-related WWW links and other information, visit *http://www.angustel.ca*. Some interesting statistics on global telephone usage are at *http://www.bt.com/global_reports/bt_mci/index.html*. Some history of the telephone is at *http://www.cybercom.com/~chuck/phones.html* and *http://jefferson.village.virginia.edu/albell/homepage.html*. Northern Telecom is at *http://www.nortel.com*.

See **S800**, **ADSL**, **BUTT SET**, **C.O.**, **DID**, **DN**, **CALLER ID**, **CARRIER**, **CPE**, **CTI**, **DTMF2**, **FAX**, **INBAND**, **ISDN**, **ISP**, **MODEM**, **PBX**, **RBOC OR RBHC**, **REN**, **SEALING CURRENT**, **SIT**, **SWITCHED 56**, **TAPI**, **TSAPI**, and **TIP AND RING**.

PowerOpen

A new UNIX-like operating system created by the Apple-IBM Alliance (then again, not much has been said about this lately, it may just remain "vaporware").

Will run on the PowerPC platform. Combines IBM's AIX and Apple's AUX and will have a Macintosh-like GUI.

See **AIX**, **APPLE/IBM ALLIANCE**, **A/UX**, **GUI**, **POWERPC**, **OPERATING SYSTEM**, and **UNIX**.

PowerPC

The RISC-based processor created by Apple, IBM, and Motorola all working together (through their joint-venture called Somerset). (They started this effort in 1991 when they realized they could not compete with Intel by continuing to work separately and competing with each other.)

Based on IBM's RS/6000 and manufactured by Motorola. Versions of Microsoft's Windows NT, Apple's Mac OS, IBM's AIX and Sun's Solaris operating systems are available for it. Recent IBM AS/400 minicomputers (which run OS/400) also use 64-bit PowerPC processors.

Some details of the available processors are listed below (listed in order of the ship dates), and in the subsequent table:

▲ 601: the first PowerPC processor (announced in 1991, first available in September 1993), executes three instructions per clock cycle, and has 2.8 million transistors. First units were available in 50, 66 and 80 MHz versions. 100 MHz version available in October 1994, 110 MHz in April 1995, and 120 MHz in November 1995.

▲ Uses a 3.6 V supply voltage. Executes up to 3 instructions per clock cycle. Can emulate a Motorola 68000 processor, so PowerPC-based Macintoshes can run software compiled for pre-PowerPC Macintoshes (which used Motorola 68000-family CPUs). That is, software has *binary portability* between the older Macintoshes and the new PowerPC-based Macintoshes.

▲ The PowerPC was first used in the IBM RS/6000 model 250, which was introduced in September 1993, and later used in Apple Macintoshes. 110 MHz versions are similar in performance to Pentium processors.

▲ 603: low-power version with power management features, for battery-operated portable computers and low-end computers. Similar in power to a high-end 486. First shipped in June 1994, executes up to 3 instructions per clock cycle. First versions ran at 66 MHz, later ones at 80 MHz.

▲ 603e: an improved 603 (runs at 100 and 166 MHz, uses a 2.5 V supply voltage). Has a faster 68040 emulator. First shipped in May 1995, and later versions run at 180 MHz.

▲ 604: high-speed (executes up to 4 instructions per clock cycle). Uses a 3.3 V supply voltage, and has 3.6 million transistors. Similar in performance to Pentium Pro processors. The 100, 120 and 133 MHz versions were available in June 1995. The 150 MHz version was available in October 1995, and the 166 and 180 MHz version in April 1996. The 604e version runs as fast as 300 MHz.

▲ 602: for consumer multimedia applications, such as games and PDAs (which need fast integer multiplication and logarithms for handwriting recognition and other advanced functions). Clock speed is 66 MHz, supply voltage is 3.3 V, and can execute up to 2 instructions per clock cycle.

▲ 620: really high-performance (133 MHz clock speed, executes up to 4 instructions per clock cycle, uses 3.3 V supply voltage). IBM is developing a different processor for the AS/400 minicomputer and RS/6000 workstations, so this may never become popular. Available in late 1996.

Processor	Clock Speed (MHz)	Transistors (Millions)	Width (bits)			L1 Cache (kbytes)		Pins
			Register	Address Bus	Data Bus	Code	Data	
601	50, 66, 80	2.8	32	32	64	32		304
601v	100	2.8	32	32	64	32		304
602	66	1.0	32	32	64[a]	4	4	144
603	66	1.6	32	32	32/64	8	8	240
80	1.6	32	32	32/64	8	8		256
603e	100	2.6	32	32	32/64	16	16	256
166	2.6	32	32	32/64	16	16		256
604	100, 120, 166, 233	3.6	32	32	64	16	16	256
620 604e	133 166, 187.5, 200, 233	7.0 5.1	64	40	128	32 32	32 32	625

a. 32-bit bus time-multiplexed to provide 64-bit transfers.

PowerPC Reference Platform

When running Windows NT, the PowerPC can run WINDOWS NT application code compiled for Intel processors by using *software emulation* of the Intel processor. This emulation capability immediately provides lots of application software for the PowerPC, but also provides poor performance relative to code compiled for the PowerPC processor).

For more information, see *http://www.mot.com/PowerPC/*. Also, Apple Computer, Inc. and International Business Machines Corporation (IBM) have WWW servers at *http://www.apple.com* and *http://www.ibm.com.*, respectively.

See **88OPEN, ACE, AIX, CACHE, CHRP, MOTOROLA, OPERATING SYSTEM, PDA, PORTABILITY, PREP, RISC, SOMERSET, SPEC,** and **SUPERSCALAR.**

PowerPC Reference Platform

See **PREP.**

PPM
Pulse Position Modulation

The method used by standard television (and other) remote controls to send their commands, using pulses of infrared light from an infrared LED. Typically, 880 to 950 nm wavelength light is used. This is a longer wavelength than us humans can see, and is chosen partly so that the light from the room lights can be filtered out, so the receiver is not overwhelmed by light. The receiver (typically a phototransistor, which is turned on by light—it gets really excited about it) typically has a dark red plastic filter over it, and this is the actual place you should be pointing your remote control.

Of course, how do you know there's really infrared light coming out of that little LED at the front of the remote control—maybe its actually magic. Well, if you aim your TV remote control at a wall (from a distance of a few inches) and hold down a button while viewing the wall through a video camera, you'll see the infrared light. (Well, it's not X-ray vision, but I thought it was neat.)

Anyway, back to our regularly scheduled program . . .

While there is no standard, it turns out that NEC makes the encoder IC used for most remote controls, so there is therefore a de facto industry standard, which is described below.

The actual message that is sent each time you press the button to flip (yet again) to the next channel is as follows (actually, this is sent at least twice, with a 40 ms gap (that is, about 100 ms total per command) before the repetition—though some remotes send the initial command only once, and then send a command indicating that the first should be repeated):

▲ A header or leader, which consists of 9 ms of the infrared LED being pulsed at 38 kHz, followed by 4.5 ms of no light (though the repetition has only 2.25 ms of no light).

▲ An 8-bit *customer code*, which is a unique manufacturer ID (such as one for Sony, another for RCA, and so on), assigned by NEC. This ensures that remote controls from one manufacturer won't affect another's equipment.

▲ A repeat of the customer code, but with each bit inverted (this is for error-checking).

- ▲ The 8-bit data code, representing which button you pressed on the remote control—as assigned by the manufacturer.

- ▲ A repeat of the data code, with each bit inverted.

- ▲ A trailing high bit.

The infrared light is pulsed at about 38 kHz (so that receivers can reject interference from other sources of infrared light—such as the sun which does not pulse like that). The binary bits of the customer and data code are sent as follows (this is the PPM part):

- ▲ A binary 0 is 0.6 ms of the 38 kHz pulsed infrared light (about 22 pulses), followed by 0.6 ms of no light (for a total of 1.2 ms).

- ▲ A binary 1 is 0.6 ms of the 38 kHz light, followed by 1.7 ms of no light (for a total of 2.3 ms).

After the header, there will always be a total of 16 0 bits and 16 1 bits—since there is a total of 32 bits sent, and of these half are what we wanted to send, and the other half is the complement of that. The message is therefore (16×1.2 ms + 16×2.3 ms =) 56 ms. Including the header, results in a total of about 69.5 ms. The maximum possible channel surfing rate is therefore about 14 channels per second (now there's something to aspire to). Actually, due to the entire message being repeated, and the 40 ms before the repetition, the minimum transmission time after a button push is (69.5 + 40 + 67.25 ms =) 176.75 ms, so you can only surf about $5\frac{1}{2}$; channels per second.

Also, when you hold down a button on the TV remote control, the message is automatically repeated a few times per second, in case the receiver didn't hear you the first time. The receiver ignores repeated messages of the same button press if there's too short a gap between them (though I really try to flip channels as fast as the receiver will go, just to be sure I'm not missing something really good on another channel). So unless you had a turbo-charged television (that did not ignore repeated messages of the same type), you could not actually surf $5\frac{1}{2}$ channels per second.

NEC is at *http://www.nec.com*.

See **CATV**, **ENCODING**, **IRDA**, and **NTSC**.

PPP
Point-to-Point Protocol

A full-duplex link layer protocol which is very popular for carrying TCP/IP traffic from your PC to your ISP, and also for connections between routers and connections between bridges.

PPP provides a standard way for routers (and also for bridges) and computers connected over a synchronous (typically using HDLC), asynchronous (using 8 data bits and no parity per character) or ISDN WAN link to establish, monitor, and terminate a session (and, of course, exchange data in between).

Initially, PPP only supported HDLC encapsulation, and required a synchronous leased-line connection (such as a dedicated 56 kbit/s link).

The PPP standard was later extended to support frame relay, ISDN, SONet, as well as asynchronous connections (so you can use it with your V.34 modem to dial into your Internet service provider).

PPP has largely replaced SLIP as the encapsulation method to carry IP over dial-up connections. Some advantages of PPP (compared to SLIP) include:

▲ IP header compression (though CSLIP can do this too)

▲ Data compression (see CCP)

▲ Error correction

▲ Packet sequencing

▲ Authentication

When a connection is first established, a negotiation is started to set configuration options (starting with defaults established as part of the starndard). The first negotiation uses the *link control protocol* (LCP, which is defined in RFC 1548)). This negotiates link layer options, such as throughput, packet size (maximum 1,500 bytes maximum), data encapsulation format, link quality (a 2-byte CRC is used) and authentication. After this, the *network control protocol* (NCP) negotiates which protocols will be multiplexed over the link. Protocols are identified by a 16-bit field (leaving lots of room for expansion). PPP is usually used to carry IP (its so popular these days). However, using the Bridge Control Protocol (BCP)—since bridging is protocol independent—PPP can also carry other protocols, such as: Apple AppleTalk, Banyan VINES, DEC DECnet, IBM APPN and LLC2, Novell IPX, ISO OSI, and Xerox XNS.

The PPP standard specifies that PAP and CHAP may be negotiated as authentication methods, but other methods can be added to the negotiation and used as well. New methods of data compression can also be added to the negotiation (which uses the *compression control protocol*—CCP). Handling compression at the end stations ensures that intermediate equipment doesn't waste time and computing resources compressing (and possibly decompressing and compressing multiple times as the data traverses many links) the data.

Even with the negotiation phase, there are enough implementation subsets that interoperability problems may occur (good PPP software includes diagnostics, to facilitate troubleshooting).

The RFCs defining PPP include those shown in the following table below.

	Specification	Supports
BCP	Bridge Control Protocol	Transparent bridging
IPCP	IP Control Protocol	Routing of IP encapsulated in PPP
IPXCP	IPX Control Protocol	Routing of IPX encapsulated in PPP
NBCP	NetBEUI Control Protocol	Routing of NetBEUI encapsulated in PPP
ATCP	AppleTalk Control Protocol	Routing of AppleTalk encapsulated in PPP

Defined in RFCs 1331 through 1334, 1661 through 1663 and others.

See **ASYNCHRONOUS, AUTHENTICATION, CCP, CHAP, ENCAPSULATION, HDLC, ISDN, PAP, POTS, MLPPP, PPTP, SLIP, SYNCHRONOUS, V.8** through **V.120,** and **WAN.**

PPTP
Point to Point Tunelling Protocol

A method developed by Microsoft and U.S. Robotics to create a connection between two PCs (initially, running Windows NT) where all data is encrypted. PPTP runs on top of a PPP session (which is first established), so PPTP can be used anywhere PPP is, such as anywhere over the Internet.

RSA RC-4 or DES encryption is used, and IP, IPX or NetBEUI can be transported.

See **DES**, **ENCAPSULATION**, **ENCRYPTION**, **PPP**, **RSA**, and **VPN**.

PREP
PowerPC Reference Platform

An attempt by IBM (alone) to specify a standard hardware platform that would be able to run OS/2, AIX, Windows NT, and Apple's Macintosh operating system. The requirements were the following:

▲ 8 Mbytes (minimum) and 16 Mbytes (standard) of RAM, with room for 32 Mbytes of RAM

▲ 4 kbytes (minimum) nonvolatile configuration RAM

▲ 120 Mbytes (minimum) hard disk, either local (expandable to 200 Mbytes) or network-accessible

▲ 1.44-Mbyte $3\frac{1}{2}$" floppy diskette drive

▲ CD-ROM drive (strongly recommended)

▲ SCSI-2 (preferred method of attaching additional peripherals)

▲ Keyboard and mouse

▲ 16-bit audio (soundblaster-compatible)

▲ $1,024 \times 768$ resolution monitor

▲ Serial communication ports

But Apple and Motorola wanted some say in the specification, so it has been replaced by CHRP.

See **CHRP** and **POWERPC**.

PRI
Primary Rate ISDN

An ISDN service that provides (for example):

▲ In North America and Japan, Primary Rate ISDN is typically implemented on a T1 circuit (from the telephone company CO to the customer premises), and the service provided can be any of the following:

▲ 23 B channels plus one D channel (typically, the D channel is the 24th time slot), but sometimes 24 B channels and no D channels if the D channel information can be carried over another PRI circuit)

▲ One H_{11} channel (1.544 Mbits/s) and no D channel

▲ Three H_0 channels (where each H_0 is 384 kbits/s) plus one 64-kbits/s D channel

▲ In Europe and Australia, Primary Rate ISDN is typically provided on an E1 circuit, and can be any of the following:

▲ 30 B channels plus one D channel

▲ One H_{12} channel (1.920 Mbits/s) plus one 64-kbits/s D channel

▲ Five H_0 channels (where each H_0 is 384 kbits/s) plus one 64 kbits/s D channel

The H_0 ("H" is for *hyperchannel*) channel's bit rate is equal to the aggregate of six 64-kbits/s B channels and fast enough to support full-motion, full-color video conferencing. The H_{11} (pronounced "H, 1, 1") and H_{12} channels are a full "unchannelized" T1 (or E1).

Note that these rates each add up to a full (or almost full) T1 (or E1).

In North America, PRI is implemented using a standard T1 circuit which uses B8ZS to provide *clear channel* 64,000-bits/s channels. The actual link between the customer premises and the telephone company central office will typically be either a two-pair copper link (one pair receives, the other pair transmits) or fiber-optic cabling (two strands per T1).

Typical uses are for connecting PBX (Private Branch Exchanges) to central office switches, and receiving multiple, simultaneous ISDN calls at:

▲ Companies supporting telecommuting, through dial-in routers accessing their in-house LAN

▲ *Internet service providers* supporting callers who use ISDN to access the Internet.

See **B8ZS**, **BRI**, **ISDN**, **ISP**, **PBX**, **T1**, and **VIDEO**.

Printer Command Language

See **PCL**.

Prioritization

A feature implemented in multiprocotol router software that ensures that time-critical protocols do not time-out when there is a temporary peak in the traffic load on the WAN link.

Usually needed most for *legacy* protocols (such as SDLC), which were designed to work on dedicated, single-protocol links—where the delays are known and predictable. When a router combines many protocols onto a single WAN link (to reduce communication costs), the delay between networks will depend on the WAN loading (due to the other protocols). Since some protocols cannot tolerate delays, (at best, there may be retransmissions, needlessly further loading the WAN link, and at worst, users may be unceremoniously disconnected), a method is needed to give them priority over other protocols.

Two methods are common:

▲ *Bandwidth Reservation* (sometimes called *Custom Queuing*), in which each protocol is assigned a percentage of the total WAN bandwidth, so that regardless of the total WAN traffic load, a predetermined amount of bandwidth is available for the time-critical protocol. When a protocol does not need all of its reserved bandwidth, then other protocols can use it. A problem is that if a time-critical protocol temporarily needs more than its assigned priority (and the other protocols also need all of theirs), then the time-critical protocol may still time-out.

▲ *Protocol Priority* or *Priority Queuing*, in which each protocol is assigned a relative priority. The most time-critical protocol gets the highest priority. A problem is that if the time-critical protocol needs all of the bandwidth, the other protocols get no bandwidth.

Of the two methods, bandwidth reservation is best for most applications, as long as the amount of bandwidth reserved for each protocol is the minimum required to provide acceptable service. One potention difference in implementation is that some routers require a separate PVC for each priority level between two locations—and on public frame relay networks, this costs extra money each month.

See **IPV6**, **FRAME RELAY**, **LEGACY SYSTEM**, **MLPPP**, **RSVP**, and **SDLC**.

PU
Physical Unit

An IBM data communications device that is physically connected to an FEP (typically through Token Ring or an EIA-232 connection) and directly takes part in SNA protocols (such as responding to SDLC polling).

Also referred to as a *Node Type*, and involves the lower layers of the SNA protocol, where functions such as error-detection and correction are handled.

See **FEP**.

PU 2
Physical Unit Type 2

IBM's traditional 3274- or 3174-based *cluster* (or *communication*) *controller* and the protocol for communication between it and the *front end processor* driving it.

See **S3174 AND 3274** and **FEP**.

PU 2.1
Physical Unit Type 2.1

A simple implementation of IBM SNA's APPN, also called *Low Entry Networking* (LEN). Used by the AS/400.

See **S5250**, **APPN**, and **LEN**.

PU 3
Physical Unit Type 3

There is no Node Type 3. Nobody knows why IBM skipped it (maybe they watch Monty Python).

PU 4
Physical Unit Type 4

The part of SNA that is responsible for routing, and for polling PU 2 devices (that is, *communication controllers*, such as the 3174). Typically, this will be an IBM SNA *front end processor*

PU 5

(FEP—such as a 3745). PU 4 is also the protocol is used to communicate with other FEPs. FEPs are also called an *SNA intermediate network node*.

See **S3174 AND 3274**, **CHANNEL**, and **FEP**.

PU 5
Physical Unit Type 5

An IBM SNA mainframe (such as a System/370, System/390, or 3090). Runs VTAM to handle data communications.

See **MAINFRAME** and **VTAM**.

PUC
Public Utilities Commission

The U.S. agencies (one for each state) that regulate telephone tariffs, electric power rates, and other utility rates.

See **CRTC** and **FCC**.

Push Technology

The opposite of pull (over the Internet in this case). That is, a world wide web server sends you information (hopefully, according to some criteria you have set in advance). In contrast, previously (and in my opinion most usefully) most people "pull" information, usually by specifically going to a web site (typing in the URL into Netscape for example) and then simply clicking on what you want.

Examples of Push technology include news and advertising sent to your PC, from some server elsewhere on the Internet.

A *push client* on your PC may display the information in a small window on your screen, or you may do this with a *screen saver* (which puts a moving pattern onto your monitor when your PC has been idle for some pre-set time so that your CRT's phosphor doesn't get a burned-in pattern, and to hide what you were doing from nosey people).

A push server allows you to select what information you'd like to receive, often by subscribing to "channels".

Very popular push clients and servers are from PointCast Inc., at *http://www.pointcast.com* and Marimba Inc. at (*http://www.marimba.com*).

See **IP MULTICAST**, and **RTP**.

Q

QLLC
Qualified Logical Link Control

IBM's method of supporting SNA over X.25 packet-switching networks. Usually, NPSI will be installed on the FEP to provide the X.25 support.

SNA frames are mapped to X.25 packets. For SNA frames that do not have corresponding X.25 packets, the X.25 Q bit is set to indicate a nonstandard use of the packet.

See **DLC**, **FEP**, **NPSI**, **SNA**, and **X.25**.

QOS
Quality of Service

The network requirements (latency, maximum packet loss, and so on) to support a specific application.

Different types of multimedia traffic have different requirements. It is important for networks to know these so that the networks can be efficiently used—for example, some applications require guaranteed bandwidth, some need only to use bandwidth that is left over after all guaranteed traffic has been carried).

Therefore, protocols must support carrying this QOS information, and applications must have a away of specifying it (this could be a big problem for existing applications).

See **ATM** (*Asynchronous Transfer Mode*), **CA*NETII**, **COS2** (*Class of Service*), **MULTIMEDIA**, **IGRP**, **IP MULTICAST**, **RSVP**, and **WINSOCK**.

QTC
QuickTime Conference

Apple Computer's cross-platform, video conferencing, collaborative computing, and multi-media communications technology.

Supports sharing, over LANs and WANs, of real-time (that is, not necessarily instant response time but predictable response time) data, images, and sound.

Three types of connections can be established:

▲ Point-to-point: two people interactively communicate

▲ Multipoint: many people interactively communicate

▲ Multicast: one person broadcasts to many

See **APPLE**, **IP MULTICAST**, **MULTIMEDIA**, and **SMRP**.

QWERTY

The beginning letters (from left to right) on a standard keyboard, so this term is used to describe the layout of a standard keyboard. There are other layouts, such as ABCD order which some think is easier for people who don't touch-type, and Dvorak (named after August Dvorak) which is designed for faster touch-typing.

The QWERTY layout was first used on a typewriter designed by C. L. Sholes, and called the Sholes & Glidden. It was manufactured by Remington (the gunmaker) from 1873 to 1878, and only had the upper-case (capital) letters. The keys hit the paper from under the platen, so you could not see what you typed until you lifted the printing carriage—so it was sometimes called a *blind-writer* (typewriters did not become widely popular until "visible" typewriters became widely available, such as the Underwood in 1895.

While some say the layout was designed specifically to slow typists so they would not jam the mechanics of the typewriters, it may simply have been the easiest way to lay out the keyboard, given the restrictions of an entirely mechanical deisgn, the many levers and linkages required, and where your strongest fingers are.

R

RADIUS
Remote Authentication Dial-In User Service

A centralized user-authentication security scheme developed by Livingston Enterprises Inc. Dial-in users (to a router or RAS) are required to log-in to a RADIUS client (the dial-in server), which then verifies the log-in with a RADIUS server elsewhere on the network. The server has a database of what network resources each dial-in user can access.

RADIUS is defined in RFC 2138, and further information is at *http://www.livingston.com*.

See **AUTHENTICATION**, and **RAS**.

RAID
Redundant Array of Inexpensive Disks

A disk subsystem (that appears as a single large, fast, super-reliable disk drive) composed of more than one (usually equal-sized) disk drives (called an *array*) to provide improved reliability, response time, and/or storage capacity.

Several techniques are used:

▲ *Spanning* or *Software Striping*: splits the data from a single write operation into several parts, each written to a different physical disk drive. This increases the input and output capacity of the disk drive system, however any failed drive causes the entire stripe-set (or volume) to be unavailable.

▲ *Mirroring*: duplicates the data from one disk onto others so that the data are still available if a drive fails. This doubles the number of disk drives required for a given amount of data.

▲ *Duplexing*: duplicates both the disks and the disk controllers (the printed circuit board that goes between the PC's bus and the disk drive). This doubles both the number of disk drives and the number of disk controllers required.

▲ *Deferred write-back cache* (also called *lazy writes*), where the disk write initially goes to cache memory, and is written later when the disk is available. The cache memory may be battery backed-up.

▲ During this wait, the data may be changed (thereby avoiding an unnecessary write) or there may be more data to write to the same sector or cylinder (which can very efficiently be combined into a single write operation). These can dramatically improve the performance of a disk system.

All of these techniques speed response times during periods of heavy loading, since more than one physical disk drive is supplying data simultaneously.

RAID arrays may also support the following:

▲ *Hot Swapping*: a failed disk drive can be removed and replaced, and the data can be automatically restored to the new disk while the subsystem is powered up and continues to operate in production service

▲ *Hot Sparing*: an extra disk drive in the array is automatically put into service (no need to manually plug in a new one) when a failure occurs (ideally, the copying of the data to the spare disk begins before a failing disk completely fails—that is, when the error rate on a failing disk increases)

▲ *Spindle Synchronization*: synchronizes the rotation of all drives in an array, so that data can be written simultaneously, speeding the disk operations.

Originally, levels 1 through 5 were defined as part of the RAID concept. However, as shown in the table below, people now also refer to levels 0 and 6.

RAID Level	Functionality	Comments
0	Data are striped across available disks drives (called *multiple spindles*, to sound more esoteric), to improve access times and throughput. There is no redundancy.	Was already in use when the RAID concepts were developed. Not really RAID, since there is no redundancy, just better performance.
1	Two disk drives are mirrored (both store the same data), using a single disk controller. Data can be read off both drives simultaneously (either drive can service any request), providing improved performance for reads (but not for writes), and redundancy.	Often implemented in software. Doubles the number of disk drives required, therefore suited only to smaller storage requirements. Provides faster write times than RAID 4 or 5.
2	Data are spanned (striped, bit-by-bit) across multiple disks, and additional disks are used to store *Hamming codes* (to detect and correct errors or recover from failed drives). Four data disks would require three additional error detection and correction disks.	Offers the greatest redundancy but is not currently commercially offered because of the high cost (too many extra disk drives are required).
3	Data are *striped* (sometimes called *interleaved*) either bit-by-bit or (more commonly) byte-by-byte across two or more (four is apparently best) data disks (for example, first byte to first disk, second byte to next disk, and so on—written in parallel to all disks). A parity byte is constructed from the corresponding bytes on the data disks and is written to one additional disk, which is dedicated as a *parity disk*. The contents of a failed disk can be reconstructed from the other disks. However, the use of a single parity disk creates a performance bottleneck.	Considered best for larger transfers, such as graphics or imaging files. High-performance workstations therefore often use RAID 3.

(table continued on next page)

RAID Level	Functionality	Comments
4	Same as RAID 3, but data are striped (and parity is constructed) in disk *sectors* (which is the smallest unit of disk storage allocation) rather than bits or bytes.	Since small data reads (a sector or less) still go to only a single disk drive, performance is not improved compared to a non-RAID single disk. Also, the use of a single parity disk creates a performance bottle-neck. This RAID level provides redundancy, but performanced is improved only on larger transfers. Therefore, this RAID level is seldom used or available.
5	Data are striped sector by sector across two or more disks. Parity information sectors are striped along with the data on each disk, and there is no dedicated parity disk. Since both parity and data are striped, simultaneous writes are possible (depending on where the data has to go).	Considered best for smaller transfers and transfers to sequential disk sectors. Offers better write (and the same read) performance as RAID 4. Since all information is spread among the redunandant drives, often considered the most robust, and therefore well-suited to servers and other *mission-critical* machines.
6	Not originally defined as part of RAID, but was developed as performance problems were understood. Uses RAID 5, but adds a *log-structured file system*. This provides a mapping (called a *logical track image*) between a disk's physical sectors and their logical representation, so that writes will go to sequential physical disk sectors (which is really fast) even the data is not sequential. During quiet times, disk sectors are automatically shuffled around to free-up entire cylinders, to speed later writes. Also, data is compressed before being written. This both speeds the writing (there is less to write) and increases the capacity of the disk system.	

Some vendors make up new names. For example, RAID 0/1 combines the striping of RAID 0 with the mirroring of RAID 1. The result is that at least 4 drives are used, and there should be both performance and reduandancy improvements.

RAID is typically provided by a hardware subsystem (which may appear as a single, super-reliable disk drive with a single SCSI ID). But some Operating Systems provide RAID. For example Windows NT workstation provides RAID levels 0 and 1, and the server version also supports RAID level 5.

The figure below summarizes the RAID levels.

```
Raid
                                                                    Raid
                                                                    Level
                    -- Spanning (no redundant data)                  0

                    -- Entire disk duplicated (mirrored)             1

                    -- Bit-by-bit (separate hamming code disks)      2

    Data Split      -- Bit-by-bit, or byte-by-byte (separate
    Across Disk ---|   parity disk)                                  3
    Drives by       |
                    |             -- (separate parity disk)          4
                    -- Sector --|
                                  -- (parity sectors mixed with data) 5
```

The initial concepts for RAID were developed by David Patterson, Randy Katz and Garth Gibson who were at the University of California at Berkeley at the time. They presented these at a conference in June 1988, as a proposal that smaller and cheaper disks in an array could be less expensive and of at least similar performance than single, large and expensive disks (SLEDs). The paper's comparison was between a 7.5 Gbyte mainframe disk drive (an IBM 3380 Model K, which costed over $100,000), and a 100 Mbyte Conner Peripherals disk drive intended for use in PCs (about $800 in those days—these prices include the disk controller).

As RAID has proven to be best-suited to providing high-reliability (and not lower-cost or necessarily better performance), some say that RAID is now an abbreviation for *Redundant Array of Independent Disks*. Also, the individual disk drives used are usually high-end—anything but inexpensive. RAID disk arrays are usually installed for their fault tolerance, and ability to rebuilt lost data while the array is in service. They usually do not cost less (implementing redundancy turns out to be very expensive—you also need redundant power supplies, fans and so on), or perform significantly faster than SLEDs (because of the parity write operations needed for RAID).

To control the use of RAID numbers, claims and terminology, the *RAID* Advisory Board (in St. Peter, Minnesota) was created. They are at *http://www.raid-advisory.com*.

See **DISK DRIVE**, **ECC**, and **SLED**.

RAM
Random Access Memory

A type of computer memory that can be quickly (we're talking nanoseconds here) written and read.

The "random" is in contrast to linear types, such as tape drives, in which you cannot read any location at any time (you first need to spin the tape to where your data are stored).

As processors get faster, faster types of RAM (such as EDO RAM) are required.

See **CACHE**, **DIMM**, **DRAM**, **ECC**, **EDO RAM**, **FPM**, **PC**, **RAMDAC**, **RDRAM**, **SHADOWED BIOS**, **SHARED MEMORY**, **SIMM**, **SRAM**, and **VRAM**.

RAM Mobile Data

Ram Mobile Data USA is a company jointly owned by RAM Broadcasting, Inc., Ericsson, and BellSouth Corp. that provides a cellular-radio-based packet data service called *Mobitex*.

Competes with Ardis and CDPD. Ericsson encourages others to manufacture compatible equipment (people prefer an open standard).

More information is available at *http://www.ram.com*.

See **ARDIS**, **CDPD**, and **MOBITEX**.

RAMBUS

See **RDRAM**.

RAMDAC
Random Access Memory Digital-to-Analog Converter

The integrated circuit that converts the digital information stored in a video adapter's *frame buffer* (which has an image of what is to be displayed on the screen) to the analog signals needed to drive the monitor.

At a refresh rate of 75 Hz (that is, the entire screen must be rewritten 75 times per second), a resolution of $1,024 \times 768$ pixels, and 24-bit color (3 bytes of RAM per pixel), the RAMDAC must be able to handle ($75 \times 1,024 \times 768 \times 3$ =) 176,947,200 bytes per second over 170 Mbytes/s. The frame buffer RAM must be able support this data transfer rate plus the CPU accesses needed to create and change the display.

See **COLOUR**, **RAM**, **VESA**, and **VIDEO**.

RAS
Remote Access Server

A router that supports dial-in (typically an analog auto-answer modem or ISDN connection), so that *remote nodes* (computers remote from the LAN) can have dial-in access to a LAN. RAS units may have 4 or more dial-in connections, and larger units directly support T1 or ISDN PRI connections to support 24 or 23 users per connection, without requiring separate modems or terminal adapters (just a single DSU/CSU).

The routing function may be built-in to a file server (such as Windows NT remote access service), or may be a hardware unit (such as a Shiva LANrover).

Typically, at least IP is supported, though many products support IPX. Some support DECnet, AppleTalk, VINES and NetBEUI as well.

The data link layer protocol (which encapsulates the above network layer protocols, to provide error and flow control) is typically PPP, though it may also be SLIP.

Some products with PRI interfaces support the following:

▲ Remote users that have both analog modems and ISDN access—through the same PRI to the RAS.

▲ MLPPP, to allow multiple B channels to be dynamically aggregated to provide faster LAN access to remote users.

Many products include security features such as CHAP, PAP and dial-back.

See **S56K MODEM**, **MLPPP**, **RADIUS**, **PPP**, **REMOTE NODE**, **ROUTER**, and **WAN**.

Rasterize

The process of converting an image which may be described by a series of straight-line segments (often called vectors) or curves (described with an equation) to a raster image (which is a series of horizontal lines of varying intensity and possibly color).

Many display devices (such as laser printers and television and computer screens) create their output by scanning a beam from left to right across each row (starting at the top left corner), and then repeating this process for each row down the screen.

▲ For television and computer screens, the beam is a focused stream of electrons that bombards and excites colored phosphors. This causes them to glow briefly—the *persistence* of the phosphor is chosen so that the glow lasts until the next scan (which is typically $\frac{1}{30}$ to $\frac{1}{70}$ of a second). The beam is moved using precisely-controlled electromagnets.

▲ For laser printers, the beam is often a red or infrared (770 to 795 nm wavelength) high-intensity (5 mW) light beam produced by a *laser diode* (hence the name "laser printer"). The beam is focused by lenses and reflected off of a rotating mirror—this creates the required scanning. The paper is advanced by an accurately-controlled motor.

By electronically varying the intensity of the beam as it scans, any image can be displayed.

While a raster is a very efficient method of displaying an image, it is often not the best way to store (it requires too much memory) or create the image (raster images scaled to other resolutions only look nice if the other resolutions are integral multiples of the original).

For example, fonts are best described using mathematical descriptions of the shape of their outlines. Once the font has been scaled to the desired size (and the color and pattern to be used to fill the outline has been generated), a rasterizing process (such as that done by the Adobe Type Manager) is then used to create the image needed for the display device.

See **ATM1** (*Adobe Type Manager*), **INTERLACED**, and **OUTLINE FONT**.

RBDS
Radio Broadcast Data System

Another name for the Radio Data System.

See **RDS**.

RBOC
Regional Bell Operating Company

One of the seven U.S. holding companies that were formed to own the *Local Exchange Carriers* (LECs) created by the *divestiture* of AT&T (also called *the breakup of Ma Bell*), which occurred in 1984. Now that SBC Communications Inc. and Pacific Telesis Group have merged (final approval from the California Public Utilities Commision was granted in April 1997), there are now only 6 RBOCs. Nynex and Bell Atlantic's merger would reduce this to 5.

RBOCs are sometimes called *Regional Bell Holding Companies* (RBHC), *Bell Operating Companies* (BOCs), and *Baby Bells*. Each owns the previously AT&T-owned telephone companies in a specific geographic region, as shown in the following table.

RBOC	Owns These Local Exchange Carriers	Which Are in These Geographic Areas
Ameritech	Illinois Bell, Indiana Bell, Michigan Bell, Ohio Bell, and Wisconsin Telephone	Illinois, Indiana, Michigan, Ohio, Wisconsin
Bell Atlantic	Bell of Pennsylvania, Chesapeake and Potomac of Maryland, C&P of Virginia, C&P of Washington, D.C., C&P of West Virginia, Diamond State Telephone, and New Jersey Bell	Delaware, Maryland, New Jersey, Pennsylvania, Virginia, Washington, D.C., West Virginia
BellSouth	South Central Bell, Southeastern Bell, and Southern Bell	Alabama, Florida, Georgia, Louisiana, Kentucky, Mississippi, North Carolina, South Carolina, Tennessee
Nynex	New York Telephone	Massachusetts, Maine, New Hampshire, New York, Rhode Island, Vermont
Pacific Telesis Group (merged with Southwestern Bell)	Nevada Bell and Pacific Telephone	California, Nevada
SBC Communications (was Southwestern Bell Communications until 1994), and now owns Pacific Telesis Group		Arkansas, Kansas, Missouri, Oklahoma, Texas
U.S. West	Mountain Bell, Northwestern Bell, and Pacific Northwest Bell	Arizona, Colorado, Idaho, Iowa, Montana, Minnesota, Nebraska, New Mexico, North Dakota, Oregon, South Dakota, Utah, Washington, Wyoming

Southern New England Telephone was formed in 1878, was never part of the Bell System, and is still independent. It provides local and long distance service for all of Connecticut.

Greater-distance calls within an RBOC's territory may be *toll calls*, but RBOCs were initially prevented from offering long-distance services (that is, calls between different RBOCs or to other countries). Similarly, the IXCs were initially generally restricted from offering local service.

As is the case with a company deciding to support the development of a standard, most RBOCs have decided that it is better to have some of a big thing (where you can always fight for more market share), rather than all of a little thing (where the market growth potential is low, and stagnant things seldom prosper).

Therefore, the U.S. *Telecommunications Act of 1996* (which became effective on February 8 of that year) changed the rules. Some examples are listed below.

▲ RBOCs can offer long-distance telephone service (that is, interLATA service) outside of their georgraphic region. RBOCs can offer interLATA service for customers within their region if the RBOC gives up their monopoly on providing local telephone service (also called local exchange service).

▲ RBOCs can offer cable TV service, and the incumbent cable TV company gets their rates deregulated.

▲ RBOCs (through affiliates for the first 3 years) can manufacture telecommunications and customer premisis equipment.

▲ Bellcore cannot manufacture equipment, and any standards they develop must be through an open process.

The RBOCs maintain a WWW server at *http://www.bell.com*. Some information on the Telecommunications Act and other related subjects is at *http://www.technologylaw.com/techlaw*.

See **ATT**, **BELLCORE**, **CARRIER**, **CPE**, **IXC OR IEC**, **LATA**, **LEC**, and **POTS**.

RBHC
Regional Bell Holding Company

Another name for RBOC, since an RBOC can be considered a holding company for the telephone companies (also called Local Exchange Carriers) which it owns.

See **LEC** and **RBOC OR RBHC**.

RDRAM
Rambus DRAM

A technology developed by Rambus Inc. in conjunction with Intel to provide the next generation memory architecture for PCs. Most DRAM manufacturers have licensed the technology (for about 2% of their sales revenues), and Intel is expected to provide support for RDRAMs in their chipsets beginning in 1999.

A subsequent extension to RDRAM is *Direct RDRAM*, and it provides the following features:

▲ Data transfers are 2 bytes per transfer, at 800 Mtransfers/s (using a 400 MHz clock, with a transfer on both clock edges). The peak throughput is therefore 1.6 Gbytes/s. (The original RDRAM specification supported only 1 byte transfers). In contrast, a 16-bit wide SDRAM-based memory system on a 66 MHz memory bus in a current conventional PC has a peak throughput of 133 Mbytes/s.

▲ Each "byte" can be implemented as either 8 or 9 bits. The extra bit can be used for parity or ECC, or for additional data storage, such as for a graphics overlay.

▲ A bus architecture (hence the name "Rambus") is used for the memory ICs, with the memory controller at one end of the bus, and resistor bus terminations at the other end. Up to 32 ICs can be directly attached to the bus, and this is called a channel. Using an expansion buffer, each channel can support up to a total of 64 memory ICs. A computer system can have multiple channels to increase throughput or storage capacity.

▲ DRRAM ICs are defined for 32 Mbit through 1 Gbit each.

▲ Memory can be increased in units of as little as 4 Mbytes (that is, by units of 1 IC, using the 32 Mbit ICs).

▲ Memory is built of RIMMs, which are similar in size to DIMMs. Each side of a RIMM can hold up to 8 RDRAM ICs, for a RIMM capacity of 128 Mbytes when using 64 Mbit RDRAMs. The RIMMs have 35 active signal pins (plus a few for ground), which are: 16 for data, 2 pairs for clock, 3 for memory row commands, 5 for memory column commands, 4 for memory initialization purposes, 1 for the memory reference voltage and 2 for power.

▲ Several power-down and power-reducing modes are defined. Also, RDRAMs use only a 2.5 V supply voltage and a 800 mV signal swing (on a 1 V reference voltage, producing a 1.8 V maximum output signal). This also helps to reduce power consumption.

▲ Memory transfers are in packets of 16 bytes (4 clock cycles per packet, which is 8 clock edges, which is 16 bytes). Using mask bits in the row and column control lines, the actual data transferred can be as little as 1 byte per packet (if that's all you need to transfer, though this reduces the efficiency).

Rambus is at *http://www.rambus.com*.

See **DIMM**, and **DRAM**.

RDS
Radio Data System

A method of transmitting data simultaneously with a standard FM stereo (or monophonic) radio broadcast. Applications implemented already include sending song titles and signaling when traffic or weather reports are being broadcast, to enhanced radios, as well as broadcasting to pagers.

Bits are continuously sent at 1,187.5 bits/s (chosen partly because the data's 57-kHz carrier frequency and the standard 19-kHz *stereo pilot* frequency are integral multiples).

The data are sent in blocks of 26 bits: 16 data bits plus 10 *forward error correction* bits (the error correction code used can correct an error burst of 5 or fewer bits in each block of 26 bits without requiring a retransmission). *Groups* of four blocks of 26 bits are used, each group therefore contains 64 data bits, and 104 bits total.

Four bits are reserved to designate the *group type* (which identifies what the subsequent data are). Some defined group types are:

▲ Station name (the four *call letters*)

▲ Time and date (in UTC format, sent on the zero-second each minute)

▲ Radio paging (rather than using a separate transmitter, why not use an existing radio station's?)

▲ Emergency warning messages

▲ Program type (drama, rock, etc.)

▲ Text messages (called *radio text*) of up to 64 characters, sent as 4 characters per group

Ream

Another bit sent in every group indicates whether music or speech is currently being broadcast.

Originally developed by Swedish Telecom (and called MBS) in 1976 as a method of sending data to radio pagers. Developed by the European Broadcasting Union (in the early 1980s, with widespread use beginning in 1985) into RDS. Standardized in 1993 by the U.S. National Association of Broadcasters (Washington, D.C., phone 202-429-5373).

In the U.S., RDS is called the Radio Broadcast Data System (RDBS). It is being promoted by the EIA and the National Association of Broadcasters.

A vendor of RDS equipment is at *http://www.ADSTECH.com.*

See **ECC, GSM,** and **UTC.**

Ream

Now defined as 500 sheets of paper, but some related definitions are shown in the following table.

Number of Sheets of Paper	Called	Comments
480	Short ream	Old definition of ream
500	Ream	Used to be called a long ream
516	Printer's ream	Also called a perfect ream

See **PAPER.**

Recommended Standard 232

See **EIA/TIA-232.**

Regional Bell Operating Company

See **RBOC OR RBHC.**

Registered Jack 45 (RJ-45)

See **RJ-45.**

Remote Bridge

One of (usually) a pair of (usually Ethernet) bridges that connects two (or more) LANs over a WAN. Token Ring remote bridges are usually called *split bridges.*

See **LAN, LOCAL BRIDGE, TOKEN RING,** and **WAN.**

Remote Control

See **REMOTE NODE.**

Remote Imaging Protocol Script Language

See **RIPSCRIP.**

Remote Network Monitoring MIB

See **RMON**.

Remote Node

A method of remotely accessing a LAN, typically over a dial-up connection. That is, you need to access your office's LAN, using your PC, from home or while travelling. Your PC is a node (just like any other computer on the LAN), but it is remote from the LAN (hence the name).

A device directly connected to the LAN accepts these calls (usually over a standard dial-up voice telephone line, or sometimes ISDN), and is typically called a *remote access server* (RAS).

Remote node is a good solution if the executable program and large data files don't need to be transferred over the WAN (that is, they are already on the remote PC). This requires much configuration and testing (to get all the files and the mapping to them set up properly), and is sometimes not possible (additional copies of the software may be too expensive, or the data file is large is maintained at the central site). In this case *remote control* is often the best solution.

Remote control basically uses two PCs to do the job of one. The PC at the central location (let's call it the host—there is no standard name) does all of the actual work, but runs a program that permits the remote PC to control it. Whatever is displayed on the host PC is sent to the remote (actually, just the *changes* in the display, to reduce the transfer requirements. Whatever is typed on the remote PC's keyboard is sent to the host PC and appears to have been typed at the host.

The host PC may be one of the following:

▲ an actual PC (or perhaps a stack of them, all sharing a single display, keyboard and mouse, using a switch)

▲ a PC implemented on a card, in a special chassis (this is a good solution when more than a few simultaneous remote control users need to be supported)

▲ one of many tasks run by a multi-user operating system, such as Microsoft Windows NT

Some RAS devices support both remote node and remote control (so you can switch, according to your requirements). In this case, the remote control is of a PC elsewhere on the LAN, and the RAS just routes your dial-in traffic to it.

Some vendors include Citrix Systems Inc. at *http://www.citrix.com* and *http://www.microcom.com*, *http://www.travsoft.com*, and *http://www.shiva.com*.

See **RAS**.

REN
Ringer Equivalency Number

A two-part description of the electrical characteristics of the ringer (which used to be a mechanical bell) in telephones.

Repeater

The first part is a number which indicates how much current is required to make the phone ring (an 86 V, 20 Hz signal is standard). Typical telephone company COs allow a load of up to 5, so you add the numbers for all your telephones (that have the ringer turned on), and so long as they add to 5 or less, you can be sure that all your phones will ring properly. ISDN modems that can generate ringing voltage for attached POTS devices will specify their REN, such as "2.0".

The second part indicates the frequency of the ringing voltage. Different frequencies are used in different countries, and also to ring only selected telephones on a party line (a 20 Hz signal is typically used for your standard home telephone that is not on a party line). The letter A indicates a frequency of 20 Hz or 30 Hz. B indicates any frequency from 15.3 Hz to 68 Hz. The letters starting with C are for narrow selective-ring frequencies, such as 15.3 to 17.4 Hz.

My fax machine manual says its ringer equivalence is "0.7A, 0.9B" (that is, it draws more current at some frequencies allowed in the B range).

See **BRI**, and **POTS**.

Repeater

An electronic device typically used to *regenerate* binary signals (such as those for T1 or Ethernet). For example, an Ethernet repeater typically has the following functions

▲ Input signals greater than a pre-set *threshold* (according to the type of signal) are boosted to the full voltage for that type of signal. This allows the physical size of the network to be extended.

▲ Signals less than the threshold are set to the other binary voltage, so noise induced into the cable is eliminated (so long as the noise is not greater than the threshold voltage—which is the case for properly designed networks).

▲ Signals are *re-timed*, in that they are sent with the bit-edge transitions at exactly the right place (for example, noise can randomly shift bit-edge transitions—this is called *edge jitter*).

▲ *Anti-jabber* (also called *anti-streaming*), where a defective station (which is transmitting constantly) is automatically *partitioned* from the rest of the network.

▲ *Fragment extension*, where illegally-small Ethernet frames (likely caused by collisions) are extended to frames large enough that all stations will recognize that there was a collision.

For a 10 Mbit/s Ethernet network, a maximum of 4 repeaters are allowed between any two stations, although some manufacturers allow more (such as 5), if you use only their repeaters in the network. The cable distance allowed between repeaters (or between a station and a repeater) depends on the type of Ethernet and cabling used. For example, in 10BASE-T, the maximum distance is 100 m of UTP cable.

An Ethernet repeater is also called a *multi-port repeater* (since it typically has 8 or more ports), a *hub* (since it is the center of a star-wiring topology, where all connections radiate from the hub), and a *concentrator* (since all signals are often funneled into a single backbone connection).

All devices connected to an Ethernet repeater share the same bandwidth (that is, when one station is transmitting, others cannot transmit). As more stations transmit more data, the *utilization* (percentage of time when the LAN is not idle) increases, which increases the probability that two stations will transmit at the same time (which is called a *collision*)—which requires both stations to stop transmitting, wait a random amount of time, and attempt to transmit again (hopefully not colliding with themselves or other stations). Therefore, as the network gets busier, more bandwidth is lost to collisions, which makes the network busier, and so on. Therefore, some people (especially IBM-types) say that Ethernet is unstable. This is true, but only on overloaded Ethernets. That is, for a typical office installation Ethernet LAN with many stations, the utilization should be kept less than about 40%, and preferably less than 25%.

One of the easiest ways to reduce network utilization is to *segment* the network (that is, divide it into separate segments, which are linked by switches, bridges or routers). The reduces the number of stations in the *collision domain* (the stations that share bandwidth, and who can collide with each other). The ultimate is to have only one station in each collision domain (this is often called *micro-segmentation*)—so there will never be bandwidth lost due to a collision. This is one of the features of ATM.

See **ETHERNET, SWITCHED LAN,** and **T1.**

Resource Reservation Protocol

See **RSVP.**

RFC
Request for Comments

RFCs define and document the network protocols, procedures and concepts of the Internet, and for TCP/IP in general. This process began in 1969, and procedure is roughly to do the following:

▲ Detail the proposed standard in a document

▲ Make the document available on the Internet for all to download and read

▲ Request comments

The document is therefore called a *Request For Comments* and is given a number (RFC numbers are assigned by the Network Information Center—InterNIC), for example, RFC 1149 (which is titled *A Standard for the Transmission of IP* Datagrams on Avian Carriers—a hint: this particular document's date is April 1, 1990). After comments have been considered and the document has possibly been changed, the resulting standard (after approval from the IETF) retains the original name (such as RFC 1149).

From *http://www.cis.ohio-state.edu/hypertext/information/rfc.html* , RFCs can be searched (by keyword or RFC number), and viewed or retrieved. A chronological listing of all RFCs (beginning with the most recent) is at *http://www.cis.ohio-state.edu/htbin/rfc/rfc-index.html*. Any specific RFC can be viewed at, for example, *http://www.cis.ohio-state.edu/htbin/rfc/ rfc1882.html* for RFC 1882. A mirror site is at the University of Waterloo, so you could also go to *http://www.uwaterloo.ca/rfc/rfc1882.html* or the higher-level interface at *http:// www.uwaterloo.ca/uw_infoserv/rfc.html*. Another mirror site is at *http://www.isi.edu/rfc-editor.*

Using ftp, RFCs are available from *ftp://ds.internic.net/rfc,* or by using a WWW browser from *http://ds.internic.net/rfc/.* When using this method, RFC 1597 (for example) is file `RFC1597.txt` (in ASCII text) and `RFC1597.ps` (in PostScript format—these look nicer, but you need a PostScript printer or viewer). So to receive RFC 1597 as an ASCII text file, go to *ftp://ds.internic.net/rfc/rfc1597.txt.*

A list of all RFCs and their length and status (for example, many are obsolete) is at *http://ds.internic.net/rfc/rfc-index.txt* (this file is about 250 kbytes). You can search for RFCs at *http://www.internic.net/ds/dspg1intdoc.html.*

Drafts of RFCs are at *http://ds.internic.net/internet-drafts* and *http://www.ietf.org/1id-abstracts.html.* The charters for groups working on new RFCs are at *http://www.ietf.org/html.charters/.* Searching for specific RFCs and drafts can be done at *http://www.cabletron.com/support/internet/.*

See **IETF**, **INTERNIC**, and **POSTSCRIPT PAGE DESCRIPTION LANGUAGE**.

RFC 1577
Classical IP over ATM

A method of supporting IP traffic over an ATM network (both PVCs and SVCs are supported).

The RFC defines the following:

▲ The encapsulation of IP packets into ATM AAL 5 *protocol data units* (PDUs) is defined. The default maximum packet size is 9,180 bytes (this is more efficient than Ethernet, which requires hosts to segment their data into 1,500-byte frames), but any packet size up to AAL 5's maximum of 64 kbytes is allowed, so long as all other stations on the IP subnet have been configured to support that packet size. The IP packet gets a LLC/SNAP header, which identifies the protocol (just as the type/length field of an Ethernet frame does).

▲ A mapping of IP addresses to ATM addresses (and rules on when to establish a new ATM SVC connection). For ATM networks that support only PVCs, the mapping is done by manually creating a local address table on each IP host.

▲ Since IP hosts can typically only communicate directly with other hosts on the same subnetwork, all hosts are typically given IP addresses on the same subnet (so the entire ATM network appears as a single large IP subnet). This is referred to as a *logical IP* subnet (LIS). For hosts on different subnets—but even if they are on the same ATM network—a conventional router is still required for them to communicate (and this will usually be a performance bottleneck). Each subnet can be configured to have a different QOS.

▲ For ATM networks that support SVCs, each LIS typically requires an ATM *address resolution protocol* (ARP) server. This replaces the broadcast method used for LAN-based ARP, so that end stations can determine what ATM address to use for a given destination IP host. Each host then establishes an SVC connection to the ATMARP server (typically, the address of the ATMARP server must be manually configured into the hosts) and registers itself. The ATMARP server then sends an inverse (or reverse) ARP to the calling host to determine its IP address. The ATMARP server then makes this mapping information available to other hosts.

▲ The ATMARP server may be software running on a file server or workstation, or may be built-in to an ATM switch or router.

As you might suspect from the name, this method only supports IP, and no other protocols, such as IPX or AppleTalk.

RFC 1577 was published in January 1994.

See **ARP**, **ATM** (*Asynchronous Transfer Mode*), and **LANE**.

RFC 1918

A method for dealing with the problem that no more worldwide unique Class A IP addresses and very few Class B addresses are available for new networks.

While lots of Class C addresses are available (for a while anyway), many (most?) organizations have more than 254 hosts (which is all that a single Class C IP address can address).

Sounds like a problem, doesn't it? Lots of large companies need lots of addresses, but large blocks of addresses are not available. One solution is based on the observation that while an organization may need a large number of IP addresses for internal use (one per host computer) the following is also true:

▲ Only a small number of users (that is, hosts) will need to simultaneously access the outside world (the Internet)—most of a company's TCP/IP traffic is between hosts within a company's network

▲ While everyone needs to be able to send and receive Internet mail, this only requires that one host for an entire organization (and not each individual user) needs a worldwide unique IP address.

▲ Most companies use a *firewall* between the Internet and their internal network. When using a firewall to access the Internet, all internal users' ftp, telnet, and WWW (for example) traffic usually shares the single IP address of the firewall. Each user does not need their own external IP address, since the connections are initiated by the users, who need only a unique *socket number*, not IP address.

The approach described in RFC 1918 is for the organization to obtain a (usually Class C) worldwide unique (or "external") address for each host that requires direct communication with the Internet (for example, to provide a WWW or ftp server). Internally, the organization uses any IP addresses it wishes. An *address translation gateway* (which is usually part of the software in a router) then translates the worldwide unique external addresses from the Internet to the internal addresses used by the organization.

RFC 1918 reserves some IP addresses for this private internal use. Since these particular addresses can never be valid Internet addresses, routers know whether to do a translation or not.

These reserved addresses are listed in the following table.

Bits in Address Range	Address Range Size and Type	IP Address Range	
		From	To
24	One *Class A*	10.0.0.0	10.255.255.255
20	16 *Class B*	172.16.0.0	172.31.255.255
16	256 *Class C*	192.168.0.0	192.168.255.255

A problem with this method is the administration required for the address translation gateway (manually mapping the reserved, internal RFC 1918 addresses to the registered external addresses).

RFC 1597 was the predecessor to RFC 1918.

Another method of handling the Class A and B IP address shortage is called CIDR. In fact, most ISPs are required to use CIDR, and therefore require their customers to use ranges of IP addresses from the ISPs CIDR block—which is yet another reason for customers to have to map (using *network address translation*—NAT) their addresses into the ISP's. The customer uses a convenient internal, private addressing scheme, and uses the NAT feature of their firewall to map to whatever their ISP requires. If they change ISPs, then they continue to use the same internal IP addressing scheme, and just change the NAT configuration.

See **CIDR, FIREWALL, IP ADDRESS, ISP**, and **SOCKET NUMBER**.

RFS
Remote File Sharing

The capability of locally mounting a disk drive which is physically located elsewhere on a network. That is, the remote disk drive appears to be part of the local computer system—and files can be created, opened, and deleted (subject to the access permissions) on the remote disk, using the same commands as if it were a disk on the local computer.

Developed by AT&T for their implementation of UNIX. Not as flexible as Sun Microsystems' (far more widely used) NFS.

See **NFS** and **SUN**

RGB
Red, Green, Blue

A method of sending or specifying color video information, typically to a video monitor.

Uses a separate cable for each of the red, green, and blue color signals (the connectors are the RCA-type or, more commonly, a BNC-type connector—especially in professional video equipment). Typically, the green also carries the synchronizing and blanking information, but this may be on a fourth cable.

RGB provides more accurate color than composite video does, since the color is usually generated as three separate signals in the first place, so the signals don't need to be converted (which would reduce the quality—as they say, "something always gets lost in the translation").

See **BNC, COLOUR, COMPOSITE VIDEO SIGNAL**, and **VIDEO**.

RIP
Routing Information Protocol

A method that routers use to communicate network connectivity status and determine the best path over which to send traffic.

Many protocols have their own incompatible implementation, as shown in the following table, so DECnet's RIP is incompatible with TCP/IP's RIP, which is incompatible with Novell's RIP, and so on.

Protocol	RIP Router to Router Protocol	
	Acronym	Name
AppleTalk	RTMP	Routing table maintenance protocol
DECnet	RIP	Routing information protocol
IP	RIP	Routing information protocol
Novell IPX	RIP	Routing information protocol
Vines IP	RTP or SRTP	Routing table protocol (original) or sequenced routing table protocol (newer and improved, since it sends only a short message indicating that nothing has changed, if nothing has changed)

In RIP, paths are rated by *hop counts* (from 0 to 15); a hop count of 16 means that the node is unreachable. The protocol therefore imposes a network limitation of a maximum of 15 routers between any two hosts.

Other weaknesses include the following:

▲ Factors other than hop count, such as link speed and delay, are (usually) not included in the calculation to find the "best path" between two hosts.

▲ Each router's entire table is broadcasted every (for example) 10 (Apple's RTMP) to 60 (Novell's NetWare's RIP) seconds, whether there are changes from the last broadcast or not (this wastes precious WAN bandwidth).

A new and improved (!) method with many advantages (of course) is called *link-state*. The TCP/IP implementation of this is called OSPF.

The TCP/IP implementation of RIP is UDP-broadcast-based and uses the *well-known port* 520 (so the recipient knows to expect RIP information in the packet). It has a 4-bit field where a cost can be entered, so that a route can be manually configured to be more or less desirable to be used (perhaps because it runs slower than others). A slightly improved version of RIP for IP is called RIP II. One feature is that is supports variable length subnet bit masks. However OSPF is far more popular.

Novell's RIP includes a field to indicate the speed of each link so that routers can find the fastest path.

The algorithm used for RIP is also called *Distance-Vector* and *Bellman-Ford*.

See **IGRP**, **IP MULTICAST**, **LINK STATE**, **OSPF**, **TCP**, and **TTL1** (*Time-to-Live*).

RIPSCRIP
Remote Imaging Protocol Script Language

A method of providing a graphical user interface for bulletin board systems.

The protocol supports 16-color, 640 × 350 pixel resolution graphical environments, including mouse and on-screen clickable button support, fonts, icons, and graphical primitives (such as elliptical arcs, pie slices, and bezier curves).

Uses 7-bit ASCII (rather than requiring 8-bit transparency), so the communications are compatible with X.25 networks and all computing platforms (that is, it never uses reserved ASCII characters, such as the X-ON or *data link escape* character as part of its protocol).

Is usually supported by newer bulletin board systems.

Callers' communication software must support the protocol and graphics to take advantage of the interface. A royalty-free freeware program (RIPterm) is available. It provides features such as pull-down menus, file transfer using the popular PC protocols, dialing directory, keystroke macros, and support for COM1 through COM4.

A separate program (RIPaint) is used to develop the graphical screens and mouse-clickable menus for the user interface.

Developed by TeleGrafix Communications, Inc.

See **BBS** and **GUI**.

RISC
Reduced Instruction-Set Computer

A central processing unit technology that is supposed to provide faster and lower-cost processing than the other way of doing things: *Complex Instruction-Set Computing* (CISC, which is used by Intel PCs, IBM mainframes, and most other computing platforms).

The technology was pioneered by IBM in the 1970s and resulted in a processor architecture called POWER *(Performance Optimized With Enhanced RISC)*, which was initially implemented in the first IBM RS/6000 (RISC System/6000) workstation (introduced in February 1990) and eventually formed the basis for the Apple/IBM/Motorola PowerPC processor.

The idea is that by simplifying the logic needed to implement a processor (by making it capable of executing only very simple instructions and addressing modes), the processor can be smaller, less expensive, and faster—and maybe use less power too. By using a smarter compiler, the processor can still handle any task required (by efficiently combining simple instructions at compile time).

Major requirements for the success of RISC processors include the following:

- ▲ A high-quality, efficient compiler and development environment.

- ▲ Getting important existing application programs recompiled (for the processor's *native* mode). Often RISC processors have an *emulation* mode that enables them to run code compiled for other non-RISC processors (such as the Motorola 68000)—that is, the 68000 code is *binary portable* to the RISC processor's emulation mode. This capability is intended to get past the "chicken-and-egg" problem of why would I buy a processor for which there are no application programs, and why would I develop application programs for a processor that doesn't have an installed base?

▲ However, the emulation mode usually runs more slowly than (the competing) existing processors (in their native CISC mode), so compiling programs to produce efficient and native RISC processor code is required. This creates a tough problem. If the emulation mode runs software too slow, it is useless, and no one uses it. If the emulation is fast enough, no one converts their software, so there is no incentive to recompile the software, and the new processor is simply another way to run the software, so the new processor does not get accepted or get native software written for it. Just ask IBM about their OS/2 operating system and its support for Windows software (hint: you don't find many popular programs that run natively under OS/2).

Ideally, all RISC processor instructions (for example, adding two registers) are the same length (usually 32-bits) and execute in one clock cycle. In actual practice, some instructions (such as multiplication and division) require additional clock cycles. Depending on the implementation, other instructions (such as shifts and register loads from memory) may require more than one clock cycle. Also, some "RISC" processors have some instructions that are more than 1 32-bit word. This makes the distinction between RISC and CISC somewhat gray (sort of like defining *user-friendly*).

Due to their use in high-power workstations which often do complex mathematical functions, RISC processors are usually designed to have very good floating-point math performance.

Also, RISC processors usually do not support complex addressing modes. Instructions typically load data directly from memory to one of a large number of "orthogonal" registers (all registers can do the same functions), then operate on the data, and then return the data to memory (as three separate instructions). CISC processors often have single instructions (with lengthy execution times) that can do all these steps.

In addition to the PowerPC, other popular RISC-based processors include DEC's Alpha, HP's PA-RISC, SGI's MIPS, and Sun's SPARC.

While RISC was supposed to be a better idea than CISC, Intel architecture PCs (which are definately CISC) have kept CISC much more popular. In 1997, Intel, AMD and Cyrix together had about 93% of the microprocessor market. PowerPC is next at about 3.3%, then MIPS at about 2%, SPARC at about 1% and Alpha at about 0.1%.

See **S88OPEN**, **ALPHA AXP**, **PA RISC**, **P7**, **POWERPC**, **PORTABILITY**, **SPARC**, **SPEC**, and **SUPERSCALAR**.

RJ-45
Registered Jack 45

More-correctly called an 8-pin modular plug (the male connector), or jack (or receptacle—the female connector), this clear-plastic connector is very popular as it is used for all UTP LAN cabling, as well as other uses, such as EIA-232.

The connector is usually used for 4-pair cable, where each pair is two insulated copper conductors twisted to each other (both wires are used to carry one signal, as a *differential signal*).

When looking into the jack (female connector), with the channel for the locking tab at the bottom, pin 1 is at the top left, as shown in the figure below.

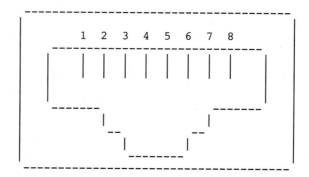

The pin-out for various uses is shown in the table below. These are shown for the end user connector (on your PC). Network equipment (for example, the hub or concentrator in the wiring closet) generally is the opposite (for example, has Rx+ instead of Tx+), so that the users can be directly connected (that is, the cabling used between the PCs and wiring closets is *straight-through*—no cross-overs required). Also, generally, two PCs (both with FDDI, or both with 100Base-T, for example) can be directly connected (no hub or repeater required) if a cross-over cable is used. For example, a cross-over cable for 100Base-T would connect the user pin 1 and 2 to the remote pins 3 and 6 (respectively). And user pins 3 and 6 would connect to the remote pins 1 and 2 (respectively).

Network Type	Pin Number							
	1	2	3	4	5	6	7	8
10BASE-T and 100BASE-TX	Tx+	Tx-	Rx+			Rx-		
Token Ring			Tx+	Rx-	Rx+	Tx-		
FDDI TP-PMD and ATM OC-3 SONet on Category 3[a] or 5 UTP	Tx+	Tx-					Rx+	Rx-
ISDN	P3+	P3-	Tx+	Rx+	Rx-	Tx-	P2-	P2+
POTS, first line				Ring	Tip			
POTS, second line			Tip			Ring		

a. Uses a modulation method that has 6 bits per symbol, so that Category 3 UTP can be used for the 155.52 Mbit/s signal.

Tx+ and Tx- are the two wires of the twisted pair that carry the data transmitted by the workstation to the hub (or network). Rx+ and Rx- are the two wires of the twisted pair that carry the data recieved from the network, to the workstation. P2 and P3 are the optional power sources on an ISDN S/T (also called S Bus) interface.

The EIA/TIA-568 *Commercial Building Telecommunications Wiring Standard* specifies the wire pairing and colors, as shown in the table below (sometimes called the EIA/TIA-568A, or *preferred* pin-out).

Pin Number	Pair	Wire Name	Wire Color
1	3	Tip 3	White (with optional green band)
2	3	Ring 3	Green (with optional white band)
3	2	Tip 2	White (with optional orange band)
4	1	Ring 1	Blue (with optional white band)
5	1	Tip 1	White (with optional blue band)
6	2	Ring 2	Orange (with optional white band)
7	4	Tip 4	White (with optional brown band)
8	4	Ring 4	Brown (with optional white band)

Depending on the manufacturer, the optional band may actually be a stripe or spiral, and shows the color of the other wire of the pair.

Looking at the pin-outs, one might wonder why the same pairs and pin-out was not used for all. As always, there is some (historical) reason for the way things are.

▲ Standard telepone RJ11 telephone jacks (like you have at home) use the center two contacts for the telephone's connection (these are officially called a CA11 in Canada). To reduce the chance of a telephone network being connected to an Ethernet network, 10BASE-T and 100BASE-T do not use the center pair (which is pins 4 and 5). The two pairs (pair 2 on pins 3 and 6, and pair 3 on pins 1 and 2).

▲ The next question is; why is pair 3 not symmetric around pairs 1 and 2 (using pins 2 and 7). There is a connector pin-out that does this—called USOC (*United States Order Code*), and this is sometimes used for voice applications. But the greater separation of the wires required to connect to those pins causes problems (such as *reflections* caused by the increase in impedance) for high-speed signals (such as Ethernet), so pair 3 was assigned to pins 1 and 2.

▲ FDDI, being a very high-speed network only uses pairs 3 (pins 1 and 2) and 4 (pins 7 and 8) because they are both the farthest from each other (to reduce cross-talk between them), and the pins of each pair are close together).

▲ Token Ring could use the 6-pin RJ11 connector, since it does not use the two outside pins.

8-pin modular jacks are typically rated for 500 to 1,000 mating cycles. The connector is standardized in ISO 8877.

See **CONNECTOR, EIA/TIA-232, POTS, T1, TIP AND RING**, and **UTP**.

RJE
Remote Job Entry

IBM's batch-oriented (as opposed to interactive) computing capability.

RLE

Uses the 2780/3780 (which was pre-SNA) and 3770 (part of SNA) family of peripheral equipment and protocols. Jobs can be submitted (originally, using 80-column card readers) and monitored, and print output and files can be retrieved. Runs on SNA/SDLC but is otherwise completely incompatible with 3270 protocols and equipment (which are interactive-oriented).

See **S3270** and **LU-1**.

RLE
Run Length Encoding

A type of data compression that looks for repeated bytes (such as many sequential ASCII space characters) and represents this in a shorter sequence.

For example, RLE could encode 5 space characters (which would be 20 20 20 20 20 in hexadecimal) as 05 20.

LZW is another type of data compression.

See **DATA COMPRESSION**, **LZW**, **MNP**, and **V.42BIS**.

rlogin

Berkeley UNIX's remote terminal facility, which provides the capability to log in to a machine that is LAN- or WAN-connected to the local one (the one on which you are typing).

The remote machine must be running the `rlogin` *daemon* (which is called `rlogind`). Similar to telnet, except that `rlogin` uses your username from your current session on your local machine (so you don't need to re-type it).

See **TELNET** and **UNIX**.

RMON
Remote Network Monitoring MIB

A way of monitoring the loading and performance of LAN segments at the MAC (*media access control*) layer—that is, frame statistics, such as who is sending to whom, and how many errors there were.

An SNMP MIB (first described in RFC 1271 for the Ethernet implementation, which was first released in 1991, and then as RFC 1757 which was released in 1995) that specifies the types of information listed in the following table. The token ring RMON group is specified in RFC 1513.

RMON MIB Group	Holds Information on
Statistics	Network performance: number of packets, bytes, errors (by type), broadcasts, multicasts, collisions, bandwidth utilization, and the packet size distribution.
History	Automatic time interval (by default at 30-second and 30-minute intervals—though many change this to 30 seconds and 5 minutes) recording of statistical performance data (from the above statistics group) for trend and repeated symptom tracking. This should facilitate proactive network planning (what a concept).

(table continued on next page)

RMON MIB Group	Holds Information on
Alarms	Generated when preset rising or falling thresholds (absolute or delta) are exceeded (for any MIB statistic maintained by the agent). Alarms can trigger other actions through the *events* group.
Hosts Table	Automatically updated list of all nodes (by MAC address) on the network and statistics related to them (such as frames and bytes sent and received, broadcasts and multicasts sent, and errors).
Hosts Top *n* Table	A sorted list of nodes (selected from the Hosts Table group, specifying how many are to be included—hence the "*n*"), with the highest specified parameters (for example, highest number of errors or highest usage)—possibly by protocol.
Matrix	Traffic and number of errors between pairs of nodes (by MAC address), for example, frames and bytes exchanged. This group requires more resources to implement than most others, so not all products include this important group.
Filters	Specifies which frames are to be captured by the packet capture group (for example, by protocol or source or destination address).
Events	Records (and time-stamps) specific network errors and user-defined events as log entries and can send alerts (SNMP traps) when thresholds are exceeded, or trigger other actions.
Packet Capture	Captures entire frames for later forwarding to, and decoding by, software running on the management station. Capture can be of full frames or only specified number of bytes of each frame, started when a trigger condition is met, specified to wrap around or halt when capture memory fills. Captured data are uploaded to a management station on request, after the capture has completed (RMON does not provide real-time capture and display). This group requires more resources to implement than most others, so not all products include this important group.
Token Ring only	Statistics on Token Ring specific parameters, such as isolating errors (those that cause a station be removed from the ring, such as burst and access control errors), non-isolating errors (such as error frames, and frame copy errors), beaconing, source routing details, ring order, and active monitor selection.

Vendors can implement any subset of these groups, and claim RMON MIB compliance. It is important to verify which groups a product supports (hopefully all). However, if a vendor implements a group, then all features of that group must be implemented. Also, implementation of some groups requires that other groups be implemented (for example, the packet capture group requires the filter group to be implemented as well).

Many devices support only the first 4 RMON groups (statistics, history, alarms and events), since these are the easiest to support (least CPU power required to gather). Some devices support 7 RMON groups. These typically are all groups except the last two (which are filter and packet capture), since those two groups require the most CPU and memory resources in the probe.

RMON information may be gathered by:

- ▲ Dedicated hardware devices (sometimes called *probes* or *pods*) or PCs running special software

- ▲ Software built in to data communications equipment, such as routers, bridges, switches, or Ethernet concentrators (this built-in software is sometimes called an *embedded agent*)

- ▲ Software built in to file servers (also an embedded agent)

RMON probes are configured to run tests by entering tasks into a *control table* (from a *management station*). Each task is a row of the table and specifies the type of data, frequency of collection, and other details of the task. Each task produces its own results, which can be retrieved by the management station. Standardization of the method of entering, monitoring, and deleting these tasks is not as advanced as are the details of the data collection itself.

Also, the complexity of the actions may differ between products. For example, some products may be able to show the Hosts Top *n* group only after a utilization threshold has been exceeded, or implement some hysteresis on alarm reporting.

Some devices with many ports that can each have different traffic (particularly Ethernet switches) support a "roving analysis port" (or something with a similar name). Rather than providing a full RMON agent for each port (which is expensive), an SNMP-controllable switch connects a special extra port to any of the other ports. An RMON probe (either an external unit, or one built-in to the device) is then connected to the port.

Since SNMP generally works only with TCP/IP, users would need to support TCP/IP to get this information back to an SNMP management station—even if they don't otherwise use (and route) TCP/IP.

RMON support is very popular for 10BASE-T and 100BASE-T Ethernet devices. It is also used for Token Ring devices. There are no standards yet for RMON for FDDI, 100VG-AnyLAN or ATM (though Token Ring is similar enough to FDDI, that some FDDI RMON probes are available).

See **MIB**, **RMON II**, and **SNMP**.

RMON 2 OR RMON V2 OR RMON II
Remote Network Monitoring MIB, Version 2

New remote LAN diagnostic and monitoring capabilities which are complementary to RMON (which basically was created to monitor the performance of LAN segments, such as collecting traffic statistics by MAC addresses—such as the Ethernet address of the device which most recently sent the frame, or the one to which the frame is now going). RMON 2 gathers higher-level (than OSI layers 1 and 2) protocol information, so end-to-end traffic flows can be monitored.

Examples of enhancements over RMON include the following:

▲ Examining router ARP caches to determine the original source of packets (in contrast, RMON for example, would only show the router from which the packet was received, not the address of the station that initially generated the packet)

▲ What applications (telnet, WWW, and so on) are being used by (for example) examining the port number in TCP and UDP packets

▲ Support for protocols other than TCP/IP (which is all the first version of RMON supported), and showing the protocol distribution (by examining the frame header information)

▲ Incremental retrieval, which reduces network traffic by only sending information that has changed since the last retrieval

▲ Mapping network connectivity by requesting *hop table* information from routers

While RMON is best deployed on each segment of a switched LAN, RMON 2 is expected to be deployed at servers, where applications are run.

Specifically, RMON 2 adds 11 function groups to the 10 defined for RMON (RMON 2 devices generally collect RMON statistics as well). Example function groups are as follows:

RMON 2 MIB Group	Holds Information on
Network Layer Hosts Table	Counts of bytes and packets, by network layer address that sent them.
Network Layer Top *n* Table	The "top talkers", that is the network addresses of the nodes sending the most traffic.
Application Layer Host Table	Bandwidth use by protocol (actually, by port number), such as http, ftp and telnet).
Application Layer Matrix	Traffic between pairs of nodes, by protocol.

As used in RMON 2, "application layer" means any layer above the network layer. So the TCP port number is considered application layer information. Therefore, an application layer probe may only monitor the transport layer (that is, layer 4), or it may monitor Lotus Notes and SQL response times. Also, a probe can be described as supporting RMON 2, and it may support only IP, or it may support IP, IPX and AppleTalk.

As for RMON, RMON 2 probes (whether they are stand-alone devices or built-in to network equipment) can only provide useful information if they are located where the traffic to be monitored exists. If the probes are on a router or switch segment that does not see all traffic of interest (because the source and destinations of the traffic are on different segments), then RMON 2 won't tell you anything.

Also, as for RMON, RMON 2 is only defined for Ethernet and Token Ring. However, there are proprietary implementations for other networks, such as FDDI and WAN connections (such as T1). And it would be nice if ATM was supported, but this is also not in the initial RMON 2 specifications.

RMON 2 is specified in RFC 2021.

See **RMON**, and **TCP**.

Rockwell International

A really big company that, in addition to big military-type stuff, makes 70% of the fax and data modem ICs in the world.

They have a WWW site at *http://www.nb.rockwell.com/*.

See **FAX** and **MODEM**.

Rockwell Protocol Interface

See **RPI**.

ROFL
Rolling on the Floor, Laughing

A common email abbreviation indicating that something is very funny (unlike this definition).

root

The UNIX account used by the system administrator (who is sometimes called the *super-user*). Once logged in to it, you can read or write to any directory and file, mount new file systems, change ownership of files and do everything else possible to the operating system.

See **SU**, **TCP**, and **UNIX**.

Router

The key building component in most large (either geographically or by number of computers) networks, as they connect networks (sometimes called subnetworks) to other networks—the result is sometimes called an internet. Typically, routers are used to interconnect LANs (which are usually within buildings), using WANs (which can span any distance, for example between cities). A modem or CSU/DSU is usually needed to connect the router to the WAN.

```
LAN  --------       -------                      -------      --------  LAN
----| Router |---|CSU/DSU|--- WAN ---|CSU/DSU|---| Router |-----
     --------       -------                      -------      --------
             ..                           cloud
```

Routers usually have one or more LAN interfaces (though they may have none), so they can connect to the LAN(s)—just as any other device on the LAN connects to it. LANs typically carry more than one protocol, and it is usually desired to carry more than one protocol over the WAN as well. A *multiprotocol router* is therefore used. Typical protocols are TCP/IP and Novell's IPX, though there are many other protocols that may be supported as well.

Because there is usually more than way to get from a source to a destination (just as there is when you are driving somewhere), routers commuinicate with each other (through the same network that is used to carry the user data) using a router to router protocol.

Every protocol has its own implementation of a router to router protocol (for example, TCP/IP can use OSPF). The router to router protocol communicates the networks, the number of hops (router to router connections) between them and often many other metrics needed for routers to make routing decisions. The figure below shows these three main components of a multiprotocol router.

```
          -------------------------------------------------------
          | None, one or more | Routing    | None, one or more  |
          | LAN interfaces    | software   | WAN interfaces     |
          | such as ....      | such as ...| such as ...        |
          -------------------------------------------------------
          |                   |            |                    |
   LAN    | Ethernet          | AppleTalk  | Analog leased line |
          | Fast Ethernet     | DECnet     | Auto-dial modem    |  WAN
 ------- | Token Ring        | IPX        | F-T1               |  -----
          | FDDI              | TCP/IP     | ISDN               |
          |                   | VINES      | Frame Relay        |
          |                   |            | SONET              |
          |                   |            | T1                 |
          |                   |            | X.25               |
          |                   |            |                    |
          -------------------------------------------------------
```

Routers range from $1,000 cards in PCs, to fixed 2-port devices to large chassis with many optional plug-in boards—resulting in a router that costs $100,000 or more.

Routers operate at layer 3 (the network layer) of the 7-layer OSI reference model. This means they read and understand the packets carried by frames. They can therefore re-encapsulate packets (so an IPX packet arriving on a Token Ring LAN (and encapsulated by a Token Ring frame) can be emitted on an Ethernet port, encapsulated in an Ethernet frame. Routers can also segment packets into multiple frames (for example, since Token Ring supports larger frame sizes than Ethernet). Routers can change some fields in the packet header (decrementing the TTL field for example), but they do not change the packet itself. An IPX packet coming in to a router, comes out as an IPX packet (though it may be split into multiple frames of a different type, Ethernet to Token Ring for example).

Routers can also perform prioritization (sending some packets ahead of others, on congested WAN links). This prioritization can be based on port number (for IP routers), so that telnet traffic gets higher priority than HTTP traffic, which gets higher priority than FTP traffic (for example).

Packets contain the address of the original source of the message, and its final destination—in the format of the packet's protocol. For example, a TCP/IP packet uses a 32-bit IP address. This address is usually manually configured when the TCP/IP software is installed or first run (or it may be automatically set, through the bootp or DHCP protocol).

Currently, routers are usually *hardware routers*. That is, they are a specialized box, designed for that purpose. Cisco Systems, Inc. has the largest market share of this market. Standard PCs, with specialized software can also be routers. These are sometimes called *software routers*. In fact, before hardware routers were developed, all routers were software routers—they were part of the software running on the computer which used that protocol. So a DEC VAX routed DECnet, and a Novell NetWare file server routed IPX (either to other LAN segments, or to a WAN connection). But these only routed their own protocol, and were useless if you wanted to support multiple protocols, so multiprotocol hardware routers became popular.

Now, software routers may become more popular again. Partly because processors are fast enough to support the traffic (for Internet access, for example), and partly because there are not as many protocols which need to be supported any more (IP for sure, and possibly IPX is most of what people need). Microsoft's *Routing and Remote Access Service* (RRAS) is an example of this.

Packets are carried by frames, and frame headers also have addresses. The frame address is the MAC (*media access control*) address for the frame. For example, an Ethernet frame has a 48-bit address, which is usually guaranteed-worldwide-unique, and is permanently assigned when the Ethernet adapter is manufactured. This address is the immediate source and destination for the frame (for example, if the frame is going from one intermediate router to another, then the source and destination MAC addresses are those of the source and destination routers' Ethernet ports—not the original source, and final destination of the packet.

Since every protocol puts its packet address, time-to-live and other network layer information in different positions (and with different interpretations) in the packet header, routers need to understand every protocol they are to carry. Most routers are therefore *multiprotocol routers*.

Some protocols are *non-routable*, in that they have no network layer (there is no packet inside the frame, just the user data). Examples are DEC's LAT (local area transport), IBM's NetBIOS and SNA, and Microsoft's NetBEUI. These protocols were intended to be used on a single network, so there would be no intermediate devices, such as routers. Since there is no place in the protocol for such intermediate addresses, these protocols cannot be handled by routers.

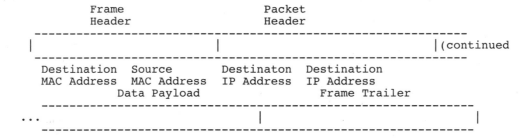

A common way to carry such non-routable protocols (and routable ones too) over WANs (and larger LANs) is to use *bridges*. A bridge is a layer 2 (link layer) device that only examines the frame header information (and does not know or care if there is a packet being carried by the frame). Ethernet and Token Ring handle bridging differently. Ethernet bridges will be described first.

Ethernet bridges are often called *transparent bridges*, MAC-layer bridges, learning bridges and spanning tree algorithm bridges (for reasons that will be described below). Bridges are usually two-port devices. They can be *local bridges* (which typically have two Ethernet ports), or *remote bridges* (which have one Ethernet port and one WAN port). Remote bridges are used in pairs—one at each end of a WAN link.

Bridges examine all frames on the network, and learn which stations are on which sides. They then only forward frames (pass them through from one of their ports to the other) if

best way, but you will get to the destination. Every time you take the trip, you may take a different path.

▲ Or, you can call the auto club, get maps, determine the best path and then start on your trip. All you need is signage showing the names of the streets and exits. This is what Token Ring does, in that the source of the message determines the route to take. You then take the same path every time (even if a better way becomes available).

To determine the best path, the sending station first sends out a *route discovery frame*, which every bridge forwards. The route discovery frame then floods the entire network (usually being replicated many times). As each frame passes through a bridge, a route information field (RIF) in the frame header is updated with the bridge's number. The frames that reach the destination are sent back to the sender along the exact path in which it arrived (according to the RIF). The sender typically receives many such replies, and records the route taken by the first reply received (since it had the shortest round-trip, so likely took the best route) in a *route cache*.

That route is then used for all subsequent communication with that destination, until the sender's Token Ring driver is unloaded (or the entire station is powered off and then on again), or until that path no longer works (due to a link along the way not being available)—at which time the route discover process is repeated.

This method has the advantage (over Ethernet's method) of utilizing all available links between bridges, and of choosing the fastest route. Disadvantages are that a change in network connectivity (that is, a link become unavailable (perhaps due to networking equipment failure), then the user usually looses their session without first havng a chance to save and close their files, so they may loose some of their work.

Some networks (such as Ethernet, especially when using ATM—and LANE—as a backbone) can have multiple subnets on a single physical LAN. For example, one building could be subnet 192.168.1.0 and ATM could be connecting it to another building, which is subnet 192.168.15.0. If the ATM backbone is configured as a bridge, then PCs in different buildings can send frames to each other, but they won't since they can tell (by checking their subnet bit mask) that they are in different subnets, which normally means the packets must go through a router. To allow such PCs to send packets to each other, a *one-armed router* is used. This is a router with a single Ethernet (for example) interface, and the Ethernet port in the router is configured with 2 IP addresses (and a single Ethernet MAC address)—one IP address for each subnet. PCs send packets destined for the other subnet to the router (using the router's IP address for the sender's subnet), and the router outputs the packet on the same single LAN interface on which it arrived, but destined for the final destination on the other subnet. Such silliness is typically only required in special situations. The router required for this example would likely (depending on the features required) be eliminated through the use of MPOA and PNNI (which were not available when LANE was first released).

Routing packets is a very CPU-intensive task. That is, it requires much processing for each packet, and often for handling the analysis of the network connectivity to build the routing tables as well. As the connections to routers increase in speed (such as for ATM), faster routers (which are typically rated in *packets per second*—commonly *PPS*, but more correctly *packets/s*) are required. And simply using faster processors is not expected to be enough (high-end conventional routers typically handle from 250,000 to 1,000,000 packets/s). Several new

approaches to routing millions of packets per second are being developed. These are sometimes referred to as *multilayer switches*, and some approaches are summarized below:

▲ *Routing switches* operate like conventional routers, but implement as much router processing as hardware (to be cool you say "in silicon"), rather than software. Typically, these have less functionality, and handle fewer protocols (typically only IP) than conventional routers (which have megabytes of code to provide a seemingly endess list of functions), and hardware routing is less flexible (bug fixes and enhancements are really expensive).

▲ The name is derived from the implementation. That is, LAN switches are implemented entirely in hardware (except for management, such as SNMP support), and can handle millions of packets per second. However, rather than the destination of packets being determined by layer 2 information (the destination MAC address), the destination is determined by routing tables created through information learned from adjacent routers (using OSPF and other routing protocols).

▲ *Flow Switching* uses conventional layer 3 (software-based) routing for packets until the "router" (flow switch) detects a *flow*—that is, more than a few packets going between a specific source and destination (for example, a file transfer or a larger web page). The flow switch then sets up a switched connection (that is, handled at layer 2, in hardware) for the duration of the transfer. ATM's MPOA is a form of flow switching.

▲ *Tag Switching* has *tag-edge routers* that add information (called a *tag*) to each packet so that subsequent *tag switches* can quickly read the tag to determine where to send the packet. Cisco has developed this method, and has submitted to the IETF in the hope that it will become an RFC.

▲ A proposed (to the IETF) standard way of doing this is *Multiprotocol Label Switching* (MPLS).

There are other proprietary methods as well. All attempt to do the hard work (such as route calculation) at the edge of the network, and let the core be really fast and dumb. Hopefully only one of these will become the standard and interoperable way of doing this.

"Router" is pronounced to rhyme with *doubt*-er, though people from the U.K. pronounce it *rooter.*

See **BOOTP, COS2** (*Class of Service*), **CISCO SYSTEMS, CSU, DHCP, DSU, IGRP, INTERNET1, IP ADDRESS, LINK STATE, MAC, MODEM, MPOA, OSPF, PACKET, PNNI, RAS, REPEATER, RIP, SOCKS, SWITCHED LAN,** and **TTL1** (*Time-To-Live*).

RPC
Remote Procedure Call

A method of program-to-program communications, usually for implementing cross-platform distributed computing.

Generically, RPC is an inter-process communication API whose strength is communication between different computing platforms, using multiple protocol stacks simultaneously. Most often used with TCP/IP, in which there are (unfortunately) two incompatible standard RPC implementations:

▲ OSF's DCE

▲ Sun's ONC+ (probably the more widely implemented of the two)

To an application program, RPCs are local procedure calls that happen to start processes on remote machines. Communication is *synchronous* (sometimes called *blocking*), in that the requester must wait for a response before continuing.

An alternative to this concept is called *messaging*.

See **API**, **DCE2**, **MESSAGING**, **ONC**, **OSF**, and **SUN**.

RPI
Rockwell Protocol Interface

A method of reducing the cost of modems by having the PC's CPU handle the error correction (V.42) and data compression (V.42*bis*), rather than a modem's own processor.

Rockwell International (who make almost all the modem and fax machine modem ICs) make low-cost versions of their modem ICs used anywhere by anyone that support this interface.

The assumption is that people seldom actually use their PCs for multitasking, so the CPU has time to handle these extra tasks while doing data communications.

The argument goes like this: Most file transfer protocols have their own error correction, so the modem's V.42 is redundant. And while RPI's software-based data compression may be slower than that implemented in a modem, most file transfers (which is possibly the most common application that requires high throughput) are of precompressed files (for example, using `pkzip`, etc.), so V.42*bis* "on-the-fly" data compression is not used anyway.

Communication software (or the operating system) must support RPI to get the benefit of error correction or data compression on RPI modems (which do not do any error correction or data compression themselves). Without RPI software, RPI modems behave like standard modems that have no error correction or data compression.

A modem with built-in error correction and data compression is a stand-alone box with known capability (that's a good thing). RPI introduces dependencies (never a good thing), so that your computer's data communications capabilities are dependent on many factors. For example:

▲ What if the PC's processor is not fast enough to support this extra work?

▲ What if several communication software packages, or operating systems, are used with the modem—and not all support RPI?

▲ What if the modem is being used with something other than a PC, for which there is no RPI communication software available?

▲ What if the data traffic is not precompressed? That is, while it is true that most files on bulletin board systems and the on-line services (such as CompuServe) are precompressed, dial-up data communications requirements are rapidly changing. For example, now that "surfing the Internet" is becoming very popular, downloading uncompressed (but highly compressible) files (such as WWW pages and USENET news) is much more common (and never fast enough).

The idea is that you buy an RPI modem if these concerns are of no concern to you. Otherwise, spend the extra money and get a modem with built-in error correction and data compression.

For more information, see Rockwell's site at *http://www.nb.rockwell.com*.

See **MODEM, MNP, PC, ROCKWELL INTERNATIONAL, V.42**, and **V.42BIS**.

RS-232
Recommended Standard 232

See **EIA/TIA-232**.

RS-422
Recommended Standard 422

See **TIA/EIA-422**.

RS-449
Recommended Standard 449

See **EIA-449**.

RS-485
Recommended Standard 485

See **EIA-485**.

RS-530
Recommended Standard 530

See **EIA/TIA-530**.

RSA
Rivest, Shamir, Adleman Public Key Encryption

A patented *public key* (also called *dual-key* or *asymmetric*) *data encryption* scheme that can provide both encryption and *authentication*.

Uses a pair of (40- to 1,024-bit) keys: the public key and the *private* or *secret key*.

When one key (either one) is used to encrypt a message, the only way to decrypt it is by using the other key of the pair. Each participant in secure exchanges has his or her own pair of public and private keys. The private key is kept secret, and the public key is distributed to anyone who wants it.

▲ When a recipient's public key is used to encrypt the message, then the message is unreadable to everyone but the holder of the secret key. Therefore the message content is kept secret.

▲ When a sender uses his or her secret key to encrypt the message, then anyone (with a copy of the sender's public key) can decrypt the message, with the assurance that only the holder of the secret key could have encrypted it. Therefore the message has been authenticated.

Combining these methods provides both authentication (analogous to someone's written signature) and encryption. (Now what else could you ask for?)

The technique was developed at Stanford University in 1977, but is named after three professors who were at the Massachusetts Institute of Technology (MIT) at the time. (Ronald L. Rivest, Adi Shamir, and Leonard M. Adleman), who made it a useful system and started a company (RSA Data Security, Inc., though only Rivest is still with the company, which was bought by Security Dynamics in 1996 for $200 million) to license the technology and sell software toolkits for application developers so that they can add these capabilities to their software.

Some of the most ingenious ways to break encryption codes have come from people outside the usual security community. To get the best exposure to people with new ideas on code breaking (so that the encryption methods can be improved) there are often open competitions (sometimes with rewards) for code breaking. At *http://www.npac.syr.edu/factoring.html* is an on-going project to evaluate (and perhaps break) 512-bit key RSA-encryption.

RSA maintains a WWW server at *http://www.rsa.com/*.

See **S802.A11**, **AUTHENTICATION**, **DES**, **ENCRYPTION**, **MIME**, **PGP**, **SET**, and **SHTTP**.

RSN
Real Soon Now

A outsider's cynical summation of when a product will be available, especially when a company has been promising it for some time, with repeated delays.

RSVP
Resource Reservation Protocol

A standard for application programs to specify the resources required for an end-to-end communication in each network (there could be many networking technologies involved) along an end-to-end path so that a (likely multimedia) application receives the *quality of service* (QOS) required. If the resources cannot be reserved, then the connection is refused. This is supposed to provide QOS guarantees even for networks based on routers (that is, protocols and networks other than ATM, such as Ethernet).

Each packet gets a label (a few header bytes) that specifies its payload.

Applications (such as video-conferencing) that cannot tolerate varying network throughput and latencies are often called *inelastic*. *Elastic* applications that can usually tolerate varying QOS include file transfer and most WWW surfing.

The receiving end-user's equipment (since it knows best what network resources are required for it to operate properly) periodically specifies the bandwidth (in bits/s) and maximum network latency (delay, in milliseconds) acceptable for the flow of data it receives. Each router along the path would attempt to reserve this capacity. When the flow of data has finished, the receiver should send a *tear-down* message saying it no longer requires the QOS. Or it can simply stop requesting the reservation (and the bandwidth reservation times-out). Note that the bandwidth reservation times-out only after the reservation messages cease—regardless of whether there is data being transmitted or not.

Conversely, if an errant application (or somebody with a malicious sense of humor) continuously sends bandwidth reservations without ever sending any data, then the network may not be able to accept additional reservations, even though it is not carrying any traffic. That is, the authorization enabling users to request bandwidth will become as important as system administrators' current responsibilities such as allocating file server disk storage quotas and assigning process priorities. If these reservations can be across the Internet, then the difficulty of controlling the use of this capability, and the potential for abuse is even greater. An important aspect of RSVP is therefore *policy control* includes determining which users can make a reservation (an authentication and access control function), and what the implications of this are (such as costing money).

The reservation is for the specified direction only (if bandwidth in the opposite direction must also be reserved, then a separate request—for that direction—must be made.

RSVP does not specify how routers and other network equipment along the path allocate bandwidth and resources, only how the resources are specified. Vendors can choose their own prioritization and queueing methods, which is good, because it allows flexibility, but bad because this is a completely important part of the solution, but is not standardized.

RSVP is defined for IP, IPX and Appletalk.

More information on RSVP is at *http://www.isi.edu*, such as at *http://www.isi.edu/div7/rsvp/rsvp.html*. RSVP version 1 is defined in RFC 2205.

See **MULTIMEDIA**, **QOS**, **RTP**, and **PRIORITIZATION**.

RTFM
Read the F_ _ _ _ _ _ Manual

Commonly expressed by technical support personnel (*almost* inaudibly) when the information that a user seeks is already in the manual (which surprises users, since they think that manuals never have the information needed—at least, not so you can find it without reading the whole thing, word by word).

Nonetheless, users usually think that only wimps (need to) read manuals.

If I may expand: It used to be that real programmers used assembler language (you know, LOAD this memory location, MOVE that register—tough, brain-busting work). Most people now concede that it is rarely necessary to use assembler, so the only way to distinguish yourself is by doing your job without reading the manual. Perhaps someday people will write more complete manuals, and users will take (or have) the time to read the manual. Then again, who would need consultants if everyone read (or had the time to read) the manual?

See **FAQ**.

RTMP
Routing Table Maintenance Protocol

Apple's older (but still widely used) distance-vector–based routing protocol. The link-state replacement is AURP (excuse me).

See **AURP**, **LINK STATE**, and **RIP**.

Computer Dictionary

RTP
Real-time Transport Protocol

A protocol developed for handling multimedia traffic over an unreliable transport, such as UDP. It supports multicasting, mixing of digitized and compressed audio and video on the same connection, and includes timing information and a sequence number in each packet, which are used for both reconstruction (to maintain synchronization of the audio and video—even if some of the packets have been lost) and for feedback on the reception quality (to determine how many packets have been dropped by the network). It also supports identification of multicast receivers and types of data compression used.

A major use of RTP is expected to be for the play-back of digitized audio, over networks with wide variations in the network latency (this is sometimes called *jitter*). At the remote end, the play-back device will buffer as much audio as the maximum expected network latency, and output the audio according to the timestamps accompanying the bits. This allows the speech to be played back at a constant rate, even though it will arrive at the destination in bursts.

While it is expected that RTP will most often be used over UDP, it can also be run over other protocols and transports, such as IPX and ATM. RSVP complements the capabilities of RTP.

The *Real-Time Control Protocol* (RTCP) enables applications to adjust to detected changes in network performance. For example, a receiver that senses that a network is getting congested (greater latencies and more lost packets) could reqest the sender to use a lower bit-rate (and lower quality, but hopefully still better than gaps in the audio), audio CODEC.

RTP and RTCP are defined in RFCs 1889 and 1890.

See **H.320, IP MULTICAST, LATENCY, MULTICAST, MULTIMEDIA, RSVP**, and **UDP**.

S

SAA
Systems Application Architecture

An application-layer effort (that is, the APIs) to enable a program to run, and communicate with others, on all of IBM's platforms.

It is a guideline for uniform languages, file structures, and processes. Builds on LU 6.2 and is therefore peer-to-peer (and not *terminal-emulation*) oriented.

See **API**, **CLIENT/SERVER**, **HLLAPI**, **LU-6.2**, and **SNA**.

SAP
Service Advertising Protocol

Novell NetWare's *multicast* (that is, a *broadcast* to a specific group of workstations—in this case, those running the IPX protocol) oriented protocol for making file, print, communication, and other servers' capabilities, LAN address, and network number known to workstations.

Runs on top of IPX. Periodic *SAP information broadcasts* are automatically generated by servers (usually every 60 seconds).

A *SAP service query* can be sent by a workstation any time it wishes to learn of available servers—without waiting for up to 60 seconds for the next periodic SAP information broadcast. For example, when the Netx shell is loaded, a SAP service query is sent. Servers then immediately reply with a *SAP service response* frame, which contains the same information as the periodic SAP information broadcast.

If a *preferred server* has not been set in the Net.cfg file, or specified on the command-line, then login is attempted to the first responding server.

See **IPX**, **NLSP**, **NOVELL**, and **RIP**.

Satellite

A complicated, typically multi-hundred million dollar, electronic and mechanical wonder hundreds or thousands of miles up in space, put there by some rocket or space shuttle, often to provide communications services.

Communications may use satellites because satellites have a *line-of-sight* (that is, direct—no trees, buildings, mountains, or horizon in the way) view of large geographic areas, due to their height (no, the satellites are not tall, they are just really high up in the sky). This is important, since the microwave frequencies that are used won't bounce off objects—the transmitter and receiver must be able to "see" each other.

Satellites have some number of *transponders*, each of which receives a signal, amplifies it, and retransmits it (typically at 8.5 to 60 watts—though the new direct broadcast satellites use up to 120 watts so that very small receiving antennas can be used) on a different (so that the satellite does not transmit to its own receiver) frequency.

Transponders typically have a bandwidth of 36 to 72 MHz each (though newer satellites have up to 108-MHz transponder bandwidths).

For comparison, an NTSC standard analog television video (with audio) signal requires 24 to 36 MHz of transponder bandwidth, so each transponder typically carries one, two, or three television signals (two for a 54-MHz transponder, three for a 72-MHz transponder). Video signal digitization and compression schemes allow up to eight television signals to share the bandwidth required by a single uncompressed 6-MHz bandwidth video signal. However, there is no single standard compression scheme, and this is preventing wider adoption of compression.

Launching a satellite typically costs $45 million to $120 million (this pays for the launch rocket, the facilities and the technicians).

Renting satellite time (for example, for a company's nationwide one-way satellite broadcast to its employees) costs about $1,000 per hour. This is for a standard analog, uncompressed video signal.

The bandwidth required by a single television signal can carry about 960 telephone conversations.

Television Receive Only (TVRO) is a very common use of satellite dish antennas (your standard back yard installation, for example).

Traditionally, communication satellites have been placed in a *geostationary* orbit called the *"Clarke Belt"* or *"Clarke Orbit"*—named after Arthur C. Clarke, who thought of geostationary communications satellites back in 1945 (and also wrote the screenplay of *2001: A Space Odyssey* in 1968—and also over 70 books). The Clarke Orbit is where the gravitational force of the earth (which pulls down) exactly counters the centrifugal force (which pulls out), because of the satellite's rotating around the earth (it does this at the same speed at which the earth rotates).

The Clarke Belt is 22,225 miles (more precisely, 35,767.0 km, ± 0.6 km or 35,898 km depending on how you determine where the surface of the earth at the equator is) above the equator (sea level at the equator is about 6,378,137 m from the centre of the earth, but varies by tens of meter due to differences in the earth's crust). Satellites are typically placed about 2° apart (which is about 1,500 km at that height) to prevent signals to and from the adjacent satellites from interfering with each other (satellites using different frequency bands, typically C and K_u, can be much closer together). Also, this separation eliminates any chance of the satellites bumping into each other. (Satellites actually drift slightly and need short bursts from their thruster rockets to keep them in the right place. The amount of thruster propellant is often what limits a satellite's life—usually about 10 to 15 years.)

The first geostationary satellite was the Syncom 3, which was launched on August 19, 1964.

Interestingly, the U.S. Space Shuttle (and the Russian Mir Space Station) can only get to an orbital height of about 300 to 400 km, so geosynchronous satellites put in orbit by the Space Shuttle need to have their own rocket to get them from the Space Shuttle's orbit to the geosynchronous orbit height.

Geosynchronous satellites must orbit the earth at a great height (for the physics to work out so that the satellite can "float" at exactly the same location, so the ground-based satellite antennas don't need to move to track the satellite). Also, the speed of light (in a vacuum) is about 299,792,458 m/s (usually rounded-off to 3×10^8 m/s), which is about 186,282 miles per second.

In air, light slows down a bit (to about 99.97% of this). And radio waves travel at the speed of light (since they are the same thing: electromagnetic waves).

Therefore, to travel from the earth to a geosynchronous satellite, a signal has to go 22,225 miles (usually slightly more, since the satellite is not likely directly above you and the destination), at 186,227 miles per second—which takes 120 ms. While this delay does not matter for a television broadcast (though that does mean that you are not getting your CNN news *exactly* as it happens), the round-trip delay for a satellite-based data communications circuit will be four times that (up and down again to get from one end of the satellite-based data communication circuit to the other, up and down to get back), which is almost $\frac{1}{2}$ second (479 ms to be more precise).

For protocols with a window size of 1 (which cannot send a second frame until the first is acknowledged), this means that only one frame of data can be sent every 479 ms (just over two frames per second), regardless of the actual data's bit rate. In contrast, the width of North America is only about 5,500 miles. The round-trip delay would be only about 91 ms (even assuming that the signal would travel in fiber-optic cable, which propagates signals at "only" 65% of the speed of light). Humans cannot perceive delays of under about 100 to 200 ms.

Therefore, switching to a satellite-based data communications circuit can reduce network throughput, even if the bit-rate is the same.

Satellite is however, an excellent communications solution in the following situations:

▲ Many remote sites, that need to receive the exact same information (such as price lists, or background music).

▲ Remote sites that are remote—that is, not in a metropolitan area (so that terrestrial communication circuits would be very expensive, or not even available).

▲ Video is required (for example, to broadcast business TV to many sites. For example, to train an automobile dealer's mechanics).

A ground-based satellite antenna is usually a large (2.1 to 3.6 m for C-band users, 1 to 1.8 m for K_u-band users, 4.5 to 10 m at the central site), parabolic-shaped dish which gathers lots of signal from the satellite and aims it all at the dish's receiver, usually located at the parabola's focus. The dish points exactly at the satellite from which it is receiving (you can't see it, but that satellite is certainly exactly where its receiving antenna is aimed). One of the jobs of the technician running the transmitter that sends signals to a satellite is to adjust the transmitter's power (typically up to 60 watts maximum for K_u-band) so that the signal coming back from the satellite (which varies, depending on the temperature and weather) is enough to "saturate" a typical-sized receiving dish antenna (too much, and the satellite's amplifiers may distort the signal, not enough, and people won't get a clear picture).

Since there are (only) 360° in a full circle, a 2° separation between satellites allows for 180 geosynchronous communications satellites (of which each must be somewhat above the area to which it is to provide communications—this area is called the satellite's *footprint*). Space may be infinite and the final frontier, but when it comes to geosynchronous satellites, there is room up there for only about 180 of them! (Actually, since many satellites do use different frequency bands, there can be much more than this, however, in 1997 there were about 178 for geosynchronous telecommunications satellites in orbit.) Also, if you want to broadcast to North America, getting a satellite position above some ocean won't help you—that is, satellite slots over North America are extremely valuable and completely sold out. Occasionally, a good satellite location will become available and be auctioned off for hundreds of millions of dollars.

Two frequency bands are commonly used for satellites carrying video (television signals):

▲ The C-band has been used for many years, requires a larger receiving antenna, and receivers are often only able to receive C-band signals (especially for older receivers).

▲ The use of K_u-band frequencies for satellites is newer, and requires more careful aiming of the satellite antenna. K_u-band receivers (that is, most new ones) can usually also receive C-band.

The table below shows the actual frequencies used. The *uplink* is from the source of the signal, up to the satellite. The *downlink* is from the satellite, down to all of the receiving satellite dish antennas on the earth.

	Frequency Band			
	C		K_u	
	Lower (GHz)	Upper (GHz)	Lower (GHz)	Upper (GHz)
Defined frequency range for entire band	4	8	12	18
Defined frequency range for satellite use	3.40	6.425	10.95	14.5
Typical North American satellite uplink frequency	5.945	6.405	14.04	14.44
Typical North American satellite downlink frequency	3.72	4.18	11.7	12.1

The type, designation, and location of the geosynchronous satellites above North America are listed in the slightly out-of-date table below (for reference, the *Continental U.S. (CONUS)* extends from about 65° to 125° of longitude, west of Greenwich, England). The table also shows the number and bandwidth of the transponders. As shown, many satellites (especially the newer ones) have both C-band and K_u-band capability.

Satellite Name	Designation	Location[a]	Transponders			
			C-band		K$_u$-band	
			No.	Bandwidth (MHz)	No.	Bandwidth (MHz)
GE Americom Satcom SpaceNet 2	S2	69.0	6	72	6	72
			12	36		
Comsat SBS 2	SBS2	71.0			10	86
Hughes Communications Galaxy 6	G6	74.0	24	36		
Comsat SBS 3	SBS3	74.0			10	42
Hughes Communications SBS 4	SBS4	77.0			10	42
GE Americom	K2	81.0			16	54
AT&T Telstar 302	T2	85.0	24	36		
GE Americom (Primestar DBS)	K1	85.0			16	
GE Americom Satcom SpaceNet 3R[b]	S3	87.0	12	36	6	72
			6	72		
Hughes Communications Galaxy 7	G7	91.0	24	36	24	108
GE Americom GStar 3	GST3	93.0			16	108
Hughes Communications Galaxy 3	G3	93.5	24	36		
Hughes Communications SBS 6	SBS6	95.0			19	42
AT&T Telstar 401	T401	97.0	24		16	54
Hughes Communications Galaxy 4[c]	G4	99.0	24	36	24	54
GE American Satcom 4	S4	101.0	12	36	6	72
			6	72		
Hughes Communications DirecTV	DBS2	100.8			16	
Hughes Communications DirecTV	DBS1	101.3			16	
GE Americom GStar 1	GST1	103.0			16	54
GE Americom GStar 4	GST4	105.0			16	54
TMI Communications MSat II		106.5				
Telesat Canada Anik E2	E2	107.3	24	36	16	54

(table continued on next page)

| Satellite Name | Designation | Location[a] | Transponders | | | |
| | | | C-band | | K$_u$-band | |
			No.	Bandwidth (MHz)	No.	Bandwidth (MHz)
Solidaridad 1	SD1	109.2	12	36	16	54
			6	72		
Telesat Canada Anik E1[d]	E1	111.0	24	36	16	54
Solidaridad 2	SD2	113.0	12	36	16	54
			6	72		
Telesat Canada Anik C3	C3	114.9			16	54
Morelos 2	M2	116.8	12	36	4	108
			6	72		
AT&T Telstar 303	T3	123.0	24	36		
Hughes Communications SBS	SBS5	123.0			10	42
					4	108
Hughes Communications Galaxy 5	G5	125.0	24	36		
GE Americom GStar 2	GST2	125.0			16	54
GE Americom Satcom	C3	131.0	24	36		
Hughes Communications Galaxy 1R	G1	133.0	24	36		
GE Americom Satcom	C4	135.0	24	36		
GE Americom Satcom	C1	137.0	24	36		
GE Americom Satcom (Aurora)	C5	139.0	24	36		

a. Degrees West longitude
b. The "R" designation means Replacement—usually because the original one didn't make it into orbit and start working successfully.
c. Supports the Hughes DirecPC Internet access by satellite service. The raw bit-rate is 400 kbit/s to 3 Mbits/s (shared among many users, and is download only—your "uplink" to request files is through a traditional ISP).
d. In 1996, Anik E1 lost half its capacity (and very nearly all its capacity) due to sunspot activity)

Many new communication satellite systems use (or are being designed for) lower orbits—*Low Earth Orbit* (LEO—about 700 to 780 km up) and *Medium Earth Orbit* (MEO)—because almost all geosynchronous orbit slots are filled (and all of the ones over North America are taken). Also, using lower-orbiting (closer to the earth) satellites permits lower-power transmitters (so they can be battery-operated) and smaller, non-directional antennas (that is, not parabolic dish antennas pointed directly at the satellite) to be used. This is important for mobile communications—nobody wants to carry a 10-foot satellite dish in their pocket (mind you, think of the prestige—wouldn't I be the most important person in the restaurant?). With omni-directional antennas, the transmitter power must be increased to the square of the distance to the receiver—so to transmit to a satellite only 1/10 the distance away, your handset's transmitter can be 1/100 the power.

Satellite

By switching between satellites (similar to how cellular telephones hand-off between cell sites), a receiver can provide continuous communication service. Since LEO satellites are constantly appearing and dissapearing over the horizon, many of them are needed to provide continuous communication.

Some LEO satellite systems are listed below:

▲ Iridium LLC's system, which uses 66 Satellites, and is estimated to cost $5 billion. It is largely backed by Motorola, and is to provide voice and data communication services to international business travelers, and people who are often not within the coverage areas of traditional cellular services.

▲ Globalstar, which will use 48 satellites, and more than 100 ground stations (costing $5 million each). It is estimated to cost $2.5 billion, and operated by Globalstar LP, and backed by Loral Space & Communications Ltd. and Qualcomm Inc. The main service to be provided is telephone service for regional business travellers (since communication will need to be through land-lines), and telephone service in developing countries.

▲ Teledesic Corp.'s system which was initially to have used 840 satellites, but they decided the job could be done with only 288 satellites, each orbiting at an altitude of 250 km. Still, they system is estimated to cost $9 billion. It is backed by Microsoft's Bill Gates and cellular telephone star Craig O. McCaw (who sold his McCaw Communications Inc. to AT&T for $11.5 billion in September 1994). This system is planned to mainly provide Internet access (so it is sometimes call an "Internet in the sky")—at 16 kbit/s to 2 Mbits/s, as well as other business and interactive media applications. Service is planned for the year 2002.

▲ TRW Inc.'s $3.4 billion system of 19 satellites which will provide very high-speed data services for multimedia applications and private data networks.

Medium earth orbit (MEO) satellite systems are also being implemented. Ico Global Communications is building a system of satellites that will orbit 10,000 km up. This allows fewer satellites to provide coverage (12 in this case), but the satellites and handsets will require higher power. Expected use is mainly providing communications service in developing countries.

Satellites are sometimes (with respect and affection) called *birds*.

Many satellites are owned by two international satellite organizations—INTELSAT (which owns 24 satellites) and INMARSAT. They were created to link the world's democratic countries in the 1960s. The U.S.'s portion of ownership is through Comsat Corp., which is a public company created in 1962, but is controlled by the FCC. In 1996, Comsat owned 19% of INTELSAT and 24% of INMARSAT.

Some excellent satellite information is available from Robert Smathers' WWW Satellite Page at *http://www.nmia.com/~roberts/roberts.html* (especially his South Scanner Satellite Services Chart). The satellite TV FAQ is at *http://www.cis.ohio-state.edu/ hypertext/faq/usenet/Satellite-TV/ faq/faq.html* . Less information can be found at *http://www.xmission.com/~keycom/ KC_terms.html*. TeleSat Canada has a WWW home page at *http://www.telesat.ca*, INTELSAT has one at *http://www.intelsat.int:8080/*, and INMARSAT has their's at *http://www.inmarsat.org/ inmarsat/*. Comsat is at *http://www.comsat.com*, and Hughes Networking Systems has information on DirecPC at *http://www.hns.com*.

See **AMPS, ANIK, CATV, COMPOSITE VIDEO SIGNAL, FEC, FCC, GPS, IRIDIUM, MOTOROLA, MSAT, NTSC, TELEGLOBE INC, VIDEO,** and **VSAT.**

SBD
Smart Battery Data

Part of an effort initiated by Duracell and Intel to define a method to monitor a rechargeable battery pack (see SMBus for the other part).

A specialized IC (which is part of the battery pack) monitors the batteries' voltage, current, and temperature, and interfaces to the SMBus to report information such as the battery pack's:

▲ Type, model number, manufacturer, and characteristics

▲ Discharge rate, and the predicted remaining capacity (so you know how much longer you have)

▲ Almost-discharged alarm (so that the PC can gracefully shut down before the battery is exhausted)

▲ Temperature and voltage (required by the battery charger so that it can provide fast charging while ensuring the batteries are not damaged)

See **BATTERIES** and **SMBUS.**

SCADA
Supervisory Control and Data Aquisition

The term used for systems that gather information, such as temperatures, pressures and voltages) from remote locations—usually for the purpose of controlling and tuning industrial processes.

The data transmission often uses EIA-485.

See **EIA485.**

Scalable Architecture

A computer system or data communications network design (some would say *architecture*) in which an increase in processing power or capacity (for example, adding processors to an MPP computer or increasing the speed or number of data communications circuits) is transparent to users and their applications.

Upgrading a nonscalable architecture often requires a *"fork-lift upgrade."* The entire system is replaced, usually at high cost, great disruption, and embarrassment (that the system you installed only a short while ago is now good for nothing).

See **MPP.**

Scalable Font

Another name for an outline font.

See **BITMAP FONT** and **OUTLINE FONT.**

Scale

The standard musical scale is based on an *equally tempered* (also called a *12-tone chromatic*) *scale*. In this scale, an *octave* consists of 12 equally spaced frequencies, each note being $2^{1/12}$ (which is called the twelfth root of 2, which is roughly 1.059463) from the previous note, as shown in the following table for the A440 musical scale. Therefore, the twelfth note is double the frequency of the first note.

Musical Note	Frequency		Koday Equivalent
	Equation	Hz	
A	440	440.00	do
A#	$440 \times 2^{1/12}$	466.16	
B	$440 \times 2^{2/12}$	493.88	re
C	$440 \times 2^{3/12}$	523.25	
C#	$440 \times 2^{4/12}$	554.37	mi
D	$440 \times 2^{5/12}$	587.33	fa
D#	$440 \times 2^{6/12}$	622.25	
E	$440 \times 2^{7/12}$	659.26	sol
F	$440 \times 2^{8/12}$	698.46	
F#	$440 \times 2^{9/12}$	739.99	la
G	$440 \times 2^{10/12}$	783.99	
G#	$440 \times 2^{11/12}$	830.61	ti
A2	$440 \times 2^{12/12}$	880.00	do

As shown, your standard "do re mi" scale (as in the movie *The Sound of Music*) is eight notes from the 12, and this is called the *diatonic scale*.

See **MIDI**.

SCAM
SCSI Configured Auto-Magically (or Configuration Automatically)

Provides *Plug and Play* support for SCSI devices (such as CD-ROMs). For example, SCSI peripherals have their *Device ID*s automatically set to a unique number, and the SCSI bus should be automatically terminated correctly.

The SCSI controller will also support Plug and Play for itself, so it will automatically have its I/O addresses, interrupts and the like, assigned—and should load the correct driver for each of the devices on the SCSI bus.

See **PLUG AND PLAY** and **SCSI1**.

SCC
Standards Council of Canada

A Canadian Crown Corporation with the responsibility of administering the voluntary standards of the National Standards System in Canada. This includes selecting organizations to actually do the testing, certification and quality system assessments.

The actual standards are drafted by one of the following:

▲ Canadian Standards Association (CSA)

▲ Canadian General Standards Board

▲ Canadian Gas Association

▲ Underwriters' Laboratories of Canada

▲ Bureau de normalisation du Québec

Standards they approve become National Standards of Canada.

See **ISO**, and **STANDARDS**.

SCI
Scalable Coherent Interface

A very high-speed data communications link intended for server to server connections. Well-suited to high-performance clustering (SMP). The link runs at 8 Gbits/s (which is 1 Gbyte/s), and is expected to be used to link multiple processors together, for example to support multiprocessing (for example, a feature is that it supports *cache coherency*, which keeps each processor's cache aware of relevant changes in other processors' caches).

SCI is standardized by ANSI.

See **ANSI**, **CACHE**, **SMP2** (*Symmetric Multiprocessing*).

SCO
Santa Cruz Operation, Inc.

A company that makes several popular UNIX operating systems that run on Intel-type PCs, as described below:

▲ OpenServer was developed by SCO (so is usually simply called "SCO"), and is based on UNIX System V Release 3.2.

▲ UnixWare is based on UNIX System V Release 4.2MP. It was initially developed by USL (which was owned by AT&T). When Novell bought UnixWare from USL Univel (which used to be owned by USL, then by Novell). The sequence of development and ownership is therefore AT&T to USL to Univel to Novell to SCO.

▲ Xenix is an older UNIX operating system based on work done long ago, by Microsoft.

Screen Pop

OpenServer Release 5 is the current version (or at least it once was), and has many major enhancements over the previous Open Desktop 3.0 (which was sometimes abbreviated ODT). These include the following:

▲ a journaling file system (which logs all changes to the file system), so the disk can be restored if there is a power failure

▲ integrated symmetric multiprocessing support

▲ improved NetWare integration

▲ new graphical management tools

OpenServer supports DOS applications (through Locus's Merge utility) and a few Windows applications (within an X Window, through SunSoft's WABI support).

OpenServer Competes with other multitasking PC-based operating systems such as Microsoft's Windows NT, SunSoft's Solaris *x86* and UnixWare too.

OpenServer and UnixWare are being combined into a single product, which is (so far) called "Gemini".

Make sure you pronounce "cruz" as "cruise" (like on a ship); otherwise, you'll feel as silly as I did when I asked for a *La Jolla burger* (what a tourist!) on my first business trip to San Diego (say "hoya," not "jawla").

SCO's web site is (where else, but) *http://www.sco.com/*.

See **COSE, GUI, IBCS, UNIVEL, UNIX, WABI, X WINDOW SYSTEM,** and **XENIX.**

Screen Pop

The information that is automatically displayed on the computer monitor of a call center telephone operator, when a new telephone arrives—and before the call is answered. Based on the caller's telephone number (provided by the telephone company, over the D Channel of a PRI ISDN line to their CO), information such as the caller's name and buying and payment history could be displayed, so the operator can more quickly handle the call.

See **CTI, ISDN, TAPI,** and **TSAPI.**

SCSI
Small Computer System Interface

A method of linking disk drives, tape drives (and more) to a computer, such as a PC, Macintosh or workstation. SCSI is a *parallel bus*, in that the data is transferred 8- (*narrow SCSI*) or 16-bits (*wide SCSI*) at a time.

The original version of SCSI is now sometimes called SCSI-1 to differentiate it from the subsequent SCSI-2 and (eventually) SCSI-3.

SCSI is based on IBM's *selector channel*, which IBM designed for the IBM System/360 computers. It was later (in 1981) adapted by Shugart Associates and called the *Shugart Associates Systems Interface* (SASI). (Shugart Associates was started by Alan F. Shugart in 1972, and was a leader in floppy disk drives. Shugart left Shugart Associates in 1974, and started Seagate Technology in 1979.) In 1982, ANSI began work on what is now called SCSI, and the first version of the ANSI standard was released in 1986, as SCSI-1.

Originally SCSI supported only hard disk drives but now includes functions for other peripherals, such as tape and CD-ROM drives, scanners, high-speed printers, and Group 4 fax machines.

Predecessor disk drive interface specifications (such as ST506 and ESDI—*enhanced serial data interface*) were bit-serial (only 1 data bit was transferred at a time) and had very limited functionality—they supported only data transfer and had specific signal wires dedicated to each disk control function. For example, a specific signal line (wire) stepped the disk drive's read/write head, another wire indicated the step direction, another indicated read or write operation, and another carried the data—in the same format as used by the disk drive, such as MFM (*Modified Frequency Modulation*) or RLL (*Run Length Limited*). Therefore the controller used was very dependent on the type of disk drive being controlled. New disk drive technologies required new controllers to be developed, purchased and installed—and all disks on a controller had to be the same technology.

SCSI removed this headache, as it handles higher-level commands, such as asking what types of devices are on the bus (Inquiry) and Read or Write a block of data. That is, in addition to specifying the physical characteristics of the bus (the type of connector, voltages used, and so on), the SCSI standard specifies the commands available (usually about 12) and expected responses, for each type of peripheral (hard disk, CD-ROM, and so on) supported. In addition, SCSI commands can be proprietary.

For SCSI-1 the standard commands are grouped into six *device types*, as shown in the following table.

Device Type	Name	Typical Function
1	Write/read random access (hard disk)	Logical block address, length of block to be written
2	Sequential access (tape drive)	Read next record
3	Printer	Page layout control
4	Processor	Simple send and receive
5	WORM (recordable CD-ROM)	Large size, removable
6	Read-only random access	Logical block address, length of block to be read

The SCSI bus supports more than one type of peripheral connected to a single SCSI controller. This requires having more than one software driver for the SCSI controller—for example, disk driver software and tape driver software. A way of sharing the SCSI controller among the software drivers is therefore needed, and the most popular method uses Adaptec Inc.'s ASPI software. The controller and all drivers using the controller must be configured for the same type of such sharing software.

Each peripheral (device on the bus) is manually assigned a *SCSI* ID (usually by setting jumpers or a switch on the device), which is a number from 0 through 7. The number of devices supported per bus is limited by the width (in bits) of the data bus—since the arbitration process when more than one device is contending for the bus at the same time depends on each device identifying its request for the bus by controlling its corresponding bit on the data bus. This is why narrow SCSI supports a maximum of 8 devices (including the controller) per bus. Wide SCSI supports a maximum of 16 devices per bus.

SCSI also supports up to eight *logical unit numbers* (LUNs) per peripheral (that is, they all share the same SCSI ID). This feature is used (for example) to select individual CD-ROMs in a *CD-ROM* jukebox (which is a CD-ROM drive with a cartridge of perhaps 6 CD-ROMs).

The SCSI controller in the host PC is usually assigned the highest SCSI ID (ID number 7)—because the highest number wins a *bus arbitration* (when more than one device attempts to gain control of the bus for a transfer) and it is best to have the host able to control the bus when it needs to.

In fact, ID 7 (and not ID 15) has the highest priority even for wide SCSI—since the IDs 0 though 7 are defined to have higher priority than 8 through 15. This ensures that narrow and wide SCSI devices can be on the same bus, and you can set narrow and wide devices to be higher or lower priority than the others.

SCSI peripherals are usually assigned IDs starting at zero, though slower devices (such as tape and CD-ROM drives) should get higher IDs so that the faster devices (hard disks) can't hog the bus (also, it is relatively fast for them to re-try an operation).

SCSI *initiators* send commands, and *targets* respond to these commands. Usually, the SCSI controller (sometimes called the host adapter) is the initiator ("get me some data, please"), and the peripherals are targets. For some commands, this is reversed—for example, when a CD-ROM has been changed or a tape drive has finished rewinding, it sends an indication of this.

Previous to SCSI, at the lowest level, data on disks was address according to its *cylinder, head* and *sector* (CHS). That is, disk drives consist of one or more disks with a magnetic coating. There is a read/write head for each disk surface (usually two per disk—top and bottom, though some disks use one surface for timing or calibration information). The data is stored on each disk surface in concentric tracks, and each track is divided into sectors. Sectors store some number of bytes, such as 512 bytes. The tracks on all of the disks at a given distance from the center of the disk are called a cylinder. By specifying which disk surface (the head), and which cylinder (distance from the center of the disk) and which sector, a block of data is addressed, for reading or writing.

The problem with this method is the computer needs to know the geometry of the disk (how many disk surfaces, how many sectors per track, and so on). In a PC, this is why you need to identify the drive type in the CMOS memory.

SCSI avoids this mess by simply giving every sector of data a *logical block address* (LBA)—that is addressing every sector of data with a sequential number, starting at 0. The drive itself figures out which cylinder, head and sector holds the data, but the computer only sees the SCSI disk, regardless of its exact geometry, as a long string of blocks that can be written or read.

A SCSI command (`Read Capacity`) even lets the computer automatically determine how many logical blocks are on the disk.

SCSI allows more than one SCSI controller per bus. For example, two computers can be connected to the same SCSI bus (each with its own controller), and both can therefore control the same peripheral. This is usually only an available option for some super-reliable, high-end minicomputers and workstations.

SCSI data transfers can be either of the following:

▲ *Asynchronous*: There is a `Request` and `Acknowledge` control line handshake for each transferred byte to ensure that the data are not sent too fast. Data transfer is typically at about 2 Mbytes/s.

▲ *Synchronous*: The sender is allowed to transfer data over the SCSI bus at a fixed data rate (with no feedback from the receiver), such as 3.33, 4, or 5 Mbytes/s. For SCSI-1 devices, the fastest rate supported (and the most common rate) is 5 Mbytes/s.

Synchronous transfer is faster than asynchronous, especially for longer SCSI buses. To use synchronous data transfers, both the initiator and the target peripheral must support synchronous transfers. That is, there is no need for all peripherals on a bus to support synchronous transfers, just the pair (initiator and target) that want to use it. Also, the initiator and target must support the same synchronous data rate used. Therefore, part of the configuration of a SCSI controller is specifying for each SCSI ID; will asynchronous or synchronous transfers be used (though this is usually negotiated automatically between the SCSI controller and each peripheral), and at the speed (typically the fastest speed supported by both).

The SCSI bus transfer rate is different than the rate that a disk drive actually reads data from the disk itself. Older SCSI disk drives have a typical maximum sustained transfer rate of 1.5 to 2.5 Mbytes/s. So if more than a few disk drives are on a 5 Mbyte/s SCSI bus, then the bus will likely be a performance bottle-neck (if the computer is a server with many simultaneous users).

Nondata SCSI transfers (such as commands, status responses, and the like) use asynchronous transfers. However the data portion of a response to an asynchronous command can use a synchronous transfer. For example, the `Inquiry` command requests an ASCII string identifying the peripheral (this response is often displayed on a PC's monitor when the SCSI drivers are loaded), and this response can use a synchronous transfer. This is one reason why some misconfigured SCSI devices can identify themselves but can't read or write data (other reasons are that the synchronous transfer rate is set too high, or the drive has not been formatted).

SCSI can use several types of connectors, as listed below:

▲ For Macintosh computers, a DB-25 25-pin connector

▲ For SCSI-1 devices connected to PCs, an RJ-21 TelCo (also called Amp or Centronics) style 50-pin connector, is usually used.

▲ For SCSI-2 devices connected to PCs, the smaller "HD" (high-density) connector is usually used.

A SCSI bus cannot have a "T" connection, it can only be one string of daisy-chained cables between the peripherals on the bus (each peripheral has two SCSI connectors—one connects to the cable to the previous device, the other to the next). Each of the two physical ends of a SCSI bus must be *terminated*. That is, they must have a *resistor* connected from each signal line (wire) to a common ground point, to absorb the signal so it does not reflect (echo) back into the signal line. All other devices on the SCSI bus (even if it is the SCSI controller—which can be located at an end, or anywhere in the middle of a SCSI bus) must have their termination resistors disconnected or removed. The termination resistors:

▲ May be electronically switchable. Enabling these termination resistors may be done by from a configuration program supplied with the SCSI controller or peripheral, or they may be enabled automatically (the controller or peripheral automatically senses if it is at the end of the bus).

▲ May be a big plug that looks like the connector on the end of an external SCSI cable, but with no cable coming out. If the last SCSI peripheral on the bus (at that end) is an external device, then this plug is plugged into the empty SCSI connector of that last peripheral on the bus. It is important to ensure that that peripheral is not already terminated inside its enclosure.

▲ May be a little *Single In-line Package* (SIP—which has one row of pins) or *Dual In-line Package* (DIP—which has two rows of pins, and looks like a 16-pin IC). These are called *resistor networks*, and are plugged directly into the printed circuit board of the peripheral. Some important points concerning these resistors are listed below:

▲ The resistor packages typically have 8, 10, or 16 pins, and plug into sockets.

▲ A dot or indent at one end or corner of the package identifies pin 1, which *must* be plugged-in to pin 1 of the socket. Pin 1 of the socket may be identified by a dot silk-screened on the component side of the printed circuit board, or failing that, it will most certainly have a square solder pad (this is easiest to see on the solder side of the PCB).

▲ Note that there are different pin-outs and values for these resistor networks. Make sure you record the socket and orientation before removing them (and tape them inside the case so that they don't get lost or switched with those from other peripherals). Before using resistors from one device in another, verify that the resistance values (by reading the part number, or testing with an ohm-meter) and pin-out match.

SCSI buses can use either *single-ended* or *differential* electrical signals. Since these use different pin-outs for the connectors, all devices on a bus (*including* the termination resistors and the cables) *must* be the same type. Note that the same TelCo and HD-type connectors can be used for both single-ended and differential SCSI. So you can't tell what kind you have by looking at the cable (if you're not sure what you have, read the manual or check the vendor's web site to find out).

SCSI buses for PCs (and some UNIX workstations) use single-ended electrical signals (negative-logic, open-collector 7438-type TTL drivers) and are limited to 6 meters total length (because of the poor noise immunity of single-ended buses).

There are two types of single-ended termination resistors:

▲ *Passive termination* is a 220-Ω pull-up resistor to a 4.25 to 5.25-V supply (called the *termination power*) and a 330-Ω resistor to ground, for each signal line.

▲ *Active termination* has a *voltage regulator* that provides a 2.85-V output (using power from the termination power supply) and a 110-Ω resistor from each signal line to this 2.85-V source.

Although these two types of terminations are electrically the same (the latter is the *Thévenin equivalent* of the former), the active termination (which is typically a larger, connector-like device) is recommended, because of its better noise immunity.

A bus can mix these types of termination (one type at one end of the bus, the other type at the other end) or have ends using the same type of termination.

SCSI buses for minicomputers and UNIX workstations may use the higher-cost *differential* electrical interface, which:

▲ Uses balanced EIA-485 voltages rather than unbalanced TTL voltages. While this costs more to implement (two wires, and therefore two electrical drivers, are required for each signal), the bus can be up to 25 meters in length (and longer if lower transfer rates and good quality cables are used).

▲ Uses passive termination—again, one at each end of the bus. In this case, the termination is a 330 Ω pull-up resistor (to the termination power) for the "–" wire of each signal, and a 220 Ω resistor to ground for the "+" wire of each signal.

▲ The two wires of the signal pair are then tied together with a 150 Ω resistor.

SCSI peripherals (and the cables to them) can be either *internal* or *external* (the controller is always internal). Internal devices are inside the computer's enclosure (guess where the external devices are).

SCSI controllers usually have both an internal and an external connector (the external connector is available at the back of the PC).

For internal devices, the SCSI bus cabling is *flat ribbon cable*. (The National Aeronautics and Space Administration—NASA—is happy to point out that ribbon cable was an invention for spacecraft, and is a very successful commercial benefit from the space program.) The ribbon cable used is a 50-conductor cable that has all the wires bonded in parallel, and is very flat and flexible. It uses a two-row rectangular connector (sometimes called a *header*) directly on the PCB of each SCSI device.

For external devices, the SCSI bus cabling is a 1 cm thick, round cable. Inside, it must not only use twisted pairs of wires for each signal (for good noise immunity), but also should be built in three concentric layers:

▲ The center has three pairs: Request, Acknowledge, and Ground.

▲ The next layer (the control signals) has the pairs twisted in the opposite direction (as compared to the other layers) to reduce the capacitive coupling between layers.

▲ The third (outside) layer (the data and *parity* wires) has its pairs twisted in the opposite direction (compared to the middle layer).

Putting the control signals in the middle layer ensures that the data and Request/Acknowledge signals do not interfere with each other.

The individual wires should not use PVC insulation, since PVC has electrical characteristics that are too temperature-dependent and has too high a capacitance (though the overall cable jacket can be PVC).

These detailed requirements show why SCSI cables are so expensive, made differently for single-ended and differential use (since their pin-outs are different), and are a bad place to save money (by buying no-name cheapo cables, which may not follow these rules—for example, each signal conductor should be twisted with a separate ground conductor, but to save money, manufacturers may use a single ground conductor).

SCAM is a specification that provides automatic *Plug and Play* configuration (and other features) for SCSI devices.

A draft of the SCSI-1 specification is at *ftp://ftp.cs.tulane.edu/pub/scsi/area07/*.** (see the file `files.bbs` there for a description). Som information is also at *ftp://ftp.symbios.com/pub/standards/io/x3t10*.

Major SCSI adapter manufacturers include Adaptec (*http://www.adaptec.com*) and BusLogic Inc. (*http://www.buslogic.com*). For web sites of some SCSI disk manufacturers, see the entry for **DISK DRIVE**.

See **ASPI**, **BUS**, **DB25**, **DISK DRIVE**, **EIA485**, **FAT**, **FAX**, **IDE**, **PARITY**, **PLUG AND PLAY**, **SCAM**, **SCSI2 TTL2** (*Transistor-Transistor Logic*), **TWAIN**, and **WINCHESTER**.

SCSI-1
Small Computer System Interface-1

The first version of SCSI.

SCSI-2
Small Computer System Interface-2

An enhancement to the SCSI-1 specification that provides more of the following:

Compatibility—the SCSI-1 specification left much room for (incompatible) interpretation by vendors, so (for example) specific disk drivers would work only with specific SCSI controllers.

Types of devices supported, as the specification defines the command sets for devices other than disk drives, such as tape drives, CD-ROM drives, and so on.

Speed—faster transfer rates.

While SCSI-2 is an official standard (ANSI X3.131, which is over 400 pages in length, and was released in 1994), the SCSI-3 standard has taken much longer to produce than expected. Many of the enhancements intended for SCSI-3 are therefore being used in advance of SCSI-3 as enhancements to SCSI-2. So there are many names and features that are not part of SCSI-3 (was not standardized when the features were available and needed), and not part of SCSI-2 either. Many of the features described in this entry are therefore not officially part of SCSI-2, but are used with, and are enhancements to SCSI-2.

Fast SCSI refers to a SCSI bus that transfers data at 10 Mtransfers/s. *Wide SCSI* refers to a 16-bit-wide SCSI bus—so, it transfers 2 bytes (16 bits) per transfer). Therefore narrow SCSI transfers at 5 Mbytes/s, fast SCSI transfers at 10 Mbytes/s and wide fast SCSI transfers at 20 Mbytes/s.

Fast-20 is ANSI's name for what many people call *UltraSCSI* (and was to be part of SCSI-3). Fast-20 SCSI buses run at 20 Mtransfers/s. Wide fast-20 SCSI (also called wide UltraSCSI or ultra wide SCSI) therefore transfers 40 Mbytes/s, since it does 20 Mtransfers/s of 16 bits each.

For a while there was talk of a 32-bit wide bus, but the industry is moving to faster, rather than wider transfers, for increased throughput. This allows smaller—and more importantly, the same as for earlier SCSI—connectors to be used.

Also, the 16-bit wide bus (wide SCSI) was initially specified to use two cables— an *A* (the original-8 bit) cable and a *B* cable (which provides the additional 8 bits for the 16-bit-wide bus).

The two cables were to use the same type of high-density (HD) connector. This was too expensive and awkward, so the 16-bit-wide bus is instead implemented using the 68-pin *P-cable*, which will be in the SCSI-3 specification. This provides a 16-bit-wide bus using a single connector and 34-pair cable.

SCSI-2 specifies that parity must be used. There is an *odd parity bit* for every 8 data bits—so wide SCSI has 2 parity bits. Parity was optional for SCSI-1, so some older SCSI devices require it to be disabled. This is done with a switch setting or configuration program.

Narrow and wide SCSI SCSI controllers and drives can be interconnected, and will automatically use narrow SCSI. Connectors and cables to do this are widely available. However, if (for example) a wide drive is connected in the middle of a bus, to a narrow controller, then the high bits must be terminated on the wide drive. Also, if a narrow drive is connected in the middle of an otherwise wide bus, wide drives farther from the controller will only be able to operate in narrow mode.

SCSI-2 also introduced the *disconnect* and *reconnect* commands. This enables a peripheral to work on a command (for example a disk drive Seek to a new cylinder position) while the SCSI bus is freed-up (the SCSI controller releases its connection to the peripheral) so the SCSI controller can communicate with other devices on the bus. Therefore, the first peripheral is doing a Seek while data is written to another disk that has previously finished its Seek.

As for other performance-enhancing options (such as synchronous data transfer support), this must be supported by both the initiator and the target.

Also, many of these performance-enhancing options are only helpful if there are many simultaneous reads and writes being sent to many disk drives. Since a single-user computer usually does not do this (there's only so much one person can do), an IDE interface (such as E-IDE or Fast ATA) usually provides the best performance at lower-cost for desktop computers. SCSI (which typically costs more than IDE) is best-suited for multiuser computers, such as file servers and UNIX workstations.

SCSI-2 also supports *command queuing*, which allows the SCSI controller to send many commands to a peripheral. The peripheral can then reorder the commands to optimize performance. The famous *elevator algorithm* (named after a good way of servicing the many calls an elevator in a building gets) specifies that all read/writes that can be satisfied as the disk drive's read/write head seeks in one direction should be completed before reversing direction. Since only the disk drive knows where exactly the data resides for a series of read requests, it is best to give the drive all the requests, so that it can service them in the most efficient sequence. Command queuing must be supported by both the host adapter and the peripheral for it to be used.

SCSI-2 recommends that active termination, with the termination power provided by the SCSI controller, be used for single-ended buses. This results in less line noise and less signal attenuation than the passive termination often used for SCSI-1 buses.

SCSI-2 specifies a smaller connector than the 50-pin TelCo style used for SCSI-1 (though both use the same type of springy clip locks to ensure the connector does not pull-out of the receptacle). For narrow SCSI, a 0.050" pitch, 50-pin Micro-D type connector is specified. It is also called a *high-density*, or HD connector, and is basically a miniature version of the TelCo-style connector used for SCSI-1. As stated above, wide SCSI uses a 68-pin P-type connector, as will be specified in SCSI-3.

SCSI-2

As for SCSI-1, each device on a SCSI-2 bus can communicate at a different speed. Common synchronous speeds are 5.7, 6.7, 8 and 10 Mtransfers/s (you don't get to set the speed for asynchronous transfers, they happen as fast as the handshaking proceeds). Most recent devices support the full 10 Mtransfer/s speed.

The following table summarizes peak data transfer rates for different disk drive interfaces.

Available	Disk Drive Interface	Data Transfer Bus Width (bits)	Data Transfer Rate (Mtransfers/s)	Peak Transfer Rate (Mbytes/s)
1978	8" floppy diskette (250 kbyte, single-sided)	1	0.25	0.03125
1979	8" floppy diskette (500 kbyte, single-sided)	1	0.5	0.0625
1981	$5\frac{1}{4}$" floppy diskette (160 kbyte)	1		
1981	ST-506[a] (interleaved[b] 2:1)	1	2.5	0.3125
	ST-506 (MFM[c], noninterleaved)	1	5	0.625
	ST-506 (RLL[d])	1	7.5	0.9375
1982	$5\frac{1}{4}$" floppy diskette (360 kbyte[e])	1	0.125	0.015625
1984	$5\frac{1}{4}$" floppy diskette (1.2 Mbyte)	1	0.25	0.03125
1984	$3\frac{1}{2}$" floppy diskette (720 kbyte)	1	0.25	0.03125
1988	$3\frac{1}{2}$" floppy diskette (1.4 Mbyte)	1	0.5	0.0625
	ESDI (10 MHz)	1	10	1.25
	ESDI (20 MHz)	1	20	2.5
1986	SCSI-1 (asynchronous)	8	2	2
1986	IDE (on an 8-bit ISA bus)	8	4	4
1990	IDE (on a 16-bit ISA bus)	16	4	8
1990	SCSI-1 (synchronous)	8	5	5
1993	SCSI-2 (narrow fast SCSI)	8	10	10
	SCSI-2 (wide fast SCSI)	16	10	20
	SCSI-2 (narrow fast-20[f])	8	20	20
	SCSI-2 (wide fast-20[g])	16	20	40

a. The ST-506 disk interface was developed by Seagate Technology for their Winchester disk drives. See the entry for **WINCHESTER**.

b. Interleaving (which is no longer used) places sequential sectors of data in every second (for 2:1 interleaving) sector on the disk to give the host computer enough time (while the next sector goes by the disk's read/write head) to process the sector just read. As shown, this reduces the transfer rate.

c. *Modified frequency modulation* (MFM) stores twice as many bits in the same space as *frequency modulation* (FM).

d. Note that many current IDE and SCSI disk drives actually use RLL internally (at a much faster transfer rate), but this is not the interface used to the outside world.)

e. The increase in storage capacity over the 160 kbyte diskettes was made possible by storing data on both sides of the diskette ("double-sided"), and supporting 9 (rather than 8) sectors (of 512 bytes each) per track.

f. The "20" refers to 20 Mtransfers (in this case, of 8-bits each) per second. Fast-20 is also called UltraSCSI.

g. Also called wide UltraSCSI or Wide Ultra-SCSI.

Note that the above rates are burst rates (while the data are actually being transferred on the bus). The actual throughput will be much slower, because of disk drive seek and latency times, SCSI bus protocol overhead, computer bus contention, CPU processing times, and other factors.

SCSI-2 and SCSI-3 devices start in 8-bit (narrow, not wide) mode, 5 Mtransfers/s (not fast) mode, and in asynchronous (not synchronous) mode—to ensure that initial communications will work. Then negotiations between the initiator and the target are supposed to work out the maximum mutual capabilities (though this does not always work, and these may need to be set manually).

SCSI-2 defines an additional five device types (that is, in addition, to those defined for SCSI-1), as shown in the following table.

Device Type	Name	Typical Function
6	CD-ROM	Replaces the read-only random access defined in SCSI-1
7	Scanner	A printer in reverse
8	Magneto optical	
9	Medium changer (also called a jukebox; for example, can select one of many CDs loaded into a cassette or magazine)	Controls selection of medium
10	Communication	

A draft of the SCSI-2 specification is in the directory *ftp://ftp.cs.tulane.edu/ pub/scsi/area08/ *.**. See the file index for a description of the directory's contents.

See **IDE, PARITY, SCSI1, SCSI3,** and **WINCHESTER.**

SCSI-3
Small Computer System Interface-3

Some of the enhancements planned for SCSI-3 are listed below:

▲ 16-bit transfers on a single cable, which is called the *P-cable*. A 68-pin Micro-D (also called HD, for high-density) connector with 2-56 or (less commonly) 4-40 thread screw locks is used. The connector has pins on 0.050" centers.

▲ A serial option, called *serial storage architecture* (SSA). It uses a 6- (inside a computer) or 9-pin connector (when connecting to peripherals external to a computer), and supports high-speed communication.

▲ Data integrity improvements.

▲ Up to 32 devices per SCSI bus. Though, this would likely only be supported by a 32-bit wide SCSI bus, and it is unlikely that this will every be standardized or implemented.

SCSI Configuration Automatically

A subset of SCSI-3 is called *Fast-20* (and is also called UltraSCSI). It supports up to 20 Mtransfers/s (providing 20 Mbytes/s transfers over the original (8-bit-wide) narrow SCSI bus and 40 Mbytes/s for transfers over a wide SCSI bus).

SCSI-3 requires active termination. Also, single-ended Fast-20 devices have an optional *active negation* feature that actively drives selected signals high (rather than waiting for the termination's pull-up resistors to do it).

Fast-20 controllers can talk different rates to each device on the SCSI bus, enabling newer (and faster) devices to reside on the same bus as older (slower) devices.

The total bus lengths allowed are as follows:

▲ For single-ended, narrow, fast-20 SCSI-3 buses (these run at 20 Mtransfers/s) that have a maximum of 4 devices (in addition to the controller), the bus can be up to 3 m in total length. A fully-loaded bus (with 7 devices on it) can be a maximum of 1.5 m in length (that's about 20 cm for each cable). Wide fast-20 buses can have 8 devices for bus lengths of up to 3.0 m, and up to 16 devices for 1.5 m buses (but check with your vendor).

▲ In contrast, a fully-loaded (with 7 devices) single-ended fast SCSI-2 bus (10 Mtransfers/s) can be up to 6 m in length.

▲ A fully-loaded differential fast-20 SCSI-3 bus can be up to 25 m in length (this is the same as for differential fast SCSI-2).

While SCSI-2 was compatible with, and has largely replaced, SCSI-1, many features of SCSI-3 are different enough (and more expensive) that it will not replace SCSI-2.

The SCSI-3 standard has taken long-enough to produce that some of its more immediately required features have been implemented as extensions to SCSI-2. These are described in the entry for **SCSI2**.

See **SCSI2**, and **SSA**.

SCSI Configuration Automatically

See **SCAM**.

SCTP
Screened Twisted Pair

Twisted pair cable with some characteristics better than Category 5 UTP; therefore some people used to refer to it as Category 6 (but there is no official Category 6 UTP).

Has four twisted pairs (as UTP does) but has a foil shield (unlike UTP).

Used in Europe (some say more for political than technical reasons). Unlikely to become a standard in North America.

See **CABLE** and **UTP**.

SD
Super Density

The technology promoted by Toshiba and Time-Warner that became part of DVD.

A double-sided, CD-ROM-like (but incompatible), play-only disk that is intended to store full-length movies and computer games. The capabilities are:

▲ 5 Gbytes stored per side. Two 0.6-mm-thick disks are bonded back-to-back for a 10-Gbyte total capacity. The 10 Gbytes provides 180 to 270 minutes (total) of compressed audio (including at least three different language tracks) and video.

▲ A "parental lockout" feature so that playback skips past violent or risqué scenes.

Developed by Toshiba, Matsushita (maker of the Panasonic, Technics, and Quasar brands), Hitachi, Pioneer, and Time-Warner. Supported by Denon, Hitachi, JVC, Mitsubishi, Samsung, Thomson (maker of the RCA brand), and Zenith, with content from movie producers Warner Brothers, MCA, MGM/UA, Toshiba/EMI, Turner Home Entertainment, and WEA.

A typical two-hour movie requires 3.5 Gbytes. The additional 1.5 Gbytes of capacity could be used for interactive applications, advertising, or another movie. The audio includes five Dolby Digital surround-sound channels plus a subwoofer channel (low frequencies are very nondirectional, so only one such channel—and speaker—is needed). Multiple language soundtracks and subtitles can be stored as well.

Was to compete with Sony and Philips' Video-CD (which was intended more for the computer market, and sacrificed capacity for compatibility with conventional CD-ROMs), but the two groups (under great industry pressure) merged their two efforts in late 1995.

See **CDROM** (*Video CD*) and **DVD**.

SDH
Synchronous Digital Hierarchy

The SONet-like, really high-speed transmission standard used outside of North America (for example, in Europe, and other far-away places such as Vietnam).

SDH uses multiples of 155.52 Mbits/s, so SDH's STM-1 rate (of 155.52 Mbits/s) is the same bit rate as SONet's OC-3 rate (and so on).

SDH has some additional features, such as improved *operation and maintenance* (OAM) capabilities—making STM-1 and OC-3c slightly incompatible for some maintenance and diagnostic functions.

Of the 155.52 Mbits/s bit rate of STM-1, 5.72 Mbits/s (3.7%) is SDH framing overhead, leaving 149.8 Mbits/s for user data.

Standardized by the ITU-T in G.707 through G.709.

See **E1**, **SONET**, and **STM**.

SDK
Software Development Kit

The software (typically APIs, utilities, and documentation) that an application programmer needs to create programs using a particular platform (hardware, operating system, and/or protocol).

See **API**.

SDLC
Synchronous Data Link Control

IBM's name for *High-level Data Link Control* (HDLC).

A bit-oriented, link-layer protocol usually used by SNA on synchronous data links.

Unlike HDLC, IBM usually uses SDLC in a *polling* mode (a *front end processor* continually asks whether the peripherals have any data to send).

IBM's predecessor protocol is BISYNC.

See **BISYNC, DLC, DLSW, ENCAPSULATION, FEP, HDLC, IBM, PRIORITIZATION, SNA**, and **SYN-CHRONOUS**.

SDRAM
Synchronous Dynamic Random Access Memory

A 3.3 V only, faster (than EDO and BEDO DRAM) type of DRAM. It supports system memory bus speeds of 66 MHz (initially), and up to 100 MHz (with no wait states).

As for BEDO DRAM, on a 66 MHz memory bus, it can support a burst of 5-1-1-1 (the first memory access of the burst requires 5 clock cycles, and the subsequent ones use an on-chip column-address counter to access the next sequential memory locations in a single clock cycle). However, the output of more than one bank of memory is coordinated by a clock signal, hence the name. Also, the ICs have an on-chip mode register, which can be set to support bursts of 2, 4, 8 or 512 accesses.

Each IC outputs 8-bits at a time, and the initial ICs have a capacity of 16 Mbits each (which is 2 Mbytes). Memory modules are typically rated by the bus speed they can support, such as 83 or 100 MHz for DIMMs.

SDRAM became popular for PCs in 1997 (after Intel released their 440LX chip set, which was their first to provide such support, for the Pentium Pro and Pentium II processors). RDRAM is expected to be a still-faster type of DRAM, to be widely commercially available in 1999.

See **DIMM, DRAM, EDO RAM, RDRAM**, and **SGRAM**.

SDTV
Standard Definition Television

The name for the current standard, traditional television format and resolution, now that HDTV is finally getting closer to a commercial reality.

With the data compression methods developed for HDTV, 3 to 6 SDTV channels can be transmitted in the 6 MHz of bandwidth currently required by a single NTSC broadcast.

See **HDTV**, and **NTSC**.

Sealing Current

A DC current sent through copper leased-lines (such as DDS circuits) to prevent corrosion of spliced connections.

Sealing currents are usually between 4 and 20 mA (depending on the line length), with a typical value of 5 mA.

Sealing current is not needed for dial-up circuits, since the ringing voltage (which is a 90 V signal) clears any corrosion.

See **DDS**, **HDSL**, **POTS**, and **T1**.

SECAM
Séquentiel Couleur Avec Mémoire

The analog color television broadcasting standard that is used in France, Eastern Europe and Russia.

There are many different implementations, with names like SECAM-B (which requires 7 MHz per channel) and SECAM-L (which requires 8 MHz per channel—and, one hopes, can produce a better picture).

While SECAM has completely different timings than NTSC, SECAM has the same 4:3 aspect ratio, 2:1 interlacing and 1 V p-p signal as NTSC.

See **HDTV**, **NTSC**, and **PAL**.

Secure Hypertext Transfer Protocol

See **SHTTP**.

Secure Sockets Layer

See **SSL**.

Semiconductor Chip Protection Act

See **INTEGRATED CIRCUIT TOPOGRAPHY ACT**.

Sequenced Packet Exchange

See **SPX**.

Serial Bus

A serial bus is a bus that uses serial data communications for the data and control signals. This is in contrast to parallel buses (such as ISA or SCSI) that may have higher transfer rates, but require 8 or 16 wires for the data, plus more for the control signals.

Serial buses are becoming popular as PCs need to connect to more devices.

See **S1394**, **ACCESS.BUS**, **ADB**, **BUS**, **DDC**, **EIA485**, **GEOPORT**, **SMBUS**, **SSA**, and **USB**.

SET
Secure Electronic Transactions

A method of supported secure transactions over the Internet. It is based on RSA's encryption technology, and also uses the widely-accepted (and U.S. government mandated) data encryption standard (DES).

Since this method is supported by both MasterCard and Visa (and IBM, Microsoft, Netscape and others), it is likely to be more widely accepted than the many other proposed methods.

See **ENCRYPTION**, and **RSA**.

SESAME
Secure European System for Applications in a Multivendor Environment

A European Computer Manufacturers Association (ECMA) security specification that is similar to, but more comprehensive than, Kerberos.

Definitely one of the nicer (and more descriptive) acronyms you'll see anywhere.

See **AUTHENTICATION** and **KERBEROS**.

SGML
Standard Generalized Markup Language

An open standard (ISO 8879) for describing the structure and content of a document.

A nonproprietary, ASCII (so the document is portable across operating systems and hardware platforms) document format.

It facilitates referencing external data, which simplifies maintenance (since information can then be stored once, in a central database, rather than being duplicated).

SGML documents have three parts:

▲ The *Declaration* is a header file that contains system-specific information that is needed to enable the document to be used and modified by the target system (for example, that ASCII is used and which characters from that character set may be used).

▲ The *Document Type Definition* (DTD) or *Style Sheet* is a hierarchical tree-structured definition for the document's *elements* (or *style specifications*). Elements are assigned *attributes*, which (for example) can customize which paragraphs are displayed for different uses of the document.

▲ The DTD specifies the order allowed for the elements (title, heading, paragraph, and so on). *Tags* (which are delimited with angle brackets) assign *element names* (main title, title, paragraph, and so on) to the content of the document, for example:

```
<MONTH>January</MONTH>
```

Thousands of DTDs have been defined. HTML is a (currently) very popular document type, since it is used for every WWW page. The source for this entire book is in SGML, and uses a DTD called DocBook 2.2.1.

The DTD also specifies the type and use of non-SGML *external entities*, such as graphics (and, using an SGML extension called *Hypermedia/Time-based Structuring Language*—HyTime—other objects such as video and audio), that are referenced and not embedded in the *compound document*.

▲ The *Document Instance* is the actual text (with tags) of the document, in the sequence allowed by the DTD (SGML editors include *validating parsers* to ensure this).

A *transformer* then takes the SGML document instance as input and produces formatted output ("*publication*"). This output is called the *Format Output Specification Instance* (FOSI) and is used (finally) for viewing or printing the document (it includes indents, fonts, and character sizes). SGML does not include or specify a method of producing formatted output.

SGML includes *hypertext* capabilities to enable a reader to easily view a glossary or section reference, or even run a program to accept input to fill in a form in the document.

SGML is based on *Generalized Markup Language* (GML), which was developed by IBM in the 1960s.

XML is a proposed new method of describing WWW pages. Like SGML, XML allows new DTDs to be defined.

Some SGML resources include SGML/Open's Web site at *http://www.sgmlopen.org*, SGML On The Web at *http://www.ncsa.uiuc.edu/WebSGML/WebSGML.sgml* and *http://www.sil.org/sgml/sgml.html*.

See **HTML**, **WWW**, and **XML**.

SGRAM
Synchronous Graphics RAM

An enhancement to SDRAM that provides features for the graphics memory on video adapters. It supports the following:

▲ *Masked writes*, where rather than doing a read-modify-write cycle, the data written to memory can be masked so that only certain bits (as specified in the mask) are changed.

▲ *Block writes*, where blocks of memory can be quickly filled with the same value (as would be needed for filling-in the background of a displayed image), or cleared (3-dimensional imaging often requires clearing the entire memory 30 to 40 times per second).

While SGRAM is not *dual-ported*, it does allow two pages of memory to be accessed simultaneously (to support updating the graphic image, while displaying it).

Typically faster (especially for 3-dimensional graphics adapters) than VRAM.

See **DRAM**, **SDRAM**, and **VRAM**.

Shadowed BIOS

Typically, EPROM (*Erasable, Programmable, Read-Only Memory*) has a much slower access time than RAM (*Random Access Memory*). Therefore BIOS code that is executed out of EPROM executes relatively slowly (*wait states* are inserted to delay a few clock cycles until the EPROM can provide the next byte of code).

Many PCs copy the BIOS code from EPROM to RAM ("shadowing") and re-map that RAM to be at the same location as the original BIOS. The BIOS code then executes faster, without any changes made to it.

See **BIOS**, **PC**, and **RAM**.

Shared Memory

A method of transferring data from a PC to a LAN or video adapter (for example).

For LAN adapters, usually, 8 to 32 kbytes of memory on the LAN adapter is mapped to a location in the PC's upper memory area (typically in the $C000_{16}$, $D000_{16}$, or $E000_{16}$ page).

For video adapters, the $A000_{16}$ and $B000_{16}$ pages are reserved for this memory mapping (which is why PCs are limited to 640 kbytes of conventional memory—the 64 kbytes of the $A000_{16}$ page starts at 640 kbytes).

A memory-mapped LAN adapter's memory is usually dual-ported. This method causes less interruption (delay while waiting for memory access) to the PC, since (for example) the memory is written (with data received from the LAN) while the PC is doing other things. A problem is that less upper memory is then available for loading device drivers, and other software, high. Western Digital (now SMC) LAN adapters use this technique.

See **DMA**, **IRQ**, **PC**, **RAM**, and **PLUG AND PLAY**.

S-HTTP
Secure Hypertext Transfer Protocol

A method that is used to support the encryption and decryption (and authentication) of specific WWW documents sent over the Internet (so that people can't watch what you are doing).

Uses RSA public-key encryption. A main use is expected to be for commerce (payments).

An alternative method is SSL, which encrypts all traffic for specific TCP/IP ports.

Supported by America Online, CompuServe, IBM, Netscape, Prodigy, SPRY (at *http:// www.spry.com,* and now owned by CompuServe), and Spyglass.

Designed by Allan Schiffman, then at EIT (which is now working with Terisa Systems).

More details are at *http://www.commerce.net:8000/cgi-bin/textit?/information/standards/dra fts/ shttp.txt* .

See **ENCRYPTION**, **RSA**, **SOCKET NUMBER**, **SSL**, **TCP**, **TERISA SYSTEMS INC.**, and **WWW**.

SI
Le Système International d'Unités (The International System of Units)

The international agreement on metrification and other standards to facilitate trade between countries (and get rid of ridiculous units of measure).

All quanties are defined in terms of 7 fundamental units, which are; meter, kilogram, second, ampere, kelvin, mole and candela.

Also defined are the standard *prefixes* for numbers (such as 4 kg and 2 ms, for 4 kilograms and 2 milliseconds, respectively). Note that there should be a space after the number, but not between the prefix and the abbreviation of the unit (the one exception to this is there are no spaces used for degrees Celsius—20°C for example).

Multiplying Factor		Prefix	Symbol
Decimal form	**Exponential form**	**Prefix**	**Symbol**
1 000 000 000 000 000 000 000 000	10^{24}	yotta	Y
1 000 000 000 000 000 000 000	10^{21}	zetta	Z
1 000 000 000 000 000 000	10^{18}	exa	E
1 000 000 000 000 000	10^{15}	peta	P
1 000 000 000 000	10^{12}	tera	T
1 000 000 000	10^{9}	giga	G
1 000 000	10^{6}	mega	M
1 000	10^{3}	kilo	k
100	10^{2}	hecto	h
10	10^{1}	deca	da
0.1	10^{-1}	deci	d
0.01	10^{-2}	centi	c
0.001	10^{-3}	milli	m
0.000 001	10^{-6}	micro	μ
0.000 000 001	10^{-9}	nano	n
0.000 000 000 001	10^{-12}	pico	p
0.000 000 000 000 001	10^{-15}	femto	f
0.000 000 000 000 000 001	10^{-18}	atto	a
0.000 000 000 000 000 000 001	10^{-21}	zepto	z
0.000 000 000 000 000 000 000 001	10^{-24}	yocto	y

As can be seen for the more extreme prefixes, the big ones use an upper-case letter for the abbreviation, and the tiny ones use a lower-case letter. Also, the names chosen are based on the Greek word for the number produced by dividing the exponent by 3. For example, the prefixes for 10^{21} and 10^{-21} are based on the Greek word for "7", which is *septem*, and the prefixes for 10^{24} and 10^{-24} are based on the Greek word for "8", which is *octo*.

Typically, countries adopt their own slightly-customized metric practice standards. In the U.S. it is called the *American National Standard for Metric Practice* (IEEE/ANSI 268). In Canada it is the Canadian Standard Association's *Canadian Metric Practice Guide* (CAN/CSA-Z234.1).

As can be seen from the table below, there is good reason to use standard multipliers, as the U.S. and Canada use the same word to mean different things than the U.K. and other European countries.

Multiplying Factor	Common Name	
	North America	Europe
10^{googol}	googolplex	
10^{600}		centillion
10^{303}	centillion	
10^{100}	googol [a]	
10^{60}		decillion
10^{54}		nonillion
10^{48}		octillion
10^{42}		septillion
10^{36}		sextillion
10^{33}	decillion	
10^{30}	nonillion	quintillion
10^{27}	octillion	
10^{24}	septillion	quadrillion
10^{21}	sextillion	
10^{18}	quintillion	trillion
10^{15}	quadrillion	
10^{12}	trillion	billion
10^{9}	billion	gillion
10^{6}	million	
10^{3}	thousand	

a. It has been estimated that there are 10^{79} electrons in the universe, so this is a really big number. The idea for a googol was suggested by U.S. mathematician Edward Kasner, who was describing large numbers to a kindergarten class, and one of the children suggested 1 followed by 100 zeros. When asked, Kasner's 9-year-old nephew suggested calling that number a googol, after Barney Googol, a comic-strip character (from the 1930s and 1940s) with bulging eyes. The nephew went on to suggest that a googolplex should be 1 followed by writing zeros until you get tired, but uncle chose a more precise definition.

Computer Dictionary

As can be seen, Europe uses multiples of 10^6 (a million) for the sequence of name, whereas the U.S. and Canada use multiples of 10^3 (a thousand) for the same sequence of names. Therefore, international publications should use unambiguous terms such as "thousand million", rather than "billion".

The U.S. is one of the last countries in the world to adopt the SI units of measurement (often called "metric"). The IEEE has committed to the following schedule:

▲ Including metric in standards developed or revised after January 1, 1996.

▲ Preferring metric (that is, placing the metric measurement first, and the inch-pound units in parenthesis after the SI) after January 1, 1998.

▲ Using metric exclusively (though footnotes of annexes may use inch-pound units) after January 1, 2000.

The metric prefixes are decided by the General Conference on Weights and Measures (CGPM) at an international conference held every few years.

Russ Rowlett has information on units at *http://www.unc.edu/~rowlett/units/index.html*.

See **PAPER**, **STANDARDS**, and **WINCHESTER**.

SIMM
Single In-line Memory Module

The type of memory module usually used in a PC and laser printer, to hold the DRAM. Has a single row of pins (actually, they are electrical contacts etched from the printed circuit board), so guess where the name comes from. There are usually electrical contacts on both sides of the little printed circuit board, but the contacts on each side are electrically connected to each other (the little hole at the top of each gold-plated contact is a *plated through hole*, which means that copper has been deposited on the inside of that drilled hole), so electrically, there is only a single row of contacts.

The older 30-pin SIMMs typically had capacities of 256 kbytes or 1 Mbyte of DRAM. Newer 30-pin SIMMs have capacities up to 16 Mbytes per module. 30-pin SIMMs read or write 8-bits per memory operation. For Macintosh computers there are 8 bits per byte. For PCs there are usually 9 bits per byte of data stored, with the extra bit used for parity (for a total of 36 bits per memory access).

The 72-pin SIMMs can have a capacity of 1 to 128 Mbytes, but are usually 4 Mbytes to 32 Mbytes per module. In newer PCs, 8 Mbyte and larger modules will typically be a faster type of DRAM, such as EDO-DRAM, FPM or BEDO DRAM. Each memory access is 32-bits wide, which provides four times the bandwidth (for the same speed memory ICs) as the older 30-pin SIMMs.

One of the characteristics for any type of memory is the *access time* (also called *speed*). This is typically the number of nanoseconds (billionths of a second) from when the address has been specified until the memory location is ready to be read or written. Typical DRAM has an access time of 60 or 70 ns (the faster versions cost more).

Another characteristic of SIMM memory is the number of bits read or written per memory access. Older 30-pin SIMMs support 8 bits (possibly with another bit for parity). Newer PCs and memory modules increase the memory bandwidth (amount of data that can be read or written per second) by reading or writing 4 or 8 bytes (typically plus 4 or more bits for ECC) per memory access. 486-based PCs have 32-bit memory buses, so SIMMs can be added one at a time. However, Pentium-based computers (these have 64-bit memory buses) must have SIMMs added in pairs. Or DIMMs can be added singly.

SIMM memory is often described with a notation such as "8x36-60ns", which means the module has 8 million 36-bit memory locations, which have an access time of 60 nano-seconds. The 36 bit memory locations are 4 bytes for data storage, plus 4 bits for error detection and correction—so the module has a capacity of (8 × 4 =) 32 Mbytes.

Another characteristic of all ICs is that the pins (electrical contacts) are typically plated with either tin or gold—the contact itself is typically copper, but this oxidizes ("rusts") too much. This results in several restrictions:

▲ Excessive removal/insertion cycles will wear off the plating, resulting in an unlreliable connection (often intermittent, possibly according to temperature cycles, or some other impossible-to-troubleshoot symptom)

▲ Gold contacts are more reliable (and therefore more desirable), since it does not oxidize as tin can (ha ha, I made a funny—*tin can har, har, har, he, he, ho, ho, ho*). But most recommend that more important than that, you match the type of metal on the two mating surfaces. So if your SIMM socket has tin-plated contacts, then you should use SIMMs with tin-plated contacts as well. There are to reasons for this. Firstly, mixing metals usually results in a *galvanic reaction* (a voltage is produced, that results in a chemical reaction that creates some type of crud, which usually is not conductive). Secondly, one metal will be harder than the other (tin is harder than gold), and will scratch off the other metal, and that contact will corrode since it is no longer protected by the gold plating (or whatever).

Some devices, such as Hewlett-Packard LaserJet printers use some of the SIMM's 72 pins to identify the speed and capacity of the SIMM module. They call these pins (pins 67 to 70, where pin 1 is the pin closest to the notched end of the SIMM) the *presence detect* pins. By shorting some of these pins to ground (which is pin 72), the module indicates its speed (70, 80 or 100 ns access time), and capacity (1, 2, 4, 8, 16 or 32 Mbytes). Without at least one of these pins shorted to ground, the printer will not recognize the SIMM as valid.

A DSIMM is two SIMMs connected together to provide a higher-density (and larger) module.

These are examples of why you need to get the right module for a specific device—not just the right speed and capacity.

See **CONNECTOR**, **DIMM**, **DRAM**, **ECC**, **EDO RAM**, **PARITY**, and **ZIF**.

Simplex

Communication that goes one way only. Examples are:

▲ Radio and television broadcasts

▲ Sending data to printers (though many newer printers have bidirectional communications to report status and problems)

▲ Stock trade and other financial data feeds

See **S1284**, **HALFDUPLEX**, and **FULLDUPLEX**.

SIT
Special Information Tone

A series of three internationally standardized (by the ITU) tones preceding recorded messages ("network provided announcements") used by telephone companies to inform callers that a call could not go through and why (for example, the tones you hear after dialing a 1-800 call that cannot be reached from the caller's area).

These ensure that automated calling equipment (or people that don't speak the language of the subsequent recording) can determine what the problem is (and avoid clogging up the telephone network with guaranteed-fruitless retries). Also, it is a good clue that you are about to hear a recording, so any attempt at interactive conversation will be somewhat one-sided.

Four of the defined messages are listed below.

▲ Intercept (IC)—The particular number you called has been redirected (perhaps because the destination's telephone service was discontinued).

▲ No Circit (NC)—No circuit is available to complete the call.

▲ Reorder (RO)—The call cannot go through because (at least some part of) the network is congested. Often, a *fast busy* tone (which is 120, rather than the usual 60 tones per minute) is used instead.

▲ Vacant Code (VC)—The area code or exchange dialled is not assigned.

SIT can also be an abbreviation for *Standard Information Tones*, which are the in-band tones sent to a payphone to indicate (for example) that the call has been answered (whereafter it drops your coins into its little safe, so you can't get it to fall into the coin return bin, if you hang-up the phone).

See **S800**, **DTMF2**, **INBAND**, and **POTS**.

SIX-σ QUALITY
Six Sigma Quality

A specification of the number of parts that can be outside of specification (see **NFG**).

A concept that was popularized by Motorola (beginning in 1987) for defining the (acceptable—and very low) number of electronic components that can have characteristics outside of the components' specifications (that is, that are defective).

If a histogram showing the deviation of the actual measured characteristics of individual components compared to their target specifications is made, then a curve such as the one shown in the accompanying graph will be constructed.

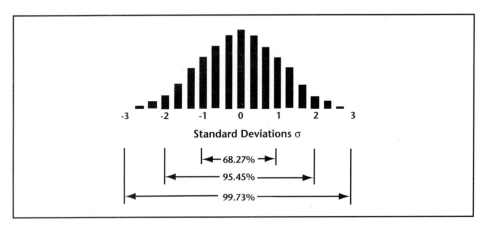

Six-σ Quality-1

This shows that many components are very close to specification and fewer components deviate farther from specification. For many physical processes, the shape of this curve is close to a *normal curve* (because the variation of the components' characteristics follows a *normal distribution*), which is defined by the equation

$$y = \frac{1}{\sqrt{2\pi}} e^{-\frac{\left(\frac{x-\mu}{\sigma}\right)^2}{2}}$$

where y is the height (number of components), μ (the Greek letter *mu*) is the mean, σ (the Greek letter *sigma*) is the *standard deviation*, and x is the particular component's measured characteristics.

As shown in the graph, and integrated numerically (using the integral below—in this example, for six standard deviations)

$$\int_{-6}^{6} \frac{1}{\sqrt{2\pi}} e^{-\frac{\left(\frac{x-\mu}{\sigma}\right)^2}{2}} \, dx$$

for such normal curves, 68.27% of all components will have characteristics within one standard deviation of the mean, 95.45% will have characteristics within two standard deviations of the mean, and so on.

This means that (100% – 95.45% =) 4.55% of the components will have characteristics that are more than two standard deviations from the target specifications. Fortunately, fewer and fewer components have specifications even farther from the target, as shown in the following table.

Computer Dictionary

For This Many Standard Deviations from the Target	This Percentage of Components Are Good	Which Leaves This Many Components Defective (per Million[a])
1	68.27	158,650.0000
2	95.45	22,750
3	99.73	1,350
4	99.99366	31.7
4.5	99.99932	3.4
5	99.9999426	0.287
6	99.99999976	0.0012

a. Actually, there will be twice this number—to include *both* the components that are more than (for example) +6σ greater than *and* those that are less than –6σ less than the target specification.

While the Motorola manufacturing targets are that ±6Σ of the components will be within the mean, they allow for the process mean to shift from the target specification by up to 1.5σ. Therefore fewer than 3.4 per million (4.5Σ) will be outside of specification.

See **ISO 900X** and **MTBF**.

SLED
Single Large Expensive Disk

The opposite of the RAID concept (though in practice, RAID also uses expensive disk drives).

The idea is to use a single, fast disk drive for a storage subsystem when fast access time is a priority, rather than a complicated array of disk drives. (RAID systems often have a relatively slow access time, though they may have a higher reliability.)

See **DISK DRIVE** and **RAID**.

SLIP
Serial Line Internet Protocol

A protocol for carrying IP over an asynchronous serial communications line (for example, a 14,400-bits/s dial-up or leased line connection).

In general, PPP is preferable to SLIP, since SLIP:

▲ Does not include a protocol identifier field (so it can be used only with IP)

▲ Requires each end to have an IP address assigned before data transfer begins (rather than assigning one as part of the connection process)

▲ Has no initial negotiation to ensure interoperability

▲ Does not support error detection or correction

▲ Supports only asynchronous data communication (which is typically 20% less efficient than synchronous data communication because of the need for start and stop bits in asynchronous data communication)

▲ Does not support data compression

Small Form Factor Committee

Since PPP has solutions to these requirements, it is now far more popular.

SLIP is defined in RFC 1055.

See **ASYNCHRONOUS**, **CSLIP**, **IP**, and **PPP**.

Small Form Factor Committee

A group that was initially formed to standardize the location of the mounting screw holes in PC disk drives.

The group's function has now expanded to include specifying data transfer rates and timings for new IDE-type disk drive interfaces, such as E-IDE and Fast ATA.

For example, it is no coincidence that the new data transfer rates (such as the *mode 3 PIO* rate of 11.1 Mbytes/s) are faster than IDE's main competitor, SCSI-2 (which supports a transfer rate of 10 Mbytes/s transfers for the 8-bit-wide implementation—currently the most widely installed).

See **EIDE**, **FAST ATA**, **IDE**, and **SCSI2**.

SMART
Self-Monitoring, Analysis and Reporting Technology

A method initiated by Compaq, with input from IBM, and now supported by disk drive manufacturers to predict disk drive failures—hopefully before they happen :).

Based on changes in a disk drive's; read/write head flying height, spin-up time, read/write head seek time and error rate, reallocated sector count (when a drive determines and marks a sector as bad, and uses an alternate location for that data), and other factors, many disk drive failures can be predicted. Vendors choose which factors are significant (and that can be economically monitored) for the technology used in their drives, and establish thresholds for acceptable performance. When these thresholds are exceeded, an alert message is sent (for example, using the DMI).

The technology is most widely supported for IDE (ATA) disk drives, but some vendors support it for their SCSI drives as well.

See **DISK DRIVE**, **IDE**, **DMI**, and **SCSI1**.

Smart Card

The credit card sized cards that have a rectangular gold star-pattern electrical contact, often used for payphone cards and other storage and identification purposes. For payphone and GSM handset use, these are called *subscriber identity modules* (SIMs). For point-of-sale and other payment use, they are called *security access modules* (SAMs).

There are 8 (or sometimes only 6) gold-plated electrical contacts, that are rated for 10,000 insertion/removal cycles. The cards are either 0.076 mm (0.030"—usually cardboard) or 2 mm (0.079"—like a standard credit card) thick.

Standardized in ISO 7810 through 7816.

The Smart Card Forum is at *http://www.smartcrd.com/*.

See **GSM**, and **NC**.

SMB
Server Message Block

The application-layer protocol used by Microsoft's *LAN* Manager and *Windows for Workgroups* (WFW) products. Runs over NetBEUI.

See **NETBEUI**.

SMBUS
System Management Bus

A two-wire bus to enable more intelligent handling of rechargeable batteries (of any technology) in portable equipment such as laptop PCs. For example, identifying the type of battery pack, monitoring its charging and discharge rates and its temperature are supported.

The bus carries clock, data, and instructions between a PC, the battery charger, and the battery pack. Other peripherals could also be attached to the bus (for example, so that they can receive commands to power down in an orderly way before the battery runs down).

The bus is based on the I^2C bus developed by Philips and Signetics, and ACCESS.bus.

Vendors using SMBus would be required to pay royalties (which may turn out to be a substantial deterrent to SMBus being widely accepted).

Proposed by Duracell and Intel and supported by:

▲ Benchmarq Microelectronics and Microchip Technology (they make the ICs)

▲ Phoenix Technologies and SystemSoft (they make PC BIOSes)

▲ Canon (they make battery-operated devices that would benefit from this technology)

Benchmarq Microelectronics, Inc., has a WWW server at *http://www.benchmarq.com*.

See **ACCESS.BUS**, **BATTERIES**, **SBD**, **SERIAL BUS**, and **USB**.

SMDS
Switched Multimegabit Data Service

A carrier-oriented (the specification was written by Bellcore), cell-relay-based, connectionless, WAN-oriented (no distance limitations) data service. That is, it is a completely specified commercial implementation, including usage-based billing, and not just a data switching and formatting scheme (in contrast, for example, the ATM and frame relay specifications do not include billing methods).

All implementations should therefore be interoperable (avoiding the problems that ISDN encountered).

Much more limited than B-ISDN. For example, it does not have an isochronous channel for voice and video (this is a major limitation).

Access is through DS-0, T1, T3, or SONet (though currently, most often at T1 or T3). Because of cell relay's large protocol overhead, a T1 carrying SMDS traffic provides only 1.17 Mbits/s service (the remaining 374 kbits/s are network overhead), and a T3 provides only 34 Mbits/s. The access speeds supported are listed in the following table.

Access Class	Access Speed (Mbits/s)	Same Speed as
1	4	Token Ring
2	10	Ethernet
3	16	Token Ring
4	25	ATM
5	44.736	T3

Higher access speeds (based on SONet) will likely be defined in the future. More features (such as usage-based billing and network management) are defined than for ATM.

In Europe, SMDS is more popular than frame relay. E1 accesses to SMDS provide data transmission speeds of 0.5, 1.5 or 2 Mbits/s. E3 accesses can provide 4, 10, 16 or 25 Mbit/s service.

Uses telephone-type 10-digit DNs (*Directory Numbers*—CCITT's E.164 defines these) and charging (per-call or per-byte and dependent on call duration and distance).

User data (up to 9,188 bytes) are first *encapsulated* in an SMDS packet, which has a 36-byte header plus a 4-byte trailer, so CUGs (*Closed User Groups*) and other features can be provided. Data are then segmented into the 48-byte (plus 5 bytes of overhead) cells—though only 44 bytes per cell are available for payload data.

SMDS is based on the IEEE 802.6 *Metropolitan Area Network* (MAN) standard. For example, SMDS uses the DQDB access method, though there is no contention for the bus, since the only other station is at the carrier's central office).

SMDS is exptected to be superseded by ATM (though ATM was initially expected to be used only inside a B-ISDN network switch) for high-speed use, and frame relay for lower-speed use.

Can use ATM (AAL 3/4) for its switching.

Concerns are the following:

▲ Unknown latency (causing possible protocol time-outs, though intra-LATA delays are specified to be kept to less than 20 ms)

▲ Unsuitable for many digitized voice and video services (again, because of the unknown latency)

▲ The difficulty of trouble-shooting connectionless services

▲ Fair allocation of bandwidth

While offered commercially (for example, there is both carrier and router support), little development has occurred recently, and the technology is unlikely to be popular.

Of course, that viewpoint might not be shared by the SMDS Interest Group, who have a WWW server at *http://smds-ig.org*.

See **ATM** (*Asynchronous Transfer Mode*), **BELLCORE**, **B-ISDN**, **CARRIER**, **CONNECTIONLESS**, **DN**, **DQDB**, **DS0**, **E.164**, **ENCAPSULATION**, **T1**, **T3**, **SONET**, and **WAN**.

SMP
Simple Management Protocol

Another name for SNMP2.

See **SNMP2**.

SMP
Symmetric Multiprocessing

A type of *multiprocessing*, in that it uses more than one CPU to handle data processing (to speed things up). In SMP, any processor can handle any task (or process or thread)—so the processors are considered "symmetric". Also, in SMP, ideally all resources are shared, including access to and the use of I/O devices, such as the disk drives and communication ports.

However, in actual implementations, some operating systems have some restrictions, such as one processor handling interrupts for all processors, or one processor handles the complete execution of a processing thread (OS/2 SMP 2.11 has both these characteristics). Some SMP implementations don't require this, but perform better if one task always executes on the processor on which it was started (for example, because that processor's CPU and disk caches only have data for that task).

An SMP computer requires support from the following components:

▲ The operating system, which must be *reentrant*. That is, temporary storage for all operating system APIs must be process-specific, so that the API can be simultaneously called by many processes, and not get their variables and parameters overwritten.

▲ The computer hardware (such as having an EISA or PCI bus), to support multiple processors and the sharing of interrupt and DMA requests.

▲ Possibly the CPUs (such as the Pentium Pro)—which simplifies the other support required. Intel's MPS describes the hardware support needed for SMP for up to 4 processors.

Popular operating systems that have SMP support include IBM's OS/2, Microsoft's Windows NT, Novell's NetWare 4.1 SMP and many UNIX implementations.

Most importantly, support is often needed from the application software, in order to get the best utilization and improvement in performance (so that tasks can be split between more than one processor).

The multiple processors need to communicate, to coordinate their work, and share information. Some categorize SMP implementations according to how this communication is performed:

▲ *Shared memory*. This provides the fastest communication between processors, and is often the simplest to implement, since it often appears as a multitasking operating system, with the new feature that the tasks can execute simultaneously. One disadvantage is that it is typically restricted to a small number of processors (such as 2 to 8), due to complexities of cache memory and limitations due to hardware bus loading and maximum throughput. It is the most widely implemented, for example, by Pentium II PCs running Windows NT.

▲ *Shared disk*. This uses data on a disk drive as the communication mechanism (often called messaging, where one process—and processor—sends another a message by

leaving it on the disk). This is more scalable (though there is still a small number of processors—perhaps around 10—that can be connected to a single disk drive), and provides more redundancy (the processors don't share a common power supply or even chassis) than shared memory implementations. Sun Microsystem's UNIX-based servers and Oracle databases support this method, for example. Business transaction applications are typically well-suited to this type of system.

▲ *Shared nothing*. This again uses messaging for inter-processor communication, but uses a high-speed network, which is typically dedicated to this communication—such as Fibre Channel or SCI (in addition, a traditional network, such as Ethernet is typically used to communicate with users). This method has the most scalability (more than 10 processors can be interconnected), higher performance (networks are faster than disk drives), and usually the highest cost as well. IBM's chess-playing Power parallel Systems SP2 is an example of this method. Other number-crunching and scientific data-mining applications are well-suited to this type of system.

An SMP system is also called a *cluster*.

See **EISA**, **FIBRE CHANNEL**, **LATENCY**, **MPP**, **MPS**, **PCI**, **PENTIUM**, **PENTIUM PRO**, **SCALABLE ARCHITECTURE**, **SCI**, and **WINX WINDOWS APIS**.

SMR
Specialized Mobile Radio

A two-way, analog radio technology used to cover a specific georgraphic area (such as a city). Used for dispatching of trucks, taxi cabs, emergency service vehicles, and couriers and by the construction industry. Individual radios can be addressed, so only the selected radio(s) will be part of a particular conversation. The capability to select groups (rather than single radios) is an important advantage compared to traditional AMPS cellular telephone.

An SMR operator is like a public carrier for radio dispatch services.

SMR (pronounced smur) typically uses the 800 MHz frequency band.

See **ESMR**.

SMRP
Simple Multicast Routing Protocol

A protocol that was developed to support conferencing.

An Apple Computer AppleTalk routing protocol that sends only a single copy of multicast traffic to a router, which then splits it and sends it out to all (and only those) downstream ports that need a copy of the traffic.

Competes with several other TCP/IP-based multicast routing protocols.

See **APPLE**, **IP MULTICAST**, and **QTC**.

SMTP
Simple Mail Transfer Protocol

The protocol used in TCP/IP networks for transferring electronic mail messages between *mail servers* (which can be message transfer agents or post offices—which store mail for users not currently connected to the network. SMTP can also be used to transfer mail between users (clients) and servers. That is, SMTP is used by a user to send mail to a post office, but a post office protocol is used to retrieve mail from a post office.

Popular freeware SMTP mail programs for user workstations are `Elm` and `Pine`.

The SMTP protocol was designed to work over a communication channel that only carries 7 bits per character (such as is provided by an auto-dial modem and asynchronous communications with 7 data bits and one parity bit per character). The SMTP protocol therefore only allows the mail message to include characters with decimal values from 0 to 127 (that is, 00000000_2 through 01111111_2). To send binary files (that is, bytes which can have any value from 00000000_2 through 11111111_2), some conversion must first be done. Traditionally, this has required the sender to first run a separate program (such as `uuencode`) to convert the binary data to 7-bit data, but this is now often done automatically by the user's e-mail program (if it has support for MIME built-in).

To SMTP, there are two types of computers:

▲ *Mail User Agents* (MUAs) are the initial source, and the final destination for mail. The e-mail software package on a PC (such as Qualcomm's Eudora) is a typical MUA. These let you build e-mail messages with the necessary header lines, such as `To:`, `Subject:`, `Reply-To:`, `Errors-To:`, `Date:` and `From:`. Not all of these are mandatory, but can be helpful in special situations. For example, `Reply-To:` if you want a reply to the e-mail message to go to a different address than initial message came from (perhaps because of Internet firewall routing requirements). `Errors-To:` is used to specify an address for e-mail forwarding error messages.

▲ *Mail Transfer Agents* (MTAs) are the servers (sometimes called *gateways*) which receive e-mail from MUAs, transfer it accross the Internet (or whatever), and finally send it to the destination MUA. MTAs typically each add a line of text for mail messages they handle. This line typically includes a time-stamp (often including the offset from UTC) and indentification of the MTA (its IP address and DNS name). There is no standard for what gets added, so the format and contents of the line is often meaningful only to the MTA's administrator. The sequence of these at the top of mail messages it helpful to track mail forwarding problems, but cryptic junk to most people (and many MUAs therefore don't display this information to users).

e-mail addresses have two components, separated by the @ character (the commercial *at sign*, as in these apples are *4 @ 99¢*). This convention was adopted in 1971 by Ray Tomlinson. The right side is the DNS name of the destination user's mail server. Since the DNS is case-insensitive, upper- or lower-case can be used. The left side is an identification for the user, which needs to have meaning to the destination mail server (only—therefore, different conventions are used, such as Mitchell_Shnier, MitchellShnier, Mitchell.Shnier, and so on). The left side may or may not be case-sensitive, this is determined by the destination's mail server.

SMTP only supports the immediate transfer of messages. The SMTP protocol includes commands only for immediately sending e-mail messages. If the destination MUA will not continuously be ready to receive mail (for example, because the destination is a PC that dials in periodically to an ISP), then a *post office* must be used to receive and temporarily store the mail for the MUA. The destination then uses a post office protocol (such as IMAP or POP) to retrieve the mail.

X.400 is a more secure, but (now) much less popular e-mail protocol.

RFC 821 defines SMTP (the message transfer procedure itself), and RFC 822 defines the format and headers of the messages. These specifications were developed in 1982.

See **ACAP**, **DNS2** (*Domain Name System*), **IMAP**, **ISP**, **MIME**, **POP2**, **TCP**, **UTC**, **UUCP**, and **X.400**.

SMPTE
Society of Motion Picture and Television Engineers

While these people produce standards for digitized video (for example), used by itself SMPTE (pronounced *simpty*) usually refers to the SMPTE's standard for numbering video frames, encoding this information with the video information, and sending this *timecode* to other devices (typically for synchronizing them to the video).

When this timecode is sent over MIDI, it is called *MIDI* timecode (MTC).

Some futher information is at *http://www.sfoundry.com/pages/tech/smpte.htm*.

See **MIDI**, and **VIDEO**.

SNA
Systems Network Architecture

IBM's proprietary data communication protocols.

▲ Original SNA (introduced in 1974) is now sometimes called *Subarea SNA*. It was *Mainframe-centric*, since all communications were directly from your dumb 3270-type terminal to a mainframe (running *Advanced Communication Facilities/Virtual Telecommunications Access Method*—ACF/VTAM).

▲ APPN is the "new SNA" (but you can't call it that for long, because what do you call the thing after the "new SNA"?). APPN, or new SNA, is therefore sometimes called second-generation SNA. It supports *peer-to-peer* communications (for example, between AS/400 midrange computers and/or workstations without the involvement of mainframes) initiated by either party.

For WAN traffic, traditional SNA data communication circuits (BISYNC or SDLC) require a dedicated data communications circuit. This was no problem when many companies were "IBM shops" (they only had IBM mainframe computers). However most companies with IBM computers now have other types of computers as well, and they have WAN traffic other than SNA. To save money and simplify their WAN, companies now want to have each WAN link carry the IBM SNA traffic along with TCP/IP, IPX or whatever other traffic they have. Several methods have been developed to do this, as listed below:

▲ Token Rings can be interconnected using source routing bridges. These bridges carry any type of Token Ring frame. *Split bridges* (that is, a pair of bridges with a WAN link between them), can be used to carry LLC2 (the type of frame used for SNA traffic on Token Rings), TCP/IP, IPX or any other type of frame.

▲ Generally, bridging is undesirable for WAN links since source route bridging requires that users connections be lost while a new path is found if a link in the path used fails.

▲ *Gateways* (which used to be called *protocol converters*) typically convert the SNA frames to other protocols, such as TCP/IP or IPX.

▲ *Data Link Switching* (DLSw), which encapsulates an SNA frame into an TCP/IP packet.

▲ *Dependent LU* Requester/Server DLUR/S, which uses APPN at the transport protocol.

▲ *Frame Relay*, using encapsulation as defined in RFC 1490.

See **S3270**, **APPC**, **APPN**, **DLC**, **FEP**, **FRAME RELAY**, **LU-6.2**, **MAINFRAME**, **SDLC**, **SAA**, **SNI**, **TOKEN RING**, and **VTAM**.

SNAFU
Situation Normal: All F_ _ _ _ _ Up

Another one of those cynical and colorful terms that was originated by the military during the second world war. It means that things are running as well as they usually do. Unfortunately, many now use the term to indicate a problem.

See **FOO.BAR**.

SNAP
Subnetwork Access Protocol

A frame format often used for TCP/IP and Apple's EtherTalk on 802.3 ("Ethernet") LANs.

See **S802.3**.

SNI
SNA Network Interface

The old way of connecting different company's IBM mainframe computers (TCP/IP might be a better way today).

See **MAINFRAME**, and **SNA**.

Sniffer
Network General Sniffer

"Sniffer" is the trademarked name for the LAN protocol analyser made by Network General Corp.

Before RMON and powerful PCs which are now able to do a good job of packet capture and analysis, the Sniffer was *the* high-end LAN analysis tool to have. It consists of a powerful portable PC with a custom-designed LAN adapter. The adapter gave the Sniffer the capability of capturing illegally short or long frames (which are typically discarded by standard LAN adapters).

Network General is at *http://www.networkgeneral.com*.

See **RMON**.

SNMP
Simple Network Management Protocol

A query/command/response protocol to examine and change configuration parameters and counters of LAN- and WAN-connected repeaters, bridges, routers, and other devices.

Agents (software running in the monitored/controlled equipment) communicate with *management stations* (usually using TCP/IP over an Ethernet LAN). Agents store and update their

information and parameters as counters, arrays or tables of values. Devices that have such SNMP agents are often called *managed*—such as a *managed bridge* or a *managed repeater*.

Proxy agents are used to manage devices that have a non-SNMP management protocol. For example, a CSU/DSU or modem that has an EIA-232 interface cannot talk TCP/IP over Ethernet (which is the usual way to carry SNMP information). Therefore a PC or stand-alone box (the proxy agent) is used. It talks the proprietary protocol over EIA-232 to the device, and converts this to SNMP and TCP/IP over Ethernet (for example).

The SNMP protocol supports only the following functions (which is why it's called a *simple* network management protocol!):

▲ `Get` (a specified variable's current value from an agent)

▲ `GetNext` (get the next variable's value)

▲ `Set` (a variable)

▲ `Trap` (the agent sends a message when a threshold is exceeded)

All variables are defined by MIBs (*Management Information Bases*), though most equipment has manufacturer-specific extensions. These extensions are described by using a subset of a language called *Abstract Syntax Notation One* (ASN.1), which is described in the *Structure of Management Information* (SMI—see RFCs 1155 and 1212). A *MIB compiler* is then used to integrate the extensions into the management station's SNMP software.

Uses TCP/IP's UDP connectionless transport. (IPX, AppleTalk, and OSI transports have been defined but are seldom used or implemented.) IBM is working on an SNA implementation.

Very little security is defined. All communicating agents are assigned a *community string* (sort of a weak password), which is not encrypted when it is sent over the network. By default, the read-access community string is `public`, and the write-access community string is `private`. These default passwords are a security problem because many installations do not change them. A common work-around that provides a slightly better level of security is that devices are configured (initially, usually from a directly-attached console) so that further configuration changes are only accepted from SNMP management stations with certain IP addresses. The problem with this is that if someone learns the IP address of the management station (not a difficult thing to do), they could program their PC to use that IP address.

A recent extension S-SNMP (*Secure SNMP*) adds security features such as user authentication and data encryption (DES) but adds significant network overhead. This extension has been bogged-down for years in the standards-setting process.

The major UNIX-based management stations (in decreasing order of number of installations and third-party applications available) are:

▲ Hewlett-Packard Co.'s *OpenView Network Node Manager*, running on an HP Apollo (running HP-UX), Sun (running SunOS), or Microsoft Windows platform

▲ Sunsoft Inc.'s *Sunnet Manager*, running on a Sun SPARCstation (used to be the most popular)

▲ IBM's *Systemview* or *Netview/6000* (which is based on HP's Openview), running on an IBM RS/6000 workstation (running AIX), Sun, or Microsoft Windows platform

A problem with SNMP is that it requires continuous polling (which loads the network—especially for larger networks), and most MIBs provide only current information. To get historical information, the management station must continuously poll and archive the current information. RMON is a widely implemented and accepted improvement to this.

SNMP was developed by Jeff Case (along with others), who was a network manager and computer science professor at the University of Tennessee in Knoxville. They developed the management station, and Proteon (a popular Router vendor at the time) developed agent software for their equipment. The first implementation of the protocol was called simple gateway monitoring protocol (SGMP—routers were often called gateways then), and was completed in the summer of 1987. SNMP was accepted as an interim standard for TCP/IP networks in February 1988 (it was expected that CMIP would replace it). SNMP is standardized in RFCs 1098 and 1157.

Information and further links to network management can be found at *http://smurfland.cit.buffalo.edu/netman/index.html*.

See **CMIP**, **DMI**, **DMTF**, **MIB**, **RMON**, **SNMP2**, and **UDP**.

SNMP V2
Simple Network Management Protocol version 2

A proposed enhancement to SNMP and Secure SNMP to support larger and faster networks (for example, 64-bit counters are supported) with more complex reporting while causing less network traffic (more than one variable can be retrieved per query, for example).

SNMP v2 can run over AppleTalk, IPX, and OSI transport layer software, in addition to TCP/IP.

Other enhancements include:

▲ A get_bulk command is supported, to enable more parameters to be retrieved in a single packet.

▲ Agents can be *locked*, so only one management station can configure it at a time

▲ Better error reporting is supported

▲ A single station can be both a manager and an agent, allowing for hierarchical management

▲ Proxy agents are supported, so one TCP/IP management station can report on many non-TCP/IP agents

▲ DES or public key encryption is used for passwords passed over the network, there are no default passwords, and authentication is supported

Sometimes called *Simple Management Protocol* (SMP).

Originally specified in RFCs 1441 through 1444, which were replaced by RFCs 1902 through 1908.

Major disagreements over the handling of security in the standards development process have delayed the standard, and the availability of products. One group proposed something called *User Based Security* (USEC), and called the resulting standard SNMP v2u. Another group called their version SNMP v2*.

As a result, a less ambitious effort called SNMP v2c was developed that continues to use the basically useless security of SNMP v1, while offering most of the new functionality of SNMP v2. SNMP v2c is specified in RFC 1901 through 1904.

These should all be superceded by SNMP v3, which provides for user athentication and data privacy, as well as proxies to perform polling of data.

A draft of SNMP v3 is at *http://www.ietf.org/html.charters/snmpv3-charter.html*.

See **DES**, **SNMP**, and **TCP/IP**.

SNPP
Simple Network Paging Protocol

A TCP/IP-based protocol to send alphanumeric messages to a *gateway computer* connected to a paging system.

Messages can be up to 900 characters in length.

Support is included for transmitting pagers so that confirmation that the recipient received the page can be sent to the original sender.

See **TCP/IP**.

SNTP
Simple Network Time Protocol

See **NTP**.

Sockets

A nonstandardized software interface (API) between a user application program and a TCP/IP protocol stack.

Initially developed (in 1984) for the 4.2BSD version of UNIX. The programming interface is somewhat like that of a file and has the following functions:

- ▲ accept (an incoming connection)
- ▲ bind (an address to an outbound call)
- ▲ initiate (a connection)
- ▲ listen (for an incoming connection)
- ▲ receive (a message from a socket)
- ▲ send (a message to a socket)
- ▲ socket (create one)
- ▲ close, read, and write, too

See **API**, **BSD UNIX**, **TCP**, **UNIX**, and **WINSOCK**.

Socket Number

In TCP/IP, the socket number is the concatenation of the sender's (or receiver's) IP address and *port numbers* (the service being used). The pair of these (the sender's and receiver's socket numbers) uniquely specifies the connection in the entire internet.

See **INTERNET1**, **TCP**, and **TCP/IP**.

SOCKS
TCP/IP Sockets Interface

While Winsock is a widely implemented standard interface for Microsoft Windows applications to utilize TCP/IP, Winsock works only with Microsoft Windows applications and requires TCP/IP to be used on the LAN.

Socks offers the same type of application program interface, but is available for other platforms, such as Macintosh, Unix and OS/2 (that is, it is *cross-platform*). Also, Socks utilizes other transport protocols (such as Novell's IPX) from the workstation to a *proxy server* which then translates the IPX to IP. Therefore, the workstations can continue using whatever LAN protocol they always have used, and this is converted to IP at the gateway, which is then connected to the Internet (or whatever). In addition to the administrative benefit of not having to install TCP/IP, not running TCP/IP on desktop machines improves security since there is no way the desktops could be accessed from the Internet (which only runs TCP/IP).

To utilize Socks, application software must support the Socks interface. Unfortunately, for Windows applications the Socks interface is not the same as Winsock, so even Windows applications must support and be configured for Socks to utilize it, and the gateway.

See **ROUTER**, and **WINSOCK**.

Software Development Kit

See **SDK**.

SOHO
Small Office and Home Office

The name given to the group of (hopefully) purchasers who have small offices, either in an office building, or in their house. These people buy lots of stuff (computers, office equipment and supplies, and so on) that businesses used to. Manufacturers realize that they often need to advertise differently, or design products differently to sell to this important (and growing) market.

These people are often telecommuters, who work from home, and need fast, reliable and secure data communications to their head offices or clients.

Solaris

Usually considered to be Sun's newer Operating System, but Sun would say Solaris 1.*x* is SunOS 4.1.*x* (which has been around for a long time), and Solaris 2.*x* is Sun's newer and SVR4-based operating system.

Somerset

The Intel platform version of Solaris runs on the 80386 (and up) processors and uses parts of Interactive Systems' *Interactive UNIX*, which is derived from a *Big Endian* version of SVR3.2. Sun liked Interactive UNIX so much, they bought the company, and Sun still enhances and sells Interactive UNIX as a separate product (currently Version 4.2).

A current version of Solaris is 2.4, and it is available for both SPARC and Intel platforms. All important features are implemented consistently on these two platforms.

See **BIG ENDIAN, IBCS, INTEL, ONC, SUN, SUNOS, SVR4**, and **UNIX**.

Somerset

The company formed by the IBM-Motorola joint venture to develop the PowerPC processor. Named after the place where King Arthur's knights put aside their swords to join the Round Table (which was round so no one was at the head of the table). This Somerset Design Center, however, is in Austin, Texas.

See **POWERPC**.

SONET
Synchronous Optical Network

A synchronous data framing and transmission scheme for (usually single-mode) fiber-optic cable—hence the "optical" in the name. SONet defines an interface option for high-speed devices (such as ATM switches). SONet's transmission rates are based on multiples of 51.84 Mbits/s. This base rate (called OC-1) can carry any of the following:

▲ 672 DS-0s (voice conversations, or 64 kbit/s data channels)

▲ 28 T1s

▲ 21 E1s

▲ 7 T2s

▲ 7 digitized television channels (typical for submarine fiber-optic cables)

▲ 1 T3

In addition, any combination of these can be carried (as fits into the bit rate). The framing format includes capacity for an *order-wire* (a digitized-voice intercom for technicians to use), equipment control information, error detection, and framing and bit-rate matching.

The 51.84 Mbits/s rate is derived from the basic frame format of 810 bytes (formatted as nine rows of 90 columns of bytes each), which is sent 8,000 times per second. The data are sent one row at a time (starting at the top left), with each byte sent most significant bit first). The first 3 (of the 90) columns are used for SONet protocol overhead, as shown in the figure below. Section overhead is 9 bytes per frame, and is comprised of the bytes which are required for section elements (such as regenerators and other line terminating equipment).

```
              Column
           1    2   3 |<----------- 87 more columns -------------------->|
          -------------------------------------------------------------
Row 1 |  Section       |  |  |                                          |
Row 2 |  Overhead      |  |  |                                          |
Row 3 |_____        |  |  |                                          |
Row 4 |                |  |  |                                          |
Row 5 |    Line        |  |  |                                          |
Row 6 |                |  |  |                                          |
Row 7 |  Overhead      |  |  |                                          |
Row 8 |                |  |  |                                          |
Row 9 |                |  |  |                                          |
          -------------------------------------------------------------

       |<- Trans ->|<------     Synchronous Payload Envelope    ------>|
       |    port   |
       |  Overhead |
```

The 87 columns not used by the transport overhead comprise the *synchronous payload envelope* (SPE). One of the columns (of 9 bytes) in the SPE is used for path overhead.

Each of the bytes of transport and path overhead is reserved for a specific function—such as an orderwire byte (which produces a 64 kbit/s digitized audio channel) and a parity byte (to monitor the bit error rate). SONet overhead permits automatic identification of problems to the specific section (sometimes called a *span*).

Speeds up to 9.6 Gbits/s (OC-192) are currently standardized. An equivalent scheme for copper media (called STS-1) has identical rates, formats, and features.

SONet can be used to carry ATM traffic as well as any other type of traffic (for example, it can be a "faster point-to-point T1").

T1 and T3 are *plesiosynchronous*, since there is no central common clock for all signals. Therefore interconnecting (for example) T1 signals from different equipment often has the problem of *clock slip*, where the clock rates do not exactly match (typically, by a few tens of bits per second). One will be sending data faster than the other can receive it (and the other will not be supplying data as fast as the one needs to take it). This is a problem for voice (though the loss in voice quality is typically imperceptable), and a big problem for data. SONet solves this by supporting a pointer (to the end of the valid new data) for links that are running faster than the rate at which the source data is being supplied. For links that are running too slow to carry the supplied data, an extra byte is provided in the frame format, and it is used to carry this occasional extra data.

Good SONet products will provide a smooth clock rate for such slightly slow and fast data. The clock should match the long-term rate of the data—not the SONet rate (with jumps everytime an extra or missing byte of data must be accomodated).

Another advantage of SONet is that it can be implemented as a *dual ring* for redundancy (this is sometimes called *dual counter-rotating rings*, since the backup ring carries data in the opposite direction to the primary ring). Traffic travels around the backup ring to temporarily bypass the problem. The reconfiguration to using the backup ring causes a maximum of a 60-ms disruption to the traffic (though typically only 15 to 20 ms). This maximum is important, as longer disruptions may cause T1s being carried by the SONet to loose synchronization (causing them a longer service outage—until they resynchronize). In contrast,

switching defective T1 circuits to backup circuits must usually be done manually or using proprietary methods. SONet rings can be set for revertive or non-revertive switching. That is, does the path revert back to the original one after the fault is repaired (this may simplify administration, but result in another brief service disruption).

The ring architecture is also good for reducing the equipment requirements for interconnecting many geographic locations—only a single ring to all locations is requires, rather than many separate T1s (or whatever) between pairs of locations.

In addition to a ring architecture, SONet has a flexible *protection switching* capability, where one SONet channel can be a backup for 1 to 14 other SONet channels.

SONet is similar to SDH. However, SDH is used outside of North America, is based on multiples of 155.52 Mbits/s and uses the maintenance bits of the SOnet frames of data differently).

Common ATM and SDH bit rates currently used are shown in the table below (actually, OC-1 is seldom used, since it is so close to T3).

SONet		SDH	Data Rate (Mbits/s)	Number of Digitized Voice or 64,000-bits/s Data Circuits
Optical Fiber	Copper			
OC-1	STS-1	STM-0	51.84	672
OC-3	STS-3	STM-1	155.52	2,016
OC-12	STS-12	STM-4	622.08	8,064
OC-48	STS-48	STM-16	2,488.32	32,256
OC-192	STS-192	STM-64	9,953.28	129,024

Virtual tributaries are used for signals less than the OC-1 rate. An OC-1 can carry 7 VT-6s. A VT-6 can be comprised of 3 VT-2 (E1 signals) or 4 VT-1.5 (T1 signals).

Tributaries are also defined for FDDI, ATM (ATM does the 53-byte segmentation, SONet does the overhead and column stuff) and SMDS.

SONet rates higher than OC-1 byte-interleave the data from the individual OC-1 SPEs (this reduces the latency for the data).

SONet systems typically include one or more of the following components:

▲ *Regenerator.* This boosts the signal strength (and defines the boundaries of a *section* of a SONet connection). Typically, signals are transmitted at 0 or -2 dB, and receivers can receive signals down to -26, -30 or -34 dB. Fiber optic cabling has a typical attenuation of 1 dB per km, so there is typically about 30 km between regenerators. Up to 30 regenerators are allowed per path.

▲ *Terminal Multiplexer.* This terminates a *path* (so is sometimes called PTE—*path terminating element*), and provides a connection point for ATM, DS-1 and DS-3 signals. It is generally one end of a SONet connection.

▲ *Add/Drop Multiplexer* (ADM). This is in-line in a SONet ring, and provides ATM, DS-1 and DS-3 interfaces to add or terminate other SONet signals.

▲ *Digital Cross-connect System* (DCS). This can be the center (hub) of a SONet signals connected in a star-wired topology. Signals from one port can each be selectively mapped to other ports.

With these building blocks, the following can be built (listed in increasing order of complexity):

▲ Point-to-point connections—using a terminal multiplexer at each end, and (optionally) one or more regenerator(s) in the middle.

▲ Point-to-multipoint—using a terminal multiplexer at each end, one or more add/drop multiplexers in the middle (and perhaps some regenerators between those).

▲ Hub (or star-wired)—using a DCS at the center.

▲ Ring—using ADMs connected in a ring (up to 16 ADMs are permitted per SONet ring). ATM, DS-0 and DS-3 signals can be added and terminated at each ADM.

The scope of SONet connections are defined as *path* (from the point of entry of a signal to its exit), *line* (between multiplexing devices) and *section* (between signal regeneration equipment, which occurs all equipment except an optical amplifier). This is shown in the following figure.

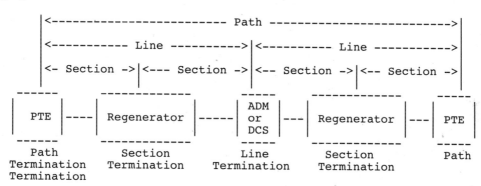

A major reason for the development of SONet was as a standard for the "mid-span meet" between equipment from different vendors.

SONet was initially developed by Bellcore in 1985 (who still make some of the relevant standards), it is now standardized in ANSI T1.105 (Rates and Format), T1.106 (Optical Parameters), T1X1.5 (OAMP Communications and Line Switched Ring) and T1.102 (Electrical Interfaces).

Synergy Semiconductor makes SONET transceivers. They have some information at *http://www.synergysemi.com*.

See **ATM** (*Asynchronous Transfer Mode*), **CARRIER**, **E1**, **SDH**, **STM**, **STS**, **T1**, **T2**, and **T3**.

SPARC
Scalable Processor Architecture

Sun's RISC-based processor family used in their workstations.

In an effort to make the processor less proprietary and more widely supported, Sun formed an industry group (including Amdahl, Cypress, Fujitsu, LSI Logic, and Texas Instruments) in which each vendor can design its own implementation of the chip. (This has not turned out to be a popular thing to do.)

The first SPARC processor was available in 1987, and had 50,000 transistors.

See **RISC**, **SPEC**, and **SUN**.

SPCI
Small PCI

An effort initiated by IBM to "develop an extension to the PCI local bus standard that would define a small PCI add-in card and connector aimed at meeting the nees of the small platform marketplace." That is, so you can get PCI card performance in a laptop computer.

Uses the same size cards as PCMCIA. The connector is also the same size, but has more pins (108 versus 68)—there are two rows of pins with 0.8 mm spacing.

Work began in 1994, and was initially also supported by Berg Electronics Inc. (they make connectors) and Western Digital, then Adaptec, AMD, Bell, Intel, AT&T, AMP and others. Adopted as part of the PCI standard in September, 1995. Initially, the interface only defines a 32-bit interface. A 64-bit interface is expected to be added in the future.

By supply voltage, three types of cards are defined. Cards can use 5 V, 3.3 V or both (called UNIVERSAL). *Keying* (plastic notches and tabs) is used to ensure that the wrong voltage card, nor a PCMCIA is not inserted into the connector.

Two styles of cards are defines. Style A has 5.5 mm height allowed for internal components. Style B has 10.5 mm allowed. Unlike PCMCIA, cards are not hot-pluggable (the system must be powered-off before inserting or removing cards). It is therefore expected that cards will typically be mounted inside devices (parallel to the main circuit board), with no covering over the components.

For SPCI cards to connect to the outside world, two types of card connectors are defined:

▲ 2 rows of 17 pins (each), spaced 2 mm apart.

▲ 1 or 2 rows of 41 pins (each), spaced 0.8 mm.

Initially, only 3 I/O options are supported for these card connector options: 9, 15 or 33 signals.

SPCI supports all the throughput, functions and signals of the original 120-pin PCI bus, except for 5 signals used for factory testing (these use a system called JTAG, which is specified in IEEE 1149.1).

See **BUS**, **PCI**, and **PCMCIA**.

SPEC
Standard Performance Evaluation Corporation

A nonprofit organization formed in 1989 to "establish, maintain and endorse a standardized set of relevant benchmarks that can be applied to the newest generation of high-performance computers." The goal is to enable the speed of different computer processors and system designs to be compared. Since the benchmark *source code* is available, it can be compiled and run on machines with different architectures.

The most frequently quoted SPEC benchmarks are as follows (these names are trademarked, so that they will only be used as defined and allowed by SPEC):

▲ *SPECint92*, which measures integer arithmetic performance, expressed as the geometric mean of the time required to run six integer-math-intensive application programs

▲ *SPECfp92*, which measures floating point math performance and is expressed as the geometric mean of the time required to run 14 floating-point math-intensive application programs.

Both results are expressed as the *SPECratio* —that is, relative to the time required to run the same benchmarks on a DEC VAX-11/780 minicomputer.

Also, while both benchmarks are very CPU-intensive (so operating system overhead and disk access time are not significant factors), the results are also dependent on:

▲ The size (and implementation) of the computer system's *Level 2 cache* (which may be different for different models of computer systems, even those based on the same CPU)

▲ The optimizations or efficiency of code generated by the computer system's compiler, since the benchmarks are distributed as C or Fortran source code

Therefore, because of a faster cache, more effective compiler optimizations selected, or a compiler that produces faster code, the same CPU, operated at the same clock frequency, will often be reported with different SPEC ratings—often by 10% or more.

There are other SPEC benchmark tests:

▲ *SPECrate_int92* and *SPECrate_fp92* are the same benchmark tests, but multiple copies (the benchmark results will quote how many) are simultaneously run (using a multi-tasking operating system). The number of times the benchmark tests can be completed in a week (yes, a *week*) is expressed as the ratio to the number that a DEC VAX-11/780 could complete in a week. The test attempts to show the multiuser characteristics of a computer—again, reflecting more real-world results, since some computers share their CPU time among many users.

▲ Tests for frequently used (at least by software developers) UNIX commands

▲ Tests of NFS performance

The previous *SPECint89* and *SPECfp89* benchmarks were replaced, since they:

▲ Ran too quickly (making small timing errors more significant)

▲ Had a total of only 10 application programs (it was thought that they did not include a wide enough range of types of computations)

▲ Had some portions that could be optimized to the point of becoming meaningless

In August 1995, SPEC released a new suite of benchmarks to prevent some "optimizations" some manufacturers had developed to enhance their processor's ratings. The new benchmarks are described below.

▲ CINT95, which measures integer math performance. It consists of 8 programs.

▲ CFP95, which measures floating-point math performance. It consists of 10 programs.

A feature of the new programs are that they are larger than the previous programs—purposely too large to be held in a processor's cache (so a computer system's main memory performance will be part of the benchmark as well). Also, the testing tools that are part of the benchmark software ensures that results are the median of a series of runs (rather than a single result from a run that went unusually well).

The *SPEC*int_base95 and *SPEC*fp95 are *baseline* measurements. These are the same benchmark tests but with *conservative optimization*. This means that the compilers are not be optimized differently for each application program in the benchmark (that is, the same compiler optimizations must be selected for all benchmark tests). The intent is to provide results that are closer to what actual users would see, rather than best-case results.

A problem with the SPEC series of benchmarks is that they require the UNIX operating system to run. If this is not the operating system which an end user will be running, then the benchmark results will not be as meaningful as they could be.

SPEC membership is composed of over 33 organizations in the computer industry, including semiconductor manufacturers, system manufacturers, and academic institutions. SPEC can be contacted at *spec-ncga@cup.portal.com*.

A copy of the SPEC FAQ is at *http://performance.netlib.org/performance/html/specFAQ.html* (that WWW server has lots of other interesting computer performance–related information too).

More SPEC results (than are shown in the table below) are available by ftp from *ftp.cdf.toronto.edu* in /pub/spectable (or try using your WWW browser specifying a URL of *ftp://ftp.cdf.toronto.edu/pub/spectable*).

Processor (L2 Instruction and Data Cache Size in kbytes)	Speed (MHz)	SPECint92	SPECfp92
DEC Alpha AXP 21066	233	94	110
DEC Alpha AXP 21164	266	302	452
	300	341	513
HP PA-RISC 7100 (64/64)	50	37.1	71.8
HP PA-RISC 7100 (256/256)	99	109.1	167.9
	125	132.8	195.7
HP PA-RISC 7100LC	64	66.6	96.5
	80	83.5	120.9
	100	100.1	137.0
HP PA-RISC 7150	99	109	168
	125	136	201

(table continued on next page)

Processor (L2 Instruction and Data Cache Size in kbytes)	Speed (MHz)	SPECint92	SPECfp92
HP PA-RISC 7200		250[a]	
HP PA-RISC 8000	200	360	
Intel 486SX	33	14.9	[b]
Intel 486DX2	25/50	30.1	13.9
Intel 486DX2	33/66	39.6	18.8
Intel DX4	100	51.4	26.6
Intel Pentium (256)	60	70.4	55.1
	66	78.0	63.6
Intel Pentium (512)	25/75	89.1	68.5
	60/90	106.5	81.4
Intel Pentium (1,024)	110.1	84.4	
Intel Pentium (512)	66/100	118.1	89.9
Intel Pentium (1,024)	121.9	93.2	
Intel Pentium (512)	60/120	133.7	99.5
Intel Pentium (1,024)	140.0	103.9	
Intel Pentium	133	155	116
	180	200[a]	
Intel Pentium Pro	66.5/133	200[a]	
	166	250	
	231	350	
Motorola PowerPC 601	80	85	105
Motorola PowerPC 601v	100	105	125
	120	125	150
Motorola PowerPC 602	66	40	
	80	40	
Motorola PowerPC 603	66	60	70
	80	75	85
Motorola PowerPC 603e	100	120	105
	133	160	140
Motorola PowerPC 604	100	160	165
	133	200	200
	150	225	250
Motorola PowerPC 620	133	225	300
	200	330	410
Sun microSPARC	50	26.4	21.0

(table continued on next page)

Processor (L2 Instruction and Data Cache Size in kbytes)	Speed (MHz)	SPECint92	SPECfp92
Sun microSPARC-II	60	47.5	40.3
	85	65.3	53.1
	110	78.6	65.3
Sun microSPARC-IIe	125	85	70
Sun SuperSPARC	50	76.9	81.8
	60	98.2	107.2
Sun hyperSPARC	75	125.8	121.2
	125	131.2	153.0
Sun UltraSPARC-1	167	240	350

a. Estimated.
b. Has no floating-point unit.

Some SPECint95 and SPECfp95 results are shown below.

Processor (L2 Instruction and Data Cache Size in kbytes)	Speed (MHz)	SPECint95	SPECfp95
DEC Alpha AXP 21164	600	18.0	27.0
HP PA-RISC 8000	160	10.4	16.3
	180	11.8	20.2
Intel Pentium Pro (256)	200	8.20	
Intel Pentium II (512)	233	9.49	
	266	10.8	
Motorola PowerPC 604	233	9.41	6.01
Motorola PowerPC 604e	233	9.24	5.75

SPEC is at *http://www.specbench.org/*.

See **ALPHA AXP**, **CACHE**, **ICOMP**, **INTEL**, **FLOP**, **MIPS**, **NFS**, **PA-RISC**, **PC**, **POWERPC**, **SPARC**, **SUPERSCALAR**, and **TPS**.

Speedo

A font technology from Bitstream, Inc. (and has nothing to do with ball-hanger bathing suits). Font file functions are shown in the following table.

Font Filename Extension	Function	Comments
*.SPD	Scalable font	Can be used in Windows using Bitstream's Facelift font-rasterizing software
*.BCO	Bitmapped (non-scalable) fonts	
*.CSD		
*.TDF		

Bitstream has a WWW server at *http://www.bistream.com*.

Competes with PostScript and TrueType.

See **BITMAP FONT, FONT, OUTLINE FONT, POSTSCRIPT PAGE DESCRIPTION LANGUAGE**, and **TRUETYPE**.

SPF
Shortest Path First

The routing algorithm used in OSI.

Each node determines its immediate connectivity and broadcasts this information to all other nodes, which then build their own topological map of the entire network so that they can determine the best routes independently.

Better than distance-vector (the most common current method) for larger networks, since SPF finds alternate routes faster and is more secure, and the entire network learns of connectivity changes faster (that is, it *converges* faster).

See **LINK STATE, OSI**, and **RIP**.

SPID
Service Profile Identifier

A number assigned by your telephone company, to each ISDN B channel. While it can technically be any 20-character string, typically telephone companies require it to be the full 10-digit telephone number for the B channel, followed by some combination of two to four 0s and 1s. You usually need to enter this number as part of configuring your ISDN equipment (or else it won't work).

The purpose of the SPID is to uniquely identify each of the devices and their capabilities on an ISDN BRI—since a single BRI can support up to 8 physical devices, and up to 64 different telephone numbers. And (for example), some devices can make or receive only data, only voice, or both types of calls. Incoming ISDN calls from the telephone network address specific ISDN devices using the SPID.

"SPID" rhymes with bid.

See **ISDN**.

Spoofing

A technique often used to get a network device (which was not designed to work over a WAN) to work over; a slower or larger network than originally intended, or over a switched WAN connection (such as ISDN).

For LANs with *polling* (continuously asking devices if they have data to send), the technique usually involves *local polling* and *acknowledgments* (also called *local termination*). In this case, a fake acknowledgment to polls is created by the local device and the polls are recreated at the remote device so that the polls don't load the WAN and the acknowledgments arrive fast enough.

For LANs with periodic broadcasts (such as Novell NetWare's RIPs and SAPs, or IP's RIPs), the technique usually blocks the broadcasts from going over WAN, but recreates them at the far end of the link. *Triggered updates* (best for networks with few changes, such as smaller LANs) are only sent when there is a change (such as a new file server being started, or a print server going down). These change the content of the broadcasts being recreated at the remote network(s). *Piggyback updates* are sent only when the WAN link is reestablished (for data transfer). This technique is usually used for larger networks, where changes are frequent.

A good and useful implementation of spoofing will support all types of periodic messages for all protocols to be supported. For example, for NetWare IPX support, the spoofing (typically implemented in routers) will locally generate the following.

▲ *Serialization packets*, which are sent by servers, and contain the software's (hopefully unique) serial number, other servers can discover whether their software has been illegally copied and used elsewhere on a network.

▲ SPX acknowledgements.

▲ Replies to the GetNearestServer requests, which are sent when each user logs-in.

▲ Keep-alive messages (typically generated every minute when a workstation has no other traffic to send).

See **DLC**, **DLSW**, **DLUR AND DLUS**, **IPX**, **LLC2**, and **RIP**.

SPOOL
Simultaneous Peripheral Operation On Line

Another one of those acronyms that may have been made up after the term was already in use—like ping.

Often used to mean that something (such as a print job) is *queued* (temporarily stored in a disk file so that many users can share a resource "simultaneously") until the peripheral (often a printer) is available (finished printing the previous job or finally has been powered on or has more paper loaded).

In the old mainframe days (before large disks were popular—that is, inexpensive), this spooling was to a reel of $\frac{1}{2}$-inch-wide magnetic tape. Since this is a spool of tape, perhaps that is the original source of the name.

See **PING**.

SPX
Sequenced Packet Exchange

An optional (and used by only a few applications, such as print servers and RConsole) Novell NetWare protocol layered on their IPX that supports connection-oriented data transfer and window sizes larger than 1.

See **IPX** and **NCP1**.

SQL
Structured Query Language

An English-like (as long as you talk like a programmer), ASCII text, standardized language that is used to define and manipulate data in a *database server*.

The format of the requests is standardized, but the APIs that are used to generate the queries are not part of the SQL standard. Also, most database vendors provide desirable nonstandard SQL extensions (making SQL implementations less portable still).

The four main data manipulation statements are:

▲ Select (retrieve data)

▲ Delete

▲ Update

▲ Insert

Data are stored in two-dimensional *tables* (each *database record* being a *row* in the table). Tables can be *joined* (according to their *keys*) on the fly, as needed to service queries.

A typical query could be the following:

Select *Temperature, Pressure* From *Table_3* Where *Temperature < 160*

SQL database suppliers usually provide an API that provides application programmers with the interface they need to submit these queries to a database (which is usually elsewhere on a LAN or WAN). For example, two of the industry-leading SQL database software suppliers are Oracle Corporation and Sybase, Inc., which have Pro*C and OpenClient, respectively.

An *atomic* (smallest useful) sequence of data manipulations (terminated by a commit statement) is called a *transaction*.

A good SQL implementation will automatically *roll back* an uncompleted transaction (a less-good implementation may require the application program to check a *transaction log* at start-up and reverse the first steps of uncompleted transactions).

Application programs usually make use of SQL database servers utilizing *embedded SQL*, in which a high-level language (such as C or FORTRAN) is used to generate the SQL statements.

Call it "sequel" (not "s, q, l") if you want any respect from programmers.

Initially developed by IBM Research in the 1970s. First standardized as NIST FIPs 127 in 1987, then as ANSI X3.135 in 1989.

SQL2

The SQL standards home page is at *http://www.jcc.com/sql_stnd.html*. Oracle Corporation and Sybase, Inc., have WWW servers at *http://www.oracle.com* and *http://www.sybase.com*, respectively.

See **API**, **CLIENT/SERVER**, **DBA**, **ODBC**, **LAN**, **OLTP**, **PORTABILITY**, **SQL2**, **WAN**, and **XBASE**.

SQL2
Structured Query Language 2

A new version of SQL that, among other changes, provides enhanced error reporting and troubleshooting support, as well as new data types, such as bit. To reduce SQL's problematic nonportability due to proprietary vendor extensions, it includes three defined levels of conformance: *entry* (similar to the current SQL), *intermediate*, and *full*.

See **SQL**.

SRAM
Static Random Access Memory

A type of computer memory that remembers stored data until the power is turned off (that is, it is *volatile*), or until new data is written to the memory. The *static* is in contrast to *dynamic*, in that the memory does not need to be periodically refreshed.

SRAM is much more expensive, but has a much faster access time than DRAM. SRAM is typically used for a computer's Level 1 (which is usually part of the processor die) and Level 2 cache (which is typically external to the processor, and SRAM is used for both the L2 cache RAM itself, and the associated *Tag SRAM* which is used to identify what is cached in the cache RAM). DRAM is typically used for the main memory (that is, for your "64 Mbytes of RAM").

Asynchronous SRAM used for cache memory typically supports a burst of 3-2-2-2 or 4-2-2-2 on a 66 MHz memory bus. This allows 2 cycles to present each half of the accessed memory location, and 1 or 2 cycles to access the memory. The three subsequent accesses (if they are for the sequential memory locations) require only 2 cycles (one to check whether the requested data is in the cache, and the other to retrieve it).

The newer *synchronous SRAM* has a faster access time (typically 7 or 8 ns) than asynchronous SRAM (which usually has an access time of as fast as 12 or 15 ns) because it can latch a memory address to be accessed, and begin retrieving the data while outputting the previously-retrieved data. Synchronous SRAM is becoming popular for Level 2 cache, and will run at the memory bus speed of (for example) 66.5 MHz for a 133 MHz Pentium, with a burst of 2-1-1-1.

See **CACHE**, **DRAM**, and **RAM**.

SRB
Source Route Bridging

The type of bridging that is used in Token Ring networks. The sender determines the best route to the destination. This usually is done by first broadcasting (along all possible paths) a request for the destination to respond (this is called a route discovery frame). The path taken by the fastest round-trip response is the path that is used for subsequent communication (even if that path later becomes slower than others, because of network loading, for example).

See **REMOTE BRIDGE** and **TOKEN RING**.

SSA
Serial Storage Architecture

A high-speed method of connecting disk, tape and CD-ROM drives, printers, scanners and other devices to a host computer. Competes with SCSI (and even can use SCSI commands, to make it easier for vendors to adopt SSA), but offers many additional features, such as those listed below:

▲ Serial communications, so that much smaller connectors can be used. This should reduce costs. Also, a fibre optic cable option is available, allowing much greater distances.

▲ Actual data transfer on the cable is at 200 Mbits/s, using fibre channel's 8B/10B encoding. This encodes 8 bits of user data as 10 bits on the media. The reason for the additional bits is to provide data transparency, with start and end delimeters, and DC balance (which is important for coupling the signal through transformers). The user bit rate is therefore 160 Mbits/s, which is 20 Mbytes/s. Since data transfer is full-duplex, this is sometimes called 40 Mbytes/s.

▲ Devices are typically dual-port, to support strings of up to 129 nodes, and rings of up to 128 nodes. Since each connection between devices is a point-to-point link (unlike SCSI, which is a shared bus), multiple messages can be one a string at a time, and devices can communicate in different directions over a loop simultaneously. Therefore, SSA is sometimes described as running at 80 Mbytes/s.

▲ Using switches (which can have up to 96 ports each), multiple loop configurations can be built with a theorectical maximum of over 2 million nodes.

▲ A link layer of software provides flow control (to ensure that a sender does not send faster than the receiver can receive) and error correction (through the use of sequence numbers, a 4-byte CRC and time-outs and retransmissions).

▲ Using shielded twisted pair cabling, cable lengths can each be up to 20 m. The signals require 2 pairs of electrical connections—1 pair for transmit, and the other pair for receive. There is also a logic ground and optional chassis ground (often used for the shield connection).

▲ When used internal to a computer, there are three types of connections defined. A 6-contact connector is used for the actual communication. A optional 10-contact connector is used for features such as activity LEDs, synchronization, fault indication and factory testing (many of these signals are not standardized). A 16-contact connector is used to supply power to the device (3.3, 5 and 12 V DC), and to indicate power failure (at least 10 ms before the power fails).

▲ When used for peripherals external to a computer, a miniature DB-9 connector is used. It is similar in shape, but smaller than the DB-9 connector often used for the COM ports on a PC. A flatter version of an 8-pin modular jack ("RJ-45") can also be used, and is called an HSSDC connector. The signals on this connector are the 2 pairs for the transmit and receive, plus logic ground and optinally a chassis ground and a 5 V DC at up to 1 amp, to power the peripheral.

▲ Using optical fibre, cables lengths can be up to 680 m.

▲ For device addressing, each device gets a factory-assigned unique ID. One node is manually designated the master node.

▲ There is no bus contention, and no need for bus arbitration, since all links are point-to-point (1 transmitter and 1 receiver).

SSA was initially developed by IBM as a proprietary disk drive interface for their 9333 I/O channel, but was proposed to be an option for SCSI-3 in 1991 (so SSA is sometimes called serial SCSI). IBM offers an SSA option for the disk drive interface on their RS/6000. In 1994, the development of the standard was turned over to ANSI, and in 1995 SSA was assigned to ANSI's X3T10.1 group.

The Serial Storage Architecture Industry Association has a web server at *http://www.ssaia.org*. Other information is at *ftp://ftp.symbios.com/pub/standards/io/x3t10.1*.

See **CRC**, **RAID**, **S8B-10B**, and **SCSI3**.

SSL
Secure Sockets Layer

A standard initially developed by Netscape Communications for providing secure WWW (and other applications, such as mail, ftp, and telnet) service over the Internet. However, SSL was developed primarily for handling commerce (payments) over the Internet.

Uses both RSA's *public-key encryption* and their secret key RC4 encryption for all traffic on specified TCP/IP ports. Both methods are used for the same reasons that they are in PGP—public key encryption methods encrypt and decrypt 1,000 to 10,000 times slower than private key methods. This makes public key systems best-suited for short messages, such as authentication and secret key distribution.

SSL version 2.0 provides the following features:

▲ encryption (and therefore integrity), though only a 40-bit encryption key is used (so that it can be exported), and some consider this too short to provide a useful level of security

▲ authentication, though only server authentication is provided, so the server does not have assurance of who the user really is

Netscape requires that companies incorporating SSL 2.0 into their products pay a licensing fee to use the technology. Also, you need a digital ID (certificate) from a *certification authority* (such as Verisign) to use SSL.

SSL 3.0 has additional features, such as authentication of who the client is.

The SSL specification is at *ftp://ftp.psy.uq.oz.au/pub/Crypto/SSL/*. Verisign is at *http://www.verisign.com*.

An alternative method is Secure-HTTP (S-HTTP), which is used to encrypt specific WWW documents (rather than the entire session).

See **AUTHENTICATION**, **ENCRYPTION**, **PGP**, **RSA**, **SHTTP**, **TCP**, **TERISA SYSTEMS INC.**, and **WWW**.

SST
Spread Spectrum Transmission

A form of digital radio communications that trades off speed for improved reliability (immunity to noise and interference).

Originally developed by the military, since it can be made to be very resistant to *jamming*, which is the enemy transmitting at high power on your frequency to disrupt your radio communications.

SST typically uses one of the ISM frequency bands. These can be used without obtaining licenses, so long as certain rules are followed. For example, the maximum transmit power is 1 watt.

The *frequency hopping* method continuously changes the frequency of the carrier signal (about every 10 bit-times—though some expensive military *fast-hopping* systems can hop frequencies faster than the bit rate), in a pattern known to both the sender and the receiver. The pattern can be dynamically changed to avoid detected noisy frequencies. Most important, by using different frequency hopping patterns (*hopping sequences*), several pairs of conversations can simultaneously use the same bandwidth (range of frequencies over which the frequency hops).

So that many users can share the same bandwidth with little interference with each other, the U.S. FCC requires the following for frequency hopping SST:

▲ The transmitted signal bandwidth (while dwelling at one frequency) is limited to 500 kHz (at 900 MHz) and 1 MHz (at 2.4 GHz).

▲ The total RF bandwidth available is divided into 1 MHz channels, and transmitters cannot dwell in a channel for more than 400 ms every 20 seconds (at 900 MHz) or every 30 seconds (at 2.4 GHz). Typical systems hop every 100 ms.

▲ The frequency hop pattern must include at least 50 channels (at 900 MHz) or 75 channels (2.4 GHz).

Perhaps the most interesting point about the frequency-hopping method is that it was invented by the 1930s-era (especially that one in 1933) movie actress Hedy Lamarr (who learned about radio from her first husband) and music composer George Antheil. In the hope that the technology could be used for torpedos, to help the war effort, they gave the patent (which was awarded in 1942) to the U.S. government—and they received no payment or profit.

The other spread spectrum method is *direct sequence*. Actual products typically have a range of up to only 250 m, but performance drops off more slowly with distance. In general, this method is:

▲ Usually performs better, and is more commonly implemented

▲ More resistant to the *multipath interference* which is common indoors (that is, the received signal interferes with itself, as it bounces off many surfaces between sender and receiver)

- ▲ Usually larger, more expensive to implement, and requires more power for a given level of performance

- ▲ More sensitive to external interference, and best for smaller networks (since fewer channesl are available, and multiple *access points* are usually not supported)

Direct sequence changes each one-bit to be transmitted into a many-bit (each bit is called a *chip*) pattern which is known to the receiver (and each zero-bit is transmitted as the complement of that pattern). The bit pattern (called the *spreading code* or *chip sequence*) may repeat every bit-time, or (more commonly) may be much longer. For example, the CDMA cellular telephone standard uses a pseudo-random sequence $2^{41}-1$ bits long. CDMA also uses:

- ▲ A *chip rate* (which is also called the *processing gain*—the rate that the spreading code, which in this case amounts to a pseudo-random bit pattern `exclusive-ored` with the data) of at least 10 (as required by the FCC), and up to 1,000 times the data rate (limited by the available RF bandwidth). This limits the data rate to 2 Mbits/s (when using the 900-MHz band) or 8 Mbits/s (when using the 2.4-GHz band). The faster the chip rate, the wider the bandwidth used by the transmitter, making it more immune to interference at specific frequencies, but resulting in a lower data rate.

- ▲ Only a portion of the available bandwidth per conversation, so that more than one conversation can occur simultaneously.

Actual products (which use the full 1 W transmit power—though battery-operated units may use less to conserve power) typically have a range of up to 50 to 300 m (perhaps 50 m through offices with drywall/sheetrock walls, and greater distances if there are only free-standing cloth partitions). Performance drops rapidly after the signal begins to fade.

Frequency hopping implementations have a typical user-data bit-rate of 0.25 to 0.6 Mbit/s, and direct sequence has a typical user bit-rate of 1 to 1.5 Mbits/s. Actual file transfers (which then depend on the protocol used and other real-world factors) may have actual user-data throughputs of only 200 kbits/s.

Traditional radio transmission (that is, not using SST) is often called narrowband transmission.

IEEE 802.11 is a standard for SST.

Proxim Inc. is major manufacturer of SST equipment for PCs, they are at *http:// www.proxim.com*.

See **S802.A11**, **CDMA**, **ISM**, and **PCCA**.

Stac, Inc.

A company that is big on data compression. Their method is the de facto standard for ISDN (BRI and PRI) connections. Similar to V.42*bis*, it usually has a best-case data compression ratio of 4:1.

In 1996 Stac created a wholly-owned subsidiary called Hi/fn, Inc. to market data compression and other communications-enhancing hardware and software solutions directly to equipment manufacturers. The Stac LZS compression scheme is therefore often called Hifn now.

Microsoft's competing, incompatible, and also proprietary compression technology is called Microsoft Point to Point Compression (MPPC).

Stac is at *http://www.stac.com*, and Hi/fn is at *http://www.hifn.com*.

See **CCP, DATA COMPRESSION, ISDN,** and **LZS.**

Standards

Standards are important to end users for the following reasons:

▲ They create documented interfaces between equipment. Therefore, other companies can then make test and diagnostic equipment. Also, more personell will be available that understand the technology, reducing staff and support costs.

▲ They ensure that vendors cannot keep customers captive, by keeping interface details proprietary. Captive customers usually perceive that they are not getting the best price, performance or service from vendors of proprietary systems and equipment (whether they really are or not).

▲ They create an international market for similar equipment, which can reduce costs (through competition and economies of scale), and facilitate international systems and networks.

Standards are usually one or more of the following.

▲ Long-established practices, proven to be good solutions to problems

▲ Documentation for the design, manufacture, procurement and testing of goods or services, to ensure quality and safety

▲ Agreements to ensure interoperability and compatibility for products from different suppliers

Many organizations produce standards with different mandates, authorities, and emphases. The following table lists some of these.

Group	Produces	Emphasis	Standard Designations	
			Format	Example
ANSI	American national standards	Standardization of existing industry standards. Coordinates U.S. voluntary standards system.		X3.135, X3.T9
ITU-T	Recommendations	International communications	*letter.numbers*	X.25, H.320
CSA	National standards of Canada (after they are approved by the Standards Council of Canada)	Health, safety, building and construction, and the environment	Canada/CSA-*standard-date*	Can/CSA-Z234.1-89
EIA	Recommended standards	Electrical and electronics	RS-*numbers-version* or EIA-*numbers-version*	RS-232-C, EIA-485

(table continued on next page)

Group	Produces	Emphasis	Standard Designations	
			Format	**Example**
IEEE	Standards	Development of new standards, which are the best technical solution, optimized for quality, maintenance, ease of maintenance and reliability	IEEE-*numbers.number*	IEEE-802.3
ISO	International standards	Promoting international trade, so standards are often minimum requirements to permit import	ISO *numbers*	ISO 7498
TIA	Recommended standards	Telecommunications	TIA-*numbers-version* or EIA/TIA-*numbers-versio n*	EIA/TIA-568

Standards however, also have a dark side. Standards mean sales to vendors, so they dedicate resources to creating standards that are easy for them to implement (especially if they own the patented technology specified in the standard), but difficult for their competitors. ADSL is an example of this. Conversely, this may encourage vendors to attempt to slow or prevent the approval of standards that would benefit their competitors (and end users!). SNMP v2 is an example of this. Vendors may promote the approval of competing standards, so they don't loose market share—but this creates confusion for end users, and fragments the market (100BASE-T and 100VG-AnyLAN is an example of this). Finally, standards may be approved before the real world is taken into account, created new versions of standards that have major differences. This results in quickly-obsoleted products, proprietary workarounds, and user (and vendor) frustration. ATM is an example of this.

Not involving vendors also is a problem. Users may create designs that meet all requirements, but cost too much (either in dollars, CPU time, or implementation complexity) to be feasible. OSI is an example of this.

Also, standards may specify *patented* technologies, in which case standards-setting organizations (such as the IEEE) require companies owning such patents to file a *letter of intent* showing that they will license the technology for a reasonable fee. The fee is negotiated and paid directly between the patent owner and the manufacturer. The IETF method for dealing with this issue is in RFC 2026.

Companies owning patents that are specified in standards may be obligated to collect such royalties; otherwise, the patent could be declared invalid (since the company is not enforcing it). The royalty may be included as part of the cost of purchasing a crucial IC needed to implement the technology, and the IC manufacturer would pay the royalty (or could be the owner of the patent).

Different standards organizations have different rules for who may be members, attend meetings and vote. Also the costs, and rules for how the voting process (what percentage must approve for a standard to be accepted), and how to deal with dissenting opinions and appeals are different for each organization.

Some standards bodies (such as the ITU) charge for the standards according to the number of pages in the standard—which some say influences the standards to be longer.

Obtaining standards documents is often the best way to verify details of a technology. While Internet-related standards (for example, all of the RFCs) are available at no cost over the Internet, most standards-setting organizations fund much of their work from standards sales.

Sources of standards are listed in the following table.

Standards Organization	Phone Number
ANSI	212-642-4900 (ANSI can also supply ISO standards)
EIA, ISO, ITU-T (CCITT), and TIA	1-800-854-7179 or 303-792-2181—for Global Engineering Documents, which supplies these (and many more, such as ANSI's) standards under royalty agreement with the standards organizations. Standards ordered through Global usually cost more, but arrive faster than if ordered directly from the standards organizations (then again, some standards organizations won't even deal directly with you).
CSA	416-747-4044
IEEE	1-800-678-4333 or 732-981-0060

Global Engineering Documents (owned by Information Handling Services) has a web site at *http://global.ihs.com*. You can search among over 20,000 standards by number or name, and find out the full name, release date, number of pages and prices for each standard. (They also have military standards, many of them concerning atomic weapons—try searching for fuze—but you have to call for pricing on those, I wonder who tracks who requests these standards). The Standards Council of Canada (*http://www.scc.ca*, telephone 1 800 267-8220) also has lots of standards.

All-encompassing references to on-line standards documents are at the site *http://www.cmpcmm.cc.com/cc/standards.html*.

Equally fantastic references to standards organizations are at *http://www.nssn.org/stds.html* and *http://dsys.ncsl.nist.gov/nssn/search/index.html*, and while you're clicking, try *http://www.dsys.ncsl.nist.gov/nssn/others/index.html*.

Some telecommunications references are at *http://ippsweb.ipps.lsa.umich.edu/telecom/telecom-info.html* , and there are still more at *http://www.rpi.edu/Internet/Guides/decemj/icmc/organizations-standards.html* .

Pacific Bell has some brief technical information and excellent cost information at *http://www.pacbell.com/Products/fastrak.htm*. Of course, the costs are applicable only for Pacific Bell's serving area, but a rough idea of relative costs is always an important thing to know when comparing alternatives.

See **CARRIER**, **COMPATIBLE**, **COMPLIANT**, **DE FACTO**, **DE JURE**, **IEEE**, **IEC2** (*International Electrotechnical Commission*), **ISO**, **ITU**, **ITUT**, **OCTET**, **PATENT**, **RBOC OR RBHC**, **RFC**, **SI**, **TIA1** (*Telecommunications Industry Association*), and **TSB**.

Stentor

An alliance of the nine major Canadian telephone companies, that collectively have about 90% of the market:

▲ Bell Canada (Ontario and Québec)

▲ BC Tel

▲ Telus Corp—which bought AGT Limited (Alberta Government Telephones) from the Alberta government and Edmonton Telephone from the City of Edmonton in 1995

▲ MTS Netcom (was called Manitoba Telephone Systems until 1997)

▲ SaskTel

▲ Maritime Telephone and Telegraph

▲ New Brunswick Tel

▲ Island Tel

▲ NewTel Communications (was called Newfoundland Telephone Company until 1996)

Stentor's purpose is to deliver national (such as maintaining the 7,000 km cross-Canada fiber optic cable based network) and international telecommunications solutions (since individual telephone companies are regional). Consists of several parts:

▲ *Stentor Canadian Network Management* is an unincorporated association of carriers, and is responsible for managing and monitoring the phone companies' interprovincial networks and their connections to the U.S. and Mexico. It is also responsible for handling the division of revenue among the members—which include the above nine telephone companies plus Telesat Canada (a full member) and Québec Tel (an associate member). Stentor's previous name (until March 1992) was Telecom Canada—which was previously (until the 1970s) was called Trans Canada Telephone System, which was formed in 1931).

▲ *Stentor Resource Centre, Inc.* provided product and service research and development functions for the nine telephone companies. It has these groups: Marketing and Development, Engineering and Research, and Signature Strategic Management. As of January 1, 1997, this was changed so that only Bell Canada, BC Tel and AGT Ltd. provide funding, control the organization, and comprise SRCI's board of directors.

▲ *Stentor Telecom Policy, Inc.* is the government relations advisory arm, providing national lobbying functions.

Stentor has ties to the MCI (for example, for its frame relay service) and to British Telecom (for international services).

Mobility Canada is the homologous affiliation of telephone company related wireless carriers accross Canada.

Stentor maintains a WWW server at *http://www.stentor.ca*.

See **CARRIER** and **TELEPHONE COMPANIES**.

STM
Synchronous Transport Module

SDH's 155.52 Mbits/s speed units. STM-4 is therefore 622.08 Mbits/s.

See **SONET** and **SDH**.

STP
Shielded Twisted Pair

The *IBM* Cabling System defined many aspects of the cabling infrastructure required for a *structured wiring sytem* in a building (up to then, building cabling was typically a disorganized mess). The IBM Cabling System defined several types of cable, which they called *Type 1* through *Type 9* (though I've never seen anything on what type 4 was), as summarized in the table below.

Type	Description	Use
1	22-gauge, 2 twisted pair, solid copper, 150 Ω characteristic impedance, with each pair individually foil shielded, with an overall braid shield	The *horizontal cabling* (in the walls and ceilings, between the data jack in an office and the wiring closet) in a building. This is standardized in ISO/IEC 11801.
2	Type 1 and 22-gauge Type 3, all in one jacket	Horizontal cabling, where the data and telephone pairs are in the same jacket (this was supposed to be easier to install, but was a big mess in the wiring closet).
3	22- or 24-gauge, 4 twisted pair, solid copper, 105 Ω, unshielded	IBM intended this to be used only for voice (your telephone), so they also call it *Voice Grade Media* (VGM), but many found that it often all you need for data applications as well.
5	Two strands of 100/140 μ (core and overall cladding diameter) optical fiber cable	Longer cable runs, or outdoor cabling.
6	26-gauge, 2 twisted pair, stranded copper, 150 Ω, with each pair individually foil shielded, with an overall braid shield	Patch cables (in a wiring closet), drop cables (from a workstation to a wall jack).
7	1 twisted pair, copper, 150 Ω, shielded	Rarely used.
8	26-gauge, 2 parallel pair (not twisted), solid copper, 150 Ω, with each pair individually shielded	Flat under-carpet cabling.
9	26-gauge, 2 twisted pair, stranded or solid copper, 150 Ω, with each pair individually shielded, with an overall braid shield	Flat under-carpet cabling.

The term STP usually refers to IBM's Type 1 cable. It is frequently used for Token Ring LAN cabling.

When the IBM Cabling System was first released in 1984, it specified the cable's electrical characteristics for frequencies of up to 20 MHz—which was adequate for all uses then required or envisioned. When IBM added the specifications necessary for Type 1 and 2 cables to support the much higher bit rate (125 Mbits/s—and therefore higher frequency components) of FDDI, these cables were called Type 1A and 2A.

Now that IBM does not scare users into thinking that STP is required to provide reliable data communications, it is not very popular for new installations because of its:

▲ Higher cost for cable and connectors (much more complex than those for UTP)

▲ Larger size of cable and connectors (compared to UTP)

▲ Longer installation time for connectors (compared to UTP)

▲ Additional problems of *ground loops*, where the ground voltage at each end of a cable run is different, causing current to flow in the cable's shield, which creates a magnetic field, which in turn induces current (noise) into the same cable that the shield was supposed to protect!

Also, while some may say that STP cable provides a higher-quality signal, STP cable runs are still limited to 100 m runs (same as for UTP) by EIA 568 (the *Commercial Building Telecommunications Wiring Standard*). Also, STP is limited to use for data communications for IBM computers and Token Ring communications—that is, there is no standard for STP for ISDN, Ethernet, and analog telephone (but there is for UTP).

STP cabling uses an IBM *universal data connector* (for wall plates and hubs) or a DB-9 connector (for the back of PCs, since the IBM universal data connector is too wide).

See **CABLE, CONNECTOR, NEXT, FIBER, TOKEN RING,** and **UTP.**

Structured Query Language

See **SQL** and **SQL2.**

Synchronous Transport Signal

STS

The standard for SONet data transmission over copper (usually coaxial) cables. The rates correspond to the SONet OC-*x* rates (so STS Level 1 is the same speed and bit format as OC-1, etc.).

See **SONET.**

su

A UNIX command (su) that enables someone knowing the root account password to log in as if he or she were another user. Once this person is logged in as the superuser, the command-line prompt changes from "%" to "#".

See **ROOT** and **UNIX.**

Subnet Bit Mask

To facilitate intra-network routing, a single IP network can be divided into many *subnets* by using some of the MS bits of the *host* address portion of the IP address as a subnet ID.

For example, Network 129.5.0.0 has 16 bits assigned as the network ID (specifically 129.5, in dotted decimal, which is 10000001.00000101 in binary) as it is a *Class B* address (the first number is between 128 and 192).

This leaves the lower 16 bits as the host address.

Using a *Subnet Bit Mask* of 255.255.255.0 (which in binary is 11111111.11111111. 11111111.00000000), specifies that the upper 24 bits (those that are set to a 1) are the network plus subnet address—that is, the 16 bits that we already expected *plus* the upper 8 bits of the host address. Therefore the network 129.5.0.0 (in this example) would consist of up to 254 subnets (129.5.*1*.0 through 129.5.*254*.0) of up to 254 hosts each.

This is useful for subdividing networks, for example, to reduce the number of stations that must receive broadcasts.

See **MS** and **IP ADDRESS**.

Subrate

A data communications access line that runs at less than the DS-0 (56,000-bits/s) data rate. Usually, several subrate lines can be multiplexed into a DS-0.

See **DS0**, **T1**, and **WAN**.

Sun

Multibillion-dollar (annual sales) maker of UNIX workstations and software (second fastest company to reach $1 billion in annual sales—Compaq Computer Corporation was the fastest—so far!). Scott G. McNealy is a co-founder, and is now chairman and CEO.

Sun's workstations have had several generations of hardware:

▲ The initial workstations (Sun 1 and Sun 2 product lines) used Motorola 68000 processors

▲ The next products used Intel processors (Sun 386i product line)

▲ The Sun 4 product line used a custom LSI (Large Scale Integration) processor

▲ The first SPARC-based product was the SPARCstation 1

Subsequently, there have been many other products, such as X terminals, really fast workstations, and multiprocessor-based devices that are intended as multiuser database servers and the like.

The announcement dates and speeds of the SPARC processors are listed below.

▲ MicroSPARC. The 50 MHz version was announced in October 1992.

▲ SuperSPARC. The 50 MHz version was announced in February 1993, the 60 MHz version in August 1993.

▲ MicroSPARC II. The 85 and 110 MHz versions were announced in October 1993.

▲ SuperSPARC II. The 85 MHz version was announced in January 1995.

▲ UltraSPARC I. The 200 MHz version was announced in March 1995, and 147 and 167 MHz versions in October 1995.

SunConnect

▲ UltraSPARC II. 250, 300 and 336 MHz versions were announced in January 1997, June 1997 and February 1998, respectively.

▲ UltraSPARC IIi. 270, 300 and 33 MHz versions were announced in January, January and March 1998, respectively.

▲ UltraSPARC III. 600 MHz version announced in October 1997 (as for most announcements, the actual product delivery dates are typically 2 to 8 months after the announcement date).

Sun has a WWW server at *http://www.sun.com*.

See **COSE, MOTOROLA, SPARC, SUNCONNECT, SUNOS, SOLARIS, OPENLOOK, OPERATING SYSTEM, OSF, UNIX,** and **X TERMINAL**.

SunConnect

A subsidiary of Sun that has a *port* (a version that runs on a different platform) of Novell's NetWare. SunNet Manager (SNMP support) is also a product.

See **PORTABILITY, SNMP,** and **SUN**.

SUNOS
Sun Operating System

Usually refers to Sun Microsystems' older UNIX-like operating system, which is based on BSD UNIX.

But officially, SunOS can also refer to Sun's (newer) Solaris operating system—Solaris version 1.*x* is usually the same as SunOS version 4.1.*x* (but only your Sun guru knows for sure).

See **SOLARIS, SUN,** and **UNIX**.

Super Density

See **SD**.

SUPERATM
Super Adobe Type Manager

A version of ATM that uses one of Adobe's two *multiple master* fonts to generate characters for fonts that are not otherwise available to the destination printer (or other display device).

See **ATM** (*Adobe Type Manager*) and **MULTIPLE MASTER**.

Superscalar

A processor (such as Intel's Pentium or NexGen's Nx586) that can execute more than one instruction per clock cycle by using more than one *instruction execution unit* (sounds rather serious to me), and a pipelined architecture.

The execution units may not be identical; for example, only one of the Pentium's two execution units (or *pipelines*) can execute floating-point instructions.

In a CISC processor, instructions require several steps (and clock cycles) to execute (for example; fetch the instruction from memory, decode the instruction to decide what to do, fetch any data specified from memory, execute the instruction, and fianlly write the results to a register or memory location). While this takes several steps, an instuction execution unit can have many stages so that while one instruction is being decoded the next one is being fetched. Having as many stages in the *pipeline* as there are steps to process an instruction allows an average of about one instruction to be executed per clock cycle.

All of this makes comparing the clock speed (to determine processing power) of different processors meaningless. The following table shows how superscalar recent processors are.

Processor Family	Average Clock Cycles per Instruction ($\leq$1 Is Not Superscalar)[a]	Instructions per Clock Cycle (>1 Is Superscalar)
DEC Alpha AXP 21164	0.25	4
Motorola PowerPC 604	0.25	4
Sun UltraSPARC-1	0.25	4
DEC Alpha AXP 21164	0.25	4
Motorola PowerPC 601	0.33	3
Intel Pentium Pro and Pentium II	0.33	3[b]
Intel Pentium and Pentium MMX	0.50	2 [c]
Intel 486	1.95	0.51
Intel 80386	4.90	0.20
Intel 80286	4.90	0.20
Intel 8086	12.00	0.08

a. For clock-doubled processors (such as the 486DX2), this is relative to the internal (faster) clock.
b. Intel calls this Superscalar Level 3.
c. Intel calls this Superscalar Level 2.

See **ALPHA AXP, ICOMP, INTEL, PENTIUM, PC, POWERPC, RISC,** and **SPEC.**

SVD
Simultaneous Voice and Data

Supporting (though for some methods, only somewhat) simultaneous dial-up voice and data communications between two parties. Usually refers to *single-line SVD*, which uses the same dial-up telephone line for voice (a normal interactive telephone conversation) and data (for example, sending a file or fax, using *electronic whiteboard* software) at the same time.

Several *classes* of support for simultaneous voice and data have been (informally) defined, as shown in the following table.

Class	Support for Voice and Data
0	*Out-of-band SVD.* Two separate circuits are established, one for voice and the other for data (for example, a 2B+D ISDN interface offers this).
1	One circuit is established, and the users somehow agree on when to switch between voice mode and data mode. This can be done currently, with standard fax machines (for example).
2	*Alternating* (or *analog* or *switched*) *SVD.* One circuit is established, and the equipment determines when to switch between voice mode and data mode—voice waits for the current data use of the line (sending a file or a fax) to complete, so this is not suited to continuous streams of data (such as digitized video conferencing) or large file transfers. Radish Communications Systems' VoiceView equipment uses this method, which is built in to Windows 95 and licensed to Rockwell (for implementation in their modem ICs), Boca Research, and others.
3	One circuit is established, and voice and data can be carried simultaneously (either by splitting the analog bandwidth or, more commonly, by digitizing the voice and multiplexing it in with the data, by packetizing each). Typically, the data are transferred more slowly while the talking occurs (voice gets priority). MultiTech System's *Supervisory Protocol* (MSP, which supports its *Talk AnyTime* feature) and AT&T Paradyne's VoiceSpan both use the latter method.

Class 3 is preferable to Class 2 but costs more to implement (voice digitizing is required).

Digital SVD sends voice and low-rate video on top of data (promoted by Intel).

Sometimes called *voice/data integration*.

The future of this technology will likely be ISDN-oriented.

ITU V.70 and V.75 describe the handshaking used for SVD.

See **DSVD, EIA/TIA-232, ISDN, MODEM, MPMLQ, PCM, ROCKWELL INTERNATIONAL,** and **WAN.**

SVID
System Five Interface Definition

A *de facto* standard established by *UNIX* Systems Laboratories describing the functions application programmers can expect at the programming level.

A predecessor of POSIX. Originated features such as interprocess communication.

A copy of issue 4 of SVID is at *ftp://ftp.usl.com/unix-standards/svid/issue4/*.

See **DE FACTO, OPERATING SYSTEM, POSIX OSE, UNIX,** and **USL.**

SVR4
UNIX System Five Release 4

The version of UNIX that *UNIX* System Laboratories supports (or did, when it was still around).

Intel, Sun, and ACE (ha!—now there is something that never was) use it. It attempts to unify several of the major variants of UNIX, including AT&T UNIX System V, University of California at Berkeley BSD 2.0, and Sun SunOS.

Generally considered to be the mainstream of UNIX implementations.

See **ACE**, **BSD UNIX**, **SUNOS**, **UNIX**, and **USL**.

SVVS
System Five Verification Suite

A POSIX-conformance test suite.

See **POSIX OSE**.

SWATS
Standard Wireless AT Command Set

An extension to the *AT command set* to support wireless modems, such as those used with standard AMPS analog cellular telephones.

See **AMPS**, **AT COMMAND SET**, and **PCCA**.

Switched 56

A full-duplex, wide area, digital data communications service offering 56-kbits/s service on a dial-up basis.

Tariffs are usually the same as for voice calls: local calls are free (if local voice telephone calls in your area are free); long-distance calls are at standard per-minute voice long-distance rates.

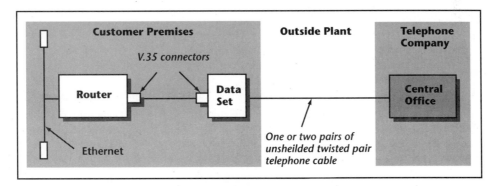

Switched 56-1

A *data set* provides the conversion between the telephone company's one or two pairs of wires (to the central office) and the customer's digital equipment (such as a router or video conferencing CODEC), as shown in the accompanying figure. The interface between the customer equipment and the data set is usually V.35.

Three *service types* are defined in EIA/TIA-596 according to the number of cable pairs (two wires are twisted together to make a pair) to the central office and the method of signaling the telephone number dialed. These service types are described in the following table.

Service Type	Characteristics	Comments
I	Four-wire	Developed and used by AT&T. Connects to something called a USDC in an AT&T 4ESS or 5ESS central office switch. 18,000-foot 26-gauge cable distance maximum.
II	Two-wire with in-band signaling	Call setup uses DTMF tones. Developed and used by AT&T. Also used by GTE. Not popular. 13,100-foot 26-gauge cable-distance maximum.
III	Two-wire with out-of-band signaling	Developed and used by Northern Telecom in its Datapath equipment. Licensed to many DSU manufacturers. Most popular technology. Supports switched 64-kbits/s clear channel service (in addition to an 8 kbits/s full-duplex channel used for call setup and signaling). Maximum cable distance to central office is 4.3 km (14,100 feet) on 26-gauge cable and 5.5 km (18,000 feet) on 22- or 24-gauge cable (repeaters can extend this). Usually limited to 56 kbits/s by central office equipment. Speeds of 9,600 bits/s and lower send each byte of data more than once (since the link between DSUs still runs at 64,000 bits/s). This provides *forward error correction* (using the redundant information, many errors can be corrected without retransmissions).

Note that for the cable distances given in the above table, it is assumed that the cable is *nonloaded* (also called *metallic*) cable. That is, the cable is simply a pair of copper wires with:

▲ No *loading coils*—these are *inductors*, and improve the voice frequency response (this is called *conditioning* the circuit, but is only beneficial for voice frequencies)

▲ No *amplifiers* (which are used to boost the signal, but only work for signals up to 3,000 Hz)

▲ No digitizing (such as going through a T1 circuit)

The two-wire service types use *Time Compression Multiplexing* (TCM, or "Ping-Pong"), in which a faster *half-duplex* communication speed (144 kbits/s for Type II and 160 kbits/s for Type III) is used, rapidly switching the direction, providing the appearance of *full-duplex* service.

DSUs of the same service type must be used at both ends of the cable. Since carriers use DS-0 channels to carry this traffic over their network, different types of DSUs can be used at each end of a data communications circuit. For example, the DSU at the customer side in City A must be compatible with the DSU used in the telephone company central office in City A. However, in City B, at the other end of the circuit, the pair of DSUs can be a different service type.

There are several ways to specify the number to be dialed, as shown in the following table.

Method	Works by	Commonly Used by
Manual dial	Manually dialing the number, using a keypad on the unit	People's fingers
RS-366	A separate connector is used to send the number to be dialed to the DSU	Video conferencing CODECs
V.25*bis*	In-band signaling over the synchronous link to the DSU	Bridges and routers
Hayes AT	In-band signaling, asynchronous data communications (either DSU subsequently handles asynchronous traffic or it switches to synchronous mode once a connection is established)	PCs

Switched 56 is mostly obsolete now that ISDN is widely available and supported (ISDN is faster, and supports neato features, such as Caller ID, call forwarding an other features mostly useful for voice calls, such as conferencing and call waiting). Also, Digital 800 service is an (optionally) much higher-speed alternative to Switched 56.

See **AT COMMAND SET, B8ZS, BONDING, CODEC, DIGITAL 800, DS0, DSU, FULLDUPLEX, HALFDUPLEX, INBAND, ISDN, OUTOFBAND, V.25BIS, V.35**, and **WAN**.

Switched LAN

A local area network in which, rather than all users sharing the media's bandwidth, a central switch forwards traffic between only those ports that require it. Each port of the switch may be connected to one of the following.

▲ A single computer (a heavily used file server, for example).

▲ A concentrator which shares that port's bandwidth among many users.

▲ Another switch.

The first switches were for Ethernet LANs and from Kalpana (which has since been bought by Cisco Systems). Now there are many suppliers—and some Token Ring and Fast Ethernet switches as well. Switches usually dynamically learn which MAC-layer addresses are on which ports, and forward messages only on the one port to which the destination is connected. *Broadcast* (to all stations) and *multicast* (to a group of stations) traffic is typically forwarded on all ports (this is sometimes called *flooding*).

In contrast, traditional Ethernet often uses a *shared media* concentrator (which is also called a *hub* or *multiport repeater*).

In addition to providing increased capacity, switches (rather than concentrators) must be used for many new technologies, such as full-duplex Ethernet (often called FDSE), 3Com's multimedia support (called PACE) and virtual LANs (called VLANs). *Multilayer switches* include many of the functions of routers, and are described in the entry for **ROUTER**.

While LAN adapters have built-in processing capacity to only receive frames addressed to them, multicast and broadcast traffic must typically be handled by the main processor of the receiving computer. Therefore, as the number of workstations and servers increases on a LAN (switched or not), the multicast and broadcast traffic received by all computers (and the

processing time they spend checking each of these frames to determine if they should be further processed or discarded) increases. Routers or VLANs are needed to reduce the size of these *broadcast domains* (the number of stations that receive multicast and broadcast traffic).

More attention is finally being given to the *latency* (the delay from first bit in to first bit out) of switches. Ethernet concentrators (also called *hubs* or *multiport repeaters*) have a latency of about 2 µs, since they basically only need to amplify (actually, *repeat*) the received signal.

In contrast, a bridge must receive the entire Ethernet frame (so it can examine the trailing CRC, to ensure the frame is not corrupted) before it reads the destination address to determine whether to *filter* (block) or *forward* the frame (to the destination port). Since this *store and forward* operation depends on the length of the packet, a bridge will have a latency of at least 57 µs to 1.2 ms (for the 64-byte to 1,518-byte Ethernet frame—plus the 8-byte preamble), plus the table look-up time of the bridge (perhaps another 50 µs to 300 or more µs).

Some Ethernet switches also operate in store-and-forward mode, since this ensures that corrupted packets are never forwarded to another LAN segment. Store-and-forward mode is also used by switches that have different speed ports (such as a switch with both Ethernet and Fast Ethernet ports), so that there is no chance that a frame is forwarded out faster than it is coming in. Switches operating in store-and-forward mode often have a latency just a few more microseconds (for example, 8 µs) than the duration of the received frame, since the address look-up is all done in hardware (bridges usually do this in software, since they do more functions, such as supporting the spanning tree algorithm for redundant connections between bridges).

There are other modes of operation supported by some switches, as listed below.

▲ Cut-through—this begins forwarding an Ethernet frame as soon as the destination address (which is the 9th through 14th bytes—including the 8-byte Ethernet preamble) has been received. This results in a latency of 11.2 µs (for the 112 bits which must first be read) plus the address look-up time. The fastest cut-through mode Ethernet switches have a latency of about 20 µs to 40 µs.

▲ Automatic (or adaptive cut-through)—these automatically change modes from cut-through to store-and-forward according to the number of corrupted frames on the LAN. If there are many corrupted frames, then the slower store-and-forward method is used.

▲ Fragment-free—this works in cut-through mode, but waits until 64 bytes of a frame have been received before deciding whether to forward the frame. This ensures that frames smaller than 64 bytes (which must be corrupted, since the minimum size for Ethernet frames is 64 bytes) will not be forwarded. Such illegally small frames (often called *runts* are one of the most common types of corrupted frames on an Ethernet, since they are often produced when two stations transmit at the same time (this is called a *collision*), and they both sense this and stop transmitting (this is required). Typical first-bit-in to first-bit-out latencies for switches operating in fragment-free mode is 64 µs.

If many switch ports are simultaneously transmitting to a single switch port (and all ports are 10 Mbits/s Ethernet, for example), then the switch will be receiving more data than it can forward. LANs may have bursts of such traffic that are too long for the switch's internal buffer memory to handle. One technique often used is called *backpressure*. In this case, the switch generates a fake collision indication (a *jam* signal) on the ports that are transmitting too much data. This prevents the stations on that Ethernet port from transmitting (this is a characteristic of Ethernet—if one station is transmitting or a collison occurs, then other stations must wait before tranmitting). Backpressure is not the best solution; it prevents all stations on that port's LAN segment from transmitting—even if the frame is to go to a port other than the switch's. Also, a transmitting station's Ethernet adapter will give-up trying to send a frame if it encounters 16 consecutive "collions" when it tries to transmit a frame.

Forward pressure refers to methods to give priority to an Ethernet port (such as that on a switch). For example, if the switch does not use the standard *binary exponential backoff* (which doubles the range from which a random number of timeslots to wait before retransmitting), then it could get priority over other standard devices.

An effort to standardize (as 802.5r) switched Token Ring (with just one Token Ring station per switch port) is called *Dedicated Token Ring* (DTR). Token Ring switching has the problem that there is no higher-speed Token Ring standard, so what is the high-speed connection to a backbone from a Token Ring switch. The answer (ATM for example) is more difficult than for Ethernet (which has 100BASE-T), which is one reason Token Ring switches are less popular than Ethernet's.

Kalpana (the manufacturer of the first Ethernet switches) has a WWW server at *http:// www.kalpana.com/kalpana* (they are now owned by Cisco Systems).

See **S10BASET, CISCO SYSTEMS, COS2** (*Class of Service*), **CRC, ETHERNET, MAC, PACE, REPEATER, ROUTER, TOKEN RING,** and **VLAN.**

Symmetric Multiprocessing

See **SMP2**.

Synchronous Data Transmission

When referring to data transmission, the characters or bytes of data are sent with no gaps between them. That is, they are synchronized in that there is a defined timing between them (that is, exactly no time at all between them). This is possible when all the data (a full frame) have already been prepared and stored—ready for sending.

The frame of data is prefaced by synchronization information: two or more sync characters for BISYNC and one or more flag characters for HDLC.

Once synchronization is achieved, one of the following methods is used so that the receiver can stay "locked on" to the transmitter's exact bit rate:

▲ A separate *clock* signal is made available (usually by the modem or DSU, on its EIA-232 or V.35 side)

▲ *Encoding* (such as *NRZI, Manchester,* or *Differential Manchester*) is used to combine both the clock and data into a single signal (usually by the modem or DSU, on its WAN side)

Synchronous data links usually use a protocol (such as BISYNC or HDLC) that provides error detection, error correction (usually through retransmission), and flow control.

See **ASYNCHRONOUS, BAUD, BISYNC, DSU, EIA/TIA-232, ENCODING, FLOW CONTROL, HDLC, MODEM, PARITY, SDLC,** and **WAN.**

Synchronous Function Calls

When referring to process to process communication within, or between computers, synchronous communications means that the requesting process waits for the response before it continues processing. Such synchronous calls are therefore also called *blocking*, since the calling process is blocked from further execution until the reply is received. When using synchronous calls, multitasking operating systems are therefore required so that the entire computer is not stuck waiting for a response (that may never come).

See **ASYNCHRONOUS FUNCTION**, and **WINSOCK**.

System 7

Apple's Macintosh operating system (called Macintosh System Software, Version 7.*x*, or simply Macintosh OS 7.*x*). Supports file sharing (*shared folders*) without a dedicated file server (any user can make their files shared—*published*).

See **OPERATING SYSTEM** and **TRUETYPE**.

System Five Interface Definition

See **SVID**.

System Five Verification Suite

See **SVVS**.

Système International d'Unités (International System of Units)

See **SI**.

T

T
Tesla

The metric (SI) unit for *magnetic flux density*, used (for example) to measure the *Electromagnetic Field* (EMF) radiation from computer video monitors. For comparison, the earth's magnetic field has a strength of about 50 μT.

100 nT (0.1 μT) is equal to 1 mG (milligauss).

Named after Nikola Tesla, who did a lot with electrical generators and transformers.

See **EMF**, **MPR-II**, **SI**, and **TCO**.

T1
Digital Transmission Rate 1

A point-to-point digital communications circuit that carries 24 64,000-bits/s (though sometimes only 56,000 bits/s are accessible to end users) *channels*, each of which may be used for data or digitized voice.

The bits on the T1 circuit are sent as *frames*, and each T1 frame of data is 24 *time-slots* (or channels—one from each user) of 8 bits each. That is, there are (24 channels × 8 bits/s per channel =) 192 bits of data per frame. This is called *time division multiplexing* (TDM) or *synchronous transfer mode* (STM), since the bandwidth of the circuit is split according to time.

The frames are sent 8,000 times per second, for an aggregate payload data rate of (192 × 8,000 =) 1,536,000 bits/s. A *framing bit* is required for synchronization (so that the other end can determine which bit is the beginning of each frame). This produces a total of 193 bits per frame, so the actual T1 bit rate is 8,000 bits/s more than this: 1.544 Mbits/s.

The user data rate will be 1.536 Mbits/s (64,000 × 24), if *clear channel* 64,000-bits/s DS-0 channels are supported (so the only overhead is the framing bit). If clear channel DS-0s are not supported (that is, each channel only supports 56,000 bits/s of user data), then the user data rate is 1.344 Mbits/s (56,000 × 24).

The framing bit cycles through a pattern, and by looking for that pattern, the receiver can be sure that it has found the framing bit, and synchronization has been achieved.

T1 was developed by AT&T Bell Labs, and the first commercial installation was in New Jersey in 1962. It was intended to be a method to improve the signal-to-noise ratio of multiplexed links—as compared to the analog *frequency division multiplexing* that was then being used. The type of framing (called "D1") that was first used (a framing bit pattern of 01010101...)

was too easily confused by repetitive digitized audio, such as the 1,000-Hz test tones that telephone companies commonly used (1,004-Hz test tones were adopted because of this problem).

Framing evolved to D4 (also called *Superframe* or *SF*) and then (beginning in 1979) to ANSI's *Extended Superframe* (ESF). D4 framing is immune to the 1,000-Hz problem, supports robbed-bit signalling (RBS—for *line supervision*), and is very widely deployed. The newer ESF framing also provides features such as continuous bit-error monitoring and an FDL.

This is called *channel associated signalling* (CAS), since each 64 kbit/s timeslot carries its own signalling information. In contrast, ISDN uses *common channel signalling* (CCS), since all channels, for example) share a single channel for supervision (for example, an ISDN PRI typically uses timeslot 24 for the signalling information for all the other 23 timeslots on the T1).

Line supervision involves signaling whether the telephones at each end of the link are *on-hook* (hung up) or *off-hook*. (Also, dial-pulse dialing is basically hanging up and going off-hook 10 times per second, so dial-pulse can be sent.)

Since this signaling on the *local loop* (the pair of wires from a central office to a customer's site) uses DC current (for example, greater current flows when the phone is off-hook, and some trunks reverse polarity to indicate certain functions), a different method of providing line supervision is required for voice conversations digitized and sent over a T1 link. (The digitizing process represents only frequencies from about 300 to 3,300 Hz and ignores DC.)

For voice circuits carried by T1 links, line supervision is often carried by using *robbed-bit signalling* (RBS). Every sixth and twelfth frame, the speech is digitized into only 7 bits rather than 8 bits. The eighth bits are called the A bits and B bits, depending on which frame in the 12- or 24-frame D4 or ESF framing sequence it is in. Combinations of these indicate on-hook, off-hook, and other supervisory information.

Instead of the intrusive and limited bit-robbing method, newer T1 circuits use the *Common Channel Signaling standard number 7*. This is a protocol running over a separate packet-switching network, which carries line supervision and other information—such as the phone number of the caller (so phone companies can offer Caller ID and other advanced services and charge lots of money for them).

The actual T1 line usually consists of two (often shielded) twisted pairs of copper conductors, which cannot have any *bridge taps* (that is, *T connections*, where a pair of wires is connected somewhere in the middle of another pair).

The *Line Build-Out* (LBO, which provides selectable attenuation) of the *Line Interface Unit* (LIU) of a T1 transmitter (for example, in a CSU) can usually be configured for *short-haul lines* (up to 655 feet), typically within a building, and *long-haul lines* (up to 6,000 feet), typically between buildings.

At greater distances than these a *T1 repeater* is required to boost the signal. Along rural roads, you will often see the weatherproof enclosures housing these—they are usually painted white or bare stainless steel (to reflect the heat from the sun) cylinders, about 30 cm in diameter and 50 cm high, mounted at waist height on telephone poles or short posts. They are typically installed every 6,000 feet (1.83 km)—something to check for next time you are cruising in the country. 6,000 feet of the 22-gauge copper-conductor cable typically used for T1 has an attenuation of 26.6 dB (at 772 kHz, which is the highest frequency component of a T1 signal), which someone decided is the the quietest a T1 signal should be. To allow for cabling within buildings, repeaters are usually installed within 3,000 feet of central offices and customer sites.

The actual cable used has a 100 Ω characteristic impedance, and is shielded twisted pair (for longer and outdoor runs), with each pair separately shielded. This cable is often called *T-Screen* or *ABAM*. It is typically terminated on a DB-15 connector, or an RJ-48 (sometimes called an RJ-48C) 8-pin modular jack, at a customer premises. This signal is often called a DSX-1. The pin-outs are shown in the following table.

ignal	DB-15 Pin	RJ-48 Pin	Comments
Tip 1	1	2 and 5	Transmit (to network)
Ring 1	9	1 and 4	
Tip	3	7 and 3	Receive (from network)
Ring	11	8 and 6	
Frame ground	2 and 4		

SA *Digital Access and Cross-connect System* (DACS, which is AT&T's name, the more generic term is *Digital Cross Connect*—DCC) can split out and recombine DS-0 channels into different T1 (or T3) circuits.

To ensure that the bits from each original T1 are running at exactly the same rate, a central (and super-duper accurate) 1.544-MHz frequency standard is maintained in Hillsboro, Missouri (which is at the geographic center of the U.S.), to minimize the phase difference of the signal throughout the U.S.

T1 circuits can be either of the following:

▲ *Wet*, which means that the central office provides 60-mA or 140-mA *span power* on the same pairs of wires that carry the data—to provide power to the CSUs or repeaters (this ensures that even if there is a local power failure at a customer site, the CSU will still provide valid ones density data). Such a *constant current* type of power supply is used to accommodate the very long cable distances. (The power supply automatically adjusts its output voltage to maintain this current—regardless of the cable length or number of repeaters—within design limits, of course.)

▲ *Dry*, which has no span power. T1 equipment outside the C.O. is powered by local power.

Current T1 circuits to customers are typically dry, and modern central office equipment doesn't get that upset if it does not receive valid ones density data (apparently, with not enough ones, central office alarms used to go off, and T1 repeaters could start oscillating and interfere with other circuits).

A T1 (or fractional T1) circuit is a digital point-to-point dedicated leased line service. It has only 2 ends, and you pay for it per month, whether you use it or not. It cannot be dialled-up—it always connects the user at one end to the user at the other end.

Channelized T1 refers to a T1 where each of the timeslots comes from a different remote location. A multiplexer at the carrier's central office combines (typically) 56 or 64 kbit/s dedicated circuits from the remote sites to a single T1 at the central site. This is desirable, since fewer data sets and connections to the carrier are required at the central site.

The term "T1" is usually used interchangeably with "DS-1," though strictly speaking T1 refers to the medium (the bit rate and the copper transmission system described above) and DS-1 refers to the bit format and framing.

T1 is also called *T-carrier*, or simply *carrier*. Some T1 characteristics are specified in G.733.

T1 is used in Canada and the U.S., but not Mexico. The similar European service is sometimes called E1.

See **ADSL, B8ZS, CSU, DS0, DS1, DSU, DSX, E1, ENCODING, ESF, FT1, HDSL, PCM, POTS, PRI, SEALING CURRENT, SONET, SUBRATE, T3, TDM,** and **WAN**.

T1C

A communications circuit that supports two T1s. The actual bit rate is 3.152 Mbits/s.

Rarely implemented.

See **T1** and **T3**.

T.120

ITU-T's series of standards for multivendor, multipoint document conferencing between several users.

Typically, one PC runs an application, and everybody gets to take control of it and the data. T.120 capabilities include the following:

▲ Sharing and editing (on your PC) a document in real-time

▲ Multipoint binary file transfer (everybody gets a copy of the file)

▲ The *still image* feature enables participants to transfer bitmaps and graphics, regardless of their type of computer or operating system, or conferencing software vendor

▲ Shared "whiteboards" (everybody gets to annotate and draw on a shared drawing)

▲ Multipoint communications, including camera and microphone control, and remote computer keyboard and mouse control as well

T.120's General Conference Control (GCC) is used by conferencing application software as a standard way of creating, controlling and terminating a conference. The General Application Templace (GAT) is used to ensre that all participants use a compatible subset of the protocols.

The document conference may be data-only, or may be part of an H.320 video-conference. Dial-up, asynchronous communication is initially supported, with other types of WAN connections to be supported in the future.

Additional information is at *http://www.csn.net/imtc/t120.html*.

See **H.320, MULTICAST,** and **PCS** (*Personal Conferencing Specification*).

T2
Digital Transmission Rate 2

A communications circuit that supports four T1s.

The actual bit rate is 6.312 Mbits/s.

Rarely implemented.

See **T1** and **T3**.

T3
Digital Transmission Rate 3

A communications circuit that supports 28 T1s, which is a total of 672 DS-0 channels. Each DS-0 carries 64,000 bits/s of data (which could also be a digitized voice conversation).

The actual bit rate is 44.736 Mbits/s.

The physical interface is as follows:

▲ Within buildings: usually two 75 Ω coaxial cables (one for receive, the other for transmit), each with a BNC connector. For RG-59B/U coaxial cable, the length can be can be up to 250 feet. Other types of coaxial cables support lengths up to 450 feet or longer.

▲ Outside: usually fiber-optic cable (two strands—one for receive, the other for transmit).

Like T1, the term "T3" is usually used interchangeably with "DS-3," though strictly speaking:

▲ T3 refers to the medium (the copper transmission system described above)

▲ DS-3 refers to the bit format

T3 circuits are very popular among those that can afford them (and need them), such as telephone companies (though SONet is becoming much more popular).

See **COAX**, **DS0**, **DS3**, **HSSI**, **PCM**, **SONET**, **T1**, and **WAN**.

T4

A communications circuit that supports six T3s (which is a total of 168 T1s, which is 4,032 DS-0s).

The actual bit rate is 274.176 Mbits/s.

Rarely implemented.

See **T1** and **T3**.

TA
ISDN Terminal Adapter

A device that connects a device with a non-ISDN interface (such as EIA-232) to an ISDN network.

Homologous to a modem, in that they are both the box you need to connect your computer's EIA-232 (for example) port to the wide area network. But it is not a modem, since there is no modulation, and there are no analog circuits.

Taligent

Using EIA-232 to connect to ISDN is usually a performance limitation, since many serial ports have a maximum speed of 115,200 bits/s, and they are asynchronous (so they add a start and stop bit for every 8 bits of user data). The maximum bits per second of user data is therefore 92,160. This is slower than a 2B ISDN connection, and too slow for a 1B connection with data compression enabled (so long as the data is compressed by at least 1.4:1—which is common).

Using an ISDN router (rather than a TA) is more flexible, in that it can connect more than one device to ISDN—but then you need an Ethernet port on each device. Also, the router must handle all the protocols you need. IP support is most common, with few vendors supporting Novell IPX and Apple AppleTalk. Using an Ethernet port connection from your equipment to the ISDN router (even if it the only device to be connected) has the advantage that it is not a performance limitation. Also, ISDN routers will typically have more a more flexible method for automatically establishing a second B channel connection.

Terminal adapters can also be internal devices (they plug directly into the PC's bus). If they use their own driver (as a LAN adapter would—rather than emulating a standard COM port), then there is typically no performance limitation. However, installation is typically more complicated as you then get into driver installations and interrupt assignments.

Some suppliers of TAs include Adtran, Inc (*http://www.adtran.com* and Ascend *http://www.ascend.com.*

See **S16550A**, **BRI**, **EIA/TIA-232**, **ISDN**, **LZS**, and **WAN**.

Taligent

The operating system software company formed from the Apple-IBM alliance to create an *object-oriented* (everything is supposed to be object-oriented these days) operating system. It is based on Apple's work on a portable operating system with the codename *Pink*. It was to run on PowerPC, 680*x*0 and Intel architecture processors.

The name comes from the words *talisman* and *intelligent*.

Like Kaleida, it eventually went into vaporware heaven (where software does what is was dreamt to do).

Taligent was officially closed, and any remaining activities transferred to IBM in early 1996.

See **APPLE/IBM ALLIANCE** and **PINK**.

TAPI
Telephony Application Programming Interface

Microsoft Corp.'s and Intel Corporation's method of integrating telephone services and computers so that your computer can control your telephone (first released in 1993).

The API supports functions such as:

▲ Controlling a telephone from a computer (dialing the telephone, answering calls, transferring calls, conferencing, and other functions you could do directly on your office telephone)

▲ Receiving caller ID information into a computer (so that a customer's name or account information can be displayed before the call is answered)

▲ Interfacing to fax boards, modems, ISDN adapters and other communications equipment

TAPI supports the data, fax and voice communications required to build application programs which are independent of the specific type of network used. For example, for modem communications, TAPI interfaces with *UniModem*, which is a device-independent *service provider* for POTS (the specific details of the type of modem used do not affect the application). An installed minidriver for each type of modem then translates these UniModem commands into the specific commands for each modem. Application programs therefore do not need to be modified for each type of modem to be supported.

A *desktop-centric* method (not a surprise, considering who developed the interface), in which a desktop PC (or Macintosh, or whatever) is directly connected to the telephone on the desktop. TAPI includes the specification for the physical link between the telephone (not the telephone's PBX) and its controlling computer (typically the telephone user's PC). The physical link is typically EIA-232, or a proprietary interface. The PC does not need to be LAN-connected (that's good), but every PC needs its own interface to its telephone (that's bad).

Emphasizes *first-party control*. That is, the telephone that is one end of the call (and not the PBX), controls the call. Also, once a call is transferred away, it is out of the original answerer's control (just like when you transfer a call—once someone else gets the call and you hang up, you don't know what they do with the call).

TAPI is part of Microsoft's WOSA, and TAPI support is available for Windows 95 (in Microsoft's Exchange software).

Competes with TSAPI, though TSAPI is server-based, rather than desktop-centric. TAPI is simpler, and is best-suited to smaller installations (perhaps less than 100 workstations), without complex requirements.

TAPI 2 supports native third-party control (so it can be server-centric, just like TSAPI), and supports sophisticated functions, such as *automatic call distribution* (ACD)—which is required for distibuting calls among telephone call center staff.

Stardust Technologies has an ftp server at *ftp://ftp.stardust.com/pub/tapi/* with lots of TAPI information.

See **CTI**, **DN**, **ECTF**, **FAX**, **SCREEN POP**, **TSAPI**, **WINSOCK**, and **WOSA**.

TAXI
Transparent Asynchronous Transmitter/Receiver Interface

An obsolete 100-Mbits/s ATM interface. It used multimode optical fiber, FDDI encoding and light levels, and SC fiber connectors, but has now been replaced by SONet.

See **ATM** (*Asynchronous Transfer Mode*) and **SONET**.

TCL/TK
Tool Command Language/Tool Kit

This programming system for building graphical user interfaces and systems controlled from them has become very popular over the last few years. It was initially developed for (and is most popular under) UNIX, but implementations for Windows are available, and implementations for Macintosh are in development.

Tcl (pronounced "tickle") is an interpreted (that is, not compiled) command language (also called a scripting language). It is:

▲ A programming environment

▲ A method of controlling and extending application programs; includes generic programming facilities such as variables, loops, and procedures

▲ Extensible (using the C language, end-users can add new features to the core library functions)

▲ Easy to learn, powerful, and has many sophisticated functions

Tcl code is called a *script*.

Tk is an X11 (X Window System) toolkit based on Tcl, providing a "graphical scripting language." It is a C language extension of Tcl, and it can be used for easily creating Motif-like graphical user interfaces under the X Window System, often without writing C code. In contrast, writing in C (which is much more difficult) is required to use the X Window System through other interfaces (most frequently Motif).

Together with an extension called WISH (Windowing Shell), Tcl/Tk can be used for facilitating application development by providing features such as:

▲ Linking applications and running subprocesses

▲ Hypertext and hypergraphics

Developed by John Ousterhout, beginning in 1988. He has since been hired by Sun and continues his work there.

Some WWW information is available at *http://cuiwww.unige.ch/eao/www/TclTk.html* and *http://www.sunlabs.com/research/tcl*.

See **GUI**, **MOTIF**, **PERL**, **SUN**, **X WINDOW SYSTEM**, and **UNIX**.

TCO
Swedish Confederation of Professional Employees

A 1992 standard developed by people concerned about the maximum strength of the *Electromagnetic Field* (EMF) emissions from computer monitors. The standard also includes the European NUTEK power-down specification.

TCO requires lower levels of emissions than the *MPR II* standard allows.

For ELF (*Extra Low Frequencies*), less than 200 nT, measured 50 cm around the monitor and 30 cm in front of it are allowed (since users, or at least parts of them, are often this close). In contrast, for MPR II, measurements are 50 cm in front of the monitor.

For VLF (*Very Low Frequencies*) the same levels as for MPR II are allowed.

See **ELF**, **EMF**, **MPR-II**, **T**, and **VLF**.

TCP
Transmission Control Protocol

UNIX's *connection-oriented* layer 4 (also called *transport*) protocol, which provides an error-free connection between two cooperating programs, which are typically on different computers, connected by a LAN or WAN.

That is, a connection must be established (using the `connect` and `accept` functions) before communication begins. This is similar to a telephone call—you can't just pick up the phone and start talking (well, you can, but you would be talking to a dial-tone—which some would consider a waste of time).

A TCP-based communication between programs is often called a *stream service* (or even a *reliable stream service*), in that the receiving program is guaranteed to receive all the data, with nothing corrupted, and no duplicates, and nothing lost, and in the same sequence as sent. The data will be received as a stream of bytes—the actual packaging (the number and boundaries of packets of data) of the bytes received may be different from how it was sent.

Expanding on that last sentence: if a sending process sends a packet with 100 bytes of data, it may be received as a 100-byte packet or as a 75-byte packet followed by a 25-byte packet. (I could go on for some time with more examples, but we'll just leave it at that.)

In any case, the receiving program does not see the packet boundaries; it simply asks (its TCP stack) for a specified number of bytes from the input queue, and up to that number of bytes is given to the receiving program, regardless of whether those bytes happen to span more than one incoming packet or not. The application protocol must therefore have a protocol for identifying the boundaries of the data structures exchanged (since the TCP protocol does not provide this service).

TCP/IP performs flow control by detecting if packets have not been acknowledged for more than about 1 second, and if not, then sending slower—because either the packets are being lost and will need to be retransmitted later (so why keep sending new ones), or the network is congested so slow down so the network does not get completely overloaded.

The TCP packet header has a 16-bit field for the *port number*. This identifies which process on the destination machine should handle a received packet (by convention, port numbers are always shown in documention in decimal). Some of the more commonly used port numbers are shown in the following table. Note that some connections use the TCP protocol, some use UDP and some can use either.

Service	Port	Protocol
ping echo	7	UDP
ping echo	7	TCP
FTP data	20	TCP
FTP control	21	TCP
telnet	23	TCP
SMTP	25	TCP
DNS	53	UDP

(table continued on next page)

Service	Port	Protocol
DNS	53	TCP
TFTP	69	UDP
finger	79	TCP
HTTP	80	TCP
POP, version 2	109	TCP
POP, version 3	110	TCP
NNTP	119	TCP
IMAP	143	TCP
SNMP	161	UDP
route	520	UDP
UUCP	540	TCP
NFS	2,049	UDP

A complete list of port numbers for a specific UNIX computer is in that computer's /etc/ services file (unless the computer is using NIS, in which case the local services file is ignored, and the information is obtained over the network from the YP services map.

The official list of port assignments is at *ftp://ftp.isi.edu/in-notes/iana/assignments/port-numbers*.

Up until 1992, the assignments of port numbers from 0 through 255 was specified in RFC 1340, and these were therefore called *well-known port numbers*. And the use of port numbers from 256 to 1023 were defined through their use by the UNIX operating system. Typically, only privileged user processes (such as system, also called root processes) can allocate (that is, bind) ports between 0 and 1,023. The use of port numbers from 1,024 through 65,535 are not controlled by the IANA, and on most computers are available for allocation by non-privileged user processes.

In 1992, the *Internet Assigned Numbers Authority* (IANA) expanded the range for their assigned port numbers to 0 through 1,023 (these are therefore often referred to as *reserved ports* or *assigned ports*).

Port numbers from 1,024 to 49,151 are referred to as *registered*, and the use of many of them are are listed as a convenience to the community by the IANA. For example, HTTP often uses port 8,080.

Port numbers from 49,152 to 65,535 are for dynamic and private use (that is whatever programmers wish to use them for). For example, networking software will choose an available port number from this range when a client process requests one. So, for example, a client will call from port 1,515 (the port it was temporarily assigned) to a server's port 25 (it specifies this well-known port number). The server will know the client wants to talk about mail (and use the *sendmail* protocol), since the call arrived on the SMTP well-known port (the server therefore knows how to parse the received message). When the server replies, it will specify a destination of port 1,515, so the initiating client process (which has attached itself to port 1,515) will receive the reply (and know how to parse the reply, since it was expecting a sendmail reply).

Computer Dictionary

The nomenclature for specifying a connection to a specific host and port is 199.12.1.1, 23 (or sometimes 199.12.1.1 23 or 199.12.1.1:23).

TCP was initially proposed and designed (by Vinton Cerf and Robert Kahn) in 1973 as the standard protocol for the (then-called) ARPAnet (which is now called the Internet). The proposal was titled "A Protocol for Packet Network Intercommunications", and was presented to the IEEE. In 1976, the protocol was divided into TCP and IP, and in 1978 the address space was expanded from 8 bits to 32 bits.

What we now call TCP is officially defined in RFC 793.

See **CONNECTIONORIENTED**, **CONNECTIONLESS**, **DNS2** (*Domain Name System*), **FINGER**, **FTP**, **HTTP**, **HOME PAGE**, **IANA**, **INTERNET2**, **NIS**, **NTP**, **PING**, **POP2**, **RFC**, **ROOT**, **SMTP**, **SOCKET NUMBER**, **SOCKETS**, **TCP/IP**, **TELNET**, **TFTP**, **UDP**, **USENET**, **UUCP**, and **WINSOCK**.

TCP/IP
Transmission Control Protocol/Internet Protocol

A very popular data communications protocol, since it is available for most operating systems and hardware platforms—so these computers (UNIX workstations; PCs running MS-DOS, Windows, or OS/2; Apple Macintoshes, IBM Mainframes; DEC Minicomputers; and so on) can all communicate.

A protocol *suite* (or *stack*, since it involves more than one protocol) endorsed by the U.S. Department of Defense in 1978 as a data communications standard and was specified as the required protocol on Arpanet and Milnet by the U.S. Office of the Secretary of Defense in 1983.

Usually refers to the applications that are commonly run on TCP/IP as well, such as ftp, SMTP, telnet, DNS, RPC, rexec, and tftp. The protocols are well suited to providing communications between dissimilar computer systems.

Network congestion control is usually by discarding packets. Does not support fair sharing of bandwidth by applications nor congestion control by *class of service*.

While TCP/IP comes built in to most versions of the UNIX operating system, it is usually purchased as separate software for DOS and other older operating systems. Some popular packages are listed in the following table.

Software	Company	WWW server
PCTCP	ftp Software, Inc.	*http://www.ftp.com*
PC-NFS	Sun Microsystems, Inc.	*http://www.sun.com*
PathWay Access	The Wollongong Group, Inc.	*http://www.twg.com*
Reflection	Walker Richer & Quinn	*http://www.wrq.com*

Since TCP/IP is now built-in to Microsoft's Windows 95 and NT, TCP/IP stacks from such third-parties are less common now.

When configuring a TCP/IP stack, the following is usually required (though they may be automatically provided by a DHCP server, which centralizes the administration of these parameters):

▲ IP address. This is like your telephone number—you need a unique one.

▲ Subnet bit mask. This specifies how many of the 32 bits of the IP address specify the network (the rest of the bits specify a specific host on that network). The TCP/IP protocol stack needs to know this so it can determine whether a destination computer is on the same network (that is, the destination network bits are the same as your own) or not. If the destination is on the same network, then your computer sends the message directly to the destination. Otherwise, the message is sent to the default gateway.

▲ Default gateway (or default router). This is the IP address of a router on the same network as your computer. Routers can connect networks together, so a router is the way to get from one network (your's) to another (the one for which your message is destined). Routers communicate with each other (using RIP, OSPF or another router-to-router protocol), so routers can learn which networks other routers can access (such as all networks in your company). Routers typically have a *gateway of last resort* or *default gateway* of their own (typically at an Internet Service Provider), to which they send messages destined for networks that are unknown to them and the routers they communicate with.

▲ Domand Name Server. This is the IP address of a server that can translate DNS names (such as yahoo.com) to IP addresses.

TCP/IP was first standardized in U.S. Department of Defense MIL STD 1777 and MIL STD 1778.

A tutorial on TCP/IP is in RFC 1180.

See **ARP, ARPANET, BOOTP, DHCP, DNS1** (*Domain Name System*), **FINGER, IP, NETSTAT, OPERATING SYSTEM, OSI, PING, QOS, RLOGIN, SMTP, SNMP, TCP, TELNET, TFTP, UDP, UNIX, VJ,** and **WINSOCK**.

TDM
Time Division Multiplexing

A way to share bandwidth, where it is split according to time (a time slot is reserved for each user). Well-suited to multimedia traffic, since each user gets guaranteed bandwidth.

A T1 circuit is an example of this technology. Sometimes called *synchronous transport mode* (STM)—which is completely unrelated to, and is a different technology than, SDH's *Synchronous Transport Module* speed units. The TDM multiplexing method used in Europe (among other places) for E1 (and the faster circuits in the hierarchy) is called *plesiochronous* (which means "nearly synchronous" or "partially synchronized"—its amazing what there are words for, like refenestration or avuncular) *digital hierarchy* (PDH).

Other ways to share bandwidth include the following.

▲ Frequency Division Multiplexing (FDM)—this divides the bandwidth by frequency (a range of frequencies is reserved for each user). CATV (Cable television) is an example of this technology.

▲ Asynchronous Transfer Mode (ATM)—this divides the bandwidth by time, but time slots can be allocated according to the type of traffic each users has (for example, delay-sensitive traffic will be taken first, when the network gets too busy).

▲ Syncrhonous Digital Hierarchy (SDH) is the homologous European technology, which is the successor to their PDH.

See **ATM, CATV, E1, INVERSE MULTIPLEXER, MULTIMEDIA,** and **T1**.

TDMA
Time Division Multiple Access

Generically, it means that many stations share a medium by cooperatively using a portion of the transmit time. However, the term is usually used to refer to the TIA/EIA IS-54 method of improving on AMPS (standard cellular telephone service) to provide more capacity.

With significant *base station* changes, it uses a standard AMPS 30-kHz frequency pair (one 30-kHz channel for receive, the other for transmit). For standard AMPS, this is one full-duplex conversation, but for TDMA, it provides a 48,600-bits/s (24,300 bits/s per direction) data stream of 40-ms frames (6.667 ms per timeslot, current speech encoders use 2 timeslots per conversation), which is shared among the users on a *round-robin* basis (each gets a turn, in a fixed sequence).

Current implementations digitize speech at 8,000 bits/s, providing up to three conversations (or 8,000-bits/s data channels) where only one was supported before (since $3 \times 8,000$ bits/s is all that fits into 24,300 bits/s—the rest is framing overhead, control and synchronization information).

It therefore triples (actually more than that—a factor of 3.4, because of the advantages of *trunking*) the number of simultaneous conversations supported by a given number of AMPS frequency pairs.

Future *"half-rate"* speech digitizers (4,000 bits/s per direction) will enable six conversations to be carried in one AMPS 30-kHz frequency pair, providing a capacity increase of 7.2 times (720%)—assuming that the voice is intelligible—there are already many complaints about the current 8,000-bits/s voice quality.

TDMA is currently widely installed (typically a few channels per base station site) but not widely accepted, because of:

▲ Poor voice quality

▲ No new features (for example, it had been expected that Caller ID would be offered sooner and more widely)

▲ Insufficient testing (there was no large-scale test as AMPS had)

▲ The potential for greater efficiency (that is, capacity improvements) of other schemes, such as CDMA (still in development) and GSM (currently not used in North America). Sometimes this is called the FUD (*fear, uncertainty, and doubt*) factor.

EIA/TIA IS-54 (Interim Standard 54) was released in 1990. While the speech is digitized, it uses an analog control channel (for example, for call set-up). IS-54A (revision A) added Caller ID. IS-54B added improved Caller ID, voice encryption and handset eletronic serial number (ESN) authentication.

A user data rate of 13 kbits/s is supported, and voice is normally digitized at 8 kbits/s (allowing 3 timeslots per channel). The standard supports a doubling of capacity, using 4 kbit/s voice digitizing (so, there would be 6 timeslots per channel). Both 4 kbit/s and 8 kbit/s voice could be used in the same system at the same time, but it is unlikely that 4 kbit/s voice will ever have acceptable quality.

TDMA is also called *North American Digital Cellular* (NADC) and *Digital AMPS* (or D-AMPS or AMPS-D).

Up-banded TDMA (sometimes called D-AMPS 1900) is a version of TDMA that operates at the PCS frequencies of about 1.9 GHz (which is 1900 MHz–hence the name). It is standardized as TIA/EIA IS-136 and is an implementation of PCS that is simpler and lower cost than CDMA and GSM. It uses a digital control channel (when operating in the 1.9 GHz band), and supports some features from GSM, such as *short message service* (SMS—as is popular for GSM), which can be used for enhanced alphanumeric paging type services. AT&T's PCS service uses IS-136.

It is expected that IS-54 and IS-136 will always be operated *dual-mode*—that is, they will be operated along with standard analog AMPS. Handsets automatically use AMPS when TDMA service is not available, and base station sites can be equipped to assign different bandwidths to AMPS and TDMA services.

See **AMPS**, **CDMA**, **FUD**, **GSM**, and **PCS1** (*Personal Communications Service*), and **TIA1** (*(Telecommunications Industry Association)*).

Teflon

DuPont Corporation's trademarked name for fluorinated ethylene propylene.

See **FEP CABLE** (*Fluorinated Ethylene Propylene*).

Teleglobe Inc.

Their wholly-owned subsidiary Teleglobe Canada Inc. is a carrier that has a legal monopoly of providing overseas satellite communications services for Canada. The company was privatised in 1991, and guaranteed a monopoly on its overseas switching services (which go to about 230 countries and territories—but not including the U.S.) until March 1997 (this was later extended to October 1, 1998).

They have a WWW server at *http://www.teleglobe.ca*.

See **CARRIER**, **SATELLITE**, and **TELESAT CANADA**.

Telephone Companies

The three main telephone companies in Canada are listed in the following table.

Phone Company	Associated with
Stentor	Uses MCI's billing software, Intelligent Networking (permitting Stentor and U.S. MCI customers to establish virtual networks), and frame relay technology.
AT&T Canada[a]	20% owned by AT&T.
Sprint Canada	25% owned by Sprint (U.S.). Owned by, and was called, Call-Net Enterprises before this purchase.

a. Was called Unitel until 1997

See **CARRIER**, **POTS**, and **STENTOR**.

Telephony Application Programming Interface

See **TAPI**.

Telephony Services Application Programming Interface

See **TSAPI**.

Telesat Canada Corporation

The carrier created to have a legal monopoly of providing geostationary satellite communication services within Canada. It was established in 1969 by an act of the Canadian parliament.

As part of a February 1997 World Trade Organization (WTO agreement among 69 countries, this monopoly must end by March 1, 2000.

They have a WWW server at *http://www.telesat.ca*.

See **CARRIER**, **SATELLITE**, and **TELEGLOBE INC.**

telnet

Terminal emulation with communications to the host over a network (rather than through an EIA-232 connection).

That is, typing `telnet servername` connects you to the host `servername`. Your session then continues as if your terminal (likely actually a PC running a data communications program that makes your PC emulate a terminal) was directly connected to the remote host. You are prompted for a username and a password.

The actual data stream between computers consists of a data and control information intermixed on port 23. To distinguish control commands from data, control commands are prefaced by a special escape character, which is called IAC (*Interpret as Control*). The IAC character is a single byte with the decimal value 255 (FF in hexadecimal). The second byte of the command defines the type of command. For example, if the second byte has the decimal value 246 (as defined in RFC 854), then it is interpreted as an `Are You There (ayt)` command (to which a reply is expected as a confirmation).

Teradata

Some say telnet is a contraction of *telephone networking*. telnet is defined in RFCs 854 through 861.

See **AYT, EIA/TIA-232, RLOGIN, TCP, TCP,** and **TN3270.**

Teradata

A company that makes large SQL-based database servers. Bought by NCR, which was then bought by AT&T. Then AT&T changed changed NCR's name to Global Information Solutions, and in the 1995 AT&T "trivestiture", split GIS off into its own company.

See **ATT** and **SQL.**

Terisa Systems, Inc.

A joint venture, formed in 1994, of Enterprise Integration Technologies (EIT), which developed S-HTTP, and RSA Data Security, Inc. (which is big on encryption).

With some (equal) investments by America Online, CompuServe, Netscape (which developed the competing SSL), and IBM/Prodigy (IBM's on-line service), it is working to combine the S-HTTP and SSL methods of providing secure (*authenticated* and *encrypted*) transactions over the Internet.

Terisa Systems maintains a WWW server at *http://www.terisa.com*. It has good technical information on S-HTTP and SSL.

See **AUTHENTICATION, ENCRYPTION, RSA, SHTTP, SSL,** and **WWW.**

TFT
Thin-film Transistor Liquid Crystal Display

A type of LCD display.

See **LCD.**

TFTP
Trivial File Transfer Protocol

A simple file transfer protocol (a simplified version of ftp) that is often used to boot diskless workstations or load configuration files (to routers for example) over a network (typically a LAN).

Each packet of the download includes a check character and a sequence number, to support error detection.

tftp uses UDP, requires no login, and has no password security. The tftp server can be turned off by commenting-out the loading of the tftp server process (often called the "daemon"—tftpd), which is started by specifying it in the file /etc/inetd.conf.

tftp is defined in RFC 1350.

See **BOOTP, FTP,** and **UDP.**

Thread

One execution of software by one user's process or task.

Modern multiuser (which means that it requires some level of security) and multitasking (which means that it can do more than one thing at a time) operating systems support multiple threads, which would allow many activities to execute (almost) simultaneously (for example, searches on many remote databases all launched by one task).

Three Letter Acronyms

See **TLA**.

TIA
Thanks In Advance

A common email abbreviation. Sometimes you see MTIA—much thanks in advance.

TIA
Telecommunications Industry Association

A trade association which was a section of the EIA. In January 1992, TIA received their own accreditation from ANSI, so they now get their name first on standards which they develop.

Old standards developed by TIA had an RS designation (just as EIA standards did). After EIA stopped using the RS designation in 1984, standards developed by the TIA would be called EIA/TIA (such as EIA/TIA-530, which was last revised in 1992), since the TIA was not yet accredited (so EIA's name came first). Since about 1992, standards TIA produces are called TIA/EIA (such as TIA/EIA-422), since the TIA is still affilated with the EIA.

Part of the accreditation process is that all ANSI standards must be reaffirmed every 5 years, or recinded.

Some TIA standards are considered *trial use standards*, so that they can be published as soon as possible. These are designated IS (*Interim Standard*, such as IS-95, the PCS CDMA standard), and are not ANSI standards. These must be reafirmed every year, and such standards can only exist for 3 years, then they must be made ANSI standards or recinded.

As of September 1997, the TIA also has responsibility for assigning the *electronic serial numbers* (ESNs) used in cellular telephones (the FCC used to have this job).

The TIA represents providers of communications and information technology products, and have a web site at *http://www.tiaonline.org*.

See **ANSI**, **EIA**, **STANDARDS**, and **TSB**.

TIA/EIA-422

A balanced (that is, uses two electrical conductors per signal, and they each have an equal impedance to ground), differential (that is, the signalling voltages used are equal, but opposite on each conductor, and the relative polarity of the voltages indicates a binary 0 or 1), digital interface standard.

The generator (signal driver) is specified to have the following characteristics:

▲ a 100 Ω output impedance

▲ be able to produce at least a 2 V (differential—that is across the two conductors) signal into a loaded (with up to 10 receivers in parallel and a cable termination resistor) cable

▲ produce no more than 6 V *open circuit* (that is, with nothing connected to the generator)

▲ produce no more than 150 mA when the conductors are shorted to each other, or to ground

When the A lead is more positive than the B lead, a binary (logic) 0, *space condition* and on state are being conveyed.

The receiver is specified to have the following characteristics:

▲ have an input impedance of 4 kΩ or more

▲ accept differential input signals of up to ±10 V, and reliably receive signals as small as ±0.2 V (±200 mV)

The receiver for EIA/TIA-422 is identical to that required for EIA/TIA-423.

A termination resistor (which best reduces reflections if its resistance matches both the driver's and the cable's impedance—generally 100 to 120 Ω) at the receiver is optional, and has been found to generally have little effect for bit rates less than about 200 kbits/s.

The standard specifies a maximum bit rate of 10 Mbits/s, but does not specify a maximum cable length at that or lower bit rates. However, an appendix to the standard does give some very conservative guidelines for maximum cable lengths. For 24 gauge twisted pair cable, which has a 52.5 pF per meter (16 pF per foot) capacitance and a 100 Ω termination resistor, the following is suggested:

▲ 1,200 m (4,000 feet) maximum (limited by the 6 dBV maximum signal attenuation desired) at bit rates of 100 kbit/s and slower

▲ 120 m maximum for signals up to 1 Mbit/s

▲ 15 m maximum for signals of up to 10 Mbits/s.

Officially called *Electrical Characteristics of Balanced Voltage Digital Interface Circuits*. The most recent version was released in 1994. It is electrically the same as the interfaces specified in ITU's V.11 and X.27.

See **GEOPORT**, **TIA/EIA-423**, **EIA449**, and **TIA1** (*Telecommunications Industry Association*).

TIA/EIA-423

An unbalanced (that is, each signal uses its own single electrical conductor, with all signals referenced to a single reference conductor, which is typically called *signal ground*), single-ended (that is, the signalling voltage is applied to a single conductor) digital interface standard.

The generator (signal driver) is specified to have the following characteristics:

▲ a 50 Ω output impedance

▲ be able to produce at least a 4 V (relative to the signal ground) signal into a loaded (with a receiver) cable

▲ produce no more than 6 V *open circuit* (that is, with nothing connected to the generator)

When the signal is positive (relative to signal ground), a binary (logic) 0, *space condition* and on state are being conveyed.

Computer Dictionary

The receiver has a sensitivity of ±0.2 V (±200 mV). The receiver for EIA/TIA-423 is identical to that required for EIA/TIA-422.

The standard suggests a maximum bit rate of 100 kbits/s, but does not specify a maximum cable length at that or lower bit rates. However, an appendix to the standard does give some very conservative guidelines for maximum cable lengths, as follows:

▲ 1,200 m (4,000 feet) maximum at bit rates of 3,000 bit/s and slower

▲ 350 m maximum for signals up to 10 kbit/s

▲ 35 m maximum for signals of up to 100 kbits/s.

Officially called *Electrical Characteristics of Unbalanced Voltage Digital Interface Circuits*. The most recent version was released in 1996.

See **TIA/EIA-422**, **EIA-449**, and **TIA1** (*Telecommunications Industry Association*).

TIC
Token Ring Interface Coupler

A Token Ring LAN adapter (especially the one in an IBM FEP).

The *printed circuit board* in a computer that connects the computer to the LAN cabling.

See **CABLE**, **FEP**, **IBM**, **LAN**, **NIC2**, and **TOKEN RING**.

Tick

Microsoft's DOS operating system sets a PC's hardware timer to interrupt about every 54.925 ms (which is about 18.2065 times per second). This is therefore the finest resolution available through DOS for timing things.

See **IRQ**, **PC**, and **UTC**.

TIES
Time Independent Escape Sequence

For standard asynchronous dial-up modems, a method of *escaping* from data to command mode (so that the modem will interpret and act on the commands you send it, rather than sending them as data to the remote modem). It does not use the Hayes Microcomputer Products' *Improved Escape Sequence with Guard Time* method and therefore avoids having to pay royalties to Hayes, while remaining compatible with existing communications software.

TIES uses a specific string of characters (usually +++AT), with no requirement for idle time between them and the rest of the data, to cause the modem to escape from data mode to command mode.

The problem with TIES is that the data (or a CRC in it) may contain this escape sequence, so the file transfer will fail.

MultiTech Systems and Maxtech/GVC use TIES—which is simply the Hayes method with the "Guard Time" removed—the AT following the +++ is the AT that precedes almost all AT commands.

Around 1992, when Hayes began enforcing their patent, there was some controversy (initiated by Hayes) about the reliability of TIES (to pressure vendors using TIES to pay royalties, by telling the public that file transfers may fail occasionally).

See **AT COMMAND SET**, **CRC**, and **MODEM**.

TIFF
Tagged Image File Format

One of many standard methods of storing digitized graphic images. TIFF supports up to 24 bits of color per pixel, and images up to 232-1 × 232-1 pixels.

"Tagged" refers to the method TIFF uses to store information about the image, such as the image's height and width (in pixels) and the color table.

When stored as files, TIFF images typically have filename extensions of `.TIF`.

Many TIFF file formats and capabilities are defined, including fax Group 3 and Group 4, and many data compression methods can be used for the images.

See **EPS** and **FAX**.

Time-stamp

Most UNIX systems provide the current time and date as a 32-bit value representing the number of seconds since midnight January 1, 1970, *Greenwich Mean Time* (sometimes written as 1970-1-1 00:00:00 GMT), though in 1972, UTC replaced GMT as the time reference.

Since this is a *signed integer* (that is, 1 bit is used to indicate whether the value is negative or not), only 31 bits are available for the date. 2^{31} is 2,147,482,648 seconds, which is about 68 years and 18 days. The UNIX software clock will therefore overflow on about January 18, 2038 (hopefully all the year 2000 software problems will be cleared up by then, so they can get to work on the year 2038 problems!).

The UNIX Time Server Protocol (RFC 868) provides the time as a 32-bit integer as the number of seconds since January 1, 1900 (GMT). This uses either TCP or UDP, and port 37.

The UNIX Daytime Protocol (RFC 867) provides the time as a human-readable ASCII string (though the exact format of the string is not standardized). This uses port 13.

DOS's FAT also uses a 32-bit value but in a different format and relative to a different time:

▲ A 16-bit time value of the time since the most recent midnight, with the bits representing hhhhhmmmmmmsssss—as in hours:minutes:seconds (each in binary)

▲ A 16-bit date offset from January 1, 1980 (this is the base date for DOS, and also for most PC BIOS hardware clocks), with the bits representing yyyyyyymmmmdddddd—as in year:month:date (each in binary)

The DOS scheme overflows when the year 2108 begins. (I hope DOS files are not used any more by then!)

See **FAT**, **GMT**, **NIST ACTS**, and **UTC**.

Tip and Ring

The name for the two wires on a telephone line, derived from the electrical contacts on old-style telephone plugs (which are similar to $\frac{1}{4}$-inch headphone plugs). One electrical contact is at the *tip* of the plug, and the other is a *ring* just above it (and there is a *sleeve* above that), as shown in the accompanying figure.

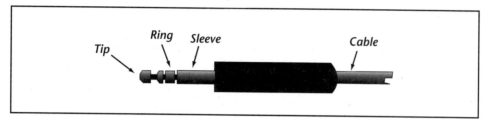

Tip and Ring-1

The following table lists some characteristics of Tip and Ring wiring.

		Wire Name	
		Tip	Ring
$\frac{1}{4}$-inch phone jack electrical contact		Tip	Ring
Voltage (DC volts)		0	−48
Residential wiring (pair)	1	Green	Red
	2	Black	Yellow
	3	White	Blue
RJ-11 pin (pair)	1	3	4
	2	5	2
	3	1	6
Office wiring (pair)	1	White with blue band	Blue with white band
	2	White with orange band	Orange with white band
	3	White with green band	Green with white band
	4	White with brown band	Brown with white band
RJ-45 pin (pair)	1	5	4
	2	3	6
	3	1	2
	4	7	8

See **CABLE**, **CONNECTOR**, **POTS**, and **RJ45**.

TLA
Three-Letter Acronym

An acronym for the acronyms, showing that there are too many acronyms. (Some people refer to an EFLA—*Extended Four-Letter Acronym*, too.)

Some Internet-accessible acronym look-up servers are at *http://curia.ucc.ie/cgi-bin/ acronym*, *http://slarti.ucd.ie/inttelec/top_level.html*, and *http://www.ucc.ie/htbin/acronym*.

TN3270
Telnet 3270

A *terminal emulation* capability for UNIX workstations and TCP/IP-capable PCs that permits them to access an IBM mainframe. The workstation or PC appears to the mainframe as a 3270 terminal.

The 3270 data stream from the terminal emulator is encapsulated in telnet TCP/IP packets. Emulation of a 3287 printer (TN3287) is also supported. These are standardized in RFC 1646. The IBM mainframe requires one of the following:

▲ TCP/IP and telnet support, often in the form of an IBM 3172 interconnect controller (which is a souped-up IBM PS/2 PC)

▲ An SNA gateway, typically located at the mainframe site, or near the users. It converts the TCP/IP traffic (typically on an Ethernet LAN) to SDLC, for connection to the mainframe's FEP.

An enhancement, called TN3270E emulates a 3278 model 2 terminal. It is standardized in RFC 1647, and has support for additional features, such as the following:

▲ file transfers between the PC and host computer

▲ host-controlled guaranteed print

▲ end-to-end acknowledgement of data

▲ the system request and attention keys

▲ response time monitoring (RTM)

See **S3172**, **S3270**, **FEP**, and **TELNET**.

Token Ring

A LAN commercialized by IBM and standardized as IEEE 802.5 (which was approved in late 1984).

Was initially conceived and is patented by Olof S. Söderblom (who gets *lots* of licensing fees—even from IBM) when he was an MIS (*Management Information Systems*) manager for a bank in Sweden (he later moved to Holland).

A Token Ring is a series of workstations connected by twisted pair cabling, with the output of one workstation being the input to the next—forming a ring. A bit in the Token Ring frame header indicates whether the frame is a *token*. A station wishing to transmit must first get the token. Since there is only one token per ring, there is no chance of wasted transmission time due to collisions (more than one station attempting to transmit at the same time). Token Ring therefore performs well, even under heavy loading.

Therefore, Token Ring is often described as being best suited to larger frames of data and heavier loading than Ethernet. The maximum frame size is about 4,500 bytes (4-Mbits/s Token Ring) and 17,800 bytes (16-Mbits/s Token Ring); the maximum frame size is actually defined by the amount of time a station is allowed to hold the token (while it is transmitting its frame)—which is 10 ms. While larger frame sizes result in lower protocol overhead, larger frame sizes also require larger buffers in the end stations. A common Token Ring frame size is therefore 4,096 bytes.

Token Ring uses three types of connectors, as described below.

▲ An IBM *Universal Data Connector* for STP cabling—everywhere except the back of a PC

▲ 9-pin D-subminiature connector for STP—at the back of a PC (since the slot is too narrow for a Universal Data Connector)

▲ 8-pin modular jack for UTP cabling

The connector pin-outs are shown in the following table.

Signal Name	Universal Data Connector wire color	9-pin D-subminiature connector pin	8-pin modular plug pin
Transmit- (from workstation)	Black	5	3
Receive+ (to workstation)	Red	1	4
Receive- (to workstation)	Green	6	5
Transmit+ (from workstation)	Orange	9	6

High Speed Token Ring (HSTR) is an upgrade for Token Ring announced in mid-1997, but is unlikely to get many buyers. IBM plans 100, 128 and 155 Mbit/s versions.

Lots of Token Ring vendor information is at *http://www.astral.org*.

See **ASTRAL, CONNECTOR, ENCODING, ETHERNET, LAN, LLC2, REMOTE BRIDGE, SRB, STP, SWITCHED LAN,** and **TIC.**

Token Ring Interface Coupler

See **TIC.**

Toolkit Without An Interesting Name

See **TWAIN.**

TPC
Transaction Processing Council

A group that defines benchmark tests for transaction-oriented database applications. Results are often measured in *Transactions Per Second* (TPS). The TPC-A benchmark is a debit/credit type that is best for demonstrating commercial I/O type loads and indicates the number of users that could be supported. TPC-B is more of a CPU and disk load test.

See **OLTP** and **TPS.**

TP-PMD
Twisted Pair–Physical Medium Dependent

An unshielded twisted pair medium option for FDDI.

See **FDDI** and **UTP.**

A common unit when measuring the performance of transaction-oriented systems.

See **MIPS**, **SPEC**, **SQL**, and **TPC**.

Trade Secret

A (usually not recommended) alternative to a *patent* (patents require full disclosure of the information—which is unpalatable to some) to protect inventions (including those that are not protectable by patents) or business information from competition.

There is no *registration* (that is, you don't have to file any forms with some government office). It is simply up to the owner of the information or invention to actively keep the information or process from the public—for example, by having everyone who is exposed to the secret sign a *nondisclosure agreement* (acknowledging that the information is a *trade secret*).

If you are trying to sue someone who (allegedly) blabbed your secret, you would have to show a court that the person had access to your secret and that you took every reasonable precaution to keep your secret secret.

If the invention or information is discovered independently or by analyzing publicly available (including by accident from the owner) information, then the trade secret protection and status are lost (people can no longer be bound to keep what they know a secret).

Such independent discoverers can use or publish the information, and even file a patent application—potentially preventing the original trade secret user from using their own invention.

Trade secret protection is therefore a silly idea for things that can be *reverse-engineered* (figured out by analyzing it). Manufacturing processes and other procedures that cannot be surmised from the finished (and sold) product are well suited to trade secret protection.

See **INTELLECTUAL PROPERTY PROTECTION**, **NDA**, and **PATENT**.

Trademark

A trademark is a word, phrase, symbol, design, or a combination of these, and is used to identify the source of products or services, so they can be distinguished from others.

Trademark legislation is a form of *intellectual property protection* that protects:

▲ Slogans

▲ Names of products (including names for computer programs and games)

▲ Distinctive packages and unique product shapes (actually, these are covered by a subset of trademark law called *trade dress*)

Restrictions generally involve not being able to trademark words that:

▲ Would be deceptive (the name claims that a product is from a certain country or city, and it is not, or that a product has certain features that it does not actually have)

▲ Would restrict others from fair business (for example, the name claims product features that all other products would also have)

▲ Are common descriptive words or names in other languages

▲ Are similar to, or would commonly be confused with, another company's (or institution's, government agency's, and so on) name or trademark

Registering provides legal title to the trademark (which can then be *assigned* to others, as can any other property).

Under *common law*, a trademark that is used for a certain length of time (an un-registered trademark) establishes ownership for *most* purposes (an exception is that precious metals shipped between countries require a *registered trademark*), but registration is highly recommended in all cases. For example, common law trademark rights protect you only in the geographic area where the trademark is used. Also, someone who registers your unregistered trademark may be able to force you to stop using "yours"—and just think of the legal costs of arguing common law use (lawyers love that sort of thing).

Products using the trademark must be on the market before registration can occur (so that the trademark becomes *associated* with the product), though the *trademark application* can be filed before this (based on *proposed use*).

There are three types of trademarks:

▲ *Ordinary marks* are words or symbols that distinguish the products or services of a specific person or company

▲ *Certification marks* are owned by a standards setter and show that the products or services that are *licensed* and using that certification mark meet a defined standard.

▲ *Distinguishing guise*, which provides protection for a product or package with a unique shape

There is no requirement to *mark* the use of the trademark, but these can be used:

▲ "™" indicates that the item is a registered or unregistered trademark

▲ "®" indicates that the item is a registered trademark

As for *copyrights* and *patents*, it is up to the owner of a trademark to find cases of *infringement* (this includes both uses of the trademark and of similar trademarks that might cause confusion) and to obtain an injunction. It is also the responsibility of the owner of a trademark to ensure that the trademark is used correctly (that is, to ensure that the term does not become part of normal conversation to refer to other similar products or services—from competitors).

Trademark protection is lost if it is not used (that is, products using it must be available on the market).

In Canada, trademarks are administered by the *Trademarks Office*, which is part of the CIPO. Registration provides 15 years of protection, which can be renewed at 15-year intervals, and requires filling out an application form and submitting a fee.

In the U.S., trademarks are registered with the U.S. Patent and Trademark Office (*http://www.uspto.gov*). The U.S. Patent Court adjudicates disputes (such as whether a term can be trademarked).

Transmission Control Protocol

The Cornell Law School has a WWW page on U.S. trademark law at *http://www.law.cornell.edu/topics/trademark.html*. For a fee, you can search trademarks (both pending and registered) in several countries at *http://www.thomson.com/thomthom.html*.

See **CIPO** and **INTELLECTUAL PROPERTY PROTECTION**.

Transmission Control Protocol

See **TCP** and **TCP/IP**.

Transparent Asynchronous Transmitter/Receiver Interface

See **TAXI**.

TrueType

Apple and Microsoft's *scalable* (or *outline*) font format, which describes characters and other symbols (each character and symbols is called a *glyph shape*). Each glyph consists of one or more *contours* (a closed path of some shape). Example contours of a glyph include; the outside edge of a period, the ovals of the inside and outside edges of the letter "o", and the triangle-like shape inside an "A" (and the more complicated curve of the outside edge of the letter "A".

TrueType support is included with Windows 3.1 and Apple's System 7, enabling the same fonts to be used for both display and printing, so the printed output matches that displayed (in the dark, old days of PCs, your carefully crafted document would print differently than it showed on your display because the printer font was an entirely different thing than your display's font).

Most laser and some ink-jet printers have built-in TrueType fonts, and those that it does not have can usually be downloaded (so after the downloading, the printer can print the new fonts as fast as its resident fonts—until you power-off the printer). For printers that do not support downloadable fonts, TrueType will *rasterize* the page, and send it to the printer as a graphics image. This takes a long time.

Windows TrueType fonts are not resolution-independent, so a change in printer resolution may produce different pagination, because of mathematical rounding errors when adjusting the font size.

Supports *hinting* (see *Outline Font*) and competes with *PostScript*—though PostScript is a general-purpose *page description language* and TrueType is more flexible but is limited to font scaling and hinting.

On a PC, the actual font files are in the `c:\windows\system` directory. Windows font files such as `VGA*.FON` and `EGA*.FON` are screen fonts (nonscalable fonts that provide optimal screen display for each video resolution). The following table shows the font filename extensions used by TrueType fonts.

Font Filename Extension	Function	Comments
*.FOT	Font header file	Required to provide font support under Windows
*.TTF	Actual font information	
*.TT	Temporary file	Can likely be deleted

The *.FOT files are automatically generated (by Windows) when the font is "installed" (that is, when you install the Wingding font that is already on your disk as WINDING.TTF, Windows creates a WINGDING.FOT file. Among the information included in the created *.FOT files is a pointer to the location of the corresponding *.TTF file. The location of the *.FOT files is specified in the [fonts] section of the WIN.INI file. The *.FOT file is deleted when the font is removed (uninstalled).

Installed TrueType fonts will be identified with (TrueType) and an extension of *.FOT, in the [fonts] section of the c:\windows\win.ini file (for example).

See **SPEEDO**, **OUTLINE FONT**, **POSTSCRIPT PAGE DESCRIPTION LANGUAGE**, and **SYSTEM 7**.

Trunk

There are two main types of copper (as opposed to fiber) interfaces to a telephone company central office switch—*trunks* and *lines*.

Trunks are usually used between switches, are usually 4-wire (one pair of conductors for the receive-direction conversation, and one pair for the transmit) and provide a D.C. voltage or current indication (such as a wire being grounded) of when either side hangs-up.

Lines are usually used to connect a telephone to a switch. They are usually 2-wire (the same pair handles both receive and transmit—just like the telephone line you have at home). Also, there is usually no easily-sensed way of knowing when the switch-end has hung-up (people know this when the other person says goodbye and you hear a click—but automated devices cannot reliably detect this).

Examples of telephone switch interfaces include the following.

▲ E&M (*Ear and Mouth*)—This 2- or 4-wire trunk interface (one pair later to an earpiece, the other to the mouthpiece of a telephone) uses combinations of grounding of wires to indicate on-hook, off-hook and dialling information. It is the most common copper method of interconnecting telephone switches. Unfortunately, there are five types of DID trunks (Types I, II, III, IV and V), but they are well-documented and standardized.

▲ Some say that E&M actually is an abbreviation for earth (as in *grounding*) and magneto (the device that used to be used to generate ringing voltage to ring a remote telephone).

▲ FXO (*Foreign Exchange Service - Office*) and FXS (*Foreign Exchange Service - Subscriber*) are the two ends of the same trunk (the *office* referring to the central office, and the *subscriber* referring to the customer). *Foreign* Exchange refers to a central office other than

the one that is closest to you. That is, this type of trunk is used to connect a customer to a central office other than your usual one—typically so you can receive a service only offered by that central office, such as a special telephone number.

▲ Loop Start is a type of 2-wire trunk that can be used to provide FSO and FXS service. There are many variations for the signalling (such as battery reversal and ground start) which need to be worked out before installing such a trunk.

See **C.O.**, **DID**, and **PBX**.

TSAPI
Telephony Services Application Programming Interface

AT&T Corp.'s and Novell Inc.'s method of integrating telephone services and computers (first released in 1994).

Emphasizes *third-party* control and more complex functions than the competing TAPI. For example, the PBX can initiate transferring a call and keep track of where the call is, and has been. And software can choose where to route a call, according to how full call queues are, or what type of expertise is required.

All interaction between a workstation and the PBX is through a LAN connection, so additional equipment is not needed for each workstation (however, the PBX needs to have TSAPI support). Better-suited to larger installations.

TSAPI performs *first-party* type control (see TAPI) from the PBX (Private Branch Exchange—the telephone switch), rather than from the telephone. For example, to make a call the PBX rather than the telephone would dial the phone number, and the call would then be transferred to the telephone.

TSAPI specifies the physical link between a server (for example a Novell NetWare file server running the *NetWare Telephony Services* NLM) and a PBX (such as an AT&T Definity 3Gi). The link may be an EIA-232 connection, ISDN link (requiring ISDN boards and software support for both the file server and PBX) or other connection (such as Ethernet or X.25).

TSAPI is supported by the Macintosh Mac OS, OS/2, UnixWare and Microsoft Windows operating systems. In contrast, TAPI only runs with Microsoft Windows.

Functions supported include:

▲ Placing outgoing calls

▲ Answering, transferring, and conferencing incoming calls

▲ Viewing the status of a current call (such as Caller ID, ringing, or on-hold)

CTI Encyclopedia is a new version of TSAPI, and was developed by the Versit vendor forum, which was founded by Apple Computer Inc., IBM, Lucent Technologies (formerly AT&T), the IBM Networking Hardware and Networking Systems divisions, and Siemens AG). New features include connectivity to more types of clients, such as PDAs and payphones, and more types of networks (wireless for example).

See **CTI**, **ECTF**, **EIA/TIA-232**, **ISDN**, **NLM**, **PBX**, **PDA**, **SCREEN POP**, and **TAPI**.

TSB
Technical Service Bulletin

A document from the EIA or TIA which is a "compilation of engineering data or information useful to the technical community, and represents approaches to good engineering practices." Often these are later included in updated versions of related standards.

See **EIA**, **EIA/TIA/TSB-37A**, **STANDARDS**, **TIA1** (*Telecommunications Industry Association*), and **UTP**.

TSO
Time Sharing Option

An IBM mainframe user interface providing an editor and program driver that are well-suited to software development. Runs under MVS. An alternative is CICS.

See **CICS**, **MAINFRAME**, and **MVS**.

TTL
Time-To-Live

An 8-bit field in an IP packet header that is set to the maximum number of routers a message could pass through to reach a destination. Traditional UNIX TCP/IP software usually sets this field to 15, DEC Pathworks to 30, and Microsoft Windows 95 and NT uses 32 (though all these can be changed).

The field is decremented by each router that handles the packet. If it is decremented to zero, that router discards the packet and should send an ICMP *TTL* exceeded message back to the sender. This capability ensures that packets cannot get stuck in a loop (therefore creating significant network loading) because of a network problem such as (possibly temporarily) incorrect routing tables.

A list of TTL settings for different operating systems is at *http://www.switch.ch/switch/docs/ttl_default.html*.

See **ICMP**, **IP**, **RIP**, and **ROUTER**.

TTL
Transistor-Transistor Logic

An old *logic family* (method of making basic binary logic circuits, such as and, exclusive-or, and nand) that uses a 5-volt DC power supply and represents the two binary states as follows:

▲ Anything from 0 to 0.8 V DC is considered off or a binary (or logic) 0.

▲ Anything from 2.0 to 5 V is *on* or a binary (or logic) 1. Voltages between 0.8 and 2.0 V are allowed only while quickly going from one state to the other.

TTL is the classic logic family referred to as *bipolar* (as that is the type of transistor it uses). Rarely used now (TTL is too slow and too high in power consumption), but the voltage levels have become an industry standard. For example, PC parallel printer ports and *single-ended* SCSI use TTL voltages.

Tunneling

There are now many variations of TTL logic families newer than the original TTL. These have names like STTL (Schottky TTL) and LSTTL (low-power Schottky TTL), and feature lower power consumption, faster propagation times, and other advantages, and are typically TTL-compatible.

Newer computers (even mainframes) usually use logic components which use a technology based on CMOS (*complementary metal oxide semiconductor*).

TTL also refers to the voltage used for the interface to the *monochrome display adapter* (MDA) monitors used for the original PCs—so these monitors were sometimes called *TTL* monitors. These supported 25 rows of 80 columns of characters. Each character has a 9 × 14 pixel matrix, so the display had a resolution of (9 times 80 × 14 times 25), which is 720 × 350 pixels (horizontal × vertical). Just to complete the story, the *color graphics adapter* (CGA—which is also now ancient history) supported color graphics or text. In text mode it also supported 25 rows of 80 colums of characters, but the characters had an 8 × 8 pixel matrix, so the display resolution was 640 × 200 pixels.

See **DE FACTO**, **PARALLEL PORT**, **SCSI1**, and **VGA**.

Tunneling

See **ENCAPSULATION**.

TWAIN
Toolkit Without An Interesting Name

A standard software interface for the imaging data from *raster image*–generating devices (for example, from document scanners, video frame grabbers, and digital cameras, which produce horizontal scans digitizing the intensity and possibly the color of the image) so that they can be input into graphics application software.

Requires a SCSI interface on both the computer and the digitizing device and is platform-independent (Macintosh and PCs) and operating system–independent (Macintosh and Windows, later OS/2 and UNIX).

Each device manufacturer must provide a TWAIN-compliant driver (which may be a stand-alone program) and SCSI interface with their scanning hardware. The application software (that supports TWAIN) can then receive the data (typically by starting the driver program by using the *Scan Acquire* command, after specifying the input device, using the Select Source command). Sometimes the transfer between the driver and application software instead uses OLE.

Before this, applications software had to supply drivers for each digitizing device it supported.

TWAIN was developed by Aldus, Caere, Kodak, Hewlett-Packard, and Logitech.

The newer ISIS (Image and Scanner Interface Standard) has better support for scanning multiple pages and graphics.

See **OLE**, and **SCSI1**.

Typeface Family

A font family, such as Times or Helvetica. Within each family, there are usually variations, such as the following:

▲ Different weight strokes: Helvetica bold

▲ Character width: Helvetica narrow

▲ Style or posture: such as slant; Helvetica italic or oblique (which only slants the font, but does not modify it), or being an *italic* font (which is both slanted, and the font is modified)

These variations are sometimes referred to as *font styles*.

Fonts can be printed or displayed in different sizes, usually specified in point size.

The spacing between characters can be *fixed* (also called *monospaced*) or *proportional* (which uses less space for narrow characters, therefore packing in more text in a given line—always a good idea for wordy books like this one). The characters spacing of monospaced fonts (which you could also call *non-proportionally spaced* or *fixed-pitch*) is usually described in characters per inch. A 10-pitch font is therefore 10 characters per inch, and every character takes exactly 1/10". Monospaced fonts are usually shaped differently (for example, so the "i" is wider than it needs to be, but looks nicer since it is closer to the width of other characters).

Two main categories of fonts are *serif* and *sans-serif*. Serifs are the little lines that extend (usually horizontally) from the top and bottom of characters. While they make the text more "flowing" and therefore easier to read, the original reason for them is likely that it is difficult to *not* make serifs when writing with a fine feather quill pen.

Font names are often copyrighted by the typeface designer. For example, *Bembo* (the serif font used for this text) and *Gill Sans* (the font used for WWW references in this book) are copyrighted by The Monotype Corporation plc, and *Helvetica* is copyrighted by Linotype AG. Therefore similar (but different) names are used by other manufacturers who copy the shape of fonts (often with minor variations, so they won't need to have unpleasant conversations with the original copyright owner's lawyers). So you see names like Times New Roman, instead of Times Roman, or Univers instead of Helvetica.

Some font suppliers license the fonts from the original designer, so the name and font shape may be identical to the original.

Also, some popular font names are not copyrighted (such as *Garamond*) so anybody can use the names, for any similar (at least to them). Therefore, there may be significant variations in the font (such as a heavier stroke or slightly different character spacing or shape) from different manufacturers (who will use names like Adobe Garamond, ITC Garamond, and Monotype Garamond for their products).

See **BITMAP FONT**, **FONT**, **OUTLINE FONT**, and **POINT**.

U

UA
User Agent

The software that interacts with a *message transfer agent* to retrieve, display, and send X.400 messages on behalf of a user.

See **MTA** and **X.400**.

UART
Universal Asynchronous Receiver Transmitter

The *Integrated Circuit* (IC) that handles the data communications for a computer.

It converts the parallel data (so called because they are stored, retrieved, and transferred 8 or more bits at a time) in a PC (for example) to serial *asynchronous data communications* (in which data are sent and received 1 bit at a time) for transmission over a data link, such as an EIA-232 cable or modem connection. It is always less expensive (and usually simpler) to send data 1 bit at a time, especially on links that are longer than a few meters.

Also, a UART converts received serial data to parallel for further processing by the receiving computer.

Other UART functions include the following:

▲ Generating the bit-rate clock

▲ Adding start and stop bits to the transmitted data so that the receiver's UART can synchronize with the sender (that is, so that it can know where the bit edges are and which bit is the first bit of data)

▲ Adding and checking a parity bit, for error-detection

▲ Generating a hardware interrupt when a character is received and when the UART is ready for another character to send

▲ Controlling and reading the status of the modem signals (RTS, CTS, and so on)

If the UART also supports *synchronous data communications*, then it is sometimes called a *Universal Synchronous/Asynchronous Receiver Transmitter* (USART); other times, it is simply called a UART. The USART would then be able to support BISYNC and HDLC and provides features such as:

▲ *Sync* (for BISYNC) or *flag character* (for HDLC) detection and generation

▲ Zero-bit stuffing (for HDLC)

▲ CRC generation and checking

See **S16550A, ASYNCHRONOUS, BISYNC, CRC, EIA/TIA-232, ESP, HDLC, IRQ, MODEM, OUT-OFBAND, PARITY,** and **SYNCHRONOUS.**

UDP
User Datagram Protocol

A connectionless transport protocol that runs on top of IP (instead of TCP).

Provides an *unreliable datagram* service. "Unreliable", in that packets may be lost, duplicated, or received in a different order than the order in which they were sent. "Datagram" means that a connection does not first need to be established—just like sending a letter or telegram, there is no assurance when you send the message that the message is correctly addressed, or the recipient ready to recieve it. Sometimes UDP is also referred to as a *streaming* protocol (for different reasons than TCP is), in that the sender can send as many packets as desired, as there is no protocol feedback for flow control. The sender can send a constant stream of UDP packets, without having to "waste" bandwidth on acknowledgements and flow control with the recipient. UDP is therefore well-suited to sending streams to many recipients (one stream to each)—unfortunately, since there is no built-in flow control mechanism, transmitters can easily overload networks (and the receiving stations—unless there is some application-level flow control implemented). Most audio-over-the-Internet technologies (such as video-conferencing, Progressive Networks' RealAudio and Internet telephone calls) use UDP (and this is a big concern, since they are a quickly growing percentage of Internet traffic).

In contrast, a connection-oriented protocol (such as TCP) is like making a telephone call—it ensures that the message is correctly addressed, and the recipient ready to receive it (you don't start talking business on the telephone until you get the person you intended).

In UDP, the receiving program requests a number of bytes (up to the number in the received packet). If less that the full packet is read, then the remainder is discarded, and the next read is from the next packet. That is, the boundaries of the original packet are preserved (which is different than for TCP). The application program must handle error correction.

UDP is best suited for small, independent requests, such as requesting a MIB value from an SNMP agent, in which first setting up a connection would take more time than sending the data. Less efficient than TCP, since the full address must be sent with each packet.

Used by DNS, NFS, ping, RIP, RPCs, SNMP, and tftp (the /etc/services file on a UNIX computer has a complete list for that computer).

UDP is defined in RFC 768. The other transport-layer protocol that can run on top of IP is TCP.

See **CONNECTIONLESS, DNS1** (*Domain Name System*), **FLOW CONTROL, NFS, PING, RIP, RPC, SNMP, TCP, TCP/IP, TFTP,** and **WINSOCK.**

UI
UNIX International

A now defunct consortium of over 200 vendors and users (including AT&T, Sun, NCR, and SCO) that promoted UNIX System V systems.

They promoted something called UI-ATLAS—a "comprehensive architecture for the development, operation and management of distributed multivendor applications in mixed computing environments." It was to compete with OSF's DME. But like so many other efforts, you don't hear much about this one any more.

See **DME**, **OSF**, **UNIX**, and **X-OPEN**.

UIFN
Universal International FreePhone Number

A toll-free (to the caller) international 800-type telephone number ("800" service is called *FreePhone* by much of the world). Callers can then dial 011 800 xxx-xxxx from anywhere in the world (this example uses North America's "011" *international access code* prefix—callers from the UK would use the UK's IAC of 00, and so on).

This service is called international freephone service (IFS), and is administered by the ITU. In an attempt to prevent the abuse of hoarding desirable numbers (for example, that spell memorable things), the ITU takes back any numbers not activated within 90 days.

For more information, see *http://www.itu.ch/uifn*.

See **S800**.

Ultra DMA

A 33 Mbyte/s, DMA-based transfer method between disk drives and computer systems.

See **ATA-3**, and **IDE**.

UltraSCSI

See **SCSI2**, and **SCSI3**.

UMA
Unified Memory Architecture

See **USDA**.

UMTS
Universal Mobile Telephone Services

The third generation of mobile telephone service (after AMPS and PCSin North America, and GSM for Europe *et al*). Services dreamed of include surfing the Internet, watching movies and receiving compact disc quality music.

For North American users, it might use CDMA. For European users, the European Commission has contracted ETSI to develop a system, so it will may be some extension of it.

So far, nobody knows what technologies will be used (maybe ATM—the ATM Forum has a *wireless ATM* working group called WATM, maybe they can help), just that it would be nice if such mobile services could be offered.

Sometimes pronounced *UMMpts* (that may not help you pronounce it though).

See **DECT**, **GSM**, and **PCS1** (*Personal Communications Service*).

UNI
User-to-Network Interface

The specification for the interface between a user's equipment (a router with an ATM interface, for example) and an ATM network (likely a SONet OC-3, or slower link, to an ATM switch).

See **ATM** (*Asynchronous Transfer Mode*), **DXI**, and **SONET**.

Unicode

A character coding scheme designed to be an extension to ASCII.

It uses 16 bits (2 bytes) for each character (rather than ASCII's 7), so virtually every character of every language, as well as many symbols (such as "•"), can be represented in an internationally standard way, and the current complexity of incompatible *extended character sets* and *code pages* should be eliminated.

The first 128 codes of Unicode correspond to standard ASCII.

Unicode is a subset of ISO/IEC 10646. ISO/IEC 10646 uses 1 to 4 bytes to represent each character.

Further information is at *http://www.stonehand.com/unicode.htm*.

See **ASCII**, **BAUD**, **EBCDIC**, **HTML**, and **JAVA**.

UniForum

A nonprofit trade association dedicated to the promotion of the UNIX operating system and other efforts that are important to the acceptance of UNIX—such as POSIX.

Formally though, their mission statement is much more broad and does not even mention UNIX: "UniForum is a vendor independent, not-for-profit professional association that helps individuals and their organizations increase their information system's effectiveness through the use of open systems, based on shared industry standards. Central to UniForum's mission is the delivery of high quality educational programs, trade shows and conferences, publications, on-line services, and peer group interactions."

Formerly /usr/group.

They have a WWW server at *http://www.uniforum.org/*.

See **POSIX-OSE** and **UNIX**.

Univel

When Novell bought UnixWare from (along with USL) in 1993, Novell created the Univel subsidiary to continue UnixWare development. In late 1995 and early 1996, Novell sold UnixWare and all of USL to SCO.

UnixWare integrates USL's UNIX System V Release 4.2 with Novell NetWare client software.

See **COSE**, **NOVELL**, **SCO**, **UNIX**, and **USL**.

UNIX
Uniplexed Information and Computing System

A usually non-real-time (for example, most implementations don't support task preemption) operating system, now written in the C language. Popular because it is available for so many hardware platforms and because it is well documented (but cryptic), with much source code available. Also popular because it is widely used at universities, so graduates are comfortable with it.

The initial development was by Ken Thompson and Dennis M. Ritchie, two programmers for AT&T. UNIX was developed starting in 1969 as a file system and some utilities on a DEC PDP-7 minicomputer to assist in the porting (from a GE 635 computer) of a game called *Space Travel*. Development continued on a DEC PDP-11/20 computer, and *UNIX* Version 1 was completed in 1971. It was written in assembler, was documented in *"Edition 1"* of the manual (so this version of UNIX was sometimes referred to as Edition 1). Initially, UNIX was used as a text processing tool for the preparation of patents.

During most of the mid-life of UNIX (the 1980s), there were three main "flavors" that were popular. The list below shows the approximate time line of when all this UNIX stuff happened, and where some of the version names and numbers come from.

▲ AT&T UNIX System V

▲ System V was first available in 1983. It supported many types of interprocess communication, such as message queues, semaphores and shared memory.

▲ System V Release 2.0 ("System five, release two point zero") was available in April 1984.

▲ System V Release 2.0 enhancement release (November 1984). Two important added features were demand paging and advisory file and record locking.

▲ System V Release 3.0 was available in 1986. It supported remote file sharing (RFS), shared libraries and mandatory file and record locking.

▲ System V Release 3.1 was released in 1987.

▲ System V Release 3.2 was available in 1988. This release supported the Intel 80386 processor, and had binary compatibility for programs written for Xenix.

▲ System V Release 4.0 (1989) was a merge of SVR3.2 with Sun Microsystems' SunOS, with features from Microsoft's Xenix, and an ANSI C compiler (which is specified in ANSI standard X3J11).

▲ System V Release 4.2 ("SVR4.2") versions are currently the most popular UNIX implementation.

▲ Berkeley Software Distribution (from the Computer Systems Research Group at the University of California at Berkeley). Initially, these were tapes of new utilities for the System V version of the operating system. These grew to be an entire operating system, though there were parts used from the System V operating system, so a license from AT&T was still required (4.4BSD-lite was the first "totally-un-AT&T-encumbered" version).

▲ 4.1BSD and 4.2BSD were released about 1982 and 1983. They were the first popular versions with good network support (TCP/IP and Ethernet, and the BERKELY SOCKETS programming interface to them.

▲ 4.3BSD was released in April 1986, and ran on a DEC VAX minicomputer. This version of UNIX is still very common today.

▲ 4.3BSD Tahoe (which refers to this version's support for the computer called Tahoe, which was made by Computer Consoles, Inc.) was released in June 1988. The University of California permitted the networking source code to be used or modified in any manner (so long as credit is given). Many commercial implementations (for other platforms) were therefore based on this software (for example, the *Berkeley sockets* interface is still the basis for most UNIX networking software).

▲ Microsoft Xenix was first a port (to DEC PDP11, Apple Lisa and PC platforms) of AT&T UNIX Version 7, then was updated to System III, and finally to System V Release 2.0. The version of Xenix that runs on PCs (Intel 8086 and up) was (and still is) widely installed.

A gross simplification of the many UNIX variants is shown in the accompanying figure. The solid lines show that the source code from one version was used in the next, or that specific features from one version were implemented in the next. The dashed lines indicate more of a design influence, rather than actual use of the source code to create the new variant.

Some important variations on UNIX are the following:

▲ Linux, which is a public domain version of UNIX.

▲ QNX, which is a real-time UNIX.

One of the cryptic features of command-line UNIX is that you type man to get help. This man is as in "manual", and typing man accesses the on-line version of the manual. The manuals for both System V and 4.3BSD UNIXes had 8 sections, and references to entries in the manuala included the section number. For example, *socket(2)* indicates that the socket function is documented in section 2 of the manual.

As to the name, the story goes that there was once an effort to make an all-singing, all-dancing operating system. It was to do everything and was called *Multiplexed Information and Computing System* (*Multics*), and initially ran on a GE 635. Although Multics was used on a small percentage of Honeywell mainframe computers in the late 1970s and early 1980s (the larger percentage used GCOS—General Comprehensive Operating System), the Multics effort mostly failed.

So the Multics developers tried something simpler (the "opposite") and therefore called it *Uniplexed Information and Computing System*—that is, "Unics." This was later written UNIX, as it is today (then again, some say that that UNIX is as in *eunuch*, that is, a "castrated Multics").

UNIX System Laboratories (USL) is responsible for the ongoing development of the original AT&T UNIX. USL was bought from AT&T by Novell in early 1993 (along with AT&T's portion

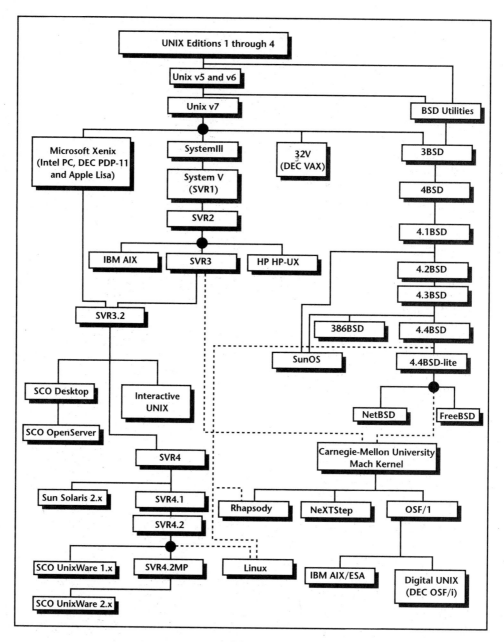

UNIX-1

of the Novell-AT&T joint-venture called Univel). In 1996, Novell sold USL to SCO for about $70 million plus on-going royalties. About of the approximately 300 USL employees (from their office in Florham Park, New Jersey) joined SCO, at their Murray Hill office (the rest went to Hewlett-Packard or stayed with Novell).

In late 1993, Novell gave the rights to the UNIX name to the X/Open Company Ltd. (which licenses it to others to use).

The UNIX and Advanced Computing Systems Professional and Technical Association has a WWW server at *http://www.usenix.org/*, and Michigan State University maintains some WWW pointers at *http://clunix.msu.edu*. QNX Software Systems Ltd. is at *http://www.qnx.com*.

A wide range of UNIX information is at *http://www.stokeley.com*. Some UNIX manuals are available at *http://www.cis.ohio-state.edu/hypertext/ man_pages.html/*. Some history of UNIX is at *http://www.cis.ohio-state.edu/hypertext/faq/ usenet/unix-faq/faq/part6/faq-doc-2.html*.

See **AIX, A/UX, BSD UNIX, CDE, COSE, DEC, FINGER, GOPHER, IBCS, IRC, LINUX, MACH, MOTD, MOTIF, NIS, NFS, NEXTSTEP, NOVELL, OPENLOOK, OPERATING SYSTEM, OSF, POSIX-OSE, SCO, SOCKETS, SOLARIS, SVID, SVR4, UI, UNIFORUM, UNIVEL, USL, WABI, X-OPEN, X WINDOW SYSTEM, XENIX,** and **XPG.**

UPC
Universal Product Code

The numbering and barcode system used for items commonly found in grocery stores. First used in 1973.

The most common UPC used is UPC-A which has a total of 12 numeric digits, as described below.

▲ The left-most digit (printed to the left of the bar code) is the *number system character*. It indicates which numbering system follows. A 0 typically indicates a grocery-type item, a 2 indicates items sold per kg or pound, and a 3 indicates the numbering system used for drugs.

▲ The next 5 digits are the *manufacturer identification number*. Actually, 6-digit manufacturer IDs are assigned, but currently the leading digit is always a zero, and this leading zero is omitted from the barcode. These 5 digits are printed below the barcode. To be assigned a manufacturer ID, you need to become a member of the Uniform Code Council, which costs $300 to $10,000, depending on the annual sales of your company.

▲ Anticipating that all manufacturer IDs will be assigned over the next decade or so, it has already been announced that the 12-digit UPC-A format will be replaced by the 13-digit EAN-13 system in the year 2005. The supressed leading 0 of the manufacturer ID will then be non-zero and assigned.

▲ The next 5 digits are the *item code number*, and these are uniquely assigned by each manufacturer for their own products (this allows 100,000 products). These 5 digits are also printed below the barcode.

▲ The last digit is the *check character*. It is calculated from the other 11 digits, and helps ensure that the barcode was read properly. The digit is printed to the right of the barcode.

A block of 35,000 UPC codes (using the 0 number system character) is reserved for stores to assign themselves, for in-house items and multiple packs of other items.

The other commonly-seen UPC system is UPC-E, which is used for smaller packages such as soft drink cans. The middle zeros (last digits of the manufacturer ID, and leading zeros of

the item number) are omitted, and an added digit at the end indicates which zeros were omitted.

Administered by the Uniform Code Council, who are at *http://www.uc-council.org*. The full UPC-A specification is available on-line there. More information on bar codes is at *http://www.adam1.com/pub/russadam/upccode.html*.

See **EDI**, and **ISBN**.

URL
Uniform Resource Locator

An addressing format commonly used by web browsers. The figure below shows the components of a URL.

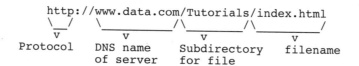

Each section of the address is described below:

▲ The first part specifies the protocol to use. Since world wide web servers provide their HTML pages using the hypertext transfer protocol, this is typically *http*, but it could be *ftp:* (for file transfers, as shown in the example below), *mailto:* (to send mail), *nntp:* (for usenet news), *gopher:*, or others as well.

▲ The next part is the full DNS name of the server to contact. Any valid DNS name can be used (such as *noodle.froodle.toodle.com*), but most organizations choose *www* followed by their registered domain name, as the name for their public WWW server. Similarly, most choose *ftp* followed by their domain name for their FTP server. These may in fact be the same machines, but provides the flexibility of using two separate servers in the future.

▲ The next part specifies the subdirectory (if any) to access when looking for the file to send to you.

▲ The next part is also optional, and specifies the file to send to you. If none is specified, then a default filename (such as *index.html*) is sent to you. Since DOS and Windows 3.1 computers (on which the pages may have been prepared) only support 3-character filename extensions, *.htm* is often the filename extension used.

Sometimes, it can make a difference whether there is a trailing "/" appended, when no HTML file is specified (such as *ftp://ftp.data.com/Tutorials/*). The trailing / indicates that the URL specifies only a subdirectory, and not a filename (that happens to have no extension). In this case, and ftp accesses would display all the files in that directory, rather than complaining that there is no file with the name *Tutorials*.

The URL can also contain a TCP *port number* to be used by the caller, instead of the default of 80 (for HTTP). For example, *http://www.ora.com:8080*.

URLs are specified in RFC 1738.

Additional information is at *ftp://ftp.isi.edu/in-notes/iana/assignments/url-schemes* .

See **DNS1** (*Domain Name System*), **GOPHER**, **HOME PAGE**, **HTML**, **HTTP**, **NNTP**, **TCP**, and **WWW**.

USB
Universal Serial Bus

A 12-Mbit/s (with an optional 1.5 Mbit/s low-cost version), daisy-chain, bi-directional, half-duplex, *serial bus* first proposed by Intel (and now with wide industry acceptance), with the intent of facilitating:

▲ the connection of a PC to telephones (for control, as well as transferring voice and data)—as required for some types of CTI

▲ the connection and rearranging of peripherals

▲ the addition of new types of peripherals

The bus supports connecting a PC to as many as 127 physical devices—and each physical device can have multiple logical devices (this is also called a *compound device*. An example of a compound devices is a keyboard with a built-in trackball.

Examples of devices include: USB hubs (which permit the connection of more devices—one device per hub port), backup tape drives, CD-ROM drives, joysticks, keyboards, mice, printers, voice-digitizing telephones, scanners, digitized cameras and other digitized audio devices. A major motivation is that all these peripherals would require only a single port on the PC. This would be a dramatic cost savings over the current situation, in which a PC needs separate ports (electronics and connectors) for each of these devices.

USB is also intended to replace the use of EIA-232 for modem connections (EIA-232 isn't fast enough, and a PC often does not have enough serial ports).

The cabling starts at the *USB* host. Only one host is currently allowed per system (your PC for example). The host has an integrated *root hub*, which presents one or more USB connectors to the outside world. Cabling then goes to other *USB* devices, which are other hubs, and "functions". Functions provide capabilities, such as a modem or speakers. Hubs are frequently built-in to monitors and keyboards (which results in a typical compound device—a hub and a function all in one). Hubs typically have 7 or fewer downstream ports.

The USB signal is carried by two-pair cable, that uses a four-pin shielded connector. The connector and the port into which is connects is marked with the USB logo, which is the letters USB, overwritten with a horizontal line with a plug on the right end (they started with a branching tree-looking thing, with a circle, arrow and square on the three ends, but like all such language-independent identifiers, it was never clear what it meant). One pair of wires (the outside two on the connector) is non-twisted, uses 20 to 28 gauge conductors, and carries 5 V DC power (from the upstream device—which may shut-off power when it is idle). Devices may be *bus-powered* (maximum allowed current draw is 500 mA) or *self-powered*.

Commands and data are carried on the other pair (of 28 gauge wire), which supports bi-direction, half-duplex communications. The individual wires are called D+ and D–. For full speed devices, the pair of data conductors is twisted, and has a 90Ω characteristic impedance. For low speed devices, this pair is not twisted. For data transmision, differential voltages (about 0 V and 3 V) are used (for noise immunity), and NRZI encoding is used (so a

separate pair of wires for the clock signal is not needed). The 1.5 Mbit/s speed (called a *low speed sub-channel*) is intended for devices such as mice and keyboards that do not need the full 12 Mbits/s speed (which is called *full speed*). Both speed devices can communicate on the same bus (hubs determine the speed by sensing which of the function's 2 data wires has a 1.5 kΩ pull-up resistor, and hosts communicate with each accordingly).

All hubs must support both full speed and low speed devices on their downstream ports, and hubs block full speed data from reaching low speed devices. Hub upstream connections are always full speed, and hubs do a speed conversion for low speed devices. Full speed devices require shielded cable. Low speed devices can use unshielded cable (which allows the cable to be thinner, and therefore more flexible). The length of each cable is a maximum of 5 m (for full speed devices) and 3 m (for low speed devices)—but may need to be less, depending on the gauge of the power conductors in the cable and the amount of power drawn by downstream bus-powered USB devices. A maximum of six hubs (and seven 5 m cables) are allowed between a function and the host (mostly for maximum signal propagation time limitations).

The term *upstream* refers to cabling and connectors that goes towards the USB host. Hubs provide upstream connectors to which devices attach. These hub connectors are called *series A*, and are for downstream connections to peripherals. Devices with permanently attached cables (such as a mouse) will also use a series A connector (at the hub-end of the cable), which will plug-in to the hub. Devices that have detachable cables (such as a printer) are built with an integral *series B* connector at the peripheral end. The two types of connectors won't mate (series A connectors are flat rectangles, and series B are higher, with bevelled top edges), so there is no chance of connecting things in a loop. Connectors are rated for at least 1,500 connect and disconnect cycles.

Bus-powered hubs can draw a maximum of 500 mA from their upstream connection, and can provide a maximum of 100 mA (which is called a *unit load*) to each downstream port. Self-powered hubs can supply a maximum of 500 mA per downstream port.

The host learns of the new connection of a device (or that a device has been reset) through a message from the hub (this is called *bus enumeration*). The host then communicates with the new device using the *USB* default address—this is address 0, so only 127 device addresses are available (from the 7-bit device address field) for other devices. The host then assigns a unique USB address to the device. If the device is removed from the USB, then the address is made available for other devices.

A 4-bit endpoint field is used to individually address each function in a compound device. Low speed devices have a maximum of two endpoint addresses per function (endpoint 0 is for used for USB configuration, status and control of the function, and the other endpoint is for whatever the function actually does). Full speed devices can have up to 16 endpoints, again endpoint 0 is reserved for USB configuration, status and control.

The host polls all devices, and gives them permission to transmit (by sending a *Token Packet*). Devices cannot talk directly to other devices, only to the host, which can then forward data to other devices. Transfers over the bus occur at 1 ms intervals.

Four types of data transfers are supported, as listed below.

▲ *Control transfers* are used to configure newly-attached devices (such as assigning a USB address), and for other device-specific functions. Full speed devices can be configured for 8-, 16-, 32- or 64-byte maximum control message payload data sizes (8-bytes is the default). Low speed devices can only use 8-byte maximum control message sizes.

▲ *Bulk data transfers*, which are large, individual, bursty transfers. Examples would be data to a printer, or from a scanner. Transfers can be up to 1,023 bytes. Low speed devices cannot use this type of transfer.

▲ *Interrupt data transfers*, such as keyboard data, mouse movements or speech echo (such as your own voice you hear in the earpiece of your telephone when you talk—this is officially called *sidetone*). These must be transferred fast enough that the time delay is imperceptible (to users). USB is designed so latency is less than a few milliseconds.

▲ *Isochronous* (also called ISO and *streaming real-time*) *data transfers*. The bandwidth and delivery latency are negotiated before the transfer begins. Isochronous data is not covered by error-correction (since the time required to get the retransmission is usually much greater than the allowable latency). Transfers are up to 1,023 bytes in length. Low speed devices cannot use this type of transfer.

▲ USB can provide reserved bandwidth from 1B+D to a full T1, or even the full bandwidth of the USB. USB bandwidth can only be reserved for a new connection if it will not adversely affect bandwidth already reserved.

Intel is providing USB support built-in to its PCI bus controller ICs. This somewhat guarantees that it will be accepted. USB was also first promoted by Compaq, DEC, IBM, Microsoft, NEC and Northern Telecom.

For lower-speed applications, USB competes with ACCESS.bus (actually, USB demolished ACCESS.bus, because USB is more powerful, as is Intel). For higher-speed requirements (as might be required for remote disk drive access, or digitized video), would compete with 1394.

The USB Implementors Forum is at *http://www.usb.org*, and Intel has information at *http://developer.intel.com/design/USB/index.htm*.

See **S1394, ACCESS.BUS, BUS, CTI, DDC, EIA/TIA-232, EVC, ISOCHRONOUS, ENCODING, MPC, PCI, PLUG AND PLAY**, and **T1**.

USDA
Unified System Display Architecture

A proposed method of sharing 64-bit-wide memory between that needed for a PC's main memory (which is used for programs, data, and disk caching) and video display memory. The intent is to both enhance performance and avoid wasting memory not needed for a particular display resolution.

For example, a 1,024 × 768 pixel display using 256 colors requires 768 kbytes of RAM. If the video board has 2 Mbytes of RAM (more of which would be needed for higher resolutions or more colors), then 1,280 kbytes would be wasted. USDA would permit this otherwise-wasted memory to be used for other PC requirements (nice big caches for example).

Has nothing whatsoever to do with the U.S. Department of Agriculture.

Usenet

Sometimes called *Unified Memory Architecture* (UMA)—for example, by Silicon Graphics. AGP and the graphics controller built-in to the Cyrix MediaGX also use system DRAM for display memory.

Silicon Graphics has a web site at *http://www.sgi.com*.

See **AGP**, **CACHE**, **PC**, and **VESA**.

Usenet

One of the main things people read and contribute to on the Internet. Equivalent to a worldwide BBS (*bulletin board system*) with over 20,000 newsgroups (which a BBS would call forums or sections), and many new ones every day.

The *network news transfer protocol* (NNTP) is used to distribute updated news (about a gigabyte per day in 1997) between news servers, and to clients. A news reader (which may be built into your WWW browser) is required to interract with news servers to send and receive news items. Since the protocol (as for SMTP) does not support binary data, encoding (such as uuencode and Base64) must be used for binary files attached to news items.

Usenet news servers (located at ISPs) typically open a connection to their *feed sites* every 15 minutes (or whatever the administrator sets) and exchange updates.

Usenet newsgroups are named in a hierarchical method, with each level separated by a period (just as domain names are)—but the sequence is in the opposite order. The left-most word is the major category (such as *news://comp.os.dos*—where the *comp* subcategory *os* has a newsgroup dedicated to the DOS operating system). In contrast, the DNS has the top-level domain as the right-most word (such as *http://www.ora.com*).

To form a new newsgroup in one of the eight original main categories (*comp, news, rec, sci, soc, talk, humanities* and *misc*) requires a proposal (called a *request for discussion*), which is eventually the subject of a vote. Such votes are announced in the *news://news.announce* and *news://news.groups* usenet newsgroups.

Other usenet hierarchies were created with different rules. For example, the *alt* hierarchy does not require a vote to form new groups, just a *control message* (a specially formatted message which can automatically instruct a news server to create, modify or delete newsgroups) which will convince the news administrators to accept the new group. And the *biz* hierarchy allows advertisments.

In addition to the usenet hierarchy, there are other hierarchies, such as local newsgroups and Clarinet, which is a fee-based (paid by the news server's administrator—typically an ISP) news feed from United Press International.

Newsgroup rules are posted in *news://news.announce.newusers*.

Since useful FAQs are often posted to newsgroups but scroll off (as the newsgroups servers need the disk space), they are archived on Usenet FAQ servers such as *http://www.cis.ohio-state.edu/hypertext/faq/usenet/faq-List.html* .

Usenet was created by Tom Truscott, Steve Bellovin, and Jim Ellis in 1979 as an experiment to create a method to post and read news messages and notices—initially primarily UNIX bug reports. It initially used UUCP (a dial-up and store-and-forward type of networking) to transfer the updates between servers. The format of usenet messages (the header fields, and their interpretation) is defined in RFCs 822 and 1036.

See **BBS**, **BUGS**, **DNS2** (*Domain Name System*), **FAQ**, **INTERNET2**, **IMAP**, **ISP**, **TCP**, **UNIX**, **UUCP**, and **UUENCODE**.

USL
UNIX System Laboratories

The previous owners of the UNIX name and source code.

USL (along with the UNIX name and the UNIX software development rights) was bought (in early 1993) by Novell Inc. from AT&T and renamed *Summit UNIX* System Group (the company is in Summit, New Jersey). The X/Open Company now owns the UNIX name. In 1995, Novell sold the UNIX business to Santa Cruz Organization for about $84 million.

There is still an ftp server at *ftp://ftp.usl.com* with some useful information.

See **ATT**, **COSE**, **NOVELL**, **SCO**, **UNIX**, and **X-OPEN**.

UTC
Universal Time Coordinated

UTC is the SI replacement for *Greenwich Mean Time* (GMT). GMT is (was) defined as the time in Greenwich, England (actually, at a lovely old observatory there), and used to be the basis for timekeeping.

In 1972, *International Atomic Time* (IAT) was adopted, as part of the SI metric stuff.

An example of IAT is that rather than the year being defined in terms of the earth's rotation around the sun (or was that the other way around?), the year is now defined as exactly 31,556,926 seconds (or one of a few other slightly larger numbers, depending on what definition for a year is used). In any case, in 1967 a second was defined to be 9,192,631,770 oscillations of the Cesium 133 atom, which (most people who care agree) is accurate to about 1 second in 300,000 years.

That is, the stars have been replaced by an oscillator; and for good reason—the earth does not rotate at a constant rate!. This is partially due to the earth wobbling a bit, and to the sloshing of the earth's liquid center. Also, the earth's rotation is slowing by a few milliseconds each day. The slowing is due to tidal drag (the ocean's tides are caused by the gravitational pull of the sun and moon) and the melting of the polar ice caps (which allows more water to go to the equator). Since the slowing will accumulate to a total of about 12 hours over 3,000 years, without these leap-seconds added (a full second added to a day—typically once every 6 to 30 months), the day would be slowly shifted so that sun would be overhead at midnight in the year 5,000. That is, the earth's rotation is only accurate to about 1 second in 1 year, and we need to adjust our clocks to keep them in sync with the earth's slowing rotation. The leap second is added when the difference between UTCand UT1 (the name for astronomical time—which is based on the stars) reaches 0.7 seconds, though typically the second is not added until the beginning of the next year. The current difference between UTC and UT1 is shown by NIST's dial-up time service.

Now *that* was a bit of a digression. Now back to things that matter more today.

UNIX computers maintain their time-of-day clocks as a 32-bit counter of the number of seconds since midnight January 1, 1970, UTC. The counter will overflow after 136 years (around February 4 in the year 2106)—I just can't wait to see the havoc). The same 32-bit counter method is used by YModem's file `datestamp`.

On some computer systems, "Time 0" is defined as midnight January 6, 1980, UTC. Many time-of-day clocks count the number of microseconds since this time. There are about 3×10^{13} µs per year, so a 64-bit counter ($2^{64} \approx 2 \times 10^{19}$) can count about 600,000 years (maybe that one I won't see wrap-around).

English grammar would dictate that UTC should have been called *coordinated universal time*. However in the interest of having the same acronym for both the English and French names, the more awkward (but equally so in both languages) *universal time coordinated* and *temps universel coordonné* was chosen by the ITU.

The Canadian National Research Council has broadcasts of the super-accurate time (both spoken, and as data in a really weird format) from CHU Canada (which transmits from Ottawa, Canada) at 3.33, 7.335 and 14.67 MHz on your short-wave (actually, I think that is medium wave) radio dial. They also have a web site at *http://www.nrc.ca/inms/whatime.html*.

The U.S. National Institute of Standards and Technology runs courses on time (now that's just begging for some punny jokes to be made). Check them out at *http://www.boulder.nist.gov/timefreq/*. They also have radio STATIONS—WWV and WWVH (which is in Hawaii). The United States Naval Observatory (USNO) maintains UT1, and they are at *http://www.usno.navy.mil/*.

See **DAYLIGHT SAVINGS TIME**, **GMT**, **GPS**, **LEAP YEAR**, **NIST ACTS**, **NTP**, **SATELLITE**, **SI**, **PC**, **TIMESTAMP**, **YMODEM**, and **UNIX**.

UTP
Unshielded Twisted Pair

A popular type of cable for LANs and other in-building voice and data communications applications.

It turns out that there are advantages to the following:

▲ Using two wires, rather than one for each signal. This permits *differential signaling* to be used, which is more immune to the effects of external electrical noise.

▲ Twisting each pair. This keeps the wires of a signal's pair as close together as possible, and periodically exposes the opposite side of the pair to the noise. Both of these factors help to cancel out the effects of outside interference. Also, each pair has a different *twist pitch* (so the pairs also appear twisted to each other), and the pairs are each moved somewhat randomly relative to the other pairs in the cable jacket. Both of these help to reduce cross-talk between the pairs.

▲ Not using cable *shielding* (a foil or braided metallic covering). While this can increase the effects of outside interference, not using shielding reduces the cost, size, and installation time of the cable and connectors and eliminates the possibility of *ground loops* (which is current flowing in the shield because of the ground voltage at each end of the cable not being exactly the same—and this current inducing interference into the cable that was supposed to be better protected through the use of the shield).

Unshielded twisted pair implements all of these.

While any cable with twisted pairs of conductors and no shield could be referred to as unshielded twisted pair, the term "UTP" usually refers to unshielded twisted pair cable as specified in the EIA/TIA-568 *Commercial Building Telecommunications Wiring Standard*. This standard (first released in 1991) specifies the electrical and physical requirements for UTP, STP, coaxial cables, and optical fiber cables. For UTP, the requirements include:

▲ Four individually twisted pairs per cable

▲ Each pair has a *characteristic impedance* of 100 Ω ± 15% (when measured at frequencies of 1 to 16 MHz)

▲ 24 gauge (0.5106-mm-diameter) or optionally 22 gauge (0.6438 mm diameter) copper conductors are used

Additionally, EIA/TIA-568 specifies the color coding, cable diameter, and other electrical characteristics, such as the maximum:

▲ *Cross-talk* (how much a signal in one pair interferes with the signal in another pair— through *capacitive, inductive,* and other types of coupling). Since this is measured as how many *decibels* (dB) quieter the induced signal is than the original interfering signal, larger numbers are better.

▲ *Attenuation* (the most a signal can get quieter for a given length of cable, measured at several specific key frequencies). Since this is measured as dB of attenuation, smaller numbers are better.

An important feature of UTP is that it can be used for Ethernet, Token Ring, FDDI, ATM, EIA-232, ISDN, analog telephone (POTS), and other types of communication. This enables the same type of cable (and connectors) to be used for an entire building—unlike STP.

EIA/TIA-568 (and the subsequent TSB-36, also first released in 1991) defines five *categories*, as shown in the following table. These are used to quantify the quality of the cable (for example, only Categories 3, 4, and 5 are considered "datagrade UTP").

Category	Characteristics specified up to (MHz)	Use
1	None	Alarm systems and other noncritical (as far as frequency response is concerned) applications.
2	None	Voice (such as the 25-pair cables with TelCo connectors used for telephones), EIA-232, and other low speed data.
3	16	10BASE-T Ethernet, 4-Mbits/s Token Ring, 100BASE-T4, 100VG-AnyLAN, basic rate ISDN. Is the minimum standard for new installations. Equivalent to IBM Cabling System Type 3 cable.
4	20	16-Mbits/s Token Ring. Not widely used.
5	100	TP-PMD, SONet, OC-3 (ATM), 100BASE-TX. The most popular for new data installations.

Cat 5 is what those on a first-name basis with cable would call Category 5 cable.

Some vendors use the terms *Enhanced Category 5* to refer to cable which can work at frequencies up to 350 MHz, and Category 6 for frequencies up to 600 MHz (these cables use a foil shield—and are sometimes called SFTP, shileded foil twisted-pair—so are not actually "UTP"). Since there is no standard specifying the test procedures used, or the test results, such terms are mainly marketing mumbo jumbo. Also, there are no standards for patch panels, wall jacks and all the other equipment required for such frequencies, having cable but not the rest of the infrastructure rated for such frequencies is somewhat useless in real life. Finally, even 155.52 Mbit/s ATM traffic uses an encoding method that results in most of the highest frequency components being about half of the raw bit rate—about 77 MHz, which is well below 100 MHz (less than 5% of the signal energy is at frequencies above 100 MHz, so it is unlikely that cable problems at frequencies above 100 MHz could cause bit errors). Higher speed communications, such as Gigabit Ethernet will likely split the traffic among all 4 cable pairs and use multilevel encoding methods to keep the maximum frequencies below 100 MHz.

In September 1997, the ISO approved specifications for Category 7 cabling. It uses individually shielded pairs (so you couldn't call it UTP), and specifies electrical characteristics up to 600 MHz.

Underwriter's Laboratory defines a *level* system, which has minor differences from EIA/TIA-568's category system. For example, UL requires the characteristics to be measured at various temperatures. However, generally (for example), UL Level V (Roman numerals are used) is the same as EIA's Category 5, and cables are usually marked with both EIA and UL designations.

Typically (for example, Token Ring and 10BASE-T Ethernet), only two of the four pairs of wires per cable are used (one pair for the receive data, one for the transmit data). The additional two pairs per cable would then be available so that the cable could be used for other types of data communications. For example, ISDN sometimes requires the third and possibly fourth pair to provide power to the networked devices; 100BASE-T4 and 100VG-Any-LAN can split the data among all four pairs to reduce the bit rate on each pair so that a lower-quality cable (Category 3) can be used instead of Category 5, which would normally be required for 100-Mbits/s data communications (this is supposed to reduce costs); and some sites use the extra pairs for other signals, such as a second 10BASE-T connection or a telephone line or for future uses.

A Category 5 cable installation requires more than just Category 5 cable. For example, installation practices (such as not untwisting a pair more than $\frac{1}{2}$ inch when terminating it onto a connector) must be met. All components (such as data jacks, cross-patch panels, and patch cables) must be certified for Category 5 installations and to work together to make a Category 5 installation (this usually restricts an installation to components from a single vendor).

It is anticipated that many sites that spent extra money to install Category 5 cable will be disappointed when they learn (likely the hard way) that they still can't carry (for example) 100BASE-TX Fast Ethernet because either the installation practices were not adequate or some components were not Category 5 compliant. The correct components, but also the correct design and installation practices are needed for a successful Category 5 UTP cable installation.

Some vendors are offering *enhanced Category 5* cable. There is no standard for how "enhanced" such cables (and connectors) are, but the vendors get to charge more, so they think its a good idea. Though there is no assurance that the cable will meet any future specifications, the vendors claim it is still a good idea because the cables provide more margin for poor installations.

Rather than (or perhaps in addition to) ensuring that all components and the installation practices meet the Category 5 requirements, some say that an end-to-end *certification test* should be used.

EIA/TIA's TSB-67 (Technical Systems Bulletin) details the tests required and accuracy needed for (usually) hand-held Category 5 cable *certification testers*. TSB-67 defines two types of testers:

▲ *Level I* testers are accurate to 4 dB and are not accurate enough for certification (but would be good low-cost field diagnostic tools)

▲ *Level II* testers are accurate to 2 dB and are suitable for Category 5 certification

In addition, there are two definitions of the links (the UTP cable connection from the workstation area to the wiring closet):

▲ The *basic link* is the cable from the wall outlet in the workstation area to the first patch panel connection in the wiring closet.

▲ The *channel* is the basic link plus the connection from the user's wall outlet to their equipment (the cable to your PC) plus all the patch cables and equipment cables in the wiring closet that are needed to connect to the concentrator. This is the more meaningful and complete measurement.

TSB-40 describes the electrical characteristics required for Category 3, 4 and 5 8-pin modular jack outlets.

See **S100BASETX, S100VG ANYLAN, S10BASET, ATM1** (*Asynchronous Transfer Mode*), **CABLE, CONNECTOR, EIA/TIA-232, ETHERNET, FDDI, ISDN, NEXT, POTS, RJ45, SCSI1, SCTP, STP,** and **TSB.**

UUCP
UNIX-to-UNIX Copy

The method popular years ago to transfer files (such as e-mail and usenet news) between UNIX computers—originally using asynchronous data transmission over auto-dial modem connections late at night, when long-distance telephone charges were low.

Along with the destination of messages, the route to get there would typically be provided, as a string of host machine names separated by exclamation marks (which UNIX people call bangs).

So, `froodle.noodle!bigcompany.com!mail.compuserve.com!isp.com` would specify that the mail message from `isp.com` should first go to the computer at `mail.compuserve.com` (you would have had to know in advance that these two computers can directly communicate). That computer has a direct (or dial-up) connection to the computer `bigcompany.com`, and would forward the message to it. Finally, there is a user with username (or alias) `froodle.noodle` on the `bigcompany.com` computer.

Newer mail systems often support such "source-routed" addressing, but use a % for all but the first-encountered !—an @ is used instead of the right-most !. So you'd use `froodle.noodle%bigcompany.com%mail.compuserve.com@isp.com` to test specific paths for your e-mail messages.

See **ASYNCHRONOUS, AT COMMAND SET, INTERNET 2, MODEM,** and **USENET.**

UUDECODE
UNIX-to-UNIX Decode

Converting a UUENCODEd file back to what it was originally.

See **UUENCODE**.

UUENCODE
UNIX-to-UNIX Encoding

A method of converting binary files (that is, files that have bytes that can be any combination of 8-bits—including reserved bit-patterns, such as those indicating the end of the file) so they can be transmitted through systems that reserve certain characters for special meaning—such as the end of a file.

The conversion is done by running a program (often called UUENCODE) and specifying the file to be converted. Other parameters can often be specified, to control the conversion. The UUENCODE function may be done automatically by an e-mail or other program.

Sometimes this conversion is called converting a file to ASCII, since the resulting file only has the printable ASCII characters in it (basically the lower- and upper-case characters plus the numbers and punctuation).

UUENCODEd files look like this:

```
section 1 of uuencode 5.20 of file 386step.com
begin 644 386step.com
MZS]3=&amp;;5P&lt;;&amp;;EN9R!L979E;"`D0C`@;W(@96%R;&amp;;EE&lt;B1<">,21$,<"
      >!O&lt;;B!H:6=H
M`>LG_(S(CL!FOP(!``<">Z@`!FNO$```!0\VQ89@0)#X0%`+H@`>L#NB,!M`G-
&amp;;(;@`3,TA
`
end
sum -r/size 22401/410 section (from "begin" to "end")
sum -r/size 51379/276 entire input file
```

The output file of UUENCODE typically has an extension of .UUE, and these files are limited to some number of lines (and therefore size)—which is usually specified as a parameter to the UUENCODE program (it often defaults to 950—which limits the file to less than 60 kbytes). If the file is larger than that, then many .UUE files will be created, with a sequential number appended to the filename—corresponding to the section number in the first line of each output file.

The keyword begin is on the line just before the actual UUENCODEd text and is followed by the file's *access mode* or *filesystem permission bits*, in UNIX format. That is, the digits (644 in the example above) represent the file access allowed for the file's owner, the file's group, and everyone else (in that order, from left to right). Each of the digits represents three binary bits. From left to right, the bits allow read, write and execute privilege. Therefore, 644 allows the file's owner to read or write the file (but not execute it), and allows everyone else to only read it.

After the permission bits is the file's orginal name and extension.

Lines beginning with M indicate that more lines follow. At the end of the file is the keyword end, usually followed by the checksums and sizes of the UUENCODE output file section, and the input file.

See **ASCII**, and **MIME**.

V

V.8

A method used by V.34 modems to negotiate connection features and options.

Using V.21 modem modulation (which is 300 bits/s FSK—the same as the initial negotiation done by Group III fax machines), the calling modem sends its *calling menu* (a message containing a list of the features it supports). The answering modem replies with a *joint menu*, which is a list of the features it supports in common with the calling modem.

Previous modem negotiations (for example, that used by V.32 modems) used tones. This method became too slow and inflexible for the large number of options that V.34 needs to negotiate.

See **FAX**, **MODEM**, **V.21**, and **V.34**.

V.17

A modem modulation standard that provides *simplex* 14,400-bits/s data transfer over a standard one-pair (that is, two-wire) POTS dial-up telephone line.

Has a *fallback* (used when the line is too noisy) speed of 12,000 bits/s. In addition, most V.17 modems can do V.29 modulation, so fallback speeds of 9,600 and 7,200 bits/s are also supported.

The most popular use of V.17 modulation is for Group III facsimile communications—especially for fax boards and data/fax modems (as most Group III fax *machines* are still V.29 only).

V.17 uses a type of modulation called *Trellis Code Modulation* (TCM).

See **FAX**, **POTS**, **SIMPLEX**, and **V.29**.

V.21

A modem modulation standard that provides full-duplex, asynchronous, data transfer at any speed from 0 to 300 bits/s (though usually at 300 bits/s) over a standard one-pair, dial-up telephone line.

Currently used by fax machines and also by V.34 modems during their negotiations. Was also used (a long time ago) in Europe (as Bell 103 was in North America) for everyday dial-up terminal to computer data communications (though the faster recent standards, such as V.32*bis* and V.34, have made V.21 all but obsolete for this application).

Similar to (in that they both use *frequency shift keying* modulation), but incompatible with, Bell 103 (they use different frequencies); that is, they are homologous. (Now there's a word you don't get to use often.)

See **ASYNCHRONOUS**, **BELL 103**, **FAX**, **FULLDUPLEX**, **MODEM**, **V.8**, and **V.34**.

V.22

A modem modulation standard that provides full-duplex, 1,200-bits/s data transfer over a standard one-pair, dial-up telephone line. Handles synchronous or asynchronous data. (Data transfer between modems is synchronous, but the modems have a built-in converter, so DTEs can use asynchronous data communications).

Is an older method, which was used mostly in Europe (and the similar technology but slightly different Bell 212A was used in North America). In general, V.22 and Bell 212A modems are compatible. The only difference is that V.22 modems can output a 1,800 Hz tone (along with whatever modem modulation is going on), which is required in some countries to suppress in-band telephone signalling (which otherwise might disrupt the V.22 modem's communication).

The symbol rate is 600 baud, and 2 bits are encoded per symbol (which is sometimes called a *dibit*). The bit rate is therefore 1,200 bits/s.

See **ASYNCHRONOUS**, **BELL 212A**, **DTE**, **MODEM**, and **SYNCHRONOUS**.

V.22*bis*

A modem modulation standard providing full-duplex, 2,400-bits/s data transfer over a standard one-pair, dial-up telephone line. In a manner similar to that of V.22 modems, both *asynchronous data communications* and *synchronous data communications* are supported.

As for V.22, V.22*bis* uses 2 tones—the call originator uses 1,200 Hz and the answerer uses 2,400 Hz. For V.22*bis*, the user data is encoded as a particular phase and amplitude combination of the tone. Sequential chunks of 4 bits of user data are converted into one of 16 phase and amplitude combinations (that is, the signal *constellation* has 16 points), so a symbol rate of 600 baud results in a user data rate of 2,400 bits/s.

See **ASYNCHRONOUS**, **MODEM**, **SYNCHRONOUS**, and **V.22**.

V.25*bis*

A serial, in-band (that is, the commands are sent on the same wires as are used to carry data) command language for auto-dialing modems and data sets (so the DTE can specify the phone number the modem should dial).

V.27ter

The standard is specified for three types of serial links:

▲ Character-oriented (BISYNC) synchronous

▲ Bit-oriented (SDLC) synchronous (for example, for CSU/DSUs, such as those for switched 56 service), in which case it uses NRZI (*Non-Return to Zero, Inverted*) encoding

▲ Asynchronous (for standard asynchronous modems)

However, V.25*bis* is usually used only for synchronous data communications, as the *AT command set* is usually used on asynchronous links.

Common uses include enabling computer or communications equipment to request that a particular number be dialed for a Group IV fax machine, synchronous auto-dialing modem, or switched 56 backup data link.

RS-366 is a rarely used out-of-band (that is, a separate connector to signal the dialing information) alternative.

See **ASYNCHRONOUS**, **AT COMMAND SET**, **BISYNC**, **CSU**, **DSU**, **EIA/TIA-232**, **DTE**, **ENCODING**, **FAX**, **INBAND**, **MODEM**, **OUTOFBAND**, **SDLC**, **SWITCHED 56**, and **SYNCHRONOUS**.

V.27*ter*

A full-duplex (on four-wire leased lines) or half-duplex (on two-wire dial-up lines) synchronous 4,800- and 2,400-bits/s modem modulation standard.

Currently used mostly for lower-speed (4,800 and 2,400 bits/s) Group III facsimile communications. (V.29 and V.17 are higher-speed modulation methods.)

Typically, V.27*ter* is used only to reduce the cost of the fax's modem or because the communication line for that call was too noisy to support higher-speed communications. Uses a type of modulation called *Differential Phase Shift Keying* (DPSK).

See **FAX**, **SYNCHRONOUS**, and **V.29**.

V.29

A full-duplex (on four-wire leased lines) or half-duplex (on two-wire dial-up lines) synchronous 9,600- and 7,200-bits/s modem modulation standard.

The two-wire, 9,600-bits/s version is used for standard Group III facsimile machines—which fall back to 7,200 (and to 4,800 and 2,400 bits/s, using V.27*ter*)—if the communication line cannot handle 9,600 bits/s (for example, because the line is too noisy or is being digitized at less than 64,000 bits/s).

Uses a type of modulation called *Quadrature Amplitude Modulation* (QAM).

See **FAX**, **FULLDUPLEX**, **HALFDUPLEX**, **MODEM**, **PCM**, **V.17**, and **V.27TER**.

V.32

A modem modulation standard providing full-duplex, 9,600-bits/s data transfer over a standard one-pair, dial-up telephone line. It was released in 1986.

Asynchronous (through the use of a built-in asynchronous-to-synchronous converter) and synchronous data communications are supported.

However, to save money, some modems (low-end) do not provide synchronous user-data support, which at first glance seems strange, since the modem uses synchronous data communications to the remote modem and requires (and has) extra circuitry to handle asynchronous data communications. One would expect that it would be easy to provide synchronous user-data support (by simply bypassing the asynchronous converter). The bottom line is that it costs more money to support synchronous user-data, since it requires extra signals—the clocking—on the EIA-232 interface. And very few users require it, especially in the home-PC market, in which saving money is more important than seldom-used features.

Also, *internal modems* (the modem is a card in the PC rather than an external box) usually do not support synchronous data communications. This is because the built-in COM port required by internal modems uses a standard PC UART, and these UARTs do not support synchronous data communications.

The above discussion concerning synchronous data communications support applies to all modems from Bell 212A through to V.34.

A fallback speed of 4,800 bits/s is included in the V.32 standard.

See **ASYNCHRONOUS, BAUD, EIA/TIA-232, MODEM, SYNCHRONOUS, UART, V.42**, and **V.42BIS**.

V.32*bis*

A modem modulation standard providing full-duplex, 14,400 bits/s data transfer over a standard one-pair, dial-up telephone line. It was released in 1991.

Synchronous and asynchronous data communications are supported. Fallback speeds of 12,000, 9,600, 7,200, and 4,800 bits/s (using fewer bits per symbol) are included in the standard.

Modulation handshaking can take up to 8 seconds, and subsequent V.42 and V.42*bis* handshaking can require an additional 10 to 20 seconds.

See **BAUD, V.32, MODEM, V.42**, and **V.42BIS**.

V.33

A modem modulation standard providing synchronous, full-duplex, 14,400 bits/s data transfer over a 2-pair leased line. A fall-back speed of 12,000 bits/s is used on lower-quality lines.

V.34

One-pair leased lines can be used to provide half-duplex operation.

See **MODEM**, and **SYNCHRONOUS**.

V.34

A modem modulation standard providing full-duplex, 28,800-bits/s data transfer over a standard one-pair, dial-up telephone line.

Synchronous and asynchronous data communications are supported. A handshaking method based on V.8 provides faster (it was supposed to be under 5 seconds, but this doesn't seem to really happen) call setup negotiation than V.32*bis*, V.FC, or V.*terbo*.

Other enhancements over V.32*bis* (and its predecessors) include the following:

▲ *Line Probing* (choosing a *carrier frequency* between 2,400 and 3,429 Hz) at call setup time. The choice is based on detected line impairments and which frequencies the line best carries—perhaps because of telephone company digitizing. Previous modem modulation methods specify only a single carrier frequency. V.34 modems are supposed to perform line probing continuously after a connection is established, to adjust to changing line conditions. A good implementation will make these adjustments quickly.

▲ *Precoding*—the receiving modem tells the transmitting modem about detected line distortion (for example, because of PCM digitization of the analog phone line) so that the transmitting modem can precompensate for these deficiencies in the communications channel (for example, by boosting the frequencies that are attenuated more than the others).

▲ *Preemphasis*—precompensating for suspected line impairments (such as boosting frequencies that get greater attenuation on the analog line) when the signals are transmitted, so they arrive with less distortion.

▲ *Retrain/Entrain* during a data call to adjust the transmitting modem's precoding, receiving modem's *equalization* (compensating for the communication line's deficiencies), or the data transmission rate (faster and slower) as required because of changing line conditions. Data transfer is suspended during the few seconds that this occurs.

▲ A half-duplex version (which could, for example, be used in Group III fax machines).

▲ Smaller fallback (due to noisy lines) data transmission speed increments (or should that be decrements?) of 2,400 bits/s (many previous modems have 4,800-bits/s increments). A total of 12 speeds (from 2,400 to 28,800 bits/s) are therefore available.

The modulation scheme maps up to 9 data bits to each *symbol* (baud) sent over the telephone line. Therefore, a bit rate (data bits into the modem's EIA-232 connector) of 28,800 bits/s results in a baud rate of 3,200 (9-bit) symbols per second out the analog phone line (since $3,200 \times 9 = 28,800$ bits/s).

Implementation options are listed in the following table.

Feature	Provides
Asymmetrical Transmission Rates	Sending and receiving data rates can be different so that they can each be as high as the communication circuit supports.
Auxiliary Channel	Supports a 200-bits/s in-band data channel for diagnostics, line quality monitoring, and modem configuration.
Baud Rate	The standard baud rates are 2,400, 3,000, and 3,200 symbols per second. Optional rates of 2,743 and 2,800 baud may be the highest that work for links that use ADPCM (for example, satellite data links usually can't handle the 3,000-baud rate). This provides a higher data rate than if the 2,400-baud rate was used. An optional baud rate (implemented by Motorola) of 3,429 9-bit symbols per second results in a data rate of 33,600 bits/s.
Nonlinear Encoding	Allows better operation over PCM-digitized analog communication circuits by using amplitudes that are less sensitive to *quantization* noise (it moves the symbols farther apart at the perimeter of the constellation to accomodate the nonlinear digitizing—μ-law and A-law—of audio by CODECs).
Precoding	Reduces high-frequency noise and reduces inter-symbol interference—important for noisier analog communication circuits.
Trellis Coding	Modems must be able to transmit using 16-, 32-, *and* 64-state codes. Modems only need to be able to receive using any one (though optionally two or all three) of these Trellis codes. Higher-state codes provide better operation on noisier communication circuits—ideally, avoiding the need to drop to a lower baud rate. This is a form of *forward error correction* (FEC).

Note that vendors can call the modem a "V.34 modem" if it implements none, any, or all of these options. Also options will be used only if both modems in a session support the option.

Other implementation options (which are entirely up to the vendor and not part of any standard) include the following:

▲ How the modem's software (sometimes called *firmware*, because it is more like hardware that is built in to the modem) is upgraded (Flash ROM with downloading from a bulletin board system is best; plugging in a new EPROM is next best)

▲ Configuration by the front panel, a management system, or remotely (in addition to *AT Commands*)

▲ *Distinctive ringing* detection

▲ *Caller ID* detection

Other differences between V.34 modems include the quality of the data compression algorithm (not that errors will occur, but that the data will not be compressed as much as possible) and the processing power available (if it is inadequate, transmission may slow significantly if data are sent full-duplex).

V.34+

See the discussion about synchronous data communications support in the entry for **V.32**, as this applies to all modems from Bell 212A through V.32.

During its lengthy standards development process, V.34 was called "V.*fast*" (since it was expected to be the modem modulation standard that provided the fastest possible data rate over standard POTS analog telephone lines).

See **ADPCM**, **AT COMMAND SET**, **BAUD**, **BBS**, **EIA/TIA-232**, **FEC**, **INBAND**, **MODEM**, **PCM**, **POTS**, **V.8**, **V.32**, **V.34BIS**, **V.42**, **V.42BIS**, **V.FC**, and **V.TERBO**.

V.34+

An enhancement to the V.34 modem modulation standard that supports full-duplex 31,200 and 33,600 bit/s (in addition to all the speeds and features of V.34) data transfer over a standard one-pair, dial-up telephone line.

The increased speeds are possible through the new baud rate of 3,429 symbols per second (V.34 has a maximum baud rate of 3,200 symbols/s).

Other enhancements are listed below:

▲ Additional combinations of encoding methods and baud (symbol) rates were defined to support the 26,400 and 28,800 bit/s bit rates, so these speeds may be possible, using V.34+ modems, on (slightly poor) connections that would not support these speeds with V.34 modems.

▲ A faster negotiation, so connections can be established (after the telephone network connection) in about 10 seconds, rather than the 15 seconds needed by V.34 modems.

It was not enough of an enhancement to be called V.34*bis*, so it is just an extension of the V.34 standard.

See **MODEM** and **V.34**.

V.35

A 48,000-bits/s *group modem* defined by the (then) CCITT (now ITU) standard V.35—which is officially called *Data Transmission at 48 kbps Using 60-108 kHz Group-Band Circuits*. The modem is no longer used (it used a 100 kHz carrier with sideband suppressed carrier modulation, to limit the bandwidth needed), but the *interface* (voltages, connector type, pin-out, and so on) specified is frequently used to interconnect other high-speed devices (for example, a router to a DSU).

V.35 is the most popular interface (in North America) for serial data at speeds greater than EIA-232's official maximum of 20,000 bits/s. Specifically, V.35 is typically used for 56,000-bits/s to 1.544-Mbits/s (T1) data communications, using cables up to about 200 feet in length.

The connector is a squarish block about 5 cm high × 2 cm wide × 4 cm deep that has two large knurled retaining thumbscrews (to keep the connector from unplugging). The connector can accommodate 34 pins, but several are usually not used. The connector is sometimes called an *M34*, an *M-series*, or a *Winchester* connector (as it is often made by a company called Winchester Electronics)—and it is defined in ISO-2593.

The M34 connector is quite expensive and wide. Therefore, a DB-25 connector is sometimes used (with an adapter cable that has a DB-25 for the equipment, and a standard M34 for the outside world). This is really confusing, since DB-25 connectors are also used for EIA-232 (and EIA-530), and these two uses for a DB-25 are completely incompatible (different voltages, different pin-outs). For that matter, DB-25 connectors are also used for PC parallel ports and SCSI too—and all of these are completely incompatbile, its just a reliable low-cost connector that everybody chooses.

The actual voltages used are a combination of V.28 (the voltages used in EIA-232) for low-speed signals, and differential voltages for the high speed signals (the data and clock). The differential voltages are ±0.55 V DC, ±20%. A space (binary 0) is indicated by the A lead of a pair being more positive than the B lead.

The table below shows the V.35 pin functions with the M34 connector pin-outs, and the *de facto* DB-25 pin-outs (these are industry practice, but are not standardized). Not all functions (especially the test functions) will be implemented by all data sets.

M34 Pin Number	DB-25 Pin Number	Direction DTE	DCE	Pin Function
A	1	↔		Protective ground
B	7	↔		Signal ground
C	4	→		Request to send
D	5	←		Clear to send
E	6	←		Data set ready
F	8	←		Carrier detect
J	18	→		Local loopback
K and NN	25	←		Modem is in a test mode
L	22	→		Transmit a test pattern towards network
M	12	←		No signal is being received from network
N and BB	21	→		Send signal to put remote data set into loopback
P	2	→		Transmit data +
R	3	←		Receive data +
S	14	→		Transmit data -
T	16	←		Receive data -
U	24	→		External transmit clock +
V	17	←		Receive clock +
W	23	→		External transmit clock -
X	19	←		Receive clock -
Y	15	←		Transmit clock +
AA	13	←		Transmit clock -
EE	11	→		Remote digital loopback
JJ	9	←		+12 volts
KK	10	←		-12 volts

V.35 is usually used only for carrying *synchronous* data. High-speed asynchronous data are not very common. The most common application for higher-speed asynchronous data communications is from a PC to a V.34 modem, and EIA-232 is typically used here (the cables are short enough that it usually works, even though using EIA-232 at this speed is outside of the EIA-232 specification).

V.35 competes with these other (incompatible) high-speed serial interfaces:

▲ EIA-449, which uses a DB-37 connector and an optional DB-9 as well. It is used in Europe and by the military (and by some North American video-conferencing equipment too).

▲ EIA-530, which uses a DB-25 connector and is being implemented (but slowly—people just don't seem to order it when it is offered as an interface option, because the rest of their equipment is V.35).

V.35 was first standardized in 1976, and an appendix to the standard suggested a serial interface to use for the modem. IBM used the M34 connector on its equipment, and this became the *de facto* connector to use (though, for a while other vendors assembled the connector in the opposite way, with the male screw-lock at the top of the male connector, which created lots of finger-pointing about who was wrong). V.35 was omitted from the ITU standards documents beginning in 1988, as the V.35 modem was never accepted by industry.

While a V.35 interface would be a better way (than EIA-232) to handle high-speed from PCs, USB and IEEE 1394 allow multiple devices to be connected so are a far better choice.

See **S1394, DCE1, DTE, DSU, EIA/TIA-232, EIA449, EIA/TIA-530, SYNCHRONOUS, SWITCHED 56, T1, USB**, and **WAN**.

V.42

A standard for *error detection and error correction* (through retransmission) that is often implemented in modems.

Compliance with V.42 requires support for two error correction protocols:

▲ LAPM. This is usually the preferred protocol.

▲ MNP level 4, which is usually used only as a fallback, when the remote modem does not support LAPM. MNP level 4 includes support for MNP levels 3 and 2.

See **CRC, HDLC, LAPM, MNP, MODEM**, and **RPI**.

V.42*bis*

A *data compression* capability that is often implemented in modems. (Both communicating modems must support V.42*bis* for it to be used—this is detected and negotiated at the beginning of a dial-up modem connection.)

The data compression algorithm:

▲ Can compress data by more than an 8:1 ratio (though this high compression ratio would occur only for extremely redundant data, such as 10,000 consecutive "A"s in the data stream). The compression ratio is more often quoted as 4:1, to represent more real-world data, but is actually about 2.5:1 if you (and I mean you, not your modem supplier) actually measure it.

▲ Requires V.42 (so that the link is known to be error-free).

▲ Usually works with asynchronous data only (because of the necessity for flow control if the data are not compressible enough to match the DTE speed used with the modem throughput).

As a fallback, modems usually also support the older MNP *Level 5*, which has a maximum compression ratio of 2:1 and can actually increase the transfer time of files that are already compressed. Therefore, V.42*bis* is preferred.

Uses an implementation (developed by British Telecom) of the *Lempel-Ziv* data compression method, which is called BTLZ (not to be confused with a bacon-lettuce-tomato sandwich, which is quite a different thing—though a BLT may require compression if there is too much lettuce).

A continuously-updated *dictionary* (512 to 2,048 bytes in length) of frequently occurring strings of (usually up to six, but the Lempel-Ziv algorithm supports up to 32) characters is constructed by the transmitting modem and sent to the receiving modem. The transmitter then uses up to 11-bit patterns (depending on the size of dictionary used) to represent the most-common *strings* (or *sequences*) of characters.

A variation of BTLZ developed by Hayes Microcomputer Products (and therefore sometimes called HBTLZ) is actually used. If it detects that the data are not compressible, then compression is temporarily disabled.

The length of the dictionary and the speed at which data compression occurs are determined by the transmitting modem's design (and therefore designers). For example, while the V.42*bis* standard documents the compression algorithm by using the C language, a good implementation will re-code this for efficiency and speed. Therefore, different (and compatible) V.42*bis* modems can have significantly different compression ratios (for the same data!) and throughput (expressed in bits/s transferred) rates.

Note that the serial port speeds of the PCs (or whatever is sending the data) at both ends of the link should be set to at least four times (which is the maximum compression ratio) the modem data-pump speed (the bit rate at which the modems are actually sending data); otherwise, you don't get the full (or any) benefit of data compression.

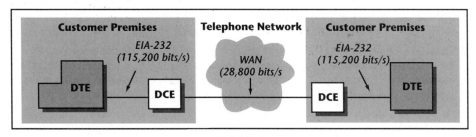

V.42bis-1

For example, PCs using V.34 modems (with V.42*bis* data compression) should have their serial ports set to $4 \times 28,800$ bits/s = 115,200 bits/s, as shown in the accompanying figure. Not all PCs support this speed.

Also, the PC's communication software used must be configured to enable *flow control* (either `x-on/x-off` or RTS/CTS—whatever matches the modem's configuration). Flow control is required so that the PC does not send data too fast when the data are not very compressible. Also, flow control is required to stop the data from the PC while the modem retransmits during error correction.

Finally, only very short EIA-232 cables (since EIA-232 is specified to work only at speeds up to 20,000 bits/s) should be used, and the serial port UARTs should be 16550s (at both ends).

See **S16550A, ASYNCHRONOUS, DATA COMPRESSION, EIA/TIA-232, FLOW CONTROL, INBAND, LZW, MNP, OUTOFBAND, RPI**, and **V.42**.

V.54

The ITU-T standard that describes where *loopbacks* (referred to as *L1, L2, L3*, and *L4*) should be supported for troubleshooting.

The standard does not specify how to enable the loopbacks or whether they can be enabled *remotely* (that is, from the other end of the link). Therefore each device that supports V.54 should specify which loopbacks it supports and how to enable them. (You will need to dig through the manual to figure this out—usually an *AT command* or a front-panel button-push sequence.)

The accompanying figure shows an example of the loopback locations for the classic DTE (terminal) to DCE (modem) to DCE (remote modem) to DTE (host) connection.

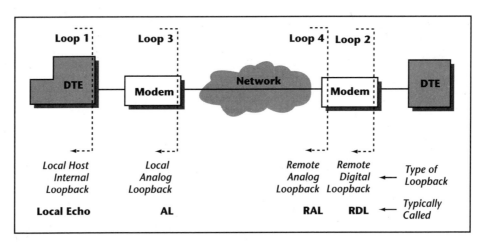

V.54-1

By first testing a single component (by enabling *Loop 1*), that part of the network can be tested (in this case, that the transmitting terminal can receive its own data). If the terminal is shown to be working, then removing Loop 1 and enabling *Loop 3* will test more of the network (the digital receiver of the local modem, and its modulator and demodulator).

Loop 3 is called a *local analog loopback*, since the local device (to where the tests are initiated) takes the digital data from the local DTE, converts it to analog (suitable for transmission over the network), redirects it back to the DCE's input from the network, and converts the signal back to digital. The loopback occurs at and exercises the analog portion of the DCE.

Loop 4 (usually only used in 2-pair analog leased-line circuits) involves connecting the circuit pair bringing data from the network, back to the pair taking data back into the network. The network administrators can then test the quality of the circuit from the network to the remote customer site.

Loop 2 is called *remote digital loopback*, since the demodulated (that is, digital) data is looped back at the remote modem's digital interface.

This standard troubleshooting technique (start by testing a small, isolated component and then add more components of the system—one at a time) is continued until the problem is identified.

See **AT COMMAND SET, DCE1, DTE, EIA/TIA-232, MODEM, RTFM,** and **WAN**.

V.56BIS
V.56bis Intercontinental Network Model

A standard describing many typical analog communication circuit impairments (delays, attenuations, and other distortions).

The purpose is to characterize a wide range of real-world less-than-perfect data communication circuits (short, long, noisy, satellite, digitized, etc.) so that modems can be designed to work well on them. Modem evaluations (and the benchmark test results that are published in magazines) often use these types of lines in their throughput and connection-success comparisons.

Builds on the EIA/TIA TSB-37a.

See **EIA/TIA-232, EIA/TIA/TSB-37A, TSB, MODEM, PCM, SATELLITE,** and **TSB**.

V.64

The standard for DSVD.

See **DSVD,** and **SVD**.

V.70

A standard for simultaneously combining digitized voice and data on an analog dial-up connection. It is based on DSVD and V.34+ modems.

Uses 8 kbits/s for voice, and the remainder of the 33.6 kbits/s (or whatever the modems were able to connect at) for data.

See **DSVD,** and **V.34**.

V.110

A standard for ISDN *Terminal Adapters* (TAs to provide EIA-232 interfaces (which will typically connect to the serial COM port of a PC). ISDN refers to such non-ISDN interfaces as an *R interface*.

Provision is made for the following:

▲ Sending (or receiving) on the ISDN circuit the status of the following EIA-232 interface signals: request to send (RTS), clear to send (CTS), data carrier detect (DCD), data set ready (DSR), and data terminal ready (DTR). The remote ISDN device can then control the user's TA so that its EIA-232 interface signals react just as those on a modem would.

▲ Carrying either asynchronous or synchronous EIA-232 port data.

▲ *Rate adaption*, which means enabling the 64 kbit/s speed of the ISDN B channel to communicate with the (lower) speed of the EIA-232 port. EIA-232 speeds of 600, 1,200, 2,400, 4,800, 7,200, 9,600, 12,000, 14,400, 19200, 48,000 and 56,000 bits/s are supported. 48,000 bits/s and 56,000 bits/s are only supported for synchronous data.

For all but the two highest speeds, up to 48 user data bits (plus bits indicating the EIA-232 port speed, the status of the interface signals, synchronous data clocking and frame synchronization) are put into an 80-bit frame of data, which is sent at 64,000 bits/s to the ISDN network.

V.110 is much more popular in Europe than in North America. Instead, V.120 is usually used in North America.

See **ASYNCHRONOUS**, **EIA/TIA-232**, **ISDN**, **SYNCHRONOUS**, and **V.120**.

V.120

A standard for ISDN terminal adapters (TAs) to (among other functions) provide an asynchronous interface for PCs, so the PCs can communicate over an ISDN network, using only the standard PC COM port. The PC data is *encapsulated* into ISDN B channel data. This is sometimes called *rate adaption* (since the bit rates of the PC's asynchronous (likely 115,200 or 230,400 bits/s) and the ISDN's synchronous (64,000 or 128,000 bits/s) serial communications are different.

The TA may be either internal or external to a PC.

This data communications alternative to the equivalent analog method (a modems connected to a standard POTS analog telephone line) is expected to become quite popular, since ISDN has a much faster call setup time (about 2 seconds compared to at least 20 seconds) and a faster data transmission rate (64,000 or 128,000 bits/s compared to, for example, 28,800 bits/s).

Instead of V.120, in Europe V.110 is usually used (V.110 does not support as many functions, for example, V.110 cannot multiplex more than one conversation over a circuit-switched B channel, as V.120 can). Also, V.120 can carry an asynchronous *break* indication.

Broadly, V.110 gets the ISDN network to understand and communicate with an EIA-232 interface. V.120 gets the PC to talk native ISDN.

V.120 is a modification of the LAPD link layer protocol used for ISDN. LAPD is defined in ITU standard Q.921. V.120 carries the EIA-232 signals: request to send, clear to send, carrier detect, and data terminal ready.

V.120 supports three modes of operation:

▲ Synchronous. The data from the EIA-232 interface is already encapsulated in an HDLC frame. The V.120 TA checks the CRC, strips-off the HDLC flags, and removes the zero-bit stuffing. The rest of the HDLC frame (the HDLC address, control and data fields) and any error indications are translated into the modified LAPD frame, for transmission to the remote device.

▲ Asynchronous. In this case, the V.120 strips-off the start and stop bits (and may also check the parity bit) from the EIA-232 interface data.

▲ Transparent. The V.120 TA encapsulates every bit received on the EIA-232 interface, and sends it to the remote device.

V.120 also supports D channel signalling for ISDN call setup and clearing, using a subset of ITU's standard Q.931, for ISDN signalling.

See **ASYNCHRONOUS**, **ENCAPSULATION**, **HDLC**, **ISDN**, **MODEM**, **SYNCHRONOUS**, **UART**, and **V.110**.

V.fast

The name that was used for V.34 before it was approved as a standard.

See **MODEM** and **V.34**.

V.FC
V.Fast Class

A modem modulation scheme (promoted by Rockwell International) that is based on an early, not yet standardized version of V.34.

Transmits data at the same speeds as V.34, but a significant difference is that V.FC has a less powerful handshaking method (V.FC does not use the V.8 scheme).

Now made obsolete by V.34.

See **MODEM**, **ROCKWELL INTERNATIONAL**, **V.8**, and **V.34**.

V.terbo

A nonstandard enhancement to V.32*bis* (promoted by AT&T Microelectronics).

Transmits data at up to 19,200 bits/s (with fallback speeds down to 4,800 bits/s, in decrements of 2,400 bits/s).

Now made obsolete by V.34.

See **ATT**, **MODEM**, and **V.34**.

VBI
Vertical Blanking Interval

While the electron beam that scans the CRT is returning to the upper-left corner of the screen (called *vertical retrace*), it is turned off (*blanked*). During this *vertical blanking interval*, the electron beam does about 22.5 horizontal scans (per field, and two interlaced fields make a frame, and there are 29.97 frames per second). Field 1 has lines 1 through 262, and field 2 has lines 263 through 525. Binary information can be sent during the blanking intervals, and this is used for time codes (90 bits of information, typically during lines 7, 11, 270 or 274), closed-caption text (this uses one scan line), signalling between television stations and other purposes.

About 350 bits of information can be sent during each scan line (the additional bits that can be carried per scan line are used for error-correction).

One really useful recent addition is that public broadcasting stations send the current time of day, as part of the *television data service* (other uses include sending detailed program listings as an extra-cost service). Televisions and VCRs that look for this information can then always have the correct time, even if daylight savings time or a power failure has occured.

The format of the information in the VBI is defined by the National Association of Broadcast Transmission Standards (NABTS). 10 lines are left unused, so the 350 bits per scan line produces a total capacity of about 104,895 bits/s. Some companies are trying to use this to send WWW-type pages to the PC of integrated television/PC devices, to augment the information on the television.

See **CRT**, **DAYLIGHT SAVINGS TIME**, and **NTSC**.

VAN
Value Added Network

A communications network that offers more than just carrying your data (or voice).

For example, a network may do protocol conversion (for connecting ASCII terminals to an IBM computer), store-and-forward and format checking of messages (such as often required for EDI) or provide customized addressing and security features

A *value added reseller* (VAR) is a company that retails (typically computer) equipment, as well as other services, such as design, installation and management—all for a fee, of course.

See **EDI**.

VESA
Video Electronics Standards Association

The group that has developed many of the important PC hardware standards, such as the following:

▲ The *VESA* local bus standard (also called *VL*-bus and *VLB*).

▲ The recommended video display refresh rate. Until 1994, VESA recommended that a computer monitor have at least a 72 Hz *refresh rate* (also called the *vertical scan rate*— the number of times per second that the entire screen is rewritten). They then increased this recommendation to 75 Hz at all resolutions from 640 × 480 to 1,280 × 1,024 (horizontal × vertical pixels)—it is easier to support faster refresh rates at lower screen resolutions. The current recommendation is 85 Hz at 1,024 × 768 resolution. Therefore, you want to ensure that the refresh rate *at the resolution you are planning to use* is acceptable.

Super VGA (that is, screen resolutions of 800 × 600, and higher) signal timings, so that any monitor can work with any video adapter.

Plug and Play support for monitors—which is called the *display data channel* (DDC) standard).

The Flat Panel Display Interface (FPDI), first released in 1995. It defines the connector, signal names and timing, power and other aspects of LCD (or other technology) displays for laptop PCs. The intent is to define standard displays to facilitate competition, and the introduction of new technologies.

See **DDC**, **DPMS**, **EVC**, **LOCAL BUS**, **PLUG AND PLAY**, **RAMDAC**, **USDA**, **VGA**, **VIDEO**, and **VLBUS OR VLB**.

VFD
Vacuum Fluorescent Display

A type of display often used for when only a few numbers (such as on a clock) or letters (such as the status display of some laser printers). It usually produces a blue or blue-green display, made up of dots (for example, in a 5 × 7 matrix, for an alpha-numeric display) or rectangles (usually 7 segments, to display the digits 0 through 9 only).

The dots or rectangles are phosphor-coated, and can be electrically switched to be about 100 V to 200 V DC more positive than some very fine wires (the cathode), which are usually about 1 or 2 cm apart, across the display. The entire display is in a glass enclosure which has been sealed after drawing a vacuum in the display. The wires are heated slightly (you can usually see them faintly glowing red, if the room is really dark. When the positive voltage is applied to a segment, electrons are pulled from the cathode (which is facilitated by its heating), and when they hit the phosphor illuminates (fluoresces). Since each segment is individually controlled (usually in a matrix), any display can be generated.

An advantage over LCD is that VFD produces its own light. LCD only reflects existing light, or must be back-lit.

See **CRT**, and **LCD**.

VGA
Video Graphics Array

A graphics standard for PCs that provides a resolution of 640 × 480 (that is, 480 rows of 640 pixels per row). A 15-pin D-subminiature connector is used (the shell size of the connector is the same as a standard COM port type DB-9, but the pins are closer together).

VGA was first introduced with the IBM PS/s PCs, which were announced in April 1987.

While the initiall VGA could support a maximum of 256 colors (8 bits per pixel), this required (640 × 480 × 1 =) 307,200 bytes of video memory. Since 256 kbit/s DRAM memory ICs were common then, most video controllers had only 256 kbytes of memory (1 bank of 8 ICs), so could only support 16 colors. VGA+ referred to controllers that had 512 kbytes of

memory, so they could support 256 colors. Since virtually all video controllers support more than VGA+ now, the more generic term VGA (or S-VGA) is used instead.

Some common graphics-mode (as opposed to character mode) screen resolutions are shown in the following table. Note that beginning with VGA (except for the seldom implemented 1,280 × 1,024), the pixels are "square"—that is, the ratio of the number of horizontal to vertical pixels is the same as the size of computer monitors (and standard televisions)—that is, as *aspect ratio* of 4:3.

Name	Resolution (pixels)		Comments
	Horizontal	Vertical	
Color graphics adapter (CGA)	640	200	Used with the very first IBM PCs, in 1981. Supported 4 colors (2 bits) per pixel. Designed so a standard television monitor could be used.
Enhanced graphics adapter (EGA)	640	350	IBM released this in 1985. Supported 16 (4 bits) colors per pixel.
Video graphics array (VGA)	640	480	First available in 1986 for the IBM PS/2 models 50, 60 and 80 as an IC that handled most video functions.
Super VGA (S-VGA)[a]	800	600	IBM released this in 1985.
	832	624	Some Macintoshes support this.
Extended graphics adapter (XGA)	1,024	768	Actually IBM's never-widely-accepted improvement to their never-widely-accepted 8514/a. But the term is often used for anything at this resolution.
	1,152	864	Some Macintoshes support this.
	1,280	1,024	
	1,600	1,200	

a. Some would say that S-VGA (also written as SVGA) includes all resolutions from 800 × 600 to 1,280 × 1,024.

See **CRT**, **DDC**, **EVC**, **LCD**, **MPC**, **PIXEL**, **TTL2** (*Transistor-Transistor Logic*), and **VESA**.

VHS
Video Home System

The video and audio $\frac{1}{2}$" magnetic tape cassette recording and playback method used by standard home VCRs (*Video Cassette Recorders*). Developed by JVC (which is officially called Victor Company of Japan, Limited), and first sold in 1976.

VHS competed with Sony Corp.'s *Betamax* format (which was developed in 1975), and VHS won (largely for marketing and timing reasons, though Beta is better technically and as a result is still very popular for professional recording).

When VHS was first developed, the acronym was for *video helical scan*, since that is the trick that was used to provide high-quality video with a slow moving tape (so you could get hours of video on a tape). The tape is spiral-wrapped around a short cylindrical recording and playback head which rotates as the tape moves. Each field of the video is recorded as a diagonal stripe on the tape, which is read quickly as the head rotates. When the tape is paused, the head continues to rotate so the fields can be read (this rapidly wears out that spot on the tape).

See **DVD**, **NTSC**, and **VIDEO**.

Video

A standard broadcast (and CATV) NTSC video signal uses 6 MHz of bandwidth to carry 29.97 frames per second of color picture information (as well as the audio).

One of the measures of the quality of a picture is the horizontal resolution, measured as the number of vertical lines which could be displayed and discerned. Some video technologies and their horizontal resolutions are shown in the table below (along with some others, for comparison).

Video Technology	Horizontal Resolution (vertical lines)
Average consumer VHS videocassette player or Hi-8 8mm camcorder	240 to 250
Good VHS videocassette player	270 to 320
Professional (broadcast) quality NTSC or PAL Betacam camcorder	330
Typical NTSC	350
Laser-disk player and direct broadcast satellite (DBS)	400
High-end Super-VHS (also called S-VHS and S-Video) videocassette player or Hi-8 8mm camcorder	400 to 425
NTSC theoretical maximum	485
DV (digital video) camcorder	500
RS-170A (monochrome) or high-end color television (using S-Video[a] direct video input, bypassing tuner)	550 to 700
DVD Player	720
35 mm film	2,500[b]

a. S-Video's cable contains 2 miniature coax cables, and uses one for the luminance and the other for the chrominance information. Since the luminance and chrominance information are not combined (as NTSC must do, to fit into a 6 MHz channel), the luminance information can have a higher frequency, resulting in the higher horizontal resolution.
b. Standard Kodak Kodachrome film has a resolution of about 2,500 lines per inch.

A line of horizontal resolution is usually defined as the maximum number of closely-spaced vertical lines that can be discerned—for example, by having a black vertical line adjacent to a white vertical line, which is adjacent to another black vertical line, and so on. Note that there would actually be twice as many lines on the screen as the resolution, since a black *and* a while line are required to *see* a line of resolution (all while lines is a bit like saying there's a white polar bear in a snowstorm, when all you can see is solid white). A better way of stating this is to call the horizontal resolution as the maximum number of *visible vertical line pairs*.

Video

Several *studio-quality* (also called *broadcast-* or *production-quality*) digitization schemes are available, as shown in the following table.

System	Data rate at 10 bits per sample (Mbits/s)
SMPTE 240 M (HDTV at 1,150 scan lines per frame)	1,485
ITU 601 (525 scan lines per frame)	270
NTSC (composite signal)	143.2

ITU Recommendation 601 used to be called CCIR 601, and is very popular in television production environments. For NTSC use, it has 525 horizontal lines total per frame, but only 483 lines are *active* (that is, visible). For European use, it has 625 lines, of which 576 are visible. Both formats have 720 pixels horizontally, per line (that is, vertical lines of resolution).

Note that even for the same video format and without using data compression, the digitized video data rate will depend on the number of samples per horizontal scan line, usually 400 to 720 (for production-quality NTSC video), and the number of bits per sample (typically 8 or 10).

A 640 × 480 pixel, full-color (24-bit), full-motion (30 frames per second digitized video signal (from standard NTSC) requires a data rate of about 27 Mbytes/s (before compression), which is about 216 Mbits/s. Using only 256 colors (8-bit digitizing), requires a data rate of about 72 Mbits/s.

PC-quality video often uses one of the following screen resolutions (in pixels).

Standard	Horizontal	Vertical
NTSC	352	240
PAL	352	288

Several compression schemes are available, as shown in the following table.

Feature	JPEG	MPEG-1	MPEG-2	Px64
Full-color, still images	✓			
Full-color, motion video	✓	✓	✓	✓
Broadcast quality	✓		✓	
Resolution (horizontal × vertical, in pixels)	65,536 × 65,536	352 × 240	1,920 × 1,152 1,440 × 1,152 720 × 486 352 × 288	
Compression ratio	5:1 to 80:1	Up to 200:1	Up to 100:1	100:1 to 2,000:1
Compressed data rate (Mbits/s)	10 to 48	1.544	4 to 80	0.064 to 2
Optimized for	Interlaced or noninterlaced	Non-interlaced	Interlaced	Noninterlaced

3 = Suitable for

Current "studio-quality" broadcast video typically uses the MPEG-2 720 × 486 resolution and has a compressed data rate of 15 Mbits/s. For home use, MPEG-2 compressed video at 3 to 6 Mbits/s is typically adequate. Lower VCR-quality video requires about 1.5 Mbits/s, using MPEG-1 compression.

The P×64 scheme is a video-conferencing standard that is specified in the H.320 standard.

Different video formats have different *frame rates*, as listed in the following table.

Standard	Frame Rate (frames/s)	Comments
Film	24	Standard movies—but each frame is projected twice (resulting in a 48-Hz flicker rate), so the flicker is not noticeable
PAL	25.17	*Phase Alternate Line*, the method used in Europe
NTSC	29.97	Standard broadcast and cable TV
RS-170A	30	Monochrome video
Desktop video	30	Such as that produced from MPEG-1 and .avi files

To display movies on North American NTSC televisions, a process called *telecine* is used. This displays the first frame of the movie 3 times, and the next frame 2 times (then the next frame 3 times, and the next 2 times, and so on). This *3:2 pull down* produces a 60 Hz frame rate (5 television frames for every 2 movie frames), which matches the NTSC field rate of 59.94 Hz close enough (within 0.1%) that the difference is not noticable. Though it does mean that movies on television are being shown slightly too slow, and a 90 minute movie shown on television actually lasts about 5.4 seconds longer than in a movie theatre (not including the copious commercials).

A common production-quality 35 mm movie film digitizing process uses 2,664 lines of 3,656 pixels each, using 36 bits of color information for each pixel (12 bits per primary color). This resolution will be used for studio production work.

See **S1394, CATV, CCIR, COLOUR, COMPOSITE VIDEO SIGNAL, DV, DVD, JPEG, H.261, H.320, HDTV, LOSSY DATA COMPRESSION, MONITORS, MPEG, NTSC, PAL, PCS** (*Personal Conferencing Specification*), **PRI, RAMDAC, SMPTE, VESA,** and **VHS.**

VIM
Vendor Independent Messaging

An effort sponsored by Novell, WordPerfect (which was bought by Novell, then by Corel), IBM, Lotus (which is now owned by IBM), Apple, and Borland to provide application-level APIs for all popular computing platforms, to send and receive messages between application programs.

Used mostly by Lotus 1-2-3 and cc:Mail, and OS/2 messaging.

Competed with MAPI and XAPIA's CMC. Microsoft's MAPI won.

See **API, CMC, MAPI,** and **XAPIA.**

Virus

A computer program (or macro or script) that causes your computer to do something undesirable. Part of the function of a virus is often to try to copy itself to other computers, hence the name.

Time was, smart people knew that the only way to have your computer affected by a virus was to actually run the infected program—just reading an e-mail message or opening a text file from your word processor was entirely safe—despite alarmist news stories to the contrary.

This all changed with the Microsoft Word macro virus. This is simply a Microsoft Word document file that has an attached macro which runs automatically when the document is opened. This macro adds itself to Word's global document template (which is called `normal.dot`), so it gets added to any subsequent documents created or edited.

Often steps taken when you think you have a virus are more destructive than a virus might have been.

A list of virus-detection software products certified by the National Computer Security Association can be found at *http://www.ncsa.com*. Details of hundreds of viruses are at *http://www.llnl.gov/ciac/CIACVirusDatabase.html*. Further information is at *http://www.security.org.il*. Interesting reading is also at *http://www.infowar.com* and *http://www.digicrime.com*. Some major virus software vendors are at *http://www.symantec.com* and *http://www.commandcom.com*.

A major cost of Viruses are the many hoaxes that scare people into wasting time and resources. A list of hoaxes is at *http://www.llnl.gov/ciac/CIACHoaxes.html#naughty*.

See **CERT**, **CIAC**, **HACKER**, and **INBAND**.

VJ
Van Jacobson

Someone who did lots of work on the TCP protocol and has been immortalized by having his TCP header compression method named after him (Van is his first name). This method does not compress the data in TCP packets, nor any part of UDP packets. Nor does it affect the link layer protocol which carries the TCP, so it can be used with PPP or proprietary (for example, Cisco's "HDLC") layer 2 protocols.

Same as *CSLIP*, and defined in RFC 1144

See **CSLIP**, and **TCP/IP**.

VLAN
Virtual LAN

VLANs define which LAN stations can directly broadcast to others. Since broadcasting is typically required for communication (for example, to learn what an IP address's MAC address is), VLANs determine which stations can directly communicate with each other.

A VLAN is a switched LAN technology (which can be implemented using ATM) that uses an *administrative console* (typicallly using a drag-and-drop type GUI) to determine which traffic gets forwarded on which ports (which is the most common type of VLAN—but VLANs can also be defined by IP address, user, and so on, depending on the capabilities of the switch).

The requirement is that it is important to keep users grouped according to some plan (for example, by job function or company department, or protocol or network number) for the following reasons:

▲ *Administrative*: for example, the computers on a single IP subnet must usually be kept together (typically on one floor of a building) so that they all connect (through a *concentrator*) to one port of a router—but typical company reorganizations usually result in people being moved all over a building, which would require new IP addresses to be assigned.

▲ *Network loading*: LAN protocols typically use broadcasts for many functions, and these cause substantial network load.

▲ *Security*: LAN troubleshooting and management tools can trap information that is intended for other users.

The idea is that since user locations physically move frequently (reorganizations, project changes, and so on), rather than trying to keep up with these *moves, adds, and changes* using patch panels, how about putting all the traffic on a high-speed backbone and using ATM (and other switching technologies) to forward traffic for each *group* only on those switch ports that have at least one member of that group?

Also, VLANs can be implemented to limit broadcast and multicast traffic, since a VLAN defines a *broadcast domain* (the locations to which broadcasts are forwarded). Limiting such traffic is important for the following reasons:

▲ Since broadcasts and multicasts are forwarded through bridges and switches, these frames load all LAN segments, reducing the bandwidth available for other traffic.

▲ Every broadcast and multicast frame must be examined by every PC on the LAN. This uses CPU time on people's PCs, and slows their compter's response times.

Each port of a switch which supports VLANs may be connected to an individual PC (such as a server or a user), or the port may be connected to an Ethernet concentrator (also called a hub), so that all the users share the port's bandwidth and VLAN assignment.

VLANs can be implemented by LAN switches, in which case a router is required to move traffic between different VLANs. VLANs can also be implemented by ATM networks, in which case routers (which are typically too slow and expensive) or ATM's MPOA can be used to route traffic between VLANs.

A method of implementing VLANs will be standardized as IEEE 802.1Q, and uses a 4-byte header before a standard Ethernet frame.

See **S802.A10**, **ATM** (*Asynchronous Transfer Mode*), **COS2** (*Class of Service*), **MPOA**, **ROUTER**, and **SWITCHED LAN**.

VL-BUS
VESA Local Bus

A 16- or 32-bit wide bus that was introduced in 1992 and can be used to connect a PC's motherboard to video, SCSI-2, LAN, or other adapters (though the original intent was, and most available adapters are, video adapters) at the processor's full speed.

Was very popular for 486-based PCs but rarely implemented on Pentium-based PCs. PCI is typically used for Pentium-based PCs.

Peak theoretical throughput is 130 Mbytes/s, but a more typical rate is 66 Mbytes/s (which is two bus cycles on a 33-MHz bus per 32-bit word transfer). A *burst mode* of one address cycle followed by four data cycles results in 105 Mbytes/s on a 33-MHz bus.

Can be implemented as a chip-level bus implemented on a motherboard (no connectors) or by using an MCA-style connector (112 pins) in-line with an ISA connector, so the slot can be used for either an ISA or VL-Bus card; if used for VL-Bus, then the card uses the ISA bus for power, interrupts, DMA, and I/O.

Up to three cards can reside on the bus (though most PCs require only one or two cards), which is basically a 486 processor's local system bus (and the bus runs at the same speed as the processor).

Runs at 16 to 33 MHz (higher speeds would require wait states or fewer devices on the bus).

Two types of *programmed I/O* transfers are supported: a single block of 512 bytes, or multiple blocks of 512 bytes (this requires an enhanced BIOS and device driver support).

Some limitations of the version 1.0 standard are that 3.3-volt devices are not supported, it does not support *Plug and Play* automatic configuration, burst mode is not supported, and while it supports *bus mastering DMA*, the CPU cannot run concurrently with bus-mastering peripherals (and it does not support non-bus master DMA).

Version 2.0 of the specification supports:

▲ A 64-bit bus (this requires an additional in-line connector)

▲ 50-MHz operation (resulting in a peak speed of 320 Mbytes/s)

▲ *Plug and Play*

However, VL-Bus 2.0 will likely never be widely implemented, owing to PCI.

A compatibility testing effort should result in "VESA-compatible" stickers on products. (Currently, there is no compatibility testing or assurance.)

Competes with PCI, though PCI won for Pentium-based PCs—since PCI is less 486-specific and already has Plug and Play support.

See **BUS**, **LOCAL BUS**, **MCA**, **PCI**, **PIO**, **PLUG AND PLAY**, and **VESA**

VLB
VESA Local Bus

Another name for VL-Bus.

See **VLBUS OR VLB**.

VLF
Very Low Frequency

Frequencies from more than 300 Hz (300 cycles per second) up to (and including) 30,000 Hz (30 kHz).

See **ELF**, **EMF**, and **MPR II**.

VLIW
Very Long Instruction Word

A proposed new technology (for example, being worked on through an alliance between Hewlett-Packard and Intel) for increasing the processing capacity of CPUs.

Many simple and independent operations are specified simultaneously by fixed-length (such as 128-bit) instructions. These are then executed in parallel (as determined by the compiler), to speed program execution.

VLIW is a mix of CISC and RISC architectures. For example, all "instructions" are the same length—as in RISC, but can be somewhat complex operations—as in CISC.

The P7 from Intel might use this technology.

See **HP**, **INTEL**, **P7**, and **RISC**.

VLM
Virtual Loadable Module

Novell's newer workstation shells (the software that redirects disk drive and other local resource calls to networked devices).

Supports:

▲ Running the shell software out of extended memory (to leave the 640 kbytes of conventional memory available for application programs)

▲ More customization of features supported (you need only to load those functions required, to reduce memory usage)

▲ Features needed for NetWare 4.*x* (for example, support for NetWare Directory Services)

The VLMs replace (for example) the NetX TSRs.

See **NDS** and **NOVELL**.

VM
Virtual Machine

IBM's most recent mainframe operating system (which is many years old).

Suited to more casual and interactive use than MVS. Partitions a machine into multiple *virtual machines*, each running native VM or MVS (VM's predecessor) applications.

See **CMS**, **MAINFRAME**, and **MVS**.

VMS
Virtual Memory System

DEC's minicomputer operating system that initially ran only on DEC's VAX (*Virtual Address Extension*) CPUs. The newer portable version (*OpenVMS*) runs on other platforms, such as DEC's Alpha processor.

See **ALPHA AXP**, **DEC**, **OPENVMS**, and **OPERATING SYSTEM**.

Voice/Data Integration

See **SVD**.

VPIM
Voice Profile for Internet Mail

A proposed open standard for exchanging voice and fax traffic using TCP/IP, over Ethernet or the Internet. Support for prioritization and confirmation of delivery is included.

Developed by Centigram Communications Corp, Lucent Technologies, Northern Telecom Ltd., Octel Communications Corp. and Siemens Rolm Communications Inc.

See **INTERNET2**.

VPN
Virtual Private Network

A (usually IP-based) network which uses special router configurations (such as filters and static routes) so that users see only their own traffic, though the network carries traffic from many users.

For example, a company with 4 offices nation-wide could have a T1 connections to each office (from the IP network cloud), and the offices would only be able to exchange data with each other (and not other users physically connected to the same cloud).

Of course, a prime candidate for the IP network is the Internet.

One concern is end-to-end network latency, since the network operator may be tempted to put more users on the network than it can handle—so user traffic waits in buffers (hopefully) until a shared link is available. Some vendors provide maximum end-to-end delays, such as 150 ms one-way.

Protocols used to create encrypted point-to-point connections (also called *encrypted sessions*) across networks (some provide support for distributing the encryption keys) include the following:

▲ Microsoft's proprietary PPTP

▲ Cisco's proprietary L2F (*layer 2 forwarding*)

▲ a combination of the above two, called L2TP, which may be a public standard approved by the IETF someday

▲ IPSec (IP security) is a method which will be an IETF-approved method

▲ *Simple Key Management for Internet Protocols* (SKIP)

VPNs are sometimes called *Virtual Private Data Networks* (VPDNs).

See **FIREWALL**, **INTERNET2**, **IPSEC**, and **PPTP**.

VRAM
Video Random Access Memory

Memory optimized for use on video adapters.

It is *dual-ported*, in that there are two ports. The PC can write into the memory (to change what will be displayed), while the video adapter continuously reads the memory (to refresh the monitor's display).

Usually needed only when the display has high resolution (more than 1,024 × 768 pixels), more than 65,536 colors, and a high refresh rate (more than 70 Hz).

WRAM (Window RAM), is also dal-ported, but a better buffering scheme and other improvements provide about a 25% faster throghput than VRAM. And both are faster and more expensive than EDO RAM. SGRAM typically has better performance that all of these.

See **EDO RAM**, **RAM**, **SGRAM**, and **VESA**.

VRML
Virtual Reality Modeling Language

Basically a way to encode 3-dimensional graphic images, to support simulation and modeling. It allows users to describe a 3-D scene's elements, such as polygonal (cubes, cylinders and cones, and other shapes) rendered objects (called *nodes*) and transformation effects on them, lighting, surface textures and other ambient properties and effects.

Version 1.0 was released in April 1995, and is based on the *Open Inventor* ASCII file format developed by Silicon Graphics Inc. It defines how to render 3-D images, and basic support for linking objects and scenes.

Version 2.0 (sometimes called *moving worlds*) was released in 1996, and is standardized by ISO/IEC 14772. It includes support for sound, video, motion, dynamics and backdrops, and is not compatible with version 1.0.

URLs for VRML documents typically end with `.FLR`, `.WRL` or `.WRZ`.

VMRL was initially an abbreviation for *Virtual Reality Mark-up Language*.

Pronounced *VER-mal*.

Two important WWW resources for VRML information are the VRML Repository at *http://www.sdsc.edu/vmrl* and the VMRL standards site, at *http://www.vmrl.org*. IRC and VRML resource information is available at *http://www.internetuser.com*.

See **HTML**, and **MPEG**.

VSAT
Very Small Aperture Terminals

Small (0.75 to 2.4 m) ground-based satellite dish antennas, used to communicate with a large, central satellite dish antenna, and from there to a central computer system. The link from the remote end users, up to the satellite and back to the central satellite dish (sometimes called the *hub*) is called the *inroute*. It typically runs at 256 kbits/s.

A *backhaul* connection (usually a terrestrial link) connects the user's main data center to the service provider (who usually has a really big dish—typically 7 m in diameter).

The service provider can then broadcast up to the satellite, and back to the user's many (often hundreds of) remote sites. This is called the *outroute*, and typically runs at 512 kbits/s.

While there are relatively high data rates, this "bandwidth" is shared among many users.

In addition to the small satellite dish antennas, the remote sites each have "magic boxes" (often called the *indoor unit*—guess where it is located) that:

▲ Provide users with a standard interface, such as SDLC or X.25 (for example)

▲ Support many methods of prioritizing and scheduling bandwidth among the users (as controlled by the service provider, and ultimately, according to how much money you pay). For example, fixed bit-rate per remote site (constantly, or for a pre-determined duration), and fixed bit-rate shared by a group of sites are common. Also, prioritizing based on protocol or end user computer address can also be done.

▲ Ensure that users cannot adversely affect other users and get only the capacity they have arranged for

▲ Provide error-correction (through retransmission)—though the bit error rate of satellite links is usually so low that the system is typically configured so protocols such as TCP/IP often use TCP's error-correction (performed by the TCP protocol running in the end users computers) instead.

▲ Provide network diagnostics and control functions for the service provider

Using *time division multiple access*, permits many such groups of users to share the same satellite capacity (each gets a coordinated slice of communications time).

Networks are run by *service providers* (such as Telesat Canada), which (typically) lease large blocks of capacity from satellite owners (such as Hughes Network Systems) and provide a *point-to-multipoint* architecture to the end users.

See **SATELLITE** and **SDLC**.

VTAM
Virtual Telecommunications Access Method

IBM's communications method for linking user applications running under any of their (S/370 and S/390) mainframe operating systems (VM and MVS, for example) to user terminals and printers (such as the 3270 series). Supports SNA and APPN (OSI layers 3, 4, and 5) and SDLC (layer 2).

See **S3270**, **DLC**, **MAINFRAME**, **PU-5**, **SDLC**, and **SNA**.

VTOA
Voice and Telephony over ATM

An extension to the *circuit emulation service* (CES) which allows circuits up to T1 (and E1) speeds to use a simplified version of AAL 1 (including the sequence number byte, to improve reliability).

Support includes forwarding and transferring calls, signalling and identifying voice channels, as well as for transmitting tones and recorded announcements, such as those needed for voice-mail systems.

See **ATM** (*Asynchronous Transfer Mode*).

W

WABI
Windows Applications Binary Interface

Sun Microsystems' SunSelect operating unit's software that converts documented Microsoft Windows function calls to X Window System calls—so that Windows programs can run on Sun and other UNIX computers (such as SCO's).

Included with Sun's Solaris operating system and licensed by SunSelect to other UNIX vendors (including HP and IBM).

Sounds like a great idea, but you don't hear much about this anymore (perhaps because non-Windows calls and instructions are interpreted, which provides very slow performance).

See **SCO**, **SUN**, **UNIX**, and **X WINDOW SYSTEM**.

WAIS
Wide Area Information Service

A method for searching for information on the Internet. The process involves three components:

▲ An *indexer*, that generates seven indices from the indexed documents; for example, an index of the words in the documents, an index of the words in the document abstracts (which are called "headlines"), and an index of the file names.

▲ A link to this index is established from the central servers.

▲ Servers store the documents and indices and are referenced from gopher menus or WWW links in HTML documents.

▲ Client software runs on user PCs or is accessed by WWW or gopher browsers.

For more information, see *http://www.wais.com*.

See **GOPHER**, **HTML**, **INTERNET2**, and **WWW**.

WAN
Wide Area Network

A data communications network that spans any distance and is usually provided by a public carrier. You get access to the two ends of a circuit; the carrier does everything in between—which is typically drawn as a "grey cloud," since you don't know (or usually care) how the carrier implements it. In contrast, a LAN typically has a diameter (the maximum distance between any two stations) limited to less than a few kilometers and is entirely owned by the user.

With a leased line service, the line connects locations specified when the service is ordered. The carrier charges by the month, regardless of how much data is transferred over the leased line circuit.

A circuit switched service allows the customer to choose where the line connects on a per-call basis. Usually, the entire circuit is connected to one location until the call is terminated (just like a normal phone call). The carrier charges by the month for the connection of the circuit to their switched network. In addition, there may be per-minute charges for the cumulative duration of established connections (whether you are sending data or not). That is, local calls may be free, and long-distance calls charged—again, just like for normal telephone service).

Packet, frame and cell switched services can be either of the following.

▲ *Permanent virtual circuit* (PVC) based, where the connection is established as *subscription time* (that is, when the service is ordered from the carrier).

▲ *Switched virtual call* (or *circuit*—SVC) based, where the connection is established on a per-call basis, just like a normal telephone.

WAN options are shown in the figure below. Most carriers have marketing names for each service, which is different from the technical name. Sometimes this is to create some brand distinction for the carrier's offerings, sometimes because the offering has fewer or more features than the corresponding standard, or maybe its just to create more difficulty for customers to do comparative shopping. In the figure, some Stentor Canada and AT&T marketing names for the services are shown in *italics*.

Many studies have shown that the monthly costs for WAN services from carriers are usually 60% to 80% of an organization's communications budget (the other 40% to 20% is used for the purchase of routers and other equipment). It is therefore important to ensure that the WAN services are tailored to the requirements—so you don't use more resources that you need, since you can be sure you'll pay dearly for these. The table below summarizes some of the services and the reasons for using them.

Type of Service	Best used for ...
Dedicated circuit (or leased line)	Constant traffic, or when security is very important.
Circuit switched	Heavy traffic for a well-defined, and relatively brief, time. Examples are facsimile transmission, video-conferencing and file transfer.
Packet switched (X.25)	Transaction-oriented exchanges of relatively short amounts of data, which may be in bursts, spread over the whole day. Expecially where many locations may need to connect to any other locations, and network latencies of a few hundred milliseconds is no problem. Examples are financial transactions, e-mail, inventory inquiries and telemetry and data gathering.
Frame Relay	Connection of many locations to a fixed set of locations, where data is somewhat bursty throughout the entire day and shorter network latencies than X.25 are required. Examples are LAN to LAN connections between the remote offices of a company.
Cell switched	Interconnection of LAN equipment at very high speeds, and (eventually) with different required throughputs and latencies, to support multimedia traffic.

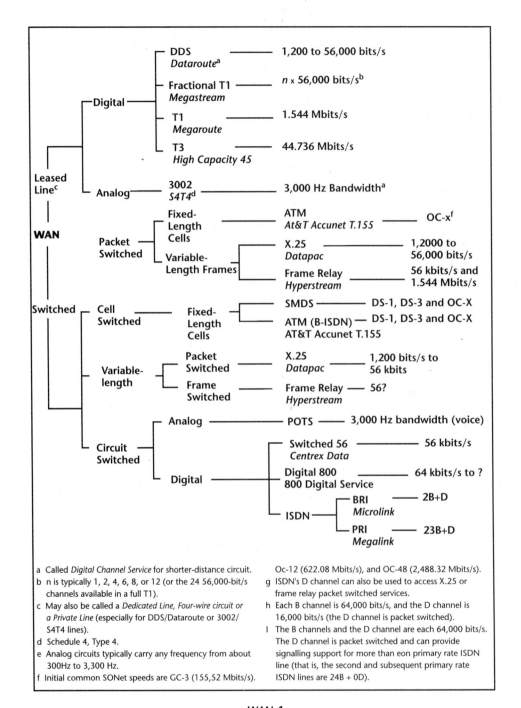

a Called *Digital Channel Service* for shorter-distance circuit.

b n is typically 1, 2, 4, 6, 8, or 12 (or the 24 56,000-bit/s channels available in a full T1).

c May also be called a *Dedicated Line, Four-wire circuit or a Private Line* (especially for DDS/Dataroute or 3002/S4T4 lines).

d Schedule 4, Type 4.

e Analog circuits typically carry any frequency from about 300Hz to 3,300 Hz.

f Initial common SONet speeds are GC-3 (155,52 Mbits/s).

Oc-12 (622.08 Mbits/s), and OC-48 (2,488.32 Mbits/s).

g ISDN's D channel can also be used to access X.25 or frame relay packet switched services.

h Each B channel is 64,000 bits/s, and the D channel is 16,000 bits/s (the D channel is packet switched).

I The B channels and the D channel are each 64,000 bits/s. The D channel is packet switched and can provide signalling support for more than eon primary rate ISDN line (that is, the second and subsequent primary rate ISDN lines are 24B + 0D).

Networks often use a transmission method different than used for the original source of the information, so some type of an adapter is needed to connect the two. The table below shows (for example) that an amplifier is used if both the source and network are analog, but a CODEC is used if the source is analog, but the network is digital.

	Network is . . .	
Information is . . .	**Analog**	**Digital**
Analog	Amplifier	CODEC
Digital	Modem	Terminal Adapter (ISDN) Transceiver (Ethernet) DSU/CSU (T1) Data Set (Dataroute/DDS)

One might wonder what "adapting" is needed if the information is digital, and the network directly handles digital data. Below are some examples of the functions these devices perform.

▲ An ISDN *Terminal Adapter* is needed to convert protocols and signalling rates, as well as to do network signalling (dialling the number to establish an ISDN connection).

▲ An Ethernet transceiver (*transmitter/receiver*) is needed to provide impedance matching for the different cable types and provide collision detection.

▲ For a T1 or fractional T1 circuit, a CSU/DSU (which is often simply called a DSU) converts the signalling (for example V.35 to T1's AMI), enforces the 1s-density requirement, has lightning and over-voltage protection, and provides status LEDs and loopback control (for trouble-shooting assistance).

▲ A data set is a generic term for the device needed to connect to a digital leased line. The type needed must match the data set in the telephone company's central office. It usually does most of the same functions as a CSU/DSU. For example, these circuits usually use a different signalling method than AMI, trouble-shooting functions are still required, but 1s-density enforcement is usually not required.

See **ATM** (*Asynchronous Transfer Mode*), **CARRIER, C.O., CODEC, CSU, DCS, DDS, DSU, DATAROUTE, DIGITAL 800, EIA/TIA-232, FRAME RELAY, FT1, HDLC, INVERSE MULTIPLEXER ISDN, LAN, MAN, MODEM, POTS, SATELLITE, SONET, STENTOR, SWITCHED 56, T1, T3, TA,** and **V.35.**

WCS
Wireless Communications Services

Frequencies in the 2.3 GHz band set aside for any uses other than commercial broadcasting or satellite communications. Data communications at 50 kbits/s to 100 kbits/s is one expected application.

The frequencies were first made available through an auction (which resulted in total accepted bid of $13.6 million) by the FCC in the spring of 1997.

See **WIRELESS.**

WIMP
Windows, Icons, Multitasking and Pointing Device

See **GUI**.

Winchester

In the late 1970s, IBM developed a disk drive read/write head technology that was initially used in its *Winchester* disk drives and has since become the standard for all hard disk drives. In fact, for several years in the early 1980s, all hard disk drives were called Winchester drives.

The technology uses very lightweight read/write heads that "fly" just above (less than the thickness of a piece of paper) the disk surface (the air moves at almost the disk surface's speed so close to it—about 100 km/h). The entire disk assembly is sealed to ensure that no dirt particles can get between the read/write head and the disk surface—a common cause of *disk head crashes*, which is when the read/write head touches the spinning disk surface, scraping off the magnetic stuff where all the bits live.

The next question is why IBM called their initial disk drive a Winchester. One influence is that IBM's first random-access disk drive (introduced in 1956, with a capacity of 5 Mbytes, using 24" platters) was called the *Rochester*. The model introduced with the flying read/write head technology had two 30-Mbyte sections (one might have been a removable cartridge, as was common then), and this "30-30" reminded someone of the famous Winchester 30-30 repeating, lever-action rifle.

The rifle's "30-30" refers to the type of *cartridge* (which is the assembly of a lead bullet, its brass case, and the black powder inside) for which the rifle was *chambered* (the same type of rifle can be built to accept different sizes of cartridges). The 30-30 cartridge uses a .30 caliber bullet (that is, the diameter of the bullet itself is 0.30 inch), and 30 *grains* of black powder (there are 7,000 grains to a pound, and a diamond's carat-weight is 3.17 grains per carat—these pre-metric units of weight are so quaint).

The cartridge was designed for the Winchester model 1894, which was introduced a long time ago, in the year—you guessed it—1894. (It seems they were not very imaginative in their product naming then and were confident that they would not introduce more than one new product per year!)

For its time, this was a high-tech rifle. It was the first to use a smokeless round (cartridge), and this required a nickel-steel barrel.

See **DISK DRIVE**, **IDE**, **SCSI1**, **SI**, and **V.35**.

Windows 3.0

Released in May 1990. Was the first popular version of Windows, since it had a good-looking user interface (previous versions were criticized as having colors that looked as though they were selected by computer nerds—I wonder why), computer hardware was finally powerful enough, and good development and debugging tools were available. Also, it used the protected mode of the 80286 processor, which provided access to 16 Mbytes of memory and a more robust environment (that is, it crashed less often).

The first version of Windows (version 1.0) was released in November 1985, and the very popular version 3.1 was released in April 1992.

See **GUI**, **OPERATING SYSTEM**, **WINDOWS 95**, and **WINDOWS NT**.

Windows 95

The successor to Microsoft's Windows 3.1 and Windows for Workgroups. Code-named (for marketing purposes) "Chicago" during development (though other code names were selected for other countries where "Chicago" doesn't mean anything). First released in August 1995 (due to a few announcement delays, there was some concern it wouldn't be ready until 1996, which might have required a name change).

Does not run over DOS, but is bootable itself. Requires an 80386 or faster Intel-architecture PC. Offers:

▲ A 32-bit memory space

▲ Long filenames

▲ Preemptive multitasking (but not symmetric multiprocessing)

▲ Multithreading and memory protection (as OS/2 and Windows NT do already)

▲ Support for *Plug and Play*

Windows 95 can use the 16-bit "real-mode" device drivers from Windows 3.1, but 32-bit protected-mode drivers have many advantages, such as they can be dynamically loaded and unloaded, support Plug-and-Play, and they don't use conventional memory.

My favorite feature is that to get the "Designed for Windows 95" logo, a product must come with an uninstall feature.

See **DLL**, **FUD**, **PC-95**, **OPERATING SYSTEM**, **PLUG AND PLAY**, **WINDOWS 3.0**, **WINDOWS NT**, and **WINX WINDOWS APIS**.

WINDOWS NT
Windows New Technology

This effort initially was to produce OS/2 3.0, but when IBM and Microsoft separated their development efforts, Microsoft renamed it to this (possibly because the development is being led by Dave Cutler, who had a lot to do with DEC's VMS, and the next letters after *v, m,* and *s* are *w, n,* and *t*).

Runs on other platforms—DEC's Alpha AXP, MIPS R4x00 series and the PowerPC). Will not replace Windows 3.x and Windows 95 but is a higher-end product requiring a more powerful platform. The initial version was released in 1993, and required a PC with at least 8 Mbytes of RAM (a large amount at the time), though most would say that it required at least 16 Mbytes (a huge amount at the time).

Has peer-to-peer networking built in. Is single-user but multitasking. Add-on products provide it with POSIX 1003.1 and NFS. The original version has 4 to 5 million lines of code and required 200 software developers years to develop.

Windows NT 4.0 has 16.5 million lines of code, and Microsoft says they spent over $400 million on Windows NT development by the time version 4.0 was released.

See **ALPHA AXP, CAIRO, CDE, DEC, MIPS COMPUTER SYSTEMS, NFS, OPERATING SYSTEM, POSIX-OSE, POWERPC, VMS,** and **WINX WINDOWS APIS.**

WINISDN
Windows ISDN APIs

A set of 18 APIs developed by NetManage, PSI, and ISDN*tek to enable Windows applications to communicate over ISDN lines, using synchronous PPP (which is more efficient than asynchronous PPP, which is used over dial-up modem lines).

See **ISDN, MODEM, PPP,** and **SLIP.**

WINSOCK
Windows Sockets Interface

The standard APIs (often called the *socket interface*) between Microsoft Windows (3.1, 95, and NT) application software and TCP/IP protocol software (often called a protocol stack).

Winsock enables any vendor's Winsock-compliant application to work over any vendors' Winsock protocol stack (before this, applications that ran over TCP/IP had to have drivers for each vendor's TCP/IP protocol stack it could use). Winsock version 1.1 was released in January 1993. Functions include `connect` and `accept` (for requesting and accepting a connection) and `send` and `recv` (for sending and receiving data).

Winsock is based on the *Berkeley Sockets* APIs (version 4.3), which was developed for TCP/IP communications on UNIX-based computers. Changes required to these BSD sockets APIs for Winsock include the following:

▲ Unlike Microsoft Windows 3.1, UNIX does *preemptive multitasking* (that is, a task can be waiting for data to be sent, and other tasks will still run). Since Windows 3.1 supports only *cooperative multitasking* (one task with nothing to do but wait for input must periodically call the operating system, which will then give CPU time to the other tasks), *blocking* (also called *synchronous*) calls (which don't return until the function, such as a read, completes) therefore cannot be used under Windows 3.1.

▲ Winsock therefore includes *asynchronous* functions that return immediately (and other functions that are used to check the status of the pending asynchronous function).

▲ There is no support for UNIX-style interprocess communication on the same computer.

Winsock development work is done by the Winsock Group (which was formed in the fall of 1991 and included Microsoft from the start). It is now called the Winsock Forum. Much of the original development work was done by Martin Hall, now of Stardust Technologies, Inc., which is an "independent testing, research, and consultancy organization providing services, facilities and tools to developers and users of Winsock software." The goal is to "provide an independent center of high quality information, services, and facilities dedicated to promoting the development of fast, high-quality, interoperable communications software for Microsoft Windows." Their offices include the *Winsock Interoperability Laboratories*, where testing is done.

A early and very popular public-domain version of Winsock is *Trumpet Winsock*, which is often provided free by *Internet service providers* (along with other public-domain and shareware software such as Eudora Mail and Netscape). Trumpet Winsock was written by Peter

WINSOCK 2

Tattam (*peter@psychnet.psychol.utas.edu.au*) in Hobart, Tasmania (Australia). The ftp site is *ftp.utas.edu.au*, and the files are in `/PC/trumpet/wintrump/*`. The actual TCP/IP protocol stack is implemented by a *dynamic link library*, perhaps with the file name `wsock32.dll`.

Now that Microsoft supports Winsock as part of its WOSA, and both 16- and 32-bit versions are included in Windows 3.1 and Windows 95, other Winsock implementations are not as frequently used.

Stardust Technologies (now called Stardust Winsock Labs Inc.) has a WWW server (with lots of Winsock information) at *http://www.stardust.com*. A copy of version 1.1 of the Winsock specification is at *http://www.microsoft.com/bussys/winsock/spec11*. Lots of pointers to Winsock-compatible software are at *http://www.tucows.com* (which is "The Ultimate Collection of Winsock Software") and *http://dwsapps.texas.net*.

See **API**, **BSD UNIX**, **DLL**, **ISP**, **NETSCAPE**, **PCCA**, **SOCKETS**, **SOCKS**, **SYNCHRONOUS FUNCTION**, **TAPI**, **UNIX**, **WINSOCK 2**, and **WOSA**.

WINSOCK 2
Windows Sockets Interface, version 2

A 32-bit implementation of Winsock 1.1, with lots of new features.

Winsock version 2 adds support for:

▲ Protocol stacks in addition to TCP/IP—such as Novell's IPX, DEC's DECnet, and OSI protocols

▲ Media other than LANs (for example, wireless)

▲ A wide range of WANs (such as ISDN, frame relay, and ATM)

This enables an application to work over many protocols (even simultaneously), with no additional development effort.

Application programs to specify a *quality of service* (QOS)—the average and peak bandwidth required, and latency and the latency variation acceptable. This is called a *flow*. Also specified is one of 3 levels of service, as described below.

▲ *Guaranteed service* means that the application requires exactly that QOS, and no less for the duration of the connection. Also, it would not benefit from better service. If the application sends more traffic, then the network can delay or discard the excess. Real-time applications are expected to use this service.

▲ *Predictive service* provides a minimum guaranteed throughput, but the delay may have occasional wide variations. Again, traffic levels above that specified in the flow may be discarded by the network. Video applications are expected to use this service, as it makes very efficient use of the network (it can be temporarily busy) while offering a high-throughput service.

▲ *Best effort service* is similar to ATM's *available bit rate* (ABR) service in that the application specifies a flow (which the network can use to allocate resources, but there are no service guarantees from the network. All networks are expected to provide this level of service, but some may only implement one or none of the other two above.

Networks can inform users during a connection of changes in network loading, and if it is necessary to change their level of service.

Eventually, a cost (as in dollars and cents) will be offered by some networks in response to the requested level of service specification. Users can then decide whether to proceed with that level of service, or perhaps track the cost of the service on a per-call and immediate basis.

Bandwidth requirements are specified using a credit-based method which uses a bucket analogy. As with all buckets, it has a maximum volume (in this case, a number of bytes, which is called the *token bucket size*), and is filled at a certain rate (in bytes per second, and called the *token rate*). Once full, it cannot be filled any more. As an application sends data to the network, it reduces the number of token bytes left in the bucket (and the bucket continues to fill). Therefore, if the application has not been sending recently, it is allowed to send a large burst (the token bucket size). If it has been sending constantly, then it can send at the token rate. If it has been sending faster than its token rate, then when it runs out of token bytes, it must stop transmitting (or risk having the network discard the excess data).

Winsock 2 applications can request special services, such as multicasting. New features include API functions to reply to the application program with information such as the following:

▲ Whether the link is currently available (for example, a wireless link may currently be out of range of the home office network),

▲ Whether modem battery power available

▲ Time delay (that is, the *latency*) and congestion of the link (which may affect how the use of the link is optimized), or how much traffic it generates (for example, reducing the frame rate for a video conference when the network is temporarily overloaded)

▲ Wireless signal strength and base station identification

As shown in the figure, Winsock 2 is comprised of 3 components, each with their own API functions.

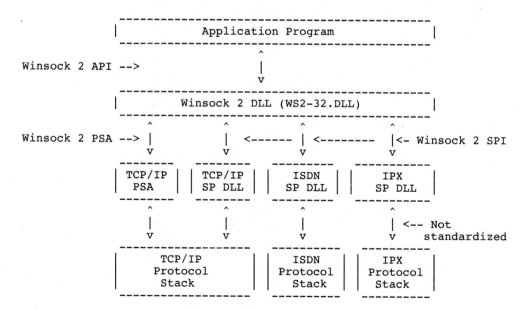

The 3 components, and their interfaces are described below:

▲ The Winsock 2 API is used by the application program for all communication functions (that is, when the people writing the application program need a communication function, they use those available in the Winsock 2 API). The library of Winsock 2 functions is implemented as a Windows *dynamic link library* (DLL) called `WS2-32.DLL`.

▲ For each protocol supported, there is also a Winsock 2 *service provider* (SP) DLL. The API between the main Winsock 2 DLL and each of the SP DLLs is called the *service provider interface* (SPI). The interface between the SP DLL and the actual protocol stack is not standardized (which means that the protocol stack vendor provides the SP DLL as part of their product).

▲ Some protocol functions are specific to a protocol (such as IP's ping and multicast). The interface between the main Winsock DLL and these protocol-specific functions is called the *protocol specific annex* (PSA).

Winsock version 2 protocol stacks are be binary-compatible with applications written for Winsock version 1.1. Specification and development of the standard is done by the *Winsock 2 Forum*, and work on the specification was completed in January 1996.

Winsock 2 information is available at *http://www.stardust.com* and *http://www.intel.com/IAL/winsock2*.

ATM (*Asynchronous Transfer Mode*), **IP MULTICAST**, **PING**, **QOS**, **WINSOCK**, and **WIRELESS**.

WINTEL
Windows/Intel Architecture

A common name used to refer to the standard office-environment personal computer that has an Intel (or clone) processor (usually simply called a PC), and runs some variant of Microsoft Corporation's Windows.

See **INTEL**, **MICROSOFT**, **NC**, and **PC**.

Winx Windows APIs

Microsoft has defined several *Application Program Interfaces* between application programs and the different versions of Windows. These are listed in the following table in increasing order of capability.

API	Use
Win16	The 16-bit programming model API used for Windows 3.1 (therefore sometimes called the Windows 3.1 API, or simply Win31).
Win32s	A 32-bit version of Win16 that has virtually none of the enhancements of Win32 (so this API is a *subset* of Win32, hence the "s" in Win32s). Mostly handled by a DLL that converts the 32-bit application calls to 16-bit calls supported by Windows 3.1. Only runs on 80386 or better. Intended for (likely math-based) applications that need 32-bit code but need to run on both Windows 3.1 and Windows NT. Hoping to hasten the demise of 16-bit Windows applications (and Windows 3.1), as of mid-1996, Microsoft's compilers no longer support Win32s.

(table continued on next page)

API	Use
Win32c	The API used by Windows 95 that is almost as extensive as Win32 (so this API is supposed to be *compatible* with Win32, hence the "c" in Win32c). Sometimes called Win95.
Win32	The 32-bit API used for Windows 95 and Windows NT. Mostly a superset of Win16 and Win32c. This is supposed to be the standard API for the near future. Has about 2,000 API functions (calls). Including MAPI, TAPI OLE and other extensions, it includes over 3,000 function calls.
Win32CE	The 32-bit API Microsoft developed to support hand-held computers (HPCs) and other "embedded" applications (that are mostly small applicance-type devices, rather than computers). Only about 500 calls (API (functions) are supported, for example, it doesn't support printing, but has extensive communication capabilities, such as PPP, TCP/IP, IrDA, TAPI, WinSock and NDIS.

Using the 32-bit API ("Win32") provides many advantages, some are listed below.

▲ The "32-bit" refers to the *flat* 32-bit address space supported by the API (and the operating system and processor). This means that (for example) program references to memory locations use a 32-bit pointer, which can therefore access any memory location in 2^{32} bytes (this is 4,294,967,296 bytes, which is 4 Gbytes)—and that's a big program. Predecessor processors (and therefore operating systems, and therefore APIs) supported 16-bit operations, and could therefore only directly access memory in blocks of 65,536 (2^{16}) bytes. Segment registers, offsets and other headache-producing and performance-slowing work-arounds were used to support larger programs and data.

▲ Also, applications can be *preemptively multitasked*. The operating system takes control of the computer when it needs or wants to—to handle some external event (such as data received from a modem connection or disk drive read) or to give CPU time to another process or thread.

▲ In contrast, Windows 3.1 only supports *cooperative multitasking* (or *cooperative scheduling*), where the application must periodically give control back to the operating system (so that it can handle external events and give CPU time to other programs).

▲ Preemptive multitasking is better, because it ensures that an "errant" application cannot hang your PC.

▲ *Multithreading* is supported, in that a single task (usually called a *process*) can start (sometimes called *spawn*) one or more other paths through its code. These *threads* inherit the *context* (access to the same open files and variables for example) as the initial instance of the program, so they can work in the background helping the main program (for example, by printing a document in the background, while doing text editing in the foreground). This capability is also very useful for many types of server functions.

▲ In UNIX, the operating system call that starts a thread is called a `fork`, and the threads are called *child processes*.

▲ Easy access to filenames longer than DOS's "8.3" format.

See **API**, **HPC**, **SMP2** (*Symmetric Multiprocessing*), **WINDOWS 3.0**, **WINDOWS 95**, and **WINDOWS NT**.

Wireless

A long, long time ago, the radio was called *the wireless*. Then the name went away, but now its back. Now it usually refers to two-way communication, often including data communication.

There are many options, as shown below.

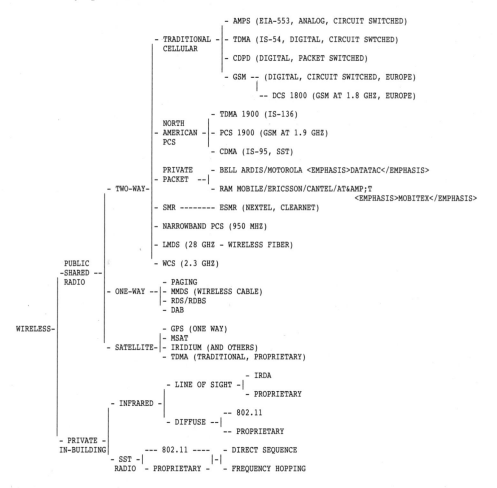

```
                                              - AMPS (EIA-553, ANALOG, CIRCUIT SWITCHED)

                               - TRADITIONAL -|- TDMA (IS-54, DIGITAL, CIRCUIT SWTCHED)
                                 CELLULAR
                                              |- CDPD (DIGITAL, PACKET SWITCHED)

                                              |- GSM -- (DIGITAL, CIRCUIT SWITCHED, EUROPE)
                                              |
                                                      -- DCS 1800 (GSM AT 1.8 GHZ, EUROPE)

                                          - TDMA 1900 (IS-136)
                               NORTH
                             - AMERICAN -|- PCS 1900 (GSM AT 1.9 GHZ)
                               PCS
                                          - CDMA (IS-95, SST)

                               PRIVATE    - BELL ARDIS/MOTOROLA <EMPHASIS>DATATAC</EMPHASIS>
                             - PACKET  --|
                   - TWO-WAY-|            - RAM MOBILE/ERICSSON/CANTEL/AT&AMP;T
                             |                                           <EMPHASIS>MOBITEX</EMPHASIS>
                             |- SMR ------- ESMR (NEXTEL, CLEARNET)

                             |- NARROWBAND PCS (950 MHZ)

                             |- LMDS (28 GHZ - WIRELESS FIBER)

           PUBLIC            |- WCS (2.3 GHZ)
          -SHARED --|
           RADIO            |            - PAGING
                           - ONE-WAY --|- MMDS (WIRELESS CABLE)
                           |            |- RDS/RDBS
                           |            - DAB
 WIRELESS-|                |
          |                |            - GPS (ONE WAY)
          |                |            |- MSAT
          |                - SATELLITE-|- IRIDIUM (AND OTHERS)
          |                            - TDMA (TRADITIONAL, PROPRIETARY)

          |                               - IRDA
          |                - LINE OF SIGHT -|
          |              - INFRARED -|       - PROPRIETARY
          |              |           |
          |              |           |       -- 802.11
          |              |           - DIFFUSE --|
          - PRIVATE -|                           -- PROPRIETARY
            IN-BUILDING|      --- 802.11 ----  - DIRECT SEQUENCE
                       - SST -|          |-|
                         RADIO  - PROPRIETARY -  - FREQUENCY HOPPING
```

CDPD, Ardis and RAM Mobile used to be happy competing with each other, but PCS has them worried enough that they are working on a plan for interoperability.

While wireless is becoming much more prevalent, there is still a haunting concern that some study (or worse yet—a court of law) someday may find that radio frequency transmissions can adversely affect one's health, or that the increasing use of wireless will more commonly and seriously affect airplane control systems, pacemakers and other important things. Some therefore consider wireless best left to niche markets, where wire- and cable-based systems are not possible (for example, because mobility is required).

Some standards for wireless communinication are at *http://www.industry.net/tia*, and some links are at *http://www.wlana.com/index.html*. The Personal Communications Industry Association is at *http://www.pcia.com*.

See **S802.A11, AMPS, ARDIS, DAB, ESMR, IRDA, GSM, LMDS, NARROWBAND PCS, PAGING, PCS, RDS, SMR, SST, TDMA, WCS,** and **WINSOCK 2.**

WORM
Write Once, Read Mostly (or Many)

A storage device that can be written to by an end user—but only once (it is nonerasable, but sometimes it can be written to incrementally until it is full). Examples include nonerasable optical and CD-R storage media (often used for archival backup).

See **CDROM.**

WOSA
Windows Open Services Architecture

Microsoft's framework (and APIs) for providing services (such as receiving real-time stock market data or supporting retail banking transactions) for Windows applications.

WOSA services consist of two parts:

▲ The APIs required for the service (so programmers have access to the function calls required to use the service)—, which are independent of the actual type of connection or network used to access the service.

▲ The service-providers interface to the required network or network service (one for each type of connection or network required). For example, TAPI may communicate over an EIA-232 connection to a telephone, or it may use an ISDN connection to receive caller ID information.

WOSA services include Winsock (which replaces NetBEUI as Microsoft's preferred communications API), and Microsoft's ODBC and TAPI support.

See **API, CALLER ID, MAPI, ODBC, TAPI, WINSOCK,** and **WINX WINDOWS APIS.**

WWW
World Wide Web

The network of *servers* on the Internet, each of which has one or more hypertext *home pages*, which provide information and links (by clicking on them) to other documents on that and (usually) other servers.

First proposed in March 1989 by Tim Berners-Lee at the *European Laboratory for Particle Physics*, which is usually called "CERN" as it was previously called *Conseil Européen pour la Recherche Nucléaire*. (It is near Geneva, Switzerland, and many people speak French there.) It was originally intended as a method of making scientific papers and graphical images available on the Internet (for other scientists).

Tim Berners-Lee developed HTML, HTTP, and URLs, and thought of the name world wide web. In September 1990, he finally got his project approved, and he selected the NeXT workstation as a platform, since it had built-in support for many of the capabilities he needed. He wrote the first WWW server and the first text and graphical client, though the graphics were not embedded with the text (Netscape was the first to do that), graphics were in a separate window. The software included an HTML editor too. The browser was operational by late 1990, and the software was made available on the Internet in the summer of 1991.

Previous attempts at hypertext used centralized databases of the links for each hypertext entry. While this ensured that all links for all documents could be easily updated (so that if a document was moved, all references to it on other pages would be updated correctly), such centralized systems could not be scaled to large (and Internet) sizes. That is, common wisdom at the time was that a useful hypertext systems required that all links be guaranteed to be current. However, Tim Berners-Lee's insight was that while having the links for each hypertext entry embedded in the link, it was possible (nay, likely) that the links on some pages will point to non-existent documents (sometimes called *dangling links*), at least such a system can easily be used on networks as large as the Internet. And as we all know now, the system works quite well, and is far better than nothing.

Servers communicate with *clients* by using the *Hypertext Transfer Protocol* (HTTP). A secure version (S-HTTP) is currently under development.

WWW server addresses (*Uniform Resource Locators* or URLs) are typically of the form *http:// www.orgname.com,* where `orgname.com` is the DNS name of the organization running the server.

Sources for WWW server software can be found by snooping around, starting at *http:// www.w3.org*, for example, or *http://emwac.ed.ac.uk/html/internet_toolchest/top.html*.

The first popular browser (or client) was written by Marc Andreessen, Eric Bina and others, while they were undergraduate students and working at the National Center for Super-computing Applications at the University of Illinois. Marc Andreesen called it *Mosaic* because it could combine different aspects of the Internet—text, graphics and audio into a single page (and because he thought there already too many acronyms). It was initially written over the winter of 1992 and 1993, for Silicon Graphics workstations, though others soon had versions for Microsoft Windows and Apple Macintosh computers. The first public beta version was released in March, 1993. This package's ease of use is what made the Web quickly become extremely popular. It is available from *http://www.ncsa.uiuc.edu/SDG/Software/Mosaic/ NCSAMosaicHome.html* . Marc Andreessen and Jim Clark (a founder of Silicon Graphics) started Netscape Communications Corp. in April 1994. Most people now use either Netscape Communications Corporation's Navigator or Microsoft Corporation's Internet Explorer.

The operation of a WWW server is determined by a configuration file (also called a rule file), by default `/etc/httpd.conf`.

For WWW servers, the document `Welcome.html` is returned when no document is specified (though this can be changed to any other filename, using the `Welcome` directive). This `Welcome` file is located in a directory pointed to in the configuration file (using the `ServerRoot` directive).

By default, a trailing "/" is not required in the URL. If one is not in the URL, then the server software adds one, and the default document name (typically `Welcome.html`) is appended to this (to construct the full URL for the document to be returned). This behavior can be changed by setting the `AlwaysWelcome` directive to `Off`. This permits URLs that do not specify a document (and specify only a directory—perhaps the `ServerRoot` directory that is used when no directory is specified) to be used to retrieve a directory listing rather than the Welcome document (so now you—and I—know why only sometimes a trailing "/" is required).

By default, the *well known port* 80 is used for HTTP, but the WWW server's configuration file can specify another port to be used (with the `Port` directive). Optionally, this default port can be specified in the URL (for example, *http://ds1.internic.net:80/rfc/rfc-index.txt),*. If a non-standard port is required (sometimes 8000, 8001, or 8080 is used instead, since ports less than 1024 can have only services provided by the root user), then it must be specified in the URL (unless the WWW server does a redirect to the correct port).

The tilde character is often used in subdirectory names (e.g., */~pcmag*), since it marks a *user-supported directory*. This is a subdirectory (specified with the `UserDir` directive, typically set to `www`) below each user's home directory on the WWW server that is *exported* (made available to the calling public) where users (with accounts on the WWW server) can maintain their own HTML pages. This is a standard UNIX convention, supported by the C and Korn shells.

Heavily used servers (such as those for popular Internet search engines, such as Excite) are actually many servers operating in parallel. This provides more throughput, as well as redundancy in case a server develops a problem. Specialized hardware splits incoming requests according some algorithm, such as rotating the requests equally among the available servers, or the least-loaded server gets the next request. In 1997, the Excite search engine (often called a *server farm*, since there are many actual servers) could handle 30,000 simultaneous sessions, by using such load splitting.

In January 1995, CERN handed over its development of the WWW to the *World Wide Web Consortium* ("W^3" or "W3C"), which "promotes the Web by producing specifications and reference software, and is funded by industrial members but its products are freely available to all."

The Consortium is run by MIT's LCS (the *Massachusetts Institute of Technology's Laboratory for Computer Science*) in Cambridge, Massachusetts, with INRIA (*Institut National de Recherche en Informatique et en Automatique*—which is France's National Research Institute for Computer Science and Control, in Roquencourt) acting as European host, in collaboration with CERN.

The W3C maintains a WWW server at *http://www.w3.org* (which replaces *http://info.cern.ch* as the main source of WWW information). The W3 server has:

▲ Specifications for HTML and HTTP

▲ Lists of WWW servers by country and city (see *http://www.w3.org/hypertext/DataSources/www/servers.html*)

▲ The status of new developments

▲ Lots of other useful WWW information

A FAQ is at *http://sunsite.unc.edu/boutell/faq/www-faq.html.*

Pointers to many browsers are at *http://www.ski.mskcc.org/browserwatch/* and *http://www.nln.com.*

WXModem

Companies that produce server software include O'Reilly & Associates (*http://www.ora.com*), Silicon Graphics (*http://www.sgi.com*), and Sun Microsystems (*http://www.sun.com*).

See **CGI**, **DNS1** (*Domain Name System*), **HOME PAGE**, **HTML**, **HTTP**, **NEXTSTEP**, **SHTTP**, **SSL**, **TCP**, **URL**, **WAIS**, and **YAHOO**.

WXModem

The XModem file transfer protocol with a *window size* of 4 (that is, up to 4 frames of data can be outstanding before the sender must stop sending and wait for an `ack`).

Improves throughput on communication links with longer delays.

See **XMODEM** and **YMODEM**.

X

X
X Window System

A very popular standard for the low-level functions required to support graphical user interfaces in the UNIX environment.

A *de facto* standard, initially developed by the Massachusetts Institute of Technology, for sending graphics primitives to a display server. This display server can be either a dedicated X terminal or a more general-purpose computer, such as a workstation or PC (with the necessary software). The X Window System was preceded by a system called "W," perhaps as in "Window" (and since "X" is the next letter in the alphabet, maybe that's where the name came from).

The X Window System usually uses TCP and sockets for communications. The standard is maintained by the *X Consortium* at MIT.

The functions (or *user interface library*) that are available to the host computer (which is the *client* and runs the application software) are defined by and referred to as *Xlib* (a series of C language APIs). However, the exact program interface (APIs) to generate the Xlib commands is not specified.

The communication over a network is specified as the *X-wire protocol*.

X11R6 is a typical name of a version of the standard—this means "X version 11, release 6".

The higher-level toolkit for generating menus, scroll bars, push buttons, and other basic elements of a GUI is called *Widgets*.

Any user interface (that is, the look and action of push-buttons, the menu scheme, and so on) can be built by using the Xlib and the Widget functions.

A *style guide* specifies how the application should react to the user's manipulation of Widgets and therefore describes the look and feel of the GUI. The *window manager* controls the interface elements in accordance with a set of rules that specify the allowable sizes and positions of Windows and Widgets. The most common user interface (sometimes called a *window manager*) is *Motif*.

The X Window System is an example of *server-centric* computing, where everything but the actual display of the data is done at the server (just like the old mainframe days!).

See **CDE, CLIENT/SERVER, DE FACTO, GUI, LBX, MOTIF, OPENLOOK, OSF, TCL-TK, TCP, WABI,** and **X-TERMINAL.**

X-10
X-10 Powerhouse

A patented, by X-10 (USA), Inc., method for sending control signals (ON, OFF, DIM, and so on) through 110 A.C. wiring (this is sometimes called *Power Line Carrier*), typically to modules into which are plugged the appliances and lights to be controlled.

While there are many weaknesses to the system (poor error detection and correction, limited command set and address range, etc.), there are too many proposed new methods, so manufacturers are not building in this capability to new appliances and electronic equipment.

There are two main types of X-10 devices—transmitters and receivers. A transmitter sends the X-10 commands, and may be a small box with a button, or a timer which sends commands at predetermined times, or due to other inputs (such as it detecting that it is getting dark outside).

A receiver usually controls the power to a household device. Two types are the most common. *Light modules* are solid-state (there are no moving parts), can only control incandescent lights, and can dim the lights. *Appliance modules* have a relay to switch the power (they cannot "dim"), so they can control devices that have motors (such as fans) and fluorescent lights.

X-10 commands are 9-bit messages, consisting of:

▲ A 4-bit "house code", which identifies a group of X-10 devices. The initial idea was that each house would use a different house code, so they would not turn on and off each others' lights. However, there is no problem in using more than one house code within a single house. The 16 available house codes are usually designated by the letters A through P.

▲ A 5-bit "key-code". The first 16 of the 32 key-codes (the "Unit Code") designate which device within a house-code group is being addressed (numbered 0 through 15). Key codes 16 through 31 specifies which function is being requested, as shown in the table below.

Function Code	Function	Comment
16	All units off	Turn off all light and appliance modules in housecode
17	Hail request	
18	Dim	Dim specified light module by one step
19	Extended data	
20	On	Turn on specified light or applicance module
21	Preset dim low	Set specified light module to a specific setting (rarely implemented)
22	All lights off	Turn off all light modules in house code
23	Status = off	
24	All lights on	Turn on all light modules in house code
25	Hail acknowledge	
26	Bright	Brighten specified light module by one step
27	Status = on	
28	Off	Turn off specified light or appliance module
29	Preset dim high	Set specified light module to a specific setting (rarely used)
30	Extended code	
31	Status request	

The bits of the X-10 command are sent just after the zero crossings of the 60 Hz 110v a.c. signal (there are 120 of these each second). Commands are preceeded by the bit sequence 1110, and each of the 9 command bits is followed by its complement (for error detection). The entire 22-bit sequence is then repeated (a receiver will use the second copy if the first was corrupted). Each 1 bit is actually sent as a 5 V, 1 ms burst of a 120 kHz signal right after the zero-crossing, and again 1.77 ms later, and a third time 1.77 ms later (these subsequent bursts correspond to the zero-crossings of 3-phase power). A 0 bit is indicated when there is no burst. The data rate is therefore basically 60 bits/s.

X-10 was initially developed by the Scottish company Pico Electronics in 1976 (they had 9 unrelated predecessor products code-named X-1 through X-9), and marketed through established audio equipment maker BSR.

A competing, much more powerful, but very slow to be standardized and developed technology is called CEBus. Further information on it is at *http://www.cebus.org*.

Further information on X-10 is available from X10 USA Inc. at *http://www.x10.com*. The Home Automation Association is at *http://www.hometeam.com/haa.shtml*. Circuit Cellar magazine (a great magazine for electronic designers) has some X-10 pointers at *http://www.circellar.com/hasites.html*. Some X-10 equipment vendors are at *http://www.hometeam.com/homenet/home.htm* and *http://www.smarthome.com*. The *news://comp.home.automation* usenet FAQ is at *http://www.cs.ualberta.ca/~wade/HyperHome*.

X.25

A packet-switched WAN.

That is, rather than having dedicated bandwidth (such as a circuit-switched or leased line, which you pay for by time, regardless of how much data you send), your packets of data go onto a high-speed shared connection (just as your driveway eventually leads to a highway). You pay only for the bits you send.

Charging is typically by the *packet* (usually up to 128 or 256 bytes of data per packet), *segment* (which are billing units of up to 64 bytes of data in a packet), or *character* (byte of data).

Different networks have different charging methods (which makes it very difficult to compare rates—you need to know your packet-size distribution).

A connection-oriented protocol, in that you need to establish a connection before exchanging data—analogous to a telephone call.

See **CONNECTIONORIENTED, EDI, NPSI, QLLC, WAN, X.400**, and **ZMODEM**.

X.400

The OSI messaging (electronic mail—and some day more) standard.

The connections between MTAs (*Message Transfer Agents*) and service providers (each of which is an *administrative domain*) are usually X.25. A hierarchical addressing scheme is used to create a *distinguished name* (DN), with at least the field names listed in the following table.

X.400 Address Field Name	Meaning	Comments
C	Country	Such as USA
ADMD or A	Administrative Domain	The internationally registered service provider, to which a private organization connects for X.400 mail service
PRMD or P	Private Domain	The name of the MTA to which the service provider forwards mail
O	Organization	Periods (".") can be used in fields to give the appearance of additional levels of hierarchy. These fields are optional.
OU	Organization Unit	
D or DDA	Domain-Defined Attribute	A user identifier for a user on a non-X.400 mail system. For example, an Internet address or a CompuServe ID. This field is optional.
PN	Personal Name	Could be MShnier, but is usually divided into S (Surname), G (Given Name), and I (Middle Initial) fields

Unfortunately, the use of optional fields (and whether they are optional for a specific installation) is determined by the *private mail domain's* X.400 mail administrator (that is, the guy who sets up your company's X.400 software). Therefore you can never guess or figure out someone's X.400 mail address. They have to tell it to you (or put it on their business cards, or maybe the X.500 directory service will help some day).

X.400 messages cannot be routed through intermediate X.400 service providers, so there must be direct connections between them (X.25 or a leased line).

There are (or at least, there used to be) about 12 U.S. service providers, including ATTMail, CompuServe, GEIS, IBM, MCI, and Sprint (Telemail).

Sample X.400 addresses are

```
C:USA,A:Telemail,P:Internet,"RFC-822":<72567.3304(a)CompuServe.com
```

and

```
(C:USA, A:Telemail, O:LearnTree, FN:Mitchell, SN:Shnier)
```

Not a very user-friendly thing (especially compared to Internet mail addresses).

A site with X.400 messaging capability uses a *message transfer agent* (software on a computer) to send and receive messages from a service provider. *User agents* run on user computers to assist with composing, viewing, sending, and retrieving messages to and from a message transfer agent.

SMTP is the homologous e-mail protocol in the TCP/IP and Internet world. However, compared to SMTP, X.400 has far better security (for example, support for authentication and encryption) and delivery confirmation. But X.400 service providers usually charge per

X.400 e-mail message (compared to SMTP e-mail, which is almost free, due to the low fixed-price most ISPs charge for Internet access, which includes unlimited e-mail).

Some further information is at *ftp://FTP.u.uwashington.edu/pub/user-supported/reader/text/standards/X.400/ /*

See **DNS2**, **MTA**, **OSI**, **SMTP**, **UA**, **X.25**, and **X.500**.

X.500

Refers to a series of standards, some of which define the *directory services* specification originally intended to be used with X.400 messaging (electronic mail). It is a database system with the following features:

▲ The database (which they call a *directory*) is distributed and hierarchical, so that the database servers can be located near their administrators (for example, each company would maintain their own data on their own database server). The database can be searched without users having to know where the retrieved data is stored.

▲ The database servers can be implemented on different platforms.

▲ The database can be customized to store most any type of information about any type of object. For example, users' email addresses, PGP encryption keys, locations, telephone numbers and photos, or descriptions of the applications and printers available on file servers could be stored.

A simple use would be to respond to queries ("find me all the people with first name Mitchell who work for Integrated Intelligence's Toronto office"), likely posed with a clicky-mousey kind of user interface. Other capabilities include:

▲ The ability to search on different fields

▲ Storing what type of computer a mail message recipient has so that the correct file format will be automatically used (or generated) when sending a file as an attachment to a mail message

▲ Storing public keys for secure mail messaging

Improvements of the 1993 version of the specification over the original version (1988) include:

▲ *Replication* (storing multiple copies of the information for improved response time, capacity, and availability—and specified in X.525)

▲ *Certificate Management* (a security feature that tracks which users have access to which resources—and specified in X.509)

▲ Additional TCP/IP support functions

X.500 defines two *agents* (implemented in software):

▲ *Directory Service Agent* (DSA), which is the part that resides in an X.500 server, which communicates with clients and other X.500 directory servers (through their DSAs)

▲ *Directory User Agent* (DUA), which is the part that resides in a client and communicates with DSAs to get directory information for the client

As shown in the figure, the data communication uses these OSI-based protocols:

▲ *Directory Access Protocol* (DAP)—used by the client (through its DUA) to request and obtain directory information from a DSA

▲ *Directory Service Protocol* (DSP)—used by the X.500 server (through its DSA) to communicate with other servers

▲ *Directory Information Shadowing Protocol* (DISP)—used to replicate the data between servers

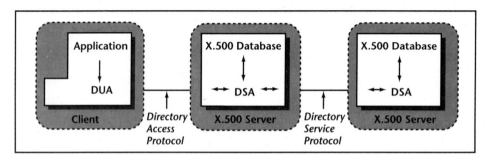

X.500-1

Since most clients will not have an OSI protocol stack, the IETF has defined the Lightweight Directory Access Protocol (LDAP), which uses TCP/IP rather than OSI. Since OSI-based communication is currently required for the DSP, X.500 database servers will require an OSI protocol stack.

The IETF has also defined how certain types of information are to be stored, to facilitate interoperability between X.500 servers. For example, RFC 1274 defines how to store and reference telephone numbers.

Directory entries are identified by a *Distinguished Name* (DN), which is a concatenation of the *values* for (for example) these *attributes* (which are standardized for X.400 electronic-mail use). Some examples are shown in the following table.

Attribute		Typical Value
Abbreviation	**Name**	
CN	Common Name	
	Mitchell Shnier	
OU	Organizational Unit	
	Engineering	
O	Organization	Integrated Intelligence
ST	State/Province	On
C	Country	Canada

A single distinguished name can match to more than one value for a specific attribute (for example, Mitchell Shnier and M. Shnier).

Access Control Lists (ACLs) determine who can access which entries and which fields of those entries. For example, only the engineering department can see the workstation type attribute values, and outside users can see only the sales department's telephone extensions.

Predecessor directory services have been proprietary, or unique to specific platforms (such as Novell's NetWare MHS and Directory Services, or Banyan's Intelligent Messaging Architecture and StreetTalk)—a big problem when an organization has multiple platforms, as information might need to be entered multiple times or might not be available from certain platforms.

Implementations will likely always support TCP/IP, since the OSI protocols that were initially expected to be used for X.500 are not widely accepted (now there's a big understatement).

See **ENCRYPTION, LDAP, NDS, OSI, TCP/IP, PGP, X.400**, and **X.509**.

X.509

A standard (developed by Northern Telecom) for defining *authentication certificates* (also called *digital ID*s. These are used to hold the information necessary provide assurance of the identity of the sender or receiver in an electronic communication.

See **AUTHENTICATION**, and **PGP**.

X/OPEN
X/Open Company Ltd.

A not-for-profit consortium of end users and open system vendors (originally mostly European) that specifies user requirements for open systems and selects the standards and most suitable options to achieve interoperability. The goal is to increase the number of open applications that are available.

OSF is, and UI was, a member. Produces the XPG and provides a certification service. Conforming products receive a stylized "X" brand.

X/Open was formed in 1988 and is also the owner of the UNIX name. It controls the licensing of the name. For example, vendors using the name must comply with X/Open's "SPEC 1170," which describes the common API which all UNIXes must support.

See **CDE, OSF, UI, USL, UNIX**, and **XPG**.

X/Open Portability Guide

See **XPG**.

X-stone

A graphics performance benchmark.

See **SPEC**.

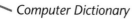

X Server

An *X Window System* display server—that is, an X terminal (since the X terminal is doing the actual processing and therefore displaying of the commands). The client typically executes on a computer elsewhere on the network, using the X server (that is, X terminal) for the display functions (just as the database server would be used for the database functions).

See **X-TERMINAL**.

X Terminal

A graphics terminal (usually with an integrated Ethernet interface) that is an *X Window System* display server. Has a keyboard and mouse. The monitor may be color or monochrome.

See **X WINDOW SYSTEM**.

X Windows

An incorrect name for *The X Window System*.

See **X WINDOW SYSTEM**.

XAPIA
X.400 Application Program Interface Association

A standards-setting organization that has published an interface specification for X.400 systems. Lotus, Microsoft, and Novell are members. They are also working on the *Common Mail Calls* (CMC) API.

See **CMC**, **MAPI**, **VIM**, and **X.400**.

XBase

Database systems and application environments derived from Ashton-Tate's (now owned by Borland) dBase systems.

See **SQL**.

Xenix

Microsoft's UNIX-like operating system for the Intel platform, first released in 1979.

It was initially a port of AT&T UNIX Version 7, then System III, then System V. Versions used to be available for the DEC PDP-11 and Apple Lisa, but the PC version is all that is available today.

Microsoft owns Xenix (and some of the copyrights on parts of Xenix), and did some of the initial Intel 8086-based port. Since then, all ports have been done by SCO, under contract to Microsoft. SCO became a Xenix reseller, has continued to develop the product and for many years has been the only serious seller of the product. That is why SCO is sometimes considered a SCO product, and sometimes a Microsoft product.

See **SCO**, and **UNIX**.

XGA
Extended Graphics Adapter

IBM's improvement on its 8514/a (a superset). While IBM's XGA implementation was never widely accepted, the term is often used to refer to the maximum monitor resolution it supported—1,024 ×768 pixels.

See **S8514-A** and **VGA**.

XML
Extensible Markup Language

A proposed enhancement to HTML, which allow new tags to be defined. Where HTML allows a specific set of tags to be used, XML allows new tags to be defined (as does SGML).

Drafts of XML are at *http://www.w3.org/pub/WWW/markUp/SGML/Activity.*

See **SGML**, and **HTML**.

XModem

The original XModem file transfer protocol. Uses a PC's COM port to transfer files to another PC (usually through modems).

It has many limitations and weaknesses (but was state-of-the-art in its day—there was no other way to transfer files error-free between two microcomputers using their serial ports):

▲ The size of transferred files must be a multiple of 128 bytes (the program was first written for the CP/M operating system, and this was the disk *sector size*), so sent files may be longer than the original files.

▲ Frames are always (only) 128 bytes in length (larger frames would improve the efficiency of file transfers).

▲ Since data are sent exactly as they appear in the file being sent (they are not encoded), a transparent 8-bit (that is, any 8-bit value must be carried) communications channel is required. This can be provided by a direct dial-up modem connection between PCs, but is a problem for many operating systems and networks (such as X.25). These often have the restriction that they can only carry 7-bit data, or that they reserve certain *control* characters (such as Carriage Return or DLE—*Data Link Escape*) for their own use, or for software flow control (which requires use of the x-on and x-off ASCII control characters—11_{16} and 13_{16}). Even PCs need flow control, so they should be configured for hardware flow control (or a very slow data rate).

▲ It does not transfer the file's name or any other file attributes.

▲ The *window size* is limited to 1—that is, a second frame cannot be sent until the first is acknowledged (this significantly reduces throughput on high-speed and long-delay data links, as the sender must stop sending until the ack arrives).

▲ Recovery of synchronization is difficult, since the data and the checksum characters could be the same as the beginning of frame character (which is soh).

XModem-CRC

▲ The `ack` response is a single character and is not covered by an error check, so a *spurious* (generated by line noise) `ack` could be generated by noise on a poor communications link.

▲ The checksum is only 8 bits, which does not provide very robust detection (1 in 256 errored frames will not be detected, as it will have the same checksum as an uncorrupted frame).

Was originally developed, and the Intel 8080 *source code* was placed in the public domain, by a nice guy named Ward Christensen. The first implementation was in his `Modem` program, which was developed for CP/M (*Control Program for Microcomputers*, which was popular in the late 1970s and early 1980s) computers. An improved version (`Modem2`) was released in August 1977. The program permitted two computers running the program to transfer binary or text files through their serial ports (and typically, through modems), with a simple error check.

Others added features (to the program and protocol) and incremented the program's name until `Modem7` was released (it could handle transferring more than one file at a time and was able to run unattended and have the dialing-in computer control the file transfers).

The XModem protocol uses an 8-bit sequence counter (to check for lost frames), which is repeated (as the one's complement, in which each bit is inverted) so that a corrupted (and lost) frame or a 7-bit data channel will be detected reliably and immediately.

File transfers can be aborted by typing an ASCII `can` (`Control-X`) twice. (YModem and ZModem require `Control-X` to by typed more times.)

Sometimes called *XModem-Checksum* to differentiate it from a subsequent version (called XModem-CRC) that used a more reliable form of error detection.

Subsequent improvements (XModem-CRC, WXModem, XModem-K, YModem, YModem-G, ZModem, and ZModem-90) address the shortcomings described above.

See **CHECKSUM, DISK FORMATTING, INBAND, KERMIT, OUTOFBAND, XMODEM CRC, WXMODEM, XMODEM K, YMODEM, YMODEM G, ZMODEM**, and **ZMODEM 90**.

XModem-CRC

XModem with better (and unfortunately more CPU-intensive) error detection. (But who cares? CPUs are powerful-enough to handle this now.)

It uses the standard 16-bit CCITT CRC, rather than an 8-bit checksum (which is simply an `Exclusive-or` of the data).

XModem-CRC programs can detect and work with programs that support only XModem-Checksum (by using the 8-bit checksum for that file transfer).

See **CRC, XMODEM**, and **YMODEM**.

XModem-K

XModem with support for 1,024-byte frames (file transfers can use any mix of the 128 or 1,024 byte frames).

The larger frame size improves the protocol efficiency, though on noisy lines, efficiency will be worse than with XModem, since more data must be retransmitted—and there is a greater chance of errors in each frame.

See **XMODEM** and **YMODEM**.

XModem-1K-G

See **YMODEM G**.

XNS
Xerox Network System

A LAN protocol developed a long time ago by Xerox Corporation. Has (only) a 576-byte maximum packet size.

Is also the basis for Novell's, 3Com's, and Ungermann-Bass's (OSI) layers 3 and 4 LAN protocol, which explains why those protocols (IPX, NetBEUI, etc.) also (at least initially) had a small maximum packet size.

See **IPX** and **NETBEUI**.

XPG
X/Open Portability Guide

A guide (for example XPG4, which would be the fourth edition) produced by the *X/Open Company Ltd.* that specifies the standards to be used to ensure cross-platform, vendor-independent interoperability and compatibility. It specifies the requirements of systems, such as the commands, interfaces, utilities, and languages.

See **X/OPEN**.

Y

YAHOO
Yet Another Hierarchical Officious Oracle

A WWW index created in April 1994 by two Stanford University Ph.D. candidates (David Filo and Jerry Yang), who then started Yahoo! Corp.

See *http://www.sun.com/cgi-bin/show?950523/yahoostory.html* for an interview with them.

Their search engine is at *http://www.yahoo.com/search.html*. Other search engines include; *http://www.altavista.com, http://opentext.uunet.ca:8080/omw.html*, and *http://lycos.cs.cmu.edu/*. Some sites automatically submit your query to several other sites, these include; *http://www.cs.colostate.edu/~dreiling/smartform.html   http://www.intbc.com/sleuth/*, and *http://www.albany.net/~wcross/all1srch.html*.

While most search engines let you manually add web sites to their database, there are web sites that will automatically add web sites to multiple search engines. One such site is at *http://www.hometeam.com/tools/submital.htm*.

Directories of companies that have web sites are at *http://www.ais.net:80/netsearch/* and *http://www.directory.net*.

See **WWW**.

YModem

A very popular file transfer protocol in the PC environment.

XModem-K with the addition of an initial frame that specifies the file's name, length, and date (so the file name gets transferred automatically), and support for sending more than one file in a session (often called a *batch* capability), by using wildcards in the filename (for example *.doc).

Like XModem-K, YModem supports both 128- and 1,024-byte frames and checksum or CRC error detection. Also, many YModem implementations will work with XModem at the other end of the link.

Still has a *window size* of 1, resulting in poor throughput.

Called YModem either because it succeeded XModem or because it is based on YAM (Yet Another Modem), which was written by Chuck Forsberg.

Sometimes called *YModem-batch* to emphasize that more than one file can be sent during a file transfer session, by using a wildcard character in the filenames specified (for example, `*.tmp` would result in sending all files with a filename extension of `tmp`).

See **KERMIT**, **UTC**, **XMODEM**, **XMODEM-K**, and **YMODEM-G**.

YModem-G

YModem with CRC error detection, but acknowledgments are only expected for the initial file information (name, length, and date) frame and after the entire file has been transferred successfully.

That is, there is no error correction (only error detection), so an error-free data link must be used. Modems with V.42 or MNP Level 4 error correction or an X.25 network provide this—but these were rare when YModem-G was released (early 1980s). The transfer is aborted if errors are detected.

See **YMODEM** and **ZMODEM**.

YP
Yellow Pages

The previous name for NIS.

See **NIS**.

YUV
Luminance (Y), Chrominance (UV)

A method of representing color information.

See **COLOUR**, and **COMPOSITE VIDEO SIGNAL**.

Z

ZIF
Zero Insertion Force

Integrated circuits (ICs) usually have pins for their electrical connections. This pins can either be soldered directly into a *printed circuit board* (PCB), or they can be inserted into a socket. For more expensive ICs, or those that may need to be removed, a socket is typically used. A socket usually has spring-loaded electrical contacts, which will require that some pressure be applied to insert or remove each pin.

The force needed to insert or remove an IC is therefore force per pin times the number of pins. For ICs with many pins (such as a Pentium, which has 273 pins), the force is so great, that damage to the IC or PCB becomes likely—especially if the person doing the forcing is an untrained consumer (or a hasty technician).

A zero insertion force socket is one that has a lever that moves each spring-loaded contact so that the IC can simply be dropped-in to the socket, and then the lever closed to secure the IC and make the electrical contacts.

ZIF sockets are very expensive. For example, Digikey at *http://www.digikey.com* shows that for single quantities, a 273-pin ZIF socket costs about $61, and a regular socket costs about $13 (these prices drop to about half in large quanties).

See **CONNECTOR**, and **SIMM**.

ZModem

A very popular file transfer protocol in the PC environment.

Whereas YModem was a slight improvement on XModem, ZModem is a dramatically different protocol from YModem. Enhancements include the following:

▲ Character encoding (usually only for 7 to 10 of the ASCII control characters), so that control characters, such as the x-on (11_{16}), x-off (13_{16}) and Carriage Return ($0D_{16}$) characters are sent as other characters that X.25 networks can carry—specifically, for these examples, can Q (18_{16} 51_{16}), can S (18_{16} 53_{16}) and can M (18_{16} $4D_{16}$) are sent.

▲ Support for both 16-bit and 32-bit CRCs.

▲ Acknowledgments are covered by error detection, so there is little chance of a *spurious* ack, and are sent only when the sender requests them—of benefit, since some error correcting modems work faster if they don't need to process data in both directions (that is, the data plus acknowledgments) at once.

▲ Data are sent as a constant stream, with CRCs (covering all the data since the previous CRC) sent at least every 1,024 bytes. If the sender wants an ack, then this request is included in the CRC frame, to which the receiver replies with the file position (a count of the bytes that have been successfully received so far, where byte 0 is the start of the file). This capability of having more than one unacknowledged frame of data outstanding is often called *sliding windows*. This improves file transfer throughput—especially on networks with long round-trip delays.

▲ If the receiver detects an error, whether it was requested to ack or not, the receiver requests the sender to back up to the last successfully received file position for error recovery.

▲ An initial negotiation to confirm that both sides are capable of the normal full-duplex (or *streaming*) file transfer, in which acks are sent during the file transfer, as requested by the sender.

▲ If both sides cannot support this, then a half-duplex (or *segmented streaming*, where the window size is set to 1) mode is used, and only one frame (of a negotiated size, called the *burst-length*) is sent, with a pause until the mandatory acknowledgment is received by the sender.

▲ *Crash Recovery*—restarting aborted file transfers (for example, because the communication line became noisy and the modem abruptly hung up) where they left off (once the connection is reestablished). This is a really nice feature when someone elsewhere in the house picks up the phone to make a call when you have almost completed a multi-megabyte download.

▲ Commands to:

  – Determine how much available disk space the destination computer has—a good thing to check before sending a large file.

  – Specify what the receiver should do with a file if it already has one with the same name. For example, replace it always, or only if the sender's file is newer or longer or has different contents, or append it to the existing one. Determining whether the contents of the files are different is done by comparing the 32 bit CRCs for each of the files.

  – Request that a (usually user-typed) command be sent to the remote computer's ZModem program or its operating system's command interpreter.

▲ Data compression, using LZW, though this is seldom implemented (since the algorithm is patented).

Developed by Chuck Forsberg under contract with the operator of a large U.S. X.25 packet-switched network (GTE Telenet, now called SprintNet). X.25 networks typically have low error rates but long time delays (500 ms and longer) and a few reserved characters, so it was in Telenet's interest to have a PC (and other platform) file transfer protocol widely available that would work well with their network. It was therefore part of the contract that the protocol details and source code would be placed in the public domain.

See **FULLDUPLEX, HALFDUPLEX, KERMIT, LZW, X.25, YMODEM,** and **ZMODEM 90.**

Computer Dictionary

ZModem-90

A proprietary enhanced ZModem (developed by Chuck Forsberg's company, Omen Technology) that supports additional features, such as:

▲ Operation over 7-bit data channels

▲ Data encryption

▲ *Run-length encoding* data compression, which is good for files with bytes that are repeated (contiguously) many times

See **RLE** and **ZMODEM**.

INDEX

Numbers

A

A cable, 578
A-law, 483
A/UX, 26
ABAM, 643
Abandoned, 469
Absolute names, 190
Absolute novelty, 467
Abstract, 468
Abstract Syntax Notation One, 604
Academy format, 304
ACAP (application configuration access protocol), 26, 328
Accelerated Graphics Port (AGP), 32–33
Acceptable use policy (AUP), 72, 337
Access channels, 121
Access Control Lists, 741
Access fees, 364
Access lines, 279
Access mechanisms, 197
Access methods, 160
Access mode, 690
Access points, 624
Access time, 124, 591
ACCESS.bus, 26–27, 170
ACE (Advanced Computing Environment), 28
Acknowledgment, 181, 376, 618
Acrobat, 28
Active, 179, 305, 443, 710
Active-matrix, 380
Active negation, 582
Active termination, 576
Adaptation layers, 28–29, 207
Adaptec SCSI, 49
Adapters, 98
Adaptive answering, 253
Adaptive clock recovery, 133
Adaptive differential pulse code modulation (ADPCM), 29
Adaptive Equalization, 303
Adaptive Packet Assembly, 406
Adaptive Transform Acoustic Coding, 395
ADB (Apple Desktop Bus), 29
Add/Drop Multiplexer, 611
Additive primary colors, 146
Address, 340

Address classes, 340
Address resolution, 375
Address resolution protocol (ARP), 46–47, 108, 538
Address translation gateways, 539
Adjacency Database, 439
Administration, 60
Administrative, 713
Administrative consoles, 712
Administrative domain, 737
Adobe, 29
Adobe Type Manager (ATM), 55, 277, 512
ADPCM (adaptive differential pulse code modulation), 29
ADSL (asymmetric digital subscriber line), 30–32
Advanced ATA, 53, 321
Advanced Communication Facilities/Virtual Telecommunications Access Method, 602
Advanced Computing Environment (ACE), 28
Advanced Interactive Executive (AIX), 34
Advanced mobile phone service (AMPS), 36–40
Advanced Peer-to-Peer Internetworking (APPI), 43
Advanced Peer-to-Peer Networking (APPN), 44–45
Advanced power management (APM), 42
Advanced Program to Program Communications (APPC), 42–43
Advanced Research Projects Agency Network (ARPAnet), 47
Advanced SCSI Programming Interface (ASPI), 49
Advanced Technology (AT), 51, 352
Advanced television (ATV), 72
Advantage Networks, 32, 430
Adverse channel enhancements, 407
AFP (AppleTalk Filing Protocol), 32
Agents, 603, 739
AGP (Accelerated Graphics Port), 32–33
Air blown fiber, 270
Airplane magazine syndrome, 33–34
AIX (Advanced Interactive Executive), 34
Alignment errors, 239
Alliance for Strategic Token Ring Advancement and Leadership (ASTRAL), 49
Allocations units, 245
Allowed cell rate, 68
Alpha, 506
Alpha AXP, 34–35
Alternate mark inversion, 75, 161, 302
Alternate mark-space, 88
Alternating SVD, 634

Altitude, 292

American National Standard Code for Information Interchange, 48

American National Standard for Metric Practice, 589

American National Standards Institute (ANSI), 41

American Standard Code for Information Interchange (ASCII), 47–49

American Telephone and Telegraph, 70–71

Amorphous-silicon, 380

Amount, 397

Amplifiers, 636

Amplitude, 147, 148

Amplitude modulated, 148, 444

AMPS (advanced mobile phone service), 36–40

Analog-overlay, 204

Analog SVD, 634

Analog-to-Digital converter, 483

Anchor frames, 419

Anik, 40

Anomalistic year, 380

Anonymous ftp, 282

ANS Communications Inc. (ANS), 40–41

ANSI (American National Standards Institute), 41

Anti-jabber, 536

Anti-streaming, 536

Aperture grilles, 159

API (application program interface), 41–42, 728

APM (advanced power management), 42

APPC (Advanced Program to Program Communications), 42–43

APPI (Advanced Peer-to-Peer Internetworking), 43

Apple Computer, Inc. (Apple), 43–44

Apple Desktop Bus (ADB), 29

Apple-IBM Alliance, 44

Apple Update-Based Routing Protocol (AURP), 72

AppleTalk Filing Protocol (AFP), 32

Applets, 366

Appliance modules, 736

Application configuration access protocol (ACAP), 26, 328

Application-level gateways, 272

Application program interface (API), 41–42, 728

Application protocol, 27

Application proxy, 273

Application Server 400, 210

Application specific integrated circuits, 187

APPN (Advanced Peer-to-Peer Networking), 44–45

APPN+ (APPN Plus), 45

APPN++ (APPN Plus Plus), 45

APPN Implementor's Workshop, 181

APPN Plus (APPN+), 45

APPN Plus Plus (APPN++), 45

Architecture, 393, 569

ARCnet (Attached Resource Computer Network), 45–46

Ardis Company, 46

Are you there (AYT), 74

Area codes, 188

ARnet, 104

ARP (address resolution protocol), 46–47, 108, 538

ARP caches, 46, 108

.arpa, 190

ARPAnet (Advanced Research Projects Agency Network), 47

Arrays, 525

Ascender, 509

ASCII (American Standard Code for Information Interchange), 47–49

Aspect ratio, 708

ASPI (Advanced SCSI Programming Interface), 49

Asserted, 218

Assigned ports, 650

Assigning, 154, 331, 665

Associated, 665

ASTRAL (Alliance for Strategic Token Ring Advancement and Leadership), 49

Asymmetric data encryption, 233, 558

Asymmetric digital subscriber line (ADSL), 30–32

Asynchronous, 6, 85, 86, 90, 219, 252, 410, 575, 725

Asynchronous communications, 12

Asynchronous data communications, 150, 672, 693

Asynchronous data transmission, 49–51

Asynchronous function calls, 51

Asynchronous mode, 133

Asynchronous transfer mode (ATM), 55–70, 507

Asynchronous Transfer Mode Forum (ATM Forum), 70

AT (Advanced Technology), 51, 352

AT Attachment 2 (ATA-2), 53

AT Attachment 3 (ATA-3), 53–54

AT attachment packet interface (ATA-PI), 54, 227, 321

AT attachment software programming interface (ATASPI), 54

Because It's There (Time) Network (BITnet), 91
Bell 103, 85–86
Bell 202, 86
Bell 202S, 86
Bell 202T, 86
Bell 212A, 86
Bell Ardis, 87
Bell Operating Companies, 531
Bellcore (Bell Communications Research Inc.), 87
Bellman-Ford, 541
Bembo, 671
Bently Nevada Corporation, 92
Berkeley Internet Name Daemon, 191
Berkeley sockets, 677, 725
Berkeley Software Distribution UNIX (BSD UNIX), 98
Berne Convention for the Protection of Literary and Artistic Works, 154, 335
BERT (bit error rate test), 87–88
Best effort service, 67, 726
Betamax, 708
Bézier spline, 456
BGP (border gateway protocol), 88
Bi-endian switching, 459
Bi-Tronics, 10
Big endian, 88–89, 399, 459, 608
Binary coded decimal (BCD), 63, 85
Binary compatible, 453
Binary exponential backoff, 639
Binary File Transfer, 254
Binary large objects (BLOB), 91
Binary portability, 318, 510, 515, 542
Binary synchronous communications (BISYNC), 90–91
Binder, 303
Bindery, 433
BIOS (basic input/output system), 89–90, 224
Bipolar, 310, 669
Bipolar, with 8-Zero Substitution (B8ZS), 75–77
Bipolar 7, with Zero Code Suppression, 75–76
Bipolar violations, 76
Birds, 568
BISYNC (binary synchronous communications), 90–91
Bit-block transfer, 176
Bit error rate test (BERT), 87–88
Bit error rates, 278

Bit errors, 87
Bit-oriented, 91, 302
Bit-rate allocation signal, 299
Bit rates
    available, 66, 68, 426, 726
    constant, 57, 64, 359, 426
    unspecified, 66
    variable, 65, 426
Bit synchronization, 50
Bitmap fonts, 91, 277
BITnet (Because It's There (Time) Network), 91
.biz, 684
Blanking, 147, 305, 443, 706
Blind PIO, 226
Blind-writers, 524
Blit, 176
BLOB (binary large object), 91
Block, 36
Block check characters, 136
Block errors, 87
Block mode, 224
Block writes, 587
Blocking, 557, 640, 725
Blue Book, 128
Blue boxes, 329
Blue Lightning, 91
Bm, 296
BNC (Bayonet Nut Connector/Bayonet Neill Concelman), 92
Body, 313
Bold, 313
Bonding (bandwidth on demand interoperability group), 92
Bookmark, 313
Boot managers, 179
Bootable, 93
Bootp (bootstrap protocol), 93
Bootstrap, 93–94
Bootstrap protocol (Bootp), 93
Border gateway protocol (BGP), 88
Boundaries, 468
Boundary Scan, 368
Branch prediction, 94
Branches, 12
Break, 704
Break signals, 50
Breakup of Ma Bell, 530

Calling line identification service, 111

Calling menu, 692

Calling number identification (Caller ID), 109–111, 697

Calling Subscriber Identification, 251

Calling tone, 250

Calls, 41

Canadian Intellectual Property Office (CIPO), 139

Canadian Internet (CA*NET), 103–104

Canadian Internet II (CA*NETII), 104

Canadian ISBN, 353

Canadian Metric Practice Guide, 589

Canadian Network for the Advancement of Research, Industry, and Education (CANARIE), 111–113

Canadian open systems application criteria (COSAC), 156–157

Canadian Patent Act, 470

Canadian Patent Office, 470

Canadian Radio-Television and Telecommunications Commission (CRTC), 160

CANARIE (Canadian Network for the Advancement of Research, Industry, and Education), 111–113

CA*NET (Canadian Internet), 103–104

CA*NETII (Canadian Internet II), 104

Canonical form, 188

CAP (carrierless amplitude phase), 30, 31

Capacitive, 687

Card Information Structure, 486

Card services, 485

CardBus, 113, 485

Cards, 476

Carriage return, 47

Carrier amplitude, 30

Carrier extension, 290

Carrier frequency, 696

Carrier phase, 30

Carrier Sense, 20

Carrier sense, multiple access with collision avoidance (CSMA/CA), 160–161

Carrier sense, multiple access with collision detection (CSMA/CD), 161

Carrierless amplitude phase (CAP), 30, 31

Carriers, 113–114, 644

Carterfone, 70

Cartridge, 723

CAS (Communicating Applications Specifications), 114, 254

Cascade, 479

Cascading Style Sheets Level 1, 315

Cat 5, 687

Categories, 687

Cathode ray tubes (CRT), 147, 159–160

Cathodes, 159

CATV (community antenna television), 114–118

CCD (charge-coupled device), 118–119

CCIR (Comité Consultatif International Radio), 119

CCITT (Comité Consultatif International Télégraphique et Téléphonique), 119

CCP (compression control protocol), 119, 518

CD-ROM (compact disc, read-only memory), 123–131, 574

CDE (Common Desktop Environment), 120

CDMA (code division multiple access), 120–122

CDPD (Cellular Digital Packet Data), 122–123

Ceephones, 84

Cell delay variation, 67

Cell delay variation tolerance limit, 64

Cell directories, 168

Cell loss priority, 60

Cell loss rate, 64

Cell rate decoupling, 67

Cell relaying function, 59

Cell transfer delay, 67

Cells, 77, 131–132

Cells in Frames (CIF), 139

Cellular Digital Packet Data (CDPD), 122–123

Central directory servers, 45

Central offices (CO), 142, 169, 512

Central processing units (CPU), 107, 158
    486DX, 17
    486DX2, 17
    486SX, 17
    486SX2, 17
    80386DX, 24
    80386SX, 24
    Alpha AXP, 34–35

Centronics interface, 464

Centronics port, 7

CERT (Computer Emergency Response Team Coordination Centers), 132

Certificate Management, 739

Certification authority, 622

Data authentication, 72

Data circuit-terminating equipment (DCE), 167–168, 218

Data communications, 165

Data communications equipment, 218

Data compression, 166, 200, 700

Data country codes, 62

Data encryption standard (DES), 172–173

Data Exchange Interface (DXI), 207

Data Link Connection Identifier, 280

Data link control layer protocol (DLC), 179–180

Data link escape, 542, 743

Data Link Switching (DLSw), 180–182, 603

Data Link Switching Plus (DLSw+), 183

Data multiplexing, 101

Data over circuit switched voice, 356

Data service unit/channel service unit (DSU/CSU), 200–201

Data service unit (DSU), 200

Data set, 635

Data sources, 446

Data-strobe encoding, 13

Data terminal equipment (DTE), 167, 201, 218

Data transfer rates, 124

Data Transmission at 48 kbps Using 60-108 kHz Group-Band Circuits, 698

Data VPN, 281

Database, 369

Database administrators (DBAs), 167

Database records, 619

Database servers, 619

Dataphone Digital Service (DDS), 171

Dataroute, 166

Daylight Savings Time, 166

DB-25, 166–167

DBA (database administrator), 167

DBS (digital broadcast service), 167

DCE (data circuit-terminating equipment), 167–168, 218

DCE (Distributed Computing Environment), 168

DCI (Display Control Interface), 168–169

DCS (Digital Channel Service), 169, 721

DDC (Display Data Channel), 169–170, 707

DDE (Dynamic Data Exchange), 170

DDS (Dataphone Digital Service), 171

De facto standards, 171, 253, 258, 385, 491, 634, 699, 700, 735

De jure standards, 171, 281

Deasserted, 219

DEC (Digital Equipment Corporation), 171–172

Decibels, 687

Decided, 364

Decision to Put to Ballot, 363

Declaration, 586

DECnet/OSI, 172

DECnet Phase IV, 172

DECT (Digital European Cordless Telecommunications), 172, 492

Dedicated, 264

Dedicated circuits, 166

Dedicated data circuits, 169

Dedicated Line, Four-wire circuit, 721

Dedicated Token Ring, 639

Default gateways, 652

Defense Advanced Research Projects Agency, 47

Deferred write-back cache, 525

Delta frames, 74

Demand priority, 6, 7

Demand priority access method (DPAM), 6

Demarc, 157

Demodulators, 292

Dependent LU Requester/Server (DLUr/DLUs), 183, 603

DES (data encryption standard), 172–173

Descender, 509

Design patents, 173, 330, 470

Deskset tools, 120

Desktop-centric, 647

Desktop management, 187

Desktop Management Interface (DMI), 185–187

Desktop Management Task Force, Inc. (DMTF), 185, 187–188

Destructive interference, 261

Det Norske Veritas, 359

Determined, 363

Deutsche Instustrie Normen, 372

Device address, 11

Device ID, 10, 570

Device types, 573

DFT (distributed function terminal), 173

DHCP (dynamic host configuration protocol), 174

Diagonal viewable image, 159

Dial pulse, 174

Diatonic scale, 570

Dibit, 693

Distinguishing guise, 665

Distorted, 445

Distributed computing, 168

Distributed Computing Environment (DCE), 168

Distributed Computing Object Model, 156

Distributed function terminal (DFT), 173

Distributed LANE, 376

Distributed Management Environment (DME), 185

Distributed processing, 42

Distributed queue dual bus (DQDB), 197

Divestiture, 71, 530

Divx, 206

DLC (data link control layer protocol), 179–180

DLL (dynamic link libraries), 180, 726, 728

DLSw (Data Link Switching), 180–182, 603

DLSw+ (Data Link Switching Plus), 183

DLSw Working Group, 181

DLUr (Dependent LU Requester), 183, 603

DLUs (Dependent LU Server), 183, 603

Dm, 296

DMA (direct memory access), 183–185, 476, 505

DME (Distributed Management Environment), 185

DMI (Desktop Management Interface), 185–187

DMS (Digital Multiplex Switching), 187

DMTF (Desktop Management Task Force, Inc.), 185, 187–188

DN (directory number), 188–189, 208, 598

DNS (Digital Naming Service), 190

DNS (domain name system), 190–196

Document Instance, 587

Document Type Definition, 586

Dolby Digital Surround sound, 203

Domain name servers, 174, 190

Domain name system (DNS), 190–196

Dot pitches, 159

Dots per inch (DPI), 197

Dotted decimal, 340, 345

Double-clocking, 33

DoubleDensity, 275

Downlink, 565

Downstream channel, 30

DPI (dots per inch), 197

DPMS (Display Power Management Signaling), 197

DQDB (distributed queue dual bus), 197

DRAM (dynamic random access memory), 197–199, 215

Drawings, 468

Drivers, 506

Drop-and-insert, 200

Dry, 643

DS-0 (digital signal level 0), 199

DS-1 (digital signal level 1), 199

DS-3 (digital signal level 3), 199

DSP (digital signal processing), 18, 199, 405, 409

DSU/CSU (data service unit/channel service unit), 200–201

DSU (data service unit), 200

DSVD (Digital Simultaneous Voice and Data), 201, 634

DSX-1 (digital signal cross-connect level 1), 201

DTE (data terminal equipment), 167, 201, 218

DTMF (Dual-Tone Multi-Frequency), 201–202

Dual Attachment Stations, 259

Dual counter-rotating rings, 609

Dual homing, 259, 374

Dual in-line memory module (DIMM), 175–176

Dual In-line Package, 576

Dual-key data encryption, 558

Dual-mode, 488, 654

Dual-ported, 587, 717

Dual processing, 495

Dual ring, 259, 609

Dual ring-of-trees, 259

Dual-scan twisted nematic, 379

Dual-Tone Multi-Frequency (DTMF), 201–202

Duplex, 30, 150

Duplexing, 525

DV (digital video), 11, 203

DVD (digital versatile disc), 203–206

DX4, 206–207

DXI (Data Exchange Interface), 207

Dynamic, 134, 197, 342, 620

Dynamic branch prediction, 94

Dynamic data exchange (DDE), 170

Dynamic execution, 497

Dynamic host configuration protocol (DHCP), 174

Dynamic link libraries (DLL), 180, 726, 728

Dynamic memory allocation, 511

Dynamic random access memory (DRAM), 197–199, 215

Dynamic rate conversion, 267

Dynamic reconfiguration, 508

E

E-IDE (Enhanced IDE), 54, 224–227, 322, 323
E-SMR (Enhanced Specialized Mobile Radio), 209
E1, 209
E2, 209
E3, 210
E4, 210
E5, 210
E.163, 208
E.164, 208–209
Ear and Mouth, 667
Early packet discard, 67
Easter egg, 210
Eastern Daylight Time, 166
EBCDIC (Extended Binary Coded Decimal Interchange Code), 210–212
ECC (Error-Correction Code), 212–213, 466
Echo cancellation, 303
ECP (Extended Capabilities Port), 8, 213
ECTF (Enterprise Computer Telephony Forum), 213–214
Edge devices, 69, 421
Edge jitter, 536
EDI (Electronic Data Interchange), 214–215, 500
Edition 1, 676
EDO DRAM (extended data out dynamic random access memory), 215
.edu, 190, 339
EIA-449, 216–217
EIA-485, 217–218
EIA (Electronic Industries Association), 216
EIA/TIA-232, 218–223
EIA/TIA-530, 223–224
EIA/TIA TSB-37a, 224
EISA (Extended Industry Standard Architecture), 227
Elastic, 559
Electric fields, 229
Electrical Characteristics of Balanced Voltage Digital Interface Circuits, 658
Electrical Characteristics of Unbalanced Voltage Digital Interface Circuits, 659
Electrical loads, 479
Electrically erasable, programmable read only memory, 274
Electrodes, 77
Electroluminescent, 379

Electrolytes, 77
Electromagnetic compatibility (EMC), 228–229
Electromagnetic fields (EMF), 228, 229, 641, 648
Electromagnetic interference (EMI), 229, 230, 231
Electron beam, 336
Electronic Data Interchange (EDI), 214–215, 500
Electronic Funds Transfer, 500
Electronic Industries Association (EIA), 216
Electronic Industries Association/ Telecommunications Industry Association Recommended Standards
    EIA/TIA-232, 218–223
    EIA/TIA 530, 223–224
    EIA/TIA TSB-37a, 224
    TIA/EIA-422, 657–658
    TIA/EIA-423, 658–659
Electronic Mail Broadcast to a Roaming Computer (EMBARC), 228
Electronic serial numbers, 136, 488, 657
Electronic whiteboard, 633
Element names, 586
Elements, 586
Elevator algorithm, 579
ELF (extremely low frequency), 228
EMBARC (Electronic Mail Broadcast to a Roaming Computer), 228
Embedded agents, 548
Embedded SQL, 619
EMC (electromagnetic compatibility), 228–229
EMF (electromagnetic field), 228, 229, 641, 648
EMI (electromagnetic interference), 229, 230, 231
EmPower, 230
Emulated LANs, 375
Emulation, 542
Encapsulated PostScript (EPS), 235–236
Encapsulated security payload, 344
Encapsulation, 180, 230–231, 423, 598, 704
Enciphering, 233
Encoding, 231–232, 259, 270, 639
Encrypted session, 716
Encryption, 233–234, 254, 501, 656
End nodes, 44, 382
End-system address, 62
End system (ES), 236
Energy Star, 197, 234
Enhanced BIOS, 224, 322
Enhanced Category 5, 687, 688

Enhanced IDE (E-IDE), 54, 224–227, 322, 323
Enhanced IGRP, 326
Enhanced Parallel Port (EPP), 8, 234–235
Enhanced serial data interface, 573
Enhanced Serial Port (ESP), 238
Enhanced Specialized Mobile Radio (ESMR/E-SMR), 209, 237–238
Enhanced throughput cellular, 39
Enhanced Video Connector (EVC), 241–242
Enhanced write performance, 481
Enterprise Computer Telephony Forum (ECTF), 213–214
Enterprise Network Roundtable, 70
Enterprise systems connection (ESCON), 236, 263
Enterprise wireless transmission, 492
Entertainment units, 204
Entries, 245, 620
Enumeration, 508
Enumerators, 508
EPP (Enhanced Parallel Port), 8, 234–235
EPROM, 198, 588
EPS (Encapsulated PostScript), 235–236
Equal, 358
Equalization, 696
Equally tempered scale, 570
Equipment, 467
Equivalent, 175
Erasable, Programmable, Read-Only Memory, 198, 588
Error-Correcting Mode, 252, 254, 410
Error-Correction Code (ECC), 212–213, 466
Error Detection and Correction, 213
Error detection and error correction, 700
Error-free seconds, 87
Error terms, 419
Errored-seconds, 87
ES (end system), 236
Escape sequences, 482
Escaping, 659
ESCON (enterprise systems connection), 236, 263
ESF (extended superframe), 237, 642
ESMR (Enhanced Specialized Mobile Radio), 237–238
ESP (Enhanced Serial Port), 238
Essential features, 468
Ethernet, 239–240
Ethernet II, 240

ETSI (European Telecommunications Standards Institute), 240
Eunuch, 677
Eureka 147, 164
Euro-ISDN, 437
European Article Numbering, 352
European Laboratory for Particle Physics, 731
European Telecommunications Standards Institute (ETSI), 240
EVC (Enhanced Video Connector), 241–242
Even, 466
Events, 547
Examination fees, 331, 469
Excess information rate, 279
Exchange, 28
Exchanges, 169
Exclusive, 423
Execute in place, 395, 485
Exercising, 83
Explicit Forward Congestion Indication, 60, 68
Explicit rate, 68, 139
Explicit rate marking, 68
Exported, 733
Extended Binary Coded Decimal Interchange Code (EBCDIC), 210–212
Extended Capabilities Port (ECP), 8, 213
Extended character sets, 49, 675
Extended data out dynamic random access memory (EDO DRAM), 215
Extended Display Identification Data, 169
Extended Four-Letter Acronym, 661
Extended Graphics Adapter (XGA), 743
Extended Industry Standard Architecture (EISA), 227
Extended MAPI, 393
Extended partitions, 179
Extended superframe (ESF), 237, 642
Extenders, 115
Extensible Markup Language (XML), 743
Exterior gateway protocol, 88
External, 577
External caches, 108
External clock, 220
External dial-up modems, 410
External entities, 587
External gateway protocols, 317
Extinction ratio, 270
Extra Low Frequencies, 648

G

MIDI (musical instrument digital interface), 398–399, 602

MIF (management information format), 399

.mil, 190

Millions of instruction per second (MIPS), 402

Milnet, 399

MIME (multipurpose Internet mail extension), 399–402

MIME type, 400

Mini disc (MD), 395

MiniCard (Miniature Card), 274, 395–396

Minimum cell rate, 66

Minimum length trees, 455

MIPS (millions of instruction per second), 402

MIPS Technologies Inc., 402–403

Mirroring, 525

misc., 684

Mission-critical, 527

Mixed mode, 128

MLPPP (multilink point-to-point protocol), 403–404

MMDS (Multichannel Multipoint Distribution System), 404

MMS (manufacturing message specification), 404

MMX (Matix Math Extensions), 405

MNP (Microcom Networking Protocol), 406–408

Mobidem, 409

Mobile IP (Mobile Internet Protocol), 408

Mobile MIB, 397

Mobile Satellite (MSAT), 423–424

Mobitex, 408–409, 529

Mobitex Operators Association, 409

Modal dispersion, 269

Mode 1 (CD-ROM), 124, 130

Mode 1 (DXI), 208

Mode 1 Multiword DMA, 226, 245

Mode 2 (CD-ROM), 124, 130

Mode 2 (DXI), 207

Mode 2 Multiword DMA, 226

Mode 3 PIO, 226, 596

Mode 4 PIO, 226

Modems (modulator/demodulator), 409–411

Modified, 423

Modified frequency modulation, 573, 580

Modified Huffman Encoding, 251

Modified Julian date, 438

Modified Modified Read, 252

Modified Read, 251

Modulator/demodulator (modem), 409–411

Monitors, 411–412

Monochrome, 445

Monochrome display adapters, 670

Monospaced, 671

Moore's Law, 412–413

Moral rights, 154

Mosaic, 732

Most significant bit, 386

Most significant (MS), 423

MOTD (message of the day), 414

Motherboard speed, 475

Motif, 298, 414, 450, 735

Motion vectors, 419

Motorola, Inc., 414–415

Motorola Integrated Radio System, 237

Mouse, 415

Moves, adds, and changes, 713

Moving Picture Coding Experts Group (MPEG), 417–420

Moving worlds, 717

MP-MLQ (Multipulse Maximum Likelihood Quantization), 421

MP (multilink point-to-point protocol), 415

MPC (Multimedia PC), 415–417

MPEG-1, 417

MPEG-2, 417

MPEG-2 audio stream layer-3 compression, 415

MPEG (Moving Picture Coding Experts Group), 417–420

MPIM (Voice Profile for Internet Mail), 716

MPOA (multiprotocol over ATM), 421

MPP (massively parallel processing), 421

MPR II, 422

MPS (Multiprocessing Specification), 423

MPTN (Multi-Protocol Transport Network), 423

MS (most significant), 423

MSAT (Mobile Satellite), 423–424

MTA (message transfer agent), 424, 672, 737, 738

MTBF (mean time between failures), 424–425

Mu (μ), 594

μ-law, 483

Multi-Protocol Transport Network (MPTN), 423

Multi-transaction timer, 481

Multi-vendor integration protocol (MVIP), 427

Multicast, 46, 390, 425, 562, 637

Multicast IP (Internet protocol multicast), 425

Multicast Open Shortest Path First, 343

Multichannel Multipoint Distribution System (MMDS), 404

Multifrequency tones, 174

Multilayer switches, 556, 637

Multilevel Transmit, 5

Multilink point-to-point protocol (MLPPP/MP), 403–404, 415

Multimedia, 359, 425–426

Multimedia Extensions, 405

Multimedia PC (MPC), 415–417

Multimedia Video File, 205

Multimode fiber, 268

Multipath interference, 122, 623

Multiple Access, 20

Multiple Master, 28, 426, 632

Multiple read, 224

Multiple service interconnect, 266

Multiple spindles, 526

Multiple Sub-Nyquist Encoding, 307

Multiple Virtual Storage (MVS), 427

Multiple write, 224

Multiplexed, 479

Multiplexed Information and Computing System, 677

Multiplexer, 340

Multipoint control unit, 301

Multipoint Distribution Service (MDS), 395, 404

Multiport repeaters, 536, 637, 638

Multiprocessing, 599

Multiprocessing specification (MPS), 423

Multiprotocol brouter, 553

Multiprotocol Label Switching, 556

Multiprotocol over ATM (MPOA), 421

Multiprotocol routers, 550, 552

Multipulse Maximum Likelihood Quantization (MP-MLQ), 421

Multipurpose Internet mail extension (MIME), 399–402

Multirate ISDN, 340, 356

Multisession, 127, 129

Multistation access units, 150

Multithreading, 452, 729

Multiword DMA, 322

    Mode 1, 226, 245

    Mode 2, 226

Musical instrument digital interface (MIDI), 398–399, 602

Musicam, 164

MVIP (multi-vendor integration protocol), 427

MVS (Multiple Virtual Storage), 427

Mylar, 178

Mythical Instructions Per Second (MIPS), 402

N

Name caching, 108, 181

Name resolver, 192

NAP (network access point), 361, 428–429

Narrow SCSI, 572

Narrowband ISDN, 429

Narrowband PCS (narrowband personal communications service), 430

NAS (Network Application Support), 430

National destination codes, 208

National Institute of Standards and Technology Automated Computer Telephone Service (NIST ACTS), 438–439

National ISDN-1 (NI-1), 436–437

National ISDN-2 (NI-2), 437

National ISDN-3 (NI-3), 437

National Library Act, 154

National prefixes, 208

National Research and Education Network (NREN), 337, 441

National Science Foundation Network (NSFNet), 441

National Science Foundation (NSF), 441

National Security Agency, 172

National significance numbers, 208

National significant numbers, 208

National Television System Committee (NTSC), 443–445

National treatment, 335

Native, 542

Native Signal Processing (NSP), 441–442

Navstar (Navigation Satellite Timing and Ranging), 294, 430

nb*net, 104

NC (network computer), 141, 430–432

NCP (NetWare Core Protocol), 432

NCP (Network Control Program), 432

NDA (non-disclosure agreement), 432, 664

NDIS (Network Device Interface Specification), 432–433

Remote procedure calls (RPC), 168, 398, 556–557

Remote Source Route Bridging, 183

Remote Terminal, 220

REN (ringer equivalency number), 535–536

Rendezvous point, 504

Repeat, 638

Repeaters, 536–537

Replication, 739

Request, 273

Request for Comments (RFC), 537–538

Request for discussion, 684

Request to send, 222

Request to Send/Clear to Send, 456

Reselling, 364

Reservation, 174

Reserved ports, 650

Resistor networks, 576

Resistors, 575

Resource arbitrators, 508

Resource management, 60, 68

Resource reservation protocol (RSVP), 559–560

Response, 273

Retrain/Entrain, 696

Reverse channels, 115

Reverse-engineering, 332, 664

Reverse-path forwarding, 504

RFC 1577 (classical IP over ATM), 538–539

RFC (Request for Comments), 537–538

RFS (remote file sharing), 540

RGB (red, green, blue), 540

Right of integrity, 154

Ring-in-a-box, 259

Ringer equivalency number (REN), 535–536

Ringing indicator, 222

Rings, 513, 661

RIP (routing information protocol), 541

RIPscrip (Remote Imaging Protocol Script Language), 541

RISC (Reduced Instruction-Set Computer), 542–543

RISQ, 104

Rivest, Shamir, Adleman Public Key Encryption (RSA), 558–559

RJ-45 (Registered Jack 45), 543–545

RJE (Remote Job Entry), 545–546

RLE. See Run length encoding (RLE)

Rlogin, 546

RMON 2 (remote network monitoring MIB, version 2), 548–549

RMON II (remote network monitoring MIB, version 2), 548–549

RMON (remote network monitoring MIB), 546–548

RMON V2 (remote network monitoring MIB, version 2), 548–549

Roaming, 23, 39, 296

Robbed-bit signalling, 133, 642

Rochester, 723

Rockwell International, 550

Rockwell Protocol Interface (RPI), 557–558

Rods, 144

ROFL (rolling on the floor, laughing), 550

Roll back, 619

Rolling on the floor, laughing (ROFL), 550

Root, 11, 455, 550

Root hubs, 6, 681

Root mean square, 293

Root storage, 448

Rotary, 175

Rotational latency, 124

Round robin, 653

Route caches, 108, 555

Route discovery frames, 555

Route Information Field, 182

Route server, 421

Routers, 337, 550–556

Routing, 180

Routing algorithm, 383

Routing and Remote Access Service, 552

Routing codes, 188

Routing information protocol, 541

Routing switches, 556

Routing Table Maintenance Protocol (RTMP), 560

Rows, 619

RPC (remote procedure call), 168, 398, 556–557

RPI (Rockwell Protocol Interface), 557–558

RSA (Rivest, Shamir, Adleman Public Key Encryption), 558–559

RSN (real soon now), 559

RSVP (resource reservation protocol), 559–560

RTFM (read the f_____ manual), 560

RTMP (Routing Table Maintenance Protocol), 560

RTP (real-time transport protocol), 561

Rubber bandwidth, 403

Run length encoding (RLE), 25, 213, 251, 388, 546, 750

Run Length Limited (RLL), 573
Runts, 239, 638

S

S/390 server, 392
S bus, 94, 442
S-HTTP (secure hypertext transfer protocol), 588
S-Video, 445
SAA (systems application architecture), 562
Samples, 50
Sans-serif, 671
Santa Cruz Operations, Inc. (SCO), 571–572
SAP information broadcasts, 562
SAP (Service Advertising Protocol), 562
SAP service query, 562
SAP service response, 562
SASK#net, 104
Satellites, 562–569
Saturating arithmetic, 405
Saturation, 146, 148
SBD (Smart Battery Data), 569
SBus, 442
SCADA (supervisory control and data acquisition), 569
Scalable, 56, 425, 507, 666
Scalable architecture, 569
Scalable coherent interface (SCI), 571
Scalable fonts, 277, 456, 569, 666
Scalable Processor Architecture (SPARC), 612
Scales, 570
SCAM (SCSI configured auto-magically/configuration automatically), 570
Scan Acquire, 670
Scatter/gather, 184
Scatter/gather DMA, 480
SCC (Standards Council of Canada), 571
sci., 684
SCI (scalable coherent interface), 571
SCO (Santa Cruz Operations, Inc.), 571–572
Screen pops, 162, 572
Screen saver, 522
Screened twisted pair (SCTP), 582
Scripts, 314, 648
SCSI-1 (small computer system interface-1), 578
SCSI-2 (small computer system interface-2), 578–581

SCSI-3 (small computer system interface-3), 581–582
SCSI configured auto-magically/configuration automatically (SCAM), 570
SCSI (small computer system interface), 572–578
SCTP (screened twisted pair), 582
SD (Super Density), 583
SDH (synchronous digital hierarchy), 583
SDK (software development kit), 584
SDLC (Synchronous Data Link Control), 179, 183, 302, 584
SDLC-to-LLC2 conversion, 183
SDRAM (synchronous dynamic random access memory), 584
SDTV, 584–585
Sealing current, 585
SECAM (séquentiel couleur avec mémoire), 585
Second-level, 6
Secondary caches, 108
Secondary master, 191
Secret key, 233, 500, 558
Sections, 611
Sector size, 743
Sectorizing, 37
Sectors, 124, 179, 245, 363, 527
Secure data exchange, 22
Secure electronic transactions (SET), 586
Secure European System for Applications in a Multivendor Environment (SESAME), 586
Secure hypertext transfer protocol (S-HTTP), 588
Secure SNMP, 604
Secure Sockets Layer (SSL), 622
Security, 713
Security access modules, 596
Security association ID, 345
Seek time, 124
Seeking, 54, 225
Segment, 90, 537, 737
Segmentation and reassembly, 28, 57, 60, 207
Segmented look-ahead, 107
Segmented streaming, 749
Segmented virtual source/virtual destination, 68
Selective Availability, 293
Selector, 62
Selector channels, 318, 572
Self-declare, 228
Self-monitoring, analysis and reporting technology (SMART), 596

Structured data transfer, 133
Structured DS, 133
Structured Query Language 2 (SQL2), 620
Structured Query Language (SQL), 619–620
Structured storage, 448
Structured wiring system, 629
STS (synchronous transport signal), 630
Studio-quality, 710
Study groups, 363
Style guides, 735
Style Sheet, 586
Style specifications, 586
Su, 630
Sub-band ADPCM, 285
Sub-carrier, 461
Subarea SNA, 602
Subminiature D-shell, 9
Subnet Bit Mask, 630–631
Subnets, 630
Subnetwork access protocol (SNAP), 603
Subpackages, 110
Subrate, 631
Subroutines, 41
Subscribe, 342
Subscriber, 667
Subscriber connectors, 150
Subscriber identity modules, 296, 596
Subscriber Information Module, 488
Subscriber numbers, 208
Subscription time, 279, 720
Subsets, 728
Subsystem IDs, 481
Subtractive primary colors, 146
Subtype, 400
Suite, 651
Summarization, 138
Summit UNIX, 685
Sun, 631–632
SunConnect, 632
Sunnet Manager, 604
SunOS (Sun Operating System), 632
Super Density (SD), 583
Super-pipelined, 497
Super twisted nematic, 380
SUPERATM (Super Adobe Type Manager), 632
Superframe, 237, 642
Supernet/NII, 357

Superscalar, 319, 494, 632–633
Superuser, 550
Supervisory control and data acquisition (SCADA), 569
Supervisory Protocol, 634
Surround sound, 164
Suspend mode, 234
Sustainable cell rate, 65
SVD (simultaneous voice and data), 633–634
SVID (system five interface definition), 634
SVR4 (UNIX System Five Release 4), 634–635
SVVS (system five verification suite), 635
SWATS (standard wireless AT command set), 635
Swedish Confederation of Professional Employees (TCO), 648
Switched, 55, 264
Switched 56, 635–637
Switched LAN, 637–639
Switched multimegabit data service (SMDS), 597–598
Switched SVD, 634
Switched virtual calls, 279, 720
Switched virtual circuits, 279, 720
Switching fabric, 56
Switchless configuration, 227
SX, 17
Symbols, 259, 696
Symmetric, 172, 233
Symmetric multiprocessing (SMP), 599–600
Sync, 673
Sync channels, 121
Synchronizing, 147
Synchronous, 48, 86, 90, 219, 252, 410, 557, 575, 700, 725
Synchronous bandwidth allocation, 261
Synchronous data communications, 48, 51, 231, 672, 693
Synchronous Data Link Control (SDLC), 179, 183, 302, 584
Synchronous data transmission, 639
Synchronous digital hierarchy (SDH), 583
Synchronous dynamic random access memory (SDRAM), 584
Synchronous function calls, 640
Synchronous graphics RAM (SGRAM), 587
Synchronous mode, 133
Synchronous Optical Network (SONet), 608–611
Synchronous payload envelope, 609

Transmit, 14
Transmit clock, 220
Transmit data, 219
Transmit Station Identification, 251
Transmitter/receiver, 722
Transparent, 296
Transparent asynchronous transmitter/receiver
    interface (TAXI), 647
Transparent bridges, 552
Transparent spanning tree, 553
Transponders, 563
Transport, 649
Transport mode, 344
Tree, 504
Trellis code modulation, 84, 261, 692
Trial use standards, 657
Trickle-charge rate, 82
Triggered updates, 618
Triple DES, 173
Trivial file transfer protocol (TFTP), 656
Tropical year, 380
True, 218
True Color, 506
TrueImage, 512
TrueType, 277, 666–667
TrueType Fonts, 277
Trumpet Winsock, 725
Trunks, 653, 667–668
TSAPI (Telephony Services Application
    Programming Interface), 668
TSB (technical service bulletin), 669
TSO (Time Sharing Option), 669
TTL (time-to-live), 669
TTL (transistor-transistor logic), 464, 669–670
Tunnel mode, 344
Tunneling, 231
Tunnels, 393
Tuples, 486
TWAIN (toolkit without an interesting name), 670
Twist pitch, 686
Twisted, 379
Twisted pair, 512
Twisted Pair Physical Medium Dependent
    (TP-PMD), 258, 663
Two-dimensional, 251
Two-way glueless SMP, 497
Two-way set-associative caches, 107

Type, 400
Type 1, 426, 512, 629
Type 9, 629
Type Foundries, 512
Type of service, 383, 455
Typeface family, 277, 671
Types of devices, 578
Typical, 352

U

U interface, 442
UA (user agent), 672, 738
UART (universal asynchronous receiver
    transmitter), 672–673
UDP (user datagram protocol), 673
UI (UNIX International), 674
UIFN (universal international FreePhone number),
    674
.uk, 190
ULF (very low frequency), 648, 714
Ultra DMA, 674
UltraSCSI, 578
Ultrathin client, 366
UMTS (universal mobile telephone services),
    674–675
Unbalanced, 464
Underwriter's Laboratory, 688
Unhinted, 512
UNI (user-to-network interface), 56, 326, 675
Unicast, 376, 390
Unicode, 675
Unified, 206, 474
Unified caches, 108
Unified Memory Architecture, 684
Unified System Display Architecture (USDA),
    683–684
Uniform resource locator (URL), 680–681, 732
UniForum, 675
UniModem, 647
Uniplexed Information and Computing System
    (UNIX), 634, 676–679
Unit loads, 217, 682
United States Order Code, 545
Univel, 676
Universal asynchronous receiver transmitter
    (UART), 672–673
Universal Copyright Convention, 154
Universal data connector, 630, 663

V

X